A HISTORY OF
ENGLISH DRAMA
1660–1900

A HISTORY OF
ENGLISH DRAMA
1660-1900

BY
ALLARDYCE NICOLL
*Formerly Professor of English Language and Literature
in the University of Birmingham*

VOLUME IV
EARLY NINETEENTH
CENTURY DRAMA
1800–1850

SECOND EDITION

CAMBRIDGE
AT THE UNIVERSITY PRESS
1963

PUBLISHED BY
THE SYNDICS OF THE CAMBRIDGE UNIVERSITY PRESS

Bentley House, 200 Euston Road, London, N.W. 1
American Branch: 32 East 57th Street, New York 22, N.Y
West African Office: P.O. Box 33, Ibadan, Nigeria

First Edition 1930
Second Edition 1955
Issued as Volume IV of
A History of English Drama 1660–1900
Reprinted 1960
1963

First printed in Great Britain at the University Press, Cambridge
Reprinted at The Whitefriars Press Ltd, Tonbridge

PREFACE

In this volume I have endeavoured to bring up to date the study of early nineteenth-century English drama originally issued, in two volumes, in 1930. For the most part, the pages of the main text have been left standing, but numerous small corrections or modifications have been made throughout: supplementary notes provide references to books and articles published on the theatre of this period during the past twenty years.

The chief contributions recently made to dramatic history during this half-century have been concerned with identifying authors of dramas which I had listed as anonymous and with adding titles not recorded; and as a result in the Handlist of Plays I have been forced to fall back on a compromise. Both from new material which I personally have gathered and from the contributions of others many alterations are here introduced into the Handlist itself, and at the same time nearly a hundred pages of supplementary information have been added.

In the preparation of this supplementary information and in correcting the main Hand-list some dozen articles have proved particularly useful. One or two of these are concerned with the work of individual authors, such as James Sandoe's study of the plays written by T. J. Dibdin (*University of Colorado Studies*, 1940, i, 205–20) and W. P. Bowman's study of the plays written by George Soane (*Modern Language Notes*, 1939, liv, 278–9). The majority, however, are more generally devoted to correcting or adding to the Hand-list. Among these, the most important are the several contributions made by Allan Wade and Sir St Vincent Troubridge in *Theatre Notebook*. To Sir St Vincent I am also greatly indebted for his kindness and courtesy in offering me the use of his additional extensive collection of card entries: the supplementary notes in this volume owe a very great deal to the information he has provided. Of considerable value, too, have been the two articles by R. Crompton Rhodes on 'The Early Nineteenth-century Drama' (*Library*, 1935–6, xxi, 91–112 and 210–31), where special attention is given to the standard collections of printed texts. On one such collection M. W. Stone has some notes in 'Unrecorded Plays Published by William West' (*Theatre Notebook*, 1946, i, 33–4); other notes on the "juvenile drama" appear in the same journal by Stone (1946, i, 41; 1947, i, 80), T. Walton (1949, iii, 64–6) and H. D. Spencer (1950, iv, 37–8), while George Speaight has issued a book, *Juvenile Drama* (1946), on this subject.

Among other lists particular reference may be made to Majl Ewing's 'Notes on Nicoll's *Hand-list* for 1800–1850' (*Modern Language Notes*, 1943, lviii, 460–4) and 'The Authorship of Some Nineteenth-century Plays' (*id.* 1942, lvii, 466–8); J. E. Tobin's 'Early Nineteenth-century Drama' (*Notes and Queries*, April 21 and May 5, 1945) and 'More English Plays: 1800–1850' (*Philological Quarterly*, 1944, xxiii, 320–32); and Arnold Biella's 'Additions and Corrections to the Bibliography of Nineteenth Century British Drama' (*Philological Quarterly*, 1942, xxi, 298–332).

An indispensable tool has now been provided by Dougald MacMillan in his *Catalogue of the Larpent Plays in the Huntington Library* (San Marino, California, 1939). Further notes on individual plays in this collection are provided by L. F. Peck ('M. G. Lewis and the Larpent Catalogue', *Huntington Library Quarterly*, 1941–2, v, 382–4) and Ethel Pearce (*id.* 1942–3, vi, 491–4). For the study of operas during the period equally indispensable is Alfred Loewenberg's *Annals of Opera*, 1597–1940 (Cambridge, 1943).

In the supplementary notes several contractions and symbols have been used in order to save space. Under the names of individual authors the symbol "[+from *UA*..." indicates titles of plays in the Unknown Authors section which may certainly or probably be assigned to these playwrights. In the Unknown Authors section corresponding references are given, with an "=" sign preceding the authors' name. Any titles added in the supplementary notes to those mentioned in the Hand-list are preceded by a "+" sign, and a similar sign is placed before the names of authors not elsewhere recorded. The abbreviation "L", followed by an appropriate number, refers to the entries in Dougald MacMillan's Larpent catalogue, and "LND" refers to the Hand-list which forms part of *A History of Late Nineteenth Century Drama*.

It should be observed that I have not included all the material enumerated in the articles cited above. Occasionally the information did not correspond with my own findings, and on occasion, too, the sources of this information did not seem to me sufficiently trustworthy to warrant its acceptance. It must fully be realised, in dealing with the early nineteenth-century drama, that quite frequently attributions of plays to particular authors which appear in one contemporary source conflict with attributions given in another source, that often the minor theatres advertised as "new" dramas which had already been elsewhere on the boards and that often the same title was given to entirely different plays. For these reasons alone it is obvious that a very long time must elapse before a definitive record can be made of all productions and publications of dramas between 1800 and 1850: the present Hand-list and the supplementary notes are to be regarded merely as a contribution towards that record.

Owing to the fact that this volume consists partly of the text presented first in 1930 and partly of supplementary material, there is a certain inevitable inconsistency in the citing of the earlier volumes of *A History of English Drama* and of the volume which follows. Thus references appear both to *A History of Late Eighteenth Century Drama* and to *A History of English Drama*, vol. iii, while sometimes *A History of Late Nineteenth Century Drama* appears under its full title and sometimes (to save space) under the contraction 'LND'. As will be realised, such inconsistencies, in view of the composition of this book, have proved unavoidable.

A.N.

THE SHAKESPEARE INSTITUTE
(UNIVERSITY OF BIRMINGHAM)
STRATFORD-ON-AVON

June 1953

CONTENTS

PART I

Chapter One

THE THEATRE

Chapter Two

THE DRAMATIC CONDITIONS OF THE AGE

Chapter Three

THE ILLEGITIMATE DRAMA

Chapter Four

THE LEGITIMATE DRAMA

Chapter Five

THE STILL-BORN DRAMA

Chapter Six

CONCLUSION . . . 211

Appendix A

THE THEATRES, 1800–1850

PART II

CHAPTER I

THE THEATRE

I. *Introductory*

IN the year 1801 there was billed to appear at one of the "minor" theatres a certain precocious child named as "Master Carey, the Pupil of Nature." While never rivalling the attraction later exercised by "the infant Roscius" (young Betty), Master Carey seems to have caused a little sensation among the novelty-loving audience of the period, and that sensation was no doubt stimulated when it was noised abroad that the clever child was a great-grandson of no less a person than the facetious Harry Carey, author of *Chrononhotonthologos* and of the still more famous *Sally in our Alley*, both still played or sung in those years. The sensation, however, would have been yet greater had the spectators of the period possessed a divining insight to display to them the future glory of the dark-eyed child-actor. Many of those who saw the boy Carey acting in 1801 at a minor theatre no doubt flocked to the patent houses in 1814 to witness the same boy, now grown into a man, seize with the powerful hand of a master upon the emotions of the playhouse and interpret Shakespeare in a manner all his own. The Master Carey of 1801 had returned to gain mature triumph under the name of Edmund Kean.

This concrete example serves to indicate how close, in time and generation, were the ties between the early nine-teenth century and the days when first the sprightly rimes and dainty tunes of *The Beggar's Opera* charmed the fashion-able society of London. It serves, moreover, to show how much closer even are the ties which bind the age of Coleridge with the twentieth century. Edmund Kean himself to modern youth lives in an antiquity not nearly so far removed as that in which Garrick shone. His son, Charles Kean, was acting till 1868, and with Charles Kean we are at least stepping on to the threshold of the theatre of today. In a

word, linked as the early nineteenth century may be with
the life of the preceding Georgian era, there is something
which tells us that a passage over the year 1800 will carry us
at once into the midst of an epoch which seems to be, or at
least gives the definite foundation for, that which we call
modern. The connections are everywhere apparent. The
gayer costumes, wrought in brocade and delicate with silk,
give way to sober pantaloons and dress-coats. Victoria
ascends the throne in 1837 and carries her reign on to 1901.
Ellen Terry first appeared as Mamilius in *The Winter's Tale*
on April 28, 1856; Dame Madge Kendal preceded her by
playing the Blind Child in *The Seven Poor Travellers* in 1852;
both were born in the same year, 1848. Definite links, some
literary, some historic, some by personal relations, easily
carry the mind back to this half-century, and the mental
picture has a certain nearness and precision lacking in the
more artificial revisualisations of Augustan or Caroline
times[1]. This fact gives a peculiar charm to a study of the age,
and as a result the drama and theatre of the period have
for us an interest greater than, and distinct from, that which
we feel for the efforts of previous eras.

On the other hand, to counter this impression of modernity
and this apparent interest, there confronts us the almost total
ignorance displayed by theatre-lovers of today concerning
the fortunes of the theatres during those fifty years. There are
numbers who have read the poetic plays written by the
romanticists; a few have penetrated as far as Sheridan
Knowles or Douglas Jerrold; one or two dramas of this time,
such as *Money* and *Box and Cox*, have come down to us
in living form[2]; some of the older generation may remember

[1] One instance of the material bonds connecting the present period with
the earlier illustrates this clearly. About 1928, a friend of mine informed
me that his father had a play performed in 1820 at Drury Lane. He had
been born in the same year as Shelley.

[2] Occasionally stock companies in minor theatres, or those touring the
lesser circuits, make use of the early nineteenth century repertoire. Some
old melodramas have lately been revived at the Elephant and Castle,
while one or two of Colman's comedies are still performed in the provinces.
Amateurs, too, ransacking French's and Dicks' old stock sometimes
find here treasure-trove.

their fathers' accounts of the days of Phelps and Macready; but of deeper knowledge concerning the progress or retrogression of the theatres there is practically nothing save among a few enthusiasts. The age seems nearer, yet theatrically it is in some ways further off, than the period when the elder Colman and Foote produced their now seldom remembered comedies. It is the object of the present book to outline at least the main features of the playhouse and dramatic development during those years, and to provide a general background for the possible study, along more specialised lines, of particular plays or of particular movements in the world of the theatre.

As the publication of many volumes of anecdotal character show, the theatre of this time exercises an undoubted fascination, even when exacter knowledge be lacking. Little space, of course, can be devoted here to the careers of the famous actors and actresses who thronged the boards, but, even when we leave the Macreadys, the Keans and the Ellen Trees aside, we find in the playhouse itself ample materials for our careful and interested consideration[1]. The

---

[1] The lives of the more famous actors of this time have been often told, and naturally many of these biographies contain matter of considerable general value. Among the more important volumes the following may be specially noted as contributing towards the history of the theatre: James Boaden, *Memoirs of the Life of John Philip Kemble* (2 vols. 1825); James Boaden, *Memoirs of Mrs Siddons* (2 vols. 1827); Barry Cornwall, *The Life of Edmund Kean* (2 vols. 1835); F. W. Hawkins, *The Life of Edmund Kean* (2 vols. 1869); J. W. Cole, *The Life and Theatrical Times of Charles Kean, F.S.A. Including a Summary of the English Stage for the last Fifty Years* (2 vols. 1859); *Macready's Reminiscences...edited by Sir Frederick Pollock* (2 vols. 1875); W. Archer, *W. C. Macready* (1890); *The Life of Charles James Mathews....With Selections from his Correspondence....Edited by Charles Dickens* (2 vols. 1879); *Memoirs of Joseph Grimaldi. Edited by "Boz"* (2 vols. 1838); and C. E. Pearce, *Madame Vestris and her Times* (1923). Details concerning other works are included in R. W. Lowe, *A Bibliographical Account of English Theatrical Literature* (1888). The newspapers of the age contain very full accounts of production and of acting. Hazlitt's reviews were collected together in one volume as *A View of the English Stage; or, A Series of Dramatic Criticisms* (1818; reprinted 1821, 1851, and, with an important introduction by W. Archer and edited by R. W. Lowe, in 1895 as *Dramatic Essays*). The reviews of Leigh Hunt likewise appeared as *Critical Essays on the Performers of the London Theatres, including general Observations on the Practise and Genius of the Stage* (1807). Some valuable *obiter dicta* occur in *Oxberry's*

age, it is true, but carries on traditions started towards the
end of the eighteenth century, but pioneer work is always
of less permanent interest than the full development of that
which before has been but vaguely prophesied. The greatest
event of the time was, of course, the Act "for regulating
theatres[1]," by which the monopoly held since 1660 by Drury
Lane and Covent Garden was definitely ended. This, like
all the innovations of the fifty years, was not unheralded
in earlier times. In the eighteenth century, apart from the
opera-house licences, the Haymarket had secured a limited
warrant, the minor houses at Sadler's Wells and elsewhere
were producing their musical and spectacular shows, and an
ill-fated attempt had been made at the Royalty to break
down the patent monopoly[2]. The final victory of the "minors"
was secured by following up the lines of the earlier attack.
The "burlettas[3]" permitted to them were widened as far as
the laws allowed, and persistent efforts were made to raise
at least a third patent playhouse in London. In 1808 a Bill
was for this purpose introduced in the House of Commons,
but was defeated[4]. Two years later a fresh effort was

Dramatic Biography, and Histrionic Anecdotes (1825–7), and in *Oxberry's Dramatic Biography, or The Green-Room Spy* (1827).

It may be advisable here to mention also some books and articles which are of special value for the study of the drama during this period. The survey of E. B. Watson, *Sheridan to Robertson* (1926), contains much matter of interest both on players and playwrights. Harold Child has an important, though short, study on *Nineteenth-Century Drama* in the *C.H.E.L.* vol. xiii. Important for its critical judgments is A. Filon, *The English Stage* (1897; translation of *Le théâtre anglais*, 1893). Genest, of course, carries his account down to 1830. On the poetic drama see E. Gosse, *The Revival of Poetic Drama* (*Atlantic Monthly*, xc), and U. C. Nag, *The English Theatre of the Romantic Revival* (*Nineteenth Century*, Sept. 1928). There are, also, several important Memoirs or Autobiographies by dramatists of the time, such as Blanchard, Fitzball, Dibdin and Reynolds. These are cited later. Fuller bibliographies are to be found in E. B. Watson, *op. cit.*, and the *C.H.E.L.*

[1] Statutes 6 and 7 of Victoria c. 68. Comment on this Act appears in nearly all the later memoirs of the period. Among other recent works Ernest Bradlee Watson's *Sheridan to Robertson* (1926) and Watson Nicholson's *The Struggle for a Free Stage* (1906) should be consulted.

[2] See *A History of English Drama*, iii. 230.

[3] On this term see *infra*, pp. 137–40.

[4] See Frederick Howard, Earl of Carlisle, *Thoughts upon the present Condition of the Stage, and upon the Construction of a new Theatre* (1808).

made[1], and was again unsuccessful. In 1813 another Third Theatre Bill was defeated in the Commons[2]. Legal defeat, however, simply urged the lesser managers to renewed efforts; burlettas were produced not far different from the ordinary dramatic fare in the major houses, and persistent attempts were made to question the validity of the old patents. The consequences were a formal decision on the part of the Solicitor-General that the vaunted strength of the original grants made to Killigrew and D'Avenant in 1660 was purely a fiction[3], and a series of meetings designed to bring the matter once more before Parliament. T. J. Thackeray had stirred men to review the whole subject[4], and as a result at the Albion Tavern on Dec. 4 and 31, 1831, and at the City of London Tavern on Feb. 24, 1832, there gathered together groups of dramatists and others interested in the theatre for the purpose of drafting a fresh petition. Lord Lytton brought in a Bill the same year, and the *Report* of a Select Committee[5], produced on Aug. 2, 1832, gave it approval. The Bill, however, after passing the Commons, was defeated in the Lords (1833). The failure, on the other hand, was by no means so complete as had been that of earlier endeavours of a similar kind, so that the adoption of the later Act of 1843 need affect us with no surprise. Here was no sudden decision, but the triumph of long effort, the reward of the hard and devoted labour of years. It may seem that, while the new Act marks a great turning-point so far as theatrical legislation is concerned, there is little change in the drama after that date; we may draw attention to the fact that, while many new

---

[1] See the *Account of the Proceedings before His Majesty's most Hon. Privy Council, upon a Petition for a Third Theatre in the Metropolis* (unpublished, 1810). A petition was sent by the trustees of Drury Lane protesting against the proposed erection of the third playhouse. See also *The London Chronicle*, March 17 and 20, 1810.

[2] See James Lawrence, *Dramatic Emancipation* (1813).

[3] For the granting of the original patents see *A History of English Drama*, i. 293-4. The value of the patents had been destroyed (1) by the Union of the Companies in 1682 (*id*. pp. 296-7), (2) by the granting of a licence to Betterton in 1695 (*id*. p. 301), and (3) by the formal surrender of one of the patents in the eighteenth century in return for a licence.

[4] See his *Theatrical Emancipation* (1832).

[5] Moved by Lytton on May 31, 1832.

theatres were erected in the early years of the century, none was built from 1845 to 1866; but, if there was no immediate change, there was unquestionably laid the foundation of that theatrical liberty which permitted the production later of our modern dramatic literature. The earlier efforts are a heritage of eighteenth century striving; the Theatre Regulation Act belongs to the period which carries us on to our own days.

Besides this truly epoch-making change, there were many movements in the half-century which proved to be the origins of later tendencies. The eighteenth century had inaugurated the correct costuming and setting of historical plays, but Macklin's Scots attire for *Macbeth* was only a tentative experiment; archæology did not take full possession of the theatre until the days of Macready and of Kean. These actor-managers, although they worked in gas-light and in ignorance, had the ideals which resulted in the better-known efforts of Irving and of Tree. Dramatically, the age produced, out of the welter of melodrama, the origins of that form which, adopted and perfected by Tom Robertson, marked the beginnings of the modern realistic movement. Technically, it gave scene painters and machinists who proved to be the masters of those of later years. In regard to material arrangements, it introduced stalls and reserved seats and a dozen other little theatrical conveniences which are familiar in the playhouses of today.

This period is, above all others, the period of change in the theatre. The eighteenth century, in spite of its numerous innovations, clung to traditions which had their original being in the Elizabethan age. In acting, in dramatic workmanship, and in management Garrick and his companions joined hands with Alleyn and Shakespeare. About the year 1800 the new age was born, and, while in many ways the lyric poets of the Romantic era seem nearer to Sidney and Spenser than to Pope and Prior, the theatre and all connected with the theatre broke the bonds of the past and established that playhouse which exists among us today. For evil or for good, the old had given way to the new. We may easily trace the stages by which the journey was made, for this, like all changes in the world of art, was not the affair of a moment. We may even go back and see in Lillo the father of realistic drama, in the innovations of 1770–90 the genesis of Kemble's and Macready's efforts; but fundamentally the fifty years after 1800 are modern, the fifty years before are ancient.

Considering this modernity of the period and also the wealth of critical matter contained in books of anecdotes, in biographies, in playbills and in newspapers[1], it will be understood that only a comparatively small proportion of the evidence available for the student can be presented here. Descriptions abound of the performances and productions of the major actor-managers, but in this survey we must be content to review certain selected and typical notices. The same is true of the drama. Texts of melodramas and farces are included in the many invaluable but often eye-straining collections of Cumberland, Lacy, French and Dicks, but to discuss even one-tenth of the plays produced during these years would be far beyond the scope of this volume. The Hand-list given as an appendix preserves the titles; the text must present only the chosen few which seem most symbolic of tendencies in the age. What we want is not a confused conglomeration of unassimilated facts, but a broader survey of the period as a whole, into which we may fit those individual facts observed in the course of our researches.

II. *The Audience*

The nineteenth century theatre opened badly. Conflagrations which destroyed the two patent theatres within

---

[1] This period saw the appearance of the definitely theatrical newspaper. There are a number of earlier periodicals of the first decades, mention of which will be made later. Here may be noted the establishment of *The Era* in 1838, and of *The Theatrical Times* in 1847. Among other similar publications *The Dramatic Magazine* (1829–31), *The Dramatic Gazette* (1830–1), *The Dramatic and Musical Review* (1842–4), *The Theatrical Inquisitor* (1812–21), *The Theatrical Observer* (1821–76), *The Theatrical Examiner* (1823–8), and *The Theatrical Journal* (1839–73) will be found of special value.

a space of twelve months were serious enough[1], but worse for the drama was the audience which playwright and player alike had to appeal to and please. All contemporaries are agreed on one thing; the spectators in the larger theatres during the first decades of the century were often licentious and debased, while those in the minor playhouses were vulgar, unruly and physically obnoxious. The tumult in a nineteenth century theatre was one of those things which bound it to the theatres of the past. *The Theatrical Repertory; or, Weekly Rosciad* for Monday, Dec. 28, 1801, describes, without too much horror, a disturbance which took place at a Covent Garden performance of *Richard III*:

A ruffian in the Two Shilling Gallery threw a quart bottle upon the Stage, which fell so near Mr Betterton as to strike the hat which he held in his hand, but fortunately did no injury either to that gentleman or any of the other performers.

There was a "Tailors' Riot" at a benefit of the actor Dowton at Haymarket on Aug. 15, 1805[2]. "There was much fighting," says a critic of a performance of *The Pirate's Doom* at the Adelphi on Feb. 12, 1827[3], "which probably would have been more effective, but for a real battle in the pit, to which the screams of the women imparted a truth and reality, that quite spoilt the effect of the stage combats." A riot during a performance of a French play at Drury Lane in 1848 recalls the earlier "Chinese Festival" disturbances[4]. These riots and disturbances, which thus remind us of the theatres of Dryden and of Cibber, were set in a constant noise and confusion. Here is Hazlitt's picture:

Everything...has its draw-backs; and the Little Theatre in the Haymarket is not without them. If, for example, a party of

[1] On the theatres see Appendix A. R. W. Lowe in his *Bibliographical Account*, p. 98, mentions a pamphlet entitled *An authentic account of the fire which destroyed Drury Lane Theatre*; this apparently he had not seen and I have failed to discover an extant copy. A similar *Account* (1808) of the burning of Covent Garden (*op. cit.* p. 72) seems also to have disappeared. A description of the old and new theatres there will be found in the interesting *Covent Garden Journal* of 1810.

[2] See Thomas Gilliland, *The Dramatic Mirror* (1808), I. 154–5, and R. B. Peake, *Memoirs of the Colman Family* (1841), ii. 309.

[3] *The Theatrical Observer*, T. 13/2/1827.

[4] See *A History of English Drama*, iii. 5–6.

elderly gentlewomen should come into a box close at your elbow, and immediately begin to talk loud...your only chance is either to quit the house altogether, or...to remove to the very opposite side of it....At the great Theatres, it is sometimes very difficult to hear, for the noise and quarrelling in the gallery; here the only interruption to the performance is from the overflowing garrulity and friendly tittle-tattle of the boxes. The gods...at Drury-lane and Covent-garden, we suspect, "keep such a dreadful pudder o'er our heads," from their impatience at not being able to hear what is passing below; and, at the minor theatres, are the most quiet and attentive of the audience[1].

At both the major and the minor theatres, companies of "*would-be* young men of fashion" would indulge in

the witty explosion of six-penny crackers. This is now an old joke as well as a bad one,—but it still affords amusement to some courageous and gallant Gentlemen, for it never fails to frighten the women; and, from the difficulty of detection, they feel perfectly secure from the angry indignation of those who could resent it[2].

Colman the younger, who had experienced the difficulties involved by such behaviour, has his comment upon it:

Whence arise the deafening vociferations, when there is a full house, of "turn him out!" and "throw him over?" Why is a vocal performer so often kept on a see-saw, called back, sent off, called back again, about the *encore* of a song, and at last, after ten minutes, perhaps, of confusion, obliged to sing it in the midst of the "tumult and disorder" of a divided audience?

Again, why is a play, on the first exhibition of a Christmas Pantomime, acted almost in dumb-show, like the mummery that is to follow it, in consequence of the "tumult and disorder" of the spectators?...Why, during the intervals, is the stage strewed with apples, and orange-peels, accompanied in their descent thither, by the shouts, groans, whistles, catcalls, yells, and screeches of the turbulent assemblage which has so elegantly impelled its vegetable projectiles from the upper regions?...Why are disturbances in the upper boxes, and lobbies, among black-guards and women of the town, by no means rare?[3]

[1] W. Hazlitt, *op. cit.* ed. 1821, p. 133.
[2] Newspaper cutting in Shaw Collection, Harvard, dated 25/9/1814. I have failed to identify the original paper.
[3] R. B. Peake, *Memoirs of the Colman Family* (1841), ii. 364-5.

The notorious "O.P. Riots" were thus in no ways exceptional[1], and probably Thomas Dibdin was right when he declared in his *Harlequin Hoax* (Lyc. 1814) that only at a pantomime were the spectators "very silent and attentive" while "tragedies, comedies, operas, and farces are doom'd to suffer all the complicated combinations of 'Pray ask that gentleman to sit down,' 'Box Keeper, where's my fourth row on the second circle?' 'Take off your hat,' and 'Keep quiet in the lobby.'...In a Pantomime...the moment the curtain goes up, if any unfortunate gentleman speak a word, they make no reply but throw him over directly[2]." Various actor-managers attempted to make improvements, but not always with success; even in 1841 Macready found opponents in the press when he tried to stem the "improper intrusion" associated with certain parts of Drury Lane[3]. "The feelings of performers," says a writer in *Oxberry's Theatrical Inquisitor*[4], speaking of Easter pieces, "are martyred by playing to a noisy, drunken set of auditors, who are impatient throughout the play, from an anticipation of the 'glorious pageantry' that a specious program-matical play-bill has prepared them for," while Sir Walter Scott reflects grimly that the theatres in general are "destined to company so scandalous, that persons not very nice in their taste of society, must yet exclaim against the abuse as a national nuisance"—"prostitutes and their admirers usually" forming "the principal part of the audience[5]." Even the ordinary

[1] The history of this long and clamorous warfare between indignant spectators and the managers of the new theatre at Covent Garden has often been told. The pamphlets and books issued in connection therewith are detailed in R. W. Lowe's bibliography, occupying no less than four pages (pp. 72–6). In addition to the works cited there see *The Theatrical Journal* for 1846 and 1862, William Dunlap's *Memoirs of George Fred. Cooke* (1813), ii. 101–17, and *The Life and Times of Frederick Reynolds* (1827), ii. 380–6.

[2] The speaker is Miss Kelly in the opening scene. One may note the references to the hat trouble and the implication that there were reserved rows, if not reserved seats.

[3] William Archer, *William Charles Macready* (1890), p. 111, and *The Theatrical Observer*, Oct. 6, 1841. *The Theatrical Journal* for July 27, 1844, styled the theatres "great public brothels." [4] 1828, p. 109.

[5] *Essay on Drama* (originally published in 1819), *Prose Works* (Edinburgh, 1834), vi. 392.

critics of the newspapers took constant notice of these abuses. "We regret to observe," says the dramatic correspondent to *The Times* in 1801[1], "that no measures have been yet taken to prevent the indecent and scandalous conduct of the loungers, both male and female, who infest the lobby of the Theatre," and his remark is but one of many. There can be no doubt, when thus we find anonymous critics, playwrights, theatre-lovers and actors all united, that the auditorium of an early nineteenth century playhouse was a place lacking both in taste and in good manners, a place where vulgarity abounded, where true appreciation of the drama was subordinated, not to witty if somewhat improper badinage as in the Restoration theatre, but to rude and foolish practical jokes, to the roaring of a drunken bully, to the besotted solicitations of a prostitute. Such an audience necessarily reacted both upon actor and upon dramatist, and a good deal of the roughness in texture in the histrionic art and in the ordinary theatrical fare of the time must be credited to these spectators who were, in the opinion of Sir Walter Scott, nothing less than "a national nuisance."

So far as the general appearance of the theatrical auditorium in which these spectators sat was concerned, there was but little general change from the conditions established in the preceding century, although in a hundred small ways approach was being made towards the present-day playhouse. As some of the extracts quoted above go to show, the sharp division into pit, box and gallery was retained from the earlier years, and, in spite of the fact that the rudeness of the "gods" seemed to have descended upon those who occupied the more fashionable portions of the theatre, the distinctions in taste seem also to have been retained. This division is expressly mentioned, with some variations, in Dallas' *Not at Home* (Lyc. 1809):

In saying the PUBLIC, I am glad of this opportunity of stating what I mean by that word at a Theatre. I mean that cultivated Company who usually occupy the circle of dress boxes; I mean those judicious Critics who take their station in the Pit; I mean

---

[1] *The Times*, Monday, Aug. 3, 1801, regarding the Little Theatre or Theatre Royal in the Haymarket.

my worthy friend John Bull, who is to be found in either Gallery.
...I do not mean the self-conceited, ephemeral Pseudo-critics
of the age, who, after attempting in vain to foist their writings on
the public, have sunk into the critics immortalized by Pope....
Neither do I mean those rare spirits who love to make a noise in
the slips of a theatre, and to condemn what they do not understand[1].

Pit, box, and gallery—as Planché lilts:

> Ye belles and ye beaux,
> Who adorn our low rows
> Ye gods, who preside in the high ones;
> Ye critics, who sit
> All so snug in the pit,—
> An assemblage of clever and sly ones![2]

There were no stalls in the earlier days, and the pit served
alternately for "Fops' Alley[3]" and for its more regular "sage
grave rulers" who were the "Imperial arbitrors of taste
and wit[4]." Stalls came gradually towards the end of the
period, ousting the severer critics and causing a change of
orientation in the acting, but throughout the greater part
of this period the fundamental distinctions divided the
audience into clearly marked groups[5]. Gradually, however,
the changing conditions made themselves felt, and Professor
Watson is undoubtedly right in tracing to the introduction

[1] Preface.   [2] *Olympic Revels* (Olympic, 1831).
[3] See note to Planché's *Success* (Adel. 1825) in the 1879 edition of his
Extravaganzas (i. 34). The term descends from Restoration days (see
A History of Restoration Drama, p. 11).
[4] Dimond's *The Sea-Side Story* (C.G. 1801), Prologue.
[5] G. C. D. Odell in his *Shakespeare from Betterton to Irving* (1921),
ii. 242–3, quotes a Haymarket bill of 1843 which, he thinks, marks the
beginning of the stalls and of reserved seats. Watson, *op. cit.* p. 87, cites
as the earliest reference to stalls a French Lyceum advertisement in *The
Companion* on Jan. 31, 1828. There is an interesting note in *The Dramatic
Magazine* of 1829 (pp. 159–60) regarding the Theatre Royal at Liverpool.
"A new regulation has been adopted at the box-keeper's office....On
taking places in the boxes, a slip of paper is given to the party, containing
the date on which places were taken, the name of the parties, the number
of places, and the number of the box. This arrangement is well
calculated to put an end to these clamorous altercations and appeals to
the box-keeper, by which an audience is so often annoyed while the first
act of the play is proceeding." Evidently the provinces were well abreast
of, if they did not actually anticipate, the metropolis. The "dress-circle"
is referred to in *The London Magazine*, Feb. 1822, p. 180 and the Edinburgh *Dramatic Review*, Nov. 16, 1822.

of stalls a change in histrionic technique during the last years of this period[1]. These stalls, more highly priced, were frequented by people of society, and there were thus removed from the reflected glow of the footlights and the stage-lighting those front rows of old "pittites," critical and eager to appreciate at its full worth the play that was being enacted before them. The robust performances that had pleased in 1810 began to fall flat and, after an indeterminate period when those actors who had been trained in earlier standards found to their amazement that the tricks which pleased of yore now met with no applause, there gradually came into being a fresh style of acting, simpler and less inclined towards exaggeration, which provided the material upon which a Lytton and, in other years, a Robertson were to work. Perhaps, too, the introduction of the stalls, added to the severer moral tone of a Victorian epoch, aided in reforming the general character of the playhouse. The presence of fashionable and respectable women in the front of the old pit must have aided at least in subduing the more clamorous denizens of that region and in establishing that highly decorous tone which distinguishes the theatre of today[2].

That these various portions of the playhouse demanded, as in previous years, the careful attention of the managers, the playwrights and the actors, may well be imagined, and there is plentiful evidence remaining to testify to the nature of their tastes. One thing we notice at the very start—the comparative simplicity of the average spectator. This is exemplified in the popularity of the melodrama, which, in spite of a number of travesties and burlesques, seems to have been accepted in a serious spirit. Even more typical is the patriotic enthusiasm of the day. In earlier times classic tragedies might contain many an overt significance; Whigs and Tories applauded vigorously during the first performance of *Cato* because each believed that individual sentences bore reference to their political ideals. Nothing of this do we

[1] *Op. cit.* p. 89.
[2] Vocal disapprobation of a new play may yet be heard in London theatres; but obviously such outbursts are rare and are in any case confined to occasional first nights.

find in the early nineteenth century; veiled reference gives place to direct and simple exposition. Audiences enjoyed, not the vaguely symbolic or allusive drama, but the "spectacle" which presented to them national facts unadorned save by the trappings of the patriotic imagination. It was in such pieces as *The Battle of the Nile* (S.W. 1815), *The Battle of Trafalgar; or, The Death of Nelson* (Cob. 1824), or *The Naval Victory and Triumph of Lord Nelson* (H.[1] 1805) that they delighted. They loved to see the military and naval events of their own and of immediately preceding generations presented to them in mimic form upon the stage.

This political note is accompanied by another which may be styled the domestic, or, more precisely, the familiar. Here as evidence can be adduced the innumerable "domestic dramas" which crowd the pages of the appendix to this survey; it is all part of that movement towards realism which accompanies the visionary flights of the Romantic imagination. What, however, most surely characterises the age is not merely the domestic subject matter, for that we had in Heywood and Lillo and have still in many authors, but the familiarity of some of the themes. "My," "You" and "Our" appear in hundreds of play titles—*My Album* (St J. 1838), *My Friend from Town* (Queen's, 1831), *Our House* (S.W. 1842), *Our New Governess* (Lyc. 1845), *You can't marry your Grandmother* (Olym. 1838), *You Know What* (S.W. 1842)—and when we add these to others of the "How" type—*How to Live without Money* (S.W. 1830), *How to Settle Accounts with your Laundress* (Adel. 1847)—we realise that here we have a highly typical feature of the dramatic tastes of the time. Immediately, this produced nothing but melodrama and rather trivial farce; ultimately it was to have its importance in the building up of the foundation for the deeper and more profound domestic drama of today.

Most characteristic of all, however, is the moral sentiment of the time. Exemplified among critics, dramatists and spectators, this "Victorianism[1]," which subtly differs from

[1] It is, of course, marked long before the actual accession of Queen Victoria.

the sentimentalism of the preceding decades, must be taken fully into account when we consider the failure of contemporary tragedy and comedy. Sentimentalism of the older sort gave us the many sympathetic dramas of the period; all the "Dumb Girls" and "Blind Boys[1]" are the progeny of this mood. The "Victorian" morality exercised an influence more negative than positive, and succeeded rather in killing free expression than in producing something entirely new. A few examples may serve to make this clear. *The Double Dealer* was revived, almost certainly in an altered form, at Drury Lane on Saturday, Feb. 27, 1802, and *The Theatrical Repertory* on the first of the following month came forth with weighty fulminations:

Such a trough-full of villainy and lewdness was surely never before kneaded together...down, down with it to the lowest pit of hell; and there let devils act the parts, and devils only be the auditors![2]

Well: one cannot say much more than that, and, if the critics took this lead, what wonder if the spectators and, after them, the playwrights, followed? There is nothing very seriously wrong with Lacy's *The Two Friends* (H.[2] 1828), but both reviewers and audiences saw it as "one of the most immoral and dangerous dramas" that had ever been written, "loudly demanding the censure of all who regard the well-being of society[3]." It is one of the jests of literature that, in this age of such decorous and sentimentally moral dramas, a reviewer could declare that "now it is almost dangerous to take a young person to a play-house[4]." One can imagine the indelicate sallies this must raise among the shades of Etherege and Wycherley as they sit wittily over their ambrosial wine. For the dramatists the aim naturally was to please by inculcating some moral, to avoid offending public taste.

---

[1] E.g. Farrell's *The Dumb Girl of Genoa* (Bath, 1823) and the anonymous *The Blind Orphan* (Surrey, 1833).

[2] No. xxiv.

[3] *The Dramatic Magazine* (1829), p. 194. It must be confessed, however, that the reviewer in *Oxberry's Theatrical Inquisitor* (1828), p. 194, saw nothing improper in the play.

[4] *Id.*

"In all," Mrs Inchbald's "anxious hope" in writing *To Marry, or Not to Marry* (C.G. 1805)

> was still to find
> Some useful moral for the feeling mind[1].

One Lumley St George Skeffington, who wrote the prologue to Dimond's *Adrian and Orrila* (C.G. 1806), found this morality the greatest achievement of the nineteenth century theatre:

> Long has the Stage, determined to impart
> Such scenes alone as meliorate the heart,
> Barr'd from all avenues, with rigid sway,
> Plots which corrupt, and maxims that betray...
> Proud of no praise, of no distinction vain,
> Unless distinguish'd in the moral train...
> Licentious follies rarely intervene,
> And truth and sense, and honour claim the scene!

Truth and honour, perhaps—but the dramatists often seemed to lose their sense of humour in their frantic endeavours to be polite. In Somerset's *A Day after the Fair* (Olym. 1829) Jerry has to come in as Mademoiselle Dumplino, but as that *diva* is supposed to be only 3½ feet tall, Jerry is made to kneel on a little stool on rollers. In the course of the scene he rises to his own six feet of height, and at this point the author deems it necessary to give us a footnote:

> The little stool on rollers is fastened round Jerry's waist, and, of course, when he rises, is concealed by his wide petticoats. The effect is exceedingly comic, for, when he stands on his legs, his female garb only extends to his knees, *yet there is no indecency in this, as he has stockings, &c. on underneath.*

I am glad of the presence of that "&c."

Perhaps the morality, however, was only specious, after all. It is, at least, noticeable that both dramatists and audiences, even if they would have nothing to do with Wycherley and his peers, seemed to take a sneaking interest in the affairs of the Restoration court. Jerrold produces his *Nell Gwynne* (C.G. 1833), where, of course, the one-time orange-girl and the king's mistress plays a most becoming

---

[1] Prologue.

part; Wilks pens *The King's Wager* (Vic. 1837) with Charles himself as a central figure; Moncrieff writes his *Rochester; or, King Charles the Second's Merry Days* (Olym. 1818), in which two court ladies gull the witty rakes; and Knowles deals with a Charles II theme in *Woman's Wit* (C.G. 1838). Perhaps more than one spectator and more than one author of the age inwardly echoed the desire expressed by a stage damsel a century before and wished that he had been born in good King Somebody's days[1].

The censor, for his part, was determined that the audience should get nothing of good King Somebody's merriment. When the century opened, the official reader of plays was that John Larpent who quietly converted to his own uses the dramatic manuscripts submitted to him in the course of his long career. On his death, George Colman the younger was appointed to the post on Jan. 19, 1824, and in his turn was followed by Charles Kemble (appointed on Nov. 2, 1836) and John Mitchell Kemble (appointed Feb. 24, 1840). Concerning the ways of Larpent and Colman we have ample information. Both were officious rather than official in their duties. The one, guilty of what is tantamount to larceny, and the other, often licentious in his own early plays, forgot their own peccadilloes and insisted on the utmost decency, piety and loyalty from the miserable dramatists whose lords they were. The best account of Larpent's methods is told in the preface to Theodore Hook's *Killing No Murder* (H.[2] 1809). In the course of his enquiries Hook discovered

that John Larpent, Esq. was *clerk* at the Privy Seal Office, that John Larpent, Esq. was *deputy* to John Larpent, Esq. and that the *deputy's secretary* was John Larpent, Esq.

This gentleman had censored the character of a Methodist in Hook's play, declaring that the "Government did not wish the Methodists to be ridiculed." The author found later that the official reader was "not only a rigid methodist himself, but...had even built a little tabernacle of his own." Happily

[1] See *A History of English Drama*, ii. 160.

for Hook, however, he was able to add an advertisement to his printed play, thanking Larpent

for refusing his licence, and creating an interest for the farce[1].

Colman was no less particular. Not only did he object to any play the plot of which concerned rebellion, but he imposed a rigorous censorship upon all kinds of expletives. "Oh Gods" were anathema to him, and the dramatic lovers were not even permitted to call their mistresses angels. From Jerrold's *The Rent Day* (D.L. 1832) this official cut out several "Gods" and "damns" together with the following sentences:

"Heaven be kind to us, for I've almost lost all [other] hope."
"Isn't that an angel?" "I can't tell; I've not been used to such company."
"I love you, and may heaven pardon and protect you[2]."

A few other examples may be cited from the original evidence provided by the copies of plays in the possession of the Lord Chamberlain[3]. First may be taken a *Jack Sheppard* (1839) sent in from the Theatre Royal at Hull. Here two sentences were cut out which read:

Jack. Oh God! In thy Mercy either restore my mother or destroy the Son!
Mrs Sheppard. I will not pray for my poor Jack's soul! I know it is wicked to do it.

Two years later the same licenser (Kemble) ordered the omission from *Sixteen String Jack* (Olym. 1841) of the following fragment of conversation:

Mary. Is Life the price of Gold?
Jack. So says the Law.
Mary. But not *his* Law.

Even French plays suffered heavily. In 1840 a *Clémence* was denuded of a sentence spoken by Duvernay:

Et si l' on rend compte un jour de toutes les péchés inutiles, notre époque aura terriblement à faire.

Sometimes, too, the wrath of the licenser and of the Lord

---

[1] On Larpent's methods see also T. J. Dibdin's *Reminiscences* (1827), ii. 25.
[2] W. Jerrold, *Douglas Jerrold* (1918), i. 193–4.
[3] See Appendix B.

Chamberlain rose to a higher pitch. In 1844 some of the "saloons" submitted three plays, *The Murder House, The Thieves' House* and *George Barrington; or, The Life of a Pickpocket*. The Lord Chamberlain was out of town, so Kemble sent on the dramas to him with an accompanying note. The reply came back within a few days, with the heavy intimation that the plays were to be rejected and that the erring managers should come to answer for their sins at the official headquarters. The Lord Chamberlain confesses he is "astonished at the *audacity* of the Managers of the Britannia and Albert Saloons in soliciting a Licence for *such* Pieces[1]."

It is clear, of course, that the licenser's injunctions were not always attended to in the theatres, whatever nominal submission was made as regards the text. Fitzball has a record of a visit paid by Colman to a performance of the popular drama, *The Pilot*:

> Cooke, who never failed of making an excellent point of "No, if I do I'm d——d," on coming to the proscribed line in question, and suddenly perceiving the Licenser in the boxes, proceeded, "No, if I do I'm ——" and placing his thumb with great ludicrous quaintness on his nose, stopped short, with a look so comic, that the immortal George laughed heartily himself, at a manœuvre, which told better than words, how, on other occasions, the critic's professional morality had been attended to[2].

This registers one method of escape open to the players; the presence of the minor theatres provided another for the dramatists. Thus a licence was denied to Bunn's *The Minister and the Mercer* (D.L. 1834) until the author quietly but firmly pointed out that, should the denial be final, his play, perhaps with the inclusion of a few songs, would be performed as a burletta[3] at the lesser theatres and would achieve there special popularity because of the action of the licenser[4]. Such devices, however, were obviously not entirely sufficient to set the stage free, and ample evidence has been given to make us realise, first, the intense pruriency which was deemed

---

[1] Letters in the Lord Chamberlain's Department, St James's Palace.
[2] Edward Fitzball, *Thirty-Five Years of a Dramatic Author's Life* (1859), i. 161.
[3] On this term see pp. 137–40.   [4] Introduction to the play.

necessary by those holding office, and, secondly, the confusion which was bound to arise from the conflict between the extraordinary strictness of the licensers and the practice in the playhouses themselves.

This moral sensibility in the audience—for the licenser may have been stricter than the average spectator, but did not move in any very original direction—itself peculiar because of the vulgarity of ordinary playhouse life, was coupled with a tasteless following of fashion. The "bucks" of the Regency period were nothing if not stupid, and even the vaunted learning and critical taste of contemporary blue-stockings led to little beyond the affected worshipping of popular idols. The two groups, so excellently depicted in Scott's *St Ronan's Well*, were equally dull, and in the theatre Sir Bingo Binks and Lady Penelope roared or simpered along the lines taken by the mob that was society. The domination of fashion is to be seen nowhere more clearly marked than in the notorious Betty furore. This youth, William Henry West Betty, appeared on Dec. 1, 1804, in London, at the age of thirteen, achieving for two years a popularity which cast even Mrs Siddons and her brother into the shade. Everyone crowded to see the "Young" or the "Infant Roscius" so that "he drew all public attention from the real actors of the time, and was alone the magnet of both the London theatres, and the theme of the writers whose principal attention is turned to the stage[1]." The craze, as stated, lasted for two years. Thereafter although "some twenty or thirty *young wonders*, or *infant prodigies*, under the title of Infant Billington, seven years old Roscius and Billington, Infant Columbine, Ormskirk Roscius, Young Orpheus, Infant Vestris, Infant Clown, Comic Roscius, Infant Degville, Infant Hercules, and Infant Candlesnuffer[2]," were followed for a time by those

[1] W. Dunlap, *Memoirs of George Fred. Cooke* (1813), i. 276. Pamphlets and books in scores appeared on Betty during 1804 and 1805. In particular should be noted G. D. Harley, *An Authentic Biographical Sketch of the Life, Education, and Personal Character, of William Henry West Betty, the Celebrated Young Roscius* (1804), T. Harral, *The Infant Roscius* (1805), *The Life of Wm. Henry West Betty* (1804), and *The Young Rosciad....By Peter Pangloss, Esq., LL.D. and A.S.S.* (1805).

[2] W. Dunlap, *op. cit.* i. 281.

who had not realised that fashion had swept on to some other fancy, the infant frenzy died away. Perhaps the most amusing account of one of these Infant Phenomenons— which incidentally shows how fashion, having blinded its eyes to the follies of Betty, had awakened to comparative sanity—appears in *The Percy Anecdotes* (1822)[1]:

The success of Master Betty, if it did not raise juvenile emulation, at least excited the cupidity of parents, and a host of nursling Richards, and pigmy Macbeths, were preparing to feed the public rage for infant actors, when the mania received a fatal check.

In November, 1805, a Miss Mudie, called "The Theatrical Phenomenon," a child apparently about eight years of age, but with a figure remarkably diminutive, even for her years, who had, in the preceding season, played the first rate comic characters at Birmingham, Liverpool, Dublin, and other theatres, made her debut at Covent Garden, as Miss Peggy, in the "Country Girl." She repeated the words correctly, and her performance, as an infant, was surprising; but as an infant, the illusion was completely lost....When Miss Peggy came to be talked of as a *wife*, as a *mistress*, as an object of love and jealousy, the scene became so ridiculous, that loud hissing and laughing ensued. The little child was also contrasted with the fine person of Miss Brunton, now Countess of Craven, who, in the character of Alithea, wore a plume of three upright ostrich feathers on her head, constituting altogether a figure of nearly seven feet high. When Peggy was with her guardian, Mr Murray, who was not very tall, he was obliged to stoop to lay his hand on her head; to bend himself double to kiss her; and where she had to lay hold of his neckcloth to coax and pat his cheek, he was obliged to go almost on all fours. In the third act, Miss Peggy is seen walking in the Park, dressed in boy's clothes, when, instead of appearing a young man who ought to be "shown the town," she looked shorter than before, and even too little to be safely put into jacket and trowsers. Yet Mr Brunton, as her lover Belville, pursues her, and is transported to find her under this disguise, while Mr Murray, her pretended husband, is thrown into an agony of despair, at the idea of another man taking her by the hand.

The absurdity was too great to be endured; and there was a burst of censure from all parts of the house....A loud cry for the manager succeeded, when the first tragedian of his day, Mr Kemble, appeared to supplicate that the child might be allowed

[1] pp. 156–8.

to finish the play; the audience, however, were inexorable; the part of Miss Peggy was transferred to a young lady, whose age corresponded with the character, and Miss Mudie was withdrawn.

The audience perhaps acted rightly in this instance, but it is important to observe that it had been the rapturous adoration of Betty on the part of this very same audience which induced Kemble to put Miss Mudie on the stage. Had not even the veteran Home declared that he had never seen Norval more perfectly acted than when the boy of thirteen took that part? Maturer judgment, no doubt, reversed this decision; Betty was no different, was no more talented than the others—he had only the good fortune to be one of the first and so to catch the rising tide of fashionable enthusiasm.

Nor was the Betty craze the only one which indicated the contemporary power of fashion. Italian opera, which had always been a society diversion since first it was introduced in the days of *The Spectator*, still, with ebbing and flowing, sang its syren-songs to those who would be thought polite. French plays, too, came in for their share of popularity, and private theatricals, already a craze in the late eighteenth century[1], attracted youthful Pizarros and coquettish Juliets[2]. With one attraction after another the regular theatres had to fight, combating dulness and insipidity, vulgar sentiment and hypocritical morals, fashionable fancy and tastes, rude, petty and insincere.

III. *The Theatre*

Somewhat of the same confusion which is manifested among audiences and governing officials is indicated by a study of the actual playhouse conditions of the time. There is, first of all, the general struggle between the major and the minor playhouses. Until 1843 Drury Lane and Covent Garden retained their patent rights, although a stricter

---

[1] See *A History of English Drama*, iii. 19–22.

[2] On this subject there is an interesting set of correspondence (relating to the New Theatre in Tottenham-street) in *The Theatrical Repertory; or, Weekly Rosciad*, No. xxvi, Monday, March 15, to Monday, March 29, 1802.

examination of their claims showed that those rights were indeed based but on flimsy authority. Mere rights, however, do not always bring prosperity. The history of these two houses in the early nineteenth century is one long tale of vicissitudes. Committees of *dilettanti*, including among their number no less a person than Lord Byron, are succeeded by actor-managers; actor-managers are followed by adventurers like Bunn—and always the tale is one of disaster and despair. Frantic efforts are made to make ends meet. Prices are lowered to 4s., 2s. and 1s. during the Osbaldistone management of Covent Garden; at another time the two great theatres are run under one government, with the same troupe of players, so that actors and actresses may be seen on dark nights scurrying from one house to the other, playing a part in the opening piece at Drury Lane and performing again in the concluding farce at Covent Garden. All these efforts fail, and by 1850 Drury Lane is in a serious way, while Covent Garden has entirely abandoned the spoken drama and is turned into an opera-house.

The reason of this failure is to be traced partly to the presence of many other theatres in the metropolis, but also partly at least to bad management and bad architecture. Hazlitt confesses that the gods cannot hear at the two patent theatres, and the complaint, which had already been uttered in the earlier period[1], was echoed again and again in this age.

> "I think," says Syntax, looking round,
> "It is not good, this vast profound:
> I see no well-wrought columns here!
> No attic ornaments appear;
> Nought but a washy wanton waste
> Of gaudy tints and puny taste:
> Too large to hear—too long to see—
> Full of unmeaning symmetry![2]"

Other more serious critics uttered the same complaint; it was agreed by all that a spectator in the further parts of the house "cannot see the countenances of the performers without the

[1] See *A History of English Drama*, iii. 22–4.
[2] W. Combe, *Doctor Syntax's Three Tours* (1808), p. 92.

NED

aid of a pocket telescope, he cannot hear any thing except the
ranted speeches[1]." It is certainly true that Reynolds thought
that audiences really preferred theatres of a large size[2], and
that Macready professed the same opinion when before the
Select Committee of 1832[3], but such views, it would seem,
were exceptional or misguided. Sir Walter Scott seems to
have been in the right when, speaking at the Edinburgh
Theatrical Fund Dinner in 1827 and referring to the project
for a new playhouse in that city, he expressed the hope that
"wherever the new theatre is built...it will not be large,"
that "it should be one in which we can hear our old friends
with comfort." "It is better," he added, "that a moderate-
sized house should be crowded now and then, than to have
a large theatre with benches continually empty[4]." The evils
of the large theatre are patent enough now; they were
rendered trebly worse in a time when lighting was not so
brilliant and when endless alterations had ruined the acoustic
properties of the houses.

Still, the large theatres were a tradition and had to be
used. They were the homes of "legitimacy" and many actors,
after having made names for themselves elsewhere, thought to
advance their positions by performing in the "majors." The
results may easily be foreseen. When an audience could not
see or hear, it was inevitable that actors should coarsen their
methods of performance and that managers should indulge
in greater and greater spectacular effects. This tendency
towards show was, of course, aided by the activities of the
minor houses. In the eighteenth century Sadler's Wells and
its companions had been the homes of musical and pantomimic entertainment; Astley had made his name through
his historic spectacles enacted in an extended circus ring;
and it was natural that this tradition should be continued in
an epoch when the minor theatres rose to a position of still

[1] F. G. Tomlins, *A Brief View of the English Drama, from the Earliest
Period to the Present Time: with Suggestions for elevating the present
Condition of the Art, and of its Professors* (1840), p. 73.
[2] *The Life and Times of Frederick Reynolds* (1827), ii. 378.
[3] On this subject see E. B. Watson, *op. cit.* p. 138.
[4] *Edinburgh Weekly Journal*, Wednesday, Feb. 28, 1827.

greater glory and importance. Fitzball tells of the way in which the better authors and the better scene painters, including Stanfield himself, brought the minor playhouses "to a pitch of grandeur and excellence, little or never anticipated by old stagers."

The theatres, in their interior, became so magnificent as to elicit both wonder and astonishment; the Surrey Theatre being, at one time, decorated with gold and velvet, a Genoa velvet curtain covering the stage. The Coburg...decorated with one sunny glitter of gold braided mirrors, with a superb looking-glass curtain, which drew up and let down in the sight of the audience, and reflected every form and face in that gorgeous house[1].

Show and spectacle, then, were the order of the day at both camps. Fitzball's own drama of *The Flying Dutchman* (Adel. 1827) was, according to its author, "not by any means behind even Frankenstein, or Der Freischütz itself in horrors and blue fire[2]." Such sights delighted

> In this hobgoblin'd and be-spectre'd age,
> Where all that's wond'rous occupies the stage:
> Where oceans foam without a single wave,
> And colour'd beards enchant that never shave...
> Where living objects, too, supply our wants,
> Cows, camels, steeds, pigs, apes, and elephants![3]

The "living objects" were both plentifully introduced and plentifully satirised in the period. Reynolds' *The Caravan* (D.L. 1803) brought success to Drury Lane at a moment of impending disaster, not by reason of its characters or its wit, but because a real dog, Carlos, after a good deal of coaxing, was persuaded nightly to rescue a heroine from a tank of water. Fitzball introduced into *Paul Clifford* (C.G. 1835) "a stage coach, and six *real* horses, determined to have a *run* of some kind[4]." During the rehearsals of *Thalaba the Destroyer* (C.G. 1836) Osbaldistone, the manager, told the author that he

had *luckily*...engaged *superior* strength....He told me, with a gust of satisfaction, that he had engaged the Burmah bulls,

---

[1] E. Fitzball, *op. cit.* i. v–vi.   [2] *Op. cit.* i. 169.
[3] T. J. Dibdin's *Of Age To-morrow* (D.L. 1800), Prologue.
[4] *Op. cit.* ii. 24.

elephants, ostriches, I think, and heaven knows what besides, from the Surrey Zoological Gardens[1].

Nor were these by any means uncommon. It is certainly at no rare intervals that we run across notices such as the following in the daily and monthly press:

An oriental spectacle, entitled, *Hyder Ali, or the Lions of Mysore*, was this evening produced, in which the principal actors were the inhabitants of the menagerie at Paris[2].

All efforts were made to secure novelty. Mazurier, a French pantomimic actor, had made a hit in *Jocko, ou le Singe de Brézil*, and was engaged by Kemble for Covent Garden, where, in *Jocko, or, The Brazilian Monkey* (C.G. 1825), he won such unmeasured applause that Planché could make Success, the heroine of his "revue," *Success* (Adel. 1825), declare that "A monkey...is the man for me!"—

> There's fifty young men have told me their fine tales,
> And called me their fairest she;
> But of all the gay fellows that sport on the green,
> Young Jocko's the lad for me.
> He tumbles and capers, and climbs up a tree;
> He scratches himself with his toes;
> He looks to a monkey as like as can be,
> When he puts on his pasteboard nose!

Satire of the introduction of such attractions was, apparently, indulged in also by Colman in his *Quadrupeds of Quedlinburgh* (H.[2] 1811), based on Canning's *The Rovers*. Quite naturally, under these conditions, the playwright became of less importance than the machinist. Moncrieff in the Advertisement to his *Zoroaster* (D.L. 1824) explains that

the necessity of transposing, curtailing, and lengthening many Scenes of this Piece, to suit the capabilities of carpenters and scene-shifters, nearly wholly deprived it of any pretensions to Dramatic construction it might originally have possessed.

---

[1] *Op. cit.* ii. 81–2.
[2] *The Gentleman's Magazine*, Nov. 1831, regarding a production at Drury Lane on Oct. 17, 1831.

We can understand for what audiences went to this play
when we read a stage direction in the first act:

The back part of the Scene disappears, and discovers

THE

ΕΙΔΟΦΥΣΙΚΟΝ,

or,

Καλοσκηνητεκνηφυσικινεων

[which includes] The Great Desert by Twilight; A Caravan of
Merchants; The Pyramids; The Great Temple of Apollinopolis
Magna; The Colossus of Rhodes; Mount Vesuvius by Moonlight;
The Grand Falls of Tivoli; The City of Babylon; The Destruction
of Babylon——

the directions and description occupy four closely printed
pages. Few there were who could repeat Dimond's declaration:

> No scenic shew he boasts to bribe the eye;
> No dance, procession, elephant and car,
> No ghost, no dungeon, no alarms of war[1].

Dimond, and a few others, such as the author of *My Uncle
Gabriel* (D.L. 1824), who would not indulge in the aid of "*a
matchless stud of horses, splendid scenery*" or "*costly dresses,*"
might endeavour "to return to those golden days, when a
good Tragedy or Comedy, followed by a lively Farce, used
to gratify the Patrons of the Drama[2]." Even Shakespeare
had to bow to the prevailing mood and spirit of the time.
Bunn, in his work *The Stage: Both before and behind the
Curtain* (1840), comments on the attractiveness of Stanfield's
"Pictorial Illustrations" to *Henry V*[3]. In *The Tempest*
Macready had an Ariel who

floated in air across the stage, singing or mocking as she floated—
while a chorus of spirits winged after her higher in the air. Now
amidst the terrors of the storm she *flamed amazement*; now with
the gentle descent of a protecting god she hung over the slumbers
of Gonzalo.... The masque is given as Shakespeare wrote it,
with beautiful landscapes, brown and blue, such as Titian would
have beheld with pleasure[4].

---

[1] *The Sea-Side Story* (C.G. 1801), Prologue.
[2] Address to the reader.   [3] iii. 102–3.
[4] Quotation from *The Examiner* in W. Archer, *W. C. Macready*,
p. 119.

There were adverse critics, of course, some blaming the public, some the managers. In his Advertisement to *The Antiquary* (C.G. 1820) Daniel Terry is quite frank about the matter, confessing that

how materially the Artist and Machinist contributed to the support of this piece, is manifest by the applause bestowed upon Scenery, justly entitled to the highest praise for appropriate beauty of design and uncommon excellence of execution.

If the public thus applauded scenic effects, the rhetorical question in *The Covent Garden Journal*[1] does not seem to be justified. "Who," asks the author, "who called upon [the managers] to produce their Pizarros, their Blue-Beards, their Sleeping Beauties, and Cinderellas?" The answer, I fear, must be—the British Public.

The chief charge against the managers is on the score of rivalry. Rivalry arises usually in an endeavour to secure an audience, but even in Garrick's time there had been a not very dignified struggle over *Romeo and Juliet* which left the spectators disgusted[2]. In this half-century the struggles were continuous and bitter. "Rivalry," says *The Theatrical Repertory*[3], "has already commenced at the two theatres... Braham and Storace, are to play at Covent Garden, against Mrs Billington, the nights she performs at Drury Lane, and it is reported Madame Mara, is to stand forward at Drury-lane, when Mrs B. appears at the other house." "According to the courteous custom which has prevailed time out of mind in English theatricals," Planché tells us,

an Easter piece on the subject of "Oberon" had been rushed out at Drury Lane in anticipation of Weber's opera, and, in addition to this, Bishop was engaged to write an opera to be produced in opposition to it, the libretto by George Soane being founded on the popular story of "Aladdin, or the Wonderful Lamp[4]."

Some older writers looked back upon a—perhaps not very accurate—vision of past times. "We then had a stage,"

---

[1] i. 28.
[2] See *A History of English Drama*, iii. 45.
[3] No. ii. S. 26/9/1801.
[4] J. R. Planché, *Recollections* (1872), i. 86. On this question of rivalry see T. J. Dibdin, *Reminiscences* (1827), ii. 208–11.

thought Fitzball[1], "now we have not. The reason is obvious—
there were then certain people for certain things, and certain
theatres for certain performances: everyone had a chance.
Now they seem always on the look-out to snap up each other's
ideas, to eat up each other's thoughts." Chapter IV of Bunn's
third volume of *The Stage* is headed "War, war, no peace,"
and under Dec. 3, 1838, he notes that his production of
William Tell "was attempted to be forestalled and injured
by another of those disgraceful efforts which had been made
the preceding season at Covent Garden Theatre, in the
instance of *Joan of Arc*[2]." The public, or at least a certain
part of the public—perhaps not uninfluenced by pecuniary
associations—banded themselves into parties, so that there
were Drury Lane and Covent Garden "party-men," and
ordinary members of an audience on first nights might hear
the cries of "Turn out those noisy fellows from Drury Lane"
and *vice versa*[3]. Sometimes the rivalry failed, as when *The
Love Charm*, which had been hurriedly rushed to performance in order to forestall *Fra Diavolo* at Covent Garden,
was damned, but, successful or not, the "absurd and illiberal
opposition" persisted. Obviously it is necessary to take this
wide-spread rivalry into account both when we are studying
the repertoires of the various houses and when we are
occupied with the spectacular tendencies in the theatres of the
time.

From the earlier stage the nineteenth century adopted
a certain limited number of conventions, but many of these,
as decades passed by, were ignored or were supplanted by
others. The ancient practice of giving out a play endured till
the close of the half-century. "The drama was announced by
Mr C. Kemble for repetition with applause[4]," is a typical
record of the time, and the persistence of the custom gives
point to a criticism on one of Fitzball's early dramas, that he
had

displayed a precosity of tact by leaving one person living at

---

[1] *Op. cit.* i. 85–6.   [2] *Op. cit.* iii. 111.
[3] R. B. Peake, *op. cit.* ii. 363.
[4] *The Dramatic Magazine* (1829), p. 19.

the end of [his] tragedies, to give out the play for the ensuing night[1].

So, too, died slowly the convention of the prologue. In 1842 Robert Bell, trying to imitate an older style in his comedy of *Marriage* (H.[2] 1842), tacked on to it a prologue, but its wording shows clearly that it was an unusual performance:

> The good old custom of an elder day,
> When Prologue raised the curtain to the play,
> And sprightly Epilogue came tittering after,
> To draw it down again with roars of laughter,
> Has been abandoned in this railroad age,
> That you might steam more quickly o'er the stage.

Nearly two decades before Bell's time, George Croly had voted the prologue

> a horrid great bore
> Half a puff for the House, half a rant for the Nation;
> In short,—'tis—a *Prologue*. A grand Botheration![2]

There is some question, it seems, concerning the dramatist to whom we should give the credit for first boldly daring a pit with an unprologued play. Saxe Wyndham in his records of Covent Garden[3] gives the palm to Miss Mitford, instancing her *Julian* (C.G. 1823), yet Planché, who, conceited as he was, did not often bear borrowed feathers, distinctly states that the first drama to abandon the practice was his own *A Woman never Vext* (C.G. 1824), adding some apparently realistic details concerning the episode:

> At one of the last rehearsals Fawcett asked me if I had written a prologue. "No." "A five-act play, and no prologue!—they'll tear up the benches!" They did nothing of the sort. The play... was a great success, and the custom for prologues to
>
> > "—Precede the piece in mournful verse,
> > As undertakers strut before the hearse,"
>
> was broken through for the first time, without the slightest notice being taken of it by the public[4].

---

[1] E. Fitzball, *op. cit.* i. 59. On this now vanished convention see Clement Scott, *The Drama of Yesterday and Today* (1899), i. 72. The practice is still in being among the recently revived "tent theatres" of the American Middle West.

[2] *Pride shall have a Fall* (C.G. 1824), Prologue. Already in 1804 we find this tendency; in that year Holt introduced a "Prelude" instead of a prologue in his *The Land We Live In* (D.L. 1804).

[3] ii. 24.   [4] *Recollections* (1872), i. 63.

The probability is that the credit must be shared by a number of daring spirits and that there was a general feeling about the middle of this period that the prologue and the epilogue had run their day.

The same conflict between traditionalism and the spirit of a new age is to be seen in the attitude of the period towards the proscenium doors. An attempt to remove them was made on the rebuilding of Drury Lane at the close of the first decade, but actors' prejudices demanded their return. By 1822, however, they had gone once more, and Colman's address written for the reopening of the theatre draws attention to the innovation:

> Nor blame him [the manager] for transporting from his floors
> Those old offenders here—the two stage doors—
> Doors which have, oft', with burnish'd panels stood,
> And golden knockers, glitt'ring in a wood;
> Which on their posts, through every change remained,
> Fast as Bray's Vicar, whosoever reign'd;
> That served for Palace, Cottage, Street, or Hall—
> Used for each place, and out of place in all;
> Station'd, like watchmen, who in lamp-light sit,
> For all the business of the night unfit[1].

Gradually the apron crept back. Still we may get the old-fashioned stage directions:

> Mrs HAMILTON, *discovered sitting in a musing posture, after a pause, rises and comes forward*[2]—

yet the action of dramas was slowly but surely moving behind the proscenium pillars. The age of the picture-frame stage has come.

The question of the actual scenic effects in these theatres is a large one, and one concerning which there is much more information to be gathered than that which may be brought together to illustrate the eighteenth century stage. No detailed analyses can be entered into here; for those reference must be made to other volumes; but an attempt may be

---

[1] *The Theatrical Observer* of Oct. 16, 1822, draws attention to the fact that, with the removal of the doors, the actors were more blended with the scenery than they had been in earlier times.

[2] Marianne Chambers' *The School for Friends* (D.L. 1805), II. (i).

made to indicate at least a few of the more peculiar and influential of the movements of the time[1]. The age teems with great scene painters, who, be it observed, by no means confined their activities to Drury Lane and to Covent Garden alone. The great Stanfield worked for the minor theatres, as did the Grieves. Roberts, Charles Marshall, Tomkins, Wilson ably supported their still more talented colleagues, achieving what must often have been real beauty, and devising new methods of securing their effects. It must not, of course, be imagined that the results were always fine. In the early years of the period they were often exceedingly clumsy and even by 1850 no sort of perfection had been attained. As an illustration, two or three excerpts may be made from *The Theatrical Repertory*:

We could not help smiling on observing that the scene on the Sierra de Ronda presented nothing but barren rocks, without a tree or shrub, although Sadi says, "there are eatables on every bush"; and the front of the Goatherd's cottage, instead of the residence of humble poverty, wore the semblance of the stone front of a superb monastery, with the figure of St Dominick in a niche over the door...[2].

New scenery; though by the by, the latter article is often *vox et preterea nihil*, for although it be a standing line at the bottom of the Advertisement of almost every new production, he must have keen eyes who can discover, except in a pantomime, above two scenes out of twenty, that have not slept in the scene-room, or become familiar to the sight, for several years past...[3].

Even the Scene-shifters seem ashamed of the cause which calls forth their exertion.... The wings representing woods, are pushed on to the flat of a chambre, and so *vice versa*...[4].

Some illuminated boats are introduced at the close of the Opera, which came down the stage. We could not but smile at the invention—they display astonishing mechanical powers—The painted canvases intended to represent the waves, have the

---

[1] G. C. D. Odell in his *Shakespeare from Betterton to Irving* has sections on the staging of this period, and something is said of it in my *Development of the Theatre* (1927). Contemporary accounts are innumerable; among them might be mentioned G. Scharf, *Scenic Effects at Covent Garden* (1838).

[2] No. VIII. S. 7/11/1801, regarding *The Mountaineers* at Drury Lane.

[3] No. XXII. M. 15/2/1802.

[4] No. XXIII. M. 22/2/1802, regarding *The Pirates* at Drury Lane.

appearance of the bottom part of double doors left on their hinges, which very conveniently open for the boats to pass[1].

Leigh Hunt found the same weaknesses in contemporary settings, and noted

The alteration of scene, so badly managed at the theatre, where you see two men running violently towards each other, with half a castle or a garden in their grasp[2].

These notes may serve to indicate the failures of the time. The words of Leigh Hunt and of the editor of *The Theatrical Repertory* are amply supported by other contemporary evidence, for audiences were growing more critical now, and were less inclined to let pass those many inconsistencies which had seemed but natural to their forefathers. If theatrical managements did not keep abreast of the popular demand, that simply indicated, first, the gradual growth of this desire for consistency and for realism, and, secondly, the impoverishment of the playhouses which could not at once bring the new methods full-formed into operation. The ways of the early producers are well indicated by the manuscript notes, evidently from the hand of a prompter, in the Harvard Library copy of Pocock's *Woodstock* (C.G. 1826), and these notes form a fitting commentary upon the critical passages quoted above. In the second scene of the first act of this play we discover a demand for "Madge Wildfires Cot—Hovel Wings 3^d Gr^s [3]." After a "Library" with "Gothic Wings" and an "Antique Chamber" with similar wings, we get "Magpie Cottage," which, I suggest, is simply the stock setting taken from the chief scene of Pocock's *The Magpie, or the Maid*, originally produced at Covent Garden in 1815 but retained for years in the regular repertory. Indication of the same practice is provided in the peculiar printed list of "Scenery and Properties" given at the beginning of Peake's *The Three Wives of Madrid* (Lyc. 1844). These obviously come from the prompter, and for their interest some at least may be quoted here. The first scene in act I is described in the

---

[1] No. xxiii. M. 22/2/1802, regarding *The Cabinet* at Covent Garden.
[2] *Critical Essays* (1807), p. 22.
[3] "Gr^s " obviously stands for "Grooves."

text as "*A beautiful Public Garden*"; in the list it is given as "Telbin's Garden in the Panorama Groove. Fountain in front. Basin in front of fountain." Evidently, as in days gone by, special flats came to be known by the names of their artists, and Telbin is immortalised here as Harvey was in an eighteenth century inventory[1]. "*A Chamber in the House of* GELOSO" in the second scene is marked as "Yeoman's Daughter, chamber 1st groove"; in other words the chamber scene from one of the *Yeoman's Daughter* plays is set immediately behind the proscenium pillars. Perhaps the "*Exterior of the villa of Diego de Morales*" (scene iii) was specially painted, for its description is more detailed: "Stone house and wing to join wing 2nd; wing groove. House oblique to join do. Window piece in 3rd flat grooves. Mill landscape in panorama groove." The next scene, however, introduces us to an old friend. In the text the locality indicated is "*A chamber in the house of* NICHOLAS. *Table, &c.*," but the prompter carries us off to Eastcheap with his "Boar's head, flats, 1st grooves." In the second scene of act II the "*Room in the House of* GELOSO" is once more the "Yeoman's Daughter" but with the "chamber removed to the 3rd groove," while the final picture, which should be "*A Cemetry belonging to* ISIDORE'S *Monastery*," is simply the "Last scene of Romeo and Juliet, tomb, &c."

In spite of the repetitional use of stock flats and wings, however, and in spite of a certain clumsiness of effect, this age theatrically was an age of innovation. The introduction of gas meant that new devices could be employed undreamt of before. Candles, it is true, along with the ever-faithful lamps, continued at the Haymarket till 1843[2], while at Covent Garden and Drury Lane there were still qualms about the use of gas at the end of the second decade of the period[3]. At first the experiment was tried only in the auditorium[4],

---

[1] See *A History of English Drama*, iii. 31.
[2] See a bill of Friday, March 28, 1843, quoted in Clement Scott, *op. cit.* i. 5.
[3] On this subject see G. C. D. Odell, *Shakespeare from Betterton to Irving* (1921), ii. 157, and E. B. Watson, *op. cit.* pp. 92–5.
[4] At the Olympic in 1815.

and then, later, the new form of lighting was carried to the stage[1]. Complaints were made regarding the danger, the odour and the colour of this illuminant, but, once managers realised the ease with which the gas-taps could be manipulated, there was opened up the possibility of great scenic advance; gas had come to remain until its later rival, electricity, disestablished it in our own times. It must not be thought, of course, that the introduction of gas in itself led to any very great changes. Ample contemporary evidence is available to show that, for the greater part of this period, the auditorium remained fully illuminated during the performance of a play, and that a fierce glare of light ascended from the footlights to make deep upward shadows on the countenances of the performers. On the other hand, gas is a more manageable illuminant than either candles or lamps, and we must presume at least a certain progressive development in the art of theatre lighting. Perhaps too much may be made of those who, critical by nature, saw fit to animadvert against the ways of the producers.

In other respects, at least, the early nineteenth century proved itself ambitious and experimental. Scenic devices which had already been tried tentatively in the preceding age were now brought to perfection. Thus the use of gauze, known to Loutherbourg and his successors, appears more frequently than before for the purpose of securing pleasant effects. In Planché's *Telemachus* (Olym. 1834), Calypso

waves her sceptre—Music—A gauze to imitate smoke covers the stage . . music—Gauze rises and discovers the figure of ULYSSES *leaning on a pedestal.*

Similarly in a pantomime performed at Covent Garden Prince Pückler-Muskau describes "a thick mist" covering the stage "and gradually rolling off." "This," he says, "is remarkably well managed by means of fine gauze[2]." "Practicable Mountains" is the heading to the ninth scene of Cross's

[1] Drury Lane introduced auditorium and stage lighting by gas in 1817.
[2] *A Tour in England of a German Prince* (1832), iii. Letter 7.

Rinaldo Rinaldini (R.C. 1801), and we know from prints and from other stage directions that Loutherbourg's innovations in this way were eagerly followed by many scenic artists[1]. The age, however, had passed far beyond Loutherbourg; its panoramic and interior effects could never have been dreamt of in the preceding century. The old Eidophusikon, it is true, still continued its career[2], but it was outdone by other and more startling devices. The panoramic effects were specially popular. In September 1823 Daguerre and Bouton first exhibited their diorama in Regent's Park, the device being patented the following year in the name of J. Arrowsmith[3]. Apparently the diorama presented in a kind of optical illusion a series of pictures which were moved either on separate canvases or on the roller system. The lighting employed was borrowed from the Eidophusikon. Both in its elaborated form and in the simpler panorama system the diorama was used freely in the theatres. Thus a stage direction from Planché's *Paris and London* (Adel. 1828) describes the scene as the

Deck of the Steamer—Moving Panoramic View from Calais to Dover, by various Painted Flats to the Scene[4].

We can almost hear the rollers creaking and look into the rapt eyes of the spectators.

This burletta of Planché's furnishes us with another interesting description. The fifth scene of act I is

A Diagonal View of the Stage of the Odeon...seen through the wings—the proscenium boxes, L.—at the end of the float a section of the audience and part of the theatre is visible...the sham curtain falls, amidst applause from behind, and the characters advance through the wings to the front of the real stage.

This, truly, is a modern effect, but even its revolutionary tendencies are outshadowed by the setting of Fitzball's *Jonathan Bradford* (Surrey, 1833), where the interiors of four rooms were placed upon the stage at one time[5]. It is said

---

[1] See *A History of English Drama*, iii. 29.
[2] See *id.* p. 27. *Supra*, p. 27, and G. C. D. Odell, *op. cit.* ii. 164-5.
[3] Patent No. 4899.   [4] II. iv.
[5] See E. Fitzball, *op. cit.* i. 238-40.

that Fitzball had been anticipated by Colman, who had shown two rooms simultaneously in *The Actor of All Work* (H.[2] 1817)[1]; he was certainly followed by Edward Stirling, in whose *Above and Below* (Lyc. 1846) two floors were presented on the stage. Whoever was responsible for its introduction, we realise that we are well on the way to modern times. The setting of Eugene O'Neill's *Desire under the Elms* is at least a century old. It will be noticed that both Fitzball and Planché worked largely for the minor theatres, and it is once more at a minor—Astley's Royal Amphitheatre —that we find another interesting innovation. When that house reopened on Monday, March 23, 1818, after "improvements," it displayed "a contracted and progressive extension of the New Proscenium, which with the stage doors will move and remove in sight of the audience[2]." Here, instead of O'Neill, we are reminded of Germany and Reinhardt.

One might continue enumerating the various stage inventions of the period, drawing attention to device after device which, like Fitzball's "vampire-trap[3]," have continued as stock machines, but such innovation in regard to stage appurtenances is really of less importance than the gradually altering tendency in the sphere of scenic design. Already in the late eighteenth century there had been movements towards realism of setting and towards a certain historical accuracy[4]; but these movements up to 1800 had been but feebly tentative. It is clear that this period opened with a scenic art which was largely conventional and largely inconsistent. Such devices as the diorama, however, were teaching men the art of the realistic setting, so far at least as landscape was concerned, and Capon continued his archæo-

---

[1] It seems also that two cells with a partition appeared in Lewis' *Venoni* at Drury Lane in 1808.

[2] Note from the playbill.

[3] The "vampire-trap" was a two-leaved trap, with springs, constructed either on the stage floor or in the flats. It permitted a supernatural figure to disappear more rapidly than the older traps had allowed, the springs drawing the two leaves of the trap-door close once more and so concealing the aperture.

[4] See *A History of English Drama*, iii. 29–30, and *The Development of the Theatre* (1927), pp. 174–6.

logical researches, translating these to terms of the stage. Slowly, but surely, the older conventionality began to disappear; its place came to be occupied by spectacular, historically "accurate," settings for tragedies placed in the past and by "realistic" interiors for modern comedies. The full development of these tendencies does not, of course, arrive until the Shakespearian productions of Charles Kean and the comedies of Robertson in the fifties and sixties of the century, but a great deal had already been accomplished even before 1850. Planché was interested in more than costume; he sought at once to give distinction, accuracy and realistic effect to the scenes of his later plays, and his efforts began to be copied by other theatrical workers of the time. "A beautifully painted plafond...lighted by an immense skylight" is distinctly mentioned by *The Theatrical Observer*[1] in referring to the Drury Lane production of Bunn's *The Minister and the Mercer* (D.L. 1834), showing that the full box-set, with ceiling complete, had been evolved by 1834. This was a "royal" apartment, but a similar movement is to be traced also in the setting for humbler interiors. Mathews and Vestris, who had been originally responsible for many of the changes in scenery and costume, evidently caused a stir when in 1841 they produced Boucicault's *London Assurance* (C.G. 1841) at Covent Garden, using there "not stage properties, but *bona fide* realities[2]." The domestic melodrama, too, must be held responsible for a further change of tone, scenes such as those presented in Buckstone's *Luke the Labourer* (Adel. 1826) calling for a very different setting than had been accorded to the "genteel" comedies of the eighteenth century. In every way we see an approach towards modern ideas and modern conventions. It is in this period that the detailed "accuracy" of later producers found, if not its birth, at least its boyhood. J. P. Kemble, with his passion for Shakespeare, endeavoured to set and dress the plays more carefully than had ever been done before. We need not stop to argue that Kemble's "accuracy" was often exceedingly inaccurate; the important point is

[1] Feb. 10, 1834.   [2] *Id.* March 5, 1841.

that his aim was in the direction of later effort. In achievement he may have failed, but the lordly mantle he wore was assumed by all his successors. Macready, perhaps with not such whole-hearted enthusiasm but at least dominated by popular predilections, continued in the same path, and the task was brought to completion in the very midst of the century by Charles Kean, who, almost more of an archæologist than an actor, ransacked every available "authority" for materials on which to work. Even the botany in his scenes was historically correct[1]. Nor must we assume that these endeavours were confined to the major theatres and the better-known managers. Already it has been seen how the tendency towards realism in comedy owed much to the Olympic, and when we read that T. J. Dibdin for the Surrey production of his *Heart of Midlothian* "consulted every well-authenticated accessible authority for the *vrai costume*[2]," we realise how far the new movement had penetrated. A new type of historical accuracy, too, was born, or at least suggested in this period. The eighteenth century had imagined the costuming of a *Henry V* in garments not too far distant from those worn in that monarch's reign; it was left to the following century to imagine the performance of old plays in what at least purported to be the original methods of production. We thus hear of a semi-Grecian rendering of a Sophoclean drama and of the presentation of an Elizabethan play without the usual scenery, curtains being employed to give something of that effect which even this period realised belonged to Shakespeare's theatre. Even at Edinburgh, in 1847, the scene for Garrick's *Catherine and Petruchio* was "laid in the Baron's Hall, fitted up for a temporary theatre as in the days of yore[3]." Not only Irving, but William Poel, was anticipated before 1850. It is impossible in this volume to do more than outline general tendencies, but, from such few facts as have been given, it must be apparent how "modern" were becoming the views of the age. In this

---

[1] See *The Development of the Theatre*, p. 193.
[2] T. J. Dibdin, *Reminiscences* (1827), ii. 179.
[3] J. C. Dibdin, *The Annals of the Edinburgh Stage* (1888), p. 407.

connection it is interesting to note that it is in this period
we first hear of the fourth wall[1]. Speaking of Bannister,
Leigh Hunt informs us that

the stage appears to be his own room, of which the audience
compose the fourth wall: if they clap him, he does not stand still
to enjoy their applause[2].

Truly are we standing here on the threshold of the twentieth
century.

Costume kept steady pace with this scenic art, which
aimed, now at spectacle, now at realism, now at historical
accuracy. Already in the eighteenth century attempts had
been made to clothe the Shakespearian plays in a fitting
manner; Macklin and Garrick, aided by such artists as Capon,
had set an ideal which all later managers to Irving's time
were to follow. For several decades of the nineteenth century,
of course, there were serious lapses from perfection. In 1801,
at Covent Garden, *Richard III* came upon the stage

headed with a Grecian casque and plume of feathers, and wearing
glaves or gauntlets, with a corselet. The casque had more sense
than the property man who invented it, for it was ashamed of its
post, and fell off Richard's head in his second scene of the act[3].

Professor Odell chronicles the failures as well as the successes
of J. P. Kemble's efforts[4], which, in spite of many inconsistencies, were the first real attempts to secure upon the
stage the semblance of historical accuracy. In order to
understand aright both the general movement of the time
and the results secured, we must turn to J. R. Planché's
interesting *Recollections*. "In 1872," he says,

it may surprise many persons to learn that forty or fifty years ago
our greatest painters, poets, and novelists were, as far as regarded
a correct idea of the civil and military costume of our ancestors,
involved in Cimmerian darkness. To Sir Walter Scott the honour
is due of having first attracted public attention to the advantages
derivable from the study of such subjects, as a new source of
effect as well as of historical illustration[5].

---

[1] The first reference to this term—as those to many others discussed
here—in the *N.E.D.* is very much later than that given here.
[2] *Op. cit.* p. 60. [3] *The Theatrical Repertory*, No. VI. S. 24/10/1801.
[4] *Op. cit.* ii. 98–101. [5] i. 224.

That this statement is fundamentally true we have no reason to doubt; indeed, as will be indicated later, Scott's influence in the direction of "Götzism" upon the theatre of his time cannot be over-exaggerated. The actual achievement, however, both in drama and in scenic art, he left to other men. In 1823, Planché tells us, he had a casual conversation with Kemble respecting a production of *King John*. After Planché had pointed out to the manager the inconsistencies in previous performances of Shakesperian plays,

> Mr Kemble admitted the fact, and perceived the pecuniary advantage that might result from the experiment. It was decided that I should make the necessary researches, design the dresses, and superintend the production of "King John," *gratuitously*, I beg leave to say....That I was the original cause of this movement [towards historical accuracy] is certain[1].

King John, therefore, produced at Covent Garden on Monday, Jan. 19, 1824, and *Henry IV*, produced on Thursday, May 6 of the same year, were duly billed as being re-dressed, and the advertisements gave ample space to a list of "Authorities for the Costumes." One may note, in Planché's account, the reference to Kemble's recognition of "the pecuniary advantage" to be derived from the innovation. Indeed, the author informs us that

> receipts of from 400*l*. to 600*l*. nightly soon reimbursed the management for the expense of the production[2].

Boldly, H. G. Tomlins in his *A Brief View of the English Stage* (1840) declares that

> "Correctness of costume" was a phrase invented to excuse pageantry, as was "accuracy of locality" for spectacle. 'Hamlet,' 'Lear,' 'Macbeth,' 'Coriolanus,' 'The Tempest,' 'Othello,' 'Henry the Fifth' were now "revived[3]."

Unquestionably, although Planché himself was sincere, the Kembles indulged in the new fashion, partly because it allowed them to rival the spectacles of the minor theatres while still crying their watchword of "Shakespeare and Legitimate Drama," partly because they realised, from the

---

[1] Planché, *op. cit.* i. 52–7.   [2] *Op. cit.* p. 57.   [3] *Op. cit.* p. 79.

box-office receipts, that the age as a whole, sharing the general romantic fervour, was full of a desire to see these past ages brought upon the stage realistically. The "conventional dress" of Mrs Siddons, which Planché ridicules, was out of favour. Indeed, in spite of the gorgeous spectacle indulged in by the Kembles, the Keans and the Irvings, we are not far from the efforts of the present day. It is to be observed that Planché himself would have preferred *King John* "or any other play...acted in plain evening dress" rather than performed in the Augustan modes of the past age, and that the close of this period saw the production of *The Taming of the Shrew*, in a modified "Elizabethan" setting, the actors playing against curtains and title-boards[1]. For the moment, however, Shakespeare in modern dress is but a fanciful dream and Elizabethan staging only a peculiar experiment; the period is dominated by the desire for historical accuracy and splendour. Even in a "fairy extravaganza," Planché's *The Invisible Prince* (H.[2] 1846), "the Amazonian Guards of the Princess" have to be "dressed and armed... from accurate drawings of Mexican costumes as published in the magnificent work of Lord Kingston[2]." This is from the close of the period; how realism was used in the service of spectacle in earlier years is not unamusingly illustrated in the bills issued by Sadler's Wells Theatre during April and May 1804 for a show entitled Ὠκεάνια, otherwise known as *The Siege of Gibraltar*. This performance, we are told, was

a grand Naval Spectacle, presenting that memorable monument of British Glory, the Siege of Gibraltar; with an exact representation of the armament both by Land and Sea, of the combined forces of France and Spain, with real Men of War and Floating Batteries, built and rigged by professional men from his Majesty's Dock Yards, and which float in a receptacle containing nearly 8000 cubic feet of real water[2].

Evidently it was considered by the management advisable to emphasise still further the accuracy of the show, for on

[1] See Clement Scott, *op. cit.* i. 74, and *supra*, p. 39.
[2] *Note on the Costumes*.
[3] Bill of Monday, April 2.

May 28 the bills altered their wording for the purpose of drawing attention to the

real ships of 100, 74, and 60 guns, &c. built, rigged, and manœuvred in the most correct manner, as every nautical character who has seen them implicitly allows, which work down with the wind on their starboard beam, wear and haul the wind on their larboard tacks, to regain their situations, never attempted at any Theatre in this or any other country: the ships firing their broadsides, the conflagration of the town in various places, the defence of the garrison, and attack by the floating batteries, is so faithfully and naturally represented, that when the floating batteries take fire, some blowing up with a dreadful explosion, and others, after burning to the water's edge, sink to the bottom; while the gallant Sir Roger Curtis appears in his boat to save the drowning Spaniards, the British tars for that purpose plunging into the water, the effect is such as to produce an unprecedented climax of astonishment and applause.

These two extracts indicate well the theatrical tendencies of the time. Everything must be spectacular, must be correct, must be decorous—for "many persons disliked the appearance" of "naked feet represented (in silk fleshings, of course)" even in a Greek tragedy of *Orestes* at Covent Garden[1]. We are near, yet far, from the twentieth century.

The note regarding this wonderful Ὠκεάνια[2] has led us somewhat away from the subject of costume, but its obvious insistence on naturalism may serve to emphasise the importance of studying, in the realm of stage dress, that movement which accompanied archæological precision. If this historical accuracy had a considerable influence on tragedy and melodrama, comedy unquestionably was guided and admonished by the simpler naturalistic effects.

Comedy in general has and had nothing to do with costumes of the past, and the gradual adoption of un-exaggerated garments *à la mode* had probably as great an influence as had the other in the tragic sphere. Prints and

---

[1] E. Fitzball, *op. cit.* i. 69.

[2] That the realisation of effect was as fine or as "natural" as the word picture may be questioned. The "receptacle" for water at Sadler's Wells measured 40 feet by 100 feet, and, large as it was, hardly offered much room for a number of men of war, floating batteries and "et ceteras."

written records tell us surely enough that comic persons
in plays of the late eighteenth century and in the early
years of the nineteenth were characterised not only by
oddities of dress but by serious inconsistencies of garment,
while in the companion field, that of burlesque, exaggeration
was the rule unalterable. Coats of the Georgian period met
with pantaloons; rude contrasts were secured by the use of
the most blatant colouring; the low comedians clowned it,
not only in the delivery of their lines, but in the clothes they
assumed. The little sketches by Robert Cruickshank given
as frontispieces to some plays of the period were perhaps
not overfar from theatrical "nature." Again, the reform
instituted in the later years must be credited to J. R. Planché,
who, since he is an entertaining witness, may once more
be allowed to tell his own tale. It was the production of this
writer's *Olympic Revels* (Olym. 1831) which marked out an
epoch, and Planché declares that "the extraordinary success"
of his play "was due not only to the admirable singing and
piquante performance" of Vestris, "but also to the charm of
novelty imparted to it by the elegance and accuracy of the
costumes, it having been previously the practice to dress a
burlesque in the most *outré* and ridiculous fashion."

My suggestion to try the effect of persons picturesquely attired
speaking absurd doggerel, fortunately took the fancy of the fair
lessee, and the alteration was highly appreciated by the public,
but many old actors could never get over their early impressions.
Liston thought to the last that Prometheus, instead of the Phrygian
cap, tunic, and trousers, should have been dressed like a great
lubberly boy, in a red jacket and nankeens, with a pinafore all
besmeared with lollipops; others that, as in "Midas," the costume
should be an incongruous mixture of the classical and the farcical[1].

Directly, of course, this innovation led towards the further
development of historical accuracy, but indirectly it had its
influence upon comic dressing. Although Liston and his
contemporaries remained unconvinced, younger actors saw
that Planché's experiment was a success, and as a result they
were willing to put aside their low comedians' over-exag-

---

[1] *The Extravaganzas of J. R. Planché* (1879), i. 40–1.

gerated costumes in favour of others of a more "naturalistic" kind. Not at once was the reform effected, but within a few decades at least it became customary to habit a comedy in the prevailing garments of the period with no further oddities than might be met with in ordinary life. The effect of this change on drama must at once be appreciated. Neither a *Money* nor a *London Assurance* would have been possible in 1810. These, and other plays of a similar cast, were inspired by the new schools of scenic design, of costuming and of acting, both Lytton and Boucicault realising that there was now the possibility for the suitable interpretation of comedies based, not like the earlier comedy-farces upon theatrical types and conventions, but upon the manners and men of contemporary life. The stage Irishman, the stage butler, the stage friend with his blundering ways, all are with us yet in pale replica—relics of the past; but fundamentally we may say that the whole tendency of the writing of comedy since 1840 has been towards realism, and that tendency in its turn is dependent upon the gradual movements in scenic and in costume design which, traceable in the preceding century, first became dominant and popular in the age of Victoria.

It is interesting to notice how soon after Planché's experiment the newer style became acclimatised. We hear in 1820 of ridiculous combinations in the dress of different ages and nations, but when, about the thirties of the century, "D. G." set about to write an introduction for Cumberland's edition of Macfarren's *Lestocq*, based on the homonymous opera of Scribe, he saw fit to contrast favourably the English with the French setting. One can see from his words how closely the new realism and the popular spectacle were bound together in the contemporary mind:

The contracted size of the French theatres, and the parsimonious economy of their managers, forbid anything like a magnificent *spectacle*. Nothing can be more trumpery than their scenery and stage appointments; while their costume displays a heterogeneous jumble of all nations and times. A marble wig, stone helmet, steel waistcoat, and a pair of tin breeches for the ghost, would hardly astonish a Parisian audience.

This truly is a swinging back of the pendulum, and, even if we make some allowance for patriotic sentiment, we must believe that "the superadded charms of scenery and decoration so magnificently lavished upon *Lestocq* by the English manager" strove at least towards due correctness.

Naturally, with this elaboration of scenic and kindred effects, the curtain is brought into greater play than it was in past times. There are still plays which obviously move from scene to scene without its aid, but they are fewer in number than we may discover in the previous half-century. The stage directions to be found in Pocock's *Alfred the Great* (C.G. 1827) are almost unique: at the end of the first scene there is a note

[*March strikes up, and continues till the Stage is occupied in Scene the Second,*

while at the close of this scene, which represents a "Forest Country," the text runs

[*Music striking at the same time, which is continued in*

SCENE III.

Corfe Castle on an eminence.

The clicking flats of older times are mentioned in Hoskins' *De Valencourt* (Norwich, 1842):

Two side scenes close in, and hide the parties[1],

while in the extravaganza of *Valentine and Orson* (Lyc. 1844):

As the Chorus is going on, they rise and disperse about the Scene.... The flats close in[2].

References, however, to the curtain at the end of acts are now frequent. Thus the "*Curtain falls*" at the end of the first acts of Dimond's *Æthiop* (C.G. 1812) and *The Young Hussar* (D.L. 1807). With this use of the curtain must be associated that practice of final groupings and tableaux which is indicated in so many of the acting texts of the period. Perhaps *The Theatrical Repertory* is right in tracing the tradition to the German plays where

all the characters are arranged in a picturesque manner, and

---

[1] I. ii.　　　　　　　　　　　[2] I.

stand in fixed attitudes, like images on pedestals, when the curtain drops[1].

By the twenties of the century the "images on pedestals" had become thoroughly English. *"The Curtain falls upon the picture"* and *"The Characters form into a Picture of mute attention and the drop falls"* are two stage directions in Dimond's *The Bride of Abydos* (D.L. 1818), and *"all the characters dispose themselves into cheerful groups, when the Curtain falls"* is another from the same author's *The Peasant Boy* (Lyc. 1811). This tendency towards the tableau is itself part of the spectacular movement of the early nineteenth century and is to be connected, too, with the miming indulged in so freely by the makers and producers of the melodrama[2]. Those "pictures" were loved by the spectators almost as much as the dialogue and the dramatic action, and the more successful effects were loudly applauded. As some recent productions have demonstrated, the tradition is not dead even in our own days.

IV. *Actors, Authors, Managers and Publishers*

As regards acting talent the early nineteenth century was at once weak and strong. We can point to the Kembles and the Keans and the Robsons and find in the age a fine genius. We can peruse the dramatic reviews, and, noting the attention given to the performances, we can picture the age as an age of the actor. On the other hand, we may study certain other records of the half-century and discover a surprising lack of skill and originality, a sterile sameness which speaks of an age of decay. Above all, we may look at the actor-manager star system and see there elements of danger for the theatre. It is perfectly true that in previous periods dramatists had deliberately written tragedies and comedies for particular players; instances of this abound[3]; but usually the playwrights cast their gaze beyond one individual. Up to 1800

[1] No. IV. S. 10/10/1801.   [2] See *infra*, pp. 102–4.
[3] See *A History of English Drama*, i. 53–4; ii. 40–1; iii. pp. 39–41.

the stock companies, varying though they did from season to season, were comparatively constant, and an author would realise that, on taking his work to Drury Lane or to Covent Garden, a certain dozen performers would be used for his play. In the nineteenth century, the companies were constantly changing; a multitude of lesser stars, continually flashing up and flickering away, clustered round the planets of greater magnitude—the Keans and the Macreadys. When, therefore, Talfourd declares that he wrote his *Glencoe* (H.² 1840) and *The Athenian Captive* (H.² 1838) for Macready, we are to understand that for Macready and for Macready alone he wrote them. No thought of another performer would enter his mind. So Mathews is the predominating influence in Colman's mind when he pens *The Actor of All Work* (H.² 1817), and Kean and Kemble similarly dominate other dramas. The consequence of this, itself one of the causes of theatrical doctrine in the age, must be treated later[1]; here the bare facts alone must be noted. In addition to this, one may observe the carelessness with which even more important productions were prepared. The actor-manager was sure of his part, probably sure of his patronage among the audience, and as a result the rehearsals were permitted to take care of themselves. Perhaps the lesser actors, knowing that all eyes would be on the star, and losing heart, chose the primrose path of easy dalliance. At any rate, newspaper criticisms show us that frequently the ensemble of productions left much to be desired. The weaknesses of the star system are well outlined in a comment by William Archer upon Macready the manager. After noting the actor's "artistic scrupulousness," the biographer has to confess that

this artistic scrupulousness...was accompanied by a large amount of the inartistic unscrupulousness of the typical "star." His own part was everything; the opportunities of his fellow-actors, and even the poet's text, must all give place to the complete development of his effects. "When he played Othello," says George Vandenhoff, "Iago was to be *nowhere*!...Iago was a mere *stoker*, whose business it was to supply Othello's passion

---

[1] See *infra*, pp. 68–9.

with fuel, and keep up his high-pressure. The next night, perhaps, he took Iago; and lo! presto! everything was changed. Othello was to become a mere puppet for Iago to play with; a pipe for Iago's master-skill to 'sound from its lowest note to the top of its compass'." He would probably have glozed the egoism of this policy by arguing that the opportunities should be to him who can make use of them, and that, with country companies, it was useless to strive for an "all-round" effect. But the tendency, alas! was dominant whatever his surroundings. Even Fanny Kemble, as Lady Macbeth, had to sacrifice her legitimate opportunities to his self-aggrandizement[1].

The way of the ordinary actors was made the simpler because of the type-characterisation in so many dramas of the time, this type-characterisation being both a result and a cause of the methods of performance in the theatres. *The Actors' Hand-Book*, published by Dicks, although it is a "Guide to the Stage for Amateurs," provides us with much interesting information. At the very opening of this little pamphlet we are somewhat surprised to learn that "a good stock of tights, boots, hats, swords, &c., &c., often procures a young man an engagement when he could not obtain one on his merits[2]." This is truly an instance of clothes making the actor. And what is the actor? He is a man who must abstain from originality[3]; he is a man who must learn how to express some two-score emotions in a conventional manner. Thus rage demands

rapidity, interruption, rant, harshness, and trepidation. The neck is stretched out, the head forward, often nodding, and shaken in a menacing manner against the object of the passion...the mouth open, and drawn on each side towards the ears, showing the teeth in a gnashing posture; the feet often stamping; the right arm frequently thrown out and menacing, with the clenched fist shaken, and a general and violent agitation of the whole body[4].

One example is sufficient; there is no need to go through the pitys and the fears and the jealousies. We have seen enough to realise the conventionality imposed upon the ordinary performer, to see both the simplicity and the torture of his part.

[1] W. Archer, *W. C. Macready* (1890), pp. 210–11.
[2] p. 8.   [3] p. 26.   [4] p. 22.

If, however, the styles of acting were rapidly becoming more and more conventionalised, the audiences as a whole, probably because of the general weakness in dramatic effort, looked rather towards the histrionic performance than towards the piece presented. The constant backslidings of the drunken Cooke were easily forgiven because of this fact. Leigh Hunt in his *Critical Essays on the Performers of the London Theatres* (1807) has no doubt on the matter. "If any man," he says,

not very fond of music, will reflect a little between the acts of one of the modern comedies, he will find that his chief entertainment has arisen from the actors totally abstracted from the author[1].

The same critic then affords us a glimpse of the reflex influence upon dramatic authorship which this condition of affairs naturally induced. "The authors," he continues,

know this as well as anybody...If there is a countryman, it must be adapted to EMERY; if an Irishman, to JOHNSTONE; if a gabbling humourist, it must be copied from nothing but the manner of FAWCETT....The loss of LEWIS...whose gaiety of limb is of so much benefit to modern comedy, would be a perfect rheumatism to MR REYNOLDS; and the loss of MUNDEN, who gives it such an agreeable variety of grin, would affect him little less than a lock-jaw[2].

Should we need further proof regarding the interdependence of the drama and the stage in those years, we have only to listen a little more to Hunt's criticism:

If the principal characters of REYNOLDS and of DIBDIN are always out of nature, their representation...must be unnatural also; and as our comic actors are perpetually employed upon these punchinellos, as they are always labouring to grimace and grin them into applause, they become habituated and even partial to their antics, and can never afterwards separate the effect from the means, the applause from the unnatural style of acting[3].

This is putting the cart before the horse, it is true, but it serves to illustrate one great weakness in the period. Only in the very last decades of this period is a change to be discovered. Occasionally, in the earlier years, an individual such as Bannister seemed to reach a conception of art beyond

[1] Introduction, p. vi.　　　　[2] *Id.* pp. vii and viii.
[3] *Id.* p. 81.

that of his time[1], but it was not until the late thirties and the forties of the century that any general movement is to be traced towards a more naturalistic style of performance. This newer naturalistic style, of course, must be closely associated with the changes in stage settings and in costume designs. When Liston had to abandon his awkward boy's suit in burlesque[2], he had naturally to cultivate a style more in keeping with his new habiliments, and when the stock comic actor lost his inconsistent and crudely exaggerated garments he had to make himself appear what he now seemed, a man of real life and not a figure in a harlequinade. Realism may not be the highest type of theatrical art, but this realism had to be before anything of a higher type could be evolved on the stage. The expressionism of today is based on the realism of yesterday; it could not have been founded on the primitive and vulgar conventions of the early nineteenth century playhouses.

Turning from the actors to the authors themselves, we find once more ample causes for decline. It has been seen that throughout the course of the eighteenth century the income of the average dramatist was rising[3]. At first, it seemed as if the nineteenth century was to carry on this forward movement, but, in spite of the fact that the authors later won some hard-wrung privileges, the passing by of the earlier decades shows nothing but a retrograde movement. The records of Reynolds' life indicate clearly that the income derived from the dramatist from the theatre was, in the very first years, as good as, if not better than, that which a dramatist was accustomed to receive in 1790. For *The Caravan* (D.L. 1803), successful because of its dog and tank effect, this author received £350[4]; for a damned play and two successful afterpieces made out of the condemned material he got £740 in all[5]; £300 for *Out of Place* (C.G. 1805), £500 for *The Delinquent* (C.G. 1805), £500 for *Begone Dull Care* (C.G. 1808)[6], £600 for *The Exile* (C.G. 1808)[7] and £700

---

[1] See *supra*, p. 40.
[2] See *supra*, p. 44.
[3] See *A History of English Drama*, iii. 46–8.
[4] *Life and Times* (1823), ii. 351.
[5] *Id.* ii. 354.
[6] *Id.* ii. 365.
[7] *Id.* ii. 377.

for *The Free Knights* (C.G. 1810)[1] are thoroughly representative. In passing it is to be noted that the highest gains came from the afterpieces and from the musical three-act *Free Knights*, precisely those plays which, as Reynolds himself tells us, were the easiest to write. The effect of this can readily be imagined. Five-act comedies became rarer and rarer, the dramatic authors quite naturally preferring to earn their money by the less arduous paths of operatic farce and melodramatic spectacle. Dibdin's profits were about the same as those of Reynolds. In 1800 this author cleared £200 for his comedy *Liberal Opinions* (C.G. 1800)[2], £630 for the operatic *Family Quarrels* (C.G. 1802) in 1802[3], 300 guineas (and 60 guineas for the copyright) for *Thirty Thousand* (C.G. 1804) in 1804[4], £200 for the operatic *White Plume* (C.G. 1806) in 1806[5], £270 with a copyright free of £100 for the comedy *Five Miles Off* (H.[2] 1806)[6], and £300 with a copyright fee of £60 for the opera *Two Faces under a Hood* (C.G. 1807)[7]. The declining receipts, to be discussed later, are indicated by the fact that for *What Next?* (D.L. 1816) in 1816 Dibdin received only £100 with £40 for the copyright[8]. These records of Reynolds and Dibdin are corroborated by the notes provided by Peake concerning the theatrical income of George Colman the younger. Thus £550 each was received by that playwright for *The Poor Gentleman* (C.G. 1801) and for *Who Wants a Guinea?* (C.G. 1805), this "being the customary price for a five-act comedy" at the rate of £300 for the first nine nights, £100 on the twentieth night and £150 for the copyright[9]. For a special success, such as *John Bull* (C.G. 1803), the playwright might expect even higher fees; this comedy brought in to Colman £1200 in all.

The change, however, was soon to come. After chronicling these prices, Peake indulges in a lament:

Alas! times are sadly changed for authors; but in those days there were no ruinous salaries, nor was the star system in vogue (the stepping-stone to the downfall of the drama of England)....

[1] *Life and Times* (1823), ii. 387. [2] *Reminiscences* (1827), i. 267.
[3] *Id.* i. 347.   [4] *Id.* i. 387.   [5] *Id.* i. 390.
[6] *Id.* i. 396.   [7] *Id.* i. 413.   [8] *Id.* ii. 91.
[9] R. B. Peake, *op. cit.* ii. 413.

At that period, an author could write for a company, but now it must be for an individual; and the individual is paid such a monstrous sum for his nightly performance that the manager is incapacitated from giving a proper remuneration to the author[1].

Fitzball suggests another reason. The managers, he thinks, prefer to pay 3 francs for a French play instead of providing £300 for an English author. Unless this is changed,

how else are men gifted, perhaps, as Sheridan Knowles, Bulwer, or many others of great genius, blushing unseen, languishing under a cold sun, ever to add a literary lyric glory to their country? while on the other hand, we are sneered at by our continental, dramatic allies, who believe, and not unjustly, that we have no dramatists of our own[2].

Only the outstanding author, then, could command a fair price for his play, and even that fair price was below what had once been paid for similar efforts. Miss Mitford received only £200 for her *Julian* (C.G. 1823); Knowles got £400 for *Virginius* (C.G. 1820); Boucicault, for the most famous play of the age, *London Assurance* (C.G. 1841), pocketed only £300. Apparently £50 was considered a good price for a melodrama produced at the Surrey in 1829[3]. A few writers of the earlier decades, like Thomas Dibdin, may have been "Play-wrights in ordinary" with annual fees at one theatre or another[4], but even that method of remuneration seems to have been wiped out in later years.

If, however, in one way the authors found their incomes considerably smaller than had been those of their fathers, they succeeded in winning one great victory which was to be the foundation of the future prosperity of dramatic

---

[1] *Op. cit.* ii. 414.

[2] E. Fitzball, *op. cit.* ii. 42–3.

[3] *The Dramatic Magazine* (1829), pp. 246–7.

[4] *The Theatrical Repertory*, No. xxii. M. 15/2/1802. Interesting notes regarding Dibdin's position are given in his *Reminiscences* (1827). His salary at C.G. in 1801 was £260, but he succeeded in increasing this to £543 for the season (i. 277). In 1804 he cleared £1515 in all (i. 368). Later he acted as author and manager at the Surrey for £15 a week (i. 433). In 1823 and 1828 Jerrold may have been the Coburg playwright. In 1829 he got £5 a week from the Surrey for his services as author (W. Jerrold, *Douglas Jerrold* (1918), i. 72, 83, 92, 106). Planché at one time agreed to write solely for the Adelphi (*Recollections*, i. 44).

authorship. Although a playwright could count on a "reward" of only a hundred pounds for his labours, the dramatists of this time, by virtue of concerted action, prepared the path for that age we now enjoy, when an author, through the successful run of one single play, may look forward to a life of ease, and perhaps of indolence. It is well known that up to this time piracy of various kinds ruled on the theatrical high-seas. Planché informs us that, when a youth, he was an actor in a troupe playing at the Theatre Royal, Greenwich. The play chosen for performance was Colman's *The Actor of All Work* (H.[2] 1817), which had never been printed. However, Planché's "memory was in those days really marvellous," and "he wrote the whole piece out after one night's hearing at the Haymarket, going a second night to correct errors, and scarcely finding a word to add or to alter[1]." Planché's theft illustrates one form of piracy in practice at this period; a petition of Charles Bucke, author of *The Italians* (D.L. 1819), presented on June 4, 1829, illustrates another[2]. Quite clearly the petitioner states the general view of the age, that, when a dramatist had published a play, he made it thereby "amenable to the appropriation of all licensed theatres throughout the kingdom." Such a state of affairs, while it was good for the manager, obviously was very unfair to the author, and we are by no means surprised when we find, in the thirties of the century, active opposition to the reigning beliefs of the time.

Peculiarly enough, it was Planché himself who was the instrument by which the liberty of the dramatic author was secured. A certain play of his had been successful in London, and application was made by Murray of the Edinburgh Theatre Royal for a text (it had not then been published). Planché demanded a fee of £10, which Murray declined to pay. The manager now resorted to underhand devices. Surreptitiously he obtained a manuscript copy of the play and produced it at his theatre. Planché, knowing the legal difficulties, called a number of fellow-dramatists to his rooms

---

[1] *Recollections* (1872), i. 24–5.
[2] Printed in *The Dramatic Magazine* (1829), pp. 148–50.

to talk the matter over and, as a result of their conference, the Hon. George Lamb was induced to bring a Copyright Bill before Parliament. This, which gave the dramatic writer "indisputable control over his own property," received the Royal assent on June 10, 1833[1]. In order to render the Act operative a *Dramatic Authors' Society* was formed, "with a secretary...authorised by the members generally to grant conditional permission as the agent of the author." As Planché confesses, it was less easy to enforce the law than to make it, but "the first step was...gained by English dramatists...to place themselves on a footing with their continental brethren[2]."

One great blow was received during the dramatists' jubilation over their triumph. At first sight, it seemed that certain copyrights were worth a considerable sum of money. Shortly after the passing of the Act, Fitzball, who had had many of his many dramas published by Cumberland, imagined that El Dorado was opening before him. His hopes, however, were dashed when he discovered that Cumberland claimed the right of collecting the acting fees and when a legal judgment was given in the latter's favour[3]. It is to this case Planché refers in his pessimistic note to the 1879 edition of *High, Low, Jack, and the Game* (Olym. 1833)[4]. Still further, in spite of the benefits accruing from the acting fees for dramas written after June 1833, it was found that a great source of income was taken away from the playwright. All through the eighteenth century the reading public had been growing. Popular plays went into many editions; and the printed texts, if they were not dignified quartos or aristocratic folios, were at least octavos of decency and gravity of demeanour, for which a reader was prepared to pay anything

---

[1] *Recollections*, i. 148–50.
[2] *Id.* i. 196–200. An interesting comparison of French and English conditions appears on pp. 201–10. On the position of the French dramatists and Pixérécourt's activities in connection with the Comité des Auteurs, see P. Ginisty, *Le Mélodrame* (Paris, 1910), pp. 104–8. The English Dramatic Authors' Society is discussed in W. Jerrold, *op. cit.* i. 226–9.
[3] E. Fitzball, *op. cit.* i. 271–2.
[4] In *Extravaganzas*, i. 119.

5 NED

from two to five shillings. Undoubtedly the publishing of a popular play at this price must have been exceedingly profitable, and a bookseller was prepared to take a risk and to give an author—even an unknown author—a substantial lump sum for the copyright. The democratisation of literature, however, passed into a still further stage in the nineteenth century. For the most part the drama ceased to be a fancy of the *élite*, and grubby hands fumbled over that which had lain by oriental-perfumed fans and dandyishly tasselled canes. Except for a few works by the dramatists of the poetic school, the plays of the nineteenth century had to be produced at low prices. In olden days, we are informed once more by Planché, "successful dramas had a certain sale,"

but these days are fast disappearing, and booksellers were becoming chary of purchasing the copyrights of any dramatic pieces whatever, unless at such low prices that they were able to publish them in a small size at sixpence or a shilling, instead of, as formerly, in 8vo, at three or five shillings[1].

Truly a Scylla and a Charybdis—on the one hand, wary and astute provincial managers who refused to make payment to an author, who even refused to be caught and to answer for their sins; on the other, Cumberlands and Lacys and Dicks and Frenchs, willing to publish perhaps, but unable to give more to the writer than a Marlowe or a Fletcher may have received from an Elizabethan bookseller.

Complaints, naturally, are to be found on all sides. Perhaps we may take as typical the words of Douglas Jerrold uttered in 1832[2].

Were we asked what profession promised, with the greatest show of success, to form a practical philosopher, we should on the instant make reply, "The calling of an English dramatist." There is in his case such a fine adaptation of the means to the end that we cannot conceive how, especially if he be very successful, the dramatist can avoid becoming a first form scholar in the academy of the stoics. The daily lessons set for him to con are decked with

[1] *Op cit.* i. 154–5.
[2] Review of T. J. Thackeray's *On Theatrical Emancipation and the Rights of Dramatists* in *The New Monthly Magazine* (May, 1832). On this and on other connected matters see Walter Jerrold, *op. cit.* i. 201–6.

that "consummate flavour" of wisdom, patience; they preach to him meekness under indigence; continual labour with scanty and uncertain reward; quiescence under open spoliation; satisfaction to see others garner the harvest he has sown; with at least the glorious certainty of that noble indigence lauded by philosophers and practised by the saints—poverty, stark-naked poverty, with grey hairs; an old age exulting in its forlornness! If, after these goodly lessons, whipped into him with daily birch, he become no philosopher, then is all stoicism the fraud of knaves, and even patience but a word of two syllables. But we are convinced of the efficacy of the system. English dramatists *are* stoics, and not in the speculative sense, but in the hard practical meaning of the term. Time has hallowed their claim to the proud distinction, it is consecrated to them by the base coats of their prime, and the tatters of their old age; not only endured without complaint, but enjoyed as "their charter."

Under these conditions the nineteenth century melodrama, farce and extravaganza took their rise. As is perfectly obvious, a whole series of hindrances were operative calculated to retard the development of higher drama. The coarseness of the audience, the vagaries of the actor-manager, the pruriency of the censor, the activities of the "pirate" and the niggardliness of the publisher—all these cast their clouds over the playwriting profession during the course of the half-century. As we shall see, this bare statement of fact does not completely exonerate the literary men of the period for failing to produce something more worthy of the ancient traditions in the English theatre; yet it cannot be denied that, in spite of the vast amount of pioneer work which was being done during these years in every branch of dramatic and theatrical activity, a survey of the general conditions under which the dramatists worked makes but pitiful reading. The consequences of those conditions must now be studied.

CHAPTER II

THE DRAMATIC CONDITIONS OF THE AGE

I. *The Reasons of Decline*

IN the preceding sections many matters of interest have been rapidly hurried over. It is now time to consider the relations of some of the facts observed to the general dramatic debility of the half-century. Concerning the existence of this debility no one was, or is, in doubt. On all sides we can hear the cries, now monstrous pitiful like Bottom's roar, now stern-lipped with would-be grandeur, declaiming on the weakness of the time. The difficulty is not to recognise the phenomena but to trace to their sources the underlying causes. It is not sufficient to talk glibly of the general retrograde movement in drama from the times of Shakespeare; the day has passed for such generalisations. Nor may we hastily label the Romantic era as "lyric" as distinguished from the "dramatic" spirit of Elizabethan England. The Romantic poets may have been intensely lyrical in the sense that they were continually writing and speaking of themselves, but the lyric poets were not the only authors of that age, and their failure is only part of the general failure of the age as a whole.

On surveying this period, one fact strikes us at once; the presence of three distinct types of authors, or rather the production of three distinct types of plays. The great mass of nineteenth century dramas are the melodramas, farces, spectacles and extravaganzas turned out in their hundreds by the Planchés and the Fitzballs. These are the dramas which were successful both at the larger and at the smaller theatres. Besides these, however, there were the various plays written by more pretentious authors—the *Ions* and the *Moneys*—

which made attempts to secure something of an older and higher tone. Sometimes these plays were tragedies, sometimes comedies, sometimes tragi-comedies, but in all the effort was made to provide something better than that ladled out promiscuously to the spectators in melodrama and in farce. Finally, there were the "poetic plays," those dramas written by the romantic poets, sometimes with the stage in view, sometimes with no thought but the publisher, which never saw actual embodiment in the theatre. It is difficult at times to make a clear distinction between this and the second type, for such plays as Coleridge's *Remorse* (D.L. 1813) and Joanna Baillie's *De Monfort* (D.L. 1800) secured sympathetic managers, but there is at least some distinction to be made between them.

The problem of the decline of the drama is more easily studied, it seems to me, when we split it into a series of independent yet connected questions, which might be framed in some such wise. (1) Why was there not a greater connection between the true poets of the time and the theatre? (2) Why did those more talented men who wrote for the stage fail to pen works of a truly permanent value? (3) Why did not other non-poetic writers embrace a stage career more willingly? (4) Why did the "theatre-authors" indulge in such crude farce and extravaganza and melodrama? Putting the questions in this way, we may gain at least some dim idea of the genuine causes of the failure. Personally, I can find no absolute authority for Professor Watson's statement[1] that the contemporary answers to the general query regarding dramatic decline differed from decade to decade. It is critically comforting, perhaps, to say that from 1800 to 1810 the size of the theatres was blamed, from 1810 to 1820 the paucity of good authors and managers, from 1820 to 1830 the star system and spectacle, from 1830 to 1840 the patent monopoly and the vagaries of the adventurer Bunn, and from 1840 to 1850 the French companies and opera. As a matter of fact, the contemporary explanations are varied and perhaps in the end do not give us all the information we desire.

[1] *Sheridan to Robertson*, p. 136.

It may be well to turn from these to the questions proposed above, and try to answer each, both from the point of view of contemporaries and from the point of view of the present century.

(1) There can be no question concerning the sharp cleavage between the poets and the theatre. Coleridge succeeded in getting one of his plays acted; Byron was director of a patent theatre for a number of years and brought several of his plays on the stage; Browning, it is well known, wrote for Macready; but the vast mass of the dramas penned by those poets who are now so famous for their lyrical work never passed beyond the stage of print, occasionally not even beyond the stage of manuscript. It is easy to find excuses for them; it is pleasant to exonerate the Wordsworths and the Shelleys by pointing the scornful finger at the Fitzballs and the Kenneys. But, after all, greater dramatists in the past have accepted the conditions of their own times. The Elizabethan theatre was in no state of perfection when Shakespeare wrote; nay more, Shakespeare as well as any of his academic contemporaries realised its failings; but the dramatic genius that was Shakespeare's subordinated the clowns and the clowneries to its own will. Jonson might sneer and pen a dull *Sejanus*; Shakespeare wrote a *Lear*. An individual author may endeavour to establish new forms, may point out inconsistencies, may show his dissatisfaction with this or with that, but, if he be great, he will do so, not by turning away in contempt, but by remoulding the evil conditions set before him. An impartial survey of the romantic poetry reveals the fact that the poets—with the possible exception of Byron—were at least tinged with the brush of priggism. There is a certain clergymanlike superiority about Wordsworth which is lost only in his more imaginative moods; Shelley is undoubtedly "superior" in his own way; Keats, cockney though he was, shares the same quality. Perhaps, if the word prig offend, one might rephrase by saying that the romantic poets all took themselves too seriously. Their lyrical triumphs spring from that which, in another way, made them weak. The "I" is always intruding

into their lines; "*I* fall upon the thorns of life," "When *I* have fears that *I* may cease to be," "Strange fits of passion have *I* known"—again and again the note is struck, now meanly and low, now triumphantly and with glorious cadence. The lyric mood may exist alongside the dramatic, as Shakespeare and Webster testify, but the dramatic mood depends ultimately on a sense of humour. A sense of humour springs from the power of seeing two sides to a question, or, in other words, from the power of seeing beyond oneself. Both tragedy and comedy depend upon the ability of the author to forget for a moment his own petty loves and woes, or so to transform these that they become universal. This the romantic poets, because they were always thinking of themselves, failed to do. Wordsworth is immersed in Wordsworth; Coleridge is fascinated by Coleridge's own metaphysical cleverness; Shelley soars with his own airy spirit.

The romantic poets, therefore, are not seen in the theatre, not because they were kept out, but because they would not, or could not, go in. Perhaps they are not to be blamed overmuch; it may be that their education was to blame. A dramatic author often has to have the goad of sheer necessity or the example of some far-seeing critics. With the exception of Keats, the romantic poets were not forced to make an income for themselves, and the critics gave them little aid. What was needed at this time was a sound body of scientific, historical and appreciative interpretation of past dramatic efforts; but that type of dramatic criticism which has entirely revisualised the efforts of Shakespeare was not to be born for nearly a century. For Coleridge, the critic, Shakespeare was a pure poet and a creator of character; concerning the play-wright's dramatic construction the author of *Biographia Literaria* is silent. Hazlitt has a somewhat clearer view of what is wanted in a drama, but even he fails; while for Lamb a play is evidently good when it possesses one or two passages of lyrical beauty. Malone in those days was battling manfully forward towards a clearer conception of the Elizabethan stage, but no critic of standing collaborated with him by showing how certain features of Shakespearian drama were suited for a platform, and unsuited for a picture-frame, theatre. In their plays, therefore, the poets blindly followed the Elizabethan dramatists without capturing their tone. Soliloquies, pages in length, abound, and the language is neither the language of the older nor that of modern times. The critical bias, too, had another grave influence. The metaphysical and philosophical tone of Coleridge, merely a reflex of a general spirit, overstressed the abstract, and as a consequence those concrete elements which are of such importance in drama were more or less neglected. Joanna Baillie might have been a great playwright, but we can see one at least of the causes of her failure in her *Plays on the Passions*.

One excuse for the poets, adumbrated by Leigh Hunt[1] and warmly advocated in our own days by Professor Watson, is the thesis that a self-respecting literary man could not have been expected to undergo the tortures a nineteenth century dramatist is supposed to have undergone. It is undoubtedly true that in the theatre of the period a playwright could get very thoroughly damned indeed, and that, if he sought for success, he had to pen his play in such a way as to get the applause of the galleries. But are these such real deterrents to true dramatic production as Professor Watson and Leigh Hunt seem to imagine? Did Æschylus sit with folded arms because he had to compete in the theatre for a prize which was often awarded according to the plaudits of a vast and essentially "popular" audience? Is the hissing (which Professor Watson pictures so vividly) so terribly wrong; is it not in some ways better than the present polite acceptance of a new piece, which permits a wretched play, with the aid of

---

[1] *Op. cit.* pp. 50–2. Hunt avers that the whole endeavour of a comic writer of his age must be to pen for the galleries, and adds a recipe for the popular play:

"An inveterate love of punning;

A deformed alteration of common characters and incidents;

A dialogue either extremely flowery or extremely familiar;

An affectation of ardent loyalty, and, consequent to this affectation, a gross flattery of the audience;

Lastly...a most abject system of begging the favour of the house."

a little puffing, to poison the town for a twelvemonth? Did a great dramatist of any period disdain composition because of the presence in the theatre of the profane vulgar? Truly Kemble's remark, cited below[1], seems more worthy and more surely artistic than the attitude of the poets who are thus so deeply pitied. We must look at those Romantic poets honestly, and, if we do, we realise that, in spite of their high-sounding Pantisocracies and their revolutionary views, they were too aristocratic and affected—thin-skinned, too, preferring to write their lyrics which might be ridiculed or loved in private rather than attempt dramas the open condemnation of which might ruffle their dignity. Perhaps criticism has been overkind in the past to these Romantic poets. They have long been the spoilt children of our literature; we have been too readily inclined to bow to their pettish wills, to find excuses for their failures, instead of treating them honestly, and perhaps a little severely, as spoilt children ought to be treated.

More detailed notes we may leave till later, and, even with this brief summary, we must remember that other considerations have to be taken into account; but, viewed impartially, the question seems to demand one clear answer; the failure of romantic genius to produce a true and expressive romantic drama was due not so much to outside theatrical influences as to a weakness on the part of the poets themselves.

(2) Yet there were some poets who entered into the lists. Coleridge and Byron in the earlier years, aided by Talfourd and Sheridan Knowles and Browning towards the end of the half-century, tried hard to win popular applause for their efforts. Not one of them, however, really gripped the imagination of the age, in spite of the success of Bulwer's *The Lady of Lyons* (C.G. 1838); not one produced a dramatic masterpiece which can be looked upon as the starting-point for further art development. It will be seen, when we proceed to analyse their separate works, that each in his own way had something of a talent for the theatre, that each produced works which may, even in this century, be read

[1] *Infra*, p. 75.

with pleasure; we might even go further and declare, if one
or two of these works had been found in manuscript and the
authors had not been known, if a literary Puck had passed
them off as seventeenth century dramas, we might now be
reading them in much be-commented and limited editions—
perhaps, who knows? they might have been set as selected
texts for university examinations. All this we may confess;
but the fact remains that they did not provide that for which
the age was seeking and which it found dimly suggested by
Robertson and robustly by Ibsen.

Again, in studying this question, we must consider the
superiority of the authors. In putting forward his *Glencoe*
(H.[2] 1840) Talfourd gives us a preface in which he discusses
the lamentable state of the stage. One sometimes feels, in
reading these prefaces, that the writers hesitate between two
ideals—getting their plays accepted, and getting them rejected.
Sometimes they are positively apologetic because they have
soiled their fair hands with the dust of old Drury. "A flimsy,
flippant tribe" they are—

> Authors,—who blush to throw their pearls to swine;
> Vain of their triumphs of *rejected* Plays,
> And talents, never mortified by praise;
> Who humbly vaunt, who haughtily confess
> Their tasteful toils uninjur'd by success,—
> Seldom insulted by a *three-days run*,
> And complimented often with—*not one*:
> Glow-worms of wit, expos'd to light, they fade;
> But shine and sparkle in their native shade!
> Their boast, their proud distinction, *not* to please,
> Hooted and hiss'd they calmly sit at ease;
> While conscious Genius happily supplies
> The laurel wreaths a niggard world denies[1].

This satirical note does indeed touch upon a feature of the
age which has been, it would appear, unduly neglected by
the literary historians.

Beyond the tone of superiority, however, we have to note
the absolutely uninventive character of the various tragic

---

[1] W. R. Spencer, *Urania* (D.L. 1802), prologue by the Rt. Hon. Lord
John Townshend.

and comic efforts of those poets who descend to the play-house. Their blank-verse is Shakespeare's or Fletcher's; their themes are old; they talk in a language strange to their contemporaries, throwing in perhaps a melodramatic trick or two as a sop to Cerberus. As one looks at the audiences of the time, one seems to see them constantly thirsting, thirsting, thirsting. The French Revolution has rumbled away in Napoleon's cannons; a new social age is born; and here are the dramatists giving them Greek tragedies and "Love Chases" of Elizabethan life, and Kings and Princes of days gone by. "The subject of the drama," says a writer in *Blackwood's Magazine*[1] of Tennant's *Cardinal Beaton*, "is a conspiracy—and we are partial to conspiracies. They cannot but be interesting." The external conspiracies of the *littérateurs*, however, are one and all of the past, are artificial, are removed from the social surroundings of the period, are, above all, sentimental and decorous. The age wanted action and robustness, as the popularity of the melodramas witnesses, but the poets, restrained by their high thoughts, would not give it that for which it craved. In an article on *Modern Dramas, and Dramatic Writers* another writer in *Blackwood's*[2], signing his essay "Titus," observes that while "Vice furnished the plot for most of the Elizabethans," the romantic poets rarely treated this theme with the same freedom as had been done in earlier times. Murder was part of the stock-in-trade of the minor playwrights; the poets were too decorous to rely on such vulgar props. Another essay in *The London Magazine*, in the form of *A Letter to the Dramatists of Today*[3], calls further attention to this weakness. "*Action*," says the writer, "is the essence of drama; nay, its definition: business, bustle, hurly, and combustion dire, are indispensable to effective drama....But" [addressing the dramatists] "you seem to think that the whole virtue of tragedy lies in its *poeticity*....At any rate, if you don't think thus, you write as if you did....In short your action is nothing, and your

[1] Vol. xiv. Oct. 1823, p. 422.
[2] *Id.* p. 557.
[3] Vol. viii. July 1823, p. 85. The letter is signed "John Lacy" but is known to have been written by George Darley.

poetry every thing." These judgments are perfectly just, and, as will be seen more clearly when we contrast the poetic with the "illegitimate" plays, go far towards explaining the dulness and dramatic failure of the former. Undoubtedly, if we had lived in 1830, we should have preferred to see an honest melodrama at Sadler's Wells rather than an artificial, and therefore dishonest, masterpiece at Covent Garden. Such feelings undoubtedly swayed at least some spectators of the time, and many must have echoed the sentiments expressed by H. S. Leigh in his good-humoured verses:

> I gape in Covent Garden's walls,
>   I doze in Drury Lane;
> I strive in the Lyceum stalls
>   To keep awake—in vain.
> There's nought in the dramatic way
>   That I can quite abide,
> Except the pieces that they play
>   Upon the Surrey side[1].

One appreciates, perhaps, the efforts of the reformers; but no amount of appreciation can dim our eyes to the fact that the reform they aimed at was only the revival of antique forms which possessed not an atom of significance for the newer age.

(3) Not all the reformers were poets; among them is numbered the novelist Bulwer Lytton; but the majority had won their fame rather in the realms of verse than in the realms of fiction. One may perhaps wonder why some of those many prose writers, who had presented such living galleries of types, did not endeavour to win fame in the playhouses. Daniel Terry, in presenting his dramatisation of *The Antiquary* (C.G. 1820) to the public, had indulged

a wish, that the mysterious and powerful pen, to which the world is so greatly indebted for the immortal productions whence these plays have been extracted, had sometimes turned its powerful force directly to the Drama,—and [lamented] the causes by which it has been diverted or withheld from raising the present state of our dramatic literature to an equality with that of its brightest age[2].

---

[1] *Carols of Cockayne* (1874), p. 43.   [2] Advertisement.

Why did Thackeray not approach the theatre? Why did Dickens pen only one or two trivial farces? To find a true answer to this question one must now move beyond the failings of the authors. It is certainly true that the qualities that make a great novelist are not necessarily those which will suffice for a dramatist. When one compares Dickens' farces[1] with his fictional work one sees how firmly his style is based on the narrative method. The humour and the sympathy of Dickens are not expressed through his dialogue alone; they are conveyed to the reader by means of a subtle intermingling of dialogue and humorous or emotional comment. This we may admit, but beyond that there were many external causes which led men to other walks of literature just as external causes led many men in the Elizabethan age to the public theatres.

The first of these is the lessening rewards given to the writers of plays[2]. A successful novelist could now build up for himself a handsome fortune. Dickens attained to considerable affluence, and Scott could erect a lordly Abbotsford on the profits of the *Waverley* series. Periodical literature, too, was increasing annually. The great reviews, the more popular magazines, the comic papers, the annuals—all of these attracted bands of authors, partly because of the continual clamouring for material, partly because of the then excellent remuneration offered. "The crosses and disappointments which attend dramatic productions[3]," added to the pittance meted out to even the popular playwright, hardly offered sufficient attraction to men who elsewhere could earn money easily. The Elizabethan age and our own period have this in common, and so differ from the early nineteenth century, that the stage offered and offers the lordliest rewards to the successful author[4].

The explanation of these small sums given to dramatic

---

[1] See *infra*, p. 209. [2] See *supra*, pp. 51–3.
[3] *The Dramatic Magazine* (1829), p. 242.
[4] I do not, of course, suggest that the payment for dramatic authorship in the Elizabethan period was especially high; but clearly a man such as Shakespeare could hope to earn far more from association with the theatre than from association with the printing press alone.

authors depends upon a series of concomitant circumstances all tending to the one result, the impoverishment of the manager. In spite of large theatres, the playhouses rarely could be made to pay. All devices were tried, from raising the prices (which led to riots) to lowering them (which led to bankruptcy), but every endeavour ended in failure. Costs were much higher than they had ever been before. The then wonderful machinery of the patent theatres demanded a large corps of property men; besides, theatrical machinery requires not only a large capital expenditure, there is a constant outlay for upkeep. The audiences demanded spectacle, and so scenery and costume had to be kept rich. The Grieves and the Telbins must have taken a fair share of the theatrical profits. Most important of all was the star system and the consequent rise in salaries. In 1812 the great comic actor Mathews thought that a weekly income of £17 was "*stupendous* and *magnificent*[1]"; by 1850 the major actors were demanding salaries which vied with those which are paid today to the more distinguished performers. With this great rise for the chief actors, the amounts paid to minor players likewise increased, and, when we consider the vast size of the stock-companies, we realise what a constant drain there was on the finances of the theatre. Little could remain for the poor author.

The star-system is being constantly blamed by contemporaries for the evil state of the drama, for it not only caused greater expense but also had a pernicious effect upon the work produced. In *The Italians* (D.L. 1819) Charles Bucke indulges in a long attack on Kean, who, the author declares, demanded that "tragedy must be martyrized into a MONODRAME." If a drama without a star-part was by chance accepted, then it was given only a slovenly performance. *Oxberry's Theatrical Inquisitor* (1828) takes up the same tale:

To hope for another Shakespeare would be madness, so long as the stage continues in its present state....The croakers of the drama assert, that tragedies and comedies will not draw. Cast them strongly and try[2].

[1] Bunn, *The Stage*.   [2] pp. 110 and 147.

The actor-managers with their cuttings are blamed for much of the evil of the time[1]. Still another source of consequent iniquity is hinted at by the author of *Better Late than Never* (1824):

In these days, when every play-goer complains of the poverty of the entertainment offered by the proprietors of the two "Great Theatres" to the public, it is no wonder their theatres should cease to be frequented, and that they should not cease to be poor. At present the ostensible proprietor or lessee at either house, is both manager and actor; and although this ought not to afford any excuse for such poverty of entertainment, it will, nevertheless, be found upon examination, to be the primary cause:—but when it is observed, that at one of these theatres, the proprietor is not only actor and manager, but also author, the result is not surprising.... What sensible independent writer will attend to an ignorant manager—"Sir, you must write to please the reigning taste"—consent to get up processions for bipeds, and curvettings for quadrupeds—and become the pander to such a taste?

This passage reveals at one and the same time the two causes of failure, the importunity of the managers and the superiority of the literary authors. One can imagine a Shakespeare making joyous or sublime use even of an elephant.

While we thus seek for one of the chief explanations in the star-system and in the errors of management[2], we must, on the other hand, remember that an unsuccessful author is not always the best and most impartial of witnesses. At least one writer, George Macfarren, rebutted the charges made by so many against those in command of the theatres:

It has been a prevailing theme of late, to rail at theatrical jealousies, and the tyranny of Managers and Actors towards those servants of the Muse whose labours bring them as suitors to the door of the Green-Room. The Writer, who here appears before the Public, very confidently ventures to refute such prejudices, at least, as far as *Old Drury* is concerned: himself and his humble effort having been received, by every member of that establish-

---

[1] p. 52. See *supra*, pp. 48–9.
[2] See also R. B. Peake, *op. cit.* ii. 414–5.

ment whose talents were pressed into the service, with the utmost kindness and cordiality[1].

In addition to these deterrents (for, in spite of Macfarren's plea, we must believe that there is some truth in the complaints of others), the size of the patent theatres must have seemed an insuperable barrier to many. The large theatre was suited for no form of intimate drama, and its vastness undoubtedly hindered the development of true comedy and of domestic tragedy by frightening away those few who might have given originality to the playhouse. Everything seemed to conspire together to bring about the ruin of the stage.

It is not intended here to suggest that the drama of any period is created entirely by the force of external and economic appeals, but a study of theatrical history does convince us that such economic appeals must be largely considered when we regard, not merely dramatic activity in general, but the particular writers attracted to this form of literary art. The facts that many of the best brains of the Elizabethan period were recruited to the service of the stage, and that in our own times the theatre has once more been enriched by the application to its demands of the major writers, must be attributed partly at least to the pecuniary rewards which have been offered in these two periods and to the possibility of fame arising from theatrical authorship. On the other hand, the true dramatist is born, not made, and we are bound to believe that, in spite of the interest taken in the playhouse by such a man as Dickens, there did not live in this half-century any single individual whose primary call it was to pen dramatic dialogue. Dickens' strength lay, not in the use of dialogue itself but in the blending of dialogue with narrative. Exactly the same is true of the work of Sir Walter Scott, who, beyond that objectivity which at first sight seems to be akin to the objectivity of the greater dramatists, secures his effects very largely by the constant impression

---

[1] *Malvina* (D.L. 1826), Advertisement. This may be compared with the preface to *The Rake and his Pupil* (Adel. 1833) where Buckstone praises the magnanimity of the manager Yates.

of his own personality upon the narrative portions of his novels. In this connection another remark may be made. If it is true that the outstanding dramatic writer must be born, it is also true that an author, not necessarily qualified in the first instance for theatrical work, may, by careful application and study of stage conditions, achieve success and fame by the penning of plays; examples of such authors are common in every land. One might, therefore, have expected that, with their interest in the fortunes and dignity of the theatre, some of the many novelists or poets of the period might have given something of dramatic worth to the early nineteenth century stage. Here again, however, we come back to the prevailing weaknesses of the romantic temperament. Among those who were most enthusiastic, Scott, Dickens and Byron stand out chief; but all of these failed to study dramatic conditions in such a manner as to improve their own work. Scott was a noble patron, a good friend to players and to playwrights, but he never set himself down to analyse the essential conditions governing dramatic authorship. Attendance at the Theatre Royal, Edinburgh, acting as chairman at various theatrical functions, welcoming notable players to his house, half-heartedly scribbling a play or two—beyond these things he could not go. Dickens might well have been an actor instead of a novelist, but again his association with the stage was not such as to prepare him for a career as a dramatist. Histrionic art he loved, but the power of mastering that essential restraint and tremendous condensation required of the playwright he could not achieve. The romantic temperament loves breadth, it is feverish in its activity; dramatic art perhaps demands always a tincture at least of classic calm and of classic simplification. The same criticism may likewise be applied to Byron. For a time he liked his position on the board of directors at Drury Lane, but "milord" was too fond of his own pleasures, was too far immersed in himself, to permit of any of that severer study which has been suggested above. The fact remains that even the attempts at drama made by those writers most enthusiastic in the cause of the theatre lacked the impress of professionalism. Dickens' operatic farces are decidedly amateur, and the majority of Byron's dramas, in spite of Byron's own highly developed dramatic sense, are admittedly penned not for representation upon the stage but for leisured perusal in the study.

Through a combination of outward conditions and of inner failings, therefore—this must be our answer to the third question which we have proposed—the possibility of higher dramatic achievement was frustrated even among those who had the power of creating character, of projecting themselves into the minds of others. The outward conditions did undoubtedly mean much in this connection, but when Scott boldly declared "that the age has no reason to apprehend any decay of dramatic talent[1]," he displayed clearly that, like his companions, he had failed to grasp those genuine essentials on which "dramatic talent" must be founded, or without which "dramatic talent" cannot hope to succeed

(4) We have now reached the fourth question proposed: Why did melodrama and the like flourish so freely in this age? Again the answer, which involves many of the explanations cited above, demands the careful consideration of a variety of movements in the time. In the first place, the superiority of the more literary authors was galling, and impertinence was challenged by impertinence. Some authors, fully conscious of the superior tone, remained openly unrepentant. Thus Reynolds tells us how the critics began to attack his mannerisms and his weak plots.

Oh, ho, thought I, with Fielding when, on a first night, he heard one of his scenes hissed, "they have found me out, have they."...It is not *wholly* improbable that the above mentioned gentlemen had some grounds for their reproaches[2].

With a jest against himself, and a heart entirely unstricken by conscience, Reynolds turned gaily towards melodrama, finding that this type of play provided him with a new field for his energies while being at the same time infinitely easier to write. The reflection of the lordly affectations of the poets is to be seen in many another writer besides Reynolds. One

---

[1] *Essay on Drama, ed. cit.* vi. 380.　　　　[2] *Op. cit.* ii. 333.

of the raciest passages in the whole of Fitzball's memoirs
is a satire on the pretensions of the proud. His imagination
calls into being a manager of the Theatre Royal, Plumpton
Marsh, who, having read the superior dramatic reviews,
determines to come and save the London stage. He starts
with *Magbeth*—pronounced *Mag* "ever since he heard of
such a word being discovered, cut on a stone among the
ruins of Macbeth's castle." This is followed by "the unfailing
'Lady of Lyons.'" The newspapers are a trifle cold, so he
sends round invitations to "three of the most powerfully-
writing editors."

They, those awfully great men, all legitimitists, condescendingly
sacrifice their time, as martyrs, ready to expire in a legitimate
cause, and confidentially accept the invitation....At length, to
come to business: Terence Beak, has condescendingly brought
with him a legitimate tragedy, "Pope Pius," to be played without
scenery. Mr Neverlaugh presents him with a screaming farce,
called "A Cold Reception," entirely divested of frivolous play
upon words, or vulgar practical jokes, till, at the conclusion, the
comic man falls into a horsepond, off the stage, according to the
strict rules of the classic drama. Mr Sheridan Bowles has a
comedy for which he expects, (happy is the man, &c.,) £300
sterling. *This* comedy is all to be played seated *à la-Moliere*, and
glorifies itself with the cheering title of the "Paralytic Stroke."...
[Mr Plumpton] plays the first two of their immaculate inspirations,
which, notwithstanding the heading of the bill in large *red*,
un*read* letters—*Restoration of the Legitimate Drama*, are received
thinly and coldly by discriminating but *select* audiences. But
although his last *stroke*, the "Paralytic Stroke," is underlined, and
places *kindly* advised to be taken early, from the apprehension
of not obtaining any, luckless P., fortunately at all events for
himself, this time escapes the paralytic stroke by the timely
stroke of a writ, which cuts short, not only his anticipated triumph,
and the gratitude of the million, but the *real legitimate drama*
at the same time[1].

While all who have even the slightest acquaintance with the
drama of the early nineteenth century must appreciate the
fundamental distinction between the legitimate and the
illegitimate, every sincere lover of the theatre must agree that

[1] *Op. cit.* ii. 110–16.

the superior tone adopted by the contemporary high-brows was both irritating and ill-calculated to serve the best interests of the playhouse, and further that the general level of the dramatic work produced by these mental aristocrats was not of a type to command respect. Fitzball's satire is perfectly merited, yet it is in a way pathetic, for it reveals poignantly the antagonism which kept the two parties so unfortunately apart. The same spirit is displayed in another manner in Bunn's work on *The Stage*. In his third volume he shows, and evidently with some authority, that the legitimatists, banded together in a fanatical company, disregarded entirely some of the more patent facts of the time. He records "the yell from the beauties, calling themselves Shaksperians" when he introduced a lion-show in a spectacular *Charlemagne*, and notes that

In the blindness of their excitement they forgot that we had no Shakespearian actors alive, and that an attempt at the representation of any of the bard's immortalities would disgrace the theatre far more than any other performance. They forgot that *The Tempest*, performing at the other house with the announced quotation of "the text of Shakspeare," owed all the attraction it possessed to the novelty of Miss P. Horton, "My gentle Ariel," singing while suspended in the air[1].

If the antagonism between the legitimatists and the theatre writers was one of the main forces which drove the nineteenth century down a false path, it is hardly true to say that this cause stood alone. Indeed, we must assume once more that a series of concomitant circumstances all tended in the one direction. In attempting to assess the respective shares of responsibility, however, we must be careful to balance one statement and one fact with another. Thus an anonymous author in *The Dramatic Magazine* for 1829 comes to the decision that the failure is to be traced to the fact that

Nine nights out of ten the galleries have complete command of the house, and, generally speaking, the applause proceeds from that part. Now we are well aware that a long sentence, or a declamatory dialogue, though written with all the inspiration

[1] iii. 98; see also iii. 21.

of a Milton, would not be received with attention by them. Thus it is that the productions of our modern authors are frequently overrun with nonsense, ribaldry, and rant[1].

At first sight, the complaint would appear to be perfectly just, yet we must counter this criticism by a paragraph in Fitzball's records in which he notes the effect of Osbaldistone's lowering of theatre prices. "It might be argued," remarks the dramatist, "that he reduced the mental audience also; yet I heard Kemble, say one night, as he came off the stage in Hamlet, that he never played to a more glorious one[2]." The audience undoubtedly had something to do with the dramatic Denmark's rotten state; so had the large theatres, and the actors, and the pantomime, and the musical show, and the high salaries and the delight in spectacle—but none of these can be brought forward by itself to account for the decline as a whole.

Among these contributory causes mentioned, however, there are not mentioned two which seem of prime importance, and which in a way serve to exonerate the theatre-writers from having to share a large part of the blame. Professor Watson has suggested in his study of stage conditions from Sheridan to Robertson that the drabness of the age accounts for much, and this suggestion seems to me among the most fruitful of the many adduced, both by him and by other critics. No genuine comedy or tragedy could rise out of the level greyness of early Victorian society. The poor were struggling harshly in a period of industrial change; the rich were duller than they had been in the Augustan days. In other literary realms Thackeray could only sneer at the pretensions of the aristocracy, and Dickens, in dealing with the mob, had to resort to false pathos and melodramatic effect. The melodrama of the period, then, was largely dependent upon the social circumstances of the period. If the melodrama was of the oriental romantic kind, then it was an escape from the sordid; if it was realistic in tendency, it was so tied and fettered by the conventionalities of the melodramatic condition that, in spite of its realistic tone, it

[1] p. 150. [2] ii. 116–17.

remained false to life. It was only when a wittier spirit arose in more aristocratic circles, and when the industrial chaos began to resolve itself, that a higher drama rose in England towards the end of the century.

The playwrights, feeling unconsciously the impossibility of devising dramatic material which should be in direct harmony with the spirit of the age, naturally turned abroad for inspiration. The German drama had run its course, and now Paris once more furnished a centre of attraction. In 1859 Fitzball found that the drama was "nearly almost all composed of translations[1]," and for decades before that date the French theatres had been ransacked for plots and situations. While adaptation has ruled for generations on the London stage, facts force us to admit that never before were so many foreign dramas reworked for English audiences. It was not only the difficulty of building plots out of the social life of the time which drove the playwrights to this wholesale imitation. Already we have noted the low remuneration for dramatic work[2], and it will at once be realised that any author who attempted to live by his pen was forced to turn out many more dramas than his predecessors had done. From 1818 to 1850 J. R. Planché produced over 150 plays, an average of five per year, while Fitzball's efforts seem almost incalculable. In earlier years, thought "D.G.," the introducer to Cumberland's set of plays, "relieved by the curious and uncommon performance of" rope-dancers and similar entertainers,

a pantomime and a brace of burlettas were quite sufficient to carry a minor season through triumphantly. But now, "another and another still succeed," till their very names become a tax on our recollection[3].

This frenzied activity was, as we have seen, due to hard necessity, the poor rewards for dramatic work encouraging the production of quantity rather than quality. Some conception of the vast number of new pieces produced annually may be gained from contemplation of the fact that had any

[1] *Op. cit.* i. i. [2] See *supra*, pp. 51–3.
[3] Introduction to Campbell's *The Forest Oracle* (S.W. 1829).

newspaper wished to cover all the Easter productions played for the first time on Monday, April 4, 1831 (and this year is taken at random), it would have had to send representatives to nine theatres and to criticise no less than sixteen new dramas. The very length of the appendix provided to this study indicates, too, the enormous quantity of farce, melodrama, opera and pantomime introduced with ever-changing bills at both the "majors" and the "minors."

Careless workmanship and stolen plots were the more obvious results. The stolen plots, of course, came not only from France; Scott was a "mighty luminary which reflected its lustre upon the so-called illegitimate drama[1]." As will be seen[2], his novels were eagerly adapted by scores of needy authors, and performances of these dramatisations dominate the bills for many a season. Unfortunately Scott's themes, like so many of Dickens', are almost entirely melodramatic. A villainous Osbaldistone, a generous hero, a noble heroine, a high-souled brigand in Rob Roy, single combats, gloomy scenes, thrills, humour, ambuscades, escape—such a combination was well calculated to appeal to the age, and, at the same time, to hammer tighter yet the fetters of the melodramatic tradition.

The practice of adaptation from the French play or from the English novel did not demand the highest of talents, and we find expressed in this time what is a kind of reflex influence or subsidiary result in the realm of dramatic authorship. Thus Terry, in the Advertisements to his own and Pocock's rendering of *The Antiquary* (C.G. 1820), confesses that

The task of compressing Tales of three volumes into Plays of three Acts, is one of merely technical and mechanical drudgery, which no one would willingly undertake who could do better things; and he who performs it must be content to resign the title of *Author*, for the humbler but juster appellation of *Compiler*.

With this feeling, or with that of opposition as expressed by Fitzball, there could hardly be any advance in dramatic literature; the theatre had fallen on stony paths and no

[1] Fitzball, *op. cit.* i. iv. [2] *Infra*, pp. 92–5.

one body of men had the sagacity or the power to help it over the roughs; on all sides is a pathetic and at times almost ridiculous acceptance of the facts and a weary reiteration of "these degenerate-dramatic days[1]."

II. *General Influences on the Drama*, 1800–1850

From the rapid survey of dramatic development given in the preceding chapter, it is evident that serious drama in this age was sharply divided into three sections. The first comprised the unacted poetic plays and those not intended for the stage; the second included the poetic dramas which secured performance in the theatre; while the third was the section of melodrama. To a certain extent the first and second groups may be considered together, but here, since we are studying dramatic development from the point of view of the theatre, they must be separated. It will also be realised at once that the poetic drama section is much smaller than the melodramatic. A manager is "a very great fool" if he thinks "tragedy is likely to obtain Success, now-a-days," at least according to Planché[2]. Tragic writing, deems Bucke, is "an ART, which the world is unanimous in believing is almost totally extinct[3]." The host of melodrama, led by ghostly spirits and stock-heroes, had wellnigh vanquished the enfeebled armies of the tragic muse.

In view of this sharp division into two types, it is obvious that we cannot hope to trace in detail common influences on the serious drama of the time, yet the two types are not so fundamentally severed as to preclude the possibility of a certain harmony of atmosphere and even of aim. The poetic authors, in spite of their lordly air of superiority, were not above

---

[1] See T. Dibdin's *Harlequin Hoax* (Lyc. 1814), scene v. In the above account I have used only a small section of the various species of periodical and pamphlet literature bearing on the dramatic decline of the age. What I have taken is, however, thoroughly representative, and naturally has been chosen for its typical qualities. Among the other works special attention might be devoted to the prejudiced but well-written article by "Philo-Dramaticus" (the Rev. W. Harness) in *Blackwood's Magazine*, June 1825.

[2] *Success* (Adel. 1825).   [3] *The Italians* (D.L. 1819), preface.

indulging in the tricks of the inferior style. The *Alfred the Great* (D.L. 1831) of Sheridan Knowles is very little but a self-conscious melodrama, while Talfourd's *Glencoe* (H.[2] 1840), although it has not the regular stock characters, shows in its general atmosphere a certain kinship with the melodramatic type. It has been pointed out[1] that even Shelley's *Prometheus Unbound* has a structure not far different from that accorded to the majority of melodramas. Both species at times veered close to one another and showed spirits which were to all intents the same.

The serious drama of the early nineteenth century is fundamentally a regular development of the drama of 1780–1800. Already the melodramatic characters had been created; already the poetic authors were rushing their unactable wares to the press; already attempts were being made in the direction of a "romantic" style. All that this half-century achieved was the establishing of melodrama as a formal type, the elaboration of some special themes untouched before and the more definite introduction of the poetic play. To insist on merely terminological differences is purely pedantic, so that, while we may note that certain names, such as that of melodrama itself, are of nineteenth century origin, we must not assume that the appearance of a certain type in the period was without its premonitions in the late eighteenth century. Nor must we make too much of foreign influence, even when we note the enormous activity in adaptation which marks out the age dramatically. Leigh Hunt was not far wrong in finding Goldsmith ultimately responsible for the farce of his own times[2], and even the melodrama was as much English as Continental.

French influence, of course, and that far more widespread than in any preceding age, cannot be denied or neglected. Fully one-half of the plays written between 1800 and 1850 must have been suggested by Parisian models, and many were literally adapted by English authors. To attempt any

---

[1] Unpublished thesis by U. C. Nagchaudhuri, in the University of London.
[2] *Op. cit.* p. 54.

analysis of that influence would obviously be impossible here[1], but a few notes may not be inopportune regarding several outstanding tendencies. At the very start, we observe that the more vital efforts of the French stage made but little impression on English playwrights. To all intents Victor Hugo passed unnoticed in this age[2]. It is certainly true that *Hernani* (1830) was translated by Lord Leveson Gower and presented privately before the Royal Family at Bridgewater House in June 1831, and that two months earlier a version by Kenney had appeared on the boards of Drury Lane. It is also true that others of his dramas saw English translation or adaptation during this period—notably *Angelo* (1835), presented at the Vic. shortly after its appearance in Paris (*Angelo*, June 1835), *Le roi s'amuse* (1832) which was given by Burton as *The Court Fool* at the Royal Pavilion in August 1833, *Marie Tudor* (1833) which was staged as *Queen Mary* at the Adelphi in Nov. 1840[3], and *Lucrèce Borgia* (1833) which was translated by J. M. Weston in 1843 and in 1847 re-translated by William Young. The fact, however, remains that the plays of Hugo roused no such critical controversy as they did in France, and that with them the works of the greater French writers were fundamentally neglected. Typical of the un-understanding English attitude of this time is the critique of Lytton's *The Duchess de la Vallière* (C.G. 1837) in *The Gentleman's Magazine*[4]. This play is there condemned as being "after the unwholesome fashion of the modern French dramatic school,—vide Dumas, Hugo, &c." The explanation of this attitude, of course, is to be found in the facts that the more talented authors were too deeply immersed in their Elizabethan dramatists, while the theatre-writers sought, not

[1] Indications are given in Appendix B of sources where these are known. While I have added a few notes culled from my own reading, it must be realised that, with a subject so vast, nothing in the way of exhaustive "research" into foreign origins could have been attempted in this work.

[2] On this subject see the interesting essay of Victor E. A. Bowley on *English Versions of Victor Hugo's Plays* in *The French Quarterly* (x. 2, June 1928).

[3] This version also made use of Harrison Ainsworth's *The Tower of London*; see Bowley, *op. cit.* p. 97.

[4] 1837, i. 421.

for a new way of art, but for that which, being familiar, could hardly fail to make an appeal. As we have already seen, the majority of these theatre-writers were unrepentant. They wrote plays, as a cobbler makes shoes, for the purpose of bringing in a few pence or a few pounds, and consequently they sought in Paris, not for what was new and vital, but for what was old and sure to please. At first sight, this statement may appear to be contradicted by the fact that, in 1802, Holcroft adapted as *A Tale of Mystery* Guilbert de Pixéré-court's *Cœlina, ou l'enfant du mystère* (Paris, 1800), which is generally regarded as the first melodrama proper. As I have shown elsewhere[1], however, the contradiction is only apparent, for the formal "melodrama" of the nineteenth century merely marks the culmination of a movement which had been rapidly gathering power between 1790 and 1800. In other words, Holcroft recognised in Pixérécourt's work, not so much a new type of dramatic art, as a perfection of that which he himself, Morton and a dozen others had been blunderingly aiming at for over a decade. Holcroft knew, from experience, that Pixérécourt would be popular in London. And popular he was, giving fresh impetus to the tendency towards type characterisation, thrilling plot, contrast of dark villainy and purest innocence, helping to establish definitely on the English stage all the tricks and devices of the melo-dramatic style. We can see how eagerly he was followed, but from no adaptation of his work do we get a sense of a novel spirit or of a hitherto untried tendency.

In dealing with Pixérécourt, it may not be inopportune here to outline such versions of his plays as I have been able to trace, since he and Scribe may be taken as typical contemporary French authors and the record of adaptation may be regarded as representative of similar activity in different spheres. After *Cœlina*, *Le pèlerin blanc, ou les orphelins du hameau* (Paris, 1801) was Pixérécourt's next complete melodramatic experiment, and this appeared in an English dress as *The Wandering Boys* (S.W. 1830) by Kerr.

---

[1] *A History of English Drama*, iii. 97–107. On Pixérécourt and the *mélodrame* the works cited there should be consulted.

Thereafter many of his works were eagerly seized upon. *L'homme à trois visages, ou le proscrit de Venise* (Paris, 1801) provided four English plays[1], while *La femme à deux maris* (Paris, 1802) gave another two[2]. *Les mines de Pologne* (Paris, 1803) was the basis of the anonymous *The Mines of Poland* (Royalty, 1822), *Tékéli, ou le siège de Montgatz* (Paris, 1803) appeared in Hook's rendering as *Tekeli* (D.L. 1806), while *Les maures d'Espagne* (Paris, 1804) suggested *The Moors of Spain* acted at Sadler's Wells in 1841. Hook returned to Pixérécourt when he wrote *The Fortress* (H.[2] 1807), which is taken from *La forteresse du Danube* (Paris, 1805). Apparently *Robinson Crusoé* (Paris, 1805) provided suggestions for Mark Lemon's *Robinson Crusoe* (Olym. 1842) and for Pocock's drama of the same title (C.G. 1817). *Le chien de Montargis, ou la forêt de Bondy* (Paris, 1814) was twice rendered[3], and *Charles-le-Téméraire, ou le siège de Nancy* (Paris, 1814) four times[4]. Dibdin took *La chapelle des bois, ou le témoin invisible* (Paris, 1818) as the model for *The Invisible Witness* (R.C. 1818), *Le Belvéder, ou, la vallée de l'Etna* (Paris, 1818) was given as *Le Belvéder* at the Surrey in 1831, while the same theatre in 1822 presented a rendering of *Le Mont Sauvage, ou le duc de Bourgogne* (Paris, 1821)[5]. *Valentine, ou la séduction* (Paris, 1821) was adapted by Ebsworth[6] and Payne[7], *Le château de Loch-Leven* (Paris, 1822) became *Mary Stuart; or, The Castle of Lochlevin* (R.P. 1839), and *La peste de Marseille* (Paris, 1828) was translated thrice[8]. Lastly may be

---

[1] Elliston's *The Venetian Outlaw* (D.L. 1805), Lewis' *Rugantino* (C.G. 1805), Powell's *The Venetian Outlaw* (1805) and an anonymous *Rugantino* (Surrey, 1831).
[2] Cobb's *The Wife of Two Husbands* (D.L. 1803), and another of the same title (1803) by E. Gunning.
[3] Barrymore's *The Dog of Montargis* (C.G. 1814) and Dibdin's play of the same title (R.C. 1814).
[4] Three anonymous versions as *Charles the Terrible* (W.L. 1821; Cob. 1830; Surrey, 1837) and one by Arnold, *Charles the Bold* (D.L. 1815).
[5] As *The Solitary of Mount Savage*.
[6] *Adelaide; or, The Fatal Seduction* (Cob. 1822).
[7] *Adeline; or, The Victim of Seduction* (D.L. 1822).
[8] An anonymous play called *The Plague of Marseilles* (S.W. 1828), a play of the same title by R. J. Raymond (Cob. 1828) and Moncrieff's *The Pestilence of Marseilles* (Surrey, 1829).

cited Fitzball's *Ondine* (Queen's, 1843), derived from *Ondine, ou la nymphe des eaux* (Paris, 1830).

It is evident here that Pixérécourt's influence is by no means unimportant, but one must again emphasise the comparative lack of novelty in choice and in treatment of theme to be found in his work. The same is true of other forms of dramatic art taken from France, and at this point we may consider in brief survey the adaptations of the plays written by the popular dramatist Eugène Scribe. Of his plays it is fairly easy to trace adaptations of at least the more popular and better known. One drama (*Les diamants de la couronne*, written in collaboration with de Saint-Georges and with music by Auber, Paris, 1841) saw no less than six English versions[1], while five adaptations each were accorded to four plays—*La muette de Portici* (with Delavigne and Auber, Paris, 1828)[2], *La Juive* (with music by Halévy, Paris, 1835)[3], *Robert le Diable* (with Delavigne and Meyerbeer, Paris, 1831)[4], and *Le domino noir* (with music by Auber, Paris, 1837)[5]. Four plays were given three English versions—*Les Huguenots* (with music by Meyerbeer, Paris, 1836)[6], *Le cheval de bronze* (with music by Auber, Paris, 1835)[7], *La sirène* (Paris, 1844)[8],

---

[1] *Catarina; or, The False Jewels* (Strand, 1844), *Catarina; or, The Crown Jewels* (Vic. 1844), *The Crown Brilliants* (Grecian, 1846), *The Crown Diamonds* (Yarmouth, 1847), *The Crown Diamonds* (P'cess, 1844) and Fitzball's *The Crown Jewels* (D.L. 1846).

[2] Levius' *Masaniello* (D.L. 1829), an anonymous *Masaniello* (R.A. 1829), a ballet based on the story (H.¹ 1829), Milner's *Masaniello* (Cob. 1829) and Kenney's *Masaniello* (C.G. 1849).

[3] As *The Jewess*—Moncrieff's (Vic. 1835), anonymous (R.P. 1835), Planché's (D.L. 1835), Burroughs' (Edinburgh, 1836), anonymous (Queen's, 1844).

[4] *The Demon Duke* (D.L. 1832), *The Demon Father* (R.P. 1832), *The Fiend Father* (C.G. 1832), *Robert le Diable* (S.W. 1832), Fitzball's *Robert le Diable* (Adel. 1832).

[5] Four plays called *The Black Domino* by Wilks (S.W. 1838), Mathews (Olym. 1838), Coyne (Adel. 1838) and Morton and Kenney (C. G. 1838); *Le domino noir* (D.L. 1848).

[6] Three plays, *The Huguenots*, two anonymous (E.O.H. 1836; C.G. 1845), and one by Russell (Surrey, 1849).

[7] Fitzball's *The Bronze Horse* (C.G. 1835), an anonymous play (R.A. 1835) and Bunn's *The Bronze Horse* (D.L. 1836).

[8] Bunn's *The Syren* (D.L. 1844) and two anonymous plays (P'cess, 1844, and the Eagle, 1846).

and *La somnambule* (Paris, 1819)[1], and seven others reached two separate renderings—*La neige* (with Delavigne, Paris, 1823)[2], *La dame blanche* (with music by Boieldieu, Paris, 1825)[3], *La fiancée* (with music by Auber, Paris, 1829)[4], *Lestocq* (with music by Auber, Paris, 1834)[5], *L'ambassadrice* (with de Saint-Georges, Paris, 1836)[6], *Haydée, ou le secret* (Paris, 1847)[7], and *Michel et Christine* (Paris, 1821)[8]. Besides these, fully fifteen plays by Scribe appeared, either in directly translated or in adapted forms, on the English stage—*Valérie* (Paris, 1822)[9], *Bertrand et Raton* (Paris, 1833)[10], *Une chaine* (Paris, 1841)[11], *Le philtre* (Paris, 1831)[12], *Le prophète* (Paris, 1849)[13], *La part du diable* (with music by Auber, Paris, 1843)[14], *Une visite à Bedlam* (Paris, 1818)[15], *Rodolphe, ou frère et sœur* (Paris, 1823)[16], *La demoiselle à marier* (Paris, 1826)[17], *La belle-mère* (Paris, 1826)[18], *L'oncle d'Amérique* (Paris, 1826)[19], *L'ambassadeur* (Paris, 1826)[20], *Le mariage de raison* (Paris, 1826)[21], *Louise, ou la réparation* (Paris, 1829)[22], and *Une faute* (Paris, 1830)[23].

[1] An anonymous *Love's Dream* (E.O.H. 1820), Beazley's *La Somnambula* (D.L. 1833), Moncrieff's *The Somnambulist* (C.G. 1828).
[2] Planché's *The Frozen Lake* (E.O.H. 1824), *The Frozen Lake* (C.G. 1824).
[3] Payne's *The White Maid* (C.G. 1827), *The White Lady* (D.L. 1826).
[4] *The Husband's Mistake* (C.G. 1830), Planché's *The National Guard* (D.L. 1830).
[5] Macfarren's *Lestocq* (C.G. 1835), Moncrieff's *Lestocq* (Vic. 1835).
[6] À Beckett's *The Ambassadress* (St J. 1838), *The Ambassadress* (Grecian, 1848).
[7] *Haydee* (Strand, 1848), *Haydee* (C.G. 1848).
[8] *Michael and Christine* (S.W. 1849), *Love in Humble Life* (D.L. 1822).
[9] *Valeria* (H.² 1828).
[10] Bunn's *The Minister and the Mercer* (D.L. 1834).
[11] Rodwell's *The Breach of Promise of Marriage* (Adel. 1842).
[12] Planché's *The Love Charm* (D.L. 1831).
[13] Fitzball's *The Prophet* (R.A. 1849).
[14] Archer's *Asmodeus, the little Demon* (Surrey, 1843).
[15] Morton's *A Roland for an Oliver* (C.G. 1819).
[16] Lacy's *The Two Friends* (H.² 1828).
[17] Planché's *A Daughter to Marry* (H.² 1828).
[18] Lacy's *The Stepmother* (C.G. 1828).
[19] Poole's *A Nabob for an Hour* (C.G. 1833).
[20] Planché's *Manœuvring* (H.² 1829).
[21] *The Marriage of Reason* (H.² 1844).
[22] Bernard's *Louise* (H.² 1843).
[23] Selby's *The One Fault* (City, 1831).

This bare list of adaptations[1], which could certainly be supplemented, seems to show a deep indebtedness to the French writer's works, but in reality Scribe brought nothing thoroughly new to the theatre. He is a perfecter in style and construction rather than an innovator and an inventor. Even the vaudevilles, the revues and the fairy extravaganzas which seem so characteristically French were not so very far removed from the burlesques and the burlettas of eighteenth century England. I should by no means wish to deny the widespread Gallic influence on the dramatic work of these years, but, while admitting that influence, I should desire to stress the fact that, after all, the main theatrical movements in the period are to be traced back to the tendencies of preceding years.

It has been remarked that the French almost completely supplanted the German drama in the minds and hearts of English dramatists. In 1799 the publishers were frenziedly turning out their innumerable editions of Kotzebue and Schiller; by 1819 these editions were no doubt littering the cheaper second-hand bookstalls. Attempts were still made to furnish new renderings of the greater German masterpieces; volumes of collected works of men such as Goethe and Schiller were issued by the larger publishers[2]; but apparently

---

[1] It must be insisted that only such versions are cited here as have been noted from my own reading of Scribe. A detailed search would no doubt show that nearly all his plays had appeared on the English stage. The order of the French plays given above follows that in the *Théâtre de Eugène Scribe* (Paris, 1856–7, 18 vols.).

[2] B. Q. Morgan in his *Bibliography of German Literature in English Translation* [University of Wisconsin Studies, xvi. 1922] essays to cover the whole of this activity. The following works deal with the early nineteenth century: W. F. Hanhart, *The Reception of Goethe's Faust in England in the First Half of the Nineteenth Century* (N.Y., 1909); J. M. Carré, *Goethe en Angleterre* (Paris, 1920); Lina Baumann, *Die englischen Übersetzungen von Goethes Faust* (Halle, 1907); F. W. C. Lieder, *Goethe in England and America* (*Journal of English and Germanic Philology*, x. 1911); J. G. Robertson, *Goethe and Byron* (*Publ. of the English Goethe Society*, N.S., ii. 1925); W. Heinemann, *Goethes Faust in England und Amerika* (Berlin, 1886); E. Oswald, *Goethe in England and America, A Bibliography* (1909); J. Tait, *The Literary Influence of Goethe's Faust in England, 1832–1852* (*Trans. of the Manchester Goethe Society*, 1894); W. Macintosh, *Scott and Goethe* (1925); T. Rea, *Schiller's Poems and Dramas in England* (1906); C. Sachs, *Schillers Beziehungen zur englischen Literatur* (*Archiv,*

that wellnigh universal interest which had characterised the last years of the eighteenth century had almost completely vanished. Editions of Benjamin Thompson's *The German Theatre*[1] continued to appear; individual enthusiasts still worked at new versions of the plays of Schiller and of Goethe[2];

xxx. 1861); H. F. G. Roscher, *Die Wallensteinübersetzung von S. T. Coleridge* (1905); M. W. Cooke, *Schiller's Robbers in England* (*Modern Language Review*, xi. 2. April 1916); L. A. Willoughby, introduction to edition of *Die Räuber* (Oxford, 1922); Sprague Allen, *Analogues of Wordsworth's "The Borderers"* (*Publ. of the Modern Language Association of America*, xxxviii. 2, 1923); M. J. Herzberg, *Wordsworth and German Literature* (*id.* xl. 2, 1925); W. Sellier, *Kotzebue in England* (Leipzig, 1901); L. Bahlsen, *Kotzebues Peru-Dramen und Sheridans Pizarro* (*Archiv*, lxxxi. 1893); F. Koeppel, *Kotzebue in England* (*Englische Studien*, xiii. 1891); J. E. Gillet, *A Forgotten German Creditor of the English Stage* (*Nineteenth Century*, April 1912); W. Todt, *Lessing in England* (Heidelberg, 1912); S. H. Kenwood, *Lessing in England* (*Modern Language Review*, 1914); K. Blumenhagen, *Sir Walter Scott als Übersetzer* (Rostock, 1900); T. Zeiger, *Beiträge zur Geschichte der deutsch-englischen Literaturbeziehungen* (*Studien zur vergleichenden Literaturgeschichte*, i. 1901); F. W. Stokoe, *German Influence in the English Romantic Period 1788–1818* (1926).

[1] See Hand-list, Appendix B.

[2] *Faust* and *Don Carlos* seem to have proved particularly attractive to translators. For the former see Appendix B under Talbot (1835), Syme (1834), Swanwick (1850), Macdonald (1838), Lefevre (1841), Knox (1847), Hills (1839), Hayward (1833), Gurney (1842), Gower (1823), Filmore (1841), Blackie (1834), Birch (1839), Bernays (1839), Soane (1820), Anster (1835), Duckett (1845). Three anonymous versions appeared in 1821, 1834 and 1838. *Faustus* was presented at the Coburg in 1824; another adaptation (by Soane and Terry) appeared at Drury Lane in 1825; and a third (by Grattan) at Sadler's Wells in 1842. As an opera it was given at H.[1] in 1842. *Don Carlos* was translated by Towler (1843), Cottrell (1843), Bruce (1837), Russell (1822, acted at Surrey, 1848). As an opera it was produced (libretto by Tarantini) at H.[1] in 1844. Here may be noted Thompson's (1804) and Shoberl's (1804) renderings of Goethe's *Stella*, as well as a series of versions of Schiller's works. *Die Braut von Messina* (1803) was Englished by Irvine (1837), Lockwood (1839) and Lodge (1841); Knowles' play appeared at Covent Garden in 1840. Crescini has a *Brigands* (1836) from *Die Räuber*. An anonymous translation of *Fiesko* was issued in 1841, while Daguilar (1832) produced another. *Die Jungfrau von Orleans* (1802) was rendered by Bethune (1835), Egestorff (1836), Lucas (1841), Turner (1842), Swanwick (1843) and Thompson (1845). *Maria Stuart* (1801) was translated by Mellish (1801), Salvin (1824), Trelawney (1838), Percival (1839) and Peter (1841). An anonymous version was published in 1833, and a *Mary Stuart* play based on Schiller's appeared at Covent Garden in 1819. Coleridge's *The Piccolomini* (1800) is well known; another anonymous translation was issued in 1805 and Moir's in 1827. *Wilhelm Tell* was also popular among translators—Grosett (1812), Robinson (1825), Roche (1808), Vœux (1827), Talbot (1829), Banfield (1831), Peter (1839), Thompson (1845) and

Die Räuber and other dramas kept some of their inspiration for poetic dramatists; Kotzebue still held for a few some charm[1]; a German theatre ran for a whole season in London[2]; but for the theatre as a whole, save for a few exceptions, the German drama exerted but little direct influence. The many translations may have given pleasure to those poetically inclined, but it will be noted that, in the lists given above, only one or two plays actually found an English stage dress. There are, however, the exceptions. The first comprises the German operas. Händel had worked in England during the eighteenth century, but Händel's efforts had been all in the direction of the Italian style. Now for the first time the beauties of opera in German came to charm English audiences; Mozart and Beethoven appeared at the Haymarket, at Drury Lane and at the Princess's with both original German and adapted English libretti. This movement was not without its influence upon the London stage, for in this age of melodrama and of musical comedy there was but a slight line of demarcation between the purely dramatic and the purely operatic. The second exception includes a few melodramatic works, over which there arose tremendous furore in certain years of this period. Typical of these is Kind's *Der Freischütz*, with Weber's music, which startled and thrilled the town in the year 1824. Of this play at least five adaptations appeared in that season[3], while within a few months of the original

---

Molini (1846). A *William Tell* appeared at the Coburg in 1821. There may be noted also Clarke's *Ravenna* (C.G. 1824), based on *Kabale und Liebe*, and the anonymous translation of *Wallenstein* (1799 and 1800).

[1] The following may be noted: *Alfred and Emma* (1806) from *Die Kreuzfahrer*; Kenney's *Benyowsky* (D.L. 1826) from *Graf Benjowsky*; *The Confusion* (1842) from *Der Wirrwarr*, which also gave *All in Confusion* (German, 1806); Siber's *The Female Jacobin-Club* (1801) from *Der weibliche Jacobiner-Clubb*; *How to Die for Love* (Lyc. 1812); Cumberland's *Joanna of Montfaucon* (C.G. 1800); Kemble's *Kamtchatka* (C.G. 1811); *Kindred* (1837) from *Die Verwandtschaften*; Capadose's *The Organs of the Brain* (1838) from *Die Organe des Gehirns*; Shoberl's *The Patriot Father* (1830) from *Die Hussiten*; Kemble's *The Wanderer* (C.G. 1808) from *Eduard in Schottland*; Reynolds' *The Virgin of the Sun* (C.G. 1812) and an anonymous *Virgin of the Sun* (Norwich, 1815) from *Die Sonnen-Jungfrau*. [2] See Appendix A.

[3] Soane's (D.L. 1824), Logan's (E.O.H. 1824), Fitzball's (Surrey, 1824), Planché's (C.G. 1824), Amherst's (R.A. 1824).

7

productions "Septimus Globus" had issued a *Freischütz Travestie* and the Olympic had staged a regular burlesque. The following year appeared another burlesque, *Der Fryshot*, at the Theatre Royal, Edinburgh, to be followed by a fourth at the Adelphi in 1828. The original German libretto was played at the Haymarket in 1832. Such isolated examples, however, cannot be used to prove any widespread interest, such as existed from 1790 to 1800, in the German drama. The explanation of this neglect, no doubt, is to be traced in that moral mood which had greeted the earliest translations in the preceding age[1]. During the first decades of the nineteenth century this moral mood was growing in intensity and its decorousness would by no means accept either the problems presented by Kotzebue or the daring of Schiller. There is, of course, nothing exceptional here, for Ibsen was denied fifty years later, and only yesterday Strindberg, Toller and Hauptmann were looked on askance. One peculiarity of the English stage is that it is always accepting at a late date other people's forgotten and outworn ideas. It assumes that fresh and novel ideas originated abroad must of necessity be subversive of morality. It is not strange, therefore, that Schiller and the other German dramatists were in the early nineteenth century recognised in the main only by a few literary enthusiasts.

One great characteristic of this time is, of course, the interest in Elizabethan literature. Something has been said on this subject above, but the theme requires at least a few additional notes. This was the period when the long-buried works of the minor Elizabethans were unearthed; this, too, was the period when the criticism of Coleridge, Schlegel, Hazlitt and a host of others revealed a profundity in Shakespeare which had hardly been felt before. It is true that Shakespeare had never been for one moment forgotten in the eighteenth century, either by managers or by *littérateurs*, but rarely did the Augustans divine the psychological depth in Shakespeare discovered in the later age and comparatively rarely did the dramatists seek to imitate his works. Now,

[1] See *A History of English Drama*, iii. 121–2.

it seemed as if a whole Eldorado of poetic gold had been revealed to the poets, and they, like the adventurers of old, hesitated not to make free use of the treasures poured in front of them. The poetic dramas of the time are literally filled with Shakespearian and Elizabethan imagery. Often does Patience sit melancholy upon a monument; often do characters look in a moved sort as if they were dismayed. This wholesale borrowing is accompanied by slavish imitation of plot and character; the real gold is frequently set in a framework of tinsel. Many dramatists, "thouing" through five acts, seem physically incapable of penning a "you." Blank verse unimaginatively follows the cadences of a Shakespeare or a Fletcher. Iagos subtly insinuate their way on to the stage, and Rosalinds lisp in quivering Forests of Arden.

Clearly, such universal imitation can lead to nothing that is original, for every age, however fully it may be conscious of the beauties and the virtues of the past, must work out its own methods, its own language, its own characters and its own aim. The theme of our later survey of the poetic drama must be once more the failure of the dramatists to escape from the trammels of this Elizabethan idolisation. It is not too much to say that Shakespeare cast a blight upon the would-be higher drama of the time. Nor, in dealing with this subject, must we forget that the knowledge of the Elizabethans was by no means confined to the contemporary men of letters. Shakespeare, as has been seen, gained a new lease of life owing to the spectacular tendencies of the age[1], and of the minor Elizabethan writers there were many interesting revivals during the half-century. The audiences, therefore, had ample opportunities for hearing the works of the Immortal Bard, and the habit of playing Shakespeare against Shakespeare, of presenting the same plays with different casts or at least with changes of star-performers, undoubtedly led towards an added attention paid to the actual words spoken in the theatres. Typical examples of the extent of this interest in the earlier plays may be found in Planché's extravaganzas and burlesques. Many of these

[1] See *supra*, p. 41.

depend for their very existence upon the recognition by the audience of the Shakespearian phrases which he has cleverly interwoven into his own dialogue. Few playgoers of today could immediately distinguish the allusions, yet we must suppose that Planché's contemporaries found no difficulty in doing so. The success of his pieces seems to testify to that. Testimony, too, comes from *The Theatrical Repertory* and from Colman the younger. A protest in the former, against the operatic version of *The Tempest*[1], shows what close attention was being paid to the original text, while the latter definitely states that everyone is "perfectly aware...that a modern audience would not allow of any further meddling with the text of Shakespeare[2]." This statement, however, must be qualified so as to make it apply only to the major theatres, for the minors early discovered that Shakespeare had in him the stuff of which excellent "burlettas" and melodramas are made. It would be impossible to give a full list of such versions here, but we may note at least a few selected examples. As a burletta *Antony and Cleopatra* appeared at the Surrey in 1810. *The Battle of Bosworth Field* (Cob. 1827) is simply *Richard III*[3]. *Julius Cæsar* became a melodrama at the East London in 1818, while at the Royalty in 1812 appeared a burletta of *King Lear and his Three Daughters*. A melodrama, *The Life and Death of King Richard II; or, Wat Tyler and Jack Straw* (R.A. 1834), was indebted partly to Shakespeare, while *Romeo and Juliet* was a melodrama at the Surrey in 1813. Another melodrama called *The Royal Dane* (Surrey, 1827) is only *Hamlet* adapted. These pieces were obviously successful, as is indirectly attested by the extraordinary number of Shakespearian burlesques and travesties which this age produced[4]. *King "Leer"* was given at the Bower Saloon in 1848, while

---

[1] No. VIII. Saturday, Nov. 7, 1801.

[2] R. B. Peake, *op. cit.* ii. 434.

[3] Cf. *King Richard III and the Battle of Bosworth Field* (Royalty, 1812), and *The Life and Death of King Richard III; or, The Battle of Bosworth Field* (Surrey, 1813).

[4] See R. Farquharson Sharp, *Travesties of Shakespeare's Plays* (*The Library*, I. i, June 1920). A number of those cited here have not hitherto been noted.

a *King Lear and his Daughters Queer* was printed in 1830. Selby's *King Richard ye Third; or, ye Battel of Bosworth Field* (Strand, 1844) has clearly the melodramatic adaptations in view. There are many travesties of *Macbeth*[1] and *Othello*[2] and *Romeo*[3]. Here may be mentioned, too, C. Dibdin's *Anthony, Cleopatra and Harlequin* (S.W. 1804). In surveying the interest in Shakespeare taken by the people of this period two other things are to be observed. The first is a tendency to translate, as it were, the Shakespearian characters into terms of everyday existence. Moncrieff's *The Lear of Private Life* (Cob. 1820) and *The Othello of Private Life* (C.L. 1849) may serve as examples. It is interesting to note that Turgeniev's experiment has thus been anticipated in the early nineteenth century stage. The other concerns the numerous plays dealing with episodes in Shakespeare's life. Somerset's *Shakespeare's Early Days* (C.G. 1829), *Shakespeare and Burbage* (Strand, 1838), and *Shakespeare's Dream* (Edinburgh, 1831) show clearly a new interest in the playwright as an individual, while such pieces as Moncrieff's *Shakespeare's Festival* (Surrey, 1830) and C. Dibdin's *Shakespeare versus Harlequin* (D.L. 1820)[4] may be noted to add yet fresh weight of evidence proving the widespread interest taken by both majors and minors in the plays of the "Bard of Avon."

Alongside of this revived interest in things Elizabethan must be chronicled the interest in the contemporary novel. Fiction was rapidly becoming a dominant form of literature, and the minor dramatists found here in plenty that for which they were seeking—plots, characters and dialogues ready formed, the *scenario* (and more than the *scenario*) on which they could base their hastily written plays. The dramatisation of novels had begun in the latter half of the preceding century[5], but it was not until the time of Scott that the whole field of fiction

---

[1] Talfourd's (Oxford, 1850), Bell's (1838), an anonymous *Macbeth Travestie* (1813) and another (Strand, 1842).
[2] Anonymous (1813), Dowling's (Liverpool, 1834).
[3] Dowling's (1837), Gurney's (1812), anonymous (Edinburgh, 1841).
[4] Adapted from Garrick's *Harlequin's Invasion*.
[5] See *A History of English Drama*, iii. 71–2.

was eagerly and systematically ransacked[1]. In the Waverley Novels the playwrights found that there was for them as for the original author a mint of money. Even before the appearance of *Waverley*, Scott's work had attracted theatrical attention. The poetical romances were soon seized upon by one after another of the needy dramatists. *The Lady of the Lake*[2], *Marmion*[3], *Rokeby*[4], *The Bridal of Triermain*[5], *The Rose of Ettrick Vale*[6], and *The Lord of the Isles*[7], all appeared on the English stage, while a version of *The Lay of the Last Minstrel*, as *Border Feuds*, was published in Dublin in 1811. Of the novels, *Rob Roy* most surely captured the hearts of contemporaries. By January 1818 an anonymous version was being given at the Pantheon Theatre, Edinburgh; on February 16 of the same year was produced another at the Olympic; Pocock's rendering appeared at Covent Garden on March 12, and was followed a fortnight later by Soane's at Drury Lane; in June, Murray of the Theatre Royal, Edinburgh, brought out a revised text of the Covent Garden production. Thereafter, with minor changes in the various versions, *Rob Roy*

---

[1] H. A. White has an essay on *Sir Walter Scott's Novels on the Stage* (Yale University Press, 1927). This is a good survey of the subject, but it omits many of the versions and has no indication of the printed texts.

[2] See in the Hand-list of Plays appended to this survey. T. J. Dibdin's *The Lady of the Lake* (Surrey, 1810), E. J. Eyre's *The Lady of the Lake* (Edinburgh, 1811), T. Morton's *The Knight of Snowdoun* (C.G. 1811), as well as *The Lady of the Lake* (D.L. 1827), *The Knight of Snowdoun* (E.O.H. 1823), *The Lady of the Lake* (C.G. 1843) and Tully's *The Lady of the Lake* (Strand, 1843), all taken from Rossini's *La Donna del Lago* presented at Naples in 1819 and performed in Italian at the Haymarket in 1823.

[3] See under Unknown Authors, *Marmion* (New, 1810), *Marmion; or, The Battle of Flodden Field* (Norwich, 1811), and Macready's (Newcastle, 1814), S. Kemble (D.L. 1818), Fitzball (R.A. 1848). C. Dibdin's *The Spectre Knight* (S.W. 1810) is from the same source.

[4] Macready's version appeared at Newcastle in 1814 and Thompson printed another the same year.

[5] An operetta, *Triermain*, by Ellerton appeared in 1831, and Pocock's *King Arthur* at Drury Lane in 1834.

[6] Murray's version came out at Edinburgh in 1825; another was licensed for the Adelphi in 1829.

[7] An anonymous *Robert the Bruce* appeared at Perth in 1819; this was probably an emended version of a Coburg melodrama, 1819. An Olympic play had been prepared in 1815, Fitzball brought out an operetta at the Surrey in 1834, and an anonymous dramatisation appears in the L.C. plays for Covent Garden in 1835.

held the stage. As *Gregarach* it was presented at Astley's in 1821 and as *Roy's Wife* at the Coburg in 1825. Three separate versions seem to have been prepared thereafter, two for Corbett Ryder's company in Edinburgh (1825) and one for the Coburg (1828). North of the Tweed one may still have the opportunity of seeing it during annual revivals. Once the value of Scott from the theatrical point of view was appreciated, there was a frenzied scrambling among the playwrights for a share in the spoils. Practically every one of the *Waverley* series was seized upon, and for decades the theatres were fed with versions of *Guy Mannering*[1], *The Antiquary*[2], *Old Mortality*[3], *The Fortunes of Nigel*[4], *The Heart of Midlothian*[5], *Ivanhoe*[6], *The Legend of*

[1] The very first adaptation was that of *Guy Mannering* (C.G. 1816) made by D. Terry with the assistance of Scott himself. In 1821 the plot of the novel was combined with that of *La Sorcière* (Paris, 1821) by Dupetit-Méré and Ducange, giving Planché's *The Witch of Derncleuch* (E.O.H.), Jerrold's *The Gipsy of Derncleuch* (S.W.), *Dick Hatteraick* (Cob.) and an anonymous *Witch of Derncleuch* (Edinburgh, 1822). The dramatic fate of this novel was somewhat peculiar. With *The Monastery* it was used by Scribe for *La dame blanche* (Paris, 1825) and the French musical drama was in its turn re-dramatised in English as *The White Lady* (D.L. 1826) and *The White Maid* (C.G. 1827; by Payne), besides being played in the original French on the London stage.

[2] Pocock's *The Antiquary* appeared at Covent Garden in 1818; this was refashioned by Terry (C.G. 1820) and by Murray (Edinburgh, 1820). A Coburg version appeared in 1832.

[3] *Old Mortality* was made into a play by Farley, as *The Battle of Bothwell Brig* (C.G. 1820); a month later Dibdin produced another version (Surrey, 1820) and Calcraft revised one of these for Edinburgh production (1823). The derivative opera, *I Puritani di Scozia* (Paris, 1835), was Englished by Pocock as *Cavaliers and Roundheads* (D.L. 1835), while Marston's *Strathmore* (H.[2] 1849) was inspired by the novel.

[4] Fitzball's *The Fortunes of Nigel* appeared at the Surrey in 1822, Pocock's *Nigel* at Covent Garden in 1823. A *George Heriot* said to be by Ryder was produced at Perth in 1823, and the same year saw an homonymous version by Murray (Edin. 1823).

[5] *The Heart of Midlothian* was particularly popular. In 1819 appeared versions by Dibdin (R.C.), Terry (C.G.), Dimond (Bath), Montague and Jervis (Pantheon, Edin.), and an unknown author (T.R. Edin.). Murray's rendering was produced at Edinburgh in 1824; some unused chapters were taken over for *The Whistler* (Cob. 1833) by G. D. Pitt; while a play by Rafter (Princess, 1849) was based on Paul Duport's *La Vendéenne* (Paris, 1837), a French dramatisation. A fresh version was licensed for Edinburgh in 1841. Maclaren's *Filial Duty* (1819) is from the same source.

[6] *Ivanhoe* also made a wide appeal. No less than seven versions made their appearance in 1820: Dibdin's (Surrey), Moncrieff's (Cob.), Beazley's (C.G.), Soane's (D.L., as *The Hebrew*), anonymous (Adel.), and two printed renderings (London and Birmingham). Calcraft and Murray

Montrose[1], *Peveril of the Peak*[2], *Redgauntlet*[3], *Waverley*[4], *Woodstock*[5], *Kenilworth*[6], *The Abbot*[7], *The Bride of Lammermoor*[8],

brought out successive dramatisations for the Theatre Royal, Edinburgh, and as *The Lists of Ashby* it was given at Astley's in 1837. E. Deschamps and G. de Wailly had produced *Ivanhoé* at the Odéon in 1826, and this appeared as *The Maid of Judah* (C.G. 1829), adapted by Lacy. Jackson's *The Templar and the Jewess* (printed 1833) is a modified translation of Wohlbrück's *Der Templar und die Jüden* (1829), which was played at the Prince's in 1840 and at Drury Lane in 1841.

[1] Dibdin's *The Legend of Montrose* appeared at the Surrey in 1819, and the same year was produced *The Children of the Mist* at the Coburg. A Glasgow version followed within a few months. In 1822 at Covent Garden Pocock's rendering was produced and in 1823 at Edinburgh that of Murray. The Caledonian, Edinburgh, brought out another dramatisation in 1827, and in 1847 a second Glasgow play was printed there.

[2] Fitzball was first in the field with a *Peveril of the Peak* (Surrey, 1823) and his rendering was revised for the Theatre Royal, Edinburgh, production in the same year. At Covent Garden in 1826 appeared a fresh dramatisation by Pocock.

[3] An anonymous version of *Redgauntlet* was produced at the Surrey in 1824, and a second, no doubt by Murray, at the Theatre Royal, Edinburgh, in 1825.

[4] The Corbett Ryder company seems to have been first with a *Waverley* acted at Perth in 1822. The Caledonian, Edinburgh, followed in 1823 (with a new version four years later). Fitzball's drama appeared at the Adel. in 1824, and on this Calcraft based his production at the Theatre Royal, Edinburgh (1824). Separate versions were prepared for Covent Garden in 1824 and in 1832.

[5] Pocock's *Woodstock* was produced at Covent Garden in 1826, and the same year dramas of the same title were given in Edinburgh and at the Surrey, the latter by C. Dibdin.

[6] The year 1821 saw at least six versions of *Kenilworth*: Planché's (Adel.), Dibdin's (Surrey), Bunn's (C.G.), Dimond's (Bath), anonymous (Olym.), anonymous (Surrey, as *Elizabeth and Essex*). A seventh appeared at Edinburgh in 1822, and an eighth at the same city in 1824. Drury Lane versions came out in 1824 and 1832, while a new rendering was given at the Caledonian, Edinburgh, in 1825. A ballet, *Kenilworth*, was produced at Covent Garden in 1833. Stirling's *Tilbury Fort* was performed at Gravesend in 1829, and Heath's *The Earl of Leicester* was printed in 1843. A belated dramatisation appeared at Astley's in 1847.

[7] Beverley's *The Abbot* was given at Tottenham-street in 1820 and Murray's *Mary Queen of Scots* at the Theatre Royal, Edinburgh, in 1825.

[8] In 1819 Dibdin brought forward *The Bride of Lammermoor* (Surrey, 1819) and another was given at Astley's contemporaneously. Calcraft's version is usually cited under the year 1822, but a melodrama, *The Bride of Lammermuir, A Caledonian Romance*, was "allowed" by the Lord Chamberlain for the Theatre Royal, Edinburgh, on Oct. 27, 1819. As *The Mermaiden's Well* a dramatisation appeared at the Brunswick in 1828, and another at the Queen's in 1831. Cammarano's *Lucia di Lammermoor* (Naples, 1835), with music by Donizetti, was given at H.[1] in 1838, at Drury Lane in 1845, and (in English) at the Princess in 1843 and the Grecian in 1844. A burlesque was prepared for the Strand in 1848.

Quentin Durward[1], *The Black Dwarf*[2], *The Fair Maid of Perth*[3], *The Highland Widow*[4], *The Monastery*[5], *The Pirate*[6], *St Ronan's Well*[7], *The Two Drovers*[8], *The Betrothed*[9], and *The Talisman*[10]—they followed one after another in regular succession. The contemporary enthusiasm was given expression, also, in Knowles' *The Vision of the Bard* (C.G. 1832), a festival in honour of "The Wizard of the North." It is not to be questioned that this enthusiasm aided materially in the still firmer establishment of the melodrama. The themes of Scott's novels are themselves inclined towards that atmosphere which we have come to call melodramatic, and this atmosphere, when transferred to terms of the stage, became necessarily still more pronounced. The romantic settings, the boldly drawn type characters, the clear differentiation of virtue and vice,

---

[1] A *Quentin Durward* by Haworth was printed in 1823; the same year saw a rendering by Haines at the Coburg. A Caledonian version was presented the same year. A "grand opera" by Fitzball appeared at Covent Garden in 1848.

[2] Arnold's *The Black Dwarf*, or *The Wizard*, appeared at the English Opera House in 1817. As *The Recluse* it was re-rendered at the Theatre Royal, Edinburgh, and Drury Lane in 1825.

[3] Milner and Lacy brought out *A Fair Maid of Perth* or *St Valentine's Eve* at the Coburg in 1828. The same year the Bass company seems to have had another at Perth. A later version by Webb appeared at the Surrey in 1845.

[4] *Dougal the Piper* appeared at the Adelphi, Edinburgh, in 1836. The following year a new rendering, *The Highland Widow*, is to be found in the L.C. collection. As *Military Punishment* a third version was given at the Surrey in 1846.

[5] See *The White Lady* under *Guy Mannering*.

[6] In 1822 appeared three versions of *The Pirate*: Dibdin's (Surrey), Planché's (Olym.) and Dimond's (D.L.). Another drama was given at the Theatre Royal, Edinburgh, in 1824. I do not know whether Dibdin's pantomime, *The Pirate*, has anything to do with this novel. A later rendering came out at the Grecian in 1844.

[7] A dramatisation by Planché of *St Ronan's Well* was brought out at the Adelphi in 1824 and was used a few months later at Edinburgh. McNeill had another produced at the Princess, Edinburgh, at the same time. Still another appeared at D.L. in 1824.

[8] A Caledonian (Edinburgh) production was first in the field in 1827. This was followed by Murray's at the Theatre Royal, Edinburgh, in 1828. Goff's was given at the Surrey in 1849.

[9] See under Fitzball, *The Betrothed* (Olym. 1826) and *The Betrothed; or, The Eve of St Mark* (Queen's, 1836).

[10] *The Talisman* first appeared as *Knights of the Cross* (D.L. 1826) by Beazley. An Edinburgh playwright brought out a second version in 1825.

the innumerable adventures—all these appealed to the age
and led towards many an imitation. The enthusiasm for Scott,
too, opened up the whole field of fiction for the theatre.
Old novels were dug up again, and, above all, the bookstalls
were eagerly ransacked for any new work which might have a
stirring and popular plot. Typical of the frenzied rush which
greeted the appearance of a popular favourite is the collection
of dramatic versions of *The Cricket on the Hearth* preserved
among the Lord Chamberlain's documents at St James's
Palace. The Lyceum seems to have been first on the field
with a rendering which was licensed on Dec. 17, 1845. The
following weeks must have been busy ones for the official
Reader of Plays, for on Jan. 3, 1846, versions of the same
novel were licensed for the Princess's, the Albert Saloon,
the Adelphi, the Marylebone, the City of London and the
Haymarket. On the 16th of the month an Apollo Saloon
version was set free, and on the same day an Olympic
burlesque entitled *The Cricket on our Own Hearth* received
the official signature. This was in less than one month
from the date when the first early dramatisation had been
"allowed." By the 23rd of the month, still another adaptation
was being performed in Edinburgh.

Scores of similar examples might be taken, but this one
may be sufficient to stand as symbolic of the eagerness with
which the dramatists rushed to take advantage of the material
offered to them in contemporary fiction. Almost all novelists
were exploited, from old favourites such as Smollett[1], down
to the latest favourites of the hour. A startling romance,
such as Mrs Shelley's *Frankenstein*, could arouse tremendous
enthusiasm[2], and a tale of eccentric humours, such as Egan's
Life in London[3], could provide dramatic material for years.

[1] See Dibdin's *The Adventures of Roderick Random* (R.C. 1818) and
Humphrey Clinker (R.C. 1818). Another version of the latter appeared
at S.W. in 1828. Dibdin also wrote a *Ferdinand Count Fathom* (R.C. 1818).
[2] In 1823 versions appeared at the English Opera House, Royalty and
Coburg. Milner's rendering (Cob. 1823) and Brough's burlesque (Adel.
1849) testify to its enduring popularity.
[3] The following is not an exhaustive list: Moncrieff's *Tom and Jerry*
(Adel. 1821), *Tom and Jerry* (S.W. 1822), Dibdin's *Life in London*
(Olym. 1821), *Tom, Jerry and Logic* (Royalty, 1822), *Tom and Jerry*

Naturally there were among the novelists those who were particularly followed; popularity attended Cooper[1], Lytton[2], Ainsworth[3] and Dickens. The last-mentioned is sufficiently important to demand fuller analysis. *Posthumous Papers of the Pickwick Club* (1837) appealed because of its mixture of humour and pathos[4], and the same qualities were those which made the succeeding novels popular. Nearly all saw several adaptations—*Oliver Twist* (1838)[5], *Nicholas Nickleby* (1838-9)[6], *Barnaby Rudge* (1841)[7], *The Old Curiosity Shop* (1841)[8], *A Christmas Carol* (1843)[9], *Martin Chuzzlewit*

(Edinburgh T.R. 1823), *Tom and Jerry in Edinburgh* (Edinburgh, Caledonian, 1823), Macfarren's *Tom and Jerry in France* (Cob. 1822), *Our Future Fate; or, Tom, Jerry and Logic in* 1845 (Cob. 1823), *Tom, Jerry and Logic Hop at Brighton* (L.C. Collection, 1834), *Nautical Tom and Jerry* (Liverpool, 1843).

[1] *The Bravo*: Buckstone's (Adel. 1833), Barnett's (Surrey, 1833). *The Pilot*: Fitzball's (Adel. 1825), Bernard's (Cob. 1826), Buckstone's (Adel. 1830). *The Red Rover*: Fitzball's (Adel. 1829), anonymous (Cob. 1829). *The Wept of the Wish-ton-Wish*: Bernard's (Adel. 1831). *The Water Witch*: Bernard's (Adel. 1830). This list is, of course, by no means complete.

[2] *Paul Clifford*: Fitzball's (C.G. 1835), Webster's (Cob. 1832). *Eugene Aram*: anonymous (Edin. 1832), anonymous (R.P. 1832), Moncrieff's (Surrey, 1832). *The Last Days of Pompeii*: Fitzball's (Vic. 1835), Buckstone's (Adel. 1834). A whole crowd of "Last" this and "Last" that shows the impress of his style.

[3] Cf. *Jack Sheppard*: Buckstone's (Adel. 1839), Haines' (Surrey, 1839), anonymous (Hull, 1839), Murray's (Edin. 1840). Most of his novels were used by one or another writer.

[4] W. L. Rede's *The Peregrinations of Pickwick* (Adel. 1837), Stirling's *The Pickwick Club* (C.L. 1837), anonymous *Pickwick* (Norwich, 1838), Moncrieff's *Sam Weller* (Strand, 1837, "new edition," 1838), anonymous *Sam Weller's Tour; or, The Pickwickians Abroad* (Strand, 1838). The *Pickwickians* (L.C. Collection, 1837) is probably Rede's drama. At the Strand in 1840 appeared *Mr Weller's Watch*.

[5] Almar's (Surrey, 1838), A. Beckett's (St. J. 1838), C. Z. Barnett's (R.P. 1838), Stirling's (Adel. 1839), Murray's (Edin. 1840), Greenwood's (S.W. 1838).

[6] Stirling brought out a *Nicholas Nickleby* at the Adelphi in 1838 This was followed by an anonymous version at the Strand and by *Poor Smike* at the Vic., both in 1839. Stirling has a sequel, *The Fortunes of Smike* (Adel. 1840).

[7] Selby and Melville produced an E.O.H. version in 1841; another, by Stirling, came out the same year at the Strand, and a third followed at the Adelphi in 1842.

[8] Stirling's version appeared at the Adelphi at the end of 1840.

[9] Four dramatisations were produced in 1844: Stirling's (Adel.), C. Z. Barnett's (Surrey), anonymous (Strand) and anonymous (S.W., as *Scrooge, the Miser's Dream*).

$(1843-4)^1$, *The Chimes* $(1844)^2$, *The Cricket on the Hearth* $(1845)^3$, *The Battle of Life* $(1846)^4$, *Dombey and Son* $(1846-8)^5$ and *The Haunted Man* $(1848)^6$.

Before leaving this question of the adaptation of Dickens' novels to the stage there is one point of interest which may be rapidly discussed. One notes that, in the rush of the dramatists, one nearly always out-distances his peers by a week or two, and that occasionally a particular playwright succeeds in anticipating the end of the novel before that has made its appearance in print. Now in *The Almanack of the Month* for Jan. 1846^7, it is asserted that Dickens provided Albert Smith with the "proof-sheets hot from the press" of *The Cricket on the Hearth*. This seems to provide the true explanation of the facts outlined above, but a passage from the anonymous skit called *The Civil War of Poetry* (Olym. 1846) provides us with something more—a statement that Dickens gave his manuscript to the adapter and that he received money for the favour. In this play, after a discussion among the giants of antiquity—Shakespeare, Jonson and Otway—there enter two modern dramatists. The first is representative of those who take from the French. Says he[8]:

> I must indeed, my friend, confess
> I have at present great Success.

[1] Three versions appeared in 1844: Higgie's and Lacy's (Queen's), Webb's (Strand), and Stirling's (Lyc.).

[2] Five versions appeared in 1844: Lemon and à Beckett's (Adel.), Stirling's (Lyc.), Edwards' (Apollo) and two anonymous (Albert and Queen's).

[3] Two versions appeared in 1845: Smith's (Lyc.) and Stirling's (Adel.); and six in 1846: Archer's (Edin.), Barnett's (Albert), Rayner's (Apollo), Webster's (H.²), Townsend's (C.L.) and anonymous at Princess's and Marylebone. A burlesque by Blanchard, *The Cricket on our Own Hearth*, was given at the Olympic in 1846. See *supra*, p. 96.

[4] Smith's *The Battle of Life* was produced at the Lyceum in 1846, while six others came out in 1847; Stirling's (Surrey), Somerset's (Bower), Atkyns (Albert), Lyon's (C.L.) and two anonymous (Britannia and Norwich).

[5] Taylor's *Dombey and Son* was given at the Strand in 1847.

[6] Versions of this appeared at the Olympic, the Albert, and the Adelphi in 1848.

[7] Quoted in T. E. Pemberton, *Charles Dickens and the Stage* (1888), p. 158.

[8] This quotation is from the MS. in the L.C. Collection; the play is not printed. I have supplied punctuation, of which the dialogue is entirely innocent.

> Why! of the piece that I'm translating
> (Which now is Paris agitating)
> Four versions have been booked as yet,
> And I expect to-day to get
> An order to supply another.

Whereupon the second proceeds to account for his time:

> I'm pretty full of occupation;
> I'm working at an adaptation
> Of the great Story to the Stage,
> Which all expect will be the rage
> When it comes out. 'Tis not yet printed,
> But, as we'd have it represented
> Before our rivals, we've succeeded
> In getting Boz's leave to read it
> In Manuscript (of course you know
> That golden reasons work'd him so).

This seems to suggest an unsuspected source of income for the by no means financially careless Boz.

It will be realised that Dickens' novels helped, like Scott's, in still further developing the melodramatic tradition, and, besides this, that they contributed in preventing the development of a new and truer dramatic technique. Careless adaptation of narrative fiction can lead towards nothing but the stringing together of episodes, and it is this episodical treatment which, more than anything else, mars the workmanship of the plays of the half century. The influences on the stage of the period all tended towards the same ends. The better work of France and Germany was neglected; only the lighter and the more spectacular pieces were seized upon. Narrative poetry[1] and narrative prose of native composition were taken, not for their higher qualities, but for the thrill or force of the mere tale itself. Finer dramatic technique was lost; characterisation was not sought for; incidents alone could make a direct and a popular appeal.

[1] A long list could be given of the poems of the period which were dramatised. Naturally Byron, with his romantic lays, was popular. So was Southey with his *Thalaba the Destroyer* (Fitzball's, Cob. 1823; Fitzball's, C.G. 1836). Everywhere, however, the dramatists searched—from Burns (Ebsworth's *Tam O'Shanter*, Cob. 1820; anonymous version, R.A. 1828; Addison's, D.L. 1834) to Pope (Oxenford's *The Rape of the Lock*, Olym. 1837).

CHAPTER III

THE ILLEGITIMATE DRAMA

I. *Melodramas*

FROM the summary of playhouse conditions given in the preceding chapters, it will be realised that the illegitimate far surpassed in popularity that form of drama which Mr Plumpton Marsh vaingloriously thought to establish in London. Melodrama of a kind was to be seen before 1800; melodrama, like the poor, will no doubt always be with us; but when we think of early nineteenth century theatres we think of them as the home *par excellence* of spectacularism and of melodramatic effect. There is, accordingly, every justification for beginning a survey of the dramatic literature of the time with this type of despised and neglected entertainment.

Roughly, the melodramas of the period may be classed in three main divisions: the romantic, the supernatural and the domestic; and we may consider this dramatic form as a whole to have developed chronologically from one division to another in the order which is given above. Pixérécourt, who, as we have seen, gave the final impetus to the melodramatic movement, was primarily romantic in aim, and that romantic atmosphere was consolidated in the English theatres through the influence of Sir Walter Scott. Romanticism, however, always loves the strange and the uncanny, and we do not feel surprise when we discover ghosts and goblins freely mingling with more material personages on the romantic stage. Those ghosts and goblins, however, soon come to assume a predominant position, and thus is evolved the *Freischütz* drama, in which the interest definitely centres in the supernatural effects. Perhaps the domestic melodrama may be regarded as a kind of reaction to both these types, although in essence it is but the enunciation by illegitimacy of that realistic tendency which ever accompanies romanticism. On the one side, the fanciful kingdoms, the gloomy castles, the ruined abbeys; on the other, the dingy cottage, the slum tenement, the poverty-stricken alleys.

All of these types of melodramatic activity, of course, share certain common characteristics. As the name itself shows, all melodrama freely utilises the service of music. Not only are songs introduced at fitting (and unfitting) moments, but the action proceeds to the accompaniment of instrumental orchestration which strives always to be as "appropriate" as possible[1]. Thus Moncrieff's *Giselle* (S.W. 1841) has "*Supernatural Music*" in act II, while "*Spherical Music*" and "*Pastoral Music*" adorn the same author's *Zoroaster* (D.L. 1824). After these the merely "*Hurried Music*" of Campbell's *The Forest Oracle* (S.W. 1829) seems exceedingly tame. No doubt this music was often of a very primitive nature, and occasionally, perhaps, became perfunctory in execution, but that it formed for most of the audience at least one source of pleasure seems amply proved, not only by contemporary references, but by the fact that it persisted even after the Act of 1843 had removed the so-called "Burletta" restrictions. Perhaps an unconscious æsthetic feeling was at work, the slow or frenzied music harmonising with the artificial sentiments expressed in the dialogue and the unnatural characters introduced.

These unnatural characters form the second great characteristic of melodrama. There may be occasional deviations, but usually we can find in any specimen of the *genre* the presence of the well-known stock types: hero and heroine (almost always in distress), humorous confidant for the former and confidante for the latter, villain black as night and villainess of ruddy hue. The action varies, naturally, from one play to another, but frequently the stories are complicated by

[1] Pocock's *The Miller and his Men* (C.G. 1813) has a stage direction in act II: "*Riber, on seeing Frederick, draws a poniard.—As he raises his arm, Grindoff catches it, and prevents the blow.—Music appropriate.*"

criss-cross love emotions not unreminiscent of those presented more than a century before in Dryden's *The Indian Emperour*. Attempted seductions, wrongful accusations, disloyalties, hidden secrets, lost parentage keep the puppets in continual movement upon the stage.

The third characteristic of the type is the attention devoted to action, and this increases as the decades pass by. It is easily understood that, since the earlier romantic melodramas had usually plots full of thrilling situations, the action as such should be more deeply marked than in ordinary tragedy. This tendency towards action was without a doubt intensified by the fact that the melodrama really absorbed within itself the historic spectacle which had been one of Astley's prime attractions. In these spectacles mimetic action alone was used to convey to the audience the development of the story, the only other indication being occasional sentences scrawled (often with undue aspirates, false grammar and mangled spelling) on the "printed flags" of which we read in Cross' *Circusiana* and in Leigh Hunt's criticism[1]. Many of the melodramas were merely these historic spectacles given a certain amount of dialogue, but preserving as their prime attraction the scenic effects and the mimetic movement. Naturally, as the writers of melodrama had to turn out scores of these pieces to make a living, and as stage directions are easier to write than dialogue, this action-element was not only retained but increased. The resultant effects on dramatic composition may well be realised. Whenever a Pocock or a Fitzball comes to a really difficult situation he switches off his dialogue and turns to the italics and capitals of stage direction. This is particularly marked at the close of these plays. Thus Macfarren in *The Boy of Santillane* (D.L. April 1827), after an artificial passage of dialogue, ends his drama with action:

With a desperate effort [ROLANDO] *pulls the ring—the grating flies open—*GIL BLAS *and* DONNA MENSIA *escape—*DESPARDO *following them, encounters* ROLANDO *just as the explosion takes place, which rends the mountain, crushes the tower, and discovers*

[1] *Op. cit.* p. 31.

the cave beneath, burying ROLANDO, DESPARDO, *and the rest of the band, in the blazing ruins*—DON MARTIN *joins the hands of* GIL BLAS *and* DONNA MENSIA—ALVAREZ *and the Holy Brotherhood re-enter*—CORCUELO *exults.*—*Tableau.*

Perhaps, to show the prevalence of this custom, some further examples may not be out of place. Explosions, as providing a thrilling finale, were specially popular; one, in Campbell's *The Forest Oracle* (S.W. Nov. 1829), is planned on the same lines as that of Macfarren's:

He rushes down, followed by Aranza, Aaron, and party, with torches—general fight—Filippo catches the Child, and throws it in the torrent—Delzi knocks him down, and, mounting the bridge, looks anxiously after it—jumps in—two Men fire after him—Filippo beckons two others, who ascend the bridge, and fire—Aaron, who has received a whisper from Adriani, seizes a torch, and, firing the train, the bridge blows up with a tremendous explosion—all are struck motionless—Delzi is seen coming through the ruins with the Child— he places it in its parents' arms—Colonna rushes forward to stab it, when Delzi, catching his poniard, stabs him—the Filippo party are conquered—Picture—Curtain Falls.

Sometimes the stage directions, penned more "poetically," deal with supernatural effects, as in Moncrieff's *Giselle* (S.W. 1841):

The Dell of the Mist in the Forest of Rosenbad; a romantic thicket; wild shrubs and flowers thickly bestrew the ground; the silvery mist of the morning is seen ascending in natural incense from the earth, gilded by the first rays of the rising Sun, which is brightly piercing through the forest verdure, at the back, chasing the shades of night, and lighting up the dew drops with its beams like fairy lamps.— Supernatural Music.—LOTTA *and* WILIS *enter, slowly waltzing onwards, their movements becoming fainter and weaker, as the Sun's rays beam more strongly, 'till, staggering and apparently dying away, they disappear through the tufts of flowers at the wings.*

Sometimes it is a scene of "real life" with the poetry left far behind, as in Moncrieff's *The Scamps of London* (S.W. Nov. 1843):

Charlotte *has rushed to* Bob—Louisa *to* Herbert—*and* Eliza, *encouraged by her Father, to* Frank. *A desperate Combat then takes place between* Police, *headed by* Fogg—*and* Onion, Brindle, *and* Scamps, *headed by* Devereux—*the* Police *hastening to secure them*—

NED

pistols are fired—cutlasses crossed, 'till Onion *and* Scamps *are conquered by the* Police; *and* Devereux *receives a pistol shot from* Fogg, *who has wrested it from him in the struggle, when levelled at his own head, and, in self-defence, has lodged the contents of it in* Devereux's *body, it stretches him lifeless on the ground—with his last breath he makes a motion as if imploring pardon.* Fogg *regards him with great agitation, then turns away, as if in forgiveness, and raises his eyes to heaven in grateful thanks—he then sinks into his daughter's arms, who leaves* Herbert *to support him.* Shabner *has sneaked off in the confusion—Parties form Tableau, and Curtain falls.*

It will be noted here how much that is purely psychological is expected to be shown outwardly by the performers, and we are led back once more to those methods of acting which have been briefly referred to above[1]. All of these scenes already quoted are innocent of dialogue, hence everything is left to the player; in all, the action is of a boisterous or thrilling nature, hence no subtle effects could be employed. In a modern "discussion play," where two or three characters remain almost motionless on the stage for an entire act, the whole effect depending upon the talk itself, there may be the opportunity for more delicate outward indications of feeling on the part of the actors; but, in a large theatre, with a score of people on the stage, amid a riot of swift movement and a regular bombardment of shots and explosions, nothing but the broadest effects could be attempted. The depiction of anger, therefore, would be very much as the author of Dicks' pamphlet recommended and Fogg's expression of forgiveness would take on a very material form. It is clear that the close relationship between the player and the playwright would lead towards an intensification of these type emotions both in the histrionic sphere and in that of dramatic creation. The actors need such plays as these where the broad effects will be telling; the dramatists, for their part, knowing that only the broad effects can be secured, continue drawing their types, their stock figures, and, both for effect and for ease (to say nothing of haste), they continue to piece out their dialogue with plentiful passages of noisy stage

[1] See *supra*, pp. 48–9.

direction. They know quite well that these are as pleasing to the audience as the dialogue itself. One must not, of course, be too severe in criticising this tendency. Not only is action a very important element in any theatrical performance, but even in the greater ages action has been accepted boldly as something popular and as an instrument for securing a certain impression. Stage directions were simple in Shakespeare's time; but, had there been then the fashion of the lengthy instructions to the players, we should have had quite a considerable amount of italics in the First Folio. As any performance of *As You Like It* shows, there is not nearly enough dialogue to go round, and the wrestling bout must take place either in silence or (more modernly) amid a confused and confusing *sotto voce* murmur from the whole cast—thought by the producer to be realistic. In condemning the melodrama, we have undoubtedly to be on our guard, lest the net with which we set out to catch sparrows inadvertently entangle an eagle.

The themes of the melodramas are of varying character, but excitement, exaltation of virtue and poetic justice appear in all. Most popular, perhaps, were the romantic subjects, particularly if these were spiced with a little pathetic humanitarianism and a dash of ghostliness. Dimond's *The Æthiop* (C.G. Oct. 1812) gives us plenty of the latter; Brooks' *The Creole; or, Love's Fetters* (Lyc. April 1847) provides humanitarian sentiment in abundance. Not only is there in this last-mentioned drama a direct appeal to the audience in favour of the anti-slavery campaign, but the story itself is planned as a concrete example of the horrors of the slave-trade. Here Alphonse, the hero, meets and loves Louise, the heroine, but she, unfortunately, is found to be legally his slave. For imagined wrongs the Creole Latour plans vengeance on the hero, and, by his villainous tricks, he gets Louise sold to himself. Disaster seems imminent when the usual melodramatic *deus ex machina* arrives in the shape of an order of slave-abolition from the French Government. A similar aim is shown in *The Destruction of the Bastille* (Adel. 1842) by Benjamin Webster. The true love of Victor

Rollande and Ernestine (the latter discovers that she is the daughter of Robespierre), the jealousy of Ninon, the brutal villainy of Guillaume Le Rouge and the humorous honesty of Coco Latour, all go to make up a *mélange* of tears and laughter held together by the thin strands of the story and the predominant humanitarian aim. Themes taken from the history, or legend, of the French Revolution were popular, and sometimes, as in George Macfarren's "historical opera" (really a melodrama) of *Lestocq; or, The Fête of the Hermitage* (C.G. Feb. 1835)[1], the playwrights went further afield to treat of inhumanity and kindness and tyranny and liberal sentiment in Slavonic lands. In this play of Macfarren's we get the typical villain in Count Goloffkin, distressed innocence in low life presented by Stroloff and his Catherine, nobility in the Princess Elizabeth and a *deus ex machina* in the person of Lestocq, the clever French physician. As *Lestocq* provides another good example of the speechless scene, the last lines of the play may be quoted here:

SCENE IV.—*The Imperial Palace—the barrier-gate across from R. to L. third entrance—barracks and guard-house, R.—beyond the gates, the bridge of the Moika, C., leading to the Imperial Palace, which runs across in the distance from R. to L.—a large pile of arms near the guard-house.*

A Sentinel discovered on duty on the right of the barrier-gate.

Enter an Insurgent, peeping on cautiously, L.

He fires on the Sentinel, who falls—drums and trumpets sound an alarm—the populace rush in R. and L., armed with various weapons, and seize the arms near the guard-house—a body of the Imperial Guard charge the conspirators, and drive them back—they rally again, and drag on a cannon and ammunition, L., and storm the barrier-gate, which is carried by the people.

COUNT GOLOFFKIN *is seen in the midst of the battle—he is shot by* STROLOFF, *and borne off, L.*

The Imperial Palace and Bridge become suddenly illuminated—the Soldiers are beaten off, R. and L.—the people rush on the bridge to meet the procession, shouting, "Hurrah! hurrah!—Long live the Empress Elizabeth!"

---

[1] Adapted from the *Lestocq* of Scribe with music by Auber. The distinction between "operas" of this type and melodramas is but a slight one.

CHORUS. [*During the Procession.*]
God bless the empress!
Whose worth we proclaim:
Her life be all glorious,
And deathless her fame.

PROCESSION.
Two officers of the Novgorod Regiment.
A File of Soldiers of the Novgorod Regiment.
Band.
Hussars.
Preobajenski Guard.
LESTOCQ—EMPRESS ELIZABETH—EUDOSIA—DIMITRI.
Four Train-bearers.
STROLOFF—CATHERINE.
Maids of Honour.
Officers of the Novgorod Regiment.
Officers of the Preobajenski Guard.
Flag.
Peasantry—Soldiers—Peasantry.

That such speechless scenes were particularly loved in the
English theatre is shown by a comparison of this last portion
of Macfarren's drama with the corresponding scene[1] in his
original, Scribe's *Lestocq ou l'intrigue et l'amour* (Paris, Opéra-
Comique, May 1834). The passage is given here for purposes
of contrast, and the two may be regarded as thoroughly
typical of the nineteenth century adaptations from the
French:

(*En ce moment, le peuple se précipite sur le théâtre, mêlé aux
soldats. Les fenêtres du fond sont ouvertes. On voit en dehors, à
la lueur des torches, une des places principales de Saint-Pétersbourg.*)

CHŒUR.
Vive l'impératrice
Qui proclament nos vœux;
Que chacun obéisse
A son nom glorieux!
Vive l'impératrice
Qui proclament nos vœux!

(*Paraît Élisabeth, appuyée sur le bras de Lestocq,
et entourée de tous les conjurés.*)

[1] IV. ix.

DIMITRI.

Que vois-je! Élisabeth?

LESTOCQ.

Que le peuple couronne,
Et qui voit à ses pieds ses ennemis vaincus.

ÉLISABETH.

Grâce pour eux, qu'on leur pardonne.
Grâce pour Golofkin. (*A Strolof*) Courez vite!

STROLOF, *froidement*.

Il n'est plus.

DIMITRI, *à part, avec joie*.

Ciel! il n'existe plus!

LESTOCQ, *à Strolof*.

En as-tu l'assurance?

STROLOF, *froidement*.

Je m'en étais chargé; je l'avais retenu:
Un seul jour a payé vingt-cinq ans de vengeance.

ÉLISABETH.

Je vous dois tout, Lestocq. (*Montrant les autres conjurés*.)
Ainsi qu'à leur vaillance.
(*Apercevant Dimitri, elle fait un geste d'émotion, et
s'avance vers lui*.)
Et vous... vous dont le zèle à mon cœur est connu,
Que puis-je faire ici pour votre récompense?

DIMITRI.

J'en veux une.

ÉLISABETH, *tendrement*.

Parlez.

DIMITRI, *hésitant*.

C'est... non pas maintenant...
Mais plus tard... de daigner... me protégeant vous-même,
Vous employer pour moi près de celle que j'aime,
Près d'Eudoxie...

ÉLISABETH, *chancelant, et s'appuyant sur Lestocq*.

O ciel! (*A Lestocq, avec un regard douloureux*.)
Vous m'avez trompée!

LESTOCQ.

Oui!

Pour voir sur votre front briller le diadème!

(*Lui montrant les soldats qui lui portent les armes.*)

Votre règne commence.

ÉLISABETH, *à part, regardant Dimitri, et essuyant une larme.*

Et les chagrins aussi!

CHŒUR.

Vive à jamais, vive l'impératrice

Que sur le trône appelaient tous nos vœux!

Houra! houra! que chacun obéisse,

Et que tout cède à son nom glorieux!

Vive l'impératrice

Que proclament nos vœux!

(*Les tambours battent aux champs, les trompettes sonnent, les cloches se font entendre, le peuple agite ses chapeaux, ses mouchoirs, et les soldats leurs drapeaux.—La toile tombe.*)

It will be at once apparent how heavily the English dramatist has stressed the purely physical action, and how, in the French version, almost all the content of the scene is devoted to the development of the sentiments of the characters. It will be noted also how much more directly Macfarren has dealt with the killing of the villain Goloffkin by his former serf, Stroloff. Humanitarianism construed as poetic justice to the oppressor always appealed in English melodrama.

These humanitarian melodramas, however, much as they may use romantic incident and surroundings, nearly always aim at a certain domestic or realistic effect, and consequently do not show in fullest form that love of the strange, the outlandish and the picturesque which clearly swayed many among the audiences at the beginning of the century. Sometimes humour and exciting incident prevail, as in Frederick Reynolds' *The Caravan; or, The Driver and his Dog* (D.L. Dec. 1803), which won success mainly through the exertions of the life-saving dog Carlos, and partly through the secret-dispensing qualities of Blabbo. Sometimes the romantic qualities of the story overwhelm all else, and possibly this is the commonest type. Dimond's *The Bride of Abydos* (D.L. Feb. 1818), described as "A Tragick Play" but naught else than a melodrama, shows by its very title that love of the East which attracted so many minds, great and small, of the period. This drama is full of picturesque poses—"*The Curtain falls upon the picture*" and "*The Characters form into a Picture of mute attention and the drop falls*" are stage directions that tell their own tale. Then there is the appeal of the Middle Ages or of ages which, if not middle, are at any rate sufficiently dimly outlined to stand for all kinds of Gothicism. Kerr's *Therese, or The Orphan of Geneva* (W.L. 1821), itself adapted from the French, tells a romantic story in which Therese is pursued by the villain Valther and loved by the magnanimous Charles, Count de Senange. By the end of the play the unfortunate Valther—for he is to be pitied in spite of his villainy—thinks he has satisfactorily disposed of the heroine, but, on seeing her alive and believing her to be a ghost, miserably confesses his crimes. Music plays at each entry and stage directions freely bespatter the text. A moment spent in *Therese's* company may not be either unprofitable or unamusing. We have come to the end of the second act and there, once more, our ears are treated to music:

> (*They retire, the lightning flashes with redoubled fury, and the thunder rolls loudly awful.* Valther *enters cautiously, the night becomes still darker.*
> *Val.* All are retired—I am alone—there is but one course to pursue. 'Tis in that chamber Therese reposes—the darkness, the roar of the thunder, all favour me. Let me listen all is safe, yet I shudder, in spite of my natural courage. Conscience—psha!—she must, she must die. (*draws out the knife which he had concealed in his bosom.*) The door is open (*looks into the farm-house*)—no one appears (*pointing to the door*)—it invites my entrance—I go, and it is done.
> (*He hastily shuts the window, and enters, at that moment* Charles *and* Picard *cross the yard, as if in quest of some one. A plaintive cry is heard from the pavilion—at the same moment a thunder-bolt strikes the building, destroying a part of it.* Valther, *in a state of consternation, bursts*

through the windows, and rushes off 1st ent. L.H.; Therese
enters from the farm-house, and sees the pavilion in flames.
The. What noise—what frightful lightning. Ah! Madame de
Senange is lost. (*Enters* the pavilion, crying) Help! help!
(MUSIC. *At the same moment* Mathurin *and* Bridget, Nanette
and all the servants, enter from the farm; Charles *and* Picard
at the same instant.
Math. Ah! 'tis the thunder that has fallen on the farm. Fire!
fire! fire!
Chas. (*hastening towards the pavilion*). Heavens! the flames
engulph the pavilion. My mother! oh, my mother!
Math. Hasten—let us save Madame de Senange.
(MUSIC. *All the characters hasten to gain the burning pavilion,*
when Therese *appears at the window, her hair disordered, holding*
a Knife in her hand.
The. It is too late—Madame de Senange is murdered.
All. Murdered!
Chas. Heavens!
The. Behold, behold her blood!—'tis I, 'tis I?
(*She falls on her face.*
Chas. (*throwing himself on the stairs*). Oh, my mother!—(*the*
flames burst from every part of the edifice)—Oh, my mother!
(*Part of the spectators regard* Therese *with a fright, while the*
rest haste to prevent Charles *from precipitating himself into the*
flames; the conflagration is in its heighth when the act drop falls.

All comes right in the end, of course, and after this bustle
and noise and darkness comes the time when Valther in
terror avows his guilt, when the sorrows of Therese terminate
and when she is recognised as the Countess of Volmar. At
the conclusion the characters form themselves into a decorous
semicircle, Therese in the middle and Valther abjectly
crouching on the ground in front of her.

If we wish to find the sister of Therese, we have not far
to seek. Countless heroines possess her virtues, her sorrows
and her joys. Usually she is of unknown parentage like the
Julia of Pocock's *Twenty Years Ago!* (Lyc. July 1810) who
is defended by her own father (though both are ignorant
of their relationship) against the machinations of the evil
Count D'Essars. Often, too, as in this last-mentioned play,
her lover is the son of the villain, the former being presented
all the more whitely for his father's darkness and treachery.

In this combination of apparently friendless orphan, unknown father, villain and virtuous son we are reminded once more of the truly native element in nineteenth century melodrama. Precisely the same grouping of characters is to be discovered in *The Secret*, by Edward Morris, a play produced at Drury Lane in 1799[1].

Sometimes, of course, it is the hero who is distressed. Thus Velasco in *The Watch-Word, or Quito-Gate* (D.L. Oct. 1816) is wrongfully accused of a murderous attack upon another, nearly misses thereby his chance of marrying Louisa, is finally proved innocent and, in the last tableau, joins his hands with hers. To this type of hero belongs ultimately the virtuous brigand, who, tracing his ancestry back to *Die Raüber*, had a distinguished career during the half-century. Here, as in Campbell's *The Forest Oracle; or, The Bridge of Tresino* (S.W. Nov. 1829) there is commonly a pair of brothers, one evil and villainous who seizes the estates and makes attempts on the heroine, and the other full of all noble virtues who, cast out on a friendless cold world, joins his fortunes with those of a band of sentimental robbers and eventually wins again his own and the heroine.

Then there are the historical melodramas, ranging for setting, if not for subject-matter, over the whole field of civilised or uncivilised life. Pocock seizes on Anglo-Saxon times in *Alfred the Great; or, The Enchanted Standard* (C.G. Nov. 1827), taking some of his material from O'Keeffe's *The Magic Banner* and dealing with his material in a manner not so far distant from the treatment by Sheridan Knowles of his more pretentious *Alfred the Great* (D.L. 1831). These historical dramas naturally received especial popularity when the dramatic possibilities of Scott's novels came to be recognised. It is unnecessary here to re-comment on the various versions of *Rob Roy*, *Redgauntlet*, *The Antiquary*, *Woodstock* and the rest[2], but these innumerable adaptations played such an important part in the theatrical history of the age that they may in no wise be forgotten. Nor was Scott the only historical

---

[1] See *A History of English Drama*, iii. 138–9.
[2] See *supra*, pp. 92–5.

novelist who thus provided material for the playwrights. Other contemporary authors were ransacked, and some dramatists, like Pocock in his *Robinson Crusoe; or, The Bold Bucaniers* (C.G. April 1817), cast their glances back to the picaresque and adventurous fiction of the preceding century.

Ghosts and goblins, fiends and fairies—the stage embodiment of disembodied creatures—next must occupy our attention. Monk Lewis with *The Castle Spectre* had introduced romantic diablerie to the English boards and gloomily it continued to flourish. The German terror school naturally (or unnaturally) ruled here predominant, although generally France served as intermediary. Moncrieff's *Giselle; or, The Phantom Night Dancers* (S.W. Aug. 1841), described as "A Domestic, Melo-dramatic, Choreographic, Fantastique, Traditionary Tale of Superstition," is thoroughly typical. The "tale of superstition" comes from Germany, but the prime model of the author seems to have been a French ballet called *Giselle* danced at the Académie de Musique on June 28, 1841. The whole play is full of mysterious figures amid which move the human actors, Aloise (alias Duke Albert), a sentimental villain, Hilarion, a hero, and Giselle, a heroine. The last-mentioned is seized by the fays known as the Wilis and duly rescued at the end by her lover. Moncrieff loved this style of play, and another production of his, *Zoroaster; or, The Spirit of the Star* (D.L. April 1824), may be regarded as equally typical. This is once more derived from a ballet[1], and, like *Giselle*, abounds in scenic effects[2]. The magical devices of Zoroaster, as the title shows, form the chief interest of this "Grand Melo-dramatic Tale of Enchantment." Passing over the many Frankensteins and Freischütz we may pause for a moment on Fitzball's *The Flying Dutchman; or, The Phantom Ship* (Adel. Jan. 1826) which, according to the author, "was not by any means behind even Frankenstein, or Der Freischütz itself in horrors and blue fire[3]." The story is a perfectly simple one, narrating how Lestelle Vanhelm,

---

[1] Gardel's *L'enfant prodigue.*
[2] See *supra*, p. 101.
[3] *Thirty-Five Years of a Dramatic Author's Life*, i. 169.

who loves Mowdrey, is carried off by the spirity Vanderdecken and heroically rescued at the conclusion from his chill clutch. This, however, is the merest framework, for, as "D— G." remarks in his preface to the Cumberland edition,

the author of the Flying Dutchman has wisely catered for all palates: for those whose taste inclines them to the terrible, he has provided thunder and lightning in abundance, thrown in a grotesque dance of water imps, and served up a death's head (not according to the old adage, stewed in a lantern), but picturesquely mounted on a black flag, and garnished with cross bones; while to the laughing souls, to whom—

"A merry jest is better far
Than sharp lampoon or witty libel,"

he presents a bill of fare irresistibly comic. We may, therefore, congratulate the "*violent spirits*" of the present day on the production of a piece where mirth and moonshine—murder and merriment—fire and fun, are so happily blended!

The fun is provided by Peter Von Bummel, Toby Varnish and Mynheer Von Swiggs; the fire is contributed by Vanderdecken, nor is that fire extinguished by the watery presence of Rockalda, wearing a "sorceress's sea-green dress, trimmed with sea-weed and shells," and by that of Eight Water-Imps. At one point in the play the Flying Dutchman, with mimetic show, offers a letter to the sailors:

MUSIC.—*Peter attempts to snatch the letter, when it explodes— a sailor is about to seize Vanderdecken, who eludes his grasp, and vanishes through the deck—Tom Willis fires on R., Von Swiggs on L.—a Sailor falls dead on the deck—Vanderdecken, with a demoniac laugh, rises from the sea in blue fire, amidst violent thunder —at that instant the Phantom Ship appears in the sky behind— Vanderdecken and the Crew in consternation exclaim* "Ah! Vanderdecken! Vanderdecken!" *as the drop hastily falls.*

That is the end of act 1, and it prepares us for all the terrors that are to come. What thrills, what tremblings, when Vanderdecken covers Lestelle with a cloak and she vanishes! What sentimental feelings when Mowdrey, returning, cries, "Lestelle! my love, my life! my—horror!—lost, lost! Help,

help!" What terror when to the spectators the following is presented—

[Storm.—A mist begins to rise, through which Vanderdecken is seen crossing the sea in an open boat with Lestelle, from L.U.E.— the storm rages violently—the boat is dashed about upon the waves— it sinks suddenly with Vanderdecken and Lestelle—the PHANTOM SHIP *appears (a la phantasmagorie) in a peal of thunder.—The stage and audience part of the Theatre in total darkness.*

INVISIBLE CHORUS, L.

Vanderdecken, come.
The bridal-bark, the spectre band,
Over sea and over land,
Wait to guide this captain's lady home.
Then, Vanderdecken, Vanderdecken, come.

Let us haste from these eerie realms where horror has its being, and pass to the domestic sphere where humbler joys and sorrows (though no less thrilling) have their home.

Here Isaac Pocock may first occupy our attention, some four of his numerous plays serving as representatives of various types. *"For England, Ho!"* (C.G. Dec. 1813) gives us the patriotic note with the injured hero, Enrico Altieri, who is wrongfully persecuted by Holstein (alias the Commandant), a thorough villain. *The Magpie, or the Maid?* (C.G. Sept. 1815), one of the many adaptations from a common French original, shows us the injured heroine. Poor little friendless Annette is accused of stealing a spoon and she cannot tell the truth because of her father's danger. It is soon discovered, of course, that a magpie was the culprit and that the spoon which Annette sold in order to get money for her father was her very, very own. Then *The Miller and his Men* (C.G. Oct. 1813) and *The Robber's Bride* (C.G. Oct. 1829)—these present various treatments of the brigandage theme, the latter, however, with interesting novelty of conception. In neither of these are the robbers, Schiller-wise, virtuous. The first shows us an apparently jovial and genial miller, who is in reality the cruel leader of a cruel troup of bandits. There is a faithful lover, Lothair, and a useful *deus ex machina* in Count Friberg, who returns just in time to rescue innocence in distress. *The Robber's Bride* has a more original theme. Rose, the heroine, is married (few heroines in melodrama are married; the wedding bells are usually reserved for the close of act III) to a man who turns out to be a bold bad robber. Rose's long-lost father, Briarly, comes into the clutches of her husband; Rose succeeds in saving him, receives parental forgiveness and leaves her home of sin. This melodrama is interesting in many ways, chiefly because it shows how something at least of virtue was rising out of the domestic type. Rose's story is in one respect a problem story and, in spite of artificialities of treatment, points the way forward towards the domestic drama of late years. It is in the tradition of Heywood, Lillo and Moore; it indicates the coming of Robertson. Reading such a play as this, we realise that the melodrama, crude as it is, has more potential vitality than the long line of Elizabethan imitations which it will be our business to discuss later. Even a despised Pocock could rise out of the rut to produce something that had a direct relationship to life and that had in it at least the germ of something powerful. This impression of potential strength reappears in Buckstone's *Luke the Labourer, or, The Lost Son* (Adel. Oct. 1826). In spite of much poverty-stricken dialogue, there is something here that calls for our attention, in particular the characterisation of Luke, who, although the villain, is presented in an interesting manner. This man, a creature of evil circumstances and the victim of drink, is given a definite motive for his attempt to ruin Farmer Wakefield. Indeed his own account of his wife's death is rather effective, and deserves particular notice. "I ha' summut to say," he cries to Wakefield,

I ha' summut to say, summut at my tongue's end—it must come out. Farmer, do you recollect when you sent me away fra' your sarvice? Do you recollect when I were starving for want o' work, and, because I were at times given to drink, you turn'd your back upon me. I ha' never been a man since that time.

Wakefield. What, do you wish to rake up old affairs that ha' been gone by many a day?

Luke. If it had been gone by a hundred years, and I alive, I should never ha' forgotten it: and I must and I will tell thee on't.

I never had the chance afore; but now it do all come fresh upon
my brain, my heart do seem ready to burst wi' summut buried
in it, and I cannot keep it down. You turn'd me away, and I had
no character, because you said I was a drunkard. I were out o' work
week after week, till I had not a penny in the world, nor a bit o'
bread to put in mine or my wife's mouth. I then had a wife, but
she sicken'd and died—yes, died!—all—all along o' you.

Wakefield. You never came to me in a right way.

Luke. She wouldn't let me go to parish, because she were
daughter of as good a man as you were then; so we crept on little
by little, and bad enough it were—but at last all things went
cross; and at one time, when a bit hadn't been in my mouth for
two days, I sat thinking, wi' my wife in my arms—she were ill,
very ill—I saw her look at me wi' such a look as I shall never
forget—she laid hold o' this hand, and, putting her long thin
fingers all around it, said, "Luke, wouldna' the farmer give you
sixpence if he thought I were dying o' want?" I said I'd try once
more—I got up, to put her in a chair, when she fell, stone dead,
down at my feet!

Clara. Oh, Luke! Luke!—for mercy's sake, no more—forgive
him!

Luke [*after a pause*]. I were then quite ruin'd. I felt alone in the
world. I stood looking on her white face near an hour, and did not
move from the spot an inch; but, when I *did* move, it were wi'
my fist clenched in the air, while my tongue, all parch'd and dry,
curs'd a curse, and swore that, if I had not my revenge, I wish'd
I might fall as stiff and as dead as she that lay before me.

All the play, of course, is not written in this strain. Clara
is nearly seduced by the wicked squire who is in league with
Luke, and the noble hero, Charles Maydew, comes just in
time to save her and her father from ruin. This is in the
regular melodramatic strain—but the presentation of Luke
is not. The latter shows inventiveness on the part of the
dramatist and makes ample atonement for the poverty of the
rest. Once more we come upon what is at least potential
strength in the domestic branch of the minor and illegitimate
theatre.

The movements, naturally, towards newer things were but
tentative in this age. It was easier to write along the well-
worn lines than to strike out along new paths, and most of
the domestic melodramas, like Kenney's *Ella Rosenberg*

(D.L. Nov. 1807), which tells how Rosenberg has been immured by Mountfort, who has designs on his wife, and whose evil aims are defeated by the noble Elector, ring the changes on stock themes. If brigandage is dealt with, it is usually introduced, either to show distressed virtue driven to extremities or to provide a nice contrast with innocence. In Bird's *The Smuggler's Daughter* (S.W. Oct. 1835) the smuggler is Anker Bruce, whose daughter Margaret loves Lieutenant Paul Vincent. Bruce is found murdered and Vincent, accused of the crime, is about to be executed, when Gilbert, the real perpetrator of the deed, now stung by conscience, dashes in to receive the fire of the mariners. The only interesting feature here is the struggle in Margaret's mind occasioned by her love of her father and her love of Vincent. A trifling touch of novelty appears, too, in *My Poll and My Partner Joe* (Surrey, Sept. 1835) by J. T. Haines. Here Harry Halyard, after falling into the clutches of villains, is pressed for the navy. He returns after many years and finds that his old sweetheart, whose image has been always in his mind, thinking him dead, has married his faithful partner Joe. After a scene of conflicting emotions, old Joe dies and presumably his widow will marry Halyard. This *Enoch Arden* theme is treated with a certain psychological insight which again indicates, even though but vaguely, the possibilities inherent in the domestic type. We must remember, too, that by means of the melodrama the whole sphere of the serious play was being enlarged. Such dramas as Moncrieff's *The Scamps of London; or the Cross Roads of Life* (S.W. Nov. 1843) and Dillon's *The Mysteries of Paris. A Romance of the Rich and Poor* (Marylebone, Sept. 1844), carry pathetic sentiment and occasionally would-be-tragic situation far away from the higher fields these occupied in poetic plays. It is true that this type of melodrama is mostly French in origin—even *The Scamps of London*, described as 'A National, Local, Characteristic, Metropolitan, Melodramatic Drama of the Day," is derived from *Les Bohémiens de Paris* (Théâtre de l'Ambigu Comique, Sept. 1843)—but, whatever its origin, its importance remains. The stories are

poor, perhaps. In Moncrieff's play there is a stock villain
Devereux, a stock hero Frank, a stock heroine Louisa and
a stock comic friend Bob Yorkney. Dillon has a hero in
Prince Rodolphe who rescues innocence in distress and
finds that the said innocence, Fleur de Marie, is his long-lost
daughter. With him Mike Murphy provides the comic relief.
The scenes displayed, however, take us to new realms and
we feel prepared to recognise in those scenes another instrument, slight as it might be, by means of which drama
succeeded in the following half-century in freeing itself from
old fetters and in finding a new emancipated path.

We need not stay longer with the melodrama. Beyond
variations in setting, the other specimens of this type have
not much to offer us that we cannot find in the few selected
examples. Nor is there need to attempt any formal differentiation of the work of the various writers—Holcroft, Pocock,
Brough, Moncrieff, Campbell and the rest. All took the
same models; all worked to type; all penned their pieces
with no thought of literary glory. We may say that one had
a better style and another a more inventive gift, that one
was prolific and another penned merely a few pieces of this
kind, but the distinctions, after all, are slight and the labour
of making the critical analysis would be labour lost. At the
same time the presence of sameness and of unoriginality
must not cause us to overlook entirely this type of drama.
Apart from the fact noted above that the domestic melodrama
possessed certain premonitions of future domestic triumphs,
we have to remember that in this type consisted all that was
vital and popular in the theatrical world of the time. We may
smile at the follies of the melodramatic scene—although,
perhaps, people in glass-houses should not throw stones; we
flock today to our cinemas to see films built according to
plan precisely similar to that beloved in the early nineteenth
century. And, besides this thought, there is another which
should make us pause. Gazing drearily on the long array of
"unacted" dramas and of "poetic" dramas put forward by
well-meaning littérateurs of the age, I personally feel convinced that, had I lived in these decades, I should have loved

better the struggling actors at the minor theatres than the lordly potentates legitimately wedded at Drury Lane and Covent Garden, that I should have been in complete sympathy with H. S. Leigh, and should have firmly endorsed his advice to contemporaries:

> Look always on the Surrey side
> For true dramatic art.
> The road is long—the river wide—
> But frequent busses start
> From Charing Cross and Gracechurch Street,
> (An inexpensive ride;)
> So, if you want an evening's treat,
> O seek the Surrey side.

II. *Farces*

With the melodrama naturally goes the farce. A nineteenth century audience wanted to laugh; it wanted its comic friend in the melodramatic spectacle, and it wanted, besides, a good jolly brisk absurd after-piece to which it might give itself up in genuine whole-hearted enjoyment. The explanation of the truly enormous number of short plays, of which melodramas, farces, comic operas and pantomimes formed by far the largest part, was the lengthy return made in those years for money paid at the box-office. Performances started at 6.30 or 7 and lasted till midnight or after; special arrangements were made for those who, preferring to have a leisurely meal at a near-by tavern, did not come to the theatre till 9. Under these conditions there was therefore ample time for a three hour play, a farce and a pantomime all on the same evening. The audience demanded, and got, them all; demanded, too, and saw that it got, not stale pieces but such as bore upon them the stamp of novelty. Occasionally a particularly successful melodrama such as Fitzball's *Jonathan Bradford* (Surrey, June 1833) would continue running for months on end, occasionally a specially popular farce would reappear year after year in a theatre's repertory, but normally this flotsam and jetsam bobbed momentarily on the theatrical waves and sank without hope of recovery.

It is not strange, therefore, that the farces, like the melo-dramas, should be "made to order." There is but small real ingenuity in any one and much was left to the actors who were to interpret them. To what has already been said on this subject[1], there may be added a typical passage culled from *The London Magazine* for Oct. 1823. A critic there, writing of a Haymarket performance, declares that he looks upon

Liston's *face* in the light of a national misfortune. We consider, what we must own to be his happy infelicity of feature, a serious injury to the public stage. We are decidedly of the opinion that by the admirable scenic effect of his physiognomy, he has in-advertently precipitated the fall of drama amongst us, or rather, that the last blow has been given to English comedy, by the exquisite comicality of his visage....Writers for the stage, depending on this phenomenon of a phyz, neglect all legitimate means of pleasing, all rules whatsoever by which comedy is distinguished from the very lowest species of buffoonery,—that which depends on grimace....The whole endeavour of our playwrights is directed to exhibit, not their own wit, if they happen to possess such a rare commodity, but Liston's face under new and ludicrous aspects; the sum of their energies is applied to present us with, not a fair exaggeration of human nature, as it is found displayed in the various follies and foibles of mankind, but some fantastical mockery, some gross caricature of real existence; or, rather some burlesque extravaganza, which has no prototype in real existence, where Liston, in a pair of *unmention-ables* coming half-way down his legs, a waistcoat of the pattern of my grandmother's chinz bedgown, and a flaxen wig with the tail turn'd up behind, shall set the audience in a roar without opening his lips.

This was at the Haymarket, a small house where Liston's face could be seen; at the larger theatres, so we may well imagine, broad farcical action of the lowest type was more favoured; and both were equally inimical to a true comic spirit. Action, then, and not witty words, was what everyone demanded.

Yet even farce requires dialogue. Here again the broadest effects were aimed at. None of Congreve's gracious periods could charm this audience; none of Farquhar's delicate

[1] See *supra*, pp. 50–1.

innuendoes. The language was rough in the stylistic sense, if ultra-pure in the moral. Puns of the broadest kind obviously made their appeal. Open any comic piece of the period and these puns stare at you. Says Pacolet in *Valentine and Orson* (Lyc. Dec. 1844):

> He's hard at work inventing a new plot,

to which Oberon answers:

> *Invent* a plot! You're wrong in what you've stated.
> Plots ain't invented now: they're all translated.

An air sung by Orpheus in Planché's *Olympic Devils; or, Orpheus and Eurydice* (Olym. Dec. 1831) runs thus:

> Voulez-vous danser, while I play,
> Trees make bows and stump away,
> Lawns and meadows dance the hay,
>   And rocks to reel are fain, sir?
> Rivers join the *country*-dance,
> Streamlets in quad-*rills* advance,
> Fountains cool
> Glide through la *poole*,
>   And pastorale the plain, sir;
> Voulez-vous danser, while I play,
> Panthers paws-de-deux essay,
> And lordly lions waltz away
>   With all their might and *mane*, sirs.

The two examples given above are from extravaganzas, but prose farce was just as full of the puns. Thus in Coyne's *How to Settle Accounts with your Laundress* (Adel. July 1847), Widgetts has a long conversation with Mary the laundress in which he begs her not "to wring" his "heart and mangle" his "affections like that," while later in the same play the following speech is put into the mouth of Brown the hair-dresser:

I'm an 'airdresser, ma'am, my name's Brown, and I've a professional engagement at the Opera House, where I cultivate romance and ringlets amongst the ladies of the ballet. There I first beheld the lovely Cheri Bounce, the very image of the wax Wenus in my shop window. I loved her, not for her foreign grace, but for her native hair. Oh, she had such a head of real hair;

and oh, the showers of tears and the bottles of Macassar oil that I've poured upon it nobody would believe! Well, I toasted her for two years regularly, and at length she consented to become *Brown*. Well, we were to be married, I had bought my wedding suit, when this fellow Widgetts, came to take the curl out of my happiness. We quarrelled about him last Saturday, and grew so warm that we've been cool ever since.

Much as I am tempted, for I have a partiality for puns, I must leave this aspect of the farces of the time. A detailed survey of their other qualities is impossible within the limits of this volume, for the farces are as numerous as the melodramas; once more, therefore, a glance at some of the better and more typical examples of the type must serve to indicate the characteristics of all.

It may not be unwise to start with that neglected *jeu d'esprit* of poor Charles Lamb, *Mr. H——* (D.L. Dec. 1806). Often have been quoted Elia's words concerning his fond hopes and aspirations before the production, his bitter disappointment when the many-headed serpent hissed forth what was, in England, an irrevocable doom. *Mr. H——* well deserves modern revival[1]. Its style is easy and there are two truly excellent scenes, that between Mr H—— and the landlord and that between the former and Melesinda. The comic pathos in the latter could hardly be bettered. The whole piece, with a certain Wildesque grace although characteristically humorous in the Lamb manner, might well prove a modern success. Yet there is this contemporary damnation to be explained. Professor Brander Matthews has a "playwriting" theory that Lamb has failed because he conceals too long the name of his hero from the audience; but this theory cannot be truly maintained when we note that both at New York and at Philadelphia the farce was a notable success. Not a genuine fault in structure but two elements calculated to arouse contemporary dissatisfaction militated against it. The first was its finer tone. The language and the humour were both too subtle for the larger London theatres of its day; *Mr. H——* demands an intimate playhouse. The

---

[1] Since writing this paragraph I see that Lamb's farce has been revived with great success by a body of amateurs.

second was the name of the hero. In spite of brutality and coarseness in plenty, the audiences of Lamb's time were becoming, not only prurient, but suspicious of anything that seemed "vulgar." When Mr H—— reveals himself as Hogsflesh, the very name, we must feel, grated on the supersensitive ears of the spectators and the hissing began. The faults lay in the audience of the time and not in any inherent error on Lamb's part. It may be confessed that the theme of *Mr. H*—— is a trifle thin, but for its other virtues the farce should have been popular had these two things not caused it to be damned.

Most of the other farce-writers were careful to avoid the pitfalls into which Lamb fell. Their pieces are broad and rough in style, in expression refusing to admit anything that has the slightest tincture of vulgarity. Usually their plots are of the flimsiest. Mrs Pennyfarthing gives a masquerade in Pocock's *Cent. per Cent. or, The Masquerade* (C.G. May 1823), and her husband turns up in fancy dress unexpectedly. Ledger, in the same author's *The Omnibus! or, A Convenient Distance!* (C.G. Dec. 1830), hating visitors, takes a house ten miles from London. The fun, of course, consists in the constant succession of would-be week-enders, added to the gaucheries of Pat Rooney, the well-meaning but awkward Irish servant. These Irishmen were very popular and furnished the basis of many a farce, their stage follies ekeing out more than one dull plot and mitigating much wretched technique. Their presence, and that of other similar types, added to the consciousness that they would be fittingly interpreted, led the dramatists to write ever more and more carelessly. Here is a fairly typical exposition culled from *Each for Himself* (D.L. 1816):

ACT I.—SCENE I.

A Street.

Enter Sir HARRY FREEMAN *and Young* CANISTER, *meeting.*

Can. What!—Sir Harry Freeman!

Sir H. What! Tom Canister! Old college acquaintance, how are you? (*shake hands*).

Can. How d'ye do, my noble Baronet.—Just arrived in town, I suppose?

Sir H. Yes, Tom, here I am again at the starting post of pleasure, and eager for the race.—Well, how go Bohea, Twankay, and Congo?

Can. Nay, confound you, Sir Harry, don't put one out of countenance.

Sir H. Are you ashamed of your calling?—What, man, of a business that brings you in each year a brace of thousands!

Can. The income, certainly, is not to be despised—but then only recollect, Sir Harry, a college education unfits one—

Sir H. For enjoying a snug fortune, hey!—No, no,—stick to your Tea Chests, Tom.—Woo washerwomen and old maids, instead of the muses.

Can. Faugh!—don't mention it—Do you know I think of changing my name, merely to get rid of the odious superscription on my letters—"For Mr. *T.* Canister."

Sir H. Ha! ha!—poor Tom—Oh, pray are you as great an orator as ever, Tom?

Can. Aye, now I see you want me to deny the little reputation I obtained in that way.

Sir H. No, no, that would be unreasonable—I wish you rather to flatter yourself, for, 'pon my soul, I can't.

Can. I see you are the same satirical dog as ever.

Sir H. (*looking out*).—Hey!—An Angel!—Beautiful! By heavens, incomparable!—Curse that opaque old woman!—hey, turned the corner—oh, oh! (*runs out*).

Can. (*calls*). Sir Harry!

Sir H. (*without*). Good day, Tom.

Can. Why, he's running after my aunt, and cousin Rosa, whom he never saw in his life before! Ha! ha!—this is a good joke—I'll follow, to see how they'll take his fine speeches—Ha! ha!

The Ha, ha's! have lost their flavour now, and after this array of information gratuitously flung at the audience we well know what threadbare situations and dialogue we must expect.

The writers of farce are numerous in this time and it may be well to glance at one or two selected works from those who were most prolific or most popular. Charles Dance was both prolific and popular; from his writings the comedietta, *Delicate Ground; or, Paris in* 1793 (Lyc. Nov. 1849) may be taken here. This little play shows well the peculiar combination, fairly common in that age, of latent potentiality and frigid, groping structure. The opening, like that of *Each for Himself*, does not promise much. Pauline enters weeping and kissing a letter alternately and together; then she speaks —the comments, naturally, are mine—

Pauline, [this is to let the audience know her name] what is it that you did? [to arouse expectancy] Alas! that even when one is alone one cannot escape the searching inquiries of conscience. [sentimental appeal] Yet, after all, is not conscience a less hard taskmaster than a cold, dissembling, ironical, tyrannical husband? No doubt, no doubt. Know then, good conscience, [she means, but does not say, good spectators] that I kissed this letter, and know further, that this letter is *not* from my husband. [a very blind conscience this] Nay, start not! It is a letter of other days, and it is from him who should have been my husband—from him who, had he lived, would have been my husband; from the object of my early, my deep affection; from the long-lamented Alphonse— De—Hush! My husband!

The development, however, belies this beginning. Alphonse De Grandier is not dead, and the pair are about to elope, when citizen Sangfroid's coolness succeeds in exposing their romantic follies. Here is farce undoubtedly with the basis of a serious thought, and we learn once more, how, out of the minor "illegitimate" drama of the time, higher ideals were being formed. Indeed, it is not too much to say that in Dance we have the far-off ancestor of Bernard Shaw. That which characterises all Shaw's writings is the attack, direct or implied, at romantic assumptions. In *Man and Superman* it is the convention of the love-chase that is dealt with; in *How He Lied to Her Husband* it is the eternal triangle; in *The Dark Lady of the Sonnets* it is the nineteenth century picture of "the Bard." Now, while it would be utter folly to suggest that in Charles Dance we find anything at all comparable with Shaw's brilliant wit and destructive rationalism, we may, I think, discern in the earlier writer's work the operation of that critical mood which ultimately leads to the work of Shaw. This is made plain when we turn to the last section of the play. Alphonse has made his appearance and has succeeded in fluttering little Pauline's heart. Sangfroid, instead of flying into a romantic passion, offers her a divorce, and this rather troubles the romantic lover:

Sangfroid. Ah, there you are again! Written your letter? That's right! The carriage is ordered, and the Citizen Pauline will be ready directly.

Alphonse. Would you object to allowing me two or three minutes conversation with you in private?

Sangfroid. Certainly not. Pray go on.

Alphonse. Thank you! But the fact is, the questions I wish to ask you are of so delicate a nature that I hardly know where to begin.

Sangfroid. At the beginning, I should say.

Alphonse. Yes, I know; but that's the difficulty.

Sangfroid. Then try the middle, or the end. You have no time to spare.

Alphonse. You—you—you don't love—that is, of course, I don't wish you to love her now—but I mean you *didn't* love Pauline.

Sangfroid. I shall not contradict you.

Alphonse. Yes, but it seems to me that you couldn't bear her. Now as she has become my wife—

Sangfroid. Not yet, she's my wife at present.

Alphonse. We'll say "our wife."

Sangfroid. Excuse me, I don't mean to be rude, but I don't like the partnership. Call her Pauline.

Alphonse. As you please, but you will think it but natural that I should feel curious, not to say anxious, to know the cause of your aversion. You can have nothing to say against her personal appearance.

Sangfroid. Nothing.

Alphonse. Nor against her numerous virtues!

Sangfroid. No. Yes, stop; there is one virtue you will have to teach her.

Alphonse. What is that?

Sangfroid. Fidelity to her husband.

Alphonse. What, sir, do you imagine Pauline capable—

Sangfroid. Upon my life, you're a treat! You supposed her capable when you asked her to run away from me.

The result is that Alphonse's ardours cool as he nears his romantic goal:

Alphonse. Any communication you have to make to her now, must go through me.

Sangfroid. Must it? Then I have a favourite sword I wish to send her. Would you like *that* to go through you?

Alphonse. No; of course I don't mean anything of that sort.

Sangfroid. It's not very easy to know what you mean. But what I mean is this, you have come here like a thief, as you are—

Alphonse. A thief, sir?

Sangfroid. Don't interrupt me. You'll find I'm quite right. Like a thief as you are—to rob me of my wife. Are you ready, now, on the instant—that is to say, the instant the forms of law are complied with—to make her yours?

Alphonse. Well, I don't know.

Sangfroid. You don't know! But you must know. Do you suppose that I'll allow you to disturb the peace of a quiet, well-regulated family in this manner, to deprive a lady of a husband who is worthy the name of a husband, without being prepared to offer her the poor consolation of such a paltry, contemptible substitute as you are?

There is here, unquestionably, an interesting treatment of a domestic theme, and in it one can see how, in the very midst of romantic flamboyance, a spirit of rationalism was rising to react against the false, the rosy-coloured, conventions of a society that had long since ceased to look upon facts. It is to be confessed that portions of *Delicate Ground* are sentimentally conceived and that the exposition is thoroughly wretched; but there remains that other quality, shown in the two passages quoted above, which links the treatment of the theme to some of the prevailing tendencies in twentieth century drama[1].

These last two examples show well between what limits the farces of the time moved. It is true that a certain definite chronological advance can be traced, but absolute chronology in reality aids us little. Constantly in these decades we see the clash of opposing elements, now dominant the absurdities and the ludicrous situations, now a quality which points forward towards a more thoughtful and deliberate form of art. The follies, of course, are the more numerous and noticeable, although even the follies at times take on a

[1] It matters little whether this play or another is of French extraction or not. The fact remains that we have this attitude apparent before 1850 and expressed dramatically in the theatre.

charm all their own. *Five Hundred Pounds Reward; or, Dick Turpin the Second* (Lyc. Jan. 1847) displays the typically bustling plots of the period. Mr Dumbleton, a foolish old Dogberry, expects Dick Turpin to give himself up to justice. Valentine Honeyball (played by Wigan) is cheated into pretending he is the famous highwayman and has the uncomfortable experience of falling in with a real band of robbers, who at once accept him as their leader. It is obvious that the plot here was designed for the displayal of acting alone; nothing but the broadly ludicrous and the boisterously active is granted admission. *A Model of a Wife* (Lyc. Jan. 1845), with its punning title, is of the same character, presenting a rough and tumble plot which depends mainly upon Stump's jealousy of Bonnefoi. For the most part Douglas Jerrold's farces belong to the same genre, with, often, the addition of a semi-sentimental flavour. Thus *Gertrude's Cherries; or, Waterloo in 1835* (C.G. Sept. 1842) has the rougher element in the characters of Blague, Mr Crossbone and Mrs Crossbone, while the emotional element is freely provided for in the discovery by Willoughby of his long-lost son in Guibert and his long-lost grand-daughter in Gertrude. This seems a case of carrying ancestral discoveries just a trifle far back. To exploit ridiculous situations, too, and to provide material for low-comedy actors, Jerrold turned to write his *Paul Pry* (Cob. Nov. 1827), which, like the *Sir Martin Mar-all* of a previous age, made constant fun out of the meddlesome and intruding qualities of its hero. Peculiarly enough, yet explainably if we take into account the theatres of the time, even Planché, so neat and witty in his revues and extravaganzas, trusts in his farces to action alone. In *Hold your Tongue* (Lyc. March 1849) all the laughter comes from the embarrassing situation of Lady Ryder who has secretly attended a masquerade and who comes, through circumstances, to see the folly of her carelessly premeditated action. The only farce of this prolific author which catches a gleam from his extravaganza tinselling and which suggests a novel purpose is *A Romantic Idea* (Lyc. March 1849), where a young German author, who has come to a village in search of literary material, spends his night in a ruin and has a most uncomfortable dream of a demon-jester and similar awe-inspiring sprites. The embodiment of the dream-figures has a certain modern note, but this piece stands unfortunately alone among Planché's kindred works. Equivocal situations and threadbare characters are once more exploited in Mrs Planché's *The Welsh Girl* (Olym. Dec. 1833) which tells of an ancient story wherein a girl (Julia) secretly married to an only son (Alfred) wins the affections of her father-in-law (Sir Owen Griffiths) by pretending to be an innocent little stranger. The intrigues of lovers and their servants naturally provided a good deal of comic subject-matter. Sometimes the tricks are all imposed on the foolish old relics of Pantalone and Graziano; sometimes, as in S. Penley's *The Sleeping-Draught* (D.L. April 1818), the intriguers are caught for a time in their own traps. In the last-mentioned play Rinaldo adores Francesca while his servant Popolino loves Nonna. By mistake Popolino swallows a potent sleeping-draught made up by Doctor Vincolo and is carried off as dead in a chest. The miserly Farmer Bruno finds the chest and carries it off home. The equivocal situations which arise when Popolino wakens may be imagined.

More of sentimentalism appears in the productions of R. C. Dallas, whose *Not at Home* (Lyc. Nov. 1809) may be taken as representative. "How delightful it is to expose villainy and rescue innocence!" exclaims Fitzalban in good old eighteenth century style, and his remark may well serve as a motto for this story of Lord Sedley's evil practices, Fitzalban's heroism and Lovell's jealousy. Sentimentalism of a different kind is flaunted before us in Buckstone's *A Rough Diamond* (Lyc. Nov. 1847). Once more we seem to be breathing the air of 1780 when we find the native but un-polished honesty of the country wife Margery deeply contrasted with the refined duplicity of Lady Plato and Captain Blenheim. Rousseau still lays his hand on many a dramatic work of the period.

One after another these pieces were brought, in huddled confusion, upon the various stages, sentimentalism, bustling

action, broad jests, atrocious puns making up for any poverty
in invention or style. Heavy contrasts were beloved. Take
your hypocritical Puritans (a stage mother-in-law and an
Aminadab Sleek) and show a good-natured husband,
yearning for brighter things, in their toils, and your farce—
in this instance *The Serious Family* (H.[2] Oct. 1849) by Morris
Barnett—is done. Heap together a group of ridiculous
"humours"—Sam, a Yorkshire waiter, Fainwou'd, a wealthy
lout, Miss Laurelia Durable, a spinster, Diddler, a kind of
Jingle—and you have made a popular success. Kenney
knew the truth of this when he composed *Raising the Wind*
(C.G. Nov. 1803). Sometimes you might, with due circum-
spection, sail somewhat close to the wind and introduce a
situation bordering on the *risqué* side, telling, for example,
how a maid (Maria) poses as the wife of a friend (Selborne)
in order to deceive an old man (Sir Mark Chase). Provided
you do not overstep the mark and merely introduce distracting
ludicrosities such as the lamentable position of a stranger
(Alfred Highflyer) who is informed that a country house is a
lunatic asylum, your play will be successful: Tom Morton's
A Roland for an Oliver (C.G. April 1819), built on this
plan, proved so successful that his publisher could declare
that "no Farce ever excited more genuine laughter, and
tumultuous applause, than this has done[1]."

The disguises indulged in in earlier comic drama, exaggerated and made more ridiculous, appear in these pieces
and evidently caused constant merriment. Amelia in Moncrieff's *Tarnation Strange; or, More Jonathans* (Strand, Aug.
1838) is about to be married to a boaster, Jonathan Jonah
Goliah Bang, and is saved by the astute Cornet Wimbleton,
who assumes a multitude of disguises. Obviously that which
pleased the eighteenth century still pleases this. Moncrieff
and others harp again and again on the same theme. In
The Winterbottoms! or My Aunt, the Dowager (Strand, June
1837) both Frank Jekyll and his man Jeffrey impersonate
the Dowager Lady Winterbottom, the former succeeding
eventually in winning the hand of Celestine. The equivocal

[1] See original octavo edition of 1819.

situations may be left to the imagination; they anticipate by
half a century those which still excite laughter in *Charley's
Aunt*. It is obvious that these, as well as such farces as
J. T. Allingham's *The Weathercock* (D.L. Nov. 1805) where
Tristram Fickle moves from profession to profession, give
ample scope for low-comedy performances. Very typical
in this way is Somerset's *The Day after the Fair* (Olym. Jan.
1829). Here Old Fidget, the noise-hating ancient who carries
his ancestry back to Jonson's *Epicoene*, is presented to us in
a little cottage which he has recently bought and where he
seeks for peaceful retirement. Jerry and Polly covet this
cottage, and to gain it from him they impersonate between
them a variety of types—a noisy cobbler, a ballad-singer, a
drummer, a French singer, a maniac, a washerwoman and a
theatrical manageress. One might compare with this Joseph
Lunn's *Lofty Projects; or, Arts in an Attic* (C.G. April 1825),
written expressly for the actor Yates, designed to show him
as Versatile imitating a number of other characters. Or one
might take T. E. Hook's *The Trial by Jury* (H.[2] May 1811).
In this play Sanford disguises himself as a gardener and
Milford as a footman in order to oust the parentally-favoured
Wilkins. Complications of an intricate sort arise from the
fact that, while Sanford knows the footman to be Milford,
Milford thinks Sanford is really the gardener. As a final
example we may turn to Boucicault's *Used Up* (H.[2] Feb.
1844), derived from a French play, *L'homme blasé*. Here a
different explanation is given for the disguises. Sir Charles
Coldstream is thoroughly bored; seeking for excitement, he
finds it in a scuffle with the brawny Ironbrace. They both
fall into a river and are thought dead. Sir Charles, however,
escapes drowning, disguises himself as Joe, a ploughboy, and
succeeds in winning the heart of Mary, the charming niece
of the crotchety old farmer, Wurzel. As is clear, we are really
not so far from the present day; the outlines of this plot
are quite evidently reproduced in Arnold Bennett's modern
comedy, *The Great Adventure*.

The farces of this time have not much to offer us of real
intrinsic merit. Some are written in a sprightly style; but

even the best display a certain mechanical structure. Most of them were written for low-comedy actors who could "put across" almost anything, and consequently there is generally evident a carelessness on the part of the authors both as regards plot and form. Old themes are constantly being refurbished, and stock situations occur with irritating frequency. We may say that neither in regard to literary form nor to inventiveness did these farces bring anything of permanent worth to the theatre: yet such a judgment may hardly be final or unqualified. Here at least was a world of hearty laughter; here was a type of drama which carried on that tradition for broad merriment which can be traced back to Elizabethan days, and further. The farce stands alongside of the melodrama as the most characteristic and most popular play-form produced in the age; and as such it demands our close attention, whether our aim be to recapture and explain the theatrical tendencies of these decades or to follow the fortunes of our drama from the eighteenth century on to the modern period.

III. *Burlettas and Comic Operas*

Many of those pieces which I have included in the last section were called by a variety of names. Sometimes the old-fashioned "Farce" stood starkly on the title-page or in the printed bill, but, more commonly, a desire for novelty led the dramatists to diversify their nomenclature. "Comic Drama" and "Comic Piece" are not far out of the ordinary, but terms such as "Farcetta" and "Comedietta" are new and display the movement towards individuality of classification. That many of these terms meant nothing definite or precise cannot be denied; there seems, for example, to be no distinction between a farcetta and a farce. But in general this tendency marks a realisation on the part of the dramatists that new forms were springing into being. Constantly in drama there has been a break-down of the original "kinds," and tragi-comedies, farces, interludes, and the like have pushed their way forward and even ousted regular tragedy and comedy from the boards. This movement towards novelty of form, however, was never so marked as in this early nineteenth century. Perhaps the cause was romantic freedom, but, whatever the reason, we see on all sides the evolution of dramatic types which were either entirely new or but dimly adumbrated in preceding years. From five-act comedy of the Sheridan mould down to the shortest of farcical interludes there existed a whole series of intermediate forms, and the diversified nomenclature marks the endeavour of the playwrights to indicate at what precise stage or level their particular works stood. Comedietta, for instance, indicates that the author was aiming rather at a purely comic than at a farcical effect, but that his play was not of a full five-act form. Although it is in error in imagining that the name "comedietta" is "newly-coined," a paragraph in *The Reader* for April 8, 1865, gives a fairly clear explanation of this title:

A comedietta is a newly-coined term for a new species of drama. A name was required for that dwarf species of comedy that is not so broad as farce, nor so light as vaudeville, nor so tragic as melodrama....It ought, being a species, to be complete in itself, and not merely two or three scenes belonging to a larger comedy.

The comedietta, or *petite comédie* as sometimes it was alternatively styled, in this age when five-act comedy was mostly sentimental and farce lorded it over the lighter stage, marks a tentative endeavour to return to a social comedy, of diminutive proportions and midway between a farce of Garrick and a comedy of Congreve.

The Reader mentions as a still lighter form, the vaudeville. The name, it is said, derived originally from a *chanson du Vau* (or *val*) *de Vire*, a district in Normandy, and was applied in the sixteenth century to a certain type of pleasant, generally popular, ditty. In the nineteenth century the word was extended in meaning to include a "pièce de théâtre où le dialogue est entremêlé de couplets faits sur des airs de vaudeville, ou empruntés à des opéras-comiques[1]." To

---

[1] Definition in Littré, *Dictionnaire de la langue française*. The various types of *vaudeville-farce, comédie-vaudeville, vaudeville anecdotique* and *vaudeville intrigué* are dealt with by Eugène Lintilhac in vol. v. of his *Histoire générale du théâtre en France* (1910).

England the word came, in this secondary sense, about the thirties of the century. In 1833 Lord Lytton used it in close connection with farce and "lighter comedy[1]," while, a few years later, Moncrieff was commenting upon it in his prefaces. In *The Kiss and the Rose, or Love in the Nursery Grounds* (Vauxhall 1827), taken from the French *La servante justifiée*, the latter considered it necessary to show how the form "differs from the Burletta." This point of distinction he finds in the fact that the vaudeville was "a dramatic story in verse, rather than prose, illustrated and carried on by means of the songs and melodies of the day rather than original compositions." This commentary he continues in the preface to *Bringing Home the Bride! or the Husband's First Journey* (Adel. March 1831), derived from *Le Voyage de la Mariée*. Here he asserts that the first of the type in England was *The King of the Alps* (Adel. Jan. 1831). The vaudeville plays an important part in the refining of the English stage, and deserves to be studied in close connection with the dramatic efforts of Planché and with the endeavours of the Mathews-Vestris managements. With the vaudeville, too, must be considered the *revue*, a dramatic form which, important as it was and is, has not found a place in the *Oxford English Dictionary*. The *revue*, as its name indicates, attempts to present in a light form a survey, mingled with good-humoured criticism, of recent dramatic events; in this way it is closely connected with the extravaganza-burlesque. The *locus criticus* regarding its history in England is a passage in J. R. Planché's *Recollections* (1872), where he is discussing his earlier activities. "My theatrical labours in the year 1825," he says,

terminated with the production at the Adelphi, then under the management of Messrs. Terry and Yates, of a one-act piece on the 12th of December, entitled "Success; or, a Hit if you Like it," which I only mention because it was the first attempt in this country to introduce that class of entertainment so popular in Paris called "Revue," and of which, with one solitary exception, I believe I have been the sole contributor to the English stage[2].

[1] *Godolphin*, chap. ix; quoted in the *N.E.D.*
[2] *Op. cit.* i. 73.

In the introduction to *Success* as presented in the first volume of Planché's *Extravaganzas* (1879) the author notes that he has never found a convenient English equivalent for the French name, and gives as his definition "a 'Review' of the dramatic productions of the past season." In *Success* there are thus presented before Fashion, his daughter Success, and his officers, Pshaw and Fiddle-de-dee, a whole series of dramatic caricatures—Zamiel, from the English Opera, Brutus from Drury Lane, Polichinelle from Covent Garden, Paul Pry from the Haymarket and Long Tom Coffin from the Adelphi. The Press, the "Privy Council of Fashion, as *suit*-ably represented as the Wardrobe will admit upon so *press*-ing an occasion," naturally form an important part of the spectacle.

Success was printed among the *Extravaganzas*, and this term, extravaganza, also requires a note or two of comment. Derived from the Italian *stravaganza*, the word explains itself, and serves to indicate at one and the same time a wide field of nineteenth century dramatic activity and a general tendency of the age. As we glance over the bills and theatrical advertisements of the time, we must inevitably be struck by the composite descriptions appended to many a play, highly reminiscent of Polonius' famous divisions. This in itself indicates the "romantic" movements of the age, the neo-classical "kinds," as we have seen, being ousted in favour of novelties of all sorts. In addition to this, we note the rapid growth of two apparently contradictory tendencies—the realistic and the fantastic. The first is symbolised in the domestic melodrama, the second finds typical expression in the extravaganza. Apparently the first play to be given this name was Planché's *High, Low, Jack, and the Game; or, The Card Party* (Olym. Sept. 1833), which was styled "A Most Extravagant Extravaganza" or (this was for the sake of the Lord Chamberlain) "Rum-antic Burletta." The *dramatis personae* are the playing cards, and the settings were evidently of a rich and fantastic order. In the programme we read of

A *deal* of Machinery by Mr Mackintosh. The properties *made* and *cut* by Mr Buckley. The new scenery (painted by Mr Gordon) will be *dealt out* in regular order.

The extravaganza had a glorious career in the thirties and forties of the century. Usually it adopted themes of an allegorical or classic kind, but its looseness of style also suited the presentation of such exaggerated and plot-less "realistic" scenes as are given in W. T. Moncrieff's *Tom and Jerry; or, Life in London* (Adel. Nov. 1821). This "whimsical melange" as Cumberland's editor, "D.G.," calls it, exists simply for the purpose of providing half-fantastic, half-naturalistic glimpses of scenes of London Life—the "Chaffing Crib in Corinthian House, Tattersal's, Hyde Park Corner, Almack's, Tom Cribb's Parlour, Temple Bar, Fleet Street, a "fashionable Hell, at the west-end of the Town," "Back Slums in the Holy Land" and others. Whether realistic or romantic, however, it was always the "extravaganza," and, retaining its flourish, passed on vital traditions which, fifty years later, were taken over by Gilbert and Sullivan in their famous Savoy operas.

Of all the terms employed during this period, the burletta is by far the most difficult to define. In the eighteenth century the term was introduced with a certain exact significance[1], but by the beginning of the following century it had come to mean nothing but a play which could with safety be given at a minor, or unpatented theatre. "Ask now," says George Colman the Younger, "what is a burletta, and you will be told it is one thing at one theatre, and another at another." He notes that the lawyers failed to provide a definition, but himself finds he cannot consider it other than "as a drama in rhyme, and which is entirely musical; a short comic piece, consisting of recitative and singing, wholly accompanied, more or less, by the Orchestra[2]." This, however, as Colman himself observes, was by no means a definition capable of covering the vast number of plays included under the one title; confusion reigned in the minds of spectators, managers

---

[1] See *A History of English Drama*, iii. 194.
[2] *Op. cit.* pp. 397–8.

and officials. Writing to Colman on Feb. 22, 1824, the Lord Chamberlain thought that

Surely a Burletta must be interspersed throughout with songs at least, whatever may be the other characteristics of a Burletta[1],

while Colman, answering his chief on the 24th of the month, displayed equal uncertainty:

I think you may fairly say, that it is easy sometimes to say what is not a Burletta, tho' it may be difficult to define what a Burletta is, according to the legal acceptation of the Term, Burletta, Five or six songs in a Piece of one Act for example, where the songs make a natural part of the Piece (*and not forced into an acting piece,* to qualify it as a Burletta) may be perhaps considered so far a Burletta, as not to be refused by the Chamberlain, tho' there always remains the question, whether a Burletta must not be in verse, and the whole sung, not *said*; which makes the question dangerous.

In spite of this confusion, it is fairly easy to see how the extension of the term began and to what it led. In origin the burletta was not a minor or "illegitimate" type at all, but had begun in the patent theatres of the late eighteenth century. Minor theatres, however, were arising, and at first these specialised in the "spectacle," with plentiful music and printed flags for the text[2], but soon men like Dibdin tried the experiment of presenting musical pieces with dialogue. These were simply the "legitimate" burlettas taken over by the minors because, apart from their airs, the whole was in recitative and consequently, not spoken, but sung. Perhaps to their surprise no opposition was put in their way, and as a result still a further experiment was made. A regular play was taken, the dialogue put into blundering rimed couplets and a few songs added, the whole being presented as a "burletta." No doubt the very first attempts in this style were adaptations of comedies and farces, but continued success led to boldness, and serious plays were seized upon. When once this fashion had been established,

---

[1] This and the following passage are extracted from original letters bound up with the plays for 1824 in the L.C. Collection.

[2] See *supra*, p. 102. While I do not hold with all his conclusions, and while he omits altogether mention of the earlier "legitimate" burletta, I should call special attention to Professor E. B. Watson's excellent treatment of this question in his *From Sheridan to Robertson*, pp. 33–47.

clearly the dialogue came to assume an ever greater importance and the formal orchestra dwindled down to a single piano. 'The tinkling of the piano and the jingle of the rhyme[1]," were, therefore, the chief characteristics of the burlettas of the first decades of the nineteenth century. By this time it had become an unwritten law that anything which could be called a burletta might be presented at a minor theatre. The next movement forward was, peculiarly enough, the result of an action on the part of the patent theatres. Colman once more comes to our aid. He observes that *Tom Thumb*, as altered and provided with songs, was produced at one of the two major theatres as a burletta, that is to say as a "legitimate" burletta. He continues:

In this piece there is partly dialogue without music; and I have been recently informed from good authority, that it was inadvertently announced by the managers of Covent Garden theatre...as a burletta, and that they repent of having afforded this precedent.

Well might they repent, for the managers of the minor theatres were not slow to seize their opportunity. Now they could put on a play with a few songs, and, when challenged, point to the Covent Garden interpretation of the term. The tinkling of the piano became fainter and fainter, an occasional chord at long intervals providing merely an indication of its presence. The songs, of course, remained, and it seems that the Lord Chamberlain finally came to take the view that a three-act play—for five acts were always indicative of legitimacy—with not less than five songs could come within the burletta division. The minors were now free, to all intents and purposes, to play what they desired[2]. Even Shakespeare was swept into their net, although for the most part they found it safer and more profitable to confine their activities to melodrama, farce, extravaganza and burlesque.

In order to make quite clear the scope of this burletta

---

[1] *Theatrical Inquisitor*, Oct. 1812.
[2] Planché has a note in his *Extravaganzas* (ii. 23) explaining that by burlettas "we were desired to understand dramas containing not less than five pieces of vocal music in each act." From an examination of extant plays, it would seem that the words "in each act" are here a mistake.

tradition, it may not be unwise to glance at two typical repertories, that of the Surrey Theatre in 1810 and that of the Royalty in 1812. Shortly after opening for the spring season we find that the managers of the former present, as burlettas, both Farquhar's *The Beaux Stratagem* (May 21) and Shakespeare's *Antony and Cleopatra* (May 28), following up the production of these two plays with another of Mrs Centlivre's *A Bold Stroke for a Wife* (Aug. 27). Nothing could have been more "legitimate" than these dramas, yet the burletta conception could allow of their free performance. Even more informative is the list of new productions at the Royalty in the summer of 1812. On Aug. 3 appeared a burletta version of Charles Shadwell's *The Fair Quaker*, accompanied by *The Enchantment or Trappolin's Vagaries*, evidently derived from Cockain's *Trapolin a supposed Prince*. *Tekeli; or, the Siege of Montgatz* (Aug. 10) is obviously a burletta rendering of Hook's melodrama (D.L. 1808), while a whole series of later performances filch freely from dramas written in the last years of the preceding century. *The Battle of Hexham; or, Days of Yore* (Aug. 17) must be Colman's *The Battle of Hexham; or, Days of Old*; *No Song, No Supper* (Aug. 10) and *My Grandmother* (Aug. 13) are taken from Prince Hoare; *The Stranger* (Sept. 7) is simply the famous Drury Lane success of 1798; *Fortune's Frolic* (Sept. 24) is a version of Allingham's play; while *The Follies of a Day; or, The Marriage of Figaro* (Oct. 1) clearly is naught else than Holcroft's adaptation of Beaumarchais' comedy. These burlettas prove that the minors could, without impunity, seize upon all the more modern plays which had proved popular in the major theatres. A fictional division into three acts and the addition of those few songs could make legitimate dramas the property of whichever minor manager cared to appropriate them. Before leaving the 1812 Royalty season, moreover, it is important to observe that the last three "new" burlettas produced during the year were *The Merry Wives of Windsor* (Oct. 5), *King Lear and his Three Daughters* (Oct. 24) and *King Richard III; or, the Battle of Bosworth Field* (Dec. 26).

As is made plainly evident from the above summary account, we can with no certainty give the title burletta to any particular species of dramatic composition of the age. The word may be applied to any of the varied types produced in the minor theatres, although in general it signified most frequently the operatic farce which was so popular a form. Just as comedy bowed to the will of farce, the comic opera bowed to the farcical sketch interspersed with songs. A few more elaborate comic operas, it is true, attempt to retain the style of Bickerstaff and his eighteenth century companions, and such a man as William Dimond can present us with a genuine "confession of Operatic Faith[1]." The points made by this author deserve some attention. As to the plot of comic opera, he decides that

it may be either serious or sprightly, or it may combine both qualities, *ad libitum*, with just a sufficient interest to excite attention and to banish *ennui* during the necessary spaces between song and song, but never so vividly to stimulate the feelings of an Audience, as to make the recurrence of Music be felt as an impertinent interruption. The *Incidents* are not required to be strictly probable; nevertheless they certainly ought to be *just possible*, and at no time to degenerate into the downright extravagances of fantastic Melodrame or of buffoon Farce. The *Dialogue* should be unambitiously colloquial, yet raised above positive meanness; it should unfold whatever fable there may be, intelligibly, and come to the point with as much conciseness as possible—Above all, the MUSICAL SITUATIONS ought to spring with spontaneity out of the very necessities of the Scene; never betraying themselves to be labored introductions for the mere purpose of exhibiting vocal talent, but always to appear so many integral portions and indispensable continuations of the Story.

These remarks are interesting, but few there were who thought on this subject so curiously.

Dimond was one of the most energetic purveyors of this operatic comedy during the age, generally flavouring his pieces with a highly sentimental tone. *The Sea-Side Story* (C.G. May 1801), *Youth, Love, and Folly* (D.L. May 1805) and *The Young Hussar, or Love and Money* (D.L. March

[1] Preface to *Native Land; or, The Return from Slavery* (C.G. Feb. 1824).

1807) are among his better works, although hardly any deserve space for individual analysis. There is one point, however, concerning others besides Dimond, which warrants particular comment. In *Native Land* we find a note:

TIME—From the Hour of Noon until a few Minutes beyond the Midnight,

while in *Youth, Love, and Folly* there is this:

TIME—From Noon till the beginning of the Evening.

At first sight, these might be considered isolated examples, elements traditionally retained by an individual dramatist from the Augustan system. Further investigation of the drama of the period, however, reveals the interesting fact that Dimond's notes are by no means so isolated. Not only does a dignified dramatist such as Talfourd refuse to overstep a two-day limit[1], but quite illegitimate playwrights joined in a crusade for the retention of the Unities. Brown's *Narensky* (D.L. Jan. 1814) and Siddons' *Time's a Tell Tale* (D.L. Oct. 1807) both boast of a fictional one-day duration, and such a writer as Thomas Dibdin can present a whole series of plays with as restricted a sphere[2]. While it forms a digression, this note on these neo-classic conventions may help to show how far the age was as yet from a sure dramatic purpose. In the midst of melodrama and vaudeville the Augustan standards still weakly hold their heads aloft.

There does not seem to be much gained by any formal differentiation between the farcical and comic types of opera during this period. In any event most of the so-called comic situations descend to farcical levels. Beside Dimond, Thomas Dibdin helped to keep the operatic form popular. His plays, like Dimond's, are for the most part sentimental; *The Two Gregories; or, Where did the Money came from?* (Surrey, April 1821) may be regarded as typical. Here the plot concerns an error in name. One Mr Gregory has saved the life of John Bull, and the latter, on learning the name of his bene-

---

[1] Cf. *The Athenian Captive* (H.[2] 1838).

[2] *The Cabinet* (C.G. 1802), *The English Fleet, in* 1342 (C.G. 1803), *Morning, Noon, and Night* (H.[2] 1822). *Of Age To-morrow* (D.L. 1800), has a time-limit equal to "that of the action."

factor, sends him a thousand pounds. The money, however, gets into the hands of a second Mr Gregory and there is considerable pother before the final discovery and highly sentimental retribution.

The majority of these pieces are exceedingly slight. Moncrieff's *The Parson's Nose! or The Birth Day Dinner* (Vic. Dec. 1835), derived from Desaugiers' *Le dîner de Madelon, ou le bourgeois du Marais*, is a thoroughly representative *jeu d'esprit*. Old Bubb is to have a dinner and his house-keeper Madeleine dearly wishes that no visitors should come. Parson Chittenden arrives, and Madeleine succeeds in driving him off by declaring that Bubb is mad and has a strange propensity for "the parson's nose." Since Bubb does really love this part of a fowl, the scenes go merrily forward "in equivoque." *How to take up a Bill, or the Village Vauxhall* (City, Nov. 1833) deals with a similar subject. The idea here is taken from *L'ami bontemps, ou la maison de mon oncle* by Theauton and Mélesville. Merrycliff is seriously in debt, and, to ease his fortunes and incidentally to enable him to marry, his friends, putting bills outside, arrange his uncle's house as a kind of Vauxhall. The old uncle, of course, is very puzzled and very irate, but all ends well and Merrycliff runs away with his Cecilia. "Gulling" provides also the theme of *Rochester; or, King Charles the Second's Merry Days* (Olym. Nov. 1818). This shows us Rochester and Buckingham, bored and seeking for intrigue, in a country inn. Two gay (but of course virtuous) ladies of quality come down and cheat them finely. How unhistorical the atmosphere is may be gauged from one remark of Rochester's in the third act:

All powerful nature, how potent is thy sway? Silvia, you have conquered me.—The honour of woman should always be kept sacred, when entrusted to the honour of man.

That this admixture of sentimentality and risqué-ness was pleasing to the age is proved by a note to the 1825 edition which states that "all the fashion, and nearly all the population of London, were attracted 'by this drama' to a Theatre, previously almost wholly unknown, and unattended. The two Royal Theatres, with the whole weight of their attractions, were for the time deserted." Nor was the risqué-ness confined to dramas set in the age of Charles II. Something of this tone appears in *Maid or Wife; or, The Deceiver Deceived* (D.L. Nov. 1821), a not unamusing operatic farce by Barham Livius. Most of the comic interest here depends on equivocal situation. Sir George Rakewell makes love to Fanny while her real husband, Ready, has to stand behind his chair in his capacity as waiter. Lady Rakewell comes home thinking that her husband is unwell and addresses him under this impression while he replies, wondering whether she has discovered his philandering propensities. The risqué situations are, however, as in the other plays, covered with a veil of sentimental reflection.

Sentimentalism, too, colours the operatic farces of Isaac Pocock and James Kenney. *Yes or No?* (H.[2] Aug. 1808) by the former shows Charles Fervor slandered by his hypocritical guardian, Obadiah Broadbrim. Naturally his honesty is discovered and he is reconciled to his uncle, Sir Barometer Oldstyle. The devices by which a Janus Jumble succeeds in marrying his Clara fill out the two acts of *Hit or Miss!* (Lyc. Feb. 1810) and those by which a Prince Royal gains the affections of a Princess of Navarre provide material for *John of Paris* (C.G. Nov. 1814)[1]. Kenney's *Turn Him Out!* (Lyc. March 1812) runs on a theme just as hackneyed. The story of Maria's pretended idiocy in order to escape the attentions of Dr Truckle is derived either from Arthur Murphy's *The Citizen* or from its original, *La Fausse Agnès* of Destouches. *Matrimony* (D.L. Nov. 1804) is certainly taken from *Adolphe et Clare* and veers sentimentally close to tears. Delaval and Clara have a lovers' quarrel. Their good-natured uncle pretends to despatch them to prison, and their differences are, of course, disposed of when separation threatens. *The Alcaid; or, Secrets of Office* (H.[2] Aug. 1824) is a foolish piece, interesting only when taken along with the numerous other Oriental-set operas of the time. Of this

---

[1] This play is taken from St Just's *Jean de Paris*.

species Dimond's *Abou Hassan* (D.L. April 1825), written on the theme of O'Keeffe's *The Dead Alive*, C. E. Walker's *The Fall of Algiers* (D.L. Jan. 1825), with its blundering Timothy Tourist, and C. A. Somerset's "*Yes!*" (Surrey, 1829) may be taken as representative.

The favourite subjects were those such as appeared in some of the above-mentioned plays—"gullings," deceits, equivocal situations. James Cobb has quite an amusing piece called *A House to be Sold* (D.L. Nov. 1802), built on these lines[1]. Here we are presented to a pair of penniless gentlemen, Charles and Belfield. Wandering in the country they see a house to be sold and, after making an inspection, sign an agreement to buy it for £5000. A neighbouring Jew, alarmed at some rumours, offers them £8000, which, naturally, is accepted. Charles presents the whole of the £3000 to his friend Belfield that the latter may marry his Charlotte. Lovers' deceits occupy the attention of the author of *The Quadrille; or, A Quarrel, for What?* (E.O.H. June 1819), and these are varied in J. R. Planché's *The Loan of a Lover* (Olym. Sept. 1834). Here Gertrude, the orphan, loves Peter Spyk while Captain Amersfort loves Ernestine. Ernestine and Peter cannot bring themselves to a declaration of passion, so Gertrude and Amersfort plot together and pretend betrothal; this successfully brings the other pair to their senses. These deceits, of course, frequently provide quite fair stage situations, as in Planché's *Paris and London* (Adel. Jan. 1828). In this piece Viscount Volatil pursues the honest ballet-girl, Coraly. Lady Volatil dresses as William and succeeds in gaining him back. A sub-plot deals with the loves of Rose and the jealous little peruquier, Jean Jacques François Antigone Hypolite Frisac. A quarrel of husband and wife gives more than one amusing situation in Marie-Therese Kemble's *The Day after the Wedding; or, A Wife's First Lesson* (C.G. May 1808), while equally good episodes are provided by Mr O. P. Bustle, the strolling manager, in R. B. Peake's *Amateurs and Actors* (E.O.H. Aug. 1818).

---

[1] This is derived from *La maison à vendre*.

Other writers try an exaggerated fantastic style. J. B. Buckstone in *Nine too many* (Adel. March 1847) has a tale of a sailor, Jack Modest, who is condemned in Mexico to live with his nine wives. He escapes with one. James Kenney in *The Illustrious Stranger, or Married and Buried* (D.L. Oct. 1827) likewise has a sailor hero, one Bowbell[1]. This gentleman is wrecked on an island off Malabar and is in great glee when he is about to be married to the princess Irza. His joy turns to fear when he discovers that, in that country, a husband is buried with a dead wife, and he is only too glad to abandon his claims to Azan, the princess' lover. Another play of the same type is Shirley Brooks' *The Wigwam* (Lyc. Jan. 1847). Fondlesquaw, an Indian chief, is really Mr Lobscouse, who has fled from his wife in Bloomsbury. This lady eventually discovers him, to his discomfiture. The little opera is full of Rousseauesque sentiments in spite of its ludicrous and fantastic theme, Julia Lobscouse and her lover Pluffy Plumpton being sharply contrasted with the innocent Cora and the Indian braves.

In thus dealing with the operatic farce of the times we must not forget the work of Charles Dickens—not because Dickens' efforts are particularly fine, but because they have an interest beyond those of the Moncrieffs and the Kenneys[2]. Three of his plays in this style were performed at the St James's theatre in 1836 and 1837. *The Strange Gentleman* would have been a successful production had it not been spoiled by that common Dickensian failing—the over-employment of coincidence. The Strange Gentleman's fear of a duel is like Winkle's, and Tom Sparks, the one-eyed boots at the St James's Arms, is sworn brother to Sam Weller. Much poorer is *The Village Coquettes* (St James's, Dec. 1836), which has a duller and sentimental theme—the pursuing of Lucy by Squire Norton and the prickings of conscience that come eventually to his heart. *Is She his Wife? Or, Something Singular* (St James's, March 1837) returns to the

---

[1] This play obviously owes much to *La veuve de Malabar*.
[2] See A. Woolcot, *Mr. Dickens goes to the Play* (1922), and T. E. Pemberton, *Charles Dickens and the Stage* (1888).

world of misunderstandings. Lovetown flirts with Mrs Limbury and Mrs Lovetown with Tapkins—not because they love flirting but because they want to waken jealousy in each other. Through an error Limbury and Tapkins come to believe that Mrs Lovetown is not really Lovetown's wife, and there are considerable complications to solve at the close.

Perhaps Dickens' operatic farces, particularly *The Strange Gentleman*, have a truth to character and a literary finish denied to most of the others, but his endeavours in this kind cannot be accounted really outstanding achievements. The three plays easily fall in with the prevailing tendencies of the time, and, after a brief examination, they may be dismissed along with the whole of that teeming world of musical farce. The interest of the type is largely historical, and a few scenes of brilliance, even a few brilliant plays, cannot quite call for any general critical praise. The operatic farce of the early nineteenth century is an inheritance from the eighteenth century; it has had much to do with the forming of popular dramatic types of today; and for those two things, rather than for any great intrinsic worth, must we value it.

IV. *Burlesques and Extravaganzas*

Undoubtedly the age saw many of its own follies, and melodramatic burlesque flourished freely alongside of melodrama. It is to be questioned, however, whether that critical spirit which lies behind *The Rehearsal* and *The Critic* was chiefly responsible for the flourishing of the burlesque type in the nineteenth century. That criticism, implied if not directly stated, did enter in cannot be gainsaid, but there was something else which impelled men to applaud the burlesques which, as a glance at the play-list given to this volume will show, formed no mean part of the general repertoire of these years. That something else was the love of the fantastic, the impossibly exaggerated and the patently absurd. Most of these burlesques exist for their own ridiculous qualities, and many, especially the "travesties," have little thought of follies inherent in the original play travestied. To turn a pair of doves in a would-be poetic simile into a boar and sow implies criticism; to make Romeo speak like a navvy and Cleopatra like a Cockney flower-girl manifests only the desire for the openly absurd. In general, therefore, the burlesques of the early nineteenth century are of less intrinsic interest than those of preceding decades and must, for the most part, be treated in the mass rather than individually.

Of those which imply direct or indirect criticism may be mentioned *The Quadrupeds of Quedlinburgh, or The Rovers of Weimar* (H.[2] July 1811), described as a "Tragico-Comico-Anglo-Germanico-Hippodramatico Romance" and refashioned from Canning's earlier burlesque of the Kotze-buian school, *The Rovers*. Thomas Dibdin's *Melodrame Mad! or The Siege of Troy* (Surrey, May 1819) by its title promises well, but the rehearsal-scheme with which it starts is not sustained and the follies ridiculed are really not those of the melodrama at all. Slightly cleverer is the same author's *Bonifacio and Bridgetina; or, The Knight of the Hermitage, or The Windmill Turrett; or, The Spectre of the North-East Gallery* (C.G. March 1808), but nearly all its hits fail to find a mark. There is clever satire, it is true, in G. A. à Beckett's well-known *Scenes from the Rejected Comedies* (1844), but this is not truly theatrical. The scenes from *The Husband* by J[ame]s S[herida]n K[nowle]s, *The Humbugs of the Hour* by D[ougla]s J[errol]d, *The Templars* by Serjt. T[alfour]d, *Jane Jenkins; or The Ghost of the Back Drawing Room* by E. F[it]zb[al]l and *Credit* by Sir E. L. B. L. E. D. B[ulwe]r, Bart., have all some genuine *jeux d'esprit*.

There are, of course, innumerable topical pieces, such as *Another Maid and Another Magpie* (Olym. Nov. 1815) and *The Man and the Monkey* (Olym. Nov. 1815), both ridiculing the popular versions of *The Maid and the Magpie* (in 1815)[1] or *Black-eyed Sukey* (Olym. Dec. 1829) which makes absurdity of the well-known *Black-eyed Susan* (Surrey, 1829), but these

---

[1] See under Pocock and Arnold in the Hand-list of Plays.

have no real intrinsic value and are usually very vulgar
artistically and very dull[1].

Of all the burlesques of this time that which has survived
the longest is *Bombastes Furioso* (H.[2] Aug. 1810) by W. B.
Rhodes, but it is quite evident that in this piece there is no
satirical thought of contemporary (or other) serious drama.
The absurdity exists for its own sake. We may laugh at
the witty lines and the exaggerated rant, but it is not because
we are able to compare these lines mentally with others
from would-be dignified plays. The madness of Tilburina
has a peculiar quality of its own because it recalls other
stage madnesses; the roaring of Bombastes belongs to
himself[2].

There is, however, still to be considered the field covered
by the revue[3] and by the extravagant travestie. Already we
have met with J. R. Planché's *Success; or, A Hit if you like it*
(Adel. Dec. 1825) and an indication has been given of its
contents. In turn the various candidates for Success are led
before the royal throne, until finally comes the satirical
portrait of Masurier who made a name for himself in *Jocko,
or the Ape of Brazil* (1825). Success is charmed: to her
father she admits that he has gained her heart. This
style Planché continued in *The Drama's Levée; or, A
Peep at the Past* (Olym. April 1838) which shows us The
Drama (in a critical state of health), Legitimate Drama
and Illegitimate Drama, "her sons, on the worst possible
terms with each other," Praise, Censure and Folly, together
with a whole series of Presentations, imitations of popular
performers in all theatres from Drury Lane to Norton
Folgate. The dialogue, with its neat rimes and constant
puns, goes easily; here, for example, is the entry of the two
brothers:

---

[1] In France also the spirit of the melodrama was laughed at in spite
of its popularity. On the parodies and burlesques produced in Paris
during the early nineteenth century see P. Ginisty, *Le Mélodrame*
(Paris, 1910), pp. 184–90.

[2] On the Shakespeare travesties see *supra*, pp. 90–1, and *infra*,
pp. 151–2.

[3] See *supra*, p. 135.

Enter LEGITIMATE DRAMA *in a Roman toga.*

L. DRA.   He whom they own Legitimate is here.

DRA.   You naughty boy! when I'm so very poorly;
   You have been fighting with your brother surely.

L. DRA.   I have; because of him I can't get fed,
   Whilst he is almost sick with gingerbread.

DRA.   Will you ne'er cease this ruinous debate?
   Where's that audacious Illegitimate?

Enter ILLEGITIMATE DRAMA *in a dress half
   harlequin and half melo-dramatic.*

I. DRA.   Behold! (*striking an attitude*).

DRA.   Unnatural son!

I. DRA.   Is't thus I'm styled?
   I always thought I was your *natural* child.

L. DRA.   He puns! He'll pick a pocket the next minute!

I. DRA.   I shan't pick yours, because there's nothing in it!

L. DRA.   That is because you robb'd me long ago!

I. DRA.   Come, who began to rob, I'd like to know?
   When I was quite a child in leading string,
   Before I'd learnt to speak, or anything
   But dance my dolls to music, didn't you
   Begin to vow they were your playthings too?
   Stole from the nursery of my best hopes,
   My rocking horses and my skipping-ropes,
   And took my harlequins from loss to save you,
   And now you blame the *punches* that I gave you.

Duet—LEGITIMATE DRAMA *and* ILLEGITIMATE DRAMA—
   "*You Minicking Miss*"—"*Midas.*"

L. DRA.   You mimicking fool, do you hope with the town
   Your trumpery shows will go longer down?

I. DRA.   D'ye think they ever would come you to see,
   If it wasn't for show that you take from me?

L. DRA.   Tawdry elf!

I. DRA.   Go look to yourself!
   You've laid till you're mouldy on the shelf.

L. DRA.   You lay out in gingerbread all your pelf.
   (*they attack each other*—THEATRES *take different sides*)

DRA.   Hence both and each who either cause espouses!
   You'll drive me mad! a plague on *all* your houses!
   (*drives them all out*)
   Unless between themselves they soon agree,

Those boys, I feel, will be the death of me!
They so confound me that though I'm their mother,
I vow I sometimes can't tell one from t'other.
I'm half distracted with the horrid din!

The Drama at Home; or, An Evening with Puff (H.² April 1844) continues in the same style. Written lightly, yet in a state of profound pessimism in regard to the future of drama, it is particularly interesting as showing the impression made by the passing of the Theatres Act of 1843. These revues of Planché's are among the most delightful things the early nineteenth century theatre produced. Trivial they may be, but they have a grace and a lightness of touch which makes us esteem more highly this prolific Somerset Herald.

Among the extravagant travesties perhaps *The Enchanted Isle; or, "Raising the Wind" on the most approved Principles* (Adel. Nov. 1848) by the Brothers Brough is the best-known. Scene ii shows the

Deck of the "Naples Direct" Steam-boat, Funnel in C., Paddle-boxes R. & L., with practicable gallery from one to the other.

Here are Alonso and Ferdinand and Gonzalo, who become mightily seedy with the tossing of the waves. The scenes unfold themselves in Shakespearian order but with constantly topical dialogue. Even Caliban is affected:

Pro. Well, sir, why don't you work?
Cal. (giving the boot a single rub). Ay, there's the rub.
Pro. What! mutinous! out, vile, rebellious cub!
Cal. (with sudden vigour). Oh! who's afraid? Blow you and your
    boots together.   *[Throws boot down.*
    My soul's above your paltry upper leather.
Pro. (aside). That's democratic, and by no means moral!
    (To Caliban) Pick up that boot, unless you'd pick a quarrel.
    You'd best not raise a breeze.
Cal.   Oh! blow your breezes,
    The love of liberty upon me seizes;
    My bosom's filled with freedom's pure emotions,
    And on the "Rights of Labour" I've strong notions.
Pro. You won't work, then?
Cal.   No—up for my rights I'll stick;
    I've long enough been driven—now I'll kick.

11   NED

SONG.

TUNE—"*When the Heart of a Man.*"

When the back of a donkey's oppress'd with wares,
Which weigh rather more than his strength well bears,
Instead of submitting he stoutly—stoutly
Plucks up a spirit and shows some airs.
Stripes are administer'd—kicks also,
But his stout ribs no emotion show.
Press him,
Caress him,
Try kicking
Or licking,
The more he is wollop'd the more he won't go.

Such travesties proved popular and over half a score of Shakespeare's works were similarly treated[1]. It is not a far cry from these to the extravaganzas proper, where mythological or fairy stories were told in topical style. Here once more Planché is supreme. Starting with *Amoroso, King of Little Britain* (D.L. April 1818) he provided for Madame Vestris and others a long series of wildly fantastic burlesque pieces, some on classical legend, some on the stories of Perrault. *Olympic Revels; or, Prometheus and Pandora* (Olym. Jan. 1831) was his first real success, and this led, immediately, to *Olympic Devils; or, Orpheus and Eurydice* (Olym. Dec. 1831), and, generally, to his life-long dramatic career. Classical subjects occupied his attention for a few years and then in December 1836 at the Olympic came *Riquet with the Tuft*, derived from the French Féerie Folie *Riquet à la Houppe*. This was immediately successful and was followed by *Puss in Boots* (Olym. Dec. 1837) and many another. Sufficient has been already quoted to give an idea of Planché's style. Puns appear in every second line; colloquialisms intrude into the formally rimed verse spoken by famous characters; well-known stories are treated in familiar manner; topical allusions abound; and the whole is evidently planned for the richest possible settings. Others followed in the same path. The Brothers Brough produced their still-remembered *Camaralzaman and Badoura; or, The Peri who loved a Prince* (H.[2] Dec.

---

[1] See *supra*, pp. 90–1.

1848), which contains some rather amusing scenes. In the third part we are shown the Gardens of the Imperial Palace in China; the Emperor enters with his guards and mandarins:

Man. Long live the Emperor!
Emp.   Silence, villains! stow it!
We'll not live long, unless we like—you know it.
'Tis not for your plebeian throats to give
Orders to *us* how long you'd have us live.
                    [*They all prostrate themselves before him.*
Sons of burnt fathers! what means that position?
How dare you tumble down without permission?
        [*They rise abruptly, and stand bolt upright, in a line.*
Now, by my pigtail! by my father's nails!
By the imperial dragon's sacred scales!
My mind's so tossed about, so hurried, flurried,
Bothered, perplexed, annoyed, insulted, worried,
That soon I feel, with passion and disgust,
Within my *bosom* there will be a *bust*—
One universal smash my senses scatter—
                              [*Mildly to audience.*
Yet, stay, I'd best first tell you what's the matter.

These extravaganzas and burlesques were among the most popular of dramatic types in the thirties and forties of the century. In some ways they aided in developing something new in the theatre; in others they helped to retard the development of more serious drama. In any case, with pantomime they clearly were attractive forces. Much they took from older writers, but they had the merit of altering what they stole. Free merriment, familiar themes new treated, gorgeous settings, these they gave freely to the people of the time. If we substitute "Extravaganza" for "Pantomime" in the quotation, Thomas Dibdin's satirical remark in *Harlequin Hoax; or, A Pantomime Proposed* (Lyc. Aug. 1814) might be regarded as strictly apposite:

Manager. Pardon me, Sir, but it is *our* place to remember there have been such authors as *Gay, Steele, Congreve,*...
Patch. The best names living for Pantomime, let your beginning be *Gay*, for the middle you may, perhaps, be obliged to *Steal*, and the fire of CONGREVE will make your last scene go off like a SKY-ROCKET.

II-2

The remarks are true, however, for the pantomime itself. It was during this period that there grew up the regular tradition of the Christmas pantomime, so that by 1830 we find all the theatres in London vying with one another on Dec. 26 with their fare of the Harlequinade. Up to 1850 Harlequin —now alas! all but banished—dominated the pantomime. Usually he was attached to some sort of nursery tale, as in *Harlequin and Cinderella* or *Harlequin and Jack the Giant Killer*, but the themes of the early nineteenth century pantomime were legion. Old plays appear here, as in *Harlequin and Friar Bacon*; so too does classic legend, as in *Harlequin Bacchus*, and ancient English history, as in *Harlequin and Good Queen Bess*, and ancient English legend, as in *Harlequin and King Lud of Ludgate*, and pure extravagance, as in *Harlequin and Poonoowingkeewangflibeedeeflobeedeebuskeebang, King of the Cannibal Islands*. It is impossible, of course, to deal with the pantomime in a survey of this kind, for the history of the early nineteenth century pantomime is a history of personalities and not of dramatic achievement. At the same time, the popularity of this form of theatrical art must always be remembered as we trace the course of the other types of drama in the age. The spectacular display, the bold merriment, the constant action of the pantomime made an ever constant and ever dominating appeal to audiences not only in Sadler's Wells but in Covent Garden and Drury Lane as well.[1]

---

[1] In connection with Planché's extravaganzas may be noted an interesting paper, *Some Burlesques with a Purpose*, 1830–70 (*Philological Quarterly*, viii, 3, July, 1929) by Dougald MacMillan, which discusses the serious aim underlying these "revues."

CHAPTER IV

THE LEGITIMATE DRAMA

I. *Tragedies and Dramas*

"HE whom they own Legitimate is here," says Legitimate Drama on his entry to the stage in Planché's *The Drama's Levée*[1], and the self-conscious, self-assured tones are characteristic. The trouble with the legitimate drama was not that it was legitimate but that it was too conscious and proud of its legitimacy. It resembled some scions of our present-day aristocracy in that it trusted too much to its ancestry, and thought too little of individual worth and of individual effort; it resembled these, too, in forgetting that that from which it had sprung often had in origin the bar sinister. For Philip Sidney Shakespeare would have been as illegitimate as Pocock was for Talfourd or Sheil.

On the other hand, one must judge these men according to their lights and must endeavour to do justice to their attempts, misguided though many of them might be, to restore the ancient glories of the English stage. That their efforts were sincere enough, no one can deny; but sincerity does not necessarily imply artistry or even a right way of thinking. It is their own dramatic achievements and not the strength of their convictions which must be that by which they are judged.

As has been suggested above, it is virtually impossible to separate entirely the unacted from the acted drama, for most of those who penned the unacted plays originally intended them for the stage. On the other hand, the distinction is there for all, and many poets deliberately eschewed the theatre and professed openly that their works were for the closet alone. Within the limits of this chapter, therefore, I have included only those writers whose plays, or some of whose plays, were actually given performance, although

---

[1] See *supra*, p. 150.

I fully recognise that the harsh separation of Coleridge and Wordsworth, simply because *Remorse* happened to be acted, is not justifiable on all counts.

Something has been said in my last volume[1], both concerning the "poetic play" in general and concerning the work of one of the most interesting of the early reformers, Joanna Baillie. Not only was this Scots author first on the field, but her tireless energy drove her to produce a body of dramatic literature far exceeding the scope of that provided by any of her companions. In 1798 her first series of *Plays on the Passions* was published; a second appeared in 1802, a third in 1812; while in addition there were the *Miscellaneous Plays* of 1804 and the *Dramas* of 1836. Of her 26 dramas five were publicly performed[2]. To be perfectly just to her efforts, Joanna Baillie's critical pronouncements must, at one and the same time, be read along with and carefully separated from, her dramas themselves. It is well known how, in the *Plays on the Passions*, she endeavoured to pen comedies and tragedies on set emotions—hate, fear, jealousy, and what not, although we must admit that often her practice, particularly in her later plays, belies her own initial and theoretical purpose. Some of the *Dramas* of 1836 at least introduce a complexity of passion which is far removed from the mono-emotional note aimed at in the plays included in her first series. Taking that initial purpose at its face value, however, we find that it serves to mark at once a potentiality for dramatic advance and an unquestionably vitiated tendency. That which marred much of the early nineteenth century poetic drama was the tendency towards the abstract. A Romantic poet only too often started from a theory, attempting to discover and devise a plot which should illustrate his mental abstract, in this providing a sufficient contrast to the methods of the Elizabethan dramatists whose prime interest was in the human personality and in the story, thought of in

---

[1] See *A History of English Drama*, iii. 224–6.
[2] See M. S. Carhart, *The Life and Work of Joanna Baillie* (Yale Studies, 1923). Her connection with Scott has, of course, led to the incidental treatment of her work in most histories of romanticism.

the first place as a stirring or amusing theme. On the other hand, great drama always exhibits a central atmosphere, or dominant passion, which gives an informing purpose to the human events narrated in the course of the five acts; and it is this dominant passion which was so lamentably lacking in the dramas produced in England between the time of Otway and that of the Romantic poets. In thus stressing the necessity for the central emotion, therefore, Joanna Baillie was doing something which was of the utmost importance. The very calling attention to this fact marks out her plays as landmarks in the history of the English theatre.

As regards her positive achievement, of course, one may have considerable doubts. Her constructive power, while in the main adequate, is apt to suffer from sudden lapses. Her characters are only too often "romantically" conceived, and her dialogue has far too many echoes of Elizabethan, particularly Shakespearian, language. In atmosphere she recalls now Otway, now Shakespeare, now Kotzebue, now Schiller, almost always losing what might have been tragic effect in an outpouring of sentimentalism. These weaknesses are seen in her plays from first to last, no less indeed in the late *Romiero* than in the early *Basil*. It would be impossible here to analyse each one of the long series in detail, but a glance at several typical tragedies may serve as representative treatment. *De Monfort* (published 1798, acted D.L. April 1800), both because it was selected for stage performance, and because of its intrinsic merits, is the most important play of her earliest collection. There are faults in plenty as regards the construction; there is the inherent weakness in the presentation of the one passion; yet we feel here that there is at least the potentiality for dramatic power. Reading *De Monfort* our hopes rise for a resuscitation of true drama, for technique may, to a certain extent, be learned in the theatre and subtler characterisation may come with deeper knowledge of life. As always, however, these hopes are dashed to pieces on the rock of language[1]. Joanna Baillie

---

[1] For supplementary quotations see *A History of English Drama*, iii. 224–5.

cannot forget the Elizabethans, and ever we are in the presence
of a dialogue which is false because imitative and out of
harmony with the age. Sometimes the imitation may give
us passages of individual beauty. More often it leads to
frigid and pathetic diction. Says a Lady to a Page in *De
Monfort*[1],

> Is she young or old?
> *Page.* Neither, if right I guess, but she is fair;
> For time hath laid his hand so gently on her,
> As he too had been aw'd.
> *Lady.*   The foolish stripling!
> She has bewitch'd thee. Is she large in stature?
> *Page.* So stately and so graceful is her form,
> I thought at first her stature was gigantick,
> But on a near approach I found, in truth,
> She scarcely does surpass the middle size.

What can we hope from this?

From the second volume we may select the first part of
Ethwald for brief analysis. This play, written on the theme
of ambition, shows the same weaknesses, together with an
even more imitative tendency so far as the situations are
concerned. *Macbeth* is a general model, but *Richard III* lies
behind Ethwald's wooing of Elburga, and *King John* is not
forgotten. Such palpable reminiscences, however, do not
completely rob of value this tale of youthful innocence
turned to terrible criminality by the one passion. Again, it
is the language which gives the final blow to our wishes.
Descriptive "poetic" passages are dragged in needlessly,
giving, as in Ethelbert's speech in the first act, a tone unconsciously comic:

> When slowly from the plains and nether woods,
> With all their winding streams and hamlets brown,
> Updrawn, the morning vapour lifts its veil,
> And thro' its fleecy folds, with soften'd rays,
> Like a still'd infant smiling in his tears,
> Looks thro' the early sun:—when from afar
> The gleaming lake betrays its wide expanse,
> And, lightly curling on the dewy air,

[1] II. i.

The cottage smoke doth wind its path to heaven:
When larks sing shrill, and village cocks do crow,
And lows the heifer loosen'd from her stall:
When heaven's soft breath plays on the woodman's brow,
And ev'ry hair-bell and wild tangled flower
Smells sweetly from its cage of checker'd dew:
Ay, and when huntsmen wind the merry horn,
And from its covert starts the fearful prey;
Who, warm'd with youth's blood in his swelling veins,
Would, like a lifeless clod, outstretched lie,
Shut up from all the fair creation offers?
(ETHWALD *yawns and heeds him not.*) He heeds me not.

But who would, in a theatre? This love of tangled flowers agitating the breast of an Anglo-Saxon thane has no truth, no reality, no passion; it is an interlude, false and impertinent.

In the collection of 1804 the historical drama of *Constantine Paleologus* stands out boldly, and here, perhaps as clearly as in any of her later tragedies, we feel the potentialities of Joanna Baillie's art. Impossible speeches there are, but the conception of the emperor, with his strange mingling of heroism and effeminacy, is one which shows how her power of characterisation was developing as year passed year. For one thing in especial *Constantine Paleologus* deserves attention. In this play the authoress has most deliberately attempted to make use of that spectacular element which was so closely bound up with stage success. This spectacular element led to its successful performance, in an altered form, as *Constantine and Valeria* at the Surrey; and this too contributed to its popularity when produced at Liverpool in 1808 as *The Band of Patriots*. The endeavour shows that Joanna Baillie possessed more of the theatre sense, and of the will to the theatre, than the majority of her poetic companions.

In 1810 at Edinburgh appeared *The Family Legend*. Sponsored by Sir Walter Scott (who wrote the prologue) and with Mrs Siddons in the cast, it won a certain success. Unfortunately for its worth as a play, this drama falls into two sharply marked portions. The first, which shows Helen Campbell, now the wife of the Maclean, surrounded on all sides by hatred and suspicion, is well worked out, with less of that false verbiage so common in her other serious plays. From the end of the second act, however, we suddenly plunge into artificial melodrama. Helen is marooned on a lonely rock which is submerged at high tide. The water creeps higher and higher and she is rescued just as her last despairing cries are about to be stifled by the rising waves. This perhaps we could suffer, but there is a double rescue. Helen's child has remained in the custody of the Macleans; the following scene will explain itself.

Lochtavish. Be not so hasty, Lorne—Think'st thou indeed
Ye have us here within your grasp, and nought
Of hostage or security retain'd
For our protection?
Lorne.   What dost thou mean?
Loch. Deal with us as ye will:
But if within a week, return'd to Mull,
In safety I appear not, with his blood,
The helpless heir, thy sister's infant son,
Who in my mother's house our pledge is kept,
Must pay the forfeit.
Helen (starting up from the body in an agony of alarm). O horrible!
ye will not murder him?
Murder a harmless infant!
Loch. My aged mother, lady, loves her son
As thou dost thine; and she has sworn to do it.
Hel. Has sworn to do it! Oh! her ruthless nature
Too well I know. (*To* LORNE *eagerly*) Loose them, and let
them go.
Lorne. Let fiends like these escape?
Argyll (to Helen). He does but threaten
To move our fears: they dare not slay the child.
Hel. They dare! they will!—O if thou art my father!
If Nature's hand e'er twined me to thy heart
As this poor child to mine, have pity on me!
Loose them and let them go!—Nay, do it quickly.
O what is vengeance! Spare my infant's life.
Unpitying Lorne!—art thou a brother too?
The hapless father's blood is on thy sword,
And wilt thou slay the child! O spare him! spare him!
(*Kneeling to* ARGYLL *and* LORNE, *who stand irresolute,
when enter* SIR HUBERT DE GREY, *carrying something
in his arms, wrapped up in a mantle, and followed by*

MORTON. *On seeing* SIR HUBERT, *she springs from the ground, and rushes forward to him.*)
Ha! art thou here? in blessed hour return'd
To join thy prayers with mine,—to move their hearts—
Their flinty hearts;—to bid them spare my child!
De Grey (*lifting up the mantle, and shewing a sleeping Child*). The
prayer is heard already: look thou here
Beneath this mantle where he soundly sleeps.

(HELEN *utters a cry of joy, and holds out her arms for the Child, but at the same time sinks to the ground, embracing the knees of* SIR HUBERT. ARGYLL *and* LORNE *run up to him, and all their Vassals, &c. crowding round, close them about on every side, while a general murmur of exultation is heard through the whole.* LOCHTAVISH *and* GLENFADDEN, *remaining on the side of the Stage with those who guard them, are struck with astonishment and consternation.*)

Their astonishment, however, cannot equal ours.

Unquestionably, Joanna Baillie's art developed with maturity, and, in spite of weaknesses and foolish situations similar to that in *The Family Legend*, her later plays have a psychological strength which strongly testifies to her talent. In *Orra*, we certainly have the unnatural and " poetic " language, but there is given us something in recompense. " Nay, Orra," says Eleonora,

Nay, Orra; these wild fits of uncurb'd laughter,
Athwart the gloomy tenor of your mind,
As it has low'r'd of late, so keenly cast,
Unsuited seem and strange.

To which Orra answers:

O nothing strange, my gentle Eleonora!
Did'st thou ne'er see the swallow's veering breast,
Wing the air beneath some murky cloud
In the sunn'd glimpses of a stormy day,
Shiver in silv'ry brightness?
Or boatman's oar, as vivid lightning flash
In the faint gleam, that like a spirit's path
Tracks the still waters of some sullen lake?
Or lonely Tower, from its brown mass of woods,
Give to the parting of a wintry sun
One hasty glance in mockery of the night
Closing in darkness round it?

Yet, beyond this useless verbiage, there is a strength in *Orra* which is, as it were, a premonition of greater dramatic power to come. The terrors of her mind are well portrayed and the presentation of the supposed supernatural visitor is dealt with in what might almost be styled a modern manner. Less interesting is *The Dream*, although there is an outward attempt here to escape towards a prose medium. The hand of Elizabethanism, unfortunately, lay heavy on prose and verse alike, so that Jerome and Benedict can have this frigid conversation:

Jer. Be satisfied! be satisfied! It is not always fitting that the mind should lay open the things it is busy withal, though an articulate sound may sometimes escape it to set curiosity on the rack. Where is brother Paul? Is he still at his devotions?

Ben. I believe so. But look where the poor Peasants are waiting without: it is the hour when they expect our benefactions. Go, and speak to them: thou hast always been their favourite confessor, and they want consolation.

There is not much to be hoped for from a style such as this, yet, strangely enough, the spirit of Maeterlinck, moaning to be born, lingers in these long-forgotten pages.

There is little in Joanna Baillie's last collection, published in 1836, that presents to us anything new, although in *Romiero* and *Henriquez* (D.L. March 1836), and, to a less extent, in the prose-tragedy of *The Stripling*, she shows an increased appreciation of dramatic technique. Those plays which we have already considered may be taken as representative of her whole career, a career which, in its turn, may be taken as symbolic of literary dramatic authorship during the period. With talent and a knowledge of the stage, Joanna Baillie has failed, and the reason of that failure is easily traced to the dead hand of Elizabethanism which lies heavy on her scenes. With an originality which makes her anticipate now Ibsen and now Maeterlinck, she has been crushed by that devastating idolisation of seventeenth century dramatic effort. There was the possibility that she might have been one of our foremost dramatists, but, as her works stand, we can only account her an interesting historical figure whose works are now to be read rather for the light they throw on contemporary conditions than for any great inherent merit.

Among those who, like Joanna Baillie, stood with one foot in the eighteenth and one foot in the nineteenth century may be mentioned Lewis, Delap and Tobin, each of interest in his own way. The earlier works of Matthew Gregory, or "Monk," Lewis have been already dealt with[1], but the dramatic career of this lover of diablerie extended on to the end of the first decade of the period at present under discussion. As might be expected, Lewis' style tends towards the melodramatic, and he may be regarded as typical of a group of intelligent writers who, retaining just a touch of literary quality, wrote with the popular success of the theatre authors in their minds. In *Alfonso, King of Castile* (C.G. Jan. 1802) we get a blood-red drama of revenge, confessedly unhistorical, although "The Action is supposed to pass in the year 1345." Alfonso, the king, has, in past years, unjustly condemned Orsino, and the latter's son, Cæsario, thirsts for vengeance. Leagued with Melchior, he plans to assassinate the monarch. Complications, however, enter in from the facts that he is secretly married to Alfonso's daughter, Amelrosa, and that Orsino unexpectedly returns to aid his king. Cæsario is stabbed by his own father and Amelrosa runs decorously mad. The theme of outlawry, made so popular by *Die Räuber*, is repeated in *Adelmorn, the Outlaw* (D.L. May 1801), a "Romantic Drama" or tragi-comedy, with musical accompaniments, including a touching ditty:

The clock had toll'd "One!" all was silent and dread!

Here Adelmorn is the exile, banished for a crime of which he was, of course, entirely innocent. He is captured and about to be executed when Lodowick, the faithful friend, worms out the fatal secret of Count Ulric and all is well. We are grateful to the author for a footnote which appears in act v:

I must again request the reader to observe, that wherever Lodowick's speeches appear ludicrous, he is never supposed to intend them to produce that effect.

[1] See *A History of English Drama*, iii. 99-100.

Lewis, however, belongs more to the popular than to the literary school, and one cannot pretend—he never pretended—that he endeavoured to do aught else than give the public what it wanted. John Tobin is of far different calibre. Gifted with a sense for poetry and steeped in Elizabethan literature, he attempted to provide for the stage replicas of the dramas he most admired. That all his plays were produced posthumously is, in one way, a capital charge against the theatrical tastes and management of his times, yet that charge cannot be pushed too far. If it be taken to mean that the theatrical world was callous towards young dramatists, then it is true; but one cannot accept Tobin's works as of a truly creative kind. The imitative element mars whatever claims they might otherwise put forward. Four plays in all he has left to us, *The Honey Moon* (D.L. Jan. 1805), *The Curfew* (D.L. Feb. 1807), *The School for Authors* (C.G. Dec. 1808) and *The Faro Table, or The Guardians* (D.L. Nov. 1816). Although some of these are comedies, they may all be treated together in this section because of the poetic quality they share in common. All Tobin's dramas can be read with pleasure, yet of all can be said what was written in the prologue for his first play:

> Not new the subject of his first-born rhyme;
> But one adorn'd by bards of elder time.

For *The Honey Moon* he has gone primarily to *The Taming of the Shrew*, but he has not forgotten *Rule a Wife and Have a Wife*, *Twelfth Night*, *Romeo and Juliet* and *Henry IV*[1]. The play is interesting, and we watch the gradual subjection of Juliana with sympathy, but we can never forget the three facts, that the theme is outworn, that it has no connection with the life of the age, and that the language, beautiful though it may be, is merely a dim echo of Elizabethan diction. In *The Curfew* Tobin clearly tried to win applause by appealing to some of the dominant theatrical tendencies of the time. The scene is one of Norman days; "Gaunt Superstition" is appealed to; the prologue notes the patriotic

[1] See an unpublished thesis in the University of London by U. C. Nagchaudhuri entitled *Poetic Drama of the Nineteenth Century*.

element; there are robbers in the cast. The story is thoroughly melodramatic, with its gloomy castle-halls and its no less gloomy caves, with its hovel of high-born poverty, its strange recognitions, its final defeat of villainy and triumph of virtue. In thus abandoning himself to all the paraphernalia of the contemporary theatre, Tobin showed, clearly enough, what little stock of originality or of imagination the poetic dramatists of the time possessed.

If Lewis represents the complete submission of the literary playwright to the melodramatic tendencies so prevalent in the contemporary theatre, and if Tobin shows the wholehearted acceptance of Elizabethan standards with the occasional acceptance of elements borrowed from Kotzebue and Schiller, Dr John Delap may be taken as typical of another mood, that which would lead towards a resuscitation of classicism. In reality, of course, Delap, who knew Dr Johnson, is an eighteenth century author strayed into the world of romance, and his earlier efforts have been included in the previous volume of this history[1]. The year 1803, however, saw the appearance of four tragedies from his pen, and, in reading them, we must remember that classicism of a sort, as is exemplified even in the career of Byron, was at least one ingredient in romantic art. To the more broadly appealing tendencies of his time Delap bows by giving to *Gunilda* and *Matilda* early British settings, and by carrying that of *Abdalla* to the East, but his whole mind is set on classical standards; the Athenians and Addison are his two great models. There is, in reality, nothing in Delap's work which should call for a treatment of his plays in particular. Dulness casts a gloomy mantle over all, and, save as a prime example of that Augustanism which continued to cling to the nineteenth century stage, he may be passed by and forgotten. Delap's importance, paradoxically enough, comes, not from his own work, but from the work of others. He is an extreme representative of a school which, many years later, still held the liberal-minded Talfourd in its clutches.

---

[1] *Op. cit.* p. 80. Although unacted, Delap's plays are dealt with here because they represent better than others a certain tendency of the age.

With reminiscences of Shakespeare, with Schillerian or Kotzebuian features, with Addisonian blank-verse, legitimate drama continued during the half-century its somewhat dismal career. Attempt after attempt was made to hold the stage; successively a Maturin, a Milman, a Byron, a Knowles, a Talfourd, a Browning was acclaimed as a master-dramatist, and successively the tones of each playwright's voice grew fainter and fainter.

Sheil, Maturin and Milman were the favourites of the literary critics of the earlier decades; but when have their works been played? Who now remembers their names save faintly as echoes in some account of nineteenth century literature? What true merit is to be discovered in their dramas? The dramatic career of Richard Lalor Sheil commenced in 1814 with the production of *Adelaide, or The Emigrants* (Crow-street, Dublin, Feb. 1814; C.G. 1816) in the capital of his native land, Dublin. In spite of a few good situations, *Adelaide* must be accounted but a sorry production. Full of dismal sentimentalism which pretends to be tragic, it drags its weary length along amidst an atmosphere of tears, artificial emotions and vague, meaningless philosophisings upon honour and liberty. Kotzebue and Fletcher seem to struggle over its silly corpse. In the same strain, with the added influence of Byron, Sheil continued his theatrical career. Sometimes, as in *The Apostate* (C.G. May 1817), he succeeded in devising situations of a certain force, but his mind is too full of sentimentality and his taste lies too much in the direction of horrors for any real good to come of his writing. It is characteristic of his talent that, for the theme of *Evadne* (C.G. Feb. 1819), he passed back to Shirley's somewhat lurid drama, *The Traitor*, and that the gloomy scenes of Massinger and Field's *The Fatal Dowry* were adapted by him for the stage. It may be confessed that Sheil has in him something of dramatic power, that, in reading his works, even a modern student feels there the potentiality of something greater than he actually achieved; but, after all, it is actuality and realisation, not potentiality, which we have to deal with here.

The same, or a similar, general criticism may be made of the work of Maturin and Milman. The former, Charles Robert Maturin[1], hailed, like Sheil, from Ireland, and, again like Sheil, his mind was filled with images and ideas culled from Byron, Fletcher and Kotzebue. In *Bertram; or, The Castle of St Aldobrand* (D.L. May 1816), his first and his most famous play, the hero is a count who, after the machinations of his enemy, becomes a corsair, returns to find his love, Imogine, the wife of his greatest foe, woos her into infidelity to her husband, kills this wretched man and finally dies by his own hand. There is a certain power in many of the scenes, but the love of horror, the distracted frenzy of the plot, the pathos unduly insisted upon, take from the merit of the play. The horror, the frenzy, and the pathos appear in even more terrible forms in Maturin's later plays, *Manuel* (D.L. March 1817) and *Fredolfo* (C.G. May 1819). If Sheil and Maturin show the romantic tendency towards sensationalism, Henry Hart Milman displays the tendency towards Fletcherian fantastic "tragedy." Milman's work was not so definitely theatrical as that of his two companions. Not only was he more noted in another sphere of literary endeavour, but only one of his plays was written deliberately for the stage[2]. This was *Fazio* (Surrey, Dec. 1816), originally performed at the Surrey as *The Italian Wife*, a drama which tells of the seizure of the dead Bartolo's gold by the hero Fazio, of his betrayal by his jealous wife, Bianca, and of her final repentance. The great merit of the play is the opportunity it gives for robust and full-blooded acting. Fazio is a good "part" and there is ample opportunity for the display of talent in both Bianca and Aldabella. Possibly this quality gave it its contemporary popularity.

From this group of dramatists one passes easily to Byron, Byron who, one of the committee of management at Drury Lane, man of the world and theatre-lover, might have been expected to do so much for the fortunes of the English

---

[1] See N. Idman, *Charles Robert Maturin: His Life and Works* (1923).
[2] *The Fall of Jerusalem* (1820), *The Martyr of Antioch* and *Belshazzar* (1822), and *Anne Boleyn* (1826) were dramatic poems rather than plays.

drama[1]. It is in his work that we can see most clearly at once the power of the age and the qualities which prevented the appearance of true dramatic success. Byron has a lordly power over the emotions; he has a style calculated to provide excellent dialogue; and he has, what many of his companion poets lacked, a flair for the theatre. Yet Byron's dramas, even if we make all allowances for them, even if we agree that their value is to a certain extent underrated, just fail to reach true greatness. This failure seems to be due to three major causes. In the first place, there is Byron's preoccupation with Byron. All the romantic poets were individualists, one might almost say egoists. Rarely could they pass beyond themselves to see the world and men objectively. As a result, their heroes are themselves, and the figures set alongside those heroes are either mistily outlined or else coloured by the reflected light of the author's personality. To be great, drama demands objective treatment, and the whole structure of the stage seems to come clattering down amidst the selfish tones of these Manfreds and their peers. Secondly, there is the familiar disdain of the contemporary theatre. Byron's letters show clearly that, in spite of his association with the playhouse, he looked upon it from the height of his overweening personality and the dignified seclusion of the House of Lords. The stage for him was little more than a toy. It amused him to be directing this thing, but he had no real aspirations for its immediate improvement. And, lastly, there is the preoccupation with themes ill-calculated to express the spirit of the age. Like the others, Lord Byron looks back instead of forward. His models are Kotzebue and Schiller and Otway and the Elizabethans; his themes are the themes of past times; of conscious endeavour on his part to devise something which will grip and interpret the temper of his time there is abso-

[1] On Byron's career as a playwright see particularly S. C. Chew's essay, *The Relations of Lord Byron to the Drama of the Romantic Period* (1914), and Sir Squire Bancroft and William Archer, *Byron on the Stage* (in *Byron the Poet*, edited by W. A. Briscoe, 1924). The *Letters*, as is well known, contain many important references both to Byron's own works and to the dramatic and theatrical affairs of his time.

lutely nothing. Because of his egoism there is a sameness in his dramas; because of his disdain an untheatrical quality in many; because of his retrospective mind a lack of strength and vitality. *Manfred* (1817) and *Cain* (1821) we may leave aside as purely dramatic poems, indicating in their form that one great weakness of the age. The others have to be compared, not with plays to come, but with plays of the past. Thus *Marino Faliero* (1821) recalls at once the *Venice Preserv'd* of Otway; if not an imitation, it is at least in the same style, and, powerful as some of its scenes undoubtedly are, it is seen to want power simply because of this fact. We may assure ourselves if we desire that the plot mirrors the main facts of the Cato Street Conspiracy; but, whether this is true or not, the framework is old and the texture faded. In *Sardanapalus* (1821) Byron turns to earlier days, and tells the story of the weak, yet strong, king whose fall brought the ruin of an empire. The structure of the play is excellent, and we are led deliberately on to the final pyre-scene when Sardanapalus and his Myrrha perish gloriously; yet there is something lacking in the drama as a whole. Perhaps our main dissatisfaction arises from the pathetic sentimentalism which breathes over the drama. We do not wonder at the hero; we simply pity him, and the end seems rather a thing for tears than for admiration. Beyond this, there is the sense that we are listening here to matters untrue. When a Shakespeare told of Antony and Cleopatra, he might make his heroine play billiards and show an acquaintanceship with Elizabethan fashions; but her life and the life of her lover were essentially and terribly vital and true. Byron has his facts all right, and notes are appended to show his knowledge of the authorities, but the vitality is lacking. Sardanapalus and Myrrha are abstractions of German philosophy, not real beings. In detail, too, Byron fails. Sometimes his work reminds us of earlier "chronicle histories," for, like their authors, he often allows stage direction to do what should have been done in dialogue or by hearsay. In III. i the rebels

charge the King and SALEMENES *with their Troops, who defend themselves till the Arrival of* ZAMES, *with the Guard before mentioned. The Rebels are then driven off, and pursued by* SALEMENES, *&c. As the King is going to join the pursuit,* BELESES *crosses him.*

Beleses is wounded and disarmed, and, as the King is about to despatch him,

A party of Rebels enter and rescue BELESES. *They assail the King, who, in turn, is rescued by a party of his Soldiers, who drive the Rebels off.*

What a pother of rescuings, and what a useless movement on the stage! The wordless action recalls alike these crude Elizabethan histories and the even cruder melodramas of Byron's own time. *The Two Foscari* (1821) was originally published in the same volume as *Cain* and *Sardanapalus*, and shows a return to the historical atmosphere of *Marino Faliero.* There is not much good that can be said of it as a play; its qualities are almost wholly poetic. *Werner* (D.L. Dec. 1830) carries us to a different sphere, one familiar enough indeed, for we are in the company of Schiller's *Räuber.* A certain praise is due to this work, particularly because of the restrained close of the drama; but after all *Werner* is little more than a superior melodrama with the distressed Werner, the villain Stralenheim and the gloomy setting of the ruined palace. Once more the unreality, the lack of vital qualities, take away from the value of the drama. Thus even Byron failed; and, if he could not succeed, what hope was there from the others?

Before glancing at some independent plays, it may be well to make a rapid survey of those major writers who, in the succeeding decades, were acclaimed as masters and seemed likely to give strength to the stage. Among these, possibly the most famous is James Sheridan Knowles, author of over a dozen poetic or semi-poetic comedies and tragedies[1]. Again, a consideration of his work may help towards an understanding of the age. Knowles' early work, *Leo, or The Gypsy* (Waterford, 1810) and *Brian Boroihme* (Belfast, 1811; C.G. April

---

[1] On Knowles see the *Life* (1872) written by his son and the interesting essay in Horne's *A New Spirit of the Age* (1844). A discussion of *Virginius* appears in A. Filon, *The English Stage* (1897).

1837), was almost entirely melodramatic, but with *Caius Gracchus* (Belfast, 1815; D.L. Nov. 1823) he attempted something more ambitious. Like all the others, Knowles had to return to older models, so that his hero is simply a kind of popular Coriolanus, Cornelia is another hard Roman mother, Licinia is a second Virgilia, soft and timorous, with another Roman lady, Livia, recalling Valeria. The language on the whole is fine, and Gracchus' first entry at the Forum is undoubtedly striking. Most noticeable of all, however, is the genuine attempt to delineate a tragic flaw in the hero, the proud revenge emotions in Gracchus at once giving dignity to his character and compassing his overthrow. One feels here the undoubted possibility of true greatness, and we cannot cavil at contemporaries for discovering in the play an heroic note of majestic proportions. Having succeeded with a Roman theme, Knowles returned to the same atmosphere for his next play, *Virginius*, written for, but rejected by, Kean. After an original production at Glasgow (1820) it was soon accepted by Macready and successfully performed at Covent Garden in May 1820. Again reminiscent of Shakespeare, the play of *Virginius* retraces the same ground covered centuries before by the anonymous *Apius and Virginia* and by Webster's homonymous tragedy. The main story remains, of course, the same, telling how Appius sees Virginia, the betrothed of Icilius; how she is claimed as his slave; how she is stabbed by her father, who finally goes mad and strangles the evil Appius. There is no question that the treatment is striking, yet there is one fatal weakness accurately diagnosed by Horne in his essay on Macready[1]. "The only way," he says, "in which Mr Knowles personifies our age, is in his truly domestic feeling"—

In what consists the interest and force of his popular play of *Virginius?* The domestic feeling. The costume, the setting, the decorations are heroic. We have Roman tunics, but a modern English heart,—the scene is the Forum, but the sentiments those of the "Bedford Arms." The affection of the father for his daughter —the pride of the daughter in her father, are the main principles

---

[1] See *A New Spirit of the Age* (World's Classics edition), p. 304.

of the play, and the pit and galleries and even much of the boxes are only *perplexed* with the lictors and the Decemviri, and the strange garments of the actors.

Yet this criticism, true as it may be, indicates that Knowles was at least so far ahead of his companions that he endeavoured to treat his theme in a vivid, rather than in an artificial, manner. This domesticity, foolish as at times it may appear, is a thousandfold more to be treasured than the spurious heroicism of other authors. After *Virginius* Knowles turned to other spheres of interest. His following play, *William Tell* (D.L. May 1825), narrates, rather slightly, of the exploits of the Swiss hero; its treatment reverts to the author's earlier melodramatic proclivities. These melodramatic tendencies were continued in *Alfred the Great; or, The Patriot King* (D.L. April 1831), written on a theme obviously popular at the time[1]. We are shown here everything of interest in the life of the Saxon monarch, from the tending of the cakes to the most magnanimous and heroic actions. Obviously Knowles was suing for success along the lines of the "illegitimate" stage. This was succeeded by *The Hunchback* (C.G. April 1832), a much better production, clearly recalling the style of Middleton. The Hunchback is Master Walter, supposedly the agent of the Earl of Rochdale. His daughter, Julia, is loved by Sir Thomas Clifford, but is rejected by him on her assuming the giddy fashionable airs of town life. Eventually Julia's idiosyncrasies are cured and Walter reveals himself as the real earl. In reality the play is a serious comedy with a purpose; its characterisation prevents its being dull; and the language is not so hopelessly artificial as that of many other plays of the time. Equally well told is *The Wife: A Tale of Mantua* (C.G. April 1833), where the theme of Italian intrigue is embraced. Here Mariana (acted by Ellen Tree) finds her lost lover in Leonardo Gonzaga, rightful Duke of Mantua (acted by Charles Kean). The deposed duke, Ferrardo, plots with St Pierre to slander her, but her innocence is proved, partly through the agency

---

[1] It provided material for the plays of Mrs Faucit (Norwich, 1811), H. M. Milner (Cob. 1824) and I. Pocock (C.G. 1827).

of St Pierre, who, in his dying hours, is discovered to be her brother. Unfortunately, the long-lost lover and brother of this plot give to the whole play an air of unreality, and it is evident how far astray the Elizabethan proclivities were leading even such capable dramatists as Knowles. Finally, we reach *The Daughter* (D.L. Nov. 1836), where melodrama once more triumphs, but where contemporary themes are dealt with. Domesticity colours the whole of the play, and, in melodramatic-wise, innocence in the persons of Edward and Marian dominates, even if at times hard pressed, over villainy in the person of the murderous Norris. One feels, in reading this play, that if only Knowles could have escaped from melodrama on the one hand and from Elizabethanism on the other, he might have done something notable for the stage. As it is, many of his plays are but glorified tales of black evil and white innocence; while a *Virginius* is marred by the conflicting styles—by a desire to mirror the general tendencies of his own age and by an imposed necessity of following the masters of Shakespeare's day. Success, in Knowles' work, is near, yet is not attained.

Very similar to that of Knowles is the achievement of Edward Bulwer, Lord Lytton, who began his dramatic career in the very year of the production of *The Daughter*. *The Duchess de la Vallière* appeared at Covent Garden in January 1837, and this was followed by a series of other plays, among which *The Lady of Lyons* (C.G. Feb. 1838), *Richelieu* (C.G. March 1839) and *Money* (H.[2] Dec. 1840) are among the more important. Lytton's work in the dramatic sphere is a hesitating compromise between the legitimate and the illegitimate, with just a touch of something which seems to suggest that this author, like Knowles, was groping darkly towards something new. *The Lady of Lyons; or, Love and Pride* is, of course, his most famous drama, and it has to be confessed that it possesses something of a genuine, as opposed to a spurious, dramatic note. The story, which is well known, tells how Beauseant and Glavis, slighted by Pauline, dress the poor Claude Melnotte as a prince and get her married to him. Stung by shame when first she discovers the cheat,

Pauline comes to love the low-born youth and discovers a new humanity in her love. Here, almost for the first time, do we catch the accents of the new French style of play-writing—modern accents which well indicate the true power which Lytton possessed. The easy construction, the comparatively natural dialogue and the general atmosphere of the play all strike a new note. It is interesting to observe that the theme had been dramatised at least once before Lytton adopted it, and was also dealt with again after the production of his play. In 1824 George Croly had acted his *Pride shall have a Fall* (C.G. March 1824), "A Comedy... with Songs," where the theme of the false prince is treated farcically. One realises how little Lytton had to fear from his rival when one reads the following piece of dialogue:

Stephano [the real Prince de Pindemonte]. All is easily explained:—In the Italian wars, I sent my infant heir...to the cure of Anselmo....He was a villain....He substituted his boy for mine....Then dreading inquiry, he changed his name to Ventoso, and brought up this gallant wooer (*To* LORENZO) in obscurity. How I have obtained this knowledge so lately, how I obtained the Vice-Royalty for the purpose of a closer search, how I preserved my incognito till the search was complete, you shall hear at the banquet, to which I now invite you all.

Torrento. Your Highness! since you have the talent of finding out sons, perhaps you can find out fathers too. Whose son am I? somebody's, I suppose.

Ste. In looking for the Captain, I accidentally traced your career. I found your errors more of the head than of the heart. You have your liberty. Count and Countess, you must resign your titles.

Ven. With all my heart.

Ste. And, with them, Anselmo's estate.

Ven. Ruin! I'm not worth a sequin.

Countess. I'm thunderstruck.

Ste. Torrento, stand forth; *you* are Anselmo's heir! *You* are the banker's son!

—a fair piece of ordinary dialogue such as is to be found in hundreds of plays of this period, and one which serves as a fitting comparison for the dialogue in Lytton's play. Six years after the appearance of the latter drama Moncrieff essayed the same theme, producing *The Beauty of Lyons* (S.W. Feb. 1842), "A Domestic Drama" in which the humble bellows-mender turns out to be the real Marquis Montlimort. Here the story is dealt with seriously and there is a touch of real feeling in the crisis scenes. It will be remembered that part of the same plot is introduced into Browning's *Pippa Passes* (1841), the art students there reminding us a little of their prototypes in Moncrieff's play. For some reason this story of pride captured the emotions of contemporaries. *The Lady of Lyons* saw regular revivals up to the end of the century, and a series of later burlesques—H. J. Byron's *The Lady of Lyons; or, Twopenny Pride and Pennytence* (Strand, Feb. 1858), H. C. Merivale's *The Lady of Lyons Married and Settled* (Gaiety, Oct. 1878) and R. Reece's *The Lady of Lyons Married and Claude Unsettled* (Glasgow, Sept. 1884)—goes to prove continued popularity.

Money (H.[2] 1840), although called a comedy, has an atmosphere similar to that of Lytton's other famous play. The theme is unduly sentimental, but the dialogue is vivid and the treatment is much more natural than, let us say, that of Morris's drama with a like plot, *The Secret* (1799). Lytton knows well how to develop dramatic contrast and how to secure concentration. Making Evelyn the centre of his work he is able on the one hand to reveal the devoted tenderness of Clara and on the other the selfish ambition of Georgina. As a serious drama of manners this play also points on to Robertson. In reading it, one realises that by 1840 the age was growing just a trifle weary of melodramatic romance, was seeking at one and the same time for a return to classical precision and more ordinary themes. *Money* is modern; out of it and out of the domestic melodramas of the illegitimate theatre grew that type of drama which ultimately led to the *Strifes* and *Justices* of the present day. Perhaps, in the attention given to Lytton's novels, hardly sufficient praise has been given to Lytton as a dramatist.

Among the other dramatists who, during these decades, attempted to support the legitimate style on the stage Miss Mitford, Talfourd and Browning are the more important, but all of these carry us back from the modern note of Lytton to the "poetic" style of Maturin, Knowles and Milman. Thomas Noon Talfourd and Mary Russell Mitford[1] must inevitably be associated together, for it was the former who, with his usual unselfish encouragement, helped to guide and make known the novelist and poetess. Her first important play was *Foscari*, produced originally by provincial actors and eventually performed at Covent Garden in November 1826, after the publication of Byron's drama on the same theme. Miss Mitford, not wanting in the writer's self-esteem, saw fit to censure both Byron and his work, but her play, strong as it is in the crisis scenes, can never, for power of poetry or strength of characterisation, be compared with his. Her Doge is a lifeless creation and the hero, Francesco, is little more than a white-washed puppet. *Julian*, her second ambitious play, had already been acted at Covent Garden in March 1823, with Macready in the cast, and after the fair success of these two she again attempted an Italian theme in her best-known drama, *Rienzi* (D.L. Oct. 1828), where, as the authoress directly informs us, she has attempted to shadow forth in her hero the Napoleon of the earlier years. Unquestionably interesting and dealing capably with the contending factions of aristocrats and populace, it fails, like all her other dramas, because of the artificiality of both scene and language. Somehow, these Italian stories, to which many of the Elizabethans gave strength and dignity, collapse when treated in this later age. The reason probably lies in the altered spirit of the time. When a Webster dealt with a White Devil he was writing in an atmosphere when Englishmen could know of that Italian fever at first hand; he could take many of his characters from the life around him in the London taverns. Now, in the age of Mary Mitford, all that was far away. In the midst of the Romanised setting of *Virginius* peers forth the spirit of Victorianism, and the Julians and their companions are only mental images, not real men.

---

[1] On her work see C. Hill, *Mary Russell Mitford and her Surroundings* (1920).

Talfourd, too, in spite of his undoubted talents, followed along the same path. *Ion* (C.G. May 1836) won for its legal author an immediate literary fame. Printed in a strictly private edition, its praises were sung by Talfourd's friends, and, on its production at Covent Garden, it sprang immediately into popular esteem. Yet what is there in this drama to call for our attention now? In spite of his admiration of Wordsworth and the romantic poets, Talfourd was a classicist, esteeming Addison's *Cato* as one of the greater dramas of all time; accordingly in *Ion* he chooses a classic theme and, in its treatment, holds to the Unities. Occasional beauty there is in the language, but usually the blank verse drags wearily forward, with an irritating run-on effect which brings many passages down to the levels of awkward prose. The following is not untypical:

> I know enough to feel for thee; I know
> Thou hast endured the vilest wrong that tyranny
> In its worst frenzy can inflict;—yet think
> O think! before the irrevocable deed
> Shuts out all thought, how much of power's excess
> Is theirs who raise the idol:—do we groan
> Beneath the personal force of this rash man,
> Who forty summers since hung at the breast
> A playful weakling; whom the heart unnerves;
> The north-wind pierces; and the hand of death
> May, in a moment, change to clay as vile
> As that of the scourged slave whose chains it severs?[1]

The same style is continued in *The Athenian Captive* (H.[2] Aug. 1838), which, originally written for Macready, was eventually produced at the Haymarket under Webster. In spite of the classical tendencies of the author, the interest here is hopelessly dissipated, and our minds and attention are constantly being shifted from Ismene to Creon, and thence to Thoas, Hyllus and Creusa. In *Glencoe; or, The Fate of the Macdonalds* (H.[2] May 1840) there is an apparent movement away from this over-strict classicism, but even in *Glencoe* Talfourd fails. The love story of Helen Campbell is not told in an interesting way and nowhere are we made to

[1] II. ii.

feel either the real horrors of the massacre or the tragic emotions which Talfourd wished to arouse. Like that of the others, his manner is distant, and reality seems to rumble far off from his scenes of artificiality and meaningless talk.

And then we reach Browning, who, at first sight, like Byron, might have been expected to do so much for the fortunes of the English stage[1]. Browning was, above all other things, interested in life. His portraits of *Men and Women* show a greater catholicity of interest and a greater profundity than is to be found elsewhere in the whole poetic sphere of his time. His attitude towards style is different from that of many of his contemporaries, for his sole purpose was the expressing, as directly and as vividly as possible, what for him was truth. No purely artificial leanings towards the Elizabethans were likely to over-rule his saner judgments; no over-extravagant romanticism or over-chill classicism was likely to sway his mind. If the poetic drama were to be made something truly great, it seemed as if the person who alone could make it so was Browning. Yet Browning's dramas are, like the others, mostly unacted and perhaps unactable. We turn to *Strafford* (C.G. May 1837), written at the request of Macready, and we come away from a perusal of it with a vague, indeterminate impression. The loyalty of the title-character stands out, as does the resolute, fixed purpose of Pym, but there is no true dramatic atmosphere here. We seem to have been floating over a sea of words, words that may express personality, but cannot express dramatic personality. Most of Browning's dramas are even more verbose than *Strafford*, for many were written purely for the press and not for the stage. Moreover, with the passing of the years, his style grew harsher and his meaning less clear, so that *A Blot in the 'Scutcheon* (D.L. Feb. 1843), in spite of its unquestionably affecting scenes, is difficult to follow and often definitely obscure. Browning was not destined to be a leader of a new poetic drama.

Thus did one after another of those greater writers who attempted the legitimate stage fail; only Lytton, out of them

[1] See W. Fairfax, *Robert Browning and the Drama* (1891).

all, seemed to be pointing forward towards something new, and Lytton was the least poetic. The effort to write legitimate drama, of course, was not confined to a bare dozen authors, and many attempted in these years the so-called "higher" style. Even the illegitimates occasionally crept into the more aristocratic fold, usually creeping out again so soon as they found that they had left their bread and butter behind them. Almost all these plays are similar to those which we have already considered. The themes are all themes of the past, and little effort is made to secure anything that approaches towards vitality of treatment. The efforts are scattered well over the five decades, although it must be admitted that there is a marked improvement in characterisation and in dialogue after 1840, due, apparently, to the coalescing of naturalistic melodrama and of the legitimate type through the freeing of the minor theatres. Dimond's *Adrian and Orrila; or, A Mother's Vengeance* (C.G. Nov. 1806) may be selected as a typical prose piece of the earlier years. The story of the long-lost child and the faithful love, told with many echoes of Shakespearian dialogue[1], is one of hackneyed proportions and dismal artificiality. Alfred Bunn's "tragedy" *Conrad the Usurper* (Birmingham, 1821) provides the equally familiar Continental theme, with the usual inflated and unnatural dialogue. The Germanised sentimentalism is favoured by James Boaden in *The Maid of Bristol* (H.[2] Aug. 1803), which concentrates on the devoted love of Stella. German romance, Shakespearian dialogue and undramatic philosophy lead astray W. H. Hoskins in *De Valencourt* (Norwich, 1842), where the story is told of the ruin of Fernando de Valencourt and his fair wife Euphrania. None of these deserve lengthier attention.

There is, however, a group of plays, now wholly forgotten, of the forties of the century which occasionally strike a higher note. One of these is *The Wife's Secret* (H.[2] Jan. 1848) by George W. Lovell. Cavalier themes were fairly popular at this time, but for the most part these were dealt with in a comic-melodramatic manner and provided the usual

[1] See *supra*, p. 62.

stock persons in their distressed lovers, villains, comic serving-men and foolish but honest maids. Major Murray and Lady Somerford, Sir Richard Wroughton, John Duck and Patty Pottle in Planché's *The Jacobite* (H.[2] June 1847) may be taken as concrete examples of these. In Lovell's play, however, there is something different. The story of the drama may have a certain familiarity, but the characterisation is individual. Lady Eveline Amyott succours her Cavalier brother, Lord Arden. Her husband returns to his home from a journey and is led by Jabez Sneed to doubt her fidelity. Unfortunately the lady is bound by an oath not to reveal her brother's hiding-place and tragedy is narrowly averted at the end. The dramatic situations are good in every way, and, although one feels that the author is a trifle hampered by the blank verse tradition, this seems a drama really worthy of praise. It is certainly one of the best plays I have read in this period, and I imagine that its strength comes from the fact that the author, writing from his heart, is not misled by high-sounding but false ideals of legitimacy. There is here the union, so long desired, of the two dramatic spheres.

It has to be confessed, of course, that many of the dramas produced in this time still kept to the older themes. Kenney in *The Sicilian Vespers* (Surrey, Sept. 1840), adapting *Les Vêspres Siciliennes* of Casimir Delavigne, has remembered Otway in his story of conspiracy with love as a conflicting element, but the dialogue here is much more natural than we should have met with in 1820 and there is a certain dignity in the characters. This survey may be ended with an account of two other similar plays, one of slightly earlier date, Douglas Jerrold's *Thomas à Becket* (Surrey, Nov. 1829) and Leigh Hunt's *A Legend of Florence* (C.G. Feb. 1840). The former, written in prose, aims at, and almost reaches, true tragic effect. The absence of the Elizabethan element is noticeable, and, remembering that it was written for the Surrey, one feels again that the hope of later drama lay in the illegitimate type. Hunt's play is likewise free of reminiscences of earlier drama, and shows a power of construction and an ease of dialogue which makes us wish that its author had devoted more time to the stage. The theme is not very original. Agolanti has married Ginevra, who is loved by Antonio Rondinelli. Her husband ill-treats her, but the passion of the two lovers remains pure. Finally death seems to come to her, and she is rescued from the grave by Antonio. On Agolanti's arriving to drag her back to misery her spirit at length rebels; she refuses and, in the resulting mêlée, Agolanti is slain. The main characters, however, are well outlined and are excellently contrasted with the honest gay friends of Antonio—Fulvio da Riva, a poet, and Cesare Colonna, an officer in the Pope's guard.

Such a play as this shows how the other poets failed. The story is only a "legend of Florence" yet Hunt has been able to give it true life. We may condemn his work because of the unreality of the theme—for here he followed the others— but his production has a strength which is wanting elsewhere. Had all the legitimate poets been as Lovell and Hunt, the story of our nineteenth century drama might have been vastly different. The Milmans, the Maturins, the Talfourds— even the Byrons and the Brownings—merely led it astray.

II. *Comedies*

If the early nineteenth century failed to produce a really fine drama and a poignant tragedy, it failed even more dismally in the realm of the comic muse. Some of the illegitimate farces have rollicking fun in them; few of the five-act comedies possess the faintest spark of liveliness. This failure, too, was appreciated by the age; G. A. à Beckett in his *Scenes from the Rejected Comedies* (1844) speaks, seriously for once, of "that almost extinct species—the writer of a successful Five Act Comedy." Various styles were tried, but all are marked by restraint, by slavish imitation, by a want of that force which is so difficult alike to capture and to analyse, the *vis comica*. These styles may, for convenience, be roughly classified, and attention paid to a few examples of each. The poetic romantic comedy found a true exponent only in Tobin[1], but alongside of that romantic species, and often borrowing some of its atmosphere, there is the ordinary serious comedy, closely allied to the "dramas" which have been considered in the preceding section. Connected with these in their turn are the sentimental comedies, recalling the styles of a previous age and often mingling, Reynolds-wise, study of contemporary manners with humane and moral precepts. A few plays exist solely for their humours or their intrigue, but of this class there are not many, for humours and intrigue were more commonly drawn into the service of farce.

One may start with the serious type—perhaps that which most suited the temper of the period. Very few of these unfortunately deal with problems real enough to be interesting, and the prudery of the time prevented anything like free expression. It has been already noted[2] that contemporaries thought M. R. Lacy's *The Two Friends* (H.[2] July 1828) "one of the most immoral and dangerous dramas" they had ever witnessed, the reason being that the author had dared to show a Herbert and Elinor, apparently brother and sister, who, on discovering that they were not of kin, confessed love to one another and married. There is no suggestiveness in the treatment, yet even here the heavy hand of public opinion descended severely. Most of the plays, therefore, dealt with situations of a kind that were not likely to offend and in a manner hopelessly artificial. In *Secret Service* (D.L. April 1834), for example, J. R. Planché, adapting from a play by Mélesville and Duveyrier, tells of a plot against Napoleon, where the Curé Perrin becomes a secret service agent without being aware of it. The piece is saved by a number of equivocal situations not badly dealt with, but little praise can be given to the work as a whole. We are as far here from real life as we are in the midst of the *Ions* and the *Ethwalds*. Like Planché other "illegitimate" writers essayed the full comedy form, but none succeeded in rising above mawkish sentimentality. Buckstone's *Victorine; or, "I'll Sleep on it"* (Adel. Oct. 1831) and *The Rake and his Pupil; or, Folly, Love,*

---

[1] See *supra*, p. 164.   [2] See *supra*, p. 15.

and Marriage (Adel. Nov. 1833) are typical. In the latter Rosambert, the rake, tutors the young Chevalier de Florville in the ways of the world. Florville, throughout three-quarters of the play, proves an apt pupil, but in the end, after being severely wounded, returns to his old manner of life and his country love, Sophia. It may be observed that many of these comedy dramas are set abroad. This may be partly due to the fact that quite a considerable number were adapted from the French, but the major cause seems to have been the fear of bringing the scenes too near to actual English life. Occasionally one feels that, given more freedom and better models, an individual dramatist might have been able to produce something finer than his actual accomplishment. One notes, for example, the able portraiture of Count Bertrand de Rantzau in Alfred Bunn's *The Minister and the Mercer* (D.L. Feb. 1834)[1], but such portraits stand by themselves, isolated and lonely, and all is vitiated by the distance of the scene and the artificialised restraint everywhere apparent.

The sentimental comedies for the most part flounder and wallow in the most dismal, the most moral and the most impossible of emotions, mingling with these emotions farcical humour of a kind already popularised by Frederick Reynolds. R. F. Jameson's *Living in London* (H.[2] Aug. 1815) thus pictures a hero Count Clamorcourt, of a good heart, but supreme vanity. He is led astray by Lady Killcare, but realises his own folly in the third act. Lady Clamorcourt's virtue is, of course, doubted in the play—here because Vivid takes the name of Neville, her brother. Centum, Motley, Specious and Potiphar provide the comic element. Moncrieff in *Monsieur Mallet; or, My Daughter's Letter* (Adel. Jan. 1829) depends for his comic relief mainly on dialect and the follies of the stage-struck Indian, Oronooko. The serious part tells of the attempts of Mallet, an exiled Frenchman, to discover in America his lost daughter, who has a lover in Orlando Stapleton. Miss Marianne Chambers, for her part, provides us in *The School for Friends* (D.L.

---

[1] This is an adaptation of Scribe's *Bertrand et Raton* (1833).

Dec. 1805) with professional and class types, introducing
Mathew Daw, an honest Quaker, a neglectful Sir Edward
Epworth and a hopelessly dull gallant, Lord Belmour. Stock
characters fill out the dreary plot of Kenney's *The World!*
(D.L. March 1808), where Cheviot is a proud poet in distress,
who turns out to be the long-lost son of Davenant, after he
has relieved the distresses of his unknown mother and sister.
He is set off by Echo, a Reynoldised character who apes
the follies of fashion but possesses that which, in this age,
seemed to atone for all—a good heart. Following Morton's
line in *Speed the Plough* (C.G. Feb. 1800), the younger Colman
provided in *The Poor Gentleman* (C.G. Feb. 1801) a melodramatic comedy with a reproduction of Farmer Ashfield
in Harrowby. Here the immaculate hero Frederick succeeds
in rescuing the distressed heroine, Emily, from the clutches
of the would-be seducer, Sir Charles Cropland. A fair stage
Irishman, Dennis Brulgruddery, is all that saves the same
author's *John Bull; or, The Englishman's Fireside* (C.G.
March 1803) from sheer inanity, and this in spite of high
contemporary praise and considerable theatrical success[1].
Sometimes the themes show just a touch of an attempt to
reach a problem, but the touch is faint and hesitating. In
John Poole's *Tribulation; or, Unwelcome Visitors* (H.[2] May
1825), confessedly taken from *Un Moment d'Imprudence*,
Dorrington goes out secretly for an evening's amusement
with his friend Forrester. Mrs Dorrington, also secretly,
does the same. They meet, unknown to each other, and the
husband barely escapes throwing his wife into the arms of
Sir George Faddle. Naturally there is a sentimental reconciliation of the pair after many fears and misunderstandings.
A similar note is struck in Morton's *Education* (C.G. April
1813), a comedy which shows the almost complete ruin of
Templeton through the extravagance of his over-educated
wife and his son Vincent. The play is eked out by a group
of exaggerated characters, notably Damper, the true friend,
Aspic, the parasite, and Sir Guy Stanch, the country Squire.

[1] See particularly Dunlap's *Memoirs of George Fred. Cooke* (1813),
i. 229.

Among the sentimental dramatists, Mrs Elizabeth Inchbald, after as before 1800, stood out predominant, but her work has little save an historical value. *To Marry or Not to Marry* (C.G. Feb. 1805) is not unrepresentative of her later productions. Here Hester runs away from a disagreeable match, finding an asylum in the house of Mrs Sarah Mortland, whose bookish and hitherto anti-matrimonial brother falls in love with her. Several of the sentimental dramas, as has been seen above, deal partly at least with vice, and, as has been suggested[1], a number of the playwrights looked back with not unlonging eyes to the days of Charles II. Thus Douglas Jerrold, author of many worthless comedies but a force in his own time, penned a play on *Nell Gwynne; or, The Prologue* (C.G. Jan. 1833), in which is shown the first meeting of the king and the orange-girl, with the episode of the broad-brimmed hat prologue to *The Conquest of Granada*. Similarly Moncrieff in *The "Tobit's Dog!"* (Strand, April 1838) presents us with a fanciful adventure of the gay Rochester, who is made to sacrifice his intended, Lady Diana Clarges, to his friend Savile. Jerrold's case is not untypical of the time. He was unquestionably a wit, and in some of his lesser "illegitimate" plays there is more than a hint of true joyousness; but, whenever he essays the five-act form, his genuine laughter seems to vanish. Characters and plot in *Bubbles of the Day* (C.G. Feb. 1842) are of the most artificial substance, and the author's attempt to show sprightliness in Pamela and in Florentia has a dismal result. There is a suggestion of a "problem" in *Time Works Wonders* (H.[2] April 1845), but here again the purely comic portions are pitiful in the extreme. We cannot laugh at the "humours" either of Miss Tucker or of Professor Truffles, and even although we may feel a passing interest in this theme of youthful affection and parental opposition, we must inevitably lay the play aside as largely worthless because of its constant note of frigid sentimentalism. The same criticism is true of *The Prisoner of War* (D.L. March 1842). Here there is a trifle more of spirit, and patriotic boastfulness is not ill-painted in

[1] See *supra*, p. 17.

the figure of Pallmall, whose philosophy it is that, if the soldier's duty is to "die" for his country, it is the duty of the civilian to "lie" for it. There is, indeed, a touch of true humour in the letter written by this character, who is prepared to see everything better done in England than in France, from his prison-cell at Verdun:

Fortress of Verdun, June, 1803. My dear Polly,—I scratch you these few lines like a mole under ground. The prison is tolerably strong, but not to be spoken of after Newgate. As for their locks, they haven't one fit for a tea-caddy. The rats at night come in regiments. We're allowed no candle; but we can feel, as they run over our faces, that they must be contemptible in the eyes of Englishmen. I am teaching a spider to dance; but find the spiders here nothing to the spiders in our summer-house at Hornsey.

Such touches of humour, however, are few and far between, and are almost completely obscured by the highly sentimental affection of the secretly married lovers, Clarina and Basil Firebrace. Only in one respect does Jerrold display any quality that is vital and new. Quite clearly, he was experimenting in dramatic technique. Of this two examples may be taken. In *Time Works Wonders* his first act takes place in a "*Room in a country Inn*" and shows the arrival of a runaway schoolgirl, the entry of her pursuers and her return. The next act opens on a lodge belonging to Sir Gilbert Norman, there being supposed to have elapsed a period of five years between the two scenes. This may not seem very revolutionary, but, when we consider the familiar plan of most early nineteenth century comedies, there does indeed appear to be in this a promising note of modernity. The second example concerns dramatic dialogue. The "aside," of course, is a device of hoary antiquity, and in the drama of this period it is of constant occurrence. A reading of Jerrold's plays, however, will convince us that in his works these asides appear much more frequently than in the plays of his companions. At first sight, we are inclined to believe that they represent merely the abuse of what was a common failing, but a further examination suggests that they possess a deliberate purpose and that here Douglas Jerrold was holding forth his hand, if but weakly, to the author of *Strange Interlude*. It may be that we are mistaken here, but Jerrold must at least be given the benefit of the doubt. Like some of the stage craftsmen of the period it is at least possible that, in spite of the commonness and conventionality to be found in his work, he was groping darkly towards something new.

The commonness and the conventionality, however, are the two characteristics which dominate all others. Jerrold's sentimental comedies differ in this respect hardly at all from the many other specimens of the same *genre*. From these it is clear no real good could arise; yet there are one or two associated dramas by other authors which, however faintly, indicate a new spirit at work, which point forward towards the awakening of naturalism in the future. Two examples only need be selected, for after all the signs of promise are by no means great. The first is Peake's *The Title Deeds* (Adel. June 1847), in the main a poor comedy, yet valuable for one scene. The story deals with two themes, one of which concerns the riotous waste of Philip Fustic, and the other of which tells how some title-deeds are lost, how Haywhisp, a cabby, finding them by chance, conceals them for a year. It is the latter which concerns us, for the scenes where we are shown Haywhisp's poverty and his torments of conscience are truly affecting. There is artificiality here, it is true, but there is at least the endeavour to descend from hopeless romance and artificial clichés to the way of real life. The other play is Planché's *Not a Bad Judge* (Lyc. March 1848), which is interesting, not for its scenes of real life, but for its plot. The setting is a Swiss village where a rogue Mariano is masquerading as the Marquis de Treval. Just at the moment when this rascal, having hoodwinked everyone, is about to reap his wicked harvest, old Lavater arrives, and, because of his skill in reading faces, succeeds in unmasking the impostor. Lavater is pictured as a kind of nineteenth century Sherlock Holmes, and in *Not a Bad Judge* we have what is virtually the first of the modern detective dramas. Its importance is slight, yet once more, in the forties of the century, we discover a definite link with the present day.

A still more definite link is perhaps provided in the early work of Dion Boucicault, or Bourcicault, who started his long theatrical career with the production of *A Legend of the Devil's Dyke* in 1838 and first won fame with *London Assurance* in 1841[1]. It is possible to say many vicious things about Boucicault's plays—both those of his youth and those of his age—but we must endeavour, in estimating his worth, to place ourselves in his own time and to read his plays, not in comparison with those of Shaw but in comparison with those many wretched farces with which the mid-nineteenth century theatre was fed. Were there serious question of the influence of Boucicault now, we should have to condemn him as William Archer condemned him in 1882[2], but that time has long passed, so that we can look upon his work impartially, without the prejudicing incentive of passion. From the half-dozen plays which Boucicault wrote between 1838 and 1849, two may be taken here as representative—*London Assurance* (C.G. March 1841) and *The School for Scheming* (H.[2] Feb. 1847). With these may be remembered that shorter sketch, *Used Up* (H.[2] 1844), which has already been dealt with elsewhere[3], and which we found to possess at least a certain individuality and inventiveness. *London Assurance* has something of the same quality. The story itself is an impossible one, and, if we are to make reality our standard of judgment, then we must dismiss the play outright. The question, however, is not one entirely of reality, and there are at least a few points in *London Assurance* that call for our attention. Some of the characters are mere Reynoldised "humours," but others stand out, if not with individuality, at least with a boldness and directness which testifies to a power lacking in the majority of the earlier dramatists. Lady Gay Spanker is not a masterpiece, yet she has a vivacity of her own and a

---

[1] On his life see Townsend Walsh, *The Career of Dion Boucicault* (Publications of the Dunlap Society, Third Series, 1915, i). A good account of Boucicault's life and activities in America is given in A. H. Quinn, *A History of the American Drama from the Beginning to the Civil War* (1923), pp. 368–94.

[2] *English Dramatists of To-day* (1882), pp. 38–48.

[3] See *supra*, p. 132.

genuine comic appeal. There is, too, in Dazzle a figure of quiet fun, and the situations in which he appears are conceived with a decided sense of the theatre. There is no wonder that *London Assurance* created a slight stir in 1841, for, however near in spirit it was to the sentimental manners style of Reynolds, it yet marked an advance upon the average contemporary production and indicated that the way was being prepared for Robertson. *The School for Scheming* has similar qualities. The plot is undoubtedly sentimental, being designed to show the false standards created by money and fashion as opposed to the natural goodness in an honest and not over-civilised heart. The fashionables or would-be fashionables include Claude Plantagenet, a decrepit scion of the nobility, Lord Fipley, a brainless and rather vulgar youth of great possessions, and the MacDunnum, a man whose greatest aim in life is to be a capitalist. Opposed to these are Helen Plantagenet, whose schooling in Mrs French's academy for snobs has not reft from her some honest feelings, Craven Acton, a man of fashionable pretensions but of good purpose, and old Sykes, his father (although that fact is unknown to him), who for years has watched over the career of his only son. In the course of the play we are carried rapidly from Plantagenet's poor lodgings to Mrs French's ball-room and thence to the environs of Boulogne, accompanying the various characters in their chase through life. Much is artificial, for Boucicault has retained many of those exaggerated tricks which were inherited by the forties of the century from the twenties; the jokes are often feeble; and the painting of contemporary manners is executed in a style which exhibits false proportion and inharmonious colours. To set against this, however, we must consider the slight touches of greater subtlety in the characterisation of Helen, a girl of good heart educated in evil if fashionable surroundings and torn between obedience to her father's wishes and her slowly awakening love of Craven Acton. There is not much here that is worthy of high praise, but there is potentiality at least. An earlier dramatist would have presented this girl in the good old standard way—wholly lovable and completely opposed to the precepts of Mrs French's academy. It was a blessing that the English stage got beyond Boucicault; at the same time it was a blessing that, by 1840, it had reached his ways of art.

It is not necessary here to spend more time on the other comedies of humours and of intrigue, for universal darkness covers all. The Jonsonian style could rarely give anything more than unnatural exaggerated farcical characters, such as the talkative Lady Topple in Bell's *Temper* (H.[2] May 1847), and intrigue had lost its verve and dash. Thomas Archer in *Marguerite's Colours; or, Passing the Frontier* (Lyc. July 1847) was about as *risqué* as the nineteenth century could allow. He actually permits a married woman—Marguerite, wife of the old Duke de Croissy—to have a lover, even if he is only a rejected one, in Captain Sanspeur. Most of the type are merely dull imitations of such plays as *The Belle's Stratagem*. Charles Dance's *The Beulah Spa* (Olym. Nov. 1833), where a gay Caroline (acted by Vestris) is captured by an honest Sydney Beauchamp, may be taken as a representative example.

This is truly a vale of tears. Where laughter should sport lithesomely, we have only awkward movement, moral sentiments and the hoarse rough guffaw of unintellectual vulgarity. The eighteenth century, in the realm of comedy at least, I believe to have been unduly neglected. This age shows not the slightest spark of the true comic fire, although in other spheres of drama it was doing pioneer work for our contemporaries.

CHAPTER V

THE STILL-BORN DRAMA

I. *Tragedies*

IT has been remarked above that no sure distinction is to be made in this time between the acted and the unacted drama[1]; some dramatists such as Talfourd penned their plays with no thought of the stage and saw those plays presented on the boards; others wrote with fond theatrical ambitions and had to condescend to the printing press for making known their wares. If, however, there is no certain classification to be made along these lines, the great fact remains that this period abounds in dramas of a purely "poetic" kind which either were never performed in their own times or have never, even to this day, found actors and actresses to interpret them. There is, therefore, an insistent necessity for considering these dramas as a class, and for endeavouring to estimate their worth as dramas. It is not my purpose here to deal with such productions as the *Prometheus Unbound* of Shelley, which obviously makes no pretence towards theatrical form, but, even leaving aside such works, we find a great mass of tragedies and of comedies, written by some of our most famous poets and prose-writers, which stand completely apart from the regular fare of the playhouses. The question which is raised, therefore, in this present chapter is the same as that raised elsewhere in this book[2]. We have to consider whether the theatres or the poets were at fault that so few of their dramas were produced, and the question here must be answered, not along the lines of generalisation, but from concrete examples.

It may be convenient, in this summary, to consider these poetic playwrights, if not according to strict chronological sequence, at least according to the various groups into which

---

[1] See *supra*, p. 58.   [2] See *supra*, pp. 59–78.

they fall. We have, thus, the Wordsworth, Coleridge, Scott group, followed in the early decades by the Shelley, Byron, Keats group. This in turn gives way to the Tennyson, Browning set which leads us to the year 1850, and the arising of yet later bands of dramatic authors.

Two things served to destroy the dramatic worth of the productions of the earliest romantic poets—didacticism and the German influence. Wordsworth has written poetry of a visionary splendour and a profound emotion unequalled elsewhere, Coleridge has given us dream-pictures of a truly magical beauty, even Southey occasionally rises to a moderate poetic height—but all of these, and all of their followers, have about them a touch of the surplice. They were all so immersed in the study of philosophy and of political thought, they were all so downright in their convictions, that they felt it incumbent upon them to inform the world in direct terms of their opinions and their beliefs. This didacticism mars the lesser poetry of Wordsworth and of Coleridge alike, and, unfortunately, these poets deemed the dramatic form to be that most fitted for the inculcation of those truths they wished to spread among mankind. All these poets, too, were filled with admiration of German thought and literature. Unfortunately again they took from Germany, not its strength, but its weakness. They became immersed in a vague transcendental philosophy which often they could not appreciate or knew not how to express; they created for themselves, Southey-wise, a spurious mysticism which pretended to be Eastern and was not; they lost sight of the true power of German drama under Lessing and Schiller to dote sentimentally on innocent outlaws and gloomy goblins. Gloriously in poetry they were able to shake off their self-imposed fetters, but drama seemed to call forth only their worst qualities and dismally they trudged along a weary and uninteresting path.

We may dismiss Southey's *Wat Tyler* (1817) as an unfortunate mistake on the part of a very young man, but it is not so easy to pass by either Wordsworth's *The Borderers* (1842; written 1795-6) or Coleridge's *Osorio* (1798), which, refashioned as *Remorse*, was played at Drury Lane in January 1813. Both of these show clearly the impress of German example. *The Borderers* has for its main theme a crime committed with the best possible intentions, and *Remorse* tells of an honest hero, dominated by the most humane sentiments, who is outlawed by an evil brother. In both there is action of a kind, but the trouble with most of the romantic dramatists was that they could not think of action and of character together. These two, in all greater plays, are fused, so that, for example, we cannot think of Hamlet the man apart from the Hamlet story, or of Othello alone away from the tragic scene at Cyprus. A romantic poet, on the other hand, seemed to think of a "passion" first of all, fit that "passion" next to some quite harmless individual, and then add, as a last ingredient, a dash of action unrelated to either. Coleridge's Inquisition scenes are of this nature. At first sight they would appear to indicate that the poet-philosopher was not without his interest in the outward movements of men, but a later consideration shows that these scenes have been introduced solely because the author feels that something is necessary to enliven his lengthy soliloquies and pages of poetic narrative. Both for Coleridge and for Wordsworth it is the abstract passion that counts, Wordsworth writing his drama to prove the thesis that "sin and crime are apt to start from their opposite qualities[1]," and Coleridge, as his later title shows, dealing primarily with a "passion."

If we turn from Wordsworth and Coleridge to Sir Walter Scott, we see the other baneful influence of the German style. Characteristically, the young Scots advocate had chosen for translation at the very beginning of his career Goethe's somewhat rococo *Götz von Berlichingen*, and, as his ballads show, he fell deeply under the spell of that new literature which mingled historical setting with strange diablerie. *Halidon Hill* (1822), described as "A Dramatic Sketch, from Scottish History," may have been an experiment made in the hope of developing a dramatic kind similar to that provided

[1] Preface, *The Borderers*.

in fictional form by the Waverley novels. The usual failure of the romantic poets, however, is seen in Scott's declaration that his play was "in no particular either designed or calculated for the stage[1]," and the language follows the usual line of artificiality leading towards rhetoric and bombast. The same weaknesses are apparent in *The Doom of Devorgoil* (1830) and *The House of Aspen* (Surrey, Nov. 1829). Scott's genius, like that of Dickens, required the aid of narrative for its free expression. In the dramatic form there is lacking entirely that majestic atmosphere which makes atonement for the rigidity of heroes and of heroines and for the stiltedness of a language which, unless it be in the dialect, is unnatural and forced. His style in dramatic dialogue is dull, and he can think of naught in plot beyond a rather pitiful Götz-like presentation of historical fact and legend.

Many other writers in this early period essayed the poetic style but with the same or similar failings. William Godwin's *Antonio; or, The Soldier's Return* (D.L. Dec. 1800) and *Faulkner* (D.L. Dec. 1807), although they were staged (unsuccessfully), have the same tendency towards declamatory periods, the same insistence on a thesis, the same predominance of an abstract passion[2]. Charles Lamb, leaning more towards the Elizabethans, tried to write a drama in *John Woodvil* (1802), originally called (characteristically) *Pride's Cure*, and offered vainly to John Kemble about Christmas 1799. The very first scene gives some promise, but, as the play progresses, all the worst faults of the romantic style become apparent. The theme, which tells of a son's unwilling betrayal of his father, is slight in the extreme, and the conclusion strikes a note unutterably false. All that can be said of *John Woodvil* is that in it Lamb has played the sedulous ape to Beaumont and Fletcher and to Massinger, sprinkling his play, too, with reminiscences of Shakespearian romantic comedy. Beyond a few lines of beauty it does

[1] Advertisement.
[2] B. Sprague Allen has an interesting paper on *William Godwin and the Stage* (*Publ. of the Mod. Lang. Assoc. of America*, 1920, xxviii. 3), but this deals mainly with the fate of his plays in America.

not rise. The characters are vague and shadowy. It is a dream called forth consequent upon the reading of older plays; of value for its time it has nothing. In later years Lamb again essayed the dramatic form, publishing, after rejection by the managers, *The Wife's Trial; or, The Intruding Widow* in *Blackwood's Magazine* (Dec. 1828). Taken from Crabbe's tale of *The Confidant*, this "drama" is no more striking than the other. Mrs Frampton, the chief character, is but ill-drawn, and Selby is wholly unconvincing. Once more the sole merit of the play rests in a few blank verse lines clearly imitated from the Elizabethans.

Minor authors, of course, followed the way of their betters, but naturally with no more success. Andrew Birrell, otherwise unknown to fame, published a sentimental *Henry and Almeria* in 1802, loudly proclaiming that his wares had been stolen and brought upon the stage as *Alfonso*. Even Lewis, one feels, would not wish to filch from such work. The scene is Mexico, and the plot, which deals mainly with faithful love, parental commands, pride and vengeance, puts in contrast the ambitious greed of Europeans and the deep honesty of the savage. The influence of Kotzebue is over all, but the play has representative interest because we can trace below the German atmosphere elements clearly taken from the Elizabethans[1]. These Elizabethanised adaptations of Kotzebuian themes were popular. So too were sentimentalised chronicle histories. Of the latter type, J. Grahame's *Mary Stewart, Queen of Scots* (1801) may be taken as representative. Here there is additional pathos introduced in the unfortunate loves of Adelaide and George Douglas, although a certain strength comes to the play through the author's deliberate leaving of the Queen before her end. There are individually fine scenes and passages to be discovered in this and in many others of these dramas, but of genuine strength, of vital power, of true tragic nobility and grandeur there is nothing.

[1] Mr U. C. Nagchaudhuri may be right in tracing one episode to *The Merry Devil of Edmonton* (unpublished thesis in the University of London).

The tale was eagerly taken up by the Byron and Shelley group. Already the work of the former has been glanced at, for Byron, more than any of the others, was associated with the theatre. The weaknesses inherent in all this work, however, are to be traced in his plays. The constant disdain of the playhouse and the lofty notes prefixed to some of his published dramas show that even here the stage had failed to find its deliverer. His companion, Percy Bysshe Shelley, is, of course, entirely a closet playwright, although again careful consideration must be given to his one purely dramatic work, *The Cenci* (1819), largely because this has been so bepraised by critics and because it has been performed publicly in our own times. Are we to blame the contemporary theatre for refusing it? Are we to esteem it as the greatest play produced in England since the appearance of Otway's *Venice Preserv'd*[1]? The question seems a particular one; in reality it has a general significance, for on our answer will depend the attitude we adopt towards the dramatic work of this whole poetic school.

No one can deny that *The Cenci* possesses highest poetic worth, but the question here is not one of poetry but of drama, and on two counts at least it is in this respect defective. A great play, although like *Hamlet* it may arouse a certain amount of doubt and wonder, must sweep definitely from exposition to conclusion. The audience must understand, emotionally if not intellectually, the main atmosphere of the drama and the motives actuating the words and deeds of the characters. In *The Cenci*, however, there is no such dominant and appreciable purpose. We are puzzled—at least we are puzzled in the theatre—at the later actions of Beatrice. There is an explanation, it is true, but that explanation is not provided for us by Shelley himself; it can come only when we have studied his ideas in other works and applied his philosophic principles to this particular play. A tragedy must be a self-contained work of art if it is to

---

[1] See the discussion on *The Cenci* in *The Saturday Review* (by J. Agate, cxxxiv. Nov. 25, 1922), *The New Statesman* (by M. Baring, xx. Nov. 18, 1922) and *The London Mercury* (vii. Dec. 1922).

be great; *The Cenci* is to be understood only by Shelley enthusiasts.

Apart from this, Shelley displays in his drama that common weakness of all his contemporaries. He is so occupied with the Elizabethan theatre that he echoes and re-echoes mechanically the phraseology and the situations of Shakespearian days. "And yet I need not speak," cries Cenci,

> Though the heart triumphs with itself in words.
> O, thou most silent air, that shalt not hear
> What now I think! Thou pavement which I tread
> Towards her chamber,—let your echoes talk
> Of my imperious step scorning surprise,
> But not of my intent!—

and in these words Shelley displays, first, his failure to deal with a theatrical convention, and secondly, the imitative quality of his style. This is made even more palpable in the finest scene of the drama—the murder of Cenci. It is the finest scene, yet it is but a variation of the murder-scene in *Macbeth*. "Is it accomplished?" cries Beatrice. "What?" says Marzio, and then the "Did you not call?" of Olimpio's, the "When?" of Beatrice, and Olimpio's "Now" seem borrowed word for word from Shakespeare. The lines—"If it were done when 'tis done"—are monotonously echoed and varied.

> O, fear not
> What may be done, but what is left undone,

cries Beatrice. Lucretia wishes, "Would it were done!" and Beatrice catches the echo again when she declares to her mother that "What is done wisely, is done well." These are only a few examples, but they are sufficient to show the crushing influence of Shakespeare upon the poet. They show, too, that when an exciting *dramatic* scene has to be devised, the poet has not theatrical sense enough to invent unaided; he has to fall back on the past. *The Cenci* is perhaps the most beautiful thing given to us by the poetic dramatists, but it shares the same defects and weaknesses which are so patent in the other plays of the time.

Of the one dramatic effort of John Keats, *Otho*, written

along with Armitage Brown, hardly anything that is good
may be said. In turning to the medieval period, Keats
showed the impress of the usual romantic tendency. It is
certainly true that the abstract "passion" or "theory" is not
so marked in his play as it is in the works of many of his
contemporaries—for Keats was less intellectually inclined
than they—but both the plot and the delineation of character
are weak. The tragedy gives us a regular villain in Conrad,
a villainess in Auranthe; Ludolph is an injured hero, and
Erminia a very much distressed heroine. In spite of the
fact that the close is "tragic" (in the sense that it ends on
death and misery) Keats' play is intimately connected with
the regular melodramatic school. Nor does the language
make amends for the poverty in other spheres. Hardly
anything of the poet's magic appears in the dialogue, and
many lines are of a harshness and crudity one might little
have expected from the creator of *Isabella*.

Joining the other poets, Walter Savage Landor also
essayed the dramatic style, but hardly with greater success.
For *Count Julian* (1812) he turned to that half-mythical
theme which had already inspired Rowley's *All's Lost by
Lust* and Scott's *The Vision of Don Roderick* (1811), and was
to give, two years later, the *Roderick* (1814) of Southey.
Perhaps the very horror of the story and its lack of subtlety
appealed to these romantic poets. Landor's version compares,
as a drama, but ill with Rowley's. No critic can claim that the
earlier play is a masterpiece, but there is a certain luridness
in the colouring which stamps its characters upon our mind.
Landor's is hopelessly confused. Neither Julian nor the
sensual Roderigo is granted a personality of force and distinction, while one who did not know of the legend before-
hand would be disastrously lost amid Landor's dialogue. All
that may be said in favour of *Count Julian* is that Landor,
possessing a restraint denied to so many of his fellow writers,
has been able in one or two scenes to strike out of the hard-
ness of his imagination a power rarely seen in this age.
As we read the play we come across passages which remind
us of his more famous epigrams, and we can only regret that

such passages are lost amid the other scenes of this unequal play. The same confusion marks out the trilogy, *Andrea of Hungary*, *Giovanna of Naples* (both 1839) and *Fra Rupert* (1841), although a flash of greatness succeeds in illuminating the story of *The Siege of Ancona* (1846). Obviously, the stage was not to revive through Landor's efforts; his peculiar classicism, no more than the romanticism of his companions, failed to adapt itself to theatrical conventions.

Nor was his brother, Robert Eyre Landor, more successful. *The Count Arezzi* (1824) "was written designedly with those qualities which would render it unfit for representation" and as such is marred at the start. There is a certain ease in the dialogue here, but the story, like that of *Count Julian*, is somewhat confused, and the stabbing of Arezzi at the end seems to be purely fortuitous, a device to secure a tragic conclusion which the plot itself hardly justifies. In 1841 R. E. Landor published three other plays as *Tragedies—The Earl of Brecon*, a not uninteresting study of the conflicting claims of religion and of this earth, *Faith's Fraud*, a foolish story of the *Götz von Berlichingen* type, full of poison and medieval castles and villainy, and *The Ferryman; or The Translated Escutcheon*, an equally foolish tale of concealed identity, with impossible Counts of Altheim and vague Barons, and dark crimes and the Danube flowing by ready to receive the bodies. The claims of R. E. Landor to a place in the history of literature have been recently vindicated[1]; but as a dramatist he has no more merit than any of the others.

Once more, beside the major writers stood many who are now entirely forgotten, struggling, but struggling in vain, to gain success in the poetic sphere. Some, like J. Bird, openly declared that they would have liked to see their works on the stage; others took up the attitude of disdain. Bird's *Cosmo, Duke of Tuscany* (1822) follows the regular Byronic style, telling a dull story of the love of Giovanni, son of the usurping Duke, for Julia, and of his brother's villainy. Again we see an instance of how the poetic dramatists, when they did try

---

[1] See a volume of criticism and another of selections prepared by Eric Partridge (1927).

to introduce action, treated that action as something separate and apart from the dialogue. In the last scene Garcia, the villain, has set a convent in flames, and the stage direction, silent so far as dialogue goes, reminds us of the stage directions in the melodramas of the period:

JULIA *is seen above, enveloped in flame. A shriek of women is heard without. In a few moments,* GIOVANNI *is discovered, making his way through the flames. He catches* JULIA *in his arms, and bears her fainting on the stage. The curtain falls.*

It is as exciting as the heroic rescue in *Speed the Plough*, but what an ending for a poetic play which attempts to delineate character! The verb "attempts" is necessary here, for Bird's dialogue is much less exciting than his stage directions, and the reader is rather inclined to echo the words of a Soldier in the middle of act I:

Good night, old man!—good night!—you weary us.

Charles Bucke's *The Italians; or The Fatal Accusation* (1819) contains, like Bird's play, a long preface loudly complaining of the hardheartedness of theatrical managers. The story of *The Italians* is also one of villainy and virtue, mingled with political aspirations and a dash of horror. The loyal Fontano's eyes, like those of Gloucester, are put out, and this character wanders about the play, accompanied by a faithful Edgar, named Scipio. There is no subtlety in the delineation either of Manfredi, the villain, or of Alfonso, the Duke misled by him; and a turgid bombastic style dominates every scene. Turgid diction, too, mars Thomas Aird's *Murtzoufle* (1826), a play of Doge theme obviously influenced by Byron. How the author ever imagined that *Murtzoufle* could ever be accepted as the title of a successful tragedy only the gods can tell. Romantic folly is here summarised in one word. Byronic influence appears also in the peculiar *Duke of Mantua*, published in 1823, with a dedication to Lady Byron and bearing a frontispiece showing a figure obviously intended to be that of Byron half concealed behind a mask. In recent years it has been generally credited to John Roby[1]. This fairly poor blank verse tragedy tells of the love of a Duke for Hermione and of the love-turned-to-hatred borne by Carlos. Ruin comes to all in the end. The dialogue, broken by a number of extraordinarily long soliloquies, is stilted, and the Shakespearian prose servant scenes[2] indicate well the evil influence of the Elizabethans.

A year before the appearance of *The Duke of Mantua*, Thomas Lovell Beddoes—like Lamb full of dark thoughts culled from Jacobean drama—issued *The Bride's Tragedy*. It is peculiar that this author, whose work breathes the very spirit of Webster and Tourneur, should have been he who gave the best advice to his age—advice unhappily never followed—concerning dramatic necessity. "I am convinced," he declared in 1825 to a friend[3],

the man who is to awaken the drama must be a bold trampling fellow—no creeper into worm-holes—no reviser even—however good. These reanimations are vampire-cold—Such ghosts as Marloe—Webster &c. arc better dramatists, better poets, I dare say, than any contemporary of ours—but they are ghosts—the worm is in their pages—& we want to see something that our great-grandsires did not know. With the greatest reverence for all the antiquities of the drama I still think, that we had better beget than revive—attempt to give the literature of this age an idiosyncrasy & spirit of its own & only raise a ghost to gaze on not to live with—just now the drama is a haunted ruin.

That is genuinely inspired, thorough and profound theatrical criticism; yet all that Beddoes produced was *The Bride's Tragedy*, an immature drama redolent of the Elizabethans, and *Death's Jest Book or The Fool's Tragedy* (finished in its first form 1826; published 1850)[4], in which, more than half in love with easeful death, he brought back to life the gloomy

---

[1] See S. C. Chew, *Byron in England* (1924), p. 176. The play was reprinted in Roby's *Legendary and Poetical Remains* in 1854.

[2] Particularly I. ii.

[3] *The Complete Works of Thomas Lovell Beddoes* (Fanfrolico Press, 1929), i. 25.

[4] There are also two fragments of plays, *The Second Brother* and *Torrismond*.

and macabre conceptions of the early seventeenth century
stage.

> As sudden thunder
>   Pierces night;
> As magic wonder,
>   Wild affright,
> Rives asunder
>   Men's delight:
> Our ghost, our corpse; and we
>   Rise to be...
>
> As wake the morning
>   Trumpets bright;
> As snowdrop, scorning
>   Winter's might,
> Rises warning
>   Like a spright:
> We buried, dead, and slain
>   Rise again[1].

The "Voices in the air" who sing this ditty might be those of
Tourneur and Marston and Webster and Ford. Beddoes has
an independent style of his own; for he is a true poet: but
neither of these plays is great as a play, because both are
wanting in that constructive power and in that delineation
of character which will always accompany a determined
and inspired attempt to give to contemporary drama "an
idiosyncrasy and spirit of its own." They are remembered
today only for a few individual passages and for the lovely
lyrics which Beddoes, like so many other poets of the time,
knew so well how to write.

In Elizabethan style, too, Charles Jeremiah Wells treated
his biblical story in *Joseph and his Brethren* (1824; but
revised frequently up to 1879). Absolutely untheatrical,
Joseph and his Brethren yet attracts the modern reader as
it attracted Swinburne fifty years ago because of the high-
sounding Marlowesque verse, because of the verve and the
vision shot through every scene, because of the commanding
figure of the lustful queen, Phraxanor. Praise, however, as
we may certain qualities of Wells' drama, we yet come back

---

[1] *Op. cit.* i. 215.

to Beddoes' declaration. *Joseph and his Brethren* may have been a model for the Pre-Raphaelite Brotherhood, but it could never be a model for the stage. Its language and its characterisation alike are poetic rather than dramatic.

Among plays which have been singled out for praise by contemporary or later critics Martin Archer Shee's *Alasco* (1824) has a special interest because of the 56 page preface addressed to the Lord Chamberlain. One may, of course, thoroughly sympathise with the outraged feelings of the author, and wholeheartedly endorse his attack on a petty-minded censor. There is absolutely nothing in *Alasco* which deserved the veto which was put upon its performance. As at least one play in our own times has shown, however, the fact that a drama has been unrighteously banned does not by any means indicate that the work is one of prime dramatic worth, although in Shee's wail of indignation there is really an implication that he has suffered martyrdom as much for excellence in plot-construction as for somewhat liberal sentiments. This being so, it may be well to glance at least at the main development and treatment of his theme. And first we may start with a prefatory note which he himself prefixes to the text. "The reader is requested to observe," he comments, that

the passages distinguished by inverted commas were omitted by me, in the copy for the Theatre, in order to reduce the Play within the necessary acting limits;—*having taken the Tragedies of Shakespeare, in Johnson and Steevens's edition, as my guide, in judging of the length to which I should extend my composition; and not being aware how much they were curtailed for the stage, I was led into the error of writing nearly one thousand lines more than could be admitted within the usual limits of an acting play*[1].

The italics, of course, are my own, designed to call attention to that first and last and never-to-be-forgiven sin of the would-be dramatist—mere study appreciation of past efforts and disdain of the "acting play." Archer Shee is condemned, not because he was banned by the Censor, but, on his own count, because he had not the first requisites of a playwright.

[1] Advertisement, p. lvii.

Having read cool statement in the preface, one is not surprised to find dull realisation in the body of the play. The play opens with a daybreak scene, by a dim cavern, men standing on guard and others entering with their leaders, Conrad and Malinski. Thus they speak:

> CONRAD (*speaking to one of the Peasants*).
> Call in the scouts—
> By Heaven, the moon's a prodigal to-night,
> And showers her silver lavishly.
>
> MALINSKI.
>   'Tis the dawn
> That breaks above the hill.
>
> CONRAD.
>   Why, what's the hour?
>
> MALINSKI.
> Four, by the Abbey clock.
>
> CONRAD.
>   Then we again
> Have loiter'd at our sport.—But who comes here,
> Outstripping haste?   [*Enter a scout, hastily.*
> Why, comrade, if thy news
> Should wear but half the importance of thy face,
> We must have a gazette for it. If thou'st breath,
> Proclaim.

The needless oaths, the florid references to natural phenomena, the stilted and would-be poetic language are scattered throughout the entirety of the play, rising to a frenzy of bombast when, at the end, Alasco, his Amantha dead, breaks away from the hold of Conrad and raises his dagger on high:

> As you regard your lives, molest me not!—
> For I'm a desperate man, that frenzy grapples with.
> Think you, the dagger and the bowl removed,
> With every mortal means the wretch resorts to[1],
> That you can prison life in this frail mansion!

---

[1] It may be noted how these poetic dramatists, besides copying situations and direct phrases in Shakespeare's plays, echoed even the formation of Shakespearian sentences, as if in them lay the secret of dramatic virtue. Hamlet's "The thousand natural shocks that flesh is heir to" obviously is the model for Archer Shee's line above.

Oh! no—no, no!—the soul eludes all jailers!
Tyrants may frown—the bullying world look big—
And scowl down feebler spirits;—who dares to die,
Scoffs at the vain grimace, and sets him free!—
There is a point, at which the heart will break,—
And I have reached it!—yes—this friendly steel
But saves some useless pangs.—Had she—there cold—
Had she remained to bless me—for her sake,
I might have lived—and writhed through some sad years,
A pardoned slave!—in shackles, with my country.
But now!—
Life's load were insupportable to sense.—
Thus then, I shake the loathsome burthen off,
And fly to my Amantha!—

No; the drama could receive nothing of value, nothing of strength, from such as Martin Archer Shee.

There is no need here to continue further. One might occupy space with praise of the poetic beauty which appears in scene after scene of the *Cosmo de Medici* of Richard Hengist Horne and in those of John Westland Marston's *The Patrician's Daughter*; one might continue to quote from the follies of the period—but, in reality, such additional space devoted to the subject would not contribute more than we already know of the chief qualities of this dramatic or non-dramatic school. For, in spite of all their differences, in spite of that intense individualism fostered by lyric ideals, these men did form a school which had two things in common —a vague desire to shine in the sphere of dramatic authorship and a childish inability to take advantage of what was offered to them by the theatre itself. As we have already seen, extenuating circumstances may be brought forward in their defence, but always our researches into the causes of dramatic decline lead us back ultimately to the failure of the poets themselves, to their essential blindness regarding the facts. They could not see that true drama must always be a popular thing dependent upon the contemporary theatre; they could not see that what the age craved for was not resuscitations of past effort but something new, something that should be expressive of a changed and changing civilisation. Lord

Byron, in the pride of his intellect, may vent his spleen on the stage of his day and pompously enquire,

> Shall sapient managers new scenes produce
> From CHERRY, SKEFFINGTON, and Mother Goose?
> While SHAKESPEARE, OTWAY, MASSINGER, forgot,
> On stalls must moulder, or in closets rot?[1]

But, after all, it might have been better for the drama had Shakespeare, Otway and Massinger been forgotten or at least left out of the sphere of original creation. There were only a few men of the age who saw the real truth of things and even they failed to carry their precepts into action, even they confused the issue by paying humble obeisance to the poets. Because of their interest the opinions of Richard Hengist Horne may be taken as a conclusion to this section. Horne was wiser than most. He saw that the use of the word "legitimate" was doing evil, and realised that

> the most legitimate, because the genuine offspring of the age, is that drama which catches the manners as they rise, and embodies the characteristics of the time.

This, he found, had "taken shelter at what have been named 'Minor Theatres'," and was expressed

> in the skilful little comedies, and bright, racy dramas of Jerrold, Planché, Bernard, Buckstone, Oxenford, Dance, Mark Lemon, Moncrieff, Coyne, Leman Rede, Lunn, Peake, Poole, and others. ...They have, each and all (though in very different quantities), lavished much wit, fancy, and invention on their productions, doomed by the theatrical destinies to an ephemeral existence[2].

This reads like sound criticism, and the impression is strengthened when Horne stretches out the finger of contempt at those who have disdainfully criticised the efforts of the "illegitimate" writers. Unfortunately, however, the argument soon moves back to familiar lines. These authors of the Minor Theatres are doing as Shakespeare did, but the public has changed. No longer are there audiences of "inquiring and earnest-minded men"; the modern theatre-goers crave for lesser things. Praise may be given to a few individual

---

[1] *English Bards, and Scotch Reviewers* (3rd edn., 1810), p. 46.
[2] *A New Spirit of the Age* (1844; World's Classics, 1907), p. 307.

playwrights, but poverty is behind. And what is the result? The "unacted drama." And who then are these unacted dramatists? Horne's answer is, "Nearly all the best authors," and he proceeds to show that

there is manifestly the strongest tendency in the present age to be dramatic, but its chief authors have no means of learning the art. To go no further back than Byron, Southey, Shelley, Coleridge, the list includes almost every author eminent in works of imagination and invention. With those just mentioned we should class—because his genius ranks among them—the honoured name of Barry Cornwall, who having had a tragedy successfully produced upon the stage as long ago as 1821, has manifestly never felt it worth while to tempt again the countless troubles and unworthy annoyances attending representation[1].

In this passage, Horne has not only brought back the argument to the familiar lines, he has provided his own refutation. The poets have not the opportunity to learn the art, he thinks; and then proceeds to cite Barry Cornwall. Did Byron have no opportunities? Was not Browning asked to write for the stage by Macready himself? Did not Coleridge and Talfourd and a host of others get their pieces put upon the boards? And if these are not opportunities, what other opportunities has the stage to offer?

The truth is that the poets were lordly inclined. They would not "tempt the countless troubles and unworthy annoyances attending representation." They would not recognise that Literature is not the only thing in the theatre; that there are actors to interpret and an audience to applaud or to condemn. Their passion for the theatre, on which Horne comments, was not a passion for the theatre but a passion for themselves.

II. *Comedies*

The "unacted drama" was, of course, mainly serious in style, specialising, as we have seen, in bombastic tragic sentiment, but a further word may be said of the few comedies which the poets and novelists produced in this age. The fatal

[1] *A New Spirit of the Age*, pp. 313–4.

weakness of the period is the lack of a sense of humour, and, when this has been said, it will be at once realised that the "legitimate" comedies of the time form but a miserable and sorry show. Literature, in aristocratic wise, sneered at the pun and the witticism, but failed to give anything to take their places. The comic scenes of the "minor" plays may be feeble enough, but at least they possessed interest of action and good rough and tumble fun. There is little in the ordinary "unacted" sphere but elephantine merriment and dismal attempts at forced humour.

Comedy took equal share with tragedy in Joanna Baillie's scheme of passionate drama; her original plan was to devote one play of each kind to every passion she selected for treatment. A trifle of tragic power she possessed; of genius for comedy she had none. Only one of her many experiments in this sphere found its way to the stage—that being *The Election* (E.O.H. June 1817), a companion comedy for *De Monfort* (D.L. 1800). The subject is Hate with a capital H. We are presented to two main characters, Baltimore, an impoverished squire, and Freeman, a rich upstart. The former detests the latter heartily enough, and Mrs Freeman devotes her enmity to Baltimore. Mrs Baltimore and Freeman are, on the other hand, generously inclined; indeed Freeman actually saves Baltimore from ruin and is insulted for his pains. A duel is about to take place when it is discovered that the pair are really brothers. Sentiment colours the whole of the dialogue, and of comic force there is not, in the whole five acts, the slightest glimmer of a sparkle. There is no need here to analyse all, or even many, of Joanna Baillie's efforts in this style. Every one is stilted. Not a laugh rises from a single scene. One further example will serve for all, *The Second Marriage*, which was printed in 1802. Here the chief character is Seabright, a man who has recently lost his wife and who, out of ambition, proceeds to woo and marry Lady Sarah. The troubles and vexations that arise from his passion of Ambition dully and sentimentally fill five acts. *Requiescat in pace.*

This section, devoted to unacted comedy, may well remain

as brief as possible, and two authors only may serve as representative of the rest. Maria Edgeworth essayed the same or a similar effort as that attempted by her literary sister, but once more sentimentalism ruled and comedy was forgotten, even although, as in *Love and Law* (1817), the authoress tried to introduce local Irish humours. In this play a *Romeo and Juliet* theme appears in the enmity of the McBrides and the Rooneys—Honor of the first house loving Randal of the other. The only scene that possesses any real worth is that in which the two factions appear before the Justice of the Peace, Mr Carver. Humours, too, appear in *The Rose, Thistle and Shamrock*, particularly with the persons of the drunken Christy Gallacher and Andrew Hope, the Scots drum-major, but the main theme, in which Mabel Larkin succeeds in capturing Gilbert in spite of Florinda Gallacher's flirtatious efforts, is as sentimental as the other. This sentimentalism reaches a nadir in *The Two Guardians*. St Albans, the hero, loves the artificial and heartless Juliana, daughter of Lady Courtington, whose husband is one of his guardians. Like the Tom Joneses of earlier days, he is a thoughtless but generous youth, and his eyes are opened to the evils of the world by his faithful negro servant, Quaco. The follies of fashionable life are attacked in each scene, and due prominence is given to the generous sentiments of "the noble savage." The play is dull, and, worse than that, it is old.

Joanna Baillie and Maria Edgeworth both show the preoccupation with sentimental "messages," and this preoccupation is that which did most to kill contemporary so-called comedy of the literary kind. Another type of weakness is indicated in *The Lamplighter* (first printed 1879), by Charles Dickens. One might have thought that Dickens, with his skill in drawing peculiar and amusing figures, would have been able to produce farce of a vivid, even if exaggerated nature. *The Lamplighter*, however, is incredibly dull, and happily for our purpose there exists for comparison with it Dickens' narrative treatment of the same theme, *The Lamplighter's Story*. The latter is not one of the novelist's masterpieces, but it has a charm of its own and a direct appeal; the former has neither the one nor the other. This seems to show that even Dickens, whose heart was ever, from his earliest youth, with the theatre, could not find the true way of expressing himself in dramatic wise. When he is permitted that opening into personal revelation which is narrative, he can do great things; when he is tied down to dialogue alone, his strength fails him.

It were needless to seek further examples of the general debility usually masked in high-sounding terms which is to be discovered in almost every dramatic work produced by those authors whose fame rests mainly in their poetic or narrative achievements. Sufficient examination has been given to show that their efforts were in the main retrospective, that they never thought of producing anything which should be vitally connected with the spirit of their times and that consequently their efforts could make no true appeal, could lead towards no advance either in the sphere of dramatic craftsmanship or in that of dramatic ideas. As we have seen, while certain allowances may be made on account of the theatrical conditions, this inability to create something new was the result of a weakness in the literary authors themselves. They thought too much of their own virtues; they were dazzled by the light of Elizabethan achievements; they were loath to expend that time and toil which every great dramatist must devote to the mastering of his craft. They saw that melodramas, spectral, domestic and nautical, were popular on the boards of the stage, and they persisted in the writing of romantic Italian conspiracies; they saw that the contemporary audiences loved broad humour and boisterous fun, and they continued penning their dull "comedies" in which a laugh might seem as incongruous as in a cathedral. Instead of taking the theatric material which was given to them, they preferred to trudge along their own paths, thus indirectly dragging the stage lower and lower yet into the depth of despond.

CHAPTER VI

CONCLUSION

OUTWARDLY in 1850 the English theatre had reached almost its lowest ebb. The playhouses had been freed, but no startling dawn had sent its rays over the darkness of the dramatic horizon. It might well seem to contemporaries that the London playhouse could never recover, but would always remain a mere adjunct of the Parisian Comédie Française, even of the minor theatres of France. Its only real hope seemed to be Shakespeare; its orientation was still towards the Elizabethans and towards such men as Browning who were prepared to turn out poetic dramas.

From our twentieth century pinnacle, however, we can now see that the playhouses of London were but working out their destiny, and that the darkness of 1850 was illuminated by a light cast from the regions despised in those times. The poetic drama had been a natural form in the late sixteenth century; its essentially useful career was continued, so far as tragedy is concerned, up to the period of the Civil Wars. At the Restoration, quite naturally, the thoughts of the dramatists were turned to those models which had been produced in the decades immediately previous to their own times. A glimmering of Elizabethan emotionalism still stirred in the breasts of many, so that an Otway could yet create a passionate *Venice Preserv'd*, and a Lee, in moments of sanity, could emulate the richness of earlier times. This being so, the poetic drama had a perfect right to live. The heroic tragedy of the Restoration is a completely regular and just development of dramatic style. It presents the adaptation of the earlier model to the requirements and conditions of a changing generation, and the very fact that it was thus adapted indicates in itself the individual force and inventiveness of the Restoration stage. That inventiveness showed itself also in the sphere of comedy. Shadwell might continue to produce Jonsonian pieces, but the particular style of comic achievement which has come to be associated in the minds of most with the reign of Charles II is unquestionably a new style, born of the desire to express faithfully the ideals of the age and the result of much experimentation before perfection is reached in the comedies of Congreve.

During the eighteenth century conditions changed once more. The free and reckless audience of Caroline courtiers made way for the less aristocratic spectators of Georgian eras. Reformation of manners (outward at least) was in the air and a new type of drama was demanded. It is precisely here that we begin to trace signs of debility. The dramatic authors ought to have created a new tragic form for the new ideals, and just for a moment it seemed as if one man were to succeed in doing this. Rightly George Lillo produced a prose tragedy with themes taken from life, providing a form of expression which obviously made its contemporary appeal. Lillo is not a great artist, but, because of his inventiveness, he deserves to be counted among those English dramatists who belong to the Shakespearian line. Unfortunately, however, the dead hand had its grip upon his companions. Memories of the poetic dramas, increased by a growing enthusiasm (not always genuine) for Shakespeare, met with pseudo-classic sentiment. Few dared to follow Lillo's lead, and dull *Irenes* and duller *Abdallas* ruled predominant. In comedy, because of the escape into prose, greater vitality persisted. The eighteenth century may have forgotten how to be thrilled, but, in spite of its lachrymose men of feeling, it never quite forgot how to laugh. The line of development from Vanbrugh and Farquhar, through Gay and Fielding, on to Colman and Sheridan and Goldsmith, is fundamentally unbroken.

The nineteenth century opened with the growing love of melodrama, and this melodrama was at once the cause of dramatic decline and the expression of vital forces yet working in the theatre. In one respect, it was the unashamed demand of dramatists and spectators for thrill and action on the stage.

It was the reply of the romantics to the passionless rhetoric of *Irene*. In so far, the melodrama was a force for the good. Romanticism, however, had already called forth a group of highly philosophic poets with exceedingly lofty ideals, and the melodrama, to them, seemed naught but primitive buffoonery. These poets recognised Shakespeare as a master, and soon they were discovering Shakespeare's companions and followers, Marlowe and Massinger and Ford. Condemning the melodrama, they sought to provide a legitimate tragic drama of their own by copying the Elizabethans in style, by throwing in gratuitously a good deal of their philosophic conceptions, and by borrowing a few themes and characters from the fashionable German dramatists of the day. As has already been seen, they never escaped from these toils. From Baillie to Browning, from Wordsworth to Tennyson, the dead hand of the older poetic drama was upon them. This meant that only those authors who made no claim to the fame of authorship dared to write plays which might be popular, and as a consequence the purely literary form of drama inevitably declined. Subsidiary causes—such as the necessity of rapid production—took away even that simple polish which a Fitzball might have desired in leisure to give to his melodramas.

That, however, the melodrama possessed a monopoly of dramatic inventiveness, that through it has passed down the vital force from Elizabethan days, is proved, not only by its initial popularity, but by the fact that it constantly adapted itself to meet the needs of the time. When it started, about the year 1800, it was romantically adventurous, and introduced those elements of the supernatural which were calculated to thrill an audience which had grown once more passionate. No one could hiss a villain or cheer a hero in *Irene*; the melodrama is made to stir the galleries. After its career in the realm of spirits and romantic enthusiasm, the melodrama became domestic, and for the first time since the appearance of *The London Merchant* in 1730 there seemed to be an awakening to the need of a new type of drama. Most of the domestic pieces produced between 1830 and 1850 are crude in the extreme, but they not only suited the demands of the age, they pointed forward towards that type of domestic play which has provided the most characteristic medium of modern theatrical expression. Had it not been for the domestic dramas of 1830–50, Tom Robertson could not have produced his class plays of the sixties, and, had it not been for Tom Robertson, Ibsen could not have been accepted so soon or so enthusiastically in the last decades of the nineteenth century. It may be said, indeed, concerning the whole line of tradition, that such a play as *A Woman Killed with Kindness*, through its inventive power and endeavour to express the ideas of the time, is no unworthy successor of *Othello*; that in *The London Merchant* another endeavour is made to recreate this type of drama adumbrated by Heywood; that in the early nineteenth century a *Luke the Labourer* carries on the tradition thus established, not merely imitatively but with creative purpose; that *Caste* is a refinement upon the earlier efforts; and that Galsworthy's *Strife* or Sean O'Casey's *Juno and the Paycock* are but modern adaptations of this ideal to the requirements of the twentieth century. It is the varying of the method of expression to suit the demands of the period which proves the vital power in all the dramas mentioned here. In spite of the different spirits of classicism or romanticism, *Irene*, *Douglas*, *Abdalla*, *The Borderers*, *Remorse*, *Cenci*, *Strafford*, *Becket*, *Paolo and Francesca*—and countless others—are the same; removed from the life of their day, wilfully ignorant of the demands of contemporaries, each of these is imitative in essence, not of life, but of past literary models.

Nor is this inventive power confined to the region of melodrama in the nineteenth century minor theatre. Higher comedy always demands either the great author or the great intellectual actor. The great authors kept away from the stage, and the actors of the period seem to have lacked that quality which once made Tristano Martinelli and Tiberio Fiorilli the joyous companions of kings. As a result the comedy of Colman and Sheridan descended to farce. Action came to play a greater part in the conjuring up of laughter than did spoken dialogue. Yet even here inventiveness appeared. Already attention has been drawn to the varied nomenclature used for the lighter productions of the minor stage[1], and that varied nomenclature shows in its own way how eagerly the dramatists were experimenting in an endeavour to find those styles best suited to the age. It may be that we shall judge harshly the intrinsic merits of these works, as the late William Archer judged Boucicault, but between 1840 and 1850 at least we see traces of a renascence of pure wit, in the extravaganzas we see the beginnings of Savoy opera, in the burlesques we see a spirit of fun which has played its part in the formation of modern comedy. Like the authors of the melodramas, the authors of the farces and extravangazas were pioneer workers, changing their modes in accordance with the temper of the decades.

Here again the dead hand laid its spell over the literary dramas with results even more apparent than in the sphere of serious plays. The eighteenth century, for all practical purposes, had forgotten Shakespeare's romantic comedy, but *As You Like It* and *Twelfth Night* were rediscovered in the romantic period, with disastrous effects, for these plays led some writers to a style of blank verse play, called by the authors themselves "comedy," in which an endeavour was made to imitate Shakespeare. Tobin's efforts in this way are not to be despised, but any one of a score of farces of the period is to be preferred to his efforts. The farces are at least alive, and young; poor Tobin's plays are either senile or lifeless. Writers of wit could have given much to the contemporary theatre, but, with the exception of Lamb—and even he succumbed to the literary spirit of the times—the "comedies" of a would-be-higher sort published during these fifty years are lamentably lacking in any sparkle of merriment. That which the authors forgot was that romantic humour is a thing which must be spontaneous and that it includes within itself a true element of the ridiculous. They found much of *Twelfth Night* and *As You Like It* serious, and as a consequence they forgot that Shakespeare's genius could

[1] See *supra*, pp. 133-4.

express itself with equal propriety and success through the medium of *The Merry Wives of Windsor*.

It is not too much to say that, if the nineteenth century drama is weak, its weakness is due to Shakespeare. It was the very greatness of Shakespeare and of the other Elizabethans that dimmed the eyes of the critics and of the creative writers to the necessity of looking, not to the past, but to the present and to the future. It was the Shakespearian poetic play which provided the greatest hindrance to the development of prose drama in the age. The romantic poets thought that they could become a set of second Shakespeares; yet, if they only could have known it, the true representatives of the Elizabethan in the nineteenth century, and those whom, we feel, Shakespeare himself would have welcomed, were the writers of the melodrama and the farce. Shakespeare might have been a little out of his ease in the company of a serious Wordsworth and a metaphysical Coleridge; he could have spent many hours with a witty Planché and a cheery Fitzball.

SUPPLEMENTARY NOTES

The Theatre

THE establishment of The Society for Theatre Research has stimulated interest in early English playhouses and, in particular, has served to direct attention towards those of which remains are still to be found or concerning which nineteenth-century records preserve a clear account. Apart from the numerous short articles contributed to *Theatre Notebook*, the Society has been responsible for issuing several important books and booklets bearing on this subject. Among these special attention should be drawn to Alfred Loewenberg's "bibliography" of *The Theatre of the British Isles, excluding London* (1950). This gives reference to many of the books and articles which deal directly or indirectly with the "provincial" theatres; it must prove a necessary tool for any later researches in this area.

Two other of the Society's publications demand mention. Edited by A. C. Sprague and Bertram Shuttleworth, *The London Theatre in the Eighteen-Thirties* (1950) presents a series of manuscript "reviews" made by Charles Rice. Of particular value are his comments on audience behaviour; his account of the riots at Covent Garden on January 31, 1837, and at the Surrey on August 12 of the same year are racy and vivid. Along with this goes *Penny Theatres* (1952), reprinting certain chapters of James Grant's *Sketches in London* (1838), which gives an equally vivid record of numerous "gaffs" below even the level of the "minors."

In *The Georgian Playhouse* (1948) Richard Southern, although concerned mainly with the eighteenth century, provides valuable notes on some early nineteenth-century houses, and the same author's *Changeable Scenery* (1952) excellently surveys the altering methods of managing the scenes.

Some material dealing with this period appears in W. J. Lawrence's *Old Theatre Days and Ways* (1935). On the subject of histrionic style Alan S. Downer has an acute essay entitled "Players and Painted Stage—Nineteenth Century Acting" (*PMLA*, lxi. 1946, 522–76). In this he shows how J. P. Kemble's classic approach was challenged by the fiery Edmund Kean and the domestic Macready, and how naturalism gradually took shape on the boards. Especially interesting in this study is the examination of various contemporary actors' handbooks. H. N. Hillebrand has an acute and comprehensive study of Edmund Kean's acting style[1]. The vogue and significance of "Private Theatricals" and "Private Theatres" is indicated by James Sandoe (*Colorado-Wyoming Journal of Letters*, 1939, 77–84).

A most useful volume of *Leigh Hunt's Dramatic Criticism, 1808–1831* (1950), well edited by L. H. and C. W. Houtchens, forms another important contribution to the study of the theatre in this period.

The Drama

The general and increasing reliance placed upon the contemporary French theatre has been summarily indicated by Edith Wray in her list of "English Adaptations of French Drama between 1780 and 1815" (*Modern Language Notes*, 1928, xliii. 87–90). Although the titles recorded are only a few among many, they serve to demonstrate how eagerly English authors sought for themes and styles from across the Channel. Victor E. A. Bowley, discussing "English Versions of Victor Hugo's Plays" (*French Quarterly*, 1928, x. 86–98), examines the problems of adaptation, and Charles B. Qualia, in "French Dramatic Sources of Bulwer-Lytton's *Richelieu*" (*PMLA*, 1927, xlii. 177–84), shows how one author at least wrought a play out of several French originals.

A few among the many popular playwrights of the time have received attention. There is now a thorough study of George Colman the Younger[2], Elizabeth Inchbald's career

---

[1] *Edmund Kean* (1933) in which, from contemporary sources, he gives a vivid impression of his power and methods of interpretation.

[2] J. F. Bagster-Collins, *George Colman the Younger, 1762–1836* (New York, 1946).

has been surveyed[1], as have those of Sheridan Knowles[2] and Fanny Kemble[3]. Virgil R. Stallbaumer deals with "Thomas Holcroft: A Satirist in the Stream of Sentimentalism" (*ELH*, 1936, iii. 31–62); "The Career of George W. Lovell" is briefly outlined by Wilbur D. Dunkel (*Theatre Notebook*, 1951, v. 52–9).

A general survey of English farce from 1800 to 1900 has been provided by Werner Klemm[4]. In a couple of interesting essays Dougald MacMillan has stressed the significance of J. R. Planché's extravaganzas—"Planché's Early Classical Burlesques" (*Studies in Philology*, 1928, xxv. 340–5) and "Some Burlesques with a Purpose, 1830–1870" (*Philological Quarterly*, 1929, viii. 255–63); and A. R. Thompson has made an attempt to define the elusive quality of melodrama (*PMLA*, 1928, xliii. 810–35). One or two other essays on the minor theatre have been written, such as J. D. Gordon's "*The Red Rover* Takes the Boards" (*American Literature*, 1938, x. 66–75); and there are some related studies of subject-material, such as Nils Erik Enkvist's survey of American characters on the stage up to 1870[5]. But for the most part the orientation of those who have concerned themselves with the drama of this period has been directed towards the problems of the poetic drama.

This orientation is evident in the most important general survey—E. Reynolds' *Early Victorian Drama, 1830–1870* (Cambridge, 1936). Although this volume does pay some attention to the minor forms of nineteenth-century play-writing, it is largely concerned with the more "literary" efforts. Numerous articles have been contributed on this subject. In an interesting article on "Shakespeare and Nine-teenth-century Drama" (*ELH*, 1934, i. 163–96), A. E. Du Bois takes issue with the conclusions reached in the original text of this volume. Adopting a sociological approach, Du

---

[1] S. R. Littlewood, *Elizabeth Inchbald and her Circle* (1921).
[2] L. H. Meeks, *Sheridan Knowles and the Theatre of his Time* (1933).
[3] Leota S. Driver, *Fanny Kemble* (1933).
[4] *Die englische Farce im 19. Jahrhundert* (Bern, 1946).
[5] *Caricatures of Americans on the English Stage prior to 1870* (Copenhagen, 1951).

Bois suggests a complex series of causes for the dramatic failure of the time. Of these causes perhaps the chief, in his view, was the rejection of the cosmological in favour of the social point of view, together with a growing feeling of conflict between the individual and society. Aesthetically, there was a trend away from tragedy towards comedy, and, in particular, towards a general confusion of the dramatic genres. Undoubtedly, in any later attempts to elucidate this subject further, Du Bois' careful analysis must be given due consideration.

Where attention is given to particular playwrights, Byron and Shelley naturally take centre stage. David V. Erdman, in "Byron's Stage Fright: The History of his Ambition and Fear of Writing for the Stage" (*ELH*, 1939, vi. 219–43), attempts a psychological approach to the problem, stressing how genuine and sincere were Byron's aspirations and yet how effectively these aspirations were defeated by certain qualities of his own nature. Special weight is laid on the failure of *Marino Faliero*, which, in the critic's view, was largely responsible for Byron's fear of dramatic writing. In "Byron's *Werner* Re-estimated" (*Essays in Dramatic Literature: Parrott Presentation Volume*, ed. Hardin Craig (Princeton, 1935), pp. 243–75), it is argued by T. H. Vail Motter that this play is based on the popular drama of the time and also marks a transition from the early poetic plays to the prose dramas of a later period. The importance of the Gothic stage tradition, as opposed to that of the Gothic novel, is likewise stressed by Bertrand Evans in "Manfred's Remorse and Dramatic Tradition" (*PMLA*, 1947, lxii. 752–73), and by E. D. H. Johnson in "A Political Interpretation of Byron's *Marino Faliero*" (*Modern Language Quarterly*, 1942, iii. 417–25). E. D. H. Johnson essays to demonstrate how Byron's thoughts on contemporary politics have been shaped into dramatic form. Most significant of all attempts to rehabilitate Byron's plays, however, is G. Wilson Knight's, in "The Plays of Lord Byron" (*Times Literary Supplement*, Feb. 3, 1950) and a later book[1], where the thesis is argued that in effect these dramas are conceived in a style well adapted to the present-day radio.

[1] *Lord Byron: Christian Virtues* (1952).

For the dramatic quality of *The Cenci* St John Ervine finds high praise ("Shelley as a Dramatist" (*Royal Society of Literature: Essays by Divers Hands*, 1936, xv)). According to Kenneth N. Cameron and Horst Frenz, the play's stage history shows it to be "a genuine acting drama" (*PMLA*, 1945, lx. 1080–1105). As produced by the Bellingham Theatre Guild in March 1940, a stage text has been published (Caldwell, Idaho, 1945). K. N. Cameron discusses "Shelley's Use of Source Material in *Charles I*" (*Modern Language Quarterly*, 1945, vi. 197–210). D. L. Clark surveys the influence of Shakespeare on the dramatist (*PMLA*, 1939, liv. 261–87).

H. B. Charlton has a lecture-essay on "Browning as Dramatist" (Manchester, 1939) and W. L. Phelps prints two interesting letters bearing on the Browning-Macready quarrel (*Times Literary Supplement*, Jan. 28, 1939). J. M. Purcell seeks to explain "The Dramatic Failure of *Pippa Passes*" (*Studies in Philology*, 1939, xxxvi. 77–87), but his basic assumption is queried by J. M. Ariel in "Is *Pippa Passes* a Dramatic Failure?" (*Studies in Philology*, 1940, xxxvii. 120–9). "Robert Browning and the Experimental Drama" is discussed by J. P. McCormick (*PMLA*, 1953, lxviii. 982–91).

Among other cognate essays there should be noted M. Norton's presentation of Joanna Baillie's dramatic principles (*Review of English Studies*, 1947, xxiii. 131–43), F. S. Boas' study of "R. H. Horne: His Plays and 'Farthing Epic'" (*Royal Society of Literature: Essays by Divers Hands*, 1944, xxi. 24–45), and H. W. Donner's volume on T. L. Beddoes[1]. The stylistic weakness of the poet-dramatists is discussed in Moody E. Prior's *The Language of Tragedy* (New York, 1947), and some relevant material appears in Robert Fricker's *Das historische Drama in England von der Romantik bis zur Gegenwart* (Bern, 1940).

[1] *Thomas Lovell Beddoes: The Making of a Poet* (Oxford, 1935).

APPENDIX A

THE THEATRES, 1800–1850

I. *London and Environs*

IN this list I have included all the theatres and houses of entertainment known to me between the opening and the middle of
the century. This account, of course, could have been extended
to great length by the enumeration of managers and the occupancy
of actors, but such detail appeared not to have importance enough
for inclusion here. I have restricted myself, therefore, to the
outstanding facts, which I have endeavoured to make as accurate
as possible. It will be observed that change of name was common
in this period, and I have thought it best to tabulate the theatres
separately under their various titles rather than group these titles
under a single heading. Full cross-references indicate the history
of any single building during the half-century.

Almost all these theatres are new. In 1800 only nine theatres
were in regular use: *Drury Lane, Covent Garden,* the *Opera House*
in the *Haymarket,* the *Theatre Royal, Haymarket, Sadler's Wells,*
the *Royal Amphitheatre,* the *Royal Circus,* the *Royalty* and the
Sans Souci. Of these, practically all were rebuilt during this era,
and, as will be realised, many fresh playhouses rose in rivalry
to them in many districts of London.

The Academic Theatre (Leicester-place, Leicester-square). Under
this name the *Sans Souci* was opened in 1806 as a Dramatic
Academy[1].

The Adelphi (Strand) [Adel.]. As the *Adelphi,* the old *Sans
Pareil* was opened on Saturday, Oct. 23, 1819. This theatre was
one of the best of the minors, F. H. Yates, Daniel Terry, the
Mathews, B. N. Webster and Madame Celeste being among its
most famous managers. It was rebuilt in 1858. Noted for weird
and wonderful melodrama, it favoured the introduction of strange
"effects" and of animal performers. Towards the close of the
period it was also becoming famous for its burlesques.

The Albert Saloon, or *Royal Albert Saloon* (Shepherdess-walk,
Britannia Fields, Hoxton). This house of entertainment seems to
have been opened in 1844. In its most flourishing days it was
owned by H. Brading. A remarkable feature in it was the two

---

[1] See *The News* for March 16, 1806.

stages built at right angles to one another, one opening into a closed theatre, the other in front of an open-air auditorium.

The Albion Theatre (Windmill-street, Haymarket). Not much is known of this house. It was opened about 1832 and renamed the following year as the *New Queen's*. Its short life was ended in 1836.

The Aquatic Theatre. See *Sadler's Wells.*

The Argyll Theatre or *Argyll Rooms* (Argyll-street, Regent-street). French plays were given here by subscription between 1819 and 1823. See *The New Private Saloon Theatre.*

Astley's Pavilion. See *The Olympic Theatre.*

Astley's Theatre. See *The Royal Amphitheatre.*

The Bower Saloon (Stangate-street, Lambeth). This house of variety entertainment was opened in 1837 by Phillips. It later became the *Royal Stangate Theatre*, which was closed in 1878.

The Britannia Theatre or *Saloon* (High-street, Hoxton). Presenting the usual mixed fare of "illegitimate" drama, the *Britannia*, managed by Lane from 1841 to 1849, was directed for fifty years (1849–99) by his widow, Mrs Sarah Lane.

The Brunswick Theatre. See *The New Royal Brunswick Theatre.*

The City Theatre. See *The New City Theatre.*

The City of London Theatre. See *The Royal City of London Theatre.*

The Clarence Theatre. See *The Royal Clarence Theatre.*

The Coburg Theatre. See *The Royal Coburg Theatre.*

The Colosseum Theatre (Albany-street, Regent's Park) [Col.]. This house was opened for minor shows and variety entertainments on Wednesday, July 12, 1837.

Covent Garden, Theatre Royal [C.G.]. As rebuilt in 1792[1], Covent Garden stood unaltered until it was burned to the ground on Sept. 20, 1808. The century opened with a bitter dispute between the management and the actors (season 1799–1800)[2]. In 1803 Kemble purchased a share in the theatre and took part in its direction. On the destruction of their house the actors, in 1808, moved to the *Opera House* in the *Haymarket*. The foundation stone of a new structure, designed by Robert Smirke, was laid on Dec. 12, 1808, and this new *Covent Garden* was completed by September 18 of the following year. The old building, which had an ovoid auditorium, held 3013 persons[3]; the new building, in

---

[1] See *A History of English Drama*, iii. 229.

[2] See *A Statement of the Differences subsisting between the Proprietors and Performers of the Theatre-Royal, Covent Garden* (1800).

[3] Gilliland, *The Dramatic Mirror* (1808), i. 135–8. The pit held 632, the boxes 1200, the first gallery 820 and the upper gallery 361.

point of capacity, seems to have been a trifle smaller, but its stage
for accommodation and excellence of machinery was considered
"superior to that of any theatre in Europe[1]." On its opening,
the attempt of the managers to raise the prices led to the notorious
O.P. riots[2]. In 1823 Charles Kemble assumed full control; under
his management and with the assistance of Edmund Kean (1827–
33) there was presented here a series of elaborate Shakespeare
productions. Alfred Bunn in October 1833 took over the management of the two patent theatres; in October 1835 a new lessee,
Osbaldistone, tried the experiment of reducing prices—but without success; the Macready management lasted from 1837 to 1839;
that of Vestris and Mathews from 1839 to 1842. The next years
saw the gradual encroachment of musical shows, and on Tuesday,
April 6, 1847, the theatre was formally opened as *The Royal
Italian Opera House*. This was burned in 1856; the present
Covent Garden Opera House was opened two years later.

The Dominion of Fancy Theatre (Strand, "between South-
ampton-street and Exeter 'Change"). This was opened on Friday,
March 1, 1816, for the exhibition of "pieces of mechanism,
ombres, chinois, etc."

Drury Lane, Theatre Royal [D.L.]. The latest Drury Lane house
had been built by Holland in 1794[3]. For the seasons 1800–1 and
1801–2 Kemble was in command. On his withdrawal, the theatre
sank steadily in dignity and worth; Feb. 24, 1809, saw its complete
destruction by fire. During the period from October 1809 to
May 1812, the Theatre Royal company acted at the King's
Theatre in the Haymarket (March–May 1809) and at the Lyceum.
£400,000 was subscribed for a new building, the foundation-stone
of which was laid on Oct. 29, 1811, and which was formally
opened on October 10 of the following year. It was slightly
smaller than the 1794 structure, but still too large for the production of intimate plays. When Elliston was manager, the
interior was reconstructed under Beazley's direction; this, with
minor alterations, remains to the present day. At first managed
by Arnold and others, in 1814 it was taken over by a committee
which included Lord Byron. Edmund Kean aided in keeping
the house from bankruptcy. In 1818 Stephen Kemble became
manager and prices were lowered from 5s. and 3s. to 3s. and 2s.
The following year the theatre was leased to R. W. Elliston, who,
however, was forced to abandon it in 1823. Kean, Macready and
Liston were then its most noted actors. Various other lessees

---

[1] *Covent-Garden Journal*, i. 61.
[2] See *supra*, pp. 9–10.
[3] See *A History of English Drama*, iii. 229.

were secured, but all ended in failure. The notorious Alfred Bunn management of the two patent theatres dates from October 1833 to 1839. In 1841 Macready assumed control, but was compelled to retire in 1843, when Bunn once more took over the management, with no more successful results.

Ducrow's New National Arena (Church-street, Whitechapel). This house was opened on Monday, Jan. 27, 1834, but I know nothing more of its history.

The Eagle Saloon, also called *The Grecian Saloon* and *The Olympic Saloon* (Shepherdess-walk, Britannia Fields, Hoxton). Built by Thomas Rose about 1838, as the *Grecian*, this entertainment theatre began to present "illegitimate" dramas regularly from 1843. It was taken over by Benjamin Conquest in 1851 and rebuilt by him in 1877; now it is used by the Salvation Army. Evidently one of the most famous of the variety houses, its name is immortalised in the still-remembered song, "Pop goes the weasel."

The East London Theatre (Wellclose-square, E.) [E.L.]. Under the name of the *East London*, the *Royalty* was opened in August 1816, with considerable renovations. It had not a very distinguished career, and, after being extensively altered in 1819 (opening Wednesday, Nov. 3), was burned down in 1826. On its site was erected *The Royal Brunswick Theatre*.

The Effingham Saloon (Whitechapel). This saloon theatre was opened in 1843 and rebuilt in 1867. It was burned in 1870, re-erected and again destroyed by fire.

The English Opera House. See *The Lyceum Theatre*.

The Fitzroy Theatre. See *The Royal Fitzroy Theatre*.

Garrick's Subscription Theatre (Leman-street, Goodman's Fields). The *Garrick* had been erected on the site of the old *Goodman's Fields Theatre*, and was opened on Monday, Jan. 3, 1831. It was burned in 1846 and rebuilt by B. O. Conquest. In 1859 it was used as a music-hall.

The German Theatre (Leicester-place, Leicester-square) [German]. This is but a new name for the *Sans Souci*, used for the performance of German dramas by "Schirmer's Children" during the season 1805–6. It opened under the new title on Wednesday, July 17, 1805.

The Globe Theatre or *Rotunda* (Blackfriars-road). This was opened as a theatre in 1833; by 1838, however, it had been turned into a concert hall.

The Grecian Saloon. See *The Eagle Saloon*.

Haymarket, King's Theatre or *Opera House* [H.[1]]. A new King's Theatre had been built in 1790[1], and this, about 1801, was

[1] See *A History of English Drama*, iii. 230.

remodelled by Marinari. The stage was very large, 60 feet deep, 80 feet broad and 46 feet from box to box. Apparently at this theatre "persons could walk from the pit or boxes behind the scenes during the performance[1]." In 1809 it was used by the homeless patent companies. A reconstruction was undertaken in 1818; in 1867 a fire destroyed the building; and a new Opera House was erected in 1871-2. This was later known as *Her Majesty's* and was pulled down in 1892.

Haymarket, Theatre Royal [H.[2]]. The original "Little Theatre[2]" as built by Foote in 1766, was managed till 1820 by George Colman the Younger, under whose direction it had a highly successful career, specialising in farces and lighter pieces. On Colman's retiral, a new building was opened (on Wednesday, July 4, 1821) by Morris, near the old site. In 1837 B. N. Webster assumed the management. Here Samuel Phelps and Madame Celeste first appeared in London, while from 1839 to 1841 Macready and Helen Faucit acted as "stars." Webster retired from the management in 1853.

Little Drury Lane. On Monday, April 19, 1813, an announcement was made by the managers of the *Olympic Pavilion* that their theatre would open under this name. The patentees objected and the title was abandoned.

The Lyceum (Strand) [Lyc.]. Often described as the *Large Theatre, Lyceum*, this building had originally been erected in 1765 as an exhibition room for artists, but by 1790 it was being used for variety entertainments by Charles Dibdin. In 1794 it was rebuilt, and when the century opened it was presenting such attractions as "Musical Glasses," "Phantasmagoria" and battle pictures, with, it is interesting to note, illumination by gas. The first theatrical show I have been able to trace here appears in 1807. In 1809 S. J. Arnold received a licence to open it for musical plays, which he did on Friday, April 21, 1809. From 1809 to 1812 it housed the Drury Lane company and then once more returned to musical drama. On Saturday, June 15, 1816, still under Arnold's direction, it was formally opened as *The English Opera House* [E.O.H.], after almost complete rebuilding. This was burned down in 1830, when Arnold's company acted in various theatres, chiefly the *Adelphi*. The present *Lyceum*, as designed by Beazley, was opened on Monday, July 14, 1834, for "the representation of English operas and the encouragement of indigenous musical talent[3]." From 1844 to 1847 it was managed by Robert and Mary Keeley; in 1847

[1] Gilliland, *op. cit.* i. 167.
[2] See *A History of English Drama*, iii. 229.
[3] The present building was actually reconstructed about 1904.

Vestris and Mathews took it over, the latter retiring in 1855. In the bills, both *Lyceum* and *English Opera House* are used to describe this building.

The Marylebone Theatre (Church-street, Edgware-road) [M'bone]. Under this name the *New Royal Sussex Theatre* (or *Royal Pavilion, West*) opened, it is said, in 1837; I have been unable to discover an earlier record than 1844.

The Minor Theatre (Catherine-street, Strand). In 1829 the *Theatre of Variety* seems to have assumed this name. Here stage-struck youths were encouraged to pay for the privilege of appearing in dramatic rôles.

Miss Kelly's Theatre and Dramatic School (73 Dean-street, Soho-square) [Kelly's]. Under the patronage of the Duke of Devonshire, and fortified with a "minor" licence, Miss Kelly opened this (the first of the personally-named theatres) on Monday, May 25, 1840. It was used by her for the presentation of plays for a few years; after 1850 it became *The Soho* and *The Royalty*.

The New Theatre (Tottenham-street, Tottenham-court-road) [New]. This house, "the decorations designed and executed by Mr Greenwood" and "licensed by Act of Parliament," was opened on the site of *The New Royal Riding School* on Monday, April 23, 1810. The following season it was renamed *The Regency*.

The New City Theatre (Milton-street, Fore-street, Cripplegate) [City]. *The New City Theatre* was opened by John Kemble Chapman on Monday, April 4, 1831, and ran till 1836, when it was demolished. It was among the more respectable of the "minors," and welcomed such performers as Kean, Mrs Stirling and Webster to its boards. For a time, from November 1833, Moncrieff was its manager. An effort was made here to create a Dramatic Academy, and for one season at least the house was run in conjunction with *The Royal Coburg*.

The New Private Saloon Theatre, Argyle-street. The building was opened in July 1807, and a few old plays were performed occasionally. As the *Argyll Rooms*, it later (1819–23) witnessed the production of some French dramas.

The New Queen's Theatre. See *The Albion Theatre*.

The New Royal Brunswick Theatre (Goodman's Fields). After the burning of *The East London Theatre* in April 1826, a new theatre was erected and opened on Monday, Feb. 25, 1828, as the *Brunswick*. The following Thursday, during rehearsal, the entire fabric collapsed.

---

[1] *The Dramatic Magazine* (1829), pp. 173–4.

The New Royal Riding School, late His Majesty's Ancient Concert Rooms, Tottenham-street. I find a pantomime presented here in 1808. On the site of this building rose *The New* (later *The Regency*) *Theatre.*

The New Royal Sussex Theatre (Church-street, Edgware-road). This was apparently opened in 1832, and was later renamed as *The Royal Pavilion, West,* and the *Marylebone.*

The New Royal West London Theatre (Tottenham-street) [W.L.]. After considerable "improvements" *The Regency* (formerly *The New*) opened under this name on Tuesday, Dec. 26, 1820. In 1822 it was described[1] as "the smallest of these places devoted to the drama; and being of too humble pretensions to create jealousy, is permitted to play tragedy, comedy, or farce, in as legitimate a manner as the company is capable of doing." Later it became the *Tottenham-street Theatre* and *The Queen's Theatre.*

The New Standard Theatre. See *The Royal Standard Theatre.*

The New Strand Theatre. See *The Strand Theatre.*

The Olympic Theatre (Wych-street, or Newcastle-street, Strand) [Olym.]. As the *Olympic Pavilion* [Pav.] or *Olympic Saloon,* this house was opened by Philip Astley on Monday, Dec. 1, 1806. In 1807 it was called *Astley's New Olympic Pavilion* and in 1808 *Astley's Pavilion.* Thereafter, it was usually named *The Pavilion,* until it was taken over by Elliston in 1814, who, after failing to open it as *Little Drury Lane* (q.v.), styled it *The Olympic.* The opening day was Tuesday, Feb. 8, 1814. Rebuilt in 1818, it was, from 1819 to 1831, managed by a variety of directors, including Oxberry and Vining. At this time it specialised in melodrama. In 1831 Madame Vestris took control and, with her extravaganzas and light entertainments, made it one of the most refined theatres in London. In 1839 Vestris and Mathews moved to *Covent Garden,* leaving *The Olympic* to Samuel Butler, who in 1841 abandoned it to George Wild. In 1846 Miss Kate Howard and in 1847 Davidson undertook the direction. The theatre was burned to the ground in March 1849, and a new house, which was finally closed in 1899, was erected the following year. The importance of the Vestris management of 1831-9 cannot be minimised.

The Olympic Pavilion. See *The Olympic Theatre.*

The Olympic Saloon. See *The Olympic Theatre* and *The Eagle Saloon.*

The Orange-street Theatre (King's-road, Chelsea). This is said to have been used in 1831.

The Pantheon (Oxford-street). The older *Pantheon* had been

[1] *The Percy Anecdotes Original and Select* (1822), p. 168.

burned in 1792[1], but a new house under this name was opened on Thursday, Feb. 27, 1812. It was used only during 1812 and 1813.

The Pavilion (Wych-street, Strand). See *The Olympic Theatre*.

The Pavilion (Whitechapel). See *The Royal Pavilion*.

The Peckham Theatre (High-street, Peckham). This was used in 1828.

The Prince's Theatre (King-street, St James's) [Prince's]. The *St James's* seems to have assumed this name for a time on Monday, April 27, 1840.

The Princess's Theatre (Oxford-street) [P'cess]. The *Princess's* began its history as *The Royal Bazaar, The British Diorama and Exhibition of Works of Art* in 1828. The building was burned one year after opening and was re-erected in 1830, when various entertainments were given. In 1834 it seems to have been called *The Queen's* and, after a rebuilding in 1836, *The Court*[2]. In 1840 it became *The Princess's*, and was opened originally (on Wednesday, Sept. 30) for promenade concerts and musical shows. For a number of years foreign opera in English was its chief attraction, mainly directed by one Maddox. In 1850 the theatre was taken over by Charles Kean.

The Queen's Theatre (Fitzroy-square, Tottenham-court-road) [Queen's]. Under this title the Tottenham-street house was opened on Thursday, Feb. 3, 1831 (see *The New Royal Riding School, The New Theatre, The Regency, The Regency Theatre of Varieties, The New Royal West London Theatre* and *The Tottenham-street Theatre*). George Macfarren was its first manager. Two years later, it became *The Royal Fitzroy Theatre*, but a reversion was made to the name of *The Queen's* on Monday, Jan. 19, 1835. In 1865, under the management of the Bancrofts, it became *The Prince of Wales's*.

The Regency Theatre (Fitzroy-square, Tottenham-court-road) [Reg.]. Under this title *The New Theatre* was opened on Monday, Oct. 28, 1810, with Moncrieff as manager. It had not a very distinguished career. In 1818 it reopened, after a period of inactivity, as *The Regency Theatre of Varieties*.

The Regency Theatre of Varieties (Fitzroy-square, Tottenham-court-road). The old *Regency* was opened under this name on Thursday, July 17, 1818. In 1820 it became *The New Royal West London Theatre*.

The Royal Adelphi Theatre. See *The Adelphi Theatre*.

The Royal Albert Saloon. See *The Albert Saloon*.

The Royal Amphitheatre (Westminster Bridge Road) [R.A.].

[1] See *A History of English Drama*, iii. 230.
[2] I have been unable to verify these statements.

After the burning of the original circus-ring theatre on Friday, July 2, 1803[1], plans were immediately made for a new house, which opened on Monday, April 2, 1804. Its most famous period was between 1830 and 1841, when Ducrow was manager. In 1807 it was called *Astley's Royal Amphitheatre* and in 1808 *Astley's Amphitheatre*. Throughout its career it specialised in equestrian melodrama and spectacle.

The Royal Borough Theatre (Tooley-street, S.E.). This was used between 1834 and 1836, and then destroyed.

The Royal Circus (Blackfriars-road) [R.C.]. A rival of *Astley's*, *The Royal Circus* gained some notoriety through its "burletta" exploits[2]. In 1810 it was taken over by Elliston and renamed *The Surrey Theatre*, but, when Elliston moved to *The Olympic Pavilion* in 1814 and Thomas Dibdin became manager, it was redecorated and rebuilt "on the old plan" and once more named *The Royal Circus* (opened on Monday, July 4, 1814). Its second title (*The Surrey*) was given to it again on Monday, July 5, 1819.

The Royal City of London Theatre (near Bishopsgate Station, Norton Folgate) [C.L.]. This house was opened on Monday, March 27, 1837, by Cockerton, and made a speciality of domestic melodrama. By the middle of the century it had fallen to a very low level, and was eventually closed in 1868[3].

The Royal Clarence Theatre (King's Cross, New-road) [Clar.]. Under this name *The Royal Panharmonion* was opened on Monday, May 7, 1832.

The Royal Coburg Theatre (Waterloo-road) [Cob.]. This theatre was built by Dunn and Jones in 1816, and was opened, "under the patronage of H.R.H. Prince Leopold of Saxe-Coburg," on Monday, May 11, 1818. The architect was Rudolph Cabanal of Aachen. It had a very deep and narrow stage (94 feet by 32 feet) and in 1820 boasted the possession of a magnificent looking-glass curtain. In 1819 it was managed by Moncrieff; under him and others it indulged in melodrama of the most startling nature; performed before audiences of the "lowest kind." Occasionally, however, West End players of distinction, such as Edmund Kean and Madame Vestris, made their appearance on its boards. In July 1833 it was formally renamed *The Royal Victoria Theatre*.

The Royal Fitzroy Theatre (Fitzroy-square, Tottenham-court-

---

[1] It had been built in 1777. See *A History of English Drama*, iii, 230.

[2] See *id.* p. 230; and *supra*, p. 140.

[3] On this theatre see M. Williams, *Some London Theatres* (1883).

road). Under this title, *The Queen's* was opened in the autumn of 1833. It was renamed *The Queen's* on Monday, Jan. 19, 1835.

The Royal Kent Theatre (Kensington High-street). This theatre was opened in 1834, and, after a chequered career, was closed in 1840.

The Royal Manor House Theatre (King's-road, Chelsea). This theatre was opened about 1838 and continued its career, partly under the management of E. L. Blanchard, till 1841[1].

The Royal Marylebone Theatre. See *The Marylebone Theatre.*

The Royal Panharmonion Subscription Theatre (King's Cross, New-road). This, the first King's Cross theatre, was opened on April 18, 1831. The following year it became *The Royal Clarence Theatre.*

The Royal Pavilion, West. See *The New Royal Sussex Theatre.*

The Royal Pavilion (Whitechapel-road, Mile-End). This house, celebrated for "Newgate melodrama," was opened, under the direction of Wyatt and Farrell, on Monday, Nov. 10, 1828. It was burned to the ground in 1856, but, rebuilt, it has continued its activities to the present day, being now the home of Yiddish drama in the East End.

The Royal Princess's Theatre. See *The Princess's Theatre.*

The Royal Standard Theatre (Shoreditch) [Stand.]. This theatre was opened for various entertainments in 1835, when it seated over 2000 people. In 1845 it was remodelled and was opened in January of that year as *The New Standard.* In 1866 it was destroyed by fire and rebuilt in 1868.

The Royalty Theatre (Wellclose-square) [Royalty]. The old *Royalty* had been built in the eighteenth century by John Palmer[2]. Denied a licence for plays, its managers specialised in spectacular and musical shows. In 1800 it was owned by Philip Astley, who seems to have used it as a winter house. In August 1816 the interior was remodelled, and the new building opened as *The East London Theatre.*

The Royal Victoria Theatre (Waterloo-road) [Vic.]. *The Royal Coburg* definitely changed its name to this title in July 1833[3]. It became one of the most successful of the minors, and was "in a good way" under Abbot in 1834. It has, of course, since won fame for its Shakespeare productions as the "Old Vic."[4]

Sadler's Wells Theatre (Rosebery Avenue, Islington) [S.W.].

---

[1] See E. L. Blanchard, *Some Managerial Memories* (*The Theatre Annual*, 1885, pp. 16–21).
[2] See *A History of English Drama*, iii. 230.
[3] See *The Times* for Tuesday, July 2, 1833.
[4] See Cicely Hamilton and Lilian Baylis, *The Old Vic.* (1926).

The basic structure of this theatre dates back to 1765[1]. Under a variety of managements, and with the aid of the New River, it indulged freely in nautical melodrama, using in 1806 the title of *The Aquatic Theatre*. Charles Dibdin, Thomas King and William Siddons were among its early managers. In 1844 Samuel Phelps adopted it for his remarkable Shakespeare and other "legitimate" productions. His direction continued until 1862. The theatre as standing at present has the distinction of possessing the most ancient fabric of any playhouse in London.

The St James's Theatre (King-street, St James's) [St. J.]. This theatre was opened on Monday, Dec. 14, 1835 by John Braham and for a few years struggled on precariously with musical shows. By 1840 it was "to be let," was renamed *The Prince's* for a short time, and eventually became the home in London of drama in French. Its architect was Samuel Beazley.

The Sans Pareil Theatre (Strand) [Sans P.]. This was built by one Scott and was opened on Friday, Nov. 27, 1806. It had a fair career among the minors and in 1819 was renamed *The Adelphi*.

The Sans Souci Theatre (Leicester-place, Leicester-square) [Sans S.]. As a house of varieties, *The Sans Souci* had been opened by Dibdin in the eighteenth century. It had a chequered career in the nineteenth, sometimes presenting crude farce, sometimes (as *The German*) acting as a home of German drama, sometimes professing, as *The Academic Theatre*, to be a Dramatic Academy. Its importance is slight.

The Standard Theatre. See *The Royal Standard Theatre.*

The Strand Theatre (Strand) [Strand]. This house was opened in 1820 as "Reinagle's and Barker's New Panorama near the New Church in the Strand," which later became "Burford's Panorama." Rebuilt in 1831, the house was opened on Thursday, Jan. 26, 1832, as *The New Strand Subscription Theatre*. A varied career followed. At first extraordinary devices were used to evade the letter of the law, but in 1835 a partial licence was secured, and on April 25, 1836, the playhouse was formally opened under the direction of W. J. Hammond and Douglas Jerrold. William Farren the Younger, who assumed management in 1848, brought it to a state of unprecedented popularity, and it had later glories (after 1858) with burlesque. Even in 1840 it was praised for "its tiny spectacles...humorous burlesques...and spirited actors[2]." The theatre was eventually destroyed to make way for Aldwych Underground Station.

The Surrey Theatre (Blackfriars Road) [Surrey]. Under this

---

[1] See *A History of English Drama*, iii. 230.
[2] Tomlins, *op. cit.* p. 63.

title *The Royal Circus* was opened under Elliston's management on Monday, April 23, 1810. On July 4, 1814, it reverted to its original name, but became *The Surrey* once more on Monday, July 5, 1819. T. J. Dibdin and R. W. Elliston were its two most famous early managers. In 1827 the latter reassumed control and under his direction the theatre became exceedingly popular. Melodramas of many kinds were exhibited here; comedy and farce under Jerrold were ably interpreted by T. P. Cooke; and sporadic attempts were made in the "legitimate" way. Altogether *The Surrey* was one of the most important of the minors. It was burned down in 1865, to be rebuilt a few years later.

The Theatre of Variety (Catherine-street, Strand). I find this house exhibiting a few shows in October 1823. It was this house which in 1829 was named *The Minor Theatre*.

Tottenham-street Theatre (Fitzroy-square, Tottenham-court-road) [Tottenham]. Under this name, the *Royal West London* was presenting plays in the spring of 1830.

Vauxhall Gardens (Vauxhall) [Vauxhall]. The first records of plays produced here seem to occur in 1826, when Moncrieff became manager. Thereafter a few vaudevilles and operettas were originally produced at the Gardens.

The Westminster Subscription Theatre (Tothill-street, S.W.). Under T. W. Davenport, who had been stage-manager at *The Strand*, this theatre was opened on Thursday, May 17, 1832, and remained open until 1835.

It must be noted that, in addition to these playhouses and places of entertainment, there were a number of private theatres and of saloons where dramatic pieces were occasionally performed.

II. *The Provinces*

Aberdeen. In 1745 and 1751 there are records of outside players performing in a wooden booth somewhere without the city walls. In 1768 there was a *New Inn Theatre* in Castle-street, in 1779 another in Shoe-lane, and about 1780 another in Queen-street. The first permanent playhouse, however, was the old *Marischal-street Theatre Royal*, opened in 1795 under the management of Stephen Kemble. It held £65. Its history is traced by J. Keith Angus in *A Scotch Playhouse* (1875). Aberdeen had a stock company and was also the chief town of a Northern circuit.

Andover. The theatre at Andover, in the Thornton circuit, seems to have been opened early in 1803.

Arbroath. This was in the Ryder circuit, which embraced

Aberdeen, Glasgow, Edinburgh, and Dundee. A *New Theatre* was built in 1793 and the Trades Hall was used for plays from 1812.

Aylsham. This town had a "theatre" in 1757, and performances were given there in the nineteenth century.

Bath. A booth of some kind existed at Bath in the early years of the eighteenth century. In 1747 Hippisley started a permanent troupe, but in 1750 a certain John Palmer raised subscriptions for, and erected, a new theatre in *Orchard-street.* This house for long maintained a theatrical monopoly, although a rival theatre existed in 1753–4; and on its reconstruction in 1767 a special patent valid for 21 years was issued to Palmer's son. This was dated Nov. 26, 1767, and was operative from March 25, 1768. This Theatre Royal had a distinguished history in theatrical annals. It was closed in 1805 to give place for the *Beaufort-square Theatre.* This held £300. In 1834 Macready undertook its management, and from 1844 to 1850 Mrs Macready directed its fortunes. Until about 1817 the Bath playhouse was run in close connection with that at Bristol. A regular stock-company was maintained, which was supplemented on occasion by London "stars."

Beccles. A theatre was built here by David Fisher in 1819.

Beverley. A *Walkergate Theatre* was used in the late eighteenth century by Tate Wilkinson. Its place was taken by *The Playhouse,* opened in 1804. A *Victoria Pavilion* was erected about 1842.

Birmingham. There are records of several theatres in Birmingham in the early eighteenth century, but the first of real importance was the *King-street Theatre* opened in 1751–2. This, after a series of remodellings, was closed in 1780. In 1774–5 another and larger theatre in *New-street* was opened. Burned in 1792, it was rebuilt in 1795. This held £268. W. C. Macready managed it for a decade during the nineteenth century. A patent for a Theatre Royal was obtained in 1807. This house was burned in 1820 and rebuilt the same year.

Bridlington. A theatre, still standing, was opened here about 1803.

Brighton. In 1774 Brighton had a *North-street Theatre* which gave way in 1790 to the *Duke-street Theatre,* a small house, holding £100. This existed till in 1807 a *New-road Theatre* was opened.

Bristol. Bristol had booths in the early eighteenth century, and John Hippisley fitted out a regular *Jacob's Well Theatre* in 1729. The *King-street Theatre* was opened in 1766 and a Royal licence was secured in 1778. Until 1817 Bristol co-operated with Bath.

Bungay. A theatre was built here in 1827 by David Fisher, but a *New Theatre* had been in existence since 1773.

Cheltenham. A theatre was in existence here in the early eighteenth century; see T. Hannam-Clark, *Drama in Gloucestershire* (1928).

Chichester. A theatre was built at Chichester in 1792; it held only £50.

Cirencester. A theatre was built at Cirencester in 1794; see T. Hannam-Clark, *op. cit.* pp. 129–32.

Dereham. David Fisher built a theatre at Dereham in 1816, but the Norwich players had visited the town as early as 1758.

Doncaster. Doncaster, in the York circuit, had a theatre which was opened in 1776.

Dundee. In the Aberdeen circuit, Dundee had a booth or theatre from the second half of the eighteenth century. The Town Hall was used for performances from 1755 to 1767. A *Yeoman Shore* theatre was opened in 1800, a *Theatre Royal* in 1810, and a *Thistle Hall* theatre in 1840. See R. Lawson, *The Story of the Scots Stage* (1917).

Edinburgh. Booths existed in Edinburgh at an early date, and one in *Carrubber's Close* was fitted out by Allan Ramsay in 1736 as a permanent theatre. A *New Concert Hall* in the Cannongate about a decade later was used for dramatic entertainments. This in 1767 became a *Theatre Royal.* It held £70. A new *Theatre Royal* in Prince's-street holding £140 was opened in the winter of 1769. In 1809 a patent was secured by Henry Siddons who opened a *New Theatre Royal* in a house which had been used in 1790 as *The Amphitheatre, or Edinburgh Equestrian Circus.* In 1811 the company moved back to Prince's-street, and the "New Theatre Royal" became, first, *Corri's Pantheon,* and, later, *The Caledonian Theatre* and *The Adelphi.* The Edinburgh theatre had a notable series of managers and important stock-companies. At the *Theatre Royal* some of the finest London actors made their appearance. See J. C. Dibdin, *The Edinburgh Stage* (1888).

Exeter. In the Plymouth circuit, Exeter had an "old" theatre erected in 1749. The *New Theatre* opened in 1787 held £100. It is interesting to note that between 1811 and 1813 Edmund Kean, then unrecognised, appeared on its boards. The management seems to have been a progressive one, for as early as 1817 gas was introduced. A new theatre was opened in 1821 to take the place of the 1787 structure, which had been burned the year previous. This in turn was destroyed in 1885.

Eye. David Fisher built a theatre here in 1815.

Fakenham. A playhouse at Fakenham was in use during the nineties of the eighteenth century.

Glasgow. In 1764 a playhouse was erected, outside the borough, at the junction of Hope-street and Argyle-street. In 1782 a new house in Dunlop-street, known as *The Caledonian*, was opened. It held £90. A *Queen-street Theatre* holding £260 appeared in 1805, and this was followed by *The York-street Theatre* (opened October 1829), *The Adelphi* (opened December 1842), *The City* (opened May 1845), *The Prince's* (opened January 1849), and *The Queen's* (opened October 1849). The Glasgow theatres had important managers and some brilliant stock-companies. See W. Baynham, *The Glasgow Stage* (1892).

Gloucester. A *Barton-street* Theatre was opened in 1763; the *New Theatre* was opened in 1791.

Grantham. A theatre had been established here as early as the fifties of the eighteenth century; it formed part of the Lincoln circuit.

Halesworth. A theatre was built here by David Fisher in 1809.

Holt. In 1791 the White Lion Inn was used for dramatic performances and touring actors performed there in the early years of the nineteenth century.

Hull. Hull belonged to the York circuit. The *Lowgate Theatre* was being used in 1768. The following year a *Theatre Royal* was opened in Finkle-street. This was supplanted by a new *Theatre Royal* in Humber-street, opened in 1810 and burned in 1859. Another house, first a circus (1820), then called the *Sans Pareil* (1825), the *Minor* (1826), the *Summer* (1827) and the *Clarence* (1831), was eventually pulled down in 1836. A third playhouse, the *Adelphi*, was opened in 1827, while the *Royal Amphitheatre* (1846) and the *Queen's* (1847) added a further element of competition.

King's Lynn. St George's Hall was used for performances till a *Theatre Royal* was erected in 1815. This is still standing.

Leeds. Also in the York circuit, Leeds had a theatre by 1771.

Leicester. In 1750 the first permanent theatre was built at Leicester. A *New Theatre* was opened in 1800 and was closed in 1836.

Lewes. Lewes possessed a booth theatre in the nineteenth century.

Liverpool. Beyond a series of booths Liverpool does not seem to have had a regular theatre till on June 5, 1772, a patented house was opened in Williamson-square. In 1821 *The Royal Court Theatre*, then known as *The Royal Amphitheatre*, was opened.

Lowestoft. A theatre built here by David Fisher in 1827.

Maidstone. The first records of performances at Maidstone seem to be those connected with the performances of a summer company in 1757 led by Wignell. For a time the rude theatre there was run by a Mrs Baker. The *New Theatre*, which held £60, in the High-street was opened on April 12, 1798.

Manchester. Various booths existed in Manchester in the early eighteenth century. In 1775 was opened a *Theatre Royal* in Spring-gardens. This was burned in 1789 and a new building erected on the same site in 1790. A *New Theatre Royal* in Fountain-street was opened in 1807; this was also burned in 1844, and another *Theatre Royal* in Peter-street was opened in 1845. Macready's father was manager from 1807 to 1809. An *Amphitheatre* was opened in 1793. Manchester formed part of the Derby circuit. See W. T. Baker, *The Manchester Stage* (1903).

Margate. Margate was part of a Kent circuit which apparently was established by William Smith in 1762. At this time the performances took place in a converted barn. Charles Mate, who took over the circuit in 1779, succeeded in gaining a patent, and a *Theatre Royal*, holding £80, was opened on June 27, 1787. In the nineteenth century, Margate ceased to be part of a regular circuit and the theatre was open in the summer months only.

Newbury. A *New Theatre* was opened here in November 1802.

Newcastle. This formed part of a regular Newcastle circuit. A *Theatre Royal* was opened in 1789 and a *New Theatre Royal* in 1837.

North Walsham. A theatre was built here by David Fisher in 1828.

Norwich. This was one of the chief towns in a Norwich circuit. Plays were presented here in the early eighteenth century at the *White Swan Inn*. In 1758 Thomas Ivory opened *The New Theatre*, near Chapel Field, and a formal licence was granted in 1768. This house was enlarged in 1801. The later *Theatre Royal* (the house standing today) was opened in 1826. For this and other theatres in the circuit see T. L. G. Burley, *Playhouses and Plays in East Anglia* (1928).

Perth. This town was in Corbett Ryder's circuit. The Glovers' Hall was used for plays in 1786. A *New Theatre*, in the disused Grammar School, was opened in 1810 and closed in 1819. A *Theatre Royal* was opened in August 1820.

Plymouth. An early eighteenth century house, which held £75, was rebuilt in 1804. This formed part of a Plymouth circuit.

Portsmouth. Little seems to be known of the earlier history of the Portsmouth theatre; it formed part of the Winchester circuit.

Reading. In 1788 a theatre in Friar-street, holding £40, was erected by Thornton.

Richmond. A theatre which was regarded as "a model for

theatrical architects" was in existence here in the early nineteenth century. The town was regularly served during the summer months by the London performers.

Sheffield. Early performances were given in the yard of the Angel Inn; a permanent theatre was built in 1762. For a number of years Tate Wilkinson was manager and included the town in various circuits.

Southampton. A *New Theatre* in French-street, holding £100, was opened in 1803.

Stroud. On the theatres at Stroud and Tewkesbury see T. Hannam-Clark, *op. cit.* pp. 132–7.

Sudbury. A theatre was built here by David Fisher in 1814.

Swaffham. A theatre was built here by David Fisher in 1822.

Tunbridge Wells. Tunbridge Wells belonged to the West Kent circuit. Various early performances are chronicled for the period 1700–1800; in 1770 Mrs Baker built there a regular playhouse. A new building was opened on July 8, 1802.

Wakefield. In the York circuit, Wakefield had a theatre from the seventies of the eighteenth century.

Wells. A theatre was built here by David Fisher in 1812.

Winchester. A theatre is recorded at Winchester as early as 1760, although the first regular playhouse was not erected till 1785. This held £60.

Windsor. The Windsor theatre, erected in 1793, was a summer house only and depended largely on royal residence at the Castle. It held £70.

Woodbridge. A theatre was built here by David Fisher in 1814.

Yarmouth. Various makeshift theatres were used here in the early eighteenth century. The present *Theatre Royal*, opened in 1778, is one of the oldest theatres in England.

York. The chief town in an important circuit, York had a royal patent dating from 1759.

III. *The Old Circuits*

Aberdeen. The Northern circuit included, in addition to Aberdeen, the towns of Perth, Montrose and Dundee.

Bath and Bristol. This hardly formed a regular circuit, but until 1817 the theatrical activities of the two towns were closely associated.

Exeter. Plymouth, Weymouth and Exeter for long years were connected by a regular circuit.

Kent. The Kent circuit originally included the following towns: Margate, Canterbury, Dover, Deal, Maidstone, Faversham and

Rochester. Later there was a division made between the East and West Kent circuits.

Manchester. The Manchester circuit included, with Manchester itself, Shrewsbury, Chester, Lichfield and (usually) Buxton.

Newcastle. The earlier circuit included Newcastle, Lancaster, Chester, Whitehaven and Preston. Later the towns visited were Newcastle, Scarborough, Durham, Sunderland, South and North Shields, Stockton, Darlington and Coventry.

Norfolk and Suffolk. Organised by the Fishers; included Halesworth, Wells, Woodbridge, Sudbury, Eye, Dereham, Beccles, Swaffham, Lowestoft, Bungay, North Walsham, Thetford and Newmarket.

Norwich. The order of the Norwich circuit was usually Yarmouth, Ipswich, Norwich, Yarmouth, Bury, Colchester, Ipswich, Norwich, Lynn, Norwich and so back to Yarmouth [see also under Norwich, p. 232].

Winchester. This circuit included Portsmouth, Winchester, Southampton, Chichester and Newport.

York. One of the chief circuits, and that with which Tate Wilkinson in the eighteenth century, and J. P. Kemble in the nineteenth, were associated, included, besides the city of York, Hull, Wakefield, Leeds, Pontefract and Doncaster. [See Thomas Sheppard, *Evolution of the Drama in Hull and District* (1917).]

A few notes are added here on some of the London playhouses, but most of the additional material concerns the provincial theatres. I have found particularly useful *An Alphabetical List of Theatres in the United Kingdom, with the Names of Managers*, compiled by John Miller for the Dramatic Authors' Society in 1833. The only copy of this list I have been able to locate is in Birmingham University Library: since it was intended merely as a notebook, with columns headed "When heard from," "When Paid" and "Remarks," presumably not many exemplars are likely to have been preserved. Its value rests in the facts that it gives a complete register of theatres operative in 1833 and that its naming of managers shows well the working of the circuit system at that time. References to the list are given under the date "1833": theatres added to those recorded in the text are marked by an asterisk.

p. 221] *London Bridge*. This is recorded, under the management of Bedford, in 1833.
    Lyceum. The house was altered in 1816, and the new structure of 1834 was refashioned by Bradwell in 1847.
p. 225] *Royal Clarence*. See M. St Clare Byrne, "Supplement to the

Playbill" (*Times Literary Supplement*, 29/6/1933) and Allan
Wade, "Royal Clarence Theatre" (*id.* 6/7/1933).

р. 226] *Royal Panharmonion.* See under *Royal Clarence*, above.

p 228] *Vaudeville (Leicester-square). This is recorded, under the
management of W. Chaplin, as a theatre in 1833.

Westminster. See article by M. St Clare Byrne, cited above under
Royal Clarence.

Aberdeen. Manager, F. Ryder: 1833.

**Abergavenny.* Managers, Potter and McRoy: 1833.

**Aberystwyth.* Manager, J. Potter: 1833.

**Abingdon.* Manager, Bullen: 1833.

**Alcester.* 1833.

**Alnwick.* 1833.

**Andover.* 1833.

**Arundel.* Manager, Davenport: 1833.

**Ashborne.* Manager, G. Stanton: 1833.

**Ashby de la Zouch.* Manager, J. Bennett: 1833.

**Atherstine.* Manager, M. H. Simpson: 1833.

**Aylesbury.* Manager, H. Jackman: 1833.

p. 229] **Bakewell.* Manager, Thornhill: 1833.

**Banbury.* Manager, H. Jackman: 1833.

**Barnsley.* Manager, Smedley: 1833.

**Barnstaple.* Manager, H. Lee: 1833.

**Barton.* Manager, Smedley: 1833.

Bath. See *Theatre Notebook*, (1945), i. 4; and F. T. Woods,
"Theatrical Performances at Bath in the Eighteenth Century"
(*N.Q.* cxcii. Nov. 1, 1947, pp. 477–8; Nov. 15, pp. 486–90;
Dec. 13, pp. 539–41; Dec. 27, pp. 552–8; cxciii. Jan. 24,
pp. 38–40; March 6, pp. 92–3; June 12, pp. 253–5). In 1833
the manager was E. Barnett.

Beccles. Manager, C. Fisher: 1833.

**Bedford.* Manager, H. Jackman: 1833.

Beverley. Manager, Smedley: 1833.

Birmingham. See Percival Hinton, "The Dramatic Library of
the Old Theatre Royal, Birmingham" (*Theatre Notebook*,
1946, i. 12–13).

**Bishop's Castle.* Manager, Smedley: 1833.

**Blandford.* Manager, W. Shalders: 1833.

**Bodmin.* Manager, Dawson: 1833.

**Bolton.* 1833.

**Boston.* Manager, W. Robertson: 1833.

**Bridgenorth.* Manager, G. Stanton: 1833.

**Bridgewater.* Manager, H. Lee: 1833.

**Bridport.* 1833.

**Brigg.* Manager, Smedley: 1833.

Brighton. Managers, Vining and Bow: 1833.

Bristol. See Rennie Powell, *The Bristol Stage* (1919) and G. T.
Watts, *Theatrical Bristol* (1915).

**Buckingham.* Manager, H. Jackman: 1833.

Bungay. Manager, C. Fisher: 1833.

p. 230] **Burlington Quay.* Manager, Smedley: 1833.

**Burton-on-Trent.* Manager, G. Stanton: 1833.

**Bury St Edmunds.* Manager, J. Smith: 1833.

Buxton. 1833.
Cambridge. Manager, J. Smith: 1833. The Barnwell, Cambridge, theatre existed in 1745 and was rebuilt in 1816. After being used for a mission-hall from 1878, it was refashioned in the present century as the Festival Theatre.
Canterbury. Manager, J. Dowton: 1833.
Cardiff. Manager, H. Collier: 1833.
Cardigan. Manager, H. Collier: 1833.
Carlisle. Manager, J. H. Alexander: 1833.
Carmarthen. Manager, J. Potter: 1833.
Chelmsford. Manager, W. Harvey: 1833.
Cheltenham. Manager, W. A. Spencer: 1833.
Chester. Manager, T. Lewis: 1833.
Colchester. Manager, J. Smith: 1833.
Croydon. Manager, E. Barnett: 1833.
Deal. Manager, J. F. Saville: 1833.
Derby. Manager, T. W. Manley: 1833.
Dereham. Manager, J. Coppin: 1833. The Theatre, rebuilt in 1935, was abandoned in 1938.
Devonport. Manager, Mrs Bennett: 1833.
Doncaster. Manager, W. J. Hammond: 1833.
Dover. Manager, J. Sloman: 1833.
Downham. Manager, C. Fisher: 1833.
Drayton. 1833.
Dudley. 1833.
Dumfries. Manager, W. Copeland: 1833.
Dundee. Manager, T. Ryder: 1833.
Durham. Manager, H. Beverley: 1833.
Eastbourne. Manager, J. Robberds: 1833.
Exeter. Manager, Mrs Bennett: 1833.
Eye. Manager, C. Fisher: 1833.
Falmouth. Manager, J. Dawson: 1833.
Faversham. 1833.
Folkestone. 1833.
Gainsborough. Managers, Huggins and Clarke: 1833.
p. 23 *Gosport.* Managers, Irish and Wilson: 1833.
Grantham. Manager, Mrs T. Robertson: 1833.
Gravesend. 1833.
Greenwich. Manager, J. F. Saville: 1833.
Grimsby. Manager, Smedley: 1833.
Guernsey. Manager, Mrs Bennett: 1833.
Guildford. Manager, E. Barnett: 1833.
Haleston. Manager, J. Dawson: 1833.
Halesworth. Manager, J. Coppin: 1833.
Halifax. Manager, T. W. Manley: 1833.
Harrogate. Manager, J. E. Parry: 1833.
Hastings. Managers, C. Waldegrave and Co.: 1833.
Hemel Hempstead. Manager, Bullen: 1833.
Hereford. Manager, J. Watson: 1833.
Holt. Manager, J. Coppin: 1833.
Horncastle. Manager, Smedley: 1833.
Horsham. Manager, T. Rogers: 1833.
Howden. Manager, Smedley: 1833.

Hull. Manager, S. Downe: 1833.
*Huntingdon. Manager, W. Robertson: 1833.
*Hythe. 1833.
*Ipswich. Manager, J. Smith: 1833. See R. Southern, *The Georgian Playhouse* (1948), pp. 55–6.
*Jersey. Manager, Gibbs: 1833.
*Kendal. A theatre was built here in 1789 and closed in 1823 (*Theatre Notebook*, 1946, i. 17).
*Lancaster. Manager, W. Copeland: 1833.
Leeds. Manager, S. Downe: 1833.
Leicester. Managers, P. Penley and J. Anderson: 1833. A new theatre was built here in 1836 and altered in 1873.
Lewes. 1833.
*Lincoln. Manager, W. Robertson: 1833.
*Litchfield. 1833.
*Little Hampton. 1833.
Liverpool. Managers in 1833: (1) *Theatre Royal*, Clarke and Lewis; (2) *Liver*, Hammond and Raymond; (3) *Queen's*, Hutchinson; (4) *Sans Pareil*, W. Holloway; (5) *Circus*, Armistead and Batty. A *Pavilion* is also recorded.
*Loughborough. Manager, J. P. Cooke.
*Louth. 1833.
Lowestoft. Manager, C. Fisher: 1833.
*Lymington. Manager, Belford: 1833.
*Lynn. Manager, J. Smith: 1833.
Maidstone. Manager, J. Sloman: 1833.
*Malton. Manager, Smedley: 1833.

p. 232]   *Manchester*. Managers, Clarke and Lewis: 1833. See W. A. Hulme, "Early Manchester Theatres" (*Transactions of the North West Group: Society for Theatre Research*, 1951, i. 7–8).
*Mansfield. Manager, Smedley: 1833.
*March. Manager, Smedley: 1833.
Margate. Manager, J. F. Saville: 1833.
*Market Deeping. Manager, Smedley: 1833.
**Market Harborough*. Manager, H. Jackson: 1833.
*Matlock. 1833.
*Melton Mowbray. Manager, Smedley: 1833.
*Merthyr Tydvil. Manager, D. McRoy: 1833.
*Monmouth. 1833.
*Newark. Manager, Mrs T. Robertson: 1833.
Newbury. Manager, E. Barnett: 1833. See *Theatre Notebook* (1945), i. 3.
Newcastle-on-Tyne. Manager, S. Penley: 1833. On plans made for a reconstruction by Benjamin Green in 1836 see *Theatre Notebook* (1946), i. 15. The theatre was rebuilt in 1895 and burned in 1899. See also R. Southern, *The Georgian Playhouse* (1948), pp. 59–61.
**Newcastle-under-Lyme*. Manager, G. Stanton: 1833.
*Newmarket. Manager, C. Fisher: 1833.
*Newport (Isle of Wight). Manager, W. Shalders: 1833.
*Newport (Wales). 1833.
*Newry. 1833.
*Northallerton. Manager, J. E. Parry: 1833. The theatre was

built in 1800 and closed about 1832–3 (*Theatre Notebook* 1946, i. 17).

*Northampton. Manager, J. Scott: 1833.
*North Shields. Manager, H. Beverley: 1833.
North Walsham. 1833.
Norwich. Manager, J. Smith: 1833.
*Nottingham. Manager, T. W. Manley: 1833.
*Oswestry. Manager, G. Stanton: 1833.
*Oundle. Manager, W. Robertson: 1833.
*Oxford. Manager, E. Barnett: 1833.
*Penryn. Manager, J. Dawson: 1833.
*Penzance. Manager, J. Dawson: 1833.
Perth. Manager, T. Ryder: 1833.
*Peterborough. Manager, Mrs T. Robertson: 1833.
Plymouth. Manager, G. Sandford: 1833. See R. Southern, *The Georgian Playhouse* (1948), pp. 56–9.
*Pontefract. Manager, Smedley: 1833.
Portsmouth. Managers, S. Maxfield and H. Kelly: 1833.
*Preston. Manager, W. Burroughs: 1833.
*Ramsgate. Manager, J. F. Saville: 1833.
Reading. Manager, E. Barnett: 1833.
*Retford. Manager, T. W. Manley: 1833.
Richmond (Surrey). Manager, T. W. Jones: 1833.
p. 233] **Richmond* (Yorks). Manager, J. E. Parry: 1833. On this theatre see *Theatre Notebook* (1945), i. 3.
*Rochdale. 1833.
*Rochester. Manager, J. Sloman: 1833.
*Rotherham. 1833.
*Ryde. Manager, E. Barnett: 1833.
*Rye. 1833.
*St Albans. Manager, J. F. Saville: 1833.
*Salisbury. Manager, W. Shalders: 1833.
*Sandwich. Manager, J. F. Saville: 1833.
*Scarborough. Manager, H. Beverley: 1833.
Sheffield. Manager, W. J. Hammond: 1833.
*Shrewsbury. Manager, J. Bennett: 1833.
*Sleaford. Manager, Smedley: 1833.
Southampton. Managers, S. Maxfield and J. Kelly: 1833.
*South Shields. Manager, H. Beverley: 1833.
*Southwell. Manager, Smedley: 1833.
*Spalding. Manager, T. W. Robertson: 1833.
*Stafford. Manager, G. Stanton: 1833.
*Stamford. Manager, T. W. Manley: 1833.
*Stockdale. 1833.
*Stockton-on-Tees. Manager, H. Beverley: 1833.
*Stourbridge. Manager, J. Bennett: 1833.
*Stratford-upon-Avon. Manager, Raymond: 1833.
Sudbury. Manager, C. Fisher: 1833.
*Sunderland. Manager, H. Beverley: 1833.
Swaffham. Manager, C. Fisher: 1833.
*Swansea. Manager, J. Woulds: 1833.
*Tamworth. 1833.
*Taunton. Manager, H. Lee: 1833.

*Teignmouth. 1833.
*Tenby. 1833.
*Tenterden. Manager, D. McRoy: 1833.
*Torrington. 1833.
*Truro. Manager, J. Dawson: 1833.
Tunbridge Wells. Manager, J. Sloman: 1833.
*Upton-upon-Severn. Manager, Colewell: 1833.
*Uxbridge. Manager, H. Jackman: 1833.
Wakefield. Manager, O. E. Read: 1833.
*Walsall. 1833.
*Warwick. Manager, J. Watson: 1833.
Wells. Manager, H. Lee: 1833.
*Weymouth. Manager, Hay: 1833.
*Whitby. Manager, J. E. Parry: 1833.
*Whittlesea. Manager, W. Robertson: 1833.
Winchester. Managers, S. Maxfield and H. Kelly: 1833.
*Wisbech. Manager, Mrs T. Robertson: 1833.
*Woburn. Manager, H. Jackman: 1833.
*Wolverhampton. Manager, J. Bennett: 1833.
*Worcester. Manager, J. Bennett: 1833.
*Worthing. Manager, G. Stanley: 1833.
*Wrexham. Manager, G. Stanton: 1833.
Yarmouth. Manager, J. Smith: 1833.
York. Manager, S. Downe: 1833.

HAND-LIST OF PLAYS
1800–1850

EVERY attempt has been made to render this hand-list as comprehensive as possible. While the register of the French repertoires at the St James's Theatre has been entirely omitted because of exigencies of space, and while the records of foreign operas produced in England have been considerably curtailed, all other purely dramatic forms are here included. Ballets (when these were not merely individual dances), spectacles, pantomimes and entertainments find their places here alongside regular tragedy and comedy. It may be that some of the material gathered and presented here will not prove of much general or immediate use; but comprehensiveness has been aimed at, first, because no effort has hitherto been made to survey the theatrical activities of this half-century, and, secondly, because the correct interpretation of the dramatic movements of the period demands that full attention should be paid to the efforts—and even to the more trivial efforts—of the minor theatres. It is certain that further research will provide many additions to this hand-list, but I believe it will be found that I have succeeded in listing at least the vast majority even of the lesser pieces of the time.

The difficulties in the preparation of this 1800–1850 hand-list have been immeasurably greater than those encountered in the preparation of the lists for the years 1660–1700, 1700–1750 and 1750–1800. For the earlier plays the *Biographia Dramatica* proved a useful, if an occasionally erring and incomplete guide; at least some bibliographical work had been accomplished on a few individual authors; while attention had to be devoted in the main only to a few important theatres. During this period the theatres multiply decade by decade; practically nothing has been done in a scholarly way on the bibliography of the subject; the libraries have not troubled to make extensive collections of these minor dramas, and of reliable guides there are none. The latest issue of the *Biographia Dramatica* appeared in 1812. Genest neglects entirely the activities of the minors, and in any case ends his survey with the year 1830. Clarence in *The "Stage"Cyclopædia* (1909) is not only often inaccurate, but neglects almost entirely the pieces produced at the lesser theatres. Barely half a dozen of the numerous Coburg melodramas find mention in his pages. The same weaknesses are to be discovered in W. Davenport Adams's *A Dictionary of the Drama* (1904), which, moreover, extends only as far as the letter

246 HAND-LIST OF PLAYS

G. It will be realised, therefore, that the labour of gathering the material has been very much greater (not merely because of the multiplicity of plays) and that the possibilities of having permitted single dramas to escape the net have been markedly increased. Luckily, two main sources of information have come to my aid. The Larpent Collection of dramatic MSS., now in the Henry E. Huntington Library, which was used so largely for the 1750–1800 hand-list, preserves plays of as late a date as 1824. It was in that year that it became definitely (and illegally) private property. By the courtesy of the Lord Chamberlain I have been enabled to make use of the continuation of this official collection. In the cellars of the Office of Works there is preserved a library of plays in manuscript submitted to the licenser from the year 1824 onwards. For some reason the period from 1824 to 1832 is not so completely represented as are the later decades, but altogether we have here nearly three-quarters of the entire dramatic output during twenty-five years. Personally, I can find no explanation for the vagaries of the Larpent and Lord Chamberlain's MSS. One would have expected to find all the theatres represented in them, but in point of fact before 1832 only plays produced at the "majors," at the English Opera House, at the Pavilion (Astley's) and at the Adelphi seem to have been preserved. It is possible that the confusion then reigning in the minds of many concerning the precise power of jurisdiction possessed by the Lord Chamberlain over the minors may in some way account for these facts, but this in itself does not seem to provide a full explanation. Several of these MS. dramas appear with titles differing from those accorded to the plays when they were acted, a discrepancy which may have led to a certain small duplication. So far as was possible, I have tried to equate these double-titled plays, but here and there, perhaps, I have let a manuscript version slip in as a separate entity alongside its other self, the acted play.

The arrangement of material here follows largely the arrangement adopted in the hand-list to my last volume. A summary of the methods employed will make the system clear.

    1. First is indicated, in abbreviated form, the nature of the play itself. The asterisk used in *A History of Late Eighteenth Century Drama* has been dispensed with owing to the enormous number of unprinted plays. The abbreviations used are the following:

Ba.	Burletta	Ca.	Comedietta
Bal.	Ballet	C.D.	Comic Drama
Bal.P.	Ballet Pantomime	C.Ent.	Comic Entertainment
B.O.	Ballad Opera	C.Int.	Comic Interlude
Bsq.	Burlesque	C.O.	Comic Opera
C.	Comedy	C.P.	Comic Pantomime

C.R.	Comic Romance	O.D.	Operatic Drama
C.Sk.	Comic Sketch	O.Ent.	Operatic Entertainment
C.Spec.	Comic Spectacle	O.Ext.	Operatic Extravaganza
D.	Drama	O.F.	Operatic Farce
D.D.	Domestic Drama	O.P.	Operatic Pantomime
D.F.	Dramatic Farce	O.R.	Operatic Romance
Div.	Divertisement	P.	Pantomime
D.O.	Dramatic Opera	Pag.	Pageant
D.Past.	Dramatic Pastoral	P.Sk.	Pantomimic Sketch
D.R.	Dramatic Romance	Past.	Pastoral
D.Sk.	Dramatic Sketch	P.Bal.	Pantomimic Ballet
Ent.	Entertainment	P.C.	Pantomimic Comedy
Eques.D.	Equestrian Drama	P.F.	Pantomimic Farce
Ext.	Extravaganza	Pol.	Political Play
F.	Farce	P.R.	Pantomimic Romance
Fa.	Farcetta	Prel.	Prelude
Hist.R.	Historical Romance	R.Ba.	Romantic Burletta
Int.	Interlude	R.C.	Romantic Comedy
M.	Masque	R.D.	Romantic Drama
M.Bsq.	Musical Burlesque	R.O.	Romantic Opera
M.Ca.	Musical Comedietta	R.Spec.	Romantic Spectacle
M.D.	Melodrama or Musical Drama	Sat.	Satire
		Sk.	Sketch
M.Ent.	Musical Entertainment	Spec.	Spectacle [or Spectacular]
M.Ext.	Musical Extravaganza		
M.R.	Musical Romance	T.	Tragedy
O.	Opera	T.C.	Tragi-comedy
Oa.	Operetta	Vaud.	Vaudeville

As will readily be realised, these designations are in no way final, and are often indefinite. Thus Domestic and Romantic Dramas fall under the general heading of Melodrama, while a Burletta may be an Operatic Farce or a Burlesque or a Melodrama. Where possible, the designation employed in the original bills has here been followed.

2. The dates enclosed in round brackets after the title are those of production. The full list of theatres and abbreviations will be found in Appendix A. Here three points are to be noted:

(*a*) Where I have been able definitely to establish a date of production, the full date, with indication of the day of the week, is given. In some instances, however, I find records which I have been unable to verify; the records are then presented without indication of the day.

(*b*) Where I have found a play marked as new at a certain theatre but have a suspicion that this was merely a revival of an earlier piece, I have presented the double dates within round brackets. Occasionally I may thus have erred in identifying two distinct pieces; but in general my practice here has been conservative.

(*c*) Where no date in round brackets appears it must not be assumed that there was no theatrical production. I have given production dates only when I discovered these in original bills or when I found the dates in reliable authorities.

3. Immediately following comes the record of Larpent and Lord Chamberlain's manuscripts. L. is used for the former (with press-mark, and date of licensing in square brackets); L.C. stands for the latter (with date of licensing not enclosed in brackets).

4. Then are given indications of published editions, starting with separate octavos (if any) and proceeding to texts provided in the many collections of the period, such as:

Acting Nat. Drama [The Acting National Drama (1837–1859), edited by B. N. Webster].
Ames [Series of plays published by Ames, N.D.].
B.D. [The British Drama; 1824–1826].
Cumberland [Cumberland's British Theatre; dates from 1826 to 1861].
Cumberland Minor [Cumberland's Minor Theatre; 1828–1843].
Dicks [Dicks' Standard Plays, 1875 onwards].
Dicks B.D. [The British Drama, published by Dicks about 1880].
Dolby's British Theatre: 1823–1825.
Douglas Minor N.Y. [Douglas's Minor Theatre (*c.* 1840), published in New York].
Duncombe [Duncombe's British Theatre; 1828–1852].
Duncombe's New Acting Drama: 1821–1825.
French [French's Acting Edition (a continuation of Lacy's). *French's N.Y.* and *French's Minor N.Y.* refer to the New York edition of French's series of plays].
Inchbald's B.T. [The British Theatre (1808), edited by Mrs Inchbald].
Lacy [Lacy's Acting Edition (*c.* 1849–1855)].
L.T. [The London Theatre (1815–1818), edited by T. J. Dibdin].
L.S. [The London Stage (1824–1827)].
Mod. Eng. Com. Th. [The Modern English Comic Theatre (*c.* 1850)].
New B.T. [The New British Theatre (*c.* 1860)].
Oxberry [Oxberry's Edition (1818–1823)].
Pattie's Universal Stage [afterwards *Barth's Universal Stage*: 1839–1845].
Pattie's Play, or Weekly Acting Drama: 1838–1839.
Richardson Minor [Richardson's New Minor Drama (1828–1831), edited by W. T. Moncrieff].

The references to volumes of these collections follow the numeration of the British Museum exemplars. Sometimes the plays were bound in a different order.

5. It has been found exceedingly difficult to attribute plays correctly to their authors. The MSS. cited above have proved of considerable service in this connection but before 1838 it is but seldom that these MSS. contain indication of authorship. For the period 1840–1850, however, I have been able to add considerably to the list of works known to have been written by such men as G. D. Pitt, Edward Stirling and Tom Taylor. A few plays are admitted here which either were written in an earlier period or were produced abroad. In such instances the name of the author is preceded by a single square bracket.

I. *English Plays and Operas.*

ABBOTT, WILLIAM.
M.D. The Youthful Days of Frederick the Great (C.G. Th. 2/10/1817).
8° 1817.
M.D. Swedish Patriotism; or, The Signal Fire (C.G. W. 19/5/1819).
L. 75 S. [14/5/1819]. 8° 1819; 12° 1823 [New York].
O.F. I'm Puzzled; or, Three to One (H.² S. 31/7/1819).
[Ascribed to Abbott.]

À BECKETT, GILBERT ABBOTT.
F. The King Incog. (Fitzroy, Th. 9/1/1834).
M.Bsq. The Son of the Sun; or, The Fate of Pha'ton (Fitzroy,
S. 8/2–S. 15/2/1834).
Bsq. The Revolt of the Workhouse (Fitzroy, M. 24/2/1834). *Cumberland Minor*, vol. viii.
F. The Siamese Twins (Fitzroy, M. 14/4/1834). L.C. 1834. *Dicks* 338; *Cumberland Minor*, vol. xiv; *Lacy*, vol. lxxix.
Ba. Caught Courting; or, Juno, by Jove! (Vic. S. 2/8/1834).
F. The Turned Head (Vic. M. 3/11/1834). *Cumberland Minor*, vol. xiii; *Dicks* 338; *Lacy*, vol. lxvii.
F. Figaro in London (Strand, M. 24/11/1834).
Ba. St Mark's Eve (Olym. F. 19/12/1834). L.C. 2/12/1834.
Bsq. Man-Fred (Strand, F. 26/12/1834). *Cumberland Minor*, vol. ix.
[Apparently this is the same as the burlesque in L.C. 15/3/1836.]
F. The Man with the Carpet Bag (Strand, 1835). L.C. 7/12/1835. *Cumberland Minor*, vol. xiii; *Dicks* 959; *Mod. Eng. Com. Th.* vol. iii; *Lacy*, vol. lxviii.
Ba. The Unfortunate Miss Bailey (Strand, M. 2/2/1835). *Cumberland Minor*, vol. xi.
Bsq. The Roof Scrambler (Vic. M. 15/6/1835). *Cumberland Minor*, vol. x.
F. "The French Company" (St J. M. 14/12/1835). L.C. 14/12/1835.
F. A Clear Case (St J. M. 14/12/1835). L.C. 5/12/1835.
O. Agnes Sorel (St J. M. 14/12/1835). L.C. 5/12/1835.
[Music Mrs G. A. à Beckett.]
D. The Mendicant (St J. T. 2/2/1836). L.C. 1/2/1836. *Cumberland*, vol. xxxvii.
F. The Tradesman's Ball (St J. Th. 29/9/1836). L.C. 20/9/1836. *Dicks* 1040, *Duncombe*, vol. iiiiii.
Ba. Love is Blind (St J. Th. 5/1/1837). L.C. 11/1836 [as *L. is B.; or, Manners make the Man*]. *Duncombe*, vol. xxv.
Ba. The Postillion (St J. M. 13/3/1837). L.C. 9/3/1837. 8° [1837; Duets, Trios, Chorusses]; *Cumberland*, vol. xliii.
Ba. Jack Brag (St J. 5/1837). L.C. 10/5/1837. *Dicks* 534; *Mod. Eng. Com. Th.* vol. iii.
Ba. The Assignation; or, What will my Wife say? (St J. F. 29/9/1837). L.C. 1837. *Dicks* 452; *Duncombe*, vol. xxxiv.
Bsq. King John with the Benefit of the Act (St J. M. 16/10/1837). L.C. 1837. *Duncombe*, vol. xxxiv.
Ba. Wanted, a Brigand; or, A Visit from Fra Diavolo (St J. W. 6/12/1837). L.C. 1837. *Dicks* 613.

O. Pascal Bruno (St J. T. 26/12/1837). L.C. 19/12/1837. *Dicks* 559;
Duncombe, vol. xxxv.
[Based on Dumas' work.]

Ba. The Black Domino (St J. M. 29/1/1838). L.C. 23/1/1838. *Dun-combe*, vol. xxix.
[Based on Scribe, *Le domino noir* (Paris, 2/9/1837).]

C.O. The Ambassadress (St J. M. 5/3/1838). L.C. 3/3/1838. *Dun-combe*, vol. xxxii.
[A version of Scribe, *L'ambassadrice* (Paris, 21/9/1836), with music by Auber.]

F. The Artist's Wife (H.² S. 28/7/1838). L.C. 1838. *Dicks* 442;
Acting Nat. Drama, vol. v.

Bsq. The Yellow Dwarf; or, The King of the Gold Mines (P'cess, M. 26/12/1842).

Fairy O. Little Red Riding Hood (P'cess, M. 6/2/1843).

Bsq. The Three Graces (P'cess, M. 17/4/1843).

Ext. The Magic Mirror; or, The Hall of Statues (P'cess, T. 26/12/1843).
L.C. 23/12/1843.

Sat. Scenes from the Rejected Comedies. By some of the Competitors for the Prize of £500, offered by Mr. B. Webster, Lessee of the Haymarket Theatre, for the best original Comedy, illustrative of English Manners. 8° 1844.
[Contains the following skits: 1. *The Husband* [Knowles].
2. *Humbugs of the Hour* [Jerrold]. 3. *The Templars* [Talfourd].
4. *The Absurdities of a Day* [Planché]. 5. *Jane Jenkins; or, The Ghost of the Back Drawing Room* [Fitzball]. 6. *Floreat Etona* [Boucicault]. 7. *A Story of London* [Hunt]. 8. *The School for Sentiment; or, The Tar! The Tear!! and the Tilbury!!!* [à Beckett].
9. *Grandmother Browning* [Lemon]. 10. *Credit* [Lytton].]

Bsq. Open Sesame; or, A Night with the Forty Thieves (Lyc. M. 8/4/1844). L.C. 1/4/1844. *Acting Nat. Drama*, vol. x.
[Written in collaboration with *M. LEMON*.]

Bsq. The Wonderful Lamp in a New Light (P'cess, Th. 4/7/1844).
L.C. 4/7/1844.

D. Don Cæsar de Bazan (P'cess, T. 8/10/1844). L.C. 7/10/1844.
Dicks 800; *Lacy*, vol. xii.
[Written in collaboration with *M. LEMON*; based on the play by Dumanoir and Dennery.]

Bsq. The Knight and the Sprite (Strand, M. 11/11/1844). L.C. 9/11/1844.
[Written in collaboration with *M. LEMON*.]

D. The Chimes; or, A Goblin Tale (Adel. 19/2/1844). L.C. 18/12/1844.
Dicks 819; *Acting Nat. Drama*, vol. xi.
[Written in collaboration with *M. LEMON*. A dramatisation of Dickens' novel.]

Ext. Joe Miller and his Men (P'cess, T. 24/12/1844). L.C. 23/12/1844.

Ext. Timour the Cream of all the Tartars (P'cess, M. 24/3/1845).
L.C. 22/3/1845.

Bsq. St. George and the Dragon (Adel. M. 24/3/1845). L.C. 22/3/1845.
Acting Nat. Drama, vol xii.
[Written in collaboration with *M. LEMON*.]

Spec. Peter Wilkins; or, The Loadstone Rock and the Flying Indians (Adel. Th. 9/4/1846). L.C. 11/4/1846. *Acting Nat. Drama*, vol. xii.
[Written in collaboration with *M. LEMON*.]

Ext. The World Underground; or, The Golden Flute and the Brazen
   Waters (H.² M. 27/12/1847). L.C. 30/12/1847.
Bsq. The Castle of Otranto (H.² M. 24/4/1848). L.C. 22/4/1848.
   Acting Nat. Drama, vol. xiv.

ADAMS, SARAH FLOWER.
   D.Poem. Vivia Perpetua. 12° 1841.

ADAMSON, JOHN.
   T.   Dona Ignez de Castro. 8° 1808 [Newcastle].
       [A translation from the Portuguese of Nicola Luiz.]

ADDISON, Captain (later Lieutenant-Colonel) HENRY ROBERT.
   M.D. Lo Zingaro (Adel. S. 3/8/1833). L.C. 15/7/1833. *Duncombe*,
       vol. xii.
       [Music A. Lee.]
   Oa. Jessie, the Flower of Dumblane; or, "Weel may the Keel row"
       (Adel. M. 26/8/1833). L.C. 26/8/1833. *Duncombe*, vol. xiii.
   F.   Who would be married? (Vic. S. 28/9/1833).
   F.   Tam o' Shanter (D.L. T. 25/11/1834). L.C. 22/11/1834. 8° 1834;
       Dicks 532.
   Int. The King's Word (D.L. 20/1/1835; Lyc. M. 12/7/1847). L.C.
       19/1/1835. 12° 1835.
   D.   Sigismund Augustus (C.G. S. 13/2/1836). L.C. 8/2/1836.
   Ca. Marie, a Tale of the Pont Neuf (C.G. S. 27/2/1836). L.C.
       22/2/1836. *Dicks* 991; *Duncombe*, vol. xxi.
   D.   Abraham Parker (Adel. M. 20/7/1846). L.C. 18/7/1846.
   Ba. British Beauty; or, The Seraglio in an Uproar. L.C. Grecian
       29/3/1848.
       [Music A. Lee. A version of *Les trois sultanes*.]
   F.   A Pretty Couple. L.C. Grecian, 17/4/1848.
   O.F. Did You Ever? No, I never saw such a Babby (Surrey, Th.
       27/8/1848). L.C. 8/6/1848.
   O.F. Sophia's Supper (Surrey, M. 21/5/1849). L.C. 28/4/1849.
       Lacy, vol. xvi.
       [Addison is said to have written over sixty plays before his
       death in 1876. The above are all I have been able to trace prior
       to 1850.]

AINSLIE, Dr WHITELAW.
   T.   Clemenza; or, The Tuscan Orphan (Bath, 1/6/1822). L. 127 M.
       [22/5/1822]. 8° 1823.

AIRD, THOMAS.
   T.   Murtzoufle....With other Poems. 8° 1826 [Edinburgh and
       London].

ALBERT, —
   Bal. The Beauty of Ghent (D.L. Th. 7/11/1844).
       [Music A. Adam.]

ALLEN, ROBERT.
   T.   The Parricide (Bath, 12/5/1824). L.C. 24/4/1824. 8° 1824 [Bath].

ALLINGHAM, JOHN TILL.
   [For his earlier plays see *A History of Late Eighteenth Century Drama*,
   p. 232.]
   F.   'Tis All a Farce (H.² T. 17/6/1800). L. 38 S. [10/6/1800]. 8° 1800.

C. The Marriage Promise (D.L. S. 16/4/1803). L. 79 M. [29/3/1803].
    8° 1803 (5 editions).
F. Mrs Wiggins (H.¹ F. 27/5/1803). 8° 1803; *Dicks* 250; *Duncombe*,
    vol. i; *Cumberland*, vol. xxxix.
C. Hearts of Oak (D.L. S. 19/11/1803). L. 43 S. [14/11/1803].
    8° 1804.
F. The Weathercock (D.L. M. 18/11/1805). L. 83 M. [8/11/1805].
    8° 1805 (2 editions); 8° [1806; 4 editions]; *Dicks* 631.
C. The Romantic Lover; or, Lost and Found (C.G. S. 11/1/1806).
O.F. Who Wins? or, The Widow's Choice (C.G. F. 25/2/1808).
C. Independence; or, The Trustee (H.² 9/3/1809).
O.F. Transformation; or, Love and Law (Lyc. F. 30/11/1810).

ALMAR, GEORGE.
M.D. The Rover's Bride; or, The Bittern's Swamp (Surrey, S.
     30/10/1830). *Cumberland Minor*, vol. xi.
M.D. The Fire Raiser; or, The Haunted Tower (Surrey, M. 21/2/1831).
     Cumberland Minor, vol. ix; *Lacy*, vol. lxxxix; *Dicks* 947.
     [Also called *The Prophet of the Moor; or, The F.R.*]
R.D. Le Belveder; or, The Sicilian Exile (Surrey, M. 1/8/1831).
     [An adaptation of Pixérécourt, *Le Belvéder* (Paris, 10/2/1818).]
D.   Pedlar's Acre; or, The Wife of Seven Husbands (Surrey, M.
     22/8/1831). *Cumberland Minor*, vol. v; *Lacy*, vol. lxxiv [as *The
     W. of S. H.*]; *Dicks* 280.
D.   The False Key; or, The Locksmith of Stockholm (Surrey, M.
     29/8/1831).
R.D. The Black Eagle; or, The Lake of the Apennines (Surrey, M.
     24/10/1831).
R.D. Cinderella; or, The Fairy and the Little Glass Slipper (Surrey,
     M. 7/11/1831).
M.D. Attar Gull; or, The Serpent of the Jungle (S.W. M.
     11/6/1832).
R.D. Hallowmas Eve; or, Under the Old Church Porch (Surrey,
     M. 11/6/1832).
M.D. The Tower of Nesle (Surrey, M. 17/9/1832). *Cumberland*,
     vol. xci; *Cumberland Minor*, vol. vi; *Dicks* 234.
M.D. The Charcoal Burner; or, The Dropping Well of Knaresborough
     (Surrey, W. 26/12/1832). *Cumberland Minor*, vol. ix; *Lacy*, vol.
     lxxi; *Dicks* 767.
M.D. Don Quixote; or, The Knight of the Doleful Countenance
     (Surrey, 1833). *Cumberland Minor*, vol. xiv; *Dicks* 956.
Ba. Crossing the Line; or, The Boat Builders of Brugen (S.W. M.
     8/4/1833; Surrey, M. 24/6/1833, as *C. the L.; or, Crowded Houses*).
     Duncombe, vol. ii; *Lacy*, vol. xxxv.
M.D. The Robber of the Rhine; or, Schinderhannes of the Owl
     Forest (R.P. M. 22/4/1833; S.W. M. 29/4/1833, as *S.! the Robber
     of the Rhine*). *Cumberland Minor*, vol. x; *Lacy*, vol. lxxxvii.
M.D. Lucrece Borgia; or, The Fiend of Ferrara (S.W. M. 29/4/1833).
M.D. The Peerless Pool; or, The Early Days of Richard III (S.W.
     M. 1/7/1833).
M.D. Perinet Leclerc; or, The Red Cross of Burgundy (S.W. M.
     1/7/1833).
M.D. The Knights of St. John; or, The Fire Banner (S.W. M.
     26/8/1833). *Duncombe*, vol. xii; *Lacy*, vol. lvi.

M.D. The Clerk of Clerkenwell and the Three Black Bottles (S.W. M. 27/1/1834). *Cumberland Minor*, vol. vii.
D. The Good-looking Fellow; or, The Roman Nose (S.W. 4/1834). *Cumberland Minor*, vol. ix; *Dicks* 989.
   [This may be *The Roman Nose* (Surrey, 1835).]
M.D. The Cedar Chest; or, The Lord Mayor's Daughter (S.W. M. 11/8/1834).
M.D. The Demon of the Ganges; or, The Tiger Tribe (S.W. M. 20/10/1834).
M.D. The Shadow; or, A Mother's Dream (S.W. M. 5/3/1835).
M.D. The Seven Sisters; or, The Grey Man of Tottenham Cross (S.W. W. 29/7/1835).
D. The Battle of Sedgemoor (R.P. 2/1837). *Cumberland Minor*, vol. xiii.
D. The Earl of Poverty; or, The Old Wooden House of London Wall (Surrey, M. 5/2/1838). *Cumberland Minor*, vol. xiv.
D. Gaspardo the Gondolier; or, The Three Banished Men of Milan (Surrey, M. 9/7/1838). *Duncombe*, vol. xxx.
F. Page 21; or, The Great Cigar (Strand, M. 10/9/1838). L.C. 1/8/1838 [as *Page 21 of an Interesting History*].
R.D. The Bull-Fighter; or, The Bridal Ring (Surrey, M. 8/10/1838). *Cumberland Minor*, vol. xiv.
D. Oliver Twist; or, The Parish Boy's Progress (Surrey, M. 19/11/1838). *Dicks* 293; *Mod. Eng. Com. Th.* vol. i; *Acting Nat. Drama*, vol. vi. [From Dickens.]
Spec. Jane of the Hatchet (Surrey, M. 20/7/1840). *Duncombe*, vol. xli [as *J. of the H.; or, The Siege of Beauvais*].
D. The Pirate Minister; or, The Tiger Crew (M'bone 2/12/1844). L.C. 2/12/1844.
D. Hearts of Iron; or, The King's Watch (Albert, 17/11/1845). L.C. 19/11/1845.
D. The Witch of the Waters (Queen's, 9/1849). L.C. 3/10/1849.
   [In addition to these, the following were produced before 1850: *The Death Light*, *The Evil Eye*, *The Headsman of Vienna*, *Alfred the Great*, *Der Freischutz*, *The Mountain King*, and *Jack Ketch* (S.W. 20/9/1841). For his later work see *A History of Late Nineteenth Century Drama*, pp. 239–40.]

AMHERST, J. H.
Spec. The Black Castle (Royalty, M. 16/2/1801).
Spec. The Blood-red Knight; or, The Fatal Bridge (R.A. M. 23/4/1810).
M.D. The Death of Christophe, King of Haiti (Cob. M. 29/1/1821).
D. The Faithless Friend; or, A British Seaman's Fidelity (Cob. Th. 17/5/1821).
R.D. Almoran and Hamet (D.L. M. 8/4/1822). L. 85 S. [30/3/1822]. [Music Cooke.]
Spec. The Shipwreck of the Grosvenor East Indiaman (Royalty, M. 14/10/1822).
Ba. Married or Not? or, Puzzles and Penalties (Royalty, M. 9/9/1822).
M.D. The Infernal Secret; or, The Invulnerable (Surrey, M. 7/10/1822).
Ext. The Three Cripples and the Queen of Billingsgate (Royalty, M. 25/11/1822).
M.D. Zadoc the Sorcerer; or, The Princes of Persia (Royalty, Th. 26/12/1822).

Spec. The Battle of Waterloo (R.A. M. 19/4/1824). *Dicks* 696; *Lacy*, vol. xcviii.
M.D. Der Freischutz (R.A. M. 30/8/1824).
Spec. Buonaparte's Invasion of Russia; or, The Conflagration of Moscow (R.A. M. 4/4/1825; Bath, 6/11/1826). *Lacy*, vol. xiii.
Ext. The Six Simpletons (R.A. M. 25/4/1825).
Spec. The Burmese War; or, Our Victories in the East (R.A. M. 27/3/1826).
       [On M. 15/5/1826 the title was altered to *War in India; or, The Burmese.*]
M.D. The White Spectre; or, The Village Phantom (Cob. M. 3/3/1828).
M.D. Blood demands its Victim; or, The Convict's Flight (R.A. M. 8/9/1828; R.A. M. 27/4/1829 as *Will Watch, the Bold Smuggler; or, B. d. i. V.*).
M.D. The Death of Fair Rosamond (R.P. F. 26/12/1828).
M.D. The Attack of the Diligence (R.A. M. 3/8/1829).
M.D. The Iron Collar (S.W. W. 26/12/1832).
       [To these should be added the following: *Fifteen Years of Labour Lost, Ireland as it is, Bill Jones, The Bloodstained Banner, The Fish and the Ring, The Fall of Missolonghi, The Irish Witch, The Monk, the Mask and the Murderer, Real Life in London, The Silver Mask, Three Magic Wands* and *Three Blind Eyes.*]

AMPHLETT, —
  F. The Astronomer (Wolverhampton, 1802).

ANDERSON, JAMES R.
  T. The Robbers (L'pool, 13/3/1846). L.C. D.L. 26/12/1845.
       [On this actor-author see Davenport Adams, p. 55: *The Robbers* was not produced until 21/4/1851 at D.L.]

ANSTER, JOHN.
  D. Faustus...A Dramatic Mystery. 8° 1835.
       [An adaptation from Goethe's drama.]

ANSTRUTHER, Sir R. A.
  D. Griselda (Edinburgh, 26/1/1841). 8° 1840; 12° 1844.
       [An adaptation from the German of "F. Halm" (E. F. J. Freiherr von Münch-Bellinghausen.]

ARCHER, THOMAS.
  D. A Night at the Bastille (D.L. 4/12/1839). L.C. 25/11/1839. *Dicks* 623.
  R.D. The King's Ransom; or, The Spectre of Griefenstein (Surrey, M. 6/2/1843).
  R.D. Blood Royal; or, The Crown Jewels (Surrey, M. 17/4/1843).
       [A version of Scribe, *Les diamants de la couronne* (Paris, 6/3/1841), with music by Auber.]
  F. Asmodeus, the Little Demon; or, The Devil's Share (Surrey, M. 12/6/1843). *Duncombe*, vol. xlvii [as *A.; or, The Little Devil's Share*]; *Lacy*, vol. xlvi.
       [A version of Scribe, *La part du diable* (Paris, 16/1/1843), with music by Auber.]
  D. Don Cæsar de Bazan (Queen's, 28/10/1844). L.C. 18/10/1844.
       [Adapted from the play by Dumanoir and Dennery (Paris, 30/7/1844).]

D. The Strange Intruder (Grec. 18/11/1844). L.C. 15/11/1844.
Bsq. Monseigneur; or, The Jeweller's Apprentice (Strand, M. 20/1/1845). L.C. 18/1/1845.
F. Dick and his Double (Olym. F. 24/10/1845; S.W. M. 23/2/1846). L.C. 22/10/1845.
M.D. The Artizan and his Daughters (C.L. 26/12/1845). L.C. 20/12/1845.
D. The Black Doctor (C.L. 9/11/1846). L.C. 1846.
D. The Cricket on the Hearth (P'cess, Th. 1/1/1846). L.C. 26/12/1845. [From Dickens' novel.]
D. The Carpenters of Paris. L.C. C.L. 11/4/1846.
Ca. My Uncle's Pet (S.W. 13/4/1846). [See under UNKNOWN AUTHORS.]
D. The Cabin Boy. L.C. Garrick, 11/4/1846.
F. The Barber's Secret; or, The Invention of Powder (Grecian 19/10/1846). L.C. 17/9/1846.
Ca. Red Cap; or, The Prisoner of Vincennes (Olym. 30/11/1846). L.C. 27/11/1846.
D. The Inundation; or, The Miser of the Hill Fort (C.L. 5/4/1847). L.C. 3/4/1847. Lacy, vol. xlv.
Ca. Marguerite's Colours; or, Passing the Frontier (Lyc. M. 5/7/1847). L.C. 1/7/1847. Dicks 1020; Duncombe, vol. lxi; Lacy, vol. xlvii.
C. The Letter Box; or, The Jailor's Daughter. L.C. Grecian, 22/7/1847.
F. Our Wife. L.C. Grecian, 14/8/1847.
D. The Three Red Men (C.L. and Standard, M. 1/5/1848). L.C. C.L. 1848. Lacy, vol. xli. [A version of Les trois hommes rouges by Paul Jéval (Paris, 1847).]
O. The Daughter of the Regiment. L.C. P'cess, 20/6/1848.

ARNOLD, SAMUEL JAMES.
[For his earlier plays see A History of Late Eighteenth Century Drama, p. 234.]
C.O. The Veteran Tar; or, A Chip of the Old Block (D.L. Th. 29/1/1801). L. 40 S. [15/1/1801]. 8° 1801.
M.D. "Foul Deeds will Rise" (H.² W. 18/7/1804). L. 44 S. [16/7/1804]. 8° 1804.
C. A Prior Claim. 1805 [see H. J. PYE].
C. Man and Wife; or, More Secrets than One (D.L. Th. 5/1/1809). L. 49 S. [24/12/1808]. 8° 1809 [8 editions]; Dicks 575.
C.O. Up All Night; or, The Smuggler's Cave (Lyc. M. 26/6/1809). L. 51 S. [10/6/1809; titles reversed]. 8° 1809 [Songs, Duets, Chorusses, and Finales].
O. The Russian Impostor (Lyc. S. 22/7/1809). See H. SIDDONS.
M.Ent. Britain's Jubilee (Lyc. W. 25/10/1809). L. 89 M. [21/10/1809].
C.O. The Maniac; or, Swiss Banditti (Lyc. T. 13/3/1810). [Music Bishop.]
O. Plots! or, The North Tower (Lyc. M. 3/9/1810). [Music by M. P. King.]
C.O. The Americans (Lyc. S. 27/4/1811). L. 94 M. [12/4/1811; as The War Whoop]. [Music M. P. King and Braham.]

O.R. The Devil's Bridge; or, The Piedmontese Alps (Lyc. W. 6/5/1812). L. 55 S. [27/4/1812]. 12° 1820 [Dublin]; *Cumberland*, vol. xlii.
  [Music C. E. Horn and Braham.]

M.D. The Woodman's Hut (D.L. T. 12/4/1814). L. 59 S. [17/2/1814]. 8° 1814; *Dicks* 935.
  [Music Horn.]

Oa. Frederick the Great; or, The Heart of a Soldier (Lyc. Th. 4/8/1814). L. 59 S. [18/7/1814]. 8° 1814 [Songs, Duets].
  [Music T. Cooke.]

F. Jean de Paris (D.L. T. 1/11/1814). L. 59 S. [24/10/1814].

M.D. The Unknown Guest (D.L. W. 29/3/1815). L. 60 S. [8/3/1815; as *The State Tower; or, The U. G.*].

M.D. Charles the Bold; or, The Siege of Nantz (D.L. Th. 15/6/1815). L. 61 S. [3/6/1815].
  [The advertisements attribute this adaptation of *Charles le Téméraire; ou, le siège de Nancy* (Paris, 26/10/1814) by Pixérécourt to Wallack, but Arnold seems to have been the author.]

C.O. The King's Proxy; or, Judge for Yourself (Lyc. S. 19/8/1815). 8° 1815 [Songs, Duets, Chorusses].
  [Music T. Cooke.]

M.D. The Maid and the Magpye; or, Which is the Thief? (Lyc. M. 28/8/1815). L. 106 M. [24/8/1815]. 8° 1815.
  [A version of Caigniez, *La pie voleuse; ou, la servante de Palaiseau.*]

M.D. Two Words; or, The Silent not Dumb! (E.O.H. M. 2/9/1816). L. 62 S. [10/8/1816; under sub-title].

C.O. Free and Easy (E.O.H. M. 16/9/1816). L. 62 S. [5/9/1816]. *Cumberland*, vol. xlii.
  [Music Addison.]

M.D. The Wizard; or, The Brown Man of the Moor (E.O.H. S. 26/7/1817). L. 65 S. [21/7/1817].
  [Music Horn. A dramatisation of Scott's *The Black Dwarf*.]

B.O. Broken Promises; or, the Colonel, the Captain and the Corporal (E.O.H. T. 5/7/1825).

D. Baron Trenck; or, The Fortress of Magdeburg (Surrey, M. 11/10/1830).
  [This seems to be the same as *Baron de Trenck* (*UA*); if so the Surrey performance is a revival. The problem is further complicated by the attribution to Osbaldiston of a *Baron Trenck* (Surrey, 10/1/1831), described as a new play.]

D. The Sergeant's Wife (D.L. M. 8/6/1835).

ASHE, NICHOLAS.
T. Panthea; or, The Susian Captive. 12° 1800 [Dublin].

ASHTON, JOSEPH.
T. Retributive Justice. A Tragedy... of which a few Copies only have been printed for Private Communication. 8° 1813 [Manchester].

ASTLEY, PHILIP, Junior.
P. The Pirate; or, Harlequin Victor (R.A. M. 25/8/1800; Royalty, M. 19/10/1801).

Spec. The Iron Tower; or, The Cell of Mystery (R.A. Th. 9/4/1801).

Spec. British Glory in Egypt (R.A. Th. 4/6/1801).

Spec. The Death of Abercromby (Royalty, M. 30/11/1801).

P.   The Phœnix; or, Harlequin and Lillipo (R.A. M. 12/7/1802).
P.   The Silver Star; or, The Mirror of Witchcraft (R.A. M. 11/4/1803).
P.   The Man in the Moon; or, The Witches' Rout (R.A. M. 18/4/1808).
Spec. The Honest Criminal; or, False Evidence (R.A. M. 16/5/1808).
P.   The Magic Pagoda; or, Harlequin's Travels, East, West, North
     and South (R.A. M. 27/6/1808).

ATKYNS, SAMUEL.
D.   Walpurgis Night; or, The Wolf-hunter of the Haitzberg. L.C.
     Albert, 23/5/1844.
M.D. Wonga of the Branded Hand. L.C. Albert, 19/7/1844.
D.   The Thieves' House; or, The Murder Cellar of Fleet Ditch.
     L.C. Albert, 8/1844 [licence refused].
Spec. Tilbury Fort; or, The Spanish Armada. L.C. Albert, 15/8/1844.
D.   The Wandering Jew. L.C. S.W. 5/9/1844.
D.   The Chimes. L.C. Albert, 28/12/1844.
     [From Dickens' novel.]
D.   The Bastille. L.C. Albert, 25/1/1845.
M.D. Montrano, the Pirate Lord of Sicily. L.C. Albert, 22/3/1845.
M.D. Hoxton a Hundred Years Ago; or, The Dogs of Tipple's Farm.
     L.C. Albert, 5/4/1845.
D.   The Battle of Life (Albert, M. 4/1/1847). L.C. 26/12/1846.
     [From Dickens' tale.]
D.   Lilly Dawson. L.C. Albert, 1847.
D.   The Poacher's Wife. L.C. Albert, 21/5/1847.
D.   The Old Friends. L.C. Albert, 1/7/1847.
D.   Dark Donald, the Idiot of the Cliff; or, The Dogs of Loch Lomond.
     L.C. Albert, 30/9/1848.
M.D. Guerillas; or, The Storming of St. Sebastian. L.C. Albert,
     3/11/1848.
D.   The Life of a Labourer; or, The Emigrants, the Smuggler and
     the Bushranger. L.C. Albert, 14/12/1848.
D.   Proud Prudence. L.C. Albert, 9/1/1849.
D.   The Fire of London; or, The Baker's Daughter. L.C. Albert,
     3/2/1849.
D.   The Corsair; or, The Greek Pirates of the Gulph. L.C. Albert,
     2/4/1849.
D.   The Foresters; or, The Merry Men of Englewood. L.C. Albert,
     14/4/1849.
D.   Adeline; or, The Grave of the Forsaken. L.C. Albert, 29/9/1849.

AYTON, RICHARD.
Oa. The Rendezvous (E.O.H. M. 21/9/1818). L. Extra [11/8/1818].
     8° 1818; *Dicks* 236; *Cumberland,* vol. xvii; *Lacy,* vol. xliii.
     [Music Price.]

BAILEY, WILLIAM.
T.   Grimaldi. 8° 1822.
O.F. Sold for a Song (E.O.H. S. 5/9/1829). L.C. 26/8/1829.

BAILLIE, JOANNA.
[For her first *Series of Plays* see *A History of Late Eighteenth Century
Drama,* p. 235. *De Monfort* was acted at D.L. 29/4/1800, and is
preserved in L. 38 S. [3/4/1800.]

A Series of Plays. 8° 1802.

> [Contains: 1. *The Election* (E.O.H. S. 7/6/1817, with music by Horn; L. 66 S. [3/5/1817]); 2. *Ethwald* [in two parts]; 3. *The Second Marriage*.]

Miscellaneous Plays. 8° 1804.

> [Contains: 1. *Rayner*; 2. *The Country Inn*; 3. *Constantine Paleologus* (preserved in L. 87 M. [Liverpool, 10/10/1808], and no doubt acted in Liverpool; see also *T. J. DIBDIN*'s *Constantine and Valeria*, which is a revised version of this play).]

T. The Family Legend (Edinburgh, 29/1/1810; D.L. 29/4/1815). 8° 1810 [Edinburgh; *bis*].

> [This was originally called *The Lady of the Rock*.]

A Series of Plays. 8° 1812.

> [Contains: 1. *Orra*; 2. *The Dream*; 3. *The Siege*; 4. *The Beacon* (preserved in L. 103 M. [Edinburgh, 9/2/1815]). The three *Series* were reprinted in three volumes 8° 1821.]

T. The Martyr. 8° 1826.
D. The Bride. 8° 1828.
Dramas. 8° 1836.

> [Contains (besides *The Martyr* and *The Bride*): 1. *Romiero*; 2. *The Alienated Manor*; 3. *Henriquez* (D.L. S. 19/3/1836; preserved in L.C. 18/3/1836); 4. *The Separation* (C.G. W. 24/2/1836; preserved in L.C. 16/2/1836); 5. *The Stripling*; 6. *The Phantom*; 7. *Enthusiasm*; 8. *Witchcraft*; 9. *The Homicide*; 10. *The Match*.]

BAIN, DONALD.
C. Olden Times; or, The Rising of the Session. 8° 1841 [Edinburgh].

BALFOUR, MARY.
D. Kathleen O'Neill (Belfast, 9/2/1814). 8° 1814 [Belfast].

BALL, EDWARD. See *FITZBALL, EDWARD.*

BALL, WILLIAM.
T. Freemen and Slaves. 8° 1838.

BANFIELD, THOMAS C.
D. William Tell. 8° 1831.

> [A translation of Schiller's play.]

BANIM, JOHN.
T. Turgesius [see the *D.N.B.*].
T. Damon and Pythias (C.G. M. 28/5/1821). 8° 1821; *Dicks* 19; *Duncombe*, vol. lxi; *British Drama*, vol. iii.

> [See *The Force of Friendship* under *UNKNOWN AUTHORS*. The stage version was altered and revised by *R. L. SHEIL*.]

T. Sylla (Dublin, 1826).
M.D. The Sergeant's Wife (E.O.H. T. 24/7/1827). L.C. 25/6/1827. *Dicks* 369; *Lacy*, vol. xxiii.

> [Music Goss.]

R.D. The Ghost Hunter (Surrey, T. 26/3/1833).
D. The Duchess of Ormond (D.L. Th. 20/10/1836). L.C. 1836.

BARBER, J. H.
F. America. 8° 1805.

BARBER, JAMES.
Eccentric D. The Memoirs of the D—l; or, The Warning Bell of
  Ronguerall (Surrey, M. 8/8/1842). *Dicks* 901; *Duncombe*, vol. xlv.
Ba. Which is the Thief? (P'cess, Th. 9/3/1843).
F.   The Weaver of Lyons; or, The Three Conscripts (R.A. 24/11/1844).
     L.C. 21/11/1844. *Dicks* 969; *Duncombe*, vol. lvii; *Lacy*, vol. cx.
Ca. Rebecca (Surrey, 24/2/1845). L.C. 20/2/1845.
D.   The Dame de St Tropez (Olym. F. 21/2/1845). *Dicks* 849;
     Duncombe, vol. lii.
F.   Jonathan; or, The Man of Two Masters. L.C. R.A. 17/6/1845.
     Dicks 983; *Duncombe*, vol. lxii.

[*BARKER, JAMES N.*
M.D. Pocahontas; or, The Indian Princess (D.L. F. 15/12/1820).
     L. 78 S. [17/11/1820].
     [This is a revised version of *The Indian Princess; or, La Belle
     Sauvage* (Philadelphia, 6/4/1808)—the first Indian play put upon
     the stage. See A. H. Quinn, *A History of the American Drama*
     (1923), pp. 138–9.]

[*BARNES, CHARLOTTE M. S.* [*Mrs CONNER.*
T.   Octavia Bragaldi (Surrey, Th. 9/5/1844). L.C. 6/4/1844 [as *O. B.;
     or, The Confession*]. 8° 1848 [in *Plays*].
     [This was first acted in New York on 8/11/1837, and was
     published in 1848.]
D.   The Forest Princess; or, Two Centuries Ago. L.C. Liverpool,
     26/10/1844. 8° 1848 [in *Plays*].
     [As *The Forest Princess* was not performed in America till
     16/2/1848 (Philadelphia) it would appear that an English version
     preceded the American.]

BARNETT, C. Z.
D.   The Phantom Bride; or, The Castilian Bandit (R.P. M. 6/9/1830).
     Duncombe, vol. vii.
M.D. The Bier Kroeg; or, The Yager's Rest (R.P. M. 1/11/1830).
F.   "Swing" (Surrey, M. 14/2/1831). *Duncombe*, vol. viii.
D.   The Youthful Days of William IV; or, British Tars in 1782
     (R.P. M. 27/6/1831). *Duncombe*, vol. viii.
M.D. The Banks of Allan Water; or, The Death of Fair Eleanor
     (R.P. M. 25/7/1831).
M.D. Caesar Borgia, the Scourge of Venice (R.P. M. 8/8/1831).
     Duncombe, vol. xi.
M.D. Victorine; or, The Maid of Paris (R.P. M. 12/9/1831). *Dun-
     combe*, vol. ix.
D.   Dominique the Possessed; or, The Devil and the Deserter (R.P.
     T. 27/9/1831). *Dicks* 256; *Duncombe*, vol. ix.
M.D. The Bravo; or, The Bridge of Sighs (Surrey, Th. 21/2/1833).
     Duncombe, vol. xi.
     [From Cooper's novel.]
M.D. The Skeleton Hand; or, The Demon Statue (S.W. M. 31/12/1833).
D.   The Bell-ringer; or, The Hunchback of Notre Dame (S.W. M.
     31/3/1834).
M.D. The Loss of the Royal George (R.P. M. 8/6/1835). *Dicks* 775;
     Duncombe, vol. xlii.
M.D. The Worm of Lambton (S.W. M. 6/7/1835).

D   The Rise of the Rothschilds; or, The Honest Jew of Frankfort (St J. M. 15/2/1836).
O.   Fair Rosamond (D.L. T. 28/2/1837). L.C. 23/2/1837. 12° [1837; Songs; *Duncombe*].
D.   Oliver Twist; or, The Parish Boy's Progress (R.P. 21/5/1838). *Duncombe*, vol. xxix.
     [From Dickens' novel.]
D.   The Dream of Fate; or, Sarah the Jewess (S.W. M. 20/8/1838). *Dicks* 771; 16° [1840; *Dramatic Tales*].
D.   The Mariner's Dream; or, The Jew of Plymouth (R.P. W. 17/10/1838).
O.   Farinelli (D.L. F. 8/2/1839). L.C. 1839; 8° [1839; *Duncombe*, 3 editions; Songs, Duets, Trios]; *Duncombe*, vol. xxxiii.
     [Music J. Barnett.]
D.D. The Merchant's Daughter; or, Wealth and Pride (S.W. M. 16/9/1839).
D.   Mariette Duval (Vic. Th. 26/12/1839).
M.D. The Loss of the Royal George; or, The Fatal Land Breeze (S.W. M. 5/10/1840).
     [See above under date 8/6/1835.]
M.D. Maria Padilla; or, The Husband! the King! and the Court Favourite! (S.W. M. 7/6/1841).
D.   The Three Smugglers of Kent (Vic. M. 5/6/1843).
Ba. Marie (Adel. M. 2/10/1843). L.C. 23/9/1843 [as *M.; or, The Pear of Savoy*].
D.   The Bohemians of Paris; or, The Mysteries of Crime (Surrey, M. 27/11/1843). L.C. 16/11/1843. *Duncombe*, vol. xlviii.
     [From Sue, *Les Mystères de Paris*.]
D.   Stella de Rittersdorf (Surrey, M. 22/1/1844). L.C. 12/1/1844 [as *S. de R.; or, The Captive of Silesia*].
D.   A Christmas Carol; or, The Miser's Warning (Surrey, M. 5/2/1844). L.C. 3/2/1844. *Dicks* 722; *Lacy*, vol. xciv; *Duncombe*, vol. xlviii.
     [From Dickens' tale.]
F.   La Polka (Surrey, 6/5/1844). L.C. 30/4/1844. *Duncombe*, vol. l.
D.   Hugh the Gipsey (Surrey, 13/5/1844). L.C. 8/5/1844.
D.   Don Caesar de Bazan (Surrey, 21/10/1844). L.C. 14/10/1844. *Duncombe*, vol. li.
     [From the play by Dumanoir and Dennery.]
F.   Six Degrees of Crime (Olym. 18/11/1844). L.C. 16/11/1844.
D.   Midnight, the Thirteenth Chime; or, Old St. Paul's (Surrey, 2/1845). L.C. 12/2/1845. *Duncombe*, vol. liii; *Lacy*, vol. ci.
C.   Captain Sabertache; or, Under Arrest (S.W. M. 21/7/1845). L.C. 7/7/1845.
D.   Grace Challoner. L.C. Albert, 25/8/1845.
D.   Ship on Fire (Queen's, 1/9/1845). L.C. 25/8/1845.
D.   The Daughter of Fire (Albert, 29/9/1845). L.C. 25/9/1845.
D.   The Minute Gun at Sea; or, The Mariner's Sister (Surrey, 24/11/1845). L.C. 19/11/1845. *Duncombe*, vol. lv.
P.   Harlequin and the Magic Sirloin (Albert, 26/12/1845). L.C. 26/12/1845.
D.   The Q. of Diamonds; or, The Curse of Scotland. L.C. Queen's, 1846.
D.   The Cricket on the Hearth. L.C. Albert, 3/1/1846.
     [From Dickens' novel.]

D. Ruth Martin, the Fatal Dreamer. L.C. Albert, 9/3/1846.
D. The Midnight Torch. L.C. Garrick, 11/4/1846.
D. The World of Fashion (C.L. 1/6/1846). L.C. 28/5/1846 [as *The World in London*].
D. Amy the Skipper's Daughter; or, The Lily of Devon (Surrey, M. 3/5/1847). L.C. 1/5/1847.
D. The Bottle and the Glass; or, The Drunkard's Progress. L.C. Albert, 18/10/1847.
D. The Mercer of Ludgate. L.C. Grecian, 13/12/1847.
M.D. England's Charter; or, The Old Abbey Ruins. L.C. Albert, 16/10/1848.
D. Hearts and Homes. L.C. Albert, 18/11/1848.
D. Julie de Moin; or, The Assassin of Nantes (Vic. 11/6/1849). L.C. 12/6/1849.
   [For his subsequent work see *A History of Late Nineteenth Century Drama*, p. 249.]

BARNETT, MORRIS.
Ba. Supper's Over (Adel. M. 1/2/1830). L.C. 6/1/1830.
Da. The Bold Dragoons (Adel. T. 9/2/1830). *Dicks* 509; *Lacy*, vol. ix.
F. Tact (Queen's, M. 14/2/1831). *Duncombe*, vol. xiii.
M.Ent. Mrs G. (Queen's, M. 14/3/1831). *Duncombe*, vol. viii.
M.D. The Spirit of the Rhine (Queen's, T. 22/9/1835). *Duncombe*, vol. xix.
Ba. The Yellow Kids (Adel. M. 19/10/1835). L.C. 19/10/1835. *Dicks* 967; *Duncombe*, vol. xviii.
Ba. Monsieur Jacques (St J. W. 13/1/1836). 12° 1836; *Dicks* 503; *Lacy*, vol. xxviii.
   [From *Le pauvre Jacques* (Paris, 15/9/1835) by Cogniard.]
F. The Serious Family (H.² T. 30/10/1849). L.C. 24/10/1849. *Dicks* 1007.
   [From *Le mari à la campagne*.]
   [For his subsequent work see *A History of Late Nineteenth Century Drama*, pp. 249-50.]

BARON-WILSON, Mrs CORNWELL.
Oa. Genevieve, the Maid of Switzerland (E.O.H. M. 3/11/1834). L.C. 14/10/1834.
   [Music Sir G. A. Macfarren.]

BARRETT, EATON STANNARD.
F. My Wife! What Wife? (H.² T. 25/7/1815). L. 60 S. [17/7/1815]. 8° 1815.
   [And see under *CERVANTES HOGG*.]

BARRYMORE, WILLIAM.
P. War and Peace; or, Harlequin and the Miller's Daughter (R.A. M. 27/6/1814).
M.D. The Dog of Montargis; or, The Forest of Bondy (C.G. F. 30/9/1814). *Dicks* 163.
   [A version of Pixérécourt, *Le chien de Montargis; ou, la forêt de Bondy* (Paris, 1814). Music by Bishop.]
M.D.Spec. Trial by Battle; or, Heaven defend the Right (Cob. M. 11/5/1818). *Duncombe*, vol. viii; *New B.T.* 62.
M.D.Spec. Meg Murnoch; or, The Fatal Glen (R.A. M. 20/5/1816). *New B.T.* 382 [as *M.M., the Hag of the Glen*].

M.D   Wallace, the Hero of Scotland (R.A. M. 6/10/1817; Cob. M.
8/6/1818). *Dicks* 953; *Lacy*, vol. lxxiii.
M.D.Spec.   El Hyder, the Chief of the Ghaut Mountains (Cob. M.
7/12/1818). *Dicks* 140; *Lacy*, vol. vi.
Ba.   Country Actors; or, A Peep behind the Scenes (R.A. M. 9/7/1821).
Spec.   The Pirate of the Isles (R.A. M. 13/8/1821).
M.D.   Gilderoy, the Bonnie Boy (Cob. T. 25/6/1822). *Cumberland
Minor*, vol. viii; *Richardson Minor*, vol. ii.
M.D.   The Foulahs; or, A Slave's Revenge (Surrey, T. 26/8/1823).
D.   Aslan the Lion; or, The Seven Brazen Towers of Tepelini (Surrey,
M. 2/2/1824).
Ba.   The Secret (R.A. T. 11/5/1824). *New B.T.* 478; *Lacy*, vol. xlviii.
P.   Harlequin and the Dragon of Wantley (R.A. M. 26/7/1824).
Ent.   Jack Robinson and his Monkey. L.C. Edinburgh, 18/12/1828.
P.   The Queen Bee; or, Harlequin and the Fairy Hive (D.L. F.
26/12/1828). L.C. 18/12/1828.
[To these should be added: *The Two Sisters*; *The Blood Red
Knight*, printed in *Duncombe*, vol. lxvi; and *The Fatal Snowstorm*,
printed in *Cumberland Minor*, vol. xiii and in *Richardson Minor*,
vol. iv.]

BARRYMORE, Mrs W.
Div.   Evening Revels (D.L. 10/11/1823).

BARTHOLOMEW, B.
O.   Antigone (C.G. Th. 2/1/1845). L.C. 10/12/1844.
[Adapted from the German, with music by Mendelssohn.]

BASS, CHARLES.
D.   Lara (Dundee, 1827).

BAYLEY, PETER.
T.   Orestes in Argos (C.G. W. 20/4/1825). L.C. 18/2/1824.

BAYLEY, —, of Bath.
Ba.   The Witness (E.O.H. W. 12/8/1829). L.C. 28/7/1829.
[Music A. Lee.]

BAYLIS, HENRY.
F.   "But however —" (H.[1] T. 30/10/1838). See *H. MAYHEW*.

BAYLIS, JOHN.
F.   A House to be Sold. 12° 1804.
[An adaptation of *La maison à vendre*.]

BAYLY, THOMAS HAYNES.
F.   Perfection; or, The Lady of Munster (D.L. Th. 25/3/1830;
E.O.H. T. 7/9/1841). L.C. 23/3/1830. 12° [1830]; *Lacy*, vol. xiii;
Dicks 276.
Ba.   My Eleventh Day (Olym. 28/2/1832).
O.   Der Alchymist (D.L. T. 20/3/1832). See *E. FITZBALL*.
Ba.   Cupid (Olym. M. 10/9/1832). L.C. 1/9/1832 and 25/2/1832 [as
C.; or, My Eleventh Day].
Ba.   How do you manage? (Adel. M. 9/2/1835). *Lacy*, vol. i.
Ba.   Why don't she marry? or, The Swiss Cottage (Olym. M. 9/2/1835).
L.C. 9/2/1835. *Lacy*, vol. i.
F.   A Gentleman in Difficulties (Olym. M. 28/9/1835). L.C. 28/9/1835.
Dicks 545.

F.   Comfortable Service (Olym. M. 16/11/1835). *Lacy*, vol. i; *Dicks* 526.
Ba. One Hour; or, A Carnival Frolic (Olym. T. 12/1/1836). L.C.
     11/1/1836. *Acting Nat. Drama*, vol. iv; *Dicks* 906.
Ba. Forty and Fifty (Olym. W. 2/3/1836). L.C. 27/1/1836. 8° [1836];
     Acting Nat. Drama, vol. v; *Dicks* 462.
D.   The Daughter (Olym. 5/11/1835). L.C. 5/11/1835. *Lacy*, vol. i.
     [Based on Scribe, *La lectrice*.]
Ca. The Barrack Room (Olym. M. 7/11/1836). L.C. 1836. *French's
     Minor N.Y.*; *Dicks* 448.
Ba. The Ladder of Love (Olym. S. 16/12/1837). L.C. 12/12/1837 [as
     The Love Ladder]. *Lacy*, vol. i; *Dicks* 421.
Ba. The Culprit (St J. 18/1/1838). L.C. 30/12/1837. *Acting Nat.
     Drama*, vol. viii; *Mod. Eng. Com. Th.* vol. ii.
Ba. The Spitalfields Weaver (St J. S. 10/2/1838). L.C. 24/1/1838.
     Dicks 324; *Acting Nat. Drama*, vol. iii; *Mod. Eng. Com. Th.* vol. ii.
Ba. You can't marry your Grandmother (Olym. Th. 1/3/1838). L.C.
     25/2/1838. *Dicks* 527; *Acting Nat. Drama*, vol. iv.
F.   My Album (St J. M. 16/4/1838). L.C. 13/4/1838.
Ba. The British Legion (St J. M. 7/5/1838). L.C. 2/5/1838. *Dicks* 757;
     Acting Nat. Drama, vol. iv.
F.   Tom Noddy's Secret (H.² W. 12/9/1838). L.C. 11/9/1838.
     Dicks 462; *Acting Nat. Drama*, vol. v.
F.   Mr. Greenfinch (H.² S. 17/11/1838). L.C. 1838. *Dicks* 519
     Acting Nat. Drama, vol. vi.
F.   "My Little Adopted" (H.² W. 12/12/1838). L.C. 1838. *Dicks* 545;
     Acting Nat. Drama, vol. vi.
Ba. Friends and Neighbours (St J. M. 11/2/1839). L.C. 1839.

BEAZLEY, SAMUEL, Junior.
O.F. The Boarding House; or, Five Hours at Brighton (Lyc. M.
     26/8/1811). L. 95 M. [12/8/1811]. 8° 1811 [3 editions]; 8° 1814;
     8° 1816; *Cumberland Minor*, vol. xv.
     [Music Horn.]
Oa. Is He Jealous? (E.O.H. T. 2/7/1816). 8° 1816; *Dicks* 774; *Oxberry*,
     vol. iii; *New B.T.* 72.
     [Music T. Welsh.]
Oa. Old Customs; or, New Year's Gifts (E.O.H. M. 5/8/1816).
     L. 107 M. [17/7/1816].
Oa. My Uncle (E.O.H. M. 23/6/1817). L. 65 S. [22/5/1817]. 8° 1817.
     [Music Addison.]
Oa. Bachelors' Wives; or, The British at Brussels (E.O.H. W. 16/7/1817).
     L. 66 S. [19/6/1817; as *Tit for Tat; or, The B. in B.*].
     [Music Kearns.]
Oa. Fire and Water; or, A Critical Hour (E.O.H. T. 19/8/1817).
     L. 66 S. [4/8/1817].
     [Music Price.]
Oa. The Bull's Head (E.O.H. T. 14/7/1818).
C.O. Jealous on All Sides; or, The Landlord in Jeopardy! (E.O.H.
     W. 19/8/1818). L. 68 S. [7/8/1818]. 8° 1818.
     [Music Jolly.]
F.   Cozening; or, Half an Hour in France (C.G. S. 22/5/1819).
     L. 116 M. [20/5/1819].
C.   The Steward; or, Fashion and Feeling (C.G. W. 15/9/1819).
     L. 116 M. [23/6/1819]. *Dicks* 539.

18   N E D

M.D. Ivanhoe; or, The Knight Templar (C.G. Th. 2/3/1820).
L. 118 M. [10/2/1820].
O. Love's Dream (E.O.H. 5/7/1821). L. 77 S. [5/7/1820]. *Dun-combe*, vol. viii.
[An adaptation of Scribe, *La Somnambule* (Paris, 6/12/1819); music Moss.]
Oa. Gretna Green (E.O.H. S. 31/8/1822). L. 125 M. [17/8/1822].
C.O. Philandering; or, The Rose Queen (D.L. T. 13/1/1824).
L. 132 M. [7/1/1824]. 8° 1824.
[Music Horn.]
R.D. The Knights of the Cross; or, The Hermit's Prophecy (D.L.
M. 29/5/1826). L.C. 24/5/1826. *Cumberland*, vol. xxxiv.
[Music H. R. Bishop. A dramatisation of Scott's *The Talisman*.]
F. The Lottery Ticket; or, The Lawyer's Clerk (D.L. 13/12/1826).
L.C. 11/12/1826 [titles reversed]. *Dicks* 226; *Lacy*, vol. lxviii.
Spec. The Elephant of Siam; or, The Fire-Fiend (Adel. W. 2/12/1829).
L.C. 30/11/1829.
Ba. The Scapegrace (S.W. M. 30/1/1832).
F. The Divorce (Adel. M. 22/10/1832). L.C. 19/10/1832. *Dicks* 669.
O. Don Juan (D.L. 5/2/1833). L.C. 4/2/1833.
[Music Mozart.]
O.Bal. La Somnambula (D.L. W. 1/5/1833). L.C. 1/5/1833.
C. Hints for Husbands (H.² S. 29/8/1835). L.C. 25/8/1835.
F. Everybody's Widow (D.L. S. 8/10/1836). L.C. 1836.
Ba. The Queen of Cyprus (Adel. M. 31/1/1842). L.C. 25/1/1842.
F. You know what (S.W. M. 28/11/1842). L.C. 19/11/1842. *Dicks* 653.
[Davenport Adams, p. 131, also ascribes to him a version of
Robert the Devil.]

BECKET, ANDREW.
D. Poem. Socrates. 8° 1806; 8° 1811.
M. The Genii. 8° 1814 [in *The New B.T.*, vol. i].
[See *Dramatic and Prose Miscellanies*. 8° 1838.]

BECKINGTON, CHARLES.
Bsq. Hamlet the Dane. 8° 1847 [Newcastle]

BEDDOES, THOMAS LOVELL.
T. The Bride's Tragedy. 8° 1822.
T. Death's Jest Book, or The Fool's Tragedy. 8° 1850; 8° 1851 [in
Poems].

BEDINGFIELD, RICHARD.
T. Madeline. 8° 1847.

BELL, ARCHIBALD.
T. Count Clermont, a Tragedy; Caius Toranius, a Tragedy. 8° 1841
[Edinburgh].

BELL, ROBERT.
M.D. The Watch-word; or, Quito-Gate (D.L. S. 19/10/1816). 8° 1816.
[Genest gives this play to Bell, but the authorship is doubtful.]
Bsq. Macbeth Modernized: a most illegitimate drama. 8° 1838
[privately printed].
C. Marriage (H.² S. 29/1/1842). L.C. 17/1/1842. 8° 1842; *Dicks* 595.
C. Mothers and Daughters (C.G. T. 24/1/1843). L.C. 23/1/1843.
8° 1843; 8° 1844; *Dicks* 616.
C. Temper (H.² M. 17/5/1847). 8° 1847; *Dicks* 1018.

BENNETT, GEORGE JOHN.
D. The Soldier's Orphan; or, The Fortunes of War (Strand,
19/3/1844). L.C. 5/3/1844. *Duncombe*, vol. l.
D. The Justizia. L.C. Birmingham, 18/11/1848. 8° 1848 [as *The
Justizia; A Tale of Arragon*].

BENNETT, J. M.
D.Spec. Thirteen Years' Labour Lost; or, The Force of Nature (Cob.
M. 8/1/1821). 8° 1822.

BENTLEY, JOHN.
Sacred D. The Royal Penitent. 12° 1803.

BERARD, PETER.
F. The Uncle's Will; or, The Widow's Choice. 8° 1808.

BERNARD, WILLIAM BAYLE.
M.D. The Pilot: A Tale of the Sea (Cob. M. 17/7/1826).
M.D. Casco Bay; or, The Mutineers of 1727 (Olym. M. 3/12/1827).
L.C. 26/11/1827.
Oa. The Old Regimentals (Adel. S. 16/7/1831). L.C. 13/7/1831.
Cumberland, vol. xxxiii.
Ba. The Wept of Wish-Ton-Wish (Adel. M. 21/11/1831; Cob. Th.
1/3/1832). L.C. 12/11/1831. *Dicks* 546.
[From Cooper's novel.]
Ca. The Dumb Belle (Olym. W. 14/12/1831). L.C. 13/12/1831.
Dicks 522; *Lacy*, vol. xxiii.
D. The Metempsychosis (Surrey, M. 2/1/1832).
[I find the play recorded as performed at Tottenham-street in
1830; this I have been unable to verify.]
F. The Four Sisters; or, Woman's Worth and Woman's Ways
(Strand, M. 13/2/1832; R.P. M. 14/9/1835). *Dicks* 411; *Lacy*,
vol. xxiii.
D. Long Finn (Strand, M. 23/4/1832).
F. Wooing a Widow; or, Love under a Lamp post (Strand, F.
15/6/1832).
Ba. Rip van Winkle; or, The Helmsman of the Spirit Crew (Adel.
M. 1/10/1832). L.C. 29/9/1832.
C. The Conquering Game (Olym. W. 28/11/1832). L.C. 27/11/1832.
Dicks 676; *Duncombe*, vol. xxxvi.
C. The Nervous Man (D.L. S. 26/1/1833). L.C. 23/1/1833. *Dicks*
458; *Duncombe*, vol. xxvii; *Lacy*, vol. xxxix.
F. The Kentuckian; or, A Trip to New York (C.G. S. 9/3/1833).
L.C. 2/3/1833.
O.F. The Mummy (Adel. T. 4/6/1833). L.C. 20/5/1833. *Duncombe*,
vol. xxiv; *Lacy*, vol. xlviii.
[Music Hawes.]
D. Woman's Faith (E.O.H. M. 2/11/1835). L.C. 25/10/1835. 12°
1835; *Dicks* 536.
D. Lucille; or, The Story of a Heart (E.O.H. M. 4/4/1836; Vic. M.
4/9/1837). L.C. 31/3/1836. 12° 1836; *Dicks* 410; *Lacy*, vol. xxviii.
F. The Man about Town (E.O.H. Th. 5/5/1836). L.C. 2/5/1836.
Dicks 740; *Duncombe*, vol. xxii.
Oa. The Middy Ashore (E.O.H. M. 23/5/1836). L.C. 14/5/1836.
Dicks 349; *Duncombe*, vol. xxii.

M.D. The Farmer's Story (E.O.H. M. 13/6/1836; Vic. M. 10/7/1837; Strand, M. 9/4/1849). L.C. 6/1836. *Dicks* 434; *Lacy*, vol. xliv; *Duncombe*, vol. xxii.

Ba. The Yankee Pedlar; or, Old Times in Virginia (D.L. T. 1/11/1836). L.C. 29/10/1836.

R.D. Paulina; or, The Pass of Beresina (Adel. M. 5/12/1836). L.C. 30/11/1836. *Dicks* 516.

Ba. St Mary's Eve; or, A Story of the Solway (Adel. M. 1/1/1838). *Dicks* 382; *Lacy*, vol. xxxiii.

Ba. A Maiden's Fame; or, A Legend of Lisbon (Adel. M. 12/2/1838). L.C. 12/2/1838. *Dicks* 735; *Duncombe*, vol. xxviii.

F. A Wife for a Day (H.² M. 18/3/1839). L.C. 15/3/1839.

F. His Last Legs (H.² T. 15/10/1839). L.C. 10/1839. *Dicks* 439; *Acting Nat. Drama*, vol. vii.

F. The Happiest Man Alive (Olym. 21/3/1840). L.C. 17/3/1840. *Dicks* 965; *Duncombe*, vol. xli.

F. The Irish Attorney; or, Galway Practice in 1790 (H.² W. 6/5/1840). L.C. 26/4/1840 [as *The I.A.; or, It's Fifty Years Since*]. *Dicks* 463; *Acting Nat. Drama*, vol. ix.

D. Robespierre; or, Two Days of the Revolution (Adel. M. 5/10/1840). L.C. 21/9/1840 [as *R.; or, The Fete-day and the Fall*]. *Dicks* 610; *Duncombe*, vol. xlii.

C. The Philosophers of Berlin (Lyc. Th. 20/5/1841). L.C. 6/5/1841. *Dicks* 779.

D. Marie Ducange (Lyc. S. 29/5/1841). L.C. 25/5/1841. *Dicks* 475; *Lacy*, vol. xxxii.

F. The Boarding School (H.² W. 1/9/1841). L.C. 27/8/1841. *Dicks* 409; *Acting Nat. Drama*, vol. ix.

C. The Woman Hater (H.² T. 22/2/1842). L.C. 18/2/1842. *Dicks* 526; *Acting Nat. Drama*, vol. ix.

F. Locomotion (H.² W. 16/8/1842). L.C. 8/8/1842. *Dicks* 952; *Acting Nat. Drama*, vol. ix.

C. Louise; or, The Recompense (H.² M. 29/5/1843). L.C. 20/5/1843. *Dicks* 710.

[An adaptation of Scribe, *Louise; ou, la réparation* (Paris, 16/11/1829).]

F. The Absentee (H.² 20/5/1844). L.C. 15/3/1844.

D. Blanche de Valmy (P'cess, T. 28/5/1844). L.C. 17/5/1844.

D. The Round of Wrong (H.² S. 19/12/1846). L.C. 12/12/1846. *Dicks* 1000; *Acting Nat. Drama*, vol. xiii.

F. A Practical Man (Lyc. S. 20/10/1849). L.C. 15/10/1848 [as *Nothing to Do!*]. *Lacy*, vol. i.

[For some of his later plays see *A History of Late Nineteenth Century Drama*, p. 259. *The Passing Cloud*, cited by Davenport Adams (p. 149) as acted in 1848, seems to belong to 1850.]

BERNAYS, LEOPOLD JOHN.
D. Faust...with other poems. 8° 1839; 8° 1840 [Carlsruhe].

BERNEL, GEORGE.
T. Germanicus. 8° 1817.
[A translation from the French of A.-V. Arnault. The anonymous *Germanicus* anticipates this by three days according to a slip inserted in Bernel's edition.]

BESWICK, GEORGE.
F.　Mesmerism versus Galvanism. L.C. Albert, 1845.

BETHUNE, GILBERT.
Past.　The Gentle Shepherd; Translated into English from the Scotch of Allan Ramsay's Gentle Shepherd. 8° 1817.

BETHUNE, J. E. DRINKWATER.
D.　The Maid of Orleans. 8° 1835 [privately printed]; 8° 1848 [in *Specimens*].
　　[A translation of Schiller, *Die Jungfrau von Orleans* (1802).]

BEVERLEY, HENRY ROXBURY [or ROXBY].
M.D.　The Abbot; or, Mary of Scotland (Tottenham-street, 18/9/1820). [From Scott's novel.]

BIDLAKE, Rev. JOHN.
　　[See *A History of Late Eighteenth Century Drama*, p. 238.]
T.　Virginius; or, The Fall of the Decemvirs (D.L. M. 29/5/1820). L. 79 S. [D.L. 9/5/1820].
　　[A revised version of the *Virginia* published in 8° 1800.]

BIRCH, JONATHAN.
D.　Faust. 8° 1839 [Part I]; 8° 1843 [Parts I and II].
　　[A translation of Goethe's play.]

BIRD, JAMES.
T.　Cosmo, Duke of Tuscany. 8° 1822.
D.D.　The Smuggler's Daughter (S.W. Th. 8/10/1835). 12° 1836.

[BIRD, Dr ROBERT MONTGOMERY.
T.　The Gladiator (D.L. M. 17/10/1836). L.C. 1836. [Text in C. E. Foust, *Life and Dramatic Works of R. M. Bird* (New York, 1919).]
　　[This play also appeared in the English bills as *Spartacus*. It had been produced in New York on 26/9/1831; see A. H. Quinn, *op. cit.* pp. 229 and 435.]

BIRRELL, ANDREW.
T.　Henry and Almeria. 8° 1802.

BISHOP, Sir HENRY ROWLEY.
O.F.　Who wants a Wife; or, The Law of the Land (C.G. T. 16/4/1816). L. 64 S. [30/3/1816].
　　[Music by the author.]
M.D.　Yelva; or, The Orphan of Russia (C.G. Th. 5/2/1829). L.C. 22/1/1829.
　　[Music by the author.]
　　[For his other theatrical work see the *D.N.B.*]

BLACKET, —
C.　The Libertine Lovers. 8° 1811.

BLACKIE, J. S.
D.　Faust. 8° 1834 [Edinburgh]; 8° 1880.
　　[A translation of Goethe's drama.]

BLACKWELL, J. A.
D.　Rudolf of Varosnay. 8° 1841.

BLAKE, THOMAS G.
R.D.　The Dumb Guide of the Tyrol (Adel. 9/10/1837). *Dicks* 756.
D.　The Wreck of Twenty Years! (S.W. M. 30/7/1838).

D. Savourneen Deelish; or, The Girl of my Heart; or, The Soldier's Bride (S.W. T. 11/6/1839).
D. Life as it is l or, The Convict's Child (S.W. M. 22/7/1839).
M.D. The Cattle-stealers of the Mountain; or, The Drover's Dog (Vic. M. 7/9/1840).
M.D. Our Old House at Home (S.W. M. 26/7/1841). L.C. 2/8/1841. *Dicks* 511; *Lacy*, vol. xxv.
D. Beatrice; or, The Broken Heart (Queen's, 21/10/1844). L.C. 28/9/1844.
Ba. Poor Dog Tray (Vic. M. 7/4/1845).
F. Satisfaction; or, The Duellists. L.C. Grecian, 16/5/1845.
F. The Student's Dream; or, The Fiend of the Fountain. L.C. R.P. 25/8/1845.
D. The Dumb Driver. L.C. Apollo, 1846.
F. The Contract of St Cloud. L.C. Grecian, 26/1/1846.
F. Drawn for the Militia (Queen's, 19/1/1846). L.C. 14/1/1846.
D. Gillian the Gipsey (C.L. 8/6/1846). L.C. 11/4/1846.
D. The False Light; or, The Son of a Sailor. L.C. Albert, 24/4/1847.
Spec. The Lonely Man of the Ocean (Vic. M. 24/5/1847). L.C. R.P. 21/5/1847. *Lacy*, vol. xvi.
[To these should be added *Wapping Old Stairs* (1834), *Edith of the Marsh* (1840), *The Bridge of Kehl* (1841), *A Spanking Legacy* (1843) and *Poverty* (1844).]

BLANCHARD, EDWARD LEMAN.
F. Angels and Lucifers; or, Courtship and Congreves (Manor-house, Chelsea, 1838; Olym. 25/10/1841; Olym. M. 27/2/1843). L.C. 1841.
F. The Angel of Islington (Queen's, 12/10/1840).
F. The Artful Dodge (Olym. M. 21/2/1842). L.C. 18/2/1842. *Lacy*, vol. xlii.
F. Jack Noakes and Tom Styles (Olym. M. 10/10/1842). L.C. 7/10/1842.
Oa. Arcadia (Grecian, 1843).
Ext. Pork Chops (Olym. M. 13/2/1843). L.C. 10/2/1843. *Lacy*, vol. xlv [as *P.C.; or, A Dream at Home*].
Bsq. The Merchant of Venice (Olym. 2/10/1843). L.C. 21/9/1843.
C. The Road of Life; or, Lights and Shadows (Olym. M. 23/10/1843). L.C. 11/10/1843 [as *The R. of L.; or, Romance and Reality*].
F. Game and Game; or, Who's the Winner? (Olym. M. 20/11/1843; S.W. Th. 19/9/1844). L.C. 16/11/1843.
Ext. Cinderella; or, The Great Fairy and the Little Glass Slipper (Olym. 8/4/1844). L.C. 1/4/1844.
F. The Invisible Client (Olym. M. 6/5/1844). L.C. 2/5/1844.
P. Jack and the Bean-Stalk (Vic. M. 2/9/1844).
Bsq. Antigone (Strand, T. 4/2/1845). L.C. 1/2/1845.
Bsq. Robinson Crusoe (Strand, 12/5/1845). L.C. 8/5/1845.
D.D. Faith, Hope and Charity; or, Chance and Change (Surrey, M. 7/7/1845). L.C. 2/6/1845. *Duncombe*, vol. liv.
D. The Queen of Bohemia; or, London in 1664 (Olym. M. 6/10/1845). L.C. 15/9/1845 [as *The Q. of B.; or, L. in the Days of Charles II*].
Bsq. The Cricket on our own Hearth (Olym. Th. 15/1/1846). L.C. 16/1/1846.
P. The Birth of the Steam Engine; or, Harlequin Locomotive (Vic. S. 26/12/1846). L.C. 21/12/1846.

P.   King Alfred the Great; or, Harlequin History and the Enchanted
     Raven (Olym. S. 26/12/1846). L.C. 12/12/1846.
F.   A Wife for an Hour (P'cess, W. 28/4/1847). L.C. 5/3/1847.
P.   Eyes, Nose and Mouth; or, Harlequin Prince Perfect and the
     Birth of Beauty (M'bone, M. 27/12/1847). L.C. 13/12/1847.
P.   Harlequin Lord Lovell; or, The Mistletoe Bough; or, Lady
     Nancy Bell and the Fairies of the Oak (Surrey, T. 26/12/1848).
     L.C. 23/12/1848.
P.   William the Conqueror; or, Harlequin Harold and the Sack of the
     Saxons (Olym. T. 26/12/1848). L.C. 23/12/1848.
     [For his later plays see *A History of Late Nineteenth Century
     Drama*, pp. 262–5.]

BLOOMFIELD, HELEN.
F.   The Euston Hotel. L.C. R.P. 8/5/1845.

BLOOMFIELD, ROBERT.
D.   Hazelwood Hall. 12° 1823.

BOADEN, CAROLINE.
C.   Quite Correct (II.² S. 30/7/1825). L.C. 19/7/1825.
D.   Fatality (H.² T. 1/9/1829). L.C. 6/2/1829. *Cumberland*, vol. xxiii.
F.   William Thompson; or, Which is He? (H.² 11/9/1829). L.C.
     3/9/1829. 12° 1829; *Cumberland*, vol. xxiii.
F.   The First of April (H.² T. 31/8/1830). L.C. 3/8/1830. *Cumberland*,
     vol. xxvi.
D.   A Duel in Richelieu's Time (H.² M. 9/7/1832). L.C. 27/6/1832.
     [To these should be added: *Don Pedro the Cruel and Don
     Manuel the Cobbler.* 12° 1839; *Duncombe*, vol. iii.]

BOADEN, JAMES.
     [For his earlier plays see *A History of Late Eighteenth Century Drama*,
     pp. 238–9.]
M.D. The Voice of Nature (H.² S. 31/7/1802). L. 42 S. [20/7/1802].
     8° 1803.
     [An adaptation of Caigniez' *Le Jugement de Salomon*.]
D.   The Maid of Bristol (H.² W. 24/8/1803). L. 43 S. [2/8/1803].
     8° 1803.

BOOTHBY, Sir BROOKE.
T.   Britannicus. 8° 1803.
     [A translation of Racine's tragedy.]

BOSWORTH, J.
M.D. The Cipoy King; or, The Perilous Pass of the Cataract (Queen's,
     M. 27/3/1837). *Dicks* 654.

BOUCICAULT [or BOURCICAULT], DION.
D.   A Legend of the Devil's Dyke (Brighton, 1838). *Dicks* 1043.
C.   London Assurance (C.G. M. 4/3/1841). L.C. 1/3/1841. 8° 1841;
     Dicks 1044; *Lacy*, vol. xxxiv.
C.   The Irish Heiress (C.G. M. 7/2/1842). L.C. 27/1/1842. 8° 1842.
Ca. A Lover by Proxy (H.² Th. 21/4/1842). L.C. 12/4/1842. *Acting
     Nat. Drama*, vol. ix.
C.   Alma Mater; or, A Cure for Coquettes (H.² M. 19/9/1842). L.C.
     3/9/1842. *Acting Nat. Drama*, vol. x.
D.   Woman (C.G. M. 2/10/1843). L.C. 19/9/1843.
D.   The Old Guard (P'cess, M. 9/10/1843). *Dicks* 1056.

Ca. Used Up (H.² T. 6/2/1844; H.² M. 1/6/1846) L.C. 25/1/1844.
     Dicks 1047; *Webster*; *French's Minor N.Y.* [as by Charles Mathews
     and described as the "only published edition"]; *Mod. Eng.
     Com. Th.* vol. v.
     [Written in collaboration with CHARLES MATHEWS; based
     on *L'homme blasé*.]
Oa. The Fox and the Goose (Adel. W. 2/10/1844). See *B. N.
     WEBSTER.*
D.   Don Caesar de Bazan (Adel. M. 14/10/1844). L.C. 7/10/1844.
     Acting Nat. Drama, vol. x.
     [Written in collaboration with *B. WEBSTER*; based on the
     French of Dumanois and Dennery.]
C.   Old Heads and Young Hearts (H.² M. 18/11/1844). L.C. 14/11/1844.
     8° [1845; *bis*]; *Acting Nat. Drama*, vol. xiii; *Mod. Eng. Com. Th.*
     vol. iii.
Ca. A Soldier of Fortune (Adel. 6/2/1845). L.C. 10/1/1845.
F.   Enquire Within (Lyc. 25/8/1845). L.C. 21/8/1845.
F.   Up the Flue; or, What's in the Wind? L.C. Adel. 11/5/1846.
     [Called at first *Felo de Se*; written in collaboration with
     C. KENNEY.]
C.   The School for Scheming (H.² Th. 4/2/1847). L.C. 3/2/1847.
     Dicks 1046.
C.   Confidence (H.² 2/5/1848). L.C. 3/5/1848.
Ca. The Knight of Arva (H.² 22/11/1848). L.C. 18/11/1848. *French's
     N.Y.*
D.   The Willow Copse (Adel. 26/11/1849). L.C. 21/11/1849.
     [For his later work see *A History of Late Nineteenth Century
     Drama*, pp. 267–9.]

BRADWELL, WILLIAM.
P.   The Enchanted Hall; or, The Parthian Harlequin (R.A. M.
     20/8/1804).

BRAMSEN, J.
T.   Sappho. 8° 1820.
     [A translation from Grillparzer.]

BRANDON, ISAAC.
O.   Kais; or, Love in the Desarts (D.L. Th. 11/2/1808). L. 50 S.
     [8/2/1808]. 8° 1808 [3 editions]; 8° 1808 [Songs, Duets, Trios
     and Chorusses].
     [Music Reeve and Braham.]

BRASSINGTON, RICHARD, Junior.
F.   Tricks upon Travellers (Crow-street, Dublin, 12/11/1816).

BRAYLEY, —
F.   Wool Gathering (D.L. F. 6/1/1826). L.C. 3/12/1825.

BRECK, CHARLES.
D.   The Trust. 8° 1808.

BREWER, EBENEZER COBHAM.
T.   Charles I. 8° 1828.

BRIDGEMAN, JOHN V.
D.   The Black Doctor (C.L. 9/11/1846). L.C. 31/10/1846. *Lacy,*
     vol. xxiii.
     [An adaptation of *Le docteur noir* (Paris, 30/7/1846) by Anicet-
     Bourgeois and Dumanoir.]
     [For his later work see *A History of Late Nineteenth Century
     Drama*, pp. 274–5.]

BROADFOOT, J. W.
Spec. The Prince of Cyprus. L.C. Birmingham, 22/4/1846.

BROMLEY, GEORGE PERCIVAL.
T.C. The Rebellion; or, Norwich in 1549 (Norwich, 17/4/1815).
L. 106 M. [10/4/1815]. 8° 1815 [Norwich].

[BROOKE, HENRY.
T. Gustavus Vasa (C.G. S. 28/12/1805).
[This was apparently the first London performance of the 1745
play, which, however, had already been staged in Dublin; see
A History of Early Eighteenth Century Drama, p. 300.]

BROOKS, CHARLES WILLIAM SHIRLEY.
C. Our New Governess (Lyc. Th. 1/5/1845).
C. Honours and Tricks (Lyc. Th. 2/4/1846). L.C. 11/4/1846.
Ba. The Wigwam (Lyc. M. 25/1/1847). L.C. 16/1/1847. *Dicks* 1004.
M.D. The Creole; or, Love's Fetters (Lyc. Th. 8/4/1847). *Dicks* 1009;
Lacy, vol. i.
F. Anything for a Change (Lyc. W. 7/6/1848). L.C. 3/6/1848.
Lacy, vol. iv; *De Witt's Acting Plays N.Y.* 114; *French* 53.
F. Shave you directly (Lyc. W. 21/2/1849). L.C. 23/2/1849.
F. The Guardian Angel (H.² Th. 25/10/1849). *Lacy*, vol. v.
[For his later plays see *A History of Late Nineteenth Century
Drama*, p. 277.]

BROUGH, ROBERT BARNABAS.
Ext. The Enchanted Isle (1848). See *W. BROUGH.*
Ext. Camaralzaman and Badoura (1848). See *W. BROUGH.*
Ext. The Sphinx (1849). See *W. BROUGH.*
Bsq. Frankenstein (1849). See *W. BROUGH.*
[For his later work see *A History of Late Nineteenth Century
Drama*, pp. 277–8.]

BROUGH, WILLIAM.
Ext. The Enchanted Isle; or, "Raising the Wind" on the most
approved principles: A Drama without the smallest claim to
legitimacy, consistency, probability, or anything else but absurdity,
in which will be found much that is unaccountably coincident with
Shakspere's "Tempest" (Amphitheatre, Liverpool, 1848; Adel.
M. 20/11/1848). L.C. Liverpool, 10/8/1848. 8° (1848). *Acting
Nat. Drama*, vol. xiv.
[Written in collaboration with *R. B. BROUGH.*]
Ext Camaralzaman and Badoura; or, The Peri who loved the Prince
(H.² T. 26/12/1848). L.C. 1848; *Acting Nat. Drama*, vol. xv.
[Written in collaboration with *R. B. BROUGH.*]
Ext. The Sphinx (H.² M. 9/4/1849). L.C. 14/4/1849; *Acting Nat.
Drama*, vol. xv.
[Written in collaboration with *R. B. BROUGH.*]
Bsq. Frankenstein; or, The Model Man (Adel. W. 26/12/1849).
L.C. 19/12/1849.
[Written in collaboration with *R. B. BROUGH.*]
[For his later plays see *A History of Late Nineteenth Century
Drama*, pp. 278–80.]

BROUGHAM, JOHN.
Ba. The Demon Gift; or, Visions of the Future (E.O.H. M. 29/6/1840).
L.C. 29/6/1840.
[Written in collaboration with *M. LEMON.*]

Ext. Life in the Clouds; or, Olympus in an Uproar (E.O.H. Th. 23/7/1840). L.C. 23/7/1840. 8° [1840].
Oa. Love's Livery (E.O.H. Th. 30/7/1840). L.C. 28/7/1840.
O. The Hunter's Bride; or, The Rose of Altenheim (E.O.H. 4/6/1841). L.C. 7/6/1841.
Ba. The Enthusiast (E.O.H. 9/5/1842). L.C. 7/5/1842.
C. Romance and Reality; or, Silence gives Consent (P'cess, T. 1/6/1847). L.C. 21/5/1847. Dicks 730.
D. Jane Eyre; or, The Secrets of Thornfield Manor House (Vic. 27/1/1848). L.C. 27/1/1848. Dicks 400.
[For his later plays see A History of Late Nineteenth Century Drama, pp. 280–1.]

BROWN, CHARLES ARMITAGE.
C.O. Narensky; or, The Road to Yaroslaf (D.L. T. 11/1/1814). 8° 1814.
[Music Braham and Reeve.]

BROWNING, ELIZABETH BARRETT.
T. Prometheus Bound, translated from the Greek of Æschylus. 8° 1833.

BROWNING, ROBERT.
T. Strafford (C.G. M. 1/5/1837). L.C. 28/4/1837. 8° 1837.
D. Pippa Passes. 8° 1841 [in Bells and Pomegranates].
D. King Victor and King Charles. 8° 1842 [in Bells and Pomegranates].
D. The Return of the Druses. 8° 1843 [in Bells and Pomegranates].
D. A Blot in the 'Scutcheon (D.L. S. 11/2/1843). L.C. 16/2/1843. 8° 1843 [in Bells and Pomegranates].
D. Colombe's Birthday. 8° 1846 [in Bells and Pomegranates].
D. Luria; and A Soul's Tragedy. 8° 1846 [in Bells and Pomegranates].

BRUCE, J. W.
T. Don Carlos. 12° 1837 [Mannheim].
[A translation of Schiller's drama.]

BRUTON, JAMES.
F. Bathing (Olym. M. 31/1/1842). L.C. 21/1/1842. Dicks 949; Duncombe, vol. xliv; Lacy, vol. cviii.
Ba. Davis and Sally Dear (Olym. 7/3/1842). L.C. 5/3/1842.
F. Cut for Partners (P'cess, M. 13/5/1844). L.C. 11/5/1844. Duncombe, vol. lv; Lacy, vol. cxii.

BUCKE, CHARLES.
T. The Italians, or The Fatal Accusation (D.L. S. 3/4/1819). L. 115 M. [printed copy]. 8° 1819 [7 editions; "With a Preface; containing the Correspondence of the Author with the Committee of Drury Lane Theatre"]; 8° 1820.
[Music Cooke.]
T. Julio Romano. 8° 1830.

BUCKSTONE, JOHN BALDWIN.
M.D. The Bear-Hunters; or, The Fatal Ravine (Cob. 25/4/1825). Dicks 863; Duncombe, vol. ii.
Ba. Curiosity Cured; or, Powder for Peeping (S.W. M. 20/6/1825).
O.R. The Death Fetch; or, The Student of Gottingen (E.O.H. T. 25/7/1826). Dicks 831.
[Music C. E. Horn.]

M.D. Luke the Labourer; or, The Lost Son (Adel. T. 17/10/1826).
L.C. 16/10/1826. *Dicks* 830; *Cumberland Minor*, vol. ii; *Lacy*, vol.
lxix.

Ba. "A Card! 23 John Street, Adelphi" (Adel. T. 21/11/1826; Surrey,
M. 11/4/1836). L.C. 18/11/1826. *Dicks*, 842; *Cumberland Minor*,
vol. vii.

Ba. A Dead Shot (Adel. M. 22/1/1827). L.C. 17/1/1827. *Dicks* 808;
Duncombe, vol. ix; *Lacy*, vol. xxxiv.

D.D. Presumptive Evidence; or, Murder will out (Adel. M. 3/3/1828).
Dicks 812; *Richardson Minor*, vol. ii; *Cumberland*, vol. xxxiv;
Lacy, vol. lxxxii.

P. The Snake King. See below under date 19/8/1833.

M.D. Boyne Water; or, Oonagh of the Broken Heart (Cob. M.
7/4/1828). *Dicks* 807.

M.D. Theodore the Brigand; or, The Corsican Conscript (S.W.
14/7/1828). *Duncombe*, vol. vii.

Int. Mischief-Making (Surrey, T. 16/9/1828; S.W. W. 1/4/1846).
Dicks 804; *Cumberland Minor*, vol. iv; *Lacy*, vol. lxxix; *British and
American Theatre*, No. 7 [with German notes].

Bsq. The Absent Son (Adel. M. 29/9/1828). L.C. 24/9/1828.

Ba. Wanted a Partner; or, "A Bill due Sept. 29th" (Adel. M.
29/9/1828). L.C. 23/9/1828.

Ba. The May Queen; or, Sampson the Serjeant (Adel. Th. 9/10/1828).
L.C. 15/11/1827. 8° 1834; 8° 1835; *Dicks* 818.

M.D. The Young Quaker (Bath, 16/3/1829).

M.D. Peter Bell the Waggoner; or, Murderers of Massiac (Cob. M.
20/4/1829). *Dicks* 862; *Lacy*, vol. cx; *Duncombe*, vol. xiv.
[Davenport Adams gives to this the date 1826; 1829 is the earliest
authentic record I can discover.]

D. Vidocq the French Police Spy (Cob. 6/7/1829).

Ba. The Happiest Day of my Life (H.² W. 29/7/1829). L.C. 8/6/1829.
Dicks 844; *Cumberland*, vol. xxiii; *British and American Theatre*,
No. 10 [with German notes]; *Lacy*, vol. lxxx.

Bsq. Billy Taylor; or, The Gay Young Fellow (Adel. 11/1829).
L.C. 5/11/1829. *Dicks* 866; *Cumberland Minor*, vol. iii.

C. Snakes in the Grass (D.L. T. 3/11/1829). L.C. 5/11/1829. *Dicks*
841; *Cumberland*, vol. xxiv; *Mod. Eng. Com. Th.* vol. iii.

F. Popping the Question (D.L. 23/3/1830). *Dicks* 865; *Lacy*, vol.
lxxxvii; *Cumberland*, vol. xxxv.

Ba. Don Juan (Adel. M. 5/7/1830). L.C. 24/6/1830. *Dicks* 828;
Richardson Minor, vol. i.
[I find the date 1/12/1828 cited for this drama; quite clearly this
is wrong as the play was not licensed until 1830.]

F. A Husband at Sight (H.² F. 13/8/1830). L.C. 14/7/1830. *Dicks*
850; *Cumberland*, vol. xxvi.

Ba. The Wreck Ashore; or, A Bridegroom from the Sea (Adel. Th.
21/10/1830; S.W. M. 17/7/1837). L.C. 15/10/1830. 8° 1834;
8° 1835; *Dicks* 806; *Acting Nat. Drama*, vol. viii.
[From the L.C. copy it seems that this was first called *Miles the
Marauder*.]

R.D. The King of the Alps; or, The Misanthrope (Adel. M. 24/1/1831).
L.C. 17/1/1831. *Dicks* 854; *Lacy*, vol. vi.

R.D. The Ice Witch; or, The Frozen Hand (D.L. M. 4/4/1831).
L.C. 25/3/1831. *Cumberland*, vol. xxviii.
[Music Cooke.]

Ba. John Jones (H.² Th. 15/9/1831; Adel. M. 4/12/1848). L.C. 1/9/1831. *Dicks* 816; *Lacy*, vol. xxv.
M.D. The Sea Serpent (Adel. M. 3/10/1831). See *E. FITZBALL*.
D. Victorine; or, "I'll Sleep on it" (Adel. M. 17/10/1831). L.C. 7/10/1831. 8° 1834; *Dicks* 856; *Acting Nat. Drama*, vol. viii.
F. Damon and Pythias (Adel. 19/12/1831). L.C. 16/12/1831. *Dicks* 848; *Cumberland Minor*, vol. vi.
M.D. Robert le Diable (Adel. M. 23/1/1832). See *E. FITZBALL*.
Ba. Forgery; or, The Reading of the Will (Adel. M. 5/3/1832). L.C. 2/3/1832. *Dicks* 835.
C. Second Thoughts (H.² S. 4/8/1832). L.C. 23/7/1832. *Dicks* 839.
D. The Little Red Man; or, The Witch of the Water Snakes (S.W. M. 24/9/1832).
D. Henriette the Forsaken (Adel. M. 5/11/1832). L.C. 3/11/1832. 8° 1834; *Dicks* 821; *Acting Nat. Drama*, vol. viii.
M.D. The Bravo, A Story of Venice (Adel. M. 11/2/1833). L.C. 9/2/1833. *Dicks* 861.
[From Cooper's novel.]
Oa. The Pet of the Petticoats (R.P. M. 11/3/1833). 8° 1835; *Dicks* 824.
F. Open House: or, The Twin Sisters (H.² M. 8/4/1833). L.C. 22/3/1833 [under sub-title]. *Dicks* 838; *Cumberland*, vol. xxxi.
D. Ellen Wareham (H.² W. 24/4/1833; S.W. M. 27/5/1833). L.C. 12/4/1833. *Dicks* 837.
F. Nicholas Flam, Attorney at Law (R.P. Th. 1/8/1833). L.C. 24/7/1833. *Dicks* 840.
P. The Snake King; or, Harlequin and the Fairy of the Coral Branch (R.P. M. 19/8/1833).
[I give this to Buckstone on the authority of a MS. in the possession of Mr Crompton Rhodes which dates the pantomime "Whit Monday, 1828" at S.W. and ascribes it to "Younge alias Buckstone."]
C. Uncle John (H.² T. 15/10/1833). L.C. 12/10/1833. 8° 1833; *Dicks* 826.
C. The Rake and his Pupil; or, Folly, Love and Marriage (Adel. M. 25/11/1833). L.C. 25/11/1833 [as *The Young Rake; or, F., L. and M.*]. 8° 1834; *Dicks* 823.
D. Isabelle; or, Woman's Life (Adel. M. 27/1/1834). 8° 1835; *Dicks* 817; *Acting Nat. Drama*, vol. viii.
[Also called *Thirty Years of a Woman's Life*.]
Ba. Married Life (H.² W. 20/8/1834). L.C. 11/8/1834. 8° 1834; *Dicks* 802; *Acting Nat. Drama*, vol. v.
[Translated into German as *Eheliches Leben* in J. Wertheimer, *Dramatische Beyträge*. 12° 1833.]
C.O. Rural Felicity (H.² M. 9/6/1834). L.C. 30/5/1834. 8° 1834; *Dicks* 811.
Ba. The Christening (Adel. M. 13/10/1834). L.C. 13/10/1834. 8° 1834; *Dicks* 816.
D. Agnes de Vere; or, The Broken Heart (Adel. M. 10/11/1834). L.C. 6/11/1834. 8° 1836; *Dicks* 805; *Lacy*, vol. cvi.
M.D. The Last Days of Pompeii; or, Seventeen Hundred Years Ago (Adel. M. 15/12/1834). L.C. 10/12/1834. *Dicks* 829.
[From Lytton's novel.]
C. Good Husbands make Good Wives (H.² Th. 11/6/1835). L.C. 9/5/1835. *Dicks* 846.
C. The Scholar (H.² W. 1/7/1835). L.C. 17/6/1835. *Dicks* 834.

Ba. The Two Queens; or, Politics in Petticoats (Olym. Th. 8/10/1835).
L.C. 2/10/1835. 8° 1837; *Dicks* 848; *Lacy*, vol. i.
D. The Dream at Sea (Adel. M. 23/11/1835; Surrey, M. 2/8/1847).
L.C. 21/11/1835. 8° 1835 [4 editions]; *Dicks* 803; *Acting Nat.
Drama*, vol. viii.
R.D. Rienzi, The Last of the Tribunes (Adel. W. 3/2/1836). L.C.
1/2/1836.
R.D. The Doom of Morana; or, The Spirit of Good and Evil (Adel.
M. 3/10/1836). *Dicks* 872.
D. The Duchess de la Vaubaliere (Adel. M. 2/1/1837). 8° 1837;
Dicks 815.
D. Abelard and Heloise (Surrey, M. 8/5/1837). 8° 1837; *Dicks* 814.
C. Love and Murder; or, The School for Sympathy (H.² T. 15/8/1837).
Dicks 810.
Ba. Shocking Events (Olym. M. 15/1/1838). L.C. 2/1/1838. *Dicks*
808; *Acting Nat. Drama*, vol. iii.
F. Our Mary Anne (D.L. Th. 18/1/1838; S.W. M. 13/9/1847). L.C.
1/1838. *Dicks* 804; *Acting Nat. Drama*, vol. iii.
F. Weak Points (H.² S. 28/4/1838). L.C. 25/4/1838. *Dicks* 845;
Acting Nat. Drama, vol. iv.
F. The Irish Lion (H.² W. 13/6/1838). L.C. 6/6/1838. *Dicks* 822.
C. A Lesson for the Ladies (H.² W. 5/9/1838). L.C. 1838. *Dicks* 809;
Acting Nat. Drama, vol. v.
Ba. I will be a Duchess (Strand, M. 15/4/1839). L.C. 1839 [with
sub-title, *or, A Little Flirting*].
C. Single Life (H.² T. 23/7/1839). L.C. 21/7/1839. *Dicks* 801; *Acting
Nat. Drama*, vol. vii.
F. Brother Tom; or, "My Dear Relations" (H.² Th. 10/10/1839).
L.C. 1839. *Dicks* 822.
D. Jack Sheppard (Adel. M. 28/10/1839). *Acting Nat. Drama*, vol. vii.
C. The Banished Star (said to have been acted in America in 1840).
D. Poor Jack; or, A Sailor's Wife (Adel. M. 3/2/1840). L.C. 23/1/1840.
Dicks 813.
Ext. The Devil in London (Adel. M. 20/4/1840) See *R. B. PEAKE*.
F. A Kiss in the Dark (H.² S. 13/6/1840). L.C. 11/6/1840 [with
variant title, *Hubby's Jealousy*]. *Dicks* 852; *Lacy*, vol. vi.
F. The Snapping Turtles; or, Matrimonial Masquerading (H.² M.
14/11/1842). *Dicks* 865; *Lacy*, vol. lxix.
C.O. Josephine; or, The Fortune of War (H.² Th. 7/3/1844—2nd
performance; Surrey, M. 15/9/1845). L.C. 3/1/1844. *Dicks* 864;
Lacy, vol. xxv.
F. The Thimble Rig (H.² Th. 5/10/1844). L.C. 20/9/1844. *Dicks* 842;
Acting Nat. Drama, vol. x.
D. The Green Bushes; or, A Hundred Years Ago (Adel. M. 27/1/1845).
L.C. 22/1/1845. *Dicks* 827; *Acting Nat. Drama*, vol. xi.
F. The Maid with the Milking Pail (Adel. M. 6/7/1846). L.C.
1/7/1846. *Dicks* 866; *Lacy*, vol. x.
M.D. The Flowers of the Forest. A Gipsy Story (Adel. Th. 11/3/1847).
L.C. 5/3/1847. *Dicks* 1002; *Acting Nat. Drama*, vol. xiii.
Ba. Nine too many (Adel. Th. 11/3/1847). *Dicks* 1004.
F. A Rough Diamond (Lyc. M. 8/11/1847). L.C. 6/11/1847. *Dicks*
1006; *Lacy*, vol. xvii; *Mod. Eng. Com. Th.* vol. v.
F. An Alarming Sacrifice (H.² Th. 12/7/1849). *Dicks* 1012.
[For his later works see *A History of Late Nineteenth Century
Drama*, pp. 286–7.]

BUNN, ALFRED.
M.D. Kenilworth (C.G. Th. 8/3/1821). L. 120 M. [3/3/1821].
  8° [1821].
  [A revised version of *T. J. DIBDIN'S* dramatisation of Scott's
  novel.]
F. My Neighbour's Wife (C.G. M. 7/10/1833). L.C. 24/9/1833.
  Dicks 316.
C. The Minister and the Mercer (D.L. S. 8/2/1834). L.C. 23/1/1834.
  8° 1834.
  [An adaptation of Scribe, *Bertrand et Raton; ou, l'art de con-
  spirer* (Paris, 14/11/1833).]
F. A Good-looking Fellow (C.G. Th. 17/4/1834). See *J. KENNEY.*
O. The Bronze Horse (D.L. T. 5/1/1836). L.C. 30/12/1835.
  [An adaptation of Scribe, *Le cheval de bronze* (Paris, 22/3/1835),
  with music by Auber.]
O. The Maid of Artois (D.L. Th. 26/5/1836). L.C. 27/5/1836.
  8° [1836; Songs, Duets, Trios, Chorusses].
  [Music Balfe.]
O. Catherine Grey (D.L. S. 27/5/1837). L.C. 25/5/1837.
  [Music Balfe.]
O. Guillaume Tell (D.L. M. 3/12/1838). L.C. 29/11/1838. 8° 1838
  [Duets, Trios, Recitatives, Chorusses]; 8° 1845.
  [An adaptation of Rossini's opera (Paris, 3/8/1829), with
  arrangements by Bishop.]
O. The Bohemian Girl (D.L. M. 27/11/1843). L.C. 16/11/1843.
  [Music Balfe.]
O. The Syren (D.L. Th. 17/10/1844). L.C. 28/9/1844.
  [An adaptation of Scribe, *La Sirène* (Paris, 26/3/1844), with
  music by Auber.]
O. The Daughter of St. Mark (D.L. W. 27/11/1844). L.C. 21/11/1844.
  8° 1844.
  [Music Balfe.]
O. The Enchantress (D.L. W. 14/5/1845; Surrey, M. 1/11/1847).
  L.C. 28/4/1845. 8° (1845).
  [Music Balfe.]
O. The Crusaders (D.L. Th. 26/2/1846). L.C. 21/2/1846. 8° 1846.
O. Stradella (D.L. T. 6/6/1846). L.C. 28/5/1846. 8° 1846.
  [Music F. Flotow (Paris, 30/12/1844), arranged by Benedict.]
D. Loretta, A Tale of Seville (D.L. M. 9/11/1846). L.C. 31/10/1846.
O. The Bondman (D.L. F. 11/12/1846). L.C. 12/11/1846. 8° [1846].
  [Music Balfe.]
O. Matilda of Hungary (D.L. M. 22/2/1847). L.C. 13/2/1847.
  8° (1847).
  [Music W. V. Wallace.]

BURGES, Sir JAMES BLAND.
D. Riches; or, The Wife and Brother (Lyc. S. 3/2/1810). L. 91 M.
  [25/1/1810; as *The Mind's Magnet; or, The School for Arrogance*].
  8° 1810 [*bis*]; 8° 1814 [3rd]; *Dicks* 717; *Cumberland*, vol. xxiv.
C.O. Tricks upon Travellers (Lyc. M. 9/7/1810). L. 91 M. [30/6/1810].
  8° 1810 [Songs].
  [Music Horn and Reeve.]
Dramas. 2 vols. 8° 1817.
  [Contain: Vol. i: 1. *The Knight of Rhodes*; 2. *The Advertisement*;

3. *The Bandit*; 4. *Tricks upon Travellers*. Vol. ii: 1. *Cortez*; 2. *The Storm*; 3. *The Crusaders*; 4. *Riches*.]

BURKE, CHARLES
R.D. Rip van Winkle; or, A Legend of the Kaatskill Mountains (H.² F. 3/5/1833). L.C. 24/4/1833. *Dicks* 340.

BURKE, W.
D. The Armed Briton; or, The Invaders Vanquished. 8° 1806.

BURNABY, EDWYN ANDREW.
T. Agatha; or, The Convent of St. Bartholomew. 8° 1821.

BURNEY, FRANCES [*Madame d'ARBLAY*].
Tragic Dramas, chiefly intended for Representations in Private Families, to which is added Aristodemus...from the Italian of Vincenzo Monti. 8° 1818.

[BURNS, ROBERT.
O.F. The Jolly Beggars (Caledonian, Edinburgh, 19/3/1823).
[An adaptation of Burns's poem for the stage.]

BURRELL, Lady SOPHIA RAYMOND.
[See *A History of Late Eighteenth Century Drama*, p. 241.]
T. Maximian....Taken from Corneille. 8° 1800.
T. Theodora; or, The Spanish Daughter. 8° 1800.

BURROUGHS, WATKINS.
D. The Jewess (Edinburgh, 1/6/1836).
[An adaptation of Scribe, *La Juive* (Paris, 23/2/1835), with music by Halévy.]

BURTON, —
T. Paetus and Arria. 8° 1809 [Cambridge].
C. Right and Wrong (Lyc. Th. 2/1/1812). 8° 1812 [*bis*].
[This is the same as *A Receipt for Mirth* in *UA*. Both these plays go also under the name of *JOHN NICHOLSON*.]

BURTON, WILLIAM EVANS.
M.D. The Court Fool; or, A King's Amusement (R.P. M. 26/8/1833; S.W. 11/5/1840). *Dicks* 341.
D.D. Ellen Wareham; or, The Wife of Two Husbands (Vic. F. 12/12/1834). *Duncombe*, vol. xii; *Lacy*, vol. xxxiv.
[This author has several later plays.]

BUTLER, RICHARD, Earl of GLENGALL.
F. The Irish Tutor; or, New Lights (Cheltenham, 12/7/1822; C.G. M. 28/10/1822). L. 126 M. [20/10/1822; under sub-title]. *Dicks* 186.
C. The Follies of Fashion (D.L. S. 28/11/1829). L.C. 25/11/1829. 8° 1830; *Dicks* 729.

BYRNE, JAMES.
[See *A History of Late Eighteenth Century Drama*, p. 241.]
Bal. Auld Robin Gray (D.L. 3/6/1814).
Bal. Caledonian Laurels; or, The Highlander's Return (D.L. 3/11/1815).

BYRON, Lord GEORGE GORDON.
D.Poem. Manfred, A Dramatic Poem. 8° 1817.
[This was acted at C.G. W. 29/10/1834, and is preserved in L.C. 30/9/1834.]

T. Marino Faliero, Doge of Venice (D.L. W. 25/4/1821). L. 120 M.
[22/4/1821; printed expurgated copy]. 8° 1821.
Sardanapalus, A Tragedy. The Two Foscari, A Tragedy. Cain,
A Mystery. 8° 1821.
[*Sardanapalus* was acted at D.L. Th. 10/4/1834, and is preserved
in L.C. D.L. 13/1/1834. See *Sardanapalus, King of Assyria...
Adapted for Representation by Charles Kean* [*Lacy*]. The Two
Foscari was acted at C.G. S. 7/4/1837, and is preserved in L.C.
29/3/1837.]
D. The Deformed Transformed. 8° 1824.
D. Heaven and Earth, A Mystery. 8° 1824 [but had appeared in
The Liberal, i. 2 (1822)].
T. Werner (Bath, 10/2/1830; D.L. W. 15/12/1830). L.C. Bristol,
25/1/1830. 8° 1823.
[*Dramas* 8° 1837 (2 vols.) contain all these plays. I have not, of
course, attempted here to give more than the first edition of each
play.]

CALCRAFT [*or COLE*], *JOHN WILLIAM.*
D. The Bride of Lammermuir (Edinburgh, 1/5/1822). L. 24 L.
[16/4/1822]. 8° 1823 [Edinburgh]; *Dicks* 344; *Lacy*, vol. xxviii;
Duncombe, vol. lx.
[From Scott's novel.]
D. The Battle of Bothwell Brig (Edinburgh, 3/5/1823). L. 85 S.
[30/4/1823].
[Ascribed to Calcraft.]
D. Ivanhoe. 18° 1823.
M.D. The Pirate; or, The Reimkennar of Zetland (Edinburgh, M.
29/3/1824).
M.D. Waverley (Edinburgh, S. 22/5/1824; C.G. M. 22/10/1832).
L.C. 24/4/1824. 18° 1824 [Edinburgh].
[Music by J. Dewar.]

CAMPBELL, A. V.
M.D. The Mysterious Theft; or, Who can have taken it? (S.W. Th.
12/10/1815).
Sk. Chuneelah; or, The Death of the Elephant at Exeter Change
(S.W. M. 17/4/1826).
M.D. The Gambler's Life in London (S.W. 1/1829).
M.D. Ratheil Sullivan; or, The Feuds of Loch Lomond (S.W. M.
20/4/1829).
M.D. The Demon of the Desert; or, The Murderer's Sacrifice (S.W.
M. 29/6/1829). *Duncombe*, vol. iv; *Lacy*, vol. cx.
M.D. The Forest Oracle; or, The Bridge of Tresino (S.W. 9/11/1829).
Cumberland Minor, vol. ii.
M.D. Tom Bowling (S.W. M. 1/2/1830). *Dicks* 732; *Cumberland
Minor*, vol. iii; *Lacy*, vol. cvii.
M.D. The Mirror; or, More Scenes in Town (S.W. M. 12/4/1830).
Sk. The Bankrupt; or, Foxonian Charity (S.W. T. 10/2/1835).
Ba. The Dare-Devil; or, My Uncle Thomas (S.W. M. 16/2/1835).
D. Bound 'Prentice to a Waterman; or, The Flower of Woolwich
(S.W. T. 19/7/1836).
D. Rule Britannia! (S.W. M. 31/10/1836).
D. Don Rafaelle; or, The Returned Captive. L.C. Grecian, 9/5/1845.
D. The London Banker. L.C. Grecian, 17/6/1845. *Dicks* 723.

Spec. Trafalgar. L.C. Grecian, 25/9/1845.
Oa. Will Nobody Marry Her? L.C. Grecian, 3/5/1848.
D. The Widow of Frangny. L.C. Grecian, 2/4/1849.
F. Robson's Academy. L.C. Grecian, 2/4/1849.
C.O. The Prince's Trumpeter. L.C. Grecian, 26/6/1849.
    [For his later work see *A History of Late Nineteenth Century
    Drama*, p. 301.]

CAPADOSE, Lieutenant Colonel HENRY.
C. Kindred. 8° 1837.
    [Adapted from Kotzebue.]
C. The Organs of the Brain. 8° 1838.
    [A translation of Kotzebue, *Die Organe des Gehirns*.]

CARR, GEORGE CHARLES.
D. St. Margaret's Cave (Hull, 1805). L. 44 S. [York and Hull,
    12/1804].
D. The Towers of Urbandine. L. 1467 [York and Hull? 13/12/1805].
    [See in *UA*.]

CARR, Sir JOHN.
D. The Sea-side Hero. 8° 1804.
Patriotic Effusion. Who's Afraid? (H.² Th. 12/9/1805). L. 45 S.
    [6/9/1805; as *Who's Afraid? Ha! Ha! Ha!*].
F. First Come, First Served (H.² 22/8/1808). L. 50 S. [18/8/1808].
    [Ascribed to Carr].

CHALMERS, JOHN.
Bsq. King Leer and his Three Darters. L.C. Bower, 29/2/1848.

CHAMBERS, Miss MARIANNE.
C. The School for Friends (D.L. T. 10/12/1805). 8° 1805 [*bis*];
    8° 1806 [*bis*].
C. Ourselves (Lyc. S. 2/3/1811). L. 55 S. [15/2/1811]. 8° 1811.

CHARNOCK, JOHN.
T. Loyalty; or, Invasion Defeated. 8° 1810.

CHELTNAM, CHARLES SMITH.
C.D. The Little Madcap (S.W. M. 2/3/1846). L.C. 31/1/1846. *Lacy*,
    vol. cxiv.
    [For his later work see *A History of Late Nineteenth Century
    Drama*, p. 309.]

CHENEVIX, RICHARD.
Two Plays. 8° 1812.
    [Contains: 1. *Mantuan Revels;* 2. *Henry the Seventh*.]

CHERRY, ANDREW.
    [For his earlier plays see *A History of Late Eighteenth Century Drama*,
    p. 243.]
Ent. The Lyric Novelist; or, Life Epitomised. 8° [1804?].
C. The Soldier's Daughter (D.L. T. 7/2/1804). L. 80 M. [19/1/1804].
    8° 1804 [12 editions]; 8° 1805 ["12th"]; 8° 1809; *Dicks* 114;
    Oxberry, vol. v; *Duncombe*, vol. v; *Cumberland*, vol. xxiii.
O.F. Spanish Dollars; or, The Priest of the Parish (C.G. Th. 9/5/1805).
    L. 82 M. [29/4/1805]. 8° 1806.
    [Music Davy.]
F. All for Fame! or, A Peep at the Times (D.L. W. 15/5/1805).
C. The Village; or, The World's Epitome (H.² Th. 18/7/1805).
    L. 82 M. [10/7/1805].

19   NED

M.D. The Travellers; or, Music's Fascination (D.L. S. 22/1/1806).
L. 46 S. [14/1/1806]. 8° 1806 [9 editions]; 8° 1806 [Songs, Duets,
Trios, Chorusses]; *Oxberry*, vol. xvii; *Cumberland*, vol. xli.
[Music Corri.]

Sk. Thalia's Tears (D.L. F. 12/12/1806). L. 46 S. [4/2/1806].

C. A Day in London (D.L. Th. 9/4/1807). L. 48 S. [3/4/1807].

C.O. Peter the Great; or, The Wooden Walls (C.G. F. 8/5/1807).
8° 1807 [*bis*].

O.F. In and Out of Tune (D.L. T. 1/3/1808). See *D. LAWLER.*

M.D. Llewellyn, Prince of Wales; or, Gellert the Faithful Dog (Surrey,
M. 14/6/1813).
[Begun by Cherry and finished by *T. J. DIBDIN.*]

F. Two Strings to your Bow (D.L. 10/3/1814).

CLARANCE, JOSEPH.
F. A Curiosity; or, The Doomed Entombed. L.C. Norwich,
21/5/1847.

F. The Round of Intrigue; or, Which is the Right One? L.C.
Yarmouth and Norwich, 22/7/1847.

F. Look to your Luggage; or, A Trip by Railway. L.C. Norwich,
6/9/1847.

CLARKE, C.
C. Recrimination; or, A Curtain Lecture (D.L. Th. 22/4/1813).
L. 21 L. [9/4/1813; under sub-title].

CLARKE, JOHN BERTRIDGE.
T. Ravenna; or, Italian Love (C.G. F. 3/12/1824). L.C. 19/10/1824.
8° 1824.
[An adaptation of Schiller, *Kabale und Liebe.*]

CLARKE, Lady OLIVIA.
C. The Irishwoman (Crow-street, Dublin, 1819). 8° 1819.

CLARKE, STEPHEN.
Dramatic Romances. 8° 1809.
[Contains: 1. *The Poison Tree*; 2. *The Torrid Zone.*]
C. The Kiss; or, The Lawyer Outwitted (Lyc. Th. 31/10/1811).
8° 1811.

CLAUDIUS, Dr.
O.F. Innocence and Love; or, The Stolen Lamb (Frogmore, command
performance, 26/6/1805; German, 1805–6). 8° [1805].
[Based on *Love in the Country* and written for "Mr. Schirmer's
Children" at the German Theatre.]

COBB, JAMES.
[For his earlier plays see *A History of Late Eighteenth Century Drama*,
pp. 243–5.]
M.D. Paul and Virginia (C.G. Th. 1/5/1800). 12° [1800; Dublin;
pirated]; 8° 1800 [Songs, Duets, Trios, Chorusses]; *London Stage*,
vol. iv; *Cumberland*, vol. xxi.
[Music Mazzinghi and Reeve.]
C.O. Algonah (D.L. F. 30/4/1802). L. 42 S. [22/4/1802]. 8° 1802
[Songs, Duets, Chorusses].
[An adaptation of his own *The Cherokee* (D.L. 1794).]

O.F. A House to be Sold (D.L. W. 17/11/1802). L. 42 S. [13/11/1802],
8° 1802 [*bis*], 8° 1805.
[An adaptation of Duval, *La maison à vendre* (Paris, 1800);
music by Kelly.]
M.D. The Wife of Two Husbands (D.L. T. 1/11/1803). L. 43 S.
[24/10/1803]. 8° 1803 [3 editions]; 8° 1803 [Songs, Duets, Trios,
Chorusses]; *Inchbald's Mod. Theatre*, vol. iii.
[An adaptation of Pixérécourt, *La femme à deux maris* (Paris,
1802); music by Mazzinghi.]
C. Sudden Arrivals; or, Too Busy by Half (Lyc. T. 19/12/1809).

COBBETT, WILLIAM.
[Pol.] Big O and Sir Glory: or, "Leisure to Laugh." A Comedy.
8° 1825.

CODE, H. B.
O. The Spanish Patriots a Thousand Years Ago (Lyc. T. 22/9/1812).
L. 56 S. [11/9/1812]. 8° 1812.
D. The Russian Sacrifice; or, The Burning of Moscow. 8° 1813
[Dublin].

COLERIDGE, SAMUEL TAYLOR.
[For his earlier plays see *A History of Late Eighteenth Century Drama*,
p. 245.]
T. The Piccolomini; or, The First Part of Wallenstein....Translated
from the German of Frederick Schiller. 8° 1800.
T. The Death of Wallenstein. 8° 1800.
Int. The Triumph of Loyalty [first printed in *Poems of S.T.C.* 8° 1912,
vol. ii].
[The MS. in the B.M. has the peculiar note in the author's
hand-writing "produced D.L. 7/2/1801."]
T. Remorse (D.L. S. 23/1/1813). 8° 1813 [3 editions]. L. 98 M.
[5/1/1813].
[This is a revision of the earlier *Osorio*, written in 1797.]
Ent. Zapolyta; A Christmas Tale. 8° 1817.
[In *T. J. DIBDIN'S* rehandling, this was produced at the Surrey
in 1818.]

COLLIER, J. W.
F. Our Borough Election (M'bone, 6/12/1847). L.C. 19/11/1847.
D. Clara Charette; or, A Daughter's Sacrifice (M'bone, W. 26/12/1849).
L.C. 18/12/1849 [as *C.C.; or, Blighted Love*].

COLLIER, WILLIAM.
O.F. The Blacksmith; or, A Day at Gretna Green (Vic. Th. 23/1/1834).
Duncombe, vol. xiv.
D. The Queen's Jewel (Queen's, M. 6/4/1835). *Duncombe*, vol. xvii.
F. Is She a Woman? (Queen's, S. 26/12/1835). *Duncombe*, vol. xxi.
R.D. Kate Kearney; or, The Fairy of the Lakes (Queen's, M.
3/10/1836). *Duncombe*, vol. xxiii.
F. The Rival Serjeants (S.W. M. 5/4/1847). L.C. 3/4/1847 [as *The
R.S.; or, Love and Lottery*]. *Duncombe*, vol. lix.

COLLS, JOHN HENRY.
[For his earlier plays see *A History of Late Eighteenth Century Drama*,
p. 245.]
C. The Honest Soldier. 8° 1805.

COLMAN, GEORGE, The Younger.
[For his earlier plays see *A History of Late Eighteenth Century Drama*, pp. 247–8.]
O.F. The Review; or, The Ways of Windsor (H.² T. 2/9/1800). L. 39 S. [28/8/1800]. 12° 1801 [Dublin]; 8° 1808; 8° 1800 [Songs, Duets, and Chorusses]; *Dicks* 763; *Oxberry*, vol. xiii; *Cumberland*, vol. xxxvi; *Duncombe*, vol. lii; *Lacy*, vol. lxi. [Music Arnold.]
C.   The Poor Gentleman (C.G.W. 11/2/1801). L. 39 S. [31/12/1800]. 12° [1801]; 8° 1802; 8° 1806; 12° 1806 [Dublin]; *Inchbald's B.T.*, vol. xxi; *Duncombe*, vol. xxxix; *Cumberland*, vol. xxxvii; *Lacy*, vol. xxxix.
C.   John Bull; or, The Englishman's Fireside (C.G. S. 5/3/1803). L. 78 M. [5/2/1803]. 8° 1803 [Dublin; pirated]; 8° 1805; *Dicks* 21; *Inchbald's B.T.*, vol. xxi; *Duncombe*, vol. xxxvii; *Cumberland*, vol. xxxvi; *Lacy*, vol. xlii.
O.F. Love Laughs at Locksmiths (H.² M. 25/7/1803). L. 43 M. [18/7/1803]. 8° 1803 [Dublin; pirated]; 8° 1808; 12° 1818; *Dicks* 758; *Oxberry*, vol. xiii; *Cumberland*, vol. xxxvii; *Lacy*, vol. xciv. [An adaptation of *Une folie* by Bouilly.]
O.F. The Gay Deceivers; or, More Laugh than Love (H.² W. 22/8/1804). L. 81 M. [22/8/1804]. 8° 1808. [An adaptation of *Les événements imprévus* by Hell.]
C.   Who wants a Guinea? (C.G. Th. 18/4/1805). L. 82 M. [15/4/1805]. 8° 1805 [*bis*]; *Inchbald's B.T.*, vol. iii; *Cumberland*, vol. xx.
O.F. We Fly by Night; or, Long Stories (C.G. T. 28/1/1806). L. 84 M. [23/1/1806]. 8° 1806.
O.R. The Forty Thieves (D.L. 8/4/1806). *Duncombe*, vol. ii. [Music Kelly. Ascribed to Colman.]
Prel. Sylvester Daggerwood; or, New Hay at the Old Market. 8° 1808; *Dicks* 763; *Duncombe*, vol. i; *Cumberland*, vol. xxxvi; *Lacy*, vol. iii. [An altered version of *New Hay at the Old Market* (H.² 1795).]
M.D. The Africans; or, War, Love and Duty (H.² 29/7/1808). L. 49 S. [23/7/1808]. 8° 1808; *Cumberland*, vol. xliii. [Music Kelly.]
F.   X. Y. Z. (C.G. T. 11/12/1810). L. 91 M. [4/12/1810]. 12° 1820.
Ext. The Quadrupeds of Quedlinburgh; or, The Rovers of Weimar (H.² F. 26/7/1811). L. 94 M. [18/7/1811].
P.   Doctor Hocus Pocus; or, Harlequin Washed White (H.² F. 12/8/1814). L. 102 M. [2/8/1814].
F.   The Actor of All Work; or, First and Second Floor (H.² W. 13/8/1817). L. 110 M. [7/8/1817].
M.D. The Law of Java (C.G. S. 11/5/1822). L. 125 M. [22/4/1822]. 8° 1822. [Music Bishop.]
Int. Stella and Leatherlungs; or, A Star and a Stroller (D.L. W. 1/10/1823). L. 132 M. [27/9/1823]. [Ascribed to Colman.]

[*CONRAD, ROBERT.*
T.   Aylmere. L.C. Edinburgh, 7/2/1846. 18° 1852 [Philadelphia, as *A., or The Bondman of Kent*].

COOKE, JOHN.
P.   The Treasurers. 8° 1843.

COOKE, Mrs T. P.
D. The Forced Marriage; or, The Return from Siberia (Surrey, M. 5/12/1842). Dicks 701.

COOPER, FREDERICK FOX.
Bsq. The Elbow Shakers; or, Thirty Years of a Rattler's Life (Adel. M. 3/12/1827). L.C. 30/11/1827.
Bsq. Blackeyed Sukey; or, All in the Dumps (Olym. 12/1829). L.C. 21/11/1829. Cumberland Minor, vol. xiv; Richardson Minor, vol. iii.
F. The Spare Bed; or, The Shower Bath (Surrey, Th. 7/7/1833). Dicks 786; Cumberland Minor, vol. vii.
[A MS. of this is in the L.C. Collection dated 1842.]
Ext. Mr. Simpson, M.C.; or, Vauxhall Gardens (Vic. Th. 26/9/1833).
F. The Deserted Village (Adel. M. 28/10/1833). L.C. 29/10/1833. Dicks 727; Duncombe, vol. xv.
Bsq. Ion (Garrick, 9/10/1836). Cumberland Minor, vol. xii.
F. Hercules, King of Clubs (Strand, 28/7/1836; S.W. Th. 13/7/1837). Dicks 387; Cumberland Minor, vol. xiii; Lacy, vol. lxxxix.
Oa. Jenny Jones. L.C. 28/2/1838. Pattie's Play.
D. Master Humphrey's Clock (Vic. F. 29/5/1840). Dicks 724; Duncombe vol. xli.
D. Old Fleet Prison (Surrey, 12/5/1845). L.C. 9/5/1845.
F. Shooting the Moon (Strand, 21/10/1850). L.C. 21/10/1847. New B.T. No. 548.
[For his later plays see A History of Late Nineteenth Century Drama, p. 324.]

COOPER, J. W.
P. The Peri of the Mist. L.C. Effingham, 29/11/1845.

COOPER, WILLIAM.
D. Mokana; or, The Veiled Prophet of Khorassan. L.C. Norwich, 1/4/1843. 8° 1843 [Norwich].

CORN, G. EDWARDS.
Spec. Wars in Spain. L.C. Apollo, 15/8/1844.

CORNWALL, BARRY [BRYAN WALLER PROCTER].
Dramatic Scenes, and other Poems. 12° 1819; 8° 1820.
T. Mirandola (C.G. T. 9/1/1821). L. 119 M. [25/12/1820]. 8° 1821 [3 editions].

COTTRELL, C. H.
D. Don Carlos. 8° 1843.
[A translation of Schiller's drama.]

COURTNEY, JOHN.
F. Bounce; or, The Ojitteway Indians (P'cess, S. 10/2/1844). L.C. 8/2/1844.
F. Aged Forty (P'cess, M. 26/2/1844). L.C. 21/2/1844. Lacy, vol. lix.
F. Taken by Surprise (P'cess, 8/6/1844). L.C. 1/6/1844.
D. The Sisters of Chatillon (Surrey, 4/11/1844). L.C. 17/2/1844.
D. The Bride's Journey (Vic. 20/4/1846). L.C. 22/4/1846.
D. The Day Dream; or, The Heart's Ordeal (C.L. 31/8/1846). L.C. 5/9/1846.
D. Clarissa Harlowe (P'cess, 28/9/1846). See T. H. LACY.

D. The Gunsmith of Orleans; or, The Dead Woman's Secret (Vic. 25/1/1847). L.C. 17/1/1847.
D. Raby Rattler. L.C. Liverpool, 3/4/1847.
D. The Lighterman of the Bankside; or, The Orphan of Bermondsey (Vic. 3/1/1848). L.C. 30/9/1847.
D. Jack Frock (C.L. 3/2/1848). L.C. 3/2/1848.
D. Rose Clinton; or, The Victim of Circumstantial Evidence (Vic. M. 24/4/1848). L.C. 8/4/1848.
D. The Blacksmith of Ghent (Vic. M. 12/6/1848). L.C. 8/6/1848.
D. Leah and Nathan (C.L. 24/6/1848). L.C. 20/6/1848 [as *L. the Jewess of Constantine; or, The Arab's Sacrifice*].
D. Marion Hazleton (Vic. 26/6/1848). L.C. 29/6/1848.
D. Time tries all (Olym. M. 4/9/1848). 8° [1848]; *Lacy*, vol. i.
D. The Green Hills of Surrey (Vic. 1/1849). L.C. 23/12/1848.
D. The Heir of Ashmore; or, Time's Story (Vic. 12/2/1849). L.C. 12/2/1849.
D. The Maid of Velitri (Vic. 9/4/1849). L.C. 4/4/1849 [as *The M. of V.; or, The Last Deed of Garboni*].
D. The Outcast of Lausanne; or, Claudine of Switzerland (Vic. 28/5/1849). L.C. 26/5/1849.
D. The Soldier's Progress; or, The Horrors of War (Vic. 5/11/1849). L.C. Vic. 25/10/1849. *Lacy*, vol. i.
D. Hearts at Fault (Surrey, 4/3/1850). L.C. 9/11/1849.
[This author has many later plays.]

COYNE, *JOSEPH STIRLING*.
F. The Phrenologist (Dublin, 3/6/1835).
F. The Honest Cheats (Dublin, 7/4/1836).
F. The Four Lovers (Dublin, 14/4/1836).
F. The Queer Subject (Adel. M. 28/11/1836). L.C. 18/11/1836. *Dicks* 782; *Acting Nat. Drama*, vol. i.
Ba. Valsha; or, The Slave Queen (Adel. M. 30/10/1837). *Dicks* 702; *Acting Nat. Drama*, vol. ii.
D. All for Love; or, The Lost Pleiad (Adel. T. 16/1/1838). L.C. 13/1/1838. *Lacy*, vol. lxi; *Acting Nat. Drama*, vol. iii.
Ba. Arajoon; or, The Conquest of Mysore (Adel. M. 22/10/1838). L.C. 19/10/1838. *Dicks* 700.
M.D. Helen Oakleigh (E.O.H. T. 9/6/1840). L.C. 10/6/1840. *Dicks* 605; *Duncombe*, vol. xlii.
Bal. Satanas and the Spirit of Beauty (Adel. Th. 11/2/1841). *Lacy*, vol. xxxix.
Spec. The World of Dreams (H.² 27/12/1841). L.C. 22/12/1841.
F. My Friend the Captain (H.² T. 20/7/1841). L.C. 22/6/1841. *Dicks* 740.
Ba. The Water Witches (E.O.H. 6/6/1842). L.C. 3/6/1842. *Lacy*, vol. xli.
F. Dobson and Company; or, My Turn Next (Adel. 13/10/1842). *Dicks* 624.
D. The Merchant and his Clerks (Adel. M. 12/12/1842; M'bone, M. 12/2/1849). L.C. 3/12/1842. *Dicks* 642.
F. Binks the Bagman (Adel. M. 13/2/1843). L.C. 10/11/1842. *Dicks* 624; *Lacy*, vol. vii.
F. The Trumpeter's Daughter (H.² 7/12/1843). L.C. 2/12/1843.
Bsq. Richard III. L.C. Adel. 8/2/1844. 12° 1844.
D. The Signal (Olym. 8/4/1844). *Lacy*, vol. cx; *Duncombe*, vol. xlix.

F.   Did you ever send your Wife to Camberwell? (Adel. M. 16/3/1846).
     Dicks 955; *Acting Nat. Drama*, vol. xii.
F.   How to settle Accounts with your Laundress (Adel. M. 26/7/1847).
     L.C. 19/6/1847. *Dicks* 1006; *Acting Nat. Drama*, vol. xiv.
Ext. This House to be Sold (the Property of the Late William
     Shakespeare), Inquire Within (Adel. 9/9/1847). L.C. 1847. *Acting
     Nat. Drama*, vol. xiv.
          [Music A. Mackenzie. The same as *The Old House at Home*,
     in *UA*.]
F.   The Tipperary Legacy (Adel. M. 6/12/1847). L.C. 4/12/1847.
     Acting Nat. Drama, vol. xiv.
Spec. The Fountain of Zea; or, The Child of Air (Adel. M. 24/4/1848).
     L.C. 17/4/1848 [under sub-title].
F.   Lola Montes; or, A Countess for an Hour (H.² W. 26/4/1848).
     L.C. 17/4/1848.
F.   The Pas de Fascination; or, Catching a Governor (H.² M.
     22/5/1848). L.C. 13/5/1848. *Acting Nat. Drama*, vol. xiv.
C.   Separate Maintenance (H.² M. 12/3/1849). L.C. 5/3/1849.
     Duncombe, vol. lxiv.
          [For his later plays see *A History of Late Nineteenth Century
     Drama*, pp. 327–8.]

[CRADOCK, JOSEPH.
     [For *The Czar*, written 1776 and printed 1824, see *A History of Late
     Eighteenth Century Drama*, p. 249.]

CRAVEN, ELIZABETH, Margravine of ANSPACH.
     [For her earlier plays see *A History of Late Eighteenth Century Drama*,
     p. 249.]
Int. Nourjad (private, Brandenburg House, 1803).
F.   Nicodemus in Despair (H². W. 31/8/1803).
          [Acted at Brandenburg House in 1803 as *Poor Tony*.]
C.   Love in a Convent (private, Brandenburg House, 7/1805).

CRAVEN, HENRY THORNTON.
F.   The Card Case (Liverpool, 1844).
F.   Done Brown (Adelphi, Edinburgh, 1845). L.C. 13/10/1845.
     Duncombe, vol. lvi.
D.   Bletchington House (C.L. 20/4/1846). L.C. 18/3/1846. *Duncombe*,
     vol. lvi.
Ca. Fellow Servants (C.L. 19/10/1846).
Ca, The Little Nun; or, A Bit of Scandal (C.L. M. aa/a/1847). L.C.
     13/2/1847. *Duncombe*, vol. lviii.
F.   Tic doloureuse (C.L. 18/10/1847). L.C. 18/10/1847.

CROLY, Rev. GEORGE.
T.   Catiline. 8° 1822.
          [As adapted by H. M. Milner. 8° [1827].]
R.C. Pride shall have a Fall (C.G. Th. 11/3/1824). L.C. 14/2/1824.
     8° 1824 [4 editions].
M.D. The Enchanted Courser; or, The Sultan of Curdistan (D.L.
     Th. 28/10/1824). L.C. 23/9/1824.
M.D. Paris; or, The Massacre of the 28th (R.A. M. 9/8/1830).
          [On M. 16/8/1830 the title was altered to *France; or, The
     Massacre of Paris*.]

CROMWELL, THOMAS.
T.   The Druid...With Notes on the Antiquities and Early History of
Ireland. 8° 1832.

CROSS, JOHN C.
[For his earlier plays see A History of Late Eighteenth Century Drama,
pp. 249–51.]
Spec. The Mine; or, The Black Forest of Istria. 8° 1800.
P.   The Magic Flute; or, Harlequin Champion (R.C. M. 30/6/1800).
Spec. Sir Francis Drake, and Iron Arm (R.C. M. 4/8/1800). 8° 1800;
8° 1809 [Circusiana]; 8° 1812 [Works].
[Music Sanderson.]
Bal. Rinaldo Rinaldini; or, The Secret Avengers (R.C. M. 6/4/1801).
8° 1801 [Songs, Chorusses]; 8° 1809 [Circusiana]; 8° 1812 [Works].
[On Th. 9/4/1801 the title appeared as R.R.; or, The Black
Tribunal. Music Reeve.]
Spec. The Fire King; or, Albert and Rosalie (R.C. S. 20/6/1801).
8° 1801; 8° 1809 [Circusiana]; 8° 1812 [Works].
[Music Reeve.]
P.   The Eclipse; or, Harlequin in China (R.C. M. 10/8/1801). 8° 1801.
[Music W. Ware.]
Spec. King Caesar; or, The Negro Slaves (R.C. W. 16/9/1801).
8° [1801; Songs, Chorusses].
[Music W. Ware.]
Spec. The Jubilee of 1802; or, The Preston Guild. 8° 1802.
Spec. The Enchanted Harp; or, Harlequin for Ireland (R.C. Th.
22/4/1802). 8° 1802.
Bal. The Fatal Prediction; or, Midnight Assassin (R.C. M. 17/5/1802).
8° [1802; Songs, Chorusses].
P.   The Golden Farmer; or, Harlequin Ploughboy (R.C. M.
28/6/1802). 8° 1802.
Bal. Gonsalvo de Cordova; or, The Conquest of Granada (R.C. W.
11/8/1802). 8° 1802.
P.   The Rival Statues; or, Harlequin Humourist (R.C. M. 11/4/1803).
8° 1803.
Spec. Louisa of Lombardy; or, The Secret Nuptials (R.C. T. 3/5/1803).
8° 1803; 8° 1809 [Circusiana]; 8° 1812 [Works].
[Music Sanderson.]
Spec.P. Number Nip; or, The Elfin King of the Giant Mountains
(R.C. M. 30/5/1803). 8° 1803 [Songs].
[This seems to be the same as the Number Nip contained in
L. 50 S. [Lyc. 29/7/1809].]
Bal. Our Native Land, and Gallant Protectors (R.C. T. 12/7/1803).
8° 1803; 8° 1809 [Circusiana]; 8° 1812 [Works].
Spec. John Bull and Buonaparte; or, A Meeting at Dover (R.C. M.
8/8/1803). 8° 1803.
Spec. The Corsican Pirate; or, The Grand Master of Malta (R.C.
18/6/1803). 8° 1803.
P.   Cybele; or, Harlequin's Hour (R.C. M. 2/4/1808). 8° 1804.
Spec. Joanna of Surinam (R.C. M. 2/7/1804).
P.   Pedler's Acre; or, Harlequin Mendicant (R.C. M. 2/7/1804).
8° 1804.
M.D. The Cloud King; or, Magic Rose (R.C. M. 30/6/1806). 8° 1809
[Circusiana]; 8° 1812 [Works]; 8° 1806 [Songs].

Bal. The False Friend; or, Assassin of the Rocks (R.C. M. 25/8/1806).
8° 1809 [*Circusiana*]; 8° 1812 [*Works*].
[Music Russel and Corri, Junior. This is also in L. 58 S. [Olym.
11/1/1814; printed].]
Circusiana, or A Collection of the most favourite Ballets, Spectacles,
Melo-dramas, &c. performed at the Royal Circus, St. George's
Fields. In Two Volumes. 8° 1809.
[This was reprinted as *The Dramatic Works of J. C. Cross*.
8° 1812. Indication has been made above of its contents.]
Bal. Lethe (Bath, 7/3/1812).

CROWQUILL, ALFRED [*pseud. of ALFRED HENRY FORRESTER*].
P. Friar Rush; or, Harlequin and King Gold (D.L. M. 27/12/1847).
L.C. 22/12/1847.
[Written in collaboration with *A. SMITH*.]
P. The Moon Queen and King Knight; or, Harlequin Twilight
(Surrey, W. 26/12/1849). L.C. 18/12/1849.

CUMBERLAND, RICHARD.
[For his earlier works see *A History of Late Eighteenth Century Drama*,
pp. 251–3.]
R.D. Joanna of Montfaucon (C.G. M. 16/1/1800). 8° 1800.
[Based on a play by Kotzebue; music Busby.]
C. Lovers' Resolutions (D.L. T. 2/3/1802). L. 42 S. [24/2/1802].
8° 1813 [in *The Posthumous Dramatick Works*].
C. The Sailor's Daughter (D.L. S. 7/4/1804). L. 43 S. [21/3/1804].
8° 1804 [*bis*].
Spec. The Victory and Death of Lord Viscount Nelson (D.L. M.
11/11/1805). L. 83 M. [8/11/1805].
C. A Hint to Husbands (C.G. S. 8/3/1806). L. 46 S. [1/3/1806].
8° 1806.
C.O. The Jew of Mogadore (D.L. T. 3/5/1808). L. 49 S. [28/4/1808].
8° 1808.
[Music M. Kelly.]
M.D. The Robber (Tunbridge Wells, 15/10/1809).
C. The Widow's Only Son (C.G. Th. 7/6/1810). L. 90 M. [24/5/1810].
D. The Sybil; or, The Elder Brutus (D.L. 3/12/1818). 8° 1813 [in
The Posthumous Dramatick Works].
The Posthumous Dramatick Works of R. C. 8° 1813.
[Contains, besides those mentioned above and others acted in
the eighteenth century: 1. *The Confession*; 2. *Torrendal*; 3. *Tiberius
in Capreae*; 4. *The False Demetrius*.]

CUMMINS, —
O. The Innkeepers (Leeds, 9/1829).

CUNNINGHAM, ALLAN.
C. Sir Marmaduke Maxwell. 12° 1822; 8° 1827.

DACRE, Baroness.
[Various works published under the names of *Mrs BARBARINA
WILMOT* (*q.v.*) and *BARBARINA BRAND, Lady DACRE*.]

DAGUILAR, General Sir GEORGE CHARLES.
T. Fiesko; or, The Conspiracy of Genoa (Dublin, 22/12/1832).
8° 1832 [Dublin.]
[A translation of Schiller's drama.]

DALLAS, ROBERT CHARLES.
[For an earlier play see *A History of Late Eighteenth Century Drama*, p. 253.]
O.F. Not at Home (Lyc. M. 20/11/1809). L. 89 M. [8/11/1809]. 8° 1809.
T. Adrastus. 8° 1823.

DALRYMPLE, —
D.Spec. Celestia; or, The World in the Moon (Adel. M. 2/2/1835). L.C. 30/1/1835 [as *Eva's Bridal; or, The Land of Luna*].

DANCE, CHARLES.
Int. Manoeuvring (H.² W. 1/7/1829). See *J. R. PLANCHÉ.*
Ba. Olympic Revels (Olym. 3/1/1831). See *J. R. PLANCHÉ.*
Ba. Olympic Devils (Olym. M. 26/12/1831). See *J. R. PLANCHÉ.*
Ba. The Water Party (Olym. M. 1/10/1832; Lyc. M. 21/5/1849). L.C. 24/9/1832. 12° 1836; *Dicks* 563.
F. Kill or Cure (Olym. M. 29/10/1832; Lyc. T. 22/5/1849). L.C. 31/10/1832. *Dicks* 366.
Int. Petticoat Government (D.L. M. 12/11/1832). L.C. 3/11/1832.
Ba. The Paphian Bower (Olym. W. 26/12/1832). See *J. R. PLANCHÉ.*
F. A Match in the Dark (Olym. Th. 21/2/1833). L.C. 18/2/1833. 12° 1836; *Dicks* 852.
Ext. High, Low, Jack, and the Game (Olym. M. 30/9/1833). See *J. R. PLANCHÉ.*
Ent. The Station House (Strand, M. 30/9/1833; Queen's, M. 19/1/1835). L.C. Adel. 16/11/1835. *Dicks* 232.
    [I am not sure that only one play is indicated here; three theatres at least are mentioned.]
C. The Beulah Spa (Olym. M. 18/11/1833). L.C. 16/11/1833. 8° 1833; *Dicks* 446.
Ba. Hush Money (Olym. M. 28/11/1833). L.C. 14/11/1833. *Dicks* 330.
Ext. The Deep, Deep Sea (Olym. Th. 26/12/1833. See *J. R. PLANCHÉ.*
F. Pleasant Dreams (C.G. S. 24/5/1834). L.C. 23/5/1834. *Dicks* 590; *Lacy*, vol. lxxx.
Ba. A Little Pleasure (Olym. M. 29/9/1834). L.C. 26/9/1834.
Ext. Telemachus (Olym. F. 26/12/1834). See *J. R. PLANCHÉ.*
Ba. Tame Tigers; or, No Harm Done (Queen's, Th. 9/4/1835).
Ba. Riquet with the Tuft (Olym. 26/12/1836). See *J. R. PLANCHÉ.*
C. The Country Squire; or, Two Days at the Hall (C.G. Th. 19/1/1837). L.C. 16/1/1837. 12° [1837]; *Dicks* 326; *Acting Nat. Drama*, vol. i.
F. Advice Gratis (Olym. F. 29/9/1837). L.C. 1837. *Dicks* 590; *Mod. Engl. Com. Th.* vol. ii; *Acting Nat. Drama*, vol. ii.
C. A Dream of the Future (Olym. M. 6/11/1837). L.C. 15/4/1837. *Dicks* 359; *Lacy*, vol. xxi.
Ba. The Bengal Tiger (Olym. M. 18/12/1837). L.C. 14/12/1837. *Dicks* 366; *Mod. Engl. Com. Th.* vol. i.
Ba. Puss in Boots (Olym. T. 26/12/1837). *Acting Nat. Drama*, vol. iii.
Ba. Naval Engagements (Olym. Th. 3/5/1838). L.C. 1/5/1838. *Dicks* 351; *Acting Nat. Drama*, vol. iv.
Ba. Sons and Systems (Olym. S. 29/9/1838). *Dicks* 580; *Acting Nat. Drama*, vol. v.

Ba. The Burlington Arcade (Olym. M. 17/12/1838). L.C. 1838.
     Acting Nat. Drama, vol. vi.
Ext. Blue Beard (Olym. W. 2/1/1839). See *J. R. PLANCHÉ*.
D.   Izaak Walton...In Four Parts, Moonlight, Sunrise, Noon, and
     Sunset (Olym. M. 1/4/1839). L.C. 27/3/1839. 8°[1839]; *Dicks* 566.
F.   Alive and Merry (C.G. M. 30/9/1839). L.C. 25/9/1839. *Dicks* 927;
     Duncombe, vol. xxxviii.
Ba. A Close Siege (St J. M. 25/11/1839). L.C. 1839. *Dicks* 709.
Ba. The Lucky Stars; or, The Cobler of Cripplegate (Strand, M.
     4/7/1842). L.C. 6/7/1842. *Dicks* 564; *Duncombe*, vol. xlv.
Ba. Blue Beard; or, Fatal Curiosity. L.C. Lyc. 8/8/1842.
     [See above under 2/1/1839.]
C.   Hasty Conclusions (Lyc. M. 8/4/1844). L.C. 1/4/1844. *Dicks* 858.
C.   The Victor Vanquished (P'cess, 25/3/1845). *Lacy*, vol. xxvi.
C.   The Dustman's Belle (Lyc. M. 1/6/1846). L.C. 28/5/1846.
     12° [1846].
Ext. The Magic Horn (Lyc. 24/8/1846). 8° (1846).
Ext. The Enchanted Forest; or, The Bear, the Eagle and the Dolphin
     (Lyc. M. 22/2/1847). L.C. 13/2/1847. 8° 1847.
F.   A Morning Call. L.C. M'bone, 31/10/1847. 12° [1847]; *Lacy*,
     vol. xxii.
     [This was apparently not produced until 17/3/1851 at D.L.]
Ca. The Happy Family (Lyc. 22/3/1848). L.C. 28/1/1848.
C.   Who speaks first? (Lyc. Th. 11/1/1849). L.C. 9/1/1849. 12° 1849;
     Lacy, vol. xxiii.
C.D. A Wonderful Woman (Lyc. Th. 24/5/1849). 12° 1849; *Dicks*
     1038; *Lacy*, vol. xviii.
Ca. Delicate Ground; or, Paris in 1793 (Lyc. T. 27/11/1849). L.C.
     26/11/1849 [originally called *The Citizen's Wife; or, The Reign of
     Terror*]. *Dicks* 1008.
     [For his later work see *A History of Late Nineteenth Century
     Drama*, p. 335.]

DANIEL, GEORGE.
Bsq. Doctor Bolus (E.O.H. T. 21/7/1818). L. 70 S. [9/7/1818].
      8° 1818; *Cumberland*, vol. xiii.
O.F. The Disagreeable Surprise; or, Taken Up and Taken In (D.L.
      W. 1/12/1819). L. 74 S. [5/12/1819]. 8° 1819; *Cumberland*, vol. xiv.
      [Music Reeve.]
O.F. Sworn at Highgate (S.W. M. 1/10/1832). *Cumberland Minor*,
      vol. vi.

DARLEY, GEORGE.
D.Poem. Sylvia; or, The May Queen. 12° 1827.
D.Poem. Thomas à Becket. 8° 1840.
D.Poem. Ethelstan; or, The Battle of Brunanburh. 8° 1841.
T.   The Plighted Troth (D.L. W. 20/4/1842).

DAVIDGE, W. P.
C.   The Family Party (Norwich, 1842). L.C. 11/5/1842.

DELAP, Rev. JOHN.
[For his earlier plays see *A History of Late Eighteenth Century Drama*,
   p. 253.]
Dramatic Poems. 8° 1803.
   [Includes: 1. *Gunilda*; 2. *The Usurper*; 3. *Matilda*; 4. *Abdalla*.]

DENVIL, —
M.D. Alerame, the Knight of the Lion; or, The Hut of Sarona (R.P.
M. 4/2/1833).

DERBY, C.
Charade. Matrimony. L.C. Brighton, 19/1/1844 (printed copy).
8° 1844 [Brighton].

DEW, DYER.
T. Harold; or, The English King. 8° 1820.

DIBDIN, CHARLES.
[For his earlier plays see *A History of Late Eighteenth Century Drama*
pp. 254–6.]
Ent. Britons strike home! (Sans Souci, S. 18/2/1804).
Ent. Most Votes (Sans Souci, Th. 23/2/1804).
Ent. The Frolic (Sans Souci, M. 5/11/1804).
B.O. The Broken Gold (D.L. S. 8/2/1806). L. 47 S. [3/2/1806].
    [To these should be added the following entertainments: *The
Saloon, The Statue, She's mad for a Husband, The False Dervise,
The Land of Simplicity, The Milkmaid, Pandora, The Passions,
The Refusal of Harlequin* and *The Regions of Accomplishment*. See
Biographia Dramatica, i, 187 and 188.]

DIBDIN, CHARLES ISAAC MUNGO [CHARLES DIBDIN Junior].
Ba. Old Fools; or, Love's Stratagem (S.W. M. 14/4/1800).
P. Boadicea; or, The British Amazon (S.W. M. 14/4/1800).
P. Peter Wilkins; or, Harlequin in the Flying World (S.W. M.
    14/4/1800).
P. Blackenberg; or, The Spirit of the Elbe (S.W. W. 28/5/1800).
O.F. Moses and Mammon; or, The Devil and the Lawyer (S.W. T.
    10/6/1800).
P. Chaos; or, Harlequin Phaeton (S.W. T. 5/8/1800).
Ba. The Black Pig; or, The Lady's Hobby horse (S.W. Th. 21/8/1800).
P. The Ethiop; or, The Siege of Granada (S.W. 1801).
Spec. Egyptian Laurels (S.W. M. 1/6/1801).
P. Harlequin Benedick; or, Mother Shipton's Ghost (S.W. M.
    29/6/1801). MS. in the possession of Mr Crompton Rhodes.
    8° 1801 [Songs].
    [Music Moorhead.]
Spec. The Grand Junction Canal; or, A Trip to Paddington (S.W. F.
    31/7/1801).
Spec. The Great Devil; or, The Robber of Genoa (S.W. M. 17/8/1801;
    Cob. M. 11/2/1828). 8° 1801; *Cumberland Minor*, vol. xiv.
Ba. The Rival Tars; or, One good turn deserves another (S.W. 1802).
P. St George and the Dragon; or, The British Champion (S.W. 1802).
P. Ko and Zoa; or, The Belle Sauvage (S.W. 1802). 8° 1803 [Songs].
    [A manuscript of this is in L. 97 M. [Pav. 24/11/1812].]
P. Harlequin Greenlander; or, The Whale Fishery (S.W. 1802).
M.D. Speed the Plough; or, The Return of Peace (S.W. S. 1/5/1802).
Ba. Fox and Geese; or, The Amorous Quaker (S.W. M. 16/8/1802).
P. Wizard's Wake; or, Harlequin's Regeneration (S.W. M. 23/8/1802).
    8° [1803].
Prel. New Brooms; or, The Firm Changed (S.W. 1803). 8° [1803].
P. Jack the Giant-Killer (S.W. 1803). 8° [1803].
P. Fire and Spirit; or, A Holiday Harlequin (S.W. 1803). 8° [1803].

P. The Bower of Spring; or, Harlequin Labour (S.W. Easter, 1803).
    MS. in the possession of Mr Crompton Rhodes.
D.F. Edward and Susan; or, The Beauty of Buttermere (S.W. M.
    11/4/1803).
P. Philip Quarll; or, The English Hermit (S.W. M. 9/5/1803).
    8° [1803 ; Songs].
D.F. Red Riding Hood; or, The Wolf Robber (S.W. M. 23/5/1803).
    8° [1803].
P. Goody Two Shoes; or, Harlequin Alabaster (S.W. M. 20/6/1803).
    8° [1803].
Bsq. Claudine; or, The Basket-maker (S.W. 1803). 8° 1803.
Spec. Barbara Allen (S.W. M. 11/7/1803). 8° [1803 ; Songs].
Spec. The Old Man of the Mountain; or, A Tale of the Eleventh
    Century (S.W. M. 18/7/1803). 8° [1803].
Spec. The British Amazons; or, Army without Reserve (S.W. M.
    8/8/1803). 8° [1803].
Ba. The Serjeant's Whim; or, Village Frolics (R.C. M. 16/1/1804; not
    first performance).
Spec. Ωκεανεια (S.W. M. 2/4/1804). 8° [1804].
    [This also appeared under its sub-title, *The Siege of Gibraltar*,
    on M. 29/4/1805.]
O.F. The Little Gipsies (S.W. M. 2/4/1804). 8° [1804].
    [Music Reeve.]
Spec. Osric the Lion (S.W. 2/4/1804). 8° [1804].
C.O. Click Clack; or, The Miller's Daughter (S.W. M. 28/5/1804).
    8° [1804].
    [Music Reeve.]
P. Anthony, Cleopatra and Harlequin (S.W. M. 11/6/1804). 8°
    1805.
M.Ent. Odd Fish; or, Mrs. Scaite in the Seraglio (S.W. M. 3/9/1804).
    8° 1805.
    [Music Reeve.]
Ba. Ally Croaker (S.W. 1804).
Int. A Trip to the Danube (S.W. 1804).
Spec. Gothmund the Cruel; or, The Old Man of the Mountains (S.W.
    1804). 8° 1804.
    [An altered version of *The Old Man of the Mountain*, 1803.]
P. The Talking Bird; or, Harlequin and Perizade (S.W. 1805).
O.F. The Aquatic Prize (S.W. M. 15/4/1805). 8° [1805].
    [Music Reeve.]
M.D.Spec. Red Hands! or, The Welch Chieftains (S.W. W. 5/7/1805).
M.D. An Bratach; or, The Water Spectre (S.W. 7/1805).
P. Harlequin and Æsop; or, Wisdom versus Wealth (S.W. S.
    17/8/1805). 8° 1805.
    [Music Reeve.]
Spec. The Rival Patriots (S.W. 1806). 8° 1806.
    [Music Reeve.]
P. Harlequin and the Water Kelpe (S.W. M. 14/4/1806). 8° 1806.
    [Music Reeve.]
M.D. The Invisible Ring; or, The Water Monster and Fire Spectre
    (S.W. M. 25/6/1806). 8° 1806.
    [Music Reeve.]
P. Jan Ben Jan; or, Harlequin and the Forty Virgins (S.W. M.
    30/3/1807). 8° 1807 [Songs].

M.D. The Ocean Fiend; or, The Infant's Peril (S.W. M. 25/5/1807).
8° 1807.
[Music Reeve.]

P. The Cassowar; or, Harlequins Rouge et Noir (S.W. M. 3/8/1807).
8° 1807 [Songs].

Int. The Flitch of Bacon; or, The Custom of Dunmow (S.W. 1808).
8° [1808].

M.D. The White Witch; or, The Cataract of Amazonia (S.W. M.
18/4/1808). 8° 1808.

P. Thirty Thousand; or, Harlequin's Lottery (S.W. M. 18/4/1808).
8° [1808].

P. Harlequin's Lottery (S.W. M. 2/5/1808).

P. Harlequin High flyer; or, Off she goes (S.W. M. 4/7/1808).
8° 1808 [Songs].
[Music Reeve.]

M.D. The Magic Minstrel; or, The Fairy Lake (S.W. M. 8/8/1808).
8° 1809.

C.O. The Farmer's Boy (S.W. 1809). 8° 1809 [Recitatives, etc.].

P. Fashion's Fools; or, The Aquatic Harlequin (S.W. 1809). 8° 1809
[Recitatives, etc.].

M.D. The Wild Man; or, The Water Pageant (S.W. M. 22/5/1809).
8° 1809; 8° 1814; *Cumberland Minor*, vol. xcvi.
[Music Reeve.]

P. Castles in the Air; or, Columbine Cowslip (S.W. M. 31/7/1809).
8° 1812 [Songs].
[Music Reeve.]

M.D. Babes of the Castle; or, Mercy to the Penitent (S.W. M.
25/9/1809).

P. The Astrologer; or, Harlequin and Moore's Almanack (S.W. M.
23/4/1810). 8° 1810 [Songs].
[Music Reeve.]

M.D. The Spectre Knight (S.W. M. 4/6/1810). 8° 1810 [Songs].
[Based on Scott, *Marmion*. Music Reeve.]

P. Bang Up! or, Harlequin Prime (S.W. M. 23/7/1810). 8° 1810
[Songs].
[Music Reeve.]

F. The Three and the Ace; or, The Deuce is in it (S.W. M.
22/10/1810).

M.D. The Red Reaver (S.W. M. 15/4/1811). 8° 1811.

P. Dulce Domum; or, England the Land of Freedom (S.W. M.
15/4/1811). 8° 1811 [Songs].
[Music Reeve.]

M.D. The Council of Ten; or, The Lake of the Grotto (S.W. M.
3/6/1811). 8° 1811.
[Music Reeve.]

M.Ent. The Round Robin (H.² F. 21/6/1811). L. 54 S.
[27/5/1811].

P. Harlequin and Bluebeard (S.W. M. 15/7/1811).

M.D. The Wild Girl (S.W. M. 21/10/1811).

M.D. The Prince; or, The Illuminated Lake (S.W. M. 30/3/1812).

P. Whang Fong; or, The Clown of China (S.W. M. 11/5/1812).

M.D. Jonnie Armstrong; or, The Scottish Outlaw (S.W. W. 15/7/1812).
[Music Reeve.]

Spec. The Battle of Salamanca (S.W. M. 24/8/1812).

P. Fairlop Fair; or, The Genie of the Oak (S.W. M. 7/9/1812).
8° 1812.
[Music Reeve.]

Bsq. Castle Blarneygig! or, The Lady of the Wreck (S.W. M.
5/10/1812).

M.D. Juan Fernandez; or, The Stratagem (S.W. T. 20/10/1812).

C.O. The Lord of the Manor (C.G. 24/10/1812). *Dibdin's London
Theatre*, No. 22; *Dicks* 48.

P. London; or, Harlequin and Time (S.W. M. 19/4/1813). 8° 1813
[Songs].
[Music Reeve.]

M.D. Rokeby Castle; or, The Spectre of the Glen (S.W. M. 19/4/1813).

Int. The Spanish Gala; or, Cervantes Knight (S.W. M. 7/6/1813).

P. The Brachman; or, The Oriental Harlequin (S.W. M. 28/6/1813).
8° 1813 [Songs].
[Music Reeve.]

Bal. Spec. Vittoria; or, Wellington's Laurels (S.W. M. 12/7/1813).
8° [1813; Vocal Compositions].
[Music Reeve.]

M.D. Kaloc; or, The Slave Pirate (S.W. M. 9/8/1813). 8° 1813
[Songs].
[Music Reeve.]

Ext. Odd Fish; or, Madam Scaite in the Seraglio (S.W. 9/10/1813).

C.O. The Farmer's Wife (C.G. T. 1/2/1814). L. 98 M. [30/12/1813].
8° 1814; *Dibdin's London Theatre*, No. 17; *Dicks* 110.

P. Harlequin Wild Man; or, The Rival Genii (S.W. M. 11/4/1814).
8° 1814.
[Music Reeve.]

M.D. The Two Caliphs; or, The Palace of the Waters (S.W. M.
11/4/1814). 8° 1814.

M.D. Vive le Roi; or, The White Cocade (S.W. T. 17/5/1814).

M.D. The Corsair (S.W. M. 1/8/1814). 8° 1814.
[Music Reeve.]

P. The Fortune-Teller; or, Harlequin's Jubilee (S.W. M. 29/8/1814).
8° 1814 [Songs].
[Music Reeve.]

M.D. Oberon; or, The Magic Minstrel (S.W. M. 3/10/1814).
[Altered from his own *The Magic Minstrel*, 1808.]

Int. The Village Heiress (S.W. 1814). 8° 1814.

O.F. The Mother-in-law (S.W. 1815).

M.D. Egbert (S.W. 1815).

O.F. Brother and Sister (C.G. W. 1/2/1815).
[See *W. DIMOND*.]

O.F. Law's Two Tails; or, En-tail and Ren-tail (S.W. T. 28/3/1815).
8° 1815 [Songs].

P. The Mermaid; or, Harlequin Pearl-diver! (S.W. T. 28/3/1815).
8° 1815 [Songs].
[Music Reeve.]

M.D. The Red Hands; or, Welch Chieftains (S.W. M. 15/5/1815).
[See above under 5/7/1805].

P. Harlequin Brilliant; or, The Clown's Capers (S.W. M.
3/7/1815).

O.F. Mrs. Mullins; or, Grunt and Gaby (S.W. M. 2/10/1815).

O.F. My Spouse and I (D.L. Th. 7/12/1815; Surrey, F. 3/12/1841).

L. 61 S. [28/11/1815]. 8° 1815; 8° 1816; *Cumberland*, vol. xli; *Dicks* 180.
[Music Whitaker.]

Ext. The Boarding School Miss; or, The Fog Family (S.W. M. 15/4/1816).
[Also cited as *The Fog Family; or, The Chandler's Daughter*.]

P. London and Paris; or, Harlequin Traveller (S.W. M. 15/4/1816).

M.D. Iwanowna; or, The Maid of Moscow (S.W. M. 13/5/1816).

P. Gnomes and Fairies; or, Harlequin Hurry Skurry (S.W. M. 24/6/1816).

M.D. Phillip and his Dog; or, Where's the Child? (S.W.M. 15/7/1816).

M.D. Barsissa; or, The Hermit Robber (S.W. M. 16/9/1816).

P. Plants and Planets; or, Fairly in for't (S.W. M. 4/11/1816).

P. April Fools; or, Months and Mummery (S.W. M. 7/4/1817).
[Also cited as *M. and M.; or, Clown's Chronology*.]

M.D. The Viceroy; or, The Spanish Gipsy and the Assassin (S.W. M. 26/5/1817).

M.D. Forget me not! or, The Flower of Waterloo (S.W.M. 23/6/1817).

P. Alchymy; or, Harlequin Large and Harlequin Little (S.W. M. 14/7/1817).

M.D. The Terrible Peak; or, A Mother's Sorrows (S.W. M. 4/8/1817).

O.F. No. 2; or, The Old Figure (S.W. 22/9/1817).

O.F. A Friend Indeed (C.G. W. 5/11/1817). L. 109 M. [29/10/1817].
[Music Whitaker.]

D. Three Miles from Paris (C.G. Th. 15/1/1818). L. 113 M. [6/1/1818].

M.D. The Gheber; or, The Fire Worshippers (S.W. M. 23/3/1818).
[A dramatisation of *Lallah Rookh*.]

M.D. The Gathering of the Clans (S.W. M. 6/4/1818).

P. Salmagundi; or, The Clown's Dish of All Sorts (S.W. M. 11/5/1818).

M.D. O'Donoughue and his White Horse (S.W. M. 25/5/1818).

Ext. The Widow and her Grandmama (S.W. M. 6/7/1818).

M.D. The Seaman and the Savage (S.W. M. 3/8/1818).

Ext. Fig Hall; or, Lingo in a New School (S.W. M. 10/8/1818).

M.D. The Maniac; or, The Dark Assassin (S.W. M. 24/8/1818).

O.F. Miss Michaelmass; or, The Dog and the Shadow (S.W. M. 7/9/1818).

P. The Elements; or, Harlequin Earth, Air, Water and Fire (S.W. 1818).

Ext. Father Luke and Darby (S.W. M. 12/4/1819).
[Music Nicholson.]

M.D. The Weird Sisters; or, The Thane and the Throne (S.W. M. 12/4/1819).
[A melodramatic version of *Macbeth*.]

P. The Talking Bird (S.W. M. 12/4/1819).

Ball.P. Herman and Halstein; or, The Free Judges (S.W. M. 17/5/1819).

Ent. Jack and the Beanstalk; or, Harlequin and the Ogre (D.L. M. 27/12/1819). L. 23 L. [12/1819].

P. Shakespeare Versus Harlequin (D.L. S. 8/4/1820).
[Based on Garrick, *Harlequin's Invasion*. Music Reeve and Cooke.]

Int. The Admirable Crichton (D.L. M. 12/6/1820). L. 119 M.

O. David Rizzio (D.L. S. 17/6/1820).
[See *R. HAMILTON*.]
Prel. Let by Auction (Olym. 10/1820).
[Music Reeve.]
P. The North Pole (D.L. 26/12/1821).
Ext. Life in London; or, The Day and Night Adventures of Logic, Tom and Jerry (Olym. M. 12/11/1821). L. 126 M. [17/10/1821]; L. 128 M. [8/11/1821]; L. 127 M. [as *L. in L.; or, The Larks of Logic, Tom and Jerry*]. 8° 1822.
Int. All in the Wrong (R.A. 6/1822).
M.D. Ursa Major (R.A. 6/1822).
M.D. Alexander the Great and Thalestris the Amazon (R.A. M. 12/8/1822).
M.D. Woodriffe; or, The Smuggler's Boy (R.A. M. 26/8/1822).
Int. The Bill of Fare; or, What's to be Seen? (R.A. 9/1822).
M.D. Maurice; or, The Mysterious Host (R.A. T. 10/12/1822).
Ext. Billy Duck (R.A. 10/1822).
Bal. Yarra; or, The Rival Indians (R.A. M. 21/10/1822).
M.D. Fillebrande; or, The Female Bandit (R.A. M. 28/10/1822).
P. Harlequin Achilles; or, A Trip to Hyde Park (R.A. T. 12/11/1822).
M.D. St George and the Dragon; or, The Seven Champions of Christendom (R.A. Th. 26/12/1822).
Ba. Dunoir the Base; or, Is it a Spectre? (R.A. M. 31/3/1823).
Ba. The Wild Man, Fair Maniac and Dumb Brother and Sister (R.A. 1823).
M.D. The Female Freebooter; or, The Mysterious Host (R.A. M. 21/4/1823).
Ext. Doctor Syntax and another Doctor (R.A. M. 5/5/1823).
Ext. The Ghosts of Tom and Jerry; or, The Wind Up (R.A. M. 30/6/1823).
M.D. Bonduca; or, The British Queen (R.A. M. 4/8/1823).
Ext. Polynchinel Vampire; or, The Man in the Moon (R.A. M. 18/8/1823).
Bsq. The Furor of Friendship; or, Manslaughter by Moonlight; or, The Ghost of a Hamper of Wine (R.A. 1823).
Prel. The White Surrey; or, Saddled for the Field (Surrey, 9/4/1825).
M.D. Murder and Madness; or, A Traveller's Tale (Surrey, 9/4/1825).
M.D. Atala and Chactas; or, The Law of the Desart (Surrey, M. 4/4/1825).
D. The Colonel's Come; or, La Femme Soldat (Surrey, 18/4/1825).
M.D. Elfrida of Olmutz; or, The Child of Mistery (Surrey, 25/4/1825).
M.D. The Fatal Precept; or, The Assassin of Silesia (Surrey, 9/5/1825).
M.D. Klebir in Egypt; or, The Fanatic of Aleppo (Surrey, M. 23/5/1825).
O.F. Six Hours More (Surrey, M. 23/5/1825).
P. Horrification; or, Harlequin Preciosa, Der Fryshoots and Dr Faustus (Surrey, M. 23/5/1825).
M.D. The Orphans; or, Love, Avarice and Repentance (Surrey, 20/6/1825).
O.F. She's not to be managed; or, How to drive a tandem (Surrey, 27/6/1825).
M.D. Black Caesar; or, The Fatal Thicket (Surrey, M. 11/7/1825).

M.D. The Manslayer; or, The Mountain Smugglers (Surrey, M. 1/8/1825).

M.D. Maurice; or, The Mysterious Host (Surrey, 22/8/1825).
[See above under 10/12/1822.]

M.D. The Jew of Wilna; or, Bravery and Ingratitude (Surrey, M. 29/8/1825).

O.F. The Old Bear; or, Bound to keep the Peace (Surrey, M. 12/9/1825).

M.D. The Maid of Venice; or, The Prophet's Priest (Surrey, M. 19/9/1825).

O.F. A Cheap Bargain; or, A Little Misery and a Little Mischief (Surrey, M. 17/10/1825).

M.D. Filial Love; or, The Prisoner's Daughter (Surrey, M. 31/10/1825).

Ext. A Figure of Fun; or, Listeners hear no good of themselves (Surrey, M. 31/10/1825).

M.D. The Yellow Fiend; or, The Scorpion's Sting (Surrey, M. 7/11/1825).

P. The Seaman and la Belle Sauvage (Surrey, M. 7/11/1825).
[See above under 3/8/1818.]

Ent. Mr N'Importe; or, What does it signify? (Surrey, M. 7/11/1825).

Ext. Crom-a-boo'; or, The Ape and the Infant (Surrey, 26/12/1825).

M.D. The Foresters; or, Truth and Treason (Surrey, M. 23/1/1826).

P. The Knight and his Page; or, The Ape of the Forest (Surrey, M. 13/2/1826).

M.D. Friendship's Test (Surrey, 1826).

O.F. The Flaw in the Lease; or, What is he? (Surrey, M. 6/3/1826).

Ext. Miss Poppy; or, The Chandler's Daughter (Surrey, M. 6/3/1826).

D. The Apprentice's Opera; or, The Fate of the Fancy Lad (Surrey, M. 27/3/1826).

M.D. Bruno the Black and the Knight Champion (Surrey, M. 27/3/1826).

M.D. Isolate and the Ape (Surrey, M. 27/3/1826).

M.D. The Savage Lovers; or, The Rival Regicides (Surrey, M. 24/4/1826).

M.D. Woodstock; or, The Cavalier (Surrey, M. 15/5/1826).

Ext. The Election; or, The Casting Vote (Surrey, 12/6/1826).

F. Billy Duck; or, Old Rugg's Words (Surrey, 12/6/1826).

O. The Rake's Progress (Surrey, 10/7/1826).

P. The Monster of the Glen; or, Harlequin and the Fairy Fanciful (Surrey, 17/7/1826).

M.D. The Curse of Kavanah (Surrey, 31/7/1826).

M.D. The Victim of Malice (Surrey, 21/8/1826).

Ba. Paul Pry (Surrey, 11/9/1826).

O.F. Lodgings to Let (Surrey, 11/9/1826).

Bal. Oberon and Titania; or, The King and Queen of the Fairies (S.W. M. 9/2/1829). MS. in the possession of Mr Crompton Rhodes.

O.F. All at Sixes and Sevens (D.L. S. 21/3/1829).
[Music Whitaker.]

F. Nothing Superfluous (Hull, 5/8/1829). MS. in the possession of Mr Rimbault Dibdin.

DIBDIN, THOMAS JOHN.
[For his earlier plays see *A History of Late Eighteenth Century Drama,* pp. 256-7.]

P.   The Volcano; or, Rival Harlequins (C.G. 23/12/1799). L. 37 S. [12/12/1799]. 8° 1799 [Songs, Recitatives].

O.F. Of Age To-morrow (D.L. S. 1/2/1800). L. 75 M. [28/1/1800]. 8° 1805; 8° 1805 [Songs, Duets]; *Dicks* 278; *Cumberland*, vol. xliii. [Music Kelly.]

M.Ent. True Friends (C.G. W. 19/2/1800). L. 40 S. [11/2/1800]. 8° 1800 [Songs]. [Music Attwood.]

O.F. St. David's Day; or, The Honest Welshman (C.G. M. 31/3/1800). L. 38 S. [15/3/1800]. 8° 1801; 8° 1800 [Songs, etc.]; *Cumberland*, vol. xxxvii.

Int. The Hermione; or, Retaliation (C.G. S. 5/4/1800). L. 38 S. [25/3/1800].

C.   Liberal Opinions (C.G. M. 12/5/1800).

M.Ent. The Two Farmers. L. 75 M. [10/10/1800].

C.O. Il Bondocani; or, The Caliph Robber (C.G. S. 15/11/1800). L. 38 S. [22/10/1800]. 8° 1801; 8° 1801 [Songs, Choruses]. [Music, Attwood and Moorhead.]

P.   Harlequin's Tour; or, The Dominion of Fancy (C.G. M. 22/12/1800). L. 40 S. [16/12/1800; titles reversed].

Ent. Something New (Colchester, 1801).

C.   The School for Prejudice (C.G. S. 3/1/1801). L. 75 M. [28/4/1800]. 8° 1801; *Inchbald's Modern Theatre*, vol. iv. [This is an expanded form of *Liberal Opinions*.]

P.R. Alonzo and Imogine; or, The Bridal Spectre (C.G. W. 10/6/1801).

Ba.   Gaffer's Mistake (S.W. M. 29/6/1801).

M.Ent. The Escapes; or, The Water Carrier (C.G. W. 14/10/1801). L. 76 M. [12/5/1801].

P.   Harlequin's Almanack; or, The Four Seasons (C.G. M. 28/12/1801). L. 40 S. [14/12/1801]. 8° 1801 [Introduction, Songs, Glees, Trios, Chorusses]. [Music Reeve and Ware.]

O.F. Blind Man's Buff; or, Who Pays the Piper? (Royalty, M. 1/2/1802).

C.O. The Cabinet (C.G. T. 9/2/1802). L. 77 M. [18/1/1802]. 8° 1802 [Dublin; pirated]; 8° 1805; 8° 1810; Songs, Duets, etc. 8° 1802; 8° 1803; *Cumberland*, vol. xxi. [Music Reeve, Moorhead, Davy, Corri and Braham.]

Bal. The Brazen Mask; or, Alberto and Rosabella (C.G. M. 5/4/1802). L. 42 S. [10/3/1802]. 8° 1802 [Sketch of the Fable...with the Songs and Chorusses]. [Music Mountain and Davy.]

C.O. Family Quarrels (C.G. S. 18/12/1802). L. 77 M. [11/11/1802]. 8° 1805; 8° 1803 [Songs, Duets]; *Cumberland*, vol. xxxii. [Music Moorhead, Braham and Reeve.]

P.   Harlequin's Habeas; or, The Hall of Spectres (C.G. M. 27/12/1802). L. 42 S. [17/12/1802]. 8° 1802 [Songs]. [Music Moorhead, Braham and Davy.]

C.O. The English Fleet, in 1342 (C.G. T. 13/12/1803; Cob. M. 14/4/1828). L. 78 M. [6/12/1803]. 8° 1805 [*bis*]; 8° 1803 [Songs, Duets, and Chorusses]. [Music Braham.]

P.   Harlequin's Races; or, Time beats all (C.G. M. 26/12/1803).

C.   The Will for the Deed (C.G. S. 24/3/1804). L. 80 M. [16/3/1804].
     8° 1805.
M.D. Valentine and Orson (C.G. T. 3/4/1804). L. 80 M. [10/3/1804].
     8° 1804; *Cumberland*, vol. xxvii.
     [Music Jouve.]
C.   Guilty or Not Guilty (H.² S. 26/5/1804). L. 44 S. [20/5/1804].
     8° 1804 [4 editions].
C.O. Thirty Thousand; or, Who's the Richest? (C.G. M. 10/12/1804).
     L. 81 M. [27/11/1804]. 8° 1804; 8° 1805 [2nd]; 8° 1805 [new].
     [Music Braham, Davy and Reeve.]
P.   Harlequin Quicksilver; or, The Gnome and the Devil (C.G. W.
     26/12/1804). L. 81 M. [18/12/1804]. 8° 1804 [Songs, Trios,
     Chorusses].
Bal. Aggression; or, The Heroine of Yucatan (C.G. 4/1805).
     [The songs are by Dibdin.]
Int. Nelson's Glory (C.G. Th. 7/11/1805).
P.   Harlequin's Magnet; or, The Scandinavian Sorcerer (C.G. M.
     30/12/1805). L. 45 S. [22/12/1805]. 8° 1806 [Songs].
     [Music J. Davy.]
M.D. The White Plume; or, The Border Chieftains (C.G. Th.
     10/4/1806). L. 47 S. [25/3/1806]. 8° 1806 [Songs].
     [Music Reeve.]
C.   Five Miles Off; or, The Finger Post (H.² W. 9/7/1806). L. 47 S.
     [28/6/1806]. 8° 1806; 8° 1809; *Mod. Eng. Com. Th.* vol. ii.
P.   Harlequin and Mother Goose; or, The Golden Egg (C.G. F.
     26/12/1806). L. 46 S. [23/12/1806]; MS. in possession of Mr
     Crompton Rhodes. 8° 1806 [Songs, Chorusses]; *Lacy*, vol. liv.
     [Music Ware.]
F.   The Miseries of Human Life; or, Let us all be — unhappy
     together (C.G. T. 19/5/1807). L. 48 S. [13/5/1807].
C.   Errors Excepted (H.² Th. 13/8/1807). L. 86 M. [11/8/1807].
C.O. Two Faces under a Hood (C.G. T. 17/11/1807). 8° [1807];
     8° 1807 [Songs, Duets].
P.   Harlequin in his Element; or, Fire, Water, Earth and Air (C.G. S.
     26/12/1807). L. 48 S. [19/12/1807]. 8° [1807]; 8° [1807; Airs,
     Chorusses].
Ext. Bonifacio and Bridgetina; or, The Knight of the Hermitage; or
     The Windmill Turrett; or, The Spectre of the North-East Gallery
     (C.G. Th. 31/3/1808). L. 87 M. [19/3/1808]. 8° 1808; 8° 1808
     [Songs].
M.D. The Forest of Hermanstadt; or, A Princess and no Princess
     (C.G. F. 7/10/1808; Cob. M. 1/12/1828). L. 87 M. [17/9/1808].
     [An adaptation of Caigniez, *La forêt de Hermanstadt.*]
Int. The Jubilee (C.G. W. 25/10/1809). L. 90 M. [21/10/1809].
     [Music Reeve.]
P.   Harlequin Pedlar; or, The Haunted Well (C.G. 26/12/1809).
P.   Harlequin Basket-Maker; or, Willows Bewitched (Surrey, T.
     4/9/1810).
M.D. The Lady of the Lake; or, Roderick vich Alpine (Surrey, M.
     24/9/1810). 12° [1810; Dublin]; *Cumberland Minor*, vol. iii;
     Dicks 587.
     [A play of this title is in L. 67 S. [Olym. 1/12/1817].]
M.D. The Harper's Son and the Duke's Daughter (Surrey, W.
     12/12/1810). L. 92 M. [1810; printed copy]. 8° 1810.

P. Mirth and Harlequin; or, The Road to Bath (Surrey, M. 15/4/1811.)
Ba. Peeping Tom; or, The Mayor in a Hamper (Surrey, M. 3/6/1811).
Prel. What's a Stage without Horses? (Surrey, M. 10/6/1811).
Ba. Right of Common; or, How to get a Freehold (Surrey, M. 8/7/1811).
M.D. "Blood will have Blood!" or, The Battle of the Bridges (Surrey, M. 10/6/1811).
M.D. Lodoiska (Surrey, M. 12/8/1811).
C.O. Up to Town (C.G. W. 6/11/1811). L. 93 M. [28/10/1811; as *Up to London*].
    [Music Reeve, Condell, Welsh and Whitaker.]
M.D. America; or, The Colonists (Surrey, M. 30/3/1812).
M.D. The Secret Mine (C.G. F. 24/4/1812). L. 96 M. [2/4/1812]. 8° 1813 [Dublin].
    [Written in collaboration with *J. FAWCETT.*]
P. Harlequin Colossus; or, The Seven Wonders of the World (Surrey, M. 22/6/1812).
M.D. Java (C.G. *c.* 1812).
F. Schniederkins (C.G. F. 16/10/1812). L. 56 S. [10/10/1812].
P. Harlequin and Humpo; or, Columbine by Candlelight (D.L. S. 26/12/1812). L. 55 S [20/12/1812]; MS. formerly in the possession of R. Crompton Rhodes.
O. Haroun Alraschid (C.G. 1/1813). *Dicks* 513.
    [Based on *The Æthiop* by *W. DIMOND.*]
M.D. Llewellyn, Prince of Wales; or, Gellert the Faithful Dog (Surrey, M. 14/6/1813). See *A. CHERRY.*
P. The Highmettled Racer (R.A. 1813).
    [This appears in *UA* as *The Life, Death and Restoration of the High Mettled Racer.*]
O.F. Who's to have her? (D.L. M. 22/11/1813). L. 57 S. [15/11/1813]. 8° 1813.
    [Music Reeve and Whitaker.]
Int. Orange Boven; or, More Good News (D.L. F. 10/12/1813). L. 58 S. [6/12/1813]. 8° 1813 [Songs, Duets].
P. Harlequin Harper; or, A Jump from Japan (D.L. M. 27/12/1813). L. 58 S. [13/12/1813; as *H. Harmonist; or, A Trip to J.*]. 8° 1813 [Prospectus].
Int. Tag in Tribulation (Surrey, 1814). L. 60 S. [Surrey, 1814].
Ext. Harlequin Hoax; or, A Pantomime Proposed (Lyc. T. 16/8/1814). L. 58 S. [9/8/1814]. 8° 1814; 8° 1815 [2nd]; *Dicks* 498.
Spec. The Dog of Montargis; or, The Forest of Bondy (R.C. Th. 6/10/1814).
M.D. The Ninth Statue; or, The Irishman in Bagdad (D.L. T. 29/11/1814). L. 59 S. [17/11/1814]. 8° 1814.
P. The Valley of Diamonds; or, Harlequin Sinbad (D.L. M. 26/12/1814). L. 102 M. [19/12/1814].
    [Written in association with the clown, Kirby.]
F. Past Ten O'Clock, And a Rainy Night (D.L. S. 11/3/1815). L. 60 S. [4/3/1815]. 8° 1815; *Cumberland*, vol. xxxviii.
M.D. The Magpie; or, The Maid of Palaiseau (D.L. T. 12/9/1815). L. Extra [3/9/1815]. *Oxberry.*
    [Music T. Cooke. An adaptation of Caigniez, *La pie voleuse; ou, la servante de Palaiseau.*]

F. Twenty per Cent.; or, My Father (D.L. Th. 2/11/1815). L. 61 S. [26/10/1815]. *Dibdin's London Theatre.*

P. Harlequin and Fancy; or, The Poet's Last Shilling (D.L. T. 26/12/1815; Surrey, W. 25/2/1829). L. 61 S. [17/12/1815]. [Music Smart.]

D. Accusation; or, The Family of Anglade (D.L. Th. 1/2/1816). See *J. H. PAYNE.*

F. What Next? (D.L. Th. 29/2/1816). L. 64 S. [19/2/1816]. 8° 1816; *Dicks* 267; *London Stage,* vol. iv.

Bal.Spec. Pitcairn's Island (D.L. W. 17/4/1816). L. 64 S. [12/4/1816]. 8° [1816; Songs]. [Music Corri.]

P. The House-warming; or, The Peasant's Pic-nic (R.C. M. 1/7/1816). [Described in Dibdin's memoirs as *Harlequin Pic-Nic.*]

Bal.Spec. The Sicilian; or, The Prince and the Pirate (R.C. M. 1/7/1816).

D.R. Chevy Chase; or, The Warlocks of the Border (R.C. M. 1/7/1816).

D.R. Who's the Murderer? or, A True Tale of the Twelfth Century (R.C. M. 15/7/1816).

Spec. Slaves in Barbary; or, British Vengeance (R.C. W. 31/7/1816; R.C. M. 16/9/1816, "2nd edition" as *S. in B.; or, The Bombardment of Algiers*).

P. The Dog and the Duck; or, Harlequin in the Obelisk (R.C. M. 26/8/1816).

Ba. Love in Full Gallop; or, The Highroad to Marriage (R.C. W. 30/10/1816; S.W. M. 19/6/1826). [Based on Waldron, *Heigho for a Husband.*]

Ba. Waggery in Wapping; or, King Charles in the Royal Oak (R.C. M. 4/11/1816).

M.D. Love, Hatred and Revenge (R.C. M. 4/11/1816).

Spec. The Silver Swan; or, The Wizard's Dream (R.C. F. 22/11/1816).

Ba. Three Times Three; or, Boys, Girls and Guardians (R.C. M. 16/12/1816).

M.D. The Italian Wife (R.C. Th. 26/12/1816; 2nd performance). [This is Milman's *Fazio,* as altered by Dibdin.]

P. Pedlar's Acre; or, Harlequin in Lambeth (R.C. Th. 26/12/1816).

Bsq. Don Giovanni; or, A Spectre on Horseback (R.C. M. 26/5/1817; Lyc. 17/7/1820). 8° 1817; 8° 1818 [4th]; *Cumberland Minor,* vol. ii.

P. The Golden Axe; or, Harlequin Woodman (R.A. M. 7/4/1817).

P. The Magic Grape; or, Harlequin in the Wine Trade (R.C. M. 7/4/1817).

M.D. The Red Man and the Savage (R.C. M. 7/4/1817).

Ba. Five, Six, Seven; or, Pay me my Wages (R.C. T. 15/4/1817).

O.F. The Three Paddies; or, All of a Mind (R.C. M. 5/5/1817).

Ba. Trick for Trick; or, The Man and the Maid (R.C. M. 5/5/1817).

Spec. Waterloo Bridge; or, The Anniversary (R.C. W. 18/6/1817).

M.D. Constantine and Valeria; or, The Last of the Caesars (R.C. M. 23/6/1817). [This is Joanna Baillie's *Constantine Palaeologus* as altered by Dibdin.]

M.D. The Fatal Island (R.C. M. 28/7/1817).

P. Harlequin Patchwork; or, Tria Juncta in Uno (R.C. M. 18/8/1817).

M.D. The Vicar of Wakefield (R.C. M. 25/8/1817). L. 110 M. [25/8/1817]. 8° 1817.
[Music Sanderson.]
Int. At All in the Ring (R.C. M. 1/9/1817).
M.D.Spec. The Queen of Golconda; or, Two Places at Once (R.C. M. 22/9/1817).
M.D. The Knights of the Lion (R.C. Th. 8/1/1818, 4th performance).
Ba. Tom Jones; or, The Foundling (R.C. M. 19/1/1818).
M.D. Zapolyta; or, The War Wolf (R.C. M. 9/2/1818).
[This is Coleridge's play adapted by Dibdin.]
O. Zuma; or, The Tree of Health (C.G. S. 21/2/1818). L. 113 M. [30/1/1818]. 8° 1818.
[Music Bishop and Braham.]
Ba. Sir Launcelot Graves (R.C. M. 23/3/1818).
M.D. The Three Talismans (R.C. M. 23/3/1818).
Ba. The Duke and the Devil (R.C. W. 6/5/1818).
O.F. Rather too bad! (R.C. M. 11/5/1818).
M.D. Kouli Khan (R.C. T. 12/5/1818).
Ext. How to write an Opera! or, The Delights of Dramatic Authorship (R.C. M. 1/6/1818).
Ba. Humphrey Clinker (R.C. M. 6/7/1818). Cumberland Minor, vol. iv.
[Based on Smollett's novel.]
Ba. The Adventures of Roderick Random (R.C. M. 20/7/1818).
[Based on Smollett's novel.]
Ba. Ferdinand, Count Fathom (R.C. F. 31/7/1818).
[Based on Smollett's novel.]
Spec. Red Riding Hood; or, The Wolf of the Forest of Arden (R.C. M. 24/8/1818).
P. The Sea Serpent; or, Harlequin Yankee (R.C. M. 21/9/1818).
M.D. The Invisible Witness; or, The Chapel in the Wood (R.C. M. 21/9/1818].
[An adaptation of Pixérécourt, La chapelle du bois (Paris, 12/8/1815).]
M.D. The Murdered Guest (R.C. T. 13/10/1818).
[An adaptation of Lillo, Fatal Curiosity.]
O.F. Scraps; or, The Village Theatre (R.C. S. 26/12/1818).
[Called S.; or, Black Spirits and White in Dibdin's memoirs. It seems to be the same as Scraps; or, Fun for the Gallery given at S.W. Th. 5/10/1820.]
M.D. The Reprobate (R.C. S. 26/12/1818).
[Based on Mrs Opie's story.]
M.D.Spec. Azim; or, Wants and Superfluities (R.C. S. 26/12/1818).
M.D. The Heart of Midlothian; or, The Lily of St. Leonard's (R.C. W. 13/1/1819). 8° 1819 [3 editions]; Dicks 252; Cumberland Minor, vol. i.
[Music Erskine. Based on Scott's novel.]
M.D. The Ruffian Boy (R.C. M. 15/2/1819). Cumberland Minor, vol. iv.
[Based on Mrs Opie's story.]
M.D. The Hermit of Mount Pausilippo (R.C. M. 12/4/1819).
Ba. Florence Macarthy; or, A Tour in Hibernia (R.C. M. 31/5/1819).
Bsq. Melodrame Mad! or, The Siege of Troy. A New Comic, Pathetic, Historic, Anachronasmatic, Ethic, Epic Melange, "full of doleful mirth and right merrie conceit." The Situations and

Sentiments from Mr Homer, a blind old Ballad-singer—one Shakespeare, a Warwickshire Deer-stealer—the Language of the Gods from A Pope—and many of the Songs are Gay. The ancient Music from some of the greatest Lyres of the earliest Ages—the modern Compositions by Arne, Arnold, Attwood, Bishop, Dibdin, Reeve, Shield, Sanderson, &c.—the new Music by Mr Erskine. The Scenery taken from several Spots of Greece (and Troy); the Artists being prevented, by our present Neutrality, from attending the Siege, have left the task of Invention and Execution to the talents of Mr Wilson, assisted by his Pupils H. Wilson, C. R. Dibdin, &c. The Dresses, a la Grec, from the classic Scissars and Needles of Mr Brett and Miss Freelove. The Machinery by Ben Johnson the Carpenter. The Decorations by Artists described hereafter. The Dances by Mr. Giroux—The Heroic Action and Processions under the direction of Mr Ridgway (R.C. M. 21/6/1819). 8° 1819.

R.D. Montrose (Surrey, M. 5/7/1819).
    [Based on Scott's novel.]

M.D. The Bride of Lammermoor; or, The Spectre at the Fountain (Surrey, M. 5/7/1819).

M.D. The Abbot of San Martino; or, True Revenge (Surrey, M. 26/7/1819).

Spec. Scanderbeg; or, The Outlawed Prince (Surrey, M. 9/8/1819).

M.D. Richard the First; or, Coeur de Lion (Surrey, M. 23/8/1819).

M.D. The President and the Peasant's Daughter (Surrey, W. 1/9/1819).

Ba. The Spoiled Children; or, The Manager's Night (Surrey, S. 2/10/1819).

Ba. Small Profits do Great Things (Surrey, M. 27/12/1819).

M.D. The Force of Conscience; or, The Accusing Spirit (Surrey, M. 27/12/1819).

Ba. Mouse-traps; or, The Mountain Cottager (Surrey, M. 27/12/1819).

Ba. The Prophecy; or, The Giant Spectre (Surrey, Th. 6/1/1820).
    [An adaptation of Jephson, *The Count of Narbonne*.]

M.D. Ivanhoe; or, The Jew's Daughter (Surrey, Th. 20/1/1820). 8° 1820; *Cumberland Minor*, vol. ii; *Lacy*, vol. xcii.
    [Based on Scott's novel. This play was revived at the Coburg on M. 15/2/1830 as *Ivanhoe; or, The Knights Templars; or, Isaac the Jew of York*.]

M.D. The Fate of Calais (Surrey, M. 3/4/1820). 8° 1820; *Cumberland Minor*, vol. viii.

P. Goody Two Shoes, Fairy of the Flowers; or, Village Frolics (S.W. M. 3/4/1820).

Oa. The Widow and No Widow (Surrey, M. 10/4/1820).

M.D. The Knights of Rhodes (Surrey, M. 15/5/1820).

M.D. Old Mortality; or, Burley and Morton (Surrey, M. 12/6/1820).
    [Based on Scott's novel.]

Ba. A New Way to get Married; or, Give a Man Luck and throw him in the Sea (Surrey, S. 24/6/1820).

Ba. Wheels within Wheels (Surrey, M. 31/7/1820).

M.D. Orsino; or, The Vaulted Cavern (Surrey, M. 21/8/1820).

O.F. Stop Thief! or, The Horrors of the Forest (Surrey, F. 1/9/1820).

O.F. Everybody's Cousin (Surrey, W. 27/12/1820).

M.D. Belisarius the Roman General (Surrey, W. 27/12/1820).
[Based on J. G. A. Cuvelier and Hubert, *Bélisaire* (Paris, 19/4/1815).]

R.D. The Blue Baron; or, Over the Bridge (Surrey, M. 22/1/1821).

O.F. Tost in a Blanket; or, Law without Study (Olym. M. 22/1/1821). L. 81 S. [20/1/1821].

M.D. Elizabeth and Essex; or, The Days of Queen Bess (Surrey, W. 7/2/1821; named *Kenilworth; or, The Countess of Essex* on W. 21/2/1821). *Cumberland*, vol. xxxix; *Dicks* 334; *Lacy*, vol. xcviii. [Based on Scott's novel.]

Bsq. The Daughters of Danaus and the Sons of Ægyptus; or, Fifty Weddings and Nine and Forty Murders (Surrey, M. 5/3/1821).

M.D. Alonzo the Brave and the Fair Imogene (Surrey, M. 2/4/1821).

O.F. The Two Gregories; or, Where did the Money come from? (Surrey, M. 23/4/1821; D.L. 14/6/1826). 8° 1821; *Cumberland Minor*, vol. iii; *Lacy*, vol. lxx.
[Based on *Jocrisse valet et Jocrisse maître*.]

D. The Seven Champions of Christendom (Surrey, S. 19/5/1821).

M.D. Kedeth, the Hag of Poland (Surrey, M. 11/6/1821).

O.F. Masonry; or, The Secret Discovered (Surrey, M. 11/6/1821; 2nd performance).

O.F. Frederick and Voltaire; or, The King and the Poet (Surrey, M. 16/7/1821).

C. Rise and Fall (H.² S. 4/8/1821). L. 80 S. [30/7/1821].

O.F. The Veterans; or, The Commodore and the Colonel (Surrey, M. 22/10/1821).
[An alteration of his own *Birth-day*.]

P. Three of Them; or, Harlequin Hum, Harlequin Strum and Harlequin Mum (Surrey, M. 22/10/1821).

Bsq. Leonora; or, The Apparition on the White Horse; or, Love in all its Horrors (Surrey, Th. 22/11/1821).

Ba. Jack in the Green; or, The Family Punch-Bowl (Surrey, W. 26/12/1821).

Bsq. Animal Sympathy; or, The Sentimental Waiter; or, The Man and the Monkey (Surrey, W. 26/12/1821).

M.D. The Pirate; or, The Wild Woman of Zetland (Surrey, M. 7/1/1822). 8° 1822.
[Based on Scott's novel.]

R.C. Sir Arthur; or, The Irish Chief (Surrey, M. 28/1/1822).

M.D. Elfrid; or, The Weird Wanderer of Jutland (Surrey, T. 26/3/1822).

Ba. The Soldier's Stratagem; or, The Colonel's Contrivance (Surrey, T. 26/3/1822).

Prel. The Bill of Fare; or, For Further Particulars Enquire Within (H.² S. 15/6/1822). L. 84 M. [7/6/1822].

O.F. Love Letters (H.² M. 24/6/1822). L. 84 S. [7/6/1822].

C.O. Morning, Noon and Night; or, The Romance of a Day (H.² M. 9/9/1822). L. 83 S. [31/8/1822]. 8° 1822.
[Music Perry.]

M.D. A Tale of Other Times; or, Which is the Bride? (D.L. Th. 19/12/1822).
[An altered version of his own *Princess and No Princess*.]

P. Gog and Magog; or, Harlequin Antiquary (D.L. Th. 26/12/1822). L. 84 S. [24/12/1822].

Ent. Old Nick (Olym. 1822).

Spec. The Chinese Sorcerer; or, The Emperor and his Three Sons (D.L. M. 31/3/1823). L. 86 S. [17/3/1823; as *Whang Fong*].

O.F. Summer Flies; or, The Will for the Deed (H.² 16/6/1823).

F.   Come if you can (H.² 14/6/1824). L.C. 11/6/1824.

M.D. Beauty in a Box; or, The Foundling Prince and the Vizier's Daughter (S.W. M. 4/4/1825).

Ba. The Great Gentleman in the Little Parlour (S.W. M. 4/4/1825).
     [Also called *Under the Rose*; as such it appears in *Cumberland*.]

Ba. The Man and the Marquis; or, The Three Spectres of the Castle of St. Valori (S.W. M. 18/4/1825). *Cumberland Minor*, vol. viii.

P.   Fairy Blue and Fairy Red; or, Harlequin and the Marble Rock (S.W. M. 23/5/1825).

Ba. Here we are (S.W. 1825).

Ba. Jocko; or, The Ape of Brazil (S.W. M. 6/6/1825; named *J.; or, The Orang Outang of Brazil* on M. 27/6/1825).

M.D. Abyssinia; or, A Trip to the Nile (S.W. M. 4/7/1825).

Ba. The Devil's in Dr Faustus; or, Mephistopheles in Town (S.W. 4/7/1825).

Ba. The Lawyer, the Jew and the Yorkshireman. (S.W. M. 22/8/1825).
     [An alteration of his own *School for Prejudice*.]

M.D. The Enchanted Girdles; or, Winki the Witch and the Ladies of Samarcand (S.W. M. 5/9/1825).

O.F. Garrick and his Double (S.W. M. 10/10/1825).

P.   Merlin's Mount; or, Harlequin Cymraeg and the Living Leek (S.W. M. 26/12/1825).

M.D. The Three Crumpies; or, The Baron and his Brothers (S.W. M. 26/12/1825).

Ba. All in One Night; or, The House upon the Heath (S.W. M. 26/12/1825).
     [An alteration of his own *Five Miles Off*.]

Ba. The Spread Eagle; or, The Traveller and his Host (S.W. M. 16/1/1826).

Ent. Black Spirits and White; or, The Haunted Chamber (S.W. M. 23/1/1826).

Bsq. Peggy Larkins; or, Love in Tripoli (S.W. M. 6/2/1826).

Ba. The Duke and the Devil; or, Which is Which? (S.W. M. 6/2/1826).

Ba. Don Giovanni (S.W. M. 6/3/1826).

Ba. Mrs W.; or, Vere's my Vife? (S.W. M. 27/3/1826).

M.D. Emmeline of Hungary; or, What Will be the End of It? (S.W. M. 27/3/1826).

P.   Hot and Cold; or, Harlequin Snowball and the Sprites of the Village (S.W. M. 27/3/1826).

Ba. All her own Way; or, The Romp Reclaimed (S.W. M. 10/4/1826).
     [An alteration of his own *Rather too bad!*]

M.D. The Peacock's Feather; or, The Grand Caravan and the Saddler of Cairo (S.W. M. 15/5/1826).

M.D. Alonzo the Brave and the Fair Imogine; or, The Bridal Spectre (S.W. M. 12/6/1826).
     [See above under 10/6/1801 and 2/4/1821.]

Ba. Four Legs and Two Legs; or, The Widow and the Will (S.W. M. 12/6/1826).
     [Based on *The Horse and the Widow*.]

Bsq. All a Fetch; or, Ghosts and Apprehensions (S.W. M. 14/8/1826).

Ext. Double X.X.; or, The Islington Stage (S.W. T. 26/12/1826).
Ba. Shall I Kill Myself? (S.W. Th. 28/12/1826).
M.D. The Fatal Experiment; or, The Murdered Guest (S.W. Th. 28/12/1826).
    [See his earlier *Murdered Guest*.]
M.D. The Honest Welchman (S.W. M. 1/1/1827).
Int. Spain and Portugal; or, Huzza for Lisbon (S.W. Th. 4/1/1827).
M.D. Paul Jones; or, The Solway Mariner (Adel. M. 12/2/1827; named *The Pirates Doom; or, The S. M.* on M. 19/2/1827). *Cumberland Minor*, vol. ii; *Dicks* 1011.
    [See also *Paul Jones* under *UNKNOWN AUTHORS*.]
Ba. Jemmy for Ever; or, The Lads of the Village (S.W. M. 16/4/1827).
M.D. The White Wolf; or, The Woman in the Wood (S.W. M. 16/4/1827).
Ba. The Clown and the Captain (S.W. S. 4/8/1827).
Ba. One and Twenty; or, Love in Germany (S.W. W. 2/1/1828).
Ba. The Lady in her Sleep (S.W. M. 14/1/1828).
M.D. Suil Dhuv the Coiner (S.W. M. 14/1/1828). *Cumberland Minor*, vol. i; *Dicks* 290.
Ba. Long Cloth; or, The Lancer (S.W. M. 21/1/1828).
F. Personation (D.L. 17/4/1828).
M.D. The Banks of the Hudson (Cob. 26/12/1829). *Cumberland Minor*, vol. iv; *Dicks* 264.
Ba. Old Ones and Young Ones (Cob. M. 7/12/1829).
M.D. The Wigwam; or, The Men of the Wilderness (C.G. M. 12/4/1830). L.C. 31/3/1830. *Dicks* 570.
    [Based on Cooper's novel.]
Ext. Female Government; or, The World upside down (Vic. M. 10/3/1834). 8° 1834.
B.O. The Covenanters (E.O.H. M. 10/8/1835). L.C. 3/7/1835 [title altered from *The Trooper*]. *Duncombe*, vol. xviii.
    [Music Loder.]
Spec. Alexander the Great! in Little (Strand, M. 7/8/1837). 8° 1837; *Duncombe*, vol. xxvii.

DICKENS, CHARLES.
Ba. The Strange Gentleman (St J. Th. 29/9/1836). L.C. 1836. 8° 1837; *Dicks* 466.
O.F. The Village Coquettes (St J. T. 6/12/1836). L.C. 11/1836. 8° 1836; 8° 1837 [Songs, Choruses]; *Dicks* 467; *Mod. Eng. Com. Th.* vol. iii.
    [Music John Hullah.]
Ba. Is She his Wife? or, Something Singular (St J. M. 6/3/1837). L.C. 1/3/1837. 8° [1837]; *Dicks* 470.
F. The Lamplighter. 8° 1879 [from MS. in Forster Collection in South Kensington Museum].

DILLON, CHARLES.
M.D. The Mysteries of Paris. A Romance of the Rich and the Poor (M'bone, 2/9/1844). L.C. 28/8/1844. *Dicks* 980; *Duncombe*, vol. li.
D. Life's Highway; or, Sharps and Dupes (M'bone, 11/11/1844). L.C. 31/10/1844.
P. General Tom Thumb; or, Harlequin Punch. L.C. M'bone, 23/12/1844.
D. The Female Bluebeard (M'bone, 20/1/1845). L.C. 22/1/1844.

DILLON, JOHN.
T.	Retribution; or, The Chieftain's Daughter (C.G. Th. 1/1/1818).
L. 110 M. [27/11/1817]. 8° 1818.

DIMOND, WILLIAM.
C.O.	The Sea-Side Story (C.G. T. 12/5/1801). L. 76 M. [30/4/1801].
8° 1801; 8° 1801 [Airs, Duets, and Trios]; 8° 1806.
[Music Attwood.]
M.D.	The Hero of the North (D.L. S. 19/2/1803). 8° 1803 [7 editions];
8° 1803 [Poetry of the Songs, Choruses].
[Music M. Kelly.]
M.D.	The Hunter of the Alps (H.² T. 3/7/1804). L. 44 S. [24/6/1804].
8° 1804 [3 editions]; *Dicks* 961; *Cumberland*, vol. xxxix; *Lacy*,
vol. xci.
[Music M. Kelly.]
C.O.	Youth, Love, and Folly (D.L. F. 24/5/1805). L. 45 S. [22/5/1805;
as *L. Y. and F.*]. 8° 1805; *Cumberland*, vol. xxxix.
[Music M. Kelly.]
D.	Adrian and Orrila; or, A Mother's Vengeance (C.G. S. 15/11/1806).
L. 85 M. [2/11/1806; as *The Mountains of Saxony; or, A. and O.*].
8° 1806.
C.O.	The Young Hussar; or, Love and Mercy (D.L. Th. 12/3/1807).
L. 86 M. [2/3/1807]. 8° 1807; *Cumberland*, vol. xli.
[Music M. Kelly. The Widener Library, Harvard University
(17476.52.204) possesses the Surrey prompt copy dated 1821.]
M.D.	The Foundling of the Forest (H.² 10/7/1809). L. 89 M.
[30/6/1809; with an additional sub-title, *or, Twice the Dagger
Struck*]. 8° 1809; 8° 1814; *Dicks* 74; *Cumberland*, vol. xl; *Lacy*,
vol. xcix.
D.	The Doubtful Son; or, Secrets of a Palace (H.² T. 3/7/1810).
L. 52 S. [8/6/1810]. 8° 1810.
O.	Gustavus Vasa (C.G. Th. 29/11/1810). L. 90 M. [26/11/1810].
8° 1811.
[From *The Hero of the North, q.v.* It was announced originally
as *Gustavus of Sweden.*]
D.O.	The Peasant Boy (Lyc. Th. 31/1/1811). L. 55 S [as *The
P. B.; or, Innocence Protected*]. 8° 1811; 8° 1812; *Cumberland*,
vol. xl.
M.D.	The Royal Oak (H.² M. 10/6/1811). L. 21 L. [24/4/1811]. 8° 1811.
[Music M. Kelly.]
M.D.	The Aethiop; or, The Child of the Desert (C.G. 6/10/1812).
8° 1812; 8° 1813.
O.F.	Brother and Sister (C.G. W. 1/2/1815). L. 102 M. [19/12/1814].
8° 1829; *Lacy*, vol. xlvi.
[Lyrics by *CHARLES DIBDIN Junior.*]
M.D.	The Broken Sword (C.G. M. 7/10/1816). L. 107 M. [31/9/1816].
8° 1816 [*bis*]; *Dicks* 272; *Cumberland*, vol. xli; *Lacy*, vol. lxxxv.
M.D.	The Conquest of Taranto; or, St. Clara's Eve (C.G. T.
15/4/1817). L. 111 M. [10/4/1817; as *The Fate of T.*]. 8° 1817;
8° 1818.
[Music M. Kelly.]
M.D.	The Bride of Abydos (D.L. Th. 5/2/1818). L. 71 S. [23/1/1818].
8° 1818; *Lacy*, vol. lxx.
[Music M. Kelly. Based on Byron's poem.]

M.Ent. December and May (C.G. S. 16/5/1818). L. 114 M. [4/5/1818].
 [An adaptation of *Barnaby Brittle*.]
M.D. The Heart of Midlothian (Bath, 3/12/1819).
 [A combination of *DIBDIN'S* and *TERRY'S* versions of Scott's
 novel.]
O.F. The Lady and the Devil (D.L. W. 3/5/1820). L. 79 S. [10/4/1820].
 8° 1820; *Dicks* 435; *Lacy*, vol. xc.
 [Music M. Kelly. Derived from *La Dama Duende* of Calderon.]
C. Dog Days in Bond Street (H.² Th. 31/8/1820). L. 78 S. [28/8/1820].
 [Attributed to Dimond.]
M.D. Kenilworth; or, England's Golden Days (Bath, 15/12/1821).
 [Attributed to Dimond.]
M.D. The Pirate (D.L. T. 15/1/1822). L. 84 S. [4/1/1822].
 [Music W. Rooke. Based on Scott's romance.]
D.O. Native Land; or, The Return from Slavery (C.G. T. 10/2/1824).
 L. 132 M. [7/1/1824; as *Manumission; or, The Soldier's Welcome
 Home*]. 8° 1824; 8° 1824 [Songs].
 [Music Bishop.]
C.O. Abou Hassan (D.L. M. 4/4/1825). L.C. 23/3/1825. 8° 1825.
 [Music K. M. von Weber.]
C.O. Englishmen in India (D.L. S. 27/1/1827). L.C. 23/1/1827.
 Duncombe, vol. xlii.
 [Music Bishop. On the authorship of this play see *The Theatrical
 Observer* for W. 7/2/1827 and S. 10/2/1827.]
O. The Seraglio (C.G. S. 24/11/1827). L.C. 13/10/1827.
O. The Nymph of the Grotto; or, A Daughter's Vow (C.G. Th.
 15/1/1829). L.C. 5/11/1828. 8° 1829.
F. The Little Jockey (Olym. M. 3/1/1831). L.C. 27/12/1830. *Dicks*
 427.
F. Stage Struck (E.O.H. Th. 12/11/1835). L.C. 25/5/1835. *Dicks*
 324; *Lacy*, vol. x.
D. The Novice (C.G. W. 11/10/1837). L.C. 1837.

DISRAELI, BENJAMIN, Earl of BEACONSFIELD.
T. The Tragedy of Count Alarcos. 8° 1839.
 [This was acted on 1/8/1868 at R.A.]

DOUGLAS, THOMAS.
F. A Friend at Court; or, The King and the Cobler. 8° 1811 [Burton-
 upon-Trent].

DOWLING, MAURICE G.
Bsq. Othello Travestie (Liverpool, 3/1834). 8° 1834; *Dicks* 282;
 Duncombe, vol. xxii; *Lacy*, vol. xxxviii.
Bsq. Romeo and Juliet. 8° 1837; *Duncombe*, vol. xxvi.

DUBOIS, —
Ba. Deeds of Dreadful Note (Adel. M. 11/1/1841). L.C. 30/12/1840.
 Dicks 782.

DUCKETT, Sir GEORGE FLOYD.
D. Faust. 8° [1845].
 [A translation of Goethe's drama.]

DUCROW, ANDREW.
M.D.Spec. The Days of Athens (D.L. M. 14/11/1831).
Spec. St. George and the Dragon; or, The Seven Champions of
 Christendom (D.L. T. 24/12/1833). L.C. 20/12/1833.

Spec. Crichton (R.A. 2/7/1837).
Spec. Charlemagne; or, The Moors of Spain (D.L. 22/6/1841).

DUDLEY, Sir HENRY BATE.
[For his earlier plays see *A History of Late Eighteenth Century Drama*, pp. 235–6, under *HENRY BATE.*]
F. Fair Game; or, The First of October (C.G. T. 21/12/1813). L. 99 M. [5/12/1813].

DUGGAN, J.
D. King James and the Piper (P'cess, 25/5/1847). L.C. 13/5/1847.

DUNCAN, JOHN.
T. The Jew's Revenge. L.C. York, 2/5/1844.
T. The Spy of Venice. L.C. York, 21/4/1845.

DWYER, P. W.
C. The Soldier of Fortune. 8° [1805?].

EAMES, CHARLES CHAMBERS.
Ba. A Slight Mistake (Olym. W. 28/10/1840). L.C. 16/10/1840.

EARLE, —
C.O. Outwitted at Last (D.L. S. 13/12/1817). L. 67 S. [1/12/1817; as *O. at L.; or, The Ward and Brother*].
[Music Lanza.]

EBSWORTH, JOSEPH.
C. Keeping up Appearances. L. 62 S. [H.² 16/7/1816].
M.D. Tam o' Shanter; or, My Auld Mare Maggie (Cob. T. 18/7/1820).
Ba. Crockery's Misfortunes; or, Transmogrification (Cob. M. 11/7/1821). 8° 1821.
O. Ups and Downs; or, The Heart of a Woman. L. 123 M. [E.O.H. 8/9/1821].
M.D. Adelaide; or, The Fatal Seduction (Cob. M. 4/3/1822). 8° [1822].
[Adapted from Pixérécourt.]
M.D. The Minstrel; or, The Italian Foresters (Surrey, M. 22/4/1822).
Ba. A Widow to let; or, Marriage Prospects (Cob. M. 22/9/1823).
D. Rosalie; or, Father and Daughter (H.² T. 7/10/1823). L. 86 S. [6/10/1823; as *R.; or, The Deserted Child*]. 8° 1828 [Edinburgh; as *R.; or, The Bohemian Mother*].
[Adapted from *Louise; ou, le père juge.*]
D. The Prisoners of Lyons; or, The Duplicate Keys (Royalty, T. 9/12/1823). 8° 1824.
M.D. The Retreat of the Mountains; or, The Mysterious Protector (S.W. M. 28/6/1824).
F. The Rival Valets (H.² 14/7/1825). L.C. 4/7/1825. *Cumberland*, vol. xii.
D. Ourika, the Orphan of Senegal (H.² 1828).
D. The Tempter; or, The Gifts of Immortality (1830).
D. Saul Braintree the Poacher (Cob. T. 5/7/1831).
Ba. Quite Correct (H.² 29/7/1835).
Ba. The Glass Door; or, The Man in the Macintosh (S.W. M. 26/6/1837). L.C. 23/6/1837.
Ba. Mr Walker's Trunks (Strand, M. 3/7/1837).
O.F. Rouge et noir. L.C. Adel. 17/8/1838. 12° [1838]. *Dicks* 978; *Lacy*, vol. xxi.
Ba. Summer and Winter (Kelly's, M. 25/5/1840). L.C. 19/5/1840.

D. The Pilot's Son; or, the Father's Ransom and the False Key (S.W.
M. 16/11/1840).
D. The Crusaders; or, Emma von Falkenstein (M'bone, 11/1849).
L.C. 17/10/1849.
[For his later work see *A History of Late Nineteenth Century
Drama*, p. 353. Probably before 1850 came: *Clemence, The Cala-
brian Assassin, The Bachelor of Duddington, Commerce, The Twenty
Thieves, Youth's Vagaries, The Wreck of the Dauntless, Ranting
Roaring Willie, Roslin Castle, Legatees, Two Prima Donnas* and
The Queen's Visit.]

EDGEWORTH, MARIA.
Comic Dramas. 8° 1817.
[Contains: 1. *The Rose, Thistle and Shamrock*; 2. *The Two
Guardians*; 3. *Love and Law.* A play with the title of the last-
mentioned appears in L. 52 S. [Lyc. 23/11/1810.]

EDWARDS, —
D. Land Sharks and Sea Gulls (Queen's, 1/1841).

EDWARDS, E.
D. The Chimes. L.C. Apollo, 28/12/1844.
[Based on Dickens' novel.]
Bsq. Noureddin; or, The Fair Persian (P'cess, M. 9/4/1849). L.C.
2/4/1848.

EDWARDS, JOHN.
T. Abradates and Panthea. 8° 1808.

EDWARDS, P. H.
Pol. The Imperial Conspirator Overthrown; or, Spanish Poison for
Subjugation. 8° 1808.

EGAN, PIERCE.
Ext. Tom and Jerry (S.W. 8/4/1822). 8° 1822 (Songs).

EGESTORFF, GEORG HEINRICH CHRISTOPH.
D. The Maid of Orleans. 8° 1836.
[A translation of Schiller's drama.]

ELLENDEN, —
D. Grizzel Jamphray, the Last of the Witches; or, The Sea Captain
of Dundee (Dundee, 3/2/1846).

ELLERTON, JOHN LODGE.
O. Triermain (1831).
[Based on Scott's *The Bridal of Triermain.*]
O. Domenica (D.L. Th. 7/6/1838). L.C. 1838 [as *D.; or, The
Mother*].

ELLISTON, ROBERT WILLIAM.
Prel. No Prelude (H.² M. 16/5/1803). L. 78 M. [12/5/1803].
M.D. The Venetian Outlaw (D.L. F. 26/4/1805). L. 45 S. [23/4/1805].
8° 1805 [*bis*]; 12° 1806.
[A version of Pixérécourt, *L'homme à trois masques; ou, le
proscrit de Venise* (1801).]
T. Shakespeare's Coriolanus. 12° 1820.

EMDEN, W. S.
M.D. The Evil May Day; or, The London Apprentices of 1517
(C.L. M. 1/5/1837). *Duncombe*, vol. xxvii.

F. The Rear Admiral (St J. M. 4/3/1839). L.C. 27/2/1838. *Dicks* 985; *Duncombe*, vol. xxxvi.
Ba. New Inventions (Strand, 12/4/1841). L.C. 10/4/1841. *Dicks* 985.
Ca. Love's Labyrinth (Strand, 5/6/1843). L.C. 20/5/1843. *Dicks* 421; *Lacy*, vol. lxx.

EYRE, EDMUND JOHN.
[For his earlier plays see *A History of Late Eighteenth Century Drama*, pp. 258–9.]
C.O. The Caffres; or, Buried Alive (C.G. W. 2/6/1802). L. 77 M. [20/5/1802].
     [Music J. Davy. Ascribed to Eyre.]
D.Sk. The Tears of Britain. 8° [N.D.].
M.D. The Vintagers (H.² 1/8/1809). 8° 1809.
     [This is *Tears and Smiles*, in *UA*. Music Bishop.]
C. High Life in the City (H.² W. 25/7/1810). L. 52 S. [16/7/1810]. 8° 1810.
M.D. The Lady of the Lake (Edinburgh, 15/1/1811). L. 93 M. [2/1/1811]. 8° 1811 [Edinburgh].
     [Music J. Jones. A dramatisation of Scott's poem.]
C. Look at Home (H.² S. 15/8/1812). 8° 1812; 8° 1814.
     [This is *The Italian Husband*, in *UA*.]
M.D. The Fates; or, The Mysteries of the Black Tower (Royalty, M. 1/3/1813).
D.Sk. Hyde Park in an Uproar; or, The Don-Cossack in London (D.L. 17/6/1813). L. 97 M. [3/6/1813].
M.D. The Savage Chieftain; or, Buried Alive (Surrey, T. 10/5/1814).
     [Probably based on *The Caffres*.]

FAIRBROTHER, D. S.
P. The King of the Castle; or, Harlequin in the Land of Dreams (Surrey, S. 26/12/1846). L.C. 16/12/1846.

FARLEY, CHARLES.
P. The Magic Oak; or, Harlequin Woodcutter (C.G. T. 29/1/1799). 8° 1799 [*bis*; Songs, Recitations].
P. The Corsair; or, The Italian Nuptials (H.² 29/7/1801). L. 41 S. [28/7/1801].
     [Music Arnold.]
M.D. The Battle of Bothwell Brigg (C.G. M. 22/5/1820). L. 120 M. [11/5/1820]. 8° 1820.
     [Music Bishop. Derived from Scott's *Old Mortality*.]
P. Harlequin and Friar Bacon; or, The Brazen Head (C.G. T. 26/12/1820). L. 78 S. [15/12/1830]. 8° 1820.
P. Harlequin and Mother Shipton; or, Riquet with the Tuft (C.G. T. 26/12/1826). L.C. 19/12/1826. 8° 1826.
     [Farley seems to have been responsible for many of the C.G. annual pantomimes. I have included here only those distinctly attributed to his pen. In the others probably only the effects were arranged by him.]

FARMER, EDWARD.
O.F. Uncle Gregory. L.C. Birmingham, 23/2/1849.

C.   Hartley Manor. L.C. Birmingham, 2/12/1849.
F.   Worse than Ever. L.C. Birmingham, 2/12/1849.

FARRELL, JOHN.
O.F.   It's All a Mistake (E.L. F. 19/2/1819). 8° 1820.
M.D.   The Maid of Genoa; or, The Bandit Merchant (Cob. M.
26/6/1820). *Duncombe*, vol. v; *Lacy*, vol. xxix.
[Performed at Bath, 18/4/1823, as *The Dumb Girl of Genoa; or,
The Mountain Robber.*]
P.   Harlequin Jack of All Trades; or, Harlequin the Busy Bee. L.C.
R.P. 18/2/1844.

FARREN, WILLIAM.
M.D.   The Field of Forty Footsteps (Tottenham-street, Th. 14/1/1830;
City, M. 11/7/1831). L.C. 27/5/1833. *Dicks* 569.

FAUCIT, JOHN SAVILLE.
M.D.   Justice; or, The Caliph and the Cobbler (D.L. T. 28/11/1820).
L. 78 S. [21/11/1820].
[Music Cooke and Horn.]
M.D.   The Miller's Maid (E.O.H. Th. 16/8/1821). L. 117 M.
[18/7/1820]. 8° 1821.
[Music Jolly.]
D.   Fair Rosamond (W.L. Th. 18/10/1821). *Dicks* 788.
Ext.   "Sweep Sweep Sweep!" or, The Revolt of the Chumnies (R.P.
M. 17/11/1834; S.W. M. 24/11/1834).
D.   Newton Forster (Surrey, M. 10/8/1835). *Dicks* 938.
M.D.   Wapping Old Stairs; or, The Rover's Cruise (H.² M. 20/11/1837).
L.C. 1837. *Dicks* 966; *Cumberland Minor*, vol. xiii.
M.D.   The Floating Kingdom; or, The Last Voyage of Captain Cook
(S.W. M. 29/1/1838).
F.   The Aldgate Pump (Strand, 7/6/1841). L.C. 7/6/1841. *Dicks* 778.
Ba.   The Bump of Benevolence (Strand, M. 6/9/1841). L.C. 1/9/1841.
Dicks 778.
D.   The Last Shilling (Surrey, 3/1844). See also in *UA*.
D.   The Eve of Battle (Surrey, 7/10/1844). L.C. 28/9/1844.
D.   The Widow's Mite (C.L. 13/11/1848). L.C. 3/11/1848.

FAUCIT, Mrs J. S.
D.   Alfred the Great (Norwich, 5/1811). L. 54 S. [19/2/1811].

FAVALLI, J. A.
T.   Aristodemus. 12° 1809 [Dublin].
[From the Italian of Monti.]

FAWCETT, JOHN.
P.   Obi; or, Three-fingered Jack (H.² W. 2/7/1800). L. 38 S.
[26/5/1800]. 8° 1800; *Duncombe*, vol. lix.
[Music Arnold.]
P.   Perouse; or, The Desolate Island (C.G. S. 28/2/1801). 8° 1801
[Songs].
Ba.   The Fairies' Revels; or, Love in the Highlands (H.² S. 14/8/1802).
L. 41 S. [10/8/1802]. 8° [1802].
Bal.   The Enchanted Island (H.² W. 20/6/1804). L. 20 L. [14/6/1804].
M.D.   The Secret Mine (C.G. F. 24/4/1812). See *T. J. DIBDIN*.
C.O.   The Barber of Seville (C.G. T. 13/10/1818). L. 112 M.
[5/10/1818]. 8° 1818; 8° [1819].
[Music Bishop. Written in collaboration with *D. TERRY*.]

FEATHERSTONE, J.
   D. Cooke's Folly. L.C. Canterbury, 12/2/1840.

FENWICK, JOHN.
   F. The Indian (D.L. M. 6/10/1800). L. 38 S. [30/3/1800]. 8° [1800].

FILMORE, LEWIS.
   D. Faust. 8° 1841; 12° 1847.
      [A translation of Goethe's drama.]

FISHER, —
   O.F. The Assignation (D.L. S. 12/12/1812).

FITZBALL [or BALL], EDWARD.
   T. Edwin (Norwich, 1817). L. Extra L. [2/1817; as, *Edwin, Heir of Cressingham*].
      [Based on Miss Porter's *The Scottish Chiefs*.]
   T. Bertha; or, The Assassins of Istria (Norwich, 8/3/1819). L. 72 S. [12/2/1819].
   M.D. The Ruffian Boy (Norwich, 1819).
      [See *Thirty-Five Years of a Dramatic Author's Life* (1859), i. 60. This seems also to have been played as *Giraldi*; see T. L. G. Burley, *op. cit.* p. 36. As *Giraldi; or, The Ruffian of Prague* it appears in L. 23 L. [22/2/1820].]
   M.D. Edda (Surrey, M. 29/5/1820). 8° 1820 [as *E.; or, The Hermit of Warkworth*].
   T. Antigone; or, The Theban Sister (Norwich, 1821). L. 122 M. [8/2/1821].
   P. Alonzo and Imogene (Surrey, 2/4/1821).
   M.D. The Innkeeper of Abbeville; or, The Ostler and the Robber (Norwich, 1822; Surrey, 1826). L. 124 M. [Norwich, 6/3/1822]. 8° 1822; *Dicks* 950; *Cumberland Minor*, vol. iii; *Lacy*, vol. xc.
   M.D. The Fortunes of Nigel; or, King James I and his Times (Surrey, T. 25/6/1822). *Cumberland Minor*, vol. iv.
      [A dramatisation of Scott's novel.]
   M.D. Joan of Arc; or, The Maid of Orleans (S.W. M. 12/8/1822). *Lacy*, vol. ciii.
   C.O. The Barber; or, The Mill of Bagdad (Surrey, M. 21/10/1822). *Dicks* 975.
   M.D. Peveril of the Peak (Surrey, 6/2/1823). 8° [1823]; *Cumberland Minor*, vol. v.
      [A dramatisation of Scott's novel.]
   M.D. Nerestan, Prince of Persia; or, The Demon of the Flood (S.W. M. 19/5/1823).
   M.D. Waverley (Adel. Th. 11/3/1824). L.C. 6/3/1824 [as *W.; or, Sixty Years Since*]. *Cumberland Minor*, vol. v.
      [Music Rodwell. A dramatisation of Scott's novel.]
   Spec. The Fire-worshippers; or, The Paradise of the Peris (Surrey, M. 19/4/1824).
   M.D. The Floating Beacon; or, The Norwegian Wreckers (Surrey, M. 19/4/1824). *Cumberland Minor*, vol. ii; *Lacy*, vol. lxxv.
   M.D. The Burning Bridge; or, The Spectre of the Lake (Surrey, M. 16/8/1824).
   M.D. Der Freischutz; or, The Demon of the Wolf's Glen, and the Seven Charmed Bullets (Surrey, M. 6/9/1824). 8° 1824.
   M.D. Wardock Kennilson; or, The Outcast Mother and her Son (Surrey, M. 25/10/1824). *Dicks* 376.

M.D. Omala; or, Settlers in America (Surrey 6/6/1825). L.C. 1825.

M.D. Father and Son; or, The Rock of La Charbonniere (C.G. M. 28/2/1825). L.C. 15/2/1825.

Ba. Cupid in Disguise (Olym. 31/10/1825). L.C. 25/10/1825.

Ba. The Pilot; or, A Tale of the Sea (Adel. M. 31/10/1825). L.C. 25/10/1825 [as *The P.; or, A Storm at Sea*]. 8° 1825; *Dicks* 347; *Dicks B.D.* [1867].
      [A dramatisation of Cooper's novel.]

M.D. The Three Hunchbacks (Strand, 5/7/1847). L.C. Edinburgh, 31/1/1826. *Cumberland Minor*, vol. vi.

D. The Betrothed (Olym. 31/1/1826). L.C. 10/1/1826.

M.D. The Songs of the Birds.
      [Music Rodwell. See *Thirty-Five Years*, p. 165.]

M.D. The Flying Dutchman; or, The Phantom Ship (Adel. M. 1/1/1827). L.C. 30/11/1826. *Cumberland Minor*, vol. ii; *Lacy*, vol. lxxi.
      [Music Rodwell.]

Ba. The Libertine's Lesson (Adel. 8/10/1827). L.C. 4/10/1827. *Dicks* 598.

Ba. Nelson; or, The Life of a Sailor (Adel. M. 19/11/1827). L.C. Adel. 14/11/1827 [as *N.; or, Britannia rules the Waves*]. *Dicks* 760.

M.D. The Inchcape Bell; or, The Dumb Sailor Boy (Surrey, M. 26/5/1828). *Lacy*, vol. lxxix; *Cumberland Minor*, vol. i.

M.D. The Earthquake; or, The Spectre of the Nile (Adel. M. 15/12/1828). L.C. 22/11/1828 [as *The Phantom of the Nile*].
      [Music Rodwell.]

M.D. The Red Rover; or, The Mutiny of the Dolphin (Adel. M. 9/2/1829). L.C. 14/2/1829. *Dicks* 450; *Cumberland Minor*, vol. vi.
      [A dramatisation of Cooper's novel.]

M.D. The Devil's Elixir; or, The Shadowless Man (C.G. M. 20/4/1829). L.C. 24/3/1829.
      [Music Rodwell.]

M.D. Die Rauberbraut; or, The Robber's Bride (E.O.II. 15/7/1829).
      [Music F. Ries.]

O.F. Les deux nuits; or, The Night before the Wedding (C.G. Th. 17/11/1829).
      [Music Bishop. Based on Boieldieu's *Les deux nuits*.]

Ent. Mr Chairman (C.G. 12/1829).
      [See *Thirty-Five Years*, p. 193.]

O. Ninetta; or, The Maid of Palaiseau (C.G. Th. 4/2/1830). L.C. 14/12/1829
      [Music Bishop. Based on Rossini's *La Gazza Ladra*.]

Vaud. The Maid of the Oaks (Vauxhall, 1830).
      [A curtailment of the original comic opera; see *Thirty-Five Years*, i. 199.]

M.D. The Black Vulture; or, The Wheel of Death (Adel. M. 4/10/1830). L.C. 27/9/1830.

Ba. William and Adelaide (Adel. M. 11/10/1830).
      [This seems first to have appeared at Vauxhall earlier in 1830; see *Thirty-Five Years*, i. 199.]

M.D. The Haunted Hulk (Adel. T. 12/7/1831; Surrey, M. 21/1/1833). L.C. 11/7/1831.

O. The Sorceress (Adel. Th. 4/8/1831). L.C. 19/7/1831.
      [Music F. Ries.]

M.D. The Sea Serpent; or, The Wizard and the Winds (Adel. M. 3/10/1831). L.C. 23/9/1831.
> [Written in collaboration with *J. B. BUCKSTONE.*]

Vaud. The Fillip on the Nose (Vauxhall, 1831).
> [See *ib.* i. 213; this seems to be by Fitzball, but the reference is ambiguous.]

M.D. Robert le Diable; or, The Devil's Son (Adel. M. 23/1/1832). L.C. 21/1/1832.
> [Written in collaboration with *J. B. BUCKSTONE*. An adaptation of Scribe and Delavigne, *Robert le Diable* (Paris, 21/11/1831), with music by Meyerbeer.]

O. Der Alchymist (D.L. T. 20/3/1832). L.C. 13/3/1832.
> [Music Spohr, adapted by Bishop. Words by *T. H. BAYLY*, songs by Fitzball.]

M.D. Andreas Hofer, the Tell of the Tyrol (Surrey, M. 11/6/1832).

Vaud. The Bottle of Champagne (Vauxhall, F. 27/7/1832).
> [Music Bishop.]

Oa. The Sedan Chair (Vauxhall, M. 27/8/1832).

Bal. The Maid of Cashmere (D.L. S. 16/3/1833). L.C. 5/3/1833.
> [Music Bishop. An adaptation of Scribe, *Le dieu et la bayadère.*]

M.D. The Soldier's Widow; or, The Ruins of the Mill (Adel. S. 4/5/1833; Surrey, M. 27/8/1849). L.C. 1/5/1833 [as *The Mill of the Loire*].

M.D. Jonathan Bradford; or, The Murder at the Roadside Inn (Surrey, W. 12/6/1833). *Dicks* 370; *Lacy*, vol. lv; *Duncombe*, vol. xii.
> [Music Jolly. A play of this title is in L.C. 31/10/1835.]

M.D. Mary Glastonbury (Surrey, S. 28/9/1833).

C. Walter Brand; or, The Duel in the Mist (Surrey, M. 30/12/1833). *Duncombe*, vol. xiii.

M.D. Esmeralda; or, The Deformed of Notre Dame (Surrey, 14/4/1834; Adel. M. 17/11/1834). *Dicks* 346; *Lacy*, vol. xviii.
> [Based on Hugo's novel.]

D. Tom Cringle; or, The Man with the Iron Hand (Surrey, 26/5/1834). *Duncombe*, vol. xiv.

O. The Lord of the Isles; or, The Gathering of the Clans (Surrey, Th. 20/11/1834).
> [Music Rodwell. An adaptation of Scott's poem.]

R.D. The Last Days of Pompeii; or, The Blind Girl of Tessaly (Vic. T. 6/1/1835).
> [An adaptation of Lytton's novel.]

D. The Note Forger (D.L. M. 20/4/1835). L.C. 13/4/1835. *Dicks* 968; *Lacy*, vol. xxxviii; *Duncombe*, vol. xvii.
> [This seems to have been the play produced at S.W. on M. 26/8/1839 as *The N. F.; or, A Father's Curse.*]

D. Carlmilham (C.G. M. 20/4/1835). L.C. 13/4/1835 [as *C.; or, The Drowned Crew*].

M.D. Paul Clifford (C.G. W. 28/10/1835). L.C. 16/10/1835. *Dicks* 367. 8° 1835 [Songs]; *Duncombe*, vol. xx.
> [An adaptation of Lytton's novel. Music Rodwell.]

O. The Siege of Rochelle (D.L. Th. 29/10/1835). L.C. 23/9/1835. 8° [1835; Songs, Duets, Trios, Chorusses]; *Lacy*, vol. xcv; *Duncombe*, vol. xlvii.
> [Music M. W. Balfe.]

C. Inheritance; or, The Unwelcome Guest (C.G. T. 24/11/1835).
L.C. 25/11/1835.
[From Miss Ferrier's novel.]
D. The Carmelites; or, The Convent Belles (C.G. Th. 3/12/1835).
L.C. 27/11/1835.
[An adaptation of *L'habit ne fait pas le moine.*]
M.D. The Bronze Horse; or, The Spell of the Cloud King (C.G. M.
14/12/1835). L.C. 14/12/1835.
[Music Auber, arranged by Rodwell. An adaptation of Scribe,
Le cheval de bronze (Paris, 23/3/1835).]
R.O. Quasimodo; or, The Gipsy Girl of Notre Dame (C.G. Th.
4/2/1836). L.C. 29/1/1836. 8° [1836; Songs]; *Duncombe,* vol. xxv.
[Based on Hugo's novel; see *Esmeralda* above.]
Bsq. Za-ze-zi-zo-zu (C.G. M. 4/4/1836). L.C. 29/3/1836. *Duncombe,*
vol. xxi.
[Translated from the French.]
D.F. The Assurance Company; or, The Boarding School of Montesque
(C.G. S. 30/4/1836). L.C. 23/4/1836.
M.D. The Wood Devil (S.W. M. 9/5/1836).
O. The Rose of the Alhambra; or, The Enchanted Lute (C.G. Th.
12/5/1836). L.C. 2/5/1836.
[Music de Pinna. Fitzball seems merely to have revised this
opera.]
M.D. The Sexton of Cologne; or, The Burgomaster's Daughter (C.G.
W. 15/6/1836). L.C. 6/1836.
[Music Rodwell.]
M.D.Spec. The Hindoo Robber (C.G. Th. 29/9/1836). L.C. 26/9/1836.
F. Mutual Expense; or, A Female Travelling Companion (C.G. T.
11/10/1836). L.C. 7/10/1836.
M.D. Thalaba the Destroyer; or, The Burning Sword (C.G. M.
21/11/1836). L.C. 18/11/1836. *Cumberland Minor,* vol. v.
D. False Colours; or, The Free Trader (C.G. S. 4/3/1837). L.C.
2/3/1837. *Lacy,* vol. cx.
D. The Eagle's Haunt (St J. F. 5/5/1837). L.C. 21/4/1837 [as *The
Eagle's Nest*].
T. Walter Tyrrel (C.G. T. 16/5/1837). L.C. 15/5/1837. *Dicks* 565;
Acting Nat. Drama, vol. i.
O. Joan of Arc (D.L. Th. 30/11/1837). 8° [1837; Songs, Duets,
Trios]; *Lacy,* vol. ciii.
[Music Balfe.]
M.D. The Negro of Wapping; or, The Boat-builder's Hovel (Garrick,
M. 16/4/1838). *Duncombe,* vol. xxix.
C.O. Diadeste; or, The Veiled Lady (D.L. Th. 17/5/1838). L.C.
9/5/1838. 8° [1838; Songs, Duets, Chorusses].
[Music Balfe.]
D. Oconesto; or, The Mohawk Chief (R.P. M. 3/9/1838).
[In *Thirty-Five Years,* ii. 162, this is given to the City Theatre.]
O. The Maid of Palaiseau (D.L. S. 13/10/1838). L.C. 13/10/1838.
8° [1838; Songs, Duets, Trios].
[Music Rossini adapted by Bishop. This was a separate version
of *La Gazza Ladra;* see above *Ninette.*]
M.D. The King of the Mist; or, The Miller of the Hartz Mountains
(D.L. M. 1/4/1839). L.C. 26/3/1839. *Duncombe,* vol. xxxvi.
[Music Stansbury.]

C.O. Scaramuccia; or, The Villagers of San Quintino (E.O.H. F. 23/8/1839). L.C. 29/12/1836 and 20/8/1839. 8° [1839; Songs, Duets, Trios, Chorusses].
[Music Ricci.]

O. Këolanthè; or, The Unearthly Bride (E.O.H. T. 9/3/1841). L.C. 23/2/1841.
[Music Balfe.]

Ba. The April Fool (Olym. 17/5/1841). L.C. 17/5/1841.

M.D. The Robber's Sister; or, The Forge in the Forest (E.O.H. 7/6/1841). L.C. 7/6/1841.

Bal. Hans of Iceland (C.G. M. 27/9/1841). L.C. 24/9/1841.

D. Charlotte Hanwell; or, Sorrow and Crime (S.W. M. 10/1/1842).

R.D. Ombra; or, The Spirit of the Reclining Stone (Surrey, T. 22/2/1842).

M.D. The Trooper's Horn; or, The Goblin of the Chest (Lyc. 9/5/1842). L.C. 7/5/1842.

M.D. Jane Paul; or, The Victim of Unmerited Persecution (Vic. M. 16/5/1842).

D. The Miller's Wife (Vic. 22/8/1842).

Spec. The Owl Sisters; or, The Haunted Abbey Ruin (Adel. F. 31/9/1842). L.C. 5/10/1842.

M.D. Mary Melvyn; or, The Marriage of Interest (Adel. M. 20/2/1843). L.C. 12/2/1843. 12° 1843; Dicks 622.

Oa. The Queen of the Thames; or, The Anglers (D.L. S. 25/2/1843). L.C. 7/1/1843 [as Uncle Brayling; or, The Fisherman of the Thames]. 12° 1843.
[Music Hatton.]

D. The Ranger's Daughter (Olym. M. 27/2/1843). L.C. 18/2/1843 [as Mathew the Poacher; or, The R. D.].

Bal. Spec. Ondine; or, The Naid (Queen's, 9/11/1843). L.C. 23/9/1843. Dicks 746.
[Based on Pixérécourt, Ondine; ou, la Nymphe des Eaux (Paris, 17/2/1830).]

Bsq. Alma (Adelphi).
[See Thirty-Five Years, ii. 197.]

O. La Favorita (D.L. W. 18/10/1843). L.C. 18/10/1843. 12° 1858 [Melbourne].
[An adaptation of the opera by G. Vaez and A. Roger (Paris, 1840), with music by Donizetti.]

D. The Daughter of the Regiment (D.L. Th. 30/11/1843). L.C. 16/11/1843 [as Madelaine; or, The D. of the R.]. Duncombe, vol. lii [as Madelaine; or, The D. of the R.].
[Music J. H. Tully.]

D. Ben Bradshaw; or, A Man without a Head (Lyc. 12/1/1844).

D.D. The Momentous Question (Lyc. M. 17/6/1844). L.C. 10/6/1844 [as Rachael Ryland; or, The M. Q.]. Dicks 762; Duncombe, vol. l; Lacy, vol. xxx.

D.D. Home Again; or, The Lieutenant's Daughters (Lyc. Th. 28/11/1844; Surrey, M. 10/2/1845). L.C. 26/11/1844. Dicks 820; Duncombe, vol. li; Lacy, vol. cxi.

O. Maritana (D.L. S. 15/11/1845). L.C. 3/11/1845. 8° 1845; 12° [1860].
[Music W. V. Wallace. Based on Don Cézar de Bazan.]

O. The Crown Jewels (D.L. 16/4/1846). L.C. 18/4/1846 [as *Catarina*]. 8° [1846].
[Music Auber, adapted by Tully. An adaptation of Scribe and de St Georges, *Les diamants de la couronne* (Paris, 6/3/1841).]

Spec.O. The Desert; or, The Imanns Daughter (D.L. M. 5/4/1847). L.C. 3/4/1847.
[Music F. David adapted by Tully.]

D. The Wreck and the Reef (Surrey, 24/5/1847). L.C. 21/5/1847.

D. The Traveller's Room (Surrey, M. 1/11/1847). L.C. 31/10/1847. *Duncombe*, vol. lx.

O. The Maid of Honour (D.L. M. 20/12/1847). L.C. 20/12/1847. 8° [1847].
[Music Balfe.]

O. The Daughter of the Regiment (Surrey, 21/12/1847). L.C. 18/12/1847. *Dicks* 761.
[New version for the Surrey.]

M.D. The Lancashire Witches. A Romance of Pendle Forest (Adel. 3/1/1848). *Dicks* 1036.

D. The Crock of Gold; or, The Murder at the Hall (C.L. 5/1848; R.A. M. 25/6/1849). L.C. C.L. 31/10/1847.

Spec. Marmion; or, The Battle of Flodden Field (R.A. M. 12/6/1848). L.C. 17/4/1848. *Duncombe*, vol. lxiii.

O. Quentin Durward (C.G. W. 6/12/1848). L.C. 2/12/1848. 8° 1848.
[Music H. R. Laurent.]

Spec. Corasco; or, The Warrior's Steed (R.A. M. 12/2/1849). L.C. 3/2/1849.

Spec. The White Maiden of California (R.A. M. 9/4/1849). L.C. 20/3/1849.

D. Alhamar the Moor; or, The Brother of Valencia (Surrey, M. 9/4/1849). L.C. 2/4/1849.

Spec. The Prophet (R.A. M. 1/10/1849). L.C. 18/9/1849.
[An adaptation of Scribe, *Le prophète* (Paris, 16/4/1849), with music by Meyerbeer.]
[In addition to these the following are mentioned in *Thirty-Five Years*: *Auld Robin Grey* (written but not produced, ii. 159); *Pascal Bruno* (produced in Germany, ii. 158–9). For his later plays see *A History of Late Nineteenth Century Drama*, pp. 367–8.]

FITZGERALD, PRESTON.
T. The Spaniard and Siorlamh. 8° 1810.
T. The Siege of Carthage. 8° 1819.

FLORANCE, Mrs B. E.
M.D. The Bohemian Bandit (Olym. Th. 6/4/1843). L.C. 1/4/1843 [as *The B. B.; or, The Shrine of St. Margaret's*].

FORTESCUE, —
M.D. Gonzalo; or, The Spanish Bandit. 8° 1821.

FOX, G.
P. The House that Jack built; or, Harlequin tattered and torn (Olym. W. 26/12/1821). L. 123 M. [20/12/1821].
[A piece of this title was advertised at the Olym. on Th. 20/11/1817 as "the last new Pantomime."]

FRANKLIN, ANDREW.
[For his earlier plays see *A History of Late Eighteenth Century Drama*, p. 261.]
C.O. The Egyptian Festival (D.L. T. 11/3/1800). L. 74 M. [24/2/1800].
8° 1800; 8° 1800 [Songs, Duets, Trios, Chorusses].
[Music Florio.]
F. The Counterfeit (D.L. S. 17/3/1804). L. 80 M. [29/2/1804].
8° 1804 [*bis*].

FRAZER, T. J.
C.O. The Muleteer. L.C. Grecian, 27/4/1844.
O.F. Locked Up; or, A Day of Economy. L.C. Grecian, 30/12/1848.

FRERE, B.
T. Olympia. 8° 1821.

FRERE, JOHN HOOKHAM.
[Published several translations of Aristophanes' comedies.]

FROME, SAMUEL BLAKE.
O. Sketches from Life; or, The Wandering Bard. 8° 1809 [Songs].

FRYE, WILLIAM EDWARD.
T. Guilt; or, The Gipsey's Prophecy...followed by Schiller's Ideal
and the Cranes of Ibycus. 8° [1819].
[A translation from the German of A. G. A. Müllner.]

GALLOWAY, GEORGE.
T. The Admirable Crichton. 12° 1802.
D. The Battle of Luncarty; or, The Valiant Hays Triumphant over
the Danish Invaders. 12° 1804 [Edinburgh]; 12° 1806.

GALT, JOHN.
The New British Theatre. 8° 1814.
[Contains of Galt's: 1. *The Apostate; or, Atlantis Destroyed*;
2. *Hector*; 3. *Love, Honour, and Interest*; 4. *The Masquerade*;
5. *The Mermaid*; 6. *Orpheus*; 7. *The Prophetess*; 8. *The Watchhouse*; 9. *The Witness*.]

GANDY, E.
T. Lorenzo, the Outcast Son...founded on the Robbers of Frederick
Schiller. 8° 1823.
T. Caswallon, King of Britain. 8° 1826.

GARDINER, WILLIAM.
T. The Sultana; or, The Jealous Queen. 8° 1806 [Gloucester].

GAULTIER, B.
D. King Rene's Daughter (Strand, T. 11/12/1849). L.C. 6/12/1849
[printed]. 8° 1849 [not published].
[A translation from the Danish of Henrik Hertz.]

"GAY, BUCKRA."
O. The Black Opera (Strand, T. 1/6/1847).

[*GAZUL, CLARA pseud.*
The Plays of Clara Gazul. A Spanish Comedian. With Memoirs of
her life. 8° 1825.
[Contains: 1. *The Spaniards in Denmark*; 2. *A Woman is a
Devil*; 3. *African Love*; 4. *Ines Mendo*; 5. *Heaven and Hell*. Clara
Gazul is a pseudonym for Prosper Mérimée.]

GENT, —
F.   The Meteor; or, A Short Blaze for a Bright One. 8° 1809.

GIBBON, G. COLLINS.
C.   Right at Last (Surrey, F. 17/10/1828).

GIBSON, FRANCIS.
D.   Streanshall Abbey; or, The Danish Invasion (Whitby). 8° 1800
[Whitby].

GILBERT, —
C.   The Tender Sisters. 8° 1805 [in *The Theatrical Recorder*].

GILLIES, ROBERT PIERCE.
T.   Guilt; or, The Anniversary. 4° 1819 [Edinburgh; not published].
[A translation from the German of A. G. A. Müllner.]

GLENGALL, Earl of [see *RICHARD BUTLER*].

GLYNN, GORDON.
D.   Robert Ryland; or, The Carpenter's Family. L.C. Britannia,
7/7/1849.

GODWIN, WILLIAM.
T.   Antonio; or, The Soldier's Return (D.L. S. 13/12/1800). L. 39 S.
[9/12/1800]. 8° 1800.
T.   Faulkner (D.L. W. 16/12/1807). L. 86 M. [3/12/1807]. 8° 1807.

GOFF, HENRY.
M.D.   Second Sight; or, Prediction (Surrey, M. 4/2/1828).
M.D.   The Two Drovers. L.C. Edinburgh, 4/7/1841.
[This, as *The T. D.; or, The Prophetess of the Glen*, was acted
at the Surrey on M. 24/9/1849.]

GOLDSMITH, MARY.
C.   She Lives! or, The Generous Brother (H.² M. 7/3/1803). L. 40 S.
[28/3/1800].
C.O.   Angelina (provinces, 1804).

GORDON, F. C.
D.   The Mysterious Stranger. 8° 1812.

GORE, Mrs CATHERINE GRACE FRANCES [*née MOODY*].
D.Poem. The Bond. 8° 1824.
C.   The School for Coquettes (H.² Th. 14/7/1831). L.C. 18/6/1831.
C.   Lords and Commons (D.L. T. 20/12/1831). L.C. 8/12/1831.
M.D.   The Queen's Champion (H.² W. 10/9/1834). L.C. 28/7/1834.
Dicks 744.
C.   Modern Honour; or, The Sharper of High Life (C.G. W.
3/12/1834). L.C. 20/11/1834.
C.   The King's Seal (D.L. S. 10/1/1835). See *J. KENNEY.*
D.   The Maid of Croissey; or, Theresa's Vow (H.² M. 20/7/1835).
L.C. 19/6/1835. *Dicks* 339; *Acting Nat. Drama*, vol. vi.
C.D.   King O'Neil; or, The Irish Brigade (C.G. W. 9/12/1835). L.C.
1835. *Dicks* 461; *Acting Nat. Drama*, vol. vii.
D.   Don John of Austria (C.G. S. 16/4/1836). L.C. 15/4/1836.
[An adaptation of C. Delavigne, *Don Juan d'Autriche*.]
D.   A Tale of a Tub (H.² S. 15/7/1837). L.C. 11/7/1837.
F.   A Good Night's Rest; or, Two in the Morning (Strand, M.
19/8/1839). L.C. 8/8/1839. *Dicks* 403; *Duncombe*, vol. xxxix.

M.D. Dacre of the South; or, The Olden Time. 8° 1840.
C. Quid pro Quo; or, The Day of Dupes (H.² T. 18/6/1844). L.C.
      10/6/1844. 8° [1844]; *Dicks* 766.

GOWER, *Lord FRANCIS LEVESON.*
D. Faust. And Schiller's Song of the Bell. 8° 1823; 8° 1825.
      [A translation of Goethe's drama.]
D. Wallenstein's Camp. 8° 1830.
      [A translation of Schiller, *Wallensteins Lager* (1800).]
T. Hernani; or, The Honour of a Castilian (Bridgewater House,
      22/6/1831). 8° 1832 [with *Catherine of Cleves*].
      [An adaptation of Hugo, *Hernani* (1830).]
M.D. Catherine of Cleves (C.G. W. 18/1/1832). L.C. 15/1/1828.
      8° 1832 [with *Hernani*].
      [An adaptation of Dumas, *Henri trois.*]
T. The Paria. 8° 1836.
      [A translation from M. Beer.]
D. Alfred. 8° [1840].
T. Blue Beard. 8° 1841.

GRADY, *T. J.*
P. The Firedrake and the Fairy of the Silver Flame; or, Harlequin
      Rub-a-dub-dub and the Butcher, the Baker, the Candlestick-
      maker, all fell out of a rotten Potatoe. L.C. Effingham, 30/11/1843.

GRANT, *JAMES M.*
F. Invasion...Addressed to the Yeomanry of Ireland. 8° 1803
      [Dublin].
D.Sk. Custom's Fallacy. 8° 1805.

GRATTAN, *H. P. [HENRY WILLOUGHBY GRATTAN PLUN-
      KETT].*
D. The Dumb Conscript; or, A Brother's Love and a Sister's Honour
      (R.A. 1835). *Dicks* 429.
R.D. The Corsair's Revenge (Vic. W. 15/7/1835). *Dicks* 751.
      [See also under *UNKNOWN AUTHORS.*]
M.D. The Gold Seekers; or, The Outcasts of Anzasca (S.W. M.
      29/7/1839).
F. My Uncle's Card; or, The First of April (E.O.H. M. 13/7/1840).
      L.C. 12/7/1840. *Dicks* 419.
D. Norah O'Donnell; or, The Sybil of the Camp (S.W. M. 6/1/1840;
      Surrey, M. 6/3/1843, as *N. O'D.; or, The Fatal Prophecy*).
R.D. Faust; or, The Demon of the Drachenfels (S.W. 9/1842).
      Dicks 573.
      [For his later work see *A History of Late Nineteenth Century
      Drama,* p. 389.]

GRATTAN, *THOMAS COLLEY.*
T. Ben Nazir, the Saracen (D.L. M. 21/5/1827). L.C. 14/5/1827.
      8° 1827.

GRAVES, *JOSEPH.*
D.D. The Tempter; or, The Effects of Passion (Fitzroy, Th.
      26/12/1833). *Dicks* 712; *Duncombe,* vol. xxix [as *The T.; or, The
      Old Mill of St. Dennis*].
Ba. Cupid (Queen's, 15/6/1835). *Duncombe,* vol. xxxiv.
Ext. The Black God of Love (Surrey, M. 12/9/1836).
Bsq. The Wife: A Tale of a Mantua Maker! (Strand, M. 19/6/1837).
      L.C. 2/6/1837. *Duncombe,* vol. xxvi.

Ba. Olympic Frailties; or, The Magic Zone (Olym. 12/4/1841). L.C. 2/4/1841.

GRAY, SIMON.
The Spaniard; or, Relvindez and Elzora...and The Young Country Widow...With Three Letters to Dr Blair; and Thoughts on the Present State of the British Drama, and what seems calculated to improve it. 8° 1839.

GREENE, WILLIAM A.
T. D'Enghien. 8° 1842.

GREENWOOD, THOMAS LONGDON.
Bsq. The Death of Life in London; or, Tom and Jerry's Funeral (Cob. M. 2/6/1823). L.C. 1823. 8° [1823].
D. "Boz's" Oliver Twist; or, The Parish Boy's Progress (S.W. M. 3/12/1838).
M.D. The Lesson of Life; or, The Woodsman's Dream (S.W. T. 2/7/1839).
M.D. Paul the Pilot; or, The Wreck of the Raven in 1692 (S.W. M. 9/9/1839).
M.D. Jack Sheppard; or, The Housebreaker of the Last Century (S.W. M. 28/10/1839).
M.D. The Death Omen; or, The Wizard Tree (S.W. M. 3/2/1840).
M.D. Bianca Contarini; or, The Doge's Daughter (S.W. M. 20/4/1840).
Bsq. La Somnambula (S.W. M. 7/6/1841).
Ba. That Rascal Jack (S.W. 2/1843).
Ba. "A Row in the Buildings" (S.W. W. 29/5/1844). L.C. 22/5/1844.

GREFFULHE, —
F. The Portrait of Cervantes (C.G. T. 21/6/1808). L. 87 M. [28/4/1808].
F. Is He a Prince? (C.G. T. 7/2/1809).
F. The Budget of Blunders (C.G. F. 16/2/1810). L. 91 M. [2/1810].

GRIFFIN, GERALD.
T. Gisippus (D.L. W. 23/2/1842). L.C. 10/2/1842. 8° 1842; *Dicks* 604; 8° 1857 [in *Poetical and Dramatic Works*; reprinted 1859].

GROSETT, HENRY WILLIAM.
D. William Tell; or, The Hero of Switzerland. L. 21 L. [4/4/1812].

GROVER, HENRY MONTAGUE.
T. Anne Boleyn. 8° 1827.
T. Socrates. 8° 1828.

GROVES, Rev. EDWARD.
T. The Warden of Galway (Dublin, 1831; Coburg, M. 14/5/1832). L.C. 3/10/1834.
T. Alom Pram (Dublin, 1832).

GULLY, JAMES MANBY.
D. The Lady of Belleisle; or, A Night in the Bastille (D.L. 4/12/1839). *Lacy*, vol. xci.
[Based on Dumas, *Mademoiselle de Belleisle*.]

GUNNING, ELIZABETH.
M.D. The Wife with Two Husbands. 8° 1803.
[A translation of Pixérécourt, *La femme à deux maris* (Paris, 1802).]

GURNEY, ARCHER THOMPSON.
    T.C. Turandot, Princess of China. 8° 1836.
        [An adaptation from Schiller's drama.]
    D. Faust. 8° 1842; 8° 1843.
        [A translation of Goethe's drama.]
    D. Alboin. L.C. Edinburgh, 5/5/1846.
    D.Poem. King Charles the First. 8° 1846.

GURNEY, RICHARD.
    Bsq. Romeo and Juliet. 12° 1812.

GYPSUM, NICHOLAS.
    Int. The Architect. 8° 1807.

HAINES, JOHN THOMAS.
    M.D. Quentin Durward (Cob. M. 9/6/1823).
    M.D. The Idiot Witness; or, A Tale of Blood (Cob. M. 6/10/1823;
        Bath, 22/3/1827). Duncombe, vol. v; Lacy, vol. xlvi.
    M.D. The Haunted Hulk; or, The Rebel's Heir (Cob. M. 26/7/1824).
    M.D. The Wraith of the Lake (Cob. 26/10/1829).
    D. Eily O'Connor; or, The Foster Brother (City, M. 18/7/1831).
    M.D. Austerlitz; or, The Soldier's Bride (Queen's, M. 26/9/1831).
        Dicks 479; Cumberland Minor, vol. xiv.
    M.D. The Wizard Skiff; or, The Pirate Boy (Cob. M. 26/12/1831;
        Surrey, M. 23/7/1832).
    Ba. Love and Mystery; or, Which is my Cousin? (S.W. M. 23/1/1832).
    D. The Invisible Husband (Queen's, 2/7/1833).
    D. Jacob Faithful, the Lighter-Boy. A Tale of the Thames (Vic. T.
        16/12/1834). Dicks 507; Duncombe, vol. xvi.
        [Based on Marryat's novel.]
    M.D. My Poll and My Partner Joe (Surrey, M. 31/8/1835). Dicks 500;
        French 1058; Lacy, vol. lxxi; Cumberland Minor, vol. ix.
        [Music Jolly.]
    Vaud. A House Divided (St J. M. 4/1/1836). L.C. 31/12/1835.
        Dicks 576.
    D. The Ocean of Life; or, Every Inch a Sailor (Surrey, M. 4/4/1836).
        Dicks 634; Cumberland Minor, vol. xi; Lacy, vol. lxix.
    M.D. Rattlin the Reefer; or, The Tiger of the Sea (Vic. M. 22/8/1836).
        Duncombe, vol. xxiv.
    D. Richard Plantagenet; or, A Legend of Walworth (Vic. Th.
        1/12/1836). Dicks 449; Cumberland Minor, vol. xiv.
    Ba. Maidens, Beware! (Vic. T. 6/12/1836). Dicks 772.
    D. Breakers Ahead; or, A Seaman's Log (Vic. M. 27/3/1837).
        Duncombe, vol. xxvii.
    D. Angeline de Lis (St J. 29/9/1837; H.² F. 17/1/1840). L.C. 1837.
        Dicks 669; Acting Nat. Drama, vol. iii.
    R.D. Amilie; or, The Love Test (C.G. S. 2/12/1837). L.C. 1837.
        8° [1837; Songs, Duets, Trios, Recitatives, Chorusses]; 12° 1862.
        [Music W. M. Rooke.]
    D. The French Spy; or, The Siege of Constantina (Adel. 4/12/1837).
        Dicks 680.
    Spec. The Rye House Plot! or, The Maltster's Daughter (S.W. M.
        4/6/1838).
    D. The Charming Polly; or, Lucky and Unlucky Days (Surrey, M.
        2/7/1838). Dicks 600; Duncombe, vol. xxx.

O. Henrique; or, The Love Pilgrim! (C.G. Th. 2/5/1839). 8° [1839; Songs, Duets].
    [Music W. M. Rooke.]
D. Alice Grey, the Suspected One; or, The Moral Brand (Surrey, M. 20/5/1839). *Dicks* 354; *Lacy*, vol. xliv.
D. The Alpine Hold (Vic. 3/6/1839).
D. The Phantom Ship; or, The Demon Pilot (Surrey, M. 1/7/1839).
D. Armstrong the Shipwright; or, Saturday Night at Sea (Surrey, M. 2/9/1839).
Spec.D. King Harold; or, The Battle of Hastings (Vic. M. 16/9/1839).
M.D. Jack Sheppard (Surrey, M. 21/10/1839). 8° 1839.
      [Based on Ainsworth's novel.]
M.D. Nick of the Woods; or, The Altar of Revenge (Vic. 1839). *Duncombe*, vol. xliv.
T.   The Life of a Woman; or, A Curate's Daughter (Surrey, M. 20/4/1840). *Dicks* 468.
D.D. The Factory Boy; or, The Love Sacrifice (Surrey, M. 8/6/1840). *Dicks* 641.
D. The Wizard of the Wave (Vic. M. 7/9/1840). *Dicks* 921; *Lacy*, vol. xlvi.
D. The Yew Tree Ruins; or, The Wreck, the Miser and the Murderer (Vic. M. 11/1/1841). *Dicks* 485; *Lacy*, vol. lxxiv.
D. Claude Duval (Surrey, 3/5/1841).
D. The Queen of a Day (Surrey, 14/6/1841). 12° [1841; Songs].
    [An adaptation from the French of E. Scribe.]
M.D. The Iron Hand; or, The Dumb Carrier Boy and his Pony (Surrey, M. 18/10/1841).
D. Elizabeth Lazarus (Surrey, M. 17/1/1842).
Spec. Aslar and Ozines; or, The Lion Brothers of the Burning Zaara (Lyc. M. 16/1/1843). L.C. 27/12/1842 [with "Hunters" for "Brothers"].
M.D. Ruth; or, The Lass that Loves a Sailor (Vic. 23/1/1843). *Dicks* 925; *Lacy*, vol. xliv.
O. The Spirit's Song. L.C. E.O.H. 12/4/1843.

HALFORD, JOHN.
    Ext. Faust and Marguerite. *Lacy*, vol. lxxiii.

HALL, Mrs ANNA MARIA.
    Ba. The French Refugee (St J. M. 20/2/1837).
    Da. Mabel's Curse (St J. M. 27/3/1837). L.C. 23/3/1837. 12° 1837; *Dicks* 424; *Duncombe*, vol. xxviii.
    D. The Groves of Blarney (Adel. M. 16/4/1838). L.C. 13/4/1838. 12° [1838]; *Acting Nat. Drama*, vol. iv.
    D. Chester Fair (Queen's, 27/5/1844). L.C. 22/5/1844.
    Ba. Juniper Jack; or, My Aunt's Hobby (Queen's, 16/6/1845). L.C. 10/6/1845.

HALLORAN, L. H.
    D. The Female Volunteer; or, The Dawning of Peace. 8° 1801.

HAMILTON, Colonel RALPH.
    M.D. Elphi Bey; or, The Arab's Faith (D.L. Th. 17/4/1817). L. 68 S. [2/4/1817]. 8° 1817.
          [Music Attwood, Horn and Smart.]

O. David Rizzio (D.L. S. 17/6/1820) L. 77 S. [1/6/1820]. 8° 1820;
8° 1820 [Duets, Chorusses].
[Music Braham, Attwood, Cooke and Reeve. Songs by
CHARLES DIBDIN Junior.]

HAMILTON, W. H.
O.D. The Portrait of Cervantes (Crow-street, Dublin, 27/2/1810).
O.D. The Magician without Magic (Crow-street, Dublin, 1/3/1815).
[Music Jonathan Blewitt.]

HARDWICKE, Countess of [see *ELIZABETH YORKE*].

HART, J. P.
D. Mary le More! (S.W. T. 28/8/1838; not first performance).
D. The Freemason; or, The Secret of the Lodge Room (Queen's,
3/6/1839). *Dicks* 909.

HARVEY, MARGARET.
M.D. Raymond de Percy; or, The Tenant of the Tomb (Sunderland,
1822). 12° 1822 [Bishopswearmouth].

HASKIN, J. [of Cuckney].
T. Osburga; or, The Danish Invasion (Mansfield, F. 7/8/1829).
[See *The Dramatic Magazine* (1829), p. 214.]

HAWORTH, R.
M.D. Quentin Durward. 8° 1823.
F. Disguises; or, Two Stages from Gretna (S.W. 1824). 12° 1824.

HAYES, —
— Koranzo's Feast. 8° 1811.

HAYLEY, WILLIAM.
T. The Viceroy. 8° 1811 [Chichester].

HAYNES, JAMES.
T. Conscience; or, The Bridal Night (D.L. W. 21/2/1821). 8° 1821.
T. Durazzo (C.G. 11/1838). 8° 1823.
T. Mary Stuart (D.L. W. 22/1/1840). L.C. 20/1/1840. 8° 1840;
Dicks 749.

HAYWARD, ABRAHAM.
D. Faust. 8° 1833; 8° 1834; 8° 1838; 8° 1847; 8° 1851.
[A translation of Goethe's drama.]

HEATH, SAMUEL.
D. The Earl of Leicester. 8° 1843.
[Based on Sir Walter Scott, *Kenilworth*.]

HELME, ELIZABETH.
D. Cortez. 8° 1800.
D. Pizarro. 8° 1800.

HELPS, Sir ARTHUR.
T. Catherine Douglas. 8° 1843.

HEMANS, Mrs FELICIA DOROTHEA.
T. The Vespers of Palermo (C.G. F. 12/12/1823). L. 128 M.
[23/10/1823; as *Procida; or, The V. of P.*]. 8° 1823; *Dicks* 155.
T. The Siege of Valencia. 8° 1823.

HERBERT, —
C.   Tryal's All (Crow-street, Dublin, 1802).
      [The *Biographia Dramatica* suggests that Herbert is a pseudonym
      for Dowling.]

HERBERT, HAMILTON.
D.   Fleurs de Lys (Lyc. M. 19/7/1847). See *A. B. REACH.*

HERBERT, HENRY JOHN GEORGE, Earl of CARNARVON.
T.   Don Pedro, King of Castille (D.L. M. 10/3/1838). L.C. 16/2/1838.

HERBERT, THOMAS.
C.   Too much the Way of the World. 8° 1817 [Brighton].
C.   Hydrophobia; or, Love created Madness. 8° 1820.

HEWLETT, ABRAHAM.
C.   The Fortune Hunters (H.² Th. 23/7/1812).

HEWLINGS, —
O.F. The Nondescript (C.G. T. 5/10/1813). L. 100 M. [22/9/1813].
      8° 1813.

HIGGIE, THOMAS H.
D.   The Tower of London; or, The Death Omen and the Fate of
      Lady Jane Grey (C.L. S. 26/12/1840). *Lacy,* vol. xciv.
      [Written in collaboration with *T. H. LACY.*]
D.   Wilful Murder (P'cess, T. 18/6/1844). L.C. 14/6/1844. *Duncombe,*
      vol. li; *Lacy,* vol. xxxii.
D.   Martin Chuzzlewit (Queen's, 29/7/1844). L.C. 27/7/1844. *Lacy,*
      vol. i (new series).
      [Written in collaboration with *T. H. LACY.*]
F.   The House Dog. L.C. Vic. 15/2/1845. *Duncombe,* vol. lii.
D.   Laid up in Port; or, Sharks Alongshore (Vic. 13/4/1846). L.C.
      10/4/1846. *Duncombe,* vol. lvi; *Lacy,* vol. cv.
R.D. The Devil's Mount; or, The Female Bluebeard (Queen's,
      24/5/1847). L.C. 21/5/1847. *Lacy,* vol. lxxxviii.
Int. A Devilish Good Joke; or, A Night's Frolic (Vic. 1848). *Dun-
      combe,* vol. lxi.

HILL, ISABEL.
T.   The Poet's Child. 8° 1820.
C.   The First of May (C.G. S. 10/10/1829). L.C. 2/10/1829.
T.   Brian, the Probationer; or, The Red Hand. 8° 1842.

HILLS, JOHN.
D.   Faust. 0ⁿ 1839, 16ⁿ 1840.
      [A translation of Goethe's drama.]

HITCHENER, WILLIAM HENRY.
Ent. Love in the Desert. 8° 1802.
D.   Ivor; or, The Sighs of Ulla (Henley-on-Thames, *c.* 1808). 8° 1808.

HOARE, PRINCE.
      [For his earlier plays see *A History of Late Eighteenth Century Drama,*
      pp. 269–70.]
D.   The Children; or, Give them their Way (D.L. M. 28/4/1800).
      L. 39 S. [21/4/1800].
      [Music Kelly.]
C.   Indiscretion (D.L. S. 10/5/1800). L. 39 S. [4/5/1800]. 8° 1800 [*bis*].

C.O. Chains of the Heart; or, The Slave by Choice (C.G. W. 9/12/1801).
L. 76 M. [27/11/1801; as *C. for the H.; or, The Slaves of Centa*].
8° 1801 [Songs, Duets]; 8° 1802.
[Music Mazzinghi and Reeve.]

O.F. The Paragraph (C.G. Th. 8/3/1804). 8° 1804; 8° [1804; Songs,
Duets, and Chorus].
[Music Braham.]

C. The Partners (H.² F. 28/6/1805). L. 45 S. [6/1805].

C. Something to Do (D.L. F. 22/1/1808). L. 87 M. [16/1/1808].

HOGG, CERVANTES [pseudonym of *EATON STANNARD
BARRETT*].
Bsq. The Setting Sun...To which is added a new musical Drama;
being a Parody on the Beggar's Opera. 8° 1809.

HOLCROFT, FANNY.
[*The Theatrical Recorder* (1805) contains the following translations:
vol. i. 1. *Philip the Second* (from Alfieri); 2. *From Bad to Worse*
(from Calderon); 3. *Emilia Galotti* (from Schiller): vol. ii.
1. *Fortune Mends* (from Calderon); 2. *Minna von Barnhelm* (from
Lessing); 3. *The Baron* (from Moratin); 4. *Rosamond* (from
Weisse).]

M.D. The Goldsmith (H.² Th. 23/8/1827). L.C. 18/8/1827.

HOLCROFT, THOMAS.
[For his earlier plays see *A History of Late Eighteenth Century Drama*,
pp. 270–1.]

M.D. Deaf and Dumb; or, The Orphan Protected (D.L. T. 24/2/1801).
L. 41 S. [9/2/1801]. 8° 1801 [4 editions]; 8° 1802 [5th]. *Dicks* 263.
[An adaptation of Bouilly, *L'abbé de l'Epée*, itself based on
Kotzebue's work.]

M.Ent. The Escapes; or, The Water-carrier (C.G. W. 14/10/1801).

M.D. A Tale of Mystery (C.G. S. 13/11/1802). L. 78 M. [4/11/1802].
8° 1802; 8° 1813 [3rd, 4th, 5th and 6th]. *Dicks* 38; *Cumberland*,
vol. viii.
[An adaptation of Pixérécourt, *Coelina; ou, l'enfant du mystère*
(Paris, 1800).]

C. Hear Both Sides (D.L. S. 29/1/1803). L. 43 S. [18/1/1803].
8° 1803 [4 editions].

D. Proverbs. The Two Friends and The Play is over [in *Travels
from Hamburgh*. 4° 1804, vol. iii].

M.D. The Lady of the Rock (D.L. T. 12/2/1805). L. 45 S. [6/2/1805].
8° 1805 [2 editions].

C. The Vindictive Man (D.L. Th. 20/11/1806). L. 47 S. [16/11/1806].
8° 1806; 8° 1809 [2nd].

C.O. The Marriage of Figaro (C.G. 6/3/1819). L. 116 M. [28/2/1819].
8° 1819; 8° 1819 [Airs, Duets, Trios, Choruses].
[Music H. R. Bishop.]

HOLL, HENRY.
D.D. Grace Huntley (Adel. M. 14/10/1833; Surrey, M. 31/3/1834).
L.C. 14/10/1833. *Lacy*, vol. lxxxii; *Cumberland Minor*, vol. vii.

M.D. Wapping Old Stairs! or, The Child of a Tar (R.P. M. 7/7/1834;
Surrey, M. 13/11/1837). *Duncombe*, vol. xxviii.

Ba. The Seasons (not Thomson's) (Strand, M. 23/5/1836). L.C.
21/5/1836.

HOLLAND, W. A.
    M.D. Augustus and Gulielmus; or, The Villagers (H.² 3/1806).
    L. 47 S. [4/3/1806].

HOLMAN, JOSEPH GEORGE.
    [For his earlier plays see *A History of Late Eighteenth Century Drama*,
    pp. 271–2.]
    C.O. What a Blunder! (H.² Th. 14/8/1800). L. 75 M. [4/8/1800].
        8° 1800; 12° 1800 (Dublin); 8° 1800 [Songs, Duets, and Choruses].
        [Music J. Davy.]
    C. Love gives the Alarm (C.G. Th. 13/2/1804).
    C. The Gazette Extraordinary (C G. T. 23/4/1811). L. 94 M.
        [4/4/1811]. 8° 1811.
    O.F. Frost and Thaw (C.G. T. 25/2/1812).
        [Music Cooke. Attributed to Holman.]

HOLROYD, J. J.
    Three Comedies. 8° 1838 [Colchester].
        [Contains translations from Schiller, *Freigeist*, *Schatz* and
    Minna.]
    T. Gisela. 8° 1839.

HOLT, FRANCIS LUDLOW.
    C. The Land we live in (D.L. S. 29/12/1804). L. 81 M. [14/12/1804].
        8° 1805 [3 editions].

HONAN, MICHAEL BURKE.
    F. The Queen's Horse (Olym. M. 3/12/1838). See *J. R. PLANCHÉ*.

HOOD, THOMAS.
    O.F. Mr Sims (Surrey, W. 25/2/1829).
    M.D. York and Lancaster (Adel. 5/10/1829). L.C. 24/12/1828.

HOOK, THEODORE EDWARD.
    C.O. The Soldier's Return; or, What can Beauty do? (D.L. T.
    23/4/1805). 8° 1805; 8° [1805; Songs, Duets, Choruses].
        [Music J. Hook.]
    O.F. The Invisible Girl (D.L. M. 28/4/1806). L. 85 M. [23/4/1806;
    as *Loquacity; or, The I. G.*]. 8° 1806; *Cumberland*, vol. xl.
        [An adaptation of *Le babillard*.]
    O.F. Catch him who can! (H.² Th. 12/6/1806). L. 46 S. [6/6/1806].
        8° 1806; *Cumberland*, vol. xl.
        [Music J. Hook.]
    M.D. Tekeli; or, The Siege of Montgatz (D.L. M. 24/11/1806).
    L. 47 S. [28/10/1806]. 8° 1806; 8° 1808; 12° 1814 [Dublin];
    Dicks 542; *Cumberland*, vol. xxx.
        [Music J. Hook. An adaptation of Pixérécourt, *Tékéli; ou, le
    siège de Montgatz* (Paris, 29/12/1803).]
    M.D. The Fortress (H.² Th. 16/7/1807). L. 86 M. [9/7/1807]. 8° 1807.
        [Music J. Hook. An adaptation of Pixérécourt, *La forteresse du
    Danube* (Paris, 1805).]
    D.Sk. Music Mad (H.² Th. 27/8/1807). L. 49 S. [23/8/1807]. 8° 1808.
        [Music J. Hook.]
    M.D. The Siege of St. Quintin; or, Spanish Heroism (D.L. Th.
    10/11/1808). L. 50 S. [4/11/1808].
        [Music J. Hook.]
    O.F. Killing No Murder (H.² M. 21/8/1809). L. 89 M. [22/6/1809]
    and L. 88 M. [1809, printed]. 8° 1809 [Together with a Preface,

and a Scene suppressed by order of the Lord Chamberlain;
2 editions]; 8° 1811 [5th]; *Cumberland*, vol. xxxi.
[Music J. Hook.]
C.O. Safe and Sound (Lyc. M. 28/8/1809). 8° 1809.
[Music J. Hook.]
Ext. Ass-ass-ination (Orange House, near Windsor, 30/1/1810).
D.Trifle. The Will, or the Widow; or, Puns in Plenty (Orange House,
near Windsor, 30/1/1810).
F.   Trial by Jury (H.² S. 25/5/1811). L. 53 S. [20/5/1811]. 8° 1811.
F.   Darkness Visible (H.² M. 23/9/1811). 8° 1811 [*bis*].
F.   Oil and Vinegar (H.² M. 10/7/1820). L. 77 S. [22/6/1820].
C.   Exchange no Robbery; or, The Diamond Ring (H.² S. 12/8/1820).
L. 78 S. [8/7/1820]. 8° 1820; *Dicks* 908; *Cumberland*, vol. xxxvii.
O.F. Over the Water (H.² S. 23/9/1820). L. 77 S. [20/9/1820].
F.   A Day at an Inn (Lyc. 25/8/1823). *Dicks* 776.
[Based on *Killing No Murder*.]

HOOKHAM, —
F.   Nota Bene (D.L. Th. 12/12/1816). L. 62 S. [4/12/1816].

HOOLE, JOHN.
[For his earlier translations see *A History of Late Eighteenth Century
Drama*, p. 272.]
Dramas of the Abbé Pietro Metastasio. Translated from the Italian.
8° 1800.

HORNCASTLE, J. H.
O.   The Bayadère. L.C. Grecian, 1/3/1844.
F.   The Savage and the Maiden; or, Crummles and his Daughter.
L.C. Grecian, 31/5/1844.
[Adapted from Dickens.]
Bsq. Aladdin, in another Shape. L.C. Grecian, 12/9/1844.
O.   Ma Part; or, Carlo Broschi (Grecian, 27/4/1846). L.C. 26/1/1846.
F.   The Poddyhighs. L.C. Grecian, 13/2/1849.

HORNE, F. L.
O.F. All in the Dark (E.O.H. 1/4/1839). L.C. 17/4/1839.

HORNE, RICHARD HENGIST.
T.   The Death of Marlowe. 8° 1837; 8° 1870; *Lacy*, vol. lxxxix.
T.   Cosmo de' Medici. 8° 1837; 8° 1875.
T.   Gregory VII. 8° 1840; 8° 1849.
Miracle Play. Judas Iscariot. 12° 1848.

HORT, Major.
O.F. Love à la Militaire (Edinburgh, 4/1841).

HOSKINS, HORATIO HUNTLEY.
T.   De Valencourt (Norwich, Lynn, etc. 1842). L.C. Norwich,
7/5/1842. 8° 1842 [Norwich; as *Extremes; or, De V.*]; 8° 1842
[London].
[Written in collaboration with *WILLIAM H. HOSKINS*.]

HOSKINS, WILLIAM HENRY.
D.   Count de Denia.
T.   De Valencourt (1842). See *H. H. HOSKINS*.

HOULTON, Dr ROBERT.
[For his earlier plays see *A History of Late Eighteenth Century Drama,*
p. 273.]
C.O. Wilmore Castle (D.L. T. 21/10/1800). L. 75 M. [11/10/1800].
8° 1800 [*bis*]; 8° [1800; Songs, Airs, Duets].
[Music J. Hook.]

HOUSTON, THOMAS.
C. Term Day; or, The Unjust Steward. 8° 1803 [Newcastle].

HOWARD, FREDERIC, Earl of CARLISLE.
[For an earlier play see *A History of Late Eighteenth Century Drama,*
p. 273.]
T. The Step-Mother. 8° 1800; 8° 1812.
T. The Last of the Greeks. 8° 1828.

HUDSON, E. NEEVES.
D. The Bridge of Notre Dame; or, The Parricide's Curse (Surrey,
4/1847). L.C. 8/4/1847. *Duncombe,* vol. lix.

HUNT, LEIGH.
Scenes from an unfinished Drama [published in *The Indicator,*
1/3/1820].
D.Sk. A Father Avenged [published in *The Companion,* 28/5 and
4/6/1828].
D. A Legend of Florence (C.G. F. 7/2/1840). L.C. 30/1/1840.
8° 1840 [2 editions]; and in *Works,* 12° 1844; 12° 1849; 12° 1857
[Boston]; *Dicks* 373.
[A MS. with variants is in the Forster Collection, South
Kensington Museum.]

HYDE, GEORGE.
C. Love's Victory; or, The School for Pride (C.G. W. 16/11/1825).
L.C. 12/10/1825. 8° 1825.
[A translation from the Spanish of Moreto.]
T. Alphonsus. 8° 1825.

INCHBALD, Mrs ELIZABETH.
[For her earlier plays see *A History of Late Eighteenth Century Drama,*
p. 275.]
C. To Marry, or Not to Marry (C.G. S. 16/2/1805). L. 82 M.
[9/2/1805]. 8° 1805 [*bis*].

IRELAND, SAMUEL WILLIAM HENRY.
[For his earlier plays see *A History of Late Eighteenth Century Drama,*
p. 276.]
T. Mutius Scaevola; or, The Roman Patriot. 8° 1801.
D. The Maid of Orleans; or, La Pucelle of Voltaire. Translated into
English Verse. 8° 1822.

IRVINE, GEORGE.
D. The Bride of Messina. 8° 1837.
[A translation of Schiller, *Die Braut von Messina* (1803).]

IRWIN, EYLES.
C.O. The Bedouins; or, The Arabs of the Desert (Crow-street,
Dublin, 1/5/1801). 12° 1802 [Dublin].
[Music Sir John Stevenson.]

ISDELL, SARAH.
C.   The Poor Gentlewoman (Crow-street, Dublin, 4/3/1811).
C.O.   The Cavern (Hawkins-street, Dublin, 1825).
   [Music Sir John Stevenson.]

JACKSON, JOHN P.
D.   The Templar and the Jewess. 8° [c. 1833].
   [A version of *Der Templar und die Jüdin* (Leipzig, 1826), by
   W. A. Wohlbrück with music by H. Marschner, itself based on
   Scott's *Ivanhoe*.]

JAMES, C. STANSFIELD.
P.   Tom Tiddler's Ground (Queen's, 26/12/1846). L.C. 26/12/1846.
F.   Where's Eliza? (Strand, 18/10/1847). L.C. 19/11/1847.
P.   Fair Rosamond; or, Harlequin and the Magic Rose. L.C. Queen's,
   22/12/1847.
D.   Jonathan Wild (Queen's, 25/9/1848). L.C. 10/8/1848.
P.   The Maid and the Magpie; or, Harlequin and the Magic Spoon.
   L.C. Queen's, 23/12/1848.
D.   Faust; or, The Fiend of the Volcano (Queen's, 22/1/1849). L.C.
   22/1/1849.
D.   The Haymakers. L.C. Queen's, 14/4/1849.
D.   Seven Dials; or, The Beggars of London (Queen's, 6/6/1849).
   L.C. 6/6/1849.
   [Also ascribed to *T. TOWNSEND*.]
D.   Old London Bridge. L.C. Queen's, 7/7/1849.
D.   The Hand of Fire. L.C. Queen's, 30/8/1849.
R.D.   The Iron Grip. L.C. Queen's, 15/10/1849.
D.   Death at the Stake; or, The Jew of Eastcheap. L.C. Queen's,
   28/11/1849.
P.   The Sleeping Beauty in the Wood; or, Harlequin and the Golden
   Horn. L.C. Queen's, 18/12/1849.

JAMESON, H.
F.   A Wild Goose Chase (D.L. T. 21/11/1820). 8° 1820.

JAMESON, ROBERT FRANCIS.
C.   A Touch at the Times (C.G. M. 6/7/1812). 8° 1812.
   [This seems to be the same as *The Town*, L. 96 M. [C.G.
   15/5/1812].]
C.   The Students of Salamanca (C.G. S. 23/1/1813). L. 99 M.
   [12/1/1813]. 8° 1813.
C.   Delusion (C.G. Th. 4/3/1813).
   [A version of the preceding play.]
F.   The Invisible Bridegroom (C.G. W. 10/11/1813). L. 97 M.
   [30/10/1813].
   [Attributed to Jameson.]
C.   Love and Gout; or, Arrivals and Marriages (H.² T. 23/8/1814).
F.   The King and the Duke; or, Which is Which? (C.G. T. 6/12/1814).
   L. 58 S. [28/11/1814]. 8° 1814.
C.   Living in London (H.² S. 5/8/1815). L. 103 M. [29/7/1815].
   8° 1815.
F.   The Mail-Coach Passengers (D.L. T. 13/2/1816). L. 108 M.
   [7/2/1816].
   [Attributed to Jameson.]
C.   Exit by Mistake (H.² M. 22/7/1816).

O.F. Teasing made Easy (H.² W. 30/7/1817). L. 67 S. [24/7/1817].
[Music Bishop.]
C. Nine Points of the Law; or, Possession (H.² S. 18/7/1818).

JEFFERINI, —
M.D. Mark the Mulatto; or, The Smuggler of the Blue Crag Rock
(S.W. W. 24/8/1836).

JEFFERSON, GEORGE.
F. The Lady's Dream (Harrowgate, 12/9/1822). 12° 1823 [North-
allerton; in *Theatrical Eccentricities*].

JERROLD, DOUGLAS WILLIAM.
F. More Frightened than Hurt (S.W. M. 30/4/1821). *Dicks* 992.
[Originally called *The Duellists*.]
M.D.Spec. The Chieftain's Oath; or, The Rival Clans (S.W. M.
30/7/1821).
M.D. The Gipsy of Derncleuch (S.W. M. 27/8/1821). *Duncombe*.
[Based on Scott, *Guy Mannering*, with suggestions from *La
Sorcière; ou, l'orphelin écossais* (Paris, 3/5/1821) by Frédéric
(Dupetit-Méré) and Victor (J. H. B. Ducange).]
M.D. The Island; or, Christian and his Comrades (S.W. 1823).
[Based on Byron's poem, *The Island* (1823).]
Bsq. Dolly and the Rat; or, The Brisket Family (Olym. M. 6/1/1823).
Duncombe.
Int. The Smoked Miser (S.W. 6/1823). *Dicks* 360; *Duncombe*, vol. lii;
Lacy, vol. lviii.
D.Sk. The Seven Ages [announced in *The Mirror of the Stage*,
26/1/1824, as about to be published].
Ba. The Living Skeleton (Cob. 15/8/1825).
Int. London Characters; Puff! Puff!! Puff!!! (Cob. T. 22/11/1825).
Ba. Popular Felons (Cob. 5/6/1826).
F. Paul Pry (Cob. 27/11/1827). *Dicks* 982; *Lacy*, vol. xlvii; *Mod.
Eng. Com. Th.* No. 67.
Vaud. The Statue Lover (Vauxhall, M. 2/6/1828). *Duncombe*.
M.D. Descart, the French Buccaneer; or, The Rock of Annaboa
(Cob. M. 1/9/1828). *Dicks* 258; *Duncombe*.
M.D. The Tower of Lochlain; or, The Idiot Son (Cob. M. 1/9/1828).
Duncombe, vol. viii; *Lacy*, vol. cx.
D.Sat. Wives by Advertisement; or, Courting in the Newspapers
(Cob. M. 8/9/1828). *Dicks* 971; *Duncombe*.
M.D. Ambrose Gwinett; or, A Sea-side Story (Cob. M. 6/10/1828).
Dicks 637; *Cumberland Minor*, vol. viii; *Richardson Minor*, vol. ii;
Lacy, vol. lxxxvi.
Ext. Two Eyes between Two; or, Pay me for my Eye (Cob. M.
13/10/1828). *Dicks* 975; *Lacy*.
M.D. Fifteen Years of a Drunkard's Life! (Cob. M. 24/11/1828).
Dicks 220; *Duncombe*, vol. iii.
M.D. Vidocq! the French Police Spy (Surrey, 6/1/1829). *Duncombe*.
M.D. Bampfylde Moore Carew (Surrey, 21/5/1824). *Duncombe*.
[A play of this title appears in L. 63 S. [Olym. 12/2/1816].]
M.D. John Overy, the Miser; or, The Southwark Ferry (Surrey, M.
20/4/1829). *Dicks* 796; *Cumberland*, vol. vii; *Richardson Minor*,
vol. ii; *Lacy*, vol. lxxxvi.
F. Law and Lions! (Surrey, Th. 21/5/1829). *Dicks* 964; *Duncombe*,
vol. iv.

M.D. Black Eyed Susan; or, All in the Downs (Surrey, M. 8/6/1829). *Dicks* 230; *Lacy*, vol. xxiii; *Duncombe*, vol. iv.
M.D. The Flying Dutchman (Surrey, 15/10/1829). *Richardson.*
Ba. The Lonely Man of Shiraz (Surrey, 3/11/1829).
T. Thomas à Becket (Surrey, 30/11/1829). *Dicks* 619; *Richardson Minor*, vol. iii; *Cumberland Minor*, vol. xi.
M.D. The Witch-Finder (D.L. S. 19/12/1829).
M.D. Sally in our Alley (Surrey, M. 11/1/1830). *Dicks* 934; *Cumberland Minor*, vol. xvi.
D. Gervaise Skinner; or, Penny Wise and Pound Foolish (Surrey, M. 25/1/1830).
      [A *Gervaise Skinner* occurs in L.C. Olym. 24/10/1831.]
M.D. The Mutiny at the Nore; or, British Sailors in 1797 (R.P. M. 7/6/1830). *Dicks* 795; *Cumberland Minor*, vol. v; *Lacy*, vol. lxxviii.
M.D. The Press-Gang; or, Archibald of the Wreck (Surrey, M. 5/7/1830).
M.D. The Devil's Ducat; or, The Gift of Mammon (Adel. Th. 16/12/1830). L.C. 13/12/1829. *Dicks* 933; *Cumberland Minor*, vol. v; *Lacy*, vol. cvii.
D. Martha Willis, the Servant Maid; or, Service in London (R.P. M. 4/4/1831). *Dicks* 420.
C. The Bride of Ludgate (D.L. Th. 8/12/1831). L.C. 5/12/1831. *Dicks* 530; *Cumberland*, vol. xxx; *Lacy*, vol. xciii.
M.D. The Broken Heart; or, The Farmer's Daughter of the Severn Side (City, 1832).
D. The Rent Day (D.L. W. 25/1/1832). L.C. 23/1/1832. 8° 1832; *Dicks* 210; *Duncombe*, vol. xxv; *Lacy*, vol. xv.
C. The Golden Calf (Strand, S. 30/6/1832). L.C. 21/4/1837. *Dicks* 529; *Cumberland Minor*, vol. ix.
D.D. The Factory Girl (D.L. S. 6/10/1832). L.C. 4/10/1832.
C. Nell Gwynne; or, The Prologue (C.G. W. 9/1/1833). C.G. 29/12/1832. 8° 1833; *Dicks* 274; *Lacy*, vol. xxxvii; *Duncombe*, vol. lxv.
C. The Housekeeper; or, The White Rose (H.² W. 17/7/1833). L.C. 10/7/1833. 8° 1833; *Dicks* 294; *Duncombe*, vol. xvi; *Lacy*, vol. xxix.
F. Swamp Hall; or, The Friend of the Family (H.² W. 11/9/1833). L.C. 26/8/1833.
C. The Wedding Gown (D.L. Th. 2/1/1834). L.C. 28/12/1833. 8° 1834; *Dicks* 591; *Duncombe*, vol. xxxvii.
C. Beau Nash, the King of Bath (H.² W. 16/7/1834). L.C. 2/7/1834. 8° 1834; *Dicks* 554.
C. The Schoolfellows (Queen's, 16/2/1835). L.C. 7/2/1835. *Dicks* 525; *Duncombe*.
T. The Hazard of the Die (D.L. T. 17/2/1835). L.C. 16/2/1835. 8° 1835; *Dicks* 638; *Duncombe*, vol. xviii.
Ba. Hearts and Diamonds (Olym. M. 23/2/1835). L.C. 17/2/1835.
Ba. The Man's an Ass (Olym. M. 26/10/1835). L.C. 21/10/1835.
      [MS. also in Forster Collection.]
C. Doves in a Cage (Adel. F. 18/12/1835; Strand, M. 12/6/1837). L.C. 17/12/1835. *Dicks* 633; *Duncombe*, vol. xx; *Lacy*, vol. xcix.
D. The Painter of Ghent (Strand, M. 25/4/1836; C.L. M. 1/5/1837). L.C. 13/4/1836. *Dicks* 651; *Duncombe*, vol. xxi; *Lacy*, vol. xxix.

F. The Man for the Ladies (Strand, M. 9/5/1836). L.C. 6/5/1836. *Dicks* 652.

Ba. The Bill-Sticker; or, An Old House in the City (Strand, Th. 21/7/1836). L.C. 23/7/1836.

Ba. The Perils of Pippins; or, The Man who "couldn't help it" (Strand, Th. 8/9/1836). L.C. 26/8/1836. *Dicks* 447; *Duncombe*, vol. xxiii.

Ba. A Gallantee Showman; or, Mr. Peppercorn at Home (Strand, M. 27/3/1837). L.C. 22/3/1837.

D.D. The Mother (H.² Th. 31/5/1838). L.C. 8/6/1838.

D. The Spendthrift [written 1839, but not acted].

C. The White Milliner (C.G. 9/2/1841). *Dicks* 607; *Duncombe*, vol. xliii; *Lacy*, vol. lxxii.

C. Bubbles of the Day (C.G. F. 25/2/1842). L.C. 20/2/1842. 8° 1842; 8° 1845; *Dicks* 553.

D. The Prisoner of War (D.L. T. 1/3/1842). L.C. 10/1/1842. 8° 1842; *Dicks* 521; *Lacy*, vol. xxvii; *Duncombe*, vol. lviii.

C. Gertrude's Cherries; or, Waterloo in 1835 (C.G. T. 30/8/1842). L.C. 27/8/1842. 8° 1842; *Dicks* 656; *Lacy*, vol. lxxxviii.

C. Time Works Wonders (H.² S. 26/4/1845). L.C. 25/4/1845. 8° 1845; *Dicks* 851; *Mod. Eng. Com. Th.* Series 3; *Lacy*, vol. xcii.

F. A Honeymoon Scruple (Surrey, 26/5/1845). L.C. 24/5/1845.

[For his later work see *A History of Late Nineteenth Century Drama*, p. 436.]

JODDRELL, RICHARD PAUL.
[See *A History of Late Eighteenth Century Drama*, p. 277.]
T. The Persian Heroine (D.L. W. 2/6/1819). L. 75 S. [21/5/1819; as *Xerxes*]. 4° 1822 [stage version].

JOHNSON, —
R.D. The Castle of Wonders (D.L. M. 8/3/1819). L. 115 M. [9/2/1819]. [Music Tanza.]

JOHNSTONE, JOHN BEER.
D. The Lion of the Jungle; or, Yaldo the Remorseless. L.C. Albert, 12/9/1844.

D. The Gipsey Farmer; or, Jack and Jack's Brother (Surrey, 28/4/1845). L.C. 25/4/1845. *New British Theatre*, No. 509; *Lacy*, vol. xxxvi.

D. Gale Breezeley; or, A Tale of a Tar (Surrey, M. 8/9/1845; Queen's, Th. 26/2/1846). L.C. 6/9/1845. *Lacy*, vol. vii.

D. Jack Long of Texas; or, A Shot in the Eye (Vic. 12/4/1847). L.C. 8/4/1847.

D. Daniel Day and the Faust Child, the Oak and the Coffin (R.P. 3/7/1848). L.C. 29/6/1848.

D. The Drunkard's Children (R.P. 10/7/1848). L.C. 10/7/1848. *Lacy*, vol. xcix.

JONES, Capt. J.
D. The Philanthropist. 8° 1801.
T. Sons; or, Family Feuds. 8° 1809.

JONES, JACOB.
T. Longinus. 8° 1827.
T. The Stepmother. 8° 1829.
T. Spartacus, the Roman Gladiator (Surrey, M. 31/8/1840). L.C. Bath, 28/3/1840. 8° 1837.

T.   The Cathedral Bell. 8° 1839.
D.   The Carpenter of Rouen (Olym. 24/6/1844). L.C. 31/5/1844.
     Dicks 384.
R.D. The Surgeon of Paris; or, The Younger Days of the Carpenter
     of Rouen. L.C. Albert, 17/10/1849. *Dicks* 714.

JONES, RICHARD.
C.   The Green Man (H.² S. 15/8/1818). L. 70 S. [10/8/1818]. 8° 1818
     [*bis*]; *Dicks* 958.
     [From the French of D'Aubigny and Poujol.]
F.   Too Late for Dinner (C.G. T. 22/2/1820). L. 118 M. [29/1/1820;
     as, *Ins and Outs; or, A Little too Late*]. 8° 1820 (2 editions); 8° 1846.
F.   Peter Fin or, A New Road to Brighton (H.² Th. 11/7/1822).
     L. 83 S. [30/6/1822; as *The Retired Fishmonger; or, A N. R. to B.*].
     8° 1822 [as *Peter Fin's Trip to Brighton*].

JONES, T.
F.   Phantoms; or, The Irishman in England. 8° 1803.
F.   Confined in Vain; or, A Double To-do. 8° 1805.

JOSHUA, JOHN, Earl of CARYSFORT.
T.   The Fall of Carthage. 8° 1810.
T.   Caius Gracchus. 8° 1810.

KEAN, EDMUND.
T.C. The Merchant of Bruges (D.L. Th. 14/12/1815). See *D. J. W.
     KINNAIRD.*
D.   Richard Duke of York; or, The Contention of York and Lancaster
     (D.L. M. 22/12/1817). 8° 1817.
     [Attributed to Kean; see G. C. D. Odell, *op. cit.*]

KEATS, JOHN.
T.   Otho the Great [in *Poems*, 1883].

KEMBLE, CHARLES.
D.   The Point of Honour (H.² T. 15/7/1800). L. 75 M. [9/7/1800].
     8° 1800; 8° 1801; 8° 1805; *Dicks* 791; *Cumberland*, vol. xxviii.
     [An adaptation from Mercier, *Le deserteur*.]
D.   The Wanderer; or, The Rights of Hospitality (C.G. T. 12/1/1808).
     L. 48 S. [10/12/1807] and L. 47 S. [H.² 5/6/1806]. 8° 1808;
     8° [1809].
     [An adaptation of Kotzebue, *Eduard in Schottland*. A revised
     version appeared at C.G. Th. 26/11/1829 as *The Royal Fugitive*,
     with music by J. Stansbury. On this see *The Dramatic Magazine*
     (1829), p. 300.]
F.   Plot and Counterplot; or, The Portrait of Michael Cervantes
     (H.² Th. 30/6/1808). L. 88 M. [23/6/1808; as *P. and C.; or, The
     Spanish Valets*]. 8° 1808; 8° 1812 [2nd]; *Dicks* 503; *Cumberland*,
     vol. xli; *Lacy*, vol. xc.
     [An adaptation of Dieulafoi, *Le portrait de Michael Cervantes*.]
M.D. Kamtchatka; or, The Slave's Tribute (C.G. W. 16/10/1811).
     L. 94 M. [3/10/11; as *The Day of Tribute*, under which title it
     was first announced].
     [An adaptation from Kotzebue.]
F.   The Child of Chance (H.² W. 8/7/1812).
M.D. The Hungarian Cottage; or, The Brazen Bust (C.G. S. 29/5/1813).
     L. 100 M. [22/5/1813].

KEMBLE, FRANCES ANNE [Mrs BUTLER].
  T.   Francis the First (C.G. Th. 15/3/1832). L.C. 14/2/1832. 8° 1832
       [9 editions]; 8° 1833 [10th].
  D.   The Star of Seville. 8° 1837 [*bis*].

KEMBLE, JOHN PHILIP.
  [For his earlier plays see *A History of Late Eighteenth Century Drama*,
       pp. 278–9.]
  C.   Congreve's The Way of the World. 8° [1800]; 8° 1815.
  T.   Shakespeare's King John. 8° 1800; 8° 1808.
  C.   Congreve's The Double Dealer. 8° [1802]; 8° 1815.
  T.   Lee's Mithridates. 8° 1802.
  T.   Shakespeare's Richard III. 8° [1801]; 8° 1814.
  T.   Shakespeare's Hamlet. 8° [1802]; 8° 1814.
  T.C. Shakespeare's The Winter's Tale. 8° [1802]; 8° 1815.
  T.C. Shakespeare's Cymbeline. 8° [1802]; 8° 1815.
  T.C. Shakespeare's Measure for Measure. 8° [1803]; 8° 1815.
  D.   Shakespeare's King Henry the Eighth. 8° 1804; 8° 1815.
  T.   Shakespeare's Othello. 8° 1804; 8° 1814.
  T.C. Shakespeare's Henry V. 8° 1806; 8° 1815.
  C.   Shakespeare's The Two Gentlemen of Verona. 8° 1808; 8° 1815.
  C.   Massinger's New Way to pay Old Debts. 8° 1810; 8° 1814.
  T.   Addison's Cato. 8° 1811.
  C.   Shakespeare's Twelfth Night. 8° 1811; 8° 1815.
  C.   Shakespeare's Comedy of Errors. 8° 1811; 8° 1815.
  C.   Beaumont's and Fletcher's Rule a Wife and Have a Wife. 8° 1811;
       8° 1815.
  T.   Otway's Venice Preserved. 8° 1811.
  C.   The Follies of a Day (Holcroft's). 8° 1811.
  T.   Shakespeare's Julius Caesar. 8° 1812.
  T.   Shakespeare's Antony and Cleopatra. 8° 1813.
  T.   Moore's Gamester. 8° 1814.
  T.   Rowe's Fair Penitent. 8° 1814.
  T.   Shakespeare's Coriolanus. 8° 1814.
  T.C. Shakespeare's Merchant of Venice. 8° 1814.
  T.   Shakespeare's Romeo and Juliet. 8° 1814.
  T.   Young's Revenge. 8° 1814.
  T.   Southerne's Isabella. 8° 1814.
  T.   Murphy's Grecian Daughter. 8° 1815.
  T.   Rowe's Jane Shore. 8° 1815.
  T.C. Shakespeare's Henry IV. 8° 1815.
  C.   Shakespeare's The Merry Wives of Windsor. 8° 1815.
  C.   Shakespeare's Much Ado about Nothing. 8° 1815.
  C.   Shakespeare's The Taming of the Shrew; or, Katharine and
       Petruchio. 8° 1815.
  C.   Shakespeare's As You Like It. 8° 1815.

KEMBLE, MARIE-THERESE [née MARIE THERESE DECAMP].
  [For an earlier play see *A History of Late Eighteenth Century Drama*,
       p. 279.]
  F.   Personation; or, Fairly Taken In (D.L. M. 29/4/1805). L. 82 M.
       [21/4/1805]. *Dicks* 748.
  Int. The Day after the Wedding; or, A Wife's First Lesson (C.G. W.
       18/5/1808). L. 87 M. [12/5/1808]. 8° 1808; 8° 1811 [2nd];
       Dicks 284; *Cumberland*, vol. xxix; *Lacy*, vol. iii.

C. Match-making; or, 'Tis a Wise Child that knows its own Father (C.G. T. 24/5/1808).
[Ascribed to Mrs Kemble.]

C. Smiles and Tears; or, The Widow's Stratagem (C.G. T. 12/12/1815). 8° 1815.

KEMBLE, STEPHEN.
[For an earlier play see *A History of Late Eighteenth Century Drama*, p. 279.]

R.D. Flodden Field (D.L. Th. 31/12/1818). L. 69 S. [8/12/1818]. 8° 1819.
[Music Cooke; based on Scott's *Marmion*.]

KEMP, Dr JOSEPH.
Ent. The Jubilee. 8° 1809.

M.D. The Siege of Isca; or, The Battles of the West (New, Th. 10/5/1810). 8° 1810.

KENNEDY, CHARLES RANN.
M. Britain's Genius. A Mask. 8° 1840.

KENNEDY, WILLIAM.
T. The Siege of Antwerp; or, The Inundation (S.W. M. 14/1/1833). 8° [1833]; 8° 1838.

KENNEY, C. L.
Bsq. Aladdin; or, The Wonderful Lamp (Lyc. 1844). See *A. SMITH*.

C. Infatuation (P'cess, Th. 1/5/1845). L.C. 28/4/1845.

F. Up the Flue; or, What's in the Wind (1846). See *D. BOUCI-CAULT*.

KENNEY, JAMES.
F. Raising the Wind (C.G. S. 5/11/1803). L. 79 M. [24/10/1803; as *How to Raise the Wind*]. 8° 1803; 8° 1804 [2nd]; 8° 1805; 8° 1810; *Dicks* 208; *Cumberland*, vol. xix; *Lacy*, vol. ii (extra series).

O.F. Matrimony (D.L. T. 20/11/1804). 8° 1804 [3 editions]; *Dicks* 906; *Cumberland*, vol. xxvi; *Lacy*, vol. xxxvii.
[Music M. P. King; based on Marsollier, *Adolphe et Clare*.]

O.F. Too many Cooks (C.G. T. 12/2/1805). L. 84 M. [14/1/1805]. 8° 1805.
[Music M. P. King.]

C.O. False Alarms; or, My Cousin (D.L. M. 12/1/1807). L. 80 M. [2/1/1807]. 8° 1807 [*bis*]; 8° 1807 [Airs, Duets, Trios]; *Cumberland*, vol. xxxix.
[Music Braham and M. P. King.]

M.D. Ella Rosenberg (D.L. Th. 19/11/1807). L. 86 M. [16/11/1807] 8° 1807; *Dicks* 216; *Cumberland*, vol. xxvii.
[Music M. P. King.]

M.D. The Blind Boy (C.G. T. 1/12/1807). L. 48 S. [23/11/1807]. 8° 1807; *Dicks* 753; *Cumberland*, vol. xxv; *Lacy*, vol. lviii.

C. The World! (D.L. Th. 31/3/1808). L. 50 S. [25/3/1808]. 8° 1808.

C.O. Oh! this Love! or, The Masqueraders (Lyc. T. 12/6/1810).
[Music M. P. King.]

O.F. Turn Him Out! (Lyc. S. 7/3/1812). 8° 1812 [*bis*].

F. Love, Law and Physic (C.G. F. 20/11/1812). L. 96 M. [12/11/1812]. 12° 1821 [Dublin]; *Dicks* 673; *Cumberland*, vol. xxiv; *Lacy*, vol. i (extra series).

C.   Debtor and Creditor (C.G. W. 20/4/1814). 8° 1814.
F.   The Fortune of War (C.G. W. 17/5/1815). L. 105 M. [1/5/1815].
M.D. The Portfolio; or, The Family of Anglade (C.G. Th. 1/2/1816).
     L. 108 M. [29/1/1816]. 8° 1816.
C.   The Touchstone; or, The World as it goes (D.L. S. 3/5/1817).
     L. 66 S. [4/1817]. 8° 1817.
O.F. A House out at Windows (D.L. S. 10/5/1817). 8° 1817.
     [Music Corri.]
C.   A Word for the Ladies (C.G. Th. 17/12/1818). L. 23 L. [10/12/1818].
O.F. Match-breaking; or, The Prince's Present (H.² Th. 20/9/1821).
     L. 80 S. [18/9/1821]. 8° 1821.
C.   John Buzzby; or, A Day's Pleasure (H.² W. 3/7/1822). L. 84 S.
     [23/6/1822]. 8° 1822.
C.O. Sweethearts and Wives (H.² M. 7/7/1823). L. 85 S. [21/6/1823].
     8° 1823 [Songs, Duets, Chorusses]; 12° [1827; Philadelphia];
     Dicks 228; Acting Nat. Drama, vol. xv.
     [Music Whitaker, Nathan, T. Cooke and Perry.]
C.O. The Alcaid; or, The Secrets of Office (H.² T. 10/8/1824).
     L.C. 14/7/1824. 12° [1824]; Cumberland, vol. viii.
C.O. The Wedding Present (D.L. F. 28/10/1825). L.C. 26/10/1825.
     [Music Horn.]
R.D. Benyowsky; or, The Exiles of Kamschatka (D.L. Th. 16/3/1826)
     L.C. 6/3/1826. 8° 1826.
     [Music Sir J. Stevenson, Cooke, Horn, Livius and Kelly; based
     on Kotzebue's drama.]
O.F. Thirteen to the Dozen (H.² F. 28/7/1826). L.C. 3/7/1826.
     [An adaptation of Le conspirateur sans le savoir; ou, les manteaux.]
C.   The Green Room (C.G. W. 18/10/1826). L.C. 28/9/1826.
C.   Spring and Autumn; or, The Bride at Fifty (H.² Th. 6/9/1827).
     L.C. 29/8/1827 [with titles reversed]. Dicks 708; Lacy, vol. xxiv.
O.F. The Illustrious Stranger; or, Married and Buried (D.L. M.
     1/10/1827). L.C. 29/9/1827 [as The I. S.; or, Marriage in the
     East]. 8° 1827; Dicks 254; Cumberland, vol. xxiii; Lacy, vol. lii.
     [Music Nathan. Written in collaboration with J. MILLINGEN.]
F.   Forget and Forgive; or, Rencontres in Paris (D.L. W. 21/11/1827).
     L.C. 19/11/1827.
C.   Frolicks in France (D.L. S. 15/3/1828).
     [A revised version of the preceding play.]
M.D. Peter the Great (C.G. S. 21/2/1829). See T. MORTON.
O.   Masaniello (C.G. M. 4/5/1829). L.C. 14/3/1849. 12° 1831;
     8° 1858; Lacy, vol. xciii.
     [An adaptation of Scribe, La muette de Portici (Paris, 29/1/1828).]
T.   The Pledge; or, Castilian Honour (D.L. F. 8/4/1831). L.C.
     6/1/1831. 8° 1831; Lacy, vol. lxxvii [as Hernani].
     [An adaptation of V. Hugo, Hernani.]
F.   The Irish Ambassador (C.G. Th. 17/11/1831). L.C. 15/11/1831.
     Dicks 920.
F.   The Self-Tormentor; or, Whims and Fancies (D.L. Th. 16/2/1832).
     L.C. 11/2/1832.
Ba. Fighting by Proxy (Olym. M. 9/12/1833). L.C. 5/12/1833.
     12° 1835; Lacy, vol. lxxiv.
     [This is said to be taken from a French adaptation of More
     Frightened than Hurt (1821) by D. JERROLD.]
Ba. Dancing for Life (Olym. Th. 16/1/1834).

F.   A Good-looking Fellow (C.G. Th. 17/4/1834). L.C. 16/4/1834.
8° 1834.
[Written in collaboration with *A. BUNN*.]
C.   The King's Seal (D.L. S. 10/1/1835). L.C. 12/1/1835. 8° 1835.
[Written in collaboration with *Mrs GORE*.]
Ba. "Not a word!" (Olym. M. 26/1/1835). L.C. 19/1/1835.
C.O. The Spirit of the Bell (E.O.H. M. 8/6/1835). L.C. 9/5/1835
[as *The Magic Bell*].
[Music G. H. Rodwell.]
C.   Hush! or, Secrets at Court (D.L. 27/12/1836). L.C. 16/12/1836.
F.   Macintosh and Co. (C.G. W. 21/2/1838). L.C. 9/2/1838.
O.   Barbara; or, The Bride of a Day (C.G. S. 3/11/1838). L.C. 2/11/1838.
T.   The Sicilian Vespers (Surrey, M. 21/9/1840). 8° 1840.
[An adaptation of C. Delavigne, *Les vêpres siciliennes*.]
F.   Love Extempore (H.² T. 23/11/1841). L.C. 4/11/1841. *Dicks* 733.

KERR, JOHN.
C.   Drenched and Dried; or, Water and Fire. 8° [1820].
M.D. The Wandering Boys (S.W. 24/5/1830). *Dicks* 916; *Lacy*, vol.
xxxiv; *Cumberland Minor*, vol. iii; *Duncombe*, vol. vi.
[Music Nicholson. An adaptation of Pixérécourt, *Le pèlerin
blanc* (Paris, 1801).]
M.D. Therese; or, The Orphan of Geneva (W.L.). *Duncombe*; *Dicks* 30.
F.   The Intimate Friend; or, A Queer Guest at a Wedding (Queen's,
F. 26/12/1845). *Duncombe*, vol. i.

KIMPTON, F.
Oa. He "lies like Truth" (E.O.H. Th. 24/7/1828). L.C. 25/7/1828.
Dicks 914; *Lacy*, vol. lxxv.
[An adaptation of *Le menteur véridique*.]

KINNAIRD, DOUGLAS JAMES WILLIAM.
T.C. The Merchant of Bruges; or, The Beggar's Bush (D.L. Th.
14/12/1815). 8° 1815; 8° 1816 [2nd]; *Dicks* 103; *B.D.* vol. iv.
[Music Cooke. An adaptation of Brome's play.]

KLANERT, CHARLES MORITZ.
M.D. Elisina (Richmond). 8° 1824.

KNIGHT, —
O.F. The Sailor and Soldier; or, Fashionable Amusement (Hull,
1805). L. 44 S. [Hull and York, 30/12/1804].

KNIGHT, EDWARD P.
O.F. A Chip of the Old Block; or, The Village Festival (H.² T.
22/8/1815). L. 60 S. [15/8/1815]. 8° 1815.
[Music Whitaker.]
Int. Cry To-day and Laugh To-morrow (D.L. F. 29/11/1816).
L. 63 S. [17/11/1816; as *Sunshine after Rain*].
[Music Cooke.]
C.O. The Veteran Soldier; or, The Farmer's Sons (D.L. S. 32/2/1822,
as *The Veterans*). L. 85 S. [13/2/1822]. 8° 1822 (as *The Veteran*).
[Music Whitaker, Parry and Cooke.]

KNOWLES, JAMES SHERIDAN.
D.   Leo; or, The Gypsy (Waterford, 1810).
D.   Brian Boroihme; or, The Maid of Erin (Belfast, 2/3/1812; C.G. Th.
20/4/1837). L.C. 16/4/1837. *Dicks* 670; *Lacy*, vol. cix; *Acting
Nat. Drama*, vol. viii.

T. Caius Gracchus (Belfast, 13/2/1815; D.L. T. 18/11/1823). L. 87 S. [6/11/1823]. 8° 1823 [Glasgow]; *Dicks* 298; *Cumberland*, vol. vi.

T. Virginius; or, The Liberation of Rome (Glasgow, 1820; C.G. W. 17/5/1820). L. 120 M. [9/5/1820]. 8° 1820 [*bis*]; 8° 1823 [5th]; *Dicks* 246; *Cumberland*, vol. vi.

T. The Fatal Dowry (D.L. W. 5/1/1825; S.W. W. 27/8/1845). L.C. 27/12/1824. 8° 1825.
   [An adaptation of Massinger's drama.]

D. William Tell (D.L. W. 11/5/1825). L.C. 13/5/1825. MS. B.M. Add. 27719. 8° 1825; *Dicks* 238; *Cumberland*, vol. xxii; *Lacy*, vol. lxxxiii.

C. The Beggar's Daughter of Bethnal Green (D.L. S. 22/11/1828). L.C. 8/5/1828. 8° 1828; *Dicks* 695.

D. Alfred the Great; or, The Patriot King (D.L. Th. 28/4/1831). L.C. 14/4/1831. 8° 1831; 8° [1832]; *Dicks* 314.

D. The Hunchback (C.G. Th. 5/4/1832). L.C. 30/3/1832. 8° 1832 [*bis*]; 8° 1836 [9th]; *Dicks* 206; *Cumberland*, vol. xlii; *Lacy*, vol. lxvii.

M. The Vision of the Bard (Edinburgh, 1/10/1832; C.G. M. 22/10/1832). L.C. 20/10/1832. 8° 1832.

D. The Wife: A Tale of Mantua (C.G. W. 24/4/1833). L.C. 17/4/1833. 8° 1833 [6 editions]; *Dicks* 288; *Lacy*, vol. cix.

C. The Beggar of Bethnal Green (Vic. 1834). 8° 1834.
   [A revised version of *The Beggar's Daughter of Bethnal Green*.]

D. The Daughter (D.L. T. 29/11/1836). L.C. 23/11/1836. 8° 1837 [*bis*]; *Dicks* 313.
   [Also played as *The Wrecker's Daughter*.]

T. The Bridal (H.² M. 26/6/1837). L.C. 24/6/1837. 8° [1837]; *Dicks* 320; *Acting Nat. Drama*, vol. i.
   [An adaptation of Beaumont's and Fletcher's, *The Maid's Tragedy*.]

C. The Love-Chase (H.² M. 9/10/1837). L.C. 1837. 8° 1837; *Dicks* 322; *Cumberland*, vol. xli; *Lacy*, vol. lxviii.

D. Woman's Wit; or, Love's Disguises (C.G. W. 23/5/1838). L.C. 22/5/1838. 8° 1838; *Dicks* 302.

D. The Maid of Mariendorpt (H.² T. 9/10/1838). L.C. 11/10/1838. 8° 1838; *Dicks* 496.

D. Love (C.G. M. 4/11/1839). L.C. 2/11/1839. 8° 1840; *Dicks* 364; *Lacy*, vol. lxxiv; *Cumberland*, vol. xl.

T. John of Procida; or, The Bridals of Messina (C.G. S. 19/9/1840). L.C. 14/9/1840. 8° 1840; *Dicks* 691.
   [Also played as *The Bride of Messina*.]

C. Old Maids (C.G. T. 12/10/1841). L.C. 8/10/1841. 8° 1841; *Dicks* 629.

T. The Rose of Arragon (H.² S. 4/6/1842; Surrey, M. 17/9/1849). L.C. 3/6/1842. 8° 1842; *Dicks* 689.

D. The Secretary (D.L. M. 24/4/1843). 8° 1843; *Dicks* 665.

D. The Rock of Rome. 8° 1849.
   [The *Dramatic Works* were published in 3 volumes in 1843. For his later plays see *A History of Late Nineteenth Century Drama*, p. 445.]

KNOWLES, RICHARD BRINSLEY.

C. The Maiden Aunt (H.² W. 19/11/1845). L.C. 19/11/1845. 16° 1845.

KNOX, *Capt.*
- D. Faust. 8° 1847.
   [A translation of Goethe's drama.]

KORNER, —
- C. The Bride [1808].

LACY, *MICHAEL ROPHINO.*
- O. The Turkish Lovers (D.L. T. 1/5/1827). L.C. 26/3/1827 [as *The T. L.; or, The Faithful Infidel*].
- C. Love and Reason (C.G. T. 22/5/1827). L.C. 14/5/1827. 12° 1827.
   [An adaptation of *Bertrand et Suzette* by Scribe.]
- C. The Two Friends (H.² F. 11/7/1828). L.C. 10/6/1828. *Dicks* 679; *Cumberland*, vol. xxxvii.
   [An adaptation of Scribe, *Rodolphe; ou, frère et sœur.*]
- C. The Stepmother (C.G. W. 22/10/1828). L.C. 22/10/1828.
   [An adaptation of Scribe, *La belle-mère* (Paris, 1/3/1826).]
- C. The Soldier's Stratagems (C.G. W. 5/11/1828). L.C. 23/10/1828.
- C.O. Love in Wrinkles; or, The Russian Stratagem (D.L. Th. 4/12/1828). L.C. 22/11/1828.
   [Music by the author. An adaptation of *La vieille.*]
- O. The Maid of Judah; or, The Knights Templars (C.G. S. 7/3/1829; Vic. Th. 27/11/1834; R.P. M. 14/12/1835). L.C. 14/2/1829. *Cumberland*, vol. xxv.
   [An adaptation of *Ivanhoé* (Paris, 15/9/1826) by E. Deschamps and G. G. de Wailly.]
- C.O. The Casket (D.L. T. 10/3/1829). L.C. 3/2/1829.
   [Music Mozart. An adaptation of *Les premières amours.*]
- M.D. Robert the Devil, Duke of Normandy (C.G. T. 2/2/1830). L.C. 28/11/1829 [as *R. the D.; or, The Bridal Ring*]. *Lacy*, vol. xxxi.
   [An adaptation of *Robert le Diable*, music by Meyerbeer. Genest attributes this play to Raymond.]
- C.O. Cinderella; or, The Fairy Queen and the Glass Slipper (C.G. T. 13/4/1830). L.C. 15/3/1830. 8° 1830 [Songs, Duetts; reprinted 1840]; *Dicks* 1060; *Lacy*, vol. xviii.
   [Music Rossini. An adaptation of *La Cenerentola.*]
- D.Spec. Napoleon Buonaparte, Captain of Artillery, General and First Consul, Emperor and Exile (C.G. M. 16/5/1831). 8° 1831
   [*Programme* containing description].
- O. Fra Diavolo; or, The Inn of Terracina (C.G. Th. 3/11/1831). L.C. 17/10/1831. 8° 1831 [Songs, Duets, Chorusses].
   [An adaptation of Scribe, *Fra Diavolo* (Paris, 28/1/1830), with music by Auber.]
- O. The Coiners; or, The Soldier's Oath (C.G. S. 23/3/1833). L.C. 15/3/1833.
   [Music Auber.]

LACY, *THOMAS HAILES.*
- F. A Silent Woman (17/8/1835). 12° [1835].
- C. The Pickwickians. *Lacy*, vol. i (new series).
- D. The Tower of London (C.L. S. 26/12/1840). See *T. H. HIGGIE*.
- D. Martin Chuzzlewit (Queen's, 29/7/1844). See *T. H. HIGGIE*.
- D. Clarissa Harlowe (P'cess, M. 28/9/1846). L.C. 1/10/1846. *Dicks* 995; *Lacy*, vol. lxxvii.
   [Written in collaboration with *J. COURTNEY*; but see note

on this play under *T. H. REYNOLDSON.* Apparently Lacy had
already produced a *Clarissa Harlowe* at the Olympic on 3/1/1831.]

LAKE, JOHN.
D.   The House of Morville (Lyc. Th. 27/2/1812). L. 56 S. [8/2/1812].
       8° 1812 [*bis*].
C.   The Golden Glove; or, The Farmer's Son. 8° 1815.

LAMB, CHARLES.
T.   John Woodvil. 12° 1802; 8° 1818 [in *Works*].
       [This play, originally called *Pride's Cure*, had been offered to
       J. P. Kemble at Christmas 1799 but refused.]
F.   Mr. H—— (D.L. W. 10/12/1806). L. 84 M. [8/12/1806]. 8° 1818
       [in *Works*].
D.   The Wife's Trial; or, The Intruding Widow [published in
       Blackwood's Magazine, Dec. 1828].
D.   The Pawn-broker's Daughter [published in *Blackwood's Magazine*,
       Jan. 1830].

LAMBE, Hon. GEORGE.
C.O.   Whistle for it (private, Stanmore Priory; C.G. 10/4/1807).
          L. 49 S. [5/3/1807]. 8° 1807.
D.   Timon of Athens (D.L. 28/10/1816). 8° 1816.
       [See G. C. D. Odell, *op. cit.* ii. 77–80.]

LANCASTER, CHARLES SEARS.
Ba.   The Devil's Daughter; or, Beelzebub's Belles (Queen's, 17/11/1839).
          Dicks 940.
Ca.   Advice to Husbands (P'cess, 1846). *Duncombe*, vol. lvii.

LANDOR, ROBERT EYRES.
T.   The Count Arezzi. 8° 1824.
T.   The Earl of Brecon. 8° 1841.
       [Published with *Faith's Fraud* and *The Ferryman*.]

LANDOR, WALTER SAVAGE.
T.   Count Julian. 8° 1812; 8° 1821 [with *Gebir*]; and in *Works*
       [8° 1846; 8° 1876; 8° 1909].
T.   Andrea of Hungary and Giovanna of Naples. 8° 1839; and in
       Works, as above.
T.   Fra Rupert. 8° 1841; and in *Works*, as above.
T.   The Siege of Ancona. 8° 1846 [in *Works*].
[Scenes] Antony and Octavius. 8° 1856.

LANGSDORFF, Baron.
F.   Come and See (H.² M. 18/7/1814). L. 103 M. [12/7/1814].

LATHOM, FRANCIS.
[For his earlier plays see *A History of Late Eighteenth Century Drama*,
   p. 280; *The Dash of the Day* is there antedated.]
C.   The Dash of the Day (Norwich, 1800). L. 20 L. [25/7/1800].
       8° 1800 [Norwich; *bis*].
C.   Curiosity (Norwich, 1801). L. 74 M. [Norwich, 18/11/1800].
       8° 1801 [Norwich].
F.   Holiday Time; or, The School-boy's Frolic. L. 20 L. [Norwich,
       10/4/1801].
C.   The Wife of a Million (Norwich, 1802). L. 20 L. [Norwich,
       3/3/1802]. 12° 1803 [Norwich].

O.F. The Dash; or, Who but he? (D.L. S. 20/10/1804). L. 44 S.
[9/10/1804; as *The Denouement*.]
[An alteration of *Holiday Time* (1800) by Lathom; the alteration
may not be his. Music by Reeve.]

LAWLER, DENNIS.
O.F. In and Out of Tune (D.L. T. 1/3/1808). L. 49 S. [22/2/1808].
[Evidently the play was originally written by Lawler, who penned
it at the suggestion of Corri, the composer; the actual working-out
(Lawler says distortion) was accomplished by *A. CHERRY*. See
Biographia Dramatica, ii. 321.]
C. The School for Daughters. 8° 1808; *Mod. Engl. Com. Th.* No. 79.
M.D. Industry and Idleness (Surrey, M. 15/4/1811).
O.F. Sharp and Flat (Lyc. W. 4/8/1813). 8° 1813.
[Music J. Hook.]
Ba. The Advertisement for a Husband; or, More Blunders (Surrey,
M. 30/5/1814).

LEE, ALEXANDER.
Ba. The Fairy Lake; or, The Magic Veil (D.L. 26/10/1839). L.C.
22/10/1839.

LEE, FRANCIS.
T. The Glorious Revolution of 1688. 8° 1821.

LEE, HARRIET.
[For her earlier plays see *A History of Late Eighteenth Century Drama*,
p. 280.]
M.D. The Three Strangers (C.G. S. 10/12/1825). L.C. 28/10/1825.
8° 1826.

LEE, HENRY.
O. Caleb Quotem and his Wife! or, Paint, Poetry and Putty!...To
which is added a Postscript, including the Scene always play'd in
the Review, or Wags of Windsor, but omitted in the Edition lately
published by G. Colman, Esq. 8° [1809].
[See *A History of Late Eighteenth Century Drama*, p. 280.]

LEE, NELSON.
[Nelson Lee's productivity was enormous; often three or four Christmas
pantomimes from his pen appeared in the same year at different
theatres. The list given here is certainly not complete, record
being made only of those pieces which can quite definitely be
assigned to him.]
P. The Whitechapel Needle; or, Harlequin and the Pretty Little
Dicky Bird. L.C. R.P. 11/12/1843.
P. Harlequin Grammar; or, Murray and A. E. I. O. U. (Surrey, T.
26/12/1843). L.C. 20/12/1843.
M.D. The Maid and the Magpie. L.C. Grecian, 1844.
P. Auld Lang Syne; or, Morning, Noon and Night and Harlequin
Jack o' Daylight. L.C. Standard, 21/12/1846.
P. Forty Thieves; or, Harlequin Ali Baba and the Robber's Cave
(R.A. S. 26/12/1846). L.C. 27/11/1846.
D. Past, Present and Future. L.C. Standard, 1847.
P. Harlequin Doctor Syntax and his Dapple Grey Mare (R.A. M.
27/12/1847). L.C. 4/12/1847.
P. Battledore and Shuttlecock; or, Harlequin Trap, Bat and Ball
(Surrey, M. 27/12/1847). L.C. 22/12/1847.

M.D. The Mysteries of an American City. L.C. Britannia, 28/1/1848.
Bsq. Lady Godiva and Peeping Tom of Coventry (C.L. 30/9/1848).
L.C. 22/9/1848.
P. War, Love and Peace; or, Harlequin Gossip Chat and Beauty
(C.L. 26/12/1848). L.C. 14/12/1848.
P. Harlequin and Yankee Doodle, who came to Town upon his Little
Pony (R.A. W. 26/12/1849).

LEE, SOPHIA.
[For her earlier plays see *A History of Late Eighteenth Century Drama*,
p. 281.]
C. The Assignation (D.L. W. 28/1/1807). L. 48 S. [15/1/1807].

LEFANU, Mrs ALICIA [née SHERIDAN].
C. The Sons of Erin; or, Modern Sentiments (Lyc. S. 11/4/1812).
L. 55 S. [4/4/1812]. 8° 1812 [3 editions].
[Called on first performance, *Prejudice; or, Modern Sentiment.*]

LEFEVRE, Sir GEORGE.
D, Faust. 12° 1841; 12° 1843 [Frankfurt a. M.].
[A translation of Goethe's drama.]

LEFTLY, CHARLES.
[For *A Masque, The Corsicans* and *The Sylph* see *Biographia Dramatica*,
i. 450.]

LEIGH, JAMES MATTHEWS.
D. Cromwell. 8° [1838; privately printed].

LEIGH, LANGTON.
D. Louise (Vic. M. 19/2/1838). 8° [1838].

LEIGH, RICHARD.
C. Grieving's a Folly (Lyc. F. 21/4/1809). L. 51 S. [20/4/1809].
8° 1809.
C. Where to find a Friend (Lyc. 20/5/1811). L. 61 S. [15/11/1815].
8° 1815; 8° 1816 [2nd].

LEMON, MARK.
O.F. P.L.; or, 30 Strand (Strand, M. 25/4/1836). L.C. 13/4 1836.
Dicks 977; *Duncombe*, vol. xxii.
D. Arnold of Winkelreid; or, The Fight of the Sempach (Surrey, M.
25/7/1836). *Duncombe*, vol. xxii.
M.D. The Ancestress; or, The Doom of Barostein (C.L. M. 27/3/1837).
Duncombe, vol. xxviii.
[See below under 1840.]
Ba. Love and Charity (St J. Th. 3/5/1838). L.C. 2/5/1838. *Dicks* 963;
Duncombe, vol. xxx.
O.F. The M.P. for the Rotten Borough (E.O.H. F. 27/7/1838). L.C.
21/7/1838. *Dicks* 719.
Ba. The Grey Doublet (E.O.H. T. 28/8/1838). L.C. 8/1838. *Dicks*
719; *Duncombe*, vol. xxx.
M.D. Self-Accusation; or, A Brother's Love (E.O.H. M. 10/9/1838).
L.C. 1/9/1838. *Dicks* 483; *Duncombe*, vol. xxxi.
Ba. A Familiar Friend (Olym. S. 8/2/1840). L.C. 5/2/1840. *Dicks* 981.
Ba. The Ladies' Club (Olym. 3/1840). L.C. 25/2/1840. *Dicks* 386;
Lacy, vol. xiii.
D. Gwyneth Vaughan (Olym. W. 1/4/1840; P'cess, T. 2/7/1844).
L.C. 27/3/1840. *Dicks* 345; *Lacy*, vol. xxix.

Ba. The House of Ladies (Olym. 4/1840). L.C. 25/4/1840. 12° [1840].
F.   A Captain pro tem. (Olym. M. 18/5/1840). L.C. 18/5/1840.
Ba. Three Secrets (E.O.H. 9/6/1840). L.C. 1840.
Ba. Ins and Outs (E.O.H. F. 26/6/1840). L.C. 23/6/1840.
D.   The Demon Gift (E.O.H. M. 29/6/1840). See *J. BROUGHAM*.
D.   The Ancestress (E.O.H. M. 14/9/1840). L.C. 14/9/1840. *Dicks* 773.
     [See above under 1837 possibly the text revised in 1840.]
F.   Out of Place (H.² M. 19/10/1840).
     [See under *UA*.]
C.   Fashionable Arrivals (C.G. Th. 29/10/1840). L.C. 20/10/1840. *Dicks* 562.
F.   Bob Short (H.² S. 5/12/1840). L.C. 8/12/1840.
F.   The Gentleman in Black; or, The Loves of the Devils. L.C. Olym. 9/12/1840. *Dicks* 776.
     [See also under *W. L. REDE*.]
D.   The Brother's Sacrifice; or, Self-Accusation (S.W. T. 2/2/1841).
     [See above under 10/9/1838.]
F.   The Good for Nothing (H.² Th. 4/2/1841). L.C. 1840 and L.C. 30/1/1841.
Ba. The Little Gipsy (Olym. 12/4/1841). L.C. 2/4/1841.
Ba. The Silver Thimble (Strand, 12/4/1841). L.C. 11/4/1841.
Ba. Lost and Won. L.C. Olym. 1/5/1841. *Dicks* 594.
C.   What will the World say? (C.G. S. 25/9/1841). L.C. 24/9/1841 [as *Vanity; or, W. w. the W. s.?*]. 8° 1841.
F.   My Man Tom (Olym. Th. 27/1/1842).
Ba. Robinson Crusoe. L.C. Olym. 21/3/1842.
Ba. Dick Whittington and his Cat (Olym. M. 28/3/1842). L.C. Olym. 21/3/1842.
Ba. Robert Burns (Strand, Th. 31/3/1842). L.C. 23/3/1842.
Ba. Wax and Wonders (Strand, 1/8/1842). L.C. 1/8/1842.
C.   Grandfather Whitehead (H.² F. 31/9/1842). L.C. 21/9/1842. *Dicks* 505; *Acting Nat. Drama*, vol. x.
D.   The Adventures of a Gentleman (Olym. M. 3/10/1842). L.C. 5/10/1842.
R.D. The Turf (C.G. M. 31/10/1842). L.C. 25/10/1842. 8° 1842; *Dicks* 497.
F.   Love and War (Olym. M. 21/11/1842). L.C. 10/11/1842.
Bsq. Ils Amores da Gileso Scroggini e Molli Brownini (Olym. M. 27/3/1843). L.C. 1/5/1841.
F.   The Bashful Irishman (H.² Th. 20/4/1843). L.C. 1/4/1843.
F.   The Yellow Husband (H.² W. 17/5/1843). L.C. 11/4/1843.
D.   Old Parr (H.² M. 9/10/1843). L.C. 30/9/1843. *Dicks* 686.
Bsq. Open Sesame (Lyc. M. 8/4/1844). See *G. A. À BECKETT*.
D.   The Sempstress (H.² S. 25/5/1844). L.C. 22/5/1844. *Dicks* 759.
D.   Don Caesar de Bazan (P'cess, T. 8/10/1844). See *G. A. À BECKETT*.
Bsq. The Knight and the Sprite (Strand, M. 11/11/1844). See *G. A. À BECKETT*.
D.   The Chimes (Adel. 19/12/1844). See *G. A À BECKETT*.
Bsq. St. George and the Dragon (Adel. M. 24/3/1845). See *G. A. À BECKETT*.
Spec. Peter Wilkins (Adel. Th. 9/4/1846). See *G. A. À BECKETT*.
D.   The Old Soldier (H.² 18/6/1845). L.C. 10/6/1845.

O.F. Honesty the Best Policy (Strand, M. 11/6/1849). L.C. 6/6/1849.
D. The Three Secrets; or, The Lost Jewels (Surrey, M. 23/7/1849).
    Dicks 596.
F. Hearts are Trumps (Strand, M. 30/7/1849). L.C. 10/8/1849.
    Dicks 1058.
F. Domestic Economy (Adel. Th. 8/11/1849). L.C. 5/11/1849.
    Dicks 1034.
    [To these should be added: *The Pacha's Bridal* (1836), *My Sister Kate* (1838), *The Lady of the Lake* (1843).]

LENNOX, Lord W.
F. Incog.; or, Three Days at a Well-known Hotel (D.L.W.11/6/1817).
    L. 66 S) [2/6/1817;with "Hatchetts" for "a Well-known Hotel"].

LEVIUS or LIVIUS, BARHAM
O.F. Maid or Wife; or, The Deceiver Deceived (D.L. M. 5/11/1821).
      L. 79 S. [28/10/1821). *Cumberland*, vol. xxxiii.
      [Music by the author.]
O.   Masaniello; or, The Dumb Girl of Portici (D.L. M. 4/5/1829).
     L.C. 25/4/1829.
     [An adaptation of Scribe and Delavigne, *La muette de Portici* (Paris, 29/1/1828), with music by Auber.]

LEWIS, A.
D. Grace Clairville; or, The Coiner of Symon's Yat (Surrey, M. 20/2/1843). *Dicks* 951.

LEWIS, MATTHEW GREGORY.
[For his earlier plays see *A History of Late Eighteenth Century Drama*, p. 281.]
R.D. Adelmorn, the Outlaw (D.L. M. 4/5/1801). L. 41 S. [17/3/1801].
      8° 1801 [*bis*]; 8° 1801 [Songs; 3 editions]; 12° 1801 [*Dublin*].
      [Music M. Kelly.]
T.   Alfonso, King of Castile (C.G. F. 15/1/1802). L. 76 M. [19/11/1801].
     8° 1801; 8° 1802 [2nd].
D.   The Captive (C.G. T. 22/3/1803). [Printed in his *Life* (1839),
     vol. i. 136–41.]
T.   The Harper's Daughter (C.G. W. 4/5/1803). L. 78 M. [8/4/1803].
     12° 1813 [*Philadelphia*].
     [An adaptation of *The Minister*, itself an adapted translation of
     Schiller, *Kabale und Liebe*.]
M D Rugantino; or, The Bravo of Venice (C.G. F. 18/10/1805).
     L. 83 M. [11/10/1805]. 8° 1805; 12° [1814; Dublin]; *Oxberry*,
     vol. ix; *Cumberland*, vol. xxxiv.
     [An adaptation of Pixérécourt, *L'homme à trois visages; ou, le
     proscrit de Venise* (Paris, 1801). The original music seems to have
     been by Dr Busby, but, when acted at Crow-street, Dublin, in
     1814, the play was given out as with music by T. Cooke.]
M.D. The Wood Daemon; or, "The Clock has Struck" (D.L. W.
     1/4/1807). L. 86 M. [24/3/1807].
     [Music M. Kelly.]
T.   Adelgitha; or, The Fruits of a Single Error (D.L. Th. 30/4/1807).
     L. 85 M. [22/4/1807]. 8° 1806 [3 editions]; 8° 1817 [5th]; *Cum-
     berland*, vol. xxxix.
D.   Venoni; or, The Novice of St. Mark's (D.L. Th. 1/12/1808).
     L. 49 S. [26/11/1808]. 8° 1809; *Cumberland*, vol. xxxviii.

M.D. Raymond and Agnes. L. 89 M. [Norwich, 22/11/1809].
Cumberland, vol. xxxviii.
M.D. Timour the Tartar (C.G. M. 29/4/1811). L. 94 M. [6/4/1811].
8° [1811]; 8° [1814; Dublin]; Cumberland, vol. xxix; Lacy,
vol. lxxix.
M.D. One O'Clock! or, The Knight and the Wood Daemon (Lyc.
Th. 1/8/1811). L. 54 S. [16/7/1811]. 8° [1811]; Dicks 128;
Oxberry, vol. xix; Cumberland, vol. xxxii; Lacy, vol. xc.
[Music M. P. King and M. Kelly. See The Wood Daemon
above.]
C.O. Rich and Poor (Lyc. W. 22/7/1812). Dicks 755; Oxberry, vol. xix.

LINDOE, —
C. Forget and Forgive; or, The Road to Happiness (Newcastle, 1804).

LINLEY, GEORGE.
O. Catherine Gray (D.L. 27/5/1837).
O. The Gipsy's Warning! (D.L. Th. 19/4/1838). L.C. 6/4/1838.
8° [1838; Songs, Duets, Trios, Recitatives, Choruses].
[Music J. Benedict. Written in collaboration with R. B.
PEAKE.]

LINLEY, WILLIAM.
[For his earlier plays see A History of Late Eighteenth Century Drama,
pp. 281–2.]
M.Ent. The Ring; or, Love me for myself (D.L. 21/1/1800). L. 38 S.
[13/1/1800]. 8° 1800 [Songs].
[An alteration of his earlier play, The Pavilion.]

LISTER, THOMAS HENRY.
T. Epicharis (D.L. W. 14/10/1829). L.C. 10/10/1829. 8° 1829.

LLOYD, CHARLES.
The Tragedies of Vittorio Alfieri, translated from the Italian. 8° 1815.
T. The Duke d'Ormond. 8° 1822.

LOCKWOOD, PERCIVAL.
D. The Bride of Messina. 8° 1839 [München].
[A translation of Schiller's drama.]

LODER, EDWARD JAMES.
B.O. Robin Goodfellow; or, The Frolics of Puck (P'cess, W. 6/12/1848).
L.C. 2/12/1848.

LODGE, ADAM.
D. The Bride of Messina. 8° 1841; 8° 1863 [3rd].
[A translation of Schiller's drama.]

LONG, C.
F. False Conclusions (Grecian, 20/1/1845). L.C. 18/12/1844.
D. The Privateer; or, The Lady of St Tropez. L.C. Grecian,
22/1/1845.
Vaud. The Corporal; or, Brothers in Arms. L.C. Grecian, 22/3/1845.
C.O. The Chalet; or, Caught, not Won. L.C. Grecian, 28/10/1845.
O.F. Ernestine and Georgette. L.C. Grecian, 1846.
F. Wife and Widow. L.C. Grecian, 18/3/1846.
O. The Crown Brilliants. L.C. Grecian, 10/7/1846.
[An adaptation of Scribe, Les diamants de la couronne (Paris,
6/3/1841), with music by Auber.]
F. My Friend. L.C. Grecian, 18/9/1846.

F.   Family Arrangements. L.C. Grecian, 12/10/1846.
F.   Edwin and Emma. L.C. Grecian, 13/2/1847.
O.   Hymen's Muster Roll; or, A Marriage at the Drum Head. L.C.
     Grecian, 3/6/1847.

LONSDALE, —
P.   Puss in Boots; or, Harlequin and the Ogre (R.C. Th. 28/5/1801).

LOVEDAY, W.
F.   Modern Misses; or, Sixteen and Sixty-three (Exeter, 8/5/1812).
     8° 1812.
D.   The Castle of Morosino. 8° 1812.

LOVELL, GEORGE WILLIAM.
D.   The Avenger (Surrey, F. 13/2/1835). L.C. 20/8/1835 [licensed for
     country Theatre Royals].
T.   The Provost of Bruges (D.L. W. 10/2/1836). L.C. 1/2/1836 [as
     Bertulphe, the P. of B.]. 8° 1836; *Dicks* 681; *Cumberland*, vol. lxiv.
D.   The Trustee. 8° 1841.
D.   Love's Sacrifice; or, The Rival Merchants (C.G. M. 12/9/1842).
     L.C. 27/8/1842 [as *The R. M.; or, The Daughter's Sacrifice*].
     Dicks 650; *Lacy*, vol. lxvii.
C.   Look before you Leap; or, Wooings and Weddings (H.[2] Th.
     29/10/1846). L.C. 31/10/1846. *Dicks* 998; *Acting Nat. Drama*,
     vol. xiii.
D.   The Wife's Secret (H.[2] M. 17/1/1848). L.C. 8/1/1848. *Dicks* 1005;
     Lacy, vol. lxxxii.
     [This was first produced at the Park Theatre, New York, on
     12/10/1846.]
D.   The Trial of Love (P'cess, 7/6/1852).

LOVER, SAMUEL.
Ba. The Beau Ideal (Olym. M. 9/11/1835). L.C. 13/11/1835.
Ba. Rory O'More (Adel. F. 29/9/1837). L.C. 1837. *Dicks* 356; *Acting
     Nat. Drama*, vol. ii.
     [Based on his own novel.]
D.   The White Horse of the Peppers (H.[2] S. 26/5/1838). L.C.
     25/5/1838. *Dicks* 441; *Acting Nat. Drama*, vol. v.
Ext. The Happy Man (H.[2] M. 20/5/1839). L.C. 4/6/1839. *Dicks* 328;
     Acting Nat. Drama, vol. vii.
F.   The Hall Porter (E.O.H. F. 26/7/1839). L.C. 1839. *Dicks* 520;
     Acting Nat. Drama, vol. vii.
M.D. The Greek Boy (C.G. T. 29/9/1840). L.C. 25/9/1840. *Dicks*
     609; *Acting Nat. Drama*, vol. ix.
Oa. Il Paddy Whack in Italia. L.C. E.O.H. 22/4/1841. *Duncombe*,
     vol. xliv.

LUCAS, N. J.
D.   The Maid of Orleans. 8° 1841 [Bremen]; 8° 1845.
     [A translation of Schiller's drama.]

LUCAS, WILLIAM.
Int. The Manuscript. 12° 1809.

LUCAS, WILLIAM JAMES.
M.D. The Death Plank; or, The Dumb Sailor Boy (R.P. 7/1832).
     Duncombe, vol. xxxvii.
M.D. The Traitor's Gate; or, The Tower of London in 1553 (R.P.
     M. 31/3/1834). *Lacy*, vol. xcv.

Ca. The Widow Bewitched (P'cess, W. 13/11/1844). L.C. 14/10/1844.
Duncombe, vol. lii; Lacy, vol. cxvi.
M.D. The Rag-Picker of Paris (Queen's, 28/6/1847).

LUNN, JOSEPH.
Bsq. The Sorrows of Werther (C.G.W. 6/5/1818). L. 71 S. [28/4/1818].
O.F. Family Jars (H.² M. 26/8/1822). L. 84 S. [15/8/1822; as F. J.;
or, The Double Mistake and the Triple Discovery]. Lacy, vol. xiv;
Dicks 355.
[Music Perry.]
F. "Fish out of Water" (H.² T. 26/8/1823). L. 86 S. [17/8/1823;
with sub-title, or, Clerkship and Cookery]. Dicks 355; Lacy, vol. xvi.
M.Ent. Hide and Seek (H.² M. 25/10/1824). L.C. 16/10/1824.
Cumberland, vol. xii.
M.D. The Shepherd of Derwent Vale; or, The Innocent Culprit
(D.L. S. 12/2/1825). L.C. 1/2/1825 [as Reverses; or, The I. C.].
8° [1825]; Lacy, vol. lxxxix.
[Music Horn.]
F. Lofty Projects; or, Arts in an Attic (C.G. F. 22/4/1825). L.C.
28/3/1825. Cumberland, vol. x.
C. Roses and Thorns; or, Two Houses under One Roof (H.² W.
24/8/1825). L.C. 1825. Cumberland, vol. xii.
F. Three Deep; or, All on the Wing (C.G. T. 2/5/1826). L.C.
21/4/1826. Dolby.
F. White Lies; or, The Major and the Minor (D.L. S. 2/12/1826;
S.W. M. 6/8/1827). L.C. 2/12/1826. 8° 1826.
F. Fast and Slow (D.L. W. 18/4/1827). L.C. 14/4/1827.
Int. Management; or, The Prompter Puzzled (H.² M. 29/9/1828).
L.C. H.² 29/9/1828. 12° [1830]; Cumberland, vol. xxxviii.
[An adaptation of Le bénéficiaire by T. de Lambert and Étienne.]
F. Rhyme and Reason (D.L. T. 11/11/1828). L.C. Adel. 21/10/1826.
[I do not know whether the L.C. play is the same as that given
at D.L. or not.]
C. The Widows Bewitched (C.G. T. 3/2/1829). L.C. 16/1/1829.
F. False and Constant (W.L. M. 23/11/1829). Lacy, vol. xvi;
Dicks 646.
[Said to have been given at H.² 16/6/1823 and Queen's,
23/11/1829.]
Ba. Honest Frauds; or, Money and Music (H.² 29/7/1830). L.C.
25/5/1830.
Ba. Scheming and Seeming; or, Mimic Art and Attic Science (Adel.
Th. 7/10/1830). L.C. 1/10/1830 [as Seeming and Scheming; or,
A. S. and M. A.].
C. Capers and Coronets (Queen's, M. 4/5/1835). Duncombe, vol. xvii.
Ba. French Polish (Olym. 17/2/1840). L.C. 28/10/1839.
C. Belford Castle; or, The Scottish Gold Mine (H.² Th. 19/6/1841).
L.C. 7/6/1841. Dicks 617.
Ca. The Rights of Woman (Strand, M. 5/6/1843). L.C. 20/11/1843
[as The R. of W.; or, The Rose and Thistle].
Ba. Sharp Practice. L.C. Strand, 10/8/1843. Lacy, vol. lv.

LYON, T. E.
F. Wife Hunting; or, A Hint for Duelling. L.C. C.L. 8/5/1844.
D. The Battle of Life (C.L. M. 4/1/1847). L.C. 7/1/1847.

LYONS, CHARLES.
F. Templars' Tricks; or, Financeering (Crow-street, Dublin, 7/5/1814).

LYTTON, Baron [EDWARD GEORGE EARLE LYTTON BULWER-LYTTON].
D. The Duchesse de la Vallière (C.G. W. 4/1/1837). L.C. 2/1/1837. 8° 1836 [*bis*]; *Dicks* 847.
D. The Lady of Lyons; or, Love and Pride (C.G. Th. 15/2/1838). L.C. 9/2/1838. 8° 1839 [10 editions]; 8° 1841; 8° [1848]; *Dicks* 188; *Lacy*, vol. xxxiv.
D. Richelieu; or, The Conspiracy (C.G. Th. 7/3/1839). C.G. 1838. 8° 1839; *Dicks* 317.
D. The Sea-Captain; or, The Birth-Right (H.² Th. 31/10/1839). L.C. 28/10/1839. 8° 1839; *Dicks* 311.
C. Money (H.² T. 8/12/1840). L.C. 1839. 8° 1840; *Dicks* 318.
[For his later work see the *Collected Works* 8° 1873–5 or the *Life* by T. Cooper 8° 1873.]

MABERLEY, Mrs.
Oa. A Day near Turin (E.O.H. Th. 6/5/1841). L.C. 6/5/1841.

McALISTER, JOSEPH.
T. Winkelried. 12° 1837.
[A translation from the German of K. H. W. Völcker.]

MACARTHY, —
Ba. Charles O'Malley, the Irish Dragoon (Olym. M. 4/12/1843). L.C. 2/4/1841. *Dicks* 866.
[It is possible that this was acted in 1841, when Lever's novel, on which it is based, was published.]

MACARTNEY, CHARLES JUSTIN.
C.O. The Vow. 8° [1802?; Sheffield].

MACDONALD, W. B.
D. Faust. 12° 1838 [Dumfries]; 12° 1842.
[A translation of Goethe's drama.]

MACFARREN, GEORGE.
Bsq.O. Ah! what a Pity!!! or, The Dark Knight and the Fair Lady (E.O.H. M. 28/9/1818). L. 114 M. [14/9/1818].
Ba. Sir Peter Pry; or, Male Curiosity (Cob. W. 9/6/1819).
Int. Winning a Husband; or, Seven's the Main (Cob. 20/9/1819). *Dicks* 971; *Cumberland Minor*, vol. V.
M.D. The Horatii and Curatii (Cob. M. 3/1/1820).
O.D. Gil Blas at 17, 25, 52 (Lyc. Th. 15/8/1822). L. 127 M. [28/6/1822]. *Dicks* 698.
[Music Moss.]
D. Edward the Black Prince; or, The Glories of England in 1356 (Cob. M. 19/8/1822).
M.D. Guy Fawkes; or, The Gunpowder Treason (Cob. 9/1822). 8° 1822; *Cumberland Minor*, vol. iv; *Lacy*, vol. cxiv.
Ext. Tom and Jerry in France (Cob. 2/12/1822).
D. George III, the Father of his People (Cob. 30/8/1824).
D.O. Malvina (D.L. S. 28/1/1826). L.C. 1/1826. 8° [1826]; 8° 1826 [2nd]; *Cumberland*, vol. xxxv
[Music T. Cooke.]

Fairy Tale. Oberon; or, The Charmed Horn (D.L. M. 27/3/1826).
L.C. 23/3/1826. 8° 1826.
[Music T. Cooke.]

M.D. The Boy of Santillane; or, Gil Blas and the Robbers of Asturia
(D.L. M. 16/4/1827). L.C. 7/4/1827. 8° 1827; *Dicks* 698 [as
Gil Blas; or, The Boy of Santillane]; *Cumberland*, vol. xxxvi.
[Music T. Cooke and Blewitt.]

D. The March of Intelleck; or, Family Masquerading (Surrey, M.
27/8/1827). *Cumberland Minor*, vol. xii.

M.D. The Talisman; or, The Genii of the Elements (Surrey, M.
7/4/1828). 8° 1828.
[Music Blewitt.]

Oa. Auld Robin Grey (Surrey, S. 17/5/1828).
[Music A. Lee.]

C.O. My Old Woman (Surrey, W. 14/1/1829). *Dicks* 581.

P. Harlequin Reformer (Surrey, 1831).

D. The Danish Wife (Queen's, Th. 10/3/1831).

Oa. The Piccadilloes (Queen's, W. 13/4/1831). 8° [1831; Songs, Duets].

O. Lestocq; or, The Fête of the Hermitage (C.G. S. 21/2/1835).
L.C. 18/2/1835. 8° [1835]; *Cumberland*, vol. xxxiii.
[An adaptation of Scribe, *Lestocq; ou, l'intrigue et l'amour*
(Paris, 24/5/1834); Auber's music arranged by T. Cooke.]

Oa. Innocent Sins; or, Peccadilloes (Cob. 8/1836). L.C. 15/8/1836.
[See *The Piccadilloes* above.]

O. The Devil's Opera (Lyc. M. 13/8/1838). L.C. 8/1838. *Acting
Nat. Drama*, vol. v.

F. Latin, Love and War; or, If the Cap fits ye, wear it (H.² M.
1/4/1839). L.C. 2/4/1839. *Duncombe*, vol. xxxvi.

M. The Emblematical Tribute in Honour of Her Majesty's Nuptials
(D.L. 10/2/1840).

C.O. The Matrimonial Ladder (E.O.H. Th. 25/3/1841).
[Music A. Thomas.]

O. Don Quixote (D.L. T. 3/2/1846). L.C. 26/1/1846 [as *The
Adventures of D. Q.*].
[Music G. A. MacFarren.]

MACKENZIE, T. H.
The Spanish Father [1808].
[See *The "Stage" Cyclopedia*.]

McLAREN, ARCHIBALD.
[For his earlier plays see *A History of Late Eighteenth Century Drama*,
p. 284.]

F. The First Night's Lodging. 12° [? 1800].

M.Ent. The Monopolizer Outwitted! 12° 1800; 12° 1801.

M.Ent. The Soldier's Widow; or, The Happy Relief. 8° 1800.

M.D. The Chance of War; or, The Villain Reclaimed. 12° 1801.

M.Ent. Fashion; or, The World as it goes. 12° 1802.

M.Ent. The First of April; or, The Fool's Errand (Strolling Players in
Jersey, 1802). 12° 1802.

M.D. The Lottery Chance; or, The Drunkard Reclaim'd. 12° 1803.

M.D. Britons to Arms; or, The Consul in England. 12° 1803.

M.D. Saw ye Bony coming? or, The Female Volunteers. 12° 1804.

M.Ent. A Touch at the Times; or, An Attempt to please. 12° 1804.

M.Ent. The Coronation!! or, The British Captives in France. 12° 1804.

M.Ent. A Soldier and a Sailor. 12° 1805 [see the next play].
[An altered version of *The Soldier's Widow*.]
Bsq. The Old Roscius; or, The World for Novelty...to which is added A Soldier and a Sailor. 12° 1805.
O.F. The Highland Drover. 12° [1805].
[His earlier play of the same title altered.]
M.Ent. The Days we live in; or, A Tale of Eighteen Hundred and Five. 12° 1805.
M.Ent. A Dish of All Sorts. 12° 1806.
O.F. A Wife to be Sold; or, Who Bids Most?...to which is added The Slaves. 12° 1807.
M.D. Kenneth, King of Scots; or, The Female Archers. 12° 1807.
[A revised version of *The Chance of War*.]
M.Ent. The British Carpenter; or, The Irishman in France. 12° 1808.
M.D. Bessie Bell and Mary Gray; or, Love in the Highlands. 8° 1808.
M.D. The Spanish Heroine; or, The Female Patriots. 12° 1808.
M.Ent. How to grow wise; or, Folly exposed. 12° 1808 [Dumfries].
O.F. London out of Town; or, The Family Genius's. 12° 1809.
M.D. The Private Theatre; or, The Highland Funeral. 12° 1809.
O.F. Whimsicality; or, Great News from France. 12° 1810.
O.F. Empress and No Empress; or, Mr. Bony's Wedding. 12° 1810.
D.Sk. Spite and Malice; or, A Laughable Accident...to which is added an Humble Attempt to convert The Gentle Shepherd into English Prose. 12° 1811.
O.F. Paddy Bull; or, A Cure for the Gout. 12° 1811.
O.F. The Elopement; or, A Caution to Young Ladies...to which is added The Duelists. 12° 1811.
O.F. The Swindlers; or, Diamond cut Diamond. 12° 1812.
O.F. The Tricks of London; or, Honesty the Best Policy. 12° 1812.
M.D. The Prisoner of War; or, A Most Excellent Story. 12° 1813.
[Also known as *The Resource of War*.]
M.D. The Irish Girl; or, Cossack and No Cossack. 12° 1813.
M.Ent. Good News! Good News! or, The Case is Altered. 8° 1814.
M.Ent. Forget and Forgive; or, All made up again. 12° 1814.
M.D. The Last Shift; or, The Prisoner's Released. 12° 1814.
M.Ent. Mr. Napie's Reception in Elba. 12° 1814.
M.Ent. Retaliation; or, An Hour and a Half in Paris. 12° 1815.
M.D. The Highland Chiefs. 12° 1815; The Maid of Lorn; or, The Castle of Dunstaffnage. 12° 1815.
M.Ent. The Man in the Moon; or, Tumble Down Naps. 8° 1815.
M.Ent. The Man-Trap; or, A Scene in Germany. 8° 1816.
M.Ent. The Deceiver; or, Old Robin and his Niece. 12° 1816.
M.Ent. The Debating Club; or, The Noble Revenge. 12° 1816.
M.Ent. The Coup-de-Main; or, Love and War in Yankyland. 12° 1816.
[A revised version of *The Coup de Main* (1784).]
M.Ent. Live and Hope; or, The Emigrant Prevented. 12° 1817.
M.D. Second Sight; or, A Tale of Other Days. 12° 1817.
M.D. The Highland Robbers; or, Such Things Were...To which is added Health to the Rich and Work to the Poor: an Interlude. 12° 1817.
M.Ent. The Half-way House; or, The Battle of the Dandies. 8° 1818.
[This was also published with the titles reversed.]
M.D. Oliver Cromwell; or, The Scotch Regalia...To which is added Imitation Tea; or, Death in Disguise. An Interlude. 12° 1818.

M.D. The Siege of Berwick; or, The Brothers Devoted. 8° 1818.
M.D. Filial Duty; or, The Heart of Midlothian. 12° 1819.
[Based on Scott's novel.]
M.D. Wallace the Brave; or, The Siege of Perth. 12° 1819.
Int. The Highland Wedding...To which is added, The Highland
Funeral. A Farce. 12° 1819.
M.Ent. Females Beware! or, The Ingenious Footman. 8° 1820; The
Plagiarist Detected; or, The Ingenious Footman. 8° 1820.
M.D. The Isle of Mull; or, The Lady on the Rock. 12° 1820.
Int. Folly Exposed! or, Miss Sootie's Masquerade. A Satirical,
Ironical, Some-let-at all, None-wit-at all, Bombastical, Fantastical,
not Spurious but quite Curious Interlude. 12° 1820.
M.D. The Unfortunate Youth; or, Bear the worse, and hope for the
better. 12° 1821.
Int. Food for Mirth; or, Half an Hour in the Highlands...To which
is added A Peep at the Lord Mayor's Show. A Dramatic Piece.
8° 1821; Dead and Not Dead, or, Half an Hour in the Highlands.
8° 1821.
Int. The Royal Visit; or, All Alive in Auld Reekie. 12° 1822.
M.Ent. The New Marriage Act; or, Look before you leap. 12° 1822.
M.Ent. Juvenile Friendship; or, Ancient Animosities. 8° 1822.
O.F. All the World's a Fair; or, A Merry Day at Greenwich. 12° 1822.
O.F. The Runaway Bride; or, The New Marriage Act Repealed.
12° 1823.
O.F. The Three Wishes; or, The King's Frolic. 8° 1823.
F. Credulity; or, The Force of Superstition...To which is added
A Chip of the Old Block; or, The Pirates Repulsed. An Interlude.
12° 1823.
Int. Music has Charms; or, The Marrow-bones and Cleavers. 12° 1824.
Int. The Ups and Downs of Life; or, The Fortunate Irishman.
12° 1824.
M.D. The Beautiful Insane; or, The Rose of Morven. 12° 1824.
Int. Arrogance brought down. 12° 1824.
Bsq. The Affair of Honour; or, The Dishonourable Affair. 12° 1825.
Int. Eccentricity; or, Every One has his Whim. 12° 1826.
[Many of these were acted in Scots theatres.]

MACPHERSON, J.
D. Edward I. 8° 1845.

MACREADY, WILLIAM CHARLES.
M.D. Marmion (Newcastle, 1814).
[Based on Scott's poem.]
M.D. Rokeby (Newcastle, 1814).
[Based on Scott's poem.]
T. Macbeth (C.G. 6/11/1837).
T. King Lear (C.G. 25/1/1838). *Lacy.*
[See G. C. D. Odell, *op. cit.* ii. 194–6.]
T. Coriolanus (C.G. 12/3/1838).
[See *ib.* ii. 197–8.]
C. The Tempest (C.G. 13/10/1838).
[See *ib.* ii. 200–1.]
D. Henry V (C.G. 1839).
[See *ib.* ii. 201–2.]

C. As You Like It (D.L. 1/10/1842). *Lacy.*
　　[See *ib.* ii. 205–7.]
D. Philip van Artevelde (P'cess, M. 22/11/1847). L.C. 13/11/1847.
　　[Stage version of the play by *Sir HENRY TAYLOR.*]
D. The Bridal. *Acting Nat. Drama,* vol. i.
　　[Stage version from Beaumont and Fletcher.]

MADDOX, FREDERICK MORE.
　M.D. Infanticide; or, The Bohemian Mother (Cob. M. 15/9/1823).
　　Duncombe.
　M.D. Frederick the Great; or, The King and the Deserter (Cob.
　　15/9/1824). *Dicks* 597; *Cumberland Minor,* vol. xiii.
　D. The Violet (P'cess, T. 18/11/1845). L.C. 11/11/1845.

MAES, FERDINAND.
　M.D. Ignacio. L.C. Albert, 3/3/1845.

MALKIN, BENJAMIN HEATH.
　T. Almahide and Hamet. 8° 1804.
　　[Based on Dryden, *The Conquest of Granada.*]

MANGIN, Rev. EDWARD.
　T. Hector. 8° 1810 [Bath].
　　[A translation from the French of J. C. J. L. de Lancival.]

MANNERS, GEORGE.
　D. Edgar; or, Caledonian Feuds (C.G. F. 9/5/1806). L. 85 M.
　　[29/4/1806; as *E.; or, Northern F.*]. 8° 1806.
　　[Based on Mrs Radcliffe, *The Castles of Athlen and Dumblayne.*]

MARSTON, JOHN WESTLAND.
　T. The Patrician's Daughter (D.L. S. 10/12/1842; S.W. W. 26/8/1846).
　　L.C. 3/12/1842. 8° 1841; 8° 1842 [3 editions]; *Lacy,* vol. xliii.
　D.Poem. Gerald. 12° 1842.
　F. Borough Politics (H.² S. 27/6/1846). L.C. 24/6/1846. *Acting Nat.
　　Drama,* vol. xii.
　D. The Heart and the World (H.² 4/10/1847). L.C. 18/10/1847.
　　8° 1847.
　T. Strathmore (H.² W. 20/6/1849). L.C. 16/6/1849. 8° 1849; *Lacy,*
　　vol. lvi.
　　[Based on Scott, *Old Mortality.*]
　　[For his later plays see *A History of Late Nineteenth Century
　　Drama,* pp. 478–9.]

MASON, JAMES.
　T. The Natural Son. 8° 1805 [Liverpool].

MASTERS, MARTIN KEDGWIN.
　C. Lost and Found (Lyc. W. 2/1/1811). L. 91 M. [22/2/1810].
　　8° 1811.

MASTERTON, CHARLES.
　T. The Seducer. 8° 1811.
　T. Bentivoglio. 8° 1824.
　D.R. The Wreck. 8° 1824.
　D.R. Blighted Love. 8° 1832.
　T. The Stern Resolve. 8° 1837.

MATHEWS, CHARLES JAMES.
　Ent. Country Cousins (Lyc. M. 28/2/1820).

Ent. Christmas at Brighton (Lyc. 2/1820).
Ent. The Hypochondriac (Lyc. 1/3/1821).
Ext. Pong Wong (H.² W. 13/9/1826). L.C. 28/8/1826 [as *P. W.; or, The Horoscope*].
Ent. The Home Circuit; or, Cockney Gleanings (Lyc. 8/3/1827).
C. The Court Jester (H.² Th. 19/7/1832). L.C. 7/7/1832.
C. My Wife's Mother (H.² W. 3/7/1833). L.C. 27/6/1833. *Dicks* 659; *Lacy*, vol. xxiii.
C. Pyramus and Thisbe; or, The Party Wall (H.² W. 14/8/1833).
Ba. Truth; or, A Glass too much (Adel. M. 10/3/1834). L.C. 8/3/1834. *Acting Nat. Drama*, vol. iii.
M.D. Mandrin (Adel. M. 28/9/1835). L.C. 23/9/1835. *Dicks* 931.
F. The Hump-backed Lover (Olym. M. 7/12/1835). L.C. 7/12/1835. *Dicks* 660; *Cumberland*, vol. xii.
Ba. He would be an Actor (Olym. M. 31/10/1836). L.C. 1837.
Ba. Why did you Die? (Olym. M. 20/11/1837). L.C. 1837. *Dicks* 662; *Acting Nat. Drama*, vol. ii.
Ba. The Ring-doves (Olym. M. 11/12/1837). L.C. 9/12/1837. *Dicks* 661; *Mod. Eng. Com. Th.* Series ii; *Acting Nat. Drama*, vol. iii.
Ba. The Black Domino (Olym. Th. 18/1/1838). L.C. 1837. *Acting Nat. Drama*, vol. iii.
　　[An adaptation of Scribe, *Le domino noir* (Paris, 2/12/1837), with music by Auber, adapted by W. Penson.]
F. Patter versus Clatter (Olym. 21/5/1838; C.G. W. 15/9/1841). L.C. 19/5/1838. *Dicks* 660; *Lacy*.
Int. Two in the Morning (C.G. S. 3/10/1840). L.C. 23/9/1840. *Dicks* 946; *Lacy*, vol. xx.
F. The Dowager (C.G. S. 3/12/1842). L.C. H.² 5/12/1842. *Dicks* 662; *Lacy*, vol. xxii.
　　[An adaptation of *Le château de ma mère*.]
F. Used Up (H.² T. 6/2/1844). See *D. BOUCICAULT*.
C. A Match for a King (H.² M. 7/10/1844). L.C. 14/10/1844.
　　[A version of *Don Caesar de Bazan*.]
F. Astounding Phenomena (Lyc. M. 7/2/1848). L.C. 18/12/1847.

MATURIN, CHARLES ROBERT.

T. Bertram; or, The Castle of St. Aldobrand (D.L. Th. 9/5/1816). 8° 1816 [7 editions]; *Cumberland*, vol. xliii; *Dicks* 61.
　　[Music Cooke.]
T. Manuel (D.L. S. 8/3/1817). L. 68 S. [15/2/1817]. 8° 1817 [3 editions].
　　[Music Cooke.]
T. Fredolfo (C.G. W. 12/5/1819). L. 114 M. [19/4/1819]. 8° 1819.

MAURICE, THOMAS.

[For his earlier works see *A History of Late Eighteenth Century Drama*, p. 286.]
T. The Fall of the Mogul, Founded on an interesting Portion of Indian History, and attempted partly on the Greek Model. With other occasional poems. 8° 1806.

MAYHEW, EDWARD.

F. Make your Wills (H.² S. 16/7/1836). L.C. 14/7/1836. *Cumberland*, vol. xxxv; *Lacy*, vol. lix.
　　[Written in collaboration with *G. SMITH*.]

MAYHEW, HENRY.
F.   The Wandering Minstrel (Fitzroy, Th. 16/1/1834). *Dicks* 1040;
     Lacy, vol. xxiii.
F.   "But however—" (H.² T. 30/10/1838). L.C. 24/10/1838. *Mod.
     Eng. Com. Th.* vol. i; *Acting Nat. Drama*, vol. v; *Lacy*, Supp. vol. iii.
     [Written in collaboration with *H. BAYLIS*.]
Ba. The Young Sculptor (St J. M. 11/2/1839). L.C. 1839.

MAYHEW, THOMAS.
D.   Ambition; or, Marie Mignot (H.² M. 13/9/1830). L.C. 7/9/1830.
     12° 1830; *Dicks* 781; *Richardson; Cumberland*, vol. xxxiv.

MEADOWS, THOMAS.
F.   Who's to Blame; or, No Fool like an Old One. 8° 1805; 8° 1813
     [in *Thespian Gleanings*].
Ba. My Husband's Secret; or, Natural Magic (Adel. Th. 21/11/1822).
     L. 85 S. [19/9/1822].

[MEDINA, L. H.
D.   Nick of the Woods (Vic. M. 29/4/1839). *Dicks* 547.
     [Originally produced in New York, 5/2/1838.]

MELLERS, HENRY.
C.O. The Ambassadress. L.C. Grecian, 29/6/1848.
     [An adaptation of Scribe and de Saint Georges, *L'ambassadrice*
     (Paris, 21/9/1836), with music by Auber.]

MELLISH, JOSEPH CHARLES.
T.   Mary Stuart. 8° 1801.
     [A translation of Schiller, *Maria Stuart* (1801).]

MELVILLE, C.
D.   Barnaby Rudge (E.O.H. M. 28/6/1841). See *C. SELBY*.

MELVILLE, H.
D.   The Road to Happiness (Standard, M. 11/12/1848). L.C.
     14/12/1848.
D.   Punishment in Six Stages (Standard, M. 5/2/1849). L.C. 19/1/1849.

MENDHAM, —
D.   The Adventures of Ulysses; or, The Return to Ithaca. 8° 1811.

MENZIES, KENNETH.
T.   Tyrrel. 8° 1841 [Edinburgh]. [Written in collaboration with
     E. TAIT.]

MILDENHALL, T.
Ba. A Sprig of Shillelah; or, An Irishman in all his Glory (S.W. M.
     26/12/1836).
F.   The Post of Honour (Lyc. M. 8/4/1844). L.C. 1/4/1844 [as *The
     P. of H.; or, The Valiant Sentinel*]. *Duncombe*, vol. xlix; *Lacy*,
     vol. xlviii.
C.   The Governor's Wife (Lyc. Th. 7/8/1845). L.C. 30/7/1845.
     Dicks 990; *Lacy*, vol. xxxi.
D.   The Death Wedding (Queen's, 27/10/1845). L.C. 24/10/1845.
Ca. Sister and I (Lyc. Th. 4/6/1846). L.C. 23/5/1846. *Dicks* 383;
     Duncombe, vol. lvi.
D.   The Stolen Will; or, The Haunted House (Queen's, 7/12/1846).
     L.C. 12/12/1846.

Bsq. Joan of Arc; or, The Maid of All-he-uns (Olym. M. 5/4/1847).
L.C. 3/4/1847.
D. The Ship of Glass (Queen's, M. 5/4/1847). L.C. 3/4/1847.
F. Brigands in the Bud (Olym. M. 22/1/1849). L.C. 19/12/1848.
Duncombe, vol. lxiii.

MILLER, HORATIO.
F. The Fond Uncle. L.C. Manchester, 11/11/1843.

MILLINGEN, JOHN GIDEON.
O.F. The Bee Hive (Lyc. S. 19/1/1811). L. 53 S. [12/1/1811]. 8° 1811;
Cumberland, vol. xxx.
[Music Horn.]
Int. Ladies at Home; or, Gentlemen, we can do without you (H.² S.
7/8/1819). L. 23 L. [30/7/1819]. *Lacy*, vol. x.
O.F. The Illustrious Stranger (D.L. Th. 4/10/1827). See *J.KENNEY*.
D. The King's Fool; or, The Old Man's Curse (Vic. W. 17/7/1833).
F. Who'll lend me a Wife? (Vic. T. 22/7/1834). *Dicks* 647; *Dun-
combe*, vol. xviii; *Lacy*, vol. iii.
D. The Miser's Daughter. 12° 1835.
Ba. Borrowed Feathers (Queen's, F. 29/1/1836). *Dicks* 967; *Dun-
combe*, vol. xx.

MILLS, JOHN.
C. Sharps and Flats. L.C. Edinburgh, 9/3/1846.

MILMAN, Rev. HENRY HART.
T. Fazio (Surrey, 22/12/1816, as *The Italian Wife*; C.G. Th. 5/2/1818).
L. 113 M. [7/3/1818; printed copy]. 8° 1815 [Oxford]; 8° 1816
[Oxford; 2nd]; 8° 1818 [4 editions]; *Dicks* 22; *Lacy*, vol. lxvi.
D. Samor. 8° 1818 [2 editions].
D.Poem. The Martyr of Antioch. 8° 1822.
D.Poem. The Fall of Jerusalem. 8° 1820 [*bis*]; 8° 1821; 8° 1822.
D.Poem. Belshazzar. 8° 1822.
D.Poem. Anne Boleyn. 8° 1826.

MILNER, H. H.
F. The Philosopher. 8° 1819.
[A translation of the German play attributed (wrongly) to
Lessing.]

MILNER, H. M.
D.R. Barmecide; or, The Fatal Offspring (D.L. T. 3/11/1818).
L. 113 M. [28/10/1818]. 8° 1818.
[Music Cooke.]
M.D. The Jew of Lubeck; or, The Heart of a Father (D.L. T.
11/5/1819). L. 75 S. [25/3/1819]. 8° 1819 [*bis*].
[Music Cooke.]
Ba. Twelve Precisely; or, A Night at Dover (Olym. M. 1/1/1821;
H.² 11/10/1822). L. 23 L. [23/12/1820].
D.D. The Bandit of the Blind Mine (Cob. M. 15/10/1821). 12° [1821].
F. Bears not Beasts; or, Four Legs better than Two (Cob. M.
3/12/1821). *Dicks* 387.
M.D. The Temple of Death (Cob. W. 26/12/1821). 12° [1821].
M.D. Frankenstein; or, The Demon of Switzerland (Cob. M.
18/8/1823). *Lacy*, vol. lxxv; *Duncombe*, vol. ii [as *The Man and
the Monster*].
[Based on Mrs Shelley's romance.]

M.D. Alfred the Great (Cob. M. 9/2/1824).

M.D. Preventive Service; or, The Romance of the Coast (Cob. M. 23/2/1824).

M.D. Alonzo the Brave (Cob. 19/6/1826). *Duncombe*, vol. ii.

M.D. The Lovers of Verona; or, Romeo and Juliet (Cob. M. 4/9/1826).

C. 102; or, The Veteran and his Projeny (Cob. M. 25/6/1827; D.L. 6/6/1838). L.C. D.L. 2/6/1838 [titles reversed]. *Dicks* 651; *Duncombe*, vol. lxvi; *Lacy*, vol. xxxvi.

M.D. The Hut of the Red Mountains; or, Thirty Years of a Gambler's Life (Cob. M. 3/9/1827). 8° 1827; 12° [1830].
   [Based on V. Ducagne, *Trente ans; ou, la vie d'un joueur*.]

M.D. The Gambler's Fate; or, A Lapse of Twenty Years (D.L. M. 15/10/1827). L.C. 15/10/1827. 8° 1827; *Dicks* 308.
   [It appears that both these versions were by Milner.]

M.D. St. Valentine's Eve; or, The Fair Maid of Perth (Cob. M. 23/6/1828).
   [This dramatisation of Scott's novel also appeared as *The F. M. of P.; or, The Battle of the Inch*.]

M.D. The Spirit of the Waters; or, Undine and the Goblin Page (Cob. M. 9/3/1829).

M.D. Masaniello; or, The Dumb Girl of Portici (Cob. M. 3/5/1829). *Cumberland Minor*, vol. i.
   [An adaptation of Scribe and Delavigne, *La muette de Portici* (Paris, 29/1/1828), with music by Auber.]

F. Woman's Wit; or, Who's to have him? (Cob. M. 23/11/1829).

F. Dead Men's Shoes (Cob. M. 23/11/1829).

R.D. Mazeppa; or, The Wild Horse of Tartary (R.A. M. 4/4/1831). *Dicks* 620; *Cumberland Minor*, vol. v.
   [Based on Byron's poem.]

D. Victorine (S.W. M. 9/1/1832). *Dicks* 352.

Ba. Chevy Chase; or, The Battle of Otterburn (R.A. M. 23/4/1832).

D. The Tower of Nesle; or, The Dark Gondola (Cob. M. 3/9/1832). *Duncombe*, vol. x.

D. Gustavus of Sweden; or, The Masked Ball (Vic. F. 8/11/1833). *Dicks* 630; *Duncombe*, vol. xiii.

Ba. The Blind Beggar of Bethnal Green (Vic. W. 19/2/1834).

M.D. The Vacant Chair; or, Scotland and Algiers (S.W. T. 18/11/1834).

D. The Idiot Queen; or, The Chapel of Miracles (S.W. M. 19/1/1835).

D. The Temple of Death (S.W. M. 27/4/1835).
   [See above under 26/12/1821.]

M.D. Don Juan's Early Days (C.L. 183/). *Duncombe*, vol. xxxv.
   [Written in collaboration with *E. STIRLING*.]

Ent. Dick Turpin's Ride to York (Surrey, M. 30/8/1841). *Dicks* 632.

MINTON, ANN.

C. The Comedy of A Wife to be Lett...compressed into two Acts. 8° 1802.
   [An adaptation of Mrs Haywood's comedy.]

MITFORD, MARY RUSSELL.

T. Julian (C.G. S. 15/3/1823). 8° 1823 [*bis*]; 8° 1827 [with *Foscari*]; *Cumberland*, vol. xxxii.

T. The Foscari (C.G. S. 4/11/1826). L.C. 30/10/1826. 8° 1826; 8° 1827; *Cumberland*, vol. xxxiv; *Lacy*, vol. lxxxvi.

Dramatic Scenes. 8° 1827.

T. Rienzi (D.L. Th. 9/10/1828). L.C. 4/10/1828. 12° 1828 [4 editions];
   Cumberland, vol. xxiv; *Lacy*, vol. xc.
T. Inez de Castro. L.C. 28/2/1831. *Dicks* 672.
T. Charles I (Vic. W. 2/7/1834). 8° 1834; *Dicks* 667.
   [See copy of the *Charles I* in L.C. 15/10/1825, when a licence
   was refused, and the accompanying correspondence.]
R.D. Sadak and Kalasrade (E.O.H. M. 20/4/1835). L.C. 4/4/1835.
   8° [1835].
   [Music Packer.]

MOIR, GEORGE.
T. The Piccolomini. 8° 1827 [Edinburgh].
   [A translation of Schiller, *Die Piccolomini* and *Wallensteins Tod*.]

MOLINI, Miss.
D. William Tell. 8° 1846.
   [A translation of Schiller's drama.]

MONCRIEFF, WILLIAM THOMAS.
Spec. Moscow (Regency, 1810).
O.F. The Diamond Arrow; or, The Postmaster's Wife, and the
   Mayor's Daughter (Olym. M. 18/12/1815). L. 104 M. [14/12/1815].
   8° 1816; *Richardson Minor*, vol. iii; *Cumberland Minor*, vol. x.
   [Music G. W. Reeve.]
Ba. All at Coventry; or, Love and Laugh (Olym. M. 8/1/1816).
   L. 63 S. [2/1/1816]. 8° [1816]; 8° 1825; *Dicks* 912; *Richardson
   Minor*, vol. ii; *Cumberland*, vol. iii; *Lacy*, vol. lix.
Ba. Joconde; or, Le Prince Troubadour (Olym. M. 29/1/1816).
   L. 63 S. [23/1/1816]. *Richardson Minor*, vol. ii; *Dicks* 538;
   Cumberland Minor, vol. xii.
O.Ext. Giovanni in London; or, The Libertine Reclaimed (Olym. F.
   26/12/1817; S.W. M. 19/4/1830). *London Stage*, vol. iii; *Cum-
   berland*, vol. xvii; *B.D.* vol. iii; 8° 1825; *Dicks* 104; 8° 1818
   [Songs, Duets, Chorusses].
Ba. Rochester; or, King Charles the Second's Merry Days (Olym. M.
   16/11/1818). L. 72 S. [14/11/1818]. 8° 1819; 8° 1825; *Dicks* 528;
   Lacy, vol. lxxxiii; *Richardson Minor*, vol. i; *Cumberland Minor*,
   vol. xi.
Ba. The Dandy Family and the Ascot Jockies (R.A. M. 15/6/1818).
C. Wanted a Wife; or, A Cheque on my Banker's (D.L. M. 3/5/1819).
   L. 73 S. [27/4/1819]. 8° 1819.
   [See *A Cheque on my Banker* (D.L. 1821) under *UNKNOWN
   AUTHORS*.]
C. Pigeons and Crows (H.² S. 28/8/1819). L. 75 S. [17/8/1819].
   [This was claimed by *T. HOOK* but the bills distinctly advertise
   Moncrieff as the author.]
Ba. The Green Dragon; or, I've quite forgot (Adel. S. 23/10/1819).
   L. 73 S. [8/10/1819].
D. Ivanhoe; or, The Jew of York (Cob. 24/1/1820). 8° 1820; *Dun-
   combe*, vol. xix.
D. The Lear of Private Life; or, Father and Daughter (Cob. Th.
   27/4/1820). *Dicks* 924; *Richardson Minor*, vol. i; *Cumberland
   Minor*, vol. vii.
   [Based on Mrs Opie, *Father and Daughter*.]

M.D. The Shipwreck of the Medusa; or, The Fatal Raft (Cob. M.
 19/6/1820; R.P. M. 16/1/1831). *Richardson Minor*, vol. iv;
 Cumberland Minor, vol. xii.
M.D. The Ravens of Orleans; or, The Forest of Cercotte (Cob. M.
 3/7/1820). *Cumberland Minor*, vol. xv.
M.D. The Vampire (Cob. T. 22/8/1820). *Richardson Minor*, vol. iii.
Bsq.M.D. Teresa Tomkins; or, The Fruits of Geneva (Olym. S.
 24/3/1821). L. 83 S. [13/3/1821]. 8° 1821.
D. A Mother and Son (D.L. T. 24/4/1821). L. 79 S. [4/1821].
F. The Spectre Bridegroom; or, A Ghost in spite of himself (D.L.
 M. 2/7/1821). L. 121 M. [28/6/1821]. 8° 1821; *Dicks* 353;
 Cumberland, vol. xvi; *Lacy*, vol. xxxv.
F. Monsieur Tonson (D.L. Th. 20/9/1821). L. 79 S. [17/9/1821].
 8° 1821; 8° 1824; *Dicks* 115; *French Minor*; *French* 102; *London
 Stage*, vol. iii; *Cumberland*, vol. xvi; *Lacy*, vol. lxxiv.
C. The Lost Life (D.L. T. 13/11/1821). L. 82 S. [12/10/1821].
Ba. Tom and Jerry; or, Life in London (Adel. M. 26/11/1821).
 L. 120 M. [23/11/1821]. 8° 1826; *Dicks* 82; *French Minor N.Y.*;
 Lacy, vol. lxxxviii; *Richardson's New Minor*, vol. i; *Cumberland*,
 vol. xxxiii.
   [Based on Egan's sketches.]
F. The Adventures of a Ventriloquist; or, The Rogueries of Nicholas
 (Adel. 1822; Bath, 18/1/1823). 12° 1822.
Ba. Actors al Fresco (Vauxhall, 1823). 8° [1827; Songs].
   [Music J. Blewitt, T. Cooke and C. E. Horn.]
F. The Secret; or, The Hole in the Wall (Adel. 29/2/1823). 8° 1823;
 8° 1825; *French Minor*, vol. xvii; *Douglas Minor N.Y.* vol. iii;
 Duncombe, vol. iii [as *The Party Wall*].
M.D. Fazio (D.L. M. 27/10/1823).
M.D. The Cataract of the Ganges! or, The Rajah's Daughter (D.L.
 M. 27/10/1823). L. 86 S. [9/10/1823]. 8° 1823; *Richardson* [1830];
 French N.Y. vol. clxxx; *Cumberland*, vol. xxxiii.
M.D. Zoroaster; or, The Spirit of the Star (D.L. M. 19/4/1824).
 L.C. 13/4/1824. 8° 1824 [*bis*].
O.F. The Bashful Man (E.O.H. M. 20/9/1824). *Dicks* 100; *London
 Stage*, vol. iv; *Cumberland Minor*, vol. xv; *Mod. Eng. Com. Th.*
 vol. v; *B.D.* vol. x.
M.D. Jack Sheppard, the Housebreaker; or, London in 1724 (Cob.
 M. 18/4/1825; Vic. M. 21/10/1839, as *J. S.; or, The Progress of Crime*).
Vaud. The Kiss and the Rose; or, Love in the Nursery Grounds
 (Vauxhall, Γ. 10/8/1827). 8° 1827.
F. Home for the Holidays (Surrey, 8/1/1828). 8° 1828 [as *Old Heads
 and Young Shoulders*].
M.D. The Somnambulist; or, The Phantom of the Village (C.G. T.
 19/2/1828). 8° 1828; *Dicks* 224; *Cumberland*, vol. xviii; *Lacy*,
 vol. lxxxvi.
   [An adaptation of Scribe, *La somnambule* (Paris, 6/12/1819).]
Ba. The Irresistibles (Surrey, M. 11/8/1828). *Duncombe*, vol. xv.
D. Monsieur Mallet; or, My Daughter's Letter (Adel. Th. 22/1/1829).
 8° 1851; *Dicks* 936.
   [Music J. Barnett.]
M.D. Father and Daughter; or, The Victim of Seduction (S.W. M.
 9/2/1829).
M.D. The Pestilence of Marseilles; or, The Four Thieves (Surrey,

24   NED

M. 20/10/1829). *Richardson Minor*, vol. ii; *Cumberland Minor*, vol. xi.

[An adaptation of Pixérécourt, *La peste de Marseille* (Paris, 1828).]

Ext. Van Dieman's Land; or, Settlers and Natives (Surrey, Th. 11/2/1830). *Dicks* 918; *Richardson Minor*, vol. iv; *Cumberland Minor*, vol. x.

D. The Heart of London! or, A Sharper's Progress (Adel. M. 15/2/1830; Cob. M. 31/10/1831). L.C. 1829. 8° 1839; *Dicks* 430.

M.D. The Beggar of Cripplegate; or, The Humours of Bluff King Hal (Surrey, S. 6/3/1830; S.W. M. 21/1/1833). *Cumberland Minor*, vol. xi.

M.C. Shakespeare's Festival; or, The New Comedy of Errors (Surrey, F. 23/4/1830). 12° [1830]; *Richardson Minor*, vol. iv; *Cumberland Minor*, vol. x.

M.D. Old Heads on Young Shoulders; or, The House in the Forest (Surrey, F. 7/5/1830).

Vaud. Bringing Home the Bride! or, The Husband's First Journey (Adel. T. 1/3/1831). L.C. 7/2/1831 [with titles reversed]. 8° 1838; *Dicks* 666.

[An adaptation of *Le voyage de la mariée*.]

D. Reform; or, John Bull Triumphant (Cob. M. 14/3/1831). *Richardson Minor*, vol. iv; *Cumberland Minor*, vol. xiii.

D. Gipsy Jack (Cob. 30/5/1831). *Cumberland Minor*, vol. ix.

M.D. Eugene Aram; or, St. Robert's Cave (Surrey, W. 8/2/1832). *Dicks* 312; *Cumberland Minor*, vol. x; *Lacy*, vol. ciii.

C. Peer and Peasant (H.² T. 11/9/1832). L.C. 31/8/1832. 8° 1836; *Dicks* 639.

M.D. Lochinvar; or, The Bridal of Netherby (R.A. M. 24/9/1832).

D. One Fault (Cob. 7/1/1833).

Vaud. How to take up a Bill; or, The Village Vauxhall (City, M. 4/11/1833; Vic. T. 10/11/1835). 8° 1837.

[Based on Melesville, *L'ami bontemps; ou, la maison de mon oncle*.]

D. The Waggoner of Westmoreland (Garrick, 6/1/1834).

Ba. Lestocq (Vic. 2/3/1835). *Duncombe*, vol. xvi.

[An adaptation of Scribe, *Lestocq; ou, l'intrigue et l'amour* (Paris, 24/5/1834), with music by Auber.]

D.Spec. The Jewess; or, The Council of Constance (Vic. M. 30/11/1835). L.C. 13/11/1835. *Dicks* 416; *French N.Y.* vol. cxxviii.

[An adaptation of Scribe, *La Juive* (Paris, 23/2/1835), with music by Halévy.]

O.F. The Parson's Nose! or, The Birth Day Dinner (Vic. T. 8/12/1835). 8° 1837.

[Music G. B. Chapman. An adaptation of Désaugiers, *Le dîner de Madelon; ou, le bourgeois du Marais*. It is said that Moncrieff's play was first acted at the City, 4/11/1833; I have not found a record of this performance.]

F. The Winterbottoms! or, My Aunt, the Dowager (Strand, M. 5/6/1837). L.C. 2/6/1837. 8° 1837.

Ba. Sam Weller; or, The Pickwickians (Strand, M. 10/7/1837; "new edition," Strand, M. 16/4/1838). L.C. 6/7/1837. 8° 1837; *Dicks* 541; *Lacy*, vol. i [new series].

[Based on Dickens' sketches.]

C. The "Tobit's Dog!" (Strand, M. 30/4/1838). L.C. 27/4/1838.
    8° 1838; *Dicks* 438.
F. Tarnation Strange; or, More Jonathans (Strand, F. 3/8/1838).
    L.C. 28/6/1838. 8° 1842; *Dicks* 687.
Int. Foreign Airs and Native Graces (H.² M. 1/7/1839). L.C. 1839.
Ba. The Ballad Singer (Strand, 12/8/1839). L.C. 12/8/1839.
P. Harlequin and Jack of Newbury; or, Baa, baa, Black Sheep and
    the Old Woman of Berkeley (Vic. S. 26/12/1840).
M.D. Giselle; or, The Phantom Night Dancers (S.W. M. 23/8/1841).
    L.C. Liverpool, 6/7/1842. 8° 1842.
    [Music A. Adam. Based on a ballet of *Giselle* (Paris, 28/6/1841).]
D. Perourou, the Bellows Mender; or, The Beauty of Lyons (S.W.
    M. 14/2/1842). *Dicks* 608; *Ames* 89; *Duncombe*, vol. lviii.
D. Far Off; or, The Royal Visit to Edinburgh (S.W. M. 26/9/1842).
D. The Red Farm; or, The Well of St. Marie (S.W. W. 31/8/1842).
    Dicks 611.
M.D. The Wood Wolf of the Black Mountains; or, The Milo of
    Brittany (S.W. M. 28/11/1842).
M.D. The Scamps of London; or, The Cross Roads of Life (S.W.
    M. 13/11/1843). L.C. 9/11/1843 [under sub-title]. 8° 1851;
    Dicks 472; *French* 1213; *Lacy*, vol. lxxxi.
    [Based on Sue, *Les mystères de Paris*.]
F. Borrowing a Husband (P'cess, M. 27/11/1843). L.C. 25/11/1843.
    Dicks 699.
D. Caesar, the Watch Dog of the Castle (Vic. 29/4/1844). *Dicks* 745.
Vaud. The Mistress of the Mill (S.W. W. 17/10/1849). L.C. 5/3/1849).
    12° 1850; *Dicks* 423; *Lacy*, vol. xxi.
    [Based on Mélesville, *Meunière de Marty*.]

MONTAGUE, — and JERVIS, —
M.D. The Heart of Midlothian (Pantheon, Edinburgh, 1/2/1819).

MOORE, THOMAS.
C.O. The Gipsy Prince (H.² F. 24/7/1801). L. 40 S. [17/7/1801].
    [Music M. Kelly.]
T. Montbar; or, The Buccaneers. 8° 1804.
C.O. M.P.; or, The Blue Stocking (Lyc. M. 9/9/1811). L. 93 M.
    [30/8/1811]. 8° 1811.
    [Music by the author.]

"MORETON, LEE" [D. BOUCICAULT].
Int. Lodgings to Let (Strand, M. 6/5/1839). L.C. 5/3/1839.
MORGAN, JAMES.
Bsq. Coriolanus Travestie. 8° 1846 [Liverpool].

MORRIS, GEORGE.
O. The Maid of Saxony. 8° 1842.
D. Brier Cliff. 8° 1842.

MORTON, JOHN MADDISON.
P. Harlequin and Margery Daw; or, The Saucy Slut and the Sea-Saw
    (Adel. Th. 26/12/1833). L.C. 23/12/1833.
C.O. The Dragon (E.O.H. M. 4/8/1834). L.C. 4/8/1834.
    [Music A. Lee.]
F. My First Fit of the Gout (Queen's, M. 9/3/1835). *Lacy*, vol. xi.
F. My Husband's Ghost (H.² T. 26/4/1836). L.C. 4/4/1836. *Cumberland*, vol. xxxv; *Lacy*, vol. xciii.

Ba. The Sentinel (Olym. 23/2/1837). L.C. 10/2/1837 [as *Halt! or, The S.*]. *Acting Nat. Drama*, vol. vii.

Ext. The Spitfire (E.O.H. W. 13/9/1837). L.C. 1837. *Acting Nat. Drama*, vol. ii; *Lacy*, vol. lxii [as *Alabama*].

O.F. The Barbers of Bassora (C.G. S. 11/11/1837). L.C. 1837. *Acting Nat. Drama*, vol. ii.
      [Music J. Hullah.]

F. The Original (C.G. M. 13/11/1837). L.C. 1837. *Acting Nat. Drama*, vol. ii.

F. Chaos is come again; or, The Race Ball (C.G. M. 19/11/1838). L.C. 1838. *Acting Nat. Drama*, vol. vi.

F. Sayings and Doings; or, The Rule of Contrary (C.G. Th. 18/4/1839). L.C. 17/4/1839. *Acting Nat. Drama*, vol. vii.

F. Brother Ben (C.G. W. 9/12/1840). L.C. 7/12/1840. *Lacy*, vol. xxxiv.

F. The Wrong Man (C.G. S. 6/11/1841). L.C. 29/10/1841. *Dicks* 433.

P. Guy Earl of Warwick; or, Harlequin and the Dun Cow (C.G. S. 25/12/1841).
      [Probably the same pantomime occurs in L.C. Birmingham, 17/12/1845.]

F. The Attic Story (D.L. 19/5/1842). *Cumberland*, vol. xlii; *Mod. Eng. Com. Th.* vol. iii.

Ba. Cousin Lambkin (C.G. S. 8/10/1842). L.C. 6/7/1842. *Duncombe*, vol. xlv.

F. The Highwayman (C.G. W. 4/1/1843). L.C. 27/12/1842. 12° 1843.

F. The Thumping Legacy (D.L. S. 11/2/1843; S.W. M. 19/8/1844). L.C. 7/1/1843. 12° [1843].

F. The Double-bedded Room (H.² S. 3/6/1843). L.C. 1/6/1843. *Duncombe*, vol. xlvii.

F. My Wife's Second Floor (P'cess, Th. 22/6/1843). *Duncombe*, vol. xlvii; *Lacy*, vol. xliv.

F. The Wedding Breakfast (H.² Th. 24/8/1843). L.C. 21/8/1843. *Duncombe*, vol. xlvii.

F. My Wife's Come (D.L. W. 18/10/1843). L.C. 11/10/1843. *Duncombe*, vol. xlviii.

F. Slight Mistakes (C.G. W. 18/10/1843). L.C. 7/10/1843.

F. The Railroad Trip (H.² M. 23/10/1843). See *T. MORTON*.

F. The Milliner's Holyday (H.² S. 29/6/1844). L.C. 25/6/1844. *Duncombe*, vol. l; *Lacy*, vol. xxxviii.

F. Young England (H.² S. 30/11/1844). L.C. 26/11/1844. *Duncombe*, vol. li.

F. The Corporal's Wedding (Adel. M. 20/1/1845). L.C. 18/1/1845). L.C. 18/1/1845 [as *The C. W.; or, A Kiss from the Bride*]. *Duncombe*, vol. lii.

F. The Mother and Child are doing well (Adel. M. 24/2/1845). L.C. 1/3/1845. *Acting Nat. Drama*, vol. xi.

F. The King and I (H.² W. 4/6/1845). L.C. 2/6/1845. *Duncombe*, vol. liii; *Lacy*, vol. xl.

F. Who's the Composer? (H.² T. 28/10/1845). L.C. 27/10/1845. *Duncombe*, vol. liv.

F. Lend me Five Shillings (H.² Th. 19/2/1846). *Lacy*, vol. xxx; *Duncombe*, vol. lv.

F. The Irish Tiger (H.² S. 2/5/1846). L.C. 5/5/1846. *Lacy*, vol. xxxiv; *Duncombe*, vol. lvi.

F. Done on Both Sides (Lyc. Th. 24/2/1847). L.C. 22/2/1847.
    Lacy, vol. xxvi; *Duncombe*, vol. lxi.
F. Who did you take me for? (H.² T. 1/6/1847). *Lacy*, vol. cxi;
    Duncombe, vol. lix.
F. Who's my Husband (H.² 16/10/1847). L.C. 18/10/1847. *Lacy*,
    vol. lxxx; *Duncombe*, vol. lx.
F. Box and Cox (Lyc. M. 1/11/1847). L.C. 31/10/1847. *Dicks*
    1059; *Lacy*, vol. v; *Duncombe*, vol. lx; *Mod. Eng. Com. Th.*
    vol. iv.
    [Based on *Une chambre à deux lits;* see *The Double-bedded Room*,
    above.]
Ca. Old Honesty (H.² Th. 6/4/1848). L.C. 8/4/1848. *Duncombe*,
    vol. lxi; *Lacy*, vol. xxxviii.
F. Going to the Derby (Adel. M. 22/5/1848). L.C. 20/5/1848.
    Duncombe, vol. lxii; *Lacy*, vol. xxxvii.
F. Poor Pillicoddy (Lyc. W. 12/7/1848). L.C. 18/7/1848. *Lacy*,
    vol. xxxviii; *Duncombe*, vol. lxii.
D. The Midnight Watch. L.C. M'bone, 5/10/1848. *Lacy*, vol. xxxix;
    Duncombe, vol. lxii.
F. Slasher and Crasher (Adel. M. 13/11/1848). *Duncombe*, vol. lxii;
    Lacy, vol. viii.
F. Your Life's in Danger (H.² W. 20/12/1848). L.C. 14/12/1848.
    Duncombe, vol. lxiii; *Lacy*, vol. ix.
F. The Trumpeter's Wedding (H.² W. 21/3/1849). L.C.
    20/3/1849.
F. John Dobbs; or, A Dab at Anything (Strand, 23/4/1849). L.C.
    21/4/1849. *Duncombe*, vol. lxiv; *Lacy*, vol. vii.
F. A Most Unwarrantable Intrusion (Adel. M. 11/6/1849). L.C.
    18/5/1849. *Duncombe*, vol. lxiv; *Lacy*, vol. vii.
F. Where there's a Will there's a Way (Strand, Th. 6/9/1849). L.C.
    21/7/1849. *Duncombe*, vol. lxiv; *Lacy*, vol. ix.

MORTON, THOMAS.
    [For his earlier plays see *A History of Late Eighteenth Century Drama*,
    pp. 288–9.]
C. Speed the Plough (C.G. S. 8/2/1800). L. 38 S. [29/1/1800].
    8° 1800 [10 editions]; 8° 1805; *Dicks* 23; *Cumberland*, vol. xv;
    Lacy, vol. li; *B.D.* vol. iv.
C.O. The Blind Girl; or, A Receipt for Beauty (C.G. W. 22/4/1801).
    L. 40 S. [26/3/1801]
    [Music Mazzinghi and Reeve.]
C. Beggar my Neighbour; or, A Rogue's a Fool (H.² S. 10/7/1802).
    L. 41 S. [3/7/1802].
    [Partly based on Iffland, *Die Neffen.*]
C. The School of Reform; or, How to rule a Husband (C.G. T.
    15/1/1805). L. 83 M. [8/1/1805]. 8° 1805; *Dicks* 216; *Cumberland*,
    vol. xvii.
C. Town and Country (C.G. T. 10/3/1807). 8° 1807; 8° 1815;
    Dicks 345; *Cumberland*, vol. xxiii.
M.D. The Knight of Snowdoun (C.G. T. 5/2/1811). L. 94 M.
    [12/1/1811]. 8° 1811.
    [Based on Scott, *The Lady of the Lake*. Music Bishop.]
C. Education (C.G. T. 27/4/1813). L. 100 M. [20/3/1813]. 8° 1813;
    Cumberland, vol. xvi.

M.D. The Slave (C.G. T. 12/11/1816). 8° 1816; 8° 1816 [Airs, Duets, Chorusses]; 8° 1818 [2nd]; *Cumberland*, vol. xxii. [Music Bishop.]

F. Who's my Father? (C.G. M. 13/4/1818). L. 113 M. [5/4/1818; as *My Father! Methinks I see my Father!*].

F. A Roland for an Oliver (C.G. Th. 29/4/1819). L. 73 S. [23/4/1819]. 8° 1819; *Lacy*, vol. lxxv; *Dicks* 337. [Based on Scribe, *Une visite à Bedlam* (Paris, 24/4/1818).]

M.R. Henri Quatre; or, Paris in the Olden Time (C.G. S. 22/4/1820). L. 118 M. [7/4/1820]. 8° [1820].

C. A School for Grown Children (C.G. T. 9/1/1827). L.C. 30/12/1826. 8° 1827 [*bis*]; *Dicks* 716.

O.F. The Invincibles (C.G. Th. 28/2/1828). L.C. 27/2/1828. *Cum berland*, vol. xxxvi. [Music A. Lee.]

O. The Sublime and Beautiful (C.G. F. 5/12/1828). L.C. 10/11/1828.

M.D. Peter the Great; or, The Battle of Pultawa (D.L. S. 21/2/1829). L.C. 17/2/1829. [Music Cooke and Dr Carnaby; written in collaboration with *J. KENNEY*. An adaptation of Frédéric du Petit-Méré, *La bataille de Pultawa* (Paris, 1808).]

C. Separation and Reparation (H.² Th. 1/7/1830). L.C. 25/5/1830.

MORTON, THOMAS, Junior.

F. The Windmill (D.L. T. 25/1/1842; S.W. M. 9/8/1847). L.C. 21/1/1842.

F. The Eton Boy (D.L. S. 29/10/1842; Lyc. M. 8/2/1847). L.C. 21/10/1842.

F. The Angel of the Attic (P'cess, S. 27/5/1843). *Duncombe*, vol. xlvi.

F. The Railroad Trip; or, London, Birmingham and Bristol (H.² M. 23/10/1843). L.C. 18/10/1843. *Duncombe*, vol. xlviii. [Written in collaboration with *J. M. MORTON*.]

D. Judith of Geneva (Adel. M. 29/1/1844). L.C. 26/12/1843. *Duncombe*, vol. li.

D. The Drunkard's Glass (Lyc. M. 21/4/1845). L.C. 21/4/1845.

F. Seeing Wright (Adel. M. 29/9/1845). L.C. 25/9/1845.

F. The Dance of the Shirt; or, The Sempstress's Ball (Adel. M. 30/10/1848). L.C. 3/11/1848. *Duncombe*, vol. lxiii. [For his later work see *A History of Late Nineteenth Century Drama*, p. 497.]

MOSER, JOSEPH.

[I have not been able to find exemplars of the following plays listed in the *Biographia Dramatica* (1812) i. 527–8: *Cephisa* (1804), *The Minc'd Pie* (1806), *The Gipsies* (12° 1807), *The Upholsterer* (1807), *The Comet* (1807), *The Best Heart in the World* (12° 1807), *Arabella*, *The Barber of Pera*, *The Bubbles* (1808), *Don Quixote in Barcelona* (12° 1808), *Æsop* (1808), *Nourmahal Empress of Hindostan* (1808), *The Purrah* (1808), *Scenes in Imitation of the Rehearsal* (1809), *An Additional Scene to As You Like It* (1809), *An Additional Scene to The Alchymist* (1809), *British Loyalty* (1809), *The Gleaner* (1809), *The Revenge of Ceres* (1810), *Orbis; or, The World in the Moon* (1810), *Ingratitude* (1810), *The Freeholder* (1810), *Adelfrid* (12° 1811). I assume that the most of these were not printed.]

MUIR, JOHN F.
Int. Family Treacheries. L.C. Adel. Glasgow, 11/4/1846.

MURRAY, ARCHIBALD.
C. Fashionable Life; or, A Season at Cheltenham (Adel. Glasgow, 1845). L.C. 1/2/1845 [printed copy]. 8° 1845 [Glasgow].

MURRAY, WILLIAM HENRY.
M.D. Rob Roy (Glasgow, 10/6/1818).
    [This, like many of Murray's plays, is based on the work of Sir Walter Scott.]
M.D. The Antiquary; or, The Heir of Glen Allen (Edinburgh 20/12/1820).
M.D. Montrose (Edinburgh, 13/3/1822).
M.D. George Heriot; or, The Fortunes of Nigel (Edinburgh, 6/2/1823). L. 127 M [27/1/1823].
M.D. The Heart of Midlothian (Edinburgh, F. 5/3/1824). 18° 1823 [Edinburgh].
M.D. Ivanhoe (Edinburgh, 24/11/1824).
M.D. Redgauntlet (Edinburgh, 28/5/1825). L.C. 24/4/1825.
M.D. Mary, Queen of Scots; or, The Escape from Loch Leven (Edinburgh, 4/7/1825, as *Mary Stuart*; Olym. M. 3/1/1831). L.C. Olym. 1/1/1831. *Dicks* 408; *Lacy*, vol. iv.
C.D. Cramond Brig; or, The Gudeman o' Ballangeich (Edinburgh, 27/2/1826; E.O.H. M. 20/10/1834). *Dicks* 571; *Lacy*, vol. i [new series].
F. No (Edinburgh, 14/11/1826). *Lacy*, vol. i [new series].
D. Gilderoy (Edinburgh, 25/6/1827). *Dicks* 371; *Lacy*, vol. ix.
M.D. The Two Drovers (Edinburgh, 10/11/1828).
M.D. Dominique the Deserter; or, The Gentleman in Black (Edinburgh, 1833; S.W. T. 30/7/1844). L.C. Edinburgh, 4/4/1833. *New D.T.* No. 66; *Lacy*, vol. l.
D. Philippe; or, The Secret Marriage. A Story of the Revolution (Edinburgh, 1838). *Dicks* 372; *Lacy*, vol. lxxxii.
Int. Diamond cut Diamond (Edinburgh, 1838; Strand, M. 19/6/1843). *Dicks* 372; *Lacy*, vol. vii.
M.D. Jack Sheppard (Edinburgh, 17/2/1840).
    [Based on Ainsworth's novel.]
M.D. Oliver Twist (Edinburgh, 23/3/1840).
    [Based on Dickens' novel.]

MUSGRAVE, THOMAS MOORE.
T. Ignes de Castro. 8° 1825.
    [A version of *La Castro* (1587) by António Ferreira.]

NANTZ, FREDERIC COLEMAN.
D.D. Dennis; or, The Gibbet Law of Halifax [MS. dated 28/1/1833 formerly in the possession of R. Crompton Rhodes].

NEALE, FREDERIC.
D. Eliza Holmes (R.P. 22/9/1845). L.C. 25/8/1845.
D. The Venetian Maid. L.C. R.P. 1848.
D. The Cross of Death; or, The Day Witness (R.P. 11/9/1848). L.C. 30/8/1848.

P.   The Fish in the Ring; or, Harlequin Johnny Horner and the
Fayre Mayde of Stepney. L.C. R.P. 23/12/1848.
P.   The Two Thumbs; or, Multum in Parvo. L.C. R.P. 17/2/1849.

NICHOLSON, JOHN.
D.   The Robber of the Alps (Bradford, *c.* 1820).
D.Poem.   The Siege of Bradford (Bradford, 1821). 8° 1821 [Bradford];
8° 1831.

NOEL, M.
F.   Tea (Torquay, 11/1/1807).

O'CALLAGHAN, P. P.
Ba.   The Married Bachelor; or, Master and Man (Adel. M. 5/11/1821).
L. 124 M. [31/10/1821; as *Married or Not; or, The Married
Bachelor*]. *Dicks* 316; *Richardson Minor*, vol. i; *Cumberland Minor*,
vol. x; *Lacy*, vol. i [new series].

O'SULLIVAN, MICHAEL.
M.D.   The Corsair; or, The Pirate's Isle (Crow-street, Dublin, 1814).
[Music J. Blewitt.]
M.D.   Lalla Rookh (Crow-street, Dublin, 4/6/1818).
[Music C. Horn.]

OULTON, WALLEY CHAMBERLAINE.
[For his earlier plays see *A History of Late Eighteenth Century Drama*,
pp. 295–6.]
O.F.   The Sixty-third Letter (H.² W. 28/7/1802). L. 77 M. [24/6/1802;
as *The Joke; or, The S. L.*]. 8° 1802; 8° 1803.
[Music Arnold. The bills attribute this to *P. HOARE.*]
F.   The Middle Dish; or, The Irishman in Turkey (D.L. M.
16/4/1804).
Int.   The Farthing Rushlight. 1810.
[For this and the following play see *The "Stage" Cyclopaedia*.]
Ba.   The Fortunate Tars. 1810.
F.   The Sleepwalker; or, Which is the Lady? (H.² M. 15/6/1812).
L. 97 M. [13/5/1812; as *The Twin Sisters; or, Forgery in Love*].
8° 1812; *Cumberland*, vol. xi.
F.   My Landlady's Gown (H.² S. 10/8/1816). L. 65 S. [2/8/1816; as
One for Another; or, M. L. G.]. 8° 1816.
O.F.   Frightened to Death (D.L. Th. 27/2/1817). L. 110 M. [15/2/1817].
8° 1817.
[Music T. Cooke.]

OXBERRY, WILLIAM HENRY.
F.   The Actress of All Work; or, My Country Cousin (Olym. Th.
28/1/1819). L. 74 S. [26/1/1819]. *Duncombe*, vol. vi.
F.   The Conscript (Fitzroy, W. 19/3/1834). *Dicks* 969.
D.   The Delusion; or, Is She Mad? (Queen's, M. 1/2/1836). *Dicks*
765; *Duncombe*, vol. xxi.
M.D.   Matteo Falcone; or, The Brigand and his Son (E.O.H. M.
6/6/1836). L.C. 2/6/1836. *Dicks* 349; *Duncombe*, vol. xxiii;
Lacy, vol. lxxxiii.
Ba.   The First of September; or, Going out a-shooting (Strand, M.
2/9/1839). L.C. 22/8/1839.
[Written in collaboration with *F. L. PHILLIPS.*]
Ba.   The Swiss Huntress. L.C. Olym. 29/10/1840.

Bsq. Norma Travestie (Adel. M. 6/12/1841). L.C. 1/12/1841. *Dun-
combe*, vol. xlv; *Lacy*, vol. lv.
Bsq. Acis and Galatea (Adel. 28/2/1842). L.C. 18/2/1842.
Bsq. Lucy of Lammermoor (Strand, M. 14/2/1848). L.C. 12/2/1848.

OXENFORD, JOHN.
O.   Der Freischutz; or, The Seventh Bullet (E.O.H. F. 23/7/1824).
     L.C. 14/7/1824. *Lacy*, vol. lxix; 8° [1866].
     [Music Weber. This play is also attributed to *S. J. ARNOLD*.]
Ba. Legerdemain; or, He's no Conjurer. L.C. Adel. 22/11/1828.
     Dicks 657.
     [*Legerdemain* in *UA* is the same play.]
O.F. My Fellow Clerk (E.O.H. M. 20/4/1835). L.C. 4/4/1835.
     Dicks 558.
     [Music Tutton.]
F.   I and my Double (E.O.H. T. 16/6/1835). L.C. 30/5/1835. *Dicks*
     579; *Duncombe*, vol. xxxv.
     [Music G. A. Macfarren.]
M.D. The Dice of Death (E.O.H. M. 14/9/1835). L.C. 2/9/1835.
     Dicks 592; *Duncombe*, vol. xxviii; *Lacy*, vol. cx.
     [Music E. J. Loder.]
M.D. The Castilian Nobleman and the Contrabandista (Adel. M.
     2/11/1835).
Ba. Twice Killed (Olym. Th. 26/11/1835). L.C. 27/11/1835. *Dicks*
     531; *Duncombe*, vol. xxi; *Lacy*, vol. xxiv.
O.F. A Day well Spent; or, Three Adventures (E.O.H. M. 4/4/1836).
     L.C. 4/4/1836. 12° 1836; *Dicks* 531; *Duncombe*, vol. xxxi; *Lacy*,
     vol. xxxiv; *Mod. Eng. Com. Th.* vol. ii.
Ba. The Gunpowder Plot (not the 5th of November) (E.O.H. M.
     9/5/1836). L.C. 6/5/1836.
D.   Midshipman Easy (Surrey, 26/9/1836).
Ba. A Quiet Day. L.C. 1837. *Dicks* 987; *Duncombe*, vol. xxxiv;
     Mod. Eng. Com. Th. vol. ii.
Ba. The Rape of the Lock (Olym. M. 27/3/1837). L.C. 3/12/1836.
     Duncombe, vol. xxxiii; *Dicks* 1021.
Ba. No Followers (Strand, M. 4/9/1837). L.C. 1837. *Dicks* 987;
     Mod. Eng. Com. Th. vol. i; *Duncombe*, vol. xxxiv.
M.D. The Truant Chief (Vic. 2/10/1837).
F.   The Pacha's Pets (Vic. 10/9/1838).
M.D. The Idiot Boy (Vic. 1/10/1838).
F.   Doctor Dilworth (Olym. M. 15/4/1839). L.C. 1/5/1839. *Dicks* 558;
     Acting Nat. Drama, vol. vii.
Ba. English Etiquette (Olym. M. 2/11/1840). L.C. 27/10/1840.
     Dicks 658.
Bsq. Fair Star (P'cess, M. 8/4/1844). See *A. SMITH.*
D.   The Alchymyst's Daughter (P'cess, M. 3/6/1844). L.C. 31/5/1844.
Ca. The Cottage of Love. L.C. Lyc. 6/9/1845.
C.   The Last of the Bravoes (Lyc. M. 13/10/1845). L.C. 25/9/1845.
D.   The Reigning Favourite (Strand, T. 9/10/1849). L.C. 3/10/1849.
     Lacy, vol. i [new series].
F.   A Family Party (Strand, M. 12/11/1849). L.C. 7/11/1849.

PALMER, B.
C.   Life (Olym. 16/11/1846). L.C. 1/10/1846.

PARDOE, Miss.
D. Agnes St. Aubin, the Wife of Two Husbands (Adel. Th. 21/1/1841).

PARLBY, Major BROOKE BRIDGES.
T. Revenge, or, The Novice of San Martino. 8° 1818.

PARRY, JOHN.
O.F. High Notions; or, A Trip to Exmouth (D.L. Th. 11/2/1819).
    L. 112 M. [11/11/1818].
O.F. Helpless Animals (C.G. W. 17/11/1819). L. 72 S. [13/11/1819;
    as *H. A.; or, Bachelors' Fare*].
O.F. The Cabinet and Two Wives; or, A Hint to Husbands (D.L.
    W. 2/6/1824).
O.F. My Uncle Gabriel (D.L. F. 10/12/1824). L.C. 27/11/1824.
    8° 1824 [Songs, Duets].
O.F. A Trip to Wales (D.L. S. 11/11/1826). L.C. 27/10/1826.

PARRY, THOMAS.
Ca. Damp Beds (Strand, T. 29/5/1832). *Duncombe,* vol. xv.
F. P. P.; or, The Man and the Tiger (Adel. M. 21/10/1833; S.W.
    Th. 15/5/1845). L.C. 21/10/1833. *Dicks* 977; *Lacy,* vol. xi.
Ba. The First Night; or, My Own Ghost (Adel. M. 3/11/1834).
    L.C. 1/11/1834. *Duncombe,* vol. xv.
Ba. Meet me by Moonlight (Olym. M. 13/5/1839; Strand, M.
    30/8/1841). L.C. 11/5/1839. *Duncombe,* vol. xlv.
    [See under *UNKNOWN AUTHORS* (S.W. M. 27/3/1837).]
D.D. Woman's Trials (D.L. W. 27/11/1839). L.C. 24/11/1839.
    Dicks 523 [as *The Lucky Horseshoe; or, W. T.*]; *Lacy,* vol. xxvi.
D.D. Alice Aukland (Vic. 14/10/1843). L.C. 14/10/1843.
F. A Cure for Love (H.² T. 29/11/1842). L.C. 12/11/1842. *Dicks*
    603; *Lacy,* vol. xiii.
D. False Visions (Queen's, 14/9/1846). L.C. 17/9/1846.
D. Eugenia Claircille; or, The New Found Home (Adel. Th.
    17/9/1846). L.C. 17/9/1846. *Dicks* 994; *Acting Nat. Drama,*
    vol. xiii.
D. Harvest Home (Adel. W. 29/3/1848). L.C. 25/3/1848.

PAYNE, JOHN HOWARD.
D. Accusation; or, The Family of Anglade (D.L. Th. 1/2/1816).
    L. 64 S. [28/1/1816]. *Dicks* 267.
    [Revised by *T. J. DIBDIN.*]
T. Brutus; or, The Fall of Tarquin (D.L. Th. 3/12/1818). L. 71 S.
    [31/10/1818]. 8° 1818 [5 editions]; 8° 1819 [6th]; *Cumberland,*
    vol. xi; *Dicks* 31; *B.D.* vol. iii.
    [Music Hayward.]
M.D. Therese, the Orphan of Geneva (D.L. F. 2/2/1821). L. 84 S.
    [30/1/1821].
M.D. Adeline; or, The Victim of Seduction (D.L. S. 9/2/1822).
    L. 85 S. [10/1/1822].
    [An adaptation of Pixérécourt, *Valentine; ou, la Séduction*
    (Paris, 1822).]
D.Sk. Love in Humble Life (D.L. Th. 14/2/1822). L. 125 M.
    [26/1/1822]. *Cumberland,* vol. xi; *Dicks* 358.
    [Based on Scribe, *Michel et Christine.*]
Ba. The Armistice (Surrey, 7/1822).
M.D. Ali Pacha (C.G. S. 19/10/1822). See under *J. R. PLANCHÉ.*

M.D. The Two Galley Slaves; or, The Mill of St. Aldervon (D.L.
W. 6/11/1822). L. 127 M. [31/10/1822]. *Lacy*, vol. lxxii.
[Music Cooke and Horn.]

O. Clari; or, The Maid of Milan (C.G. Th. 8/5/1823). See under
J. R. PLANCHÉ.

F. Mrs. Smith; or, The Wife and the Widow (H.² W. 18/6/1823).
L. 87 S. [10/6/1823]. *Lacy*, vol. lxxxiv; *Dicks* 683.

C. Charles the Second; or, The Merry Monarch (C.G. Th. 27/5/1824).
L.C. 8/4/1824 [as *C. the S.; or, Royal Waggery*]. 8° 1824; 12° 1825;
Dicks 244; *Lacy*, vol. xxx.
[Based on *La jeunesse de Henri V.*]

O.F. 'Twas I (C.G. S. 3/12/1825). L.C. 11/1825 [as *T. I.; or, The
Truth is a lie*]. *Lacy*, vol. ix; *Dicks* 405.
[Based on *La rose et le baiser; ou, la servante justifiée.*]

F. Peter Smink; or, Which is the Miller? (H.² T. 26/9/1826). L.C.
24/8/1826. *Lacy*, vol. lxxv; *Dicks* 683 [as *P. S.; or, The Armistice*].
[See *The Armistice* (1822) above.]

O. The White Maid (C.G. T. 2/1/1827). L.C. 16/10/1826.
[An adaptation of Scribe, *La dame blanche* (Paris, 10/12/1825),
with music by Boieldieu, itself based on *Guy Mannering* and *The
Monastery* by Scott.]

F. The Lancers (D.L. S. 1/12/1827). L.C. 30/11/1827 [as *The L.;
or, One Coat and Two Bodies*]. *Dicks* 517; *Cumberland*, vol. xix.

C. Procrastination; or, The Late Mr. M. (H.² M. 21/9/1829).
L.C. 18/9/1829.

D. Woman's Revenge (Olym. 27/2/1832). L.C. 25/2/1832.

PAYNTER, DAVID WILLIAM.
T. Eurypilus, King of Sicily. 4° 1817 [Manchester].
T. King Stephen; or, The Battle of Lincoln. 8° 1822 [Manchester].

PEACOCK, THOMAS LOVE.
The Dramas of T. L. Peacock, edited by A. B. Young. 8° 1910.
[Contains *The Dilettanti, The Three Doctors* and *The Circle of
Loda.*]

PEAKE, RICHARD BRINSLEY.
D.Sk. The Bridge that carries us safe over (E.O.H. W. 18/6/1817).
L. 67 S. [16/6/1817].

D.Sk. Wanted a Governess! (E.O.H. M. 15/9/1817). L. 66 S.
[3/9/1817].

O.F. Amateurs and Actors (E.O.H. S. 29/8/1818). L. 68 S. [15/8/1818;
as *A. and A.; or, The Elopement*]. 8° 1818; *Dicks* 962; *Cumberland*,
vol. xvi.

O.F. A Walk for a Wager! or, A Bailiff's Bet (E.O.H. M. 2/8/1819).
L. 114 M. [14/7/1819]. 8° 1819.
[Music Pindar.]

F. The Duel; or, My Two Nephews (C.G. T. 18/2/1823). 8° 1823;
Cumberland, vol. xxii.

M.D. Presumption; or, The Fate of Frankenstein (E.O.H. M.
28/7/1823). L. 131 M. [12/7/1823].
[Music Watson. Based on Mrs Shelley's romance.]

F. The Poachers (C.G. F. 6/2/1824).

O.F. Jonathan in England (E.O.H. F. 3/9/1824). L.C. 24/8/1824.
Dicks 589 [as *Americans Abroad*].

Ba. The Life of an Actor (Adel. Th. 2/12/1824). L.C. 1/12/1824.
Dicks 582.

O.F. Before Breakfast (E.O.H. Th. 31/8/1826). L.C. 15/8/1826.
[Music Barnett.]

F. The £100 Note (C.G. W. 7/2/1827). L.C. 27/1/1827. *Dicks* 640;
Cumberland, vol. xxxiv.

F. Comfortable Lodgings; or, Paris in 1750 (D.L. S. 10/3/1827).
L.C. 17/2/1827. *Dicks* 678; *Cumberland*, vol. xxix; *Lacy*, vol. lxxxii.

O.F. Two Seconds! (E.O.H. T. 28/8/1827). L.C. 10/8/1827.

M.D. The Haunted Inn (D.L. Th. 31/1/1828). L.C. 16/1/1828.
Dicks 677; *Cumberland*, vol. xxx; *Lacy*, vol. i [new series].

M.D. The Bottle Imp (E.O.H. M. 7/7/1828). L.C. 24/6/1828.
Dicks 593; *Acting Nat. Drama*, vol. ii.
[Music G. H. Rodwell.]

M.D. The Noyades; or, Love and Gratitude (E.O.H. M. 14/7/1828).
L.C. 5/9/1826.
[Music Moss.]

O.F. The Master's Rival; or, A Day at Boulogne (D.L. Th. 12/2/1829).
L.C. 12/1/1829. *Cumberland*, vol. xxii; *Lacy*, vol. xciv.
[Music Hawes. Based on *Crispin, rival de son maître*.]

Oa. The Middle Temple; or, "Which is my Son?" (E.O.H. S.
27/6/1829). *Dicks* 692; *Acting Nat. Drama*, vol. i.
[Music G. H. Rodwell.]

M.Ent. The Spring Lock (E.O.H. T. 18/8/1829). L.C. 16/8/1829.
8° [1829; Songs]; *Acting Nat. Drama*, vol. iv.
[Music G. H. Rodwell.]

O.F. The Chancery Suit (C.G. T. 30/11/1830). L.C. 12/11/1830.
8° 1831; *Dicks* 583; *French*.

M.R. The Evil Eye (Adel. Th. 18/8/1831). L.C. 25/7/1831. *Dicks* 540;
Lacy, vol. xliii.
[Music G. H. Rodwell.]

M.D. The Climbing Boy (Olym. F. 13/7/1832). L.C. 26/6/1832.
Dicks 675.
[Music Hawes.]

D. The Smuggler Boy (C.G. T. 5/2/1833). L.C. 4/2/1833. *Dicks* 907.

F. In the Wrong Box (Olym. M. 3/2/1834). L.C. 25/1/1834. 12°
1834; *Dicks* 737.

M.D. The Dead Guest; or, The Sexton's Prophecy (E.O.H. M.
11/8/1834). L.C. 14/7/1834.
[Music A. Lee.]

Ba. The Chain of Gold; or, A Daughter's Devotion (Adel. M.
29/9/1834). L.C. 11/9/1834. *Dicks* 694.

D. Death and the Doctor (C.G. 10/2/1835). L.C. 31/1/1835.

M.D. The Steel Pavilion; or, The Charcoal Burners of the Hartz
(C.G. M. 23/5/1836). L.C. 23/5/1836.

Fa. House Room; or, The Dishonoured Bill (E.O.H. M. 8/8/1836).
L.C. 4/6/1836 [with titles reversed]. 12° 1836.

F. A Quarter to Nine (Lyc. 27/7/1837). *Dicks* 946; *Acting Nat.
Drama*, vol. ii.

M.D. Blanche of Jersey (E.O.H. W. 9/8/1837). L.C. 1837. 12° [1837];
Dicks 557; *Acting Nat. Drama*, vol. ii.
[Music J. Barnett.]

Ext. The Meltonians (D.L. M. 16/4/1838). L.C. 28/12/1837. 12°
[1838]; *Acting Nat. Drama*, vol. iv.

O.   The Gipsy's Warning (D.L. Th. 19/4/1838). See *G. LINLEY.*
O.F. Lying in Ordinary (E.O.H. Th. 28/6/1838). L.C. 1838. 12°
      [1838]; *Dicks* 768; *Acting Nat. Drama*, vol. iv.
O.F. Gemini (E.O.H. M. 2/7/1838). L.C. 1838. 12° [1838]; *Dicks*
      768; *Acting Nat. Drama*, vol. v.
Ba.   "H. B." (Adel. M. 9/12/1839). L.C. 6/12/1839. *Dicks* 703;
      Acting Nat. Drama, vol. viii.
Ba.   My Home is not my Home; or, The Nabob's Return (Olym. W.
      26/2/1840). L.C. 25/2/1840 [under sub-title].
Ext. The Devil in London; or, Sketches in 1840 (Adel. M. 20/4/1840).
      L.C. 13/4/1840. *Dicks* 718.
      [Written in collaboration with *J. B. BUCKSTONE.*]
C.   Court and City (C.G. W. 17/11/1841). L.C. 22/4/1841. *Cumber-
      land*, vol. xlii; *Dicks* 655.
      [Based on Steele, *The Tender Husband* and Mrs Sheridan, *The
      Discovery.*]
F.   Uncle Rip (Lyc. M. 13/6/1842). L.C. 3/6/1842. *Cumberland,*
      vol. xlii; *Mod. Eng. Com. Th.* vol. iii.
F.   Madelon; or, The Devil of a Dancing Master (Strand, M. 15/1/1844).
      L.C. 12/1/1844.
D.   Ten Thousand a Year (Adel. F. 29/3/1844). L.C. 11/11/1844.
      Cumberland Minor, vol. xvi; *Dicks* 445.
      [Based on Warren's novel.]
F.   The Three Wives of Madrid; or, The Diamond Ring (Lyc. Th.
      25/4/1844). L.C. 19/4/1844. 12° [1844].
C.   The Sheriff of the County (H.² M. 24/2/1845). L.C. 20/2/1845.
      Dicks 843; *Acting Nat. Drama*, vol. xi.
F.   The False Mr. Pope (H.² Th. 11/9/1845). L.C. 6/9/1845.
M.D. The Devil of Marseilles; or, The Spirit of Avarice (Adel. W.
      1/7/1846). L.C. 1/7/1846 [as *The Demon of M.*]. 12° [1846].
      [Music A. Mellon.]
C.   The Title Deeds (Adel. M. 21/6/1847). L.C. 19/6/1847. 12°
      [1847]; *Dicks* 1013; *Acting Nat. Drama*, vol. xiv.
D.   Gabrielli; or, The Bequeathed Heart (Adel. Th. 18/11/1847).
      L.C. 13/11/1847. *Dicks* 584.

PENLEY, SAMSON.
F.   The Sleeping Draught (D.L. W. 1/4/1818). L. 69 S. [6/3/1818].
      8° 1818; *Dicks* 363; *Cumberland*, vol. xxix; *Lacy*, vol. lviii.
D.   The Jew of Malta (D.L. F. 24/4/1818). L. 69 S. [29/3/1818].
      [An adaptation of Marlowe's play.]

PERCIVAL, EDWARD LOCKWOOD.
D.   Mary Stuart. 8° 1839 [Munich].
      [A translation of Schiller's drama.]

PERCY, T.
Ext. Little Offsprings; or, Babes out of the Wood (C.G. 26/4/1828).
      L.C. 14/4/1828.

PETER, WILLIAM.
D.   William Tell. 8° 1839 [Heidelberg]; 8° 1867.
      [A translation of Schiller's drama.]
D.   Mary Stuart. 8° 1841 [Heidelberg].
      [A translation of Schiller's drama.]
D.   The Maid of Orleans... and other poems. 12° 1843.

PHILLIPS, ELIZABETH [Mrs ALFRED P. PHILLIPS].
Int. Prejudice; or, A Bachelor's Vow (Strand, 27/11/1848). L.C. Brighton.
Int. The King's Choice (Strand, 27/11/1848). L.C. Brighton.
Int. Cupid in Brighton; or, A Visit from the Celestials. L.C. Brighton, 9/2/1848.
Ca. Katty from Connaught (Strand, M. 27/8/1849). L.C. 25/8/1849.

PHILLIPS, FREDERIC LAURENCE.
Ba. The First of September (Strand, M. 2/9/1839). See *W. H. OXBERRY.*
M.D. The Red Man; or, The Legend of Ravenstone. L.C. Garrick, 23/12/1844.
D. Ivan de Bassenvelt. L.C. 1845.
D. The Italian Lover. L.C. Garrick, 28/5/1846.
D. The Pastor's Daughter. L.C. Garrick, 1/7/1846.
D. The Elixir of Life; or, Revelations of London. L.C. Garrick, 1/8/1846.

PHILLIPS, MORRICE.
D. Fidelio; or, The Fortress of St. Jacques (R.P. 7/1/1837). *Duncombe*, vol. xxvii.

PHILLIPS, R.
F. The Man in the Moon (D.L. M. 8/12/1817). L. 67 S. [23/11/1817; as *The M. in the M.; or, The Striking Feature*]. 8° 1818.
M.D. The Heroine; or, A Daughter's Courage (D.L. M. 22/2/1819). L. 74 S. [24/1/1819]. 8° 1819.
[Music Cooke.]

PHIPPS, Hon. EDMUND.
Lyrical D. King René's Daughter (Dublin, 28/11/1849). 8° 1848; *Lacy*, vol. xxxvi.
[Based on the Danish of Henrik Hertz.]

PILGRIM, JAMES.
F. Paddy Miles, the Limerick Boy (S.W. 22/4/1836). *Lacy*, vol. xcv.

PITT, GEORGE DIBDIN.
Ba. My Own Blue Bell (Surrey, S. 16/4/1831). *Dicks* 515.
D. The Drunkard's Doom (Vic. 21/9/1832). *Dicks* 945.
D. The Hebrew Husband; or, The Jews' Revolt (Cob. M. 14/1/1833).
D. The Whistler; or, The Fate of the Lily of St. Leonard's (Cob. M. 28/1/1833; S.W. M. 8/4/1833). *Duncombe*, vol. xxviii; *Lacy*, vol. xcvii.
[Based on Scott, *The Heart of Midlothian.*]
M.D. The Last Nail; or, The Drunkard's Doom (Cob. M. 11/2/1833).
[See *The Drunkard's Doom*, above.]
M.D. Lurline; or, The Revolt of the Naiades (Adel. M. 13/1/1834; R.P. M. 17/2/1834). L.C. 11/1/1834.
M.D. The Monster of the Eddystone; or, The Lighthouse Keepers (S.W. M. 7/4/1834; R.P. M. 18/8/1834, as *The Eddystone Elf*). *Cumberland Minor*, vol. x; *Lacy*, vol. lxix.
M.D. The Jersey Girl; or, The Red Robbers (Surrey, M. 9/2/1835). *Dicks* 512; *Lacy*, vol. xxvi.
D. Rose Roy; or, The Valley of the Red Rose (S.W. T. 7/7/1835).
D. The Infernal Machine; or, The French Regicides (S.W. M. 10/8/1835).

D. Ankle Jack; or, The Thief's Shoe (S.W. M. 17/8/1835).
D. John Johnson, the Farmer of Fiddler's Green (S.W. Th. 3/9/1835).
D. Blue Eyed Mary (S.W. Th. 3/9/1835).
D. The Mill of Berezina (C.G. 14/11/1835). L.C. 19/10/1835.
Ba. The Twins, Paul and Philip (Queen's, Th. 21/1/1836). *Dicks* 419.
D. The Holstein Hussar; or, The Grenadier Guard (S.W. M. 15/1/1838).
   [See *The Hussars of Hesse*, below.]
D.D. Simon Lee; or, The Murder of the Five Fields Copse (C.L. 1/4/1839). *Lacy*, vol. lxxviii.
M.D. Rookwood! or, The Legend of the Old Lime Tree (S.W. M. 24/2/1840).
D.D. Susan Hopley; or, The Vicissitudes of a Servant Girl (Vic. 31/5/1841). L.C. Edinburgh, 21/9/1842. *Lacy*, vol. lxix.
M.D. The Whistler; or, The Fate of the Lily of St. Leonard's. L.C. Edinburgh, 4/7/1841.
   [See above under 1833.]
D. The Beggar's Petition; or, A Father's Love and a Mother's Care (City, 18/10/1841). *Dicks* 514; *Lacy*, vol. lxxxvii.
D. The Wrack of the Heart; or, The Story of Agnes Primrose (Vic. W. 3/11/1841).
D.D. The Last Man; or, The Miser of Eltham Green. L.C. Liverpool, 27/12/1842. *Duncombe*, vol. xxiv.
D.D. Cumberland Mary (Vic. 10/6/1844). L.C. 31/5/1844.
D. Charlotte Hayden; or, The Victim of Circumstances. L.C. Britannia, 25/6/1844.
M.D. Woman's Life; or, The Trials of the Heart. L.C. Britannia, 8/8/1844.
M.D. The Murder House; or, The Cheats of Chick Lane. L.C. Britannia, 8/1844 [licence refused].
Spec. The Greek Brothers; or, The Pirate of the Gulph (Queen's, 4/11/1844). L.C. 7/10/1844.
D. The Soldier's Oath (Garrick 11/11/1844). L.C. 28/9/1844.
P. Tom Titler's Ground; or, Harlequin and the Fairy of Old London Stone. L.C. Britannia, 10/12/1844.
D.D. Marianne, the Child of Charity; or, The Head of a Lawyer (Vic. 30/12/1844). L.C. 28/12/1844. *Dicks* 825.
D. The Black Fisherman; or, The Daughter of the Deep (Standard, 20/1/1845). L.C. 15/11/1844.
D. Belinda the Blind; or, The Stepmother's Vengeance. L.C. Britannia, 22/1/1845.
D. Bertha the Broom Girl; or, The Astrologer's Star. L.C. Britannia, 25/1/1845.
D. Feodora; or, The Dropping Well of Gedar (Vic. 24/2/1845). L.C. 22/1/1845.
M.D. Il Diavolo Duraldi. L.C. Britannia, 22/3/1845.
M.D. Ellen Mavourneen. L.C. Britannia, 21/4/1845.
M.D. The Golden Arrow; or, The Matricide of the Catacombs and the Maid of Notre Dame. L.C. Britannia, 24/4/1845.
D. Geoffrey Kurdistan; or, The Blacksmith's Daughter and the Mock Marriage (Vic. M. 28/4/1845). L.C. 22/3/1845.
M.D. The Maids of St. Michael; or, The Specre of the Mine. L.C. Britannia, 2/6/1845.

D. Ellen and Susan. L.C. Britannia, 17/6/1845.
D. The Farmer's Daughter; or, The Rajah's Vengeance. L.C. Britannia, 30/7/1845.
D. Theresa Vorschner (Vic. 10/8/1845). L.C. 10/8/1845.
D. The White Slave. L.C. Britannia, 15/8/1845.
D. Tallyho, the Modern Mephistopheles. L.C. Britannia, 6/9/1845.
D. Moyra; or, The Malediction of the Dead (Vic. 15/9/1845). L.C. 15/9/1845.
D. Japhet in Search of a Father (Vic. 29/9/1845). L.C. 29/9/1845.
D. The Primrose of Ireland. L.C. Britannia, 1845.
P. The Golden Lily; or, The Three Brothers of Bagdad. L.C. Britannia, 29/9/1845.
D. Gideon Giles the Roper; or, The Gipsey Belle. L.C. Britannia, 18/10/1845.
D. Pauline the Pirate; or, The Female Buccaniers. L.C. Britannia, 24/10/1845.
D. The Weaver's Wife; or, The First Crime. L.C. Britannia, 19/11/1845.
D. David Hunt; or, The Backwoodsman's Daughter. L.C. Britannia, 8/12/1845.
P. Chachechichochu; or, Harlequin in China. L.C. Britannia, 8/12/1845.
D. The Minstrel Boy. L.C. Britannia, 16/1/1846.
D. Margaret Maddison (Britannia, 9/2/1846). L.C. 15/8/1845.
D. Crosby Ravensworth. L.C. Britannia, 18/3/1846.
D. Poor Robin (Britannia, 13/4/1846). L.C. Britannia, 18/4/1846.
   [Based on Gray's *Elegy*.]
D. The Hussars of Hesse; or, The Third Day. L.C. Britannia, 23/4/1846.
D. Jarvis the Honest Man; or, The Merchant's Daughter (Vic. 4/5/1846). L.C. 4/5/1846.
D. The Pawnbroker; or, The Sorrows of a Sister. L.C. Britannia, 10/6/1846.
D. Toussaint l'Overture. L.C. Britannia, 23/6/1846.
M.D. The Wild Man of Andalusia; or, Don Quixote. L.C. Britannia, 10/7/1846.
Spec. The Ocean Doomed. L.C. Britannia, 5/8/1846.
M.D. Mary Livingstone; or, The Maid's Murder. L.C. Britannia, 12/10/1846.
D. Quentin Matrys; or, The Maid of Antwerp (Surrey, M. 16/11/1846). L.C. Bower, 16/10/1846.
D. Carlos Gangenelli. L.C. 1847.
D. The Battle of Life (Britannia, M. 11/1/1847). L.C. 7/1/1847.
D. Martin the Foundling. L.C. Britannia, 23/1/1847.
D. Algernon the Blind Guide; or, The Lord of the Storm (Vic. F. 5/2/1847). L.C. 30/1/1847.
D. Wildfire Dick. L.C. Britannia, 9/2/1847.
   [Also called *The Dishonour'd Bill*.]
F. The Yorkshire School; or, Life in Little. L.C. Britannia, 9/2/1847.
M.D. The String of Pearls; or, The Fiend of Fleet Street. L.C. Britannia, 22/2/1847.
   [This seems to have been produced as *Sweeney Todd*.]

D. The Prussian Brothers; or, The Victim of the Violet. L.C.
Britannia, 27/2/1847.
[Called at first *The Death of Xavier*.]

D. The Lancashire Witches. L.C. Standard, 28/2/1847.

D. The Daemon of the Drachenfalls; or, The Monk, the Friend and
the Enemy. L.C. Britannia, 5/3/1847.

D. Martin and James; or, The Adventures of a Country Girl. L.C.
Britannia, 14/4/1847.

D. The Pirate Smuggler; or, The Mad Girl of St. Martin's. L.C.
Britannia, 14/4/1847.

C. Black Bayaderes; or, Rival Serenades. L.C. Britannia,
24/4/1847.

D. The Poacher's Wife; or, Pride and Poverty. L.C. Britannia,
13/5/1847.

D. The Haunted Hall; or, The Spectre of the Quarry. L.C. Britannia,
27/5/1847.

D. The Victim of Falsehood; or, The Fruits of a Single Lie. L.C.
Britannia, 3/6/1847.

D. The Gipsey Twins (Britannia, 12/7/1847). L.C. 1/5/1847 [as
Gipsey Norris; or, Life in the Merry Greenwood].

D. The Bloodhound of Cuba; or, Caesar the Half-breed. L.C.
Britannia, 22/7/1847.

D. Phillip IV; or, The Mariner and his Monkey. L.C. Britannia,
22/7/1847.

M.D. The Maid and the Mirror. L.C. Britannia, 6/9/1847.

D. The Merchant's Clerk (Vic. 4/10/1847). L.C. 1/10/1847.

D. Ronald Dhu; or, The Black Cat of Coventry. L.C. Britannia,
18/10/1847.

D. Miles's Boy; or, The Miller of Goodwood. L.C. Britannia,
18/10/1847.

D. The Bottle Bane; or, The Drunkard's Fate (Britannia, W.
20/10/1847). L.C. 18/9/1847.
[This seems to have appeared alongside Pitt's other version at
the Queen's, S. 4/10/1847.]

P. The Yellow Dwarf; or, Harlequin and the Sun of the Sunflower.
L.C. Britannia, 22/12/1847.

D. The Revolution of Paris. L.C. Britannia, 1848.

D. Annette Carline; or, A Soldier's Gratitude (Britannia, M.
15/5/1848). L.C. 3/5/1848.

F. Lilly Laburnem; or, The Blue above and the Blue below. L.C.
Britannia, 12/5/1848.

D. The Flirt; or, False Accusation. L.C. Britannia, 29/6/1848.

D. Nat Graves; or, The Yorkshire Highwayman and the Twin
Brothers. L.C. Britannia, 10/8/1848.

P. Old Parr and the Magic Pills; or, Harlequin and the Wizard of
Ashdale. L.C. Britannia, 1848.

D. First Friendship; or, A Soldier's March from the Cradle to the
Grave. L.C. Britannia, 30/9/1848.

D. The Fine Old British Veterans; or, The Shamrock of Chelsea.
L.C. Britannia, 5/10/1848.

D. The Sikh Spy. L.C. Queen's, 5/3/1849.

D. Martin Hayward; or, The Victim of Perjury. L.C. Britannia,
5/3/1849.

D. A Wife and No Wife. L.C. Britannia, 8/10/1849.

D. The Sea Lion; or, The Frozen Ships and the Hermit of the Sea-bound Bay. L.C. Queen's, 7/11/1849.
D. The White Nun of Wakefield. L.C. Britannia, 12/11/1849.
D. The Sailor's Progress from the Press-gang to the Ocean Grave. L.C. Britannia, 15/11/1849.
D. The Sailor's Progress and the Horrors of War. L.C. Standard, 20/11/1849.
[Pitt has many dramas produced after 1850. Before this date were produced *Chartley the Fatalist*, *The Valkyre* and *Poor Susan*.]

PLANCHÉ, JAMES ROBINSON.

[The plays marked with an asterisk are not included in Planché's own list.]

Bsq. Amoroso, King of Little Britain (D.L. T. 21/4/1818). L. 70 S. [17/4/1818]. 12° 1818; *Cumberland*, vol. xliii.
[Music Cooke.]
P. Rodolph the Wolf; or, Columbine Red Riding Hood (Olym. M. 21/12/1818). L. 71 S. [19/12/1818].
O. The Troubadours; or, Jealousy Out-witted (Olym. T. 9/2/1819).
M.D. Abudah; or, The Talisman of Oromanes (D.L. T. 13/4/1819). L. 115 M. [3/1819].
[Music M. Kelly.]
M.D. The Czar; or, A Day in the Dockyards (S.W. M. 21/6/1819).
[Based on *Le bourgmestre de Sardam*.]
Ba. The Caliph and the Cadi; or, Rambles in Bagdad (16/8/1819).
Ba. Fancy's Sketch; or, Look before you leap (Adel. F. 29/10/1819). L. 73 S. [27/10/1819].
Int. Odds and Ends; or, Which is the Manager? (Adel. F. 19/11/1819). L. 115 M. [26/11/1819].
M.D. The Vampyre; or, The Bride of the Isles (E.O.H. W. 9/8/1820). L. 117 M. [25/7/1820]. 8° 1820; *Dicks* 875; *Cumberland*, vol. xxvii; *Lacy*, vol. cvii.
[Based on *Le vampire*.]
Ext. A Burletta of Errors; or, Jupiter and Alcmena (Adel. M. 6/11/1820). L. 117 M. [4/11/1820].
Ba. Who's to Father Her? or, What's bred in the Bone won't come out of the Flesh (Adel. M. 13/11/1820). L. 117 M. [8/11/1820; under sub-title].
Ba. The Deuce is in Her! or, Two Nights in Madrid (Adel. M. 27/11/1820). L. 117 M. [7/11/1820; as *Who is She? or, T. N. in M.*].
M.D. Zamoski; or, The Fortress and the Mine (Adel. M. 11/12/1820). L. 118 M. [6/12/1820].
P. Dr Syntax; or, Harlequin in London (Adel. T. 26/12/1820).
Bsq.Ba. Giovanni, the Vampire; or, How shall we get rid of him? (Adel. M. 15/1/1821). L. 121 M. [10/1/1821; "Introductory vision"].
M.D. Kenilworth Castle; or, The Days of Queen Bess (Adel. F. 9/2/1821). L. 124 M. [5/2/1821].
[Based on Scott's novel.]
Ba. Lodgings to be Let (Adel. M. 19/2/1821). L. 121 M. [14/2/1821].
Ba. Half an Hour's Courtship; or, Le chambre à coucher (Adel. W. 28/2/1821). L. 77 S. [22/12/1820].
Ba. Sherwood Forest; or, The Merry Archers (Adel. M. 12/3/1821). L. 121 M. [7/3/1821].

M.D. The Mountain Hut; or, The Tinker's Son (S.W. M. 23/4/1821;
      Olym. M. 25/11/1822). L. 126 M. [21/11/1822].
O.F. Peter and Paul; or, Love in the Vineyards (H.² W. 4/7/1821).
      L. 122 M. [28/7/1821]. Dicks 898.
M.D. The Witch of Derncleuch (E.O.H. M. 30/7/1821). L. 123 M.
      [5/7/1821].
      [Music W. Reeve. Based on Scott, Guy Mannering.]
Ba.   Capers at Canterbury (Adel. M. 1/10/1821). L. 121 M. [27/9/1821].
M.D. The Corsair's Bride; or, The Valley of Mount Etna (Adel. M.
      22/10/1821).
Ba.   Love's Alarum (Adel. Th. 8/11/1821).
M.D. Le Solitaire; or, The Recluse of the Alps (Olym. S. 24/11/1821).
      L. 121 M. [17/11/1821; as Le S.; or, The Unknown of the Mountain].
M.D. The Pirate (Olym. M. 14/1/1822). L. 128 M. [1/1822].
C.O. All in the Dark; or, The Banks of the Elbe (Lyc. W. 10/7/1822).
      L. 125 M. [20/6/1822; under sub-title]. 8° 1822; Dicks 896.
      [Music B. Livius. Based on Hasard et Folie by H. J. B. D.
      Victor.]
Oa.   The Fair Gabrielle (E.O.H. F. 6/9/1822). 8° 1822.
      [Music B. Livius.]
M.D. Ali Pacha; or, The Signet Ring (C.G. S. 19/10/1822). L. 126 M.
      [18/10/1822; as The Pacha]. 12° Dolby.
      [Written by J. H. PAYNE, altered by J. R. PLANCHÉ with
      additional songs.]
O.   Maid Marian; or, The Huntress of Arlingford (C.G. T. 3/12/1822).
      L. 126 M. [24/10/1822]. 8° [1822].
      [Music Bishop. Based on Peacock's novel.]
O.   Clari; or, The Maid of Milan (C.G. Th. 8/5/1823). L. 128 M.
      [24/4/1823; as Clari; or, The Milanese Peasant Girl]. Dicks 406.
      [Music Bishop. This also is credited to J. H. PAYNE.]
O.F. "I will have a Wife!" (E.O.H. Th. 7/8/1823). L. 131 M.
      [21/7/1823].
      [Music Reeve.]
O.F. Too Curious by Half; or, Marplot in Spain (E.O.H. W.
      27/8/1823). L. 131 M. [5/8/1823].
      [Music Reeve.]
M.D. Cortez; or, The Conquest of Mexico (C.G. W. 5/11/1823).
      8° [1823].
      [Music Bishop.]
M.D. St. Ronan's Well (Adel. M. 19/1/1824; Edinburgh, 5/6/1824).
      L. 132 M. [15/1/1824]
      [Based on Scott's novel.]
Oa.   Military Tactics (E.O.H. T. 6/7/1824). L.C. 5/7/1824.
      [Music Reeve. Based on Les projets de mariage.]
O.   The Frozen Lake (E.O.H. F. 3/9/1824). L.C. 14/8/1824.
      [Music Reeve. Based on Scribe, La neige; ou, le nouvel Éginard
      (Paris, 9/10/1823).]
M.D. Der Freischutz; or, The Black Huntsman of Bohemia (C.G. Th.
      14/10/1824). L.C. 7/10/1824. 8° 1825 [bis; as The F.; or, The
      Wild Huntsman of B.].
      [Music B. Livius, based on Weber.]
C.   A Woman never Vext; or, The Widow of Cornhill (C.G. T.
      9/11/1824). 8° [1824]; Dicks 880; Cumberland, vol. viii.
      [Based on Rowley's play.]

                                                            25-2

Pag. The Coronation of Charles X of France (C.G. 11/7/1825).
O.   Lilla (C.G. F. 21/10/1825). L.C. 30/9/1825.
M.D. Jocko; or, The Brazilian Monkey (C.G. T. 8/11/1825). L.C.
     24/10/1825.
Bsq. Success; or, A Hit if you like it (Adel. M. 12/12/1825). L.C.
     6/12/1825. 8° 1879 [in *Extravaganzas*, i].
O.   Oberon; or, The Elf-King's Oath (C.G. W. 12/4/1826). L.C. 1826.
     8° 1826 [3 editions]; *Lacy*, vol. lix; 8° [1826; Songs].
     [Music Weber; based on Wieland's poem.]
F.   Returned Killed (C.G. S. 31/10/1826). C.G. 26/10/1826. 8° 1826;
     Dicks 894.
     [Based on *Le mort dans l'embarras*.]
Int. All's Right; or, The Old School-fellow (H.² F. 15/6/1827).
     L.C. 31/5/1827.
Vaud. "Pay to my Order"; or, A Chaste Salute (Vauxhall, M.
     9/7/1827; S.W. W. 26/12/1832).
C.O. The Rencontre; or, Love will find out the Way (H.² Th.
     12/7/1827). L.C. 16/6/1827.
F.   You must be buried (H.² S. 11/8/1827). L.C. 6/8/1827.
     [Based on *La veuve de Malabar*.]
Ba. Paris and London; or, A Trip across the Herring Pond (Adel. M.
     21/1/1828). L.C. 29/12/1827. *Cumberland Minor*, vol. iii; *Dicks*
     886; 16° 1842 [Stuttgart].
C.   The Merchant's Wedding; or, London Frolics in 1638 (C.G. T.
     5/2/1828). 8° 1828; *Dicks* 879; *Cumberland*, vol. xix.
     [Based on Mayne, *The City Match* and Rowley, *Match me at
     Midnight*.]
O.   Carron Side; or, The Fête Champêtre (C.G. T. 27/5/1828).
     L.C. 28/4/1828.
F.   A Daughter to Marry (H.² M. 16/6/1828). L.C. 3/6/1828.
     [Based on *Une demoiselle à marier; ou, la première entrevue*.]
C.O. The Green-eyed Monster (H.² M. 18/8/1828). L.C. 12/8/1828.
     Cumberland, vol. xxii; *Dicks* 891; *Lacy*, vol. ci.
     [Based on *Les deux jaloux*.]
Ba. The Mason of Buda (Adel. T. 21/10/1828). L.C. 16/10/1828.
     Cumberland Minor, vol. i.
     [Music Rodwell.]
D.   Charles XII; or, The Siege of Stralsund (D.L. Th. 11/12/1828).
     L.C. 10/12/1828. *Cumberland*, vol. xxv; *Dicks* 871; *Lacy*, vol.
     lxvii.
M.D. Thierna-na-Oge; or, The Prince of the Lakes (D.L. M.
     20/4/1829). L.C. 10/4/1829.
     [Music Cooke.]
D.   The Partisans; or, The War of Paris in 1649 (D.L. Th. 21/5/1829).
     L.C. 6/5/1829.
     [Based on *La maison du rampart; ou, une journée de la ronde*.]
Int. Manoeuvring (H.² W. 1/7/1829; S.W. M. 24/8/1846). L.C.
     10/6/1829.
     [Based on *L'ambassadeur*. Written in collaboration with
     C. *DANCE*.]
O.   Der Vampyr (E.O.H. T. 25/8/1829). L.C. 20/8/1829.
     [Based on *Der Vampyr* with music by Marschner.]
D.   The Brigand Chief (D.L. W. 18/11/1829). L.C. 21/11/1829.
     Dicks 876; *Cumberland*, vol. xxiv; *Lacy*, vol. i [new series].

C.O.   The National Guard; or, Bride and No Bride (D.L. Th. 4/2/1830).
L.C. 25/1/1830. 8° 1830 [Songs, Duets].
[An adaptation of Scribe, *La fiancée* (Paris, 10/1/1829), with
music by Auber.]

M.D.   The Dragon's Gift; or, The Scarf of Flight and the Mirror of
Light (D.L. M. 12/4/1830). L.C. 8/4/1830.
[Music Cooke.]

O.   Hofer; or, The Tell of the Tyrol (D.L. S. 1/5/1830). L.C.
26/4/1830. 12° [1830].
[Based on Rossini's *Guillaume Tell*, with music arranged by
Bishop.]

F.   The Jenkinses; or, Boarded and Done For (D.L. Th. 9/12/1830).
L.C. 11/12/1830. *Dicks* 899; *Lacy*, vol. viii.

Ba.   Olympic Revels; or, Prometheus and Pandora (Olym. M. 3/1/1831).
L.C. 23/12/1830. 12° 1834; 8° 1879 [in *Extravaganzas*, i]; *Lacy*,
vol. xli.
[Written in collaboration with *C. DANCE*.]

O.   The Romance of a Day (C.G. Th. 3/2/1831). L.C. 6/1/1830.
[Music Bishop.]

F.   My Great Aunt; or, Where there's a Will (Olym. S. 5/3/1831).
L.C. 21/2/1831 [as *M. G. A.; or, Expectations*]. 12° 1846; *Dicks*
897; *Lacy*, vol. xx.

M.D.   The Legion of Honour (D.L. S. 16/4/1831). L.C. 11/4/1831
[as *The L. of H.; or, Better Late than Never*].
[Based on *Le centenaire*.]

C.   A Friend at Court (H.² T. 28/6/1831). L.C. 21/5/1831.

M.D.   The Army of the North; or, The Spaniard's Secret (C.G. S.
29/10/1831). L.C. 17/10/1831.

C.O.   The Love Charm; or, The Village Coquette (D.L. Th. 3/11/1831).
L.C. 2/11/1831.
[An adaptation of Scribe, *Le philtre* (Paris, 15/6/1831), with
music by Auber.]

Ba.   Olympic Devils; or, Orpheus and Eurydice (Olym. M. 26/12/1831).
L.C. 21/12/1831. 12° 1836; 8° 1879 [in *Extravaganzas*, i]; *Lacy*,
vol. xli.
[Written in collaboration with *C. DANCE*.]

D.   The Compact (D.L. Th. 5/4/1832). L.C. 2/4/1832.

Spec.   His First Campaign (C.G. M. 1/10/1832).

F.   My Daughter, Sir; or, A Daughter to Marry (Olym. T. 9/10/1832).
L.C. 8/10/1832. *Cumberland*, vol. xxxvii; *Dicks* 897; *Lacy*,
vol. lxxiv.
[Another version of *A Daughter to Marry* (1828).]

Ba.   The Paphian Bower; or, Venus and Adonis (Olym. W. 26/12/1832).
L.C. 24/12/1832. 8° 1879 [in *Extravaganzas*, i]; *Lacy*, vol.
xliv.
[Written in collaboration with *C. DANCE*.]

Vaud.   Promotion; or, A Morning at Versailles in 1750 (Olym. M.
18/2/1833; Queen's, Th. 23/4/1835). L.C. 9/2/1833. 12° 1852;
Dicks 893; *Lacy*, vol. xxi.

D.   Reputation; or, The Court Secret (C.G. M. 4/3/1833). L.C.
18/2/1833. 8° [1833]; *Dicks* 892.

Oa.   The Students of Jena; or, The Family Concert (D.L. T. 4/6/1833).
L.C. 8/6/1833.
[Music Chelard.]

O.   The Court Masque; or, Richmond in the Olden Time (Adel. M. 9/9/1833). L.C. 19/8/1833.
[Based on *Le pré aux clercs*.]

Ext.   High, Low, Jack, and the Game; or, The Card Party (Olym. M. 30/9/1833). 8° 1879 [in *Extravaganzas*, i]; *French's N.Y.* No. clv.
[Written in collaboration with *C. DANCE*.]

O.   Gustavus III; or, The Masked Ball (C.G. W. 13/11/1833). L.C. 12/11/1833. 8° 1833; 8° [1833; Songs, Duets, Choruses].
[An adaptation of Scribe's opera, with music by Auber, arranged by T. Cooke.]

Ext.   The Deep Deep Sea; or, Perseus and Andromeda (Olym. Th. 26/12/1833). L.C. 19/12/1833. 16° 1834; 8° [1833; Songs, Duets, Chorusses]; 8° 1879 [in *Extravaganzas*, i].
[Written in collaboration with *C. DANCE*.]

O.   The Challenge (C.G. T. 1/4/1834).
[Based on *Le pré aux clercs*; music T. Cooke.]

C.D.   Secret Service (D.L. T. 29/4/1834). L.C. 22/4/1834. 8° 1834; *Dicks* 870.
[Based on the French of Mélesville and Duveyrier.]

Vaud.   The Loan of a Lover (Olym. M. 29/9/1834). L.C. 22/9/1834. 8° 1834; *Dicks* 895; *Lacy*, vol. ix.

Vaud.   "My Friend, the Governor" (Olym. M. 29/9/1834). L.C. 22/9/1834. *Dicks* 899.

D.   The Regent (D.L. S. 18/10/1834). L.C. 18/10/1834. 8° 1834; *Dicks* 884.
[Based on *Le moulin de Javelle* by Scribe and Mélesville.]

O.   The Red Mask; or, The Council of Three (D.L. S. 15/11/1834). L.C. 28/10/1834 [as *The Bravo; or, The Red Mask*].
[Music Templeton.]

Ext.   Telemachus; or, The Island of Calypoo (Olym. F. 26/12/1834). L.C. 19/12/1834. *Lacy*, vol. li; 8° 1879 [in *Extravaganzas*, i].
[Written in collaboration with *C. DANCE*.]

Ba.   The Court Beauties (Olym. S. 14/3/1835). L.C. 7/3/1835. 12° 1835; *Dicks* 898; *Lacy*, vol. xxi.

M.D.   The Travelling Carriage (D.L. M. 26/10/1835). L.C. 28/10/1835.

O.D.   The Jewess (D.L. M. 16/11/1835). 8° 1835.
[An adaptation of Scribe, *La Juive* (Paris, 23/2/1835), with music by Halévy, arranged by T. Cooke.]

M.D. Spec.   Chevy Chase (D.L. W. 2/3/1836). L.C. 29/2/1836. 8° 1836 [Songs, Choruses].
[Music Macfarren.]

Ba.   Court Favour; or, Private and Confidential (Olym. Th. 29/9/1836). *Acting Nat. Drama*, vol. ii; *Dicks* 883.

O.   The Siege of Corinth (D.L. T. 8/11/1836). L.C. 1836.
[Music Rossini, adapted by Cooke.]

Vaud.   The Two Figaros (Olym. W. 30/11/1836). L.C. 22/11/1836. *Dicks* 888; *Acting Nat. Drama*, vol. i.

Ba.   Riquet with the Tuft (Olym. M. 26/12/1836). L.C. 14/12/1836. *Acting Nat. Drama*, vol. i.
[Based on *Riquet à la houppe*. Written in collaboration with *C. DANCE*.]

F.   A Peculiar Position (Olym. W. 3/5/1837). L.C. 1/4/1837. *Dicks* 878; *Acting Nat. Drama*, vol. i.

O. Norma (D.L. S. 24/6/1837). L.C. 3/6/1837. 8° 1848; *Lacy*, vol. xxxii.

Vaud. The New Servant (Olym. F. 29/9/1837). L.C. 1837.

M.D. The Child of the Wreck (D.L. S. 7/10/1837). L.C. 1837. *Dicks* 877; *Lacy*, vol. xxxix.
[Music T. Cooke.]

M.D. Caractacus (D.L. M. 6/11/1837). L.C. 1837.
[Music Balfe. An adaptation of *Bonduca* by Beaumont and Fletcher.]

Ba. Puss in Boots (Olym. T. 26/12/1837). L.C. 21/12/1837.

O. The Magic Flute (D.L. S. 10/3/1838). L.C. 8/3/1838. 8° [1838; Songs].
[An adaptation of *Die Zauberflöte*, with music by Mozart.]

Review. The Drama's Levee; or, A Peep at the Past (Olym. M. 16/4/1838). L.C. 6/4/1838; 8° 1879 [in *Extravaganzas*, ii].

F. The Printer's Devil (Olym. Th. 11/10/1838). L.C. 1838. *Dicks* 889; *Acting Nat. Drama*, vol. v.

F. The Queen's Horse; or, The Brewer of Preston (Olym. M. 3/12/1838). L.C. 30/11/1838. *Acting Nat. Drama*, vol. vi.
[Written in collaboration with *M. B. HONAN*.]

Ext. Blue Beard (Olym. W. 2/1/1839). L.C. 1839. 12°[1839];8°[1839; Songs, Duets and Choruses]; *Lacy*, vol. xix; 8° 1879 [in *Extravaganzas*, ii].
[Written in collaboration with *C. DANCE*.]

F. Faint Heart ne'er won Fair Lady (Olym. Th. 28/2/1839). L.C. 18/2/1839. *Duncombe*, vol. xxxix; *Dicks* 878; *Lacy*, vol. xxxv.

F. The Garrick Fever (Olym. M. 1/4/1839). L.C. 30/3/1839. *Dicks* 881; *Lacy*, vol. xxii.

M. The Fortunate Isles; or, The Triumphs of Britannia (C.G. W. 12/2/1840).
[Music Bishop.]

Ext. The Sleeping Beauty in the Wood (C.G. M. 20/4/1840). L.C. 13/4/1840. 12° [1840]; 8° 1840 [Songs, Duets, Chorusses]; *Lacy*, vol. xix; 8° 1879 [in *Extravaganzas*, ii].

C. The Spanish Curate (C.G. T. 13/10/1840). L.C. 30/9/1840. *Dicks* 874.
[An adaptation of the play by Beaumont and Fletcher.]

P. Harlequin and the Giant Helmet; or, The Castle of Otranto (C.G. S. 26/12/1840). L.C. 15/12/1840.
[Opening only.]

D, The Captain of the Watch (C,G, Th, 25/2/1841). L.C. 16/2/1841. 12° [1841]; *Dicks* 893; *French*, 270.
[Based on *Le Chevalier du Guet* by Lockroy.]

D. The Embassy (C.G. M. 22/3/1841). L.C. 8/3/1841.

Ext. Beauty and the Beast (C.G. M. 12/4/1841). L.C. 10/4/1841. 8° 1841 [Songs, Duets, Chorusses]; 12° [1841]; *Dicks* 1017; *Lacy*, vol. xix; 8° 1879 [in *Extravaganzas*, ii].

C.O. The Marriage of Figaro (C.G. T. 15/3/1842). 8° 1842 [Songs, Duets, Chorusses].
[Music Mozart.]

Ext. The White Cat (C.G. M. 28/3/1842). L.C. 25/3/1842. 8° 1842 [Songs, Duets, Chorusses]; *Lacy*, vol. xxiv; 8° 1879 [in *Extravaganzas*, ii].
[Music J. H. Tully.]

Vaud. The Follies of a Night (D.L. W. 5/10/1842). L.C. 5/10/1842.
12° 1842; *Dicks* 869; *Lacy*, vol. xiv.
C. The Way of the World (H.² S. 17/12/1842).
[An alteration of Congreve's play.]
Ext. Fortunio; or, The Seven Gifted Servants (D.L. M. 17/4/1843).
L.C. 11/4/1843. 12° 1843; *Lacy*, vol. xix; 8° 1843 [Songs]; 8° 1879
[in *Extravaganzas*, ii].
F. Who's your Friend? or, The Queensberry Fête (H.² T. 22/8/1843).
Acting Nat. Drama, vol. x; *Dicks* 882.
Ext. The Fair One with the Golden Locks (H.² T. 26/12/1843). L.C.
20/12/1843. 12° 1852; *Lacy*, vol. xix; 8° 1879 [in *Extravaganzas*, ii].
C. Grist to the Mill (H.² Th. 22/2/1844). L.C. 17/2/1844. 12° 1844;
Dicks 890; *Lacy*, vol. xx.
Review. The Drama at Home; or, An Evening with Puff (H.² M.
8/4/1844). L.C. 6/4/1844. 12° 1844; 8° 1879 [in *Extravaganzas*,
ii]; *Lacy*, vol. xx.
F. Somebody Else (H.² W. 4/12/1844). L.C. 26/11/1844. *Dicks* 895;
Lacy, vol. xi.
Ext. Graciosa and Percinet (H.² Th. 26/12/1844). L.C. 23/12/1844.
12° 1845; *Lacy*, vol. xx; 8° 1879 [in *Extravaganzas*, ii].
Ext. The Golden Fleece; or, Jason in Colchis, and Medea in Corinth
(H.² M. 24/3/1845). L.C. 22/3/1845. 8° 1845 [Songs, Duets,
Chorusses]; 8° 1879 [in *Extravaganzas*, iii]; *Lacy*, vol. xx.
F. A Cabinet Question (H.² T. 23/9/1845). L.C. 15/9/1845. 12° 1845;
Dicks 889; *Lacy*, vol. xx.
Ext. The Bee and the Orange Tree; or, The Four Wishes (H.² F.
26/12/1845). L.C. 26/12/1845. 12° 1846; 8° 1879 [in *Extra-
vaganzas*, iii]; *Lacy*, vol. xx.
F. The Irish Post (H.² S. 28/2/1846). L.C. 27/2/1846. 12° 1846;
Dicks 937; *Lacy*, vol. xx.
C. "The Birds" of Aristophanes (H.² M. 13/4/1846). L.C. 11/4/1846.
12° 1846; 8° 1879 [in *Extravaganzas*, iii]; *Lacy*, vol. xx.
[Based on *The Birds* of Aristophanes.]
C. Queen Mary's Bower (H.² S. 10/10/1846). L.C. 12/10/1846.
12° [1847]; *Dicks* 996; *Lacy*, vol. xx.
F. Spring Gardens (H.² Th. 15/10/1846). L.C. 16/10/1846. 12°
[1846]; *Dicks* 997.
F. Story-Telling; or, "Novel" Effects (H.² W. 16/12/1846).
[Partly acted on T. 8/12/1846; Farren was unable to continue
and the performance was abandoned.]
Ext. The Invisible Prince; or, The Island of Tranquil Delights
(H.² S. 26/12/1846). L.C. 26/12/1846. 8° [1846; Songs, Duets,
Chorusses]; 8° 1879 [in *Extravaganzas*, iii]; *Lacy*, vol. xx.
Ext. The New Planet; or, Harlequin out of Place (H.² M. 5/4/1847).
L.C. 3/4/1847. 12° 1847; 8° 1879 [in *Extravaganzas*, iii].
D. The Jacobite (H.² S. 12/6/1847). H.² 11/6/1847. 12° 1852;
Dicks 1015; *Lacy*, vol. xiv.
D. The Pride of the Market (Lyc. M. 18/10/1847). L.C. 1/10/1847.
12° 1847; *Dicks* 999; *Lacy*, vol. xx.
Ext. The Golden Branch (Lyc. M. 27/12/1847). L.C. 22/12/1847.
8° [1848]; 8° 1847 [Songs, Duets, Chorusses]; 8° 1879 [in
Extravaganzas, iii]; *Lacy*, vol. xix.
D. Not a Bad Judge (Lyc. Th. 2/3/1848). L.C. 29/2/1848. *Dicks* 1016;
Lacy, vol. viii.

Bsq. Theseus and Ariadne; or, The Marriage of Bacchus (Lyc. M.
24/4/1848). 12° 1848; *Lacy*, vol. xix; 8° 1879 [in *Extravaganzas*, iii].
Ext. The King of the Peacocks (Lyc. T. 26/12/1848). L.C. 23/12/1848.
12° [1849]; *Lacy*, vol. xix; 8° 1879 [in *Extravaganzas*, iii].
D. A Romantic Idea (Lyc. Th. 8/3/1849). L.C. 5/3/1849. 12° [1849];
Dicks 1010; *Lacy*, vol. xxi.
F. Hold your Tongue (Lyc. Th. 22/3/1849). L.C. 5/10/1848.
12° [1849]; *Dicks* 1010; *Lacy*, vol. xx.
Ext. The Seven Champions of Christendom (Lyc. M. 9/4/1849).
L.C. 14/4/1849. 12° [1849]; *Lacy*, vol. xxi; 8° 1879 [in *Extra-
vaganzas*, iii].
C. A Lady in Difficulties (Lyc. M. 15/10/1849). 12° [1849]; *Lacy*,
vol. xxi.
Ext. The Island of Jewels (Lyc. W. 26/12/1849). L.C. 21/12/1849.
12° [1850]; *Lacy*, vol. xix; 8° 1879 [in *Extravaganzas*, iv].
[For his later plays see *Extravaganzas* (1879), vol. v, pp. 328–30.]

PLANCHÉ, Mrs J. R. [ELIZABETH].
Vaud. The Welsh Girl (Olym. M. 16/12/1833). L.C. 28/11/1833.
12° 1834; *Dicks* 873.
D. The Sledge Driver (H.² Th. 19/6/1834). L.C. 9/6/1834. 12° 1834.
D. Ivan Daniloff; or, The Russian Mandate (Surrey, M. 16/11/1835).
Ba. A Handsome Husband (Olym. M. 15/2/1836). L.C. 5/2/1836.
12° [1836]; *Dicks* 887; *Lacy*, vol. xi.
D. The Ransom (H.² Th. 9/6/1836). L.C. 2/6/1836. 12° 1836;
Dicks 885.
Ba. A Pleasant Neighbour (Olym. Th. 20/10/1836). 12° [1836];
Dicks 873.
Ba. A Hasty Conclusion (Olym. Th. 19/4/1838). L.C. 29/3/1838.
12° 1838; *Acting Nat. Drama*, vol. iv; *Dicks* 887.

PLOWDEN, Mrs FRANCES.
O. Virginia (D.L. Th. 30/10/1800). 8° 1800.
[Music S. J. Arnold.]

PLUNKETT, HENRY GRATTAN [H. P. GRATTAN].
R.D. The Minerali; or, The Betrothed (Vic. W. 1/7/1835). L.C.
21/12/1835. *Duncombe*, vol. xxiii; *Lacy*, vol. lxxiv [both as *The M.;
or, The Dying Gift*].

POCOCK, ISAAC.
O.F. Yes or No? (H.² 31/8/1808). L. 49 S. [24/8/1808]. 8° 1809.
[Music C. Smith.]
O.F. Hit or Miss! (Lyc. M. 26/2/1810). L. 91 M. [20/2/1810];
L. 132 M. [1/9/1823; new scenes]. 8° 1810 [3 editions]; 8° 1811
[4th]; *Cumberland*, vol. xxxiv; *London Theatre*, vol. xxiv.
M.D. Twenty Years Ago! (Lyc. S. 21/7/1810). L. 52 S. [22/6/1810].
8° 1810 [*bis*].
Int. The Morning Post and the Morning Herald (Lyc. F. 31/5/1811).
L. 54 S. [25/5/1811].
O.F. Any Thing New (Lyc. M. 1/7/1811). L. 54 S. [15/6/1811].
8° 1811.
[Music C. Smith.]
O.F. The Green-eyed Monster; or, How to get your Money (Lyc. M.
14/10/1811). L. 53 S. [15/2/1811].
Ba. Harry le Roy (C.G. F. 2/7/1813). L. 99 M. [22/6/1813].
[Based on Dodsley, *The King and the Miller of Mansfield*.]

M.D. The Miller and his Men (C.G. Th. 21/10/1813). L. 99 M. [14/10/1813; as *The Bohemian Miller*]. 8° 1813; 8° 1816; 8° 1820; *Dicks* 28; *Dicks B.D.* [1867]; *Cumberland*, vol. xxvi; *Lacy*, vol. i [new series].

M.D. "For England, Ho!" (C.G. W. 15/12/1813). L. 98 M. [8/12/1813]. 8° 1814; *Cumberland*, vol. xxxix.

C.O. John of Paris (C.G. S. 12/11/1814). L. 101 M. [29/10/1814]. 8° 1814; 8° [1820]; *Cumberland*, vol. xxvi.

    [An adaptation of St Just, *Jean de Paris*, with music by Boieldieu arranged by Bishop.]

M.D. Zembuca; or, The Net-Maker and his Wife (C.G. M. 27/3/1815). L. 105 M. [13/3/1815]. 8° 1815.

M.D. The Magpie, or the Maid? (C.G. F. 15/9/1815). 8° [1815]; 8° 1816 [2nd]; *Dicks* 948; *Cumberland*, vol. xxviii; *Lacy*, vol. lxxxvii.

    [Based on L. C. Caigniez, *La pie voleuse; ou, la servante de Palaiseau*.]

F. The Farce Writer (C.G. M. 5/10/1815). L. 61 S. [3/10/1815].

M.D. John du Bart; or, The Voyage to Poland (C.G. W. 25/10/1815). L. 105 M. [19/10/1815].

M.D. The Ravens; or, The Force of Conscience (C.G. T. 28/1/1817). L. 111 M. [14/1/1817].

M.D. The Heir of Vironi; or, Honesty the Best Policy (C.G. Th. 27/2/1817). L. 111 M. [11/1/1817].

    [Music Bishop and Whitaker.]

M.D. Robinson Crusoe; or, The Bold Bucaniers (C.G. M. 7/4/1817). L. 111 M. [22/3/1817]. 8° 1817; *Dicks* 214; *Lacy*, vol. lxxxix; *Cumberland*, vol. xxviii.

    [Based on Pixérécourt, *Robinson Crusoë* (Paris, 2/10/1805).]

M.D. The Libertine (C.G. T. 20/5/1817). L. 111 M. [10/5/1817]. 8° 1817.

    [Based on Mozart's *Don Giovanni*.]

F. Husbands and Wives (C.G. W. 3/12/1817). L. 111 M. [27/11/1817; as *H. and W.; or, The Debt and the Duel*].

M.D. The Antiquary (C.G. 1818).

    [This version was a failure; see below.]

M.D. Rob Roy Macgregor; or, Auld Lang Syne! (C.G. Th. 12/3/1818). L. 112 M. [28/2/1818]. 8° 1818 [*bis*]; *Dicks* 70; *Oxberry* [1821]; *Dicks B.D.* [1867]; *Waverley Dramas* [1845]; *Lacy*, vol. iii; *B.D.* [1864], vol. ii.

    [Music J. Davy. This version of Scott's novel includes Songs by Burns and Wordsworth.]

M.D. The Antiquary (C.G. T. 25/1/1820). L. 118 M. [13/1/1820]. 8° 1820; 8° 1820 [Songs, Duets]; 8° 1829.

    [Music Bishop and T. Cooke. Written in collaboration with *D. TERRY*.]

M.D. Montrose; or, The Children of the Mist (C.G. Th. 14/2/1822). L. 127 M. [6/2/1822]. 8° 1822.

    [Music Bishop, Ware and Watson. Based on Scott's novel.]

M.D. Nigel; or, The Crown Jewels (C.G. T. 28/1/1823). L. 125 M. [31/12/1822]. 8° 1823.

    [This version of Scott's novel was hurried out to forestall another at D.L.]

F. Cent. per Cent.; or, The Masquerade (C.G. Th. 29/5/1823). L. 129 M. [10/5/1823]. 8° [1823].

M.D. Woodstock (Surrey, M. 15/5/1826; C.G. S. 20/5/1826). L.C. 15/5/1826. 8° 1826; *Dicks* 533.
[From a note in *The Gentleman's Magazine* it seems that the Surrey version was the same as that given at C.G.]

M.D. Peveril of the Peak (C.G. S. 21/10/1826). L.C. 28/9/1826. 8° 1826 [Songs, Duets, Chorusses].
[Music C. E. Horn. Based on Scott's novel.]

M.D. Alfred the Great; or, The Enchanted Standard (C.G. S. 3/11/1827). L.C. 2/10/1827 [under sub-title]. 8° 1827.
[Partly based on O'Keeffe, *The Magic Banner*.]

M.D. Tuckitomba; or, The Obi Sorceress (C.G. M. 7/4/1828). L.C. 3/3/1828.

M.D. The Robber's Bride (C.G. Th. 22/10/1829). L.C. 21/10/1829. *Cumberland Minor*, vol. xi; *Dicks* 362; *Cumberland*, vol. xxviii; *Lacy*, vol. lxix.
[Music F. Ries. Also called *The Robber s Wife*.]

M.D. The Blue Anchor; or, A Tar for All Weathers (C.G. M. 18/10/1830). L.C. 11/10/1830.

F. The Omnibus ! or, A Convenient Distance ! (C.G. M. 6/12/1830). L.C. 25/11/1830. *Duncombe; Dicks* 725; *Lacy*, vol. xxxii.
[An alteration of R. J. Raymond, *Cherry Bounce* (S.W. 1821).]

M.D. Comrades and Friends; or, Life for Life (C.G. F. 11/2/1831). L.C. 26/1/1831. *Dicks* 747.
[Based on D'Aubigny, *Les deux sergeants*.]

F. Country Quarters (C.G. T. 6/12/1831). L.C. 12/11/1831.

M.D. The Doom Kiss (D.L. M. 29/10/1832). L.C. 19/10/1832.
[Music Bishop.]

F. Clutterbucks; or, The Railroad of Love (C.G. W. 31/10/1832). L.C. 20/10/1832.
[Based on *Le père d'occasion*.]

M.D. The Ferry and the Mill (C.G. S. 19/10/1833). L.C. 4/10/1833.

F. Scan. Mag. (C.G. S. 23/11/1833). L.C. 12/11/1829 [as *S. M.; or, The Village Gossip*].

F. Anster Fair; or, Michael Scott the Wizard (D.L. M. 31/3/1834). L.C. 16/3/1834.

Ent. King Arthur and the Knights of the Round Table (D.L. F. 26/12/1834). L.C. 20/12/1834. 8° 1834.
[Based on Scott, *The Bridal of Triermain*. Music T. Cooke.]

F. The Night Patrol (D.L. Th. 1/10/1835). L.C. 2/10/1835.

M.D. Cavaliers and Roundheads (D.L. T. 13/10/1835). L.C. 12/10/1835.
[Based on Scott, *Old Mortality*.]

M.D. The King and the Duke; or, The Siege of Alençon (C.G. F. 8/2/1839). L.C. 1839.
[Music T. Cooke.]

POLACK, ELIZABETH.

D. Esther, the Royal Jewess; or, The Death of Haman (R.P. M. 9/3/1835). 12° [1835; *bis*]; *Duncombe*, vol. xvi.

M.D. St Clair of the Isles; or, The Outlaw of Barra (Vic. M. 16/4/1838). 12° [1838]; *Dicks* 794.
[This play seems to be given in *Dicks* 794 under the name of POCOCK.]

POOLE, JOHN.
Bsq. Hamlet Travestie (New, Th. 24/1/1811; C.G. Th. 17/6/1813).
  L. 55 S. [15/9/1812; printed copy]. 12° 1810; 8° 1811 [2nd and
  3rd]; 8° 1814 [5th]; 12° 1817; *Lacy*, vol. x.
Spec. The Earls of Hammersmith; or, Infant Maturity (Surrey,
  T. 1/10/1811). *Lacy* [with subtitle, *or, The Cellar Spectre*]. L. 1799.
  [Written in collaboration with *DENNIS LAWLER.*]
F. The Hole in the Wall (D.L. W. 23/6/1813). L. 57 S. [11/6/1813].
  8° 1813.
Int. Intrigue (D.L. T. 26/4/1814). L. 102 M. [2/4/1814]. 8° 1814;
  Dicks 315; *Lacy*, vol. liv; *Duncombe*, vol. vii.
F. Who's Who? or, The Double Imposture (D.L. W. 15/11/1815).
  L. 106 M. [7/11/1815]. 8° 1815.
F. A Short Reign and a Merry One (C.G. F. 19/11/1819). L. 73 S.
  [10/9/1819]. 8° 1819.
F. Matchmaking (H.² S. 25/8/1821). L. 81 S. [16/8/1821; as *Marriage
  Projects*]. *Lacy*, vol. xxvii; *Dicks* 522.
  [Based on *Les projets de mariage*.]
F. The Two Pages of Frederick the Great (C.G. S. 1/12/1821).
  L. 123 M. [20/11/1821]. 8° 1821; *Dicks* 954.
  [Based on *Les deux pages*.]
F. Old and Young (D.L. Th. 5/12/1822). L. 84 S. [29/11/1822].
C. Simpson and Co. (D.L. S. 4/1/1823). L. 85 S. [27/11/1822; as
  Mr S. and C.]. 8° 1827; *Lacy*, vol. lxxiv; *Dicks* 336.
M.D. Augusta; or, The Blind Girl (D.L. T. 14/1/1823). L. 86 S.
  [1/1/1823].
F. Deaf as a Post (H.² S. 15/2/1823). 8° [New York; N.D.]; *Dicks* 343;
  Lacy, vol. xiv.
F. A Year in an Hour; or, The Cock of the Walk (H.² Th. 17/6/1824).
  L.C. 11/6/1824. 8° 1824.
C. Married and Single; or, Belles and Bailiffs (H.² F. 16/7/1824).
  L.C. 24/6/1824 [as *M. and S.; or, Takings and Mistakings*]; L.C.
  D.L. 20/7/1824. 8° 1824.
  [Based on *L'homme à soixante ans*.]
F. 'Twould Puzzle a Conjuror (H.² S. 11/9/1824). L.C. 6/9/1824.
  Dicks 648; *Lacy*, vol. xiv.
C. Tribulation; or, Unwelcome Visitors (H.² T. 3/5/1825). L.C.
  19/4/1825. 8° 1825; *Cumberland*, vol. xii; *Dicks* 960.
  [Based on *Un moment d'imprudence*.]
C. Paul Pry (H.² T. 13/9/1825). L.C. 9/1825. 8° [New York; N.D.];
  Duncombe, vol. i; *Dicks* 321; *Lacy*, vol. xv.
F. The Scape-goat (C.G. F. 25/11/1825). L.C. 7/11/1825. 8° 1826; *Dicks*
  550; *Lacy*, vol. xcviii; *B.D.* [1864], vol. xii; *London Stage*, vol. iv.
F. 'Twixt the Cup and the Lip (H.² M. 12/6/1826). L.C. 8/5/1826.
C. The Wife's Stratagem; or, More Frightened than Hurt (C.G. T.
  13/3/1827). 8° 1827; *Dicks* 567.
  [Based on Shirley, *The Gamesters*.]
O.F. Gudgeons and Sharks; or, Piecrust Promises (H.² S. 28/7/1827).
  L.C. 12/7/1827 [with titles reversed].
C. The Wealthy Widow; or, They're both to blame (D.L. M.
  29/10/1827). L.C. 22/10/1827. 8° [1827].
  [Based on *La jeune mari*.]
F. My Wife! What Wife? (D.L. W. 1/4/1829). *Lacy*, vol. xcvi;
  Dicks 585.

F. Lodgings for Single Gentlemen (H.² M. 15/6/1829). L.C. 25/5/1829. *Lacy*, vol. cxv; *Duncombe*, vol. liv; *Dicks* 403.

D. Past and Present; or, The Hidden Treasure (D.L. T. 23/2/1830). L.C. 18/2/1830. *Lacy*, vol. xcvi.
[Based on *Antoine, ou les trois époques*.]

F. Turning the Tables (D.L. Th. 11/11/1830). L.C. 5/11/1830. *Duncombe*, vol. xiii; *Dicks* 380; *Mod. Eng. Com. Th.* No. 68; *Lacy*, vol. xl.

F. A Nabob for an Hour (C.G. Th. 21/3/1833). L.C. 9/5/1833. *Duncombe*, vol. xii; *Lacy*, vol. cviii.
[Based on Scribe, *L'oncle d'Amerique* (Paris, 14/3/1826).]

C. A Soldier's Courtship (D.L. T. 3/12/1833). L.C. 30/11/1833. 8° 1833; *Dicks* 343; 12° [N.Y. N.D.].

C. Patrician and Parvenu; or, Confusion Worse Confounded (D.L. S. 21/3/1835). L.C. 14/3/1835 [under sub-title]. 8° 1835.

D. The Atonement; or, The God-daughter (H.² T. 24/5/1836). L.C. 10/5/1836. 8° 1836; *Dicks* 160.
[Based on *Père et parent*.]

F. Delicate Attentions (St J. Th. 24/11/1836). L.C. 18/11/1836. 8° 1837; *Duncombe*, vol. xxxii.

POOLE, RICHARD.
D. Byzantium. 8° 1823.

PORTER, ANNA MARIA.
M.D. The Fair Fugitives (C.G. M. 16/5/1803). L. 43 S. [5/4/1803].
[Music Busby.]
T. Switzerland (D.L. M. 15/2/1819).

POWELL, JAMES.
D. The Venetian Outlaw, His Country's Friend. 8° 1805.
[An adaptation of Pixérécourt, *L'homme à trois visages; ou, le proscrit de Venise* (Paris, 1801).]

POWELL, THOMAS [of Monmouth].
D. The Children in the Wood. 12° 1805 [in *Works*].

POWELL, THOMAS [of New York].
D. The Count de Foix. 8° 1842.
F. The Blind Wife; or, The Student of Bonn. 8° 1843.
T. The Wife's Revenge. 8° 1842.
D. The Shepherd's Well. 8° 1844.

POWER, TYRONE.
C. Married Lovers (C.G. W. 2/2/1831). L.C. 29/1/1831. 8° 1831.
F. Born to Good Luck; or, An Irishman's Fortune (C.G. S. 17/3/1832). L.C. 24/2/1832. *Lacy*, vol. ii; *Dicks* 784.
D. St. Patrick's Eve; or, The Order of the Day (D.L. S. 24/11/1832). L.C. 22/11/1832. *Acting Nat. Drama*, vol. ii; *Dicks* 518.
[Music T. Cooke.]
F. Paddy Cary, the Boy of Clogheen (C.G. W. 29/5/1833). L.C. 25/5/1833. *Lacy*, vol. xxvi.
M.Ent. O'Flannigan and the Fairies; or, A Midsummer Night's Dream (not Shakespeare's) (C.G. 24/4/1836; H.² W. 26/12/1838). L.C. 23/4/1836.
C. Etiquette; or, A Wife for a Blunder (C.G. M. 16/5/1836).
Int. How to Pay the Rent (H.² Th. 2/4/1840). L.C. 17/3/1840. *Dicks* 407; *Acting Nat. Drama*, vol. ix; *Mod. Eng. Com. Th.* vol. i.

PRATT, SAMUEL JACKSON.
[For his earlier works see *A History of Late Eighteenth Century Drama*, p. 299.]
C.O. Fire and Frost. 8° 1805.
[For this and the following plays see *The Biographia Dramatica*.]
D. Hail Fellow, well met! 8° 1805.
C.O. Love's Trials; or, The Triumphs of Constancy. 8° 1805.

PULHAM, —
Int. Reformation (C.G. 28/6/1815). L. 61 S. [19/7/1815].

PYE, HENRY JAMES.
[For an earlier play see *A History of Late Eighteenth Century Drama*, p. 300.]
T. Adelaide (D.L. S. 25/1/1800). L. 40 S. [14/1/1800]. 8° 1800.
C. A Prior Claim (D.L. T. 29/10/1805). L. 83 M. [22/10/1805].
    8° 1805; 8° 1806 [2nd].
    [Written in collaboration with *S. J. ARNOLD*.]

RAFTER, Capt.
D.D. Pauline (C.L. 27/10/1845). L.C. 22/10/1845.
O. La Dame Blanche. L.C. Grecian, 20/6/1848.
    [An adaptation of Scribe's opera.]
M.D. The Heart of Midlothian (P'cess, W. 18/4/1849). L.C. 2/4/1849.

RAMSAY, THOMAS J.
Spec. The Skeleton Steed; or, The Phantom Knights of the Charmed
    Bay. L.C. Apollo, 26/12/1843.

RANNIE, JOHN.
O.F. The Lowland Lassie in London. L. 43 S. [D.L. 6/5/1803].
    [This seems to be the same as *The Highland Lassie; or, A Trip
    from the North*. 8° 1803 [cf. also *Musical Dramas* 8° (1806)].]
M.D. The Exiles. 8° [1806; in *Musical Dramas*].

RAYMOND, CATHERINE FRANCES MALONE.
D. The Devil's Share. L.C. Liverpool, 1843.
Vaud. The Two Sisters; or, The Godfather's Legacy. L.C. Liverpool,
    28/9/1843.
Vaud. Mariette; or, The Reward. L.C. Liverpool, 24/10/1843.

RAYMOND, RICHARD JOHN.
M.D. The Castle of Paluzzi; or, The Extorted Oath (C.G. W.
    27/5/1818). L. 71 S. [20/5/1818; under sub-title]. 8° 1818.
M.D. The State Prisoner (R.A. M. 25/10/1819). 8° 1818.
F. Cherry Bounce (S.W. M. 27/8/1821). 8° [1821]; *Lacy*, vol. lix;
    Dicks 360; *Duncombe*, vol. viii.
F. Which is my Cousin? (H.² Th. 29/9/1825). L.C. 1825. 8° [1825].
C. "The Two make a Pair"; or Manœuvring (D.L. S. 7/4/1827).
    L.C. 3/4/1827.
D. The Greek Family (D.L. Th. 22/10/1829).
    [Music Cooke.]
R.D. Robert the Devil; or, The Wizard's Ring (Cob. M. 21/6/1830).
    12° 1830 [*Richardson;* as *R. the D.; or, The Duke of Normandy*];
    Cumberland, vol. xxxiii.
F. The Deuce is in Her (Adel. 28/8/1830). L.C. 7/8/1830. *Dicks* 993;
    Duncombe, vol. vii.
F. "P.S. Come to Dinner" (Surrey, M. 22/11/1830).

D.D. The Farmer's Daughter of the Severnside; or, The Broken Heart (Cob. M. 11/4/1831). *Lacy*, vol. xxvi [with subtitle, *or, Mr and Mrs Toodles*].

M.D. The Wreck of the Leander Frigate; or, The Fatal Coral Bank (Cob. M. 23/5/1831).
[See also under *UNKNOWN AUTHORS*.]

M.D. The Old Oak Tree (E.O.H. M. 24/8/1835). L.C. 25/8/1835. *Duncombe*, vol. xviii.
[Music G. A. Macfarren.]

F. The Balance of Comfort (Adel. M. 22/2/1836). L.C. 13/2/1836 [as *The B. of C.; or, Bachelors and Married Men*]. *Duncombe*, vol. xxxi.

Oa. Mrs White (E.O.H. Th. 23/6/1836). L.C. 6/1836. *Lacy*, vol. lv; *Dicks* 360; *Duncombe*, vol. xxii.

D.D. The Village Story; or, The Farmer and his Wife. L.C. 21/4/1838.

M.D. The Emigrant's Daughter: A Tale of the Neutral Ground (E.O.H. T. 7/8/1838). L.C. 8/1838. *Duncombe*, vol. xxxi.

F. Like Father, like Son (E.O.H. Th. 13/8/1840). L.C. 11/8/1840. *Dicks* 993; *Duncombe*, vol. xlii.

D. Paul the Brazier; or, The Reign of Terror (Olym. M. 16/11/1840). L.C. 10/1840.

D. The Lone Hut (Lyc. M. 4/7/1842). L.C. 22/6/1842 [as *The Lone House; or, A Legend of Mount Blanc*]. *Dicks* 682.

D. The Discarded Daughter (Surrey, M. 5/4/1847). L.C. 3/4/1847. *Duncombe*, vol. lix.

RAYNER, BARNABAS F.

Spec. Lalla Rookh; or, The Ghebirs of the Desert (R.A. M. 13/6/1836). *Dicks* 549.

D. The Factory Assassin; or, The Dumb Boy of Manchester (R.A. M. 25/9/1837). L.C. 1837 [under sub-title only]. *Dicks* 368; *Lacy*, vol. xxvi [as *The Dumb Man of Manchester*].

Ba. The White Wolf; or, The Condemned House and the Diet of Ratisbon. L.C. Olym. 2/8/1841.

P. Harlequin, Prince of Thebes. L.C. Apollo, 19/11/1845.

Spec. The Edict of the Secret Council; or, The Exiled Plantagenet. L.C. Apollo, 17/12/1845.

D. The Cricket on the Hearth. L.C. Apollo, 16/1/1846.
[Based on Dickens' novel.]

Spec. Elizabeth of England. L.C. Apollo, 18/3/1846.

REACH, ANGUS BETHUNE.

F. Which Mr Smith? (Lyc. Th. 8/10/1846). L.C. 17/9/1846.

D. Fleurs de Lys; or, Love's Triumph (Lyc. M. 19/7/1847). L.C. 22/7/1847 [as *F. de L.; or, Well Won*].
[Written in collaboration with *H. HERBERT*.]

F. The Special (Olym. 3/5/1848). L.C. 3/5/1848.

REDE, WILLIAM LEMAN.

Spec. Sixteen String Jack (Cob. T. 18/2/1823). *Dicks* 392.

Ext. Professionals Puzzled; or, Struggles at Starting (Strand, Th. 26/1/1832).

M.D. The Rake's Progress (City, M. 28/1/1833). L.C. Olym. 3/6/1833 [not necessarily the same]. *Dicks* 240; *Duncombe*, vol. xii; *Lacy*, vol. xxxii.

M.D. Five Degrees of Crime (City, M. 11/2/1833; R.P.M. 11/11/1833).

F.   His First Champagne (Strand, M. 7/10/1833). L.C. 1/10/1832.
Dicks 212; Acting Nat. Drama, vol. vi; Lacy, vol. lxxiii.

D.   Faith and Falsehood; or, The Fate of the Bushranger (R.P. M.
6/10/1834). Dicks 548; Duncombe, vol. xxxiii.

Ba.   Wealth and Want; or, The Village Politicians (Surrey, M.
26/1/1835). L.C. 1835. Duncombe.

F.   An Affair of Honour (Olym. Th. 12/3/1835). L.C. 5/3/1835.
12° 1835; Dicks 517.

D.   The Skeleton Witness; or, The King's Evidence (Surrey, M.
27/4/1835). 12° 1835 [as The S. W.; or, The Murder of the Mount].

Ext.   Cupid in London; or, Some Passages in the Life of Love (Queen's,
Th. 18/6/1835). Duncombe, vol. xvii.

Ba.   The Old and Young Stager (Olym. M. 7/12/1835). L.C. 7/12/1835.
Dicks 728; Duncombe, vol. xx.

Ba.   Come to Town (Strand, M. 25/4/1836). L.C. 15/4/1836. Duncombe, vol. xxi.

M.D.   The Gaberlunzie Man (E.O.H. M. 26/9/1836). L.C. 26/9/1836.
Duncombe, vol. xxiii.

Ba.   A Flight to America; or, Twelve Hours in New York (Adel. M.
7/11/1836). Duncombe, vol. xxiv.

Bsq.   Douglas Travestie (Adel. 13/2/1837). L.C. 4/2/1837. Duncombe,
vol. xxv; Lacy, vol. xlvi.

Ba.   The Peregrinations of Pickwick; or, Boz-i-a-na (Adel. M.
3/4/1837). L.C. 4/1837 [as The Pickwickians]. Duncombe, vol.
xxxiii.

D.   Rosalie; or, The Exile's Daughter. L.C. H.² 1838.

M.D.   Kohal Cave; or, The Events of a Year (S.W. M. 9/7/1838).

Ba.   The Devil and Dr Faustus (Strand, M. 31/5/1841). L.C.
31/5/1841.

D.   The Rake's Progress. L.C. Edinburgh, 4/7/1841.
[See above under 1833.]

Ext.   The Frolics of the Fairies; or, The Rose, Shamrock and Thistle
(Strand, M. 12/7/1841). L.C. 21/7/1841.

Ba.   The Mission of Mercury (Strand, 12/9/1841). L.C. 12/4/1841.

D.   Sixteen String Jack; or, Ravin the Reefer (Olym. 15/11/1841).
L.C. 11/11/1841.
[See above under 1833.]

Ba.   The Conquest of Cupid; or, Lucre against Love (Strand, Th.
31/3/1842). L.C. 23/3/1842.

D.D.   Jack in the Water; or, The Ladder of Life (Olym. M. 25/4/1842;
S.W. M. 31/7/1843). L.C. 29/4/1842. Dicks 574.

Bsq.   Norval (Olym. T. 18/10/1842).
[See Douglas Travestie, 1837.]

Ba.   Loves of the Devils. L.C. Olym. 10/11/1842.

D.   Life's a Lottery; or, Jolly Dick the Lamplighter (Olym. M.
14/11/1842). L.C. 10/11/1842. Dicks 601.

D.   The Son of the Desert; or, The Demon Changling (S.W. M.
27/2/1843; Olym. Th. 16/3/1843). L.C. 14/2/1843.

D.   Our Village; or, Lost and Found (Olym. M. 17/4/1843). L.C.
21/4/1843. Dicks 711; Lacy, vol. lxxxviii [as O. V.; or, The Lost
Ship].

D.   The Gamecock of the Wilderness (Olym. M. 24/3/1845). L.C.
24/3/1845.

Ca.   Saloon and Cellar (Strand, 26/5/1845). L.C. 24/5/1845.

Ext. The Boyhood of Bacchus (Olym. M. 6/10/1845). L.C. 6/10/1845.
Spec. The Arab and his Steed (R.A. 13/4/1846). L.C. 11/4/1846.
F. The Queen's Bench (Strand, M. 13/11/1848).
C.O. La Somnambula, or, The Somnambulist (C.G. 1848). 12° [1848].

REEVE, WILLIAM.
D. Barark Johnson; or, The Blind Witness (Surrey, M. 8/4/1844).
L.C. 1/4/1844. *Duncombe,* vol. xlix.

REITHMULLER, C. G.
T. Launcelot of the Lake. 8° 1843.

REPTON, HUMPHRY.
C. Odd Whims; or, Two at a Time (Norwich and Harwich, *c.* 1803).
L. 78 M. [Norwich, 28/4/1803]. 8° 1804 [in *Odd Whims, and Miscellanies*].

REYNOLDS, FRANCIS.
F. No (Bath, 16/5/1828). *Cumberland Minor,* vol. v; *Dicks* 310.
Ba. My Grandfather's Will; or, The Man of Straw (Adel. M. 1/10/1838).
L.C. 25/9/1838. *Dicks* 480.

REYNOLDS, FREDERIC.
[For his earlier plays see *A History of Late Eighteenth Century Drama*, p. 301.]
C. Life (C.G. S. 1/11/1800). L. 38 S. [28/9/1800]. 8° 1801 [6 editions]; 12° 1801 [Dublin]; *Inchbald's Modern Theatre,* vol. i.
C. Folly as it Flies (C.G. Th. 29/10/1801). L. 76 M. [19/10/1801].
8° 1802 [*bis*]; *Cumberland,* vol. xxvii; *Dicks* 793; *Inchbald's Modern Theatre,* vol. ii.
C. Delays and Blunders (C.G. S. 30/10/1802). L. 42 S. [10/1802].
8° 1803; 8° 1805.
C. The Three Per Cents. (C.G. S. 12/11/1803).
M.D. The Caravan; or, The Driver and his Dog (D.L. M. 5/12/1803).
L. 43 S. [30/11/1803]. 8° [1803; 3 editions]; 8° 1803 [Songs, Duets, Trios, Chorusses].
[Music W. Reeve.]
C. The Blind Bargain; or, Hear It Out (C.G. W. 24/10/1804).
8° 1805; *Cumberland,* vol. xviii; *Dicks* 625.
O.F. Out of Place; or, The Lake of Lausanne (C.G. Th. 28/2/1805;
Surrey, F. 8/1/1813).
[Music W. Reeve and Braham.]
C. The Delinquent; or, Seeing Company (C.G. Th. 14/11/1805).
L. 83 M. [7/11/1805; under sub-title]. 8° 1805; *Dicks* 903;
Cumberland, vol. xl; *Inchbald's Modern Theatre,* vol. ii.
Spec. The Deserts of Arabia (C.G. Th. 20/11/1806). L. 47 S.
[18/10/1806]. 8° 1806 [Airs, Duets, Chorusses].
[Music G. Lanza.]
O.F. Arbitration; or, Free and Easy (C.G. Th. 11/12/1806). L. 46 S.
[2/12/1806].
[Music G. Lanza.]
C. Begone Dull Care; or, How will it end (C.G. M. 9/2/1808).
8° 1808.
O. The Exile; or, The Deserts of Siberia (C.G. T. 10/11/1808).
L. 87 M. [2/11/1808]. *Cumberland,* vol. xxix.
[Music Mazzinghi and Bishop.]
D.O. The Free Knights; or, The Edict of Charlemagne (C.G. Th.
8/2/1810). L. 92 M. [10/1/1810; with titles reversed]. 8° 1810.

D.R. The Bridal Ring (C.G. T. 16/10/1810). L. 92 M. [3/10/1810].
[Music Condell.]
D.O. The Virgin of the Sun (C.G. F. 31/1/1812). L. 95 M. [1/1/1812].
8° 1812 [4 editions].
[Based on Kotzebue's play.]
D. The Renegade (C.G. W. 2/12/1812). L. 96 M. [20/11/1812].
8° 1812; 8° 1813.
[Music Bishop. Based on Dryden, *Don Sebastian* and *The
Spanish Friar*.]
F. What's a Man of Fashion? or, A Match against Time (C.G. M.
27/11/1815). L. 61 S. [9/11/1815]. 8° 1815.
C.O. A Midsummer Night's Dream (C.G. S. 17/1/1816). 8°
1816.
[Music Bishop. On the alterations in the text see G. C. D.
Odell, *op. cit.* ii. 75–7.]
C.O. The Humorous Lieutenant; or Alexander's Successors (C.G.
18/1/1817). L. 109 M. [C.G. 29/12/1816]; B.M. MS. Add.
27,710.
M.D. The Duke of Savoy; or, Wife and Mistress (C.G. M. 29/9/1817).
L. 111 M. [14/9/1817]; B.M. MS. Add. 27,708.
[Music Bishop.]
M.D. The Father and his Children (C.G. S. 25/10/1817). L. 109 M.
[22/10/1817].
M.D. The Illustrious Traveller; or, The Forges of Kanzell (C.G.
T. 3/2/1818). L. 114 M. [26/1/1818].
M.D. The Burgomaster of Sardaam; or, The Two Peters (C.G. W.
23/9/1818). L. 114 M. [10/9/1818].
C.O. The Comedy of Errors (C.G. S. 11/12/1819). 8° 1819.
[Music Bishop. See G. C. D. Odell, *op. cit.* ii. 131–5.]
C.O. Twelfth Night (C.G. W. 8/11/1820).
[Music Bishop. See G. C. D. Odell, *op. cit.* ii. 135–7.]
C.O. Don John; or, The Two Violettas (C.G. T. 20/2/1821). 8°
1821.
[Music Bishop and Ware. An adaptation of *The Chances* by
Beaumont and Fletcher as altered by Buckingham.]
C.O. The Tempest (C.G. T. 15/5/1821).
[Music Bishop. See G. C. D. Odell, *op. cit.* ii. 137–8.]
C.O. The Two Gentlemen of Verona (C.G. Th. 29/11/1821).
[Music Bishop. See G. C. D. Odell, *op. cit.* ii. 138–40.]
C.O. The Merry Wives of Windsor (D.L. F. 20/2/1824).
[Music Bishop. See G. C. D. Odell, *op. cit.* ii. 140–2.]
M.D. Edward the Black Prince (D.L. M. 28/1/1828). L.C. 14/1/1828.
Musical score and lyrics in B.M. MS. Add. 27,722.
[Music Bishop. Based mainly on Shirley's play (1750).]
P. Harlequin and Queen Mab; or, The Three Glass Distaffs (C.G.
F. 26/12/1834). L.C. 20/12/1834.
P. Harlequin and Old Gammer Gurton; or, The Lost Needle (D.L.
M. 26/12/1836). L.C. 23/12/1836.
P. Harlequin Jack-a-Lantern; or, The Witch of the Dropping Well
(D.L. T. 26/12/1837). L.C. 20/12/1837.
P. Harlequin and Jack Frost; or, Old Goody Hearty (D.L. W.
26/12/1838). L.C. 1838.
P. Harlequin and the Enchanted Fish; or, The Genii of the Brazen
Bottle (Adel. S. 26/12/1840). L.C. 17/12/1840.

REYNOLDS, JOHN HAMILTON.
F.   Confounded Foreigners (H.[2] S. 6/1/1838). L.C. 6/1/1838. *Acting Nat. Drama,* vol. iii.

REYNOLDSON, THOMAS H.
D.   The Rich Man of Frankfort (Surrey, W. 31/10/1838). *Cumberland Minor,* vol. xiv.
O.   The Elixir of Love (Surrey, 1839). *Lacy,* vol. xxxvii.
C.   The Brewer of Preston; or, The Black Charger (Surrey, M. 1/7/1839). *Lacy,* vol. cxiii [as *The B. of P.; or, Malt and Hops*].
     [A play of this title is in L.C. 1848 licensed for the Grecian. It is probably an alteration by Reynoldson of his earlier work.]
R.D. The Venetian; or, The Council of Ten (Surrey, M. 20/4/1840). *Cumberland Minor,* vol. xv.
C.O. Don Pasquale. L.C. Grecian, 28/10/1843. 12° 1856.
F.   The 24th of May (Olym. 12/2/1844). L.C. 8/2/1844.
C.O. Little Red Riding Hood and the Wolf. L.C. Grecian, 27/4/1844.
C.O. The Crown Diamonds (P'cess, Th. 2/5/1844). L.C. 26/3/1844.
     [An adaptation of Scribe, *Les diamants de la couronne* (Paris, 6/3/1841), with music by Auber.]
R.D. The Pirate. L.C. Grecian, 15/11/1844.
C.D. Monseigneur; or, The Paris Robbers. L.C. Grecian, 10/12/1844.
C.O. Spirits and Water. L.C. C.L. 1845.
C.O. The Brigadier (P'cess, 29/1/1845). L.C. 25/1/1845.
     [Originally called *The Grenadier.*]
O.   Gustavus III; or, The Masked Ball. L.C. Grecian, 15/2/1845.
     [An adaptation of Scribe's opera; see under *J. R. PLANCHÉ.*]
C.O. The Duc d'Olonne (P'cess, M. 14/4/1845). L.C. 26/1/1845; Grecian, 5/1/1845.
C.   The Chevalier de St Georges (P'cess, T. 20/5/1845). L.C. 16/5/1845.
     [An adaptation from the French of Mélesville and Beauvoir (Paris, 15/2/1840).]
F.   Jack o' both Sides (P'cess, T. 21/10/1845). L.C. 13/10/1845.
D.   Manette. L.C. P'cess, 1846.
D.   A Curious Case (P'cess, 17/8/1846). L.C. 21/8/1846.
D.   Clarissa Harlowe (P'cess, M. 28/9/1846). L.C. 12/10/1846.
     [The L.C. manuscript definitely ascribes this play to Reynoldson; but it was announced as by *T. H. LACY* and *J. COURTNEY.*]
D.   Ernestine; or, The Foster Sister (P'cess, T. 14/4/1846). L.C. 11/4/1846.
     [An adaptation from the French of Dennery and Clément (Paris, 31/10/1845).]
F.   The Barber Bravo (P'cess, F. 7/8/1846). L.C. 21/8/1846.
     [In MS. called also *The Invention of Powder.*]
F.   Keeping a Place (P'cess, W. 4/11/1846). L.C. 6/11/1846.
D.   Dreams of the Heart (P'cess, W. 17/3/1847). L.C. 10/3/1847.
D.   The Drunkard's Children (Surrey, M. 3/7/1848). L.C. 29/6/1848.
     [Based on the drawings of G. Cruickshank, who directed the production.]

RHODES, GEORGE AMBROSE.
T.   Dion. 8° 1806; 8° 1820.
D.   The Fifth of November; or, The Gunpowder Plot. An Historical Play. Supposed to be written by William Shakespeare. 8° 1830.

RHODES, WILLIAM BARNES.
Bsq. Bombastes Furioso (H.[2] T. 7/8/1810). L. 51 S. [2/8/1810].
12° 1813 [Dublin]; 8° 1822 [pirated]; 8° 1822 [1st authorised];
12° 1830; *Dicks* 222; *Lacy*, vol. iii; *Duncombe*, vol. xlviii; *Cumberland*, vol. xliii.

RICE, THOMAS D.
C.O. Bone Squash Diabolo (Surrey, S. 9/7/1836).

RICHARDS, ALFRED BATES.
T. Croesus, King of Lydia. 4° 1845; 8° 1861.
D. Cromwell. 8° 1847; 8° 1873; 8° 1876.
    [This was performed at the Queen's on 21/12/1872.]
D. Isolda. 8° 1848.
D. Vandyck; a Play of Genoa. 8° 1850.

RICHARDS, GEORGE.
Poems. 8° 1804 [contains *Emma* and *Odin*].

RICHARDSON, Mrs SARAH.
T. Ethelred. 8° [1810].
T. Gertrude. 8° [1810].

RICHARDSON, WILLIAM.
[For an earlier play see *A History of Late Eighteenth Century Drama*, p. 302.]
M.D. The Maid of Lochlin. 8° 1801.

RIDGWAY, J.
D. The North Briton; or, Female Heroism (S.W. Th. 11/10/1810).
P. Lady Godiva and Peeping Tom of Coventry; or, Harlequin in Warwickshire. L.C. Birmingham, 12/12/1846.

RIPON, JOHN SCOTT [né J. S. BYERLEY].
D. Buonaparte; or, The Freebooter. 8° 1803.

ROBERDEAU, JOHN PETER.
[For his earlier plays see *A History of Late Eighteenth Century Drama*, p. 302.]
Int. The Alarmist; or, Cheerful Opinions. 8° 1803 [Chichester].
Int. The Maniac Maid; or, Euphemia's Flights (Portsmouth, 1804).
D. Thermopylae; or, The Repulsed Invasion (Gosport Naval Academy, 4/1805). *New British Theatre* [1814], vol. ii.
D. Cornelia; or, A Roman Matron's Jewels (Chichester, 1805). 8° 1810.

ROBERTS, J. F.
P. Graciosa the Fair; or, Harlequin Fairy King (Royalty, W. 28/10/1807).

ROBERTS, WILLIAM.
M.D. Magdalena and her Faithful Dog. L. 64 S. [Hull, 21/12/1816].

ROBERTSON, Mrs.
D.R. Ellinda; or, The Abbey of St Aubert (Newark, 1800)

ROBINSON, SAMUEL.
D. William Tell. 8° 1825; 8° 1834.
    [A translation of Schiller's play.]

ROBINSON-MORRIS, MATHEW, Lord ROKEBY.
T. The Fall of Mortimer. 8° 1806.

ROBSON, W.
Bsq. Babes in the Wood (Olym. M. 24/4/1843). L.C. 21/4/1843.
F.　The Tragedy Queen (Lyc. M. 13/12/1847). *Lacy*, vol. xxv [as *Comedy and Tragedy*].
　　[An adaptation from the French of N. R. Fournier (Paris, 15/4/1841).]

ROCHE, EUGENIUS.
T.　William Tell. 8° 1808 [in *The Dramatic Appellant*].
D.　The Invasion. 8° 1808 [in *The Dramatic Appellant*].

RODD, THOMAS.
T.　Zuma. 8° 1800.
　　[A translation of the play by P. F. A. Le Fevre.]

RODWELL, GEORGE HERBERT.
Fa.　Where shall I dine? (Olym. W. 17/2/1819). L. 74 S. [18/2/1819]. 8° [1819]; *Dicks* 973.
Ba.　More Blunders than One; or, The Irish Valet (Adel. M. 13/12/1824). L.C. 9/12/1824; L.C. 1/7/1825 [new scene]. *Dicks* 413.
F.　Freaks and Follies; or, A Match for the Old One (Adel. M. 5/11/1827). *Dicks* 988.
F.　Grimalkin; or, The Cat's Wife. L.C. Adel. 5/11/1828. *Dicks* 515.
F.　Teddy the Tiler (C.G. M. 8/2/1830). L.C. 1/2/1830. *Cumberland*, vol. xxv; *Dicks* 784.
　　[Based on *Pierre le couvreur*.]
Ba.　Was I to blame? (Adel. M. 13/12/1830). L.C. 18/11/1830. *Lacy*, vol. xxxii.
F.　I'll be your Second (Olym. M. 10/10/1831). L.C. 8/10/1831 [with sub-title, *or, The Note at Hand*]. *Lacy*, vol. iii.
O.F.　My Own Lover (D.L. W. 11/1/1832).
　　[Music by G. H. B. Rodwell.]
F.　The Chimney Piece; or, Natural Magic (D.L. S. 23/3/1833). L.C. 15/3/1833.
Ba.　The Mysterious Family (Adel. M. 5/10/1835). L.C. 28/9/1835. *Dicks* 857.
Ba.　The Breach of Promise of Marriage (Adel. M. 21/2/1842). L.C. Adel. 18/2/1842. *Dicks* 693.
　　[An adaptation of Scribe, *Une chaine* (Paris, 29/11/1841).]
Oa.　The Students of Bonn (D.L. M. 21/3/1842). L.C. 5/3/1842.
M.D.　Pride of Birth (Adel. M. 16/1/1843). *Dicks* 615; *Duncombe*, vol. xlvi.
F.　My Wife's Out (C.G. M. 2/10/1843). L.C. 22/9/1843. *Dicks* 699; *Lacy*, vol. xlv.
F.　The Pic Nic; or, Husbands, Wives and Lovers (Adel. M. 4/12/1843). L.C. 7/11/1843 [as *The Picnic Party*]. *Dicks* 561.
M.D.　Adèle; or, The Roué Brother (Strand, T. 26/12/1843). L.C. 23/12/1843 [as *A.; or, The Lone Farm*].
M.D.　The Seven Maids of Munich; or, The Ghost's Tower (P'cess, S. 19/12/1846). L.C. 12/12/1846. 8° [1846; Songs, Duets, Choruses].

RODWELL, J. THOMAS G.
F.　The Young Widow; or, A Lesson for Lovers (Adel. M. 1/11/1824). L.C. 29/10/1824. 8° 1824; *Dicks* 413; *Lacy*, vol. xxii.
F.　A Race for a Dinner (C.G. T. 15/4/1828). L.C. 14/3/1828. *Dicks* 973; *Lacy*, vol. cii; *Cumberland*, vol. xix.

ROGERS, WILLIAM.
M.D. Black Hugh; or, The Outlaw's Fate (R.P. M. 22/10/1832). *Duncombe*, vol. xx.
M.D. The Heart that can feel for Another! (S.W. Th. 6/10/1836).
Ba. The Mounting Sylph. L.C. Garrick, 20/3/1844.
F. Barney Buntline Ashore. L.C. R.P. 1845.
D. Luke Sommerton; or, The Renegade's Daughter. L.C. Garrick, 7/10/1845.
D. The Farmer of Inglewood Forest (R.P. 9/2/1846). L.C. 7/2/1846.
D. Frank the Ploughman; or, Love, Madness and Revenge. L.C. Britannia, 18/5/1849.

ROUSE, Miss E.
Bsq. Buy-em-dears, alias Bay-a-deres (Strand, F. 12/10/1838). L.C. 11/10/1838.

ROWE, Rev. HENRY.
M.Ent. The Montem. 8° 1808.

ROXBY, SAMUEL.
M.D. Zebroni, the Fire King; or, The Lonely Fisherman of Bagdad. L.C. Manchester, 14/3/1843.
D. The Lambton Worm. L.C. Sunderland, 17/4/1848.

RUSSELL, Lord JOHN.
D. Don Carlos; or, Persecution. 8° 1822 [6 editions].
    [A translation of Schiller's drama. This was acted at the Surrey on Th. 8/6/1848 and a copy of the acting version is in L.C. 8/6/1848.]
T. Caius Gracchus. 8° 1830.
    [A translation of Monti.]

RYAN, M. DESMOND.
Ba. One too many; or, Just in Time (Queen's, M. 4/1/1836). *Lacy*, vol. xcvii.
O. King Charles II (P'cess, S. 27/10/1849). L.C. 17/10/1849. 8° [1849].
    [Music G. A. Macfarren.]

RYAN, RICHARD.
F. Everybody's Husband (Queen's, 2/2/1831; Surrey, M. 20/10/1834). *Cumberland Minor*, vol. iv; *Lacy*, vol. xcii.
    [Acted at Edinburgh, 11/12/1834, as *E. H.; or, Bigamy, Trigamy and Quadrigamy*.]
F. Quite at Home (Strand, M. 8/12/1834; E.O.H. 5/11/1835). L.C. 5/11/1835. *Cumberland*, vol. xxxv.

RYDER, CORBETT.
M.D. George Heriot; or, The Fortunes of Nigel (Perth, *c.* 1823).
M.D. Rob Roy (Caledonian, Edinburgh, 29/3/1825).

RYLEY, SAMUEL WILLIAM.
[For his earlier plays see *A History of Late Eighteenth Century Drama*, p. 304.]
C. The Castle of Glyndower (D.L. M. 2/3/1818).

SALVIN, Rev. HUGH.
D. Mary Stuart, and The Maid of Orleans. 8° 1824.
    [Translations of Schiller's dramas. Actually issued in Dec. 1823 (see *Blackwood's Magazine*, vol. xiv. Dec. 1823).]

SANDY, E.
  D. Lorenzo, the Outcast Son. 8° 1823.
     [An adaptation of Schiller, *Die Räuber.*]

SAVILLE, JOHN FAUCIT.
  [See *JOHN SAVILLE FAUCIT.*]

SAWYER, WILLIAM.
  F. Wanted to Marry. L.C. Brighton, 25/8/1849;

SCOTT, JANE M.
  Spec. Asgard, the Demon Hunter; or, Le Diable à la Chasse (Sans P.
     T. 17/11/1812). L. 97 M. [5/11/1812].
  M.D. The Old Oak Chest; or, The Smuggler's Sons and the Robber's
     Daughter (Sans P. M. 5/2/1816; Cob. M. 19/7/1824). L. 22 L.
     [20/1/1816]. 12° [? 1825; *Lacy*].

SCOTT, Sir WALTER.
  [For an earlier play see *A History of Late Eighteenth Century Drama*,
     p. 304.]
  M.D. Guy Mannering (C.G. T. 12/3/1816). See *D. TERRY.*
  D. Halidon Hill. A Dramatic Sketch, from Scottish History. 8° 1822
     [Edinburgh]; 12° 1822 [Philadelphia].
  D. The Doom of Devorgoil. 8° 1830 [Edinburgh].
  D. The House of Aspen (Surrey, T. 17/11/1829).
     [Published in *The Keepsake* 1830, and later in the author's
     Works.]
  D. Auchindrane; or, The Ayrshire Tragedy (Caledonian, Edinburgh,
     5/6/1830). 8° 1830.

SELBY, CHARLES.
  Ba. The One Fault (City, T. M. 11/7/1831). *Dicks* 551.
     [An adaptation of Scribe, *Une Faute* (Paris, 17/8/1830).]
  O.F. A Day in Paris (Strand, W. 18/7/1832). *Dicks* 425; *Lacy*;
     Duncombe, vol. xvi.
  F. Captain Stevens (City, M. 31/12/1832). *Dicks* 957; *Duncombe*,
     vol. xi.
  F. Frank Fox Phipps, Esq. (Vic. T. 18/2/1834). *Dicks* 959; *Lacy* 1492;
     Duncombe, vol. xiv.
  D. The Heiress of Bruges (Vic. M. 4/8/1834). *Dicks* 674; *Duncombe*,
     vol. xv.
  Ba. The Unfinished Gentleman (Adel. M. 1/12/1834). L.C. 28/11/1834.
     Duncombe, vol. xv: *Dicks* 417; *Lacy* 502.
     [This was acted at Edinburgh on 10/6/1835 as *York Rag out of
     Place.*]
  C. The Married Rake (Queen's, M. 9/2/1835). L.C. 10/12/1835.
     Dicks 676; *Duncombe*, vol. xvi; *Lacy*, vol. lxxi.
  Ba. Robert Macaire; or, The Exploits of a Gentleman at Large
     (Adel. M. 2/3/1835; S.W. M. 29/10/1838). L.C. 28/2/1835.
     Dicks 325; *Lacy* 450.
     [See *The Two Murderers.*]
  F. Catching an Heiress (Queen's, W. 15/7/1835). *Dicks* 402; *Lacy*,
     vol. xxxix; *Duncombe*, vol. xviii.
  Oa. The Guardian Sylph; or, The Magic Rose (Queen's, M. 3/8/1835).
     Duncombe, vol. l.
  F. Hunting a Turtle (Queen's, M. 14/9/1835). L.C. 21/11/1835 [query;
     an error in date]. *Dicks* 402; *Duncombe*, vol. xix; *Lacy*, vol. xl.

C. The Rival Pages (Queen's, Th. 8/10/1835). L.C. 16/9/1835. *Dicks* 926; *Duncombe*, vol. xxv; *Lacy* 1400.

M.D. The Two Murderers; or, The Auberge des Adrets (City, 1835). L.C. 16/10/1835. *Duncombe*, vol. xvi.

O.F. The Widow's Victim (Adel. Th. 17/12/1835). L.C. 16/11/1835. *Dicks* 415; *Lacy* 930.

Ba. Little Sins and Pretty Sinners (Queen's, T. 12/1/1836; Strand, M. 4/6/1838). L.C. 8/6/1838. *Dicks* 957; *Duncombe*, vol. xxx.

O.D. The Fate of War; or, Adventures in Camp (C.G. F. 11/3/1836). L.C. 9/3/1836.

Ba. Frederick of Prussia; or, The Monarch and the Mimic (Queen's, M. 24/7/1837, as *The King of Prussia*). *Dicks* 423; *Lacy* 478; *Duncombe*, vol. xxvii.

D. A Father's Sacrifice (C.L. F. 3/11/1837).

Ba. The Dancing Barber (Adel. M. 8/1/1838). L.C. 5/1/1838. *Dicks* 380; *Acting Nat. Drama*, vol. iii; *Mod. Eng. Com. Th.* vol. ii.

Ba. The Valet de Sham (St J. Th. 29/3/1838). L.C. 26/3/1838. *Dicks* 770; *Acting Nat. Drama*, vol. iv.

F. I'll not have a Wife; or, Mutual Objections (S.W. M. 4/6/1838).

D.D. Jacques Strop; or, A Few More Passages in the Life of the Renowned and Illustrious Robert Macaire (Strand, M. 24/9/1838). L.C. 20/9/1838. *Dicks* 599; *Duncombe*, vol. xxxi; *Lacy*, vol. cii.

Ba. Ask No Questions (Olym. W. 24/10/1838). L.C. 20/10/1838. *Dicks* 454; *Acting Nat. Drama*, vol. v.
[Based on Bayard and Pickard, *Mathias l'invalide* (Paris, 1837).]

Ba. The King's Gardener; or, Nipped in the Bud (Strand, M. 1/4/1839). L.C. 27/3/1839; L.C. Edinburgh, 1841. *Dicks* 535; *Duncombe*, vol. xxxvi.

Ba. The Fairy Lake; or, The Magic Veil (Strand, M. 13/5/1839). L.C. 29/4/1839. *Duncombe*, vol. xxxvii.
[Based on *Le lac des fées* with music by Auber.]

Bsq. The Loves of Lord Bateman and the Fair Sophia (Strand, W. 3/7/1839). L.C. 1/7/1839. *Duncombe*, vol. xxxvii.

D. Marcelline; or, The Soldier's Legacy (Strand, M. 9/9/1839). L.C. 5/9/1839. *Dicks* 568; *Duncombe*, vol. xli.

Ba. Behind the Scenes; or, Actors by Lamplight (Strand, 12/9/1839). L.C. 18/9/1839. *Dicks* 703; *Duncombe*, vol. xxxviii; *Lacy* 1702.

Ba. The Pink of Politeness (Olym. S. 8/2/1840). L.C. St J. 5/2/1840. *Dicks* 772; *Duncombe*, vol. xli.

D. Barnaby Rudge (E.O.H. M. 28/6/1841). L.C. 30/6/1841. *Dicks* 393; *Mod. Eng. Com. Th.* vol. i; *Duncombe*, vol. xliii; *Lacy*, vol. xci.
[Written in collaboration with *C. MELVILLE*; based on Dickens' novel.]

Ba. The Lady and Gentleman in a peculiarly perplexing Predicament (E.O.H. M. 9/8/1841). L.C. 6/8/1841. *Dicks* 425; *Duncombe*, vol. xliv; *Lacy*, vol. lxix.

Ext. Punch (Strand, S. 18/9/1841). L.C. 1/9/1841. *Dicks* 618.

Ba. The New Footman (Strand, F. 28/3/1842). L.C. 21/3/1842. *Dicks* 535; *Duncombe*, vol. xlv; *Lacy*, vol. cvii.

F. The Boots at the Swan (Strand, W. 8/6/1842; Adel. W. 5/4/1843). L.C. 27/5/1842. *Dicks* 564; *Duncombe*, vol. xlv; *Lacy* 503.

Ba. Antony and Cleopatra (Adel. M. 7/11/1842). L.C. 29/10/1842. *Dicks* 602; *Duncombe*, vol. xlvi.

Ba. The Moral Philosopher (Adel. M. 9/10/1843; Surrey, W. 4/7/1849).
    L.C. 28/9/1843. *Duncombe*, vol. xlviii.
Bsq. Antony and Cleopatra Married and Settled (Adel. M. 4/12/1843;
    M. 26/2/1844). L.C. 7/11/1843. *Dicks* 748.
F. Dissolving Views; or, The Lights and Shadows of Life (Strand,
    M. 22/1/1844). L.C. 12/1/1844.
Bsq. King Richard ye Third; or, Ye Battel of Bosworth Field (Strand,
    M. 26/2/1844). L.C. 21/2/1844. *Duncombe*, vol. xlix; *Lacy*, vol. xl.
D. The Mysterious Stranger (Adel. W. 30/10/1844). L.C. 19/10/1844.
    Dicks 798; *Acting Nat. Drama*, vol. x.
D. London by Night (Strand, M. 12/5/1845). L.C. 9/5/1845.
    Dicks 721.
F. The Irish Dragoon; or, Wards in Chancery. L.C. Adel. 16/5/1845.
    Dicks 952; *Acting Nat. Drama*, vol. xi.
F. Powder and Ball; or, St. Tibb's Eve (Adel. M. 16/6/1845). L.C.
    17/6/1845. *Duncombe*, vol. liii.
D. The Lioness of the North; or, The Prisoner of Schlussenburg
    (Adel. M. 22/12/1845). L.C. 8/12/1845. *Dicks* 929; *Acting Nat.
    Drama*, vol. xii.
F. The Phantom Breakfast (Adel. Th. 15/1/1846). L.C. 16/1/1846.
    Dicks 955; *Duncombe*, vol. lv; *Lacy*, vol. ci.
    [Based on *L'omelette fantastique*.]
F. You must be married (Queen's, 8/1846). L.C. 24/7/1846.
Bsq. The Phantom Dancers; or, The Wili's Bride (Adel. M. 2/11/1846).
    L.C. 19/10/1846 [as *Giselle; or, The P. D.*].
F. Out on the Sly; or, A Fête at Rosherville (Adel. M. 12/7/1847).
    L.C. 3/6/1847. *Duncombe*, vol. lx.
F. Peggy Green (Lyc. W. 1/12/1847). L.C. 14/12/1847. *Dicks* 1012;
    Duncombe, vol. lxi; *Lacy*, vol. xlii.
Spec. The Pearl of the Ocean; or, The Prince and the Mermaiden
    (Adel. M. 20/12/1847). L.C. 13/12/1847.
Bsq. The Enchanted Tower; or, The Adventures of Prince Head-
    strong and Princess Bloomingbell (M'bone, M. 6/3/1848). L.C.
    29/2/1848.
C.D. The Witch of Windermere (M'bone, 4/12/1848). L.C.
    18/11/1848. *Lacy* 1249.
F. Taken in and Done for (Strand, Th. 10/5/1849). *Lacy*, vol. iii.
F. Chamber Practice; or, Life in the Temple (Strand, M. 25/6/1849).
    L.C. 26/6/1849. *Duncombe*, vol. lxiv.

SERLE, THOMAS JAMES.
'T'. Raffaelle Cimaro. 8° 1819.
D. Fulvius Valens. 8° 1823.
M.D. The Victim of St Vincent; or, The Horrors of an Assault
    (Cob. M. 22/8/1831; Surrey, M. 11/5/1835).
D. The Man in the Iron Mask; or, The Secrets of the Bastille (Cob.
    M. 16/1/1832; City, M. 5/3/1832). *Dicks* 428.
D. The Merchant of London (D.L. Th. 26/4/1832). L.C. 18/4/1832.
    8° 1832; *Dicks* 1033.
D. The House of Colberg (D.L. M. 1/10/1832). L.C. 29/9/1832 [as
    Colberg; or, The Bridal]. 8° 1833.
D.D. The Yeoman's Daughter (Adel. W. 17/7/1833). *Duncombe*,
    vol. xii.
D. The Gamester of Milan (Vic. M. 21/4/1834). *Duncombe*, vol. xiv.

D.   The Widow Queen (E.O.H. Th. 9/10/1834). L.C. 9/10/1834.
M.D. The Shadow on the Wall (E.O.H. M. 20/4/1835). L.C. 4/4/1835.
     [Music J. Thomson.]
D.   The Ghost Story (Adel. M. 4/1/1836; Queen's, F. 5/4/1839). L.C. 6/1/1836. 12° 1836.
M.D. The Witch's Son (E.O.H. M. 2/5/1836). L.C. 2/5/1836.
D.   The Queen of the Beggars (H.² S. 16/9/1837). L.C. 1837.
M.D. The Afrancesado; or, Secrecy and Truth (C.G. Th. 19/10/1837). [Music A. Lee.]
D.   The Parole of Honour (C.G. S. 4/11/1837). L.C. 1837. *Dicks* 1032; *Duncombe*, vol. xxxiv.
M.D. Joan of Arc, the Maid of Orleans (C.G. T. 28/11/1837). L.C. 1837. 12° 1837; *Dicks* 1029; *Duncombe*, vol. xxxiv.
D.   The Foresters; or, Twenty-five Years Since (C.G. F. 19/10/1838). L.C. 13/10/1838.
     [Music Loder.]
D.R. Agnes Bernauer, the Maid of Augsberg (C.G. S. 20/4/1839). L.C. 17/4/1839.
D.   Master Clarke (H.² S. 26/9/1840). L.C. 8/9/1840. *Dicks* 1031.
O.   Sappho (D.L. S. 1/4/1843). L.C. 11/3/1843. 8° [1843].
     [Music Pacini.]
D.   The Priest's Daughter (S.W. M. 3/2/1845). L.C. 11/1/1845.
C.   The Scornful Lady (M'bone, M. 29/11/1847). L.C. 19/11/1847.
     [Adapted from the play by Beaumont and Fletcher.]
T.   The Double Marriage. L.C. M'bone, 25/3/1848.
     [Attributed to Serle.]

SHANNON, CHARLES.
C.   The Youthful Queen, Christine of Sweden (D.L. F. 24/10/1828). L.C. 4/10/1828 [as *Christine; or, The Mysterious Protectress*]. *Cumberland*, vol. xxi; *Dicks* 483.
     [Based on *La reine de seize ans* by Bayard.]
F.   My Wife or my Place (H.² S. 20/8/1831). See *T. J. THACKERAY*.
F.   Jealousy (C.G. S. 20/10/1838). L.C. 17/10/1838. 12° [1838]; *Dicks* 928; *Duncombe*, vol. xxxii.
     [Written in collaboration with *Mrs F. S. SHANNON*.]

SHANNON, Mrs F. S.
F.   Jealousy (C.G. S. 20/10/1838). See *C. SHANNON*.

SHEE, Sir MARTIN ARCHER.
T.   Alasco (Surrey, M. 5/4/1824). 8° 1824.
     [This play was banned for the regular theatres, but was acted at the Surrey without a L.C. licence.]

SHEIL, RICHARD LALOR.
T.   Adelaide; or, The Emigrants (Crow-street, Dublin, 19/2/1814; C.G. Th. 23/5/1816). 8° 1814 [Dublin]; 8° 1816 [2nd].
T.   The Apostate (C.G. S. 3/5/1817). L. 110 M. [27/4/1817]. 8° 1817 [4 editions]; 8° 1818 [5th].
T.   Bellamira; or, The Fall of Tunis (C.G. W. 22/4/1818). L. 113 M. [16/4/1818]. 8° 1818 [3 editions].
T.   Evadne; or, The Statue (C.G. W. 10/2/1819; S.W. M. 10/11/1845). L. 114 M. [30/1/1819]. 8° 1819 [5 editions]; *Dicks* 25; *Oxberry*, vol. xiv; *Lacy*, vol. xxiv; *B.D.* vol. iv.
     [Based on Shirley, *The Traitor*.]

D. Montoni; or, The Phantom (C.G. W. 3/5/1820).
T. Damon and Pythias (C.G. M. 28/5/1821). See *J. BANIM.*
D. The Huguenot (C.G. W. 11/12/1822).

SHELLEY, PERCY BYSSHE.
T. The Cenci. 8° 1819 [and later].
[This drama, as is well known, was first acted by the Shelley Society on May 7, 1886; there have also been recent modern revivals.]
Lyrical D. Prometheus Unbound. 8° 1820.
Bsq. Œdipus Tyrannus; or, Swellfoot the Tyrant. A Tragedy. 8° 1820.
Lyrical D. Hellas (1822). 4° 1886 [ed. for Shelley Society by T. J. Wise].

SHEPHERD, Capt. HENRY.
O. The Orphans; or, The Generous Lovers. 8° 1800 [*bis*].

SHERIDAN, T.
M.D. The Russian (D.L. Th. 13/5/1813). L. 98 M. [9/4/1813].

SHOBERL, FREDERICK.
D. Stella. 8° 1804.
[A translation of Goethe's play.]
D. The Patriot Father. 8° 1819 [Truro]; 8° 1830.
[A translation of Kotzebue, *Die Hussiten.*]

SIBER, J. C.
C. The Female Jacobin-Club. 8° 1801 [Liverpool]; 8° 1802.
[A translation of Kotzebue, *Der weibliche Jacobiner-Clubb.*]

SICKLEMORE, RICHARD.
[For his earlier plays see *A History of Late Eighteenth Century Drama,* p. 307.]
C. Sketches from Life (Brighton, 1802).
Int. A Birthday Tribute (Brighton, 12/8/1805).

SIDDONS, HENRY.
[For his earlier plays see *A History of Late Eighteenth Century Drama,* p. 307.]
D.R. A Tale of Terror (C.G. Th. 12/5/1803). L. 79 M. [27/4/1803]. 8° 1803.
C. Time's a Tell-Tale (D.L. T. 27/10/1807). 8° 1807; *Inchbald's Mod. Th.* vol. x.
O. The Russian Impostor; or, The Siege of Smolensko (Lyc. S. 22/7/1809). L. 50 S. [17/7/1809].
[With alterations by *S. J. ARNOLD.*]
C. The Friend of the Family (Edinburgh, 24/2/1810).
C. Policy; or, Thus runs the World away (D.L. S. 15/10/1814). L. 59 S. [3/10/1814; under sub-title].

SIMEON, Y. FELIX ST ANGE.
D. Idela (Liverpool, 1802). L. 78 M. [2/11/1802]. 8° 1803.

SIMPSON, —
M.D. The British Captain and the Indian Chief (Royalty, M. 4/11/1822).

SINNETT, EDWARD.
T. Atreus and Thyestes. 8° 1821; 8° 1822.
[A translation from the French of Crébillon.]

SKEFFINGTON, Sir LUMLEY ST GEORGE.
C.   The Word of Honour (C.G. W. 26/5/1802). L. 77 M. [20/5/1802].
C.   The High Road to Marriage (D.L. F. 27/5/1803).
M.D. The Sleeping Beauty (D.L. F. 6/12/1805). L. 83 M. [22/10/1805].
C.   Maids and Bachelors; or, My Heart for Yours (C.G. F. 6/6/1806).
      L. 84 M. [31/5/1806].
      [An alteration of *The High Road to Marriage.*]
D.   The Mysterious Bride (D.L. W. 1/6/1808). L. 88 M. [29/5/1808].
D.R. The Magic Bride (Lyc. W. 26/12/1810). L. 52 S. [12/12/1810].
C.   Lose No Time (D.L. F. 11/6/1813). L. 57 S. [5/6/1813].

SLADDEN, DILMOT.
T.   Montezuma. 8° 1838.

SLOUS, FREDERICK L.
T.   Francis the First; or, The Curse of St Vallier. 8° 1843.
      [*Le Roi s'amuse! A Tragedy...by Victor Hugo. Translated by
      F. L. S., and entitled F. the F.; or, The C. of St V.*]
      [*Le roi s'amuse* was produced in Paris, 22/11/1832.]

SMIBERT, THOMAS.
D.   Condé's Wife. L.C. Edinburgh, 11/3/1843.

SMITH, ALBERT RICHARD.
D.   Blanche Heriot; or, The Chertsey Curfew (Surrey, M. 26/9/1842;
      M'bone, M. 18/9/1848). *Dicks* 586; *Lacy* 1083.
Bsq. Aladdin; or, the Wonderful Lamp (Lyc. 5/8/1844). L.C.
      27/7/1844.
      [Written in collaboration with *C. KENNEY.*]
Bsq. Fair Star; or, The Singing Apple and the Dancing Waters
      (P'cess, M. 8/4/1844). L.C. 26/3/1844 [as *Princess Fair Star*].
      [Written in collaboration with *J. OXENFORD.*]
D.   The Cricket on the Hearth; or, A Fairy Tale of the Home (Lyc.
      S. 20/12/1845). L.C. 17/12/1845. *Dicks* 394.
      [Based on Dickens' novel.]
P.   The Enchanted Horse; or, Prince Firoaz, Schah of Persia and the
      Princess of Bengal (Lyc. F. 26/12/1845). L.C. 20/12/1845.
      [Written in collaboration with *T. TAYLOR.*]
Bsq. Hop o' my Thumb (Lyc. M. 16/3/1846). L.C. 9/3/1846.
D.   The Battle of Life (Lyc. M. 21/12/1846). L.C. 16/12/1846.
      12° [1846]; *Dicks* 1001.
      [Based on Dickens' novel.]
P.   Friar Rush (D.L. M. 27/12/1847). See *A. CROWQUILL.*
D.   The Headsman (Olym. 4/1/1849). L.C. 4/1/1849.
Bsq. Guy Fawkes; or, A Match for a King (M'bone, M. 9/4/1849).
      12° [1849].

SMITH, CHARLES.
[For his earlier plays see *A History of Late Eighteenth Century Drama,*
p. 308.]
O.F. A Trip to Bengal. 8° 1802.

SMITH, G.
F.   Make your Wills (H.¹ S. 16/7/1836). See *E. MAYHEW.*

SMITH, HORACE.
C.   First Impressions; or, Trade in the West (D.L. S. 30/10/1813).
      L. 100 M. [25/10/1813.] 8° 1813 [*bis*].
D.   Amaranthus; or, The Nympholept. 8° 1821.

SMITH, J.
D.   Ralph de Bigod, Earl of Norwich (Norwich, 1829). L.C. 1829.
[This writer is described as the author of *The Siege of Colchester.*]

SMITH, JAMES and HORACE.
F.   The Absent Apothecary (D.L. W. 10/2/1813). L. 98 M. [5/2/1813].

SMITH, JOHN FREDERICK.
Ba. Sir Roger de Coverley (Adel. M. 17/10/1836). L.C. 1836.
Duncombe, vol. xxiv.
[Another play of this title appears in L.C. 7/5/1834.]
D.   Wolsey (Surrey, M. 27/1/1845). *Duncombe*, vol. liv.

SMITH, O.
M.D.Spec. Lolonois; or, The Bucaniers of 1660 (R.C. Th. 6/8–
F. 21/8/1818).

SMITH, T.
Bsq. The Highgate Tunnel; or, The Secret Arch (Lyc. Th. 2/7/1812).
L. 21 L. [24/6/1812]. 8° 1812.

SMITH, WILLIAM.
T.   Athelwold (D.L. Th. 18/5/1843). L.C. 11/5/1843.

SOANE, GEORGE.
M.D. The Peasant of Lucerne. 8° 1815.
T.   The Bohemian. 8° 1817.
M.D. The Innkeeper's Daughter (D.L. M. 7/4/1817). L. 66 S.
[17/3/1817]. 8° 1817; *Duncombe*, vol. xliii; *Lacy*, vol. cxiv.
[Music Cooke.]
M.D. The Falls of Clyde (D.L. W. 29/10/1817). L. 22 L. [17/10/1817].
8° 1817; 8° 1818 [2nd]; *French* 1894; *Cumberland*, vol. xxxi.
[Music Cooke.]
M.D. Rob Roy, the Gregarach (D.L. W. 25/3/1818). L. 69 S.
[2/3/1818]. 8° 1818; *Cumberland*, vol. xxxvi.
[Based on Scott's novel.]
Ent. The Dwarf of Naples (D.L. S. 13/3/1819). L. 116 M. [4/3/1819].
8° 1819.
M.D. Self-Sacrifice; or, The Maid of the Cottage (E.O.H. M.
19/7/1819). 8° 1819.
[Music Reeve.]
—   Extracts from Goethe's Tragedy of Faustus. 4° 1820.
D.   The Hebrew (D.L. Th. 2/3/1820). L. 77 S. [9/2/1820; as *The
Pilgrim from Palestine*]. 8° 1820.
[Based on Scott, *Ivanhoe.*]
O.   Der Freischutz (D.L. 10/11/1824). L.C. 9/11/1824. 8° 1825.
[Music Bishop. Based on the libretto by J. F. Kind.]
D.   Masaniello, the Fisherman of Naples (D.L. Th. 17/2/1825).
L.C. 27/1/1825.
[Music Bishop.]
R.D. Faustus (D.L. M. 16/5/1825). L.C. 3/5/1825. 8° 1825. *Cumberland*, vol. xxxiii.
[Music Bishop, Horn and Cooke. Written in collaboration
with *D. TERRY.*]
O.   Aladdin (D.L. S. 29/4/1826). L.C. 25/4/1826. 8° 1826.
[Music Bishop.]

M.D. Pride shall have a Fall; or, The Ladder of Life (Cob. M. 30/7/1832). 8° 1824.
F.   The Young Reefer (Queen's, M. 27/4/1835). *Cumberland*, vol. viii.
R.D. Zarah (Queen's, M. 7/9/1835). L.C. 16/8/1835. *Dicks* 357; *Cumberland*, vol. xxxv; *Lacy*, vol. xcii.
D.   The Chelsea Pensioner (Queen's, Th. 29/10/1835). *Duncombe*, vol. xix.
D.   Lilian, the Show Girl (Surrey, M. 10/10/1836). *Dicks* 739; *Duncombe*, vol. xxiv.
C.O. The Syren (P'cess, M. 14/10/1844). L.C. 19/7/1844. 8° [1844].
      [Based on *La Sirène* by Scribe with music by Auber (Paris, 26/3/1844).]
R.D. The Wilis; or, The Night Dancers (P'cess, W. 28/10/1846).
      L.C. 23/10/1846 [as *Giselle*]. 8° 1846 [*bis*; as *The Night Dancers*].
Oa. The Young Guard (P'cess, Th. 20/1/1848).
O.   Haydee; or, The Secret (Strand, M. 3/4/1848). L.C. 29/3/1848.
      12° 1848 [*Davidson's Dramatic Operas*].
      [Based on Scribe, *Haydée* (Paris, 28/12/1847), with music by Auber.]

SOMERSET, CHARLES A.
M.D. Crazy Jane (Surrey, T. 19/6/1827; S.W. S. 3/7/1830). *Cumberland Minor*, vol. ii.
D.   The Roebuck; or, Guilty and Not Guilty (Surrey, M. 1/10/1827). *Dicks* 544; *Duncombe*, vol. ii.
O.   Sylvana (Surrey, T. 2/9/1828). *Cumberland Minor*, vol. iii.
      [Based on the opera by F. K. Hiemer (Frankfort, 16/9/1810).]
Int. "Yes!" (Surrey, 1829). *Dicks* 310; *Cumberland Minor*, vol. ii.
O.F. The Day after the Fair; or, The Roadside Cottage (Olym. M. 5/1/1829). L.C. 15/12/1828. *Cumberland Minor*, vol. iii; *Dicks* 415; *Lacy*, vol. lxxvi.
M.D. Maurice the Woodcutter (R.P. M. 9/2/1829). *Duncombe*, vol. vi.
M.D. Home Sweet Home! or, The Ranz des Vaches (C.G. Th. 19/3/1829). L.C. 17/2/1829. 12° 1829; *Duncombe*, vol. iii; *Dicks* 296.
      [Music Bishop.]
Ba. Shakespeare's Early Days (C.G. Th. 29/10/1829). L.C. 17/10/1829 [called at first *The Life of William Shakespeare*]. *Dicks* 792; *Lacy*, vol. xciii; *Cumberland*, vol. xxviii.
M.Ent. The Female Mascaroni; or, The Fair Brigands (Surrey, S. 12/2/1831). *Cumberland Minor*, vol. xiii.
M.D. The Mistletoe Bough; or, The Fatal Chest (Garrick, 1834). *Cumberland Minor*, vol. xii [as *The M. B.; or, Young Lovel's Bride*]; *Lacy*, vol. c.
M.D. Yorick, the King's Jester (Vic. 9/1836).
Ba. A Dey and a Knight (Adel. M. 22/10/1838). L.C. 19/10/1838 [as *A D. and a K.; or, Four and Twenty Hours in Algiers*].
Ba. The Turn among the Knights of Chivalry in the Days of Not Lang Syne (E.O.H. M. 9/9/1839). L.C. 7/9/1839.
Ext. Charles O'Malley (Olym. 10/4/1841). L.C. 10/4/1841.
Ba. The Bay of Biscay; or, The Modern Adonis (Olym. 25/10/1841). L.C. 14/10/1841.
Ba. Young Maids; or, The Witcheries of Wych Street (Olym. 22/11/1841). L.C. 19/11/1841.

D. The Sea. L.C. Olym. 18/5/1842. *Cumberland Minor*, vol. vii; *Lacy*, vol. cv.
D. The Union Jack; or, The Sailor and the Settler's Daughter (Surrey, M. 7/11/1842).
M.D. Bibboo; or, The Shipwreck. L.C. Liverpool, 5/12/1842.
Spec. Nautical Tom and Jerry. L.C. Liverpool, 7/1/1843.
P. Harlequin and the Singing Mouse. L.C. M'bone, 11/12/1843.
M.D. The Shadow of Death; or, Captain Hawk in the Coffin Cell. L.C. Bower, 12/10/1846.
M.D. Amy; or, Love and Madness. L.C. Bower, 18/3/1847.
D. The Battle of Life. L.C. Bower, 7/1/1847.
[Based on Dickens' novel.]
D. The Lady in Black; or, The Nun of the Bank. L.C. Bower, 29/6/1848.
[Various later plays.]

SOTHEBY, WILLIAM.
D. The Cambrian Hero; or, Llewelyn the Great. 4° [1800?].
[Ascribed to Sotheby.]
T. The Siege of Cuzco. 8° 1800.
T. Julian and Agnes; or, The Monks of the Great St Bernard (D.L. S. 25/4/1801). L. 41 S. [17/3/1801]. 8° 1801.
T. Orestes. 4° 1802; 8° 1802.
M. Oberon; or, Huon of Bordeaux. 12° 1802 [Bristol].
T. Ivan. 8° 1816.
T. Ellen; or, The Confession. 8° 1816.

SOUTHEY, ROBERT.
D. Wat Tyler. 8° 1817 [3 separate editions].
[Written in the eighteenth century.]

SPENCER, WILLIAM ROBERT.
F. Urania; or, The Illuminé (D.L. F. 22/1/1802). L. 42 S. [18/1/1802] 8° 1802.

SPICER, HENRY.
D. Lost and Won. 8° 1840.
D. The Steward. 8° 1844 [in *The Night Voices, and Other Poems*].
D. Honesty (C.G. M. 27/1/1845). L.C. 24/1/1845. 8° 1845 [*bis*].
D. Judge Jeffreys (S.W. W. 15/4/1846). 8° 1846 [as *Jeffreys; or, The Wife's Vengeance*].
D. The Lords of Ellingham (Olym. W. 17/5/1848). L.C. 13/5/1848 8° 1839; 8° 1843; 8° 1848.
Ca. Cousin Cherry (Olym. M. 20/11/1848). L.C. 18/11/1848. 8° [1848].
[See also *Cousin Matthew* under *UNKNOWN AUTHORS*.]
D. The Witch-Wife: A Tale of Malkin Tower (M'bone, M. 18/6/1849). L.C. 18/5/1849. 12° 1849.
[Various later dramas.]

STAFFORD, JOHN JOSEPH.
D. My Uncle Toby (Surrey, F. 22/2/1828). 12° [1835].
D. The Pretender; or, The Rose of Alvey (Surrey, M. 8/12/1828). 12° [1828]; *Dicks* 976.
F. The Frenchman in London. 12° [1834].
M.D. Love's Frailties (Lyc. M. 9/11/1835). L.C. 5/11/1835. 12° [1835]; *Dicks* 713.
[Music Jolly.]

STANLEY, —
F.   Rejected Addresses; or, The Triumph of the Ale King. 8° 1812.

STARKE, MARIANA.
[For her earlier plays see *A History of Late Eighteenth Century Drama,* pp. 308–9.]
T.   The Tournament...Imitated from the Celebrated German Drama entitled Agnes Bernauer. 8° 1800.
[An adaptation of J. A. von Törring und Kronsfeld, *Agnes Bernauer.*]

STEPHENS, GEORGE.
T.   Gertrude and Beatrice; or, The Queen of Hungary. 8° 1839.
D.   Martinuzzi; or, The Patriot (Lyc. 26/8/1841). L.C. 6/8/1841.
[See *Dramas for the Stage,* 2 vols. 8° 1846.]

STIRLING, EDWARD.
F.   A Figure of Fun; or, An Evening at Richmond (C.G. F. 16/2/1821). L. 122 M. [1/2/1821]. 12° [1821].
M.D.   Tilbury Fort (Gravesend, 1829).
[Based on Scott, *Kenilworth.*]
Ba.   A Lucky Hit; or, Railroads for Ever. L.C. 23/4/1836. *Lacy,* vol. iii.
M.D.   Don Juan (C.L. 1837). See *H. M. MILNER.*
M.D.   Carline, the Female Brigand (R.P. 16/1/1837). *Duncombe,* vol. xxvi.
Ba.   The Pickwick Club; or, The Age we live in (C.L. M. 27/3/1837). *Duncombe,* vol. xxvi.
[Based on Dickens' sketches.]
F.   Bachelors' Buttons (Strand, M. 29/5/1837). L.C. 27/5/1837. *Duncombe,* vol. xxvi.
Ba.   Woman's the Devil; or, A Masked Ball (Vic. Th. 3/8/1837). *Duncombe,* vol. xxvii.
D.   The Rose of Corbeil (C.L. M. 13/11/1837). *Duncombe,* vol. xxix; *Lacy,* vol. cxi.
F.   Dandolo; or, The Last of the Doges (C.L. M. 8/1/1838). *Duncombe,* vol. xxxv.
F.   The Bluejackets; or, Her Majesty's Service (Adel. M. 15/10/1838). L.C. 13/10/1838. *Duncombe,* vol. xxxi; *Lacy,* vol. xlvii.
Ba.   Nicholas Nickleby (Adel. M. 19/11/1838). L.C. 16/11/1838. *Mod. Eng. Com. Th.* vol. ii; *Acting Nat. Drama,* vol. v.
[Based on Dickens' novel.]
D.   The Wreck at Sea; or, The Fern Light (Adel. M. 3/12/1838). *Lacy,* vol. cvi [as *Grace Darling; or, The Wreck at Sea*]; *Acting Nat. Drama,* vol. vi.
D.   Oliver Twist (Adel. 25/2/1839). L.C. 21/2/1839.
M.D.   Jane Lomax; or, A Mother's Curse (Adel. M. 4/2/1839; Surrey, M. 4/6/1849). L.C. 1839. *Acting Nat. Drama,* vol. vi.
R.D.   The Silver Crescent (Lyc. M. 1/4/1839). L.C. 17/3/1839.
Ba.   Out of Luck; or, His Grace the Duke (S.W. M. 1/4/1839).
F.   The Little Back Parlour (E.O.H. 17/8/1839). L.C. 19/8/1839. *Duncombe,* vol. xxxviii; *Lacy,* vol. cxi.
D.   The Knight of the Dragon and the Queen of Beauty (Adel. M. 18/11/1839). *Duncombe,* vol. xxxix [as *The Dragon Knight*].
Ba.   The Devil's Daughters; or, Hell's Belles (Surrey, M. 4/11/1839). *Duncombe,* vol. xli.

D.   The Fortunes of Smike; or, A Sequel to Nicholas Nickleby (Adel.
     M. 2/3/1840). *Mod. Eng. Com. Th.* vol. i; *Acting Nat. Drama*,
     vol. ix.
Ba. Mister Horatio Sparkins (Olym. F. 6/3/1840).
Ba. The Serpent of the Nile (Adel. M. 20/4/1840). L.C. 9/3/1840.
     Duncombe, vol. xli.
M.D. Guido Fawkes; or, The Prophetess of Ordsall Cave (Queen's,
     Manchester, 6/1840; E.O.H. M. 24/8/1840). L.C. 29/8/1840.
     Duncombe, vol. xlii.
Ba. The Old Curiosity Shop; or, One Hour from Humphrey's Clock
     (Adel. M. 9/11/1840). L.C. 3/11/1840. *Duncombe*, vol. xlviii;
     Lacy, vol. lxxvii.
     [Based on Dickens' novel.]
Ba. Teddy Roe (Strand, M. 19/4/1841). L.C. 18/4/1841. *Duncombe*,
     vol. xliii.
Ba. The Rubber of Life; or, St. James's and St. Giles's (Strand,
     10/5/1841). L.C. 6/5/1841. *Duncombe*, vol. xliii.
D.   Barnaby Rudge (Strand, 9/8/1841). L.C. 6/8/1841.
     [Based on Dickens' novel.]
Ba. The Pawnbroker's Widow. L.C. Adel. 10/1/1842.
Spec. The Miser's Daughter (Adel. 24/10/1842). L.C. 21/10/1842.
     Duncombe, vol. xlv; *Lacy*, vol. xcix.
F.   Yankee Notes for English Circulation (Adel. S. 24/12/1842). L.C.
     21/12/1842. *Duncombe*, vol. xlvi.
Ba. Captain Charlotte (Adel. M. 6/3/1843; S.W. W. 5/8/1844). L.C.
     Adel. 1/3/1843. *Duncombe*, vol. xlvi; *Lacy*, vol. xxxix.
Ba. Nice Young Ladies (Strand, M. 19/6/1843). L.C. 10/6/1843 [as
     N. Y. L.; or, The Home Service]. *Duncombe*, vol. lxii.
Ba. Auld Lang Syne; or, The Flower of Ellerslie. L.C. Strand,
     8/7/1843.
D.   Aline; or, The Rose of Killarney (Strand, M. 10/7/1843). *Dun-
     combe*, vol. xlvii; *Lacy*, vol. xciv.
Ba. Wanted, a Wife; or, London, Liverpool and Bristol (Adel. M.
     23/10/1843). L.C. 18/10/1843 [under sub-title].
D.   The Bohemians; or, The Rogues of Paris (Adel. M. 6/11/1843).
     L.C. 30/10/1843. *Dicks* 98; *B.D.* vol. x.
     [Based on Sue, *Les mystères de Paris*.]
Int. Beds for Two. L.C. Liverpool, 11/12/1843.
D.   A Christmas Carol (Adel. M. 5/2/1844). L.C. 27/1/1844.
     [Based on Dickens' tale.]
Ba. The Young Scamp; or, My Grandmother's Pet (P'cess, T.
     27/2/1844). *Duncombe*, vol. xlix.
D.   Martin Chuzzlewit (Lyc. T. 9/7/1844). L.C. 4/7/1844. *Duncombe*,
     vol. l.
     [Based on Dickens' novel.]
D.   The Sealed Sentence. L.C. Surrey, 9/11/1844. *Duncombe*, vol. li.
D.   The Chimes, A Goblin Tale (Lyc. 2/1/1845). L.C. 23/12/1844.
     [Based on Dickens' novel.]
D.   Margaret Catchpole (Surrey, M. 24/3/1845). L.C. 22/3/1845,
     Duncombe, vol. lii; *Lacy*, vol. iii.
D.   The Secret Foe (Surrey, 12/5/1845). L.C. 9/5/1845. *Duncombe*,
     vol. liii.
Sk. Mrs. Caudle's Curtain Lectures (Lyc. 10/7/1845). L.C. 2/7/1845.
     .*Duncombe*, vol. liii.

Ca. By Royal Command (Lyc. 25/8/1845). L.C. 15/8/1845. B.D. vol. xi; *Lacy*, vol. cvi.

D. Lestelle; or, The Wrecker's Bride (Surrey, Th. 21/8/1845). L.C. 1845. *Duncombe*, vol. liv.

D. Clarisse; or, The Merchant's Daughter (Adel. M. 1/9/1845). L.C. 21/8/1845. *Acting Nat. Drama*, vol. xi.

D. The Rover's Secret (Surrey, 29/9/1845). L.C. 6/9/1845.

F. The Railway King (Olym. Th. 30/10/1845). L.C. 27/10/1845. *Duncombe*, vol. liv.

Ca. Who is She? (Adel. 20/11/1845). L.C. 19/11/1845. B.D. vol. xi.

D. The Mendicant Son; or, The Jew of Southwark (Surrey, 26/12/1845). L.C. 17/12/1845. *Duncombe*, vol. lv.

D. The Cricket on the Hearth (Adel. W. 31/12/1845). L.C. 3/1/1846. *Acting Nat. Drama*, vol. xii.
[Based on Dickens' novel.]

D. The Sea King's Vow; or, A Struggle for Liberty (Surrey, 16/2/1846). L.C. 14/2/1846. *Duncombe*, vol. lv.

D. The Cabin Boy (Adel. M. 9/3/1846). L.C. 9/3/1846. *Lacy*, vol. civ; *Acting Nat. Drama*, vol. xii.

D. Industry and Indolence; or, The Orphan's Legacy (Adel. Th. 9/4/1846). L.C. 11/4/1846 [as *Indolence and Industry*]. *Duncombe*, vol. lx.

F. On the Tiles (Surrey, 13/4/1846). L.C. 12/2/1845. *Duncombe*, vol. lvi.

D. The Last Kiss; or, A Soldier's Grave (Surrey, Th. 30/4/1846). L.C. 22/4/1846. *Duncombe*, vol. lvi.

D. Above and Below (Lyc. Th. 16/7/1846). L.C. 10/7/1846. *Duncombe*, vol. lvii.

F. Mrs. Harris (Lyc. Th. 22/10/1846). L.C. 19/10/1846. *Duncombe*, vol. lvii.

Ext. The Jockey Club (Adel. M. 19/10/1846). L.C 12/10/1846. *Acting Nat. Drama*, vol. xiii.

D. The Hand of Cards (Surrey, W. 30/12/1846). L.C. 16/12/1846. *Duncombe*, vol. lvii.

D. The State Prisoner (1847). B.D. vol. iv.

D. Raby Rattler; or, The Progress of a Scamp (Surrey, W. 3/2/1847). L.C. 23/1/1847. *Duncombe*, vol. lviii.

D. The Battle of Life (Surrey, 1/1847). L.C. 9/1/1847.
[Based on Dickens' tale.]

D.D. Lilly Dawson; or, A Poor Girl's Story (Surrey, 8/3/1847). L.C. 27/2/1847. *Duncombe*, vol. lviii.

F. Kissing goes by Favour (Surrey, M. 5/4/1847). L.C. 3/4/1847. *Duncombe*, vol. lviii.

F. Buffalo Girls; or, The Female Serenaders (Surrey, 17/4/1847). L.C. 14/4/1847 [as *B. G.; or, Can't ye come out tonight?*]. *Duncombe*, vol. lix.

D. The Anchor of Hope; or, The Seaman's Star (Surrey, 19/4/1847). L.C. 14/4/1847. *Duncombe*, vol. lix; *Lacy*, vol. cxi.

D. Long Beard, Lord of Londano (C.L. 24/5/1847). L.C. 23/10/1846.

D. The Ragpicker of Paris (Surrey, Th. 24/6/1847). *Duncombe*, vol. lix [as *The R. of P. and the Dress-maker of St. Antoine*]; *Lacy*, vol. lxxxi.

D. Mary of Manchester; or, The Spirit of the Loom. L.C. Manchester, 13/12/1847.

D.　The Gold Curse; or, The Liverpool Merchant. L.C. Amphitheatre, Liverpool, 30/8/1847.

F.　The Bedroom Window (Olym. W. 15/3/1848). L.C. 11/3/1848.
Duncombe, vol. lxi.

M.D. The Idiot of the Mill. L.C. C.L. 10/8/1848. *Duncombe*, vol.
lxxxiii.

D.　Nora Creina (Surrey, M. 11/9/1848). L.C. 7/2/1846. *Duncombe*,
vol. lv.

M.D. Jeannette and Jeannot; or, The Village Pride (Olym. 26/10/1848;
Strand, M. 6/11/1848). L.C. 15/10/1848. *Lacy*, vol. cvi.

F.　The Bould Soger Boy (Olym. M. 6/11/1848). *Lacy*, vol. cxi.

D.　The Lost Diamonds (Olym. 12/2/1849). L.C. 13/2/1849. *Duncombe*, vol. lxiii.

F.　Family Pictures (M'bone, 11/3/1849). 12° [1849]; *Lacy*, vol. cvi.

D.　Clarence Clevedon, his Struggles for Life or Death (Vic. 9/4/1849).
L.C. 2/4/1849. *Duncombe*, vol. lxiv.

D.　The Mother's Bequest (Strand, M. 7/5/1849). L.C. 28/4/1849.
Duncombe, vol. lxiv.

D.　The Lily of the Desert; or, The Arab Spy (Surrey, M. 28/5/1849).
L.C. 26/5/1849. *B.D.*, vol. iii.

D.　The White Slave; or, The Flag of Freedom (Vic. 10/8/1849).
L.C. 30/6/1849. *Duncombe*, vol. lxvi.

STOCQUELER, JOACHIM HAYWARD.
F.　An Object of Interest (Lyc. M. 14/7/1845). L.C. 27/1/1845.
Lacy, vol. xvi.

F.　The Fortress (Olym. 2/1848). L.C. 12/2/1848.

STOMAN, CHARLES.
Bsq. Cherry and Fair Star. L.C. Queen's, 16/5/1845.

STONEHOUSE, JAMES.
Oa. Marinette; or, The Wolf of St Ange. L.C. Liverpool, 1/3/1843.
[Music George Hargreaves.]

STRAYCOCK, J.
C.　The Loyal Peasants. 8° 1804.

STREATFIELD, Rev. T.
T.　The Bridal of Armagnac. 8° 1823.

STRUTT, JOSEPH.
D.　The Test of Guilt; or, Traits of Ancient Superstition. 4° 1808.
D.　Ancient Times. 16° 1808.

STYRKE, ISSACHAR.
Bsq. Euripides's Alcestis burlesqued. 8° 1816.

SULLIVAN, ROBERT.
O.F. The Beggar on Horseback (H.² S. 21/3/1846). L.C. 22/3/1846.
C.　Family Pride (H.² Th. 18/11/1847). L.C. 19/11/1847.

SWANWICK, ANNA.
D.　The Maid of Orleans. 8° 1843 [in *Selections from the dramas of
Goethe and Schiller*].
　　　[A translation of Schiller's drama; a complete translation
appeared in 1870.]

SYME, DAVID.
D. Faust. 12° 1834.
[A translation of Goethe's drama.]

SYMMONS, CAROLINE.
D. The Sicilian Captive. 12° 1800.

TALBOT, Hon. ROBERT.
T. The Serf; or, The Russian Brothers (C.G. W. 23/1/1828). L.C.
5/11/1827. 12° 1828; *Cumberland*, vol. xix.
[An adaptation from the German of E. B. S. Raupach.]
D. William Tell. 8° 1829.
[A translation of Schiller's drama.]
D. Faust. 8° 1835; 8° 1839.
[A translation of Goethe's drama.]

TALFOURD, FRANCIS.
Bsq. Sir Rupert the Fearless (Strand, 24/4/1848). L.C. 22/4/1848.
Bsq. The Merchant of Venice. 8° 1849 [Oxford]; 8° 1853 [expanded
version]; *Lacy*, vol. xi.
Bsq. Hamlet. 8° 1849 [Oxford].
Bsq. Macbeth Travestie. 8° 1850 [Oxford]; *Lacy*, vol. viii.

TALFOURD, Sir THOMAS NOON.
T. Ion (C.G. Th. 26/5/1836). L.C. 25/5/1836. 8° 1835 [privately
printed]; 8° 1836; 8° 1836 [2nd]; 8° 1836 [3rd]; 8° 1837 [4th];
Dicks 319.
T. The Athenian Captive (H.² S. 4/8/1838). L.C. C.G. 13/4/1838.
8° 1838; *Dicks* 327.
[The play was to have been presented at C.G. but Mrs Warner's
indisposition caused it to be taken to H.².]
T. Glencoe; or, The Fate of the Macdonalds (H.² S. 23/5/1840;
Surrey, T. 2/10/1849). L.C. 19/5/1840. 8° 1839 [privately
printed]; 8° 1840; *Dicks* 323.

TAYLOR, Dr.
Allegorical D. Prabod'h Chandro' daya; or, The Rise of the Moon of
Intellect.
[A translation from the Sanskrit and Prakrit.]

TAYLOR, G. F.
D.D. The Factory Strike; or, Want, Crime and Retribution (Vic. M.
7/5/1838). *Dicks* 790.

TAYLOR, GEORGE [GEORGE WATSON].
C. The Profligate. 8° 1820.

TAYLOR, Sir HENRY.
D. Isaac Comnenus. 8° 1827.
D.R. Philip van Artevelde. 8° 1834; 12° 1844 [3rd]; 12° 1846 [4th];
8° 1852 [6th].
[A stage version of this drama appeared at the Princess's, M.
22/11/1847; see under *W. C. MACREADY*.]
D. Edwin the Fair. 8° 1842; 8° 1845; 12° 1845.
[For his other plays see *The Works*, 5 vols. 8° 1877–8.]

TAYLOR, THOMAS PROCLUS.
D. The Miser's Daughter (D.L. T. 24/2/1835). L.C. 17/2/1835 [as
    The Miser and his Daughter]. *Dicks* 612.
    [Based on Ainsworth's novel.]
M.D. The Chain of Guilt; or, The Inn on the Heath (S.W. M.
     3/10/1836). *Dicks* 904; *Cumberland Minor*, vol. xii; *Lacy*, vol. cx.
M.D. The Knights of St. Albans; or, The Chrystal Cross and Glittering
     Fountains (S.W. M. 18/9/1837).
M.D. The Light of Other Days; or, The Last Leaf of the Tree (S.W.
     T. 31/10/1837).
Bsq. Fair Rosamond, according to the History of England (S.W. 1838).
     Duncombe, vol. xxv.
Ext. Jim Crow in his new Place (Adel. M. 31/12/1838). L.C. 1838.
M.D. The Wine House; or, The Valley of the Soldier's Curse (S.W.
     M. 25/11/1839).
F.   Claude Duval (C.L. 8/5/1842). *Dicks* 613.
D.   Herne the Hunter; or, The Royal Stag Hunt of Windsor Forest
     (R.A. M. 5/6/1843). *Dicks* 309.
D.   George Barrington; or, The Life of a Pickpocket. L.C. Garrick,
     8/1844 [licence refused].
Bsq. Cinderella (Lyc. 12/5/1845). L.C. 8/5/1845.
D.   The Gipsy Bride; or, A Sister's Love. L.C. Bower, 31/10/1845.
P.   The Enchanted Horse (Lyc. F. 26/12/1845). See *A. SMITH.*
     Vanderdecken; or, The Flying Dutchman (C.L. 24/11/1846).
D.   The Village Outcast (Brit. 20/7/1846). *Dicks* 444.
D.   Dombey and Son (Strand, M. 2/8/1847). L.C. 1/8/1847.
D.   The Bottle (C.L. M. 18/10/1847). L.C. 1/10/1847. *Lacy*, vol.
     xvii; *Dicks* 333.
D.   Frank Heartwell; or, Fifty Years Ago (C.L. 17/1/1848). L.C.
     17/1/1848.
D.   The Drunkard's Children; or, A Sequel to the Bottle (C.L. M.
     10/7/1848). L.C. 10/7/1848.
D.   The Waits (Standard, 8/1/1849). L.C. 9/1/1849.

TAYLOR, TOM.
F.   A Trip to Kissingen (Lyc. 14/11/1844). L.C. *Dicks* 881.
D.   To Parents and Guardians (Lyc. 14/9/1846). L.C. *Dicks* 997.
Ext. Diogenes and his Lantern; or, The Hue and Cry after Honesty
     (Strand, 26/12/1849).
     [For his later work see *LND*, 592–4.]

TEMPLETON, JAMES.
T.   The Shipwrecked Lovers. 12° 1801 [in *Poems*, Dublin].

TENNANT, WILLIAM.
T.   Cardinal Beaton. 8° 1823 [Edinburgh].
D.   John Baliol. 8° 1825 [Edinburgh].
     Hebrew Dramas. 16° 1845 [Edinburgh].

TERRY, DANIEL.
M.D. Guy Mannering; or, The Gipsey's Prophecy (C.G. T. 12/3/1816).
     L. 107 M. [26/2/1816; as *Right and Might; or, The Castle of
     Ellangowan*]. 8° 1816 [*bis*]; 8° 1817 [3rd]; 8° 1818 [4th]; *Oxberry,*

vol. xii; *Dicks* 80; *Waverley Dramas* (1845); *Cumberland*, vol. xliii; *Lacy*, vol. xviii; *B.D.* vol. i.
[Music Bishop. Written in collaboration with *Sir WALTER SCOTT*.]
C.O. The Barber of Seville (C.G. 13/10/1818). See *J. FAWCETT*.
M.D. The Heart of Mid-Lothian (C.G. S. 17/4/1819). L. 115 M. [31/3/1819]. 8° 1819; 8° 1819 [Airs, Chorusses]; *Waverley Dramas* (1845).
[Music Bishop.]
M.D. The Antiquary (C.G. T. 25/1/1820). See *ISAAC POCOCK*.
R.D. Faustus (D.L. M. 16/5/1825). See *G. SOANE*.

THACKERAY, THOMAS JAMES.
F. The Barber Baron; or, The Frankfort Lottery (H.² M. 8/9/1828) L.C. 23/8/1828. 8° [1828]; 12° 1830 [*Richardson*].
M.D. The Executioner; or, Vanrick of Voorn (Cob. M. 2/2/1829) *Richardson Minor*, vol. iii.
C. The Force of Nature (H.² F. 16/7/1830). L.C. 2/7/1830. 8° 1834; *Dicks* 970.
F. My Wife or my Place (H.² S. 20/8/1831). L.C. 22/7/1831. 8° 1831.
[Written in collaboration with *C. SHANNON*.]
O. The Mountain Sylph (E.O.H. M. 25/8/1834). L.C. 9/8/1834. *Duncombe*.
[Music J. Barnett.]

THELWALL, JOHN.
[For an earlier play see *A History of Late Eighteenth Century Drama*, p. 311.]
D.R. The Fairy of the Lake. 8° 1801 [in *Poems*, Hereford].

THOMPSON, BENJAMIN.
[For his earlier plays see *A History of Late Eighteenth Century Drama*, p. 311.]
The German Theatre. 8° 1800; 8° 1801; 12° 1811 [4th].
[Contains the following translations: vol. 1. i. *The Stranger* (Kotzebue, published 1798); 2. *Rolla* (Kotzebue); 3. *Pizarro; or, The Death of Rolla* (Kotzebue); vol. 2. i. *Don Carlos* (Schiller, published 1798); ii. *Count Benyowsky; or, The Conspiracy of Kamtschatka* (Kotzebue); vol. 3. i. *Lovers' Vows; or, The Natural Son* (Kotzebue); ii. *Deaf and Dumb; or, The Orphan* (Kotzebue); iii. *The Indian Exiles* (Kotzebue); iv. *False Delicacy* (Kotzebue); vol. 4. i. *Otto of Wittelsbach; or, The Choleric Count* (Babo); ii. *Dagobert, King of the Franks* (Babo); iii. *Adelaide of Wulfingen* (Kotzebue, published 1798); vol. 5. i. *The Robbers* (Schiller); ii. *The Happy Family* (Kotzebue, published 1799); iii. *Conscience* (Iffland); vol. 6. i. *The Ensign* (Schröder); ii. *Count Koenigsmark* (Reitzenstein); iii. *Stella* (Goethe); iv. *Emilia Galotti* (Lessing).]
T. Ignes de Castro. 12° 1800.
[A translation from the Portuguese of Domingo Quita.]
M.D. Godolphin, the Lion of the North (D.L. T. 12/10/1813). L. 58 S. [28/9/1813].
[Music Horn.]
M.D. Oberon's Oath; or, The Paladin and the Princess (D.L. T. 21/5/1816). L. 65 S. [8/5/1816]. 8° 1816.
[Music Parry.]

THOMPSON, or THOMSON, C. PELHAM.
  M.D. Rokeby; or, The Buccaneer's Revenge. 8° 1814 [Dublin].
     [A dramatisation of Scott's poem.]
  M.D. Jack Robinson and his Monkey (Surrey, M. 14/7/1828). L.C.
     28/3/1828; as, *Monkeyana; or, The D. S.*]. *Duncombe*, vol. xxvii;
     Lacy, vol. xxxi.
       [On the authorship of this piece see *The Dramatic Magazine*
     (1829), pp. 246–7; *The Gentleman's Magazine* ascribes it to
     BARRYMORE.]
  F. Nothing Superfluous (H.² W. 5/8/1829). L.C. 8/6/1829. *Dun-
     combe*, vol. v.
  M.D. The Shade; or, Blood for Blood (Surrey, S. 22/8/1829).
     Duncombe, vol. vi.
  M.D. The Dumb Savoyard and his Monkey (Cob. M. 5/7/1830).
     Duncombe, vol. vi; *Lacy*, vol. xcviii.
  D. The King's Command (Adel. M. 26/10/1835). *Duncombe*, vol. xix.

THOMPSON, HENRY.
  D. The Maid of Orleans. 8° 1845 [*Burns' Fireside Library*].
  D. William Tell. 8° 1845 [*Burns' Fireside Library*].
     [Both translations from Schiller.]

THOMSON, JAMES.
  O.F. A Cure for Romance (E.O.H. M. 30/8/1819). 8° 1819.
     [Music Jolly.]
  F. Mr. Tibbs (D.L. Th. 8/3/1821). L. 82 S. [3/3/1821]. 8° 1821.
  F. An Uncle too many (Brunswick, M. 25/2/1828). 8° 1828 [*A Brief
     Narrative of the Opening and Sudden Destruction of the Royal
     Brunswick Theatre... To which is subjoined...An Uncle too many*];
     Cumberland, vol. xi; *Richardson Minor*, vol. i.

THOMSON, JAMES.
  Ba. Follow my Leader (Strand, 17/8/1843). L.C. 10/8/1843.

THORNE, R. L.
  P. The Cobbler's Apprentice of Whitechapel; or, Harlequin and the
     Queen of the Fairy Palace of Crystal Fountains. L.C. R.P.
     6/11/1847.

TOBIN, JOHN.
  F. All's Fair in Love; or, A Match for a Lawyer (C.G. F. 29/4/1803).
     L. 79 M. [23/4/1803].
  C. The Honey Moon (D.L. Th. 31/1/1805). L. 82 M. [25/1/1805].
     8° 1805; *Cumberland*, vol. xiii; *Dicks* 14; *Lacy*, vol. xvi.
  D. The Curfew (D.L. Th. 19/2/1807). L. 48 S. [3/2/1807]. 8° 1807
     [7 editions]; *Cumberland*, vol. xliii; *Dicks* 102; *B.D.* vol. iv.
     [Music Attwood.]
  C. The School for Authors (C.G. M. 5/12/1808). L. 87 M.
     [17/11/1808]. 8° 1808.
  O.F. Yours or Mine? (C.G. M. 23/9/1816). L. 107 M. [12/9/1816;
     as *The Hue and Cry; or, Y. or M.?*].
  C. The Faro Table; or, The Guardians (D.L. T. 5/11/1816). L. 84 M.
     [13/10/1816]. 8° 1816.
  M.D. The Fisherman's Hut (D.L. W. 20/10/1819).

TOMLINS, FREDERICK GUEST.
  C. Garcia; or, The Noble Error (S.W. W. 12/12/1849). 12° [1849].

TOWLER, JOHN.
D. Don Carlos. 8° 1843 [Karlsruhe]; 12° 1844.
[A translation of Schiller's drama.]

TOWNSEND, W. THOMPSON.
M.D. John Stafford; or, The Murder at the Black Farm (R.P. M. 8/6–M. 22/6/1835). *Duncombe,* vol. xxii.
M.D. Mary's Dream; or, Far, far at Sea (R.P. 24/7/1837). *Duncombe,* vol. xxix; *Lacy,* vol. cvii.
M.D. Topsail Sheet Blocks; or, The Gunner and the Foundling (S.W. M. 1/10/1838).
M.D. One Crime (S.W. M. 28/1/1839).
M.D. The Bell-Ringer of St. Paul's and his Daughter; or, The Huntsman and the Spy (S.W. M. 25/2/1839). *Duncombe,* vol. xxxvi.
M.D. The Court of Spain; or, The Queen of a Day (S.W. M. 20/5/1839).
D. Temptation (Surrey, M. 12/12/1842). 12° [1842].
D. The Lost Ship; or, The Man o' War's Man and the Privateer (Surrey, M. 16/10/1843). 12° [1843]; *Dicks* 705; *Lacy,* vol. xx.
R.D. Whitefriars; or, The Days of Charles II (Surrey, M. 8/4/1844). *Duncombe,* vol. xlix; *Dicks* 742; *Lacy,* vol. xl.
Spec. Spirit Haunted (Surrey, 31/3/1845). L.C. 22/3/1845.
F. United Service (C.L. 10/11/1845). L.C. 1845.
D. The Doom Light; or, The Bridal Eve. L.C. Garrick, 31/10/1845.
D. The Witchfinder and his Mother (R.P. 17/11/1845). L.C. 19/11/1845.
D. The Cricket on the Hearth (C.L. 5/1/1846). L.C. 3/1/1846. *Duncombe,* vol. xxv.
[Based on Dickens' novel.]
D. The Midnight Watch; or, The Death Signal. L.C. Britannia, 12/12/1846.
M.D. The Murder on the Thames. L.C. R.P. 16/1/1847.
D. The Life of a Ship from her Cradle to her Grave (C.L. 22/2/1847). L.C. 13/2/1847.

TRAVERS, W.
M.D. Cartouche, the Renowned Robber of France (Surrey, M. 22/6/1840).

TRELAWNEY, ANNE.
D. Mary Stuart. 12° 1838 [Devonport]; 12° 1838.

TROUGHTON, RICHARD ZOUCH S.
T. Nina Sforza (H.² M. 1/11/1841). L.C. 17/9/1841. 8° 1840; 8° 1841; *Dicks* 635.

TRUEBA, JOAQUIN TELESFORO DE, Y COSÍO.
O.F. Call again to-morrow (Olym. Th. 2/8/1832). L.C. 26/7/1831 [as *I promise to pay; or, C. a. to-m.*]. *Duncombe,* vol. x.
C.Ent. Mr and Mrs Pringle (D.L. T. 9/10/1832). L.C. 8/10/1832. *Cumberland,* vol. xxxi.
C. Men of Pleasure (D.L. T. 11/12/1832). L.C. 29/11/1832.

TULLY, JOHN HOWARD.
Ba. The Lady of the Lake (Strand, 3/7/1843). L.C. 22/6/1843. 8° [1843].
M.D. The Forest Maiden and the Moorish Page (Surrey, M. 31/5/1847). L.C. 21/5/1847.

TURNER, E. S. and F. J.
D.   The Maid of Orleans. 12° 1842.
     [A translation of Schiller's drama.]

TWISS, HORACE.
T.   The Carib Chief (D.L. Th. 13/5/1819). L. 75 S. [22/4/1819].
     8° 1819 [3 editions].

UPTON, —
Spec. The Inquisition; or, The Maid of Portugal (R.A. M. 14/7/1800).
Spec. Fair Rosamond; or, Woodstock Bower (R.A. M. 27/7/1801).
Spec. Zittau, the Cruel; or, The Woodman's Daughter (R.A. M.
       2/4/1804).
       [Music M. Lawrence.]
Spec. 1588; or, The Spanish Armada (R.A. M. 28/5/1804).
       [Music Broad.]
Ba.   There he goes (R.A. M. 15/4/1805).
Spec. The Spanish Patriots; or, A Nation in Arms (R.A.M. 15/8/1808).

VALPY, Dr RICHARD.
[For his earlier works see *A History of Late Eighteenth Century Drama,*
     p. 313.]
T.   King John...Altered from Shakespeare (Reading School, 1800;
     C.G. F. 20/5/1803). 8° 1800; 8° 1803.
     [See G. C. D. Odell, *op. cit.* ii. 70–2.]
D.   The Second Part of King Henry IV. 8° 1801.
D.   The Merchant of Venice. 8° 1802.

VANE, WILLIAM.
D.   Love's Systems (Fobsey Magnus, seat of Sir J. Knowles,
     22/12/1807).

VERE, Sir AUBREY DE.
D.Poem. Julian the Apostate. 8° 1822.
D.   The Duke of Mercia...and other Poems. 8° 1823.
T.   Mary Tudor. 8° 1847.

VERNIER, ISABELLA.
F.   The Barber and the Bravo; or, The Princess with the Raven
     Locks (Surrey, M. 31/8/1846). *Duncombe,* vol. lvii.

VŒUX, CHARLES de.
D.   William Tell. 8° 1827.
     [A translation of Schiller's drama.]

WADE, THOMAS.
D.   Woman's Love; or, The Triumph of Patience (C.G. W. 17/12/1828).
     L.C. 10/12/1828. 12° 1829.
F.   The Phrenologists (C.G. T. 12/1/1830). L.C. 30/11/1829.
     12° 1830.
T.   The Jew of Aragon; or, The Hebrew Queen (C.G. W. 20/10/1830).
     L.C. 29/10/1829. 12° 1830.
M.D. The Forest of Ardennes; or, The Minstrel (R.P. T. 2/7/1833)

WALDRON, FRANCIS GODOLPHIN.
[For his earlier plays see *A History of Late Eighteenth Century Drama,*
     pp. 313–14.]
C.O. The Miller's Maid (H.² S. 25/8/1804). L. 44 S. [14/8/1804].
      [Music Davy.]

WALKER, C. E.
M.D. Sigesmar the Switzer (D.L. S. 26/9/1818). L. 69 S. [19/9/1818].
8° 1818.
[Music Cooke.]
T. Wallace (C.G. T. 14/11/1820). L. 119 M. [6/11/1820]. 8° 1820;
Oxberry.
M.D. The Warlock of the Glen (C.G. S. 2/12/1820). L. 120 M.
[28/11/1820]. *Duncombe,* vol. iv; *Lacy,* vol. xlvi.
M.D. Geraldi Duval, the Bandit of Bohemia (D.L. S. 8/9/1821).
L. 81 S. [3/9/1821; under sub-title].
[Music Cooke.]
Bsq. Rumfustian Innamorato; or, The Count of Quodlibet (D.L. T.
24/2/1824). L.C. 20/7/1824.
[Originally called *The Prince of Pimlico.*]
O. The Fall of Algiers (D.L. W. 19/1/1825). L.C. 20/12/1824.
Cumberland.
[Music Bishop. This opera is also attributed to *J. H. PAYNE.*]
T. Caswallon; or, The Briton Chief (D.L. M. 12/1/1829). L.C.
5/1/1829. 8° [1829].

WALKER, JOHN.
M.D. The Wild Boy of Bohemia (Olym. M. 12/2/1827). L.C.
10/1/1827; *Lacy,* vol. cxiv.
[This is no doubt the same as *The W. B. of B.; or, The Force
of Nature* acted at the Garrick, T. 1/11/1831.]
D. Napoleon; or, The Emperor and the Soldier (S.W. M. 15/9/1828).
Dicks 961; *Duncombe,* vol. iii.
D.D. The Factory Lad (Surrey, M. 15/10/1832). *Duncombe,* vol. xi;
Dicks 930.
D. Nell Gwynne, the Orange Girl (Surrey, M. 4/2/1833). *Duncombe,*
vol. x.

WALLACE, JOHN.
D. Cælina; or, A Tale of Mystery. 8° 1802.
[An adaptation of Pixérécourt, *Cælina; ou, l'enfant du mystère.*]
D. The Merchant of Guadeloupe (Margate, 5/10/1802). L. 20 L.
[26/9/1802]. 8° 1802.
[From the French of L. S. Mercier.]
F. Simple Simon. 8° 1805 [Madras].
C. The Slanderer. 8° 1823.
[From the French of É. Gosse.]
T. Abdalla. 8° 1845.

[WALPOLE, HORACE, Earl of ORFORD.
C. The Fashionable Friends (D.L. Th. 22/4/1802). L. 42 S.
[16/3/1802]. 8° 1802.
[Found among Walpole's papers.]

WARD, C.
O. The Circassian Bride (D.L. Th. 23/2/1809). L. 51 S. [20/2/1809]
[Music Bishop.]

WARD, HENRY RICHARD.
F. The Masquerade Ball. L.C. R.P. 18/3/1846.
F. Rival Tinkers; or, The Maid of the Fountain. L.C. Albert,
3/11/1848.

WASTELL, WILLIAM.
O.F.   A West Wind; or, Off for London (Lyc. T. 29/9/1812). 8° 1812.

WATKINS, WILLIAM.
T.   The Fall of Carthage (Whitby, c. 1801). 8° 1802 [Whitby].

WATTS, WALTER.
Ba.   Which is the Uncle? L.C. Strand, 1/5/1841.
F.   The Irish Engagement (M'bone, 21/9/1848). L.C. 22/9/1848.
F.   Which is the King? (M'bone, M. 6/11/1848). L.C. 3/11/1848.
   12° [1848].
M.D.   The Dream of Life (M'bone, 1849). L.C. 17/2/1849. 12° [1849].

WEBB, CHARLES.
D.   Robert le Grange; or, The Night of the French Revolution (S.W.
   M. 4/9/1843).
C.O.   The Syren. L.C. Grecian, 1844.
D.   The Old Man's Bride (Garrick, 22/4/1844). L.C. S.W. 4/1/1844.
D.   Martin Chuzzlewit (Strand, 15/7/1844). L.C. 15/7/1844.
   [Based on Dickens' novel.]
D.   Bianca di Molino. L.C. Garrick, 1845.
D.   The Fair Maid of Perth (Surrey, 26/5/1845). L.C. 16/5/1845.
   [Based on Scott's novel.]
D.   The Story of a Feather (Strand, M. 23/6/1845). L.C. 21/6/1845.
D.   The Secretary (Surrey, T. 26/12/1848). L.C. 23/12/1848.

WEBSTER, BENJAMIN, the Younger.
D.   The Yule Log; or, Christmas Eve (Olym. 22/2/1847). L.C.
   13/2/1847. *Lacy*, vol. xcviii.

WEBSTER, BENJAMIN NOTTINGHAM.
F.   Highways and Byways (D.L. T. 15/3/1831). L.C. 28/2/1831
   [as *H. and B.; or, The Two Husbands*]. *Cumberland*, vol. xxviii.
   [Based on *Monsieur Rigaud* and *Partie et Revanche*.]
D.   Paul Clifford, the Highwayman of 1770; or, Crime and Ambition
   (Cob. M. 12/3/1832). *Cumberland Minor*, vol. vi.
   [Based on Lytton's novel.]
Ba.   The Old Gentleman (Olym. M. 19/11/1832). L.C. 17/11/1832.
   Duncombe, vol. xiii.
M.D.   The Golden Farmer; or, The Last Crime (Cob. W. 26/12/1832).
   Cumberland Minor, vol. vi; *Lacy*, vol. lxxvi.
Ent.   Webster's Wallet of Whims and Waggeries (Adel. 1836). L.C.
   20/2/1836.
F.   The Modern Orpheus; or, Music the Food of Love (C.G. S.
   15/4/1837). L.C. 13/4/1837. *Acting Nat. Drama*, vol. i.
F.   My Young Wife and my Old Umbrella (H.² F. 23/6/1837).
   L.C. 13/6/1837. *Mod. Eng. Com. Th.* vol. i; *Acting Nat. Drama*,
   vol. i.
Oa.   The Swiss Swains (H.² Th. 5/10/1837). L.C. 1837. *French;
   Acting Nat. Drama*, vol. vi.
   [Music A. Lee.]
C.D.   The Village Doctor (H.² W. 24/7/1839). L.C. 21/7/1839 [with
   sub-title; *or, The Hind's Disease*]. *Acting Nat. Drama*, vol. vii.
Ba.   Hobbs, Dobbs and Stubbs; or, The Three Grocers (H.² Th.
   26/3/1840). L.C. 18/3/1840. *Acting Nat. Drama*, vol. ix.
F.   The Unfortunate Youth (H.² Th. 1/10/1840). L.C. 25/9/1840.
D.   The King's Barber (H.² Th. 25/2/1841). L.C. 11/2/1841.

C. Foreign Affairs; or, The Court of Queen Anne (H.² W. 11/8/1841).
L.C. 14/8/1841.
C. Peter and Paul (H.² M. 11/7/1842). *Acting Nat. Drama*, vol. ix.
M.D. The Destruction of the Bastille (H.² 19/12/1842). *Dicks* 1014.
C. The Little Devil (H.² T. 16/5/1843). L.C. 28/4/1843.
F. Caught in a Trap (H.² S. 25/11/1843). L.C. 27/10/1843. *Acting
Nat. Drama*, vol. x.
Oa. The Fox and the Goose; or, The Widow's Husband (Adel. W.
2/10/1844). *Acting Nat. Drama*, vol. x.
[Written in collaboration with *D. BOUCICAULT.*]
D. Don Caesar de Bazan (Adel. M. 14/10/1844). See *D. BOUCI-
CAULT.*
F. The Miseries of Human Life (H.² Th. 27/11/1845). L.C.
29/11/1845. *Acting Nat. Drama*, vol. xi.
D. The Cricket on the Hearth (H.² T. 6/1/1846). L.C. 3/1/1846.
C. The Black Domino; or, A Night's Adventure (H.² 10/6/1846).
L.C. 10/6/1846. *Acting Nat. Drama*, vol. xii.
Oa. The Wonderful Water Cure (H.² W. 15/7/1846). L.C. 10/7/1846
[as, *The Miraculous Cold Water Cure*]. *Acting Nat. Drama*,
vol. xiii.
F. Mrs. Sarah Gamp's Tea and Turn-out (Adel. M. 26/10/1846).
L.C. 23/10/1846. *Acting Nat. Drama*, vol. xiii.
Ca. The Roused Lion (H.² M. 15/11/1847). *Acting Nat. Drama*,
vol. xiv.
Ba. Pierrot (the Married Man) and Polichinello (the Gay Single
Fellow) (Adel. M. 27/12/1847). L.C. 30/12/1847. *Acting Nat.
Drama*, vol. xiv.
Bsq. The Devil's Violin and the Revolt of the Flowers (Adel. Th.
10/5/1849). L.C. 5/5/1849.
F. A Bird of Passage (H.² M. 10/9/1849). L.C. 31/8/1849.

WELLS, CHARLES JEREMIAH.
D.Poem. Joseph and his Brethren. 8° 1824; 8° 1876; 8° 1908 [Oxford].

WEST, Mrs JANE.
[For her earlier plays see *A History of Late Eighteenth Century Drama*,
p. 315.]
T. The Minstrel; or, The Heir of Arundel. 8° 1805.
[See also her *Poems and Plays*. 8° 1799–1805, 4 vols.]

WEST, Rev. MATTHEW.
T. Female Heroism...Founded on Revolutionary Events that
occurred in France, in the Summer and Autumn of 1793 (Dublin,
19/5/1804). 8° 1803 [Dublin].
Ent. The Muse's Chaplet; or, The Feast of Thalia (Lyc. 9/4/1822).

WESTMACOTT, CHARLES MOLLOY.
F. Nettlewig Hall; or, Ten to One (D.L. Th. 7/4/1831). L.C.
23/3/1831. 12° [1831]; *Cumberland*, vol. xxxv.
D. Othello, the Moor of Fleet-street (Adel. 28/1/1833). L.C.
19/1/1833.

WESTON, FERDINAND FULLERTON.
T. St. Aubert; or, The Hour of Retribution. 8° 1808 [in *The Dramatic
Appellant*].
O.D. The Castle of Udolpho. 8° 1808 [in *The Dramatic Appellant*].
T. The Barons of Ellenbergh. 8° 1808 [in *The Dramatic Appellant*].

WESTON, J. M.
O. Lucrezia Borgia (P'cess, S. 30/12/1843). L.C. 23/12/1843. *Dicks* 378.

WHARTON, F. F.
M.D. Albert and Rosalie. 8° 1808 [in *The Dramatic Appellant*].

WHITE, Rev. JAMES.
T. The Earl of Gowrie. 8° 1845.
D. The King of the Commons (P'cess, W. 20/5/1846). L.C. 9/5/1846.
D. Feudal Times (S.W. Th. 18/2/1847). L.C. 23/1/1847 [as *F. T. or, The Court of James III*]. 8° 1847.
D. John Savile of Haysted (S.W. W. 3/11/1847). L.C. 31/10/1847. 8° 1847.

WHITE, R. MANNERS.
Ca. The Colonel's Belle; or, The Non-marriables (P'cess, Th. 14/5/1846). L.C. 5/5/1846.

WHITEHEAD, D. CHARLES.
D. The Cavalier (H.² Th. 15/9/1836). L.C. 5/9/1836. *Dicks* 644; *Duncombe*, vol. xxvi.
D. Richard Savage (Surrey, M. 26/12/1842).
D. Woman's Worth; or, The Three Trials. L.C. Surrey, 5/5/1846.

WHITEHEAD, JOHN CRAWFORD.
D.Poem. King James the Second; or, The Revolution of 1688. 8° 1828.

WIGAN, ALFRED SYDNEY.
Ca. Watch and Ward (Lyc. M. 28/10/1844). L.C. 22/10/1844.
F. A Model of a Wife (Lyc. M. 27/1/1845). L.C. 18/1/1845. *Dicks* 1008; *Lacy*, vol. lxi.
Ca. Luck's All (Lyc. M. 23/6/1845; Olym. M. 13/11/1848). L.C. 17/6/1845.
F. The Loan of a Wife (Lyc. M. 29/6/1846). L.C. 21/6/1846. *Duncombe*, vol. lvi.
F. Five Hundred Pounds Reward; or, Dick Turpin the Second (Lyc. Th. 28/1/1847). L.C. 30/1/1847. *Dicks* 1003; *Duncombe*, vol. lviii.
      [Based on *Le capitain des voleurs*.]
F. The First Night (P'cess, M. 1/10/1849).
      [Based on *Le père de la débutante*.]

WILCOX, W. T. W.
D. A Trial of Skill (S.W. W. 15/2/1837).

WILD, JAMES.
Dramas adapted to the English Stage. 12° 1804–5.
F. Maids; or, The Nuns of Glossenbury. L. 55 S. [Lyc. 28/5/1812; licence refused].
      [Based on *Les dragons et les Bénédictins* of Le Brun.]

WILKINS, JOHN H.
D. The Village Belles (C.L. 24/11/1845). L.C. 19/11/1845.
D. Our Own Hearth at Home; or, A Tale of a Reaper's Fireside (C.L. 19/2/1849). L.C. 27/1/1849.
D. Haps and Hazards. L.C. C.L. 20/3/1849.
O.D. The Prophet (C.L. 22/9/1849).
D. Pride and its Fall; or, The Jacobite and the Man of Warsman. L.C. C.L. 29/9/1849.

D. The Swiss Girl; or, The Parricide, the Lover and the Avenger
(C.L. 5/11/1849). L.C. 19/10/1849.
[The L.C. manuscripts mention him as author likewise of *The
Queen of the Hills*, *The Green Hills of the Far West*, *Kate of
Colerane* and *The Eve of Waterloo*.]

WILKS, THOMAS EGERTON.

C. The Wolf and the Lamb (H.² S. 23/6/1832). L.C. 22/6/1832.
Dicks 968; *Duncombe*, vol. xxxii [as *The Brothers; or, The W. and
the L.*].
M.D. Wenlock of Wenlock; or, The Spirit of the Black Mantle (S.W.
M. 30/6/1834). *Duncombe*, vol. xvii.
M.D. The Red Crow; or, The Archers of Islington and the Hog of
Highbury (S.W. M. 30/6/1834). *Duncombe*, vol. xiv.
M.D. The Golden Cornet; or, The King's Wager (S.W. M. 15/9/1834).
D. The Seven Clerks; or, The Three Thieves and the Dreamer
(Surrey, M 3/11/1834). *Dicks* 923; *Duncombe*, vol. xv; *Lacy*,
vol. xl.
M.D. Raymond the Rebel; A Tale of the Irish Rebellion (S.W. M.
5/1/1835).
M.D. The Raven's Nest; or, The Bride of the Grave (S.W. M.
12/1/1835).
M.D. The Castle Cauldron; or, The Scourged Page (S.W. Th.
1/10/1835).
D. Rinaldo Rinaldini (S.W. Th. 7/1/1836). *Duncombe*, vol. xx.
O.F. The Captain is not A-Miss (E.O.H. M. 18/4/1836). L.C.
16/4/1836. *Dicks* 417; *Duncombe*, vol. xxi; *Lacy*, vol. xxix.
Ba. State Secrets; or, The Tailor of Tamworth (Surrey, M. 12/9/1836).
L.C. Edinburgh, 4/7/1841. *Dicks* 914; *Duncombe*, vol. xxiii; *Lacy*,
vol. liii.
D. The Death Token (Surrey, M. 15/5/1837). L.C. 1837. *Duncombe*,
vol. xxvi.
D. Lord Darnley; or, The Keeper of the Castle Hill (Surrey,
11/9/1837). L.C. Olym. 2/8/1841. 12° 1837; *Dicks* 715; *Dun-
combe*, vol. xxxii; *Lacy*, vol. lxxviii.
F. Sudden Thoughts (C.L. 21/10/1837). *Dicks* 407; *Mod. Eng. Com.
Th.* vol. i; *Duncombe*, vol. xxxiv; *Lacy*, vol. xxxiii.
Ba. The King's Wager; or, The Camp, the Cottage and the Court
(Vic. T. 5/12/1837). 12° [1837]; *Dicks* 501; *Duncombe*, vol. xxxv;
Lacy, vol. lxii.
[See *The Golden Cornet*, above.]
C. The Black Domino; or, The Masked Ball (S.W. T. 6/2/1838).
Duncombe, vol. xxviii; *Lacy*, vol. lxxxviii.
[Based on Scribe, *Le domino noir* (Paris, 2/9/1837), with music
by Auber.]
Ba. 'Tis She; or, Maid, Wife and Widow (St J. T. 6/2/1838). L.C.
1837. 12° 1838; *Duncombe*, vol. xxxv.
O.F. The Jacket of Blue (R.P. 14/2/1838). *Dicks* 552; *Duncombe*,
vol. xxviii; *Lacy*, vol. cviii.
Ba. The Crown Prince; or, The Buckle of Brilliants (S.W. M.
16/7/1838). *Dicks* 484; *Duncombe*, vol. xxx; *Lacy*, vol. xxvi.
M.D. Gentleman Joe (S.W. M. 3/9/1838).
F. The Wren Boys (C.L. 8/10/1838; M'bone, M. 9/10/1848). *Dicks*
404; *Duncombe*, vol. xxxii; *Lacy*, vol. lii.

F. My Wife's Dentist; or, The Balcony Beau (H.² S. 4/5/1839). L.C. 1/5/1839. *Dicks* 524; *Duncombe*, vol. xliii; *Lacy*, vol. xxxv.
D. Tortesa the Usurer (Surrey, Th. 18/7/1839).
D. The Ladye of Lambethe; or, A Bridal Three Centuries Back (Surrey, M. 5/8/1839). *Duncombe*, vol. xxxviii.
D. Ben the Boatswain; or, Sailor's Sweethearts (Surrey, M. 19/8/1839). *Duncombe*, vol. xxxviii; *Lacy*, vol. xxviii.
F. A Scene of Confusion (Vic. M. 16/9/1839).
R.D. Michael Earle, the Maniac Lover (Surrey, Th. 26/12/1839; S.W. M. 17/7/1843). *Dicks* 685; *Duncombe*, vol. xl; *Lacy*, vol. xxxiii.
M.D. The Ruby Ring; or, The Murder at Sadlers Wells (S.W. M. 22/6/1840). *Duncombe*, vol. xli.
Ba. The Railroad Station (Olym. S. 3/10/1840). L.C. 30/9/1840. *Dicks* 524; *Duncombe*, vol. xlii; *Lacy*, vol. xlvii.
C.D. The Serjeant's Wedding (Prince's, Th. 26/11/1840). L.C. 17/11/1840. *Dicks* 627; *Duncombe*, vol. xliii; *Lacy*, vol. xci.
C.D. Cousin Peter (Olym. 11/10/1841). *Dicks* 552; *Duncombe*, vol. xliv.
D. Raffaelle the Reprobate; or, The Secret Mission and the Signet Ring (Vic. W. 3/11/1841). *Dicks* 401; *Lacy*, vol. x.
Ba. The Ladies Seminary (Olym. 8/11/1841). L.C. 4/11/1841.
F. Bamboozling (Olym. 16/5/1842). L.C. 5/5/1840 [as *B.; or, My Wife Polly*]. *Dicks* 627; *Duncombe*, vol. xli; *Lacy*, vol. xxviii.
D. The Welcome Home (Surrey, M. 5/9/1842).
F. My Valet and I (Olym. M. 31/10/1842). L.C. 26/10/1842. *Dicks* 770; *Duncombe*, vol. xlvi.
M.D. Sixteen String Jack; or, The Knaves of Knaves Acre (S.W. M. 28/11/1842). *Duncombe*, vol. lxiii; *Lacy*, vol. cv.
D. The "Old Blue Lion" in Gray's Inn Lane; or, Death on the Tavern Stairs (S.W. M. 16/1/1843).
C. The Devil's in it (P'cess, T. 9/5/1843).
D. Halvei, the Unknown; or, The Doom at Midnight (S.W. M. 12/6/1843). *Dicks* 690; *Lacy*, vol. xlii.
R.D. The Dream Spectre (Vic. 24/7/1843). *Dicks* 913; *Lacy*, vol. xl.
R.D. The Ambassador's Lady; or, The Rose and the Ring (Strand, M. 7/8/1843). L.C. 8/1843. *Dicks* 707; *Duncombe*, vol. xlvii.
M.D. The Watchmaker of Clerkenwell; or, A Drum of the Olden Time (S.W. M. 2/10/1843).
M.D. The Roll of the Drum (Adel. M. 16/10/1843). L.C. 11/10/1843 [as *Military Marriage; or, The R. of the D.*]. *Dicks* 706; *De Witt's Acting Plays* (N.Y.) 77; *Duncombe*, vol. xlix; *Lacy*, vol. ciii.
F. A Mistaken Story (P'cess, W, 1/11/1843). L.C. 24/10/1843 *Dicks* 736; *Duncombe*, vol. xlix; *Lacy*, vol. xx.
F. Out for a Lark (P'cess, T. 21/11/1843). L.C. 18/11/1843.
F. The Fairy Lady; or, The Cabinet of Bronze (Vic. 15/1/1844). L.C. 11/11/1843.
D. Woman's Love; or, Kate Wynsley, the Cottage Girl (Vic. T. 22/4/1845). 12° [1845]; *Dicks* 414; *Lacy*, vol. iv.
D. The Strange Legacy; or, The Man with Three Coats. L.C. C.L. 18/9/1847.
Spec. The Battle of the Amazons. L.C. R.A. 12/2/1848.
R.D. Kennyngton Crosse; or, The Old Farm House on the Common (Surrey, 12/6/1848). L.C. 8/6/1848. *Lacy*, vol. lxxv.

[Wilks has several later plays; some, such as *Crichton of Clunie*, may have appeared before 1850.]

[*WILLIS, NATHANIEL P.*
  T.   Bianca Visconti. 1843.
      [Originally acted at the Park Theatre, New York, 25/8/1837.]
WILMOT, Mrs BARBARINA [afterwards BRAND, Baroness DACRE].
  T.   Ina (D.L. S. 22/4/1815). 8° 1815 [3 editions].
      Dramas, Translations, and Occasional Poems. 2 vols. 8° 1821.
WILSON, —
  The Isle of Palms. 1812.
      [See *The "Stage" Cyclopedia.*]
WILSON, GEORGE.
  F.   Male and Female Serenaders; or, Native Talent Best. L.C. Albert,
      7/5/1847.
WILSON, JOHN.
  D.   The City of the Plague. 8° 1816.
WOOD, GEORGE A. F.
  F.   The Irish Doctor; or, The Dumb Lady Cured (Queen's,
      19/11/1844). L.C. 15/11/1844 [as *A Cure for Dumbness; or, An
      Irish Diploma*]. *Dicks* 949; *Lacy,* vol. xxvii.
      [An adaptation of Molière, *Le médecin malgré lui.*]
WOODROOFFE, Miss SOPHIA.
  Buondelmonte, The Zingari, Cleanthes, and the Court of Flora;
      Four Dramatic Poems. 8° 1826.
  F.   A Sovereign Remedy (P'cess, Th. 1/7/1847). L.C. 26/6/1847.
WOOLER, JOHN PRATT.
  F.   Founded on Facts (Olym. M. 7/8/1848). L.C. 10/8/1848. *Lacy,*
      vol. xlv; *Duncombe,* vol. lxii.
  F.   Plots for Petticoats (S.W. M. 17/9/1849). L.C. 7/9/1849. 12°
      [1849]; *Lacy,* vol. cii.
WORDSWORTH, WILLIAM.
  D.   The Borderers. 8° 1842.
      [Written 1795–6. See C. Wordsworth, *Memoir of W. W.* i. 96–7,
      113.]
WORGAN, THOMAS DANVERS.
  C.O. The Villagers. 8° 1808.
  F.   Look before you leap. 8° 1808 [in *The Dramatic Appellant*].
WROUGHTON, RICHARD.
  T.   Richard II (D.L. Th. 9/3/1815). 8° 1815.
      [On this alteration of Shakespeare's play see G. C. D. Odell,
      op. cit. ii. 72–5.]
YARNOLD, Mrs EDWIN.
  D.   Marie Aintoinette; or, The Queen's Lover (Vic. M. 5/10/1835).
      [This seems to be the same as the play contained in L.C. R.P.
      2/4/1849.]
YORKE, ELIZABETH, Countess of HARDWICKE.
  D.   The Court of Oberon; or, The Three Wishes. 4° 1831; *Lacy,*
      vol. xvii.
      [Written before 1800.]
YOUNG, —
  T.C. The Key of the Garden. 12° 1801 [Dundee].
  F.   Water's Water. 12° 1801 [Dundee].

YOUNG, —
[See also *A History of Late Eighteenth Century Drama*, p. 318.]
Ent. The Haunted Village; or, The Way to be happy (Gainsborough, 1800).

YOUNG, A.
F.   The First of May (S.W. F. 26/10/1849). L.C. 24/10/1849.

YOUNG, H.
D.   Varney the Vampyre. L.C. Bower, 5/9/1846.

UNKNOWN AUTHORS.
T.   Abarbance the Hebrew; or, Raymond the Betrayer. L.C. Britannia, 10/8/1849.
M.D.   The Abbey Lands; or, Arden of Faversham (Cob. T. 30/11/1824). [Apparently an alteration of Lillo's play.]
P.   A. B. C.; or, Harlequin Guy Earl of Warwick and the Dun Cow (Vic. Th. 26/12/1833).
Spec. Abd el Kador, the Napoleon of Algeria. L.C. Britannia, 28/1/1848.
D.   The Abdication of Ferdinand; or, Napoleon at Bayonne. 8° 1809.
Bal.   Abelino; or, The Robber's Bride (R.C. M. 15/4/1805).
D.   Abigail; or, The Second Witness. L.C. Woodbridge, 2/4/1849.
Ba.   Abou Hassan; or, The Sleeper Awake (Pav. T. 20/11/1810). L. 92 M. [10/10/1810].
F.   Above and Below. L.C. P'cess, 13/12/1847.
Ba.   Absent without Leave. L.C. 1824.
Ba.   Absent without Leave (Strand, M. 28/8/1837).
P.   Abudah; or, The Talisman of Orosmanes (R.A. W. 1/10/1817).
D.   Accusation; or, La Famille Laffarge. L.C. Adel. 19/11/1840.
O.   Acis and Galatea. L.C. D.L. 15/6/1838.
Bal.   Acis et Galathe (H.¹ S. 31/1/1818).
P.Bal. Acteon and Diana (D.L. S. 25/10/1800).
Ba.   Acting Mad (Adel. W. 6/12/1820). L. 77 S. [5/12/1820]. [Formerly called *The Apprentice*.]
Ba.   Acting Run Mad; or, The Dunstable Actor (Lyc. 26/12/1835).
F.   The Actor in Distress; or, How to Raise your Salary? (Cob. M. 1/5/1820).
F.   The Actress of All Work; or, My Country Cousin. L. 110 M. [D.L. 4/12/1817]. [See *OXBERRY*, 1819.]
M.D.   Adalna; or, The Tartar Hordes (Olym. M. 27/1/1823).
Vaud. Adelaide; or, The Royal William (Vaux. M. 26/7/1830).
M.D.   Adelaide of Wulfingen; or, The Dreadful Secret (Cob. M. 30/1/1832). [Based on Kotzebue's drama.]
D.   Adele; or, The Mystery (Surrey, M. 17/9/1849). [See *RODWELL*, 1843.]
Oa.   Adeline. L.C. Grecian, 22/2/1847.
R.D.   Adelmorn, the Outlaw (S.W. T. 26/12/1843). [See *LEWIS*, 1801.]
Ba.   The Adelphi Academy; or, The March of Intellect. L.C. Adel. 10/2/1842.
D.   Admiral Benbow; or, The Earthquake of Jamaica (Surrey, M. 16/4/1838).

28

C.O. Adolf and Clara; or, The Two Prisoners (German, S. 26/10/1805). 12° 1812 [in *Kleine Deutsch-Englische Opern*].

M.D. Adolph Arnal; or, The Death Spell (Vic. M. 27/3/1837). [This is also cited as *Albert Arnall*.]

Bal. Adolphe et Matilde; ou, le pouvoir de l'amour (H.[1] S. 1/5/1819).

C. Adolphus and Clara; or, The Two Prisoners. Translated from the French of J. B. Marsollier by Eleanor H—— [in *The Lady's Magazine*, 1804].

M.Ent. Adolphus Count Zelmar. L. 55 S. [C.G. 15/2/1812].

— Adolphus Pumpernickel. L.C. Norwich, 15/5/1830.

Ba. The Adopted Child (Royalty, M. 10/12/1810). [From the play by S. Birch, 1795.]

D. Adorni, the Deformed, and Beraldo, the Profligate (Cob. M. 5/12/1831).

Bal. Adrian and Louisa (W.L. Th. 18/1/1821).

Ba. The Advantages of Lying; or, How to give a Rout (Surrey, M. 24/5/1824).

D. The Adventures at an Inn (C.L. M. 8/5/1837).

D. The Adventures of a Shilling (Queen's, 27/1/1845). L.C. 18/1/1845.

Ent. The Adventures of a Ventriloquist. L.C. D.L. 11/5/1826.

P. The Adventures of Charley-wag, who eat the Pudding. L.C. Effingham, 16/12/1846.

Ext. The Adventures of Jerry Abbershaw, the Rum-Padder of Ninety-Five (Cob. W. 18/1/1826).

P. Æsop's Fables; or, Harlequin from Elysium (Olym. T. 26/12/1826). L.C. 11/12/1826 [as *Harlequin from the Shades*].

M.D. The Æthiop's Oath; or, The Child of the Desert (Royalty, T. 4/3/1823).

Bal. Ætius et Fulvie (H.[1] S. 10/1/1818).

F. An Affair of Honour. L.C. Grecian, 17/7/1845.

Spec. The Afghanistan War; or the Revolt at Cabul and British Triumphs in India (R.A. M. 17/4–M. 24/4/1843).

M.D. Afloat and Ashore; or, The British Tar in Storm and Sunshine. L.C. Albert, 17/2/1849.

M.D. The African; or, Slave Trade Cruelty (Cob. M. 6/1/1823).

Ent. Agamemnon, the Faithful Negro (R.A. M. 7/6/1824).

D. Agnes de Meranie. L.C. Albert, 13/10/1845.

— The Agony Bill (Pav. M. 27/10/1834).

Bal. L'agréable re-union (H.[1] 30/12/1806).

Ba. The Air Balloon; or, All in the Clouds (S.W. M. 16/7/21).

M.D. Aladdin (R.A. F. 20/9/1833).

D. Aladdin; or, The Wonderful Lamp. L. 93 M. [Norwich, 6/4/1810].

M.D. Aladdin; or, The Wonderful Lamp (New, M. 13/5/1811).

M.D. Aladdin; or, The Wonderful Lamp (C.G. M. 19/4/1813). L. 100 M. [5/4/1813].

R.Spec. Aladdin; or, The Wonderful Lamp (C.G. 1826).

R.D. Aladdin and his Cloud Palace; or, The Dumb Slave and the Sorcerer (R.A. T. 21/9/1830).

Spec. Alaric and Eliza; or, The Merciless Marauder (R.C. W. 15/6/1808).

F. Alarming Accidents. L.C. P'cess, 20/12/1845.

Bal. Alasnum and his Cottage Queen; or, The Adventures of a Night (Sans P. Th. 31/10/1816).

M.D. Albert and Elmira; or, The Dumb Boy and his Horse (S.W. M. 26/6–M. 3/7/1820).

D. Alberto and Lauretta; or, The Orphan of the Alps. L. 46 S. [H.² 15/12/1806].

Bal. Alcide (H.¹ S. 21/7/1821).

D. Alexander Selkirk (Vic. 3/11/1845). L.C. 7/11/1845.

— Alexis. L.C. 30/5/1831.

D. Alfred and Emma. 8° 1806.
    [A translation of Kotzebue, *Die Kreuzfahrer*.]

M.D. Alfred and Matilda; or, The Test of Guilt (S.W. M. 25/4/1825).

Bal. Alfred le Grand, roi d'Angleterre (H.¹ S. 8/3/1823).

D. Alfred the Great. 8° [1829].

M.D. Alfred the Great; or, England Invaded (Surrey, W. 8/5/1811).
    [By *D. LAWLER*.]

M.D. Alfred the Great; or, The Battle of Eddington (S.W. Th. 16/10/1823).

— Ali Baba; or, The Forty Thieves. L. 46 S. [D.L. 4/4/1806.]
    [This is *The Forty Thieves*, by *G. COLMAN*; see p. 282.]

M.D. Ali Baba; or, The Forty Thieves (New, M. 15/4/1811).
    [This is probably the same as the *Ali Baba* printed at Dublin in 1814.]

— Alice Gray. L.C. E O.H. 1833.

M.D. Alice Home; or, The Revenge of the Blighted One. L.C. Garrick, 23/12/1843.

Spec. Alina. L.C. Queen's, 5/11/1844.

Bal. Aline, reine de Golconde (H.¹ F. 16/5/1823).

D. Ali Pasha; or, The Signet Ring (Surrey, M. 3/10/1836).
    [See *PLANCHÉ*, 1822.]

R.D. Alive or Dead; or, The Lover's Signal (S.W. 1/1/1844). L.C. 26/12/1843.

— All about Love and Jealousy (Olym. S. 11/4/1846).

F. All a Mistake (C.G. S. 2/7/1825). L.C. 11/6/1825, as *All's a Mistake*.

— All at Home; or, The Irish Nieces. 8° 1804 [Dublin].

F. All for the Best (P'cess, W. 28/10/1846). L.C. P'cess, 15/10/1845.

R.D. All Hallows' Eve; or, The Spirit of the Lake (Surrey, M. 22/1/1838).

M.D. All Hallows' Even; or, The Brownie of the Brig (Cob. M. 31/1/1831).

C. All in Confusion (German, M. 10/3/1806).
    [From Kotzebue.]

— All in One; or, What's the Result? L.C. 1826.

Ba. All in One Night; or, The Charter of the Forest (W.L. M. 2/3/1829).
    [See *T. J. DIBDIN*, 1825.]

Ba. All's Right (Olym. M. 21/1/1833). L.C. 4/12/1832.

C. All's Well that Ends Well [altered version with music and songs] (C.G. F. 12/10/1832). L.C. 1/10/1832.
    [This included a masque, *Oberon and Robin Goodfellow*.]

F. All the World's a Stage (D.L. M. 31/5/1819).

D. Almahar, the Moor (Surrey, M. 9/4/1849).

M.D. Almazaide; or, The Fortress of Astracan (Surrey, M. 30/8/1824).

T. Almeyda; or, The Neapolitan Revenge. 8° 1801.

Spec. Alonzo and Imogine; or, The Bridal Specter (Pav. M. 15/2/1808)

D. Alonzo of Castile; or, The Treacherous Moor (R.P. M. 27/5/1833).

M.D. Alonzo the Brave; or, The Spectre Bride (R.P. M. 29/10/1832).

T. Alonzo the Patriot; or, The Moors in Grenada (S.W. M. 11/10/1830).

D. Aloyse; or, The Forester's Daughter (Edin. T. 9/12/1828). L.C. Edin. 11/12/1828.
[Music Pindar.]

M.D. Alp, the Renegade; or, The Moslem's Oath (Cob. M. 4/10/1824).

M.D. Alp, the Tartar Khan; or, The Mountain Pass (R.P. M. 20/6/1831).

M.D. Alvarez; or, Father and Son. L.C. 31/10/1835.
[This may be *The Castilian Nobleman* (Adel. 1835).]

Ba. Always Wrong and Try Again (S.W. M. 2/2/1829).

R.D. Alwyn and Bertholdy; or, Predestination (Surrey, M. 11/4/1831).

Spec. Alzira; or, The Algerine Corsair (Pav. M. 6/11/1809).

Bal. Alzora and Nerine; or, The Fairy Gift (Cob. M. 11/5/1818).

D. Amalderac, the Black Pirate; or, The Rock of Death (R.P. M. 13/1/1840).

Ba. Amanthis; or, The Child of Nature (Surrey, M. 16/10/1820).

C.O. The Amber Box (Dublin, 1800).

D. Ambition. L.C. 1836.

D. The Amethyst Ring; or, The Boy of the Alps (Vic. M. 4/6/1838).

Bal. Amintas et Sylvie; ou, l'épreuve réciproque (H.¹ S. 2/1/1802).

Bal. Aminte et Sylvie (H.¹ T. 12/4/1814).

Bal. L'amour; or, Wine and Passion (Adel. F. 5/11/1819).

Bal. L'amour et la folie (H.¹ T. 18/2/1817).

Bal. Les amours de Glauque et Circe (H.¹ F. 6/1/1809).

Bal. Les amours de Mars et Vénus (H.¹ T. 30/4/1811).

Bal. Les amours de Paris. L.C. 14/7/1834.

M.D. Anaconda; or, The Boa-Constrictor and the Buffalo (R.C. M. 1/6/1818).

M.D. The Anaconda, the Terrific Serpent of Ceylon (W.L. M. 30/9/1822; Adel. M. 23/1/1826). L.C. Adel. 18/1/1826.
[This seems to have been by *R. A. MILLIKEN*.]

Bal. Anacreon; ou, l'amour fugitif (H.¹ Th. 17/5/1810).

M.Int. Anacreontics Revived (C.G. 6/5/1800).

M.D. The Anchorite; or, Forest Bandit (Surrey, M. 27/6/1825).

D.D. The Anchor's Weighed. L.C. Standard, 29/9/1849.

D. Andrea Hofer. L.C. 26/3/38.
[See *FITZBALL*, 1832. This is probably *The Guide of the Tyrol* (Adel. 1838).]

R.D. Androcles, the Slave; or, The Wounded Lion (Cob. M. 8/6/1829).

Ba. Angeline (Olym. Th. 19/3/1840; P'cess, M. 15/3/1847).

T. Angelo; or, The Tyrant of Padua (Vic. M. 15/6/1835).

Bal. The Angler; or, Sport after Rain (E.O.H. T. 17/6/1817).
[Music M. Solly.]

Ba. The Animated Effigy (Sans P. T. 12/2/1811). L. 94 M. [29/1/1811].

Ba. The Animated Fig (Sans P. M. 25/2/1811).

Bal. The Animated Portrait (E.O.H. T. 30/7/1816).

M.D. Anna; or, The Black Spectre (Cob. M. 10/12/1821).

M.D. Anne Boleyn, the Second Queen of King Henry VIII (Cob. M. 22/8/1825).

Ca. Anne Bracegirdle. L.C. Lyc. 4/12/1847.
[This may be *The Tragedy Queen* (Lyc. 1847).]

— Ann Grandet. L.C. 27/5/1835.
Sk. Ann Jane Thornton, the Female Sailor (R.P. M. 23/2/1835).
F. Anonymous. L.C. C.G. 8/6/1838.
Bsq. Another Maid and Another Magpie (Olym. F. 3/11/1815).
    L. 106 M. [18/10/1815].
Bsq. Another Mummy (R.P. M. 14/10/1833).
Bsq. Another Piece of Presumption (Adel. M. 20/10/1823). L. 128 M.
    [18/10/1823].
M.D. Antigone; or, The Theban Brothers (Surrey, M. 11/8/1823).
    [See FITZBALL, 1821.]
M.D. The Antiquary and the Bluegown Beggar; or, The Storm of
    Mussel Craig (Cob. M. 2/7/1832).
F. Antiquity. 8° 1808.
M.D. Antoine, the Savage; or, The Outcast (Cob. M. 4/8/1828;
    S.W. W. 23/5/1832).
Bal. Antonio and Leonora (Sans P. 26/12/1814).
Ba. Antony and Cleopatra (Surrey, M. 28/5/1810).
Bal. Apelles et Campaspe; ou, la générosité d'Alexandre (H.¹ Th.
    2/7/1818).
Ba. Apollo Daggerwood (Adel. M. 6/12/1819). L. 117 M. [10/12/1819].
Bsq. Apollo's Choice; or, The Contest of the Aonides. 8° 1815.
— Apollo's Festival (D.L. 18/5/1814).
D. The Apostate Moor (Cob. M. 31/12/1832).
Ba. The Apparition (S.W. M. 17/11/1828).
T. The Appeal (Edin. M. 16/2/1818). L. 112 M. [4/2/1818].
    [By J. GALT: see supplementary notes.]
F. An Appeal to the Public (Lyc. M. 27/11/1848).
    [By J. OXENFORD.]
Bal. Appel des Fées; or, Fairy Call (S.W. M. 8/8/1831).
D. The Appointed Spot (Vic. M. 31/3/1845).
O.F. An April Fool. L. 126 M. [E.O.H. 19/6/1822].
P. The Aquatic Harlequin; or, Fashion's Fools (S.W. M. 3/4/1809).
Spec. The Arab. L. 96 M. [Pav. 24/11/1812].
Spec. The Arab; or, The Freebooters of the Desert (R.A. M. 5/6/1809).
D. The Arab Boy (Queen's, 27/4/1846). L.C. 31/1/1846.
Spec. The Arabian Night's Entertainments (Strand, M. 26/4/1847).
M.D. The Arab of the Desert; or, The French Spy (R.P. M. 2/1/1831).
    [See The French Spy.]
M.D. An Arab's Faith; or, The Seven Towers of Jaba (Royalty, M.
    8/4/1822; Cob. M. 24/1/1825).
D. Arabs of the Desert; or, The Dumb Bedouin (C.L. M. 29/5/1837).
Lyric D. Arcadia; or, The Freaks of the Passions. L.C. Britannia,
    29/9/1849.
F. The Arctic Story (D.L. S. 1/10/1842).
Bsq. The Area Sylph (E.O.H. M. 7/9/1840).
F. Are You Coming to Bed? (Strand, M. 26/4/1847).
Bal. Argus and his Hundred Eyes (R.A. T. 28/8/1821).
Mono D. Aristodemus. 8° 1802 [in The Poetical Register].
D. Armand; or, The Peer and the Peasant (M'bone, Th. 18/1/1849).
    L.C. 9/1/1849 [as A.; or, The Days of Louis the XV].
    [This drama was written by Anna Cora Mowatt (Mrs Ritchie)
    in America, and had been produced at the Park Theatre, New
    York on 27/9/1847.]
F. An Armful of Bliss (Olym. M. 6/11/1843). L.C. 1/11/1843.

D. The Armourer of Paris; or, The Cross of Blood (Surrey, M. 24/7/1837).

M.D. The Armourer's Forge; or, The Rebellion of Lowland's Creek (R.A. M. 14/4/1834).

Oa. Arrangement (Adel. M. 15/8/1831). L.C. 28/7/1831.

Ba. Arrivals; or, Three Days at Long's (Olym. M. 10/12/1821).

F. Arrived at Last (S.W. M. 19/5/1823).

D. The Arrogant Boy. 8° 1802.

Ba. Artaxerxes (Surrey, Th. 19/9/1811).

Ba. Artipadiades, King of Queeramania (R.A. M. 15/4/1822).

Mus. Piece. The Artisan's Daughter. L.C. Lyc. 6/8/1842.

D. The Artist of Cas. L.C. Glasgow Adel. 22/3/1846.

— Asancesado. L.C. C.G. 1837.

Ba. The Ashantee Prince. L.C. Lyc. 18/5/1842.

Ba. Asleep or Awake; or, Who am I? (Surrey, M. 6/10/1823).

T. Asprand (Salisbury, W. 20/3/1805).

M.D. The Assassin. L. 108 M. [D.L. 9/10/1816].

M.D. The Assassin Labourer; or, The White Farm (R.A. M. 14/5/1827).

M.D. The Assassin of Dijon; or, The Beggar and the Soldier (R.A. M. 18/4/1831).

— The Assignation. L.C. C.G. 21/11/1826.

D. Assignation, Dissipation and Starvation (Surrey, M. 21/6/1830).

O.F. Assumptions. L. 131 M. [E.O.H. 23/8/1823].

F. Astonishment. L. 71 S. [D.L. 9/10/1818].

C. As You Like It (C.G. F. 10/12/1824).
[Altered, with music by Bishop.]

O.F. At Home (C.G. Th. 25/2/1813). 8° 1813 (bis). L. 98 M. [20/2/1813].
[Ascribed to Sir H. B. DUDLEY.]

M.D. The Attack on the Convoy. L.C. Argyll Rooms, 2/12/1828.

D. At the Madonna's Shrine. L.C. R.P. 19/4/1847.

D. The Auberge des Adrets; or, The Two Murderers (Vic. W. 3/12/1834). L.C. 19/1/1835.

Sk. August First; or, The Opening of London Bridge (S.W. M. 1/8/1831).

Int. Augustus Buggins (Strand, M. 8/12/1834).

Bal. Aurora; or, The Flight of Zephyr (C.G. F. 7/2/1817).

Ba. The Automaton; or, The Whims of Love (Strand, M. 27/2/1832).

T. The Avenger; or, The Leaguers of Austria (Pav. M. 1/10/1838).

M.D. The Avenger; or, The Moor of Sicily (Cob. M. 28/6/1824).

M.D. The Avenger; or, The Moor of Sicily. L.C. Britannia, 23/10/1846.

C.O. Un' Avventura di Scaramuccia (E.O.H. Th. 29/12/1836).

Ent. The Awkward Recruit (Royalty, M. 7/1/1805).

M.D. Ayesha; or, The Maid of Kars (R.P. M. 4/1/1836).

O. Azor and Zemira; or, The Magic Rose (C.G. T. 5/4/1831). L.C. 22/2/1831 [as The M. R.; or, Beauty and the Beast].
[Music Spohr, arranged by Sir G. Smart.]

M.D. The Babes in the Wood; or, The Cruel Uncle (Surrey, M. 5/1/1824).

T. Babington. L.C. Newcastle, 10/1/1826.

Bal. P. The Baboon of Paraguay (Cob. M. 22/3/1830).

Ba. Bachelors' Miseries; or, The Double Disappointment (Sans P. M. 19/10/1818). L. 111 M. [7/10/1818].
— The Bachelor's Vow (Strand, Th. 10/5/1849).
F. The Back-Biter (Surrey, M. 18/4/1836).
Ba. Bad Business; or, A Meeting of Managers (Adel. M. 19/11/1832). L.C. 19/11/1832.
Ba. Bad Customers; or, Who Pays the Piper? (Pav. M. 26/3/1810).
C.O. Bad Neighbours; or, The Earl and the Baron. L. 52 S. [Lyc. 30/8/1810].
    [This may be *Plots! or, The North Tower* (Adel. 1810), by *ARNOLD*.]
Spec. Baghran-Ho; or, The Tartars Tartar'd (Pav. M. 20/1/1812).
M.D. Bakarak, the Miser; or, The Crazy Old Slippers of Bagdad (Surrey, M. 26/7/1824).
F. The Bald Head (Olym. M. 30/3/1840). L.C. 27/3/1840.
Ba. The Balloon (Royalty, M. 9/11/1812).
    [Altered from *A Mogul Tale* (1784) by Mrs Inchbald.]
Ba. The Balloon in Turkey (R.A. M. 3/7/1837).
— Bal Masqué; or, What shall I do for a Ticket? (Olym. 12/7/1848). L.C. 10/7/1848.
O. The Bandit. 8° 1814.
D. The Bandit Innkeepers. L.C. Brighton, 20/2/1832.
M.D. The Band of Death; or, The Robber's Mother (Royalty, M. 29/10/1821).
M.D.Spec. The Banished Brother; or, The Secret Enemy (Cob. M. 25/5/1818).
C.O. The Bankrupt Cobbler (German, Th. 27/2/1806).
Ent. Bannister's Budget with the Shipwreck; or, Two Ways of Telling a Story (D.L. M. 30/5/1814).
M.D. Bannockburn; or, The Ghost Seer (Cob. M. 5/2/1827).
Ba. The Barber and his Brothers (Adel. T. 7/11/1826). L.C. 1826.
Ba. The Barber and the Hairdresser. L.C. Adel. 14/10/1828.
F. The Barber Barrister. L.C. H.² 17/5/1838.
    [Presumably this is *The Irish Barrister* (H.² 1838).]
F. The Barber Bravo. L.C. Surrey, 5/9/1846.
Ext. The Barber of Bagdad; or, "Pay me for being shaved" (Cob. Th. 26/1/1826).
Mus.D. The Barber of Paris. L.C. 6/7/1842.
C.O. The Barber of Seville (E.O.H. S. 3/7/1824).
    [This was an altered version of Rossini's opera, with additional music from Mozart, Fioravanti, Dibdin and others.]
C.O. The Barber of Seville. L.C. 5/12/1831.
Ba. The Barbers at Court (Olym. M. 21/12/1835). L.C. 30/11/1835.
O. Barcarolle (P'cess, M. 5/4/1847). L.C. P'cess, 3/4/1847.
Ba. Barnaby Brittle; or, A Wife at her Wit's End (Royalty, M. 16/9/1811).
    [An alteration of the farce (1781) made out of T. Betterton's *The Amorous Widow*.]
D. Barnaby Rudge (Adel. 20/12/1841). L.C. 10/12/1841.
    [This is, of course, an adaptation of Dickens' novel.]
D. The Barn Burners (City, M. 8/4/1833).
C.O. Barney Brallaghan; or, "Meet Me by Moonlight" (Surrey, M. 19/4/1830).
O.F. Barney Brallaghan's Courtship. L.C. C.G. 26/6/1827.

F.   Barney Burke; or, The Devil's in the Room (M'bone, Th. 18/12/1845).

M.D. Barnwell, the London Apprentice; or, Fatal Love (Cob. Th. 26/12/1822).
       [A version of Lillo's play.]

M.R. The Baron de Trenck (E.O.H. M. 4/9/1820). L. 119 M. [29/7/1820].
       [Music Reeve.]

C.   The Baronet; or, Female Society (C.G. W. 1/4/1840). L.C. 26/3/1840.

Bsq. Baron Munchausen (Edin. M. 7/12/1840).

P.   Baron Munchausen; or, Harlequin and the Genii of the Green Island (Vic. Th. 26/12/1839).

D.   Barrington, the Pick-Pocket (Surrey, M. 21/10/1833).

F.   The Bas-Bleu. L.C. Edin. 14/12/1835.

Spec. The Bashaw; or, Eastern Fete (R.A. M. 31/8/1801).

M.D. The Bashaw; or, Midnight Adventures of Three Spaniards (Sans P. M. 23/1/1809).

Ba.   The Bashful Irishman; or, The Dublin Adventure. L.C. Adel. 23/1/1843.

D.D. Basil and Barbara, Children of the Bottle; or, The Curse Entailed. L.C. Britannia, 10/7/1848.
       [By *G. D. PITT*.]

Tale. The Basket-Maker; or, The Palace of Plenty (Cob. M. 18/4/1831).

Naut. Spec. Basque Roads (R.A. W. 26/4/1809).

D.   The Bastille (H.¹ M. 19/12/1842). L.C. 21/12/1842.

Int. The Bath Road (D.L. Th. 14/10/1830).

M.D. The Battle of Agincourt; or, The Fight of St. Crispin's Day (R.A. M. 15/9/1834).

M.D. The Battle of Agincourt; or, The Parricide (Cob. Th. 2/6/1825).

Spec. The Battle of Barnet; or, The Last of the Barons. L.C. R.A. 24/10/1845.

Eques.D. The Battle of Blenheim; or, The Horse of the Disinherited (Surrey, M. 20/9/1841).

M.D. The Battle of Bosworth Field (Caledonian, Edinburgh, M. 16/2/1824).

M.D. The Battle of Bosworth Field; or, The Life and Death of Richard III (Cob. M. 29/1/1827).

M.D. The Battle of Cronstad. L.C. Argyll Rooms, 2/12/1828.

Ba.   The Battle of Hexham; or, Days of Yore (Royalty, M. 17/8/1812).
       [A version of G. Colman's play (1789).]

D.   The Battle of Life. L.C. Norwich, 23/1/1847.
       [Adapted from Dickens' tale.]

Spec. The Battle of Navarino; or, The Arab of the Red Desert (R.A. M. 26/5/1828).

D.   The Battle of Pultawa; or, The King and the Czar (C.G. M. 23/2/1829). L.C. C.G. 20/2/1829.
       [From F. du Petit-Méré, *La bataille de Pultawa* (Paris, 1808).]

M.D. The Battle of Telavera (Royalty, M. 21/8/1809).

P.   The Battle of the Fairies (Adel. S. 2/1/1836).

Spec. The Battle of the Nile (S.W. T. 28/3/1815).

Spec. The Battle of Trafalgar (S.W. M. 14/4/1806).

M.D. The Battle of Trafalgar; or, The Death of Nelson (Cob. M. 7/6/1824).

Spec. The Battle of Vittoria (Royalty, S. 10/7/1813—3rd performance).

Spec. The Battle of Waterloo (Royalty, W. 15/11/1815).

M.D. The Battle of Waterloo. L.C. Hull, Davis's Royal Amphitheatre, 25/4/1825.

M.D. The Battle of Worcester; or, King Charles in the Royal Oak (Cob. M. 18/4/1825).

Bal. La Bayadère (H.¹ T. 14/6/1831).
    [Music Auber.]

Bal. La Bayadère (D.L. Th. 20/2/1845).

D. The Bayonet; or, The Murder of the Old Stone Quarry (Vic. M. 10/10/1836).

Hist.R. The Beacon of Liberty (C.G. W. 8/10/1823). L. 129 M. [1/2/1823].
    [Music Bishop.]

F. Bears not Beasts; or, Four Legs better than Two. L. 132 M. [Norwich, 5/5/1823].
    [See *H. M. MILNER*, 1822.]

M.D. The Beauty and the Beast (Surrey, W. 22/4/1812).

P. Beauty and the Beast; or, Harlequin and the Magic Rose (Adel. W. 26/12/1821). L. 121 M. [1821].

M.D. Beauty and the Beast; or, The Magic Rose (Cob. M. 29/11/1819).

Spec. Beauty and the Bey; or, Sidi Hamet Muley Ben Ismael and Peggy Larkins (Surrey, W. 27/12/1820).

Spec. The Beauty of Bruges. L.C. Adel. 27/12/1842.

Ba. The Beaux' Stratagem (Surrey, M. 21/5/1810).
    [A version of Farquhar's comedy (1707).]

Ba. The Beehive (S.W. M. 20/8/1827).
    [See *J. G. MILLINGEN*, 1811.]

M.D. The Beggar's Bush.
    [A new "address" for this play is preserved in L. 105 M. [D.L. 12/1815].]

M.D. The Beggars of Toulouse (R.A. M. 30/4/1832).

Ba. The Beggar's Opera (Royalty, M. 4/2/1811).
    [A new version of Gay's opera (1728).]

Bsq. The Beggar's Opera Burlesqued (Adel. M. 16/11/1840; Strand, Th. 9/9/1841).

Int. Be Guarded. L.C. Sheffield, 2/12/1848.

F. Belford and Minton; or, There and Back Again (H.² F. 13/8/1819). L. 23 L. [10/8/1819; as *The Chase; or, T. and B. A.*].

R.D. The Belgian Patriot; or, The Silent One (Surrey, M. 3/9/1838).

T. Bellamere, Earl of Carlisle. 8° 1807.

M.D. Bella Ridstone; or, Love, Hatred and Revenge. L.C. Garrick, 18/10/1845.

Ba. The Belle of the Hotel; or, American Sketches (H.² M. 17/11/1842; Strand, M. 26/6/1843).
    [This is apparently an American piece. It was acted at Niblo's Garden, New York, in August, 1842; and had probably been written to display the versatility of Fanny Fitzwilliam, who was there on a visit.]

F. Belles Have at Ye All; or, More Flirts than One (H.² Th. 1/9/1831). L.C. 30/7/1831.
    [An adaptation of Cibber's *The Double Gallant*.]

Oa. Belles without Beaux; or, The Ladies among themselves (E.O.H.
F. 6/8/1819).
[Music G. Ware. Adapted from the French.]
F. Belles and the Ring (P'cess, W. 5/5/1847). L.C. 5/3/1847.
C.O. Belmont and Constance; or, The Elopement from the Seraglio
(D.L. W. 23/6/1841).
[Music from Mozart.]
M.D. Belmonti; or, The Vulture of the Apennines (R.A. M. 19/4/1830).
D. Ben Block; or, The Veteran and his Son (R.P. M. 21/9/1835).
M.D. Ben Brace; or, The Last of Lord Nelson's Agamemnon (R.A.
M. 6/6/1836; Surrey, M. 9/1/1837).
D. Benedetto Mangone; or, The Old Log House (Vic. M. 15/8/1836).
F. The Benefit Night; or, Lovers and No Lovers. L.C. Hull,
12/9/1844.
Bsq. The Benevolent Cut-throat. 8° 1800 [in *The Meteors*; under the
pseudonym of "Fabius Pictor"].
M.D. The Benevolent Jew; or, The Gamester, the Seducer and the
Murderer (Royalty, M. 17/12/1821).
Ba. The Benevolent Tar (Surrey, M. 24/11/1823).
M.D. Ben Nazir, the Saracen (Surrey, M. 5/9/1842).
[See *T. C. GRATTAN*, 1827.]
M.D. Bertha and Durimel; or, The Soldier's Father (Surrey, M.
2/7/1821).
D. Bertrand and Burkenstaff; or, The Conspiracy of Copenhagen.
L.C. 3/4/1834.
F. The Best of Husbands (Strand, Th. 7/6/1832).
Ca. Betly. L.C. Lyc. 1/1838.
C.O. Betly (Lyc. 9/3/1841). L.C. 27/2/1841.
[Music Donizetti.]
M.D. The Betrothed; or, The Eve of St. Mark (Queen's, F.
16/12/1836).
M.D. Bianca; or, The Three Trials (S.W. M. 4/5/1846).
D. Bibboo; or, The Island Ape (R.P. M. 25/2/1839).
Ext. Billy Button's Disaster on his Journey to Brentford (R.A. M.
16/2/1807).
Ba. Billy Snivel and Sally Sly (R.P. M. 10/3/1834).
Ba. Billy Taylor, the Gay Young Fellow (S.W. M. 2/1/1831).
[See *BUCKSTONE*, 1829.]
F. Binks the Bagman. L.C. H.² 22/6/1842.
[See *COYNE*, 1843.]
M.D. The Bird of Paradise (R.C. M. 22/9/1800).
Ba. Birds of Paradise (Queen's, Th. 5/3/1835).
O.F. Birds without Feathers (H.² F. 1/10/1824). L.C. 30/9/1824.
Bsq. The Birmingham Girl (Strand, M. 15/4–M. 22/4/1844). L.C.
19/4/1844.
Ba. The Biter Bit; or, Cut your Coat according to your Cloth (S.W.
W. 26/12/1827).
D. The Bivouac of the Hills; or, The Bridal Gift (Surrey, M.
29/1/1849). L.C. 19/12/1848 [as *The Bridal Gift*].
F. The Blackamoor's Head (D.L. S. 16/5/1818). L. 70 S. [7/5/1818].
Ca. Black and White (P'cess, M. 20/2/1843).
Ba. Black and White; or, Which is Thomas? (Surrey, M. 18/8/1823).
C.Sk. The Black Band; or, The Bravoes of Calabria (R.P. M.
16/3/1835).

M.D. The Black Banner; or, The Tribunal of Blood (Cob. M. 24/10/1825).

Ba. The Black Domino (C.G. F. 16/2/1838). L.C. 9/2/1838.
[This and the following play are adaptations of E. Scribe, *Le domino noir* (Paris, 2/9/1837), with music by Auber.]

Ba. The Black Domino. L.C. 20/1/1838.

M.D. The Black Dwarf; or, The Reiver of Westburn Flat (R.A. M. 5/5/1817).

F. The Black Eagle; or, The Female Captain (R.A. M. 19/4/1841).

D. Blackeyed Susan. L.C. C.G. 23/11/1829.

M.D. Blackeyed Susan; or, The Lovers' Perils (Cob. M. 1/6/1829).
[These two pieces seem to be distinct from that by *JERROLD*, 1829.]

F. Blackeyed Susan at Dunstable; or, A Company in One (R.P. M. 13/9/1830).

Bal. The Black Festival; or, Love in America (S.W. W. 28/5/1800).

D. The Black Flag of Toraldi. L.C. R.P. 27/2/1847.

M.D. The Black Forester; or, The Children of Mexico (Cob. M. 21/2/1831).

R.D. Black Friday; or, The National Star (Surrey, M. 16/4/1838).

O. The Black Gentleman; or, A Match for the Devil. L.C. Lyc. 27/5/1842.

Spec. The Black Hand; or, The Dervise and the Peri (Adel. M. 29/9/1834). L.C. 11/9/1834.

M.D. Black Hugh the Outlaw; or, The White Boys of Ireland (S.W. M. 2/5/1836).

M.D. The Black King; or, The Gold Dreamer (Vic. M. 1/4/1839).

M.D. The Black King; or, The Three Brothers (Cob. M. 29/11/1830).

D. The Black Law of Martinique (Surrey, M. 14/11/1842).

D. The Black Legend; or, The Horse and the Murderer (R.A. M. 7/8/1837).
[Evidently given later as *The Horse and the Murderer; or, Barnet Fair.*]

D. The Black Legend of Rotherhithe; or, The Horse and the Ostler (Vic. M. 5/2/1838). 8° 1838.

M.D. The Black Musket; or, The Twins of the Tyrol (R.P. M. 2/2/1835).

M.D. The Black Phantom; or, The Smuggler and the Jew (S.W. M. 26/5/1828).

Ba. The Blacksmith of Antwerp (D.L. 1816). L. 63 S. [17/9/1816]. 8° 1816.
[Altered from the play by O'Keeffe.]

Bsq. The Black Somnambulist. L.C. 19/8/1848.

R.D. The Black Spider; or, The Field of Terror (Cob. M. 4/4/1831).

D. The Black Tower; or, A Tartar's Vengeance (R.P. M. 12/3/1832).

Spec. The Black Tower and the Spanish Patriots; or, The Downfall of Saladin (Cob. M. 3/3/1823).

M.D. The Black Valley; or, The Tomb of St. Aubin (Royalty, M. 11/3/1822).

M.D. The Black Woodsman; or, The Devil and Tom Walker (Cob. T. 3/7/1827).

M.D. Blanca Rubea, the Heroine of Padua (Surrey, M. 12/7/1824).

F.   Blasé; or, The Man in Search of a Sensation (P'cess, S. 17/2/1844).
     L.C. 3/2/1844.
     [Derived from the same source as *BOUCICAULT's Used Up*
     (H.² 1844)—*L'homme blasé*.]
Ba. Bletchington House; or, The Warning Voice (St J. M. 26/12/1836).
     L.C. 23/12/1836.
M.D. The Blighted Willow; or, The Shepherd's Heir (S.W. M.
     14/10/1839).
D.   The Blind Beggar of Moorfields (City, W. 27/6/1832).
Ba. The Blind Father; or, The Peasant Marchioness (Strand, M.
     18/9/1837). L.C. 1837.
O.F. Blind Man's Buff; or, Who Pays the Bill? (R.A. M. 18/9/1815).
     [See *T. J. DIBDIN*, 1802. A play of this title is in L.C.
     18/8/1836.]
M.D. Blindness; or, The Peasant Prince (Cob. M. 20/8/1821).
     [Presumably the same as *The Blind Prince* (Cob. M. 22/12/1828.]
D.   The Blind Orphan (Surrey, M. 7/1/1833).
O.   The Blind Sister (P'cess, Th. 10/5/1849). L.C. 21/4/1849 (as *The
     B. S.; or, The Mountain Farm*).
D.   The Bloodhound; or, The Orphan's Grave (Vic. M. 31/3/1845).
D.   Blood Royal; or, State Jewels. L.C. C.G. 27/10/1843.
Ba. Blood will have Blood. L. 98 M. [Pav. 18/4/1813].
M.D. The Blue Anchor; or, Neptune the Smuggler's Friend (Cob.
     M. 23/4/1832).
M.D. The Blue Anchor; or, The Life of Spritsail Jack. L.C. Apollo,
     23/12/1844.
Int. The Blue Devils (Kelly's, M. 9/5/1842).
D.   Blue-eyed Mary; or, The Lily of the Village (R.P. M. 8/6–
     M. 22/6/1835).
M.D. The Blue Man; or, The Punishment of Sacrilege (S.W. M.
     1/12/1834).
P.   The Blue Mountain Spirits; or, Harlequin Aerial (R.C. W.
     1/10/1800).
P.   Bluff King Hal; or, Harlequin and the Enchanted Arrow (P'cess,
     T. 26/12/1848). L.C. 2/12/1848.
F.   The Boarder (H.² Th. 14/6/1832). L.C. 2/6/1832.
Int. The Board of Conviviality; or, Fun and Harmony (C.G.
     13/5/1806).
M.Ent. Bobinet the Bandit; or, The Forest of Monte-Scarpini (C.G.
     F. 4/12/1815). L. 61 S. [29/11/1815].
O.F. The Bogle of the Clyde; or, The Bailie Bewitched (Perth, 1836).
D.   The Bohemian Mother (Surrey, M. 18/4/1831).
D.   The Bohemians; or, The Thieves of Paris (C.L. M. 20/11/1843)
     L.C. 18/11/1843.
     [This and the following piece are derived from Sue's *Les
     mystères de Paris*. See under *STIRLING* and *BARNETT*.]
D.   The Bohemians; or, The Thieves of Paris (Queen's, M. 4/12/1843).
Spec. The Bold Bucaniers; or, Caribs (Cob. M. 15/5/1826).
P.   Bold Robin Hood; or, The Pretty White Horn and the Enchanted
     Princess of Sherwood Forest (R.A. T. 26/12/1848). L.C. 30/9/1848.
     [By *N. LEE*.]
Ba. A Bold Stroke for a Wife (Surrey, M. 27/8/1810).
     [An adaptation of Mrs Centlivre's comedy.]
P.   Bonafaiso; or, Harlequin King of Epirus (R.A. M. 4/6/1804).

Ba. Bone Squash. L.C. 5/11/1839.
    [See *RICE*, 1836.]
M.D. The Boor's Hut; or, Russian Perfidy (R.A. M. 26/6/1820).
D. Border Feuds; or, The Lady of Buccleuch. 8° 1811 [Dublin].
M.D. Borrachio, the Outlaw; or, The Child of Mystery (Surrey, M. 23/2/1824).
F. The Bosom Friend. L.C. H.² 7/10/1844.
D. The Bottle (Strand, M. 25/10/1847).
    [Attributed to *F. F. COOPER*.]
D. The Bottle. L.C. R.P. 18/10/1847.
D. The Bottle (Vic. S. 11/10/1847).
D. The Bottle (Standard, S. 18/10/1847).
Ba. The Bottle of Champagne (Olym. Th. 8/1/1835). L.C. 5/1/1835.
Bsq. A Boudoir of Burlesque. L.C. Vic. 24/8/1844.
D. Bourbons and Bonapartists; or, First Love (Surrey, M. 23/10/1837).
D. The Boy and the Bandits (Adel. M. 16/4/1838).
Ent. The Boyhood and Old Age of Mr. Yates (C.G. Th. 13/6/1822).
D. The Boy King (Adel. 28/8/1845). L.C. 25/8/1845.
Ba. The Boys of Horsley Down; or, Girls of Chelsea Reach (Cob. M. 3/12/1827).
M.D. The Brahman's Curse; or, The Gentoo's Daughter (R.P. M. 20/4/1829).
M.D. Branksome Castle (Surrey, M. 4/2/1811—3rd performance).
Bal. The Brave and the Fair (Lyc. Th. 11/7/1816).
Spec. The Brave Cossack; or, The Secret Enemy (R.A. M. 30/3/1812).
M.D. The Bravo and the Venetian Conspirators (R.A. M. 15/11/1819).
    [Acted later at the same theatre as *The Conspirators; or, The Venetian Bravo*.]
M.D. The Bravo's Son. L. 115 M. [Bath, 4/3/1819].
F. Brazen Nose College; or, The Oxford Scholar (City, M. 12/12/1831).
M.D. The Brazen Water-Tower; or, The Doubtful Child (S.W. M. 7/6/1824).
M.D.Ent. Brazilian Jack; or, The Life of an Ape (S.W. M. 19/5/1834).
Ba. Breach of Promise. L.C. Olym. 12/12/1841.
Ba. The Breakfast of Love; or, The Rover Reclaimed (Royalty, M. 7/1/1822).
Int. A Breeze in the Baltic; or, The Danes in the Dumps (Edinburgh, 1801).
T. Brennus: or The Downfall of Tyranny...By Britannicus. 8° 1832 [Edinburgh and Glasgow].
M.D. Brian Boroihme, the Victorious; or, The Battle of Clontarffe (Cob. M. 28/2/1820).
Ba. The Bricklayers' Arms (Adel. T. 9/2/1830). L.C. 25/1/1830.
D. The Bridal Eve; or, Innocence Rewarded (Strand, M. 14/6/1847).
Bal. The Bridal of Flora (D.L. S. 9/11/1816).
O. The Bridal Promise (Olym. 10/6/1833). L.C. 29/5/1833.
Bal. The Bride and Bridegroom; or, The Dandy Drenched (S.W. M. 25/8/1828).
M.D. The Bride and the Proscribed; or, The Widow's Nuptials (S.W. T. 17/3/1840).
Spec. The Bride of Abydos (R.A. M. 5/4/1847). L.C. 10/3/1847.
M.D. The Bride of Lammermuir; or, The Mermaid's Well (R.A. M. 12/7/1819).
    [Adapted from Sir Walter Scott's novel; see also the following plays.]

M.D. The Bride of Lammermuir. L. 76 S. [Edinburgh, 27/10/1819].
[By *T. J. DIBDIN*, acted previously at the Surrey Theatre.]
D. The Bride of Lammermoor (Queen's, M. 9/5/1831).
O. The Bride of Lammermoor (M'bone, S. 9/10/1848).
D. The Bride of the Bleeding Heart; or, The Soldier of Vietri (R.P.
M. 31/12/1832).
D. The Bride of the Nile. L.C. R.A. 20/12/1845.
[Another appears as a spectacle in L.C. R.A. 25/8/1845, acted
on 1/9/1845.]
D. The Bride of the Prairie (Queen's, M. 13/9/1847). L.C.
13/9/1847.
O. The Brides of Venice (D.L. M. 22/4/1844). L.C. 14/4/1844.
[By *A. BUNN*. Music Sir Julius Benedict.]
D. The Bride's Journey. L.C. Vic. 22/4/1846.
D. The Brigand Monk and the Dog of Mount St. Bernard (Vic. M.
28/4/1845).
Spec. The Brigands of Ancona (R.A. M. 8/12/1845).
Spec. The Brigands of Ancona; or, The Attack of the Dragoons. L.C.
Apollo, 17/2/1844.
D. The Brigand's Daughter. L.C. Albert, 24/10/1845.
Ba. Brighton Cliff; or, The White Hawk Lady. L.C. 30/7/1831.
Bsq. The Brisket Family; or, The Running of the Rat (Olym. W.
9/1/1822). L. 85 S. [3/1/1822].
Bal.Spec. Britain's Allies (Pantheon, M. 27/12/1813).
Ent. Britain's Jubilee (Pav. Th. 26/10/1809). L. 51 S. [18/10/1809].
C. The British Admiral and the Seaman's Son. L. 97 M. [Norwich,
28/8/1812].
Spec. British Courage (R.A. M. 8/7/1805).
Spec. British Heroes; or, The Defeat of Junot (Royalty, M. 19/9/1808).
F. The British Lion. L.C. Adel. 4/11/1848.
M.D. The British Lion; or, The French Prison (Cob. M.
29/11/1830).
D. The British Queen. L.C. Hull, 1/2/1840.
D. A British Sailor Abroad and at Home (S.W. M. 19/7/1830).
C. The British Soldier; or, Life's Campaign (Norwich, S. 16/3/1805).
L. 82 M. [16/2/1805].
M.D. Britons at Navarino; or, The Destruction of the Turko-
Egyptian Fleet (Cob. M. 26/11/1827).
Ba. Broadbrim and Co. (S.W. M. 11/2/1828).
Int. Broad but not Long; or, The First Night of a New Piece (C.G.
15/6/1814). L. 102 M. [1/6/1814].
Ext. Broad Grins; or, Harlequin Mag and Harlequin Fag (Olym. T.
7/2/1815). L. 105 M. [1/2/1815].
Ba. Broad Grins; or, The Laughing Philosopher (Cob. M. 2/2/1829).
M.D. Broadsea Cliffs; or, A Tale of the Seaside (Surrey, M.
26/1/1835).
D. The Broken Chain; or, The Lady of Nuremberg (Surrey, M.
15/10/1838).
D. The Bronze Horse; or, The Flying Palfrey of China (R.A. M.
8/6/1835).
[Adapted from E Scribe, *Le cheval de bronze* (Paris, 23/3/1835),
music by Auber]
C.O. Brother and Sister (City, M. 24/10/1831).
[See *DIMOND*, 1815.]
D. The Brothers. L.C. Manchester, 2/12/1843.

Ba. The Brothers in Arms; or, The Wolf and the Lamb (St J. M.
16/4/1838). L.C. 13/4/1838.
[See *The Wolf and the Lamb* (H.² 1832) by *T. E. WILKS*.]
C. The Brothers of Cordova. L.C. 28/2/1826.
[An adaptation of Fletcher's *The Spanish Curate*.]
M.D. The Brothers of Turin; or, The Children of the Alps (S.W. M.
18/4/1831).
D. The Brown Devil; or, The Charmed Pirate. L.C. 16/1/1830.
M.D. Brown Fanny; or, The Teaman's Car (Vic. M. 31/3/1834).
F. Brown, Jones and Robinson, a Legend of the Hackney Road
(C.G. Th. 27/9/1838). L.C. 25/9/1838.
O. The Brown Man (E.O.H. Th. 19/8/1819). L. 117 M. [29/7/1819].
[Music Reeve.]
Ba. The Brown Man (Olym. 4/12/1820). L. 77 S. [29/11/1820].
Ba. Bruno; or, The Sultan's Favourite (Adel. M.8/10/1821). L. 123 M.
[2/10/1821]. [Acted at Bath in 1822 as *The Bashaw and the
Bear*.]
M.D. Brutus; or, The Fall of Tarquin (Surrey, M. 23/2/1829).
[See *PAYNE*, 1818.]
O. The Buccaneer. L.C. Lyc. 2/6/1824.
[Based on Sir Walter Scott's *Rokeby*.]
F. The Budget of Blunders (E.L. M. 11/1/1819).
[Adapted from *GREFFULHE*, q.v.]
Ext. Buonaparte Burnt Out; or, The Allies Victorious (Surrey, M.
18/10/1813).
Spec. Buonaparte's Destiny (Cob. M. 31/1/1831).
Spec. Buonaparte's Fatalities (R.A. M. 15/9/1828).
[Made up from previous spectacles at R.A.]
M.D. Burgundy the Bold (Surrey, S. 22/9/1832).
D. Burgundy the Bold; or, The Fate of the Raven of Rheinfeldt
(Cob. M. 24/9/1832).
Spec. A Burlesque Steeplechase (R.A. M. 13/7/1835).
P. The Burning Mountain; or, Neptune's Gift (R.C. M. 6/2/1804—
3rd performance).
Spec. The Burning of the Kent East Indiaman (Cob. M. 8/8/1825).
P. Butcher, Butcher, Kill an Ox. L.C. R.P. 17/12/1845.
O.Bsq. The Butterfly Ball; or, The Jealous Moth (Adel. T. 19/11/1833).
L.C. 16/11/1833 [as *The B. B.; or, Loves of the Plants*].
P. The Butterfly's Ball (Lyc. S. 26/12/1846). L.C. 21/12/1846.
Ext. "Buy a Broom?"; or, How many were Bavarians (Cob. M.
12/2/1827).
F. By Special Appointment. L.C. Vic. 21/7/1849.
D. The Cabin Boy (D.L. 28/6/1836). L.C. 25/6/1836.
F. The Cabinet; or, Much Ado about Nothing (German, Th.
16/1/1806).
M.D. The Cabinet Secret (S.W. M. 11/6/1832).
F. The Cady. L. 106 M. [D.L. 21/5/1815].
D. Caesar, Bob and Lucy Neal. L.C. Bower, 21/5/1847.
Bal. Cantata. Caesar's Triumph over the Gauls (H.¹ Th. 6/7/1815).
Oa. The Caid. L.C. St J. 17/12/1849.
D. The Caitiff of Corsica; or, The Universal Bandits. 8° 1807.
T. Caius Marius. L.C. 4/5/1837.
D. Calaf. 8° 1826.
M.D. Calas; or, Father and Son (S.W. M. 3/4/1820).

D. Caledonia; or, The Thistle and the Rose (Edinburgh, W. 23/12/1812). L. 97 M. [12/11/1812].

M.D. The Caledonian Assassin; or, The Recluse of the Monastery (Surrey, Th. 26/2/1824).

Bal.O. Le Calife de Bagdad (H.¹ Th. 11/5/1809).
[By T. J. DIBDIN, based on the opera by Godard d'Ancour de Saint-Just, music Boieldieu (Paris, 16/9/1800.)]

Bal. Le Calife voleur (H.¹ Th. 2/6/1814).

M.D. The Caliph and the Slave; or, Dead Alive (R.P. M. 12/4/1830).

M.D. The Caliph Haroun Alraschid; or, The Arab of the Desert (Surrey, M. 2/8/1824).

Spec. The Caliph Vathek; or, The Career of Crime (Cob. F. 26/12/1823).

F. The Cameleon. L. 111 M. [Edin. 1/1817].

M.D. Camelford; or, Three O'Clock (Royalty, M. 23/9/1822).

M.D. Camilla the Amazon; or, The Mountain Robber (Sans P. Th. 6/2/1817). L. 110 M. [23/1/1817].

Spec. The Camp (D.L. T. 25/10/1825).

F. The Camp and the Convent; or, The Devil and St Dunstan (Cob. W. 1/11/1820).

O.F. Il Campanello (Lyc. Th. 30/11/1837). L.C. 2/12/1837.

Spec. The Camp of Silesia; or, The Gipsy Queen (R.A. M. 8/11/1847). L.C. 6/11/1847.

Ba. Can Love Kill? (St J. Th. 10/3/1836). L.C. 7/3/1836.

Ext. The Cannibal (Strand, M. 7/5/1838). L.C. 4/5/1838.

D. Canonburg; or, The Merchant's Vow. L.C. 16/1/1834.

D. Canonburg Tower; or, The Fair Maid of Islington (S.W. M. 20/6/1831).

Ext. Cannon-mouth and Pistol-shot; or, A qu le victoire? (S.W. M. 6/10/1828).

Ba. Can't I do what I like with my own? (R.P. M. 8/8/1831).

Spec. The Cape of Good Hope; or, Caffres and Settlers (R.A. M. 20/10/1819).

D. Captain Bertram; or, The Seaman's Fireside (Surrey, M. 13/6/1836).

D. Captain Bertram and Jack Junk (Surrey, Th. 1/6/1837).
[This may be a variant title for the above.]

C.O. Captain MacShane; or, The White Bear. L. 41 S. [Norwich, 25/1/1802].

Ba. "Captain (Query?)" (Prince's, M. 30/11/1840).

M.D. Captain Ross; or, The Hero of the Arctic Regions (R.P. M. 28/10/1833).

F. Captain Stevens. L.C. Adel. 19/9/1838.

F. Captain Tarradiddle; or, What will the World say? (H.² W. 20/8/1845).

Spec. The Captive Mariner; or, The Generous Turk (Royalty, M. 3/12/1804).

M.D. The Captive Princess; or, The Book of Fate (R.C. Th. 6/10/1814).

Bal. Caractacus (D.L. F. 22/4/1808).
[Arranged by D'Egville with music by Bishop.]

Ba. The Caravan; or, The Driver and his Dog (E.L. F. 20/9/1816).
[See REYNOLDS, 1803.]

C. Carbonari; or, The Bride of Parma (P'cess, M. 10/2/1845). L.C. 27/1/1845.

M.D. Card-Drawing; or, Presumptive Evidence (S.W. M. 11/5/1829).
D. Card-Drawing; or, The Knave of Clubs. L.C. C.G. 27/2/1828.
M.D. Cardillac, the Terror of Paris; or, The Ruins of St Paul (Cob. M. 29/1/1827).
F. The Cardinal's Letters (S.W. W. 28/8/1844). L.C. S.W. 22/8/1844.
F. The Careful Servant and the Careless Master (C.G. T. 29/10/1816). L. 107 M. [23/10/1816].
Ba. The Caribee; or, Travellers from Threadneedle-street (Cob. M. 2/4/1827).
F. Cariboo; or, The Prude. L.C. Bristol, 20/2/1842.
D. Carl Carlsruhe; or, The Seven Adventures (Surrey, M. 27/1/1840).
Bal. Carl et Lisbeth; ou, le déserteur malgré lui (H.¹ M. 16/5/1814).
M.D. Carline; or, The Last of the Vendeans (City, M. 17/10/1831).
Ba. Carlo; or, The Watch Dog (Olym. Th. 16/11/1837). L.C. 1837.
M.D. Carlowitz and Orloff (R.P. M. 31/1/1831).
Spec. Carl Zeitter and his Bride; or, The Devil and the Rider (R.A. M. 20/7/1835).
Bal. Le carnaval de Venise (H.¹ Th. 31/5/1821).
D. The Carnival at Naples (C.G. S. 30/10/1830). L.C. 23/10/1829. [Music J. Barnett.]
P.Sk. The Carnival of Venice; or, The Return of Harlequin (Cob. M. 11/10/1824).
D. The Carpenters of Lambeth; or, The Bride of the Thames (Vic. M. 30/8/1847). L.C. 28/8/1847.
D. Casanova. L.C. 13/4/1837.
D. Casper Hauser; or, The Wild Boy of Bavaria (Queen's, M. 9/1/1837).
M.D. Casper the Doomed; or, The Victim of the Vault (Vic. M. 22/11/1841).
M.D. The Castellan's Oath (C.G. F. 4/6/1824). L.C. 15/5/1824.
Bal. The Castilian Minstrel (Lyc. F. 8/6/1810).
C.O. The Castle of Andalusia (H.² S. 26/7/1817).
    [O'Keeffe's opera reduced to two acts; music by Arnold.]
C.O. The Castle of Aymon; or, The Four Brothers (P'cess, W. 20/11/1844). L.C. 15/11/1844.
    [Adapted from Les quatre fils Aymon (Paris, 15/7/1844) by Leuven and Brunswick; music by Balfe.]
O.F. The Castle of Lausanne; or, The Tricks of Timothy. L. 84 M. [C.G. 23/2/1805].
Ba. The Castle of Limburg (Olym. Th. 22/10/1840).
Ba. The Castle of Limburg; or, Man or Wife (Surrey, Th. 7/3/1822).
    [Adapted from Matrimony.]
T. The Castle of St Aldobrand. L. 63 S. [D.L. 29/4/1816].
D. The Castle of St Aldobrand (Cob. W. 22/2/1832).
M.D. The Castle of Steinberg (Olym. M. 17/1/1831). L.C. 13/1/1831.
M.D. The Castle of Tarento; or, The Prisoner's Escape (Cob. T. 27/7/1819).
Ba. The Castle of Wolfenstein; or, The Accusing Spirit (Olym. M. 10/11/1828). L.C. 6/11/1828.
C. Castles in the Air. L. 69 S. [D.L. 20/2/1818].
F. Castles in the Air (Surrey, W. 29/2/1832).
D.R. Castle Walstenfurth. 8° 1801.
D. Caswallon, the King of Britain. L.C. Plymouth, 13/12/1826.

M.D. The Cataract of Sostenza; or, The Heir of Valvoni (Cob. W. 8/6/1825).

O. Catarina; or, The Crown Jewels L.C. Vic. 22/8/1844.
   [An adaptation of E. Scribe and de Saint-Georges, *Les diamants de la couronne* (Paris, 6/3/1841), with music by Auber. See the following play also.]

O. Catarina; or, The False Jewels (Strand, 10/6/1844). L.C. 10/6/1844.

T. Catherine de Medicis. 8° 1820.

Bsq. The Cat in the Larder; or, The Maid with the Parasol. L.C. Edinburgh, 21/9/1842.

Ext. The Cat of Kilkenny; or, The Forest of Blarney. L. 104 M. [Olym. 18/2/1815].

P. Cat's Castle; or, Harlequin, the King of the Rats (Adel. T. 24/12/1844). L.C. 18/12/1844.

Ba. Caught and Caged. L.C. H.² 12/8/1830.

O.F. Caught at Last (S.W. M. 23/3/1818).

F. Caught Napping (C.G. Th. 7/10/1841). L.C. 8/10/1841.

M.D. The Cavaliers; or, The Fight of Marston Moor (Cob. M. 26/3/1832).

P. The Cavern in the Rock; or, The Midnight Assembly (R.C. M. 9/1/1804).

P. C. D. I. T. D. Now Find it Out (Cob. M. 30/6/1823).

M.D. Celeste; or, The Emperor's Victim (S.W. M. 7/10/1839).

D. Celeste, the French Spy. L.C. Liverpool, 19/7/1831.

D. The Cellar Spectre (Adel. S. 11/7/1833). L.C. 1/5/1833.

Bal. C'est l'amour (H.¹ T. 6/6/1820).

Ba. C'est l'amour, l'amour, l'amour; or, Who can help it? (R.A. M. 1/9/1828).

R.D. The Chains of the Heart; or, The Milesian Mother (Surrey, M. 8/6/1835).

F. Chalk Farm; or, Pistols and Petticoats (Adel. M. 13/2/1832). L.C. 8/2/1832.

Int. The Challenge; or, A Glass too much (S.W. Th. 7/4/1836).

F. The Chamber of Horrors (S.W. W. 17/11/1847). L.C. 6/11/1847.

F. Champagne (M'bone, T. 15/2/1848). L.C. 12/2/1848.

Spec. The Champ de Mai; or, The Hundred Days of Buonaparte (R.A. M. 20/9/1824).

Ba. Changed at Nurse; or, A Fish out of Water (S.W. T. 29/5/1821).

O.F. Change Partners (D.L. Th. 10/3/1825). L.C. 28/7/1825 [as *Turn Hands and C. P.*].
   [Music Horn; *J. M. MORTON* had a play of this name.]

Ba. The Changes (Olym. M. 16/10/1843).

F. Change upon Change; or, The Yorkshire Lover (Leeds, 1805).

F. Changing Servants. L.C. 6/7/1836.

Oa. The Chaplain of the Regiment. L.C. Grecian, 27/1/1849.

F. The Character of Solomon Swop. L.C. 17/11/1832.

M.D.Spec. The Charioteers; or, The Bacchanalian Festival. L. 51 S. [Pav. 21/11/1810].

Spec. Charlemagne (D.L. M. 22/10/1838). L.C. 19/10/1838.
   [Music Eliason and Stansbury.]

C. Charles II (Kelly's, M. 9/5/1842).

M.D. Charles XII and Peter the Great; or, The Battle of Pultawa (Cob. M. 26/5/1828).

D. Charles Edward, the Last of the Stuarts (Edinburgh, M. 21/4/1828).
D. Charles Edward Stuart the Pretender in Scotland; or, The Misfortunes of an Exile. L. 130 M. [Exeter, 20/2/1823].
D. Charles Ganganelli; or, The Bravo of Castille. L.C. Britannia, 14/4/1847.
M.D. Charles the Terrible; or, The Siege of Nancy (W.L. W. 26/12/1821).
    [Adapted from Pixérécourt, *Charles le Téméraire, ou le siège de Nancy* (Paris, 26/10/1814).]
M.D. Charles the Terrible; or, The Siege of Nancy (Cob. M. 12/4/1830; Surrey, M. 10/4/1837).
    [See above.]
D. Charley over the Water (Surrey, S. 7/5/1831).
Spec. Charlotte and Werther; or, Love and Madness (Pav. M. 26/3/1810). L. 92 M. [16/3/1810; as *W. and C.; or, Love's Victim*].
D. Charlotte Corday; or, The French Revolution (S.W. Th. 25/10/1832).
D. Charlotte Corday; or, The Bleeding Rose of Normandy (Albert, M. 19/10/1846). L.C. 1/10/1846.
Legend. The Charmed Charger; or, Nipkins and the Spectre Steed (R.A. M. 21/7/1834).
D. The Charter; or, Death and Liberty (S.W. M. 23/8/1830).
D. The Charter; or, The Bastard Brother (Cob. M. 14/3/1831).
Bal. La Chasse (C.G. T. 28/4/1818).
Ca. The Chasseurs (Surrey, M. 26/9/1831).
Ba. The Chaste Salute (Olym. W. 19/1/1831). L.C. 15/1/1831.
C. Check to the King; or, The Queen's First Move (S.W. F. 13/2/1846). L.C. 7/2/1846.
D. Chelsea; or, The Pensioner's Bride (Surrey, S. 10/3/1832).
F. A Cheque on my Banker (D.L. M. 13/8/1821).
    [An abbreviated version of *MONCRIEFF*'s *Wanted, a Wife*.]
M.D. The Cherokee Chief; or, The Dogs of the Wreck (Cob. M. 25/2/1833).
M.D. Cherry and Fair Star; or, The Children of Cyprus (C.G. M. 8/4/1822). L. 124 M. [29/3/1822].
Spec. Cherry and Fair Star; or, The Orphans of Cyprus (R.P. M. 23/4/1832).
D. Cherry Chance; or, The Wild Days of Haggeston Bill. L.C. Britannia, 8/1/1848.
C. The Chevalier d'Epsonne. L.C. Grecian, 3/6/1848.
C. Le Chevalier d'Epsonne. L.C. 1848.
O. Chiara in Rosenberg (Lyc. M. 23/1/1837).
    [Music Ricci.]
Ba. Chi Chu Ali, the Charmed Pirate (Garrick, M. 7/2/1831).
M.D. The Chieftains of Scotia; or, Malvina and Calmar (Royalty, M. 6/2/1809).
D. The Child of Air. L.C. H.[2] 11/5/1844.
O. The Child of Concealment; or, The Forest of Picardy. L. 107 M. [Norwich, 22/3/1816].
M.D. The Child of Mystery; or, The Ruby Cross (Olym. Th. 1/2/1821). L. 80 S. [25/1/1821].
P. The Children in the Wood; or, Harlequin and Nobody (Adel. S. 24/12/1842). L.C. 21/12/1842 [as *Harlequin and the C. in the W*.].

M.D. The Children of the Mist; or, A Legend of Montrose (Cob. T. 13/7/1819).
[A dramatisation of Sir Walter Scott's *A Legend of Montrose*.]
D. The Chimes. L.C. Queen's, 11/1/1845.
[Adapted from Dickens' tale.]
Bal. The Chinese Divertisement (D.L. T. 6/4/1824).
P. The Chinese Exhibition; or, The Feast of Lanterns (Strand, 26/12/1844). L.C. 23/12/1844.
D. The Chinese Junk; or, The Maid and the Mandarin. L.C. Britannia, 22/9/1848.
Spec. The Chinese War; or, The Conquest of Amoy by British Arms (R.A. M. 27/5/1844). L.C. 17/5/1844 [as *Wars in China; or, The Battle of Ching Ho*].
Spec. Chinese Wonders; or, The Five Days Fête of Pekin (R.A. M. 27/5/1833).
F. A Chip of the Old Block (Olym. T. 12/11/1844).
[See *KNIGHT, E.*, 1815.]
M.D. Chiverton Hall; or, Neil Jagger's Cave (Cob. F. 26/12/1828).
Sk. The Cholera Morbus; or, Love and Fright (Cob. M. 7/1/1831).
M.D. Christians and Moors (Royalty, M. 2/2/1824).
D. Christine; or, The Poisoner of Paris (S.W. M. 28/3/1842).
Ba. Christmas Boxes (Adel. M. 19/12/1825). L.C. 6/12/1825.
Ext. Christmas Capers; or, The Jewess in the Show Room (Queen's, S. 26/12/1835).
D. A Christmas Carol; or, A Dream of the Past, Present and Future (Strand, M. 12/2/1844). L.C. 8/2/1844.
[A dramatisation of Dickens' tale.]
D. Christmas Eve. L.C. 1840.
P. The Christmas Gossips; or, Harlequin's Birth (Pav. S. 26/12/1812).
D. The Christmas Log. L.C. Standard, 26/12/1846.
Ent. A Christmas Tale (R.C. F. 26/12/1817).
[An adaptation of the play (1773) by David Garrick.]
T. The Cid. 8° 1802.
[A translation of Corneille by "A Captain of the Army."]
Ba. Cinderella (C.L. W. 21/2/1838).
P. Cinderella (Edinburgh, S. 11/1/1809).
P. Cinderella; or, Harlequin and the Little Glass Slipper (Surrey, M. 24/4/1848). L.C. 17/4/1848.
C.O. Cinderella; or, The Fairy Slipper (D.L. M. 9/1/1837).
[Music Rossini, *La Cenerentola*.]
P. Cinderella; or, The Little Glass Slipper (D.L. S. 14/1/1804). L. 43 S. [17/12/1803].
Spec. Cinderella; or, The Little Glass Slipper. L. 23 L. [Norwich, 1818].
F. Circumstances alter Cases. L.C. R.P. 11/5/1846.
Ba. The Citizen (Cob. M. 30/8/1819).
Ba. The Citizen of Paris; or, The Prince's Stratagem (Cob. M. 3/5/1824).
Spec. The City Apprentice (Surrey, M. 2/3/1840).
D. The City Madam (S.W. W. 30/10/1844). L.C. 19/10/1844.
[This was Phelps' revival of Massinger's drama.]
Spec. The City of the Plague and the Great Fire of London (Cob. M. 26/12/1825).

C. The City Rivals. L. 101 M. (C.G. 4/3/1814).
Spec. Ciudad Rodrigo (Surrey, Th. 20/2/1812).
Bsq. The Civil War of Poetry (Olym. S. 17/10/1846). L.C. 1/10/1846.
F. Clairvoyance (Strand, M. 12/5/1845). L.C. 8/5/1845 [as *C.; or, Double Delusions*].
Spec. Clara; or, The Mysterious Recruit (Pav. M. 27/11/1809). L. 51 S. [18/11/1809].
Ba. Clarissa Harlowe (Olym. M. 3/1/1831). L.C. 1/1/1831.
    [This and the following play are adaptations of S. Richardson's *Clarissa*.]
D. Clarissa Harlowe. L.C. St J. 18/3/1847.
T. Clavigo [an English rendering of Goethe's play appeared in *The Literary World*, vol. ii. 1847].
Vaud. Clementine. L.C. St J. 9/11/1843.
F. Clifford Castle (Glasgow, May, 1809).
Ba. The Cloak and the Bonnet (E.O.H. **Th.** 26/8/1841). L.C. 27/8/1841.
Bal. Clodpole's Mistake (Cob. M. 22/6/1818).
P. The Clown's Fireside; or, A Tour through France (R.A. M. 26/6/1809).
Ext. The Clown's Trip to the Moon (Surrey, M. 11/5/1829).
M.D. The Coast Blockade; or, The Kentish Smuggler (Cob. M. 10/4/1826).
M.D. The Cobbler of Munich (Surrey, 23/4/1831).
F. Cocknies in California (Adel. M. 26/2/1849). L.C. 28/2/1849.
F. Cockorico; or, My Aunt's Bantam (Adel. M. 11/10/1841). L.C. 8/10/1841.
Pol. The C[ogglesha]ll Volunteer Corps. 8° 1804 [Colchester].
    [Written "by an Inhabitant of Coggleshall."]
D. Colomba, the Corsican Sister (Adel. S. 26/12/1846). L.C. 21/12/1846.
F. The Colonel (C.G. T. 4/5/1830). L.C. 26/4/1830 [as *The C.; or, The Female Travellers*].
D. Colonel Blood; or, The Robbery at the Tower of London (Vic. M. 24/8/1846).
Ba. Come of Age; or, The Happy Return. L.C. 30/3/1837.
Sk. The Comet (Vic. M. 28/9/1835).
P. The Comet; or, Harlequin Planet-struck (S.W. T. 13/11/1832).
D.F. Comfortable Lodgings. L.C. E.O.H. 30/6/1831.
    [See *PEAKE*, 1827.]
Ba. The Comic Robbers; or, The Escape upon the Common (S.W. M. 11/10/1830).
Ba. Coming Up, Sir! or, He Would be a Sailor (S.W. T. 16/10/1827).
Ba. The Committee; or, The Irishman in Distress. L. 126 M. [Olym. 18/1/1822].
Ba. Completely Successful; or, The Undutiful Father. L.C. Olym. 27/10/1827.
D. The Comrades, an Anecdote of the Spanish War (Adel. M. 20/3/1848). L.C. 21/3/1848.
M. Comus: A Masque (C.G. 28/4/1815). 8° 1815.
F. The Confederacy. L.C. 1827.
F. The Confusion; or, The Wag. 12° 1842 [Cambridge].
    [A translation of Kotzebue, *Der Wirrwarr*.]
C. Coningsby. L.C. Lyc. 30/3/1845.

F. Conjectures; or, The Man in the Camlet Cloak (H.² T. 15/6/1830).
L.C. 25/5/1830.
Ba. The Conjuror; or, Blaize in Amaze (Sans P. M. 30/10/1815).
L. 22 L. [20/10/1815].
M.D. Conlath of the Isles; or, The Spectre on the White Horse
(Cob. W. 17/10/1827).
T. The Conquest of Granada (New, Th. 10/1/1811).
M.D.Spec. The Conquest of Mexico; or, The Days of Ferdinand
Cortez (R.A. T. 7/8/1832).
M.D.Spec. The Conquest of Scinde; or, The Siege of Hyderabad
(R.A. M. 28/7/1845). L.C. 24/7/1845.
Spec. The Conquest of the Golden Pagodas; or, The Triumph of the
Tartar Cham (R.A. M. 20/8/1827).
Ba. Conrad and Christine. L.C. Adel. 19/1/1828.
M.D. Conrad, the Robber Chief; or, The Benevolent Israelite (S.W.
M. 10/11/1828).
T. Conrad the Usurper...And The Kinsmen of Naples. By the
Author of Tancred. 8° 1821.
D. Conrad the Usurper; or, The Templars of Fortune. L.C.
Britannia, 8/6/1848.
Spec. The Conscript (R.A. M. 11/11/1839).
R.D. The Conscript; or, The Veteran and his Dog (D.L. W.
17/11/1830). L.C. 12/11/1830 [as *The Counterfeit; or, The V. and
his D.*].
L.C. 12/11/1830 [as *The Counterfeit; or, The V. and his D.*].
M.D. The Conscript's Bride; or, Englishmen in Corsica (Cob. M.
25/10/1830).
D. The Conscript's Sister (Olym. T. 21/8/1832). L.C. 13/8/1832.
C.O. The Consequences; or, Safe and Sound. L. 50 S. [Lyc.
14/8/1809].
M.D. Conspiracy (Surrey, M. 27/3/1826).
Ext. Constellations and Cauliflowers; or, The Old Maid's Almanack
(R.A. M. 13/1/1823).
Bal. The Contrabandist (Lyc. M. 28/6/1847).
Int. Contrarieties; or, All at Cross Purposes (D.L. Th. 29/5/1817).
Ba. Conundrums (S.W. M. 9/7/1827).
O. The Convent; or, The Pet of the Petticoats (S.W. M. 9/7/1832).
L.C. 29/9/1832.
[Music J. Barnett.]
C.O. The Convent Belle (Adel. M. 8/7/1833). L.C. 6/7/1833.
T. The Convict. L. 127 M. [C.G. 18/1/1822].
D. The Convict (C.L. 11/1838).
M.D. The Convict Ship (Cob. T. 9/5/1826).
[On W. 1/4/1829 at the same theatre this was given as: *The
Convict Ship; or, John Howard, the Philanthropist.*]
Ba. The Cook; or, The Wedding Dinner (Surrey, M. 11/10/1824).
Ba. The Cook and the Secretary (Olym. F. 15/11/1833). L.C. 4/2/1833.
[This was an adaptation of *Changed at Nurse; or, A Fish out of
Water* (S.W. 1821).]
Ba. The Cook of Kennington; or, No Followers Allowed (Vic. M.
9/2/1846). L.C. Vic. 26/1/1846.
Bal. Coquilla; or, The Shell Spirit (Olym. Th. 23/3/1848).
T. Coriolanus (D.L. T. 25/1/1820).
[A cut version of Shakespeare's tragedy, brought forward by
Kean and Elliston; see G. C. D. Odell, *Shakespeare from Betterton
to Irving*, ii. 149-51.]

Kean and Elliston; see G. C. D. Odell, *Shakespeare from Betterton to Irving*, ii. 149–51.]

Ba.　Cork Legs; or, What a Coincidence! (City, M. 14/1/1833).

Spec.　Cormac and Swaran; or, The Chiefs of Erin (Pav. M. 12/2/1810). L. 51 S [2/2/1810].

Ba.　The Cornet (St J. W. 4/10/1837). L.C. 1837 [as *The C.; or, Orders from Head Quarters*].

M.D.　The Cornish Miners (E.O.H. M. 2/7/1827). L.C. 25/6/1827. [Music G. H. Rodwell.]

Pag.　The Coronation (D.L. W. 1/8/1821). [By *R. W. ELLISTON*.]

Pag.　The Coronation of King George IV (R.A. M. 27/7/1821).

O.　The Corsair! (D.L. M. 21/3/1836). L.C. 15/3/1836. Programme of the Songs, etc. 8° [1836]. [Music of Hérold's *Zampa*.]

M.D.　The Corsair's Revenge (R.P. M. 25/8/1834). [By *H. P. GRATTAN*, 1835.]

R.D.　The Corsair's Revenge (E.O.H. Th. 9/7/1840). L.C. 4/7/1840 [as *The Corsair*].

M.D.　The Corsair's Son; or, The Fall of Otranto (Royalty, M. 10/12/1821).

D.　The Corsican Maid; or, The Queen of the Hills (C.L. M. 23/7/1849). L.C. 14/7/1849.

Ba.　Cosimo (St J. M. 7/5/1838).

Ba.　The Cottage and the Court; or, The King's Wager. L.C. St J. 6/4/1839.

Spec.　The Cottage of the Lake; or, My Vassal's Dog (S.W. M. 3/4/1820).

M.D.　Could the Murder? or, The Fatal Thicket (Surrey, M. 4/7/1825).

M.D.　The Council of Ten; or, The Giant Staircase (Cob. M. 24/8/1829).

[Adapted from the French with the utilisation of some passages from Byron's *Marino Faliero*.]

M.D.　Count Bertram; or, The Pirates (Cob. M. 29/9/1823).

T.　Count Egmont. 8° 1848. [A translation of Goethe's play.]

O.F.　The Counterfeits (Olym. 12/11/1827). L.C. 12/11/1827. [Identical with *Touch and Take*, below.]

C.　The Countess of Lilliput; or, The Fair Old Maid of 1725 (R.A. M. 25/8/1828).

R.D.　The Count of Anjou; or, More Marriages than One (D.L. Th. 2/5/1816). L. 63 S. [28/4/1816]. [Music Cooke.]

Ba.　Country Actors; or, The Manager's Son (Olym. M. 22/1/1827). L.C. 10/1/1827 [as *Strolling C. A.; or, The M. S.*]. [See *BARRYMORE*, 1824.]

Ba.　The Country Girl (Surrey, T. 8/9/1812).

D.　The Country Squire (Olym. F. 29/9/1837). L.C. 1837. [By *C. E. DANCE*.]

M.D.　La Coupe Gorge; or, The Black Inn of the Heath (R.A. W. 25/5/1836).

Ba.　A Court Ball in 1740 (P'cess, M. 16/6/1845).

Ca.　Court Favourites. L.C. Lyc. 5/3/1847.

Ca. The Court Guide (Lyc. M. 3/7/1848). L.C. 1/7/1848.
    [This seems to be the same play as *The Tutor's Assistant* given
    at the Lyceum on T. 4/7/1848.]

O.F. Courting by Mistake; or, A Trip to the Coronation (City, T.
    20/9/1831).

Ba. The Court of Old Fritz (Olym. Th. 22/11/1838).

D. The Court of Queen Anne; or, The Prince and the Breeches
    Maker (Vic. M. 19/5/1834).

Ba. The Court of Queen's Bench (Olym. M. 22/10/1832). L.C.
    18/1/1832.
    [Music J. Barnett.]

T. The Court of Tuscany. 8° 1822.

F. Cousin Campbell's Courtship (Strand, M. 7/8/1843). L.C.
    20/7/1843 [as *C. C. C.; or, All Fair in Fair Time*].

O.F. Cousin Joseph (E.O.H. S. 23/5/1835). L.C. 4/4/1835.
    [Music S. Nelson.]

D. Cousin Matthew; or, Proof Impression. L.C. Olym. 4/9/1848.
    [See *Cousin Cherry* (Olym. 1848) by *H. SPICER*.]

P. Cowardy, Cowardy Custard; or, Harlequin Jim Crow and the
    Magic Mustard-Pot (Adel. M. 26/12/1836). L.C. 12/12/1836 [as
    The M. M.].

C. The Cow Doctor. 8° 1810.

M.D. Cramond Brig; or, The Gudeman of Ballangrich (S.W. M.
    4/7/1831).
    [See *MURRAY*, 1826.]

F. Crank the Clockmaker. L.C. Adel. 17/3/1846.

Bal. Crazy Jane (H.¹ Th. 4/4/1805).

Ba. The Crazy Old Slippers; or, The Miser of Bagdad (S.W. M.
    7/4/1828).

D. Creon, the Patriot. L.C. Norwich, 12/5/1828.

Ba. Crichton. L.C. 15/11/1839.

Spec. Crichton; or, The Royal Bull-fight and the Dark Days of
    Catherine de Medicis (R.A. M. 3/7/1837).

D. The Cricket on the Hearth (M'bone, 5/1/1846). L.C. 3/1/1846.
    [Based on Dickens' novel.]

M.D. The Criminal; or, The Old Oak Tree (R.P. M. 28/1/1839).

Ba. Crimson Crimes; or, The Blood-stained Bandit (Adel. M.
    19/11/1832).

Int. Croaking; or, "Heaven send we may all be alive this day three
    months" (Lyc. W. 2/5/1810).
    [Adapted from O. Goldsmith, *The Good Natur'd Man*.]

D. Crohoove-na-Bilhoge (Surrey, M. 27/5/1833).

M.D. Croohove of the Bill-Hook (Cob. M. 21/7/1828).

O. The Crown Diamonds. L.C. Yarmouth, 6/9/1847.

D. The Crown Prince (M'bone, M. 28/8/1848).
    [See *WILKS*, 1838.]

Ext. The Crumlesses; or, A Rehearsal Rehearsed (Strand, W.
    15/3/1848).

M.D. The Crusaders; or, Jerusalem Delivered (Cob. M. 3/4/1820).

Vaud.Ext. Crusoe the Second (Lyc. M. 5/4/1847). L.C. 3/4/1847.

M.D. The Cry of Blood; or, The Juror Murderer (Cob. M.
    17/9/1821).

F. Cuffs and Kisses (S.W. M. 10/8/1846). L.C. 18/7/1846.

D. Cullin, King of Scotland. L.C. 26/4/1836.

Ba.   The Culprit (S.W. M. 23/10/1848).
      [See *BAYLY*, 1838.]
Bal. Cunning against Art; or, Love in Scotland (Royalty, M. 28/1/1805).
Ba.   The Cupboard and the Cabinet (Adel. M. 9/12/1822). L. 84 S.
      [3/12/1822; as *Cooking and Copying; or, The C. and the C.*].
Bsq. Cupid (Adel. 1832).
Bal. Cupid and Flora (Royalty, M. 13/6/1814).
Bal. Cupid and Folly; or, The Court of Love (D.L. W. 1/10/1820).
Ca.   Cupid and Psyche. L.C. P'cess, 22/4/1848.
P.   Cupid and the Woodcutter (Pav. T. 26/1/1813).
D.   Cupid's Diplomacy; or, Royal Woes and Royal Wooing (D.L. T.
      7/1/1840). L.C. 7/1/1840.
Ba.   Cupid turned Physician (S.W. M. 26/9/1831).
Bal. Cupid Wanderer (R.A. M. 18/5/1818).
Oa.   A Cure for Coxcombs (Lyc. Th. 30/8/1821). L. 123 M. [3/8/1821].
      8° 1821.
      [Music Watson.]
Bal. A Cure for the Heartache (Regency, M. 27/1/1812).
D.   The Curia (D.L. M. 3/6/1822).
      ['This is a scene from Massinger's *The Roman Actor*.]
F.   Curiosities of Literature (H.² S. 24/9/1842). L.C. 21/9/1842.
F.   Curiosity; or, The Doomed Entombed (R.A. M. 5/3/1849).
      [See *CLARANCE*, 1847.]
Spec. The Curse of Mammon; or, The Earl's Son and the Citizen's
      Daughter (Surrey, M. 1/4/1839).
M.D. The Curse of St. Vallier; or, The Jester's Daughter (S.W. W.
      13/5/1840).
F.   A Cutlet for Two (P'cess, T. 19/12/1848). L.C. 14/12/1848.
O.   Cymon (Surrey, M. 1/2/1813).
      [Apparently an adaptation of Garrick's play (1767).]
M.D. The Czar of Muscovy; or, The Three Ambassadors (Cob. M.
      25/11/1822).
D.   The Daemon of Daneswall. 8° 1802.
M.D. The Daemon Owl; or, The Rosicrucian Student (R.P. M.
      22/8/1831).
P.   The Daemon's Tribunal; or, Harlequin's Enterprises (Royalty,
      M. 16/11/1801).
M.D. Daft Meg of the Cliff; or, The Seventh Night (R.A. M.
      28/6/1824).
Bal. The Dairy Maids; or, Generous Tars (D.L. W. 9/6/1802).
Bal. Dalmaviva and Rosina; or, The Lover's Disguise (R.A. F.
      27/5/1814).
Bal. La Dama di Spirito in Napoli (H.¹ T. 13/2/1810).
D.   Dame Blanche. L.C. Vic. 24/5/1845.
D.   Damp Fire; or, The Murder in the Mine (S.W. M. 14/11/1842).
Bal. Les Danaides (D.L. T. 4/2/1845).
Bal. The Dancing Master (Olym. M. 2/1/1815).
F.   The Dangerous Neighbourhood (German, Th. 13/2/1806).
P.   Daniel O'Rourke; or, Harlequin from Killarney. L.C. Adel.
      15/12/1826.
P.   Darby and Joan (R.C. Th. 28/5/1801).
P.   Darby and Joan; or, Harlequin and Robin Goodfellow (Vaux. S.
      14/7/1827).
O.F. Darby and Joan; or, The Dwarf (Royalty, M. 1/2/1802).

M.D. The Dark Diamond (C.G. M. 5/11/1832). L.C. 31/10/1832.
[Music Adam.]

F. Dark Events; or, The Mis-adventures of a Night (Lyc. M. 1/4/1839).

Spec. The Dark Falcon; or, The Magic Goblet (Surrey, M. 1/6/1846).

M.D. The Dark Pandour; or, The Fatal Armour (Cob. M. 11/8/1828).

M.D. Darnley, the Knight of Burgundy; or, The Field of the Cloth of Gold (Cob. M. 21/6/1830).

M.D. The Daughter; or, The Triumph of Innocence. L. 104 M. [D.L. 7/9/1815].

Bal.P. The Daughter of Air (S.W. M. 25/8/1800).
[Adapted from the German.]

T. The Daughter of the Air. 12° 1831.
[Translated from the German of E. B. Raupach.]

Ext. The Daughter of the Danube (D.L. 21/11/1837).
[Music A. Adam and A. Pilati.]

O. The Daughter of the Regiment. L.C. Norwich, 13/5/1848.

Ba. A Daughter to Marry. L.C. Lyc. 30/7/1827.

Ba. A Daughter to Marry (Surrey, M. 17/4/1837).
[See PLANCHÉ, 1828.]

P. Davy Jones; or, Harlequin and Mother Carey's Chickens (D.L. M. 27/12/1830). L.C. 21/12/1829.

P. Davy Jones's Locker; or, Black-eyed Susan (Sans P. W. 23/12/1812).

P. Davy Jones's Locker; or, Harlequin and Black-eyed Susan (Cob. M. 11/7/1825).

Int. A Day after the Fair (Surrey, M. 27/11/1826).
[See SOMERSET, 1829.]

F. Day and Night. L. 104 M. [Edinburgh, 7/6/1815].

D. A Day at Dover (P'cess, M. 8/5/1845).

C. A Day in the Country; or, A Meeting of Friends. L. 109 M. [Edinburgh, 20/1/1817].

Ba. A Day's Fun; or, "All's Fair in Fair Time" (Adel. Th. 30/10/1828). L.C. 21/10/1828.
[Adapted from Je fais mes farces.]

Spec. The Days of Chivalry; or, The Champion Horse and the Saxon Knight (S.W. M. 2/8/1841).

Ba. The Days of Edward IV. L.C. Adel. 23/10/1835.
[This is probably The King's Command (Adel. 1835) by C. P. THOMSON.]

Ba. The Days of Old; or, The Houses of York and Lancaster (Surrey, W. 12/2/1812).

Ba. A Day's Training (St J. M. 1/4/1839). L.C. 30/3/1839.

Vaud. A Day up the River (Vaux. M. 29/6/1829).

F. The Dead Alive (Cob. T. 13/7/1819).

Ba. Dead and Buried; or, How to Raise the Wind (Surrey, Th. 27/9/1827).

M.D. Dead or Not Dead; or, The Spectre Bridegroom (S.W. M. 25/5/1829).

M.D. The Dead Wife; or, Marmaduke the Smuggler (R.P. M. 3/12/1838).

M.D. Deaf and Dumb; or, The Abbé de l'Epée. 8° 1801.
[A translation of Bouilly's play.]

F. Dealings with the Firm of Gasup and Harris. L.C. Queen's, 27/11/1846.

F. Dearest Elizabeth (H.² S. 22/1/1848). L.C. 28/1/1848.
D. The Death Dealer (Vic. M. 19/10/1840).
R.D. The Death Doom; or, A Soldier's Honour (Vic. M. 19/6/1843).
M.D. The Death Fetch; or, The Fatal Warning (Cob. M. 14/8/1826).
M.D. The Death Fetch; or, The Supernatural Warning (City, W. 26/12/1832).
Spec. The Death of Caesar; or, The Battle of Philippi (Surrey, F. 26/12/1823).
Sk. The Death of General Mortier; or, The Infernal Machine and the Massacre of Paris (R.A. M. 10/8/1835).
M.D. The Death of General Woolfe; or, An Indian's Honour (Cob. M. 18/2/1833).
Bsq. The Death of Giovanni; or, The Shades of Logic, Tom and Jerry (Olym. M. 8/12/1823). L. 132 M. [3/12/1823].
Spec. The Death of Iturbide, Ex-Emperor of Mexico (Cob. M. 11/10/1821).
M.D. The Death of Mary Queen of Scots (Surrey, M. 10/11/1823).
M.D. The Death of Rolla (S.W. T. 18/9/1821).
D. The Death of Sir John Moore and the Defeat at Corunna (R.A. M. 19/5/1834).
D. The Death of the Queen of France. L. 80 M. [Norwich, 7/5/1804; licence refused].
Spec. The Death of the Race-Horse; or, The North Steamer (R.A. M. 7/4/1828).
D. The Death of Tom Moody (R.A. M. 31/5/1830).
T. The Death of Virginia; or, The Last of the Decemviri (Caledonian, Edinburgh, 15/5/1829).
D. The Death Secret; or, The Heart and the Key (Surrey, M. 22/10/1849).
M.D. De Bassenvelt; or, The Green Rider. L.C. Garrick, 22/3/1845.
P. The Deceitful Steward; or, The Orphans Protected (Olym. M. 9/2/1807).
F. The Deceiver Deceived. L.C. C.G. 28/2/1826.
D. Deception; or, The Hour of Midnight (S.W. M. 7/12/1835).
F. Decorum; or, Very Suspicious (D.L. S. 5/3/1831). L.C. 18/2/1831.
F. A Deed without a Name. L.C. Olym. 5/10/1824.
D. The Deer Stalker; or, The Outlaw's Daughter (E.O.H. M. 12/4/1841). L.C. 5/4/1841.
Bal. Les déguisements amoureux (H.¹ T. 1/7/1817).
Bal. Les déguisements imprévus (H.¹ T. 16/6/1829).
R.D. De la Perouse; or, The Desolate Island (D.L. M. 7/11/1825). [Music Davy and Moorhead.]
Ba. The Delights of the Diligence; or, The Paris Drag (S.W. M. 7/5/1827).
M.D. De l'Orme; or, The Priest of Saragossa (Cob. M. 14/2/1831).
Ca. Delusions (Queen's, Th. 10/3/1831).
M.D. Demetri the Outcast; or, The Klepht of the Evil Eye (Vic. M. 9/11/1835).
T. Demetrius the Impostor. 8° 1806.
[Translated from A. Sumarakov, Дмитрн.]
O. The Demon Duke; or, The Mystic Branch (D.L. M. 20/2/1832). L.C. 14/2/1832.
[Adapted from E. Scribe, *Robert le Diable* (Paris, 21/11/1831), with music by Meyerbeer.]

M.D. The Demon Dwarf. L.C. Liverpool, 5/12/1842.
  [A play of this name seems to have been produced at the Vic.
  in January 1839.]
Ba. The Demon Father; or, The Devil and his Son (R.P. M. 12/3/1832).
Spec. The Demon Horse; or, The Twelve Wishes and the Charmed
  Bit (R.A. M. 9/11/1846). L.C. 1/10/1846.
M.D. The Demon Knight; or, The Doom Kiss (S.W. M. 27/3/1837).
D. The Demon Lord (Queen's, 15/11/1847). L.C. 1/10/1847.
M.D. The Demon of Jealousy; or, The Modern Iago (S.W. M.
  26/4/1830).
P. The Demon of the Mystic Dart; or, Harlequin and the Ladybird
  Sprite (R.P. M. 31/3/1834).
M.D. The Demon of the Woods; or, The Clock has Struck. L. 21 L.
  [1807].
P. The Demon's Calendar; or, Harlequin Leapyear and the Fairy
  Lunar. L.C. Effingham, 2/12/1844.
P. The Demon's Tribunal; or, Harlequin's Enterprises (R.A. W.
  16/4/1800).
R.D. The Demon's Trumpet and the Magic Ring (R.A. Th. 21/9/1826).
C. A Deserted Wife in Search of a Husband. L.C. Newcastle,
  21/7/1849.
O. The Deserter (P'cess, M. 28/5/1849). L.C. 18/5/1849.
M.D. The Deserter; or, Royal Clemency (Royalty, M. 26/1/1801).
M.D. The Deserter of Naples (Lyc. Th. 10/7/1817).
Ba. Le Deserteur (E.L. M. 28/9/1818).
D. Desrues the Deceiver; or, The Territor of St Faust (Clarence,
  M. 5/8/1833).
Bal. Detection; or, The Merry Cobbler (Royalty, M. 7/1/1805).
Bal. Les deux âges; ou, les quadrilles (H.¹ S. 7/6/1817).
Ba. The Devil and the Lady; or, The Widow and the Rake (Cob.
  M. 26/2/1827).
P. The Devil in a Bottle; or, Harlequin's Oddities (Royalty, M.
  26/1/1801).
P. The Devil at Dunmow; or, Harlequin and the Flitch of Bacon
  (S.W. M. 20/6/1831).
Bal. The Devil in Love (D.L. M. 20/11/1843).
Bal. The Devil on Two Sticks (D.L. Th. 1/12/1836).
  [Music C. Gide.]
P. The Devil on Two Sticks; or, The Miracles of the Moon (R.A.
  M. 23/5/1836).
M.D. The Devil's Brother (D.L. T. 1/2/1831).
  [Music from Auber's Fra Diavolo, arranged by A. Lee.]
M.D. The Devil's Punch Bowl; or, St. Patrick's Oak (R.P. M.
  27/1/1834).
M.D. The Devil's Ship; or, The Pirate of the Charmed Life (R.P. M.
  6/8/1832).
  [See The Money Diggers (Cob. 1829).]
Ext. The Devil's Walk; or, Pluto in London (Surrey, M. 4/10/1830).
Bal. The Devil to Pay (D.L. S. 22/11/1845).
Ba. A Dey and a Knight; or, Twenty Four Hours in Algiers (Olym.
  M. 6/11/1843).
  [See SOMERSET, 1838.]
F. Le Diable à Quatre (P'cess, Th. 30/10/1845).
F. Le Diable à Quatre; or, Dancing Mad. L.C. Garrick, 6/11/1846.

Ba. Diamonds and Clubs (W.L. M. 2/3/1829).
D. Diane de Chivri, the Blind Girl (Surrey, M. 29/7/1839).
Bal. Il Diavolo Abruzzi; or, The Brigand Chief and the Dog of the
Chateau (R.A. M. 7/7/1845).
M.D. Dick Hatteraick, the Dutch Smuggler; or, The Sorceress of
Derncleuch (Cob. M. 29/10/1821).
[Adapted from *PLANCHÉ, The Witch of Derncleuch*, and
La Socière.]
M.D. Dick Whittington and his Cat; or, London in 1370 (Cob. M.
19/5/1823).
F. Did you ever take your Wife to Broughty Ferry? (Dundee, T.
23/6/1846).
M.D. The Dillosk Gatherer; or, The Eagle's Nest (Olym. M.
30/7/1832). L.C. 13/7/1832.
M.D. Dinas Bran; or, The Prince of the Black Mountains (Cob. M.
25/1/1830).
O.F. Dine at my Villa. L. 80 M. [C.G. 24/2/1804].
P. Ding Dong Bell, Pussy's in the Well; or, Harlequin and the Magic
Cat (Vic. F. 26/12/1834).
Ba. The Dinner of Madelon (Olym. M. 22/12/1828).
Ba. The Dinner of Madelon; or, The Sportsman and the Shepherd
(Sans P. T. 17/12/1816). L. 108 M. [25/10/1816].
Spec. Dionysius; or, The Force of Friendship (Cob. Th. 2/6/1825).
D. Diplomacy; or, Private and Confidential. L.C. 1836.
O. Dirce; or, The Fatal Urn (D.L. S. 2/6/1821). L. 81 S.
[29/5/1821].
[Adapted from Metastasio's *Demofoonte*; music by C. E.
Horn.]
Ba. The Disappointments; or, Love in Castile (Sans P. M. 3/12/1810).
L. 93 M. [28/11/1810].
F. Discharge your Tiger (Lyc. M. 29/10/1849). L.C. 6/6/1849.
C. The Discontented Man. 8° 1804.
D. Discounting a Life; or, The Gentleman in Paris. L.C. Adel.
14/10/1844.
P. The Discovery; or, Harlequin's Salutation to John Bull (R.A. M.
23/4/1810).
Bsq. The Discreet Princess. L.C. P'cess, 16/10/1848.
Oa. The Disguises (Lyc. M. 8/9/1817). L. 68 S. [20/8/1817].
[Music Jolly.]
P. Disputes in China; or, Harlequin and the Hong Merchants (Cob.
M. 15/7/1822).
D. Distraining for Rent (S.W. M. 20/2/1832).
P. The Diving Bell; or, Neptune's Gift (R.A. M. 19/8/1805).
O.F. Doctor and No Doctor (S.W. M. 25/2/1828).
Ba. Doctor Bolus (S.W. M. 7/3/1831).
[This may be a revival of the similarly named play by *G.
DANIEL* (1818).]
P. Doctor Faustus and the Black Demon; or, The Seven Fairies of
the Grotto (Adel. F. 26/12/1823). L. 130 M. [1823].
F. Doctor Poker. L. 62 S. [D.L. 21/9/1816].
Bal. Doctor Sangrado (C.G. M. 26/9/1814).
Ext. Doctor Syntax in London (S.W. M. 31/3/1823).
M.D. The Dog of the Convent (Surrey, M. 4/4/1831).
D. The Dog of the Pyrenees (R.A. M. 29/12/1845). L.C. 17/12/1845.

C.O. Domestic Arrangements; or, The Bachelor, the Maid, the Wife and the Widow (E.O.H. M. 10/8/1835). L.C. 17/7/1835. [Music S. Nelson.]

Ca. Domestic Bliss (P'cess, T. 2/5/1848). L.C. 5/5/1848.

D. Dominique; or, It is the Devil! (D.L. S. 8/10/1831).

D. Dominique; or, The Devil and the Deserter (S.W. M. 31/10/1831).

D. Dominique, the Resolute; or, The Possessed (Cob. M. 26/9/1831).

C.O. Le Domino Noir (D.L. M. 10/8/1848). [From the opera by E. Scribe (Paris, 1837), with music by Auber.]

Bal. Donald and Peggy; or, Love in the Highlands (Pav. M. 9/11/1812).

M.D. Donald McClean, the Highland Robber (S.W. M. 8/5/1820).

Ba. The Don Cossack in London (R.C. W. 13/7/1814).

O. Don Giovanni (P'cess, M. 1/10/1849). L.C. 22/9/1849.

O. Don Giovanni; or, The Spectre on Horseback. L. 112 M. [C.G. 4/6/1819].

T. Don John of Arragon (Surrey, M. 11/5/1840).

O. Don Juan (D.L. 10/1838). 8° 1838 [Songs].

F. Donkey Races. L.C. 1826.

Ba. Donna Aurora; or, Adventures at Salamanca (R.A. M. 2/7/1821).

Ba. Donne Cambiate. L. 96 M. [Pantheon, 26/2/1812].

C.O. Don Pasquale (P'cess, M. 23/10/1843). L.C. 18/10/1843. [Music Donizetti.]

Bal. Don Quichotte; ou, les noces de Gamache (H.¹ T. 14/2/1809).

Bal. Don Quixote; ou, la finesse de l'epée (Cob. M. 6/7/1818).

R.D. Don Quixote, the Knight of the Wonderful Countenance; or, The Humours of Sancho Panza (Adel. M. 7/1/1833). L.C. 9/1/1833.

Ba. Don Quixotte and his Man Sancho Panza (R.A. T. 13/9/1831).

M.D. Don Sebastian, King of Portugal (Royalty, M. 14/4/1823).

F. Don't be Frightened (C.G. S. 9/11/1839). L.C. 12/11/1839.

D. The Doom'd Child (S.W. T. 13/11/1832).

D. The Doomed House; or, The Parricide's Return (R.P. M. 29/4/1839).

Spec. Dorothee; or, Love and Hatred (Olym. Pav. M. 28/3/1808).

Spec. The Double Defeat; or, British Tars and Austrian Troops (Sans P. Th. 6/7/1809).

Ba. The Double Dilemma (Olym. M. 26/12/1836). L.C. 12/12/1836.

F. The Double Mark (German, S. 7/9/1805).

F. Double or Quits (Queen's, M. 4/4/1831).

M.D. Douglas (R.C. M. 12/4/1819; City, M. 24/10/1831).

M.D. Douglas; or, The Noble Shepherd (Regency, Th. 17/9/1818).

F. A Down East Bargain; or, Love in New York (Queen's, Th. 26/1/1837).

F. Down the Area; or, Mistress and Maid (Adel. M. 10/11/1823). L. 126 M. [12/11/1822].

P. The Dragon of Wantley; or, Harlequin Knight and the Fairy Queen. L.C. Birmingham, 18/12/1844.

F. Dramatic Cookery; or, How to Dish up a Farce (Adel. M. 2/8/1845). L.C. 4/8/1845.

Ca. The Dreamer (P'cess, S. 21/3/1846). L.C. 27/10/1845.

D. The Dream Haunted (Vic. M. 11/6/1838).

Bal. Drive Love out at the Door, He'll get in at the Window (D.L. T. 16/5/1815).

Ba. Dromio the Drinker; or, The Bath Struggle (S.W. T. 15/9/1835).
F. Drop the Curtain (Lyc. M. 26/11/1849).
C. The Drunkard (German, W. 17/7/1805). 8° 1805.
    [Adapted from Kotzebue.]
D. The Drunkard's Children (Queen's, M. 10/7/1848).
D. The Drunkard's Children (Vic. M. 10/7/1848).
F. The Drunken Cobbler (R.A. M. 25/10/1819).
Ba. The Drunken Recruit (S.W. T. 29/5/1821).
D. La Duchesse de Guise (Olym. M. 7/4/1845). L.C. Olym. 5/4/1845.
Ba. The Duel (Olym. F. 3/11/1837).
M.D. Dugald the Drover; or, The Cattle Stealers and the Rover's
    Dog (S.W. M. 21/11/1842).
Ba. The Duke; or, The Night before the Battle (Edinburgh, 1/7/1837).
Ba. Duke and No Duke (Surrey, M. 17/2/1812).
Ba. The Duke and the Policeman; or, The Night Guard (Cob. M.
    1/11/1830; Surrey, M. 24/4/1837).
Ba. The Duke for a Day (Olym. Th. 24/2/1831).
T. The Duke of Florence...By One of the Medici. 8° 1843.
T. The Duke of Mantua. 8° 1823.
    [On the title-page is an emblematical figure clearly intended to
    be Byron, with a mask; the play is dedicated to Lady Byron.]
T. The Duke of Milan (D.L. S. 9/3/1816). 8° 1816 ("Revived...
    with Alterations and Additions").
    [An adaptation of Massinger's drama.]
Ba. The Duke of Shoreditch (Vic. M. 15/11/1841).
Ent. The Duke's Coat; or, The Night after the Battle (R.A. M.
    3/5/1824).
Ent. The Duke's Coat; or, The Night after Waterloo. A Dramatick
    Anecdote; prepared for Representation at the Theatre-Royal,
    Lyceum, and Interdicted by the Licenser of Plays. 8° 1815.
    L. 106 M. [29/8/1815; licence refused].
    [This play was advertised at the Lyceum on 6/9/1815.]
M.D. The Dumb Boy (S.W. M. 20/8/1821).
    [Also acted as The Deaf and Dumb Boy, rightful Count of
    Harancour.]
Ba. The Dumb Boy of Avignon (Olym. T. 17/8/1841). L.C. 4/8/1841.
R.D. The Dumb Brigand (Strand, M. 12/3/1832; City, M. 8/4/1833).
M.D. The Dumb Driver (R.A. M. 12/3/1849).
    [A play of this name, licensed for York, appears in L.C. 1/2/1845.]
Ent. The Dumb Norwegian and his Pony of Iceland (S.W. M.
    22/8/1842).
D. The Dumb Recruit (C.L. 16/1/1840).
Oa. A Dun a Day (E.O.H. W. 10/9/1823). L. 131 M. [19/8/1823].
    [Music Reeve.]
F. Duprez (P'cess, W. 22/3/1843).
Ba. Dutch Law. L.C. Adel. 20/10/1835.
Ba. The Dutchman's Dream; or, Karl Pietrehl. A Tale of the Vettle
    King (R.P. M. 20/4/1835).
M.D. The Dutch Pirate (S.W. M. 27/5/1822).
M.D. The Dwarf; or, Malvesi the Deformed (R.P. M. 15/10/1832).
    [On M. 3/12/1832, this was given as The Deformed; or, The
    Profligate Reclaimed.]
Vaud. Dying for a Kiss (P'cess, F. 9/7/1847). L.C. 1/7/1847.
O.F. Each for Himself (D.L. Th. 24/10/1816). 8° 1816.

T. Earl Harold. 8° 1837.
M.D. The Earl of Essex, the Unhappy Favourite; or, The Days of
    Queen Bess (Cob. W. 8/6/1825).
T. The Earl of Ross. 8° 1823.
F. Early Closing; or, A Night at the Casino (P'cess, S. 24/7/1847).
    L.C. 19/6/1847.
P. Earth, Air, Fire and Water; or, Harlequin Gas and the Flight of
    the Fairies. L.C. Vic. 14/12/1848.
M.D. The Earthquake; or, The Mysterious Visit (S.W. M. 28/1/1828).
P. Easter Fair; or, The Monkey and the Murder (Cob. M. 12/4/1830).
Ext. Easter Hunting; or, Johnny Newcomes at Epping (S.W. M.
    23/4/1821).
P. The Easter Offering; or, Harlequin's Golden Harvest (S.W. M.
    19/4/1824).
O. The East Indian. L. 57 S. [Lyc. 11/7/1812].
Tale of Enchantment. The Ebon Wand: or, The Charmed Man and
    the Charming Woman (Cob. M. 11/6/1832).
D.D. Ecarté; or, The Saloons of Paris. L.C. Surrey, 17/2/1844.
Ba. Eccentricities; or, Mistakes in Madrid (Sans P. M. 26/12/1814).
    L. 103 M. [19/12/1814; with sub-title, *or, The Witch of the
    Village*].
M.D. The Echo of Westminster Bridge (Vic. M. 6/7/1835).
D. Edgar. L.C. 13/3/1834.
Bal. Edgar and Effie; or, The Highland Robber (Adel. M. 22/11/1819).
T. Edward the Second...with Other Poems. By Theophilus Mac,
    of No Temple. 8° 1809.
D. Edward III. 8° 1814.
Spec. Edward the Black Prince; or, The Battle of Cressy (Olym.
    Pav. M. 9/11/1807).
Spec. Edward the Black Prince; or, The Hero of England (Royalty,
    M. 7/1/1805).
D. Edwin. L. 124 M. [Edinburgh, 25/4/1822].
P. Edwin of the Green; or, Harlequin Hunchback (R.C. W.
    29/7/1807).
D. Egmont. 16° 1848.
    [A translation of Goethe's play.]
Ent. Egrirophadron; or, Polysceine Pasticcio (D.L. Th. 8/6/1815).
D. The Egyptian Boy. L. 77 M. [C.G. 3/5/1802].
P. The Egyptian Oracle; or, Harlequin's Punishment (Royalty, M.
    23/1/1804).
F. "£8. 10. 1, if Quite Convenient" (D.L. W. 14/5/1823). L. 79 S.
    [5/5/1823].
R.D. Eily the Banshee; or, The Shrieking Woman (R.P. M. 9/3/1835).
D.Poem. Eitha and Aidallo. 8° 1801.
C. The Elder Brother. L.C. Bath, 1/3/1844.
Ext. The Election; or, Billy and Mrs. Button's Journey to and from
    London and Brentford (R.A. M. 7/6/1813).
Ext. The Election; or, Candidates for Rottenburgh (Cob. M.
    13/7/1818).
C. The Election; or, The Rival Brothers. L. 79 M. [Norwich,
    23/3/1803].
Local Bagatelle. Electioneering; or, Village Politicians (Surrey, S.
    7/8/1830).
P. The Elements; or, Where is Harlequin? (S.W. M. 23/3/1818).

Spec. The Elements—Earth, Air, Fire, Water; or, The Monster Ballroom of 1837 (R.A. M. 15/5/1837).
O.   Elena Uberti (C.G. S. 15/1/1842). L.C. 10/1/1842. 8° [1842]. [Music Mercadante.]
Spec. The Elephant of Siam (Amphi., L'pool, 26/12/1829).
Spec. The Elephants of the Pagoda (C.L. 16/2/1846). L.C. 14/2/1846.
F.   The Eleventh Day (D.L. 20/7/1835).
D.   The Eleventh Hour. L.C. Queen's, 29/1/1844.
M.D. The Eleventh Hour; or, Sixteen Years Since (Cob. M. 26/6/1826).
D.   The Elfies' Son (Surrey, M. 9/7/1832).
Spec. The Elfin Queen (Adel. S. 26/12/1835). L.C. 23/12/1835.
Spec. The Elfins of the Ice; or, The Heroes of the Frozen Land (R.P. M. 4/4/1836).
D.Legend. The Elfin Sprite; or, The Grim Grey Woman (C.G. M. 8/4/1833). L.C. 20/3/1833.
M.D. Elfrid; or, The Weird Wanderer of Jutland (Surrey, T. 26/3/1822).
M.D. Elfrida; or, The Faithless Favourites (R.C. W. 11/5/1808).
R.D. Elfrida; or, The Female Macbeth (R.P. M. 10/11/1834).
Spec. El Hyder (Surrey, M. 23/5/1836).
O.   L'Elisir d'amour (E.O.H. Th. 15/12/1836, "last time"). [Donizetti's opera (Milan, 1832).]
M.D. Elizabeth; or, The Exile of Siberia (Cob. M. 26/5/1828).
Bal. Ellen and Alberto; or, The Yorkshire Miller (Surrey, M. 26/10/1812).
D.D. Ellen Ray; or, A Brother's Doom (R.P. M. 30/12/1833).
M.D. Eloise; or, A Woman's Constancy (R.P. M. 25/2/1839).
F.   The Elopement. L.C. Leeds, 8/9/1826.
O.F. The Elopement Extraordinary. L. 102 M. [D.L. 3/6/1814].
M.D. The Elshie; or, The Wizard of the Moor (Royalty, M. 29/9/1823).
D.   Emigration (Olym. M. 21/11/1836).
M.D. Emigration; or, The Village, the Voyage and the Bush (R.P. M. 4/5/1835). L.C. 1836.
D.   Emigration—the Remedy (Olym. M. 24/7/1848). L.C. 24/7/1848.
M.D. Emilie de la Roche; or, The Bride of the Bleeding Heart (S.W. M. 24/11/1834).
Bal. Emily; or, Juvenile Indiscretion (D.L. 2/1807).
O.   The Emissary; or, The Revolt of Moscow (D.L. F. 13/5/1831). L.C. 13/5/1831.
      [Adapted from Le colporteur, by F. A. E. de Planard, music Onslow (Paris, 22/11/1827).]
D.   Emma Wingrove; or, Crime Slumbers. L.C. Queen's, 27/4/1844.
Bal. Emmeline; ou, la Valée de Griswald (H.¹ Th. 20/6/1816).
Ext. The Emperor of Queerumania (S.W. M. 28/10/1805—3rd performance).
Spec. The Emperor of Russia; or, The Deserter of Moscow (R.A. M. 10/6/1844).
D.   The Emperor's Joke (Surrey, M. 28/11/1836).
P.   The Enchanted Beauties of the Golden Castle; or, Harlequin and he One-eyed Genii (P'cess, S. 26/12/1846). L.C. 21/12/1846 with "Ogre" for "Genii" in title].
Bal. The Enchanted Bell (P'cess, S. 9/11/1844).
Spec. The Enchanted Castle; or, The Sleeping Beauty in the Wood (Cob. M. 27/5/1822).

M.D. The Enchanted Fire of the Invisible Island; or, The Golden Galley (Cob. M. 27/12/1824).
P. The Enchanted Garden (Riding School, Tottenham-street, M. 25/1/1808).
Ext. The Enchanted Girdles; or, The Witch, the Sprite, the Prince and the Barber (Cob. M. 7/1/1828).
[See T. J DIBDIN, 1825.]
P. The Enchanted Gondola. L.C. Albert, 23/5/1846.
P. The Enchanted Grove; or, Harlequin and the Fairy of the Silver Lake (Queen's, M. 27/3/1837).
P. The Enchanted Grove; or, Harlequin and the Spirit of the Enchanted Waters (Surrey, M. 4/4/1831).
Ba. The Enchanted Horn (St J. M. 26/12/1836). L.C. 3/12/1836.
P. The Enchanted Horn; or, Harlequin Prince of Persia (R.A. M. 23/3/1818).
P. The Enchanted Hull; or, The Parthian Harlequin (Royalty, M. 28/1/1805).
P. The Enchanted Island; or, Love among the Roses (Sans P. Th. 26/12/1816).
M.D. The Enchanted Raven; or, The Saxon King (R.A.W. 28/4/1841).
D. The Enchanted Ring; or, The Demon Knight and the Baron's Daughter (R.P. M. 18/1/1836).
P. The Enchanter; or, Harlequin Cymon (Olym. F. 26/12/1828). L.C. 24/12/1828.
P. The Enchanters; or, Harlequin Sultaun (D.L. F. 26/12/1806).
Ba. The Enchantment; or, Trappolin's Vagaries (Royalty, M. 3/8/1812).
F. The End of June (Lyc. M. 3/8/1846). L.C. 24/7/1846.
Bal. L'enfant prodigue; ou, les fêtes de Memphis (H.¹ Th. 8/6/1815).
Spec. England's King; or, A Soldier's Gratitude (R.A. M. 20/8/1827).
Spec. England's Monarch; or, The Battle of Worcester and the Royal Oak (R.A. M. 24/7/1843).
M.D. England, the Anchor and Hope of the World (Cob. M. 14/1/1828).
M.D. The English at Paris; or, Events in 1821 (Cob. M. 23/4/1821).
Ba. English Plum-Pudding; or, Two Masters Better than One (Surrey, M. 23/2/1824).
Ba. Enjoyment (E.O.H. T. 7/9/1841). L.C. 16/9/1841.
Ba. The Enraged Musician; or, Intrigue on the House-Top (Olym. M. 11/2/1828).
C.O. The Epaulette (H.² S. 22/10/1825). L.C. 26/9/1825 [with sub-title, or, Love and Friendship].
Bal. L'épouse persane (H.¹ W. 30/5/1810).
Sk. Epsom Downs; or, All Alive at the Races (Cob. M. 1/6/1818).
D. Ernestine; or, A Woman's Love (E.O.H. M. 10/8/1840). L.C. 11/8/1840.
P. The Erroneous Fortune-tellers; or, Harlequin's Judgment (R.A. M. 18/6/1810).
D. The Escape of Latude; or, The Prisoner of the Bastile (Vic. T. 27/10/1835).
Ba. Esdale Hall; or, The Times of Oliver Cromwell (Kelly's, S. 23/7/1842). L.C. 12/11/1842.
M.D. The Essex Rover; or, The Bridegroom of the Wave (R.P. M. 10/1/1831).
Ba. Estelle. L.C. E.O.H. 28/8/1829.
Ba. Estelle. L.C. 27/5/1835.

D. Estelle Dumas; or, Love and War (S.W. M. 18/4/1842).
Ba. Etchings and Sketchings. L.C. St J. 5/10/1836.
T. Ethelwolf; or, The Danish Pirates (Cob. M. 10/12/1827).
M.D. Etheldrida Princess of Norwich; or, The Kings of Mercia and East Anglia, and the Wild Woman of Mosswold Heath (Adel. Norwich, 1837).
M.Ent. Etiquette Run Mad (Tottenham-street, W. 25/8/1830).
D. Eugene Aram. L.C. Edinburgh, 13/3/1832.
M.D. Eugene Aram (S.W. M. 14/5/1832).
M.D. Eugene Aram; or, The Cave of St. Robert (R.P. M. 13/2/1832).
    [This and the preceding plays are taken from the novel by Lord Lytton.]
Ba. Eugenia; or, The Unknown Female (Cob. M. 18/10/1819).
M.D. Eugenia; ou, la Place du Palais (S.W. M. 11/6/1832).
M.D. Eugenio; or, The Secrets of the Abbey. L. 132 M. [Norwich, 7/3/1823.]
O. Euphemia. L.C. 19/12/1836.
O. Euryanthe (Prince's, W. 3/6/1840).
    [An English version of Weber's opera (Vienna, 1823).]
T. Eurypilus, King of Sicily. L. 22 L. [Manchester, 1817].
D. Eveline; or, The Well of Love (Surrey, M. 18/9/1843).
C. Everybody's Relation (Surrey, M. 18/5/1840).
C. Everyday Characters. 8° 1805.
Ba. The Exeter Mail; or, Three Days at Hatchett's (S.W. T. 9/9/1828).
M.D. The Exiled Minister; or, Father and Son (Cob. T. 26/12/1820).
M.D. The Exile of Genoa (E.O.H. M. 4/9/1837). L.C. 27/6/1837.
D. The Ex-Minister. L.C. 10/1/1834.
C. The Exquisites (C.G. F. 29/4/1831). L.C. 27/4/1831.
Bsq. "Eye-on!" (Queen's, F. 16/12/1836).
Bal. The Faggot Makers (Sans P. M. 11/12/1809).
O.F. Fair Cheating; or, The Wise Ones Outwitted (D.L. 15/6/1814).
    [Music Parry.]
O. The Fair Crusader. 8° 1815 [New British Theatre].
F. The Fair Deserter (H.² S. 24/8/1816). L. 63 S. [20/8/1816].
Ba. The Fair Intriguers; or, The Masquerade Frolic (R.A. M. 11/5/1835).
C. The Fair Lady. 8° 1807.
    [A translation from Calderon.]
D. The Fair Maid of Perth (Perth, T. 23/9/1828).
    [This seems to have been a distinct dramatisation of Scott's novel, as used by the company of Charles Bass in Perth, Dundee and Edinburgh.]
M.D. The Fair Maid of Tottenham Court; or, The Charcoal Burner of Charing (S.W. M. 26/10/1840).
Ba. The Fair Penitent (Royalty, M. 6/9/1813).
C. Fair Play. L. 88 M. [C.G. 28/1/1808].
Ba. The Fair Quaker; or, The Humours of the Navy (Royalty, M. 3/8/1812).
D. Fair Rosamond. L. 57 S [Norwich, 12/2/1813].
Spec. The Fair Slave; or, The Moors and Africans (R.A. M. 19/5/1806).
P. The Fairy; or, Britannia's Triumph. L. 44 S. [Hull, 10/1/1804].
P. The Fairy; or, Harlequin Prisoner (R.A. M. 13/6/1801).
P. The Fairy Gnomes of the Golden Caves; or, Harlequin and the Imp of the Great Mountains. L.C. C.L. 23/12/1844.

Spec. The Fairy Lake; or, The Enchanted Veil (S.W. M. 20/5/1839).
    [See *SELBY* (1839).]
P. Fairy Land; or, The Wandering Magician (R.A. M. 3/4/1809).
Ba. Fairy Legends; or, The Moonlight Night (Sans P. M. 7/12/1818).
    L. 112 M. [18/11/1818, as *Fairy Records; or, Days of Yore*].
Bal. The Fairy of the Fountain; or, Cupid and the Giant (Sans P.
    M. 22/11/1813).
P. The Fairy of the North Star; or, Harlequin at Labrador (Adel.
    M. 27/12/1819).
P. The Fairy of the Oak; or, Harlequin's Regatta (R.A. M. 2/9/1811).
D. A Fairy Tale (P'cess, 9/5/1848). L.C. 8/5/1848.
F. Faith and Hope; or, A Basement to Let (Grecian, 2/10/1848).
    L.C. 20/6/1848.
D. The Fallen Spirit; or, Leon of Marana. L.C. 1836.
Spec. The Fall of Badajoz (Surrey, M. 27/4/1812).
M.D. The Fall of Fair Rosamond (Surrey, T. 13/3/1821).
M.D. The Fall of Fair Rosamond; or, Woodstock Bower (R.P. W.
    26/12/1832).
M.Ent. The Fall of Montevideo (R.A. T. 28/4/1807).
T. The Fall of Portugal; or, The Royal Exiles. 8° 1808.
    [Attributed to Dr John Walcott, "Peter Pindar."]
D.Past. The Falls of Clyde; or, The Fairies (Edinburgh, 1806).
    8° 1806.
M.D. The Falls of Clyde (Cob. M. 24/9/1827).
    [See *SOANE*, 1817.]
P.R. False Accusation (R.C. M. 15/6/1818).
M.D. False Accusation; or, The Soldier's Peril (R.A. T. 9/9/1828).
C. False and True; or, The Irishman in Italy (D.L. M. 26/5/1806).
    [An amended version of *False and True* (1798), by Moultrie.]
C.O. False Appearances; or, My Cousin. L. 49 S. [D.L. 2/1/1807].
D. False Delicacies. 8° 1803.
    [A translation by J. T. from the French.]
Bal. The False Friend; or, The Two Prisoners (R.A. M. 13/6/1803).
M.D. False Friendship; or, The Irish Traveller (Surrey, F. 28/8/1829).
    [An abridgement of *False and True* (D.L. 1806).]
M.D. The False Marriage; or, Brother and Sister (S.W. M. 1/9/1828).
Spec. The False Penitent; or, The Monk of Palluzi (R.A. M. 22/7/1805).
C. False Shame. L. 41 S. [Norwich, 17/3/1801].
D. False Visions. L.C. Queen's, 17/9/1846.
Ca. Family Jars Mended (Surrey, Th. 26/12/1839).
Ba. The Family Likeness (Strand, M. 10/6/1839). L.C. 8/6/1839.
F. The Family Man; or, How Many More Wives? (Surrey, M.
    28/3/1842).
Ba. The Family of Genius. L.C. Bristol, 19/9/1826.
Int. The Family Party; or, The Philosopher Puzzled (R.P. S.
    26/12/1835). L.C. 4/12/1835.
Ba. Family Peculiarities; or, The Sisters Three (Queen's, F. 13/2/1835).
    L.C. 2/12/1835.
M.D. The Family Picture; or, The Sailor's Legacy (W.L. M.
    7/10/1822).
C. Family Politics. 8° 1814 [*New British Theatre*].
Ba. The Fancy's Opera (Adel. M. 27/1/1823). L. 87 S. [19/1/1823].
Ba. Fanny Sims, Mistress of Arts (Adel. M. 8/10/1838).
Ba. Farmer and Pheasant. L.C. Strand, 1836.

D. The Farmer Emigrant; or, The Blessings of Peace. L.C. Manchester, 14/4/1847.

C. The Farmer of Labian; or, The Blessings of Peace (Cob. M. 11/7/1825).

P. The Farmer's Boy; or, Harlequin's Zodiac (R.C. M. 18/4/1808).

D. The Farmer's Daughter; or, The Broken Heart (Surrey, M. 3/7/1837).

M.D. The Farmer's Gun; or, The Murder on the Heath (S.W. T. 25/11/1834).

M.D. The Farmer's Knife (Surrey, M. 17/9/1827).

B.O. The Farmer's Son (Queen's, M. 19/1/1835).

C. The Farmhouse Story. 8° 1803.

M.D. The Farm of Sterwick; or, The Signal (Royalty, M. 6/10/1823).

F. The Fast Man (Lyc. Th. 18/5/1848). L.C. 12/5/1848.

D. Fatal Accusation; or, Albanio. L.C. 1825.

D. The Fatal Attachment (Surrey, Th. 11/8/1831).

D. The Fatal Duel of the Glacis; or, The Advocate's Wife (Cob. M. 11/6/1832).

D. The Fatal Error; or, Woman's First Fault (Cob. M. 7/1/1833).

M.D. The Fatal Floodgate; or, The Lock-keeper's Daughter (R.P. M. 19/5/1834).

M.D. The Fatal Island and the Hour of Four; or, Lovers and their Friends (S.W. M. 23/8/1824).

M.D. The Fatal Marksman; or, The Demon of the Black Forest (Cob. M. 23/2/1824).

M.D. The Fatal Pass (S.W. M. 12/4/1830).

D. The Fatal Passion; or, The Unnatural Combat (Vic. Th. 8/5/1834).

Spec. The Fatal Pile; or, Virtue Revenged (Royalty, M. 6/2/1804).

R.D. The Fatal Ravine; or, The Hunters of the Pyrenees (S.W. M. 16/6/1828).

Spce. The Fatal Rock (Edinburgh, M. 29/12/1828).

M.D. The Fatal Sandbank; or, The Shipwreck of the Leander [see *The Wreck of the Leander Frigate*].

Ba. The Fatal Secret (St J. S. 24/2/1838). L.C. 21/2/1838 [as *The F. S.; or, Why did I listen?*].

M.D. The Fatal Shaft; or, The Murder of the Mine (R.P. M. 4/4/1836).

D. The Fated Ship; or, The Wife and the Mistress. L.C. C.L. 20/3/1849.

M.D. The Fate of the Gambler; or, The Wife of the Broken Heart (R.P. M. 13/10/1834).

P. The Fates; or, Harlequin's Holyday (S.W. M. 31/5/1819).

C. Father and Son. 8° 1814 [*New British Theatre*].
[An adaptation of Kotzebue, *Die beiden Klingsberg*.]

M.D. Fatherless Fanny; or, The Fair Mendicant and the Spirit of the Rock (R.P. M. 21/4/1834).
[A play of this name is in L.C. R.P. 28/5/1846.]

D. Father Matthias; or, Ask no Questions (Strand, M. 23/4/1849).
[A revised version of the play by *C. SELBY*.]

D. The Father Murderer; or, A Voice from the Grave (R.P. F. 26/12/1834).

M.D. A Father's Crime (E.O.H. M. 6/7/1835). L.C. 29/6/1835.
[An adaptation from the French of E. Cresnier and St Hilaire.]

M.D. A Father's Curse; or, Guilt Discovered (S.W. T. 26/9–Th. 5/10/1820).

M.D. A Father's Curse; or, The Dumb Minstrel Boy (R.P. M. 27/5/1833).

M.D. The Father's Curse; or, The Murder of the Old Oak Wood (Garrick, M. 15/2/1836).

R.D. The Father's Curse; or, Twenty Years Ago (Cob. M. 23/8/1830).

M.D. A Father's Guilt; or, The Victim's Tomb (Cob. M. 30/6/1823).

D. A Father's Plea (Fitzroy, Th. 16/1/1834).

D. Faustus. 4° 1821; 4° 1832.
[An abridged translation of Goethe's play. The following two dramas are versions of the same original.]

D. Faustus. 12° 1834.

D. Faust...rendered into English verse. 12° 1838.

M.D. Faustus; or, The Demon's Victim (Cob. M. 7/6/1824).

D. The Favourite of the Derby; or, The Life of Man and Horse. L.C. R.A. 23/9/1844.

Ext. Favourites in Town; or, Stage Arrivals (Adel. M. 12/12/1831).

Bsq. Fayre Rosamond. L.C. Vic. 21/8/1846.

Int. The Feast of Apollo (D.L. 8/6/1829).

P. The Feast of the Statue; or, Harlequin Libertine (D.L. F. 26/12/1817). L. 65 S. [16/12/1817].
[This was called later *Harlequin's Vision; or, The F. of the S.*]

Bal. La Fée Urgele (H.¹ S. 11/4/1818).

M.D. The Felon of New York (Surrey, S. 24/8/1833).
[When given at S.W. on W. 20/4/1836, said to be by the author of *The Brigand, Baron Trenk, The Returned Pirate* and *The Twin Brothers.*]

M.D. The Felon's Hate; or, The Valley of Chamouni (R.A. M. 3/10/1825).

D. The Felon's Son; or, Woman's Wrongs. L.C. Vic. 4/9/1848.

D. The Female Bluebeard. L.C. L'pool, 10/2/1845.

C. The Female Cavaliers (Fitzroy, M. 17/2/1834).

Spec. Female Courage; or, The Bandit of the Rock (Sans P. Th. 6/7/1809).

F. The Female Freemason; or, The Secret Blabbed (Queen's, M. 21/3/1831).

Spec. The Female Hussar; or, The Heroic Serjeant (R.A. M. 9/8/1802).

Ent. The Female Lancers (City, 2/1833).

D. Female Politics (Surrey, M. 31/5/1841).

Bal. The Female Sentinel (H.² M. 15/6/1829).

F. The Female Tournament. L.C. Newcastle, 21/7/1849.

Ba. The Female Volunteer (Fitzroy, M. 28/4/1834).

Ba. The Female Waterman's Society; or, The Ran Dan Club (Vic. M. 30/11/1840).

Bal. La Femme Sentinelle (D.L. T. 7/2/1832).

Spec. Ferdinand of Spain; or, Ancient Chivalry (R.A. M. 19/4/1813).

— Ferguson. L.C. 1837.

R.D. The Ferry of the Guiers (C.G. Th. 13/11/1823). L. 129 M. [23/10/1823].

Bal. The Festival of Bacchus (D.L. M. 4/1/1802).

Bal. The Festival of Fancy (R.A. M. 7/10/1805).

Bal. The Festive Cottagers (D.L. 25/6/1823).

Ca. La Fête Champêtre. L.C. H.² 16/8/1843.

M.D. The Feudal Lady (Adel. M. 4/7/1831). L.C. 3/9/1830.

D. Fidelio; or, The State Prisoner of the Iron Den (Vic. T. 22/4/1845).
M.D. The Field of the Cloth of Gold; or, The Knight of Burgundy (R.P. M. 23/5/1831).
Spec. The Fiend; or, The Gold Curse (S.W. M. 31/10/1842).
O. The Fiend Father; or, Robert of Normandy (C.G. T. 21/2/1832). L.C. 9/2/1832.
   [An adaptation of E. Scribe and G. Delavigne, *Robert le Diable* (Paris, 21/11/1831), with music by Meyerbeer.]
Spec. The Fiend King; or, The Ruby Cross and the Last of the Magi (Vic. M. 16/4/1838).
M.D. The Fiend of the Watch; or, The Fatal Purchase (S.W. M. 15/2/1830).
T. Fiesco; or, The Conspiracy of Genoa. 8° 1841 [Edinburgh].
   [A translation of Schiller's drama.]
Bsq. Fi, Fi; or, The King of the Conjugal Islands (S.W. M. 12/5/1845). L.C. 9/5/1845.
C. The Fifteenth Carbineers; or, The White Goat (R.A. M. 5/5/1834).
M.D. Fifteen Years of a British Seaman's Life; or, The Perils of the Ocean (R.P. M. 9/8/1830).
D. Fifteen Years of a Soldier's Life; or, Scenes at Home and Abroad. L.C. Queen's, 19/4/1848.
Ent. Fifty Years below the Sea; or, The Diver and the Ocean Fiend (R.A. M. 26/8/1833).
D. Figaro. L.C. E.O.H. 27/8/1841.
Bal. Figaro (H.¹ 23/1/1816).
P.Bal. Filial Love; or, The Double Marriage (S.W. M. 14/4/1800).
D.Poem. Fingal; or, Erin Delivered. L. 99 M. [H.¹ 3/7/1813].
P. Fire and Spirit; or, A Holiday Harlequin (S.W. M. 11/4/1803).
R.D. The Fire Fiend; or, The Castle of Sunderwald (Cob. M. 1/3/1830).
   [Often called in subsequent bills *The Elf of the Flame; or, The C. of S.*]
P. The Fire Goblin; or, The Three Charcoal Burners (Sans P. S. 26/12/1818).
Ext. The Fire King; or, The Frenchman Puzzled (S.W. M. 15/2/1830).
P. The Fire King, Harlequin, and the Water Queen (E.L. M. 27/12/1819).
R.D. The Fire-Raiser; or, The Blighted Moor (R.P. M. 11/7/1831).
Ba. First Champaigne (Olym. M. 10/3/1845).
M.D. First Claim; or, The Brigand Deserter (S.W. M. 23/11/1835).
F. The First Floor (II.¹ M. 7/9/1818 and performance; S.W. M. 28/7/1845).
   [An Interlude of the same name was evidently played at Edinburgh on 1/1/1829.]
Ba. First Impressions (City, M. 4/4/1831).
Ba. First Love (Adel. M. 21/1/1828).
   [By *I. POCOCK*.]
F. The First Night (P'cess, 1/10/1849). L.C. 22/9/1849 [as *The Debutante; or, Her First Night*].
F. The First Night of my Wedding (M'bone, M. 13/11/1848). L.C. 4/11/1848.
F. The Fisherman. L. 22 L. [D.L. 17/10/1819].
M.D. The Fisherman's Daughter (P'cess, F. 6/1/1843).

F. The Fitzpatricks; or, Lovers from Tipperary (Strand, M. 16/4/1838). L.C. 13/4/1838.
F. Five Hundred Pounds (D.L. T. 28/8/1821). L. 82 S. [23/8/1821].
Int. Five Minutes too Late; or, An Elopement to Rheims (D.L. T. 5/7/1825).
[Music Horn, Bishop and Cooke.]
F. Flat and Sharp. L. 57 S. [Lyc. 23/7/1813].
F. The Flexible Man (Queen's, F. 3/7/1835).
Ba. The Flip Flap Footman (Adel. M. 5/10/1840).
D. Flitting Day; or, The Farmer's Daughter (Vic. 1/6/1846). L.C. 4/3/1846.
D. The Floating Beacon; or, The Norwegian Wreckers. L.C. Adel. 16/10/1829.
[See *FITZBALL*, 1824.]
Bal. Flora's Sports (New, T. 27/11/1810).
Bal. Florenski and Nina; or, A New Way to Obtain Consent (Surrey, Th. 7/10/1819).
T. The Florentines (S.W. M. 2/6/1845). L.C. 2/6/1845 [printed copy]. 8° [1845; Dublin].
M.D. Florinda Salviati, the White Devil; or, The Traitors of Ferrara (Cob. M. 27/10/1828).
Bal. The Florist; or, The Arcades of Flora (Royalty, M. 8/2/1802).
D. The Flower of Lucerne (P'cess, W. 29/11/1843). L.C. 25/11/1843.
D. The Flower of the Mill (Vic. M. 1/2/1836).
Ba. The Flowers of Loveliness (Queen's S. 26/12/1835).
C. Flying Colours; or, Crossing the Frontier (Adel. W. 26/5/1847). L.C. 27/5/1847 [under sub-title].
P. The Flying Dutchwoman; or, Harlequin and the Enchanted Bay (R.A. M. 4/6/1827).
M.D. The Flying Fish; or, The Water King (S.W. M. 8/6/1835).
P. The Flying Island of Laputa; or, Harlequin Gulliver (R.C. M. 28/7/1806).
Bal. La Foire de Batavia (H.¹ F. 7/1/1803).
Ba. The Follies of a Day; or, The Marriage of Figaro (Royalty, Th. 1/10/1812).
Ba. Folly and Friendship (Olym. 23/1/1837). L.C. 19/1/1837.
Ba. Folly as it Flies; or, The Modern Student (Cob. M. 15/12/1828).
[See *F. REYNOLDS*, 1801.]
Ba. Fontainebleau; or, Our Way in France (Royalty, M. 13/6/1814).
M.D. Fontainville Abbey; or, The Phantom of the Forest (Surrey, T. 9/3/1824).
F. The Fools of Fashion. L. 20 L. [Norwich, 14/4/1802].
T. The Force of Friendship. L. 122 M. [C.G. 22/5/1821].
[This is *Damon and Pythias*, by *R. L. SHEIL*.]
— The Foreign Prince. L.C. Adel. 16/2/1839.
M.D. For England Ho! (E.L. T. 8/12/1818).
[See *I. POCOCK*, 1813.]
M.D. The Forester of Savoy (Cob. M. 16/2/1829).
Ba. The Forest Knight; or, Harry le Roy (Cob. M. 16/8/1824).
Ba. The Forest Knight; or, The King Bewildered (Sans P. Th. 4/2/1813). L. 98 M. [30/1/1813].
M.D. The Forest Savage; or, The Torrent of La Charbonnière (Cob. M. 9/5/1825).
Bal. La Forêt Enchantée (H.¹ S. 4/12/1802).

D.   The Forgery. 8° 1814.
M.D.   Forgery; or, Le Roy. L.C. 1824 [licence refused].
M.D.   The Forgery; or, The Fugitives' Wedding (Cob. M. 15/12/1828).
Ca.   Forgive and Forget (D.L. S. 31/10/1835). L.C. 31/10/1835.
Ba.   Forgive and Forget (Olym. M. 22/10/1838). L.C. 16/3/1838.
D.   The Fortress of Ganzbrough; or, The State Prisoner of Austria (C.L. M. 24/3/1845).
M.D.   The Fortress of Paluzzi; or, The Mysterious Monitor (Cob. M. 18/11/1822).
M.D.   The Fortress of Pressburg; or, The Hut of the Danube (Cob. M. 11/3/1822).
D.   The Fortunate Departure. 8° 1810.
Prel.   The Fortunate Youth; or, Newmarket Hoax (Sans P. W. 7/1/1818). L. 112 M. [5/1/1818].
Ba.   The Fortunate Youth; or, The Force of Credulity (Olym. Th. 29/1/1818). L. 71 S. [14/1/1818].
P.   Fortunatus; or, The Magic Wishing Cap (Olym. F. 26/12/1845). L.C. 17/12/1845.
Spec.   Fortunatus and his Sons; or, The Magic Purse and Wishing Cap (C.G. M. 12/4/1819). L. 73 S. [1/4/1819].
     [Music Bishop. An adaptation of Dekker's play.]
F.   The Fortune Hunter; or, A Morning at Margate (H.² Th. 1/10/1846). L.C. 24/7/1846.
P.   Fortune's Favourite; or, Harlequin's Harvest (R.A. M. 23/8/1813).
Ba.   Fortune's Frolic; or, The Ploughman turned Lord (Royalty, Th. 24/9/1812).
     [Apparently an adaptation of Allingham's comedy (1799).]
O.F.   Fortune's Frolics (H.² 1806?).
P.   Fortune's Gift; or, Harlequin Mad Tom (Sans P. M. 28/5/1810).
O.F.   The Fortune Teller (D.L. Th. 29/9/1808). L. 48 S. [6/10/1807].
     [Music Reeve.]
P.   Fortunio and Harlequin (C.G. 1815).
P.   Fortunio and his Gifted Servants. L.C. Norwich, 12/12/1846.
P.   Fortunio and the Seven Gifted Men; or, Harlequin and the Horse (Cob. M. 8/5/1820).
M.D.   The Forty Thieves (Surrey, M. 16/3/1812).
M.D.   The Forty Thieves (S.W. T. 18/9/1821).
M.D.   The Forty Thieves (Lyc. M. 16/11/1835—1st time at this theatre).
F.   Forty Winks; or, The Birmingham Bagsmen (Surrey, M. 27/7/1835).
Oa.   Foster Brothers (Adel. Th. 2/9/1830). L.C. 28/8/1830 [as F. B.; or, The Conscript].
M.D.   The Foul Anchor; or, Love Me, Love my Dog (Cob. M. 6/12/1830; R.P. M. 18/2/1833).
F.   Found £100. L.C. P'cess, 31/10/1847.
P.   The Four Gates; or, Harlequin's Way (R.A. M. 19/4/1813).
F.   Four in Hand. L. 53 S. [H.² 10/9/1811].
     [This is Darkness Visible (H.² 1811), by T. E. HOOK.]
Oa.   Four Inside; or, Off by the Night Coach (Surrey, M. 5/1/1824).
Ba.   Four Sisters. L.C. E.O.H. 5/7/1833.
     [See W. B. BERNARD, 1832.]
O.   The Four Sons of Aymon (P'cess, 11/1844).
     [See The Castle of Aymon, above. Music Balfe.]

P.   Fox and Geese; or, Harlequin, the White King of Chess (Surrey, F. 26/12/1823).
Int. The Fox and the Wolf; or, The Biters Bit (R.P. M. 30/12/1839).
O.   Fra Diavolo. L.C. D.L. 26/1/1831.
     [See *LACY*, 1831.]
O.   Fra Diavolo. L.C. Olym. 13/1/1831.
D.   Fra Diavolo; or, The Brigand Chief (Tottenham-street, W. 24/11/1830).
     [These three dramas are derived from E. Scribe, *Fra Diavolo* (Paris, 28/1/1830), with music by Auber.]
M.D. France; or, Heaven points to the Murderer (Cob. M. 2/12/1822).
O.   Francesca Doria; or, A Tale of the Abruzzi (P'cess, S. 3/3/1849). L.C. 23/2/1849.
O.   Francis I (D.L. T. 6/11/1838). L.C. 30/10/1838.
     [Music Loder.]
M.D. Frankenstein; or, The Danger of Presumption (Royalty, M. 22/9/1823).
     [See *PEAKE*, 1823.]
Bsq. Frank-in-Steam; or, The Modern Promise to Pay (Olym. 13/12/1824). L.C. 26/11/1824.
D.   Frank Wildeye; or, The Spendthrift Husband (Vic. 9/10/1848). L.C. 22/9/1848.
D.   The Fratricide; or, The Devil's Wood (R.P. M. 3/2/1840).
Ba. Freaks in an Attic (Strand, M. 20/9/1841). L.C. 24/9/1841.
M.D. Frederick of Bavaria (Cob. M. 25/11/1822).
M.D. Frederick of Bavaria; or, A Husband's Vengeance (Royalty, M. 22/4/1822).
Ba. Frederick of Prussia; or, The King and the Comedian (Queen's, 24/7/1837). L.C. 1837.
M.D. Frederick the Great and the Deserter; or, The Assassins of the Forest (Cob. M. 19/2/1821).
O.   The Freebooters (E.O.H. M. 20/8/1827). L.C. 24/7/1827.
M.D. The Freebooters of Vienna; or, The Jew and his Family (Cob. M. 19/7/1824).
O.   Freedom and Slavery. L. 109 M. [C.G. 2/11/1816].
Ba. The Free Nigger of New York (Vic. M. 29/6/1840).
Bsq. Der Freischutz (Olym. M. 4/10/1824). L.C. Olym. 30/9/1824.
Bsq. Der Freischutz Travestie. By Septimus Globus. 8° 1824.
Bsq. Der Freischutz. L.C. Adel. 11/11/1828.
M.D. The French Expedition; or, The Fall of the Sea Robbers (R.A. T. 24/8/1830).
Spec. The French Forest (Royalty, M. 26/12/1803).
D.   The French Libertine (C.G. S. 11/2/1826). L.C. 28/1/1826.
     [Called at first *Richelieu*, then *Rougemont*.]
Bal. The French Milliners (S.W. M. 12/7/1802).
D.   The French Revolution; or, The Massacre of Paris on the 27th, 28th and 29th of July (R.P. M. 30/8/1830).
Spec. The French Spy (Queen's, M. 4/4/1831; Scarborough, T. 13/9/1831; Cob. M. 12/12/1831).
     [Music Auber.]
D.   The French War; or, The Soldier's Bride (Cob. M. 23/4/1832).
F.   Fricandeau; or, The Coronet and the Cook (H.² T. 9/8/1831). L.C. 10/6/1831.
Ba. Fridolin (Prince's, Th. 26/11/1840). L.C. 22/11/1840.

F. A Friend at Court. L.C. C.G. 9/12/1830.
    [See *J. R. PLANCHÉ*, 1831.]
F. A Friend Indeed! (Lyc. M. 27/4/1846). L.C. 11/4/1846.
Ca. A Friend in Need (Strand, M. 23/4/1832).
Ba. A Friend in Need (Olym. M. 13/10/1834). L.C. 13/10/1834.
C. Friends at Court (Lyc. M. 9/6/1845). L.C. 10/6/1845.
C. Friendship in Fashion; or, Adventures in Vienna (Cob. M. 23/2/1829).
C. Friendship, Love and Duty; or, The Prussian Soldiers. L. 97 M. [Edinburgh, 29/11/1813].
Ba. The Frightened Ghost; or, The Spanish Painter (R.A. W. 7/10/1835).
M.D. Fritz the Outlaw; or, The Mysterious Wife (Surrey, M. 20/9/1813).
M.D. Fritz the Outlaw; or, The Wife of Two Husbands (R.P. M. 17/12/1838).
Ext. Frolics in "Forty-Five" (D.L. W. 10/2/1836). L.C. 2/3/1836 [as *The Empty Cottage; or, F. in F.-F.*].
F. The Frolics of Fortune; or, The Lordly Ploughman (said to have been "revived" at Lyc. W. 30/12/1835).
    [Seemingly this is *Fortune's Frolic* (Royalty, 1812).]
Spec. The Frolics of the Fairies; or, Puck in a Pucker (Fitzroy, M. 31/3/1834).
P. Frost Fair; or, Harlequin frae the North (Olym. M. 28/2/1814).
M.D. The Frozen Cliff; or, The Exiles in Siberia (R.A. M. 3/9/1827).
M.D. The Frozen Hands; or, The Sea-King's Daughter (S.W. M. 23/5/1831).
M.D. The Frozen Lake (C.G. F. 26/11/1824). L.C. 13/11/1824.
    [Music Reeve. An adaptation of E. Scribe and G. Delavigne, *La Neige* (Paris, 9/10/1823).]
P. The Frozen Mountain; or, Harlequinade Exile (Pav. M. 13/11/1809).
M.D. Frozen Regions; or, The Treacherous Esquimaux (R.A. M. 13/5/1822).
Bsq. Der Fryshot (Edinburgh 26/8/1825).
Ba. Fun and Fright; or, How to Gain Consent (Adel. W. 10/11/1819). L. 115 M. [14/11/1819].
D. The Funeral Pile (W.L. M. 15/10/1821).
P. Furibond; or, Harlequin Negro (D.L. M. 28/12/1807).
C.O. Il Furioso (E.O.H. S. 17/12/1836). L.C. 17/12/1836.
Oa. Gabrielle; or, The Incog. (Queen's, M. 26/4/1835).
M.D. Gabrielle de Belleisle; or, The Libertine's Wager Lost (S.W. Th. 28/11/1840).
Oa. Galatea (Queen's, Th. 3/2/1831).
C. Gallantry; or, Adventures in Madrid (D.L. S. 15/1/1820). L. 76 S. [30/12/1819].
Ba. The Gallery of St Nicholas. L.C. 30/7/1832.
Int. The Gallopade; or, Horse and Foot (H.² W. 15/5/1833).
Bal. The Galloping Lover; or, Ellen the Bride of Young Lochinvar (R.A. T. 3/10/1815).
F. A Galvanic Ring (Surrey, 6/3/1845). L.C. 3/3/1845.
M.D. Gambia; or, The Slave (S.W. T. 13/11/1832).
M.D. The Gamblers (Surrey, M. 17/11/1823).

M.D. The Gamblers; or, The Murderers at the Desolate Cottage
(Cob. M. 17/11/1823).
[On T. 18/12/1823 the title was changed to *The Inseparables;
or, The Spectre of the Desolate Cottage.*]
D. The Gambler's Life in London; or, Views in the Country and
Views in Town (S.W. F. 26/12/1828).
Ba. The Gamester (Royalty, S. 20/3/1813).
[A version of Moore's play (1753).]
Ba. The Gamester Father; or, Precept without Practice (Adel. M.
6/3/1837). L.C. 2/3/1837.
D. The Gamester's Son; or, The Last of his Race. L.C. Surrey,
21/3/1848.
D. The Gaming Table (Fitzroy, M. 3/2/1834).
P. Gammer Gurton; or, Harlequin and the Magic Needle (R.P. M.
23/4/1832).
[A pantomime of this title appears in L.C. 24/12/1829.]
O.F. The Garland. L. 83 M. [D.L. 28/3/1805].
[This is identical with *The Soldier's Return* (D.L. 23/4/1805) by
T. E. HOOK.]
Bal. The Garland of Love; or, Jack's the Lad (Olym. F. 24/11/1815).
M.D. Gaspard Hauser (Surrey, M. 24/9/1838).
D. Gaul, King of Ragah. 8° 1813.
D. Gay Gracer of Three Wives. L.C. Grecian, 19/11/1845.
O. La Gazza Ladra (D.L. Th. 4/6/1835).
[English version of Gherardini's opera with music by Rossini.]
Bal. The Generous Farmer; or, Harvest Home (Adel. W. 31/1/1821).
D. Geneviève; or, A Romance of Real Life (Surrey, M. 8/5/1843).
M.D. Geneviève; or, The Murderer of the Pyrenees (Surrey, M.
7/6/1824).
R.D. Geneviève de Brabant; or, The Hall of Torture (S.W. M.
1/4/1824).
D. Genevra, the Scourged One; or, The Convict of Munich (Vic. M.
17/8/1846).
P. The Genii of Paloguam; or, Harlequin the Sagacious Ape (Cob.
M. 4/3/1822).
P.Sk. The Genii of the Lake; or, Harlequin Ploughboy (Cob. W.
19/9/1821).
P. The Genii's Tomb; or, Harlequin Robber (R.A. M. 27/6/1803).
F. A Genius Wanted; or, The Left Wing (C.G. W. 19/10/1831).
M.D. Gentleman Joe (Garrick, M. 16/4/1838).
[See *T. E. WILKS* (S.W. M. 3/9/1838).]
Ba. The Gentleman Rover (Surrey, W. 13/6/1827).
[An adaptation of O'Keeffe's *Wild Oats*.]
Ba. Geoffrey Dunstan; or, Who'll buy a Duck? (Cob. M. 21/1/1828).
Spec. George and the Crocodile (R.P. M. 27/1/1834).
T. George Barnwell; or, The London Merchant (New, W. 29/5/1811).
[Obviously a reworking of Lillo's drama.]
Bsq. George Barnwell; or, The London Merchant Tailor (Surrey,
27/5/1844). L.C. 17/5/1844.
Bsq. Georgey Barnwell (Surrey, Th. 7/7/1833).
[There was probably a new version of this at the Surrey on
M. 27/5/1844.]
C.O. Geraldine; or, The Lover's Well (P'cess, M. 14/8/1843).
[Music Balfe.]

F. A German Blunder; or, Prince and No Prince. L. 89 M. [H.²
26/1/1809].
T. Germanicus...Translated into English, from the French of
A. V. Arnault. 8° 1817.
[See *BERNEL*, 1817.]
D. The German Jew; or, The Deserter from Orleans (S.W. M.
16/8/1830).
O.F. The German Patrol (R.A. M. 12/4/1830).
D. Gertrude of Elsinore (Surrey, M. 19/9/1836).
Ba. Gervase Skinner (Olym. M. 24/10/1831).
[See *JERROLD*, 1830.]
M.D. The Giant; or, Dunois in the Dark (R.P. M. 11/2/1839).
Spec. The Giant Horse; or, The Siege of Troy (R.A. M. 8/4/1833).
Ba. The Giant of Palestine (Adel. M. 31/12/1838). L.C. 1838.
D. The Giant's Castle; or, The Well of Marble Water (Surrey, M.
1/4/1839).
P. The Giant's Causeway. L.C. C.G. 13/12/1829.
D. The Giant's Causeway; or, The Slumber of Wonders (Queen's,
9/4/1844). L.C. 22/3/1844.
P. Gil Blas; or, Harlequin Everywhere (S.W. M. 30/6/1823).
M.D.Spec. Gil Blas de Santillane; or, The Horse Banditti (R.A. M.
11/6/1821).
Ba. Giovanni in Botany; or, The Libertine Transported (Olym. T.
12/3/1822). L. 124 M. [16/2/1822].
Ba. Giovanni in Ireland (W.L. W. 31/1/1821).
Ext. Giovanni in Ireland (D.L. 22/12/1821). L. 82 S. [11/12/1821].
[Music Cooke.]
O.F. Giovanni in the Country; or, A Gallop to Gretna Green (R.A.
M. 31/7/1820).
[On T. 15/8/1820 the title was changed to *G. in the C.; or, The
Rake Husband*.]
Ba. The Gipsey Daughter; or, The Cupid of Clerkenwell (Adel. T.
16/3/1824). L.C. 12/3/1824.
D. The Gipsey of Milan (S.W. 22/1/1844). L.C. 13/1/1844.
M.D. The Gipsy Dumb Boy (Cob. M. 22/9/1823).
Ba. The Gipsy Girl (Sans P. M. 9/1/1815).
Ext. The Giraffe; or, The Cameleopard (S.W. M. 1/10/1827).
Bal. Giselle; or, The Wilis (P'cess, M. 9/10/1843).
Spec. Giselle; or, The Phantom Night Dancers (Surrey, T.
24/11/1846).
D. The Glass; or, The Dangers of the Gin Palace (Queen's, 24/11/1847).
L.C. 19/11/1847.
Ba. The Gleaners (Surrey, M 23/9/1811).
Ba. The Gleaners; or, Harvest Frolic (Pav. T. 26/12/1809). L. 51 S.
[12/12/1809].
M.D. Glenarvon (Cob. T. 13/7/1819).
[The title was altered on M. 3/12/1821 to *Glenarvon; or, The
Murdered Heir*.]
D. Glendwyr of Snowdon; or, The Rock of Death (Surrey, M.
19/2/1849).
Tale of Enchantment. The Gnome Fly (Adel. W. 31/1/1838).
D. The Gnome King. L.C. 27/1/1838.
P. The Gnome King; or, Harlequin of the Giant Mountains (Royalty,
F. 26/12/1823).

R.D. The Gnome King; or, The Giant Mountains (C.G. M. 4/10/1819).
L. 73 S. [29/9/1819]. 8° 1819.
[Music Bishop.]
P. The Godolphin Arabian; or, The Race-horse of the Desert (R.A.
M. 12/5/1845). L.C. 28/4/1845.
Ba. Going to Execution; or, The Spanish Princess (Royalty, M.
20/5/1822).
F. Going to my Uncle's; or, My Wife's Husband (City, M. 14/1/1833).
P. The Golden Axe; or, Harlequin and the Fairy Lake (D.L. M.
6/1/1823).
D. The Golden Bell. L.C. Standard, 26/12/1845.
M.D. The Golden Days of Good Queen Bess; or, The Destruction
of the Spanish Armada (Cob. T. 26/12/1826).
P. The Golden Dream; or, Harlequin Animation (R.A. M. 18/5/1812).
P. The Golden Dream; or, Harlequin and Plutus (Royalty, M.
14/1/1805).
Ba. The Golden Farmer; or, When the Clock Strikes (R.A. M.
11/6/1821).
Spec. The Golden-footed Steed; or, The Charmed Horse of the Black
Valley (R.A. M. 24/5/1847). L.C. 7/5/1847.
P. The Golden Goose; or, Harlequin, the Goblin of the Mine
(Surrey, F. 26/12/1828).
M.D. The Golden Shield; or, The Day of Numa Pompilius (R.P.
M. 7/1/1836).
D. The Gold Seekers; or, The Dying Gift (Vic. 17/12/1838).
D. The Gold Seekers of Alasca (S.W. T. 1/2/1842).
F. Gone to Texas (P'cess, W. 13/3/1844). L.C. 9/3/1844.
Bal. Gonsalve de Cordoue (H.¹ T. 2/4/1816).
D. Gonzaga. 8° 1814.
Ba. Goodman's Fields in the Olden Time; or, The Benevolent Jew of
St Mary Axe (R.P. T. 27/12/1831).
F. A Good Name (Lyc. Th. 24/4/1845). L.C. 21/4/1845.
P. Goosey, Goosey Gander; or, Harlequin, the Fairy of my Lady's
Chamber (R.P. W. 26/12/1832).
Spec. Gordon Gray; or, Scottish Outlaws (Royalty, T. 2/4/1811).
M.D. Gordon the Gypsey (E.O.H. M. 5/8/1822). L. 126 M. [2/8/1822].
[Music Watson.]
Ba. The Gossip; or, Mischief Making (S.W. M. 14/2/1831).
D. Grace Gayton (Surrey, M. 7/9/1846).
D. Grace Rivers; or, The Merchant's Daughter (R.P. 5/2/1844).
L.C. 27/1/1844.
M.D. The Graeme; or, The Wizard of the Black Moor (Surrey, M.
16/8/1824).
M.D. Graham, the Regent of Scotland (Cob. M. 7/5/1827; R.P. M.
18/5/1829).
D. Gramachree Molly; or, The Bodagh of the Boyne (Surrey, M.
5/8/1844). L.C. 8/8/1844.
D. The Grand Army; or, The Attack on Monterreau (S.W. M.
29/1/1838; C.L. 15/10/1838).
F. Grandmother's Pet. L.C. P'cess, 12/2/1844.
F. Grandpapa (D.L. W. 25/5/1825). L.C. 14/5/1825.
Spec. Grand Sabre, the Traitor (S.W. M. 12/1/1829).
F. The Grand Tour; or, Stopped at Rochester (C.G. T. 22/5/1821).
L. 121 M. [11/5/1821].

Spec. Grand Venetian Carnival (Cob. M. 12/3/1821).
C. The Grave. 8° 1802 [in *The Metrical Miscellany*].
Ba. A Grave Subject; or, The Gentleman in Black (Cob. M. 2/6/1828).
O.F. The Great Alexander. L.C. C.G. 5/4/1828.
D. The Great Metropolis; or, Last Century (Queen's, 24/3/1845). L.C. 22/3/1845.
Ent. The Great Steeplechase; or, Harvest Home (R.A. M. 1/7/1844).
F. The Great Unknown (H.² T. 9/9/1823). L. 87 S. [1/9/1823].
F. The Great Unknown. L.C. Olym. 4/3/1840.
M.D. The Greek Amazon; or, The Santon's Cave (Cob. M. 14/1/1833).
C. The Greek Captive; or, A Peep into the Seraglio. L.C. Liverpool,
C. The Greek Captive; or, A Peep into the Seraglio. L.C. Liverpool, 5/3/1844.
Spec. The Greek Renegade; or, The Fall of Missolonghi (R.A. M. 9/6/1845).
M.D. The Greeks and the Turks; or, The Intrepidity of Jemmy, Jerry and a British Tar (Cob. M. 19/11/1821).
Ba. The Green Dragon; or, The Dead Men taken Prisoner (Cob. M. 3/11/1828).
Da. Green Gosling; or, The Poacher (S.W. M. 12/5/1828).
Ba. Green in France; or, Tom and Jerry's Tour (Adel. M. 6/1/1823). L. 83 S. [1822].
D. The Green Mantle; or, The Beggar Girl of Lambeth Marsh (Vic. M. 1/5/1837).
C. The Green Room; or, Intrigues and Disasters. L.C. H.² 12/9/1825. [See *J. KENNEY*, 1826.]
Bal. Greenwich Fair; or, The Petticoat Lancers (Garrick, M. 4/4/1831).
D. The Greenwich Pensioner (Surrey, W. 1/12/1830).
M.D. The Greenwich Pensioner; or, The Seaman's Oath (R.A. M. 7/5/1832).
D. The Greenwich Railway; or, Two to One on the Winner (R.P. M. 8/6/1835).
Spec. Gregarach, the Highland Watchword (R.A. M. 14/5/1821).
Ba. The Grenadier (Olym. M. 24/1/1831). L.C. 15/1/1831.
R.D. Grey the Collier (Olym. F. 3/11/1820). L. 77 S. [28/10/1820].
P. Grimalkin the Great; or, Harlequin and the King of the Cats (Adel. M. 27/12/1830). L.C. 23/12/1829.
M.D. Grim Will, the Collier of Croydon; or, The Death of the Red King (Cob. M. 24/10/1825).
Ba. Gripe in the Wrong Box; or, The Biter Bit (S.W. M. 11/7/1831).
D. Griselda. 12° 1844.
    [From the German of "F. Helm"; see *ANSTRUTHER*.]
M.D. The Guard House (Queen's, M. 6/7/1835).
C. The Guardians; or, The Man of my Choice. 8° 1808 [Bath].
Ba. The Guardians off their Guard (Olym. Th. 20/2/1840).
C.O. The Guardians Outwitted; or, A Bold Stroke for a Wife (E.O.H. M. 1/9/1823).
    [An adaptation of Mrs Centlivre's play; music Reeve.]
D. The Guardroom Slave (H.² T. 26/10/1841).
D. The Gude Man of Ballangeich (R.A. M. 23/7/1849).
D. The Guerilla Chief (E.O.H. 6/7/1826).
    [A dramatisation of John Doe, *Tales of the O'Hara Family*. A later version appeared at the Surrey in 1829 as *Montalto; or, The Mountain Pass*.]

D. The Guerilla Chief and his Daughters (D.L. M. 19/11/1827).
    [Music R. Hughes.]
D. The Guide of the Tyrol (Adel. M. 26/3/1838).
    [This is probably *T. G. BLAKE, The Dumb Guide of the Tyrol*.]
Ba. Gulliver among the Lilliputians. L. 102 M. [Olym. 26/3/1814].
F. Gun Cotton (Lyc. M. 26/7/1847). L.C. 22/7/1847.
D. Gunpowder Tom; or, A Seaman's Duty. L.C. Britannia,
    10/12/1844.
D. The Gunsmith of Orleans; or, The Dead Woman's Secret. L.C.
    Vic. 17/1/1847.
D. Gustave Dubarry; or, A Night in La Berlandiere (Olym. M.
    11/1/1847). L.C. 7/1/1847.
D. Gustavus of Sweden. L.C. Hull, 6/2/1834.
F. Gutta Percha (Surrey, 20/3/1848). L.C. 18/3/1848.
Bsq. Guy Fawkes. A Gingerbread Tragedy. L. 122 M. [E.O.H.
    8/9/1821].
M.D. Gwinett Bremmel; or, The Harpooner of Fish Hook Bay (R.P.
    M. 28/4/1834).
M.D. Hafed the Gheber; or, The Fire Worshippers (D.L. M.
    29/11/1824). L.C. 27/11/1824.
    [A dramatisation of *Lalla Rookh*.]
M.D. The Hag of the Glen; or, The Bandit's Bride (Cob. M.
    8/11/1819).
M.D. The Hag of the Lake; or, The Castle of Monte Falcon (Royalty,
    M. 14/9/1812).
R.D. The Hag of the Storm; or, The Doomed Knight (R.A. M.
    27/5/1833).
P. Hags of Mischief; or, Harlequin Ploughboy (Pav. M. 17/11/1806).
F. Half an Hour in England, without Cozening (C.G. Th. 1/7/1819).
Ba. The Half Pay Officer (Sans P. M. 18/1/1819). L. 117 M. [14/1/1819;
    as *The H. P. O.; or, Love and Honour*].
P. The Hall of Mischief; or, Harlequin and Maggy Lawder (Surrey,
    M. 11/4/1814).
Ent. Hallowe'en; or, The Vampire and the Water Kelpie (Perth, 1821).
Bal. The Halt of the Caravan (D.L. S. 30/11/1822).
Bsq. Hamlet. 8° 1838.
    [No extant copy of this has been traced.]
M.D. Hamlet Prince of Denmark (Cob. M. 4/2/1828).
F. The Handsell Penny (Lyc. Th. 13/5/1841). L.C. 6/5/1841.
Ba. The Handsell Penny (Olym. M. 10/6/1844).
Spec. Hans of Iceland; or, The Iron Casket (Olym. M. 28/11/1825).
    L.C. 17/11/1825.
M.D. Hans of the Iron Hand; or, The Blacksmith of Warsaw (R.P.
    M. 8/10/1832).
C. Happy at Last; or, Sigh No More, Ladies (Margate, 13/9/1805).
Bal. The Happy Return (Brunswick, M. 25/2/1828).
Ba. The Hard Frost; or, London in 1814 (R.A. M. 15/4/1833).
P. Harlequin Achilles; or, A Trip to Hyde Park (R.A. T. 12/11/1822).
P. Harlequin Amulet; or, The Magic of Mona (D.L. M. 22/12/1800).
    L. 75 M. [22/12/1800]. [By *CORDAL POWELL*.]
P. Harlequin and Æsop; or, Wisdom versus Wealth (S.W. S. 17/8/1805).
P. Harlequin and a Happy New Year; or, The White Cat and the
    King and his Three Sons (S.W. S. 26/12/1846). L.C. 16/12/1846.

P. Harlequin and Asmodeus; or, Cupid on Crutches (C.G. W. 26/12/1810).

P. Harlequin and Cinderella; or, The Little Glass Slipper (C.G. M. 3/4/1820). L. 79 S. [22/3/1820].

P. Harlequin and Cinderella; or, The Little Glass Slipper (S.W. M. 27/12/1841).
     [By *T. GREENWOOD*.]

P. Harlequin and Cock Robin; or, The Babes in the Wood (D.L. W. 26/12/1827). L.C. 21/12/1827.

P. Harlequin and Cupid; or, Love in an Humble Shed (Surrey, M. 20/4/1829).

P. Harlequin and Don Quixote (Pav. M. 11/1/1813).

P. Harlequin and Don Quixote; or, Sancho Panza in his Glory (C.G. M. 17/12/1819). L. 75 S. [17/12/1819].

P. Harlequin and Duke Humphrey's Dinner; or, Jack Cade and the Lord of London Stone (D.L. M. 27/12/1841). L.C. 12/12/1841.

P. Harlequin and Fair Rosamond; or, Old Dame Nature and Fairy Art (C.G. W. 26/12/1838). L.C. 12/1838.

P. Harlequin and Flora (Pav. T. 20/11/1810).

P. Harlequin and Fortunio; or, Shing-moo and Thun-Ton (C.G. T. 26/12/1815). L. 104 M. [11/12/1815; as *Harlequin and Fortunio; or, The Treasures of China*]. 8° 1815.

P. Harlequin and Georgey Barnwell; or, The London Prentice (C.G. M. 26/12/1836). L.C. 19/12/1836.

P. Harlequin and Golden Eyes; or, The Golden Wood (Olym. M. 26/12/1825). L.C. 8/12/1825.

P. Harlequin and Good Queen Bess; or, Merry England in the Olden Time (D.L. W. 26/12/1849). L.C. 18/12/1849.

P. Harlequin and Guy of Warwick (C.G. M. 27/12/1841). L.C. 12/12/1841.

P. Harlequin and Hardyknute; or, The Knight and the Wooden Demon. L.C. M'bone, 23/12/1848.

P. Harlequin and his Eleven Brothers; or, Little Puck and the Magician of the Hermitage (Vic. S. 26/12/1835).

P. Harlequin and Hop o' my Thumb; or, The Seven Leagued Boots and the Ogre's Seven Daughters (S.W. T. 26/12/1843). L.C. 16/12/1843.

P. Harlequin and Hot Codlins; or, The Little Old Woman and the Demon of the Metal Mine (Vic. Th. 26/12/1844). L.C. 23/12/1844.

P. Harlequin and Jack the Giant-Killer; or, The Golden Castle (Cob. F. 26/12/1828).

P. Harlequin and King Lud of Ludgate. L.C. C.L. 20/12/1845.

P. Harlequin and King Pepin; or, Valentine and Orson (D.L. T. 26/12/1843). L.C. 16/12/1843.

P. Harlequin and Ladybird's Bower (Surrey, M. 26/12/1836).

P. Harlequin and Little Bo-Peep; or, The Old Woman that Lived in a Shoe (Adel. M. 26/12/1831). L.C. 22/12/1831.

P. Harlequin and Little Great Britain; or, Jack and the Bean-Stalk and the Ogre's Wife (S.W. M. 27/12/1847). L.C. 22/12/1847.

P. Harlequin and Little King Pippin; or, The Golden Crown and Goblin of the Apple (Surrey, M. 29/12/1834).

P. Harlequin and Little Red Riding Hood; or, The Wizard and the Wolf (C.G. F. 26/12/1828). L.C. 15/12/1828.

P. Harlequin and Little Thumb; or, The Seven Leagued Boots (D.L. M. 26/12/1831). L.C. 21/12/1831.

P. Harlequin and Little Tom Tivy; or, The Fairy Queen and the Great Sea Snake. L.C. Albert, 23/12/1848.

P. Harlequin and Mother Bunch; or, The Yellow Dwarf (C.G. W. 26/12/1821). L. 81 S. [14/12/1821].

P. Harlequin and Mother Red Cap; or, Merlin and the Fairy Snow Drop (Adel. Th. 26/12/1839). L.C. 12/1839.

P. Harlequin and My Lady Lee; or, Goosey, Goosey Gander and the Spell-bound Goslings (Surrey, S. 26/12/1840).

P. Harlequin and Number Nip; or, The Giant Mountain (C.G. W. 26/12/1827). L.C. 8/12/1827.

P. Harlequin and Old Cocker; or, Arithmetic Hall and the Rule of Three (Olym. M. 26/12/1842). L.C. 21/12/1842 [as *The R. of T.; or, H. Arithmetic*].

P. Harlequin and Old Daddy Long Legs; or, Mary, Mary Quite Contrary (Surrey, S. 26/12/1835).

P. Harlequin and Old Dame Trot; or, The Fairy and the Comical Cat (Surrey, T. 26/12/1837).

P. Harlequin and Old Father Æsop; or, Little Cock Robin and the Children in the Wood (S.W. Th. 26/12/1839).

P. Harlequin and Padmanaba; or, The Golden Fish (C.G. Th. 26/12/1811). L. 53 S. [19/12/1811].

P. Harlequin and Peeping Tom of Coventry; or, The Ladye Godiva and the Witch of Warwick (C.G. T. 26/12/1837). L.C. 14/12/1837.

P. Harlequin and Poonoowingkeewangflibeedeeflobeedeebuskeebang, King of the Cannibal Islands (Adel. F. 26/12/1845). L.C. 17/12/1845.

P. Harlequin and Poor Robin; or, The House that Jack Built (C.G. F. 26/12/1823). L. 85 S. [5/12/1823].

P. Harlequin and Riddle me, Riddle me Ree; or, You Can't Guess what this may be. L.C. Olym. 22/12/1841.

P. Harlequin and St. Crispin's Day; or, The Merry Old Woman in the Shoe (R.P. M. 8/4/1833).

P. Harlequin and St. George and the Dragon (D.L. S. 26/12/1846). L.C. 21/12/1846.

P. Harlequin and the Astrologer of Stepney; or, The Enchanted Fish and Fated Ring (Surrey, W. 26/12/1827).

P. Harlequin and the Book of Life; or, Health, Wealth and Content (R.P. M. 30/12/1839).

P. Harlequin and the Cygnet; or, The Fairies of the Silver Lake (Olym. Th. 26/12/1822).

P. Harlequin and the Dandy Club; or, 1818 (D.L. S. 26/12/1818).

P. Harlequin and the Dragon of Wantley; or, More, of More Hall (C.G. M. 27/12/1824). L.C. 9/12/1824.

P. Harlequin and the Dragon of Wantley; or, Moore of Moore Hall and Mother Shipton's Black Dog (S.W. W. 26/12/1849). L.C. 21/12/1849.

P. Harlequin and the Eagle; or, The Man in the Moon and his Wife (Adel. T. 26/12/1826). 8° [1826].

P. Harlequin and the Elfin Sprite; or, The Little Grim Gray Woman (Vic. W. 26/12/1838).

P. Harlequin and the Enchanted Figs; or, The Little Yellow Man of the Golden Mountain (Surrey, W. 26/12/1838).

P. Harlequin and the Enchanter of the Coral Cavern. L.C. Grecian, 24/10/1843.
P. Harlequin and the Fairy Queen of the Magic Teapot; or, Chi, Hi, Ski, Ki!—King of the Golden Pagoda. L.C. Standard, 19/12/1849.
P. Harlequin and the Flying Chest; or, Malek and the Princess Schirine (D.L. F. 26/12/1823).
P. Harlequin and the Giant King; or, The Red Rich Mountain (R.P. M. 14/5/1832).
P. Harlequin and the Golden Branch. L.C. Grecian, 29/11/1845.
P. Harlequin and the Golden Peacock; or, The Weird Sisters and the Wizard Magician of the Glades of Glen Dell. L.C. Grecian, 2/12/1848.
P. Harlequin and the Happy New Year; or, The White Cat and the King and his Three Sons (S.W. S. 26/12/1846).
P. Harlequin and the King of the Ruby Mine; or, The Fairy Brilliant (Cob. M. 7/6/1824).
P. Harlequin and the Knave of Clubs; or, The Queen and her Syllabubs (Adel. W. 26/12/1832).
       [Also played as *H. and the King of C.; or, The Knave who Stole the Syllabubs.*]
P. Harlequin and the Lord Mayor of London; or, Fum, the Fire Fiend of Finsbury. L.C. Grecian, 18/10/1847.
P. Harlequin and the Magic Marrowbone; or, Taffy was a Welchman (Adel. F. 26/12/1828). L.C. 11/12/1828.
P. Harlequin and the Magic Rose; or, Beauty and the Beast (C.G. M. 26/12/1825). L.C. 5/12/1825.
P. Harlequin and the Merry Devil of Edmonton; or, The Great Bed of Ware (C.G. Th. 26/12/1839). L.C. 12/12/1839.
P. Harlequin and the Ogress; or, The Sleeping Beauty of the Wood (C.G. Th. 26/12/1822). L. 84 S. [17/12/1822].
P. Harlequin and the Old Witch of Teddington; or, The Golden Days of Good Queen Bess (Surrey, F. 26/12/1845).
P. Harlequin and the Red Dwarf; or, The Adamant Rock (C.G. S. 26/12/1812). L. 56 S. [11/12/1812].
P. Harlequin and the Royal Ram; or, The Brazen Dragon (Cob. W. 26/12/1832).
P. Harlequin and the Silver Dove; or, The Fairy of the Golden Ladder (Adel. W. 26/12/1838). L.C. 1838.
P. Harlequin and the Spirit of the Moon; or, Giselle and the Night Dancers. L.C. M'bone, 16/12/1846.
P. Harlequin and the Snake-King; or, The Coral Branch (S.W. M. 26/3/1828).
P. Harlequin and the Steam King; or, Perroule's Wishes and the Fairy Frog (S.W. F. 26/12/1845).
P. Harlequin and the Swans; or, The Bath of Beauty (C.G. M. 27/12/1813). L. 99 M. [15/12/1813].
P. Harlequin and the Sylph of the Oak; or, The Blind Beggar of Bethnal Green (C.G. Th. 26/12/1816). L. 62 S. [16/12/1816]. 8° 1816.
P. Harlequin and the Talking Bird, the Singing Trees and the Golden Waters (D.L. M. 27/12/1824). L.C. 15/12/1824.
P. Harlequin and the Three Sisters (Pav. F. 30/10/1807).
P. Harlequin and the White Mouse; or, A Frog in an Opera Hat (Adel. W. 26/12/1827). L.C. 17/12/1827.

P. Harlequin and the Wild Fiend of California; or, The Demon of the Diggings and the Gnome Queen of the Golden Lake. L.C. Grecian, 16/12/1849.

P. Harlequin and the Witch of Edmonton; or, Nobody and his Wife (Cob. M. 26/12/1831).

P. Harlequin and the World turned upside down; or, Number Nip and the Enchanted Fountain (S.W. T. 26/12/1848). L.C. 23/12/1848.

P. Harlequin and Tom Tyler; or, The Genii of the Golden Garden and the Silver City (R.P. M. 27/12/1830).

P. Harlequin and Wat Tyler; or, The Fairies of the Land of Flowers. L.C. Vic. 16/12/1849.

P. Harlequin and William Tell; or, The Genius of Ripston Pippin (D.L. S. 24/12/1842). L.C. 21/12/1842.

P. Harlequin at Helicon; or, Pantomime Renovated (New, M. 23/4/1810).

P. Harlequin "At Home"; or, The Magic Fountains (S.W. F. 29/6/1821—16th performance).

P. Harlequin Bacchus (R.C. M. 15/4/1805).

P. Harlequin Bluebeard; or, The Fairy of the Silver Crescent (Adel. T. 26/12/1843). L.C. 20/12/1843.

P. Harlequin Cottager; or, The Wandering Fairy (Sans P. W. 31/5/1809).

P. Harlequin Crochet and Quaver; or, Music for the Million (C.G. Th. 26/12/1844). L.C. 2/12/1844 [as C. and Q.; or, H. Sharp, Flat and Natural].

P. Harlequin Demon; or, The Moonlight Enchanters (Olym. M. 24/12/1827). L.C. 17/12/1827.

P. Harlequin Don Quixote de la Mancha; or, Sancho Panza and Dulcinea of Toboso (R.A. F. 26/12/1845). L.C. 29/11/1845.

P. Harlequin Fairy Land; or, The Princess Zela and the Magic Wishes Three (M'bone, W. 26/12/1849). L.C. 18/12/1849.

P. Harlequin Golden Farmer; or, The Fairy of the Silver Spring. L.C. Albert, 16/12/1846.

P. Harlequin Gulliver; or, Giants and Dwarfs (D.L. F. 26/12/1845). L.C. 17/12/1845.

P. Harlequin Gulliver; or, The Flying Island (C.G. F. 26/12/1817). L. 66 S. [11/12/1817].

P. Harlequin Guy Fawkes; or, The Fifth of November (C.G. S. 26/12/1835). L.C. 16/11/1835.

P. Harlequin Handy; or, The Whim of the Moment (Cob. M. 4/6/1827).

P. Harlequin Horner; or, The Christmas Pie (D.L. Th. 26/12/1816). L. 63 S. [19/12/1816]. Another MS. was in the possession of R. Crompton Rhodes.

P. Harlequin Hyacinth; or, The Golden Violet (S.W. M. 16/4/1827).

P. Harlequin in Egypt (R.C. M. 16/1/1804).

P. Harlequin in Scotland (Olym. Pav. M. 23/11/1807).

P. Harlequin Jack of all Trades (D.L. M. 26/12/1825). L.C. 13/12/1825.

P. Harlequin Jack Sheppard; or, The Blossom of Tyburn Tree (D.L. Th. 26/12/1839). L.C. 1839.

P. Harlequin Jack the Giant Killer; or, The Ogre of St Michael's Mount (Olym. T. 26/12/1843). L.C. 20/12/1843.

P. Harlequin King of Spades (Olym. Pav. M. 28/2/1808).
    [Called later, *The Card Party; or, H. K. of S.*]
P. Harlequin Lincoln Lucky of Lambeth; or, The Three Fairy
    Sisters of Witch Willow Dell (Vic. T. 26/12/1843). L.C. 20/12/1843.
P. Harlequin Mamaluke; or, The British in Egypt (R.C. Th.
    21/5/1801).
P. Harlequin Munchausen; or, The Fountain of Love (C.G. S.
    26/12/1818). L. 70 S. [17/12/1818].
P. Harlequin Othello! or, The Fairy and the Bran-new Birds-eye
    Bandana (S.W. T. 19/9/1837).
P. Harlequin Pat and Harlequin Bat; or, The Giant's Causeway
    (C.G. M. 27/12/1830). [Later called *Harlequin Fat.*]
P. Harlequin Perizade; or, The Talking Bird (S.W. M. 15/4/1805).
P. Harlequin Peter Wilkins; or, The King of the Air and the Flying
    Indian (Vic. M. 27/12/1841).
P. Harlequin Pewerite. L.C. S.W. 20/12/1845.
P. Harlequin Plagiarist; or, The Gigantic Ghost (Olym. Pav. M.
    12/1/1807).
    [Music Lawrence.]
P. Harlequin Pointer (Royalty, M. 2/11/1801).
P. Harlequin Rasselas; or, The Happy Valley (Sans P. Th. 9/2/1815).
P. Harlequin Reclaimed; or, The Magic Mentor (Surrey, W.
    26/12/1810).
P. Harlequin Robin Hood and Little John; or, Merrie England in
    the Olden Time. L.C. S.W. 23/12/1844.
P. Harlequin's Amour; or, Jupiter and Europa (R.A. M. 15/4/1811).
P. Harlequin's Ancestors; or, Mother Shipton, Mother Bunch and
    Mother Goose (S.W. M. 8/4/1822).
P. Harlequin's Banquet; or, The Magic Feast (R.C. W. 16/4/1800).
P. Harlequin's Calendar; or, The Palace of Bears (Royalty, W.
    26/12/1821).
P. Harlequin's Court of Apollo; or, Gambols Revived (R.A. M.
    8/6/1812).
P. Harlequin's Death and Revival; or, The Clown in Purgatory
    (Lyc. 9/4/1822).
P. Harlequin's Gambols; or, The Skeleton and the Clown (Royalty,
    M. 19/12/1803).
P. Harlequin's Holyday; or, The Easter Offering (Cob. M. 4/4/1831).
P. Harlequin's Holyday; or, Who Killed the Dog? (Adel. Th.
    26/12/1822). L. 125 M. [18/12/1822; as, *Who K. the D.; or, H.'s
    Triumph*].
    [Later called *H. H.; or, The Cockney Sportsman.*]
P. Harlequin's Honeymoon; or, The Antipodean Clown (Cob. M.
    15/6/1818].
P. Harlequin's Hour Glass; or, Time Works Wonders (Olym. M.
    8/1/1816). L. 62 S. [20/12/1815].
P. Harlequin Silver Penny; or, The Old Woman in the Bottle (Cob.
    M. 27/12/1830).
P. Harlequin Silver Sixpence and the Giant Penny-piece; or, The
    World of Coins (Adel. T. 26/12/1837). L.C. 17/12/1837.
P. Harlequin Simple Simon; or, The May Queen and a Voyage to
    the North Pole. L.C. Albert, 21/12/1849.
P. Harlequin Sinbad the Sailor; or, The White Gnome and the
    Valley of Diamonds. L.C. Albert, 1849.

P.   Harlequin's Olio (C.G. M. 19/2/1816).
P.   Harlequin's Punishment (Royalty, M. 5/4/1802).
P.   Harlequin's Races; or, Time Beats All (C.G. M. 26/12/1803).
     L. 43 S. [16/12/1803; as, *Harlequin at his Old Tricks; or, All for the Races*].
P.   Harlequin's Salutation. L. 92 M. [Pav. 12/12/1810].
P.   Harlequin's Trip to Paris; or, The Golden Flute (S.W. M. 31/3/1823).
P.   Harlequin Tam o' Shanter and his Steed Meg; or, The Witches of Alloway Kirk (R.A. T. 26/12/1843). L.C. 16/12/1843.
P.   Harlequin Tom the Piper's Son Stole a Pig and Away He Run (Olym. T. 26/12/1820). L. 117 M. [20/12/1820].
P.   Harlequin Traveller; or, The World Inside Out (D.L. W. 26/12/1832). L.C. 24/12/1832 [as *Europe, Asia, Africa and America; or, Harlequin Mercury*].
P.   Harlequin Vulcan and Venus. L.C. 14/12/1829.
P.   Harlequin Warrior; or, Quixotte and Sancho (Royalty, M. 16/2/1801).
P.   Harlequin Whittington; or, The Lord Mayor of London (C.G. M. 26/12/1814). L. 59 S. [10/12/1814].
P.   Harlequin Yorkshireman; or, The Fairy's Gift (Vic. T. 17/9/1833).
P.   Harlequin Zambullo; or, The Devil upon two Sticks. L. 51 S. [C.G. 14/12/1810].
Ba. Harmony Hall (St J. Th. 13/10/1836). L.C. 10/10/1836.
Bal. Harold the Renegade; or, The Red Cross Knights (C.G. T. 28/10/1823).
M.D. The Harp of Altenberg (S.W. M. 28/1/1833).
M.D. The Harpooner; or, The Ice Sea and the Monster Whale of Greenland (R.P. T. 2/7/1833).
C.   Harry le Roi; or, The Benighted Monarch (Surrey, M. 13/10/1834).
Spec. Harry of England; or, The Battle of Agincourt (S.W. M. 16/5/1842).
M.Ent. Harvest Home. L. 50 S. [Norwich, 18/3/1808].
Ent. Harvest Home; or, The Mayor Deceived (Royalty, M. 16/11/1801).
Ba. Harvest Home; or, The Tythe Sheaf (R.A. Th. 28/2/1811).
O.   The Harvest Queen (D.L. T. 22/5/1838).
       [Music Phillips.]
O.F. Hassan and Lara (R.P. M. 25/5/1829).
Ba. Hassan Pacha; or, The Arab's Leap (Adel. M. 20/2/1837). L.C. 17/2/1837.
Ba. Haste to the Wedding; or, The Marriage Portion (R.C. M. 11/6/1804).
M.D. Hate; or, The Cataract of the Mountain (Surrey, M. 3/5/1824).
D.   Hate and Love (Surrey, W. 27/1/1836).
M.D. The Haunted Chamber; or, The Crime Discovered (Surrey, M. 24/11/1823).
Ba. The Haunted Chamber; or, 'Tis Well it's no Worse (S.W. Th. 9/8/1821).
O.   The Haunted Head (Surrey, M. 11/1/1836).
M.D. The Haunted Hulk (S.W. M. 7/5/1832).
M.D. The Haunted Inn. L.C. Olym. 26/6/1832.
D.   The Haunted Man; or, The Compact with the Ghost (Adel. 20/12/1848). L.C. 20/12/1848.

D. The Haunted Man; or, The Ghost's Bargain. L.C. Albert, 30/12/1848.
F. The Haunted Man (Queen's, 1/1/1849). L.C. 1/1/1849.
    [This and the preceding plays are derived from Dickens' tale.]
Ba. The Haunted Village (R.A. M. 28/1/1811).
Ba. The Haunted Village; or, Love's Stratagem (Pav. M. 20/11/1809). L. 51 S. [24/10/1809].
C.O. Haydee; or, The Secret (C.G. S. 4/11/1848). L.C. 4/11/1848.
    [Adapted from E. Scribe, *Haydée; ou, le sécret* (Paris, 28/12/1847), with music by Auber.]
Bal. Heads and Blockheads (R.C. W. 13/1/1819).
Int. Heads and Tails (P'cess, S. 25/2/1843).
R.D. The Headsman; or, The Axe and the Sword (Surrey, M. 4/4/1841).
F. Heads versus Pockets; or, Knaves Overtrumped. L.C. 1826.
C. Hear Him Out. L. 81 M. [C.G. 9/10/1804].
    [This is *F. REYNOLDS, The Blind Bargain.*]
F. Hearing is Believing (Queen's, M. 26/10/1835).
D. The Heart (Vic. 26/6/1848). L.C. 26/6/1848 [as *The H. Test*].
D. The Heart and the Key; or, The Haunted Grange. L.C. Britannia, 5/10/1848.
M.D. The Heart of Midlothian; or, The Lily of St Leonards (T.R. Edinburgh, 9/12/1819). L. 73 S. [26/10/1819].
    [This is the play by *T. J. DIBDIN*; see p. 301.]
D. The Heart's Trials (M'bone, M. 9/4/1849). L.C. 2/4/1849.
M.D. The Hebrew Family; or, A Traveller's Adventure (C.G. F. 8/4/1825). L.C. 15/2/1825 [as *The Englishman in Spain*].
D. The Hebrew Maiden; or, The Lost Diamond (C.L. 4/1841).
M.D. The Hebrew Patriarch; or, The Unknown Knight (Royalty, M. 9/9/1822).
D. The Hebrew Twins (C.L. 22/11/1847). L.C. 19/11/1847.
Ba. The Heir at Law (Royalty, W. 10/1/1816).
D. The Heiress of Cardigan (Cardigan, 4/12/1840).
T. The Heiress of Strathearn (Edinburgh, 24/3/1813).
D. The Heir of Villeroy; or, The Palace of Palermo (S.W. T. 13/5/1835).
D. Helen Fortescue; or, The Shipbuilder's Daughter. L.C. Standard, 9/1/1847.
T. Helga; or, The Rival Minstrels. L. 21 L. [Edinburgh, 1/1812].
D. The Hemlock Draught (Olym. M. 29/1/1849).
O.F. He must be Married; or, The Miser Outwitted. 8° 1815.
Ent. Henault Forest (St J. T. 5/11/1839). L.C. 4/11/1839.
D. Henri de Rochemaine (Strand, M. 14/10/1844).
M.D. Henriette; or, The Farm of Senange (C.G. F. 23/2/1821). L. 123 M. [17/2/1821].
    [An adaptation from the French *Thérèse.*]
Int. Henri Quatre and the Fair Gabrielle. L. 125 M. [E.O.H. 19/6/1822).
D. Henri Quatre; or, The Olden Time (D.L. 21/6/1825).
T. Henry I; or, The British and Norman Feuds. L. 82 S. [D.L. 27/12/1821].
D. Henry V; or, The Conquest of France (Surrey, M. 22/3/1830).
Bal. Henry and Mary (E.L. Th. 21/8/1817).

Bal. Henry and Rosa (Cob. M. 21/6/1819).
M.D. Henry de Fleurville; or, A Mother's Sacrifice (Cob. M. 13/11/1820).
T. Henry of Transtamare (Edinburgh, 1/11/1805). L. 20 L. [24/10/1805].
Ent. Henry's Entertainment. L.C. Adel. 16/2/1828.
Ba. Henry's Table-Talk. L.C. Adel. 18/3/1825.
Ba. Henry's Table-Talk; or, Odd Sayings and Queer Doings. L.C. Adel. 2/2/1826.
O. Hermann; or, The Broken Spear (E.O.H. M. 27/10/1834). L.C. 27/10/1834.
    [Music John Thompson.]
P. The Hermetic Seal; or, Harlequin the Conjuror (R.A. T. 10/12/1822).
P. The Hermit's Altar; or, Harlequin from the Clouds (Sans P. Th. 16/8/1810).
Ext. A Hermit Wanted (Cob. M. 27/10/1828).
O. Hernando Cortez; or, The Conquest of Mexico. L. 130 M. [C.G. 13/10/1823].
T. Hernani; or, The Honour of a Castilian. L.C. St J. 24/4/1847.
M.D. Herne's Oak (R.P. M. 29/12/1834).
Ba. Hero and Leander (St J. M. 16/4/1838). L.C. 27/4/1838.
Spec. The Heroic Sergeant; or, Female Intrepidity (Cob. M. 28/2/1820).
M.D. The Hertfordshire Tragedy; or, The Victims of Gaming (Cob. M. 12/1/1824).
Ba. He's Here Again; or, No Peace for the Frenchman (S.W. M. 1/12/1828).
Ext. He's no Conjuror (Adel. M. 5/1/1829).
Ba. He's not a-miss (Olym. M. 16/1/1832). L.C. 14/1/1832.
P. He with the Hump; or, King Dick and Harlequin and the Cruel Tyrant that killed the Babbies. L.C. C.L. 21/12/1846.
Ba. He Would Be an Actor (Olym. M. 31/10/1836). L.C. 1837.
Ba. He Would Be a Player; or, The Stage-Struck Butler (Pav. M. 15/1/1810). L. 88 M. [12/12/1809].
P. Hickerty Pickerty; or, Harlequin and the Sable Hen (Surrey, M. 27/5/1833).
P. Hickety Pickety, the Black Hen; or, Harlequin and the Silver Egg (R.P. M. 7/4–M. 14/4/1834).
Int. Hide and Seek (C.G. Th. 11/11/1830). L.C. 24/10/1829.
Ba. Hide and Seek. L.C. 4/11/1833.
M.D. The Highland Cateran (E.O.H. Th. 14/9/1837). L.C. 1837.
Bal. The Highland Rivals; or, Douglas the Hero (Surrey, M. 13/5/1822).
D. The Highland Widow. L.C. 26/4/1837.
    [This is evidently the same as *Dougal, the Piper; or, The H. W.* (Adelphi, Edinburgh, 20/9/1836), taken from Scott's tale.]
F. High Life; or, Taste in the Upper Story (Hull, 1801).
    [By "a Gentleman of York."]
F. High Life in London. L.C. C.G. 1826.
C.O. The High Road to Marriage; or, Love in Full Gallop (Olym. Th. 9/11/1820). L. 77 S. [7/11/1820].
F. Hints for Painters (C.G. 10/5/1803). L. 79 M. [2/5/1803].
Ca. Hints to Wives; or, Advice to Husbands. L.C. P'cess, 29/9/1845.

F. His First Champagne (Olym. T. 25/7/1848).
F. His First Peccadillo (P'cess, 26/10/1848). L.C. 16/10/1848.
Ba. His Highness. L.C. 2/4/1832.
Ba. The Hoax (New, W. 21/11/1810).
Ba. The Hoax; or, Who's Drowned? L.C. Bath, 27/4/1826.
O. The Hoaxer; or, Vive la Bagatelle. L. 59 S. [Norwich, 5/11/1814].
Ba. Hoaxing; or, The Mayor Outwitted (Surrey, M. 3/5/1824).
P. Hocus Pocus; or, Harlequin washed White.
    [See Peake, *Memoirs of the Colman Family*, ii. 350.]
D. Hogarth's Apprentices; or, Industry and Idleness (R.A. M. 23/4/1821).
D. Hogarth's Apprentices; or, Industry and Idleness (Britannia, 27/3/1848). L.C. 28/1/1848.
P. Hokey Pokey Wankey Fum (S.W. Th. 7/1/1836).
Int. The Holidays; or, Just Broke Up. L. 97 M. [Pav. 16/12/1813].
M.D. The Hollow Way; or, The Hidden Treasure (Cob. M. 29/9/1828).
D. The Home of the Brave; or, The Child of a Soldier (Strand, M. 5/3/1832).
D. Homeward Bound; or, The Main-top Night Watch (Surrey, M. 4/6/1838).
M.D. Homeward Bound; or, The Sailor and his Wife (Pav. M. 5/8/1833).
M.D. The Homicide; or, The Dumb Boy and the Spectre Knight (Cob. M. 16/8/1824).
M.D. L'Homme Noir; or, The Executioner of Paris (S.W. M. 12/8/1839).
Ba. Homoeopathy (Queen's, M. 24/7/1837).
D. The Honest Man's Fortune (S.W. W. 28/2/1849).
Ba. Honest Thieves (Royalty, M. 4/2/1811).
O.F. Honesty the Best Policy (D.L. W. 31/5/1815).
    [Music Reeve.]
Ba. The Honey Moon (Surrey, W. 5/8/1812).
    [An adaptation of Tobin's drama.]
Ba. Hong Puf. L. 121 M. [Adel. 4/12/1821].
C. Honour; or, Arrivals from College (D.L. S. 17/4/1819). L. 74 S. [30/3/1819].
    [Music Cooke.]
D. Honour and Shame; or, The Ballet-girl and the Jew. L.C. R.P. 15/10/1849.
D. The Hooded Bridegroom (M'bone, W. 28/11/1848).
Ba. Hooking Walker; or, Eight Miles an Hour (S.W. M. 14/5/1821).
D. Hoorn, the Scourge of Norway; or, The Foundry of Kanzel (Cob. M. 18/10/1830).
Int. The Hope of Britain; or, The Twelfth of August (Brighton, 1802).
P. Hop o' my Thumb and his Brothers; or, Harlequin and the Ogre (C.G. M. 26/12/1831). L.C. 21/12/1831.
D. The Hop Pickers (Adel. M. 12/3/1849). L.C. 14/3/1849.
Ba. Hops! and Steps! (Surrey, T. 13/8/1811).
Ba. Hops without Malt; or, Equestrian Tuition (Cob. M. 14/7/1823).
D. Horatia (Olym. M. 6/1/1845).
M.D. The Horrors of the Bastile; or, The Escape of Latude (S.W. T. 15/9/1835).
M.D. The Horrors of War; or, Sixteen Years Since (R.P. W. 16/11/1831).

Spec. The Horrors of War; or, The Life of a Soldier (Cob. W. 26/12/1827).

Ba. Horse and Foot; or, The Gallopade (Surrey, 26/8/1834). L.C. 3/5/1833.

Spec. The Horse Banditti and their Forty Steeds; or, The Attack of the Caravan (R.A. M. 26/4/1830).

T. Hortensia. 8° 1815.

P. Hot Boiled Beans and the Very Good Butter; or, Harlequin and the Elfin's Supper (R.P. F. 26/12/1834).

Ext. Hot Codlings (Surrey, T. 26/3/1822).

P. The Hottentot Venus; or, Harlequin in Africa (New, M. 3/12/1810).

F. Hot Weather (Lyc. Th. 23/7/1846).

D. The Hour of Retribution (Queen's, 13/4/1846). L.C. 13/4/1846.

M.D. The Hour of Retribution; or, The Tenant of the Tomb (Cob. M. 26/2/1821).

C.O. The Hour of Twelve (S.W. M. 2/5/1836).

Ba. An Hour with Napoleon (Strand, 20/5/1844).
[See *One Hour with Napoleon*.]

P. The House-warming; or, The Peasant's Pic-nic (R.C. M. 1/7/1816).

D. How Fair the World Is! L.C. Grecian, 14/10/1843.

C.O. How happy could I be with either! L. 86 M. [C.G. 5/11/1807].

Ba. The Howlet's Haunt; or, The Story of the Skull (Adel. M. 10/12/1832). L.C. 6/12/1832.

Ba. How many Wives has he? (Strand, Th. 23/2/1832).

F. How to Die for Love (Lyc. Th. 21/5/1812). 8° 1812 [4 editions]; 8° 1816; 8° 1827.
[An adaptation of Kotzebue, *Blind Geladen*. *The Blank Cartridge* of L. 55 S. [9/5/1812] is the same play.]

Ba. How to get off (Olym. T. 25/11/1834). L.C. 22/11/1834.

Int. How to get out of a Mess; or, The Cornet in a Majority (S.W. M. 17/5/1824).

Ba. How to Live without Money (S.W. M. 9/8/1830).

Ba. How to Pay your Taxes. L. 78 S. [Olym. 23/11/1820].

C. How to Tease and How to Please (C.G. Th. 29/3/1810). L. 91 M. [16/3/1810].

C. How will it End? L. 90 M. [Manchester, 28/2/1809].

Ba. Hugo Bambino. L.C. 1824.

M.D. The Huguenots (E.O.H. M. 25/4/1836). L.C. 31/3/1836.
[An adaptation of E. Scribe, *Les Huguenots* (Paris, 20/2/1836), with music by Meyerbeer. See also the next two plays.]

O. The Huguenots (Surrey, Th. 16/8/1849). L.C. 16/8/1849.

M.D. The Huguenots; or, The Massacres of 1576 (R.P. F. 27/1/1832).

Ba. Humbug. L.C. Adel. 23/1/1827.

Ba. Humbug; or, Medecine for the Million (Olym. M. 7/4/1845). L.C. 11/3/1845.

Bsq. Humgumption; or, Dr. Frankenstein and Hobgoblin of Hoxton (Surrey, M. 1/9/1823).

Ba. The Humours of an Election (Adel. M. 9/1/1837). L.C. 6/1/1837.

O.D. The Humours of the Navy; or, A Peep at Portsmouth (Surrey, M. 6/9/1830).

Bsq. The Humpback. L.C. Edinburgh, 21/9/1843.

Bsq. The Humpback (Strand, S. 12/5/1832).

P. Humpty Dumpty; or, Harlequin Fairy of the Enchanted Egg (S.W. W. 26/12/1832).

C.   The Hunchback (Cob. M. 17/10/1831).
Ba. The Hunchback; or, Frolics in Bagdad (E.O.H. S. 8/7/1820).
     L. 24 L. [2/7/1820; as *The Little Hunchback*].
Ent. The Hunchback and his Horse Beelzebub (R.A. W. 23/5/1832).
Bal. The Hunchbacked Brothers of Bagdad (C.G. W. 25/1/1826).
P.   Hundred Eyes; or, Harlequin and Argus (R.A. M. 3/4/1820).
D.   The Hungarian Cottage; or, The Brazen Bust (Dublin, 1814).
Bsq. The Hunted Tailor's Journey to Brentford (R.A. T. 21/9/1813).
     [This is described as "a popular play."]
Ba. The Hunter of the Alps (Royalty, Th. 15/7/1813).
D.   The Hunter's Bride (Strand, M. 8/1/1844).
F.   The Husband of my Wife (Lyc. Th. 3/5/1849).
C.   Husbands Beware (City, M. 29/8/1831).
F.   The Husband's Mistake; or, The Corporal's Wedding (C.G. T.
     5/1/1830). L.C. 2/1/1830.
     [An adaptation of *La Fiancée* (Paris, 10/1/1829) by E. Scribe
     with music by Auber.]
F.   A Husband Wanted (Strand, F. 6/7/1832).
R.Ba. The Hussar; or, Love and Mercy (Surrey, F. 22/6/1821—
     2nd performance).
M.Ca. The Hussars; or, The Petticoat Colonel (Queen's, 3/11/1831).
Int. The Hustings. L. 72 S. [E.O.H. 24/6/1818; licence refused].
D.   The Hut of Valais; or, The Runaway Horse (R.A. M. 29/5/1843).
Spec. Hyder Ali; or, The Lions of Mysore (D.L. M. 17/10/1831).
     L.C. 17/10/1831.
     [Music Cooke.]
Spec. Hyder Ali; or, The Lions of Mysore (Cob. M. 23/7/1832).
Bsq. Hyder Ali; or, The Lions of Mysore (Adel. M. 24/10/1831).
     L.C. 24/10/1831.
D.   The Hydra, the Moon and the Daffodil (S.W. S. 21/8/1830).
Ba. The Hypochondriac (Surrey, M. 11/7/1825).
C.O. The Hypocrite. L. 76 S. [E.O.H. 11/7/1819].
M.D. Hypolita, Queen of the Amazons (R.A. M. 12/4/1819).
M.D. The Ice King (C.L. 23/10/1843). L.C. 18/10/1843.
M.D. The Iceland King; or, The Maid of Altona (R.P. M. 20/4/1835).
M.D. Ida of the Cottage. L. 75 S. [E.O.H. 23/6/1819].
M.D. The Idiot Heir (S.W. M. 12/7/1819).
Ba. The Idol's Birthday (Olym. M. 5/11/1838). L.C. 30/10/1838.
Bal. Ildamor and Zulcm (H.¹ Th. 30/5/1811).
F.   I'll Stay where I am. L. 129 M. [Olym. 17/11/1823].
Spec. Illusion; or, The Trances of Nourjahad (D.L. Th. 25/11/1813).
D.   The Illustrious Chief; or, The Daughter of Robert Macaire
     (Surrey, M. 23/5/1836).
Ba. The Illustrious Stranger. L.C. St J. 21/4/1837.
M.D. The Imperial Victims; or, The Caverns of Hoenhelbe (Cob.
     S. 25/9/1819).
F.   In and Out. L.C. Surrey, 31/10/1845.
Int. In and Out; or, My Landlady's Side Door (Olym. S. 24/3/1821).
     L. 81 S. [26/2/1821].
D.   The Inca; or, Peruvian Clemency (Cob. M. 28/6/1819).
M.D. The Incendiary; or, The House Burners (S.W. M. 15/12/1834).
F.   "Incog!" What's in a Name (Lyc. 20/7/1829).
Bal. The Inconstant Villager (R.A. M. 9/5/1814).
M.D. The Indian Father; or, The Bride of Mexico (Cob. M. 21/1/1822).

R.D. The Indian Girl (D.L. S. 28/10/1837). L.C. 1837.
[Music Eliason.]
M.D. The Indian Maid; or, Sailors and Savages (S.W. M. 16/6/1823).
Bal. The Indian Nuptials (D.L. M. 20/2/1815).
F. The Indians. L. 93 M. [C.G. 25/4/1810].
M.D. The Infant Heir; or, The Son of Clanronald (Cob. W. 6/2/1828).
D. Infanticide (Queen's, Th. 15/9/1831).
Bal.P. The Infant Soldier; or, Love in Miniature (R.A. M. 11/10/1802).
Ba. Inkle and Yarico (Surrey, W. 28/11/1810).
M.D. The Innkeeper's Daughter (E.L. M. 1/9/1817).
[An adaptation of SOANE's play.]
P. The Innkeeper's Disaster; or, The Vintager's Frolic (Vic. Th.
1/8/1833).
D. The Inn of Death; or, The Outcast Son. L.C. R.P. 10/3/1847.
F. In Pursuit of a Wife (Vic. M. 7/9/1840).
T. The Inquisition of 1650; or, Eugene and Maria. L. 64 S. [Glasgow,
1/1816].
Ba. The Inscription; or, The Indian Hunters (Sans P. M. 28/2/1814).
L. 22 L. [26/2/1814].
Int. In Search of a Wife; or, Love in Disguise (Olym. M. 14/1/1828).
L.C. 12/1/1828.
F. In Statu Quo! or, Romance and Romancers (Queen's, Th.
26/2/1835).
M.D. The Instrument of Torture (Surrey, M. 27/5/1844). L.C.
17/5/1844.
C. Integrity (C.G. Th. 8/10/1801). L. 40 S. [21/9/1801; as The
Garland of Truth; or, Integrity Proved].
Ba. The Interrupted Sacrifice. L.C. E.O.H. 9/6/1826.
C. Intimate Friends. L.C. D.L. 29/4/1842.
Ba. Intrigue, Love, Honour and Obey; or, The Widow (Sans P. T.
1/12/1812). L. 97 M. [27/11/1812].
C. The Intrigues of a Day; or, The Poet in Livery. 8° 1814.
Spec. The Inundation of the Nile (R.P. 13/4/1846). L.C. 11/4/
1846.
Bal. The Invasion; or, All for our Country (R.A. M. 11/7/1803).
F. The Invasion of England. 8° 1803.
Spec. The Invasion of England by William the Conqueror; or, The
Battle of Hastings (R.A. M. 8/4/1844).
M.D. The Invisible Avengers (Surrey, 1809).
F. The Invisible Client (Olym. M. 6/5/1844). L.C. 2/5/1844.
Ba. The Invisible Girl (Cob. M. 13/1/1823).
[See HOOK, 1806.]
Ext. Invisible Green (M'bone, T. 15/2/1848). L.C. 12/2/1848.
M.D. The Invisible Tribunal; or, The Guilty Son (Cob. M. 27/2/1826).
M.D. The Invisible Witness; or, The Gamester's Doom (S.W. M.
15/7/1839).
Ba. The Invitation; or, Better Late than Never (Surrey, M. 27/10/1823).
Ba. I. O. U.; or, An Old Way to Pay New Debts (R.P. W. 5/9/1832).
Ext. I. O. U. £7. 16s. 6d.; or, How to Pay Rent without Money (S.W.
M. 4/7/1831).
O. Iphigenia in Tauris (Prince's, Th. 9/7/1840).
[An English version of Goethe's Iphigenie auf Tauris.]
O. Ireland; or, The Rose of Kerry (Surrey, Th. 28/4/1831).
F. The Irish Baronet. L.C. H.² 27/5/1847.

F. The Irish Barrister (H.[2] M. 21/5/1838).
Ba. The Irish Crispin (Cob. M. 27/7/1818).
F. The Irish Gentleman (Vic. M. 13/10/1834).
M.D. The Irish Girl (Adel. Th. 9/9/1830). L.C. 9/9/1830.
C. The Irish Girl; or, The Blacksmith of Barnet. L. 23 L. [24/11/1819].
Ba. The Irish Heiress (City, M. 23/1/1832).
D. Irish Loyalty; or, The King in Dublin (R.A. T. 18/9/1821).
O.F. The Irishman in Italy (D.L. T. 15/6/1813).
Ba. The Irishman in Naples (R.A. M. 8/4/1822).
Ext. The Irishman in Windsor; or, John Bull and the Wet Quaker
     (Surrey, M. 10/4/1826; described as "a most popular comic
     entertainment").
Ba. The Irishman's Dream; or, "Am I Myself or Another?" L.C.
     Lyc. 1839.
M.Ent. An Irishman's Fortune; or, Paddy O'Rafferty (Tottenham-
     street, M. 6/9/1830).
     [Evidently the same play, as *The I. F.; or, The Adventures of
     P. O'R*, was given at the City, M. 22/8/1831.]
D. The Irishman's Home (R.A. 5/1833).
D. Irish Molly; or, The Primrose of Ireland. L.C. Britannia,
     15/9/1845.
Ba. The Irish Nigger; or, The Foreign Prince (Strand, M. 3/5/1841).
Ba. The Irish Poleander; or, The Lady and the Lawyer (Olym. M.
     27/10/1823). L. 130 M. [12/10/1823; as *The I. P.; or, Love and
     Loyalty*].
Bal. The Irish Reapers (R.A. M. 8/6/1818).
Ba. The Irish Widow. L. 81 S. [Olym. 25/10/1821].
C. The Irish Wife (C.G. S. 1/12/1832). L.C. 24/11/1832.
Ba. The Iron Chest; or, Murder Brought to Light (New, M. 25/2/1811).
M.D. The Iron Hand; or, The Dumb Carrier Boy and his Pony
     (Surrey, M. 18/10/1841).
D. Iron Heart (S.W. W. 27/1/1830).
M.D. The Iroquois; or, An Indian's Oath (Cob. Th. 13/11/1823).
M.D. The Iroquois; or, The Canadian Basket Maker (C.G. M.
     20/11/1820). L. 119 M. [14/11/1820].
     [An adaptation of O'Keeffe's *The Basket Maker*.]
D. Isabel Bertrand; or, The Wine Drinkers of Paris (Vic. M.
     10/8/1846). L.C. 1/7/1846.
D. Isabelle de Montral. L.C. C.G. 26/3/1834.
M.D. Isaure; or, The Alpine Maniac (R.P. Th. 14/2/1833).
D. Isaure; or, The Maniac of the Alps (City, Th. 10/5/1832).
F. Is He Alive? or, All Puzzled (D.L. M. 15/6/1818). L. 68 S.
     [12/6/1818]. 8° 1818.
Ba. Is He Jealous? (Surrey, M. 15/5/1820).
     [See *BEAZLEY*, 1816.]
D. Isidore and Merida; or, The Devil's Creek (D.L. Th. 29/11/1827).
     L.C. 26/11/1827.
     [Music Cooke and Braham.]
Spec. Is it a Wedding? or, Horns and Hounds (R.C. T. 9/9/1800).
F. Is it a Woman? (Vic. F. 27/9/1833).
M.D. The Island; or, Christian and his Comrades (S.W. M. 28/7/1823).
Ba. The Islanders (D.L. 4/6/1816).
Bal. The Island Nymph (D.L. Th. 12/2/1846).
     [Music Schira.]

M.D. The Island of Darkness; or, The Black Enchanter. L. 60 S.
[Olym. 13/3/1815].
F. Isn't it a Duck? (M'bone, M. 29/1/1849). L.C. 27/1/1849 [as
I. i. a D.? or, The Bird Fancier].
O. The Israelites in Egypt; or, The Passage of the Red Sea (C.G.
22/2/1833). L.C. 16/2/1833.
[Made out of Rossini's *Mosé* and Händel's *Israel in Egypt*.]
M.D. The Italian Boys; A Tale of Pisa (S.W. M. 22/4/1833).
Bal. The Italian Flower Girl (E.L. T. 7/1/1817).
Spec. The Italian Gamester; or, The Wife and Mistress. L. 92 M.
[Pav. 10/10/1810].
D. The Italian Husband. L. 56 S. [H.² 10/8/1812].
C.O. The Italians in Algiers (P'cess, 30/12/1844). L.C. 18/12/1844.
D. The Italian Sister; or, The Brigand of Albans. L.C. Adel.
21/10/1829.
M.D. The Italian Traitors; or, The Medician Brutus (Cob. M.
26/4/1830).
M.D. The Italian Wife. L. 65 S. [Olym. 28/11/1817].
[An altered version of *Fazio* by *H. H. MILMAN*.]
F. It's only my Aunt (M'bone, M. 14/5/1849). L.C. 18/5/1849.
D. Ivanhoe; or, Isaac of York. 8° 1820 [Birmingham].
M.D. Ivanhoe; or, The Jew of York (Cob. M 24/1/1820).
M.D. Ivanhoe; or, The Saxon Chief (Adel. M. 14/2/1820). L. 119 M.
[21/1/1820].
[These three plays are all adaptations of Sir Walter Scott's
romance.]
M.D. Ivan of the Mask; or, The Dumb Henchman of the Isles. L.C.
Edinburgh, 11/5/1826.
O.F. I've lost my Place (Olym. M. 30/9/1833). L.C. 26/9/1833 [as
I've left my Place; or, The Journey of Adventure].
M.D. Iwan; or, The Mines of Ischinski (Surrey, M. 22/9/1823).
Ba. I will have an Uncle (Olym. Th. 29/9/1836). L.C. 27/9/1836.
Ba. I wish you may get it (Olym. 1/10/1825). L.C. 1825.
Int. "I won't go!" or, A New Way to Keep a Place (Olym. M.
15/12/1823).
Ba. Jacintha; or, Like Master like Man (S.W. Th. 12/7/1821).
F. Jack and his Nine Wives (Surrey, M. 8/6/1840).
P. Jack and Jill; or, The Clown's Disasters (Lyc. Th. 30/7/1812).
L. 57 S. [26/7/1812].
Ba. Jack Grapplehard; or, Neptune's Love Messenger (Sans P. W.
29/8/1810).
P. Jack in the Box, And Harlequin and the Princess of the Hidden
Island; or, Heigho and Rum Go (D.L. 26/12/1829). L.C. D.L.
17/12/1829; another MS was in possession of R. Crompton Rhodes.
·Ba. Jack Junk; or, The Seaman's Fireside (Surrey, M. 3/1/1842;
R.A. M. 5/11/1849).
D.D. Jack of Paddington (M'bone, 4/3/1844). L.C. 1/3/1844.
P. Jack o' Lantern; or, Harlequin Sprite of the Dismal Swamp
(R.A. M. 30/6/1828).
D. Jack Ram; or, The Man and her Master. L.C. R.P. 8/4/1848.
D. Jack's Alive; or, The Jacobites in 1745 (Surrey, M. 27/3/1837).
Ba. Jack's Delight in his Lovely Nan (R.P. M. 12/10/1835).
D. Jack Sheppard. L.C. Hull 28/12/1839.
[A dramatisation of Ainsworth's novel.]

P. Jack Straw's Castle; or, Harlequin and Dame Durden (R.P. S. 26/12/1835).

P. Jack the Giant Killer (S.W. M. 11/4/1803).

P.Bal. Jack the Giant Killer (Lyc. M. 13/8/1810). L. 90 M. [1809].

Bsq. Jack the Giant Killer (Surrey, 13/2/1846). L.C. 11/2/1846.

D. Jacob Faithful. L.C. Edinburgh, 1/9/1841.
[This and the following play are dramatisations of Marryat's novel.]

D. Jacob Faithful; or, The Life of a Thames Waterman (Surrey, M. 8/12/1834).

Oa. James I of Scotland (Surrey, M. 7/8/1837).

T. James the Third, King of Scotland. 8° 1820.
[By the author of *Catherine de Medicis*.]

R.D. James Crichton of Clunie and Catherine de Medicis (Surrey, M. 7/5/1838).

Bal. Jamie of Aberdeen; or, Love in a Mist (Sans P. F. 20/1/1815).

D. Jane of Flanders; or, The Siege of Hennebonne. 8° 1801.
[Written by S. W.]

D. Jane Shore (Surrey, Th. 7/7/1833).

D. Jarvis the Honest Man; or, The Merchant's Daughter. L.C. Vic. 4/5/1846.

Ba. The Jealous Husband (St J. M. 22/4/1839). L.C. 15/4/1839.

F. Jeames the Railroad Footman of Berkeley Square (P'cess, W. 17/12/1845). L.C. 17/12/1845.

Ba. Jean de Paris. L.C. 19/5/1830.

D. Jeannette et Jeannot; or, The Conscript Bride. L.C. Vic. 17/4/1848.

D. Jeffery the Seaman; or, The Tar's Revenge (R.P. W. 21/4/1830).

D. Jeffreys; or, The Wife's Vengeance. L.C. S.W. 11/4/1846.

F. Jenny Lind; or, The Northern Star (Adel. 15/4/1847). L.C. 14/4/1847.

F. Jenny Lind at Last; or, The Swedish Nightingale (Lyc. W. 14/4/1847). L.C. 8/4/1847.

D. Jessie Holes; or, The Wild Herde of the Wolf's Lair (Vic. M. 16/2/1846).

Oa. Jessie the Flower of Dumblane; or, The Smugglers of the Glen (T.R. Edinburgh, 11/6/1834).

O. Jessonda (Prince's, Th. 18/6/1840).
[Libretto by E. Gehe; music Spohr. Vienna, 1825.]

M.D. The Jew and the German; or, The Devoted Daughter (Royalty, W. 9/10/1822).

M.D. The Jew and the Robbers; or, The Stage Overturned (Royalty, T. 18/12/1823).

D. The Jewess. L.C. Queen's, 1/4/1844.
[An adaptation of E. Scribe, *La Juive* (Paris, 23/2/1835) with music by Halévy. See also the following play.]

O.D. The Jewess; or, The Cardinal's Daughter (R.P. M. 23/11/1835).

M.D. The Jew of Cadiz (S.W. W. 11/9/1839).

Ba. The Jew of Canada (Cob. M. 9/11/1829).

D. The Jew of Frankford. L.C. Edinburgh, 1839.

Ext. Jim along Josey (Surrey, M. 2/11/1840).

F. Jinks the Gent (Surrey, M. 19/3/1849).

M.D. Joan of Arc (Westminster, Th. 17/5/1832).

M.D. Joan of Arc; or, The Maid of Orleans. L. 125 M. [Olym. 17/10/1822].

M.D. Joan of Arc, Maid of Orleans (Cob. T. 7/2/1826).
Ba. Job Fox, the Yankee Valet (E.O.H. 1/8/1836). L.C.
P.F. Jockey and Jenny (R.A. 29/12/1806).
Ba. The Jockey's Stratagem (R.A. T. 11/7/1843).
C.O. Joconde; or, The Adventurers. L. 68 S. [E.O.H. 7/7/1818].
F. Joe Miller; or, The Man of Few Words (City, M. 11/3/1833).
M.D. John Adams; or, The Mutineers of the High Seas (E.L. M. 30/9/1816—3rd performance).
D. John Anderson my Jo; or, The Fatal Marriage Morn (R.P. M. 27/5/1839).
F. John Brown (D.L. T. 21/2/1826). L.C. 1826.
Ba. John Brown; or, Bedlam Broke Loose (Cob. M. 6/10/1823).
Ba. John Bull in France (Surrey, W. 21/8/1811).
Ba. John Duddlestone, the Breeches Maker of Bristol; or, The Queen's Court (Surrey, Th. 13/7/1837).
F. John Gilpin. L. 104 M. [Norwich, 18/3/1815].
O.F. John Gilpin (D.L. M. 28/4/1817). L. 68 S. [21/4/1817].
Spec. Johnnie Armstrong; or, The Border Chief (Surrey, M. 13/5/1822).
Spec. Johnnie Armstrong; or, The British Captives (R.C. T. 4/10/1803).
Ext. Johnny Gilpin; or, The Calenderer's Horse (Royalty, T. 25/11/1823).
D. John of Leyden. L.C. C.L. 18/9/1849.
M.D. John of Lorne and Helen of Argyle; or, The Houses of Campbell and Maclean (Surrey, M. 31/5/1824).
F. A Joke's a Joke; or, Too much for Friendship (D.L. T. 4/5/1830). L.C. 26/4/1830.
D. Jonathan Bradford. L.C. 31/10/1835.
    [See *FITZBALL*, 1833.]
M.D. Jonathan Dobson, the Congress Trooper (Cob. M. 10/1/1831).
Ext. Jonny Gilpin; or, The Linen-draper's Tour (R.C. Th. 28/7/1808).
M.D. Joseph II; or, The Emperor and the Exile (Cob. M. 2/8/1830).
Ba. The Jovial Mourners (S.W. M. 4/4/1831).
Spec. Juan Fernandez; or, A British Seaman's Story (R.C. M. 1/6/1806).
Bal.P. Juan Fernandez; or, The Island Ape (Surrey, M. 18/7/1825).
Ext. Juan's Early Days (D.L. M. 18/2/1828). L.C. 16/2/1828.
    [Music Reeve.]
M.D. Juan the Libertine (Cob. M. 24/7/1820).
Pol. The Jubilee; or, John Bull in his Dotage. A Grand National Pantomime; as it was to have been acted By His Majesty's Subjects, on the Twenty-fifth of October, 1809. 8° 1809.
D. The Judgment of Brutus; or, Tarquin and Lucretia (Cob. M. 24/1/1820).
Ext. The Judgment of Paris (Strand, M. 23/4/1832).
Bsq. The Judgment of Paris; or, The Pas de Pippins (Adel. Th. 17/9/1846). L.C. 21/8/1846.
D. Julian. L.C. 21/1/1831.
D. Julie Ledru; or, The Goldsmith's Daughter (Surrey, 23/3/1846). L.C. 22/3/1846.
M.D. Julio of Harancour; or, The Deaf and Dumb Orphan (Cob. M. 3/5/1819).
M.D. Julius Caesar (E.L. M. 24/8/1818).
F. Jumbo Jim (R.P. W. 12/12/1838).
Ba. Justice and Quackery (Cob. M. 5/8/1822).

Spec. Justinio; or, The Bandit of Otranto (Cob. M. 30/10/1820).
— The Juvenile Dramatist; or, A Selection of Plays from the most celebrated German Writers upon Education. 8° 1801 [Hamburg].
  [A translation from J. Engel.]
D. Juvenile Friendship; or, The Holidays. 8° 1802.
Bal. The Kaleidoscope; or, Pay for Peeping (R.C. M. 8/6/1818).
M.D. Karackoo; or, The Sailor and his Dog (Vic. T. 27/5/1834).
M.D. Kasil Irmark (Cob. 9/1829).
Ba. Kate Carroway (Strand, 23/5/1842). L.C. 27/5/1842.
D. Kate Wynsley; or, The Two Wives of Clitheroe (Surrey, M. 12/2/1849).
D. Kathleen; or, The Bride of Munster (Britannia, 24/7/1848).
  [This seems to be the K.; or, The Maid of M. in L.C. 5/9/1844.]
D. Katitzka; or, The Siege of Dresden. L.C. Surrey, 29/3/1848.
Ba. Katty O'Shiel; or, The Follower of the Family (Vic. M. 25/10/1841).
C. Keep your own Secret. 8° 1807.
  [A translation from Calderon.]
C. Keep your Temper; or, Know Whom you Marry. L.C. D.L. 5/4/1829 [licence refused].
D. The Kelpie's Cave; or, The Highland Revenge (S.W. M. 19/7/1830).
D. Kenilworth. 8° 1824 [Edinburgh].
D. Kenilworth (D.L. M. 22/10/1832).
Bal. Kenilworth (C.G. S. 9/2/1833).
T. Kenilworth; or, The Days of Good Queen Bess (D.L. M. 5/1/1824).
D. Kenilworth; or, The Golden Days of England's Elizabeth (R.A. M. 8/3/1847).
D. Kenilworth; or, The Merry Days of Old England. 8° 1822 [Edinburgh].
M.D. Kenilworth (Caledonian, Edinburgh, 19/3/1825).
M.D. Kenilworth Castle (Olym. T. 27/2/1821). L. 80 S. [21/2/1821].
  [This and the preceding dramas are all derived from Scott's romance and each seems to have been a separate version.]
M.D. The Kentucky Rifle; or, The Horse and the Murderer (R.A. M. 23/4/1832).
Spec. Kerim the Pearl Diver; or, The Monster of Mysore and the Fiend of the Whirlpool (Britannia, 7/6/1847). L.C. 21/5/1847.
P. The Key of the Kingdom; or, Harlequin and the Fairy Bluebell (P'cess, F. 26/12/1845). L.C. 17/12/1845.
Ba. Killigrew; or, King Charles at Tunbridge Wells (Adel. M. 10/10/1825). L.C. 1825.
O.F. The Kind Impostor (D.L. T. 8/5/1821).
  [An adaptation of Cibber, She Wou'd and She Wou'd Not. Music Cooke and Horne.]
Ba. Kind Intentions (Adel. Th. 24/2/1831). L.C. 22/2/1831.
C. Kindred. 8° 1837.
  [An adaptation of Kotzebue, Die Verwandschaften.]
D. The King and his Crown (Surrey, M. 29/6/1835).
Ba. A King and No King; or, The Chancellor of the Exchequer. L. 82 S. [Olym. 4/4/1821].
Sk. The King and the Actor (Strand, M. 30/9/1833).
Ba. The King and the Cobler. L. 92 M. [Pav. 10/10/1810].
Ba. The King and the Freebooter; or, The Keep of Castle Hill (Surrey, M. 11/9/1837).

R.D. The King and the Piper (P'cess, T. 25/5/1847).
Sk. The King at Rheims (R.A. M. 20/6/1825).
P. King Bluebottle. L.C. Britannia, 21/12/1846.
M.D. King Charles II; or, The Battle of Worcester (Surrey, W. 7/8–S. 11/8/1821).
D. King Hal's Early Days (D.L. F. 31/3/1837). L.C. 18/3/1837 [as *The E. D. of K. Hal*].
O.F. King Henry VIII and the Cobbler (Pav. T. 27/10/1812).
P. King Jamie; or Harlequin and the Magic Fiddle (P'cess, W. 26/12/1849). L.C. 28/11/1849.
Ba. King John; or, The Origin of Horn Fair (Royalty, M. 2/6/1823).
T. King Lear (D.L. 24/4/1820).
    [A slightly altered version used by Kean; see Odell, *op. cit.* ii. 151–2. Another version appeared at D.L. on 10/2/1823; see *ib.* ii. 154–6.]
Bsq. King Lear and his Daughters Queer. 8° 1830.
    [By "Hugo Vamp."]
Ba. King Lear and his Three Daughters (Royalty, S. 24/10/1812).
Eccentric Scene. The King of Rome; or, Little Buonaparte and his Warhorse (R.A. M. 10/9/1827).
D. The King of Spain and his Barber (Surrey, W. 3/3/1812).
Ca. The King of the Brigands (P'cess, Th. 28/1/1847). L.C. 23/1/1847.
Ba. The King of the Danube and the Water Lily (Adel. M. 27/3/1837; R.P. M. 30/4/1838). L.C. 22/3/1837.
Ext. The King of the Hills; or, The Frog, the Tortoise and the Sapajou (Surrey, M. 4/6/1838).
C. King O'Neill; or, The Irish Brigade (H.² S. 11/5/1839).
C. King or Queen. L.C. Lyc. 9/3/1846.
Bsq. King, Queen and Knave; or, The Court of St. Mary Axe (Surrey, F. 15/5/1829).
D. King René's Daughter (H.² T. 18/12/1849). L.C. 16/12/1849.
Ba. King Richard III; or, The Battle of Bosworth Field (Royalty, S. 26/12/1812).
Bsq. King Richard III Travestie...with Annotations. 8° 1816.
Bsq. King Richard III. Travestie. A Burlesque, Operatic, Mock Terrific Tragedy. 8° 1823 [Duncombe].
Ba. The King's Coin; or, Home is Home After All (Surrey, M. 24/11/1823).
D. The King's Faith and the Fisher's Fealty (C.L. M. 11/12/1837; Vic. Th. 4/3/1841).
Ca. The King's Favourites. L.C. Adel. 2/12/1844.
Int. The King's Fireside (D.L. F. 17/12/1830). L.C. 11/12/1830.
F. The King's First Lesson (S.W. Th. 8/3/1849).
C. The King's Friend (S.W. W. 21/5/1845).
D. The King's Highway. L.C. D.L. 20/3/1843.
M.D. The King's Mistress; or, the Death of Jane Shore (Cob. M. 16/8/1824).
D. King Stephen; or the Wild Woman of the Fens (Surrey, M. 22/6/1835).
Ba. Kirkauld's Point; or, A Legend of the Thames (S.W. M. 15/7/1839).
C.O. The Kiss; or, Bertha's Bridal (Lyc. M. 13/6/1842). L.C. 18/5/1842.
Ba. Kiss and Be Friends (R.C. Th. 26/9/1816).

Bal. Kiss in the Ring (Sans P. M. 19/10/1818).
Vaud. The Kitchen; or, The Baker's Bride (S.W. M. 2/7/1832; Surrey, M. 17/8/1835).
Bsq. The Kitchen Sylph (Adel. M. 6/10/1834). L.C. 6/10/1834. [This is by *J. B. BUCKSTONE.*]
M.D. The Knight of Snowdoun (E.O.H. M. 14/7/1823). [See *MORTON*, 1811.]
D. The Knight of the Black Plume; or, The Fisherman's Hut (Surrey, M. 30/5/1814).
Ba. The Knight of the Boots; or, What will my Lady say? (Olym. 10/3/1817). L. 109 M. [2/1817].
Spec. The Knight of the Eagle Crest; or, The Journey of Love (R.A. T. 18/12/1849). L.C. 15/12/1849.
Spec. The Knights of St George; or, The Windsor Installation (R.A. M. 29/4/1805).
Bal. The Knights of the Garter; or, St. George's Day (R.C. M. 29/4/1805).
Spec. The Knights of the Sun; or, Love and Danger (R.A. T. 27/7/1802; Royalty, M. 18/2/1805).
M.D. The Knights of Villeroy; or, The Hermit of the Rock (Sans P. M. 17/3/1817).
Ba. Knobs and Noses; or, Gaul versus Lavater (Adel. 23/10/1820). L. 118 M. [20/10/1820].
M.D. The Kocuba; or, The Indian Pirate's Vessel (Surrey, M. 4/10/1824).
M.D. Kongo Kolo; or, Mandingo Warriors (R.A. Th. 28/2/1811). L. 92 M. [21/11/1810].
M.D. Korastikam Prince of Assassins; or, The Dreaded Harem (Cob. M. 7/5/1821).
Spec. The Koromantyns; or, Caesar and Clara (R.C. M. 19/9/1808).
Oa. Kosciusko (Prince's, W. 13/5/1840).
C. The Labyrinth Farm; or, The Fashionable Recluse. L. 21 L. [4/3/1812].
D. The Ladder across the Street; or, The Heir of Fernside. L.C. Surrey, 30/8/1848.
Ca. Ladies Beware; or, The Ultimatum (P'cess, S. 12/6/1847). L.C. 11/6/1847.
Ca. The Ladies' Matrimonial Club (Surrey, M. 15/6/1840).
D. The Lady and the Convict (Adel. 4/1/1841). L.C. 24/12/1840.
D. A Lady at Dover. L.C. P'cess, 17/4/1848.
Bsq. Lady Godiva and Peeping Tom of Coventry (P'cess, Th. 9/4/1846). L.C. 11/4/1846.
C.Spec. Lady Godiva and Peeping Tom of Coventry; or, Clearing the Toll (R.A. M. 31/7/1848). L.C. 10/7/1848.
Bal. Lady Henrietta; or, The Statute Fair (D.L. M. 15/4/1844).
Ba. A Lady in Difficulties. L.C. Olym. 13/11/1835. [See *PLANCHÉ*, 1849.]
F. The Lady Killer (Surrey, S. 15/10/1831).
Int. Lady Mary Wortley Montague; or, Courtship and Matrimony in 1712 (Lyc. M. 1/4/1839). L.C. 1839 [but marked as licence refused].
Bsq. The Lady of Lions; or, Clod, the Bellows Mender (Strand, M. 11/6/1838; Olym. Th. 22/7/1841). L.C. 8/6/1838.
D. The Lady of St. Tropez (Olym. Th. 1/1/1846). L.C. 15/2/1845.
D. The Lady of St. Tropez. L.C. Garrick, 5/2/1845.

O. The Lady of the Lake (C.G. T. 31/1/1843). L.C. 10/2/1843.
O. The Lady of the Lake and the Knight of Snowdoun (D.L. 4/1/1827). L.C. 4/1/1827.
M.D. The Lady of the Louvre; or, The Queen's Favourite (R.P. M. 11/11/1839).
Ba. The Lady of the Tower (Tottenham-street, 4/2/1811).
Ca. The Lady of the Willow; or, Wife with Two Heads. L.C. Vic. 14/4/1844.
Bsq. The Lady of the Wreck; or, Castle Blarneygig (S.W. M. 13/10/1817).
D. Laffarge; or, Self-will in Woman (Adel. Th. 29/10/1840).
M.D. The Lake of Lugano; or, Rathac the Fisherman (Cob. M. 7/5/1827).
D. Lalli Tollendal; or, The General and the Jesuit (Surrey, M. 25/2/1839).
P. The Lancashire Witches (New, Th. 27/12/1810).
M.D. The Landgrave's Leap; or, The Ancestors of Leopold (Cob. M. 8/11/1819).
D. Landlord and Tenant. L.C. R.P. 3/4/1847.
P. The Land of Enchantment; or, The Fiend of the Fated Valley and Harlequin of the Magic Horn. L.C. Apollo, 21/12/1846.
Spec. The Land Storm; or, The Sledge-Driver and his Dogs (Cob. M. 26/4/1819).
P. Langamo's Cave; or, Harlequin and the Queen of the Crystal Grot. L.C. Albert, 17/5/1844.
D. The Lapidary of Leyden (Surrey, M. 6/1/1840).
P. The Lapland Fairy; or, Harlequin's Exile (Pav. M. 9/11/1812).
D. The Larboard Fin; or, Twelve Months Since (Surrey, M. 17/4/1837).
B.O. The Lass of Gowrie (E.O.H. W. 11/9/1839). L.C. 7/9/1839.
F. The Last Act. 8° 1814.
Ba. A Last Day (Olym. W. 28/10/1840). L.C. 19/11/1840.
M.D. The Last Days of Napoleon Buonaparte at St. Helena (R.A. M. 28/4/1828).
M.D. The Last Guerilla Chief (E.O.H. Th. 6/7/1826). L.C. 13/6/1826. [Music M. Moss.]
M.D. The Last Key; or, The Dempster's Doom (R.P. M. 23/6/1834).
D. The Last Link of Love (M'bone, 24/3/1845). L.C. 24/3/1845.
D. The Last Mail (Surrey, M. 27/6/1836).
D. The Last Man (Olym. M. 10/11/1845).
Spec. The Last of the Barons; or, Warwick the King Maker and the Battle of Barnet (R.A. M. 10/11/1845). [A dramatisation of Lord Lytton's novel.]
D. The Last of the Murdakes (R.P. F. 17/9/1830).
M.D. The Last of the Romans; or, Rienzi the Patriot (R.P. F. 17/9/1830).
Ba. The Last Whistle (D.L. 6/5/1835). L.C. 9/5/1835. [A dramatisation of Burns' *Tam o' Shanter*.]
P. Laugh and Grow Fat; or, Harlequin Nutcracker (Olym. W. 26/12/1849). L.C. 18/12/1849 [as *Harlequin Jolly Nonsense*].
C. The Laughable Lover. 8° 1805. [By " Carol O'Caustic."]
P. Laugh and Lay Down; or, Harlequin King of Spades (R.A. M. 15/4/1805).

F.   The Laughing Hyena (H.² S. 3/11/1849). L.C. 26/10/1849.
Ba. Laugh when you can; or, Female Constancy (Surrey, S. 11/12/1813).
Sk. The Launch of the Good Ship William and the Royal Adelaide (Cob. M. 19/7/1830).
Bal. Laura et Linza; ou, le Troubadour (H.¹ Th. 8/5/1800).
Bal. Laurette (H.¹ T. 15/2/1803).
M.D. Laurette; or, The Lily of St. Clarens (S.W. T. 8/11/1831).
C.D. Lavater the Physiognomist and a Good Judge Too (H.² M. 27/3/1848). L.C. 25/3/1848.
Ba. Law, Latin and Love; or, All the World at Colchester (S.W. M. 16/2/1829).
       [See *Love, Law and Pugilism* (1824).]
Ba. The Law of Brahma; or, The Hindoo Widow (Adel. M. 1/10/1838). L.C. 28/9/1838.
D.   The Law of Russia (R.P. M. 25/5/1829).
D.   The Law of the Land; or, London in the Last Century (Surrey, M. 21/8/1837).
C.   The Law Suit. L. 105 M. [C.G. 27/11/1815].
Ext. Law versus Physic; or, The Clerkenwell Election (S.W. Th. 30/9/1830).
F.   Lawyers and their Clients; or, Love Suits (Edinburgh, 4/1/1815). L. 103 M. [19/12/1814].
F.   Laying a Ghost (H.² W. 15/11/1843). L.C. 7/11/1843.
Ba. Layo'ers for Meddlers (Cob. M. 3/11/1823).
       [On M. 15/3/1824 this appeared as *Sir Matthew Meddle and his Dog Turk; or, L. for M.*]
M.D. Lazaria the Greek; or, The Archon's Daughter (Cob. M. 24/11/1823).
M.D. Lazuli; or, The Demon of the Rock (Garrick, M. 3/10/1831).
Bal. Leander and Leonora (D.L. 16/2/1814).
Spec. The Learned Lions (Queen's, Th. 20/10/1831).
Ba. Leave the House; or, The Ghost's Advice (S.W. M. 3/11/1828).
Ba. Lefevre; or, The Lost Likeness (St J. S. 9/11/1839). L.C. 28/10/1839.
C.   The Legacy; or, A Thousand Pounds Reward. L. 84 M. [C.G. 6/1/1806].
       [This is *J. T. ALLINGHAM, The Romantic Lover.*]
P.   The Legacy; or, The Spendthrift (Pav. T. 23/1/1810).
F.   Legacy Hunting (Olym. W. 8/4/1840). L.C. 4/4/1840 [as *L. H.; or, An Uncle from India*].
F.   The Legal Friend. L.C. H.² 15/8/1845.
Ba. Legerdemain; or, The Conjuror's Wife (Strand, T. 30/8/1842; Surrey, M. 15/10/1849). L.C. 6/7/1842.
M.D. Leila, the Maid of the Alhambra; or, The Siege of Granada (S.W. M. 22/10/1838).
D.   Lekinda, the Sleepless Woman (Adel. M. 30/9/1833).
R.D. Lelia's Lamp; or, The Storm-Light of Anzasca (Surrey, M. 8/4/1833).
Ba. Lending your Name (R.P. M. 6/5/1833).
O.   Leocadea (D.L. S. 17/12/1825). L.C. 1825.
       [Music Auber arranged B. Livius.]
D.O. Leoline (P'cess, M. 16/16/1848). L.C. 22/9/1848.
       [Music Flotow.]

D.   Leoline; or, Life's Trials (Adel. M. 2/2/1846). L.C. 16/1/1846.
D.   Leontine. L.C. 24/5/1832.
D.   Leontine; or, Gerard the Pedlar. L.C. C.L. 11/3/1848.
D.   Leontine; or, Sixteen Years Since (Vic. M. 8/4/1844). L.C. 11/11/1843.
Ba.   A Lesson for Gentlemen; or, The City Wives (Strand, M. 1/4/1839). L.C. 4/10/1838.
P.C. A Lesson in Love (Queen's, M. 8/2/1836).
D.   A Lesson of Life; or, Three Ways of Living. L.C. C.L. 18/11/1848.
D.   Lessons of Life; or, The Lacemakers of Lisle. L.C. Surrey, 26/11/1844.
Ba.   The Liberal Candidate (P'cess, M. 16/1/1843). L.C. 7/5/1842.
Ba.   The Libertine Defeated; or, African Integrity (Cob. M. 24/10/1825).
M.D. The Libertine of Poland; or, The Colonel of Hussars (Cob. M. 11/10/1830).
P.   Liberty Hall; or, Harlequin Sportsman (Pav. S. 26/12/1807).
Ba.   Lie upon Lie; or, The Two Spanish Valets. L. 112 M. [Sans P. 26/10/1818].
D.   Life; or, The Drunkard's Children. L.C. Vic. 10/7/1848.
D.   The Life and Death of King Richard II; or, Wat Tyler and Jack Straw (R.A. M. 1/9/1834).
M.D. The Life and Death of King Richard III; or, The Battle of Bosworth Field (Surrey, T. 16/2/1813).
M.D. The Life and Reign of George III, the Father of his People (Cob. M. 30/8/1824).
P.   The Life, Death and Restoration of the High Mettled Racer; or, Harlequin on Horseback (R.A. M. 27/3/1815).
D.   The Lifeguardsman (P'cess, S. 17/11/1849).
D.   Life in America. L.C. 11/1836.
Ba.   Life in an Hotel; or, Dead, Buried and Up Again. L. 129 M. [Olym. 11/11/1823].
M.Ext. Life in Dublin (E.O.H. 5/9/1842). L.C. 3/9/1842.
D.   Life in London; or, The Day and Night Scenes of Tom and Jerry, in their Rambles and Sprees through the Metropolis (R.A. M. 17/9/1821).
Ext. Life in New York (Standard, 30/10/1848). L.C. 16/10/1848.
Ext. Life in Paris; or, Adventures of the Halibut Family (Cob. M. 8/4/1822).
D.   The Life of the Brave; or, Land and Wave (R.P. 27/5/1844). L.C. 11/5/1844.
D.   A Life on the Ocean Wave; or, A Tar Ashore and Afloat (Surrey, M. 26/11/1849). L.C. 21/11/1849.
D.   The Life Raft; or, The Two Reefers (Vic. M. 3/2/1845).
D.   Life's Luck; or, The Navvie's Wife. L.C. R.P. 17/4/1848.
D.   Light and Shade; or, The Seven Merry Maids of Marylebone. L.C. Britannia, 14/12/1848.
Ca.   The Light Dragoons (Lyc. M. 18/10/1847). L.C. 18/10/1847.
F.   The Light Troop of St. James's (H.² S. 20/3/1847). L.C. 18/3/1847.
F.   Like Father, Like Son. L. 76 M. [Norwich, 19/5/1801].
D.   The Likeness; or, The Maid of Brittany. L.C. Grecian, 7/7/1849.
R.D. Lilliput (D.L. W. 10/12/1817). L. 67 S. [2/12/1817].
Bal. Lilliputian Sports; or, Cupid's Frolic (R.A. M. 27/9/1802).
Spec. Lilliput Island (Pav. Th. 11/1/1810).

D. The Lilly of the Valley; or, The Dumb Boy of the Mill. L.C. Britannia, 23/9/1844.
Ba. Lindamira; or, The Tongue-tied Tragedian (R.A. M. 8/10/1821).
O. Linda of Chamouny (D.L. W. 12/1/1848).
Bal. Lindorf et Rosalie; ou, l'heureuse ruse (H.¹ Th. 27/5/1813).
M.D. Linishee Lovel; or, The Gipsy of Ashburnham Dell (S.W. M. 6/10/1828).
Ext. The Lion King (Vic. 6/1840).
Spec. The Lion King. L.C. E.O.H. 3/9/1842.
Spec. The Lion of the Desert; or, The French in Algiers (R.A. M. 22/6/1840; R.A. T. 10/9/1844).
Bsq. Lions for a Lark; or, The Beasts' Burletta (Adel. M. 5/11/1838).
D. Lisbeth of the Tyrol (Queen's, 10/2/1845). L.C. 12/2/1845.
Spec. Lisbon; or, Ruse de Guerre on the Banks of the Tagus (R.A. M. 7/1/1811).
Ba. Lisette. L.C. Olym. 29/1/1831.
D. Lisle Wilton; or, The Convict Steward (Vic. 20/8/1849). L.C. 10/8/1849.
D. The Lists of Ashby; or, The Conquests of Ivanhoe (R.A. M. 27/3/1837).
Ba. Little Aaron; or, The Honest Israelite (Sans P. Th. 10/5/1810).
Bal. The Little Captive (D.L. 18/12/1828).
D. The Little Corporal; or, The School of Brienne (D.L. M. 30/5/1831). L.C. 26/5/1831 [as *The L. C.; or, Buonaparte at the Military School of Brienne*].
D. Little Dawson; or, A Poor Girl's Story. L.C. Albert, 8/4/1847.
Ba. The Little Duke (E.O.H. T. 24/8/1841). L.C. 14/8/1841 [as *The Young D.*].
Bal. Little Goody Two Shoes (D.L. F. 27/2/1829). [Music R. Hughes.]
F. The Little Guardsman. L.C. P'cess, 13/11/1849.
Bal. The Little Hunchback (D.L. Th. 7/3/1839). [Music Eliason.]
Ba. The Little Innocent (Strand, M. 12/6/1843). L.C. 10/6/1843.
D. Little Joey; or, The Poacher and his Son. L.C. 21/6/1845.
M.Ent. The Little Laundress (E.O.H. M. 21/8/1837). L.C. 1837.
D. Little Ned; or, The Street-singer, the Sailor and the Noble (M'bone, 11/11/1844). L.C. 9/3/1844.
Ba. The Little Offspring (Olym. M. 2/10/1843).
P. The Little Old Woman and her Pig; or, Harlequin Pedlar and the Magic Petticoat (Adel. F. 24/12/1841). L.C. 22/12/1841.
C.Sk. The Little Pigs (D.L. 4/6/1830).
Tale of Enchantment. The Little Red Man; or, The Witch of the Water Snakes (S.W. 24/9/1832).
Bal. Little Red Riding Hood (Surrey, M. 6/1/1812).
P. Little Red Riding Hood; or, The Magician's Dream (New, Th. 14/3/1811).
D. The Little Strawbonnetmaker; or, The Old Horse Pistol (Standard, 26/11/1849). L.C. 20/11/1849.
P. Little Thumb and the Ogre; or, The Fairy Boots. L. 48 S. [C.G. 1/4/1807].
P. Little Tommy Tucker; or, Harlequin and Mother Red-cap (Queen's, F. 26/12/1845). L.C. 20/12/1845.

D. Liverpool in 1796; or, The Jew of Love Lane. L.C. Amphitheatre, Liverpool, 8/1812.
C. Living for Love. L.C. Olym. 17/1/1849.
R.D. The Loadstone of the Earth; or, Gian Ben Gian and the Elixir of Immortality (Surrey, M. 27/3/1837).
F. The Locksmith of London (Vic. M. 24/8/1846).
F. Lodgings for Single Gentlemen. L.C. D.L. 28/11/1828.
    [See *J. POOLE*, 1829.]
D. Lodovic the Corsican; or, The Vesper Bell (R.A. M. 17/4/1837).
D. Lolah; or, The Wreck Light (H.² M. 25/3/1844). L.C. 23/3/1844.
Ext. London; or, Highdays and Holydays from Tyburn to Whitechapel (Cob. M. 23/5/1825).
Ba. The London Actor; or, Four Score Years Ago (W.L. T. 13/1/1829).
F. London and Kensington (R.A. M. 22/4/1844).
C. London and the Country. L. 86 M. [C.G. 9/1/1807].
Spec. The London Apprentice; or, The Seven Towers of Constantinople (R.A. M. 3/6/1805).
D. The London Apprentice and the Woman of Pleasure (Royalty, Th. 26/12/1822).
    [An adaptation of Lillo's *George Barnwell*.]
D. The London Apprentices; or, Industry and Idleness (Cob. W. 26/12/1827).
Ba. The London Carrier (Adel. M. 28/9/1835; R.A. M. 23/4/1849). L.C. 23/9/1835 [as *The L. C.; or, The Poacher's Gun*].
Ba. The London Hermit; or, Rambles in Dorsetshire (Surrey, Th. 2/8/1810).
Int. The London Hermit (C.G. S. 7/12/1822).
F. The London Lady (S.W. M. 27/11/1848). L.C. 18/11/1848.
Ba. London Lions. L.C. Adel. 2/11/1838.
Ba. London Manners at a Country Mansion (Royalty, M. 31/3/1823).
F. London Stars; or, 'Twas Time to Counterfeit (C.G. S. 7/4/1821). L. 80 S. [3/4/1821].
D. A London Tradesman's Life; or, Fifteen Years of Prosperity and Adversity (R.P. M. 29/8/1831).
D. The Lone House on the Heath (R.A. M. 12/5/1834).
M.D. The Lone Hut of Limehouse Creek; or, The Sailor and the Miser (R.P. W. 3/10/1832).
D. The Lonely Lighthouse; or, The Prophet of the Rock (S.W. M. 15/6/1835).
D. Long Finn; or, The Treasure Seekers' Dream (Adel. 18/6/1833). L.C.
    [See *W. B. BERNARD*, 1832.]
R.D. The Long Rifle (Cob. M. 21/11/1831).
Ba. Look at Home (Olym. M. 30/9/1833). L.C. 26/9/1833.
    [See *EYRE*, 1812.]
Ba. Look before you Leap (Cob. Th. 15/8/1822).
O.F. Look before you Leap. L.C. C.G. 9/5/1829.
F. Loose Cash (Queen's, M. 24/7/1837).
M.D. Lord Byron in Athens; or, The Corsair's Isle (S.W. M. 6/2/1832).
Ba. Lord Mansfield's Wig; or, An Anecdote from the "Times" (Cob. M. 28/4/1823).
Ba. Lord Mayor's Day; or, The City Festival (R.P. Th. 11/11/1830).
    [Sub-title altered to *or, Cits and Sights* on M. 10/11/1834.]

D. The Lord Mayor's Fool; or, The Grand Secret; A Tale of 1642 (R.P. M. 29/9/1834).

D. The Lord Mayor's Fool of 1642 (R.A. M. 12/6/1837).

M.D. The Lord of the Castle (Sans P. M. 13/10/1817). L. 109 M. [7/10/1817].

M.D. The Lord of the Isles (Olym. M. 27/2/1815). L. 105 M. [18/2/1815].

M.D. The Lord of the Isles; or, The Gathering. L.C. C.G. 12/12/1835. [This is the play by *E. FITZBALL*.]

M.D. The Lord of the Maelstrom; or, The Elfin Sprite of the Norwegian Seas (Cob. M. 8/6/1829).

Ba. The Lord of the Manor. L.C. 25/1/1837.

D. Lord Ullin's Daughter; or, Love and Friendship. L.C. Glasgow, 24/8/1844.

T. Lorenzo. L. 82 S. [D.L. 10/2/1821]. [This is *J. HAYNES, Conscience*].

D. The Loss of the Alceste; or, The Sailors and the Malays (R.P. M. 23/7/1832).

Ext. Lost a Sovereign; or, Never Travel during a Revolution (Olym. M. 3/4/1848).

D. The Lost Child; or, A Villain Unmask'd (E.L. M. 7/12/1818).

D. The Lost Child; or, The Fisherman of the Lake (S.W. M. 26/8/1833).

Ca. The Lost Letter (P'cess, M. 6/2/1843; Strand, W. 15/3/1848).

D. The Lost Shilling. L.C. Surrey, 1/2/1844.

M.D. The Lost Son (Olym. T. 18/1/1831). L.C. 18/1/1831.

M.D. Louis Chaumont; or, Adventures in the Pyrenees (Cob. M. 15/9/1828).

Ba. Louise de Lignarolles; or, A Lesson for Husbands (Adel. M. 5/11/1838). L.C. 2/11/1838.

C.O. Love among the Roses; or, The Master Key (E.O.H. M. 1/7/1822). [Music Dr Kitchner.]

O.F. Love and Agility; or, The Fugitive Baron. L.C. C.G. 2/1/1830.

Ba. Love and Anatomy; or, The Skeleton Lover (Cob. M. 1/12/1828).

D. Love & Crime; or, The Mysteries of Paris. L.C. Albert, 3/1/1844.

C. Love and Impudence; or, The Fortune Hunters (H.² Th. 23/7/1812). L. 56 S. [15/7/1812].

C. Love and Jealousy. L.C. Olym. 18/4/1846.

Ba. Love and Laurel (Surrey, M. 30/3/1829).

Ba. Love and Leather; or, A Cobbler's Luck (R.P. M. 29/6/1835).

D. Love and Levity; or, The Lady's Revenge (Queen's, W. 1/4/1835).

M.D. Love and Madness; or, The Maniac of the Cave (Surrey, Th. 7/11/1811).

P. Love and Magic; or, Harlequin's Holiday (D.L. M. 27/12/1802). L. 42 S. [24/12/1802].

Ba. Love and Poverty (Olym. Th. 6/3/1817). L. 109 M. [13/2/1817; as *L. and P.; or, When Poverty comes in at the Door, Love flies out at the Window*].

Ba. Love and the Chase (Adel. M. 6/12/1819). L. 115 M. [10/12/1819].

Bal. Love and the Lancet (R.C. F. 26/12/1817).

M.D. Love and the Slave-Trade (S.W. M. 10/3/1828).

F. Love and the Toothache (C.G. F. 13/12/1816). L. 108 M. [7/12/1816].

Ba. Love a Bo-Peep; or, The Masqueraders (S.W. M. 29/6/1829).
F.   The Love Birds (Lyc. Th. 9/5/1844). L.C. 30/4/1844 [as *The
     L. B.; or, Birds of Paradise*].
Ba. Love, Debt and Fun. L.C. Adel. 26/1/1826.
Prel. Love in a Bag; or, The Flemish Tooth Drawer (Pav. M. 5/2/1810).
     L. 51 S. [16/1/1810].
Ba. Love in a Cottage (D.L. 28/6/1836).
Ba. Love in a Cottage (Olym. M. 28/9/1835). L.C. 23/9/1835.
O.   Love in Algiers. L.C. 11/3/1843.
Ba. Love in an Orchard (S.W. Th. 9/5–Th. 16/5/1805).
F.   Love in a Sack (H.¹ M. 22/4/1844). L.C. 26/3/1844.
O.F. Love in a Tub (D.L. 23/11/1808).
Ba. Love in a Village. L.C. St J. 21/1/1837.
F.   Love in Limbo (C.G. F. 31/3/1815). L. 104 M. [18/3/1815].
F.   Love in Livery (P'cess, M. 12/5/1845).
Ba. Love in the City (Sans P. Th. 4/3/1813).
Bal. Love in the Cupboard (Adel. W. 28/2/1821).
Bal. Love in the Grove; or, The Merry Lasses (Sans P. T. 1/2/1814).
Bal. Love in the Vintage (Sans P. T. 15/12/1815).
Ba. Love Laughs at Bailiffs (Adel. 9/1829).
C.   Love Laughs at Locksmiths. 8° 1803.
     [A translation of Bouilly, *Une Folie*.]
Ba. Love Laughs at Locksmiths (Regency, 11/1811).
F.   Love, Law and Pugilism; or, The Latin Scholar (S.W. M.
     14/6/1824).
     [See *Law, Latin and Love* (1829).]
Ba. Love Letters (Olym. M. 25/11/1822).
     [See *T. J. DIBDIN*, 1822.]
C.   Love makes an Irishman; or, The Double Disguise (Bath,
     3/5/1825). L.C. Bath, 21/4/1825.
Ba. Lovers on All Sides; or, Not such a Fool as he looks (Adel. F.
     7/1/1820). L. 120 M. [2/1/1820].
Ba. The Lover's Opera (Cob. Th. 25/11/1819).
F.   Love's Artifice (R.A. M. 7/5/1827).
C.   Love's Blind They Say. L.C. Strand, 7/11/1849.
Ext. Love's Contrivances (R.A. M. 18/4/1825).
F.   Love's Errors; or, The Child of Chance. L. 56 S. [H.² 18/6/1812].
D.   Love's Fetters. L.C. Lyc. 3/4/1847.
D.   Love's Frailties; or, Passion and Repentance (Surrey, W. 2/1/1828).
Oa. Love's Labyrinth. L. 117 M. [E.O.H. 17/8/1819].
C.O. Love's Mysteries. L. 52 S. [Lyc. 31/5/1810].
Ba. Loves of the Angels (City, M. 11/3/1833).
Bsq. The Loves of the Lions (S.W. T. 8/11/1831).
Ba. Loves of the Stars (Adel. M. 30/9/1833). L.C. 28/9/1833.
O.   The Love Spell (L'Elisir d'Amore) (Surrey, W. 29/5/1839).
Ba. The Love Spell; or, The Flirts of the Village (Olym. Th.
     27/10/1831). L.C. 22/10/1831.
O.   The Love Spell; or, The Mountebank of Ravenna (D.L. 24/6/1839).
     L.C. 20/6/1839.
M.D. Love's Perils; or, The Hermit of St. Kilda (R.C. M. 31/7/1809).
     L. 101 M. [Pav. 30/3/1813; this seems to be a revision of the
     earlier piece].
D.   Love's Pledge; or, A Sister's Sacrifice (Surrey, M. 19/9/1842).
Bal. Love's Puzzle (S.W. M. 28/7/1817).

D. Love's Rescue; or, The Last Hour (Queen's, 14/9/1846). L.C. 17/9/1846.
F. Love's Stratagem (Surrey, M. 20/1/1812).
C. Love's Telegraph (P'cess, W. 9/9/1846). L.C. 5/9/1846 [as *To be or not to be; or, L. T.*].
F. Love's Vagaries; or, How to Draw a Long Bow (Olym. M. 1/12/1823). L. 130 M. [28/11/1823].
D. Love's Victory; or, The Dead Woman's Secret. L.C. C.L. 5/5/1846.
D. The Loving Woman (H.[2] M. 12/12/1849). L.C. 2/12/1849.
M.D. Lowina of Tobolskoi; or, The Fatal Snow Storm (R.A. M. 30/6/1817).
Ba. The Lowland Romp; or, The Madcap (Sans P. Th. 27/12/1810). L. 91 M. [11/12/1810].
F. Lowther Arcade (Lyc. M. 24/3/1845). L.C. 22/3/1845.
D. Loyalty. L.C. Liverpool, 29/9/1845.
P. *£. S. D.*; or, Harlequin, Pounds, Shillings and Pence. L.C. Surrey, 2/12/1844.
Bal. Lubin and Laura; or, Love in a Cottage (Olym. Th. 4/12/1817).
F. Lubin Log's Journey to London; or, York, you are not wanted (Cob. M. 3/7/1820).
O. Lucia di Lammermoor (P'cess, Th. 19/1/1843).
R.D. Lucia di Lammermoor. L.C. Grecian, 5/11/1844.
M.D. Lucius Catiline, the Roman Traitor (Cob. M. 4/6/1827).
Ba. Luck in the Lottery (W.L. T. 13/1/1829).
F. Lucky Bob. L.C. H.[2] 7/7/1849.
P. The Lucky Horseshoe; or, Harlequin and the Princess of the Fairy Isle. L.C. Amphitheatre, Hull, 16/12/1846.
D.D. The Lucky Horseshoe; or, The Lone Chamber of the Silent Highway (Vic. M. 28/3/1842).
Bal. The Lucky Waterman; or, Tom of Chelsea Ferry (R.A. Th. 12/10/1820).
M.D. Lucrece Borgia; or, The Fiend of Ferrara (S.W. M. 29/4/1832).
Bal. Lucy Neal (Strand, M. 7/6/1847).
M.D. Ludolph the Fiend of Germany (R.A. T. 2/9/1823).
D. Luke Somerton (Adel. T. 19/1/1836). L.C. 13/1/1836.
C. The Lunatic Asylum; or, The Two Thompsons (Surrey, T. 13/11/1832).
Ba. Lundy. L.C. Bristol, 22/2/1840.
C.O. Lying made Easy (E.O.H. T. 1/8/1826). L.C. 24/7/1826. [Music Hawes.]
F. Lynn Wives; or, The Biters Bit. L.C. 8/5/1838.
O. Mabel; or, The Gipsy's Vengeance (C.G. S. 22/2/1840). L.C. 17/2/1840.
D. Mabel Connell (R.P. 8/9/1845). L.C. 6/9/1845.
D. Mabel Gray; or, The Eagle's Cliff. L.C. Surrey, 17/2/1844.
Bsq. Macbeth Travestie. 8° 1813 [in *Accepted Addresses*].
Bsq. Macbeth Travestie (Strand, 16/5/1842). L.C. 11/5/1842.
Int. The Mad Actor (Lyc. 8/6/1825).
C. Madame du Barry; or, A Glance at a Court (H.[2] T. 2/8/1831).
D. Madam Laffarge (Surrey, S. 25/12/1841). [See *Laffarge*, 1840.]
Ba. Mad as a March Hare (Cob. M. 14/8/1837).

D. Madelaine. L.C. H.² 7/10/1843.
Ba. Madeline. L.C. 30/12/1837.
M.D. The Mad Monarch; or, A House Besieged (Surrey, M. 20/10/1834).
Ba. Mad or Not Mad; or, The Balloon Agent. L.C. Norwich, 16/5/1837.
P. Maggie Lauder; or, Harlequin and the Wizard (Edinburgh, 26/12/1834).
D. Maggie Lawder. L.C. Britannia, 28/4/1845.
P. Magic and Fun; or, Harlequin and Oceanus (R.C. M. 22/5/1815).
P. The Magic Bell; or, Harlequin in the Haunted Hall (S.W. W. 26/12/1827).
P. The Magic Bowl; or, Harlequin Faggot-maker (Surrey, M. 15/9/1828).
Spec. The Magic Car; or, The Three Days' Trial (D.L. M. 23/4/1832). L.C. 12/4/1832.
    [Music Cooke.]
Oa. The Magic Fan (Vaux. 1832).
    [Music Bishop.]
P. The Magic Feast; or, Harlequin Renovated (Royalty, M. 3/12/1804).
O. The Magic Flute (C.G. M. 27/5/1833).
    [Mozart's *Die Zauberflöte*.]
D. The Magician (Olym. M. 14/8/1848). L.C. 10/8/1848.
P. The Magician of the Blazing Staff; or, Harlequin and the Fairy of the Wheatsheaf (R.P. T. 4/9/1832).
P. The Magician of the Ruby Mine; or, Harlequin and the Magic Amulet (S.W. M. 11/6/1832).
P. The Magicians; or, The Enchanted Bird (Sans P. S. 1/1/1814).
P. The Magic of British Liberty; or, The Disintegration of Bonaparte. L. 78 M. [York, 20/12/1803].
P. The Magic Pipe (Vic. F. 27/9/1833).
P. The Magic Pipe; or, Dancing Mad (Sans P. M. 3/12/1810).
P. The Magic Sword; or, Harlequin Warrior (R.C. M. 18/5/1807).
P. The Magic Urn (Pav. M. 30/10/1808).
P. The Magic Well; or, Harlequin Pointer (Royalty, M. 6/2/1804).
    [See *Harlequin Pointer*, 1801.]
P. The Magic World (R.A. M. 9/3/1807).
P. The Magic World; or, Harlequin's Restoration (Pav. M. 9/4/1810).
M.Ent. The Magistrate (Sans P. M. 15/2/1808).
D. Magna Charta; or, The Birthright of Britons (Vic. M. 6/1/1840).
D. Magna Charta; or, The Eventful Reign of King John (Cob. M. 28/4/1823).
M.D. The Maid and the Magpie (Surrey, T. 28/4/1846).
    [On the plays of this title see *ARNOLD, POCOCK* and *JAMES*. They are derived either from the opera, *La gazza ladra*, or from Caigniez, *La pie voleuse; ou, la servante de Palaiseau*.]
M.D. The Maiden of the Black Rock; or, The Deserter of Dresden (S.W. F. 26/12/1834).
M.D. The Maid Mariendorff (Perth, 18/4/1839).
M.D. The Maid of Canada; or, The Hag of the Rapids (S.W. W. 14/2/1838).
Ba. The Maid of Castile (Queen's, M. 19/1/1835).
D. The Maid of Grenada; or, The Tribunal of Death (R.P. M. 25/6/1832).

D. The Maid of Honour (Adel. M. 25/10/1841). L.C. 10/10/1841.
Ba. The Maid of Moffat Dale; or, The Inn of Glendery. L.C. Olym. 6/5/1825.
Spec. The Maid of Saragossa (R.A. M. 24/3/1845). L.C. 15/2/1845.
M.D. The Maid of the Forest; or, The Accusing Son (Cob. M. 5/5/1823).
M.D. The Maid of the Glen; or, Edwin and Rosalie. L. 52 S. [Pav. 7/3/1810].
T. The Maid of Warsaw (Strand, 14/9/1846). L.C. 21/8/1846.
Ba. Maids and Bachelors; or, Nettlewig Hall (Surrey, M. 16/2/1824).
C. Maids of Honour and the Night Demon (Surrey, M. 25/2/1839).
Ba. Maison à Vendre (Olym. S. 3/10/1840).
D. Maison Rouge; or, The Bouquet and Three Cards. L.C. Surrey, 13/2/1849.
C.O. Le maitre de chapelle (D.L. 12/7/1845). L.C. 21/6/1845.
   [Music F. Paer (Paris, 29/3/1821).]
C. Major and Minor (Queen's, Th. 21/5/1835).
Int. Major Domo. L.C. Queen's, 26/11/1844.
F. The Major's Daughter (P'cess, M. 15/10/1849).
M.D. Malak the Jew; or, The Bandits (S.W. M. 8/11/1830).
M.D. Malediction; or, The Deserted Priory (Cob. M. 18/1/1830).
M.D. Malak the Jew; or, The Bandits (S.W. M. 8/11/1830).
D. Malvoli; or, The Outlaw of Portugal (Surrey, M. 23/4/1849).
F. Mammon and Gammon (P'cess, T. 14/3/1848). L.C. 11/3/1848.
F. The Manager. L.C. 1/12/1834.
F. The Manager in Prosperity; or, The Actor's Comedy (Cob. M. 31/7/1820).
D. The Manager's Daughter. L.C. H.[2] 1837.
Bsq. The Man and the Monkey; or, Who Stole the Partridge (Olym. F. 24/11/1815). L. 104 M. [10/11/1815].
D. The Man and the Monster; or, The Fate of Frankenstein (Cob. M. 6/8/1827).
P. The Mandarin; or, Harlequin in China (R.A. M. 8/7/1811).
M.D. The Mandrill; or, The African Ape (R.P. M. 3/5/1830).
Spec. Manfred; or, The Castle of Otranto (R.A. M. 30/5/1803).
Ba. Manfred; or, The Mysterious Hermit. L.C. Olym. 14/8/1841.
Ba. Manfredi. L.C. 7/5/1834.
M.D. Manfredoni; or, The One-handed Monk (Cob. M. 19/3/1821).
F. The Man his Own Master (D.L. W. 12/6/1816). L. 64 S. [4/6/1816].
M.D. The Maniac; or, The Dark Assassin (Cob. M. 20/10/1823).
M.D. The Maniac Mother; or, The Forest Foundling (Olym. T. 18/2/1823).
M.D. The Maniac of the Sierra Morena; or, The Mountaineers (S.W. M. 6/9/1830).
O.F. The Man in Mourning for Himself (E.O.H. S. 20/7/1816). L. 107 M. [12/7/1816].
   [Music H. Smart and M. P. Corri.]
M.D. The Man in the Iron Mask; or, The Royal Twins (R.P. M. 30/1/1832).
P. The Man in the Moon (Strand, M. 27/12/1847).
P. The Man in the Moon; or, Harlequin Dog-star (D.L. T. 26/12/1826). L.C. 15/12/1826.
P. The Man in the Moon; or, The Magic Rose (R.C. W. 30/10/1816).
Ba. The Man in the Red Coat; or, The Duel (Cob. M. 11/5/1829).

Ba. The Man Milliner. L. 122 M. [Olym. 8/12/1821].
C. The Man of Business. L. 51 S. [Lyc. 8/12/1809].
D. The Man of Mile End; or, The Assassin of Stebonheath (now called Stepney) (R.P. M. 13/10/1834).
M.D. The Man of Mystery; or, The Fatal Precept (Surrey, M. 24/4/1826).
M.D. The Man of the Black Forest (S.W. M. 1/5/1820).
M.D. The Man of the Wood, the Fair Maniac and the Dumb Brother and Sister (R.A. M. 19/5/1823).
Ba. The Man of Two Thousand; or, An Hour before Marriage (Cob. M. 10/9/1821).
Ext. Manslaughter by Moonlight; or, The Friendly Friend; or, The Ghost of a Hamper of Wine (R.A. F. 20/9/1822).
C.O. The Man Trap (Strand, M. 26/11/1849). L.C. 16/11/1849.
F. A Man without a Head (P'cess, M. 13/10/1845). L.C. 29/9/1845 [as *A M. without a H.; or, The Pleasures of Memory*].
F. The Man with the Carpet Bag (Vic. M. 29/9/1834).
F. The Man with the Nose; or, A Cure for Love (Adel. 16/10/1837). L.C. 1837.
M.D. The Man-Wolf; or, The Loup-garcon of the Odenwald (Cob. M. 4/4/1831).
Bal. The Marble Maiden (D.L. S. 27/9/1845).
Ext. The Marble Maiden (Lyc. Th. 5/3/1846). L.C. 27/2/1846 [as *Playing at Marbles*].
Bal. Le marchand d'esclaves; ou, la fête au serail (H.¹ S. 20/3/1819).
M.D. The Marchioness de Brinvilliers; or, The Prisoner of the Seventeenth Century (Vic. M. 2/2/1846). L.C. 31/1/1846.
D. Margaret Catchpole. L.C. Garrick, 5/4/1845.
D. Margaret Catchpole, the Female Horse-stealer; or, The Life and Adventures of a Suffolk Girl (Vic. M. 24/3/1845). L.C. 22/3/1845.
M.D. Margaret of Anjou; or, The White and Red Roses, and the Robber Woodcutters of Hexham Forest (Cob. M. 21/1/1828).
D. Margaret of Regensburg. L.C. Norwich, 16/5/1837.
M.D. Margaret's Ghost; or, The Libertine's Ship (Vic. M. 14/10/1833).
M.D. Marguerite; or, The Deserted Mother (Cob. M. 18/6/1821).
M.D. Marie; or, The Manor House of Mont Louvier (S.W. M. 15/4/1839).
O. Marie, the Foundling of the Lake (P'cess, Th. 18/1/1849). L.C. 30/12/1848.
D. Marie, the Pearl of Chamouni (Surrey, M. 3/7/1843).
M.D. Marietta; or, The Hidden Treasure. L.C. Adel. 21/11/1843.
Ba. Mariette; or, The Maid of Switzerland (Surrey, M. 5/11/1821).
D. Mark Drummond; A Tale of the Past (Surrey, M. 3/9/1849).
D. Mark Fresland; or, The Citizen's Daughter (Olym. M. 21/2/1842).
D. Markham and Greenwood; or, The Brother's Career (Vic. M. 31/8/1846).
C. Mark the End On't. L. 86 M. [D.L. 9/5/1807].
D. Mark the Smuggler; or, The Coastguard of the Motherbank (Britannia, 19/3/1849). L.C. 14/3/1849.
R.D. Marmion; or, The Battle of Flodden Field (New, Th. 25/10/1810).
R.O. Marmion; or, The Battle of Flodden Field. L. 94 M. [Norwich, 24/3/1811]. 8° 1812 [Edinburgh].
Ba. Marplot in Spain. L. 121 M. [Adel. 7/11/1821].

C.R. The Marquis de Carabas; or, Puss in Boots (C.G. M. 30/3/1818). L. 113 M. [18/3/1818].
F. The Marriage Act (W.L. M. 30/9/1822).
Ba. Marriage and Murder; or, A Wife by Compulsion (Royalty, M. 9/12/1822).
F. The Marriage Certificate (P'cess, Th. 14/12/1843). L.C. 11/12/1843.
Bal. The Marriage Contract (R.A. T. 17/5/1803).
M.D. The Marriage Contract (S.W. Th. 27/4/1837).
Ba. The Marriage Contract. L.C. Olym. 18/2/1842.
Bal. The Marriage Day (R.C. M. 15/4/1805).
Bal. The Marriage Dowry (R.A. T. 22/7/1800).
C. Marriage in Miniature (Queen's, M. 9/11/1835).
C.O. The Marriage of Figaro. L.C. D.L. 9/2/1848.
Ba. The Marriage of Gamacho; or, All Correct (Cob. W. 12/8/1818).
F. The Marriage of Reason (H.² M. 4/3/1844). L.C. 1/3/1844 [as *Bertrand and Suzetta; or, The M. of R.*].
    [An adaptation of E. Scribe, *Le mariage de raison* (Paris, 10/10/1826).]
Bal. Mars et l'Amour (H.¹ S. 29/4/1815).
T. Martelli. 8° 1843.
D. Martha; or, A Mother's Crime. L.C. Norwich, 15/4/1824.
M.D. Martha the Gipsy (Surrey, M. 14/6/1824).
Ba. Martial Law (Fitzroy, T. 7/1/1834).
D. Martial Law; or, The Colonel and the Soldier (Cob. M. 6/5/1822).
D. Martin Faber; or, Who's the Murderer? (Vic. M. 11/3/1839).
M.D. Martin Rivers; or, The Emigrant Murderer (R.P. M. 29/6/1835).
D. Mary Campbell (M'bone, 10/11/1845).
D. Mary Clifford, the Foundling Apprentice Girl (Vic. 9/8/1841).
D. Mary Fenwick (Vic. 9/6/1845). L.C. 7/6/1845.
D. Mary Graham; or, A Tale of Sorrows. L.C. Vic. 3/1/1844.
D. Mary Lester (Standard, 3/11/1845).
D. Mary Lister; or, The Betrayed. L.C. R.P. 19/4/1844.
P. Mary, Mary Quite Contrary; or, Harlequin Leap-Year. L.C. Garrick, 17/12/1845.
T. Mary Stewart, Queen of Scots. 8° 1801 [Edinburgh].
T. Mary Stuart. 8° 1833.
    [This, as well as the majority of the "Mary Stuart" dramas, is a translation, or adaptation, of Schiller's play.]
M.D. Mary Stuart, Queen of Scotland (C.G. T. 14/12/1819). L. 116 M. [10/12/1819].
M.D. Mary Stuart, or, The Castle of Lochlevin (R.P. M. 21/1/1839).
Ba. Mary, the Maid of the Inn; or, The Bough of Yew (Sans P. W. 27/12/1809). L. 94 M. [11/1809].
M.D. Mary Tudor; or, The Tower of London in 1553 (Vic. M. 27/7/1835).
D. Mary White; or, The Murders of the Old Tabbard (Vic. M. 14/2/1842).
M.D. Marzovan, the Apostate (R.P. F. 3/9/1830).
Spec. Masaniello; or, The Revolt at Naples (R.A. M. 11/5/1829).
Bal. Masaniello; ou, le pecheur de Portici (H.¹ T. 24/3/1829).
    [Choruses in L.C. 25/3/1829.]
Spec. Masaniello, the Fisherman of Naples and Deliverer of his Country (Cob. M. 5/6/1826).

Ba. The Masked Battery (Strand, F. 26/12/1834).

Ba. The Masquerade; or, A Day in Spain (R.A. S. 10/6/1820).

M.D. The Massacre of Cyprus; or, The Grecian Amazon (Cob. M. 2/6/1823).

M.D. The Massacre of Rajahpoor; or, Britons in the East Indies (Cob. T. 21/2/1826).

F. The Mast and the Ploughshare; or, Britain's Best Bulwarks. L. 80 M. [C.G. 11/5/1804].

Oa. The Master Key. L. 123 M. [E.O.H. 3/8/1821].
    [This is *The Two Wives!*; see below.]

Ba. A Master's Rival; or, A Day in France (S.W. M. 9/5/1831).

Ba. The Master's Rival; or, Family Propensities (Vic. Th. 5/12/1833).

F. Match her who can! (H.² 31/10/1842). L.C. 26/10/1842.

F. Mathews and Co. (P'cess, M. 9/3/1846). L.C. 9/3/1846.

D. Matilda. 8° 1803.
    [By Eleanor H.; a translation from Mouvel.]

Ba. Mat Mizen and Tom Tiller; or, Sprees Alongshore (R.P. M. 14/1/1839).

Ba. Matrimony (Surrey, S. 22/8/1812).

Sk. Matteo Falconi (Fitzroy, T. 28/1/1834).

Ba. A Matter of Doubt; or, Seven Years Since (Adel. M. 6/10/1823). L. 130 M. [28/9/1823].

F. A Matter of Right. L.C. Adel. 2/4/1849.

Ba. Matthew Hopkins. L.C. 30/9/1829.

D. Maurice the Outcast; or, The Exile of Erin (R.P. M. 4/8/1834).

D. Maurice the Woodcutter; or, The Prince and the Peasant (S.W. F. 11/12/1835).

Ba. Maximums and Speciments of William Muggins; or, The Lights and Shadows of the World we live in (Strand, M. 16/5/1842). L.C. 11/5/1842.

P. May and December; or, Harlequin Fiddle-dee-dee! (Surrey, M. 8/6/1835).

M.D. May and December; or, My Old Woman (S.W. M. 25/6/1832).

D. May Marsden; or, Foul-weather Jack. L.C. Albert, 17/9/1846.

D. May Morning; or, The Mendicant Heir (Vic. 26/1/1850). L.C. 26/12/1849.

Ba. The Mayor and the Monkey (Adel. M. 26/3/1838). L.C. 26/3/1838.

Ba. The Mayor of Garratt. L.C. St J. 11/2/1837.

Ba. The Mayor of Garratt (Royalty, M. 3/12/1810).
    [Evidently a version of Foote's comedy.]

Ba. The May Queen (Olym. M. 13/3/1843).
    [A revival, with alterations, of the play by *J. B. BUCKSTONE.*]

Spec. Mazeppa; or, The Wild Horse of the Ukraine (Cob. M. 3/11/1823).

Ba. The Mazourka (Queen's, Th. 28/5/1835). L.C. 2/12/1835.

Ba. Medicus Borealis; or, A Day in Algiers. L. 108 M. [Glasgow, 25/1/1816].

F. Meet me by Moonlight; or, The Irish Astrologer (S.W. M. 27/3/1837).
    [See *T. PARRY* (Olym. M. 13/5/1839).]

M.D. Meg Merrilies; or, The Witch of Ellangowan (S.W. M. 7/5/1832).

T. The Melfi. L. 86 S. [C.G. 5/3/1823].
    [This is *M. R. MITFORD, Julian.*]

M.D. Melmoth the Wanderer, and Walburg the Victim (Cob. M. 14/7/1823).
F. The Melo-dramatist; or, Call me at Three (R.A. M. 4/10/1819).
Ba. The Memoirs of an Umbrella; or, The Silent Observer (Adel. M. 18/5/1846). L.C. 11/5/1846 [as *The Adventures of an U.*].
      [Music G. H. B. Rodwell, from whose tale this is taken.]
M.D. The Memoirs of the Duchess de Berri; or, The Carlists of La Vendée (Surrey, M. 6/10/1834).
Ba. Men and Women; or, Freaks of Love (S.W. M. 28/1/1828).
M.D. The Mendicant Murderer (Surrey, W. 14/4/1830).
Spec. The Merchant's Steed of Syracuse; or, The Flight of Damon (R.A. M. 20/4/1840).
P. Merlin's Cave; or, Harlequin's Masquerade (R.A. M. 11/4/1814).
P. The Mermaid; or, Harlequin-a-ground (R.C. M. 17/9/1804).
P. The Mermaid; or, Harlequin Oddfish (Cob. Th. 26/12/1822).
P. The Mermaid; or, Harlequin Fisherman (R.A. Th. 26/12/1822).
M.D. The Mermaiden's Well (Brunswick, M. 25/2/1828). [By *J. W. CALCRAFT*.]
Bal. The Merry Maidens (S.W. M. 26/9/1831).
D. Merry Terry; or, The Reefer's Wrongs (Vic. M. 18/10/1841).
O.F. The Merry Wives of Barbican (Queen's, M. 21/2/1831).
Ba. The Merry Wives of Madrid. L.C. Norwich, 8/6/1829.
Ba. The Merry Wives of Windsor (Royalty, M. 5/10/1812).
      [An adaptation of Shakespeare's play.]
D. Metamora; or, The Last of the Wampanoags (P'cess, W. 26/3/1845). L.C. 22/3/1845.
Ba. Methinks I see my Father (St J. F. 29/9/1837). L.C. 1837.
F. Methinks I see my Father. L.C. Lyc. 7/11/1849.
The Methodist. 8° 1823.
D. Michael and Christine (S.W. M. 2/1/1849).
      [An adaptation of E. Scribe, *Michel et Christine* (Paris, 3/12/1821).]
M.D. Michael Cange, the Porter of the Abbaye (Cob. M. 18/6/1832).
M.D. Michael Howe, the Terror of Van Dieman's Land (Cob. M. 23/4/1821).
Ba. Midas (Surrey, M. 15/10/1827).
Ba. The Middle Dish; or, Too Curious by Half. L. 105 M. [Olym. 7/12/1815].
D. Midnight; or, The Discovery (S.W. M. 6/2/1832).
M.D. The Midnight Attack; or, The Hut of La Vendée (Surrey, M. 12/7/1824).
P. The Midnight Bell; or, Harlequin Victim (R.A. M. 14/8/1809).
      [On M. 18/3/1811 this was performed at R.A. as *The M. B.; or, Harlequin Wanderer*. It appears in L. 95 M. [4/2/1811] as *The Last Hour; or, Harlequin Victim*.]
M.D. The Midnight Bell; or, Dunmerline Castle (Royalty, M. 28/6/1813).
M.D. The Midnight Murder (S.W. Th. 9/4/1835).
P. Midnight Revelry; or, Harlequin and Comus (Cob. M. 11/5/1818).
C. A Midsummer Night's Dream (D.L. 30/11/1833).
      [See Odell, *op. cit.* ii. 147.]
Ba. Miles's Boy (R.P. M. 16/2/1835).
F. Military Movements (Surrey, M. 3/8/1831; C.L. W. 21/6/1837).

F.   The Military Nurse; or, The Drummer and the Babies (Grecian, 7/8/1848). L.C. 10/8/1848.
C.   Military Promotion; or, The Young Colonel (H.² M. 10/7/1843). L.C. 8/7/1843 [as *M. Movements*].
D.   Military Punishment; or, The Fate of the Widow's Son (Surrey, M. 10/8/1846).
C.Ent. The Militia Muster (D.L. S. 17/11/1832). L.C. 19/11/1832.
Bal. The Millers; or, Revels by Moonlight (S.W. S. 1/5/1802).
Ba.   The Miller's Apprentice (Olym. T. 18/12/1821).
Bal. The Miller's Daughter (R.A. Th. 30/7/1818).
D.   The Miller's Dog. L.C. Albert, 10/8/1849.
Vaud. The Milliners (H.² S. 28/6/1828). L.C. 10/6/1828.
F.   The Milliners and the Lifeguardsmen (Surrey, M. 30/4/1849).
M.D. The Mill of Aldervon; or, The Unknown (Cob. M. 12/1/1829).
C.Int. The Mill of Bagdad; or, The Barber and the Olive Merchant (R.A. M. 7/7/1834).
D.   The Mill of Keben (Garrick, M. 7/2/1831).
M.D. The Mill of the Lake (Surrey, M. 4/6/1827).
M.D. The Mill of the Pyrenees (C.L. M. 16/10/1837).
R.O. Mina (P'cess, M. 3/12/1849). L.C. 28/11/1849.
Ba.   Mind your Letters (Olym. Th. 10/10/1833). L.C. 10/10/1833.
D.   The Mine Girl of Kebal; or, The Ransom of the Rose Diamond (Vic. M. 14/9/1846).
D.   The Minerali (E.O.H. M. 21/12/1835).
M.D. The Mines of Poland; or, The Castle of Minski (Royalty, M. 14/1/1822).
        [An adaptation from Pixérécourt.]
Ba.   The Miniature (St J. M. 31/10/1836).
D.   The Minister of Finance (S.W. M. 9/4/1849).
M.D. The Minstrel Boy; or, The Italian Wanderers (Cob. M. 29/6/1829).
O.   The Minstrel Maid. L. 124 M. [D.L. 22/11/1822].
        [This is *T. J. DIBDIN, A Tale of Other Times*.]
D.   The Minstrel of Lochmaben; or, The Winter Night. L.C. Edinburgh, 21/5/1827.
Spec. The Miracle; or, Afghai the Lion King (R.A. M. 14/10/1839).
D.   Miranda (R.P. 9/1/1844). L.C. 3/1/1844.
Spec. The Mirror of Fate; or, The Gnome of the Gold Mines. L.C. Albert, 20/3/1844.
M.D. Misanthropy and Repentance (Surrey, Th. 22/3/1821).
        [An adaptation of Kotzebue's drama; also called *The Recluse*.]
Ba.   Misapprehension (Olym. M. 31/1/1831). L.C. 26/1/1831.
Ba.   Mischievous Eyes (Olym. 1/10/1838). L.C. 24/9/1838.
C.   Misconception; or, The Mayor and the Three Coffins (City, T. 4/10/1831).
Ba.   The Miser of Madrid (S.W. F. 3/6/1831).
F.   The Miser Outwitted. L.C. Queen's, 13/5/1848.
D.   The Miser Reformed. L. 56 S. [Pav. 18/11/1812].
Ba.   The Miser Smoked; or, The Benefit of Hanging (S.W. M. 23/6/1823).
F.   The Misers of Smyrna; or, Mufti's Tomb (Sans P. Th. 8/3/1810).
D.   The Miser's Will (Lyc. M. 29/1/1844). L.C. 25/1/1844 [as *Dolph Heyliger; or, The M. W.*].

D. Miss Eliza Cook; or, The Felon Father and the Gipsey Child. L.C. Garrick, 5/9/1846.

Bsq. A Mission to Borneo; or, Sinbad the Sailor (Olym. M. 24/4/1848). L.C. 22/4/1848.

F. Miss Pop; or, Where is the Note? (Adel. T. 6/2/1827). L.C. 5/2/1827.

O.F. Miss Wright; or, Courting by Proxy (E.O.H. Th. 28/8/1828). L.C. 25/7/1826 [with titles reversed]. [Music Hawes.]

Ba. The Mistake; or, The G. G. (Royalty, M. 21/4/1823).

Ba. Mistake upon Mistake; or, The Irishman Bothered (S.W. M. 13/10/1828).

Ba. The Mistress of Arts. L.C. 6/10/1838.

F. The Model Couple (P'cess, 22/11/1848). L.C. 18/11/1848.

Oa. A Model of a Man (Adel. M. 12/11/1838). L.C. 8/11/1838.

D. Modern Bohemians; or, London Scamps. L.C. Britannia, 2/12/1843.

F. Modern Collegians; or, Over the Bridge (Cob. M. 9/10/1820).

D. The Modern Semiramide (Surrey, M. 23/1/1843).

Ba. Modern Travellers (Surrey, Th. 7/3/1822).

R.D. Modern Vittoria Bracciano; or, The Abbess of Santa Maria (Cob. M. 13/2/1832).

P. A Mogul Tale; or, Harlequin Wanderer (R.C. M. 3/6/1805). [See The Midnight Bell (1809).]

M.Ent. Moments of Mystery; or, The Widow Bewitched (City, M. 4/4/1831).

M.D. The Monastery; or, The White Maid of Avenel (S.W. Th. 20/4/1820).

M.D. The Money Diggers; or, The Devil's Ship and the Pirates of the Charmed Life (Cob. M. 20/4/1829).

C.P. Monkey Island; or, Harlequin and the Loadstone Rock (Lyc. S. 3/7/1824). L.C. 24/6/1824.

Ba. The Monkey that has seen the World (City, M. 10/10/1831).

O.F. Monks and Smugglers; or, Provision for the Convent (R.A. M. 4/9/1820).

M.D. The Monk's Cowl; or, The Child of Mystery (R.A. M. 14/9/1818).

D. Monomania; or, The Delusion (H.² F. 31/8/1838).

D. Monseigneur; or, Paris in 1720 (P'cess, M. 13/1/1845). L.C. 11/1/1845.

D. Monseigneur; or, Paris in 1720 (Vic. M. 20/1/1845).

Da. Monsieur Malbrouk. L.C. Olym. 17/12/1827.

M.D. Montalbert; or, The Black Tower (R.A. W. 11/10/1815).

R.D. Montaldi; or, The Black Banner (R.C. M. 29/6/1818).

T. Montalto (D.L. M. 8/1/1821). L. 81 S. [1/1821].

M.D. La Monte d'Or; or, The False Accusation (R.A. M. 16/6/1828).

D. Montrose (Glasgow, 1820).

D. Montrose (Caledonian, Edinburgh, 8/9/1827).

M.D. Montrose; or, Second Sight. L. 76 S.

D. Montrose; or, The Gathering of the Clans. 8° 1847 [Glasgow].

Spec. Mooltan and Googerat; or, The Conquest of the Sikhs (R.A. M. 28/5/1849). L.C. 18/5/1849.

D. The Moon Maiden (Surrey, M. 24/3/1845).

The Moon's Age; or, The Coroner's Inquest (Queen's, M. 26/1/1835).
C. Moonshine (H.² Th. 3/8/1843).
Spec. The Moorish Banditti; or, The Cave of Daroca (Pav. M. 1/2/1806).
[*Daroca* changed to *Plunder* at revival on M. 17/10/1808.]
D. The Moor of Toledo (Queen's, M. 15/2/1836).
Spec. The Moors of Spain; or, The Horse of the Arab Chief (S.W. M. 26/7/1841).
[This seems to be adapted from Pixérécourt, *Les Maures d'Espagne* (Paris, 9/5/1805).]
Spec. Morah, the Beast Tamer (R.A. M. 24/4/1848). L.C. 19/4/1848.
Bal. Mora's Love; or, The Enchanted Harp (H.¹ Th. 15/6/1809; C.G. Th. 4/12/1817).
F. More Ethiopians; or, Jenny Lind in New York (Grecian, 13/5/1847). L.C. 7/5/1847.
Ba. More Merry than Wise (Colosseum, M. 28/8/1837).
F. More Reform!; or, The Bill! the Whole Bill!! and Nothing but the Bill!!! (S.W. M. 23/5/1831).
Bal. More Sacks than One; or, The Miller Outwitted (Olym. M. 24/11/1817).
P. More Visitors in Town; or, The Devil's Ride to London (R.A. M. 30/7/1838).
Ba. More Ways than One; or, It's Well if it Takes (Adel. M. 29/11/1819). L. 115 M. [4/12/1819].
Ba. La Morgue; or, The Little French Doctor (Olym. M. 24/11/1828). L.C. 3/12/1827.
Int. Morilda's Wand; or, The Palace of Statues (Olym. Th. 13/12/1821). L. 120 M. [27/11/1821].
T. Moscow. 8° 1819.
D. The Mother and Daughters. 8° 1805 [in *The Theatrical Recorder*, vol. ii].
[A translation of *Les deux sœurs* by A. de St Léger de Colleville.]
D. Mother and Son (Adel. M. 30/9/1844). L.C. 23/9/1844.
P. Mother Bunch and the Yellow Dwarf (R.A. M. 30/3/1807).
D. Mother Red Cap; or, "Payable at Sight" (Surrey, Th. 23/10/1834).
P. Mother Red Cap; or, Harlequin and the Fairies of the Rose (Adel. M. 27/12/1824). L.C. 23/12/1824.
C. The Mothers. 8° 1805.
M.D. The Mother's Secret. L.C. Britannia, 17/8/1849.
P. Mother Whitecap; or, Hey up the Chimney (Sans P. Th. 2/3/1809).
M.D. The Mountain Bandit; or, The Dumb Girl of the Inn (S.W. T. 4/5/1824).
M.D. The Mountain Cataract; or, The Enchanted Spell (Surrey, M. 15/7/1844). L.C. 25/6/1844.
R.D. The Mountain Chief (D.L. Th. 30/4/1818). L. 70 S. [13/2/1818].
[Music Lanza.]
D. The Mountain Maid; or, The Beacon Tower (Surrey, M. 19/6/1837).
M.D. The Mountain Robbers; or, The Terrific Horn (D.L. 6/1806).
M.D. The Mountains of Modena; or, The Faithful Guide (Cob. M. 9/10/1826).
C.O. The Mountebank (German, Th. 26/12/1805).
Bsq.Bal. The Mount-ing Sylph (E.O.H. Th. 20/9/1838).

Bsq. The Mounting Sylph (S.W. T. 27/8/1839).
R.D. Mount St Bernard; or, The Goldsmith of Grenoble (Adel. M. 30/9/1839). L.C. 25/9/1839 [under sub-title only].
D. Mount St Bernard; or, The Headsman (Vic. T. 28/1/1834).
Ba. Mr and Mrs Grubb (Olym. 8/2/1840).
F. Mr Briggs; or, The Pleasures of Housekeeping and Horse-keeping (R.A. M. 12/11/1849). L.C. 5/11/1849.
Ba. Mr Busy (Adel. M. 3/12/1832).
D. Mr Midshipman Easy (Surrey, M. 26/9/1836).
Sk. Mr Paul Pry; or, I hope I don't intrude (Cob. M. 10/4/1826).
F. Mrs Bunbury's Spoons (Adel. M. 15/10/1849). L.C. 4/8/1849.
F. Mrs Caudle; or, Curtain Lectures (P'cess, M. 30/6/1845). L.C. 2/7/1845.
F. Mrs Caudle Abroad and at Home (Adel. M. 16/8/1845). L.C. 15/8/1845 [as *Mrs Caudle's Adventures in France*].
Ext. Mrs Caudle's Curtain Lectures. L.C. H.² 30/7/1845.
F. Mrs Gamp and Mrs Harris (Queen's, M. 16/11/1846).
C. Mrs H.; or, The White Horse (Cob. W. 26/12/1832).
Ext. Mrs Jane Shore (M'bone, 6/9/1845). L.C. 6/9/1845.
F. Mr Smith; or, Doings near Delgany. L.C. Bristol, 23/3/1831.
Bsq. Mrs Normer. L.C. Edinburgh, 21/9/1842.
F. Mrs Peaspod. L.C. R.P. 7/2/1846.
Ba. Mrs Trictrac (Colosseum, M. 14/8/1837).
Ba. Mrs Veal's Ghost (S.W. M. 18/8/1823).
F. Mr Timms. L.C. H.² 10/11/1842.
C. Mr Weller's Watch; or, The Time o' Day (Strand, M. 10/8/1840). L.C. 8/8/1840.
O. La muette de Portici (C.G. M. 23/6/1845).
Ext. The Mufti's Tomb; or, The Turkish Misers (R.A. M. 7/4/1828).
D. The Mule-driver and his Dogs (Albert, 20/4/1846). L.C. 18/4/1846.
M.D. The Muleteer's Vow (E.O.H. M. 19/10/1835). L.C. 19/10/1835.
Bal. Mulic the Slave (R.A. W. 19/5/1802).
Spec. Mungo Parke; or, The Arab of the Niger (Surrey, M. 29/6/1840).
D. Mungo Park; or, The Arab of the Niger. L.C. Liverpool and Manchester, 8/2/1841.
Spec. Mungo Park; or, The Source of the Nile (Cob. M. 21/6/1824).
Bal. Mungo Park; or, The Treacherous Guide (S.W. M. 3/5/1819).
D. Murat; or, The French Grenadier's Coat (R.A. T. 15/8/1843).
M.D. Murder and Madness; or, A Traveller's Tale (Surrey, M. 9/4/1825).
M.D. The Murdered Guest (D.L. W. 27/12/1826). L.C. 23/12/1826. [Music Horn.]
M.D. The Murdered Maid; or, The Clock Struck Four. L. 79 S. [Norwich, 25/4/1820].
M.D. The Murdered Monk; or, The Cavern of Calabria (S.W. M. 29/10/1827).
M.D. The Murderer; or, The Devoted Son (Surrey, M. 5/8/1822).
M.D. The Murderer. L. 130 M. [Edinburgh, 16/10/1823].
M.D. The Murderer's Dream; or, The Abbey of Glenthorn. L. 113 M. [Olym. 20/10/1818].
M.D. The Murderer's Dream; or, The Card Drawer (Cob. M. 29/3/1830).

M.D. The Murder of the Cliffs; or, The Smuggler's Dogs (S.W. M. 19/5/1834).
M.D. The Murder of the Courier of Naples (Cob. M. 20/5/1822).
D. The Murder of the Mount; or, Whitechapel in 1740 (R.P. M. 20/10/1834).
D. The Murders of the Round Tower Inn. L.C. 22/2/1830.
M.D. Murder will out. L. 101 M. [C.G. 19/9/1814].
F. Murphy's weather Almanac! or, Anno Domini 1838 (S.W. M. 19/2/1838).
Ba. The Muse and the Merchant (Olym. 18/3/1840). L.C. 17/3/1840.
Ba. Music hath Charms; or, The Ghost of an old Fiddle (S.W. T. 7/10/1823).
O. The Musician of Venice (St J. W. 17/1/1838). L.C. 23/12/1837.
Ba. Music Mad (Vaux. 8/1829).
Ba. The Musquetaire (R.P. M. 13/10/1834).
T. Mustapha. 8° 1814.
M.D. The Mutineer; or, The Rival Indians (R.A. M. 19/5/1817).
M.D. The Mutiny of Spithead and the Nore; or, British Sailors in 1797 (Cob. M. 16/8/1830).
        [See *JERROLD*, 1830.]
Spec. The Mutiny of the Britannia; or, The Perils of a Sailor (Royalty, M. 12/5/1823; R.P. M. 25/2/1833, with *Seaman* for *Sailor*).
Ba. My Absent Son; or, Brown Studies (Adel. M. 29/9/1828).
O.F. My Aunt (Lyc. T. 1/8/1815). L. 62 S. [25/7/1815].
        [Music Addison.]
F. My Best Friend; or, £277-7-7 (D.L. T. 23/1/1827). L.C. 23/1/1827.
Sk. My Country Cousin (D.L. 29/5/1827).
F. My Cousin the Minister (E.O.H. W. 7/8/1839). L.C. 6/8/1839.
Ba. My Eleventh Day (Olym. T. 28/2/1832).
F. "My Father did so before me" (Lyc. W. 25/10/1848). L.C. 3/11/1848.
F. My First and Last Courtship (Strand, M. 20/8/1849). L.C. 17/8/1849.
Ba. My Friend from Town (Queen's, 6/6/1831).
Oa. My Grandfather (E.O.H. M. 29/9/1834). L.C. 20/9/1834.
        [Music A. Lee.]
Ba. My Grandmother (Royalty, Th. 13/8/1812).
Ba. My Grandmother's Estate (Olym. W. 7/10/1840). L.C. 7/9/1840.
F. My Late Friend (H.² T. 18/8/1835). L.C. 4/8/1835.
Ba. My Little Brother. L.C. Adel. 23/9/1840.
F. My Lord. L. 83 S. [D.L. 30/3/1822].
C.O. "My Lord is not my Lord" (D.L. W. 29/1/1840). L.C. 15/1/1840.
        [Music Boieldieu.]
Ba. My Lord; or, The Warming Pan (Olym. M. 15/12/1843). L. 129 M. [8/12/1823].
Ba. My Lover (St J. M. 20/5/1839). L.C. 7/5/1839.
Ba. My Maiden Aunts (Lyc. 21/6/1842). L.C. 22/6/1842.
Ba. My Master's in Trouble (Queen's, F. 5/4/1839).
F. My New Boarding House; or, Five Hours in Brighton (R.P. M. 16/12/1839).
F. My Own Man (C.G. Th. 17/6/1824). L.C. 19/5/1824.

O.F. My Own Rival; or, Sophy, Lucy, and Lucy, Sophy (E.O.H. M. 28/6/1819). L. 114 M. [13/8/1818].
[Music Hart.]
C.O. My Own Twin Brother (E.O.H. T. 9/9/1834). L.C. 4/8/1834.
F. My Sister's Secret (P'cess, Th. 6/1/1848). L.C. 8/1/1848.
Ba. My Spouse and I (E.L. T. 13/8/1816).
Ba. Mysteries and Miseries; or, A Real John Bull (Royalty, M. 7/10/1822).
M.D. The Mysteries of Alviano; or, The Roman Catacombs (Cob. M. 19/1/1829).
D. The Mysteries of London (M'bone, 18/5/1846). L.C. 11/5/1846.
D. The Mysteries of Paris. L.C. Garrick, 28/8/1844.
D. The Mysteries of Paris; or, Fathers and Sons. L.C. Adel. 10/6/1844.
M.D. The Mysteries of the Cloister (W.L. M. 8/10/1821).
Spec. The Mysteries of the North; or, The Maid of Lochlin (R.A. Th. 11/10/1804—not first performance).
D. The Mysteries of the Wall; or, The Duel and the Valet (R.A. M. 20/4/1840).
Spec. The Mysterious Freebooter; or, The Days of Queen Bess (R.A. M. 14/4/1806).
M.D. The Mysterious Marriage; or, The Heir of Roselva (Surrey, M. 16/7/1821).
[This is the first performance of Harriet Lee's *The Mysterious Marriage*, printed in 1798.]
M.D. The Mysterious Stranger; or, The Cave of St Cataldo (Cob. T. 11/10/1825).
Ba. The Mysterious Tailor (R.A. M. 13/6/1831).
T. The Mystic Cavern; or, The Progress of Ambition. L. 79 M. [Norwich, 24/3/1803].
P. The Mystic Coffer; or, Harlequin the Swan Queen (Royalty, S. 26/12/1812).
P. The Mystic Tomb; or, Harlequin Restored (Surrey, Th. 7/10/1819).
C. Mystification (D.L. S. 7/4/1821). L. 81 S. [6/4/1821].
C. Mystification. L.C. E.O.H. 18/9/1826.
Ba. Mystification (Strand, Th. 26/1/1832).
F. My Two Nephews. L. 128 M. [C.G. 8/2/1823].
F. My Uncle. L. 93 M. [C.G. 30/11/1811].
Ba. My Uncle's House; or, The Bull and the Magpie (Olym. M. 2/1/1815). L. 101 M. [19/12/1814].
O.P. My Uncle's Parlour (amateurs at Sir James Knowles' house in Cornwall, 22/12/1807).
Ca. My Uncle's Pet. L.C. Olym. 18/10/1845.
[See under *T. ARCHER*, 1846.]
Ba. My Wife and Child (St J. M. 25/1/1836).
F. My Wife's Bedroom (C.G. Th. 2/10/1834). L.C. 30/9/1834.
[Later called *Bed and Board*.]
O.F. My Wife's Husband (Tottenham-street, F. 12/2/1830).
F. My Wife's Lodgings; or, Landed from China. L.C. Liverpool, 19/1/1844.
Bal. The Nabob; or, The Indian Lovers (Lyc. M. 10/7/1809).
O. Die Nachtigal und der Rabe; or, Damon and Phyllis (Surrey, Th. 8/5/1828).

O.   Das Nachtlager von Granada (D.L. W. 9/5/1849).
      [Music C. Kreutzer.]
F.   Der Nachtteufel; or, The Demon of the Night (H.² Th. 7/3/1844).
      L.C. 1/3/1844.
O.   Nadir Shah; or, The Sultan and the Soldier. L.C. E.O.H.
      21/7/1825.
D.   Naida; or, The Goddess of El Dorado (P'cess, Th. 10/2/1848).
      L.C. 9/2/1848.
Bal. La Naissance de Flore (H.¹ F. 14/4/1809).
Spec. Nameless; or, The Italian Brigand (R.A. M. 15/12/1845).
      [This is probably the same as *The Brigands of Ancona* (R.A.
      M. 8/12/1845).]
Ba.   The Namesakes; or, The Wife and the Widow (Queen's, Th.
      2/4/1835).
Ba.   Name the Winner (Olym. M. 10/11/1834). L.C. 31/10/1834.
D.   Nancy of Portsmouth (Surrey, M. 3/1/1831).
D.   Napoleon; or, The Victim of Ambition (Surrey, S. 21/5/1831).
      L.C. 21/12/1830.
Spec. Napoleon Bonaparte, General, Consul and Emperor (Cob. M.
      23/7/1821).
Ext.Spec. The Napoleon of Humble Life; or, Gipsy Jack (Cob. M.
      30/5/1831). [By *W. T. MONCRIEFF*: see p. 360 under *Gipsy
      Jack.*]
Spec. Napoleon's Glory; or, Wonders in St Helena. L.C. Adel.
      8/12/1840.
M.D. Narbonne Castle; or, The Mysterious Mother (Surrey, F.
      11/5/1821).
Ba.   The Narcotic; or, A Dose in Mistake (Cob. M. 17/5/1824).
O.   Natalie; ou, la laitière suisse (D.L. M. 16/6/1845).
Spec. National Gratitude; or, Nelson's Funeral (C.G. 15/5/1806).
      L. 47 S. [8/5/1806].
Ba.   Natural Magic (St J. Th. 26/10/1837). L.C. 1837.
Ba.   The Natural Son; or, The German Forest (Olym. T. 8/2/1814).
Ba.   Nature and Art (Vic. F. 29/5/1840).
Ba.   Nature will prevail (Surrey, M. 19/7/1824).
F.   Naughty Little Rose Pompon. L.C. Olym. 22/7/1847.
Bal. The Naval Victory and Triumph of Lord Nelson (H.¹ S.
      7/12/1805).
M.D. The Navigators. L. 68 S. [Edinburgh, 11/12/1818].
M.D. The Neapolitan Assassins (S.W. W. 26/12/1827).
Spec. The Neapolitan Pirate (R.A. W. 15/4/1807).
P.   The Necromancer; or, The Golden Key (Sans P. M. 11/12/1809).
D.   The Needle of Agony; or, The Persecuted Wife (Britannia,
      6/1849). L.C. 12/6/1848.
M.D. The Negro Murderer (R.A. M. 4/4/1831).
M.D. The Negro's Curse; or, The Foulah Son (Cob. F. 4/11/1825).
M.D. Nelson's Arrival in the Elysian Fields (German, S. 18/1/1806).
Ba.   Nelson's Monument. L.C. R.A. 26/10/1843.
Spec. Nelson's Ring. L.C. R.P. 12/10/1843.
      [A piece of this name appeared at the Standard on 10/2/1845.]
F.   Nephew and Niece (Adel. M. 26/2/1827). L.C. 13/1/1837.
Bsq. Nero, a Roman-tick Fiddler (Adel. M. 19/8/1833). L.C. 15/7/1833.
M.D. Neuha's Cave; or, The South Sea Mutineers (C.G. M. 4/4/1831).
      L.C. 18/3/1831.

Ba. The New Actress (Adel. M. 5/1/1835). L.C. 5/12/1834 [as *The N.A.; or, Poor Mr Potter*].
Ba. A New Don Juan (Adel. M. 11/2/1828). L.C. 8/2/1828.
Ba. "A New Farce"; or, A Scene of Confusion (Olym. M. 5/1/1835).
D.   Newgate Ned; or, The Prig of Pimlico (S.W. M. 30/6/1834).
Ba. The New Marriage Act; or, A Lesson for Lovers (Adel. M. 7/10/1822). 8° [1822]; L. 126 M. [30/9/1822].
F.   New Notions (H.² S. 21/7/1838). L.C. 21/7/1838.
F.   News from China (H.² Th. 7/9/1843). L.C. 6/9/1843.
F.   New Shoes ("Silk Shoes"); or, The Innocent Deception (German, W. 7/8/1805).
Ent. The Newspaper (Fitzroy, M. 3/3/1834).
F.   Newspaper Blunders; or, It's All a Mistake (Cob. M. 3/5/1824).
P.   The New World; or, Harlequin Re-animated (Royalty, M. 12/1/1801—not new; Royalty, M. 25/2/1805—revised version).
P.   The New Year's Gift; or, Harlequin Jack of Newbury (Surrey, 24/12/1830).
F.   Next Door (Lyc. Th. 2/10/1845). L.C. 25/9/1845.
Ba. Next-door Neighbours; or, A Matrimonial Noose (Surrey, M. 7/10/1822).
T.   The Nibelungen Treasure. 16° 1847.
     [A translation from the German of E. B. Raupach.]
M.D. Nicholas Mendoza (Cob. M. 7/12/1829).
D.   Nicholas Nickleby and Poor Smike; or, The Victim of the Yorkshire School (Strand, M. 20/5/1839). L.C. 17/5/1839.
D.   Nick of the Woods. L.C. Leeds, 31/10/1844.
D.   Nick of the Woods; or, The Dark Spirit of the Dismal Swamp (Edinburgh, 4/9/1841). L.C. 1/9/1841 [as *N. of the W.; or, Kentucky in* 1782].
     [*HAINES* had a drama of this title.]
Ba. The Night after the Battle; or, The Emperor and the Page (Cob. W. 8/10/1823).
Ba. The Night before the Wedding; or, Love in a Wheelbarrow (S.W. M. 14/5/1827).
Ba. The Night Errand. L.C. 7/2/1834.
R.D. The Night Hag; or, St Swithin's Chair (R.A. M. 11/9/1820).
C.O. The Nightingale (P'cess, M. 24/4/1848). L.C. 13/11/1847 [as *Phillis; or, The N.*].
O.   A Night in Granada (Prince's, W. 13/5/1840).
     [See *Nachtlager von Granada.*]
D.   A Night in the Bastile (D.L. Th. 5/12/1839—2nd performance).
D.   A Night in the Tower (Surrey, M. 22/1/1849).
Ba. A Night of Excitement (Vic. M. 26/1/1846).
F.   A Night of Horrors (Surrey, 11/11/1844). L.C. 31/10/1844.
Ba. A Night of Suspense (Strand, 21/8/1843). L.C. 16/8/1843.
C.   A Night's Adventures; or, The Road to Bath. 8° 1819 [printed, but not published, under the name of "Philo-Aristophanes"].
F.   A Night's Frolic; or, Once in a Hundred Years (Vic. M. 3/2/1845). L.C. 22/1/1845.
M.D. A Night with Punch (Strand, 23/10/1843). L.C. 18/10/1843.
Ba. Nina, the Bride of the Galley Slave (Adel. M. 26/3/1832). L.C. 10/1/1832.
C.O. Nina. L.C. E.O.H. 12/1/1837.
F.   1934; or, One Hundred Years Hence (Fitzroy, M. 5/5/1834).

Bal. Ninette à la cour (H.¹ Th. 5/6/1806).
D. The Ninth Hour (Lyc. Th. 15/7/1847). L.C. 8/7/1847 [as *From Nine till Ten*].
Bsq. The Ninth Statue; or, The Jewels of the Sun (H.² W. 26/12/1849). L.C. 21/12/1848.
R.D. The Ninth Statue; or, The Magic Mirror (Surrey, M. 24/6/1833).
Ba. Nipt in the Bud (Surrey, M. 14/6/1824).
Ba. No. L.C. Adel. 27/2/1829.
T. The Noble Heart; or, Love's Sacrifice. L.C. M'bone, 20/3/1848.
C.O. The Noble Outlaw (C.G. F. 7/4/1815).
D. The Noble Troubadour. L.C. Adel. 27/4/1840.
Ba. No Dinner Yet; or, Sponge out of Town (Adel. M. 10/2/1823). L. 130 M. [3/2/1823; as *Not Dined Yet; or, Sponge in the Country*].
Bal. Nologise, King of the Parthenes; or, The Triumph of Constancy (H.¹ M. 25/4/1803).
Ba. No, no (Surrey, T. 30/6/1846).
Oa. No Plot without Danger (E.O.H. S. 5/9/1835). L.C. 2/9/1835. [Music Mercadante.]
D. Norah; or, The Girl of Erin (C.G. W. 1/2/1826). L.C. 18/1/1826.
D. The Nore Light; or, The Smith of Sheerness (R.P. M. 9/6/1834).
D. The Norman Fiend; or, The Repentant Criminal (Cob. M. 23/10/1820).
Spec. The Northern Fleet; or, British Intrepidity Triumphant (R.C. W. 29/4/1801).
M.D. The North Pole; or, The Arctic Expedition (Cob. M. 22/6/1818).
P. The North West Passage; or, Harlequin Esquimaux (D.L. T. 26/12/1820). L. 24 L. [20/12/1820].
Ba. The Norwich Festival. L.C. 30/3/1837.
Ba. No Song, No Supper (Royalty, M. 10/8/1812).
B.O. "Not for me!"; or, The New Apple of Discord (E.O.H. S. 23/8/1828). L.C. 20/6/1828. [Music L. Maurer.]
Int. Not more than I want; or, That's Poz (S.W. M. 8/2/1830).
Ba. Nothing Like Luck (Cob. M. 19/4/1824).
F. Not Invited (S.W. W. 20/9/1820).
R.D. Noureddin and the Fair Persian; or, The "Bright Star of the Morn" (C.G. M. 27/3/1837). L.C. 23/3/1837.
Bal. Noureddin and the Tartar Robbers; or, The Rose of Balsora (Cob. M. 27/9/1819).
O. Nourjahad (E.O.H. S. 12/7/1834—public "undress" rehearsal; M. 21/7/1834). L.C. 12/7/1834. [Music E. J. Loder.]
Ca. Novel Effects. L.C. H.² 12/2/1846.
Ba. Novelty; or, New Scenes and Old Faces (Adel. Th. 29/9/1836). L.C. 20/9/1836.
F. Now or Never (D.L. T. 15/1/1839). L.C. 1839.
Bal. No Work! No Wedding! (Cob. Th. 26/2/1824).
M.D. The Noyades (Edinburgh, 24/1/1829).
M.D. Number One! or, The Hackney Coachman (City, T. 31/5/1831).
Ba. Number Two versus Number One; or, The Poppleton Court Plot at the Back of the 'Change (Cob. M. 4/2/1822).
D. The Nun; or, Marie de Rudney (Surrey, M. 20/4/1835). [This appeared later as *The Nun of the Black Convent; or, The Catacombs of St Agnes*.]

C.O. Il Nuovo Figaro (Lyc. T. 12/12/1837). L.C. 1837.
O.F. The Nursery Maid Mistress; or, The Butler in the Suds.
L. 96 M. [Pav. 24/11/1812].
Bal. The Nymph of Mount Helicon (Cob. M. 26/4/1819).
D. The Oath. L. 108 M. [Newcastle, 7/5/1816].
M.D. The Oath of Freedom; or, The Patriots of Poland (R.P. M.
15/8/1831).
O. Oberon. L.C. D.L. 16/4/1841.
Bsq. Oberon. L.C. Lyc. 21/8/1846.
M. Oberon and Robin Goodfellow (C.G. F. 12/10/1832).
[Inserted in Act 1 of *All's Well that Ends Well*.]
Ba. Oberon and the Charmed Horn (Surrey, M. 3/12/1832).
R.D. Oberon's Oath; or, The Paladin Princess (S.W. F. 3/10/1834).
M.D. An Occasional Attempt. L. 83 M. [D.L. 8/11/1805].
P. The Ocean Fiend; or, The Knights of Sicily (R.A. M.
25/8/1828).
M.D. The Ocean Fiend; or, The Wreck of the Raven (Cob. M.
13/11/1826).
D. The Ocean Grave; or, The Miner of Mexico (Surrey, M.
14/1/1833).
P. The Ocean Queen; or, Harlequin and the Enchanted Aloe (S.W.
M. 26/12/1831).
Ba. The Ocean Sylph; or, Davy Jones's Locker (R.A. M. 10/8/1840).
D. The Ocean Wolf (Strand, M. 25/10/1847).
P. O che bocconi! or, Harlequin's Vagaries (Royalty, M. 30/11/1801).
T. Octavia Bragaldi (Surrey, Th. 9/5/1844). L.C. 6/4/1844 [as *O. B.;
or, The Confession*].
Ba. Octavian; or, The Goatherd of the Mountain (Surrey, M.
9/1/1826).
Ba. Ocular Misfortunes; or, The Cadi's Flat (Surrey, T. 26/12/1837).
Ba. Odd Fish at Margate (Cob. M. 28/6/1824).
F. Odd Tricks and Rubbers (City, W. 27/6/1832).
Ext. The Odd Volume; or, There's Spirit in Punch (Surrey, M.
5/9/1831).
M.D. O'Donnell the Red; or, The Hibernian Hag and the Chief of
Kildare (Cob. M. 6/3/1826).
Ba. Of Age Tomorrow (Royalty, T. 8/9/1812).
[See *T. J. DIBDIN*, 1800.]
C. Off to the Continent (C.G. T. 20/1/1835).
[An altered version of Farquhar, *The Constant Couple*.]
C. The Old Bachelor; or, The Day after Tomorrow (Cob. M.
25/10/1830).
P. Old Beelzebub and Harlequin; or, Taffy in Holland (R.A. M.
30/3/1812).
P. Old Bogie; or, Lazy Dick of Leadenhall and Mother Leadenhall,
the Witch of Epping (Olym. Th. 26/12/1844). L.C. 23/12/1844
[as *O. B.; or, Mother Ludlam, the Witch of Epping*].
M.D. The Old Chateau; or, The Hackney Coachman of the Barrier
St Denis (Cob. M. 11/7/1831).
M.D. The Old English Baron (W.L. M. 12/3/1821; Cob. M. 12/6/1826).
Ca. The Old English Gentleman (Queen's, 2/8/1841).
P. Old Father Time; or, Harlequin and the Four Seasons (P'cess,
M. 27/12/1847). L.C. 13/12/1847 [as *Philip the Falconer; or,
H. and the F. S.*].

P. Old Harlequin's Fireside (D.L. W. 26/12/1804).

Bsq. The Old House at Home; or, A Night with Shakespeare. L.C. Adel. 6/9/1847.
[This is *J. S. COYNE, This House to be Sold.*]

M.D. The Old House on the Thames; or, Lambeth in the Olden Time (Surrey, M. 19/3/1849). L.C. 14/3/1849.

P. Old King Cole; or, Harlequin and the Fiddlers Three (Surrey, W. 28/12/1831).

Ext. Old London Bridge and New London Bridge (Cob. M. 1/8/1831).

Ba. Old Lovers and Young Lovers (Adel. S. 7/10/1826). L.C. 3/10/1826 [titles reversed].

M.D. The Old Man of the Mountains; or, The Castellan's Son (Cob. M. 27/3/1826).
[By *H. M. MILNER.*]

D. The Old Mint of Southwark (Surrey, 9/6/1845). L.C. 10/6/1845.

P. Old Mother Hubbard and her Dog (C.G. Th. 26/12/1833). L.C. 21/12/1833.

D. Old St Paul's; or, The Perils of the Plague (Queen's, 2/1841).

C. The Old School (H.² Th. 5/2/1846). L.C. 31/1/1846.

C. The Old Soldier; or, Which is Mine? L. 21 L. [Manchester, 10/1/1810].

D. Old Strike a Light; or, The Spectre of the Rising Sun. L.C. 4/3/1833.

D. The Old Swiss Church; or, The Black Robber of the Mountains. L.C. Britannia, 5/5/1849.

D. The Old Toll House; or, The Carrier and his Dog (Vic. M. 12/5/1845). L.C. 9/5/1845.

Bal. Old Turtles; or, Billing and Cooing (R.A. W. 6/10/1819).

D. The Old Willow Brook. L.C. Surrey, 14/8/1847.

P. The Old Witch of Teddington; or, Harlequin and the glorious Days of Good Queen Bess. L.C. Surrey, 31/10/1845.

P. The Old Woman Tossed up in a Blanket; or, Harlequin Arthur O'Bradley. L.C. C.L. 22/12/1847.

M.D. Olga the Dreaded Witch; or, A Caffre's Vengeance (Surrey, M. 21/11/1825).

Spec. The Olive Branch; or, The Ratification (Royalty, M. 2/11/1801).

M.D. Oliver Cromwell; or, The Days of the Commonwealth (R.P. M. 2/7/1832).

M.D. Oliver the Outlaw; or, The Old Family Legend (S.W. M. 6/10/1834).

Ba. Oliver Twist (St J. 27/3/1838). L.C. 26/3/1839.
[Based on Dickens' novel.]

M.D. Olivia; or, The Spanish Banditti (E.L. M. 14/12/1818).

Ba. The Olympic Forget-me-not. L.C. Olym. 1836.

Ba. The Olympic Pic-nic (Olym. S. 26/12/1835). L.C. 23/12/1835.

Ba. Omadhaun; or, Poor Dog Tray (S.W. T. 13/10/1835).

M.D. Omala; or, The Indian Sacrifice (Surrey, S. 6/6/1829).

F. Omnia vincit Amor (C.L. M. 10/4/1837).

Bal. Omnia vincit Amor; or, The Raw Recruits (Surrey, Th. 18/10/1810).

Sk. On Board the Mars; or, A Ball upon Deck (S.W. M. 12/4/1830).

Bal. Ondine; ou, la Naiad (H.¹ Th. 22/6/1843).

D. On Duty (Lyc. M. 7/4/1845).

Ba. One Bird in the Hand is worth Two in the Bush (H.² 5/1/1803).

C. One Fool makes many. 8° 1807.
    [A translation of De Solis, *Un Bobo hace ciento*.]
Ba. One Foot by Land and One Foot by Sea; or, The Tartars Tarter'd!
    L. 95 M. [Pav. 4/11/1811].
Int. 102; or, My Great-great-grandfather (Edinburgh, 28/11/1834).
Spec. One Hundred Battle Steeds; or, The Enchanted Arabs (R.A.
    M. 11/7/1836).
Ba. One Night at Margate (Surrey, Th. 20/11/1828).
P. One O'Clock; or, Harlequin Hardy Knute, the Knight and the
    Wood Demon (M'bone, T. 26/12/1848).
O.F. One, Two, Three, Four, Five, by Advertisement (E.O.H. S.
    17/7/1819; Bath, 21/5/1825). 8° 1819; L. 23 L. [13/7/1819; as *By
    Advertisement; or, The Immitator*].
Ext. Only Six Hours More; or, Love and Indiscretion (Surrey, M.
    23/5/1825).
F. The Opening Night; or, The Manager Hoax'd. L. 102 M.
    [Liverpool, 3/5/1814].
Ba. The Opera Buffers; or, The Dress Rehearsal (Surrey, M.
    5/11/1838).
D. The Opera Dancer. 8° 1805 [in *The Theatrical Recorder*].
Ba. Operamania; or, Music's the Language (Cob. M. 16/7/1821).
Ba. The Opiate; or, The Doctor, the Miser and the Butcher (Surrey,
    M. 9/8/1824).
Bal. Opposition; or, The Rival Dancing Masters (Adel. M. 9/10/1820).
F. O.P. Victorious; or, Who dare sneeze? 8° 1810.
P. Ora and the Red Woodman; or, The Charmed Rifle (R.P. M.
    1/7/1833).
P. The Oracle; or, Harlequin's Punishment (Royalty, M. 18/2/1805).
C.O. The Oracle; or, The Interrupted Sacrifice (Lyc. 7/8/1826).
    [An adaptation of Winter, *Das unterbrochene Opferfest*.]
Spec. The Oracle; or, The Olympic Conquest of Babylon (R.A. M.
    4/6/1838).
Ba. Orange Boven; or, The Embarcation for Holland (Surrey, S.
    11/12/1813).
P. Oranges and Lemons; or, Harlequin and the Bells of St Clements
    (Adel. F. 26/12/1834). L.C. 22/12/1834.
M.D. Ora, the African Slave (S.W. M. 19/4/1824).
F. The Organ of Order (H.² M. 24/6/1839). L.C. 23/6/1839.
Ca. The Origin of Painting. L.C. Adel. 21/8/1846.
Ba. Oroonoko, the Royal Slave (Surrey, T. 11/5/1813—2nd per-
    formance).
D. The Orphan Boy (Caledonian, Edinburgh, 24/12/1825).
D. The Orphan of Hindoostan; or, The Mine of Rubies (R.P. T.
    7/6/1831).
O. The Orphan of War. L.C. E.O.H. 27/8/1842.
M.D. The Orphan of Paris; or, The Duke's Mistress (Cob. M.
    5/9/1831).
M.D. The Orphan of Russia (Cob. M. 19/12/1831; Strand, S.
    24/3/1832).
M.D. The Orphan of the Alps (Cob. M. 31/3/1823).
M.D. The Orphan of the Pyrenees; or, The Sicilian Queen (Surrey,
    M. 2/8/1824).
M.D. The Orphans; or, Love and Jealousy (Royalty, M. 15/9/1823).
M.D. The Orphan Soldier (Cob. M. 9/7/1821).

D.   Osbert; or, The Son's Revenge. L.C. Hull, 12/12/1846.
R.D. Oscar the Bandit; or, The March of Crime (Adel. M. 20/10/1834).
     L.C. 21/10/1834.
R.D. Osric the Dane (Queen's, F. 26/12/1845).
M.D. Osric the Lion; or, The Saxon Outlaw (Royalty, M. 13/10/1823).
Bal. Ossian; ou, les bardes (H.¹ Th. 16/5/1805).
Spec. Oswald and Egberta; or, Virtue and Valour (Royalty, M.
     19/10/1801).
Bsq. Othello-Travestie...With Burlesque Notes. 8° 1813.
     [Under the pseudonym of "Ibef."]
O.   Othello. L.C. P'cess, 20/3/1844.
D.   The Othello of Private Life; or, The Curse of Jealousy. L.C. C.L.
     9/11/1849.
Ba. Our Beadle (Adel. 4/11/1839). L.C. 2/11/1839.
D.   Our Bottle; or, The Drunkard's Progress. L.C. Standard, 18/10/1847.
Ba. Our Cousin German; or, I did it for the best (Olym. M. 11/2/1839).
     L.C. 1839.
Bal. Our Dancing Days (D.L. W. 11/2/1801). 18/11/1847.
F.   Our Friend the Duke (Strand, Th. 23/11/1848).
Ba. Our Future Fate; or, Tom, Jerry and Logic in 1845 (Cob. M.
     15/12/1823).
F.   Our House; or, Lodgings in London (S.W. T. 1/2/1842).
Ba. Our Lady of the Willow (Vic. M. 24/6/1844).
F.   Our National Defences; or, The Cockshott Yeomanry (Adel. Th.
     27/1/1848). L.C. 28/1/1848.
Oa. Our Sisters (Lyc. 11/8/1834).
     [Music A. Lee.]
F.   Out-generalled; or, A Hint for Bachelors (Lyc. M. 30/9/1844).
     L.C. 23/9/1844.
D.   The Outlaws; or, The Cave of Glenmore. L.C. Albert, 28/4/1849.
M.D. The Outlaw's Oath; or, The Chieftains of the Glen (S.W. M.
     7/4/1828).
Ba. Out of his Element; or, The Cook in a Stew (Cob. M.
     23/1/1831).
F.   Out of Place (H.² M. 19/10/1840). L.C. 16/10/1840.
Sk. Out of Place; or, Flats and Sharps (R.A. M. 27/3/1826).
F.   Out of the Rain. L.C. Lyc. 25/11/1847.
Oa. The Outpost (C.G. Th. 17/5/1838). L.C. 7/5/1838.
F.   The Outside Passenger (H.² Th. 4/7/1811). L. 53 S. [26/6/1811].
R.D. Owen Ivan King of Manko; or, The Druid's Curse (R.P. M.
     29/4/1833).
T.   Owen, Prince of Powys; or, Welsh Feuds (D.L. M. 28/1/1822).
M.D. Paali; or, The Bride of Corsica (Surrey, M. 15/9/1823).
Ba. Paddy O'Rafferty (New, S. 12/1/1811).
F.   The Painter's Study; or, The Rival Valets (S.W. 2/8/1841).
Ba. Paired Off (Olym. M. 28/10/1833). L.C. 19/10/1833.
     [This is by J. PARRY.]
D.   The Palace of Geneva; or, The Spirit of the Vault (Vic. M.
     6/12/1841).
M.D. Pahdre na Mouhl; or, Peter of the Castle (R.P. M. 8/2/1830).
T.   Panthea, Queen of Susia. 8° 1809.
Bal. Panurge (H.¹ S. 19/2/1820).
Bal. Paphos assiégé lar les Scythes (H.¹ F. 18/6/1802).
D.   Paquita the Spanish Girl (Surrey, M. 17/4/1843).

F.   The Parish Beadle (S.W. M. 26/12/1831).
Bsq. The Parish Revolution (St J. M. 26/12/1836). L.C. 19/12/1836.
M.D. The Parricide; or, The Venetian Secret Tribunal (R.A. M. 14/10/1822).
O.   Le part du demon (C.G. F. 13/6/1845).
Bal. La partie de chasse d'Henri Quatre (H.¹ T. 27/2/1816).
O.   The Pasha's Bridal (E.O.H. Th. 8/9/1836). L.C. 2/9/1836.
Spec. The Passage of the Deserts; or, The French in Egypt and the Siege of Acre (R.A. M. 16/4/1838).
M.D. The Passions, Love and Jealousy (Surrey, M. 8/12/1823).
D.   Past and Present; or, What a Change! L.C. C.G. 3/1826.
Ba.   Past Four O'Clock; or, A Trip to Blackheath (Cob. M. 16/3/1829).
Past. Pastor Fido; or, The Faithful Shepherd. 8° 1809.
D.   The Pastor's Fireside (Surrey, F. 4/2/1831).
P.   Past, Present and Future. L.C. 1837.
Ba.   Past Ten O'Clock and a Rainy Night (E.L. M. 30/12/1816).
      [See *T. J. DIBDIN*, 1815.]
P.   Pat a Cake, Pat a Cake, Baker's Man; or, Harlequin and the Magic Cake. L.C. Queen's, 16/12/1843.
Ext. Pat and his Potatoes; or, The Abandoned Irishman (Adel. M. 30/4/1838). L.C. 28/4/1838.
Int.   Patent Seasons (Lyc. M. 21/8/1820). L. 119 M. [16/8/1820].
M.D. Paternal Affection; or, Welcome Home (Cob. M. 7/1/1828).
C.O. Patie and Roger; or, The Gentle Shepherd (H.² T. 10/11/1812).
Ba.   Pat in Portugal. L.C. 24/12/1837.
Ba.   Patrick's Dream. L.C. Olym. 23/11/1835.
Bal. Patrick's Return; or, Love Awake and the Guard Asleep (D.L W. 5/2/1817).
C.   Patrick the Foreigner; or, A Knight for a Day (Queen's, S. 26/12/1835).
D.   Le Patriot; or, A Bottle at Sea (Vic. M. 6/2/1837).
T.   The Patriot; or, Wallace. 12° 1806 [Edinburgh].
T.   The Patriot Prince. 8° 1809 [Calcutta].
O.D. The Patriots; or, The City Besieged (Surrey, M. 16/1/1826).
D.   Patronage (Olym. M. 16/10/1848). L.C. 16/10/1848.
D.   Patronage; or, The False Position. L.C. Surrey, 19/10/1849.
F.   Pat's Vagaries and the Road-side Inn (C.L. M. 31/3/1845).
Ba.   Paul and Virginia (New, M. 6/5/1811).
Bal. Paul and Virginia (C.G. Th. 5/11/1818).
M.D. Paul Clifford; or, The Highwayman of 1764 (S.W. M. 4/4/1836).
      [This may be Fitzball's play.]
Bal. Paul et Virginie (H.¹ S. 6/2/1819).
R.D. Pauline; or, The Phantom Lover. L.C. Ipswich, 10/8/1849.
      [See *RAFTER*, 1845.]
R.D. Paul Jones (S.W. Th. 30/8/1827).
      [See *T. J. DIBDIN*, 1827.]
Ext. Paul Pry on Horseback; or, A Peep at the Election (R.A. M. 15/5/1826).
D.D. Paul the Persecuted (R.P. 6/2/1845). L.C. 6/2/1845.
Ba.   Paul the Rich and Peter the Poor (R.A. M. 20/4/1829).
M.D. Paul the Rover; or, The Maniac Father and the Triumph of Love (Vic. M. 22/2/1841).
F.   The Pawnbroker's Sister; or, The Reprieved Man. L.C. 7/1825.
F.   Pay for Peeping (Strand, M. 18/6/1832; Fitzroy, M. 19/5/1834).

F.   Pay me; or, If you don't —— (P'cess, T. 11/7/1848). L.C.
29/6/1848 [as *Twenty Six Shillings; or, Pay me or if you don't* ——].
Ba. The Peacock and the Crow (Adel. M. 6/2/1837). L.C. 3/2/1837.
Equestrian D. The Pearl of the Harem (Surrey, W. 23/3/1842).
Ba. The Peasant Boy (Surrey, M. 26/10/1812).
     [See *DIMOND*, 1811.]
D.   The Peasant Bride (Olym. M. 17/4/1843).
C.   The Peasant Countess. L.C. Adel. 23/1/1843.
D.   The Peasant Judge (Surrey, M. 7/9/1840).
M.D. The Peasant Ruffian; or, The Rake's Progress (Cob. W. 1/4/1829).
Bal. The Peasant's Dream (Lyc. M. 23/8/1847).
P.Sk. The Peasant's Frolic; or, Harlequin and the Miller's Maid
     (S.W. M. 22/9/1823).
P.   Pease Porridge Hot, Pease Porridge Cold, Pease Porridge in the
     Pot nine Days Old; or, Harlequin Honeysuckle and the Demon of
     the Toadstool Fen. L.C. Bower, 14/12/1848.
D.   The Pedlar's Dream (R.P. T. 26/1/1836).
M.D. The Pedlar's Pack (S.W. M. 31/12/1832).
D.   Pedrillo; or, The Castle of Andalusia (St J. 9/2/1837). L.C.
     4/2/1837.
C.O. Pedrillo del Campo (Cob. M. 9/2/1829).
P.F. Pedro Lobo; or, Here He Is Again (Olym. S. 3/11/1821). L. 80 S.
     [25/10/1821].
C.   Pedro the Cruel and Manuel the Cobbler; or, The Corregidor of
     Seville (Surrey, M. 20/8/1838).
D.   Pedro the Devil; or, The Forest of Segovia (Cob. M. 13/9/1830).
C.   The Peer and the Secretary. L.C. Manchester, 5/3/1849.
D.   Peg Woffington; or, The State Secret (Adel. T. 24/6/1845). L.C.
     Adel. 10/6/1845.
P.   Pens, Ink and Paper; or, Harlequin I.O.U. Pothooks and Hangers.
     L.C. C.L. 15/12/1849.
D.   Percy's Masque. 12° 1819.
Ba. Peregrine Pickle; or, Hawser Trunnion on Horseback (R.A. M.
     27/4/1818).
F.   Perfection (Scarborough, 1839).
Bal. The Peri (D.L. S. 30/9/1843).
Spec. The Perilous Cavern; or, The Daring Brigands (R.A. M.
     6/9/1802).
D.   Perizzi; or, The Brigand, the Marchese and the Deserter (Vic. M.
     5/11/1838).
M.D. Perkin Warbeck; or, The Battle of Garra-muir (S.W. M.
     23/5/1836).
D.   The Permit; or, The Ganger's Daughter (S.W. M. 26/9/1831).
D.   Perouse; or, The Desolate Island (D.L. M. 6/4/1846).
C.   The Perplexed Husband. L. 53 S. [Lyc. 21/10/1811].
O.F. Perseverance (H.² M. 1/3/1802). L. 77 M. [12/2/1802; as *P.; or,
     He must have her*].
Ba. The Persian Ambassador and the Beautiful Circassian (Cob. M.
     26/4/1819).
P.   The Persian Festival; or, Harlequin Emperor (R.A. M. 31/8/1812).
O.   The Persian Hunters; or, The Rose of Gurgistan (E.O.H. W.
     13/8/1817). L. 65 S. [11/7/1817; as *Zodaiya; or, The R. of G.*].
     [Music Horn.]
D.   The Persian Prince and the Moorish Boy (C.G. T. 14/6/1836).

M.D. Peruvian Heroes; or, The Fate of Pizarro (Cob. T. 20/9/1825).
Bal. The Peruvian Lovers (D.L. T. 6/3/1827).
Ba. Peter Bell (Surrey, M. 8/2/1836).
F. Peter Jenkyns; or, Fibbing for a Friend (Lyc. M. 8/9/1845).
C. Peter Piper; or, Found out at home. L.C. H.² 9/5/1846.
F. Peter Priggins; or, Life in Oxford (Olym. M. 28/3/1842), L.C. 27/11/1841.
Ba. Peter Proteus; or, How to gain Five Thousand Pounds (R.P. T. 19/4/1831).
Sk. Peter Pry (Vic. 1821).
Int. Peter the Beauty; or, The Man for the Ladies (R.P. M. 10/9/1832)
M.D. Peter the Cruel; or, The Black Prince in Spain (Cob. M 11/5/1829).
M.D. Peter the Cruel; or, The Maid of Castile (Surrey, M. 18/1/1813).
M.D. Peter Wilkins; or, The Flying Indians (C.G. M. 16/4/1827). L.C. 9/3/1827.
D. La petite folle. L.C. D.L. 8/3/1825.
Bal. Les petites braconniers (H.¹ S. 28/1/1815).
Bsq.O. Les petites Danaïdes; ou, 99 victimes (H.¹ M. 18/7/1831).
M.D. Petraki Germano; or, Almanzar the Traitor (Cob. M. 1/12/1823).
Int. Petrarch and Laura. L.C. Liverpool, 11/12/1843.
Ba. The Petticoat Colonel; or, All Right at Last (City, M. 16/1/1832).
Ba. Petticoat Government. L.C. 27/2/1839.
    [See *DANCE*, 1832.]
D. Peveril of the Peak (Edinburgh, 12/4/1823). L. 128 M. [1/4/1823].
    [This is an altered version of the Surrey rendering of Scott's novel.]
M.D. The Phantom Voice; or, The Doomed One of the Hulk (S.W. W. 7/3/1838).
T. Philip. L.C. 4/5/1832.
M.D. Philip of Anjou; or, An Adventure in the Forest (Adel. M. 8/4/1833). L.C. 29/3/1833.
Ba. Philpot and Co. (S.W. M. 10/9/1827).
D. Phoebe Hersell; or, The Struggle of Seventy Years. L.C. Brighton, 19/11/1847.
D. The Physician's Wife. L.C. Garrick, 15/10/1845.
D. The Piccolomini's. 8° 1805.
    [A translation from Schiller.]
C.D. Pickwick; or, The Sayings and Doings of Sam Weller. L.C. Norwich, 8/5/1838.
Oa. The Picturesque (Adel. Th. 25/8/1831). L.C. 18/6/1830.
C. Pierre Bertrand (H.² Th. 14/12/1837). L.C. 12/12/1837.
M.D. Pierre Bonnard and his Poor Family (Cob. M. 13/1/1823).
Bal. Pietro il grande (H.¹ T. 12/12/1809).
F. The Pig and the Pepper-pot. L.C. Adel. 23/9/1844.
O. The Pilgrim. L. 106 M. [C.G. 26/3/1815].
Ba. A Pill for Portugals; or, William the Great and Miguel the Little (R.P. T. 7/6/1831).
O.F. A Pill for the Doctor (Surrey, M. 20/2/1826).
Ba. Les Pilule [*sic*] du Diable; or, The Devil's Pills (S.W. T. 2/7/1839).
Bsq. The Pilot; or, A Tale of the Thames (Adel. M. 6/12/1830). L.C. 25/11/1830.
    [This seems to have been a burlesque directed at *The Pilot*, then being given at C.G.]

P. The Pindar of Wakefield; or, Gog and Magog (R.A. M. 13/8/1810).
C.O. The Pirate of Genoa (E.O.H. F. 5/9/1828).
[An English version of Weigl's opera, *Gli amori marinari*.]
F. The Place Hunter (H.² T. 12/5/1840). L.C. 29/4/1840.
F. The Place Hunters (C.G. F. 12/2/1819). L. 74 S. [8/2/1819].
[On T. 16/2/1819 the title was altered to, *How to get a Place*.]
M.D. The Plague of Marseilles (Cob. M. 20/10/1828).
[This and the following play are versions of Pixérécourt's *La Peste de Marseille* (Paris, 2/8/1828).]
M.D. The Plague of Marseilles; or, The Horrors of 1720 (S.W. Th. 16/10/1828).
F. The Plague of Plymouth (Olym. M. 24/3/1845). L.C. 24/3/1845.
F. The Plaguy Good-natured Friend. L. 86 M. [C.G. 13/10/1807].
M.D. The Planter and his Dog; or, The Slave's Revenge (R.P. Th. 11/11/1830).
D. Sermon. The Pleasures of Anarchy. 8° 1809.
D. The Pledge; or, The Goldsmiths of Clerkenwell. L.C. Albert, 30/12/1847.
Ba. The Pledge of Love (Surrey, M. 25/9/1843).
M.D. Plots; or, The Portraits of Cervantes (Cob. M. 24/10/1831).
Ba. Plots in Madrid; or, The Painter's Study (Surrey, M. 19/4/1824).
P. The Plum Pudding Pantomime; or, Harlequin and the British Lion (Olym. M. 27/12/1847). L.C. 18/12/1847 [as *The B. L.; or, H. Panic and King Plum pudding*].
D. The Poacher and his Dog (E.O.H. M. 23/11/1835). L.C. 23/11/1835. [Music Hawes.]
Ba. Poachers and Petticoats (Strand, M. 20/6/1836).
Ba. The Pocket Book (Adel. F. 29/9/1837; Surrey, M. 16/3/1840). L.C. 1837 [as *The P. B.; or, The Two Families*].
F. Poetical Inventions (Queen's, M. 18/5/1835).
M.D. The Poisoned Goblet; or, The Knights of Castile (S.W. M. 17/10/1831).
D. The Poisoned Ring (Vic. M. 11/3/1839).
D. The Poisoner and his Victim (R.P. 17/2/1845). L.C. 15/2/1845.
P. The Poison Tree; or, Harlequin in Java (Sans P. M. 18/11/1811).
M.D. The Poison Tree; or, The Decree of Java (R.P. M. 31/1/1831).
P. The Polar Star. L.C. 24/12/1829.
Bal. Polichinel Vampire (Surrey, M. 4/8/1828).
Spec. The Polish Tyrant; or, The Woman of Ten Thousand (R.A. M. 4/8/1806; Royalty, M. 23/2/1807).
F. Polkamania (Lyc. M. 29/4/1844). L.C. 27/4/1844.
F. Polka, Polka, Polka; or, Who's to Teach? L.C. Vic. 2/5/1844.
M.D. Polly of Portsea and Joe the Marine (R.P. M. 4/7/1831).
Ext. Pong Wong (H.² W. 13/9/1826). L.C. 28/8/1826 [as *P. W.; or, The Horoscope*].
Ba. Poor and Content. L.C. 13/10/1836.
Ba. Poor Dog Tray (Vic. M. 7/4/1845).
Ba. The Poor Gentleman (Royalty, M. 16/11/1812; Cob. W. 26/10/1831).
[See *COLMAN*, 1801.]
D. The Poor Idiot; or, The Souterrain of Heidelburg (R.A. M. 8/10/1838).
B.O. Poor Jack; or, Tom Bowling's Will (Cob. M. 1/2/1830).
M.D. Poor Mary; or, The Maid of the Inn (Richmond, 24/6/1806).

O.F. Poor Relations (D.L. S. 25/2/1815). L. 22 L. [11/2/1815].
[Music Horn.]
C. Poor Relations. L. 69 S. [H.² 10/7/1818].
C. Poor Relations; or, Who's to inherit? (H.² M. 14/8/1826). L.C.
7/8/1826.
Ba. Poor Smike; or, Dotheboy's Hall (Vic. M. 20/5/1839).
[A version of Dickens' *Nicholas Nickelby*.]
O.F. Pop! or, Sparrow-shooting (Adel. T. 27/7/1830). L.C. 13/7/1830
[as *S.-s.; or, Goose Green*].
P. Pope Joan; or, Harlequin on Card Island (Cob. M. 19/4/1819).
Ba. Popolino; or, The Sleeping Draught (Vic. Th. 9/12/1841).
F. Popping the Question (D.L. T. 23/3/1830). L.C. 20/3/1830.
[See *BUCKSTONE*, 1846.]
Ba. Popping the Question (S.W. T. 18/5/1830).
[See *BUCKSTONE*, 1846.]
Ba. Popularity (Strand, M. 1/4/1839). L.C. 1839.
Ba. The Port Admiral; or, The Village Cobbler (R.A. M. 18/5/1835).
F. The Portraits; or, The Birth Day (S.W. M. 5/11/1838).
D. The Post Captain; or, Wife, Husband and Friend (Surrey, M.
10/9/1849).
D. The Post-chaise Companion (Vic. T. 17/11/1835).
M.D. The Post House; or, M. E. (R.A. W. 18/8/1819).
D. The Postillion; or, Storms by Sea and Land (Vic. M. 20/2/1837).
D. Poverty and Temptation. L.C. Vic. 19/11/1849.
Ba. P. Q.; or, Bachelor's Wives (Olym. 12/12/1832). L.C. 10/12/1832.
F. Practical Jokes; or, The Arrival of Redgauntlet. L.C. Bath,
18/8/1825.
Ext. Pranks of Puck with the Elfin King (in the Grasshoppers' Glade
by Moonlight) (Olym. M. 24/6/1844).
O. Preciosa; or, The Spanish Gipsy (C.G. Th. 28/4/1825) L.C.
2/4/1825.
[Music Weber.]
M.D. Preciosa, the Spanish Gipsy. L.C. E.O.II. 26/8/1824.
M.D. Predilection; or, The Two Drovers (R.P. M. 12/4/1830).
D. The Prediction (P'cess, M. 18/11/1844). L.C. 14/11/1844.
C. The Prescription; or, A Cure for Hysterics (H.² F. 7/6/1833).
L.C. 13/5/1833.
Int. The Pretty Girl of Dundee (Dundee, 1802).
Bal. The Pretty Sicilian (D.L. Th. 4/2/1847).
P. The Pretty White Mouse; or, Harlequin Robin Hood. L.C.
Standard, 15/11/1844.
M.D. The Pride of Kildare; or, The Dog of the Quarry. L.C.
Albert, 4/11/1844.
Aquatic D. The Prince; or, The Illuminated Lake (S.W. M.
30/3/1812).
Ba. The Prince and the Player; or, A Trifling Mistake (Adel. M.
6/10/1823). L. 130 M. [29/9/1823].
Ba. Prince Carouso. L.C. 18/11/1833.
Ext. Prince Dorus; or, The Romance of the Nose. 12° 1850 [Lacy].
Bal. Le prince et le jardinier (Sans P. T. 20/4/1813).
M.Romance. Prince Lee Boo (D.L. W. 30/10/1833). L.C. 28/10/1833.
[Music Lee.]
Spec. The Prince of Cyprus; or, The Horse of the Elements (R.A. M.
9/8/1847).

P. Princess Battledore and Harlequin Shuttlecock; or, The Island of Feathers. L.C. Birmingham, 30/11/1843.

Spec. The Princess who was changed into a Deer (D.L. M. 3/11/1845). L.C. 3/11/1845.
[Music R. Hughes.]

Bal. Le prince troubadour; ou, le double espreuve (H.[1] T. 21/2/1815).

Bsq. The Printer's Devil; or, A Type of the Old One (Adel. M. 26/3/1832). L.C. 27/3/1832.

F. The Prisoner (German, S. 21/9/1805).
[A version of Kotzebue's drama.]

C. The Prisoner (D.L. T. 8/2/1842).
[This may not be a new drama; it apparently does not appear in the L.C. collection.]

D. The Prisoner of France; or, The Fatal Brand (Surrey, M. 19/3/1849).

C.O. The Privateer (Lyc. M. 22/8/1812). L. 56 S. [16/8/1812].
[A version of Cumberland, *The Brothers*.]

Spec. The Prize; or, The Little Trader (R.A. M. 13/6/1801).

F. The Prize Wherry; or, The Sailor's Triumph (Cob. M. 9/10/1820).

F. The Problem Solved (Olym. M. 2/1/1843).

D. Procrastination; or, The Unready Gentleman. L.C. C.G. 2/3/1829.

M.D. The Prodigal (D.L. 29/4/1816). L. 63 S. [22/4/1816].

M.D. The Prodigal; or, The Horrors of Extravagance (Cob. M. 19/2/1827).

M.D. The Prodigal Son; or, The Rites of Memphis (Cob. M. 4/4/1825).

D. The Profligate (Olym. M. 29/1/1844). L.C. 25/1/1844.

M.D. The Profligates; or, The Horrors of Intemperance; being Fifteen Years' Life of a Gentleman, a Farmer and a Thief (R.P. Th. 25/6/1829).

D. The Progress of a Lawsuit; or, The Travels of a Sailor (Surrey, M. 31/5/1830).

M.D. The Progress of a Rake; or, Three Degrees of Crime (Cob. M. 4/3/1833).

M.D. The Progress of Vice (Cob. W. 23/4/1828).

Ext. The Projector (amateur performance at the Naval Academy, Cold Harbour, Gosport, 1803).

Oa. The Promissory Note (E.O.H. Th. 29/6/1820). L. 72 S. [24/7/1819]. 8° 1820.
[Music Bochsa.]

Bal.Ent. The Proof of Love (Lyc. S. 4/9/1813).

Ba. The Proof of the Pudding (Olym. W. 22/2/1832). L.C. 18/2/1832.

D. Proof Presumptive; or, The Abbey of San Marco (C.G. T. 20/10/1818). L. 71 S. [13/10/1818, as *P. P.; or, The Secret Marriage*].

P. The Prophecy (Royalty, M. 16/3/1801).

O. Le prophet (C.G. T. 24/7/1849).
[Libretto E. Scribe, music G. Meyerbeer (Paris, 16/4/1849).]

Ent. Proteus; or, Sketches of Character. L.C. 22/3/1833.

F. The Provisional Government (Olym. W. 12/7/1848). L.C. 10/7/1848.

D. The Provost of Bruges (Surrey, M. 9/6/1837).
[See *LOVELL*, 1836.]

M.D. The Provost of Paris (Vic. M. 2/10/1837).
[Also called *The Truant Chief*.]
M.D. Prussian Discipline. L. 67 S. [C.G. 24/9/1817].
[This is *W. ABBOTT, The Youthful Days of Frederick the Great*.]
P. Puck's Pantomime; or, Harlequin and Robinson Crusoe (D.L. T. 24/12/1844). L.C. 18/12/1844.
B. Pug; or, The Widow's Tears (Strand, M. 9/5/1836; E.O.H. T. 14/9/1841). L.C. 6/5/1836.
[Also called *A Widow in Tears*.]
P. Pull Devil, Pull Baker; or, Harlequin Spite and the Fairy Queen of the Sylvan Bowers. L.C. R.P. 15/12/1849.
C.O. Punch and Judy (Colosseum, W. 12/7/1837).
Ca. Punch in Italy (Strand, M. 2/7/1849). L.C. 30/6/1849.
Ext. Punchinello (Adel. M. 27/2/1843).
P. Punch's Festival; or, Harlequin's Christmas Box (Surrey, T. 24/12/1813).
P. Punch's Pantomime; or, Harlequin King John and Magna Charta (C.G. M. 26/12/1842). L.C. 21/12/1842.
Ba. The Pupil of da Vinci (St J. S. 30/11/1839).
O. I Puritani (P'cess, Th. 16/3/1843).
[An English version of Pepoli's opera (Paris, 25/1/1835), with music by Bellini.]
D. The Puritan's Plot; or, The Court of King Charles and the Cheateries of Mulled Sake (Surrey, M. 2/7/1838).
D. The Puritan's Sister. L.C. 25/5/1835.
M.D. The Purse of Almo; or, The Mendicant Monks (Vic. M. 6/10/1834).
P. Puss in Boots; or, Harlequin the Miller's Son (C.G.W. 26/12/1832). L.C. 18/12/1832 [as *H. and P. in B.*].
Ba. Puss! Puss!! Puss!!! or, Miss Metamorphoses (S.W. M. 29/10/1827).
Spec. Pyramus and Thisbe; or, The Unfortunate Lovers (R.A. M. 24/9/1804).
[Music M. Lawrence.]
D. Pyramus and Thisbe. L.C. 30/12/1831.
P. Q. in the Corner; or, Harlequin Schoolboy (Surrey, M. 23/4/1810).
Oa. The Quadrille; or, A Quarrel for what? (E.O.H. M. 14/6/1819). L. 114 M. [13/8/1818]. 8° 1819.
D. The Quadroon Slave (H.² T. 26/10/1841). L.C. H.² 19/10/1841.
Bsq. The Quadrupeds; or, The Manager's Last Kick (Lyc. Th. 18/7/1811). L. 53 S. [12/7/1811].
M.D. The Quarantine Ship. L.C. R.P. 24/3/1845.
Ba. A Quarter before Nine (E.O.H. Th. 27/7/1837). L.C. 15/7/1837.
Ba. Quarter Day; or, A New Way to Pay your Rent (Cob. M. 12/3/1821).
Ba. Quarter Day; or, Who Pays the Rent? (New, M. 15/4/1811).
Int. The Quarter Deck; or, Saturday Night (C.G. M. 13/5/1814).
Oa. The Quartette; or, Interrupted Harmony (E.O.H. Th. 18/9/1828). L.C. 17/9/1828.
Int. Quavers and Capers (D.L. 3/6/1817).
[A version of Fielding, *The Virgin Unmasked*.]
Oa. The Queen and the Cardinal (E.O.H. M. 30/5/1836). L.C. 27/5/1836.
P. The Queen Bee; or, Harlequin and Goody Two Shoes (Surrey, Th. 26/12/1839).

D. Queen Catherine and Cardinal Wolsey; or, The Life of King Henry VIII (Cob. M. 28/1/1828).
Pag. The Queen! God bless her! (R.A. M. 4/6/1838).
D. Queen Mary; or, The Tower of London (Adel. M. 30/11/1840).
Ba. The Queen of Hearts; or, The Card Party. L.C. 25/9/1833.
D. The Queen of Poland; or, The Hunters of Moldavia. L.C. Vic. 24/4/1847.
Spec. The Queen of the Abruzzi (Adel. M. 8/6/1846). L.C. 10/6/1846. [Attributed to *J. S. COYNE*.]
P. The Queen of the Butterfly Tower; or, Harlequin and Old Bogie (R.P. F. 26/12/1828).
P. The Queen of the Clover Field; or, Harlequin and "One, Two, Buckle my Shoe" (R.P. Th. 26/12/1833).
D. The Queen's Command (E.O.H. S. 14/7/1838). L.C. 9/7/1838.
D. The Queen's Lover (Kensington, 1834).
D. Quentin Durward (Caledonian, Edinburgh, 23/6/1823). [This seems to have been a distinct version of Scott's novel.]
R.D. The Questor's Steed; or, The Prophet of the Caucasus (R.A. M. 12/4/1841).
Ba. Quite Out of the Common; or, Little and Good. L.C. E.O.H. 26/7/1832.
F. Quits; or, War versus Law (C.G. M. 30/10/1843). L.C. 26/10/1843.
P. Quixotte and Sancho; or, Harlequin Warrior (R.A. M. 2/6/1800).
Ba. Quoniam. L.C. 10/2/1831.
D. Raby Rattler; or, The Progress of a Scamp (Surrey, W. 3/2/1847). L.C. 23/1/1847.
F. A Race for a Dinner (S.W. F. 19/7/1844).
Prel. A Race for a Rarity; or, The Bayaderes (Adel. M. 1/10/1838). L.C. 25/9/1838.
F. A Race for a Wife (C.G. F. 20/10/1820). L. 118 M. [9/10/1820].
Ba. A Race for a Wife; or, Win her and wear her (Olym. 21/11/1823). L. 24 L. [4/11/1823; titles reversed].
Fa. A Race to Hampstead (S.W. M. 22/6/1840).
F. The Racket Court (S.W. 19/7/1841).
D. Rafael the Libertine (Surrey, M. 8/10/1838).
F. The Railroad for Ever; or, How to get rich (H.[2] T. 10/5/1836).
F. Railway Bubbles (H.[2] S. 29/11/1845). L.C. 29/11/1845.
P. The Railway King; or, Harlequin and the Chinese Queen. L.C. M'bone, 17/11/1845.
F. Railway Mania; or, The Irish Sharebroker. L.C. Amphitheatre, Liverpool, 17/12/1845.
Int. The Railway Train (Edinburgh, 12/12/1840).
Ba. Raising the Wind (New, M. 6/5/1811).
Spec. The Rajah of Nagpore; or, The Sacred Elephants of the Pagoda (R.A. M. 9/2/1846). L.C. 26/1/1846 [as *The E. of the P.*].
D. The Ramblers; or, The Deserted Wife of Didcot (Vic. Th. 27/10/1836).
F. The Ramsbottoms at Rheims; or, The French Coronation (C.G. M. 11/7/1825). L.C. 6/1825. [This is by *R. B. PEAKE*.]
Int. Random Shots; or, Lucky Hits (S.W. M. 11/1/1830).
D. Raphael's Dream; or, The Egyptian Idol. L.C. 13/3/1834.
Spec. Raphael's Dream; or, The Mummy and the Study of Living Pictures (R.A. M. 13/9/1830).

T.   The Rash Marriage. L. 101 M. [Edinburgh, 3/1813].
Ba. Rasselas; or, The Happy Valley (St J. S. 26/12/1835). L.C. 28/12/1835.
M.D. The Rat-Trap; or, The Pass of Abruzzi (Cob. M. 23/4/1827).
D.   Ravin the Savage (S.W. M. 21/9/1807).
Ba. Raykisnah the Outcast; or, The Hollow Tree (Sans P. M. 22/11/1813). L. 99 M. [6/11/1813, as *The Outcast; or, The H. T.*].
Ba. A Real John Bull (Surrey, M. 26/8/1822).
O.F. The Reasonable Fool; or, All in Confusion (Pav. T. 17/12/1811). L. 93 M. [19/11/1811].
Ba. Rebecca and her Daughters (Vic. M. 12/6/1843).
C.   The Rebel. L.C. 28/4/1849.
M.D. The Rebel Chief (E.O.H. M. 27/6/1836). L.C. 21/6/1836.
Sat. The Rebellion; or, All in the Wrong. A Serio-Comic Hurly Burly in Scenes. 8° 1819 [2 editions].
       [This relates to the O. P. riots; see *The Theatric Count.*]
D.   The Rebellion of Norwich in 1549 (Norwich, 17/4/1815).
C.   A Receipt for Mirth. L. 54 S. [Lyc. 18/12/1811].
F.   A Recent Event. L.C. 31/10/1832.
D.   The Recluse (Edinburgh, 1825). L.C. 25/4/1825.
       [From Scott, *The Black Dwarf.* Music Caraffa, arranged by Horn.]
M.D. The Recluse; or, The Banks of the Delaware. L. 131 M. [Norwich, 16/4/1823].
O.D. The Recluse; or, The Valley of St. Gothard (D.L. 14/6/1825). L.C. 4/6/1825.
D.   The Recluse of the Cavern; or, The Triumph of Fidelity (Surrey, S. 23/10/1830).
Ba. El Recluta por Fuerza (Cob. W. 23/5/1832).
O.F. Recommendations; or, Another Fish out of Water (Olym. M. 27/10/1823). L. 132 M. [18/10/1823].
P.   The Reconciliation (D.L. 26/4/1813).
Ba. The Recruit (E.O.H. W. 9/9/1829). L.C. 18/8/1829.
       [This is said to be the same as *The Recruit* played at Dumfries in 1794; see *A History of Late Eighteenth Century Drama*, p. 341.]
M.D. The Red Banner; or, The Barons of Ubaldo (Cob. M. 25/4/1831).
D.   Redcliff. L.C. Glasgow, 11/11/1845.
M.D. The Red Daemon of the Harz Forest; or, The Three Charcoal Burners (Cob. M. 24/9/1821).
D.   Redgauntlet (Surrey, 7/1824). 12° 1824.
       [There seems to have been a separate version of Scott's novel played at the Surrey this year.]
R.D. The Red Gauntlet; or, The Piper's Receipt (R.P. M. 23/2/1835).
D.   The Red House; or, The Queen's Bouquet and the Three Cards (Surrey, M. 26/2/1849).
D.   The Red Indian; or, Selkirk and his Dog (Surrey, M. 26/8/1822).
M.D. The Red Indian; or, The Shipwrecked Mariner and his Faithful Dogs (Surrey, T. 9/3/1824).
       [Apparently a revised version of the above.]
M.D. Redland the Robber (R.P. F. 15/2/1833).
M.D. The Red Maid; or, The Renegade's Curse (R.P. M. 22/9/1834).
D.   The Red Man; or, The Sailem's Vow. L.C. Brit. 13/12/1847.
D.   The Red Man of Glatz (Vic. M. 23/4/1849). L.C. 21/4/1849.
D.   The Red Mantle; or, The Bridal of Death (Queen's, T. 14/9/1841).

M.D. Red Riven; or, The Mill of Glaris, a Canton in Switzerland (R.A. M. 19/8/1816; Cob. M. 18/4/1825).
Spec. The Red Robber; or, The Statue in the Wood (Sans P. S. 3/12/1808).
D. Red Robin. L.C. Surrey, 11/4/1846.
D. The Red Rover (Surrey, M. 7/9/1829).
D. Red Roy (Edinburgh, 7/4/1809).
Bal. Red Roy; or, Oswyn and Helen (H.² W. 10/8/1803).
D. The Red Savage; or, Sidney and his Dog (Cob. M. 6/9/1830).
P. The Red Sorcerer; or, Harlequin Captive (Surrey, M. 17/12/1810).
M.D. The Red Witch of Moravia (Cob. M. 31/7/1820).
Int. Reflection (D.L. S. 13/12/1834). L.C. 9/12/1834.
Ba. Reformation; or, Equivocal Appearances (Tottenham-street, Th. 14/1/1830).
D. The Refuge. L.C. 15/2/1837.
F. A Regiment of Tartars; or, The Pretty Girl of Stilberg (H.² M. 28/3/1842). L.C. 4/4/1842 [as *The Pretty Girl of Stilberg*].
M.D. The Reign of Terror; or, The Horrors of the French Revolution (Cob. M. 27/12/1824).
O.F. The Reign of Twelve Hours (E.O.H. Th. 5/8/1824). L.C. 31/7/1824.
       [Music G. B. Herbert.]
O. La reine de Chypre (D.L. M. 7/7/1845). L.C. C.G. 10/6/1845.
       [Music Halévy, Paris 1841.]
Bal. La reine de Golconde (H.¹ Th. 4/6/1812).
Bsq. Rejected Addresses (Clarence, M. 5/8/1833).
Bsq. The Rejected Addresses (St J. W. 24/2/1836). L.C. 22/2/1836 [as *The R. D., a Blind Bargain*].
Ext. The Rejected Addresses Received; or, The Manager in his Slippers (Royalty, S. 20/3/1813).
F. The Rejection; or, Everybody's Business (Lyc. F. W. 20/11/1811). L. 53 S. [11/11/1811, as *The Refusal; or, E. B.*].
Ba. The Renowned Mandarin, Whang Fong Long Tong Chang Song Ho; or, The Star of Destiny (Cob. M. 5/11/1821).
M.D. The Reprobate. L. 70 S. [Olym. 11/3/1821].
M.D. The Reprobate; or, The Protean Bandit (W.L. M. 9/3/1829).
M.Ent. Retaliation. L. 56 S. [Lyc. 1/9/1812].
Ba. The Retort Courteous (Olym. Th. 23/10/1834).
Bal. Returned from Trafalgar (New, S. 26/1/1811—3rd performance).
Ext. The Return of Perouse; or, The Chimpanzee in France (Surrey, M. 24/10/1836).
Ba. The Review; or, The Wags of Windsor. L.C. St J. 19/4/1837.
D. The Revolt at Sea. L.C. Adel. Glasgow, 13/9/1847.
D. The Revolt of Bruges (Olym. Th. 10/3/1842). L.C. 5/3/1842.
T. The Revolt of Flanders. 8° 1848.
       [By the author of *Richelieu in Love*.]
M.D. The Revolt of Surinam; or, A Slave's Revenge (Cob. T. 11/10/1825).
M.D. The Revolt of the Greeks; or, The Maid of Athens (D.L. Th. 10/6/1824). L.C. 29/5/1824.
Bal. The Revolt of the Harem (C.G. W. 5/2/1834).
Ext. The Revolt of the Seraglio on the other Side of the Pole (Surrey, 26/2/1834).

T. Richard III (D.L. 12/3/1821).
    [The version played by Kean; see Odell, *op. cit.* ii. 152–3.]
Bsq. Richard III. L. 106 M. [H.² 23/12/1815].
Bsq. Richard III. Travestie...with Annotations by Contrast Jumble.
    12° 1823.
Past. Richard and Betty; or, Drop a Tear to her Memory. L.C. Brit.
    18/11/1848.
D. Richard Darlington. L.C. 1836.
D. Richard Markham; or, The Brothers. L.C. Vic. 5/9/1846.
M.D. Richard Parker; or, The Mutiny at the Nore (Tottenham-street,
    M. 4/10/1830).
Spec. Richard the Lyon (R.A. M. 14/9/1801).
Spec. Richard Turpin, the Highwayman (R.A. M. 8/11/1819).
Ba. Richmond Hill; or, The Widow and the Bailiff. L.C. Olym.
    5/11/1827.
P. Riddle Me, Riddle me Ree (Olym. T. 18/1/1842).
P. Ride a Cock Horse (E.O.H. S. 26/12/1835). L.C. 24/12/1835.
Ba. Rifle Manœuvres (Adel. M. 19/2/1838). L.C. 19/2/1838.
F. The Rifles; or, Who will he have? L.C. P'cess, 18/10/1847.
Bal. The Right of Possession (Surrey, M. 18/10/1813).
D. Rimonia (Royalty, M. 19/9/1808).
M.D. Rinaldo the Remorseless; or, Philip and his Dog (Royalty, M.
    18/11/1822).
D. The Ring (Queen's, T. 29/1/1833).
P. Riquet with the Tuft; or, Dewdrop and Rosebud (R.A. M.
    15/4/1816).
Bal. The Rival Brothers; or, The Haunted Hut (R.A. W. 23/10/1816).
P. The Rival Clowns; or, Laugh if you like it (R.C. M. 17/7/1809).
P. The Rival Genii; or, Harlequin Wild Man (S.W. T. 12/4/1814).
M.D. The Rival Heroes, Charles XII and Peter the Great (S.W. M.
    29/5–M. 5/6/1820).
M.D. The Rival Indians; or, The Sailor and his Dogs (Cob. M.
    1/3/1824).
    [See *The Red Savage.*]
Ba. The Rival Queens; or, Little Alexander the Great. L.C. Rich-
    mond, 11/4/1843.
O.F. The Rival Soldiers (D.L. 8/7/1814).
Ba. The River God (Olym. Th. 26/2/1835). L.C. 21/2/1835.
M.D. The Robber of Epping Forest; or, The Man in Brown (S.W.
    Th. 10/2/1831).
M.D. The Robbers; or, The Fatal Oath (S.W. W. 20/9/1820).
R.D. The Robber's Wife (City, M. 22/8/1831).
Spec.D. The Robber's Wife; or, The Bleeding Nun of Lindenburg
    (Cob. T. 28/8/1821).
    [Also called *One O'Clock.*]
Bal. Robert and Bertrand (D.L. M. 24/3/1845).
    [Music Schmidt.]
Ba. Robert le Diable; or, The Devil's Son (S.W. M. 13/2/1832).
    [A version of Scribe and Delavigne, *Robert le Diable* (Paris,
    21/11/1831), with music by Meyerbeer.]
M.D. Robert the Bruce (Perth, 8/1819).
    [A dramatisation of Scott, *The Lord of the Isles*; this may be
    a revised version of the Coburg play.]
M.D. Robert the Bruce; or, The Battle of Bannockburn (Cob. M.
    24/5/1819).

M.D. Robert the Bruce; or, The Battle of Bannockburn (S.W. W. 10/12/1834).
M.D. Robert the Devil; or, The Terror of Normandy (R.P. T. 16/3/1830).
O.F. Robin and Marion; or, Love in a Bustle (Sans P. M. 8/2/1819).
Bal. Robin Gray (D.L. S. 2/4/1814).
Ba. Robin Hood (New, T. 27/11/1810).
Bsq. Robin Hood and Richard Cœur de Lion! (Lyc. M. 4/5/1846). L.C. 5/5/1846. 12° [1846].
     [This is by *J. H. STOCQUELER, C. W. S. BROOKS* and *C. KENNEY*.]
O.   Rob of the Fen (E.O.H. S. 7/7/1838). L.C. 22/6/1838.
Spec. Rob Roy (Pantheon, Edinburgh, S. 17/1/1818).
M.D. Rob Roy (Caledonian, Edinburgh, 3/5/1825).
     [This was the third Caledonian version of Scott's novel.]
M.D. Rob Roy; or, The Traveller's Portmanteau (Olym. M. 16/2/1818). L. 70 S. [12/2/1818].
M.D. Rob Roy McGregor (Cob. T. 8/7/1828).
Ba. Rob the Ranter; or, One Good Turn deserves another (R.A. M. 19/6/1820).
M.D. The Rock of Arpennaz; or, The Dumb Brother (Cob. T. 30/11/1824).
Bal. The Rock of Beauty (Lyc. M. 19/7/1847).
M.D. The Rock of Skulls; or, The Hidden Treasure (S.W. M. 30/1/1837).
M.D. Rodar the Raven; or, The Scourge of Denmark (S.W. M. 4/4/1831).
M.D. Roderick of Ravenscliff; or, The Black Pirate (R.P.M.11/6/1832).
M.D. Roderick the Goth; or, The Vision of the Cavern (Cob. M. 19/6/1820).
M.D. Rodolph and Rosa; or, The Queen of the Silver Lakes (R.C. M. 29/6/1807).
C.   The Roebuck. L. 128 M. [C.G. 17/11/1823].
F.   Rogues All! or, Three Generations (D.L. S. 5/2/1814). L. 103 M. [24/1/1814].
Ca. Roland; or, Carte over Arm (Edinburgh, 14/11/1835).
F.   A Roland for an Oliver (E.L. F. 30/7/1819).
     [See *MORTON*, 1819.]
D.   Rolla; or, The Peruvian Chief (Royalty, M. 26/11/1810).
C.   Rollo, the Minstrel; or, The Devil's in it (S.W. M. 26/6/1843).
Oa. Romance and Reality (Clarence, M. 12/8/1833).
M.D. The Romance of the Coast; or, The Smugglers and the Preventive Service (Cob. M. 15/11/1830).
M.D. The Romance of the Pyrenees; or, The Young Chasseur (Cob. M. 11/10/1830).
Ca. The Romance of the Rhine (P'cess, T. 5/10/1847). L.C. 18/10/1847.
Ba. The Roman Ladies (Olym. F. 6/11/1840).
F.   The Roman Nose (Surrey, M. 1/6/1835).
     [See *ALMAR*, 1834.]
C.   The Romantic Widow (H.² M. 16/10/1837).
M.D. Romeo and Juliet (Surrey, M. 22/3/1813).
Bsq. Romeo Travestie. L.C. Edinburgh, 1/9/1841.
M.Ent. The Romp (D.L. 22/5/1817).
M.D. Ronald the Reiver; or, The Devil's Cave (Royalty, M. 31/3/1823).

Ba. The Rope Ladder; or, Dissipation, Desperation and Starvation (Cob. M. 29/4/1822).
Bal. La Rose; ou, les deguisements (H.¹ T. 18/5/1819).
D. Rose Ashford; or, Woman's Love (Surrey, T. 29/2/1848). L.C. 29/2/1848.
Oa. Rose d'Amour; or, Little Red Riding Hat (C.G. Th. 3/12/1818). L. 68 S. [13/11/1818].
    [Adapted from *Le petit chaperon rouge* (Paris, 30/6/1818) by E. G. M. Théalon de Lambert, music by Boieldieu.]
D. Rose Lendin; or, The Old Chapel Ruins (S.W. M. 28/2/1842).
M.D. Rosenberg; or, The Outcasts of Molwitz (S.W. M. 9/6/1828).
D. The Rose of Ettrick Vale. L.C. Adel. 29/10/1829.
    [This is by *T. J. LYNCH*.]
P. The Rose of Stepney; or, Harlequin and Old Father Thames (R.P. W. 26/12/1838).
D. Rose Roy; or, The Valley of the White Rose (R.P. M. 11/5/1835).
    [See *G. D. PITT* (S.W. 1835).]
P. Rose, Shamrock and Thistle. L.C. Standard, 8/12/1845.
Ba. Rosine; or, Am I a Princess? (Adel. M. 31/10/1836).
Bal. The Rossignol; or, The Bird in the Bush (D.L. W. 2/2/1825).
Ba. Rouge et noir. L.C. E.O.H. 1838.
C. Rough and Smooth; or, Nature and Sentiment (Surrey, F. 20/7/1827).
Ba. A Rough Diamond (St J. M. 15/2/1836). L.C. 8/2/1836.
C. The Rout Routed. 8° 1800.
M.D. The Rover of the Isles (R.P. M. 29/7/1833).
Ba. The Row of Ballynavogue; or, The Lily of Lismore (Sans P. Th. 27/11/1817). L. 111 M. [14/11/1817; as *Ballynavogue*].
    [This is by *J. M. SCOTT*.]
Ba. Roxalana (Surrey, M. 4/10/1819).
Ba. The Royal Baker; or, The Knights of the Oven (R.P. M. 1/11/1830).
D. Royal Charlie (R.P. 24/3/1845). L.C. 22/3/1845.
Vaud. A Royal Commission from Paris (Olym. M. 20/4/1840). L.C. 27/3/1840.
M.D. The Royal Dane (Surrey, M. 25/6/1827).
    [A version of *Hamlet*.]
D. The Royal Delinquent; or, The Triumph of Justice (Vic. F. 10/1/1834).
Spec. The Royal Foxhunt; or, The Life and Death of Tom Moody. L.C. Amphitheatre, Manchester, 10/3/1847.
Ent. The Royal Jubilee (H.¹ W. 25/10/1809).
M.D. The Royal Mistress; or, The Life and Death of Jane Shore (R.P. W. 26/12/1838).
M.Ent. The Royal Nuptials; or, The Masque of Hymen (C.G. M. 6/5/1816). L. 108 M. [28/4/1816; with the titles reversed].
M.D. The Royal Scots Fusileers; or, The White Rabbit of Edinburgh Castle (R.P. M. 8/6/1835).
Ba. The Royal Twelfth Cake; or, The Queen's Court of Conscience (R.P. M. 7/1/1833).
M.D. Roy's Wife; or, The Clachan of Aberfoil (Cob. F. 4/11/1825).
    [Described as "the favourite Caledonian romance"; probably a revised version of an earlier *Rob Roy* play.]

M.D. The Ruby Cross (Cob. M. 9/2/1829).
D. Ruby Ruins; or, The Mother's Statue (Surrey, M. 14/2/1842).
Spec. Rudolph of Hapsburg; or, The Weirds of the Rhine. L.C. Adel. 24/9/1841.
P. Rudolph the Wolf; or, Columbine Red Riding Hood (Olym. M. 21/12/1818).
M.D. Rugantino, the Bravo of Venice (Surrey, M. 11/7/1831).
D. The Ruined House at Milbank (Vic. M. 26/1/1846). L.C. 3/11/1845.
M. The Ruins of Athens (P'cess, Th. 5/3/1846). L.C. 4/3/1846.
M.D. The Ruins of St. Pierre (Surrey, M. 8/10/1832).
P. Rule Britannia; or, Harlequin Old Dan Tucker and the Ocean Queen. L.C. R.P. 21/12/1846.
Bsq. Rumfuskin King of Bythnyphorbia (Olym. Th. 3/12/1818). L. 72 S. [25/11/1818].
M. The Rum Ones; or, The Club Night (Lyc. 9/4/1822).
F. The Runaway Husbands (H.² Th. 3/5/1849). L.C. 28/4/1849.
Ba. Run for your Life (Adel. M. 17/1/1820). L. 119 M. [2/1/1820].
M.Ent. Rural Visitors; or, Singularity (Sans P. F. 16/1/1807).
O. The Russian Captive (Queen's, Th. 16/6/1831).
M.D. The Russian Daughter; or, Female Heroism (Cob. M. 2/10/1820).
Bal. The Russian Festival (C.G. Th. 18/9/1817).
C.O. The Russian Village. L. 98 M. [D.L. 21/12/1813].
Ba. The Rustic Adonis (Queen's, M. 31/7/1837).
O. Ruth; or, Our Village Home. L.C. D.L. 17/2/1840.
D. Ruth of Rosedale; or, The Maid, Wife and Widow. L.C. R.P. 2/12/1848.
Ba. Ruth Tudor (Adel. M. 27/3/1837). L.C. 9/3/1837 [as *R. T.; or, The Reel Smuggled*].
Bal. Les Sabotiers; or, The Merry Woodcutters (Pav. M. 1/12/1806).
M.D. The Sacred Standard and the Chinese Prince; or, The Forest of Palms (Cob. M. 18/8/1828).
Spec. Sadak and Kalasrade; or, The Waters of Oblivion (C.G. M. 11/4/1814). L. 102 M. [25/3/1814].
Ba. The Sailor's Chest; or, The Family Picture (Cob. M. 3/2/1823).
D. The Sailor's Home. L.C. R.P. 12/7/1845.
D. St. Ann's Well! or, A Century Gone (S.W. M. 20/1/1840).
Bal. St. Bartholomew; or, Fun Alive (S.W. M. 30/8/1830).
Ba. St. Cuthbert's Eve; or, The Tomb of Monteith (Adel. M. 9/10/1820). L. 118 M. [29/9/1820].
D. St. Dru, the Accused (Edinburgh, 22/8/1836).
P. St. George and the Dragon; or, Harlequin and the Demon of the Nile. L.C. C.L. 16/12/1843.
Legendary R. St. George and the Dragon; or, The Seven Champions of Christendom (R.A. Th. 26/12/1822).
M.D. St. Gothard's Mount; or, Fatal Retribution (Cob. M. 2/8/1824).
M.D. St. Hilda's Cave; or, The Child of Crime (Cob. M. 9/8/1824).
M.D. St. John's Priory; or, Islington in the Olden Time (S.W. M. 11/2/1839).
O. St. Ronan's Well. L.C. D.L. 20/12/1824.
Spec. St. Stephen's Well; or, The Bumpkin's Dream. L.C. Brit. 10/12/1844.
Bal. La Salamandrine (C.G. T. 18/5/1847).

Spec. Salvator; or, The Invisible Brothers (Cob. M. 16/10/1820).
D. Sam Patch (H.² M. 4/11/1844). L.C. Adel. 22/10/1844 [as *S. P.; or, The Jumper*].
D. Sam Scud; or, Peril of the Sea (Surrey, M. 7/3/1842).
Ba. Sam Weller's Tour; or, The Pickwickians in France (Strand, M. 25/6/1838). L.C. 1838.
F. The Saracen's Head; or, Not at Home (H.² S. 10/9/1814). L. 59 S. [2/9/1814].
Oa. The Saracen's Head removed from Snow Hill. L. 72 S. [E.O.H. 30/6/1818].
[This is *S. BEAZLEY, The Bull's Head*.]
D. Satan; or, The Devil in Paris. L.C. 10/10/1844.
Ba. Satisfied; or, Not More than I Want (S.W. M. 31/1/1831).
M.D. The Savage Chieftain; or, The Shipwrecked British Sailor and his Dogs (E.L. M. 16/9/1816).
[See *EYRE*, 1814.]
Bal. The Savage Lovers; or, The Rival Regicides (Surrey, M. 24/4/1826).
O. The Savoyard. 8° 1815.
P. Sawney Beane; or, Harlequin and the Man Eater! (S.W. M. 1/4/1839).
Spec. Sawney Bean, the Terror of the North (Cob. T. 18/2/1823).
D. The Scamps of London (Vic. T. 26/12/1843).
Ba. The Scapegrace; or, I've been roaming. L.C. Adel. 5/3/1828.
[See *S. BEAZLEY*, 1832.]
Ca. The Scapegrace of Paris (Surrey, M. 8/4/1844). L.C. 1/4/1844.
F. Scapin in Masquerade (D.L. S. 12/11/1803).
[A version of Ségur, *Crispin Duegne*.]
F. The Scarecrow (Lyc. M. 1/5/1848). L.C. 19/4/1848.
M.D. Scenes in London; or, The Jew, the Gamester, the Seducer, the Murderer and the Thief (Cob. M. 30/7/1821).
F. The Schemer. L. 129 M. [Olym. 25/11/1823].
F. Schoolboy Frolics (P'cess, W. 13/1/1847). L.C. 7/1/1847.
Ba. The School for Fathers (Surrey, W. 29/7/1812).
C. The School for Gallantry (D.L. S. 3/5/1828). L.C. 1/5/1838.
[Music Cooke.]
F. The School for Orators; or, A Peep into the Forum. 8° 1806.
Fa. The Schoolmaster at Home (E.O.H. S. 5/9/1835). L.C. 3/9/1835.
[Music A. Wade.]
C. The Scornful Lady. L.C. M'bone, 19/11/1847.
Ent. The Scotch Ghost (D.L. W. 13/5/1801).
[This may be another form of the following.]
Bal. The Scotch Ghost; or, Little Fanny's Love (D.L. S. 8/2/1800).
Bal. The Scotch Lovers; or, The Gretna Blacksmith (R.A. M. 25/8/1800).
F. Scotch Marriage Laws; or, The Deacon and her Deputy (Edinburgh, 26/4/1823). L. 86 S. [Edinburgh, 18/3/1823].
F. Scotch Mist (Olym. 17/10/1842). L.C. 21/10/1842.
M.D. Scotland's Patriot King (W.L. M. 1/10/1820).
Ba. The Scottish Chiefs (not Miss Porter's) (Strand, M. 2/9/1839). L.C. 19/8/1839.
D. Scrooge the Miser's Dream; or, The Past, Present and Future. L.C. S.W. 27/1/1844.
Bal. The Sculptor; or, Love can move the Heart of a Stone (R.A. M. 9/7/1821).

D.   The Sculptor of Frankfort (Surrey, M. 5/2/1849).
Spec. The Sculptor's Workshop (Surrey, M. 13/11/1837).
M.D. The Sea Devil; or, The Freebooter's Boy (S.W. Th. 26/12/1839).
M.D. The Sea Devil; or, The Wandering Jew (Cob. M. 29/3/1830).
D.   The Sea Horse; or, Queen Elizabeth and the Knight of Sheppey
     (R.A. M. 15/4/1839).
M.D. The Sea Lion; or, The Corsairs of Cuba (Cob. M. 9/5/1825).
M.D. The Sea Lion's Den; or, The Idiot of the Island (S.W. M.
     29/6/1835).
Ba.   The Sea-side Story (Cob. M. 26/7/1819).
     [See *DIMOND*, 1801.]
M.D. A Sea-side Story; or, Gwinnet the Accused (S.W. M. 24/11/1828).
     [See *JERROLD*, 1828.]
M.D. The Sea! the Sea! (R.P. M. 11/8/1834).
D.   The Sea Witch; or, The Pirate's Wife (R.P. W. 10/7/1839).
R.D. Sebastian IV (Cob. M. 10/9/1821).
D.   Second Sight: A Tale of the Highlands (H.² Th. 11/8/1836). L.C.
     25/7/1836.
F.   Second Thoughts are Best. L.C. R.P. 3/4/1847.
Ba.   The Secretary and the Cook; or, Exchange No Robbery (Cob. M.
     2/4/1821).
C.O. The Secret Marriage (C.G. T. 1/11/1842). L.C. 26/10/1842.
Spec. The Secret Muse (R.A. M. 11/4/1814).
     [See *T. J. DIBDIN*, 1812.]
Ba.   The Secrets of the Night (Cob. M. 13/8/1821).
M.D. Secret Springs; or, Love and Jealousy (Surrey, M. 7/1/1811).
Bsq. The Segonde Parte of the Tragycalle Historie of Thomasse
     Thumbe (E.O.H. T. 9/6/1840). L.C. 10/6/1840.
T.   Selim and Zuleika. 8° 1815.
M.D. Selima de Gray; or, The Forsaken Daughter (R.A. F. 2/10/1818).
D.   Senekos the Greek; or, The Ensign of Freedom (R.P. M.
     14/10/1833).
Bal. The Seraglio (C.G. M. 16/9/1816).
M.D. Serbelloni; or, The Forest of Friuli (S.W. M. 7/1/1833).
Ba.   Serenading (Olym. 31/10/1836). L.C. 1837.
     [This is by *T. L. REDE*, an early version of *The Two Greens*.]
Ba.   The Serjeant's Wife (Kelly's, M. 25/5/1840).
M.D. The Serpent Lady; or, The Castle of Eberstein (R.P. M.
     27/5/1833).
Ba.   The Servant of All Work (Surrey, Th. 4/8/1831).
Ba.   Seth Slope; or, Done for a Hundred (Strand, M. 22/7/1839).
     L.C. 15/7/1839.
D.   The Seven Ages of Man (Surrey, Th. 26/12/1844). L.C.
     21/11/1844.
Spec. The Seven Capes; or, The Pirate of Algiers (R.A. S. 1/10/1808;
     Pav. M. 13/2/1809).
     [In some bills "Islands" appears for "Capes."]
R.Tale. The Seven Castles of the Passions (Lyc. M. 21/10/1844). L.C.
     7/10/1844.
Ext. The Seven Champions of Christendom (Olym. M. 24/3/1845).
P.   The Seven Champions of Christendom (R.A. 7/1829).
P.   The Seven Champions of Christendom and the Storm Demon;
     or, Harlequin and the Fiery Flying Lion, the Terror of the Land
     L.C Albert, 9/11/1844.

Bsq. Seven in One; or, The Country Actress (Royalty, W. 9/10/1822).
O.F. Seventeen and Seventy. L.C. H.³ 1837.
  [*Seven or Seventeen*, by *C. DANCE*, appeared at C.L. on 29/11/1837.]
D. The Sexton of Stepney; or, The Beggar's Grave. L.C. Brit. 18/10/1847.
D. The Shadowless Man; or, The Demon of the Crystal Rock (Surrey, M. 8/4/1833).
C.D. The Shadows on the Water; or, The Cleverest Man in China (C.G. M. 17/2/1845). L.C. 15/2/1845.
Ent. Shadrack; or, The Jew and the Sailor (Royalty, T. 5/2/1805).
Ba. Shakespeare and Burbage (Strand, M. 16/7/1838). L.C. 13/7/1838 [as *S. and B.; or, Royal Precedence*].
C.D. Shakespeare, his Life and Times (Strand, 31/8/1847).
Ent. Shakespeare's Dream (Edinburgh, 16/4/1831).
M.D. Shamacda; or, The Desert Fiend (Surrey, M. 11/4/1814).
F. The Sham Captain; or, "I want my Ma." L.C. Brit. 19/4/1848.
Ba. The Sham Fight; or, The Music-Master (R.P. M. 18/1/1836).
Ba. The Sham Prince (St J. Th. 29/9/1836). L.C. 20/9/1836.
D. The Shark of the Atlantic; or, The Fight for the Beacon. L.C. 30/10/1843.
  [Plays of this name appeared at the Queen's 27/11/1843 and at the C.L. 6/11/1843.]
F. Sharp Set; or, The Village Hotel (Lyc. M. 15/5/1809). L. 90 M. [10/5/1809; under sub-title].
O.F. Sharps, Flats and Naturals; or, The County Concert (Surrey, M. 30/5/1831).
F. Shave you directly (Lyc. W. 21/2/1849). L.C. 23/2/1849.
Ba. The Sheep Stealer; or, The Yorkshire Attorney (Cob. M. 11/8/1828).
F. The Sheep's Trotter (R.P. 4/1841).
Ent. The Sheet Anchor of Albion (Brighton, 12/8/1806).
C. She Lives; or, The Generous Brother. L. 80 M. [Margate, 2/1803].
  [See *MARY GOLDSMITH*.]
P. The Shepherd and Shepherdess; or, Harlequin Fairy Lamb and the Demon of the Wolf's Glen. L.C. Albert, 30/10/1843.
O.D. The Shepherd Boy (E.O.H. W. 7/9/1825).
  [Music Reeve.]
M.D. The Shepherd King; or, The Princely Peasant and the Peasant King (R.A. M. 1/10/1832).
O. The Shepherd of Derwent Vale; or, The Old Soldier (Cob. M. 23/5/1831).
C. She's mine for a Thousand (Strand, 6/1845). L.C. 2/6/1845.
Ext. She's not to be managed; or, How to Drive Tandem (Surrey, M. 27/6/1825). [By *C. I. M. DIBDIN*.]
D.D. She's not to Blame (P'cess, Th. 29/12/1842).
Ba. She Wants a Guardian. L.C. St J. 1837.
F. Shifts of Genius; or, Phrenological Philanthropy. L.C. Manchester, 14/12/1843.
D. The Ship Boy; or, The White Slave of Guadeloupe (Vic. M. 19/4/1847). L.C. 24/4/1847.
M.Piece. The Ship Launch (D.L. 17/5/1804). L. 44 S. [13/5/1804].
Ba. The Shipwreck (Royalty, M. 19/10/1812).

D. The Shipwrecked Mother; or, The Vow of Silence. L.C. Queen's, 10/6/1846.
Bal. The Shipwreck of Policinello; or, The Neapolitan Nuptials (C.G. M. 31/10/1825).
D. The Shoemaker of Toulouse. L.C. Brit. 30/8/1847.
Ba. Shooter's Hill; or, The First of September (R.A. M. 28/8/1826).
F. The Shop-walker (D.L. 17/12/1825).
Ba. Short Cuts and Returns; or, The Tobacconist of Bishopsgate Street (City, M. 28/1/1833).
Ba. Short Notice; or, A Husband at Sight (S.W. M. 6/8/1832).
Ba. The Shrew; or, How to Tame a Woman (S.W. M. 1/12/1828).
Spec. Siamovaindianaboo, Princess of Siam; or, The Royal Elephant (Cob. M. 4/1/1830).
Spec. The Siberian Exile; or, The Heroic Daughter (Surrey, M. 28/6/1813).
Ba. Sicilian Hussars; or, The Black Bottle. L.C. 3/10/1840.
D. The Sicilian Mother; or, The Wife of Two Husbands (Cob. M. 27/4/1829).
        [Also called *The Matron of Palermo*.]
C.D. Sidonia di Molina (Adel. M. 2/12/1844). L.C. 2/12/1844.
Spec. The Siege of Abydos; or, The Pirate of the Isles. L.C. Apollo, 15/3/1844.
Spec. The Siege of Acre; or, Britons in the East (Cob. M. 26/1/1824).
M.D. The Siege of Belgrade (Cob. Th. 17/4/1828).
M.D. The Siege of Belgrade (St J. M. 7/3/1836).
M.D. The Siege of Calais (S.W. M. 22/9/1823).
D. The Siege of Dantzig; or, The Polish Patriot (Vic. M. 5/6/1837).
Spec. The Siege of Flushing (R.A. M. 28/8/1809).
M.D. The Siege of Gibraltar; or, General Elliot in 1782 (R.P. M. 20/4/1835).
Spec. The Siege of Jerusalem; or, The Camp of the Wilderness (R.A. M. 20/4/1835).
M.D. The Siege of Londonderry and the Battle of the Boyne (R.A. M. 22/5/1820).
D. The Siege of Lynn. L.C. 8/5/1838.
M.D.Spec. The Siege of Missolonghi; or, The Massacre of the Greeks (R.A. M. 10/7/1826).
M.D. The Siege of Montgatz; or, The Mill of Keben (Cob. M. 27/9/1824).
O. The Siege of Sarragossa; or, Spanish Patriots in 1808. L. 99 M. [Norwich, 18/1/1813].
Spec. The Siege, Storming and Taking of Badajoz (R.A. M. 4/5/1812).
Spec. Sights in England and Fêtes in France (R.A. M. 22/8/1825).
        [Also called *The Coronation*.]
M.D. Sigismorn, the Danish Chieftain (R.A. M. 27/3/1815).
M.D. The Signal Fire; or, The Fortress of Kingratz (Cob. M. 18/5/1829).
D. The Signal Rocket. L.C. Olym. 1/4/1844.
Ba. The Sign Manual. L.C. 11/10/1838.
Spec. The Sikh's Invasion; or, The War in India (R.A. M. 1/6/1846). L.C. 23/5/1846 [as *Sikhs of the Punjab*].
P. The Silver Arrow; or, Harlequin and the Fairy Pari Banon (D.L. W. 6/1/1819). L. 74 S. [2/1/1819]. 8° 1819. [Airs, Chorusses.]

M.D. The Silver Knight; or, The Banquet Gallery (Cob. M. 8/11/1830).

D. The Silver Palace. L.C. R.P. 20/3/1844.

P. The Silver Quince of the Golden Valley of Dates; or, The Enchanter of the Cavern of Fire and the Fairy of the Region of Pearl. L.C. Apollo, 10/12/1844.

Spec. The Silver Valley; or, Azim and Alzira (R.P. M. 14/9/1835).

M.D. The Silver Veil; or, The Bedouin and the Fire-Worshipper (Cob. M. 11/3/1833).

Ba. A Simple Historie. L.C. 23/5/1834.

Ba. Simpson and Co. L.C. 1839.
[See *POOLE*, 1823.]

P. Sinbad the Sailor; or, The Spanish Clown (Royalty, M. 11/3/1805).

P. Sinbad the Sailor, the Genii of the Deep; or, The Clown, Emperor of China (Royalty, M. 24/8/1812).
[Probably the preceding piece revised.]

M.D. Sinbad the Sailor; or, The Valley of Diamonds (C.G. M. 16/4/1838). L.C. 13/4/1838.

F. The Singles in London. L. 76 S. [1819].

M.D. Sir Alfred the Bold; or, Sir Hildred the Black (R.A. M. 24/6/1822).

M.D.Spec. Sir Sidney Smith; or, The Siege of Acre (Cob. M. 30/8/1830).
[See *The Siege of Acre.*]

Ba. Sir Solomon Squat, the City Vampire (Cob. M. 5/1/1824).

O. The Sister of Charity (E.O.H. T. 2/7/1829). L.C. 16/6/1829.

M.D.Spec. The Sisters; or, The Heroines of Switzerland (R.A. T. 12/8/1817).

D. The Sisters Saved. L.C. E.O.H. 15/7/1824.

M.D. The Six Brigands of the Monastery de l'Annonciade; or, The Murder of Fualdes (Cob. T. 24/10/1820).

D. The Sixes! or, The Devil and the Dice (S.W. M. 4/5/1835).

O.Vaud. Six Miles from Glasgow (S.W. M. 5/7/1830).

F. Six Physicians; or, The Patient Carried Off (C.G. F. 13/11/1818). L. 70 S. [5/11/1818; as, *The Consultation*].

D. Six Steps of Punishment (Queen's, M. 5/2/1849).

O.F. Sixteen and Sixty. 8° 1815.
[By the author of *The Gondolier.*]

P. The Six Voyages of Sinbad the Eastern Mariner; or, Harlequin's Ordeal (Cob. T. 26/12/1820).

M.D. The Skeleton Lover (Adel. F. 16/7/1830). L.C. 5/7/1830.
[Music G. H. Rodwell.]

Ent. Sketches in India (S.W. W. 18/3/1846).

D. The Skimmer of the Sea; or, The Water Witch (S.W. M. 27/12/1830).

M.D. The Slave King (Surrey, Th. 7/7/1833).

Bal. The Slave Merchant (R.A. T. 6/10/1818).

M.D. The Slave of Wealth; or, The Gnome of the Gold Mines. L.C. Vic. 13/11/1844.

D. The Slave Sale (Vic. M. 30/4/1838).

M.D. The Slaves' Revolt (R.A. M. 21/5/1827).

M.D. The Slave Trade; or, African Gratitude (R.C. M. 15/3/1814).

M.D. The Sleeping Beauty (Surrey, M. 6/1/1812).

P. The Sleeping Beauty (Brighton, 1841). MS. was in the possession of Crompton Rhodes.

Ba. The Sleepless Woman. L.C. 25/9/1833.

Bsq. La Slumbernambula (Strand, M. 30/9/1844). L.C. 28/9/1844.

M.D. The Smuggler's Dog; or, The Blind Boy's Murder (Cob. M. 11/9/1820).

D. The Smuggler's Fate (Surrey, M. 15/4/1833).

D. The Smuggler's Haunt; or, The Fireside Story (Vic. M. 12/10/1835).

Ba. The Smuggler's Hut (Cob. F. 11/6/1819).

D. The Smugglers of Dieppe; or, The Beggar and the Soldier (R.A. M. 2/10/1837).

O.F. A Snake in the Grass; or, Which is He? (Surrey, M. 15/5/1826).

M.D. Snap Apple Night; or, A Kick-up in Kerry (E.O.H. S. 10/8/1839). L.C. 2/8/1839.

M.D. Sobieski; or, The Royal Fugitive (Royalty, M. 12/11/1821).

Ent. Sock and Buskin (Fishamble-street, Dublin, 27/1/1809).

Spec. The Soldier Girl; or, Albert and Louise (Surrey, M. 17/6/1822).

D. A Soldier of Fortune. L.C. Surrey, 27/2/1846.

Ba. The Soldier's Daughter (Royalty, M. 10/7/1815).

D. The Soldier's Dream; or, The Conscript's Jealousy (Cob. M. 6/3/1826; Olym. T. 21/11/1826; R.A. W. 25/3/1846).

Bal. The Soldier's Frolic (Sans P. M. 21/1/1811).

Ba. A Soldier's Honour; or, A Woman's Love (R.A. M. 8/5/1826).

Bal. The Soldier's Return; or, The Fortune-teller's Frolic (R.C. M. 3/7/1809).

D. The Soldier's Sister; or, The Child of the Army. L.C. Brit. 27/11/1847.

Ba. The Soldier's Stratagem; or, Love and Transformation (C.G. 5/11/1830).

D. The Soldier's Vow; or, The Libertine's Remorse (Vic. M. 6/3/1837).

D. The Solitary of Lambeth; or, The Murder of St. George's Fields (R.A. M. 9/7/1849).

M.D. The Solitary of Mount Savage; or, The Fate of Charles the Bold (Surrey, M. 27/5/1822).

M.D. The Solitary of the Heath; or, A Tale of Blood (Cob. M. 1/11/1830).

T. Solyman. 8° 1807.

F. Somebody's in the House with Dinah; or, The Invitation to the Nigger Ball. L.C. Queen's, 27/5/1847.

O. The Somnambula. L.C. E.O.H. 9/5/1835.

Bal. Le songe d'Ossian (H.¹ T. 9/3/1824).

F. The Son of the Navy (Strand, Th. 6/4/1848). L.C. 8/4/1848.

M.D. The Son of the Wilderness. 12° [N.D.; Lacy].
[Based on the German of F. Halm (E. F. J. Freiherr von Münch-Bellingshausen).]

D. The Sons of Mars (Adel. M. 22/10/1849). L.C. 19/10/1849.

Spec. Sons of the Ocean. L.C. Queen's, 7/11/1843.
[This is evidently the play produced as Sons of the Sea on 13/11/1843.]

D. A Son's Revenge; or, The Spaniard's Vow (Vic. M. 10/10/1836).

Spec. The Sophy of Brabant; or, The Fall of Gollo (Royalty, M. 1/3/1802).

M.D. The Sorcerer; or, The Two Brothers of Catania (Surrey, 26/12/1831).
P. The Sorcerer's Three Golden Hairs; or, Harlequin Prince of China (S.W. M. 31/5/1830).
T. The Sorceress. 8° 1814.
P. The Sorceress of Strozzi; or, Harlequin Wanderer (R.C. M. 14/4/1806).
Spec. The Sorrows and Death of Cleopatra over the Body of Mark Antony in the Roman Camp (R.A. M. 23/9/1805).
Bsq. The Sorrows of Werter; or, Love, Liquor and Lunacy (H.² M. 19/9/1825). L.C. 9/1825.
Spec. Spain and Portugal; or, Rebels and Guerillas (R.A. M. 16/4/1827).
      [See T. J. DIBDIN, 1827.]
Ba. Spain in Devonshire; or, Locks no Use (S.W. M. 11/5/1829).
M.D. The Spaniard; or, The Fatal Revenge (Cob. M. 25/1/1819).
D. The Spaniards; or, The Expulsion of the Moors. 8° 1814.
D. The Spanish Armada; or, The Golden Days of Queen Bess (R.P. M. 19/5/1834).
F. Spanish Bonds; or, Wars in Wedlock (H.² S. 2/8/1823). L. 87 S. [23/7/1823].
M.D. The Spanish Brothers; or, The Ventriloquist and the Murderer (Cob. M. 5/7/1830).
Spec. The Spanish Bull-fight (Arena, M. 27/1/1834).
Ent. The Spanish Gala; or, Cervantes Knight (S.W. M. 7/6/1813).
Bal. Spanish Gallantries (D.L. Th. 4/3/1847).
Bal. Spanish Gallants (D.L. Th. 18/3/1824).
      [Music Cooke.]
D. The Spanish Husband; or, First and Last Love (D.L. T. 25/5/1830). L.C. 22/5/1830.
Ba. The Spanish Lover (R.A. T. 5/9/1843).
Ba. Spanish Lovers. L.C. 21/12/1831.
Ca. The Spanish Marriage (P'cess, Th. 1/6/1848). L.C. 17/4/1848.
Spec. Spanish Martyrs; or, The Death of Riego (Cob. M. 13/6/1825).
M.D. Sparbuto; or, The Robber's Wife of the Apennines (Surrey, M. 9/7/1827).
F. Sparks in the Dark; or, The Three Cloaks (Vic. M. 28/4/1834).
F. A Speaking Likeness (P'cess, S. 7/3/1846; Lyc. T. 11/7/1848). L.C. 4/3/1846 [as Manette; or, The Very Picture].
R.D. The Spectre Monarch and his Phantom Steed; or, The Genii Horsemen of the Air (R A M 12/4/1830)
M.D. The Spectre of Ravenfells (R.P. M. 11/1/1830).
Ext. The Spectre on Horseback; or, Don Giovanni (D.L. 12/6/1829).
M.D. The Spectre Pilot (R.P. M. 25/5/1829).
F. Speculation; or, How to Buy a Horse without Money (Strand, Th. 7/6/1832).
F. Speculation; or, Life in Glasgow. L.C. Glasgow, 27/11/1847.
D. The Spendthrift; or, The Last Shilling. L.C. R.P. 12/1/1844.
Bal. The Spirit of Air (D.L. S. 17/11/1838; P'cess, F. 12/6/1846).
M.Ent. The Spirit of Beauty. L.C. Adel. 3/2/1841.
D. The Spirit of Gold. L.C. Vic. 29/6/1848.
D. The Spirit of the Fountain (P'cess, W. 1/11/1843). L.C. 18/10/1843.
M.D. The Spirit of the Hill; or, The Village Somnambulist (Surrey, S. 1/3/1828).

M.D. The Spirit of the Loom (Adel. Norwich, 16/11/1848).
R.Legend. The Spirit of the Mist (Queen's, M. 23/5/1831).
R.Tale. The Spirit of the Moon; or, The Inundation of the Nile
    (C.G. M. 19/4/1824). L.C. 9/4/1824.
M.D. The Spirit of the Moon; or, The Vampire and the Bride of the
    Isles (Cob. M. 23/8/1830).
M.D. Spoglioni; or, The Bandit of the Charmed Wrist (R.P. T.
    21/8/1832).
Ba. The Spoiled Child (St J. Th. 14/1/1836).
Ba. The Sportsman and the Shepherd; or, Where's the Wig? (Sans P.
    Th. 31/10/1816).
Oa. Spring-Guns and Man-Traps (Strand, M. 20/2/1832).
Ba. Spring or Autumn (H.² T. 1/10/1833).
Spec. The Sprite of the Snowdrift (Surrey, M. 27/5/1844).
M.D. The Spy of the Neutral Ground; or, The American War of 1780
    (Cob. T. 27/9/1825).
O.F. A Squeeze to the Coronation (E.O.H. Th. 19/7/1821). L. 122 M.
    [16/7/1821]. 8° 1821.
    [This is by J. THOMSON.]
Ba. A Stage Letter; or, A Bold Stroke for Success (R.C. M. 15/9/1806).
Ba. Stage-Struck. L.C. 15/4/1837.
Ba. The Stage-Struck Apothecary (S.W. M. 1/1/1827).
Ba. The Stage-Struck Lady (Surrey, M. 4/10/1819).
F. The Stage-Struck Yankee (Strand, Th. 27/2/1845). L.C.
    2/12/1844 [but licensed for Liverpool].
M.D. Stanislaus; or, The Siege of Dantsic (Cob. M. 8/9/1823).
D. Stanislaus of Poland; or, The Mill of Marimount (Vic. M.
    28/9/1835).
D. Star of my Home; or, Mother and Daughter. L.C. Standard,
    27/11/1846.
Ext. "Stars; or, A Dramatic Fête (Rehearsal)" (Queen's, S. 30/5/1835).
Bsq. State Secrets; or, Public Men in Private Life (C.G. T. 12/6/1821).
    L. 122 M. [4/6/1821].
Spec. The Statue Steed; or, The Black Hussar (R.A. M. 3/9/1832).
D. The Steel Castle (R.A. M. 17/11/1845).
T. The Step-mother; or, Fraternal Friendship. L. 22 L. [Edinburgh,
    11/2/1814].
M.D. The Stolen Sheep; or, The Distressed Peasants (S.W. M.
    23/1/1832).
D. The Stolen Sheep; or, The Pauper's Curse. L.C. Brit. 13/2/1849.
D. The Stone-Masons' Strike (Brit. 4/9/1848). L.C. 30/8/1848.
Bsq. Stoney Batter; or, The Surrey Toll-Gate (Surrey, M. 21/11/1825).
D. Stop him who can (Olym. S. 3/10/1840).
Bal. The Storm; or, The Isle of the Genii (C.G. M. 24/11/1834).
P. The Storm Fiend of the Apennines and the Arcadian Bowers; or,
    Harlequin Prince of the Blood-red Plume. L.C. Albert, 18/12/1847.
Spec. The Storming of Quito; or, The Temple of the Sun (R.A. M.
    28/9/1840).
    [Revived R.A. M. 14/6/1847 with "Warrior" for "Temple."]
Spec. The Storming of Seringapatam (R.A. M. 20/4/1829).
O.F. The Stout Gentleman (E.O.H. Th. 8/9/1825). L.C. 18/8/1825.
    [A play of this name was licensed for Bath, L.C. 18/2/1824.]
Ent. The Strand-ed Actor! or, Recollections which may or may not
    have happened (Strand, M. 25/11/1833).

C. Strange Conclusions. L.C. H.² 3/6/1848.
D. The Strange Intruder. L.C. Vic. 15/11/1844.
Ba. The Stranger (Royalty), M. 7/9/1812).
Ent. The Stratagem; or, An Exquisite at Fault (Tottenham-street, S. 20/11/1830).
D. Stratagems; or, The Lost Treasure (Sans P. M. 4/3/1816). L. 107 M. [5/3/1816].
Sk. The Striking Beauty (Queen's, M. 1/8/1836).
Ba. Strolling Players; or, Love and Mystery (Cob. M. 29/9/1823).
M.D. Strozzi; or, The Free-traders of Piedmont (Cob. M. 3/5/1824).
F. A Struggle for a Crown. L.C. H.² 14/2/1846.
D. The Student of Jena. L.C. Norwich, 3/6/1842.
   [See *PLANCHÉ*, 1833.]
Ba. The Student; or, Love, War, Physic and Latin (Surrey, T. 26/8/1823).
D. The Student of Blackfriars; or, The Descendants of Hugh Myddelton (S.W. Th. 2/5/1836).
Ba. The Students; or, The Rebel's Gauntlet. L.C. 1837.
F. Sudden Thoughts (Surrey, M. 17/4/1843).
T. Sulieman. 8° 1814.
D. Suliote; or, The Greek Family. L.C. 19/10/1829.
Ca. The Sultana (P'cess, 8/1/1848). L.C. 8/1/1848.
M.Ent. The Sultan and the Slave (Tottenham-street, Th. 9/12/1830).
Ba. The Sultan and the Slave; or, A Week in Turkey (Cob. M, 17/5/1830).
Bal. The Summer Fête (Queen's, M. 24/7/1837).
Ba. The Summer House. L. 104 M. [Sans P. 13/2/1815].
D. Sunshine and Shade (Olym. T. 4/4/1843; Surrey, M. 7/5/1849). L.C. 5/5/1849.
Ext. Supper the Night before the Coronation (Queen's, M. 12/9/1831).
Int. Sure Aim; or, The Norfolk Sharp-shooter. L. 86 M. [Norwich, 25/4/1807].
M.D. Surooj Seing; or, The Irishman in India (R.A. M. 17/1/1820).
T. The Surrender of Calais. 8° 1801 [York].
D. Suspicion; or, St. Augustine's Eve. L.C. Manchester, 1/3/1843.
D. Suzanne (H.² M. 14/5/1838). L.C. 7/5/1838.
Ba. Suzette (Clarence, M. 21/5/1832).
D. The Swedish Ferryman (P'cess, M. 12/6/1843).
Ba. Sweethearting (S.W. Th. 26/7/1827).
M.D. Sweet Revenge; or, The Mysterious Stranger (S.W. T. 24/11/1835).
M.D. The Swing Bridge (E.O.H. T. 1/7/1823).
   [Music Reeve.]
C.O. The Swiss (German, S. 24/8/1805).
M.D. The Swiss Boys; or, The Wanderers (S.W. M. 25/8/1828).
B.O. The Swiss Family; or, Home! Sweet Home! (Surrey, F. 27/6/1828).
Ba. The Swiss Father. L.C. Edinburgh, 22/8/1836.
Bal. Swiss Revels; or, The Barn in a Bustle (R.C. M. 1/6/1806).
Bal. The Swiss Villagers (D.L. M. 3/2/1823).
P. The Sylph of the Sunflower; or, Harlequin and Daddy Long Legs (R.P. M. 23/5/1831).
M.D. Sylvena! the Rose of Athlone; or, The Pass of Rathconnell (S.W. M. 29/7/1832).

Ba. Sylvester Daggerwood (Surrey, W. 28/11/1810).
O.F. Sylvester Daggerwood. L.C. C.G. 31/3/1837.
Ca. Symptoms. L.C. Lyc. 15/10/1849.
C.O. The Syren. L.C. Eagle, 6/11/1846.
     [This is derived from La Sirène by Scribe, with music by Auber
     (Paris, 26/3/1844).]
F. The Systematic or Imaginary Philosopher. 8° 1800.
O.F. Table Talk; or, Whims and Wonders. L.C. H.² 12/2/1827.
O.F. Tactic out of Place. L.C. E.O.H. 27/10/1835.
Bsq. [The Tailors.] The Devil among the Tailors; A Dramatic Bur-
     lesque, at full Length, of the Tailors; or, A Tragedy for Warm
     Weather...To which is added an Account of the Fracas at the
     Theatre, August 15, 1805. 8° [1805; 5 editions].
F. Taken by Surprise (Olym. M. 21/2/1831). L.C. 21/2/1831.
P. Take Warning! or, Harlequin in Scotland (R A. M. 24/6/1805;
     Pav. M. 20/2/1809).
Ba. Take your Choice (St J. M. 25/2/1839).
M.D. The Taking of the Bastille. L.C. C.L. 27/4/1844.
F. The Taking of the Pledge (P'cess, S. 5/10/1844). L.C. 27/7/1844.
C. Taking Possession (Lyc. M. 3/2/1845). L.C. 18/1/1845.
M.D. The Tale of Mystery (Surrey, M. 16/3/1812).
M.D. A Tale of the O'Hara Family; or, Captain John Rock (Cob. T.
     2/10/1827).
P. The Talisman; or, Harlequin's Oracle (R.A. M. 2/6/1806;
     Royalty, M. 23/2/1807).
D. The Talisman (Edinburgh, 22/6/1825). L.C. 1825.
     [Based on Scott's tale.]
Ba. "Talk of the Devil!" (Olym. S. 1/10/1831). L.C. 30/9/1831.
Ba. Tame Tigers. L.C. Olym. 20/10/1838.
O.F. Taming a Tartar; or, Magic and Mazourkaphobia (Adel. M.
     20/10/1845). L.C. 13/10/1845 [as T. a T.; or, Matrimony and
     Magic].
Spec. The Taming of Bucephalus, the Wild Horse of Scythia; or, The
     Youthful Days of Alexander the Great (R.A. M. 10/9/1827).
O.F. The Taming of the Shrew (D.L. 14/5/1828).
     [Music Rossini, Braham and T. Cooke.]
M.D. Tam o' Shanter; or, Beelzebub on Horseback (R.A. M.
     12/5/1828).
O. Tancredi (P'cess, M. 17/4/1843).
     [An English version of Rossini's opera.]
Bal. The Tarantula (S.W. M. 24/10/1831).
     [Music Gide.]
D. Tarempon and Serinda; or, The Hall of Silence (Surrey, M.
     11/6/1810).
O. Tarrare, the Tartar Chief (E.O.H. M. 15/8/1825).
     [Music Salieri.]
Bal. The Tars in Port (Royalty, M. 16/2/1801).
M.Ent. The Tars on Shore; or, Love and Jollity (D.L. 26/6/1818).
Tale of Enchantment. The Tartar Witch and the Pedlar Boy (C.G. M.
     23/4/1832). L.C. 9/4/1832 [as The Witch of the Desert].
     [A play of the same name was given as new at S.W. W.
     15/2/1837).]
M.D. The Tartar Woman; or, The Spectre Crew (Surrey, M.
     20/7/1829).

Ent. Tea and Turn Out; or, Performers and Fashionables (C.G. W. 28/5/1823).

Ba. Teaching made Easy (Royalty, M. 20/10/1823).

F. Teague; or, The Faithful Irishman (Surrey, S. 24/3/1821).

— The Tea-Room; or Fiction and Reality. 8° 1811.

M.R. Tears and Smiles. L. 89 M. [Lyc. 8/5/1809].

Bsq. Tea-totallers versus Wittelers (Adel. M. 7/12/1840). L.C. 12/11/1840.

Ba. Teddy the Tiler (S.W. M. 10/5/1830).
[See RODWELL, 1830.]

Ba. Tekeli; or, The Siege of Montgatz (Royalty, M. 10/8/1812).
[See HOOK, 1806.]

O. Telemachus (C.G. 7/6/1815). L. 105 M. [25/5/1815].
[Music Bishop.]

P. Telemachus; or, Harlequin and Calypso (R.A. T. 14/7/1807).

Bsq. Telemachus; or, The Island of Calypso (Adel. 15/10/1844). L.C. 7/10/1844.

F. Temper; or, The Domestic Tyrant (Lyc. M. 1/5/1809). L. 89 M. [27/4/1809; under sub-title].

D. The Temperance Pledge; or, A True Lesson of Life (Vic. M. 24/6/1844).

D. The Templar and the Jewess (D.L. 26/5/1841).
[A version of Der Templar und die Jüden by W. A. Wohlbrück with music by H. Marschner, itself derived from Scott's Ivanhoe.]

Ba. Temptation; or, The Vale of Sarnem (St J. S. 11/11/1837). L.C. 1837.

M.D. The Tenant of the Tomb; or, The Vampire Bride (S.W. M. 8/3/1830).

D. Ten Thousand Years (Adel. W. 17/11/1841).

Ba. A Ten Years' Blunder (Surrey, M. 2/2/1824).

D. Ten Years of a Woman's Life; or, The Fruits of Bad Advice (R.P. M. 21/4/1834).

D. The Terrible Unknown; or, The Nuns of St. Jago (Surrey, M. 2/5/1836).

F. A Terrific Register; or, Tremendous 1824 (Cob. M. 15/3/1824).

M.D. The Terrors of Conscience. L. 62 S. [C.G. 2/5/1816].

M.D. Thalaba the Destroyer (Cob. M. 11/8/1823).

M.D. Thalia's Sketch Book (St J. T. 26/2/1836; Colosseum, M. 16/4/1838). L.C. 27/2/1836.

P. The Thames Tunnel; or, Harlequin Excavator (Cob. M. 11/6/1827).

Ba. That Rascal Jack. L.C. Strand, 6/9/1843.
[See T. GREENWOOD, 1843.]

F. That Rascal Jack (M'bone, M. 14/8/1848).

O.F. That's the Manager; or, He would be a Player (R.A. M. 28/8/1815).

Sat. The Theatric Count. A Tragi-Comedy...From the Orgoglio Cupitoso, Conte Teatrino, of Gonzago Dicchieri, adapted for Representation on the English Stage. 8° 1809.
[Relating to the O.P. riots; see The Rebellion.]

M.D. Therese; or, The Maid of Geneva (Cob. Th. 8/2/1821).

M.D. Therese; or, The Orphan of Geneva (Olym. W. 21/2/1821). L. 124 M. [17/2/1821].

Bsq. Theseus and Ariadne; or, The Labyrinth of Crete (E.O.H. M. 11/7/1836). L.C. 11/7/1836.

P. They would if they could; or, The Double Surprize (R.A. W. 3/8/1803).

D. Thirty Years; or, The Life of a Gamester. L.C. C.G. 13/10/1827.

M.D. Thirty Years of a Gambler's Life (Adel. M. 15/10/1827). L.C. 12/10/1827.

M.D. Thirty Years of a Gambler's Life (Cob. M. 10/1/1831).
   [These three plays are taken from V. Ducange, *Trente ans; ou, la vie d'un joueur* (Paris, 19/6/1827).]

F. Thompson and Co. (City, T. 19/4/1831).

O.F. Three and One; or, The Colonel's Choice. L.C. 2/1839.
   [A play of this name was given at the Queen's, 2/1831.]

Ba. The Three and the Deuce (Surrey, W. 27/6/1810).

Ba. The Three Beauties of Dresden. L.C. Liverpool, 12/11/1831.

M.D. The Three Caskets; or, The Jew of Venice (Cob. M. 12/2/1827).

Ext. The Three Cripples and the Queen of Billingsgate (Royalty, M. 25/11/1822).

M.D. The Three Crumps; or, The Crooked Brothers of Damascus (Sans P. Th. 5/2/1818). L. 112 M. [5/1/1818].

C. The Three Dons; or, The Rose of Tuscany (Cob. M. 17/11/1828).

F. Three Fathers and One Son (Surrey, W. 27/6/1827).

P. The Three Fishermen; or, The Box, the Fish and the Genii (Surrey, M. 15/7/1822).

O.F. The Three Fives; or, Penny Wise and Pound Foolish (Pav. Th. 13/2/1812). L. 95 M. [4/1/1812; as *The T. F.; or, The Generous Quaker*].

Sk. The Three Fra Diavolos (Lyc. M. 10/6/1844). L.C. 10/6/1844.
   [This is by *J. H. STOCQUELER*.]

M.D. Three generations; or, Before, During and After the French Revolution (Cob. M. 22/2/1830).

P. The Three Golden Lamps; or, Harlequin and the Wizard Dwarf (Adel. M. 26/12/1825).

F. The Three Johns; or, The Miller's Wife of Charlton (Cob. M. 8/11/1819).

M.D. The Three Mutineers; or, The Devil and the Dice (Cob. M. 15/9/1828).

Ext. Threepence a Pot; or, The 10th of October (Cob. M. 11/10/1830).

D. The Three Red Men (Surrey, M. 8/5/1848).
   [See *ARCHER*, 1848.]

Ba. The Three Spectres (Queen's, Th. 7/7/1831).

C.O. The Three Suitors (German, W. 15/8/1805).

Sk. The Three Sultanas (R.A. M. 24/4/1826).

O.F. Three to One (Queen's, Th. 3/2/1831).

Ba. The Three Vampires; or, Maids Beware of Moonshine! (Cob. M. 1/9/1823).

Ba. Three Weeks after Marriage (Surrey, F. 9/10/1812).

P. The Three Wishes; or, Harlequin and Funny Island (R.A. M. 27/12/1819).

Ba. Three Yards of Broadcloth; or, The Yorkshire Attorney (Cob. T. 21/2/1826).

M.D. The Thunderbolt; or, The Burning Forest (R.A. M. 31/8/1835).

P. Tibby and Tabby (Surrey, M. 31/8/1829).

M.D. The Ticket Porter; or, The Fate of Walsingham (Cob. M. 23/5/1825).

Ba. The Tiger at Large; or, The Cad of the Buss (Strand, M. 8/5/1837). L.C. St J. 21/4/1837.

Spec. The Tiger Horde (R.C. M. 4/7/1814).

M.D. The Tiger of the North (R.P. M. 17/6/1833).

Vaud. The Timepiece (Vic. M. 15/8/1836).

Ca. "The Times" (Queen's, M. 25/4/1831).

Spec. Timour Khan; or, The Prince and the Mandarin (Surrey, M. 27/11/1826).

Spec. Timour the Tartar (R.A. 9/1829).

Ba. The Tinder Box; or, Sparks in the Dark (S.W. M. 19/5/1823).

P. Tippitywitchet; or, Harlequin Tom Bobbin and the Comical Witches of Lancashire (Vic. F. 26/12/1845). L.C. 20/12/1845.

Int. 'Tis well they are married (Brandenburgh House, 6/1804).

Oa. Tit for Tat; or, The Tables Turned (E.O.H. T. 29/7/1828). L.C. 19/7/1828 [under sub-title].

Bal. The Tithe Sheaf; or, The Cockney Sportsman (Olym. M. 10/11/1828).

P. Tit, Tat, Toe—or, Harlequin Fairy Fortune and the Three Jolly Butcher Boys all in a Row. L.C. Effingham, 18/12/1847.

D. Titus Caesar; or, The Destruction of Jerusalem (R.P. M. 1/4/1839).

Prel. To be Let by Auction (Olym. 23/10/1820). L. 78 S. [20/10/1820].

Ba. To Be or not to Be; or, Harlequin versus Shakespeare (Surrey, Th. 26/12/1811).

O.F. Tom and Jerry; or, Life in London. L. 87 S. [Edinburgh, 2/1/1823]. 8° 1824 [Edinburgh].

O.F. Tom and Jerry in Edinburgh (Caledonian, Edinburgh, 1/3/1823).

M.D. The Tomb of Sigismond; or, The Murderer's Doom (W.L. M. 3/2/1823).

Ba. The Tom Boy (New, S. 26/1/1811—3rd performance).

Ba. Tom, Jerry and Logick Hop at Brighton. L.C. 24/10/1834.

Ba. Tom, Jerry and Logic; or, Life in London (Royalty, M. 29/4/1822). 18° 1823 (Edinburgh).

Ba. Tom Jones. L.C. Olym. 21/9/1843.

F. Tom Jones; or, Coming Out. L.C. Liverpool, 16/10/1848.

M.D. Tom Moor of Fleet Street; or, The Starling of the Old Saloup House (Surrey, M. 12/4/1841).

F. Tom Smart (C.L. 12/10/1827).

D. Tom Trim (Surrey, M. 25/9/1843).

Da. Tom Tug; or, The Regatta (R.C. S. 14/9/1816).

Ba. Too Busy by Half. L.C. 27/11/1832.

Ba. Too Careful by Half; or, Who would have thought it? (Strand, M. 30/7/1838). L.C. 1838.

F. The Toodles (City, 1832).

F. Too Friendly by Half (C.G. 29/10/1807).

O.F. Too Late for Dinner (S.W. T. 12/11/1844).

Ba. Too Late for Dinner. L.C. 18/2/1835.
[See *JONES*, 1820.]

O.F. Too many Cooks spoil the Broth (P'cess, Th. 15/1/1846). L.C. 20/12/1845.

F. Top Boots; or, The Rival Quacks (R.P. M. 28/4/1834).

F. To Persons about to Marry (Lyc. M. 4/11/1844). L.C. 31/10/1844.

O. Il Torneo (St J. F. 20/7/1838).

M.D. The Torrent of the Valley; or, The Dumb Boy and the Murderer (E.L. W. 27/11/1816).

M.D. The Torrent of the Valley; or, The Speech of the Dumb Restored (Surrey, M. 6/8/1821).

Ba. Touch and Take; or, Saturday Night and Monday Morning (Olym. M. 12/11/1827).

O.F. Touch and Take; or, The Law of the Kiss (H.² M. 15/4/1839). L.C. 15/4/1839.

O. Touch not the Queen. L.C. Grecian, 10/8/1849.
[A version of Scribe, *Ne touchez pas à la reine* (Paris, 16/1/1847). It seems that this play was not produced until 14/2/1853.]

P. The Touchstone; or, Harlequin Traveller (R.C. F. 26/12/1817).
[This is the old pantomime of *The Touchstone* altered.]

O.F. The Tourist Friend. 1810.
[Music C. Smith; see The "*Stage*" *Cyclopædia*.]

Ba. Tourists; or, A Supper for Three (Strand, 17/8/1839). L.C. 11/8/1839.

Spec. The Tournament of London; or, The Spectre Champion of Ratcliff Cross (R.A. M. 4/8/1834).

Spec. The Tower of London; or, England's Dark Ages (R.A. M. 8/6/1840).

D. The Tower of London; or, Og, Gog and Magog (Adel. M. 21/12/1840). L.C. 22/11/1840 [as The T. of L.; or, Queen Mary].

D. The Tower of Nesle; or, The Black Gondola (R.P. M. 24/9/1832).

D. The Tower of Notre Dame (Surrey, M. 3/4/1837).

M.D. The Tower of Zauffen; or, The Cavern of Glotzden (Cob. M. 4/10/1830).

Ba. Town Favourites. L.C. 8/12/1831.

Bal. Tracey Castle; or, Love and Jealousy (R.A. M. 20/5/1811).

D. Trafalgar; or, The Last Days of Nelson. L.C. Brit. 12/6/1849.

Int. Trafalgar; or, The Sailor's Play. 8° 1807 [Uxbridge].

P. Transformation; or, Harlequin Navigator (Sans P. M. 25/3/1816).

Ext. Transformation; or, Six to One against you (Surrey, M. 27/5/1822).

Ba. Transformations; or, Travelling in Ireland (Olym. F. 16/2/1821).

D. The Trapper of the Hills; or, The Strong Man of the West. (R.P. 3/11/1845). L.C. 31/10/1845.

D. The Traveller; or, The Marriage in Sicily. 8° 1809.

M.D. The Travellers; or, Music's Fascination (Cob. M. 19/7/1819). [See *CHERRY*, 1806.]

M.D. The Travellers Benighted; or, The Forest of Rosenwald (H.² M. 30/9/1811). L. 95 M. [26/9/1811].

Ba. Travelling Incog.; or, A Bold Stroke for a Dinner (Cob. M. 16/2/1824).

Bal.P. The Treacherous Baron; or, Albert and Emma (C.G. W. 8/7/1812).

Ba. The Treacherous Black; or, The Monkey of the Wreck. L.C. 28/11/1829.

M.D. The Treacherous Uncle; or, The Curse of Avarice (Surrey, T. 18/4/1826).

F.   Treacle and Mustard; or, My Aunt's Tragedy (Cob. M. 11/9/1820).

F.   The Treadmill; or, The Greeks at Brixton (Olym. M. 4/11/1822).

Bal.   The Treble Lover; or, The Gentle Revenge (Sans P. M. 6/12/1813).

M.D.   Trenck the Pandour; or, The Bohemian Banditti (Surrey, M. 13/10/1823).

D.   Trevanion; or, The False Position (Surrey, M. 22/10/1849).

Ent.   Tria juncta in uno; or, Emma the Prude! Ellen the Romp! Eliza the Idiot! (Cob. M. 9/9/1822).

M.D.   The Trial of Friendship (Surrey, M. 5/12/1825).

C.   The Trial of Love (D.L. Th. 1/3/1827). L.C. C.G. 24/2/1827.

D.   The Trial of Skill (R.P. M. 7/12/1835).

Ba.   The Trials of Poverty (Adel. M. 20/3/1843).

O.F.   Trick for Trick. L.C. C.G. 17/12/1827.

O.F.   Trick for Trick; or, The Admiral's Daughter (C.G. Th. 2/7/1812). L. 56 S. [H.² 6/6/1812].

F.   Tricking's Fair in Love (C.G. Th. 26/5/1814). L. 101 M. [19/5/1814].

F.   Tricks and Blunders; or, Which is my Son? (W.L. M. 16/9/1822).

Ba.   Tricks and Blunders; or, English, Irish and Scotch (Cob. M. 3/2/1823).

Ba.   Tricks and Blunders; or, English, Irish and Scotch. L.C. Olym. 25/10/1825.

C.   The Triple Discovery. L. 75 M. [H.² 13/3/1800].

F.   A Trip to Hampton (P'cess, W. 3/11/1847).

Ba.   A Trip to Scarborough (Royalty, M. 30/8/1813).

Ba.   A Trip to the Ball; or, The Family Tutor (Cob. M. 16/6/1823).

F.   A Trip to Tunbridge; or, Do you call that nothing? (City, Th. 27/10/1831).

D.   The Triumph of Fidelity (Strand, Th. 16/2/1832).

D.   The Triumphs of the Sons of Baliol; or, Liberty Vanquished. 8° 1810.

M.Ent.   The Trophy (Colosseum, M. 31/7/1837).

Bal.   The Troubadour (Queen's, M. 14/3/1831).

Ba.   A Troublesome Lodger (St J. M. 11/2/1839). L.C. 1839.

D.   True Satisfaction; or, The Borders of the Ukraine. L. 104 M. [D.L. 29/9/1815].

Prel.   Trumps in the Dumps; or, A Peep into the House of Correction (S.W. M. 14/4/1823).
   [This appears for the Olym. in L. 127 M. [1/11/1822] as *T. in the D.; or, Diamonds in Durance*.]

C.   The Trustee. L. 89 M. [H.² 24/2/1809].

P.   Truth; or, Harlequin Touchstone (W.L. W. 26/12/1821).

Ba.   Try Again; or, Counterplots and Countermines (Olym. F. 12/1/1821). L. 80 S. [2/1/1821].

Bal.   Try before you Buy; or, Sweet Roses (R.A. M. 19/5/1806).

Pasticcio.   T. T. S.; or, The Bar and the Stage (W.L. T. 13/1/1829).

Ba.   Turn and Turn; or, The Clown and the Captain (S.W. Th. 26/7/1827).

O.F.   Turn Hands and Change Partners. L.C. D.L. 28/7/1825.

Ba.   Turning the Tables. L.C. 22/11/1836.
   [See *POOLE*, 1830.]

C.   Turns and Returns. L. 60 S. [H.² 9/8/1814].
        [This is *R. F. JAMESON, Love and Gout.*]
Spec. Turpin's Ride to York and the Death of Black Bess (R.A. M.
        3/8/1835).
M.D. The Turret Clock; or, Lovers' Signals (D.L. W. 28/1/1818).
        L. 69 S. [14/1/1818].
        [Music Lanza.]
P.   The Turret Demon; or, Harlequin and Flora. L. 92 M. [Pav.
        10/10/1810].
F.   The Twa Ghaists (Edinburgh, 1/5/1835). L.C. 4/4/1833.
Int.   The Twelfth of August (Brighton, 13/8/1805).
Ba.   The Twelve Months (Strand, Th. 18/12/1834).
F.   Twelve O'Clock; or, The Wager Lost (Olym. Th. 27/2/1823).
D.   The Twelve Pages. L.C. C.G. 2/1826.
F.   The 24th of May. L.C. Olym. 8/2/1844.
Ext.   Twenty Maids and One Bachelor (R.A. M. 11/7/1825).
Ba.   £20,000; or, London Love (Adel. M. 4/2/1833). L.C. 4/2/1833.
D.   The Twin Brothers; or, Pride and Patience (Surrey, M. 1/2/1830).
M.D.   Twm John Catty, the Welsh Rob Roy (Cob. M. 14/4/1823;
        Garrick, M. 3/1/1831).
Ba.   The Two Bears (Cob. M. 13/5/1822).
Spec. The Two Bears in Smyrna (R.A. M. 2/5/1831).
Ba.   The Two Bodkins. L.C. 2/12/1837.
M.D.   The Two Brothers of Pisa (Cob. M. 7/1/1822; Surrey, M.
        5/4/1847).
D.   The Two Clerks; or, The Merchant's Wife of Havre. L.C. C.L.
        26/1/1846.
O.F.   The Two Crispins. L.C. D.L. 1826.
F.   The Two Doctor Hobbs's (C.G. S. 1/7/1815). L. 105 M.
        [19/6/1815; as, *Love's Resurrection; or, The T. D. H.*].
M.D.   The Two Dogs of Ravensdale (Surrey, M. 3/9/1838).
D.   The Two Drovers (Caledonian, Edinburgh, 5/7/1828).
M.D.   The Two Farmers; or, The Forest of St. Vallier (Surrey, M.
        20/10/1823).
D.   The Two Fathers; or, The Inn of the Three Olive Trees (R.P.
        T. 26/1/1836).
D.   The Two Friends; or, The Liverpool Merchant. 8° 1800.
        [By C. H.; a translation from Beaumarchais.]
M.D.Spec. The Two Galley Slaves; or, The Unknown (Cob. M.
        11/8/1828).
Bsq.   The Two Gallows Slaves; or, Escaped from Brixton (Olym. M.
        9/12/1822). L. 84 S. [30/11/1822; as *Two More Slaves; or, E.
        from B.*].
Ba.   The Two Greens (Olym. Th. 20/2/1840).
C.   Two Heads better than One (Lyc. M. 27/5/1844).
C.O.   The Two Houses of Granada (D.L. T. 31/10/1826). L.C.
        27/10/1826.
        [Music Wade.]
Ba.   The Two Jack Sheppards (Olym. 26/4/1841). L.C. 26/4/1841.
Ba.   The Two Jim Crows (Vic. M. 6/2–M. 13/2/1837).
Oa.   The Two Little Savoyards (Queen's, F. 13/2/1835).
Ba.   The Two Little Savoyards (Sans P. M. 13/11/1815).
D.   The Two Locksmiths; or, Poverty and Crime (Surrey, M.
        29/11/1841).

D. The Two London Locksmiths; or, The Banker, the Thief and the Will (Vic. M. 29/11/1841).
F. Two Mr. Browns (Bath, 6/5/1825). L.C. 26/4/1825.
Ba. Two Murders but Nobody Hurt (Surrey, M. 3/6/1822).
Ba. The Two Neighbours and their Wives (Vic. Th. 19/1/1837).
D. Two Nights. L.C. C.G. 5/11/1829.
F. Twonkey and Son. L.C. Richmond, 29/10/1842.
F. Two o'Clock in the Morning (D.L. 22/6/1841).
F. Two Old Maids of Florence. 8° 1808 [in *The Dramatic Appellant*].
F. Two Owls in One Ivy Bush (Lyc. Th. 23/11/1848). L.C. 25/11/1848.
F. Two Pence (E.O.H. S. 14/7/1821). L. 24 L. [25/6/1821; as *T. P.; or, Ladies Ridiculed*].
    [Music G. Reeve and M. Pindar.]
O.F. The Two Prisoners. L. 44 S. [D.L. 12/11/1804].
D. The Two Pupils; or, The Pedagogue Puzzled (Surrey, Th. 13/1/1831).
C. The Two Rainbows (P'cess, W. 2/12/1846). L.C. 27/11/1846.
Ba. The Two Spanish Valets; or, Lie upon Lie! (Sans P. M. 2/11/1818).
Ba. Two Stages from Gretna (Surrey, W. 12/11/1828).
M.D. The Two Thieves; or, The Murderers of Grenoble (Surrey, M. 1/12/1823).
Bal. Two to One (R.A. T. 27/5/1806).
Ba. The Two Valets (Cob. M. 2/9/1822).
D. The Two Waiters (Standard, 7/5/1849). L.C. 5/5/1849.
Sk. The Two Wives! or, A Hint to Husbands (E.O.H. T. 7/8/1821). L. 123 M. [6/7/1821; as *The T. W.; or, A Hint to a Cross Husband*].
    [Music Parry.]
M.Ent. The Tyrant and Parrasite. L. 95 M. [Lyc. 25/1/1812].
D. The Tyrant of Algiers (Vic. M. 12/3/1838).
M.D. The Tyrant of Syracuse; or, The Grecian Heroine (Cob. Th. 1/3/1827).
Spec. The Tyrant Saracen and the Noble Moor (R.A. M. 15/4/1811).
O. The Tyrolese Peasant (D.L. T. 8/5/1832). L.C. 7/5/1832.
M.D. Ugolino. L. 24 L. [Norwich, 3/1822].
M.D. Ugolino; or, The Tower of Famine (Surrey, W. 26/12/1821).
D. Ulrica; or, The Prisoner of State (Adel. M. 11/3/1844).
D. Ulric the Usurper (New, M. 3/12/1810).
Spec. Ulthona the Sorceress (Sans P. 11/1807).
F. The Ultra Exquisite; or, Which is the Dandy? L. 75 S. [Edinburgh, 22/4/1819].
D. Umbroso; or, Magic Delusion (Vic. M. 31/3/1834).
Tale of Enchantment. Una and the Lions; or, The Forest Queen (Garrick, M. 21/11/1831).
Ba. Uncle and Nephew; or, Look before you leap (Royalty, M. 5/11/1821).
O.F. Uncle Jonathan; or, Independence (S.W. M. 24/9/1827).
Ba. Uncle Oliver; or, A House Divided (E.O.H. M. 20/3/1843).
F. The Unconscious Counterfeit (D.L. 9/2/1809). L. 89 M. [20/1/1809].
Vaud. Under the Oak (Vauxhall, F. 25/6/1830).
M.D. Undine; or, The Spirit of the Waters (C.G. M. 23/4/1821) L. 80 S. [12/4/1821].
Ba. Unfit for Service. L.C. Edinburgh, 4/4/1833.

Spec. The Unhallowed Templar; or, Twelve Months and a Day (Cob. M. 16/4/1827).
F. The Uniform; or, Two Men in One Coat (Surrey, W. 14/4/1841).
Bal. The United Britons (D.L. Th. 10/1/1805—2nd performance).
F. United Service (C.G. S. 11/12/1841). L.C. 11/11/1841.
M.D. The Unknown; or, Ulfrid the Dane (R.C. M. 29/3/1819).
D. The Unnatural Combat; or, The Admiral of Marseilles (R.P. M. 22/9/1834).
Ba. Up and Down; or, The Road of Life (Strand, M. 3/9/1838). L.C. 8/1838.
C. Ups and Downs; or, The Ladder of Life (D.L. T. 27/5/1828). L.C. 17/5/1828.
D. Ups and Downs of Life; or, The Scamps of London. L.C. R.P. 25/11/1843.
F. Up to Snuff; or, A Friend at a Pinch (P'cess, W. 22/3/1848). L.C. 11/3/1848 [sub-title reads, or, New Year's Gifts].
R.D. Uranda the Enchanter of the Steel Castle (R.A. M. 7/4/1817).
M.D. Urilda the Transformed (R.P. M. 28/10/1833).
Vaud. Used Up; or, L'homme blasé. L.C. York, 2/6/1845.
Ba. The Usurer's Son. L.C. Adel. 23/2/1840.
T. Valasco; or, Castilian Honour (M'bone, S. 29/9/1849). L.C. 7/9/1849.
Spec. Valdevina the Cruel (Sans P. M. 8/2/1808).
Ext. Valentine and Orson (Lyc. M. 23/12/1844). L.C. 18/12/1844. 8° [1844].
F. Valentine's Day, Dedicated to all whom it may concern. Valentine's Day; or, The Amorous Knight, and the Belle Widow. A New and Original Comedy...Prefixed by a Poetical Appeal to the Critics. By One Anonymous. 8° [1809].
F. Valentine's Day; or, Paddy Carey's Fortune (Royalty, S. 13/2/1813).
C. Valeria (H.² M. 15/9/1828). L.C. 13/9/1828.
  [A version of Scribe, Valérie (Paris, 21/12/1822).]
Spec. The Valiant Clara; or, Love and Jealousy (Pav. M. 23/11/1812).
P. The Valkyrae; or, Harlequin the Patriot Pole (Surrey, W. 26/12/1832).
D. The Valley of Wolves (Surrey, M. 20/9/1830).
Ba. The Valley of Flowers (St J. T. 14/5/1839).
Spec. Valmondi; or, The Unhallowed Sepulchre (Adel. Th. 14/10/1824). L.C. 11/10/1824.
M.D. Vanrick of Voorn; or, The Executioner of Amsterdam (S.W. M. 16/11/1835).
D. Viricatus, the Lusitanian Hero. L.C. Norwich, 30/6/1826.
Ba. Valshi. L.C. 11/3/1824.
M.D. Valvoni; or, The Knight of the Bloody Hand (Royalty, M. 31/3/1823).
M.D. Van Donderman; or, The Two Friends (W.L. W. 28/1/1829).
D. Varley the Vulture; or, A Race for Life (Brit. 10/2/1845). L.C. 10/12/1844.
M.D. The Vehme Gericht; or, The Secret Tribunal (S.W. M. 22/3/1830).
F. The Veiled Portrait; or, The Chateau de Beauvais (C.G. Th. 10/5/1838). L.C. 7/5/1838.
M.D. The Veiled Prophet of Khorossan (R.A. M. 24/7/1820).
Ba. Il Venditore d'Aceto. L. 96 M. [Pantheon, 26/2/1812].

Bal.   The Venetian Nuptials; or, The Guardian Outwitted (D.L. Th. 31/10/1822).
Ba.   Venice Preserved; or, A Plot Discovered (E.L. M. 18/8/1817).
F.   The Venison Pasty (C.G. S. 10/11/1821). L. 123 M. [6/11/1821].
M.D.   Venoni (R.P. M. 30/12/1839).
Bal.   Venus and Adonis; or, The Bower of Bliss (S.W. M. 5/5/1828).
Ba.   Venus and Mars; or, The Golden Net (Strand, M. 8/4/1844). L.C. 1/4/1844.
M.D.   Venus a Vestal (Olym. Th. 15/10/1840). L.C. 16/10/1840.
Ba.   Venus in Arms; or, What won't a Woman do? (Strand, 23/5/1836). L.C. 21/5/1836.
   [This is by *Mrs C. B. WILSON*.]
D.   The Vermont Wool Dealer (Strand, Th. 27/2/1845). L.C. 28/9/1844.
Spec.   The Veteran; or, The Mareschal de Logis (R.A. M. 8/10/1804).
Bal.   The Veteran; or, Who will get her out? (Olym. W. 31/1/1827).
D.   The Veteran Serjeant; or, The Gunner's Boy and the Foundling of the Camp (S.W. M. 15/4/1839).
Past.O.   The Vicar of Wakefield (H.² 27/9/1823). L. 199 M. [21/9/1823].
M.D.   The Viceroy; or, The Spanish Gipsy and the Assassin (S.W. M. 26/5/1817).
D.   The Victim (Adel. M. 9/12/1833). L.C. 7/12/1833.
T.   The Victim. L. 116 M. [Edinburgh, 17/12/1819].
M.D.   The Victim; or, The Mother and the Mistress (Surrey, M. 4/9/1820).
Spec.   The Victims of Tyranny; or, The Monkish Warriors (R.A. M. 23/8/1802).
D.   Victoire; or, The Fall of Constantina (Adel. M. 4/12/1837).
M.D.   Victor and Hortense; or, False Pride (H.² Th. 2/11/1843—2nd performance). L.C. 28/10/1843.
Bsq.   "Victor Dene; or, I'll sleep on it" (Surrey, 23/1/1832).
Spec.   The Victories of Edward the Black Prince; or, The Battlefield (R.A. M. 1/4/1839).
Spec.   The Victories of Joan of Arc; or, The Siege of Orleans (R.A. M. 4/11/1839).
Bal.   The Village Fête (R.A. M. 6/9/1802).
Ba.   The Village Fête (New, M. 23/4/1810).
D.D.   Village Life in France; or, The Wine Dresser's Daughter (S.W. M. 30/1/1837).
D.   The Village Outcast. L.C. Olym. 26/11/1844.
   [Qu. *T. P. TAYLOR*, 1846.]
M.D.   The Village Phantom (R.P. M. 15/4/1839).
O.   The Village Phantom; or, The Somnambulists (Vic. F. 6/12/1833).
F.   The Village Practitioner (Caledonian, Edinburgh, 1824).
T.   La Vinda de Padilla (Cob. W. 23/5/1832).
D.   The Vine-dresser's Daughter (R.A. M. 7/9/1846).
T.   Virginia (M'bone, M. 7/5/1849). L.C. 28/4/1849.
Ba.   The Virginia Mummy. L.C. 15/3/1837.
D.   The Virgin of the Sun. L. 104 M. [Norwich, 12/6/1815].
P.   Virtue and Vice; or, Harlequin's Temptation (Cob. M. 17/8/1818).
M.D.   The Vision of the Sun; or, The Orphan of Peru (C.G. M. 31/3/1823). L. 128 M. [14/3/1823].
Int.   A Visit to the Wells; or, Out of the Frying Pan into the Fire (S.W. M. 19/4/1830).

Bal. La Vivandière (H.¹ S. 20/7/1844).
D. La Vivandière; or, The Eve of Waterloo. L.C. R.P. 2/7/1845.
Ext. Vive la Bagatelle; or, Tommy and Jerry t'other Side the Water (Cob. M. 2/12/1822).
D. "Vive la Liberté"; or, The French Revolution of 1830 (Surrey, S. 14/8/1830).
Ba. The Vizier's Son, the Merchant's Daughter and the Ugly Woman; or, The Maid of Bagdad (Sans P. M. 16/12/1811). L. 94 M. [27/11/1811].
Spec. Voorn the Tiger; or, The Horse Banditti (R.A. M. 8/6/1812).
M.D. The Votaries of the Ruby Cross; or, The Treasure Seekers (Cob. M. 23/2/1829).
M.D. The Vow of Vengeance; or, The Carib Chieftain and the Irish Witch (Cob. M. 11/6/1821).
F. A Voyage to California; or, The True Test of Gold (Vic. 5/2/1849). L.C. 3/2/1849 [as A Trip to C.].
Ent. A Voyage to India (Lyc. Th. 20/8/1807).
F. The Voyage to Margate; or, Sea Bathing a Cure for Roguery. L. 78 S. [E.O.H. 20/7/1820].
F. A Voyage to the Gold Mines. L.C. Queen's, 18/5/1849.
D. A Voyage to the North. L.C. Hull, 26/12/1833.
Spec. A Voyage to the North Pole; or, The British Esquimaux (Royalty, M. 3/11/1823).
D. Waconsta; or, The Curse (Surrey, M. 12/11/1849).
M.Ent. The Wager. 8° 1808 [in The Dramatic Appellant].
Ba. The Wager; or, How to Furnish a House without Money (St J. Th. 5/1/1837). L.C. 3/1/1837.
M.D. The Wager; or, The Last Link in the Chain (S.W. M. 13/7/1840).
C.O. The Wager; or, The Midnight Hour (D.L. W. 23/11/1825). L.C. 21/11/1825.
[A version of Mrs Inchbald, The Midnight Hour.]
Bal. The Wags of Wapping (D.L. M. 16/11/1846).
Ba. The Wags of Windsor (Royalty, c. M. 26/11/1810).
M.D. Wake not the Dead; or, The Spectre Bride (Cob. M. 18/10/1824).
M.D. Walcot Castle [or Angelina]. L. 20 L. [1804].
F. Walker's Trunks. L.C. 30/6/1837.
D. Wallace (Surrey, T. 12/3/1833).
D. Wallenstein. 8° 1799; 8° 1800 [two parts].
P. Walooka and Noomahee; or, The Ape of the Island (Olym. M. 28/11/1825).
R.D. Walpurghi's Eve; or, The Doom of the Daemon Knight (Surrey, S. 17/7/1830).
D. Walsha; or, The Slave's Revolt (Vic. M. 13/11/1837).
D. Walter Lorimer; or, The Brand of Crime (R.P. 13/1/1845). L.C. 11/1/1845.
M.D. The Waltham Blacks; or, The Deer Stealer of 1623 (R.P. M. 17/9/1832).
C.O. The Waltz (Lyc. Th. 19/8/1813). L. 58 S. [7/8/1813].
[An adaptation of Wycherley, The Gentleman Dancing Master.]
Bal.P. The Wanderer of Malabar (Cob. M. 19/4/1830).
R.D. The Wandering Boys; or, The Castle of Olival (C.G. Th. 24/2/1814). L. 102 M. [11/2/1814].
[Music Bishop. An adaptation of Pixérécourt, Le pèlerin blanc (Paris, 1801).]

D.   The Wandering Jew (Queen's, Th. 5/3/1835).
M.D. The Wandering Knight (New, T. 8/12/1810).
D.   The Wandering Minstrel. L.C. 1827.
D.   The Wandering Tribe; or, The Heir of Mowbray (Surrey, M. 17/7/1837).
F.   Wanted a Bravo. L.C. S.W. 5/9/1846.
F.   Wanted a Hermit (Lyc. T. 25/5/1847). L.C. 13/5/1847.
Ba. Wanted an Actor; or, The Manager at a Nonplus (R.P. M. 27/9/1830).
Ca. Wanted a Title. L.C. Lyc. 18/5/1849.
Ba. Wards and Wardens. L.C. E.O.H. 28/8/1830.
Spec. The War in Syria; or, The Bombardment and Capture of St. Jean d'Acre (Vic. M. 7/12/1840).
R.D. The Warlock of the Glen (Surrey, M. 10/12/1827).
     [A play of this title was being played at the Caledonian, Edinburgh, in 1823.]
M.D. Warlsha; or, The Saxon Slave (Surrey, T. 27/4/1841).
Ca. A Warning to Wives (S.W. 5/11/1849). L.C. 1/10/1847.
D.   The Warrior Kings; or, The Massacre of Jerusalem (R.P. M. 30/11/1835).
D.   The Warrior's Faith; or, Love, Honour and Friendship (R.P. M. 28/4/1834).
Bal. The Warrior Slaves; or, The Miracle of Love (Vic. M. 8/2/1841).
Spec. The Wars in Spain (R.A. M. 15/5/1837).
Spec. The Wars of the Jews; or, The Fall of Jerusalem (R.A. T. 26/12/1848). L.C. 29/6/1848.
Spec. Wars of the Punjab. L.C. Amphitheatre, Hull, 1/10/1846.
Spec. The Wars of Wellington (R.A. M. 31/3/1834; M. 18/5/1840).
M.D. The War Woolf of Tlascala; or, The Mexican's Watchword (Cob. M. 4/8/1828).
D.   The Washerwoman of St. Remy (R.A. M. 19/10/1846).
D.   The Watchdog of the Castle; or, The Sword of Whitefriars. L.C. Vic. 20/3/1844.
F.   Watching the Body; or, How to Make a Will (M'bone, M. 18/12/1848).
Ba. The Watchman; or, The Army and the Navy (W.L. M. 9/2/1829).
P.Bal. The Water-carrier and the Beauty; or, The Ugly Woman of Bagdad (Garrick, M. 7/2/1831).
D.   The Water Kelpie, a Tale of the Clyde (Edinburgh, 15/9/1844).
Ent. The Waterman (S.W. M. 26/8/1844).
Spec. The Water Queen; or, The Spirits of Donan the Goblin Page (Surrey, M. 8/6/1835).
Ba. The Water Witch; or, The Skimmer of the Sea (Adel. M. 15/11/1830). L.C. 13/11/1830.
P.   Wat Tyler; or, The Lord Mayor of London. L.C. Queen's, 23/12/1844.
D.   Wat Tyler and Jack Straw; or, The Life and Death of King Richard II (Cob. M. 17/1/1831).
D.   The Wave. L.C. Vic. 19/8/1847.
D.   Waverley (Perth, 18/10/1822).
     [The version of Scott's novel used by the Corbett Ryder Company.]
D.   Waverley. L.C. C.G. 24/4/1824.

D. Waverley; or, The Forty Five (Caledonian, Edinburgh, 4/9/1827).
    [It seems that there was an earlier version given at this theatre
    on 19/7/1823.]
F. The Way of the World. L.C. R.P. 10/6/1846.
C. The Way to Win Her. 8° 1814.
Ba. The Weathercock (New. M. 18/2/1811).
F. Webster's Royal Red Book (Adel. Th. 5/7/1849). L.C. 30/6/1849.
F. The Wedding Supper (Vic. Th. 27/11/1834).
Ent. A Week at Holyrood (Edinburgh, 28/4/1832). L.C. 23/4/1832.
Ba. We Fly by Night (Royalty, S. 23/1/1813).
D. The Wehr Wolves of St. Grieux (Surrey, M. 11/2/1833).
P. The Weird Sisters; or, Harlequin in Despair (Royalty, Th.
    12/1/1804).
P. The Weird Sisters; or, Harlequin Restored (Royalty, M. 25/1/1802).
M.D. The Weird Woman of the Isles; or, Scotland's Ancient Days
    (Cob. M. 19/4/1824).
Bal. Welcome Home; or, The Return from Navarino (S.W. W.
    26/12/1827).
M.D. The Welshman; or, The Prince of Cambria (Cob. M. 15/5/1826).
Ba. West Country Wooing (Queen's, M. 8/8/1836).
Spec. The West Indian Terrific Brothers (Pav. M. 11/1/1813).
F. The Wet Nurse (Surrey, M. 20/4/1840).
F. Wet Weather (H.² T. 20/7/1819). L. 76 S. [9/7/1819].
Ba. Whackam and Windam; or, The Wrangling Lawyers (Sans P. T.
    25/1/1814; Olym. M. 26/1/1829). L. 22 L. [14/1/1814; as, Broad
    Grins; or, W. and W.].
C.O. Whang Fong; or, How Remarkable! (E.O.H. M. 21/8/1820).
    L. 79 S. [5/8/1820].
    [Music Pindar.]
F. What are you at? What are you after? or, There never was such
    Times (Cob. W. 19/4/1820).
F. What a Shocking Bad Hat! (Cob. T. 10/5/1831).
Ba. What have I done? (Olym. M. 12/3/1838). L.C. 2/3/1838.
Ba. What next? (E.L. W. 8/1/1817).
    [See T. J. DIBDIN, 1816.]
O.Ent. What's in a Name? (E.O.H. M. 20/7/1829). L.C. 1/6/1829.
Ca. What's in a Name? or, Black's White (Vic. W. 16/12/1835).
F. What! The Devil Again! (Strand, M. 30/9/1833).
F. What to Eat, Drink and Avoid (Olym. M. 4/9/1848). L.C.
    4/9/1848.
Ba. What will he do next? (Surrey, M. 5/12/1825).
F. What would the Man be at? (C.G. F. 8/5/1801). L. 76 M.
    [30/4/1801; as, Three to One; or, W. w. the M. b. a.?].
F. Wheedling; or, Love in a Snowstorm (Strand, W. 18/7/1832).
Int. When it takes Place, I shall keep my Seat and get a Place (C.G.
    F. 14/7/1820). L. 119 M. [21/6/1820; with "If" for "When"].
Spec. When the Bell Tolls; or, The Banditti of the Cavern (Cob. M.
    18/10/1819).
O.F. When the Clock Strikes; or, The Bandit Farmer (R.A. M.
    9/10/1820).
F. Where is Eliza? or, Have you seen my Sister? (Brit. 25/10/1847).
    L.C. 18/10/1847.
F. Where's Eliza? What is she at? Where can she be? (Strand, M.
    18/10/1847).

C.   Where to Find a Friend (Lyc. M. 20/5/1811). L. 54 S. [11/5/1811].
     [This is by R. LEIGH.]
Ba. Which can be the Man? The Prince or the Chimney Sweep (Cob.
     M. 8/1/1821).
F.   Which is my Love? L.C. Queen's, 18/4/1846.
     [A play of this name was produced at the Queen's, 25/2/1850.]
F.   Which is the Woman? (Vic. T. 1/10/1833).
P.   Which is Which? or, Harlequin Puzzled (Surrey, W. 6/6/1810).
D.   The Whistle (R.A. M. 6/6/1836).
M.D. The White Bard's Tower (R.A. M. 24/4/1820).
P.   The White Cat (Edinburgh, 26/1/1813).
P.   The White Cat; or, Harlequin in the Fairy Wood (Lyc. M.
     23/12/1811). L. 53 S. [18/12/1811].
M.D. The White Cross Knight; or, Martha of Mile End (R.P. M.
     19/5/1834).
M.D. The White Eagle; or, Lionel Prince of Saxony (Cob. M.
     16/6/1828).
Tale of Enchantment. The White Fairy; or, The Dove and the Vulture
     (Cob. M. 12/4/1830).
D.   The White Farm (R.A. M. 29/11/1847).
Ca. The White Feather (Lyc. M. 20/5/1844). L.C. 11/5/1844.
     [Another drama of the same title is in L.C. C.G. 19/9/1843.]
D.   The Whitefeet; or, Mabel the Maniac (R.P. M. 9/7/1832).
Spec. The White Hoods; or, The Beggars of Flanders (R.P. M.
     3/9/1838).
M.R. The White Lady; or, The Spirit of Avenel (D.L. M. 9/10/1826).
     L.C. 3/10/1826.
     [Music T. S. Cooke. A dramatisation of Scribe, La dame
     blanche (Paris, 10/12/1825), with music by Boieldieu.]
Int. The White Lion; or, Love, Lies and Literature (R.P. M. 8/7/1833).
M.D. The White Nun; or, The Heart of a True Blue (R.P. M.
     18/4/1831).
Spec. The White Pilgrims; or, The Orphans of Switzerland (Cob. W.
     1/11/1820).
D.   The White Rose and the Red Rose; or, The Battle of Bosworth
     Field (R.A. M. 10/8/1835).
D.   The White Squall; or, The Mariner's Daughter (R.P. M. 27/5/1839).
M.D. The White Surrey (Surrey, S. 9/4/1825).
D.   The White Wolf; or, The Black Walloon (R.A. M. 27/4/1840).
D.   The White Wreath; or, The Summer's Morn of 1660 and the
     Flitch of Bacon (R.A. M. 20/7/1840).
M.D. Whitsun Eve; or, The Last Link of the Chain (R.P. M.
     7/10/1839).
Ext. Whittington and his Cat. 8° [1849; Ashford].
     [By the author of Dead of Ennui and The Subaltern's Check
     Book; these I have been unable to find, but the former is evidently
     a version of L'homme blasé or Used Up.]
Bsq. Whittington and his Cat. L.C. 24/3/1845.
P.   Whittington and his Cat; or, Harlequin Lord Mayor of London
     (D.L. S. 26/12/1835).
R.   Whittington and his Cat; or, The Fairy Queen of Herne's Oak
     (H.² T. 26/12/1837). L.C. 23/12/1837.
Ba. Who am I? or, Adventures in Madrid (E.L. W. 3/11/1819).
F.   Who can I be? (C.G. M. 6/7/1818). L. 113 M. [30/6/1818].

F.   Who did it? or, What's in the Wind? (Adel. M. 11/5/1846).
F.   Who is that knocking at the Door? (Strand, T. 23/11/1847).
P.   Who killed Cock Robin? L.C. C.G. 14/12/1829.
M.D. Who kissed Jeannette; or, The Festival of the Rose (E.L. M. 22/2/1819).
F.   The Whole Hog. L.C. Adel. 9/11/1844.
F.   Who Lives at Number Nine? (Adel. W. 28/3/1849).
M.D. Who Owns the Head? or, The Monkey, the Mask and the Murderer (Cob. M. 15/1/1821).
C.Ent. Who Pays the Piper? (Royalty, M. 26/12/1803).
Int.   Who Pays the Piper? L. 92 M. [Pav. 2/2/1810].
Oa.   Who's at Home? or, Man and Wife before Marriage (E.O.H. M. 1/8/1825). L.C. 4/7/1825.
F.   Who's my Papa? (P'cess, S. 19/4/1845). L.C. 21/6/1845.
O.F. Who's the Rogue? (C.G. 15/5/1801). L. 76 M. [8/5/1801].
      [Music Florio.]
Ba.   Who's to have him? (R.P. W. 18/5/1831).
F.   Why did I marry? (Olym. M. 11/12/1820). L. 119 M. [7/12/1820; with sub-title, or, City Intrigue].
Spec. The Wicked Negro; or, A Picture of St. Domingo (Royalty, M. 15/3/1802).
O.F. The Widow; or, My Uncle's Will (Olym. 21/11/1831). L.C. 17/11/1831.
F.   The Widow Barnaby (H.² M. 18/1/1841).
C.   The Widow Bewitched; or, Love at Fault (H.² W. 15/6/1831). L.C. 21/5/1831.
Ba.   The Widow Flinn (Surrey, Th. 3/5/1810).
Ba.   The Widow of Cornhill. L.C. 25/10/1824.
      [See PLANCHÉ, 1824.]
Ba.   The Widow of Cornhill; or, London in 1444 (Surrey, T. 13/11/1832).
C.O. The Widow of Ems (Queen's, M. 7/11/1831).
O.F. The Widow's Choice L. 87 M. [C.G. 15/2/1808].
M.D. The Widow's Daughter; or, The Murder of 1694 (R.P. Th. 26/12/1833).
F.   The Widow's Frolic. L.C. H.² 10/11/1842.
      [A play of this name appeared at the Vic. 1/2/1841.]
Ca.   The Widow's Mistake (Queen's, M. 8/6/1835).
Ba.   The Widow's Mite. L.C. 4/4/1837.
Bsq.Oa. Widow's Tears (Sans P. Th. 23/10/1817).
D.   The Widow's Vow. L.C. Olym. 10/11/1840.
Ba.   The Widow's Vow; or, Mistake upon Mistake (R.A. M. 16/4/1827).
D.   The Wife (P'cess, T. 17/6/1845).
D.   Wife and Child. L.C. St J. 23/1/1836.
Spec. The Wife and Mistress; or, The Italian Gamester (Pav. T. 20/11/1810).
Ba.   The Wife at her Wit's End (R.A. W. 3/11/1819—3rd performance).
Ba.   A Wife's First Lesson (Cob. M. 23/8/1819).
Ba.   A Wife's First Lesson (Royalty, M. 3/4/1815).
D.   The Wife's Tragedy. L.C. Effingham, 1/10/1846.
M.D. A Wife with Two Husbands. 8° 1803.
      [An adaptation of Pixérécourt, La femme à deux maris (1802).]
C.Int. Wig Reforms; or, Old Times and New Times (R.P. M. 4/2/1839).

D. The Wild Dog of the Cape. L.C. Albert, 23/10/1846.
F. Der Wildfang (German, W. 13/11/1805).
Spec. The Wild Girl; or, La belle sauvage (R.C. M. 14/5/1804).
M.D. The Wild Girl; or, The Assassins of Aveyron (R.A. M. 20/9/1819).
Spec. The Wild Horse, Mazeppa; or, The Child of the Desert (Surrey, M. 9/8/1841).
C. The Wild Indian Girl. L. 106 M. [Edinburgh, 9/2/1815].
O.F. The Wild Irish Girl (Vic. T. 25/1/1842).
F. The Wild Irishman; or, O'Shatter in his Glory (Cob. W. 25/10/1820).
Bal. The Wild Islanders; or, The Court of Pekin (C.G. Th. 21/11/1805).
D. The Wild Man of the Mountain. L.C. R.P. 21/2/1846.
M.D. The Wild Woman of Languedoc (R.P. F. 1/5/1829).
Spec. The Wild Zebra Hunt (R.A. M. 24/9/1832).
M.D. Wilkins the Weaver; or, Bethnal Green in the Olden Time (R.P. M. 31/3/1834).
M.D. Will Brockman; or, The Kentish Smuggler (R.P. W. 9/11/1831).
Ent. Williams' Morsels of Mirth for Moments of Merriment. L.C. Adel. 18/2/1831.
Ent. William's London Recollections. L.C. Olym. 25/2/1830.
Bal. William's Return (Royalty, T. 2/4/1811).
M.D. William Tell, the Hero of Switzerland (Cob. M. 2/7/1821).
M.D. William Tell, the Hero of Switzerland (R.A. M. 7/6/1802).
M.D. William the Conqueror; or, The Days of the Curfew Bell (Cob. M. 17/5/1824).
Spec. William the Conqueror's Invasion of England; or, The Death of Harold. L.C. R.A. 9/3/1844.
D. Willie Armstrong; or, Durie in Durance (Edinburgh, 17/6/1829). L.C. Edinburgh, 23/6/1829. 8° 1843 (Edinburgh).
[This is by *J. POOLE*.]
P. The Will of Fate; or, Columbine Shepherdess (R.A. M. 31/8/1807).
Ba. The Willow Grove; or, The Double Blunder (Surrey, M. 1/11/1824).
Ba. Will Reckless (Queen's, S. 27/8/1836).
F. The Window Curtain. L.C. Lyc. 26/11/1849.
Oa. Windsor Castle; or, The Prisoner King (C.G. S. 7/4/1838). L.C. 5/4/1838.
C. Wine does Wonders (H.[2] 19/7/1820). 8° 1820.
[A cut version of Farquhar, *The Inconstant*.]
C.O. Win Her and Wear Her (D.L. T. 18/12/1832).
[An adaptation of *A Bold Stroke for a Wife*.]
P. The Wishing Cap!!! or, Harlequin Blue-Coat Boy (R.C. W. 1/4/1807).
P. The Witch and the Owl; or, The Palace of the Silver Lake (Sans P. T. 26/12/1815).
P. The Witch and the White Horse; or, The Old Woman of Banbury Cross (R.A. M. 18/7/1831).
P. The Witch and the Wizard; or, Harlequin's Reprieve (R.C. F. 1/7/1808).
D. The Witch of Derncleuch (Edinburgh, 25/5/1822).
[See *PLANCHÉ*, 1821.]
M.D. The Witch of Ravensworth; or, The Bridal Supper (Surrey, M. 13/1/1812).
P. The Witch of the Green Bush. L.C. Grecian, 31/10/1846.

P.   The Witch of the Volcano; or, Harlequin and the King of the Coral Isle (R.P. T. 27/12/1831).
D.   The Witch of the Whirlpool; or, The Hag's Haunt (S.W. M. 2/2/1835).
Ba. Wives and Partners; or, Mr. Wilkins (S.W. M. 3/3/1828).
D.   The Wizard of Peru; or, The Senator and the Barbary Courser (R.A. M. 28/9/1835).
M.D. The Wizard Priest; or, The Hall of Fate (R.P. M. 8/4/1833).
M.D. The Wolf Rock; or, The Five Brothers (R.P. M. 21/7/1834).
D.   Wolsey (Surrey, M. 27/1/1845).
C.   Woman (Queen's, M. 9/3/1835).
C.   Woman and Philosophy (Edinburgh, 3/4/1813). L. 100 M. [Edinburgh, 20/1/1813].
D.   Woman—Beware of Woman! (Surrey, M. 15/6/1835).
P.   The Woman of Dreams; or, The Man in the Moon (H.² M. 27/12/1841).
D.   Woman's Life. L.C. 25/1/1834.
C.   Woman's Rights. L.C. Olym. 18/7/1848.
Ba. Woman's the Devil; or, A Masked Ball (Vic. Th. 3/8/1837).
O.   Woman's Will—a Riddle (E.O.H. Th. 20/7/1820). L. 75 S. [30/6/1819].
Ba. Woman's Wit (Olym. T. 17/10/1843).
Ba. A Woman's Word; or, Imaginary Evils (Olym. F. 15/12/1820). L. 78 S. [7/12/1820].
     [Originally advertised as *Woman's Will*, evidently a misprint.]
D.   Women and Wine (Fitzroy, Th. 6/2/1834).
M.D. The Wonderful Lamp of Aladdin (Cob. M. 4/6/1827).
M.D.Spec. The Wonderful Lamp; or, The Flying Palace of Africa (R.A. M. 5/7/1830; R.A. M. 9/9/1833).
Bsq.Ext. The Wood Demon; or, One O'Clock (Lyc. 6/5/1847). L.C. 1/5/1847.
Ba. The Wood Demon; or, The Fatal Clock (Royalty, M. 8/2/1813).
O.   The Wooden Walls; or, Peter the Great. L. 84 M. [C.G. 11/10/1806].
Bal. The Woodman Prince (Sans P. M. 13/10/1817).
M.D. Woodstock; or, The Cavalier in Edinburgh, a Tale of the Year 1651 (Edinburgh, 17/6/1826).
     [Based on Scott's novel.]
C.O. Wooing a Widow (R.P. M. 25/4/1836).
Ba. Wooing a Widow; or, Love under a Lamppost. L.C. Adel. 21/10/1833.
     [See *W.BERNARD*, 1832.]
M.D. Worga; or, The Goat-herd's Oath (Cob. M. 6/12/1824).
F.   The World of Wonders; or, Harlequin Caxton. L.C. Vic. 13/12/1847.
Sat. Wortigerne. 8° 1800 [in *Monthly Magazine*].
M.D. The Wreck; or, The Bucanier's Bridal (S.W. M. 31/1/1831).
D.   The Wrecker of Cornwall; or, The Post-chaise of St. Agnes (R.A. W. 8/5/1839).
M.D. The Wrecker's Bride. L.C. Surrey, 6/6/1845.
M.D. The Wreckers of the Craig Foot; or, The Ghost with the Golden Casket (Cob. M. 15/8/1831).
M.D. The Wreck of the Leander Frigate; or, The Fatal Sandbank (Cob. M. 14/7/1828; R.P. M. 18/7/1831).
     [This is *MONCRIEFF*'s *The Shipwreck of the Medusa* (Cob. 1820) slightly altered.]

D. The Wreck of the Royal George; or, The Seaman's Chest (Surrey, M. 12/10/1840).

M.D. The Writer's Clerk; or, Life in Edinburgh (Caledonian, Edinburgh, 4/7/1828).

C. The Wrong Master (Queen's, F. 5/4/1839).

M.D. Xaia of China; or, The Fatal Flood-gate (R.A. M. 3/4/1820).

Spec. Xo Fi; or, The Hag and the Emperor (Cob. M. 26/12/1825).

Spec. The Yahrmanka nal Dhu; or, The Fair on the Ice (R.A. M. 23/7/1832).

M.D. Yamun Dhuv; or, The Hand and Word (R.P. M. 18/1/1830).

P. Yankee Doodle upon his Little Pony; or, Harlequin, how many Horses has your Father got in his Stable. L.C. R.A. 15/12/1848.

F. Yankee Land (Strand, 7/10/1844). L.C. 7/10/1844.
[This is evidently the play by *CORNELIUS A. LOGAN*, produced in the U.S.A. in 1834.]

Int. Yard Arm and Yard Farm (Surrey, T. 7/7/1812).

M.D. Yaromeer the Yager, the Hungarian William Tell (Garrick, M. 17/1/1831).

D. The Yellow Admiral; or, The Perils of the Battle and the Breeze (Vic. M. 12/5/1845). L.C. 8/5/1845.

P. The Yellow Dwarf; or, Harlequin King of the Golden Mines (S.W. M. 22/5/1820).

P. The Yellow Dwarf; or, Harlequin Knight of the Lion (Vaux. M. 29/6/1829).

F. The Yellow Husband. L.C. D.L. 7/10/1842.
[See *M. LEMON*, 1842.]

D. The Yeoman's Daughter (Lyc. 14/7/1834). L.C. 5/7/1833.
[Music Hawes.]

D. The Yeoman's Daughter (Vic. W. 4/12/1833).

M.D. The Yorkshire Grey (R.P. M. 19/8/1833).

O.F. Young at Sixty. L.C. D.L. 28/3/1829.

C.O. The Young Courier; or, The Miser of Walden (Strand, M. 1/12/1834).

Ba. The Younger Son. L.C. Olym. 24/5/1840.

Oa. The Young Friend. L.C. P'cess, 8/1/1847.

D. The Young Highwayman; or, The Gibbet of Hounslow (R.A. M. 14/5/1838).

Ba. The Young Hopefuls (Olym. Th. 15/3/1832). L.C. 8/3/1832.

D. The Young King (H.² S. 29/7/1837).

D. The Young Pretender (H.² S. 28/11/1846). L.C. 27/11/1846.

Oa. The Young Prude. L. 117 M. [F.O.H. 31/7/1819]

M.D. The Young Queen; or, Christine of Sweden (Cob. M. 3/11/1828).

O.D. The Young Queen on her Travels (Surrey, M. 3/11/1828).

F. The Young Reefer (Queen's, M. 27/4/1835).

Ba. The Young Scamp; or, My Grandmother's Pet (P'cess, T. 27/2/1844).

Ca. The Young Sculptor. L.C. Lyc. 17/5/1844.

D.D. The Young Tradesman's Progress. L.C. Standard, 19/11/1845.

F. The Young Wife and the Old Maid (R.A. M. 10/4/1826).

O.F. You're sure to be shot (Surrey, M. 29/10/1849).

Oa. The Youthful Days of Henry III, King of Castile (Surrey, M. 24/10/1831).

Spec. Zambo and Cadjoc; or, The Terrific Brothers (Pav. M. 8/1/1810).

O.R. Zameo; or, The White Warrior (Vic. M. 27/10/1834).

Bal. Zamor and Zamora; or, The Peruvian Boy (R.C. M. 6/9/1802).
M.D. Zamor the Mexican and the Black Forester (Surrey, M. 17/1/1831).
Spec. Zangarotti, the Demon of the Apennines; or, The Palace of Mystery (Royalty, T. 26/2/1822).
Bal. Zelico; or, The Rival Mexicans (R.A. M. 11/4/1803).
Bal. Zelis; ou, la forêt aux aventures (H.¹ T. 14/1/1812).
Spec. Zelma; or, The Russian Daughter (E.L. W. 3/11/1819).
Spec. Zembuca and the Net-maker of Persia; or, The Siege of Estakhar (R.A. M. 21/9/1835).
M.D. Zenaldi; or, St. Mark's Day (Surrey, Th. 25/7/1822).
Bal. Zéphyr; ou, le retour du printemps (H.¹ S. 21/2/1818).
Bal. Zéphyr inconstant, puni et fixé; ou, les noces de Flore (H.¹ T. 7/4/1812).
Spec. Zilia; or, The Child of Mystery (R.A. M. 20/9/1802).
Spec. Zingina; or, The Heroine of China (R.A. M. 22/8/1803).
O. Zohrab the Hostage; or, The Storming of Mezanderan (C.G. T. 28/2/1837). L.C. 23/2/1837.
Spec. Zomai, the Caffre Chief (Cob. W. 19/4/1820).
D. Zophyrus, the Hero of Persia (Norwich, 1844). L.C. Norwich, 8/2/1844.
P. Zora; or, La belle sauvage (S.W. M. 16/8/1802).
Ba. Zorayda (Olym. M. 19/11/1821). L. 121 M. [14/11/1821; as Z.; or, Scenes in Fashionable Life.]
Bal. Zoreida and Abdallah (Surrey, M. 17/2/1812).
D. Zorinski; or, The Salt Mine of Cracow (S.W. M. 8/1/1841).
Bal. Zulema (H.² T. 19/4/1836).
Spec. Zulema the Circassian Beauty; or, the Robbers of the Caucasus. L.C. Albert, 21/11/1844.
Bal. Zulica; ou, les Peruviens (H.¹ S. 17/5/1817).
O. Zulieman; or, Wives Incog. (Bath, 12/3/1814). L. 101 M. [4/3/1814].
Bal. Zulima and Zambourine (Adel. Th. 23/11/1826).
Spec. Zuluca and the Rival Warriors; or, The Tiger Hunt (Surrey, M. 24/5/1824).
D. Zumalacarregni, the Spanish Chieftain (R.P. M. 13/7/1835).

II. *Italian, French and German Operas*

[This list makes no pretence at completeness. It includes little more than a register of the operas preserved in the two collections cited above. While it has proved impracticable to give here a complete list of operas performed in England between 1800 and 1850, it was deemed advisable for various reasons to indicate the full MS. resources of the Larpent and Lord Chamberlain's libraries.]

O. Adelasia e Aleramo (H.¹ 10/1/1815). L.
     [Music J. S. Mayer, libretto L. Romanelli: Milan, 1806.]
O. Adelia (H.¹ 11/3/1843). L.C.
     [Music Donizetti.]

C.O. Adelina (H.¹ 19/3/1825). L.C.
      [Music Generali, libretto S. Rossi.]
C.O. Adolfo e Clara. L. [H.¹ 26/5/1814].
      [Music Puccita: Rome, 1801.]
O.   L'Agnese (H.¹ 15/5/1817). L.
O.   Alessandro e Timoteo (H.¹ 15/4/1800). L.
      [Music Sarti, revised by Perotti.]
O.   Alzira (H.¹ 28/2/1801).
C.O. Gli Amanti Consolati (H.¹ 23/6/1808). L.
      [Music Sarti: Turin, 1779.]
O.   L'Amore Fraterno (H.¹ 1805).
      [Music Winter.]
O.   Andromaque. L.C. [H.¹ 1/5/1841].
C.O. Angiolina; ossia, Il Matrimonio per Susurro (H.¹ 29/12/1801).
      L. [printed copy, as *Angelina*].
      [Music Salieri, libretto C. P. Defrancheschi, altered by Lorenzo
      da Ponte; Vienna, 1800.]
O.   Anna Bolena (H.¹ 8/7/1831). L.C.
      [Music Donizetti, libretto Romani; Milan, 26/12/1830.]
O.   Anna Boleyn. L.C. [P'cess, 7/1/1847]. 8° 1847.
      [The English version by Charles Jefferys.]
C.O. Un Anno ed un Giorno (Lyc. 31/1/1837).
      [Music Benedict, libretto D. Andreotti; Naples, Fondo,
      19/10/1836.]
O.   Gli Arabi nelle Gallie (H.¹ 12/5/1832). L.C.
      [Music Pacini, libretto L. Romanelli; Milan, 1827.]
O.   Argenide e Serse (H.¹ 25/1/1806). 12° 1807.
      [Music Portogallo; Milan, 1801.]
O.   Aristodemo (H.¹ 9/6/1814). L.
      [Music Pavesi; Naples, 1808.]
O.   Aristodemo. L.C. [H.¹ 30/4/1827].
O.   Armida (H.¹ 1/6/1802). L.
O.   L'Assedio di Corinto (H.¹ 5/6/1834). L.C.
      [Music Rossini; Milan, 26/12/1828.]
C.O. Le Astuzie Fallaci (H.¹ 21/2/1804). L.
      [Music Fioravanti.]
C.O. Le Astuzie Femminili (H.¹ 21/2/1804). L. 8° 1804.
      [Music Cimarosa, libretto G. Palomba; Naples, 1794.]
O.   Atalida (H.¹ 20/3/1810). L.
O.   Athalie. L.C. [H.¹ 9/7/1827].
O   Attila (H.¹ 14/3/1848). L.C.
      [Music Verdi, libretto T. Solera.]
O.   Aureliano in Palmira (H.¹ 22/6/1826). L.C.
      [Music Rossini, libretto F. Romani; Milan, 26/12/1813.]
C.O. Un Aventura di Scaramuccia (Dublin, 20/3/1838).
O.   Bajazet. L.C. [H.¹ 1/5/1841].
C.O. Il Barbiere di Siviglia (H.¹ 10/3/1818; C.G. 4/7/1834; D.L.
      27/7/1835).
      [Music Rossini, altered by Bishop; Rome, 20/2/1816.]
O.   Il Barone di Dolsheim (H.¹ 22/1/1822).
      [Music Pacini, libretto F. Romani; Milan, 23/11/1818.]
O.   Barsene, Regina di Lidia (H.¹ 3/6/1815). L.
O.   Belisario (H.¹ 1/4/1837). L.C.
      [Music Donizetti, libretto S. Cammarano; Venice, 4/2/1836.]

C.O. La Bella Pescatrice (H.¹ 7/4/1801).
      [Music Guglielmi, libretto S. Zini; Naples, 1789.]
O.   Boadicea (H.¹ 23/3/1813). L.
      [Music V. Pucitta.]
O.   I Briganti (H.¹ 2/7/1836). L.C.
      [Music Mercadante, libretto J. Crescini; Paris, 22/3/1836.]
C.O. La Buona Figliuola. L. [19/6/1810].
C.O. La Caccia di Enrico Quarto (H.¹ 7/3/1809). L. [3/3/1809 and,
      with alterations, 28/1/1812].
      [Music Tarchi; Naples, 1783.]
O.   Camilla; ossia, Il Sotteraneo (H.¹ 1/5/1806). L.
      [Music Paer, libretto G. Carpani.]
O.   Il Campanello (Dublin, 3/3/1838).
      [Music Donizetti.]
C.O. Le Cantatrici Villane (H.¹ 27/5/1842). L.C.
      [Music Fioravanti, libretto G. Palomba; Naples, 1799.]
C.O. La Capricciosa Pentita (H.¹ 6/1/1809). L.
      [Music Fioravanti, libretto G. Romanelli; Milan, 2/10/1802.]
O.   I Capuletti ed i Montecchi (H.¹ 20/7/1833).
      [Music Bellini, libretto F. Romani; Venice, 1/3/1830.]
O.   La Cenerentola; ossia, La Bontà in Trionfo (H.¹ 8/1/1820). L.
      [Music Rossini, libretto J. Ferretti; Rome, 1817.]
O.   La Clemenza di Scipione (H.¹ 28/3/1805). L. 8° 1805.
      [Music J. C. Bach.]
O.   La Clemenza di Tito (H.¹ 27/3/1806). L.
      [Music Mozart, libretto Metastasio. The same opera was given
      H.¹ 3/3/1812 and a separate copy is in L.]
C.O. Climene (H.¹ 25/4/1811). L.
O.   Conrado d'Altamira (II.¹ 10/8/1844). L.C.
      [Music Ricci; Paris, 15/3/1844.]
C.O. Il Consiglio Imprudente (H.¹ 9/5/1815). L.
O.   Il Conte Ori (H.¹ 28/2/1829). L.C.
      [Music Rossini, libretto based on Scribe; Paris, 20/8/1828.]
O.   La Cosa Rara (H.¹ 13/6/1805). L. 8° 1805.
      [Music Martini (Martin y Soler), libretto L. da Ponte; Vienna,
      1786.]
C.O. Così Fan Tutte; ossia, La Scuola degli Amanti (H.¹ 9/5/1811). L.
      [Music Mozart, libretto L. da Ponte; Vienna, 26/1/1790.]
C.O. Così Fan Tutte. L.C. [8/8/1842.]
O.   Il Crociato in Egitto (H.¹ 3/6/1825). L.C.
      [Music Meyerbeer, libretto Rossi; Venice, 1824.]
C.O. La Dama Soldato (H.¹ 13/5/1813). L.
      [Music Haumann, libretto C. Mazzolà; Dresden, 1791.]
O.   La Didone (H.¹ 26/1/1808). L.
      [Music Paisiello, libretto Metastasio; Naples, 1797.]
O.   Didone Abbandonata (H.¹ 7/7/1814). L.
O.   Didone Abbandonata (H.¹ 5/7/1827). L.C.
      [Music Mercadante.]
O.   Don Carlos (H.¹ 20/6/1844). L.C.
      [Music Costa, libretto L. Tarantini.]
C.O. Don Giovanni (H.¹ 12/4/1817). L.
      [Music Mozart, libretto L. da Ponte; Prague, 29/10/1787.]
O.   Don Gregorio; ossia, L'Ajo nell'Imbarazzo (H.¹ 28/7/1846).
      [Music Donizetti, libretto J. Ferretti; Rome, 4/2/1824.]

O.   Don Juan [in German]. L.C. [H.¹ 17/7/1832.]
     [Music Mozart.]
O.   Donna Caritea (H.¹ 26/7/1830). L.C.
     [Music Mercadante, libretto G. Pola; Venice, 1826.]
O.   La Donna del Lago (H.¹ 18/2/1823). L.   '
     [Music Rossini, libretto A. L. Tottola; Naples, 24/10/1819.]
Ba. Le Donne Cambiate. [See under *UA*.]
C.O. Don Pasquale (H.¹ 29/6/1843). L.C.
     [Music Donizetti; Paris, 3/1/1843.]
C.O. I Due Baroni (H.¹ 1/1/1803). L.
     [Music Cimarosa, libretto G. Palomba; Rome, Feb. 1783.]
O.   I Due Foscari (H.¹ 10/4/1847). L.C.
     [Music Verdi, libretto F. M. Piave; Rome, 3/11/1844.]
C.O. I Due Fratelli Rivali. L. [H.¹ 1800.]
     [Music Nasolini.]
C.O. Le Due Nozze e un Sol Marito (H.¹ 15/4/1806). L.
     [Music Guglielmi; Naples, 1774.]
O.   Elfrida. L. [15/5/1811].
O.   Elisabetta, Regina d'Inghilterra (H.¹ 30/4/1818). L.
     [Music Rossini, libretto G. Schmidt; Naples, 1815.]
C.O. Elisa e Claudio (H.¹ 12/4/1823). L.
     [Music Mercadante, libretto L. Romanelli; Milan,
     30/10/1821.]
O.   Eriphile (H.¹ 19/2/1805). L.
O.   Ernani (H.¹ 8/3/1845). L.C.
     [Music Verdi, libretto F. M. Piave; Venice, 1844.]
O.   L'Eroina di Raab (H.¹ 8/4/1813). L.
     [Music Ferrari.]
O.   L'Esule di Roma (H.¹ 4/2/1832). L.C.
     [Music Donizetti, libretto D. Gilardoni; Naples, 1828.]
O.   Euffemio di Messina. L.C. [6/6/1831].
O.   Euryanthe [in German] (C.G. 29/6/1833).
     [Music Weber, libretto Mme von Chézy; Vienna, 1823.]
C.O. Falstaff [in German] (H.¹ 19/7/1838). L.C.
     [Music M. W. Balfe, libretto S. M. Maggioni.]
C.O. Il Fanatico di Berlino (H.¹ 22/5/1802). L.
     [An alteration of G. Bertati, *La Locanda*.]
C.O. Il Fanatico per la Musica (H.¹ 19/6/1806). L.
     [Pasticcio; Venice, 18/10/1798.]
O.   Faust (Prince's, 21/5/1840 (in English); C.G. 15/7/1852 (in Italian)).
     [Music Spohr; libretto in English J. C. Bernard.]
O.   La Favorita (C.G. 9/6/1845 (in French); H.¹ 16/2/1847 (in Italian)).
     L.C.
O.   La Fedra; ossia, Il Ritorno di Teseo. L. [26/2/1811].
     [Music Niccolini; Rome, 1804.]
O.   Fernando in Messico (H.¹ 31/3/1803). L.
     [Music Portogallo, libretto F. Tartucci; Venice, 16/1/1798.]
O.   Le Feste d'Iside (H.¹ 21/4/1808). L.
     [Music Nasolini.]
O.   Fidelio (H.¹ 18/5/1832). L.C.
     [Music Beethoven; Vienna, 1805.]
O.   La Figlia del Regimento (H.¹ 27/5/1847). L.C.
     [Music Donizetti; Paris, 11/2/1840.]
O.   Fingal. [See under *UA*]

C.O. La Frascatana (H.¹ 9/1/1808). L.
      [Music Paisiello, libretto F. Livigni; Venice, 1774.]
O.   Der Freischutz (H.¹ 9/5/1832). L.C.
      [Music Weber, libretto F. Kind; Berlin, 1821.]
C.O. Il Furbo contra il Furbo (H.¹ 1/3/1808). L.
      [Music Fioravanti; Venice, 29/12/1796.]
O.   Gastone e Bajardo (H.¹ 26/2/1820). L.
      [Music Liverati.]
C.O. La Gazza Ladra (H.¹ 11/3/1821). L.
      [Music Rossini, libretto Gherardini; Milan, 31/5/1817.]
O.   La Gemma di Vergy (H.¹ 12/3/1842). L.C.
      [Music Donizetti, libretto E. Bidera; Milan, 26/12/1834.]
O.   Ginevra di Scozia (H.¹ 16/4/1812). L.
      [Music Mayr, libretto G. Rossi; Trieste, 21/4/1801.]
O.   Giulietta e Romeo (H.¹ 10/4/1832). L.C.
      [Music Vaccai, libretto F. Romani; Milan, 31/10/1825.]
O.   Il Giuramento [H.¹ 27/6/1840). L.C.
      [Music Mercadante, libretto G. Rossi; Milan, 10/3/1837.]
O.   La Griselda; ossia, La Vertù al Cimento (H.¹ 13/1/1816). L.
      [Music Paer, libretto A. Anelli; Parma, 1798.]
O.   La Grotta di Calypso (H.¹ 31/5/1803). L.
      [Music Winter, libretto L. da Ponte.]
O.   Guillaume Tell (H.¹ 6/3/1830). L.C.
O.   Guillaume Tell (C.G. 6/6/1845 (in French)). L.C.
      [Music Rossini, libretto V. Etienne de Jouy and H. L. F. Bis;
      Paris, 3/8/1829.]
O.   Ildegonda (H.¹ 15/7/1837).
      [Music Marliani, libretto Giannone; Paris, 7/3/1837.]
O.   Ines de Castro (H.¹ 30/5/1840).
      [Music Persiani, libretto S. Cammarano; Naples, 1835.]
C.O. L'Inganno Felice (H.¹ 1/7/1819). L.
      [Music Rossini, libretto G. M. Foppa; Venice, 1812.]
O.   L'Ingiusta Gelosia. L. [5/4/1810].
C.O. L'Isola del Piacere (H.¹ 11/6/1801). L.
      [Music Martin y Soler, libretto L. da Ponte.]
C.O. L'Italiana in Algeri (H.¹ 26/1/1819). L.
      [Music Rossini, libretto A. Anelli; Venice, 22/5/1813.]
O.   La Juive (D.L. 29/7/1846 (in French)). L.C.
      [Music Halévy, libretto A. E. Scribe; Paris, 23/2/1835.]
O.   Linda di Chamouni (H.¹ 1/6/1843).
      [Music Donizetti, libretto G. Rossi; Vienna, 19/5/1842.]
O.   I Lombardi (H.¹ 12/5/1846). L.C.
      [Music Verdi, libretto T. Solera; Milan, 11/2/1843.]
O.   Lucia di Lammermoor (H.¹ 5/4/1838). L.C.
      [Music Donizetti, libretto S. Cammarano; Naples, 26/9/1835.]
O.   Lucia di Lammermoor (D.L. 16/7/1845 (in French)). L.C.
O.   Lucrezia Borgia (H.¹ 6/6/1839).
      [Music Donizetti, libretto F. Romani; Milan, 26/12/1833.]
O.   Macbeth (H.¹ 4/7/1832).
      [Music Chélard, libretto J. Rouget de Lisle; Paris, 29/6/1827.]
O.   Malek-Adel (H.¹ 18/5/1837).
      [Music Costa, libretto C. Pepoli; Paris, 14/1/1837.]
O.   Margherita d'Anjou (H.¹ 12/1/1828). L.C.
      [Music Meyerbeer, libretto F. Romani; Milan, 14/6/1820.]

O.   Maria di Rohan (C.G. 8/5/1847). L.C.
       [Music Donizetti, libretto S. Cammarano; Vienna, 5/6/1843.]
O.   Maria Stuarda, Regina di Scozia (H.¹ 7/6/1827). L.C.
       [Music Coccia, libretto Giannone. Another *Marie Stuart* is in
       L.C. 1/5/1841.]
O.   Marino Faliero (H.¹ 14/5/1835). L.C.
       [Music Donizetti, libretto E. Bidera; Paris, 1835.]
O.   I Masnadieri (H.¹ 22/7/1847).
       [Music Verdi, libretto A. Maffei.]
O.   Matilda e Corradino; ossia, Il Trionfo della Beltà (H.¹ 3/7/1823). L.
       [Music Rossini, libretto J. Ferretti; Rome, 1821.]
C.O. Il Matrimonio per Sussuro. L. [24/5/1810].
O.   Medea in Corinto (H.¹ 1/6/1826). L.C.
       [Music Mayr, libretto F. Romani; Naples, 28/11/1813.]
O.   Merope. L.C. [9/7/1827].
O.   Merope e Polifonte (H.¹ 28/3/1802). L.
       [Music Nasolini, libretto M. Butturini; Venice, 21/1/1796.]
O.   I Messicani (H.¹ 17/3/1829). L.C.
O.   La Morte di Cleopatra (H.¹ 4/3/1806). L.
       [Music Nasolini, libretto A. S. Sografi; Vicenza, 1791.]
O.   La Morte di Mitridate (H.¹ 23/2/1802).
O.   La Muette de Portici. [See under *UA*.]
O.   Nina, Pazza per Amore (Dublin, 17/3/1838).
       [Music Coppola.]
O.   Nino (H.¹ 3/3/1846). L.C.
       [Music Verdi, libretto T. Solera; Milan, 1842.]
O.   Norma (H.¹ 20/6/1833). L.C.
       [Music Bellini, libretto F. Romani; Milan, 26/12/1831.]
C.O. Le Nozze di Figaro (H.¹ 18/6/1812). L.
       [Music Mozart, libretto L. da Ponte; Vienna, 1/5/1786.]
C.O. Olivo e Pasquale (H.¹ 31/3/1832). L.C.
       [Music Donizetti, libretto J. Ferretti; Rome, 1827.]
O.   Gli Orazi e Curazi (H.¹ 2/5/1805). L. 8° 1805.
       [Music Cimarosa.]
C.O. L'Orgoglio Avvilito (H.¹ 7/2/1815). L.
       [This is *La Capricciosa Pentita*; see above.]
O.   Otello (H.¹ 16/5/1822). L. 8° 1822.
       [Music Rossini, libretto F. Beria di Salsa; Naples, 4/12/1816.]
O.   Parisina (H.¹ 1/6/1838).
       [Music Donizetti, libretto F. Romani; Florence, 17/3/1833.]
C.O. La Pastorella Nobile (H.¹ 10/3/1801). L.
       [Music Guglielmi, libretto S. Zini; Naples, 19/4/1788.]
O.   Penelope (H.¹ 11/1/1817). L.
       [Music Cimarosa, libretto G. M. Diodati; Naples, 26/12/
       1794.]
O.   Phædra (H.¹ 5/3/1811).
O.   Pietro l'Eremita (H.¹ 23/4/1832). L.
       [Music Rossini.]
O.   Il Pirata (H.¹ 17/4/1830).
       [Music Bellini, libretto F. Romani; Milan, 27/10/1827.]
O.   Pirro (H.¹ 13/6/1809). L.
       [Music Paisiello, libretto G. de Gamerra; Naples, 12/1/1787.]
C.O. I Pretendenti Delusi (H.¹ 9/4/1822). L.
       [Music Mosca, libretto L. Prividali; Milan, 7/9/1811.]

C.O. Il Principe di Tarranto (H.¹ 23/12/1806). L.
[Music Paer; Parma, 11/2/1797.]
C.O. La Principessa Filosofa (H.¹ 5/5/1801). L.; 8° 1801.
[Music Andrcozzi, libretto A. S. Sografi, altered by S. Bonaiuti;
Venice, 6/10/1794.]
C.O. La Prova di un' Opera Seria (H.¹ 23/6/1831).
[Music Gnecco; Milan, 16/8/1805.]
O. I Puritani (H.¹ 21/5/1835). L.C.; 8° [1835].
[Music Bellini, libretto C. Pepoli; Paris, 25/1/1835.]
C.O. Le Quattro Nazioni (H.¹ 11/7/1809). L.
[Music Piccinni; Naples, 1773.]
O. Il Ratto di Proserpina (H.¹ 3/5/1804). L. 8° 1804.
[Music Winter, libretto L. da Ponte.]
O. Ricciardo e Zoraida (H.¹ 5/6/1823). L.
[Music Rossini, libretto F. Beria di Salsa; Naples, 3/12/1818.]
C.O. Rinaldo d'Asti (H.¹ 16/3/1802). L.
O. I Riti d'Efeso (H.¹ 7/3/1815). L.
[Music Farinelli, libretto G. Rossi; Venice, 26/12/1804.]
O. Il Ritorno di Serse. L. [23/1/1806 and 20/2/1807.]
[Music Portogallo; Bologna, 1795.]
O. Roberto Devereux (H.¹ 24/6/1841). L.C.
[Music Donizetti, libretto S. Cammarano; Naples, 2/10/1837.]
O. Roberto il Diavolo (H.¹ 4/5/1847). L.C.
[Meyerbeer, libretto based on A. E. Scribe; Paris, 21/11/1831.]
O. Roberto l'Assassino (H.¹ 3/2/1807). L.
[Music Trento.]
O. Romeo e Guilietta (H.¹ 20/2/1810). L.
O. Romeo e Giulietta (H.¹ 21/6/1824).
[Music Zingarelli, libretto G. M. Foppa; Milan, 30/1/1796.]
O. Romeo e Giulietta. L.C. [6/1837].
O. La Rosa Bianca e la Rosa Rossa (H.¹ 16/2/1828). L.C.
[Music Mayr, libretto F. Romani; Genoa, 21/2/1813.]
C.O. Lo Sbaglio Fortunato (H.¹ 8/5/1817). L.
O. La Schiava di Bagdad (H.¹ 30/12/1826). L.C.
[Music Pacini, libretto V. Pezzi; Turin, 28/10/1820.]
C.O. La Scomessa (H.¹ 12/12/1809). L.
C.O. La Scuffiara; ossia, La Modista Raggiratrice (H.¹ 16/12/1819). L.
[Music Paisiello, libretto G. B. Lorenzi; Naples, 1787.]
O. Die Schweizer Familie (H.¹ 25/7/1832).
[Music Weigl, libretto I. F. Castelli; Vienna, 14/3/1809.]
O. I Selvaggi (H.¹ 27/6/1815). L.
[Music Liverati.]
O. Semiramide (H.¹ 8/2/1800).
O. Semiramide. L. [13/12/1806 and 4/2/1811].
O. Semiramide (H.¹ 15/7/1824).
[Music Rossini, libretto G. Rossi; Venice, 3/2/1823.]
O. Semiramide (C.G. 1/10/1842). L.C.
O. Semiramis. L.C. [26/6/1827].
C.O. La Serva Astuta (H.¹ 10/6/1806). L.
C.O. La Serva Raggiratrice (H.¹ 16/5/1809). L.
O. Sidagero; ossia, Codononia Conquistata (H.¹ 20/6/1809). L.
O. Sidagero. L. [23/5/1811].
O. La Somnambula (H.¹ 28/7/1831).
[Music Bellini, libretto F. Romani; Milan, 6/3/1831.]

O. La Straniera (H.¹ 23/6/1832). L.C.
   [Music Bellini, libretto F. Romani; Milan, 14/2/1829.]
O. Il Tancredi (H.¹ 4/5/1820). L.
   [Music Rossini, libretto G. Rossi; Venice, 6/2/1813.]
O. Tebaldo ed Isolina (H.¹ 25/2/1826). L.C.
   [Music Morlacchi, libretto G. Rossi; Venice, 4/2/1822.]
O. Der Templer und die Jüdin (Prince's, 17/6/1840).
   [Music Marschner, libretto W. A. Wohlbrück; Leipsig, 22/12/1829.]
C.O. Teresa e Claudio (H.¹ 13/4/1809). L.
   [Music Farinelli, libretto G. M. Foppa; Venice, 9/9/1801.]
O. Titus (Prince's, 16/7/1840).
   [A German version of La Clemenza di Tito, music Mozart; Prague, 6/9/1791.]
O. Torquato Tasso (H.¹ 3/3/1840). L.C.
   [Music Donizetti, libretto J. Ferretti; Rome, 9/9/1833.]
C.O. Le Tre Sultane (H.¹ 22/1/1811). L.
   [Music Pucitta, libretto Caravita.]
O. Il Trionfo dell' Amor Fraterno (H.¹ 22/3/1804).
   [Music Winter, libretto L. da Ponte.]
Cantata. Il Trionfo di Cesare sopra i Galli. L. [6/7/1815].
   [Music Liverati.]
C.O. Il Turco in Italia (H.¹ 19/5/1821). L.
   [Music Rossini, libretto F. Romani; Milan, 14/8/1814.]
O. Gli Ugonotti (C.G. 30/6/1845).
   [Music Meyerbeer, libretto from A. E. Scribe; Paris, 29/2/1836.]
O. L'Ultimo Giorno di Pompei (H.¹ 17/3/1831). L.C.
   [Music Pacini, libretto A. L. Tottola; Naples, 19/11/1825.]
O. Das unterbrochene Opferfest (H.¹ 28/5/1834).
   [Music Winter, libretto F. X. Huber; Vienna, 14/6/1796.]
O. La Vergine del Sole (H.¹ 14/1/1804). L.
   [Music Andreozzi; Geneva, 1783.]
O. La Vestale (H.¹ 3/5/1810). L.
   [Music Pucitta.]
O. La Vestale (H.¹ 30/11/1826, rehearsal; 2/12/1826, 1st public performance). L.C.
   [Music Spontini, libretto V. J. Etienne de Jouy; Paris, 16/12/1807.]
C.O. I Viaggiatori Felici (H.¹ 1/3/1803). L.
   [Music Anfossi, libretto F. Livigni.]
C.O. I Viaggiatori Bizzari (H.¹ 31/1/1809). L.
O. Virginia. L. [C.G. 15/4/1800].
O. Virginia. L. [D. L. 25/10/1800].
C.O. La Virtuosa in Mergellina (H.¹ 7/4/1807). L.
   [Music Guglielmi, libretto S. Zini; Naples, 1785.]
C.O. La Virtuosa in Puntiglio (H.¹ 31/5/1808). L.
   [Music Fioravanti, libretto G. L. Balocchi; Paris, 26/9/1807, as I Virtuosi Ambulanti.]
O. Die weisse Frau (H.¹ 9/6/1834).
O. Zaira (H.¹ 29/1/1805). L. 8° 1805.
   [Music Winter.]
O. Zaira (H.¹ 26/12/1810). L.
   [Music Federici, libretto M. Bocciardini; Milan, 3/9/1803.]

O. Zampa (H.¹ 19/4/1833). L.C.
    [Music Hérold, libretto A. H. J. Mélesville; Paris, 3/5/1831.]
O. Die Zauberflöte (H.¹ 6/6/1811). L.
    [Music Mozart, libretto E. Schikaneder; Italian translation by
    G. de Gamerra; Vienna, 30/9/1791.]
O. Zelmira (H.¹ 24/1/1824). L.
    [Music Rossini, libretto A. L. Tottola; Naples, 16/2/1822.]
O. Zenobia in Armenia (H.¹ 22/5/1800). L.
O. Zenobia in Palmira. L. [19/5/1800].

SUPPLEMENTARY NOTES TO THE
HAND-LIST OF PLAYS, 1800-1850

p. 249] *ABBOTT, W.*
[+from *UA*: Is it a Woman?]
The Youthful Days of Frederick the Great [=*Prussian Discipline* (*UA*)].
Swedish Patriotism. [The title in L. is *Swedish Patriots; or, The Signal Fired.*]

À BECKETT, G. A.
[+from *UA*: The Gaming Table; The Twelve Months; The Parish Revolution; Oliver Twist; The Liberal Candidate; I Puritani; Geraldine.]
The King Incog. [+12° 1834.]
The Revolt of the Workhouse. [+12° 1834.]
+Bsq. Wagustavus; or, The Barn Ball (Fitzroy, 19/5/1834).
The Man with the Carpet Bag. [Apparently produced at Vic. 29/9/1834.]
+Brown's Horse (St J. 18/1/1836).
The Postillion. [Adapted from A. de Leuven and L. L. Brunswick; music by Adam (Paris, 13/10/1836), arranged by G. F. Stansbury.]
The Assignation. [+12° 1837.]
King John. [+12° 1837.]
Wanted a Brigand. [+12° 1838.]
Pascal Bruno. [+12° 1838.]
+Geraldine. [See above. Adapted from A. E. Scribe and A. de Leuven, *Le puits d'amour* (Paris, 20/4/1843). Music by Balfe.]
The Magic Mirror. [+12° (1844).]
Timour the Cream of all the Tartars. [+12° (1845).]
[For his later work see *LND*, 233.]

p. 251] *À COURT, WILLIAM, Lord HAYLESBURY.*
[+from *UA*: Montalto (8° 1821; 8° 1840).]

ADDISON, H. R.
[+from *UA*: The Moon's Age; The Last Whistle; Lost, a Sovereign.]
+The Butterfly's Ball (Adel. 11/11/1833).
[For his later work see *LND*, 235-6.]

ALBERT, —
+Bal. The Fairy Slipper (C.G. 6/5/1834).
+Bal. The Fair Sicilian; or, the Conquered Coquette (C.G. 23/6/1834).
+Bal. The Fête of Terpsichore (D.L. 28/3/1844).
+Bal. The Corsair (D.L. 30/9/1844).

+*ALBO, E. J.*
D. Rodrigo. 8° [*c.* 1846].

ALLEN, ROBERT.
T. The Parricide. [This is also recorded as written by Lucy Allen and Miss Field.]

p. 252] *ALLINGHAM, J. T.*
The Romantic Lover. [=The Legacy (1806) (*UA*). Also attributed to *J. P. KEMBLE*.]
Who Wins? [=The Widow's Choice (*UA*).]
Independence. [=The Trustee (*UA*).]
Transformation. [=Love and Law (L. 1641; first called *Love's Metamorphosis; or, Who is Who?*).]

ALMAR, G.
[+from *UA*: The Fatal Marksman; Alwyn and Bertholdy; Alp, the Renegade; Wake not the Dead; The Headsman; Rafael the Libertine; The Afghanistan War.]
+The Ashantees; or, The Adventures of Jemmy and Jerry (W.L. 24/1/1825).
+D. The Blight of Ambition; or, The Life of a Member of Parliament (Surrey, 3/1832).
Don Quixote. [+12° (1833).]
The Cedar Chest. [+*Cumberland Minor*.]
The Shadow. [+*Cumberland*.]
+The Dark Lady of Doona (Queen's, 7/1840).
+The Knight of the Sepulchre; or, The Arrow which killed the King (Queen's, 10/ or 11/1840).
Jack Ketch. [+*Dicks* 508.]
+D. Saul the Servant; or, The Hollow under the Hill (C.L. 11/1841).
+Spec. The Conquest of Granada; or, The Steed of the Silver Star and the Last Struggle of the Moors (R.A. 10/1843).

p. 253] *AMHERST, J. H.*
[+from *UA*: The Vow of Vengeance; Napoleon Bonaparte (+*Duncombe*); The Murderer (Surrey, 1822); The Wars of Wellington.]
The Three Cripples and the Queen of Billingsgate [see also under *UA*].
The Burmese War. [+*Duncombe*.]
The Battle of Waterloo. [+*Duncombe*.]
Der Freischutz. [+*Duncombe*.]
Blood demands its Victim. [There is some doubt concerning the date of this play. A piece called *Will Watch* appeared at the Royalty, 3/1/1825.]
[*Ireland as it is* appears in *French* and (as *Ireland as it was*) in *Lacy*. *The Monk, the Mask and the Murderer*, given at the National Theatre, Boston, in 1849, was acted as *Who Owns the Hand? or, The M., the M. and the M.*]

p. 254] +*ANATOLE, —*
Bal. Pandora (H.¹ 12/1/1822). [Music by Schneitzhoeffer.]

+*ANDERSON, DAVID.*
Hist.D. The Martial Achievements of Sir William Wallace. 8° 1821 (Aberdeen).

+*ANDREWS, EVAN.*
T. Gwenllian; or, The Siege of Kidwelly. 8° 1841 (Carmarthen).

ARCHER, T.
[+from *UA*: Eveline (adapted from A. E. Scribe and A. de Leuven, *Le puits d'amour*, Paris, 20/4/1843).]
+D. The Shore Devil; or, The Lone House of Marylebone (M'bone, 6/1844).

p. 255] *ARNOLD, S. J.*
[+from *UA*: Illusion; My Aunt; The Waltz; The Citizen of Paris; Tarrare; Tit for Tat; Nourjahad.]
"Foul Deeds will Rise." [Music by the author.]
The Maniac. [=Lost and Found; or, The Black Forest (L. 1617). +Songs, Duets, Choruses, &c. 8° (1810).]
[There is a problem concerning this play. As *The Maniac* it is attributed to S. J. Arnold; but a *Lost and Found*, as acted at the Lyc. 2/1/1811 and printed that year, is definitely given to *M. K. MASTERS*; see p. 343.]
Plots! [=*Bad Neighbours* (*UA*). Music M. P. King.]
Jean de Paris. [+8° 1814. Adapted from C. Godard d'Ancour de Saint Just, *Jean de Paris*.]
The Unknown Guest. [Adapted from *Zoraïme et Zulnor*.]

p. 256] +*ARNOLD, W. H.*
Marian; or, the Prisoner of Elville Castle. 8° [1825].

ASHTON, J.
+T. Conscience (Manchester, 10/2/1815). 8° 1815.

+*ASTLEY, JOHN.*
[+from *UA*: The Brave Cossack (originally, R.A. 1807, as *The B. C.; or, Perfidy Punished*).]

+*ATKINSON, —*
Montrose (Saymore's, Glasgow, 4/ or 5/1829).

p. 257] *ATKYNS, S.*
[+from *UA*: Afloat and Ashore.]
[For his later work see *LND*, 245.]

+*AUMER, —*
Bal. La Noce du Village (H.¹ 1823).
Bal. L'Offrande aux Graces (H.¹ 1823).
Bal. Cléopatre, Reine d'Egypte (H.¹ 1825).

+*BAILEY, PETER.*
[+from *UA*: The Beacon of Liberty.]

+*BAIN, DONALD.*
[+from *UA*: The Patriot.]

p. 258] *BALL, W.*
[+from *UA*: The Corsair; Azor and Zemira.]
+Belshazzar's Feast. 8° 1834.

p. 259] *BARBER, J.*
+The Dashing White Sergeant; or, The Conscript of Austerlitz (Strand, 4/10/1847).

+*BARHAM, FRANCIS FOSTER.*
D. Abdallah; or, The Arabian Martyr. 8° 1820.
D. Colonel Gardiner. 8° 1823.
T. Socrates. 8° 1842.

BARNES, C. M. S.
Octavia Bragaldi. [See also under *UA*.]

BARNETT, C. Z.
[+from *UA*: Conrad the Usurper (Britannia, 1848); Geneviève (Surrey, 1843); Mrs Caudle; The Maid of Saragossa.]
The Skeleton Hand. [+*Duncombe Minor*.]
The Bell Ringer. [+*Duncombe Minor*.]
+The Vow of Silence (Queen's, 18/6/1834). *Duncombe Minor.*
+Barnaby Rudge (S.W. 9/8/1841).
+F. Vengeance (Vic. 8/1843).
+The Cateran's Son; or, The Dread of Military Punishment. *Duncombe Minor.*
[A list of his plays, earlier than 1845, includes: *Esmeralda; The Mountain Cataran*: the latter may be the same as *The Cateran's Son*, above.]

p. 261] +*BARNETT, Miss.*
[+from *UA*: La Femme Sentinelle.]

+*BARNETT, M. BENJAMIN.*
Bal. La Génie du Globe (D.L. 6/12/1847).
Bal. L'Invitation à la Fête (D.L. 29/1/1848).

BARNETT, MORRIS.
[+from *UA*: A Husband Wanted; Double or Quits; Lefevre; Isn't it a Duck?]
+Dick Turpin and Tom King (Strand, 5/7/1847). *Duncombe Minor* (as *Richard Turpin and T. K.*).
[The title-page of the *French N.Y.* edition of *The Yankee Pedlar*, as produced at the Tremont, Boston, in 1839, gives this play to Barnett. On other authority it appears in the Hand-list under *W. B. BERNARD*.]

BARON-WILSON, Mrs C.
+C.O. Where is she gone? (advertised for Strand, 17/9/1832, but performance seems to have been postponed).

+*BARRETT, C. F.*
[+from *UA*: Britain's Jubilee; The Italian Gamester; The Turret Demon.]

+*BARREZ, Mme.*
Bal. Imelda (D.L. 20/4/1846). [Music R. Hughes.]

+*BARROW, JOHN.*
Int. King Glumpus. 12° 1837 [priv. printed].

BARRYMORE, W.
[+from *UA*: The Golden Axe (originally *The G. A.; or, Harlequin Woodcutter*, R.A. 5/1817); The Sisters (revived, Cob. 22/7/1822, as *Ida and Carelia; or, The Amazon Sisters*, and evidently the same as *The Two Sisters* cited on p. 262); The Cape of Good Hope; The Night Hag; Gregarach, the Highland Watchword; The Man in the Moon (D.L. 1826); Jack in the Box; The Conscript (D.L. 1830, with *R. J. RAYMOND*); Davy Jones; The New Year's Gift.]
Wallace. [+*Duncombe Minor*.]
Jack Robinson and His Monkey. [=The Fatal Rock (*UA*).]
The Two Sisters. [See *The Sisters* in *UA*.]

p. 262] +*BARTHOLOMEW, Mrs ANN CHARLOTTE VALEN-TINE.*
[+from *UA*: It's Only My Aunt (+*Duncombe*).]

BARTHOLOMEW, B.
(+from *UA*: The Ruins of Athens.]

BASS, C.
+The Woman of the Tree (Caledonian, Edinburgh, 13/6/1829).

BAYLEY, P.
Orestes in Argos. [+8° 1825.]

BAYLIS, J.
+M.Rom. Lodoiska. 12° 1804.
+D. The Mysteries of Udulpho. 12° 1804.
+C. The Resemblance. 12° 1804.
+F. The Valet with Two Masters. 12° 1804.

BAYLY, T. H.
[+from *UA*: The Stout Gentleman; The Grenadier; De-corum; The Picturesque; The Proof of the Pudding; The Convent Belle; My Grandfather; Love in a Cottage (Olym. 1835); The Schoolmaster at Home; Mischievous Eyes.]
+The Volunteers (Queen's, 24/3/1835).
+Picturesque and Beautiful (E.O.H., 16/5/1842). [Possibly a revised version of *The Picturesque* (Adel. 1831).]
[W. Strange printed several of his plays in series: *How do you manage?*; *Why don't she marry?*; *A Gentleman in Difficulties*; *Comfortable Service*; *One Hour*; *Forty and Fifty*; *The Daughter*; *The Barrack Room*.]

p. 263] +*BAYNEM,* —
[+from *UA*: The Sister of Charity.]

+*BAYNES,* —
F. Love and Laudanum (Woolwich, 23/2/1818). 8° 1818.

BEAZLEY, S.
[+from *UA*: The Promissory Note (adapted from *La lettre de change*); The Venison Pasty; The Militia Muster; Love among the Roses; "Talk of the Devil!"; The White Lady.]
Is he Jealous. [+L. 1927.]
Old Customs. [The title in L. is *The New Year's Gift; or, Christmas Boxes*.]
The Bull's Head. [=The Saracen's Head removed from Snow Hill (*UA*).]
The Steward. [+8° 1819. Based on T. Holcroft, *The Deserted Daughter*.]
The Lottery Ticket. [+8° 1827.]
The Scapegrace. [+*Cumberland Minor*.]
[*Wanted a Partner* (Adel. 1828) is sometimes ascribed to Beazley, but this seems to be the work of *J. B. BUCK-STONE*.]

p. 264] +*BECKWITH,* —
[+from *UA*: The Automaton.]

+*BELL, ALEXANDER.*
The Bride. 8° 1847.

BELL, R.
The Watch-word. [=The Assassin (*UA*).] [The original title was *The Beam of Fate.*]

+*BELL, WILLIAM BOSCAWEN.*
+The Queen of Argos. 8° 1823.

p. 265]   +*BENNETT, —*
F. Twelve O'Clock (Swansea, 5/10/1814).

+*BENNETT, GEORGE.*
[+from *UA*: Harvest Home (Norwich, 1808); The Siege of Sarragossa.]

+*BENNETT, WILLIAM.*
T. Panthea. 8° 1817.

BERNARD, W. B.
[+from *UA*: Delusions; The Dumb Brigand; The Water Witch; New Notions; Mungo Parke (Surrey, 1840); Long Finn; The Fortune Hunter.]
+The Servant of All Work (Tottenham, 9/10/1830). [A revival, Surrey 1831, is in *UA*.]
+St. George and the Dragon; or, The Seven Champions of Christendom (D.L. 26/12/1833).
The Yankee Pedlar. [On the authorship of this play see supplementary note under *M. BARNETT.*]

p. 267]   +*BERWICK, E. L. A.*
[+from *UA*: The Florentines.]

BEVERLEY, H. R.
[+from *UA*: Harlequin and the Silver Dove.]
The Abbot. [+8° 1820. Music by J. Kerr.]
[For his later work see *LND*, 261.]

+*BEVERLEY, —*
P. The Schoolroom in an Uproar; or, Harlequin Apple Stealer (Regency, 14/1/1815).

+*BEW, CHARLES.*
[+from *UA*: Brighton Cliff (acted as *The White Hawk Lady, a Legend of Brighton Cliffes*, Brighton, 12/9/1831); The Gallery of St. Nicholas (acted as *The G. of St. N.; or, May 17th, 1076*, Brighton, 31/12/1832).]
+Ba. The Regatta (Brighton, 25/8/1834).

BISHOP, Sir H. R.
Yelva. [Apparently *R. J. RAYMOND* had something to do with the writing of this drama.]

+*BLACK, JOHN.*
[+from *UA*: The Falls of Clyde (Edinburgh, 1806).]

+*BLACK, LAURENCE.*
C. The Gaberlunzie. 8° 1839 (Edinburgh).

BLAKE, T. G.
[+from *UA*: The Spendthrift; The Wars of the Jews.]
[Among the supplementary titles listed on p. 258 *Edith of the Marsh* was acted with the sub-title, *or, Lambeth in Olden Times*, and *A Spanking Legacy* appeared at the Queen's, 5/6/1843 (+*Lacy*). Other titles listed as Blake's are: *The Glen Girl*; *Land and Sea*; *Jack Ashore* and *A Little Tiger*.]
Life as it is! [+*Barth's Universal Stage.*]
Poor Dog Tray. [See also under *UA*.]

p. 268]   BLANCHARD, E. L.
+The Sisters of Switzerland (Queen's, 4/1840)
+The Cobbler of Coblentz (Queen's, 9/1840).
Arcadia. [With a sub-title, *or, The Shepherd and the Shepherdess*, this was acted Grecian, 19/4/1841. Music Harroway.]
The Invisible Client. [See also under *UA*.)

p. 269]   +BLINK, G.
The Beggar's Haunt; or, Fortune's Changes (M'bone, 13/11/1837).

+BLISS, HENRY Q. C.
T. Phillip the Second. 8° 1849.

+[BOKER, G. H.
T. Calaynos (S.W. Th. 10/5/1848). L.C. 5/5/1849.

+BOLOGNA, — Jr.
Bal. Poor Jack; or, The Benevolent Tars of Old England (C.G. 10/6/1807).

+BOLTON, G.
[+from *UA*: All About Love and Jealousy; The Civil War of Poetry.]

BOSWORTH, J.
+Grace Darling (Garrick, 1838).
+John Stafford (listed as Bosworth's before 1838, but see *W. T. TOWNSEND*, 1835).
+Leilia (Garrick, 1838).
+The Man of War (1838).
+The Mutineer's Widow; or, Bill Adams the Sailor (Garrick, 10/1838).
+The Post Captain (1838).
+Ten Thousand Top-sail Sheet Blocks (Garrick, 11/1838).

BOUCICAULT, D.
[+from *UA*: The Curiosities of Literature (+*Webster*).]
+Lodgings to Let (entered under *LEE MORETON*, Boucicault's pseudonym).
+M.D. Judith; or, The Maid of Geneva (Adel. 2/1844).

p. 270]   +BOUNDEN, JOSEPH.
D. The Fortress of Rotzberg; or, The Swiss Patriots. 8° [1818].

+BRADSHAW, CHRISTOPHER BROOKE.
C. Shakspere and Company. 8° 1845 [priv. printed].

BRADWELL, W.
+P. The Castle of Otranto; or, Harlequin and the Giant Helmet (C.G. 26/12/1840).

BRAMSEN, J.
Sappho. [+8° 1821.]

+*BRANDRETH, H.*
T. Sylla. 8° 1824. [From the French of Souy.]

+*BRERETON, JOSEPH LLOYD.*
T.C. Prometheus Britannicus; or, John Bull and the Rural Police. 12° 1840.

+*BRETIN, —*
Bal. The Offspring of Flora (D.L. 3/10/1846). [Music by Scaramelli.]

+*BREWER, GEORGE.*
[+from *UA*: The Outside Passenger; Martelli.]

+*BRIDEL, EDMUND PHILLIP.*
D. The Fifth of November. 12° 1807.

p. 271]   +*BROMLEY, F.*
[+from *UA*: Nicholas Mendoza.]

BROMLEY, G. P.
[+from *UA*: The Child of Concealment.]

BROOKS, C. W. S.
[+from *UA*: Robin Hood and Richard Coeur de Lion!]
The Creole. [+8° 1847 (priv.).]
Shave you Directly. [See also under *UA*.]

p. 272]   *BROWN, Major.*
C. Love's Labour Lost...Regained. 8° 1841.

BROWN, C. A.
Narensky. [=The Russian Village (*UA*).]

+*BROWN, HARCOURT.*
Ba. All in a Family Way (City, 15/10/1832).

+*BROWN, ROBERT.*
D. Mary's Bower; or, The Castle in the Glen. 8° 1811 [Edinburgh].
T. Henry, Lord Darnley. 8° [1823; Edinburgh].
T. John, Earl of Gowrie. 8° 1825 [Edinburgh].

BROWNING, ROBERT.
[See also *LND*, 283.]

BRUTON, J.
+Ba. Davis and Sally Dear (Olym. 7/3/1842). L.C.
[For later his works see *LND*, 284.]

+*BRYANT, MICHAEL.*
+M.D. Florence Macarthy; or, Life in Ireland. 8° 1823.
+M.D. Von Orenburg, the Hungarian Outlaw (S.W. 9/1824).

BUCKSTONE, J. B. [See also under pseudonym *H. YOUNGE.*]
[+from *UA*: Grimalkin the Great; Hyder Ali (Adel.); Moments of Mystery; The Little Corporal; Number One!; The Pilot; The Best of Husbands; The Kitchen Sylph; Peter Bell.]
Luke the Labourer. [+8° 1826.]
The Little Red Man. [See also under *UA*.]

Wanted a Partner. [This is also ascribed to *S. BEAZLEY, Junior.*]
+The Cabdriver (S.W. 1830). *Dicks.*
The Irish Lion. [+*Acting Nat. Drama.*]
An Alarming Sacrifice. [+*Acting Nat. Drama.*]
+My Old Woman; or, Love and Wambles (H.² 10/11/1843.)
  [A series of Buckstone's plays was printed by W. Strange between 1834 and 1837.]

p. 276] *BUNN, A.*
  [+from *UA*: Ivanhoe (Birmingham, 1820); Conrad the Usurper (1821); Hyder Ali (D.L.); The Brides of Venice.]
  Kenilworth. [+*Duncombe*, vol. x.]
  Catherine Grey. [This play seems to have been by *G. LINLEY*; see p. 346.]
  The Enchantress. [+8° 1845.]
  The Crusaders. [Music J. Benedict.]
  Stradella. [Music J. Benedict.]
  Loretta. [Music Ann Bishop.]
  [For his later work see *LND*, 287.]

+*BURGES, GEORGE.*
  D. The Son of Erin; or, The Cause of the Greeks. 8° 1823.

p. 277] *BURTON,* —
  Right and Wrong. [=A Receipt for Mirth (*UA*).]

BURTON, W. E.
  The Court Fool. [An adaptation of V. Hugo, *Le roi s'amuse.* +*Duncombe Minor.*]

BUTLER, R.
  The Irish Tutor. [+8° (1823).]

+*BYERLEY, JOHN SCOTT.* [See *J. S. RIPON.*]

BYRNE, J.
  +Bal. The Welsh Dairy; or, Suitors in Abergavenny (D.L. 21/5/1802).
  +Bal. The Black Knight; or, Perfidy Punished (D.L. 6/6/1803). [Music Bossi.]
  +Bal. The Oak and the Ivy; or, The Origin of a British Tar (C.G. 9/6/1808).

+*BYRNE, OSCAR.*
  [+from *UA*: Spanish Gallants.]

p. 278] *CALCRAFT, J. W.*
  +T. Iphigenia in Aulis (Dublin, 28/11/1846). 12° 1847 [Dublin]. [An adaptation of Euripides' play.]

CAMPBELL, A. V. [ANDREW LEONARD VOULLAIRE CAMPBELL].
  [+from *UA*: The Charter (S.W. 1830); The Wreck; Rodar the Raven.]
  Gambler's Life in London. [Produced 26/12/1828; see under *UA*.]
  Bound 'Prentice to a Waterman. [+*Cumberland.*]
  Rule Britannia! [+*Cumberland.*]

p. 279]   +*CAMPBELL, CALDER.*
[+from *UA*: Catarina (Strand, 1844).]

CAPADOSE, H.
Kindred. [An adaptation of *Die Verwandschaften.* See also under *UA.*]

+*CARD, Rev. HENRY.*
C. The Brother-in-Law. 8° 1817.

+*CARR, —*
[+from *UA*: The Railroad for Ever.]

+*CATTERMOLE, Rev. RICHARD.*
T. Becket. 8° 1832.

+*CAULFIELD, FRANCES SALLY, Mrs EDWIN TOBY.*
Sacred.D. The Innocents. 8° 1824 [Bath].

+*CAUNTER, Rev. JOHN HOBART.*
D. St. Leon. 8° 1835.

+*CHALLIS, H. W.*
[There is some confusion about a play called *A Race for a Wife.* This appears in L. 2169, was acted at C.G. 20/10/1820 (*UA*), and printed as by H. W. Challis. With slight differences, it appears in L. 2385 as *Win Her and Wear Her; or, Race for a Wife!*—attributed on the title-page to H. C. Williams: it was acted at the Olym. 21/11/1823 (*UA*).]

+*CHAPMAN, JANE.*
T. King René's Daughter. 8° 1845.

+*CHAPMAN, S. H.*
The Cream White Woman; or, The Ring, the Statue and the Tournament (W.L. 24/10/1825).

+*CHARLTON, WILLIAM HENRY.*
Ingomar, the Son of the Wilderness. *Lacy.* [An adaptation from a play by Frederick Halm.]

CHERRY, A.
[+from *UA*: The Magic of British Liberty.]
All for Fame. [This is a comic recitation, not a farce. A copy is in L. 1452.]
Peter the Great. [=The Wooden Walls (*UA*).]
+The Britons' Jubilee in Honour of Their King (Carmarthen, 26/10/1809).
+Angeline; or, Who's the Murderer? (Swansea, 16/9/1811).

+*CLAPPERTON, WILLIAM.*
Past.T.C. Il Pastor Fido; or, The Faithful Shepherd. 8° 1809 [Edinburgh]. [A version of Guarini's play. See also under *UA.*]

p. 280]   *CLARKE, J. B.*
+T. Ramiro (Dublin, 2/1822).

CLARKE, S.
The Kiss. [=The Perplexed Husband (*UA*).]

+*CLIFTON, —*
The Lion of England; or, The Talisman (Caledonian, Edinburgh, 15/12/1825).

+*CLINTON, JOHN WADE.*
The City Merchant (Brighton, 8/12/1841).

+*COAPE, H. C.*
O. The Fairy Oak (D.L. 18/10/1845). L.C. 18/10/1845.
[Music H. Forbes.]

COBB, J.
Paul and Virginia. [=Virginia, in L. 1292.]
Sudden Arrivals. [=The Man of Business (*UA*).]

p. 281] +*COCKRANE, ALEXANDER.*
Pausanius; or, The Regent of Sparta. 8° 1844.

+*COCKRILL, R.*
D. The Wrecker's Son; or, The Fate of a Matricide (Garrick,
17/3/1837). *Oxberry's Budget* (1844), no. 34.

CODE, H. B.
+The Patriot; or, The Hermit of Saxallan (Hibernian,
Dublin). 8° 1811 [Dublin]. [Music Sir John Stevenson.]
The Spanish Patriots. [Music Sir John Stevenson.]

+*COFE, —*
[+from *UA*: Flying Colours.]

COLERIDGE, S. T.
Remorse. [Music Michael Kelly.]

COLLIER, J. W.
[+from *UA*: The Kiss; Cousin Campbell's Courtship.]
+The Diary of an Exquisite (Queen's, 8/1835).
[For his later work see *LND*, 317.]

+*COLLINS, M. TERTIUS.*
D. Gertrude. 8° 1849.
D. Lost by a Head. 8° [1850; Birmingham].

p. 282] *COLMAN, G.*
Love Laughs at Locksmiths. [Original music by Méhul
(Paris, 1802); new music by M. Kelly.]
The Gay Deceivers. [Music by Grétry (Versailles, 1779),
with additions by M. Kelly.]
Who Wants a Guinea? [Originally called *Where is She?*; or,
The Charitable Quixote.]
We Fly by Night. [Adapted from Picard, *Le Conteur.*]
The Forty Thieves. [=Ali Baba (*UA*). Apparently *R. B.
SHERIDAN* and *C. WARD* had a share in it.]

+*COLOMBINE, D. E.*
T. Marcus Manlius. 8° 1837.

p. 283] *COOPER, F. F.*
[+from *UA*: Rejected Addresses (Clarence, 1833); Angelo
(from V. Hugo, *Angelo*); The Lists of Ashby.]
+Bsq. The Jewess; or, The Fatal Gridiron (Vic. 5/9/1836).
+Ba. The Queen's Visit (C.L. 11/1838). [A play of this name
is credited also to *J. EBSWORTH*.]
+D. Burnt at Sea; or, The Fate of the Falcon (C.L. 3/6/1844).
Oxberry's Weekly Budget, iii. 5.

COOPER, W.
[+from *UA*: The Student of Jena; Zophyrus.]

+*CORALLI*, —
Bal. La Tarantula (D.L. 18/3/1846). [Music Gide.]

+*CORRI, M.*
M.D. The Contraband Captain (Vic. 26/2/1835). [Later this was called *The Black Reefer; or, A New Tale of the Sea* (R.A. 1843) and printed in *Oxberry's Budget* (1844), no. 15.]
M.D. Mungo Park; or, African Treachery (acted at S.W., Surrey and R.P. before 1844). *Oxberry's Budget* (1844), no. 35.
Sir Roger de Coverley; or, The Old English Gentleman (R.P. before 1844). *Oxberry's Budget* (1844), no. 29.

COURTNEY, J.
[+from *UA*: In Pursuit of a Wife; The Spirit of the Fountain; Telemachus (Adel. 1844); Tom Trim; Paul the Rover; The Invasion of England by William the Conqueror (also acted as: William the Conqueror's Invasion of England).]
+D. Petrona; or, A Brother's Curse (Vic. 14/10/1839).
The Gunsmith of Orleans. [See also under *UA*.]
[For his later work see *LND*, 326.]

p. 284] *COYNE, J. S.*
[+from *UA*: The Humours of an Election; She Wants a Guardian; The Mayor and the Monkey; Cocknies in California; The Black Domino (L.C. 1838); Fanny Sims; Laffarge; Our National Defences (also ascribed to *B. N. WEBSTER*); Railway Bubbles (+*Barth's Universal Stage*); Mrs Bunbury's Spoons.]
Binks the Bagman. [+12° (1840).]
The Trumpeter's Daughter. [+12° (Boston, n.d.).]

p. 285] *CRAVEN, H. T.*
[For his later plays see *LND*, 328–9.]

p. 286] +*CROMWELL, THOMAS.*
[+from *UA*: Honour (and add: 8° 1820).]

CROSS, J. C.
[+from *UA*: Johnnie Armstrong (R.C. 1803).]

p. 287] *CROSS, T.*
D. Edric the Forester. 8° 1842.

CROWQUILL, ALFRED.
[For his later work see *LND*, 330 and 371.]

p. 288] *DALRYMPLE*, —
[+from *UA*: The Loadstone of the Earth.]

DANCE, C.
[Several plays recorded in the Hand-list under this author belong to *GEORGE DANCE*. Corrections are here made both under *C. DANCE* and *G. DANCE*.]
[+from *UA*: He's not a-miss; Look at Home; Misapprehension; I will have an Uncle; The Double Dilemma; Forgive and Forget (Olym. 1838); "My Lord is not my Lord" (adapted from A. F. Creuzé and E. G. F. de Favières, *Le nouveau seigneur de village*, Paris, 1813.]
Puss in Boots. [In collaboration with *J. R. PLANCHÉ*.]

p. 289] +*DANCE, GEORGE.*
[+from plays listed under *C. DANCE*: Petticoat Government; The Station House; Hush Money; A Close Siege; The Lucky Stars.]
[+from *UA*: In Statu Quo!; The Guard House; My Late Friend; Now or Never; Quits; The Duke for a Day; Major and Minor; The Emissary.]
Petticoat Government. [+*Lacy.*]
Hush Money. [+*Duncombe.*]
Pleasant Dreams. [+8° 1834.]
The Station House. [+*Duncombe.*]
+Int. Six to Four on the Colonel (Strand, 6/8/1832).

DANIEL, G.
Doctor Bolus. [+8° 1818.]

+*DANVERS, GEORGE J. B., Earl of LANESBOROUGH.*
Bust Peter (Dublin, 11/3/1826).
The Counter Charm (Dublin, 24/5/1826).
The Bohemian; or, America in 1775 (Dublin, 20/11/1833).

+*DARLEY, CHARLES.*
[*The Plighted Troth*, entered under *GEORGE DARLEY* and printed 8° 1843, was by this author.]

DARLEY, GEORGE.
The Plighted Troth. [This was by *CHARLES DARLEY*, *q.v.*]

DAVENPORT, —
[+from *UA*: The Daughter of the Regiment.]

+*DAVIS, Sir JOHN FRANCIS, Bart.*
D. Laon-Seng-Urh; or, An Heir in his Old Age. 8° 1817.
D. Hān Koong Tsew, or, The Sorrows of Hān. 4° 1829.

+*DEGVILLE, —*
Bal. Telasco and Amgahi; or, The Peruvian Nuptials (D.L. 14/5/1800).
Bal. Achille et Deidamia; or, The Education of Achilles, by the Centaur Chiron (D.L. 21/6/1804). [Music Winter.]
Bal. Terpsichore's Return (D.L. 1/11/1805).
Bal. Les Jeux Floraux (H.[1] 20/3/1809).
Bal. Paul and Virginia (Lyc. 11/5/1810).
Bal. Naissance de Venus (H.[1] 1826).
Bal. Le Siège de Cythère (H.[1] 1827).

+*DE HAYES, I. W.*
[+from *UA*: Princess Battledore and Harlequin Shuttlecock.]

p. 290] +*DELPINI, —*
P. The Life and Death of Pantaloon (H.[1] 11/3/1806).

+*DENVIL, Mrs.*
D. Emily Fitzormond (R.P. 9/1841).
D. Susan Hapley (R.P. 9/1841).
D. Wealth and Poverty (R.P. 10/1841).

+*DESHAYES, —*
Bal. L'Offrande à Terpsichore (H.[1] 10/3/1821).
Bal. Kenilworth (H.[1] 1/3/1831).

DIBDIN, C. I. M.

Jack the Giant Killer. [See also under *UA.*]
Fire and Spirit. [See also under *UA.*]
Harlequin and Æsop. [See also under *UA.*]
The Prince. [See also under *UA.*]
The Spanish Gala. [See also under *UA.*]
The Farmer's Wife. [Music Bishop.]
The Viceroy. [See also under *UA.*]
The Elements. [Acted S.W. 23/3/1818: see *UA.* Also performed with the sub-title: *Which is Harlequin?*]
Shakespeare versus Harlequin. [There is some uncertainty whether this is by *C. I. M.* or *T. J. DIBDIN.*]
Harlequin Achilles. [See also under *UA.*]
The White Surrey. [See also under *UA.*]
Murder and Madness. [See also under *UA.*]
She's not to be Managed. [See also under *UA.*]
Savage Lovers. [See also under *UA.*]

p. 296]   *DIBDIN, T. J.*

[+from *UA*: Le Calife de Bagdad (based on the play by C. Godard d'Ancour de Saint-Just, music by Boieldieu, Paris, 1800); The Victim (Surrey, 1820); Beauty and the Bey; Charles XII and Peter the Great; The Strand-ed Actor; A.B.C.]
Of Age Tomorrow. [Based on Kotzebue, *Der Wildgang.*]
Il Bondocani. [Written *c.* 1796.]
Harlequin's Tour. [+8° 1800, *Songs, Choruses, &c.*]
Something New. [Already written by 1792.]
Gaffer's Mistake. [Produced at S.W. *c.* 1795.]
The Escapes. [Dibdin acknowledges the songs only; the dialogue would seem to be by *T. HOLCROFT.*]
Blind Man's Buff. [See the Hand-list of Plays, 1750-1800).]
The Brazen Mask. [Dibdin acknowledges the songs only.]
Harlequin's Races. [See also under *UA.*]
Aggression. [The production date is 15/4/1805; songs in L. 1446.]
Two Faces under a Hood. [=How happy could I be with either! (*UA*).]
The Lady of the Lake. [L. 2000, as produced Olym. 11/12/1817, is virtually identical.]
Haroun Alraschid. [Music Bishop.]
+Int. Tag in Tribulation. L. 1840 [Surrey 1814]. [Altered from his own play of 1799.]
The Valley of Diamonds. [+8° 1814.]
The Magpie. [+8° 1815.]
The House Warming. [See also under *UA.*]
Don Giovanni. [+L. 2096, printed copy for production at C.G. 15/6/1819: see *UA.*]
The Reprobate. [The copy in L., as acted at Olym. 19/3/1821, is the same play; the full title is *The R.; or, Four by Honours*: see *UA.*]
The Heart of Midlothian. [The copy in L., as acted at Edinburgh, 9/12/1819, is a printed version of this play.]
Montrose. [This is the same as *Montrose; or, Second Sight* in *UA.*]

The Bride of Lammermoor. [This is the same as *The Bride of Lammermuir* licensed for Edinburgh, 1819: see *UA*.]
The President and the Peasant's Daughter. [An adaptation of F. Schiller, *Kabale und Liebe* (1784)].
Elfrid. [See also under *UA*.]
A Tale of Other Times. [=The Minstrel Maid (*UA*).]
Old Nick. [Although Dibdin seems to have had something to do with this piece, he himself gives the credit to one *DUBOIS*.]

p. 305] +*DIDELOT*, —
Bal. Alonzo the Brave and the Fair Imogene (D.L. 6/5/1801).
Bal. Le Bazzard d'Algier, ou, le Retour du Corsair (D.L. 27/6/1814).

DILLON, C.
+The Maid of Saragossa (M'bone, 9/1843).
+Night and Morning (C.L. 15/1/1844).
+Marco Sciarro (C.L. 6/5/1844).

p. 306] *DIMOND, W.*
[+from *UA*: Isidore e Merida; The Carnival at Naples.]
Adrian and Orrila. [Music M. Kelly.]
The Foundling of the Forest. [+12° 1818, Dublin.]
The Doubtful Son. [Based on Beaumarchais, *L'autre Tartuffe.*]
Gustavus Vasa. [Music M. Kelly.]
The Æthiop. [+L. 1734. Music Bishop.]
Brother and Sister. [Music Bishop. Based on Patrat, *L'heureuse erreur.*]
Abou Hassan. [An adaptation of the opera by F. K. Hiemer (Munich, 1811), music by Weber, adapted by T. S. Cooke.]
The Seraglio. [An adaptation of *Die Entführung aus dem Serail* (Vienna, 1782), music by Mozart, with additions by J. B. Cramer.]
+The Unknown (City, 1/11/1831).
      [T. J. Dibdin (*Reminiscences* (1827), ii. 334) refers to *The Female Jockey* as by Dimond; this I have been unable to trace.]

p. 307] +*DIXON, WILLIAM HEPWORTH.*
T. The Azamoglan. 8° 1845.

+*DOBBS, J.*
[+from *UA*: Tricks and Blunders (Cob. 1823); The Gipsy Dumb Boy; Petraki Germano.]

+*DOBELL, SYDNEY.*
D.Poem. The Roman. 8° 1850.

+*DORAN, JOHN.*
M.D. Justice; or, The Venetian Jew (Surrey, 8/4/1824).

+*DORRINGTON, W.*
Harlequin and Will o' the Wisp; or, A Midsummer Night's Ramble (C.L. 26/12/1837).

+"*DORSET, ST JOHN*" [pseudonym of *GEORGE STEPHENS*].

+*DOUBLEDAY, THOMAS.*
[+from *UA*: Babington (+8° 1825); Caius Marius (+8° 1836).]
T. The Italian Wife (Newcastle, 5/1823). 8° 1823 [Edinburgh].

DOWLING, M. G.
[+from *UA*: The Lady of Lions.]
Othello Travestie. [Acted Strand, 16/5/1836. Also called *Othello (according to Act of Parliament)*.]
Romeo and Juliet. [Acted Strand, 1/5/1837, as *R. and J., as the Law Directs*.]

+*DOWNES, JOSEPH.*
Scenic Poem. The Proud Shepherd's Tragedy. 8° 1823 [Edinburgh].

+*DRAKE, —*
The Events of Time (Exeter, 1809).

+*DUBOIS, —*
Old Nick. [For this piece see under *T. J. DIBDIN*, p. 304.]

+*DUNLAP, WILLIAM.*
D. Abaellino, the Great Bandit. 12° 1802.

p. 308] *DUNLOP, Mrs.*
[+from *UA*: The Female Cavaliers.]

+*DUPRET, —*
Bal. The Lucky Escape (D.L. 2/6/1800). [Music Bossi.]

+*DWARRIS, Sir FORTUNATUS WILLIAM LILLEY.*
D. Alberic, the Consul of Rome; or, The School for Reformers. 8° 1832.

EARLE, — [probably *WILLIAM*].
[+from *UA*: The Turret Clock.]
+D. The Exile. 8° 1804.
+The Castle of Wonders. [See under *JOHNSON*.]

EBSWORTH, J.
[+from *UA*: The Bohemian Mother; Too Careful by Half.]
+Ent. Jocko the Brazilian Ape (Caledonian, Edinburgh, 22/12/1825, 3rd time).

p. 309] *EDISON, JOHN SIBBALD.*
D. King Henry III, Part I. 8° 1840

+*EDWARDES, CONWAY.*
D. First Love. 8° 1841.

EGAN, P.
[+from *UA*: Life in Dublin (originally acted Dublin, 10/1839).]

ELLISTON, R. W.
[+from *UA*: The Coronation.]

+*ELTON, —*
D. Paul the Poacher (Surrey, 3/1832).

p. 310] +*ENGLEFIELD, Sir HENRY CHARLES.*
C. Adrian. 8° 1814 [priv.].

+*ERVINE, G.* [See *G. IRVINE*.]

+*EUSTON, J. H.*
[+from *UA*: Punch in Italy.]

+*EVANS,* —
F. The Disappointed Bachelor (Swansea, 23/9/1812).

EYRE, E. J.
[+from *UA*: The Holidays.]

FARLEY, C.
[+from *UA*: Harlequin and Asmodeus (the same as *Harlequin Zambullo*: songs printed 8° 1810); Harlequin Munchausen; Aladdin (C.G. 1813); Harlequin Pat; The Spirit of the Moon (C.G. 1824).]
The Magic Oak. [Songs by *T. J. DIBDIN.*]

p. 311] *FARRELL, J.*
[+from *UA*: An Arab's Faith.]

+*FARREN, PERCY.*
[+from *UA*: The Widow Bewitched.]

FAUCIT, J. S.
[+from *UA*: Charles the Terrible (Cob. 1834; printed in *Oxberry's Budget*, no. 24); Ben Brace (printed in *Oxberry's Budget*, no. 23); Magna Charta (Vic. 1840; printed in *Oxberry's Budget*, no. 31).]
+Bears not Beasts; or, Bruin and the Bashaw. *Oxberry's Budget*, no. 33. [See this title in *UA* and under *H. M. MILNER*, 1822.]
+D. Captain Cook; or, The Island of Owhyhee (S.W.). *Oxberry's Budget*, no. 36.
+D. The Smuggler's Son and the Exciseman's Daughter. *Oxberry's Budget*, no. 27.
+Mus.D. Oedipus (W.L.). 8° 1821.
The Aldgate Pump. [+*Pattie's Universal Stage.*]
[For his later plays see *LND*, 363.]

FAWCETT, J.
The Enchanted Island. [Music by Condell. +*Prospectus, with the Songs, Choruses &c.* 8° (1804, "For the Author").]
The Barber of Seville. [A version of *Almaviva* by C. Sterbini, original music by Rossini (Rome, 1816).]
+The Old Miner Ousted (Caernarvon, 16/10/1841). [This is probably *The Secret Mine.*]

p. 312] +*FEIST, CHARLES.*
[+from *UA*: The Recluse (Norwich, 1823).]

+*FIELD, Miss.*
T. The Parricide (Bath, 7/6/1824). In collaboration with *LUCY ALLEN.*

+*FINLAYSON, JOHN.*
Ent. Marches Day. 12° 1814 [Falkirk].

FISHER, —
The Assignation. [+L. 1848.]

+*FISHER, F. G.*
[+from *UA*: Lilliput (adapted from a play by D. Garrick).]

+*FISHER, J. B.*
Mus. Ent. The Casket. 12° 1808.

FITZBALL, E.
[+from *UA*: Iwan; William the Conqueror; The Kocuba; Hans of Iceland; Antoine, the Savage; Adelaide; The Libertine of Poland; Nina, the Bride of the Galley Slave; The Dillosk Gatherer; Margaret's Ghost (printed in *Duncombe Minor*); The Felon of New York; The Young Courier; The Black Hand; Zohrab the Hostage. Two other titles attributed to him before 1822 are: The Revenge of Taran, and Sybil's Warning]

Bertha. [+8° 1819 (Norwich).]

Antigone. [The same as *Antigone* in *UA*.]

The Innkeeper of Abbeville. [Apparently acted at the Surrey in 1822.]

The Fortunes of Nigel. [+L. 2332, printed copy; 8° 1822. Apparently produced Edinburgh, 6/2/1823 as *George Heriot*.]

Joan of Arc. [+8° (1823).]

The Barber. [+8° (1822).]

Peveril of the Peak. [+24° 1823 (Edinburgh).]

+Laurette; or, The Forest of Unterwald (Surrey, 11/8/1823).

Waverley. [+8° (1824).]

The Floating Beacon. [+8° (1824).]

Wardock Kennilson. [+*Cumberland Minor*, no. 66.]

Omala. [+8° 1826.]

Father and Son. [+*Cumberland Minor*.]

The Three Hunchbacks. [+8° (n.d., as acted at the Surrey).]

The Earthquake. [+*Cumberland Minor*.]

The Devil's Elixir. [+*Cumberland*.]

Die Rauberbraut. [+L. (23/6/1829).]

Ninetta. [The original libretto from which this is taken was by G. Gherardini, Milan, 1817; +12° (1830).]

+Hofer; or, The Tell of the Tyrol (D.L. 1/5/1830). *Cumberland Minor*. [Music by Rossini, adapted by Bishop. Also called *Andreas Hofer*: see below.]

Der Alchymist. [The original libretto from which this is taken was by K. Pfeiffer, Cassel, 1830.]

Andreas Hofer. [Originally acted D.L. 1/5/1830, as *Hofer*: see above.]

The Maid of Cashmere. [Adapted from *Le Dieu et la Bayadère* (Paris, 13/10/1830) by A. E. Scribe; music by Auber.]

Mary Glastonbury. [+*Cumberland Minor*.]

The Lord of the Isles. [See also under *UA*.]

The Bronze Horse. [+*Duncombe*.]

Thalaba the Destroyer. [This was printed 8° 1826, and probably is the same as the play of 1823 in *UA*.]

La Favorita. [+8° (1827) as *The Favourite*.]

The Daughter of the Regiment. [Music Donizetti.]

p. 317]   +*"FITZEUSTACE, RANDOLPH"* [pseudonym of *W. FRASER*.]
D. The Brides of Florence. 8° 1824.

+ *FORSTER, JOHN.*
Charles at Tunbridge Wells; or, The Cavalier of Wildinghurst (Newcastle, 2/5/1828).

p. 318] +*FRAMPTON*, —
Bal.P. The Tigers of Paris; or, The Dancing Master's Ball
S.W. 16/8/1841).

+*FRASER, W.* [See *RANDOLPH FITZEUSTACE.*]

+*FREEMAN*, —
[+from *UA*: Speculation (Strand, 1832).]

+*FRIMBLEY*, —
M.D. The Ruffian Boy (Plymouth, 11/1823).

+*GALLET*, —
Bal. Vologese, King of the Parthians (D.L. 2/5/1803). [Music Winter.]

GALT, J.
The Witness. [=The Appeal, *UA*. +8° 1818.]
+Tragedies. 8° and 4° 1812. [Contains: *Maddalen*; *Lady Macbeth*; *Agamemnon*; *Antonia*; and *Clytemnestra*.]
[For *The New British Theatre* see also *The Original and Rejected Theatre* in *UA*.]

+*GASPEY*, —
[+from *UA*: Bletchington House.]

GAULTIER, B.
[This entry should be deleted and *King René's Daughter* put under *THEODORE MARTIN*.]

p. 319] +*GIBBONS, Mrs ANNE.*
T. Mary Stuart. 12° 1838 [Devonport]. [A translation of Schiller's drama.]

GILLIES, R. P.
[+from *UA*: The Step-mother.]

GLYNN, GORDON.
[For his later work see *LND*, 382.]

+*GODFREY*, —
The Outcast of the Heath; or, Tottenham Court in 1769 (Queen's, 11/2/1840).

+*GODMOND, CHRISTOPHER.*
Vincenzo, Prince of Mantua; or, The Death of Crichton.
8° 1840 [priv.]

+*GODWIN, GEORGE, Jun.*
[+from *UA*: The Last Day (+*Webster*).]

GOFF, H.
+M.D. The Chieftain's Banquet; or, The Poisoned Cup (Royalty, 9/2/1824).

+*GOFF, RICHARD.*
[+from *UA*: The Sultana.]
The Two Drovers. [+*Duncombe*.]

GOLDSMITH, MARY.
She Lives! [See also under *UA*.]
Angelina. [=Walcot Castle (*UA*).]

p. 320] +*GOTT, H.*
[+from *UA*: The Elshie, printed 8° (1823).]
+The Four Hunchbacks; or, The Beggars of Tivoli (East London). 8° [1825].

38-2

+*GRAHAME, Rev. JAMES.*
[+from *UA*: Mary Stewart.]
T. Wallace. 8° 1799 [Edinburgh].

GRATTAN, H. P.
[+from *UA*: The Rebel Chief (printed in *Dicks* as *The White Boys*); The Omadhaun; Richmond Hill; Touch and Take (Olym. 1827.]
+The Minerali (Vic. 1835). [See under *H. G. PLUNKETT.*]
+Diana's Revenge (Vic. 7/1840).

p. 321] *GREENWOOD, THOMAS.*
[+from *UA*: Harlequin and Cinderella (S.W. 1841); Harry of England; Harlequin and Little Great Britain; Harlequin and the Dragon of Wantley (S.W. 1849); Harlequin and the World turned upside down.]
Jack Sheppard. [+*Cumberland.*]
+Adventures in Italy; or, The Frenchman at Florence (Clarence, 12/12/1833). [Described as translated by Greenwood, adapted by *S. JOHNSON.*]
[For his later work see *LND*, 393.]

GREFFULHE, —
The Portrait of Cervantes. [Based on a play by Dieulafoy.]
Is He a Prince? [=A German Blunder (*UA*).]
The Budget of Blunders. [Originally called *Madness Rules the Hour.*]

GROSETT, H. W.
William Tell. [Apparently submitted to the licenser from Norwich.]
[Two other titles by this author are recorded: *Raymond and Agnes*, and *Marmion.*]

GROVER, H. M. [Full name: *HENRY MONTAGUE GROVER.*]

GROVES, E.
The Warden of Galway. [Acted Dublin, 26/11/1831. +8° 1832 (Dublin).]

GUNNING, E.
A Wife with Two Husbands. [See also under *UA.*]

GURNEY, A. T.
[For his later work see *LND*, 397.]

p. 322] *HAINES, J. T.*
[+from *UA*: The Unhallowed Templar; The French Spy; Worga; A Son's Revenge; The Russian Captive; Adolph Arnal; The Battle of Blenheim; The Two Locksmiths; Uncle Oliver (also recorded at Vic. 7/10/1839).]
+The Spectre Knight; or, The Orphan Dumb Boy (W.L. 3/5/1825; not first performance).
+Elsie Glendinning; or, The Witch of the Coast (W.L. 3/5/1825; not first performance).
A House Divided. [+*Pattie's Universal Stage,* as *Uncle Oliver; or, A H. D.*]
Maidens, Beware! [+*Duncombe.*]

Love and Mystery. [It has been suggested that this is the same as *Mystification* (Strand, 1832) in *UA*, but the identification is doubtful.]

Alice Grey. [+*Pattie's Universal Stage.*]

Jack Sheppard. [+*Pattie's Universal Stage.*]

The Life of a Woman. [+*Pattie's Universal Stage.*]

The Wizard of the Wave. [+*Pattie's Universal Stage.*]

+The Broken Chain; or, The Circassian Maid (Vic. 17/6/1839).

Nick of the Woods. [Adapted from the play by *L. H. MEDINA, q.v.*]

+Walsha; or, The Saxon Slave (Surrey, 26/4/1841). [See *Walsha; or, The Slave's Revolt* in *UA*.]

The Queen of a Day. [Adapted from *La reine d'un jour* by A. E. Scribe and J. H. Vernoy de Saint-Georges (Paris, 19/9/1839).]

The Iron Hand. [See also under *UA*.]

+The Saucy Lass; or, The Log of a British Tar (Vic. 24/7/1843).

[Another title is recorded: *The Goldsmith of Frankfort*; while *The North Pole* is printed in *Duncombe Minor*.]

p. 323] +*HAKE, THOMAS GORDON.*
T. The Piromides. 8° 1839.

+*HALE, —*
D.Poem. Gr[envi]lle Agonistes. 8° 1807.

+*HALLAM, HENRY.*
[+from *UA*: Edgar.]

+*HALLETT, Mrs*
Juniper Jack; or, My Aunt's Hobby. 8° 1847.

+*HAMERTON, W.*
St. Arabin (Dublin, 5/1826).

+*HAMILTON, H.*
Early Closing (P'cess, 1847). [See *A. B. REACH.*]

+*HAMILTON, SARAH.*
[+from *UA*: Alfred the Great (1829).]

p. 324] +*HAMILTON, T. MENZIES.*
The Widow and her Suitors. 8° 1844.

HAMILTON, W. H.
The Magician without Magic. [Adapted from *Le magicien sans magie* by A. F. Creuzé de Lesser and J. F. Roger (Paris, 4/11/1811).]

+*HARDING, C. T.*
(+from *UA*: He's no Conjuror.]

+*HARNESS, Rev. WILLIAM.*
T. Welcome and Farewell. 8° [1837].
D. The First-Born. 8° 1844.

+*HARPER, SAMUEL BROWN.*
D. Bertrand. 8° 1837.

HART, J. P.
[+from *UA*: The Bayonet; The Postilion (Vic. 1837).]
+The Canadian War (M'bone). *Pattie's Play.*

+Jane, the Licensed Victualler's Daughter; or, The Orphan of the Almshouse (Pav.). 12° (n.d.).

+*HATCH, P. H.*
[+from *UA*: The Man Trap.]

+*HAWKES, W. R.*
[+from *UA*: Gaul, King of Ragah.]

HAYLEY, WILLIAM.
+T. The Heroine of Cambria. 8° 1811 [Chichester].

HAYNES, J.
Conscience. [=Lorenzo (*UA*).]

+*HEDDERWICK, JAMES.*
T. The Deformed. 8° 1834 [Glasgow].

HELPS, Sir ARTHUR.
+D. King Henry the Second. 8° 1843.

+*HENRY, W.*
[+from *UA*: The New Marriage Act (printed 12° 1822).]

+*HERAUD, JOHN ABRAHAM.*
D. The Roman Brother. 8° 1840.
D. Salvator, the Poor Man of Naples. 12° 1845 [priv.].

p. 325] *HERBERT, WILLIAM.*
T. The Wierd Wanderers of Jutland. 8° 1822.

+*HETHERINGTON, W. M.*
Twelve Dramatic Sketches. 12° 1829.

HEWLETT, —
The Fortune Hunters. [=Love and Impudence (*UA*).]

HIGGIE, T. H.
[For his later work see *LND*, 421.]

HILL, ISABEL.
[+from *UA*: My Own Twin Brother.]

HOARE, P.
The Children. [+*Songs, Choruses in...The C.* 8° 1800.]
The Paragraph. [=Dine at my Villa (*UA*).]

p. 326] +*HOGG, JAMES.*
M. The Royal Jubilee. 8° 1822 [Edinburgh].

HOLCROFT, T.
The Escapes. [Adapted from *Les deux journées* (Paris, 16/1/1800) by J. N. Bouilly, music by Cherubini. Songs by *T. J. DIBDIN*.]
The Marriage of Figaro. [Adapted from *Le nozze di Figaro* (Vienna, 1/5/1786) by L. da Ponte, music by Mozart. Bishop merely arranged the original music.]

HOLL, H.
[+from *UA*: Benedetto Mangone.]
[For his later work see *LND*, 424.]

p. 327] +*HOLLINGSWORTH, —*
The Exiles of France; or, The Old Hulk (Queen's, 3/1840).

HOLMAN, J. G.
What a Blunder! [Originally called *All for Error*.]
Love gives the Alarm. [This probably = False Alarms, in L. 1404.]
Frost and Thaw. [=Adolphus Count Zelmar (*UA*). +*Airs, duets, &c. &c. in...F. and T.* 8° (1812).]

HOLROYD, J. J. [Full name *JOHN JAMES HOLROYD*.]

HOOK, T. E.
[+from *UA*: A Joke's a Joke.]
The Soldier's Return. [=The Garland (*UA*).]
The Siege of St. Quentin. [Adapted from Pixérécourt, *Les mines de Pologne*.]
Safe and Sound. [=The Consequences (*UA*).]
Darkness Visible. [=Four in Hand (*UA*).]
A Day at an Inn. [+*Pattie's Universal Stage*.]
+*HOPE,* —
T. Godolphin. 8° 1843 [Hartford].

p. 328]   +*HOPKINS, THOMAS.*
T. Harold. 8° 1843 [Manchester].

HORNCASTLE, J. H.
[+from *UA*: The Chevalier d'Epsonne (Grecian, 1848); The Crumlesses.]
The Bayadère. [Performed 1/3/1844. Adapted from *Le dieu et la bayadère* (Paris, 13/10/1830) by A. E. Scribe, music Auber.]

HORNE, F. L.
[+from *UA*: Two Heads better than One. It should be noted, however, that the same title is given to *T. MILDEN-HALL* on the title-pages of Lacy's edition of *The Governor's Wife* and *The Post of Honour*.]
[For his later work see *LND*, 426.]

HORNE, R. H.
[For his later work see *LND*, 426.]

p. 329]   +*HOWARD, ALFRED.*
D. O'Donaghue of the Lakes; or, Harlequin and the Lepre-chaun. 8° 1840 [Dublin].
+*HOWARD, H. L.*
D. Joseph and his Brethren. 8° 1824.

+*HOWITT, MARY*
The Seven Temptations. 16° 1834.

+*HUIE, J. L.*
D. Quentin Durward. 8° 1823 [Edinburgh]. [This may = Q.D. (Caledonian, 1823) in *UA*.]

+*HULL, THOMAS.*
Orat. Elisha; or, The Woman of Shunem. 8° 1801.

+*HULLIN,* —
Bal. La Fête du Village (D.L. 19/6/1820).
Bal. The Chinese Wedding (Vauxhall, 6/1824).

HUNT, L.
[For his later work see *LND*, 431.]

+*HYDE, J. W.*
F. The Irish Absentee (M'bone, 2/1838).
+*IMPEY, ELIJAH BARWELL.*
T. Cumnor; or, The Bugle-Horn. 12° 1822.
C. All in the Dark; or, Ashamed to Own It. 12° 1822.
[Adapted from *Une journée à Versailles.*]
JAMES, C. S.
Where's Eliza? [See also under *UA*.]
[For his later work see *LND*, 432–3.]

p. 330] *JAMES, GEORGE PAYNE RAINSFORD.*
D. Blanche of Navarre. 8° 1839.
Fairy D. Camaralzaman. 12° 1849.
+*JAMESON, Mrs ANNA.*
T. Cadijeh; or, The Black Prince. 8° 1825.
JAMESON, R. F.
A Touch at the Times. [This is L. 1720, as *The Town*.]
Love and Gout. [=Turns and Returns (*UA*).]
Exit by Mistake. [=Keeping up Appearances, in L. 1929.]
Nine Points of the Law. [=Poor Relations (H.² 1818) (*UA*).]

p. 331] +*JAMESON, ROBERT W.*
D.Poem. The Ingrate's Gift. 12° 1830 [Edinburgh].
D.Poem. Nimrod. 8° 1848.
JERROLD, D. W.
[+from *UA*: Birds of Paradise, The Lady Killer; Mrs Caudle's
Curtain Lectures (printed 8° 1846).]
More Frightened than Hurt [+*Duncombe*.]
Dolly and the Rat. [=The Brisket Family (*UA*).]
The Island. [See also under *UA*.]
[Both *The Bill-Sticker* and *A Gallantee Showman* were
produced under the pseudonym *BROWNRIGGE* or
BROWNRIGG. Walter Jerrold (*Douglas Jerrold* (1914), ii.
662–5) lists a few other titles which I have been unable to
trace.]

p. 333] *JODDRELL, R. P.*
The Persian Heroine. [The text of 1819 differs only slightly
from that of 1786.]
JOHNSON, —
The Castle of Wonders. [Apparently — *EARLE* was also con-
cerned with this piece.]
+*JOHNSON, S.*
Adventures in Italy. [See *T. GREENWOOD*.]
JOHNSTONE, J. B.
[+from *UA*: The Old Mint of Southwark; Phoebe Hersell.]
+P. Æsop's Fables; or, Harlequin the Wolf and the Lamb
(Brighton, 26/12/1849).
[For his later work see *LND*, 438.]
+*JONES, —*
[+from *UA*: Scotch Marriage Laws (acted Edinburgh,
26/4/1823).]

+*JONES, FREDERICK.*
Tom Jones (Dublin, 6/1826).

p. 334]   *JONES, JACOB.*
 +T. Regulus, the Noblest Roman of Them All. 8° 1841.
+*JONES, MARGARET ELIZABETH MARY.*
 T. Gawyim Honor. 8° [1844].
+*JONES, RICHARD.*
 Too Late for Dinner. [This has also been attributed to
 T. E. HOOK.]
 Peter Fin. [Another variant text is in L. 2287, as *Peter Fin's
 Trip to Brighton.*]
 +M.D. Ivanhoe. [No doubt one of the plays of this title
 listed in *UA.*]
+*JONES, ROBERT ST CLAIR.*
 D. Robin Hood. 8° 1848.
 C. The Spanish Rake. 12° 1850.
 [For his later work see *LND*, 441.]
+*JOUBERT, —*
 Bal. The Millers (D.L. 18/6/1802).
+*KEAN, — (of Carlisle).*
 M.D. The Cottage Foundling. 8° 1811.
+*KEEP, W. A.*
 F. Incog; or, Three Weeks at a Well-known Hotel. 8° 1817.
 [See on p. 345 under *Lord W. LENNOX.* The play has a
 double attribution. There are two L.C. texts: L. 1976
 (manuscript) and L. 2266 (printed copy), the latter for a
 revival at the Olympic, 11/12/1821. For this see *Arrivals*
 in *UA.*]
KEMBLE, C.
 [+from *UA*: Proof Presumptive.]
 The Child of Chance. [= Love's Errors (*UA*).]
KEMBLE, F. A.
 [For her later work see *LND*, 442.]

p. 335]   *KEMBLE, J. P.*
 [For an adaptation of Joanna Baillie's *De Montfort* see L. 1287.]
KEMBLE, MARIE-THERESE.
 Smiles and Tears. [=The Law Suit (*UA*).]
KENNEDY, C. R.
 [For his later work see *LND*, 443.]

p. 336]   +*KENNEY, CHARLES.*
 [+from *UA*: Robin Hood and Richard Coeur de Lion! (in
 collaboration with *J. H. STOCQUELER* and *C. W. S.
 BROOKS*); The Wood Demon (Lyc. 1847; in collaboration
 with *A. R. SMITH*); Valentine and Orson (in collaboration
 with *A. R. SMITH* and *T. TAYLOR*).]
KENNEY, J.
 [+from *UA*: The Black Domino [adapted from *Le domino
 noir* (Paris, 2/12/1837) by A. E. Scribe, music by Auber;
 in collaboration with *J. M. MORTON* (C.G. 1838)].

Matrimony. [Adapted from *Adolphe et Clara* (Paris, 10/2/1799) by B. J. Marsollier, music by Dalayrac; =The Two Prisoners (*UA*).]

Oh! this Love! [=Love's Mysteries (*UA*).]

Turn Him Out! [=The Tyrant and Parrasite (*UA*).]

Debtor and Creditor. [=The City Rivals (*UA*).]

The Alcaid. [Music Nathan.]

Masaniello. [Adapted from the play by A. E. Scribe, music by Dalayrac (Paris, 29/2/1828). The music for the English version was adapted by T. S. Cooke and B. Livius.]

+Like Father like Son (E.O.H. 8/1840). [Ascribed to *KENNEY*; see under *R. J. RAYMOND*.]

   [For his later work see *LND*, 443.]

+*KEPPELL, —*
   [+from *UA*: The Spirit of the Mist.]

p. 338] *KERR, J.*
   [+from *UA*: Michael and Christine (printed 8° (1824).]

The Wandering Boys. [First performed C.G. 24/2/1814. This is given in *UA* and seems to be the same play; the only problem arises from the fact that the C.G. production has also been attributed to *I. POCOCK*.]

+M.D. Der Freischutz; or, Zamiel, the Spirit of the Forest, and the Seventh Bullet (Lyc. 22/7/1824). 8° (1824].

+The Monster and the Magician (W.L. 9/10/1826).
   [For his later work see *LND*, 443.]

+*KERTLAND, WILLIAM.*
   O.Rom. The Maid of Snowdon (Dublin, 5/1/1833).
   O.Rom. Shawn Long and the Fairies (Dublin, 10/1/1835).

+*KING, WILLIAM.*
   T. The Parricide. 8° 1833.

+*KNIGHT, C.*
   T. Arminius; or, The Deliverance of Germany. 8° 1814 [Windsor].

+*KNIGHT, HENRY GALLY.*
   D. Hannibal in Bithynia. 12° 1839 (3 edns.).

+*KNIGHT, T.*
   [+from *UA*: Honest Thieves (printed in *Cawthorne's Minor Drama*).]

p. 340] *LACY, M. R.*
   [+from *UA*: The Fiend Father; The Israelites in Egypt; The Blind Sister.]

The Turkish Lovers. [Adapted from *Il Turco in Italia*, music by Rossini.]

Love in Wrinkles. [Adapted from *La vieille* (Paris, 14/3/1826) by A. E. Scribe and G. Delavigne, music by Fétis.]

The Maid of Judah. [Original music by Rossini.]

The Coiners. [Adapted from *Le serment* (Paris, 1/10/1832) by A. E. Scribe and E. J. E. Mazères, music by Auber.]

Robert the Devil. [It is most probable that this version of Meyerbeer's opera is, in fact, by *R. J. RAYMOND*.]

Fra Diavolo. [+8° 1833.]

   [For his later work see *LND*, 446.]

LACY, T. H.
  A Silent Woman. [+*Lacy*.]
    [Other titles attributed to him are *Jephtha's Vow* and
    Marston Moor: he was also the adapter of *The Black Doctor*,
    translated by *J. V. BRIDGEMAN*.]

p. 341] *LANCASTER, C. S.*
  The Devil's Daughter. [This should be added to *E. R.
  LANCASTER*, below.]

LANCASTER, EDWARD RICHARDSON.
  [+from *UA*: The Manager's Daughter (printed in *Oxberry's
  Budget*, no. 11). +from *C. S. LANCASTER*, above:
  The Devil's Daughter (printed in *Oxberry's Budget*, no. 37.]
  +The Wager; or, The School Girl, the Young Wife and the
    Heroine (S.W. 1839). *Oxberry's Budget*, no. 1.
  +M.D. Amalderac, the Black Rover; or, The Rock of Death.
    Oxberry's Budget, no. 39. [This seems to be the same as
    Amalderac, the Black Pirate in *UA*.]
  +D. Claude Gower; or, The Maid of the Alder Well.
    Oxberry's Budget, no. 6.
  +F. Contrivances; or, The Bailiff and the M.P. (Queen's).
    Oxberry's Budget, no. 19.
  +F. Hereditary Honours; or, The Mysterious Stranger
    (Queen's). [Written in collaboration with *W. H. OX-
    BERRY*.]
  +D. Jared Swool; or, The Idiot of One-Tree Lane (Garrick,
    8/1843). *Oxberry's Budget*, no. 10.
  +Int. The Lapland Witch. *Oxberry's Budget*, no. 21.
  +F.Ba. My Aunt's Narcotic (Queen's). *Oxberry's Budget*,
    no. 17.
  +M.D.Ba. Petticoat Service; or, Freaks at Aboukir Bay.
    Oxberry's Budget, no. 12.
  +M.D. The Red Lance; or, The Merrie Men of Hoxton
    (Brit. 1841). *Oxberry's Budget*, no. 20.
  +F. The Tables Turned; or, Master Humphrey and His
    Clock. *Oxberry's Budget*, no. 5.
  +D. The Two Fishermen of Lynn; or, The Last of the
    Burnings. *Oxberry's Budget*, no. 8.
  +F. Ups and Downs; or, The Reverse of a Day (S.W.).
    Oxberry's Budget, no. 2. [Written in collaboration with
    W. H. OXBERRY.]
  +D. The Whytte-Chappelle Byrde Catchers; or, The Pigeon
    Fliers of Spittalfielde. *Oxberry's Budget*, no. 38.
  [Other titles recorded are: *Ruth* and *Warwick the Kingmaker*.]

+*LANE, L.*
  [+from *UA*: Richard and Betty.]

LATHOM, F.
  [+from *UA*: The Fools of Fashion.]
  The Dash of the Day. [Originally called: *Life in a Mirror;
  or, The D. of the D.*]
  Curiosity. [Originally called: *The Spanish Duel*.]
  +D. Orlando and Seraphina; or, The Funeral Pile. L. 1317
  [Norwich, 10/3/1801.]

594 SUPPLEMENTARY NOTES TO THE

p. 342] *LAWLER, D.*
[+from *UA*: The Beaux' Stratagem; The Three and the Deuce.]
+The Earls of Hammersmith (Surrey, 1811). See *J. POOLE.*
+*LAWRANCE, FREDERICK.*
[+from *UA*: Pierre Bertrand.]
+The King and the Carpenter (C.L. 1838).
+*LECLERCQ,* —
Bal. Bacchus and Ariadne (Cork, 7/6/1841).
+*LEE, E. B.*
T. Corregio [and] Sappho. 16° 1846.
[The former is a translation of Oehlenschlager's play, the latter of Grillparzer's.]
+*LEE, HERBERT.*
[+from *UA*: The Avenger (Cob. 1824).]
LEE, HENRY.
Caleb Quotem and his Wife! [+8° 1820 (Taunton).]
LEE, N.
[+from *UA*: The Queen of the Clover Field; The Little Old Woman and her Pig; Harlequin and Old Cocker; Harlequin Jack the Giant Killer; Harlequin Tam o' Shanter; Grace Rivers; Harlequin Crochet and Quaver; Pat a Cake; St. George and the Dragon (C.L. 1843); Bold Robin Hood; Mrs Jane Shore; Mrs H.]
+Robinson Crusoe (Vic. 1836).
+Marrowbones and Cleavers; or, Harlequin's Wedding Day [M'bone, 12/1838).
+The Clock House; or, The Murder at the Mansion (Vic. 19/2/1840).
+Harlequin Georgy Porgy; or, Aunty Paunty's Visits (Queen's, 12/1840).
+Harlequin and the One-Eyed Blacksmith (C.L. 26/12/1841).
+Harlequin Riddle Me Ree (Olym. 1841). [Evidently = *Riddle Me, Riddle me Ree* in *UA*, p. 527, and *Harlequin and Riddle Me, Riddle Me Ree*, p. 472.]
+Jacky Jingle; or, Harlequin and the Magic Horseshoe (Queen's, 12/1841).
+Dame Trot and her Cat; or, Harlequin and the House that Jack Built (Brighton, 26/12/1842).
+Nicholas Dunks; or, Fried Mackerel for Supper (R.P. 10/1843).
+Jerry Abershaw (R.P. 7/1844).
+Harlequin and Johnny Gilpin's Ride; or, The Black Witch of Edmonton (R.A. 12/1844).
Harlequin and Yankee Doodle. [=Yankee Doodle upon his Little Pony (*UA*).]
[For his later work see *LND*, 452–3.]

p. 343] *LEIGH, R.*
Where to find a Friend. [There are two Larpent manuscripts, 1674 (for which see *UA*) and L. 1888.]
LEMON, M.
[+from *UA*: Rob of the Fen (adapted from *Das Falkners Braut* (Leipzig, 10/3/1832) by W. A. Wohlbruck, music by

Marschner); The Pupil of Da Vinci (music by J. A. Wade);
Fridolin (songs printed 8° 1840; music by F. Romer); The
Deer Stalker; Out of Place (H.² 1840); The Lady of the
Lake (C.G. 1843).]
My Sister Kate. [Acted C.L. 1/3/1838. +*French*.]
The Three Secrets. [+*Pattie's Universal Stage*.]
The Pacha's Bridal. [See in *UA* under *The Pasha's Bridal*.]
    [In *Barth's Universal Stage* were printed: *The Ladies'
Club*; *Gwynneth Vaughan*; *Ins and Outs*; *Fashionable
Arrivals*; *Old Parr*; *The Sempstress*; *Lost and Won*; *The
Demon's Gift*. For his later work see *LND*, 455.]

p. 345] *LENNOX, Lord W.*
    Incog. [=Arrivals (*UA*). See also under *W. A. KEEP*.]

LEWIS, A. [Full name *ALEXIS LEWIS*.]
+C.D. The Hunchback and the Sutler; or, The Rival Lovers.
    Oxberry's Budget, no. 13.

LEWIS, M. G.
    [+from *UA*: The Enchanted Fire of the Invisible Island;
    Temper.]
    Rugantino. [Probably the *Rugantino* of 1831 (see *UA*) was
    this play.]
    Adelgitha. [Music M. Kelly.]
    Venoni. [Music M. Kelly. Adapted from *La victime
    cloitreé* by Bouhet.]
    Rich and Poor. [+8° 1812.] [This appears in L. 1726 as
    The East Indian; *q.v.* in *UA*.]

p. 346] +*LIGHTERNESS, WILLIAM BEATTY.*
    D.D. Mark Lawrence; or, The Farmer's Dream (Strand,
    20/11/1837). 12° [1838].
        [Other titles recorded: The Revolt of the Chummies;
    The Libertine of Paris; Hugo the Dane. See M. Summers,
    "An Unrecorded Drama?" (*Theatre Notebook*, (1945, i. 7).]

+*LINDSAY, Sir C.*
    The Black Prince. 8° 1846.
    D. Alfred. 8° 1848.

LINLEY, G.
    [+from *UA*: Mina.]
    [For his later work see *LND*, 460.]

LINLEY, W.
    The Ring. [Acted D.L. 21/1/1800.]

LODGE, A.
    [For his later work see *LND*, 462.]

+[*LOGAN, CORNELIUS A.*
    [+from *UA*: The Vermont Wool Dealer (acted U.S.A. 1840);
    Yankee Land (acted U.S.A. 1834).]

+*LOGAN, WILLIAM HUGH.*
    F. Le Bas Bleu; or, The Fall of the Leaf (Edinburgh,
    30/3/1836). 8° 1836 [Edinburgh]. [For the Lord Chamber-
    lain's manuscript see *The Bas Bleu* in *UA*.]
    Bsq. Rummio and Judy. 8° 1841 [Edinburgh].

+*LOGAN, W. McGREGOR.*
Der Freischutz. [See under *J. OXENFORD.* Music adapted by W. Hawes.]

p. 347] *LONSDALE,* —. [Full name: *MARK LONSDALE.*]
+*LOTT, W.*
D. All's Not Well That Seems So; or, The London Merchant. 8° 1843.

LOVELL, G. W.
The Provost of Bruges. [+8° 1837.]
Love's Sacrifice. [+8° 1829.]
[For his later work see *LND*, 463.]

LOVER, S.
[+from *UA*: The Olympic Pic-nic; Snap Apple Night.]
[For his later work see *LND*, 463-4.]

LUCAS, W. J.
[+from *UA*: The Cricket on the Hearth; The Man in the Iron Mask; The Hebrew Twins; She's Mine for a Thousand.]
[For his later work see *LND*, 464.]

p. 348] +*LUDLAM, GEORGE.*
M.D. The Mysterious Murder; or, What's the Clock? 12° [1817; *Birmingham*].

LUNN, J.
[+from *UA*: Hide and Seek (C.G. 1830; apparently his, although also attributed to *WESTMACOTT, Junior*); My Friend from Town; Wheedling; The Purse of Almo; Harmony Hall.]

+*LYNCH, THOMAS JOHN.*
[+from *UA*: Alberto and Lauretta; Ivan of the Mask; The Rose of Ettrick Vale (acted Edinburgh, 23/5/1825; E.O.H., 7/12/1835; *Dicks* 796); The Minstrel of Lochmaben.]

+*LYNDSAY, DAVID.*
Dramas of the Ancient World. 8° 1822 [Edinburgh].

p. 349] *LYTTON, Baron.*
The Lady of Lyons. [+8° 1851.]
Money. [+8° 1851.]
[For his later work see *LND*, 466.]

MACARTHY, —
+The Irish Absentee (Vic. 5/11/1836).

+*McCARTHY, DENIS FLORENCE.*
D. Justina. 8° 1848. [A translation of Calderón, *El magico prodigioso.*]

+*MACAULAY, Miss.*
T. Mary Stuart. 8° 1823.

+*MACDONALD,* —
[+from *UA*: Charles Edward Stuart.]

+*M'DONALD, THOMAS, Junior.*
T. Cornelia. 8° 1823 [Dublin].

MACDONALD, W. B.
Faust. [+8° 1840.]

MACFARREN, G.
George III. [See also in *UA*, under *The Life and Reign of George III*.]
Tom and Jerry in France. [+8° (1822).]
My Old Woman. [+*Cumberland Minor*. Adapted from *La vieille* (Paris, 14/3/1826) by A. E. Scribe and G. Delavigne, music by Fétis.]
+Cupid's Frolics (Queen's, 8/10/1831).
The Devil's Opera. [Music G. A. MacFarren.]
The Matrimonial Ladder. [Adapted from *La double échelle* (Paris, 23/8/1837) by F. A. E. de Planard, music by A. Thomas.]
+McKINLAN, —
[+from *UA*: Francis I.]
McLAREN, A.
The Tricks of London. [The 1812 edition also has a variant title-page, reading *The Ways of London*.]

p. 353] +MADDY, J. M.
[+from *UA*: Bluff King Hal.]
+MAGNUS, T.
D. Alfred the Great. 8° 1838.
D. Wolowski. 8° 1838.
+MALE, G.
[+from *UA*: One Foot by Land and One Foot by Sea.]
Spect. The Blood-Red Knight (R.C. 1810).
+MANSON, Dr and Mrs.
D. The Eve of St Hippolyte. 8° 1821.
+MARA, SAMUEL DELAVAL.
M.D. Brian Boroihme (Dublin, 1/1810)
+MARKWELL, W. R.
[+from *UA*: The Stage-Struck Yankee.]
+MARSTON, H.
[+from *UA*: The Highland Widow.]
+MARTIN, JOHN.
F. Fairly Hit and Fairly Missed. *Duncombe*.
[The title-page also credits him with: *My Man and the Barber*.]
+MARTIN, THEODORE.
D. King Rene's Daughter. [See under *B. GAULTIER*.]
MATHEWS, C. J.
[+from *UA*: Mathews and Co.; Methinks I See my Father; Who Killed Cock Robin?]
Country Cousins. [This has been wrongly ascribed to Mathews. See under *J. SMITH*.]
Christmas at Brighton. [This forms part of *Country Cousins*, above.]
The Hypochondriac. [This is the second part of the first "At Home" of Charles Mathews.]
+The Wolf and the Lamb. [This play, listed under *T. E. WILKS*, seems to have been by Mathews.]
The Humpbacked Lover. [+*Cumberland*.]

Pong Wong. [See also in *UA*.]
He Would be an Actor. [See also in *UA*.]
  [For his later work see *LND*, 480.]

p. 354] *MATURIN, C. R.*
Bertram. [=The Castle of St. Aldobrand (*UA*).]
+Osmyn the Renegade; or, The Siege of Salerno (Dublin,
  30/3/1830; Edin. 31/10/1831, as *The Renegate*).

MAYHEW, E.
  [+from *UA*: Martial Law; A Father's Plea; Matteo Falconi.]

MAYHEW, H.
  [+from *UA*: The Barbers at Court; A Troublesome Lodger.]
The Wandering Minstrel. [+8° 1834.]

+*MAYHEW, HORACE.*
  [+from *UA*: The Plum Pudding Pantomime.]

MAYHEW, T.
Ambition. [Adapted from *Marie Mignot*, by Bayard and
  Dupont.]

+*MAYO, Rev. ROBERT W.*
  [+from *UA*: Abdication of Ferdinand.]

MEDINA, L. H.
Nick of the Woods. [See also under *J. T. HAINES*, p. 323.]

+*MEDWIN, Capt. THOMAS*
T. Prometheus Bound. 8° 1827 [Siena]. [A translation from
  Æschylus.]

+*MENZIES, KENNETH.*
T. Tyrrel. 8° 1841. [See *E. TAIT*.]

+*MIDDLETON, —*
The Battle of Bothwell Brig (Caledonian, Edinburgh,
  9/8/1827).

MILDENHALL, T.
  [+from *UA*: The Marriage Certificate; The Eleventh Hour
  (Queen's, 1844).]
+The Red Barn; or, Mid-day Murder (Monmouth,
  23/11/1829).
+The Battle of Bovines (Queen's, 1840).
+The Witch of the White Hoods; or, The Daughter of Ghent
  (Queen's, 3/1840).
+The Demon Arab; or, The Fairies of the Silver Mines
  (Queen's, 20/4/1840).
+Old Booty; or, The Phantom of the Volcano (Queen's,
  1/2/1841; revived at C.L. 22/1/1844 as *Old Booty of
  Bishopsgate*).
+Norma; or, The Immolation (Queen's, 28/2/1842).
+Dirty Dick (Queen's, 3/1842).
The Governor's Wife. [+*Barth's Universal Stage*.]
+Blueskin (Queen's, 1846).
  [*Two Heads Better than One* seems to be by *F. L.
  HORNE*, but it is ascribed to Mildenhall in *Barth's
  Universal Stage*.]

p. 356] +*MILLAR, JAMES.*
  T. The Siege of Berwick. 8° 1824.
+*MILLETT,* —
  F. The Credulous Knight (Derby, 15/3/1800).
+*MILLIKEN, RICHARD ALFRED.*
  [+from *UA*: The Anaconda (W.L. 1822).]
MILLINGEN, J. G.
  [+from *UA*: Nero, a Roman-tick Fiddler; Name the Winner; Carlo.]
  The Bee Hive. [Adapted from P. Lebrun, *Les rivaux d'eux mêmes.*]
  Ladies at Home. [+8° 1819.]
  The King's Fool. [+8° 1833.]
MILNER, H. M.
  [+from *UA*: Rob Roy (Olym. 1818); Zangarotti; The Maid of the Forest; Dick Whittington and his Cat; The Hertfordshire Tragedy; The Enchanted Castle; Frederick of Bavaria (Cob. 1822); The Massacre of Cyprus; Stanislaus; The Caliph Vathek; A Trip to the Ball; Twm John Catty; Mazeppa; Travelling Incog.; The Siege of Acre; The Weird Woman of the Isles; The Reign of Terror; The Freebooters of Vienna; The Battle of Agincourt (Cob. 1825); The Prodigal Son; The Massacre of Rajahpoor; The Invisible Tribunal; The Old Man of the Mountains; The Coast Blockade; The Welshman; Spanish Martyrs; The Death Fetch (Cob. 1826); The Ocean Fiend (Cob. 1826); The Rat-Trap; Lucius Catiline; Bannockburn; "Buy a Broom?"; The Black Woodsman; The Man and the Monster; Britons at Navarino; The Sacred Standard and the Chinese Prince; Hamlet, Prince of Denmark; The Mysteries of Alviano; The Votaries of the Ruby Cross; The Money Diggers; The Council of Ten; The Silver Veil.]
  +The Philosopher...translated from the German of M. Lessing. 8° 1819.
  Twelve Precisely. [+8° 1821.]
  +Tipoo Sahib; or, The Storming of Seringapatan (Cob. 20/1/1823).
  +The Jew (Cob. 1/9/1823).
  Masaniello. [+8° (1824).]
  Victorine. [+*Duncombe Minor.*]
  Gustavus of Sweden. [+*Duncombe,* as *Gustavus the Third.*]
  +The Rifle-Shot; or, The Michigan Chief (Strand, 19/1/1834).
  The Blind Beggar of Bethnal Green. [+*Duncombe Minor.*]
  +The Challenge (C.G. 1/4/1834). [This version of *Le pré aux clercs,* with songs by *J. R. PLANCHÉ,* seems to have been Milner's. Music by Hérold, arranged by T. S. Cooke; original libretto by F. A. E. de Planard.]

p. 357] +*MITCHELL,* —
  [+from *UA*: The Newspaper.]
+*MITCHELL, W. A.*
  Int. No. 16 (Newcastle, 28/4/1828).
MITFORD, M. R.
  Julian. [=The Melfi (*UA*).]

39   N E D

p. 358]   *MONCRIEFF, W. T.* [A pseudonym for *THOMAS, W. T.*
The name appears occasionally as *MONTCRIEFF.*]
[+from *UA*: John Adams; The Monk's Cowl; A Cheque on
my Banker; The Actor in Distress; The Bride of Lammer-
moor (R.A. 1819); The Smuggler's Dog; Giovanni in
Ireland (D.L. 1821); The Hollow Way; Electioneering;
The Devil's Walk; The Man-Wolf; Mount St. Bernard
(printed in *Duncombe Minor*); What a Shocking Bad Hat!;
Courting by Mistake; The Monkey that has seen the
World; What are you at?; Favourites in Town; "Victor
Dene"; The Revolt of the Seraglio; The Court of Queen
Anne (+*Duncombe Minor*); The Smuggler's Haunt; What's
in a Name (Vic. 1835); A Down East Bargain; The Blind
Father; The Fitzpatricks; Harlequin and My Lady Lee;
Sam Weller's Tour; Shakespeare and Burbage; Up and
Down; Nicholas Nickleby; Popularity; An Armful of Bliss;
The Royal Foxhunt (see in *UA* under: The Favourite of
the Derby).]
Joconde. [+*Cumberland Minor*.]
Giovanni in London. [+8° 1817.]
Ivanhoe. [=Ivanhoe; or, The Jew of York (*UA*).]

p. 359]   The Lost Life. [Also called: The Posthumous Man.]
Actors al Fresco. [Sub-title: or, The Play in the Pleasure
Grounds.]
The Secret. [+8° 1823.]
The Beggar of Cripplegate [+12° (1830).]

p. 360]   Peer and Peasant. [+8° 1832.]
+The World as it Runs; or, Fancy's Freaks (Strand,
28/3/1832).
Lochinvar. [+*Duncombe Minor*.]
One Fault. [+*Lacy*.]
How to take up a Bill. [+8° 1833.]
The Parson's Nose. [+8° 1833, as The Birth Day; or, The
Parson's Nose.]

p. 361]   +The Devil's in the Room (Vic. 16/3/1840).
+The Queen of a Day (Vic. 11/5/1840). [An adaptation of
La reine d'un jour (Paris, 19/9/1839) by A. E. Scribe and
J. N. Verney de St George; music by Adam.]
+The Tribute of a Hundred Virgins (Vic. 11/5/1840).
+Love and Laugh; or, The M.P. (Strand, 12/9/1842).

+*MONNEY, WILLIAM.*
T. Caractacus. 12° 1816.

+*MONTAGUE, C.*
Bal.P. The Milliners; or, The Fairy Ball (S.W. 10/2/1838).

+*MONTIGNANI, F. A.*
Bal. The Village Doctor (Lyc. 23/4/1810).

+*MOORE, J.*
[+from *UA*: Champagne.]

+*MOREAU, —*
Bal. The Carpenter (Lyc. 3/8/1813).

+*MORETON*, —
  M.D. The Sea Devil; or, The False Beacon (Surrey, 25/11/1822).

+*MORGAN*, *Lady*.
  O. The Cavern; or, The Outlaws (Dublin, 22/4/1825). [Music Sir John Stevenson.]

+*MORRIS*, *V*.
  [+from *UA*: Francesca Doria.]

MORTON, *EDWARD*.
  [The title-pages of *The Eton Boy* (*French*) and *The Windmill* (*Lacy*) give these plays to Edward Morton. They are listed under *THOMAS MORTON*, *Junior*, to whom they are usually ascribed.]

MORTON, *J*. *M*.
  [+from *UA*: The Black Domino (C.G. 1838; in collaboration with *J*. *KENNEY*); Don't be Frightened; Harlequin and William Tell; News from China; Puck's Pantomime.]
  [For his later work see *LND*, 495–7.]

p. 363] *MORTON*, *T*.
  [+from *UA*: The King's Fireside.]
  The Blind Girl. [+8° 1801, *Airs*, *Duets*, *and Choruses*.]
  Town and Country. [=London and the Country (*UA*).]
  The Slave. [=Freedom and Slavery (*UA*).]

MORTON, *T*. *Junior*.
  [See above under *EDWARD MORTON*.]
  The Drunkard's Glass. [+*Duncombe*, as *Another Glass*.]

p. 364] *MOULD*, *J*. *WRAY*.
  O. The Marriage of Figaro (D.L. 11/2/1848). [Music Mozart. See also under *UA*.]

+[*MOWATT*, *ANNA CORA*.
  [+from *UA*: Armand (8° 1849).]

p. 365] +*MUNRO*, *Lieut*. *C*. *F*.
  [+from *UA*: The Earl of Ross.]

MURRAY, *W*. *H*.
  [+from *UA*: What! The Devil Again!; The Highland Cateran.]
  +Karfa the Slave; or, Three Fingered Jack (Cork, 3/1834). George Heriot [+8° 1823 (Edinburgh).]
  No. [+8° 1829 (Edinburgh).]

NANTZ, *F*. *C*.
  [+from *UA*: Blue-eyed Mary; St. Ann's Well!; Pickwick; The Brown Devil.]

+*NAPIER*, *N*.
  [+from *UA*: The Freebooters (from *I fuorusciti di Firenze*, libretto by A. Anelli, music by Paer; Dresden, 27/11/1802).]

+*NEALE*, *CORNELIUS*.
  Lyrical Dramas. 12° 1819.

NEALE, *F*.
  [+from *UA*: Butcher, Butcher, Kill an Ox.]
  [For his later work see *LND*, 501.]

p. 366] *NICHOLSON, JOHN.* [See under — *BURTON,* p. 277.]
  +*NOBLE, THOMAS.*
  [+from *UA*: The Persian Hunters; Cupid and Folly.]
  +*NORTON, Hon. Mrs ELIZA BLAND.*
  The Gypsy Father (C.G. 31/5/1831). L.C.
  The Martyr. 8° 1848.
  +*"ODD FELLOW, AN"* [pseudonym for *PETER MAC-
  KENZIE, JAMES WALLACE, JAMES BROWN,
  ROBERT KAY, JOSEPH SOUTER, ALEXANDER
  MᶜNEILL* and *JAMES DUNCAN*].
  F. Gotham in Alarm (Glasgow, 1816). 8° 1816 [Glasgow,
  4 editions].
  +*O'NEIL, J. R.*
  [+from *UA*: King Lear and his Daughters Queer.]
  +*OSBALDISTONE, D. W.*
  [+from *UA*: "Vive la Liberté".]
  Baron Trenck. [See under *S. J. ARNOLD,* p. 256.]
  The Brigand (Surrey, 18/11/1830).
  Naomi; or, The Peasant Girl's Dream (C.L. 1838).
  +*OSBORN, Hon. H.*
  Sketch. The Queen's Masque. 8° 1842.
  D. Fame. 8° 1850.
  +*OSWIN, CHARLES HANNAY.*
  D. Elsdale Hall; or, The Days of Oliver Cromwell. 8° [1842].
  [This is cited wrongly in *UA* as *Esdale Hall.*]
  OULTON, W. C.
  The Middle Dish. [+L. 1410.]
  OXBERRY, W. H.
  [+from *UA*: The Female Volunteer [apparently given first
  at the Clarence, 11/11/1832.]
  The Actress of All Work. [This is almost identical with the
  similarly-titled play in *UA*. The author was Oxberry the
  Elder.]
  The Conscript. [+*Pattie's Universal Stage.*]
  +Kenilworth. 8° 1824 [Edinburgh].
  +The Hackles of Hackle Hall (Fitzroy, 9/6/1834).
  +The Ourang Outang and his Double (Clarence, 9/12/1833).
  +The Truant Chief. [This, listed under *J. OXENFORD,*
  seems to have been Oxberry's work. +*Duncombe.*]
  +The Pacha's Pets. [This, also listed under *J. OXENFORD,*
  seems to have been by Oxberry. +*Duncombe.*]
  +The Three Clerks (Vic. 1838). [*Pattie's Play.*]
  +Hereditary Honours (Queen's). [See *E. R. LANCASTER.*]
  +Ups and Downs (S.W.). [See *E. R. LANCASTER.*]
    [*Oxberry's Weekly Budget* includes: The Burgraves; or,
    The Black Banner of Heppenheff (a version of Victor Hugo's
    drama); *The Lady of the Louvre; or, The Massacre of the
    Huguenots.*]
  OXENFORD, J.
  [+from *UA*: The Bridal Promise; Cousin Joseph; Dearest
  Elizabeth (+*Nat. Acting Drama*); Loose Cash; What have

I done?; The Idol's Birthday; Gone to Texas; Invisible
Green; An Appeal to the Public; The Hemlock Draught;
Virginia (an adaptation from a play by Latour de St. Ybars).]
Der Freischutz. [This piece was apparently by *W. M.
LOGAN*; music adapted by W. Hawes.]
My Fellow Clerk. [+8° 1835.]
Midshipman Easy. [See also in *UA* under *Mr Midshipman
Easy*.]
The Rape of the Lock. [+*London Acting Drama*.]
No Followers. [+8° 1837.]
The Truant Chief. [This seems to have been by *W. H.
OXBERRY*.]
The Pacha's Pets. [This seems to have been by *W. H.
OXBERRY*.]
[For his later work see *LND*, 509–11.]

p. 368] *PARDOE, Miss.*
[+from *UA*: Louise de Lignarolles.]
The Breach of Promise of Marriage. [See under *G. H.
RODWELL*.]

+*PARK, LOUISA JANE*.
D.Poem. Miriam. 12° 1849.

PARRY, J.
[+from *UA*: Paired Off; The Wager (St J. 1837).]
High Notions. [+8° 1819.]
Helpless Animals. [+8° 1819.]
The Cabinet and Two Wives. [An earlier version of this play
is listed in *UA* as: *The Two Wives!* It was printed 8°
(1821).]
+The Smuggler's Gibbet (Vic. 9/1838).

PARRY, T.
[+from *UA*: The Peacock and the Crow.]
+Omens and Coïncidences (H.¹ 3/6/1848).

PAYNE, J. H.
[+from *UA*: The French Libertine; Fricandeau.]
Accusation. [+8° 1817.]
Therese. [+8° 1821.]

p. 369] *PAYNTER, D. W.*
Eurypilus. [=similarly-titled play in *UA*.]

PEAKE, R. B.
[+from *UA*: The Man in Mourning for Himself; Two Pence;
Gordon the Gypsey; Another Piece of Presumption; My
Own Man; The Ramsbottoms at Rheims; The Cornish
Miners; Neuha's Cave; Job Fox; The Little Laundress;
The Flip Flap Footman; A Night with Punch; The Miser's
Will; The Loving Woman.]
The Duel. [=My Two Nephews (*UA*).]
The Poachers. [=The Roebuck (*UA*).]

p. 370] +Little Offsprings (C.G. 26/4/1828). [Attributed to Peake;
see under *T. PERCY*.]
+The Smuggler Count (S.W. 10/1833).

PENLEY, S.
[+from *UA*: Gallantry.]

p. 371] *PERCY, T.*
Little Offsprings. [Also attributed to *R. B. PEAKE*; see above.]

p. 372] *PHILLIPS, E. [Mrs ALFRED D.]*
Prejudice. [This was acted, Strand, 10/5/1849, as *The Bachelor's Vow*; see *UA*.]
+C. First Love; or, Uncle's Letter (Brighton, 16/1/1839). [Written in collaboration with *A. S. WIGAN*.]
[For her later work see *LND*, 522.]

PHILLIPS, F. L.
[For his later work see *LND*, 522.]

PILGRIM, J.
[For his later work see *LND*, 524.]

+*PINKERTON, JOHN.*
[+from *UA*: Woman and Philosophy.]
+The Heiress of Strathearn; or, The Rash Marriage (Edinburgh, 24/3/1813). [Listed in *UA* under both the main- and sub-title.]

PITT, G. D.
[+from *UA*: Jacob Faithful (Surrey, 1834); The Two London Locksmiths; Gunpowder Tom; Kerim the Pearl Diver; The Sexton of Stepney; Basil and Barbara; Light and Shade.]
The Last Nail. [+*Duncombe Minor*.]
Lurline. [+*Duncombe Minor*.]

p. 373] +The Leper of Leadenhall (C.L. 1838).
+The Phantom Ship (Queen's, 1/7/1839).
+Lucy Lisle (C.L. 13/9/1841).
+James Lawson; or, The Horse Poisoner (Garrick, 27/9/1841).
Susan Hopley. [+*Cumberland Minor*, no. 145.]
The Whistler. [Save for one song, the same as the play given in 1833.]
The Last Man. [Originally presented at the Surrey, 22/7/1833.]
+The Fool of Finsbury; or, The Beggar of Crosby Hall (C.L. 3/1842).
+The Wizard Schooner; or, The Twin Tars (Queen's, 9/3/1843).
Jarvis the Honest Man. [See also under *UA*.]
+The Life of a Soldier (Brit. 10/1848).
[For his later work see *LND*, 526.]

p. 376] *PLANCHÉ, J. R.*
Rodolph the Wolf. [+8° 1819.]
A Burletta of Errors. [Adapted from J. Dryden, *Amphitryon* (+8° 1820, *Songs, Duets*).]
Dr Syntax. [+L. 2191.]

p. 377] The Corsair's Bride. [=The Pirate's Bride, L. 2250.]
Le Solitaire. [+8° (1822). Originally called *The Solitaire of the Desert Mountains*.]
The Pirate. [+12° 1822.]
The Fair Gabrielle. [=Henri Quatre and the Fair Gabrielle (*UA*). +8° 1822.]

Clari. [+*Cumberland.* Apparently the songs only were pro-
vided by Planché.]
Too Curious by Half. [Adapted from Susanna Centlivre,
Marplot in Spain. An earlier version appears as *Marplot in
Spain* (*UA*).]
Cortez. [=Hernando Cortez (*UA*).]
Military Tactics. [See note on *Manoeuvring,* below.]
A Woman never Vext [+*Dolby*].

p. 378]   Manoeuvring. [+8° (1829). The title-page states that this is
adapted from *Les projets de mariage,* from which are derived
(1) *Matchmaking* and (2) *Military Tactics.* Apparently
Manoeuvring and *Military Tactics* were both by Planché;
Matchmaking is by J. Poole. A contemporary journal, however, attributes (probably by mistake) *Military Tactics* to
S. BEAZLEY.]
Der Vampyr. [This opera, libretto by W. A. Wohlbrück and
music by Marschner, appeared at Leipzig, 29/3/1828. For
the English version the music was arranged by W. Hawes.]

p. 379]   The Romance of a Day. [+8° 1831.]
+P. Little Red Riding Hood; or, The Fairy of the Silver
Lake (Clarence, 26/12/1832).

p. 380]   The Court Masque. [*Le pré aux clercs,* libretto by F. A. F.
de Planard, music by Hérold, appeared at Paris, 15/12/1832.
For the English version the music was arranged by W.
Hawes.]
High, Low, Jack and the Game. [+12° 1833.]
Gustavus III. [*Gustave III,* by A. E. Scribe, music by Auber,
appeared at Paris, 27/2/1833. For the English version the
music was arranged by T. S. Cooke.]
The Challenge. [Apparently the songs were by Planché, the
dialogue by *H. M. MILNER.*]
"My Friend the Governor." [+12° 1834.]
The Red Mask. [Adapted from *Il Bravo,* libretto by A.
Berrettoni, music by Marliani; Paris, 1/2/1834.]
The Siege of Corinth. [Adapted from *Maometto II,* libretto
by C. della Valle, music by Rossini; Naples, 3/12/1820.
For the English version the music was arranged by T. S.
Cooke.]

p. 381]   Puss in Boots. [Written in collaboration with *C. DANCE.*]
The Fortunate Isles. [+8° (1840).]

p. 382]   The Fair One with the Golden Locks. [+12° 1844.]
Somebody Else. [+12° 1845.]
The Golden Fleece. [+12° 1845.]
The Invisible Prince. [+12° (1846).]
The Jacobite. [12° (1847).]
Not a Bad Judge. [12° (1848).]

p. 383]   The Island of Jewels. [8° 1850 (*Songs*).]
[For his later work see *LND,* 527–8.]

PLANCHÉ, Mrs J. R.
[+from *UA*: Folly and Friendship.]

+*PLUNKETT, ARTHUR HUME.*
T. Beatrice of Ferrara. 8° 1837.

PLUNKETT, H. G. [see "*H. P. GRATTAN*"].

POCOCK, I.
[+from *UA*: The Wandering Boys; First Love; Oscar the Bandit.]
Twenty Years Ago! [Music J. Welsh.]
Harry le Roy. [Music Bishop.]

p. 384]   The Magpie. [=The Daughter (*UA*).]
The Farce Writer. [Originally called *Writing a Farce.*]
The Ravens. [A note by J. P. Collier in the Larpent MS. ascribes to George Colman the Younger.]

p. 386]   *POOLE, J.*
[+from *UA*: Ups and Downs; Madame du Barry; The Swedish Ferryman; The Bath Road.]

p. 387]   Turning the Tables. [Acted as *Quite the Reverse*, Queen's, 15/7/1839.]

+*POOLE, Dr RICHARD.*
[+from *UA*: Willie Armstrong (8° 1843, Edinburgh).]
D. Ethelreda (Caledonian, Edinburgh, 1829).

PORTER, A. M.
The Fair Fugitives. [+8° 1803 (*Airs, Duets, Choruses, &c.*).]

POWELL, THOMAS [*of Monmouth.*]
+D. Camillus and Columna; or, The Sleeping Beauty. 8° 1806.

POWER, T.
[+from *UA*: Etiquette Run Mad.]

p. 388]   +"*RANGER, —*" [*— BERTIE*].
[+from *UA*: The Romantic Widow.]

+*RANGER, EDWARD.*
The Gentleman and the Upstart. 8° 1848.

RANNIE, J.
[See also *A History of English Drama*, iii, 300.]

+*RAYMOND, E. M.*
[+from *UA*: Marietta.]

+*RAYMOND, GEORGE.*
[*The Lone Hut*, listed under *R. J. RAYMOND*, is ascribed to him in an edition 8° 1842.]

RAYMOND, R. J.
[+from *UA*: The Eleventh Hour (Cob. 1826); The Enraged Musician; The Wreck of the Leander Frigate; The Battle of Pultawa; The Conscript (D.L. 1830; in collaboration with *W. BARRYMORE*); Alp the Tartar Khan; The Irish Gentleman; The Plague of Marseilles; Charles the Terrible (W. L. 1821).]
The Wreck of the Leander Frigate. [See also under *UA*.]
Like Father like Son. [Also ascribed to *J. KENNEY*.]
The Lone Hut. [See above under *GEORGE RAYMOND*.]

p. 389] *REACH, A. B.*
[+from *UA*: Jenny Lind at Last; Early Closing (in collaboration with *H. HAMILTON*).]
[For his later work see *LND*, 535.]

+*READE, JOHN EDMUND.*
D.Poem. The Revolt of the Angels. 8° 1830.
D. Catiline; or, The Roman Conspiracy. 8° 1839 (priv.
printed).
D. The Deluge. 8° 1839.
D. The Drama of a Life. 8° 1840.

REDE, W. L.
[+from *UA*: The Judgment of Paris (Strand, 1832); The
Humpback (Strand, 1832); Loves of the Angels; The Barn
Burners; Loves of the Stars; "Stars"; Novelty; Serenading;
The Wandering Tribe; Hero and Leander; A Model of a
Man; The Two Greens (later version of *Serenading*); The
Irish Nigger; Sunshine and Shade (later version of *Faith
and Falsehood*); The Profligate.]
+The Dramatic Committee; or, Majors and Minors (Clarence,
28/8/1833).

p. 390]   +City Games; or, The Sports and Pastimes of London
200 Years Ago, including the Life and Death of Henry
Welby (City, 29/4/1833).
+Jupiter and Juno; or, The Roué Reformed (Strand,
26/2/1835). [Includes prelude: *The Night Rehearsal; or,
The Revolt of the Players.*]
The Peregrinations of Pickwick. [+ *The London Stage*;
London Acting Drama.]
Sixteen String Jack. [+ *Cumberland Minor*, no. 152.]
+The Gentleman in Black (City, 26/12/1842).
+The Post of Peril (Qns. 17/7/1848).
Jack in the Water. [+ *Cumberland Minor*, no. 148.]
[At the Clarence on 19/8/1833 a play by Rede called *The
Rick Burners* was given, probably *The Barn Burners*, above.]

p. 391]   +*RENNIE, J. F.*
[+from *UA*: Ethelwolf (8° 1821).]

REYNOLDS, F.
The Blind Bargain. [=Hear Him Out (*UA*).]
Out of Place. [Probably = The Castle of Lausanne (*UA*), first
called *The Lake of Geneva.*]
Begone Dull Care. [= Fair Play (*UA*).]
The Bridal Ring. [+8° 1812.]

p. 392]   The Virgin of the Sun. [Music Bishop.]
The Humorous Lieutenant. [An adaptation of the Beaumont
and Fletcher play; music by Bishop.]
The Duke of Savoy. [Adapted from *Les deux petites Savoyards*,
libretto by B. J. Marsollier, music by Delayrac; Paris,
14/1/1789.]
+The Gnome King. [This play, recorded in *UA*, has been
ascribed both to Reynolds and to *GEORGE COLMAN
the Younger.*]

p. 393]   *REYNOLDSON, T. H.*
  [+from *UA*: Mabel; The Widow Barnaby; Don Pasquale
    (from Donizetti's opera, Paris, 3/1/1843); The Dreamer.]
  The 24th of May. [See also under *UA*.]
  The Elixir of Love. [Music Donizetti.]
  Little Red Riding Hood. [Adapted from *Le petit chaperon
    rouge*, libretto by M. Théaulon de Lambert, music by
    Boieldieu; Paris, 30/6/1818.]
  The Duc d'Olonne. [Adapted from the opera by A. E. Scribe,
    music by Auber; Paris, 4/2/1842.]
    [For his later work see *LND*, 542.]

  RHODES, G. A.
  Dion. [This also includes a comedy: *The Naturalist*.]

p. 394]   *RICE, T. D.*
  [+from *UA*: The Virginia Mummy.]

  RICHARDS, A. B.
    +Runnymede; or, The Magna Charta. 8° 1846.
    [For his later work see *LND*, 542.]

  +*RIETHMULLER, C. G.* [See *C. G. REITHMULLER*.]
  +*RILEY, S. W.* [See *S. W. RYLEY*.]
  +*ROBERTS, EDWIN F.*
  D.Poem. Athanase. 8° [1847].
  +*ROBERTS, H. B.*
    [+from *UA*: Henri de Rochemaine.]

  ROBERTS, J. F.
    +P. Kelaun and Guzzarah; or, Harlequin in Asia (Royalty).
      8° [1808?].
  +*ROBERTSON, THOMAS WILLIAM.*
    [+from *UA*: The Battle of Life (Norwich, 1847).]
    D. The Chevalier de St George (P'cess, 20/5/1845). 8° [n.d.];
      Lacy.
    D. Ernestine (P'cess, 14/4/1846). *Lacy* [as *Noemi*].
    F. The Haunted Man (Queen's, 1/1/1849). L.C.
    [For his later work see *LND*, 542.]
  +*ROBINS, JOHN RADCLIFFE.*
    C. The Usurer; or, The Departed not Defunct. 8° 1833.
  +*ROBINSON, EMMA.*
    [+from *UA*: The Revolt of Flanders.]
    C. Richelieu in Love; or, The Youth of Charles I. 8° 1844.

p. 395]   +*ROBY, JOHN.*
    [+from *UA*: The Duke of Mantua.]

  RODWELL, G. H.
    [+from *UA*: A Matter of Doubt; Harlequin and Good Queen
      Bess.]
    The Chimney Piece. [+8° 1833.]
    The Breach of Promise of Marriage. [Ascribed also, probably
      erroneously, to *Miss PARDOE*.]
    [For his later work see *LND*, 548.]

  RODWELL, J. T. G.
    A Race for a Dinner. [=No Dinner Yet (*UA*).]

p. 396] *ROGERS, W.*
[+from *UA*: The Sailor's Home.]
+M.D. The Bandit Host; or, The Lone Hut of the Swamp
(C.L. 1839).
+Sketch. The Literary Dustman (R.P. 10/1840).
+Paul the Reprobate; or, The Law in 1656 (*Duncombe
Minor*).
[For his later work see *LND*, 549.]

+*ROSCOE, THOMAS.*
T. Gonzalo, the Traitor. 8° 1820.

+*ROSCOE, WILLIAM.*
T. The Conspiracy of Gowrie. 8° 1800.

+*ROSCOE, WILLIAM CALDWELL.*
T. Eliduke, Count of Yeoloc. 8° 1846.

ROXBY, S.
[+from *UA*: Shifts of Genius.]

+*RUSSELL, H.*
[+from *UA*: The Huguenots (Surrey, 1849).]
+Y. Y.; or, The Freaks of Fortune (Pav. 17/2/1842).

RYAN, M. D.
[+from *UA*: Linda of Chamouny.]

RYAN, R.
[+from *UA*: The Boarder; The Irish Girl; Second Sight.]
+Le Pauvre Jacques...Translated from the French (St J.
27/7/1836). *Cumberland.*

+*ST IVES, WILLIAM.*
[+from *UA*: Wife and Child.]

+*SALA, F.*
[+from *UA*: My Maiden Aunts.]

p. 397] +*SALMON, Mrs.*
D.Poem. Jephtha. 8° 1846.

+[*SARGENT, EPES.*
[+from *UA*: Valasco (originally, Tremont, Boston, 13/2/1837,
as *The Bride of Genoa*).]

+*SAVILLE, Mrs E. F.*
D.D. The Deserted Village (Swansea, 5/10/1835).

SAWYER, W.
[For his later work see *LND*, 557.]

+*SCOTT, HUGH.*
T. The Siege of Vienne. 8° 1838 [Edinburgh].

SCOTT, J. M.
[+from *UA*: The Animated Effigy; The Forest Knight
(Sans P. 1813); The Poison Tree (Sans P. 1811); Mary the
Maid of the Inn; Raykisnah the Outcast; The Red Robber;
Ulthona The Sorceress; The Vizier's Son; Whackham and
Windham; The Inscription; The Row of Ballynavogue;
The Two Spanish Valets.]
+O. Il Giorno Felice; or, The Happy Day (Sans P.
27/2/1812). L. 1705.

+*SCOTT, W. R.*
D. Belisarius. 8° 1846.

SELBY, C.
[+from *UA*: The Auberge des Adrets; Augustus Buggins;
Natural Magic; The Handsell Penny (Lyc. 1841); Enjoy-
ment; Maximums and Speciments of William Muggins;
Taming a Tartar; The Judgment of Paris (Adel. 1846).]
+Ruse de guerre (Strand, 5/1/1835).
Robert Macaire. [+*Duncombe*.]
+Farces and Melodramas. 16° 1835 (*Duncombe*).
+The Rifle Brigade (19/2/1838). *Webster*.
The Widow's Victim. [+*Duncombe*.]

p. 398]   Frederick of Prussia. [See also in *UA*.]
The Fairy Lake. [Adapted from *Le lac des fées*, by A. E.
Scribe and A. H. J. Mélesville; Paris, 1/4/1839.]
+Military Execution; or, The Fatal Keepsake. *Duncombe
Minor.*
[For his later work see *LND*, 560.]

p. 399]   *SERLE, T. J.*
[+from *UA*: Adelaide of Wulfingen; A Father's Crime.]
The Man in the Iron Mask. [+*Duncombe Minor*.]
The Victim of St Vincent. [+*Duncombe Minor*.]
The Shadow on the Wall. [+*Duncombe Minor*.]
The Parole of Honour. [+12° 1837.]
Master Clarke. [+12° (1840).]
The Scornful Lady. [See also in *UA*.]
[For his later work see *LND*, 561.]

p. 400]   +*SERRES, OLIVIA.*
O. The Castle of Avola. 8° 1805 [in *Flights of Fancy*].

SHANNON, C.
[+from *UA*: The Devil's Brother.]

+*SHARP, CHARLES.*
D. Zopheir. 8° 1819.

SHEIL, R. L.
[To the plays listed should be added an adaptation of *The
Fatal Dowry*, presented at D.L.]

p. 401]   Montoni. [+L. 2147, as *The Phantom*.]
The Huguenot. [=The Convict (*UA*).]

+*SHEPHERD, H.*
T. The Countess of Essex. 8° 1834.

+*SHERIDAN, R. B.*
[For his earlier works see *A History of English Drama*, iii, 305-6.]
O.R. The Forty Thieves (D.L. 8/4/1806). [See *G. COLMAN
the Younger*.]

+*SHIPP, Lieut. JOHN.*
M.D. The Maniac of the Pyrenees; or, The Heroic Soldier's
Wife. 8° 1829 [Brentford].

+*SHOBERL, F.*
The Death of Abel. 8° 1806. [A translation of the play by
S. Gessner.]

SICKLEMORE, R.
+D. The Black Armour (Brighton, 7/10/1813).
+C. Vicissitudes; or, The Daughter in Law (Brighton, 17/9/1817).

SIDDONS, H.
Time's a Tell-Tale. [=Mark the End On't (*UA*).]
+Friendship, Love and Duty. [Listed in *UA*; ascribed to Siddons.]
The Friend of the Family. [This seems to have been an early version of *Policy*, see p. 401.]

+*SIDNEY, W.*
Dombey and Son (M'bone, 6/1849).

+*SILVESTER, H.*
[+from *UA*: Humbug.]

p. 402] SKEFFINGTON, *Sir L. St G.*
The Sleeping Beauty. [+8° 1805 (*Songs, Duets, Choruses*).]

+*SLIGHT, HENRY.*
Ba. The Weir Wolf (Portsmouth, 1844).

+*SMELT, THOMAS.*
[+from *UA*: The Brothers.]

+*SMITH, —*
Bal. Love in a Sack (M'bone, 16/12/1838).

SMITH, A. R.
[+from *UA*: Valentine and Orson; The Wood Demon; The Revolt of Bruges.]
+Agnes de Vere (Brighton, 30/10/1840).
+The Pearl of Chamouni (Surrey, 7/1843).
Aladdin. [+12° (1845).]
The Cricket on the Hearth. [+12° (1845).]
Hop o' my Thumb. [+12° 1846.]
[For his later work see *LND*, 572.]

SMITH, G.
[+from *UA*: The Students.]
+The Barbers at Court (Olym. 21/12/1835). [See *H. MAYHEW*.]

SMITH, J.
[+from *UA*: Creon, the Patriot.]

+*SMITH, J. F.*
[+from *UA*: The Court of Old Fritz; A Lesson for Gentlemen; Legacy Hunting.]
+The Freemason; or, Brothers in War (Norwich, 1843).
Wolsey. [See also under *UA*.]

p. 403] +*SMITH, JOHN.*
The House of Atreus and the House of Laius. 8° 1818.

+*SMITH, Captain LEICESTER.*
P. Harlequin and the Wizard of the Steel Castle; or, The Lake of Swans (Dublin, 26/12/1846).
P. Harlequin Sulpherino; or, The Three Temptations (Dublin, 26/12/1847).
P. Harlequin Hurlothrumbo; or, The Mystic Caverns of the Metal Gnomes (Dublin, 26/12/1848).

SMITH, W.
+ Dramas. 8° 1846. [Contains, besides *Athelwold, Sir William Crichton* and *Guidone*.]

+ *SMYTH, JOHN.*
T. Evander. 8° 1847.

+ *SNODGRASS, ALFRED.*
[+ from *UA*: State Secrets.]

SOANE, G.
[+ from *UA*: Grey the Collier; The Trial of Love; Luke Somerton; Jack's Alive; The Flower of Lucerne; Othello (P'cess, 1844).]
Self-Sacrifice. [= Ida of the Cottage (*UA*).]
Masaniello. [+ 8° 1825.]
The Young Reefer. [See also under *UA*.]
+ The Lighthouse; or, The Maiden's Dream (E.O.H. 13/9/1842).

p. 404]   *SOMERSET, C. A.*
[+ from *UA*: Alonzo the Patriot; The Two Jack Sheppards; Maurice the Woodcutter (given at S.W. 6/1830 as *The Traitor; or, M. the W.*).]
+ Zelma; or, The Triumph of the Greeks (Royalty, 1830). *French.*
+ £10,000 a Year (Queen's, 11/1841).
[For his later work see *LND*, 574.]

+ *SORELLI, G.*
T. The Nun of Florence. 8° 1840.

p. 405]   *SPENCER, W. R.*
Urania. [Music J. Spencer and M. Kelly.]

SPICER, H.
Judge Jeffreys. [See also in *UA* under *Jeffreys*.]
[For his later work see *LND*, 576.]

+ *SPINK, Rev. S.*
D. Pharaoh. 8° 1848.

STAFFORD, J. J.
[+ from *UA*: Cupid turned Physician; Chelsea.]
My Uncle Toby. [+ 12° (1834).]
+ Mr B—— (Clarence, 4/11/1832).

p. 406]   *STEPHENS, G.* [*pseudonym "ST JOHN DORSET"*].
+ M.D. The Vampire. 8° 1821.
+ T. Montezuma. 8° 1823.
Martinuzzi. [+ 8° 1849, as *The Patriot*.]

+ *STERLING, J.*
T. Strafford. 8° 1843.

STIRLING, E.
[+ from *UA*: The Scottish Chiefs; The Seven Castles of the Passions (+ *Barth's Universal Stage*); The Great Unknown (Olym. 1840); Queen Mary; Barnaby Rudge; Peter Priggins; The Children in the Wood; Ulrica; In and Out (Surrey, 1845); The Demon Dwarf; The Haunted Man.]

p. 407] Woman's the Devil. [See also under *UA*.]
+Die Hexen am Rhein (Adel. 10/1841).
+The Queen of Cyprus; or, The Bride of Venice (Queen's, 2/1842).
+The Maid of Kent (Queen's 9/3/1843).
+The Love Gift; or, The Trials of Poverty (Adel. 20/3/1843).
+Ondine; or, The Water Sprite and the Fire Fiend (C.L. 17/4/1843).
A Christmas Carol. [+*Barth's Universal Stage.*]
The Young Scamp. [See also under *UA*.]
The Chimes. [+*Barth's Universal Stage.*]
The Battle of Life. [+*Duncombe.*]
+Mary Tudor; or, The Heart of a Queen (M'bone, 19/8/1849).
[Presumably a later version of *Queen Mary*.]
[For his later work see *LND*, 584.]

p. 409] *STOCQUELER, J. H.*
[+from *UA*: Polkamania; The Marble Maiden (Lyc. 1846); A Good Name; Robin Hood and Richard Coeur de Lion! (in collaboration with *C. KENNEY*); The Seven Champions of Christendom; Crusoe the Second; The Provisional Government; Emigration—the Remedy; The Three Fra Diavolos.]
+Spec. The Siege of Moultan (R.A. 1849).
[For his later work see *LND*, 585.]

+*STORY, R.*
D. The Outlaw. 12° 1839.

+*STRETTLE, Miss.*
D. The Dorias. 12° 1835 [Edinburgh].

+*STUART-WORTLEY, Lady EMMELINE.*
[+from *UA*: Moonshine.]
D. Eva; or, The Error. 8° 1840.
D. Mystery Jairah. 12° 1840.
D. Alphonzo Algarves. 8° 1841.
D. Angiolina del' Albano; or, Truth and Treachery. 8° 1841.
C. Ernest Mountjoy. 8° 1844.

SULLIVAN, R.
[For his later work see *LND*, 586.]

+*SUTER, W. E.*
F. It's All Very Well Mr Ferguson, But You Don't Sleep Here. L.C. 1837.

p. 410] +*SWIFT, EDMUND L.*
[+from *UA*: Woman's Will (8° 1820).]

+*SYMONDS, EMILY MORSE.*
D. The Parent's Progress. 8° [1850].

+*TAIT, EDWARD.*
T. Tyrrel. 8° 1841. [Edinburgh. In collaboration with *KENNETH MENZIES*.]

TALFOURD, F.
[+from *UA*: Mammon and Gammon.]
[For his later work see *LND*, 590.]

TAYLOR, G. F.
The Factory Strike. [+*Pattie's Universal Stage.*]

p. 411] *TAYLOR, TOM.*
[+from *UA*: Prince Dorus (Olym. 1850).]
Ext. Valentine and Orson (Lyc. 23/12/1844). [See *UA*.
Written in collaboration with *A. R. SMITH*.]
F. Wanted a Hermit (Lyc. 25/5/1847). [See *UA*.]

TAYLOR, T. P.
[+from *UA*: The Red Mantle.]
+The Lively Nancy; or, A Leap from the Log (Vic. 8/1838).
+The Black Lion of Finsbury (C.L. *c.* 1839).
+The Black Buccaneer; or, The Doomed of the Fiend Ship (Queen's, 12/4/1841).
+The Death Hand; or, The Shadow of the Deep (Queen's, 4/1842).
+The Ferryman of the Lone Hut (C.L. 27/11/1843).
+The Destruction of the Bastille (C.L. 6/1844).
+The Avalanche; or, The Dog of the Desert (Strand, 20/9/1847).

+*TENNANT, CHARLES.*
D. A Cobbler's Hut (Neath, 4/6/1841).

p. 412] *THACKERAY, T. J.*
[+from *UA*: The Castle of Wolfenstein; Woman; Gustavus of Sweden.]

+*THOMAS, WILLIAM LEWIS.*
T. Theresa; or, The Maid of the Tyrol. 8° 1843.

p. 413] *THOMPSON, C. P.*
[+from *UA*: Zameo; Poachers and Petticoats (in L.C. as *Farmer and Pheasant*; and acted as *Pheasant Shooting; or F. and P.*) (Strand, 13/6/1836); Ireland.]

+*THOMPSON, WILLIAM GILL.*
D. Love in the Country; or, The Vengeful Miller (Newcastle, 26/2/1830).

THOMSON, JAMES.
[+from *UA*: A Squeeze to the Coronation; The Blackamoor's Head.]

+*THOMSON, WILLIAM.*
T. Caledonia; or, The Clans of Yore. 8° 1818 [Perth].

THORNE, R. L.
[For his later work see *LND*, 599.]

+*THORNTON, BONNELL.*
The Persian Heroine; or, The Downfall of Tyranny. 8° 1820.

+*THRESHER, EDMUND HENRY.*
D. Oppression. 8° 1832 [priv.].

+*TILBURY, WILLIAM HARRIS.*
[+from *UA*: The German Jew.]

TOBIN, J.
The Fisherman's Hut. [=The Fisherman (*UA*). +8° 1819 (*Songs*).]

p. 414] *TOWNSEND, W. T.*
[+from *UA*: The Little Innocent; The Post Captain (printed in *Pattie's Play*).]

Whitefriars. [Also ascribed to *J. S. FAUCIT.*]
[For his later work see *LND*, 602.]

+*TROTTER, Dr THOMAS.*
T. The Noble Foundling; or, The Hermit of the Tweed
(Newcastle, 1/1813).

TRUEBA, J. T. DE.
[+from *UA*: The Exquisites; Arrangement.]
+The Court Delinquent (Vic. 10/1/1834).

+*TUCKER, HENRY ST GEORGE.*
T. Camoens. 8° 1832.

TULLY, J. H.
[For his later work see *LND*, 604.]

p. 415] +*TURNBALL, Mrs W.*
The Ring; or, The Farmer's Daughter (Queen's, 29/1/1833).
Duncombe Minor. [See in *UA*.]

+*TWEDDELL, H. M.*
T. Aguilhar. 8° 1820.

+*TYTLER, ALEXANDER FRASER.*
T. The Robbers. 8° 1800.

+*UPSHER, —*
F. Do you gamble? (C.L. 26/6/1837).

UPTON, —
[+from *UA*: Abou Hassan.]

+*"VAMP, HUGO."* See *J. R. O'NEIL.*

+*VANDEIGHTONE, —*
[+from *UA*: The Man in the Moon (Strand, 1847).]

+*VINING, W.*
[+from *UA*: Harlequin and the Elfin Sprite.]

WALDRON, F. G.
+D. A Trip to Marseilles; or, The Labyrinth of Love (Sans
Souci, 5/1806). L. 1487.

p. 416] *WALKER, C. E.*
[+from *UA*: The Castellan's Oath; The Revolt of the Greeks.]
The Warlock of the Glen. [+8° 1820.]
Rumfustian Innamorato. [+8° 1824.]

WALKER, J.
[+from *UA*: The Wizard Priest (*Duncombe Minor*).]

+*WALLER, JOHN FRANCIS.*
P. Harlequin Blunderbore; or, The Enchanted Faun (Dublin,
26/12/1845).

+*WALLER, WILLIAM.*
T. Mariamne; or, The Court of Herod the Great. 8° 1839
(priv.).

WARD, C.
+The Forty Thieves. [See *G. COLMAN, the Younger.*]

+*WARDE, Rev. GEORGE AMBROSE.*
T. The Flower of Yarrow. 8° 1846.

+*WARMINGTON, G.*
   D. The Fall of Leicester. 8° 1842 (Birmingham).
   D. Walter; or, The Foundling. 8° 1846 (Birmingham).
+*WARRINGTON, Rev. WILLIAM.*
   T. Alphonso, King of Castile. 4° 1813.
+*WARTON, FERDINAND FULLARTON.* See
   WHARTON, F. F.

p. 417] +*WATERHOUSE, BENJAMIN.*
   T. Annira; or, The Royal Sufferers. 12° 1822 [Sheffield].
WATTS, W.
   Which is the Uncle? [+sub-title: *or, The Errors of a Night.*]
   The Irish Engagement. [+12° (? 1848).]
+*WEAVER, R. T.*
   The Red Rover; or, The Mutiny of the Caroline (S.W.
   2/3/1829). *Duncombe.*
WEBB, C.
   [+from *UA*: The Giant; Freaks in an Attic; Alive or Dead;
   A Christmas Carol; One Hour with Napoleon (see under
   An Hour with N.); Wanted a Bravo; Our Friend the Duke;
   The Mill in the Pyrenees.]
   +The Vagrant, his Life and Family (C.L. 1838).
   Martin Chuzzlewit. [+*Barth's Universal Stage.*]
     [Webb is credited also with the following: *Lady-Bird
   Bower; Life's Morning, its Evening and its Night; Secret
   Memoirs.* For his later work see *LND*, 617.]
+*WEBB, T. H.*
   [+from *UA*: The Seven Ages of Man.]
WEBSTER, B., the Younger.
   [For his later work see *LND*, 618.]
WEBSTER, B. N.
   [+from *UA*: Pay for Peeping; The Quadroon Slave.]
   Highways and Byways. [+8° (1841).]
   +Isaure; or, The Maniac of the Alps (Pav. 14/2/1832).
   Duncombe Minor. [This seems to be the same play as that
   with similar title in *UA.*]

p. 418] +The Pretty Girls of Stilberg (H.² 9/4/1842).
   The Fox and the Goose. [Adapted from *Le panier fleuri,*
   libretto by A. de Leuven and L. L. Brunswick, music by
   A. Thomas; Paris, 6/5/1839).]
   The Black Domino. [Adapted from *Le domino noir,* libretto
   by A. E. Scribe, music by Auber; Paris, 2/12/1837).]
   The Wonderful Water Cure. [Adapted from *L'eau mer-
   veilleuse,* libretto by T. Sauvage, music by Grisar; Paris,
   30/1/1839. For the English version the music was arranged
   by T. G. Reed.]
   The Devil's Violin. [+*Acting Nat. Drama.*]
   +Our National Defences. [Listed in *UA*; ascribed both to
   Webster and to *J. S. COYNE.*]
     [For his later work see *LND*, 618.]
+*WEBSTER, FREDERICK.*
   [+from *UA*: The Place Hunter.]

+ *WEST, B.*
[+from *UA*: Melmoth; Hate; Genevieve (Surrey, 1824).]

WESTMACOTT, C. M.
[+from *UA*: Maids and Bachelors.]

p. 419] + *WHITE, G.*
[+from *UA*: Martin Faber.]

WHITE, J.
The King of the Commons. [+8° 1846.]
[For his later work see *LND*, 620.]

WIGAN, A. S.
[+from *UA*: Next Door.]
+ First Love (Brighton, 16/1/1839). [See *E. PHILLIPS.*]
Watch and Ward. [+*Barth's Universal Stage.*]
+ Law for Ladies (Olym. 24/7/1848).
First Night. [See also under *UA*.]
[For his later work see *LND*, 622.]

+ *WILKINSON, T. F.*
T.   Mustapha. 8° 1829 (priv.).
D.   Iduna, Queen of Kent; or, The Druid's Vow. 8° [1846].

p. 420] *WILKS, T. E.*
[+from *UA*: Casper the Doomed; Crichton; The Brothers
in Arms.]
The Wolf and the Lamb. [+*London Acting Drama*, as *The
Brothers.*]
Sudden Thoughts. [+*London Acting Drama.*]
+ The Golden Fox (Vic. 16/3/1840). [Apparently acted before
this date at C.G.]
p. 421] + The Gamekeeper's Gun; or, The Maid, the Murder and
the Mystery (Vic. 21/9/1840).
+ Madame Pompadour's Pearl (Olym. 10/1840).
+ The Duchess of ——! or, The Cross-Bow Letter (Strand,
30/5/1842). *Dicks.*
+ Frank the Fool; or, The Treasures of the Weeping Rock
(Surrey, 8/1843).
+ The Gold Guitar; or, the Bohemian's Prophecy (Vic.
8/1843).
| The Plank across the Street (Surrey, 8/1848).
+ A Wife's Secret (C.L. 7/10/1848).
Woman's Love. [This was originally acted, Vic. 4/1841.]

p. 422] + *WILLIAMS, H. C.*
A Race for a Wife! [See *H. W. CHALLIS.*]

| *WILLIS, A*
D.   The Broken Lily. 8° 1846.

+ *WILLS, H.*
[+from *UA*: Scotch Mist.]

+ *WILLS, J. C.*
[+from *UA*: The King and the Freebooter.]

+ *WILLS, W. H.*
[+ from *UA*: The Larboard Fin; The Law of the Land.]

WILMOT, Mrs BARBARINA, afterwards BARBARINA BRAND, Baroness DACRE.
Ina. [+ L. 1803, as *Ina of Sigiswold.*]
+ Sk. Frogs and Bulls; A Lilliputian Piece in Three Acts. 8° 1838.

+ *WILSON, Mrs C. B.*
[+ from *UA*: The Hussars (also called *The Petticoat Colonel* and *Venus in Arms*).]
+ The Maid of Switzerland. *Duncombe Minor.*

+ *WILSON, JOHN MACKAY.*
M.D. The Gowrie Conspiracy (Perth, 18/9/1828).
M.D. The Highland Widow (Perth, 3/1828).
M.D. Margaret of Anjou; or, The Noble Merchants (Caledonian, Edinburgh, 8/1829).

+ *WILSON, J. P.*
Temptation (S.W. 9/1841).

+ *WILSON, THOMAS.*
C. Plot against Plot. 8° 1821.
C. The Disappointed Authoress. 8° 1821.

+ *WILTON, F.*
Marie de Chamouni; or, The Pearl of Savoy (Pav. 8/1848).

+ *WIMBERLEY, WILLIAM CLARK.*
T. The Death Summons; or, The Rock of Martos. 8° 1832.

+ *WOODLEY, WILLIAM.*
T. Catharine de Medicis [and] James the Third. 8° 1825.

WOOLER, J. P.
[+ from *UA*: Love in Livery; A Man without a Head.]
[For his later work see *LND*, 632.]

+ *WORRELL, —*
The Ran-Dan Club (Vic. 11/1840).

+ *WYNN, HENRY W.*
D. Ravencourt. 8° 1843.

p. 423] + *YOUNG, C. M.*
[+ from *UA*: Euphemia (+ 8° 1837).]

YOUNG, H.
[For his later work see *LND*, 636.]

+ *YOUNG, WILLIAM.*
Lucrezia Borgia. 8° 1847.

+ *YOUNGE, H. [pseudonym of J. B. BUCKSTONE].*
[+ from *UA*: Harlequin and Georgey Barnwell; Sinbad the Sailor.]
+ Harlequin and "Poor Richard"; or, Old Father Time and the Almanac Maker (S.W. 26/12/1840).
+ Harlequin and the Sleeping Beauty (Garrick, 1843).

SUPPLEMENTARY NOTES TO THE LIST
OF UNKNOWN AUTHORS

A.B.C. [=*T. J. DIBDIN.*]
+Abdellac the Terrible; or, The Fisherman of Algiers (S.W.
7/1824).
Abdication of Ferdinand. [=*R. W. MAYO.*]
Abou Hassan. [=*W. UPTON.*]
Acteon and Diana. [=*J. BYRNE.*]
The Actor in Distress. [=*W. T. MONCRIEFF.*]
Adelaide. [=*E. FITZBALL.*]
Adelaide of Wulfingen. [=*T. J. SERLE.*]

p. 424] Adolph Arnal. [=*J. T. HAINES.*]
Adolphus Count Zelmar. [=*J. G. HOLMAN, Frost and Thaw.*]
The Afghanistan War. [=*G. ALMAR.*]
Afloat and Ashore. [=*S. ATKYNS.*]
Aladdin (C.G. 1813). [=*C. FARLEY.*]

p. 425] Alberto and Lauretta. [=*T. J. LYNCH.*]
Alfred le Grand. [= — *AUMER.*]
Alfred the Great (8° 1829). [=*SARAH HAMILTON.*]
Aline. [= — *AUMER.*]
Alive or Dead. [=*C. WEBB.*]
All about Love and Jealousy. [=*G. BOLTON.*]
+All Alive at Liverpool; or, The Wapping Landlady (L'pool,
18/10/1809).
+All's a Delusion. 8° 1847.

p. 426] Alonzo the Patriot. [=*C. A. SOMERSET.*]
Alp, the Renegade. [=*G. ALMAR.*]
Alp, the Tartar Khan. [=*R. J. RAYMOND.*]
+Alva; or, The Fairies of the Rhine (Queen's, 10/1840).
Alwyn and Bertholdy. [=*G. ALMAR.*]
Angelo. [=*F. F. COOPER*; adapted from the play by Victor
Hugo.]
The Angler. [= — *LECLERCQ.*]
The Animated Effigy. [=*J. M. SCOTT.*]
The Animated Portrait. [= — *BOURDEN.*]

p. 427] +Annette; or, The Old Manor House (Strand, 13/3/1837).
+Another Daughter of the Danube (Strand, 10/5/1847).
Another Piece of Presumption. [=*R. B. PEAKE.*]
Antigone. [=*E. FITZBALL.*]
Antoine, the Savage. [=*E. FITZBALL.*]
An Arab's Faith. [=*J. FARRELL.*]
+Aristodemus. 8° 1838.
An Armful of Bliss. [=*W. T. MONCRIEFF.*]
+The Armidei. 8° 1845.

p. 428] Arrangement. [=*J. T. DE TRUEBA.*]
Arrivals. [=*W. LENNOX, Incog.*]
The Assassin. [=*R. BELL, The Watch-word.*]
Assumptions. [=The Guardians Outwitted (*UA*).]
The Auberge des Adrets. [=*C. SELBY.*]
Augustus Buggins. [=*C. SELBY.*]

Aurora. [=— *NOBLE.*]

The Automaton. [=— *BECKWITH.*]

The Avenger (Cob. 1824). [=*H. LEE.*]

Azor and Zemira. [=*W. BALL.* Adapted from *Zémire et Azor*, libretto by J. J. Ihlec, music by Spohr (Frankfort, 11/4/1819). For the English version the music was adapted by G. Smart.]

Babington. [=*T. DOUBLEDAY.*]

p. 429]   The Bachelor's Vow. [=*E. PHILLIPS, Prejudice.*]

Bad Customers. [=Who Pays the Piper (*UA*).]

Bad Neighbours. [=*S. J. ARNOLD, Plots!*]

+F. Bampfyde Moore Carew; or, Harlequin King of the Beggars. L. 1910 [Olym. 12/2/1816].

+The Bandit Merchant (Strand, 23/9/1847). [This may be *The Maid of Genoa; or, The B. M.* by *J. FARRELL.*]

+The Bandit of Corsica; or, The Brigand and his Son. (Vic. 7/1840).

Bannister's Budget. [This entertainment is said to have been first produced in 1808. It has been attributed both to *G. COLMAN, the Younger* and to *T. J. DIBDIN. The Shipwreck* is an integral part of the production.]

Bannockburn. [=*H. M. MILNER.*]

The Barbers at Court. [=*H. MAYHEW* and *G. SMITH.*]

Barcarolle. [Adapted from the opera by A. E. Scribe, music by Auber; Paris, 22/4/1845.]

Barnaby Rudge. [=*E. STIRLING.*]

The Barn Burners. [=*W. L. REDE.*]

p. 430]   The Baron de Trenck. [This may be *Baron Trenck* by *S. J. ARNOLD*; if so, the performance listed *supra* p. 256 is a revival.]

+Baron Fitzarden. 8° 1845.

The Bas-Bleu. [=*W. H. LOGAN.*]

The Bath Road. [=*J. POOLE.*]

The Battle of Agincourt (Cob. 1825). [=*H. M. MILNER.*]

The Battle of Blenheim. [=*J. T. HAINES.*]

The Battle of Pultawa. [=*R. J. RAYMOND.*]

La Bayadère (H.¹ 1831). [=*DESHAYES.*]

+The Bay of Biscay (Garrick, 1/1841).

The Bayonet. [=*J. P. HART.*]

The Beacon of Liberty. [=*P. BAILEY.*]

Beauty and the Bey. [=*T. J. DIBDIN.*]

The Beaux' Stratagem. [=*D. LAWLER.*]

+The Beggar and the Soldier; or, The Thieves of Dijon (R.A. 4/1841).

p. 432]   Belles without Beaux. [=The Young Prude (*UA*).]

Ben Brace. [=*J. S. FAUCIT.*]

Benedetto Mangone. [=*H. HOLL.*]

The Best of Husbands. [=*J. BUCKSTONE.*]

Birds of Paradise. [=*D. JERROLD.*]

The Blackamoor's Head. [=*J. THOMSON.*]

p. 433]   The Black Domino (C.G. 1838). [=*J. KENNEY* and *J. M. MORTON.* Adapted from *Le domino noir* by A. E. Scribe, music by Auber; Paris, 2/12/1837.]

The Black Domino (Adel. 1838). [=*J. S. COYNE.*]
The Black Hand. [=*E. FITZBALL.*]
+Vaud. The Black Sentinel (Grecian, 8/1840).
The Black Woodsman. [=*H. M. MILNER.*]

p. 434]   Bletchington House. [= — *GASPEY.*]
The Blind Father. [=*W. T. MONCRIEFF.*]
The Blind Sister. [=*M. R. LACY.*]
+Ba. The Blister; or, A Little Piece to Draw. 8° 1814.
+M.Rom. Blue Beard (Strand, 6/9/1847).
Blue-eyed Mary. [=*F. C. NANTZ.*]
Bluff King Hal. [=*J. M. MADDY.*]
The Boarder. [=*R. RYAN.*]
The Bohemian Mother. [=*J. EBSWORTH.*]

p. 435]   +The Bosjesnans; or, Wild Bush People (Strand, 6/9/1847—
not first performance).
The Brave and the Fair. [= — *BOURDEN.*]
The Brave Cossack. [=*J. ASTLEY.* Originally given at R.A.
1807 as *The B. C.; or, Perfidy Punished.*]
The Bridal of Flora. [=*J. BYRNE.*]
The Bridal Promise. [=*J. OXENFORD.* Adapted from
Zampa, music by Hérold.]

p. 436]   The Bride of Lammermuir. [=*W. T. MONCRIEFF.*]
+The Brigands of Calabria; or, The Forest of Saint Euphemia
(C.L. 31/10/1831).
Brighton Cliff. [=*C. BEW, The White Hawk Lady.*]
The Brisket Family. [=*D. J. JERROLD, Dolly and the Rat.*]
Britain's Jubilee. [=*C. F. BARRETT.*]
Britons at Navarino. [=*H. M. MILNER.*]
The Brothers. [=*T. SMELT;* 8° 1843.]

p. 437]   +The Brothers' Duel; or, Jane of Primrose Hill (Garrick,
13/9/1841).
Brothers in Arms. [=*T. E. WILKS.*]
The Brown Devil. [=*F. C. NANTZ.*]
Butcher, Butcher, Kill an Ox. [=*F. NEALE.*]
"Buy a Broom?" [=*H. M. MILNER.*]
The Cabinet Secret. [This seems to have been given first at the
Clarence on 7/5/1832.]
The Cady. [=Honesty the Best Policy (*UA*).]
Caius Marius. [=*T. DOUBLEDAY* (Newcastle. 3/5/1837).
8° 1836.]

p. 438]   The Caliph Vathek. [=*H. M. MILNER.*]
The Cape of Good Hope. [=*W. BARRYMORE.*]
+Capers and Crushers; or, X.L. 24 (Strand, 26/4/1847).
"Captain (Query?)." [=*M. LEMON, A Captain pro tem.*]
Captain Stevens. [=*C. SELBY.*]

p. 439]   +Care Sent to Coventry (B'ham, 9/12/1800).
Carlo. [=*J. G. MILLINGEN.*]
The Carnival at Naples. [=*W. DIMOND.*]
Casper the Doomed. [=*T. E. WILKS.*]
The Castellan's Oath. [=*C. E. WALKER.*]
The Castilian Minstrel. [= — *D'EGVILLE,* music by Bishop.]
The Castle of Lausanne. [=*F. REYNOLDS, Out of Place.*]

The Castle of St Aldobrand (D.L. 1816). [=*C. R. MATURIN*.]
The Castle of Wolfenstein. [=*T. J. THACKERAY*.]
Castles in the Air (D.L. 1818). [=*S. W. RYLEY, The Castle
of Glyndower*.]
Caswallon, the King of Britain. [Probably=*E. GANDY*.]

p. 440]   Catarina (Strand, 1844). [=*C. CAMPBELL*.]
+The Cattarans; or, The Chieftains of the Orkney Islands
(Caledonian, Edinburgh, 30/11/1819).
Champagne. [=*J. MOORE*.]
Charles XII and Peter the Great. [=*T. J. DIBDIN*.]

p. 441]   Charles Edward Stuart. [=— *MACDONALD*. Adapted from
the French of A. Duval; Paris, 18/2/1802.]
Charles the Terrible (W.L. 1821). [=*R. J. RAYMOND*.]
Charles the Terrible (Surrey, 1837). [=*S. FAUCIT*.]
The Charter (S.W. 1830). [=*A. V. CAMPBELL*.]
La Chasse. [=— *NOBLE*. Music by Woolfe, Bishop and
others.]
Chelsea. [=*J. J. STAFFORD*.]
A Cheque on my Banker. [=*W. T. MONCRIEFF*.]
Cherry and Fair Star (C.G. 1822). [+8° 1822 (*Songs*).]
The Chevalier d'Epsonne (Grecian, 1848). [=*J. H. HORN-
CASTLE*. Music by Auber.]
The Child of Concealment. [=*G. P. BROMLEY*.]
The Children in the Wood. [=*E. STIRLING*.]

p. 442]   A Christmas Carol. [=*C. WEBB*.]
+T. The Cicisbeo. 8° 1837.
Cinderella (Norwich, 1818). [The date may be 1809; songs
almost identical with those of *Cinderella*, D.L. 1804.]
The Citizen of Paris. [=*S. J. ARNOLD*.]
+The Citizen's Daughter; or, The Archers of Ludgate (Strand,
27/7/1847).

p. 443]   The City Rivals. [=*J. KENNEY, Debtor and Creditor*.]
The Civil War of Poetry. [=— *BOLTON*.]
+The Clerke's Well; or, Islington in Olden Time (S.W.
13/9/1841).
The Coast Blockade. [=*H. M. MILNER*.]
Cocknies in California. [=*J. S. COYNE*.]
The Committee. [The L.C. copy is a printed text of T. Knight's
The Honest Thieves.]

p. 444]   +The Conqueror's Steed; or, The Prophet of the Caucasus
(R.A. 4/1831).
Conrad the Usurper (8° 1821). [=*A. BUNN*. +8° 1818.]
Conrad the Usurper (Britannia, 1848). [=*C. Z. BARNETT*.]
The Conscript. [=*R. J. RAYMOND* and *W. BARRYMORE*.]
The Consequences. [=*T. E. HOOK, Safe and Sound*.]
+The Conspiracy of Querini. 8° 1837.
The Convent Belle. [=*T. H. BAYLY*.]
The Convict (C.G. 1822). [=*R. L. SHEIL, The Huguenot*.]
The Convict (C.L. 1838). [Originally given at Surrey as *The
Forest of St Ange*.]

p. 445]   Cork Legs. [The City performance was not the first; it had
appeared previously at the Strand.]
The Cornish Miners. [=*R. B. PEAKE*.]

The Corsair. [=W. BALL.]
Cosimo. [From the opera by A. Villain de Saint Hilaire and P. Duport, music by Prévost; Paris, 13/10/1835.]
Could the Murder? [Evidently = T. J. DIBDIN, Black Caesar.]
The Council of Ten. [=H. M. MILNER.]

p. 446] Courting by Mistake. [=W. T. MONCRIEFF.]
The Court of Old Fritz. [=J. F. SMITH.]
The Court of Queen Anne. [=W. T. MONCRIEFF.]
Cousin Campbell's Courtship. [=W. COLLIER.]
Cousin Joseph. [=J. OXENFORD.]
+The Covenanters; or, The Battle of Drumclog (Caledonian, Edinburgh, 8/3/1825).
Creon, the Patriot. [=J. SMITH.]
Crichton. [=T. E. WILKS.]
The Cricket on the Hearth. [=W. J. LUCAS.]
+The Cricket on the Hearth (Newcastle, 13/7/1846).
+The Crowded Villa (Swansea, 19/8/1841).
The Crumlesses. [=J. H. HORNCASTLE.]
Crusoe the Second [=J H STOCQUELER.]

p. 447] Cupid and Folly. [=T. NOBLE.]
Cupid turned Physician. [=J. J. STAFFORD.]
A Cure for Coxcombs. [+8° 1821.]
Curiosities of Literature. [=D. BOUCICAULT.]
The Dæmon's Tribunal. [=The Demon's Tribunal (UA).]
+D. The Dalesman. 8° 1836.
The Dairy Maids. [=J. BYRNE.]
Les Danaides. [=— HOGUET. Music by Schmidt.]

p. 448] +Darby Kelly [M'bone, 25/9/1843].
The Daughter. [=I. POCOCK, The Magpie or the Maid.]
The Daughter of the Regiment. [=— DAVENPORT.]
Davy Jones. [=W. BARRYMORE.]
+The Days of Oliver Cromwell; or, Cavaliers and Roundheads (Strand, 4/10/1847).
Dearest Elizabeth. [=J. OXENFORD.]

p. 449] The Death Fetch (Cob. 1826). [=H. M. MILNER. +8° (1826).]
+The Death of Napoleon; or, The Rock of St Helena (Vic. 7/1840).
Decorum. [−T. H. BAYLY.]
+M.D. Deeds and Doings of the Dark House; or, Simple Bess of Billingsgate (Vic. 23/8/1841).
The Deer Stalker. [=M. LEMON.]
Delusions. [=W. B. BERNARD.]

p. 450] The Demon Dwarf. [=E. STIRLING.]
+The Denouncer; or, The Seven Clerks of Marseilles (Strand, 15/2/1848).
+De Rayo; or, The Haunted Priory. 8° 1833.
The Devil's Brother. [=C. SHANNON. Adapted from Fra Diavolo by A. E. Scribe, music by Auber; Paris, 28/1/1830.]
The Devil's Walk. [=W. T. MONCRIEFF.]

p. 451] Dick Whittington. [=H. M. MILNER. +8° (1823).]
The Dillosk Gatherer. [=E. FITZBALL.]
Dine at my Villa. [=P. HOARE, The Paragraph.]

+D. The Divorce; or, The British Socrates. 8° 1810. [By "G. M. R——D."]
Doctor Poker. [=Each for Himself (*UA*).]
Doctor Sangrado. [=— *D'EGVILLE*. Music by Bishop.]
+Doings in Bond Street (Strand, 16/5/1842).

p. 452] Don Giovanni (C.G. 1819). [The L.C. copy is a printed text of the play by *T. J. DIBDIN* (R.C. 1817) for performances at C.G. 15/6/1819.]
+Don Juan (M'bone, 28/5/1844).
Don Pasquale. [=*T. H. REYNOLDSON*.]
Don't be Frightened. [=*J. M. MORTON*.]
The Double Dilemma. [=*C. DANCE*.]
Double or Quits. [=*M. BARNETT*.]
A Down East Bargain. [=*W. T. MONCRIEFF*.]
+The Dread Sentence; or, Honour, Love and Friendship (Strand, 30/12/1847).
The Dreamer. [=*T. H. REYNOLDSON*.]
Drive Love out at the Door. [=— *ROCHFORT*.]

p. 453] +The Drover Boy; or, The Wild Herdsman of the Hills, and the Last Hope of Freedom (Britannia, 27/9/1848).
+The Druid; or, The Vision of Fingal. 8° 1815.
The Duke for a Day. [=*G. DANCE*.]
The Duke of Mantua. [=*J. ROBY*.]
The Dumb Brigand. [=*W. B. BERNARD*.]
+The Dumb Girl of the Inn (Strand, 23/9/1847).
Each for Himself. [=Doctor Poker (*UA*).]

p. 454] The Earl of Ross. [=*Lieut. C. F. MUNRO*.]
Early Closing. [=*A. B. REACH* and *H. HAMILTON*.]
The East Indian. [=*M. G. LEWIS, Rich and Poor*.]
+Ebu Bekr; or, The Emir's Edict (Queen's, 6/1840).
Edgar. [=*H. HALLAM*.]
+Edwin and Morcar. 8° 1838.
Electioneering. [=*W. T. MONCRIEFF*.]
The Elements. [=*C. I. M. DIBDIN*.]

p. 455] The Eleventh Hour (Queen's, 1844). [=*T. MILDENHALL*.]
The Eleventh Hour (Cob. 1826). [=*R. J. RAYMOND*.]
Elfrid. [=*T. J. DIBDIN*.]
+Ellen Trent; or, The Profligate (Colosseum, 6/1840).
+Elizabeth (Caledonian, Edinburgh, 26/6/1824).
The Elshie. [=*H. GOTT*. +8° (1823).]
Emigration—the Remedy. [=*J. H. STOCQUELER*.]
Emily. [=— *D'EGVILLE*.]
The Emissary. [=*G. DANCE*.]
The Enchanted Castle. [=*H. M. MILNER*.]

p. 456] The Enchanted Fire. [=*M. G. LEWIS*.]
Enjoyment. [=*C. SELBY*.]
The Enraged Musician. [=*R. J. RAYMOND*.]
Esdale Hall. [=*C. H. OSWIN*. The title should be *Elsdale Hall*.]

p. 457] Ethelwolf. [=*J. F. RENNIE*. +8° 1821.]
Etiquette Run Mad. [=*T. POWER*.]
Euphemia. [=*C. M. YOUNG*. +8° 1837.]
Eurypilus. [=*D. W. PAYNTER*.]

Eveline. [=*T. ARCHER.*]
The Exquisites. [=*J. T. DE TRUEBA.*]
+O.Bal. The Fairies' Home; or, The Test of Truth (Colosseum, 6/1840).
Fair Play. [=*F. REYNOLDS, Begone Dull Care.*]

p. 458] The Falls of Clyde. [=*J. BLACK.*]
False Visions. [=*J. PARRY*; see p. 368.]
+The Fancy Ball (Strand, 8/10/1832).
Fanny Sims. [=*J. S. COYNE.*]
Farmer and Pheasant. [Probably=*C. P. THOMPSON, Pheasant Shooting.*]

p. 459] +The Farmer's Bride; or, Love, Hatred and Revenge (Queen's, 28/12/1840).
The Fatal Marksman. [=*G. ALMAR.*]
The Fatal Rock. [=*W. BARRYMORE, Jack Robinson and his Monkey.*]
+M.D. The Father and the Son (Edinburgh, 1/11/1823). [Probably=The Murderer (*UA*).]
A Father's Crime. [=*T. J. SERLE.*]

p. 460] A Father's Plea. [=*E. MAYHEW.*]
The Favourite of the Derby. [=*W. T. MONCRIEFF, The Royal Foxhunt.*]
Favourites in Town. [=*W. T. MONCRIEFF.*]
The Felon of New York. [=*E. FITZBALL.*]
Female Cavaliers. [=*Mrs DUNLOP.*]
The Female Volunteer. [=*W. H. OXBERRY*; this was given originally at the Clarence on 11/11/1833.]
La Femme Sentinelle. [=*Miss BARNETT.*]
The Festival of Bacchus. [=*J. BYRNE.*]

p. 461] The Fiend Father. [=*M. R. LACY.*]
Fingal. [Performed in Italian.]
Fire and Spirit. [=*C. I. M. DIBDIN*; see p. 290.]
First Night. [=*A. S. WIGAN*; see p. 419.]
The Fisherman. [=*J. TOBIN, The Fisherman's Hut.*]

p. 462] The Fitzpatricks. [=*W. T. MONCRIEFF.*]
The Flip Flap Footman. [=*R. B. PEAKE.*]
The Florentines. [=*E. L. A. BERWICK.*]
The Flower of Lucerne. [=*G. SOANE.*]
Flying Colours. [=— *COFE*,]
Folly and Friendship. [=*Mrs PLANCHE.*]
The Fools of Fashion. [=*F. LATHOM.*]
The Forest Knight. [=*J. M. SCOTT.*]

p. 463] Forgive and Forget (Olym. 1838). [=*C. DANCE.*]
The Fortune Hunter. [=*W. B. BERNARD.*]
The Four Sons of Aymon. [=The Castle of Aymon (*UA*).]

p. 464] Francesca Doria. [=*V. MORRIS.* Music by G. Linley.]
Francis I. [=— *McKINLAN.*]
Freaks in an Attic. [=*C. WEBB.*]
Frederick of Bavaria (Cob. 1822). [=*H. M. MILNER.*]
Frederick of Prussia. [=*C. SELBY*; see p. 398.]
The Freebooters. [=*H. NAPIER.*]
The Freebooters of Vienna. [=*H. M. MILNER.*]

Freedom and Slavery. [=*T. MORTON, The Slave.*]
Der Freischutz Travestie. [=Der Fryshot (*UA*).]
The French Libertine. [=*J. H. PAYNE.*]
The French Spy. [=*J. T. HAINES.*]
Fricandeau. [=*J. H. PAYNE.*]
Fridolin. [=*M. LEMON.* Music by F. Romer. +8° 1840
(*Songs*).]

p. 465] Friendship, Love and Duty. [=*H. SIDDONS.*]
Frolics in "Forty-Five". [Attributed to *R. B. PEAKE.*]
The Frolics of the Fairies. [Attributed to *G. A. À BECKETT.*]
Der Fryshot. [=Der Freischutz Travestie (*UA*).]
Fun and Fright. [Attributed to *T. G. RODWELL.*]
Furibond. [+L. 1533.]
Gallantry. [=*S. PENLEY.*]
The Gallery of St Nicholas. [=*C.BEW*+Brighton, 31/12/1832.]
The Gamblers. [+8° (1824).]
Gambler's Life in London. [=*A. V. CAMPBELL*; see p. 278.]

p. 466] The Gaming Table. [=*G. A. À BECKETT.*]
Gaul. [=*W. R. HAWKES.*]
Genevieve (Surrey, 1843). [=*C. Z. BARNETT.*]
Genevieve (Surrey, 1824). [=*B. WEST.*]
The Genii of Paloguam. [=— *LECLERCQ.*]
Geraldine. [=*G. A. À BECKETT.* Another contemporary
attribution to *G. SOANE* seems to be in error.]

p. 467] A German Blunder. [=— *GREFFULHE, Is He a Prince?*]
The German Jew. [=*W. H. TILBURY.* +*Duncombe.*]
The Giant. [=*C. WEBB.*]
Giovanni in Ireland (D.L. 1821). [=*W. T. MONCRIEFF.*]
The Gipsy Dumb Boy. [=*J. DOBBS.*]

p. 468] The Gnome King. [=*F. REYNOLDS.*]
The Golden Axe. [=*W. BARRYMORE.*]
Gone to Texas. [=*J. OXENFORD.*]
+T. Gonsalvo. 8° 1822.
A Good Name. [=*J. H. STOCQUELER.*]
Gordon the Gypsey. [=*R. B. PEAKE.*]
Grace Rivers. [=*N. LEE.*]

p. 469] The Great Unknown. [=*E. STIRLING.*]
+Int. The Green Room (Olym. 21/2/1821). L. 2208.
Gregarach. [=*W. BARRYMORE.*]
The Grenadier. [=*H. BAYLY.*]
Grey the Collier. [=*G. SOANE.*]
Grimalkin the Great. [=*J. B. BUCKSTONE.*]
The Guard House. [=*G. DANCE.*]
The Guardians Outwitted. [=Assumptions (*UA*).]

p. 470] The Guide of the Tyrol. [This title is also given to *M. R.
LACY.*]
Gunpowder Tom. [=*G. D. PITT.*]
The Gunsmith of Orleans. [=*J. COURTNEY*; see p. 284.]
Gustavus of Sweden. [=*T. J. THACKERAY.*]
Guy Fawkes. [The L.C. copy is signed "J. Street".]
+Hainault Forest. [See Henault Forest (*UA*).]
Hamlet (Cob. 1828). [=*H. M. MILNER.*]
The Handsell Penny (Lyc. 1841). [=*C. SELBY.*]

Hans of Iceland. [=*E. FITZBALL.*]
Harlequin Achilles. [=*C. I. M. DIBDIN*; see p. 295.]
Harlequin and a Happy New Year. [=H. and the Happy New Year (*UA*).]

p. 471] Harlequin and Asmodeus. [=Harlequin Zambullo (*UA*). +8° 1810 (Songs).]
Harlequin and Georgey Barnwell. [=*H. YOUNGE.* Music by Blewitt.]
Harlequin and Good Queen Bess. [=*G. H. RODWELL.*]
Harlequin and Little Great Britain. [=*T. GREENWOOD.*]

p. 472] Harlequin and My Lady Lee. [=*W. T. MONCRIEFF.*]
Harlequin and Old Cocker. [=*N. LEE.*]
+Harlequin and Old Father Time (Colosseum, 6/1840).
Harlequin and the Dragon of Wantley (S.W. 1849). [=*T. GREENWOOD.*]
Harlequin and the Elfin Sprite. [=*W. VINING.*]

p. 473] Harlequin and the Ogress. [+8° 1822.]
Harlequin and the Silver Dove. [=*II. R. DEVERLEY.*]

p. 474] Harlequin and the World turned upside down. [=*T. GREENWOOD.*]
Harlequin and William Tell. [=*J. M. MORTON.*]
Harlequin Crochet and Quaver. [=*N. LEE.*]
+Harlequin Hunchback; or, The Enchanted Oak (M'bone, 26/12/1837).
Harlequin Jack the Giant Killer. [−*N. LEE.*]

p. 475] +Harlequin Libertine. L. 2004 [D.L. 16/12/1817].
+Harlequin Munchausen; or, The Fairy of the Golden Star and the Green Wizard of the Mystic Isle (Edinburgh, 26/12/1843).
Harlequin Munchausen. [=*C. FARLEY.* +8° 1818.]
Harlequin Nobody; or, Grey Eyed Greedy Guts and the Fairies of the Bilberry Hen (M'bone, 9/6/1843).
Harlequin Pat. [=*C. FARLEY.*]
Harlequin's Races. [=*T. J. DIBDIN.*]

p. 476] Harlequin Tam o'Shanter. [=*N. LEE.*]
+Harlequin Tee-to-Tum; or, The Fairy of the Silver Stream and the Demon of the Golden Mine (Amphi., L'pool, 1/1/1847).
Harlequin Zambullo. [=Harlequin and Asmodeus (*UA*). =*C. FARLEY.*]
Harmony Hall. [=*J. LUNN.*]
+M.D. Haroun Alompra; or, The Hunter Chief (Portsmouth, 19/4/1824).
+Harry Bluff; or, Look out for Squalls (Queen's, 6/1840).
Harry of England. [=*T. GREENWOOD.*]
Harvest Home. [L. 1808. =*G. BENNETT.*]
Hate. [=*B. WEST.*]
+The Haunted House; or, The Dream Girl of Devon (Strand, 17/5/1847).
The Haunted Man. (Adel. 1848). [=*E. STIRLING.*]

p. 477] The Headsman. [=*G. ALMAR.*]
The Hebrew Twins. [=*W. J. LUCAS.*]
The Heiress of Strathearn. [=*J. PINKERTON.*]

+T. The Heir of Innes. 8° 1822.
The Hemlock Draught. [=*J. OXENFORD*.]
Henault Forest. [= Hainault *Forest (UA)*.]
+MD. Hengist; or, The Fifth Century. 8° 1816 (priv.).
Henri de Rochemaine. [=*H. B. ROBERTS*.]
Henri Quatre (E.O.H. 1822). [=*J. R. PLANCHÉ, The Fair Gabrielle*.]
Henry I. [=Owen Prince of Powys *(UA)*.]
+Henry III. 8° 1840.

p. 478]   Hernando Cortez. [=*J. R. PLANCHÉ, Cortez*.]
Hero and Leander. [=*W. L. REDE*.]
The Hertfordshire Tragedy. [=*H. M. MILNER*. +8° (1824).]
He's no Conjuror. [=*C. T. HARDING*.]
He's not a-miss. [=*C. DANCE*.]
He would be an Actor. [=*C. J. MATHEWS*; see p. 354.]
Hide and Seek (C.G. 1830). [Apparently=*J. LUNN*; but also ascribed to "Westmacott Jr."]
The Highland Cateran. [=*W. H. MURRAY*.]
The Highland Widow. [=*H. MARSTON*.]
+High Notions; or, A Trip to Tenby (Cardigan, 20/11/1843).

p. 479]   His First Champagne. [This may be an altered version of the play by *W. L. REDE* (Strand, 1833).]
Hogarth's Mirror (Strand, 26/4/1847). [Acted also as *Hogarth's Marriage-à-la-mode*.]
The Holidays. [=*E. J. EYRE*.]
The Hollow Way. [=*W. T. MONCRIEFF*.]
Honest Thieves. [=*T. KNIGHT*. +*Cawthorne Minor*.]
Honesty the Best Policy. [=The Cady *(UA)*.]
Honour. [=*T. CROMWELL*.]
+The Horatii. 8° 1846.

p. 480]   An Hour with Napoleon. [=*C. WEBB, One Hour with Napoleon*.]
The House Warming. [=*T. J. DIBDIN*; see p. 300.]
How happy could I be with either! [=*T. J. DIBDIN, Two Faces under a Hood*.]
The Huguenots. [=*H. RUSSELL*.]
Humbug. (Olym. 1845). [=*H. SILVESTER*.]
The Humours of an Election. [=*J. S. COYNE*.]
The Humpback (Strand, 1832). [=*W. L. REDE*.]

p. 481]   A Husband Wanted. [=*M. BARNETT*.]
The Hussars. [=*Mrs C. B. WILSON, The Petticoat Colonel*.]
+Sketch. The Hustings (Strand, 13/3/1837).
Hyder Ali (Adel. 1831). [=*J. B. BUCKSTONE*.]
Hyder Ali (D.L. 1831). [=*A. BUNN*.]
The Hypocrite. [Acted E.O.H. 27/7/1819.]
Ida of the Cottage. [=*G. SOANE, Self-Sacrifice*.]
The Idol's Birthday. [=*J. OXENFORD*.]
I'll Stay where I am. [="I won't go!" *(UA)*.]
Illusion. [=*S. J. ARNOLD*. +8° 1814. L. 1786.]
+The Imperial Guard; or, A Soldier's Love (Strand, 11/11/1850).
+The Imp of the Brazen Spell (Newcastle, 26/12/1846).
In and Out. (Surrey, 1845). [=*E. STIRLING*.]

LIST OF UNKNOWN AUTHORS   629

p. 482]   The Indian Nuptials. [=— *ROCHFORT.*]
   In Pursuit of a Wife. [=*J. COURTNEY.*]
   The Inscription. [=*J. M. SCOTT.*]
   In Statu Quo! [=*G. DANCE.*]
   The Invasion of England by William the Conqueror. [=*J.
   COURTNEY.* =William the Conqueror's Invasion of
   England (*UA*).]
   The Invisible Client. [=*E. L. BLANCHARD*; see p. 268.]
   +The Invisible Girl (Wakefield, 20/3/1800).
   Invisible Green. [=*J. OXENFORD.*]
   The Invisible Tribunal. [=*H. M. MILNER.*]
   Ireland. [=*C. P. THOMPSON.*]

p. 483]   The Irish Gentleman. [=*R. J. RAYMOND.*]
   The Irish Girl (Adel. 1830). [=*R. RYAN.*]
   The Irish Nigger. [=*W. L. REDE.*]
   The Iron Hand. [=*J. T. HAINES*; see p. 323.]
   Isaure (City, 1832). [=*B. WEBSTER.*]
   +Is He Dead? or, Murder Will Out (Strand, 3/5/1847).
   Isidore and Merida. [=*W. DIMOND.*]
   Is it a Woman? [=*W. ABBOTT.*]
   The Island. [=*D. W. JERROLD*; see p. 331.]
   The Islanders. [=*O. BYRNE.*]
   The Island Nymph. [=— *BARREZ.*]

p. 484]   Isn't it a Duck? [=*M. BARNETT.*]
   The Israelites in Egypt. [=*M. R. LACY.*]
   +The Italian Captain. 8° 1847.
   The Italian Gamester. [=*C. F. BARRETT.*]
   The Italian Husband. [=*E. J. EYRE, Look at Home.*]
   The Italians in Algiers. [Adapted from Rossini's *L'Italiana in
   Algeri.*]
   +Its Mother's Pet (Strand, 14/2/1848).
   It's only my Aunt. [=*Mrs A. C. V. BARTHOLOMEW.*]
   Ivanhoe (Cob. 1820). [=*W. T. MONCRIEFF.*]
   Ivanhoe (Birmingham, 1820). [=*A. BUNN.*]
   Ivan of the Mask. [=*T. J. LYNCH.*]
   Iwan. [=*E. FITZBALL.*]
   I will have an Uncle. [=*C. DANCE.*]
   "I won't go!" [=I'll Stay where I am (*UA*).]
   +Jack and the Beanstalk (Newcastle, 26/12/1847).
   Jack in the Box. [=*W. BARRYMORE.*]
   Jack's Alive. [=*G. SOANE.*]
   Jack the Giant Killer (S.W. 1803). [=*C. I. M. DIBDIN*; see
   p. 290.]

p. 485]   +Jack the Giant Killer (Manchester, 26/12/1847).
   +Jack the Painter; or, The Destruction of the Dockyard
   (Queen's, 9/11/1840).
   Jacob Faithful (Surrey, 1834). [=*G. D. PITT.*]
   Jarvis the Honest Man. [=*G. D. PITT*; see p. 374.]
   Jeffreys. [=*H. SPICER*; see p. 405.]
   Jenny Lind at Last. [=*A. B. REACH.*]
   Joan of Arc (Olym. 1822). [=*E. FITZBALL.*]

p. 486]   +Joan of the Hatchet (Queen's, 6/1840).
   John Adams. [=*W. T. MONCRIEFF.*]

+Hist.D. John Churchill, Duke of Marlborough. 8° 1820.
John Gilpin. [There are only minor differences between the
two texts.]
Johnnie Armstrong (R.C. 1803). [=*J. C. CROSS*.]
+Johnnie Fa; or, Harlequin and the King of the Gypsies
(Edinburgh, 26/12/1842).
+D. John o' Armhall (Perth, 3/1828).
A Joke's a Joke. [=*T. E. HOOK*.]
The Judgement of Paris (Strand, 1832). [=*W. L. REDE*.]
The Judgment of Paris (Adel. 1846). [=*C. SELBY*.]
+D. Julia; or, The Fatal Return. 8° 1822 (Dover).

p. 487] +Bal. Kapschou, the Forest Fiend (Lyc. 4/8/1809). L. 1586.
Kenilworth (1824). [=*W. OXBERRY*.]
Kerim the Pearl Diver. [=*G. D. PITT*.]
Kindred. [=*H. CAPADOSE*; see p. 279.]
The King and the Freebooter. [=*J. C. WILLS*.]
+King Arthur: or, The Knights of the Round Table (R.A.
9/1840).
King Henry VIII and the Cobbler. [Evidently the same as *The
King and the Cobler*.]
+The King of the Mist (Caledonian, Edinburgh, 15/11/1829).
King O'Neill. [Apparently=*Mrs C. G. F. GORE*; see p. 319.]
The King's Fireside. [=*T. MORTON*.]
The King's Friend. [This may be by *R. SULLIVAN*.]
The Kiss. [=*W. COLLIER*.]
The Kitchen Sylph. [=*J. B. BUCKSTONE*.]

p. 489] The Koeuba. [=*E. FITZBALL*.]
+Ladies at Court; or, The Tale of a Palace (Strand, 9/8/1832).
Lady Henrietta. [=— *ST GEORGE* and — *MAZILIER*.]
The Lady Killer. [=*D. JERROLD*.]
The Lady of Lions. [=*M. G. DOWLING*.]
The Lady of the Lake (C.G. 1843). [=*M. LEMON*.]

p. 490] Laffarge. [=*J. S. COYNE*.]
The Larboard Fin. [=*W. H. WILLS*. +*Cumberland*.]
The Last Day. [=*G. GODWIN, Junior*.]
+P. The Last Hour; or, Harlequin Victim. L. 1662 [Pav.
4/2/1811].
+F. The Last of the Lotteries (Strand, 6/9/1847).
The Last Whistle. [=*H. R. ADDISON*.]
+The Last Witness (C.L. 10/1840).

p. 491] The Law of the Land. [=*W. H. WILLS*. +12° 1837.]
The Law Suit. [=*M. T. KEMBLE, Smiles and Tears*.]
Leander and Leonora. [=*J. BYRNE*.]
Lefevre. [=*M. BARNETT*.]
Legacy Hunting. [=*J. F. SMITH*.]
Legerdemain. [=*J. OXENFORD*.]
Leocadea. [Adapted from *Léocadie*, by A. E. Scribe and A. H. J.
Mélesville; Paris, 4/11/1824.]
Leoline. [Adapted from *L'ame en peine*, by J. N. Verney de
Saint-Georges; Paris, 29/6/1846.]

p. 492] A Lesson for Gentlemen. [=*J. F. SMITH*.]
The Liberal Candidate. [=*G. A. À BECKETT*.]
The Libertine of Poland. [=*E. FITZBALL*.]

Lie upon Lie. [=*J. M. SCOTT, The Two Spanish Valets.*]
+The Life and Almost Death of Joan of Arc, the Maid of All Work (Strand, 31/5/1847).
The Life and Reign of George III. [=*G. MACFARREN*; see p. 349.]
The Life, Death and Restoration of the High Mettled Racer. [=*T. J. DIBDIN, The High Mettled Racer.*]
The Lifeguardsman. [Evidently = The Little Guardsman (*UA*).]
Life in Dublin. [=*P. EGAN*. First produced in Dublin, 10/1839.]
+The Life of James Dawson; or, The Rebel of 1745 (Vic. 6/9/1841).
Light and Shade. [=*G. D. PITT.*]
Lilliput. [=*F. G. FISHER.*]

p. 493] Linda of Chamouny. [=*M. D. RYAN.*]
The Lists of Ashby. [Probably=*F. F. COOPER, Ivanhoe.*]
The Little Corporal. [=*J. B. BUCKSTONE.*]
The Little Guardsman. [Evidently = The Lifeguardsman (*UA*).]
The Little Innocent. [=*W. T. TOWNSEND.*]
The Little Laundress. [=*R. B. PEAKE.*]
The Little Old Woman and Her Pig. [=*N. LEE.*]
The Little Red Man. [=*J. B. BUCKSTONE*; see p. 274.]
Little Thumb and the Ogre. [Acted C.G. 16/4/1807. +8° 1807 (Songs, Choruses).]

p. 494] The Loadstone of the Earth. [=— *DALRYMPLE.*]
+F. Lock and Key; or, A Glamorganshire Story (Cardiff, 11/2/1822).
London and the Country. [=*T. MORTON, Town and Country.*]
+London Beaux and Bath Belles (Strand, 24/6/1848).
Look at Home. [=*C. DANCE.*]
Loose Cash. [=*J. OXENFORD.*]

p. 495] Lost a Sovereign. [=*H. R. ADDISON.*]
The Lost Shilling. [=*J. S. FAUCIT The Last Shilling.*]
Louise de Lignarolles. [=*Miss PARDOE.*]
Love among the Roses. [=*S. BEAZLEY.*]
Love and Impudence. [=— *HEWLETT, The Fortune Hunters.*]

p. 496] Love in a Cottage (Olym. 1835). [=*T. H. BAYLY.*]
Love in a Tub. [=— *DEGVILLE*. Music by Bishop.]
Love in Livery. [=*J. P. WOOLER.*]
+Fairy D. The Lovely Una and the Red Cross Knight. 8° 1806.
+C.Sketch. Lovers, Lawyers and Clients (Caledonian, Edinburgh, 21/12/1814).
Love's Errors. [=*C. KEMBLE, The Child of Chance.*]
Love's Frailties. [=*J. J. STAFFORD.*]
Love's Labyrinth. [=*J. THOMSON, A Cure for Romance.*]
+F. Love's Machinations (Caledonian, Edinburgh, 14/2/1825).
Love's Mysteries. [=*J. KENNEY, Oh! this Love!*]
Loves of the Angels. [=*W. L. REDE.*]
The Loves of the Stars. [=*W. L. REDE.*]
The Love Spell. [Adapted from *Le philtre,* by A. E. Scribe, music by Auber; Paris, 20/6/1831.
+D. Love's Trial. 8° 1846.

p. 497] The Loving Woman. [=*R. B. PEAKE.*]

Lucius Catiline. [=*H. M. MILNER.* +8° (1827).]
Luke Somerton. [=*G. SOANE.*]
+The McGreggors (Caledonian, Edinburgh, 20/4/1825).
Mabel. [=*T. H. REYNOLDSON.*]
Madame du Barry. [=*J. POOLE.*]

p. 498] +M.Rom. Madeleine; or, The Pearl of the Drowned (Vic. 16/8/1841).
The Magic Flute. [Performed in German.]
The Magic of British Liberty. [=*A. CHERRY.*]
+The Magic Star (Olym. Circus, L'pool, 1/1807).
Magna Charta (Vic. 1840). [=*J. S. FAUCIT.*]
+The Maid and the Monk; or, The Bravoes of Chiozza (Vic. 6/1840).
+The Maiden Lane Murder; or, Battle Bridge in 1720 (Clarence, 15/11/1832).

p. 499] +Ba. The Maid of Madrid (Strand, 7/1841).
+D. The Maid of Prague. 8° 1837.
The Maid of Saragossa. [=*C. Z. BARNETT.*]
The Maid of the Forest. [=*H. M. MILNER.*]
The Maid of the Glen. [L. 1618 is signed "G. Male."]
Maids and Bachelors. [=*C. M. WESTMACOTT.*]
Major and Minor. [=*G. DANCE.*]
Mammon and Gammon. [=*F. TALFOURD.*]
The Manager's Daughter. [=*E. R. LANCASTER.*]
The Man and the Monster. [=*H. M. MILNER.*]
The Man in Mourning for Himself. [=*R. B. PEAKE.*]
The Man in the Iron Mask. [=*W. J. LUCAS.*]
The Man in the Moon (Strand, 1847). [=— *VANDEIGH-TONE.*]
The Man in the Moon (D.L. 1826). [=*W. BARRYMORE.*]

p. 500] The Man of Business. [=*J. COBB, Sudden Arrivals.*]
The Man Trap. [=*P. H. HATCH.*]
A Man without a Head. [=*J. P. WOOLER.* +*French N.Y.*]
The Man-Wolf. [=*W. T. MONCRIEFF.*]
The Marble Maiden (D.L. 1845). [=— *ST GEORGE* and — *ALBERT.* Music by Adam.]
The Marble Maiden (Lyc. 1846). [=*J. H. STOCQUELER.*]
+D. Marco Sciarro; or, The Chief of the Arbutzi (R.P. 10/1840).
Margaret of Anjou. [See also under *J. M. WILSON.*]
Margaret's Ghost. [=*E. FITZBALL.*]
+D. Marie de Chamouni; or, A Mother's Prayer (Edinburgh, 30/9/1843). [This may=Marie, the Pearl of Chamouni (*UA*).]
Marietta. [= *E. M. RAYMOND.*]
Mark the End On't. [=*H. SIDDONS, Time's a Tell-tale.*]
Marplot in Spain. [=*J. R. PLANCHÉ, Too Curious by Half.*]

p. 501] +The Marquis of Montrose (Edinburgh, 15/1/1829). [This may =*ATKINSON, Montrose.*]
The Marriage Certificate. [=*T. MILDENHALL.*]
The Marriage of Figaro. [=*J. W. MOULD.*]
Martelli. [=*G. BREWER.*]
Martial Law (Fitzroy, 1834). [=*E. MAYHEW.*]
Martin Faber. [=*G. WHITE.*]

Mary Stewart. [=*Rev. J. GRAHAME.*]
Mary the Maid of the Inn. [=*J. M. SCOTT.*]
+D.D. Mary White, the Charity Girl (C.L. 10/1840).

p. 502] The Massacre of Cyprus. [=*H. M. MILNER.*]
The Massacre of Rajahpoor. [=*H. M. MILNER.*]
The Mast and the Ploughshare. [Evidently=The Ship and the Plough (C.G. 31/5/1804).]
+Vaud. A Match in the Dark (Grecian, 4/1841).
Mathews and Co. [=*C. J. MATHEWS.*]
Matteo Falconi. [=*E. MAYHEW.*]
A Matter of Doubt. [=*G. H. RODWELL.*]
Maurice the Woodcutter. [This may be the play by *C. A. SOMERSET.*]
Maximums and Speciments of William Muggins. [=*C. SELBY.*]
The Mayor and the Monkey. [=*J. S. COYNE.*]
Mazeppa. [=*H. M. MILNER.*]
+Ba. Me and Myself (Strand, 19/1/1834).

p. 503] Melmoth the Wanderer. [=*B. WEST.* +8° 1823.]
Metamora. [The American play by J. A. Stone (Park, New York, 1829).]
Methinks I see my Father. [=*C. J. MATHEWS.* +Lyc. 7/11/1849.]
Michael and Christine. [=*J. KERR.* +8° (1824).]
+The Midnight Hour; or, The Lost Wager (Strand, 7/2/1848).
The Militia Muster. [=*S. BEAZLEY.*]

p. 504] Mina. [=*G. LINLEY.*]
The Minerali. [+L.C.]
The Minstrel of Lochmaben. [=*T. J. LYNCH.*]
+The Minstrels of Provence; or, The Gypsie's Stratagem (Strand, 7/2/1848).
Misapprehension. [=*C. DANCE.*]
Mischievous Eyes. [=*J. H. BAYLY.*]
+D. The Miser of Lewes; or, The Restoration of Magna Charta. 8° 1823.
The Miser's Will. [=*R. B. PEAKE.*]

p. 505] A Model of a Man. [=*W. L. REDE.*]
Moments of Mystery. [=*J. B. BUCKSTONE.*]
The Money Diggers. [=*H. M. MILNER.*]
The Monkey that has seen the World. [=*W. T. MONCRIEFF.*]
The Monk's Cowl. [=*W. T. MONCRIEFF.*]
Montalto. [=*W. À COURT.* +8° 1821.]
+Montrezar; or, The Heroine of Padua (Queen's, 9/12/1840).
Montrose (Glasgow, 1820). [+12° 1820.]
+Montrose (Caledonian, Edinburgh, 8/9/1826).
Montrose; or, Second Sight. [=*T. J. DIBDIN.*]
The Moon's Age. [=*H. R. ADDISON.*]

p. 506] Moonshine. [=*Lady E. S. WORTLEY.*]
Mora's Love. [=— *DEGVILLE.*]
+P. Mother Bunch (Vic. L'pool, 26/12/1843).
+P. Mother Goose; or, Harlequin and the Golden Egg (Amphi., L'pool, 26/12/1848).
+P. Mother Red Cap (Edinburgh, 26/12/1841).
Mount St. Bernard. [=*W. T. MONCRIEFF.*]

p. 507]   +F. Moving Statues (Olym. 10/1840).
Mr Midshipman Easy. [=J. OXENFORD; see p. 367.]
+F. Mr Pep; or, The Lion and the Tiger (Strand, 23/2/1835).
Mrs Bunbury's Spoons. [=J. S. COYNE.]
Mrs Caudle. [=C. Z. BARNETT.]
Mrs Caudle's Curtain Lectures. [=D. J. JERROLD. +8°
   1846.]
Mrs H. [=N. LEE.]
Mrs Jane Shore. [=N. LEE.]
La muette de Portici. [Given in French. The opera by A. E.
   Scribe and G. Delavigne, music by Auber; Paris, 29/2/1828.]
The Muleteer's Vow. [Ascribed both to J. T. HAINES and
   T. J. SERLE.]
Mungo Parke. [=B. BERNARD.]
Murder and Madness. [=C. I. M. DIBDIN; see p. 295.]
The Murdered Maid. [+8° 1818 (Warwick), by "S. N. E."]
The Murderer (Surrey, 1822). [=J. H. AMHERST.]
The Murderer (Edinburgh, 1823). [=The Father and the Son
   (UA).]

p. 508]   Murder will out. [=W. BARRYMORE, The Dog of Montargis.]
My Aunt. [=S. J. ARNOLD.]
My Eleventh Day. [=T. H. BAYLY; see p. 262.]
My Friend from Town. [=J. LUNN.]
My Grandfather. [=T. H. BAYLY.]
My Late Friend. [=G. DANCE.]
My Lord. [=C. DANCE. Adapted from Le nouveau seigneur
   de village, by A. F. Creuzé de Lesser and E. G. F. de Favières;
   Paris, 29/6/1813.]
My Maiden Aunts. [=F. SALA.]
My Own Man. [=R. B. PEAKE.]

p. 509]   My Own Twin Brother. [=I. HILL.]
The Mysteries of Alviano. [=H. M. MILNER.]
+M.D. The Mysterious Hermit; or, The Brigands of Sicily
   (Olym. 23/8/1841).
+The Mysterious Murder; or, The Ranger of the Forest
   (Surrey, 7/1824).
+T. Mystery; or, The Monks of St Nicholas. 8° 1815.
Mystification (Strand, 1832). [Probably=J. T. HAINES, Love
   and Mystery.]
My Two Nephews. [=R. B. PEAKE, The Duel.]
The Nabob. [= — DEGVILLE. Music by H. Smart.]
Die Nachtigal und der Rabe. [Adapted from the opera by
   G. F. Treitschke, music by Weigl; Vienna, 20/4/1818.]

p. 510]   Name the Winner. [=J. G. MILLINGEN.]
Napoleon Bonaparte. [=J. H. AMHERST.]
+Vaud. Napoleon Buonaparte; or, The Deserter and his Dog
   [Albert, 7/1840).
Natural Magic. [=C. SELBY.]
+Neglected Wives; or, Petticoat Management (Clarence,
   31/5/1832).
Nero. [=J. G. MILLINGEN.]
Neuha's Cave. [=R. B. PEAKE.]

p. 511] The New Marriage Act. [= *W. HENRY.*]
New Notions. [= *W. B. BERNARD.*]
News from China. [= *J. M. MORTON.*]
The Newspaper. [= — *MITCHELL.*]
+ F. A New Way to Pay the National Debt (Cork, 6/1841).
The New Year's Gift. [= *W. BARRYMORE.*]
Next Door. [= *A. S. WIGAN.*]
Nicholas Mendoza. [= *F. BROMLEY.*]
Nicholas Nickleby. [= *W. T. MONCRIEFF.*]
The Night Hag. [= *W. BARRYMORE.*]
The Nightingale. [Adapted from *Le rossignol*, by C. G. Etienne,
music by Lebrun; Paris, 23/4/1816. For the English version
music adapted by Loder.]
A Night with Punch. [= *R. B. PEAKE.*]
Nina. [= *E. FITZBALL.*]

p. 512] The Noble Outlaw. [= The Pilgrim (*UA*). Adapted from the
play by Beaumont and Fletcher. Music by Bishop.]
No Dinner Yet. [= *J. T. G. RODWELL, A Race for a Dinner.*]
+ F. The Nondescript. 8° 1814.
Nourjahad. [= *S. J. ARNOLD.*]
Novelty. [= *W. L. REDE.*]
Now or Never. [= *G. DANCE.*]
Number One! [= *J. B. BUCKSTONE.*]

p. 513] + Rom. Fairy Tale. Oberon; or, The Charmed Horn (D.L.).
8° 1826.
The Ocean Fiend (Cob. 1826). [= *H. M. MILNER.*]
Octavia Bragaldi. [= *C. M. S. BARNES*; see p. 259.]

p. 514] The Old Mint of Southwark. [= *J. B. JOHNSTONE.*]
+ Old Mother Goose (Newcastle, 26/12/1839).
Oliver Twist. [= *G. A. À BECKETT.*]
The Olympic Pic-nic. [= *S. LOVER.*]
The Omadhaun. [= *H. P. GRATTAN.*]

p. 515] One Foot by Land. [= *G. MALE.*]
+ One Hour with Napoleon. [= An Hour with Napoleon (*UA*).]
One, Two, Three. [Ascribed both to *J. REEVE* and *J. H.
REYNOLDS.*]
+ The Original and Rejected Theatre, A Collection of Dramas,
Offered for Representation but not Accepted; including others
which have never been submitted to the Managers of the
Stage. 4 vols. 8° 1814 [1815]. [From the second volume the
title was changed to *The New British Theatre*. In the following
list of plays *UA* indicates those included separately in the
UNKNOWN AUTHORS section. Contents:—vol. i: T. The
Witness (by *J. GALT*); F. The Watchhouse (by *J. GALT*);
C. The Intrigues of a Day; or, The Poet in Livery (*UA*);
T. The Prophetess (by *J. GALT*); C. The Masquerade (by
J. GALT); T. Theodora; C. The Word of Honor; O. The
Bandit (*UA*); D. The Forgery (*UA*); M. The Genii (by
ANDREW BECKET): vol. ii: T. Sulieman (*UA*); C.
Manoeuvring; D. Villario; C. Family Politics (*UA*); T. Ther-
mopylae; or, Repulsed Invasion; F. The Sailors' Return;
F. The Last Act (*UA*); C. The Way to Win Her (*UA*);

Int. The Mermaid (by *J. GALT*): vol. iii: T. The Sorceress
(*UA*); C. A Search after Perfection; D. Gonzaga (*UA*);
O. The Gondolier; or, A Night in Venice; Heroic D. The
Spaniards; or, The Expulsion of the Moors (*UA*); C. Love,
Honor and Interest (by *J. GALT*); O. Orpheus (by *J. GALT*);
T. The Apostate; or, Atlantis Destroyed (by *J. GALT*);
C. Father and Son; or, Family Frailties (*UA*): vol. iv:
T. Selim and Zuleika (*UA*); C. Woman's Will; T. Hortensia
(*UA*); Ba. Apollo's Choice; or, The Contest of the Aonides;
Oa. He Must Be Married; or, The Miser Outwitted (*UA*);
O. The Fair Crusader (*UA*); T. Cento. Hector (by *J. GALT*);
O. The Savoyard; O.F. Sixteen and Sixty (*UA*).]

p. 516] Oscar the Bandit. [=*I. POCOCK.*]
Othello. [=*G. SOANE*. Adapted from Mercadante's opera,
Paris, 21/3/1844.]
Our Dancing Days. [=*J. BYRNE.*]
Our Friend the Duke. [=*C. WEBB.*]
+F. Our Irish Lodger (Vic. 6/1840).
Our National Defences. [Probably=*J. S. COYNE*; but
ascribed also to *B. N. WEBSTER.*]
Out of Place (H.¹ 1840). [=*M. LEMON.*]
The Outside Passenger. [=*G. BREWER.*]
Owen, Prince of Powys. [=Henry I (*UA*).]
+O.Spec. The Page of Palermo (C.L. 26/12/1837).

p. 517] The Parish Revolution. [=*G. A. À BECKETT.*]
Le part du demon. [Given in French. The opera by A. E.
Scribe, music by Auber; Paris, 16/1/1843.]
+The Partners; or, The Old House of Paris (Queen's, 12/1840).
The Pasha's Bridal. [=*M. LEMON*; see p. 345.]
Pastor Fido. [=*W. CLAPPERTON.*]
Pat a Cake. [=*N. LEE.*]
Patrick's Return. [=*O. BYRNE.*]
The Patriot. [=*D. BAIN.*]
Paul the Rover. [=*J. COURTNEY.*]
Pay for Peeping. [=*B. N. WEBSTER*. +8ᵘ 1834.]

p. 518] The Peacock and the Crow. [=*T. PARRY.*]
The Perplexed Husband. [=*S. CLARKE, The Kiss.*]
The Persian Hunters. [=*T. NOBLE.*]

p. 519] Peter Bell. [=*J. B. BUCKSTONE.*]
Peter Priggins. [=*E. STIRLING.*]
Petraki Germano. [=*J. DOBBS.*]
The Petticoat Colonel. [=*Mrs C. B. WILSON.*]
+The Phantom Corporal (Strand, 20/12/1847).
+Philip Quarl, the English Hermit; or, The Sleeper Awake
(Olym. 11/1840).
Phoebe Hersell. [=*J. B. JOHNSTONE.*]
+C. The Phrenologist (Caledonian, Edinburgh, 4/4/1825).
Pickwick. [=*F. C. NANTZ.*]
The Picturesque. [=*T. H. BAYLY.*]
Pierre Bertrand. [=*F. LAWRANCE.*]
The Pilgrim. [=The Noble Outlaw (*UA*).]
The Pilot. [=*J. B. BUCKSTONE.*]

p. 520]   The Pirate of Genoa. [Adapted from *L'amor marinaro*, by
G. de Gamerra, music by Weigl; Vienna, 15/10/1797.]
+The Pirate's Vault (Strand, 9/8/1847).
The Place Hunter. [=*F. WEBSTER*. +8° 1840.]
+The Plague of Florence. 8° 1837.
The Plague of Marseilles (Cob. 1828). [=*R. J. RAYMOND*.]
The Plaguy Good-natured Friend. [=Too Friendly by Half
(*UA*).]
The Plum Pudding Pantomime. [=*H. MAYHEW*.]
Poachers and Petticoats. [=*C. P. THOMPSON*.]
The Poison Tree (Sans P. 1811). [=*J. M. SCOTT*.]
Polkamania. [=*J. H. STOCQUELER*.]
Pong Wong. [=*C. J. MATHEWS*; see p. 354.]
Poor Dog Tray. [=*T. G. BLAKE*; see p. 268.]

p. 521]   Poor Relations (H.[2] 1818). [=*R. F. JAMESON*, *Nine Points
of the Law*.]
Popularity. [=*W. T. MONCRIEFF*.]
The Post Captain. [=*W. T. TOWNSEND*.]
The Postillion. [An opera *The Postillion* appeared at the Grecian,
28/8/1843; adapted from the opera by A. de Leuven and
L. L. Brunswick, music by Adam; Paris, 13/10/1836. *The
Postillion* (Vic. 1837) =*J. P. HART*.]
Preciosa (C.G. 1825). [Ascribed both to *G. SOANE* and
W. BALL. Adapted from the opera by P. A. Wolff, music
by C. M. von Weber; Berlin, 14/3/1821. For the English
version the music was arranged by W. Hawes.]
The Pretty Sicilian. [=— *BLASIS*.]
The Prince. [=*C. I. M. DIBDIN*; see p. 292.]
+D.   Prince Charlie; or, The Last of the Stuarts (Perth,
21/7/1830).
Prince Dorus. [=*TOM TAYLOR*.]

p. 522]   Princess Battledore. [=*W. DE HAYES*.]
+D. The Prisoner's Secret (Strand, 29/11/1847).
The Prodigal Son. [=*H. M. MILNER*.]
The Profligate. [=*W. L. REDE*.]
The Promissory Note. [=*S. BEAZLEY*.]
The Proof of Love. [=*J. BYRNE*.]
The Proof of the Pudding. [=*T. H. BAYLY*.]
Proof Presumptive. [=*C. KEMBLE*.]
The Provisional Government. [=*J. H. STOCQUELER*.]

p. 523]   Puck's Pantomime. [=*J. M. MORTON*.]
Punch in Italy. [=*J. H. EUSTON*.]
Punch's Pantomime. [By the writers of *Punch*: M. LEMON,
G. A. À BECKETT, A. SMITH, D. JERROLD and others.]
The Pupil of Da Vinci. [=*M. LEMON*. Music by J. A. Wade.]
I Puritani. [=*G. A. À BECKETT*.]
The Purse of Almo. [=*J. LUNN*.]
The Quadroon Slave. [=*B. J. WEBSTER*.]

p. 524]   Queen Mary. [=*E. STIRLING*. Adapted from *Marie Tudor*
by Victor Hugo (1833).]
The Queen of the Clover Field. [=*N. LEE*.]
The Queen's Command. [By "William Shakespeare" (i.e.
Walton).]

Quentin Durward. [See *J. L. HUIE.*]
Quits. [=*G. DANCE.*]
A Race for a Dinner. [=*J. T. G. RODWELL*; see p. 395.]
A Race for a Wife. [See *H. W. CHALLIS.*]
Rafael the Libertine. [=*G. ALMAR.*]
The Railroad for Ever. [= — *CARR.*]
Railway Bubbles. [=*J. S. COYNE.*]

p. 525]   The Rash Marriage. [=*J. PINKERTON.*]
The Rat-Trap. [=*H. M. MILNER.*]
Raykisnah the Outcast. [=*J. M. SCOTT.*]
The Rebel Chief. [=*H. P. GRATTAN.*]
A Receipt for Mirth. [= — *BURTON, Right and Wrong.*]
The Recluse (Edinburgh, 1825). [+sub-title: *or, Elshie of the Moor.* Acted 31/5/1825.]
The Recluse (Norwich, 1823). [=*C. FEIST.*]
+The Red Barn; or, The Prophetic Dream (Lincoln, 27/10/1830).
+M.D.   Red Eric, the Sea King; or, The Witch of Cullercoats (N. Shields, 1837 or 1838).
The Red Mantle. [=*T. P. TAYLOR.*]
The Red Robber. [=*J. M. SCOTT.*]

p. 526]   +B.O.   The Regatta (Strand, 16/8/1847).
+D.   A Regicide; or, Swansea Castle in 1327 (Swansea, 3/11/1842).
The Reign of Terror. [=*H. M. MILNER.*]
Rejected Addresses (Clarence, 1833). [=*F. F. COOPER.*]
The Reprobate (Olym. 1821). [=*T. J. DIBDIN.* Acted at Olym. 19/3/1821 as *The R.; or, Four by Honours.*]
Retaliation. [=*W. WASTELL, A West Wind.*]
+C.O.   Retaliation (Prince's, 30/1/1841; Lyc. 14/4/1841, amateur). [Adapted from *Così fan tutte.*]
The Revolt of Bruges. [=*A. R. SMITH.*]
The Revolt of Flanders. [=*E. ROBINSON.*]
The Revolt of the Greeks. [=*C. E. WALKER.*]
The Revolt of the Seraglio. [=*W. T. MONCRIEFF.*]

p. 527]   Richard and Betty. [=*L. LANE.*]
+D.   Richard Turpin; or, The Fate of the House of Rookwood (Vic. 7/1840).
Richmond Hill. [= *H. P. GRATTAN.*]
+D.   The Riever of Barry Hill (Alyth, Perthshire, 4/1842).
+D.   The Riever's Ransom (M'bone, 2/5/1846).
The Ring. [=*Mrs W. TURNBALL.*]

p. 528]   Rob of the Fen. [=*M. LEMON.* Adapted from *Des Falkners Braut,* by W. A. Wohlbrück, music by Marschner; Leipzig, 10/3/1832.]
Rob Roy (Olym. 1818). [=*H. M. MILNER.*]
Rodar the Raven. [=*A. V. CAMPBELL.*]
The Roebuck. [=*R. B. PEAKE, The Poachers.*]
The Romantic Widow. [= — *RANGER.*]
+T.   Rosamund. 8° 1829.

p. 529]   +The Royal Crusader; or, The Black Brand of Rome (M'bone, 1846 or 1847).

p. 530]   The Ruins of Athens. [=*B. BARTHOLOMEW.*]
+Russell. 8° 1839.

The Russian Captive. [=*J. T. HAINES.*]
The Russian Festival. [= — *NOBLE.*]
The Russian Village. [=*C. A. BROWN, Narensky.*]
The Sacred Standard. [=*H. M. MILNER.*]
+M.D. The Sailor's Grave; or, The Privateer and his Friend (City, 22/1/1834).
The Sailor's Home. [=*W. ROGERS.*]
St. Ann's Well. [=*F. C. NANTZ.*]
St. George and the Dragon (C.L. 1843). [=*N. LEE.*]
St. Gothard's Mount. [Adapted from Maturin, *Fredolfo.*]
St. Hilda's Cave. [Adapted from M. G. Lewis, *Adelgitha.*]

p. 531]   Sam Weller's Tour. [=*W. T. MONCRIEFF.*]
+Saul. 8° 1820. [Translated from Voltaire, "by Oliver Martext of Arden."]
Savage Lovers. [=*C. I. M. DIBDIN*; see p. 296.]
+D. The Saxon Maid; or, The Days of William the Conqueror (M'bone, 12/12/1842).
The Schoolmaster at Home. [=*T. H. BAYLY.*]
The Scornful Lady. [=*T. J. SERLE*; see p. 400.]
Scotch Marriage Laws. [= — *JONES.*]
Scotch Mist. [=*H. WILLS.*]
The Scottish Chiefs. [=*E. STIRLING.*]

p. 532]   Second Sight. [=*R. RYAN.*]
+D. The Secret Vaults of Tilney Castle; or, The Mysteries of the Masquerade. 8° 1806.
The Seraglio. [= — *NOBLE.*]
The Servant of All Work. [=*W. B. BERNARD.* This was acted earlier at the Tott. 9/10/1830.]
The Seven Ages of Man. [=*T. H. WEBB.*]
The Seven Castles of the Passions. [=*E. STIRLING.*]
The Seven Champions of Christendom. [=*J. H. STOCQUELER.*]

p. 533]   The Sexton of Stepney. [=*G. D. PITT.*]
Shakespeare and Burbage. [=*W. T. MONCRIEFF.*]
Shave you Directly. [=*C. W. S. BROOKS*; see p. 271.]
She Lives! [=*M. GOLDSMITH*; see p. 319.]
She's mine for a Thousand. [=*W. J. LUCAS.*]
She's not to be Managed. [=*C. I. M. DIBDIN*; see p. 295.]
She Wants a Guardian. [=*J. S. COYNE.* +sub-title: *or, They Took the Will for the Deed.*]
Shifts of Genius. [=*S. ROXBY.*]

p. 534]   +M.D. The Sicilian Outlaw; or, The Castle of Caldora (Surrey, 7/1824). [Adapted from Maturin, *Bertram.*]
The Siege of Acre. [=*H. M. MILNER.*]
+D. The Siege of Liverpool; or, The Days of Prince Rupert (Liver, L'pool, 28/4/1830).
The Siege of Sarragossa. [=*G. BENNETT.*]
+The Siege of Troy; or, The Great Horse of Greece (R.A. 8/1840).

p. 535]   The Silver Veil. [=*H. M. MILNER.*]
Sinbad the Sailor. [=*H. YOUNGE.*]
The Sister of Charity. [= — *BAYNEM.*]
The Sisters. [=*W. BARRYMORE.* Revived in 1822 as: *Ida and Carelia; or, The Amazon Sisters.*]

p. 536] The Smuggler's Dog. [=*W. T. MONCRIEFF.*]
The Smuggler's Haunt. [=*W. T. MONCRIEFF.*]
Snap Apple Night. [=*S. LOVER.*]
The Soldier's Dream. [+*Oxberry's Budget*, no. 2.]
+The Soldier's Gift (Strand, 24/6/1848).
+Some Passages in the Diary of a Physician (Strand, 11/5/1847).
A Son's Revenge. [=*J. T. HAINES.*]

p. 537] The Spanish Gala. [=*C. I. M. DIBDIN*; see p. 293.]
Spanish Gallants. [=*O. BYRNE* and — *NOBLE.*]
Spanish Gallantries. [=— *BLASIS.*]
Spanish Martyrs. [=*H. M. MILNER.*]
+D. Spanish Patriots of a Thousand Years Ago. 8° 1813.
Speculation. [=— *FREEMAN*+Tott. 20/3/30.]
The Spendthrift. [=*T. G. BLAKE.*]
The Spirit of the Fountain. [=*J. COURTNEY.*]
The Spirit of the Mist. [=— *KEPPELL.*]

p. 538] The Spirit of the Moon (C.G. 1824). [=*C. FARLEY.*]
The Stage-Struck Yankee. [=*W. R. MARKWELL.*]
Stanislaus. [=*H. M. MILNER.*]
"Stars." [=*W. L. REDE.*]
State Secrets. [=*A. SNODGRASS.*]
The Stout Gentleman. [=*T. H. BAYLY*; revised *R. B. PEAKE.*]
The Strand-ed Actor! [=*T. J. DIBDIN.*]

p. 539] The Student of Jena. [=*W. COOPER.*]
The Students. [=*G. SMITH*; for Bury St Edmunds.]
The Sultana. [=*R. GOFF.*]
The Sultan and the Slave (Tottenham-street, 1830). [This had
been acted at the same theatre, 9/3/1830, as *Who Rules? or,
The S. and the S.*]
Sunshine and Shade. [=*W. L. REDE, Faith and Falsehood.*]
Suzanne. [Apparently=*W. J. LUCAS.*]
The Swedish Ferryman. [=*J. POOLE.*]
+Sweet Poll of Horsleydown; or, Poor Joe the Marine (Vic.
23/8/1841).
+D. Sybil Clare (Queen's, 11/1840).

p. 540] The Tailors. [+L. 2202; printed copy altered for performance,
Olym. 1/2/1821.]
+Take Care of your Wife! (Strand, 3/5/1847).
"Talk of the Devil!" [=*S. BEAZLEY.*]
Taming a Tartar. [=*C. SELBY.*]
Tarrare. [=*S. J. ARNOLD.* Adapted from the play by P. A.
Caron de Beaumarchais, music by Salieri; Paris, 8/6/1787.]

p. 541] Tears and Smiles. [=*E. J. EYRE, The Vintagers.*]
Telemachus (Adel. 1844). [=*J. COURTNEY.* Also ascribed
to *J. S. COYNE.*]
Temper. [=*M. G. LEWIS.*]
Temptation. [Ascribed both to *J. G. MILLINGEN* and *G. A.
À BECKETT.*]
Thalaba the Destroyer. [=*E. FITZBALL.* +8° 1826.]
That Rascal Jack. [=*T. GREENWOOD.*]

p. 542] The Three and the Deuce. [=*D. LAWLER.*]
The Three Cripples and the Queen of Billingsgate. [=*J. H. AMHERST*; see p. 253.]

p. 543] Tit for Tat. [=*S. J. ARNOLD*. Music arranged by W. Hawes. Adapted from *Così fan tutte*.]
Tom Trim. [=*J. COURTNEY.*]
Too Careful by Half. [=*J. EBSWORTH.*]
The Toodles. [Possibly=*R. J. RAYMOND.*]
Too Friendly by Half. [=A Plaguy Good-natured Friend (*UA*).]

p. 544] Il Torneo. [Music Lord Burghersh.]
Touch and Take. (1827.) [=The Counterfeits (*UA*).]
Travelling Incog. [=*H. M. MILNER.*]

p. 545] +The Tread Mill; or, Tom and Jerry at Brixton (Surrey). 8° (1822). [Apparently the same as *The Treadmill*.]
+The Treasure Seeker; or, The Maid of Austerlitz (Strand, 6/9/1847).
Trevanion. [Ascribed to *B. BERNARD.*]
The Trial of Love. [=*G. SOANE.*]
Trick for Trick. [+8° 1812.]
Tricks and Blunders (Cob. 1823). [=*J. DOBBS.*]
A Trip to the Ball. [=*H. M. MILNER.*]
A Troublesome Lodger. [=*H. MAYHEW* and *H. BAYLIS.*]
The Trustee. [=*J. T. ALLINGHAM, Independence.*]

p. 546] The Turret Clock. [=— *EARLE.*]
The Turret Demon. [=*C. F. BARRETT.*]
The Twelve Months. [=*G. A. À BECKETT.*]
The 24th of May. [=*T. H. REYNOLDSON*; see p. 393.]
+The Twins of Warsaw (R. Pav. 30/9/1833).
Twm John Catty. [=*H. M. MILNER.*]
+M.D. The Two Galley Slaves (D.L. 6/11/1822). L. 2316.
The Two Greens. [=*W. L. REDE.*]
Two Heads better than One. [Evidently=*F. L. HORNE*; but also ascribed to *T. MILDENHALL.*]
The Two Jack Sheppards. [=*C. A. SOMERSET.*]
The Two Locksmiths. [=*J. T. HAINES.*]

p. 547] The Two London Locksmiths. [=*G. D. PITT.*]
Two Pence. [=*R. B. PEAKE.*]
The Two Prisoners. [=*J. KENNEY, Matrimony.*]
The Two Spanish Valets. [=*J. M. SCOTT*. =Lie upon Lie (*UA*).]
The Two Wives! (=*J. PARRY.*]
The Tyrant and Parrasite. [=*J. KENNEY, Turn him Out!*]
Ulrica. [=*E. STIRLING.*]
Ulthona the Sorceress. [=*J. M. SCOTT.*]
The Ultra Exquisite. [+Edinburgh, 18/5/1819.]
Uncle Oliver. [=*J. T. HAINES.*]
The Unconscious Counterfeit. [=— *GREFFULHE.*]

p. 548] The Unhallowed Templar. [=*J. T. HAINES.*]
The United Britons. [=*J. BYRNE.*]
Up and Down. [=*W. T. MONCRIEFF.*]
Ups and Downs. [=*J. POOLE.*]
+The Vagrant—his Wife and Family (Strand, 30/6/1845).

Valasco. [=E. SARGENT; originally acted at the Tremont, Boston, 1837.]
Valentine and Orson. [=A. R. SMITH.]
Valmondi. [Ascribed to J. T. G. RODWELL.]
+M.D. The Vampire Bride; or, The Tenant of the Tomb (City, 5/2/1834).

p. 549] The Venison Pasty. [=S. BEAZLEY.]
The Vermont Wool Dealer. [=C. A. LOGAN. Acted in the U.S.A., 1840.]
+The Veteran of the Old Guard; or, The Cross of Gold (Strand, 20/12/1847).
The Vicar of Wakefield. [An altered version of the play by T. J. DIBDIN.]
The Viceroy. [=C. I. M. DIBDIN; see p. 294.]
The Victim (Surrey, 1820). [=T. J. DIBDIN.]
"Victor Dene." [=W. T. MONCRIEFF.]
+Vaud. Victor Hugh; or, The Dog Friend (Albert, 8/1840).
The Village Fete (New, 1810). [+8° 1810.]
Virginia. [=J. OXENFORD.]
The Virginia Mummy. [=T. D. RICE.]
+A Vision of St Helena (Adel. 12/1840).
The Vision of the Sun. [+8° 1823 (Songs, Choruses).]

p. 550] "Vive la Liberté." [=D. W. OSBALDISTONE.]
The Vizier's Son. [=J. M. SCOTT.]
The Votaries of the Ruby Cross. [=H. M. MILNER.]
The Vow of Vengeance. [=J. H. AMHERST.]
The Wager (St J. 1837). [=J. PARRY.]
Wake not the Dead. [=G. ALMAR.]
Walcot Castle. [=M. GOLDSMITH, Angelina.]
The Waltz. [=S. J. ARNOLD.]
The Wandering Boys. [=I. POCOCK.]

p. 551] The Wandering Tribe. [=W. L. REDE.]
Wanted a Bravo. [=C. WEBB.]
Wanted a Hermit. [=I. TAYLOR.]
+D. The Warrior and his Child; or, The Blighted Flower (M'bone, 15/11/1843).
+Mil.D. The Warrior Peasant (Strand, 27/9/1847).
The Wars of the Jews. [=T. G. BLAKE.]
The Wars of Wellington. [=J. H. AMHERST.]
The Water Witch. [=W. B. BERNARD.]
+D. Waverley; or, The Bodack Glas (Caledonian, Edinburgh, 26/3/1831).

p. 552] The Weird Woman of the Isles. [=H. M. MILNER.]
The Welshman. [=H. M. MILNER.]
Whackham and Windham. [=J. M. SCOTT.]
What are you at? [=W. T. MONCRIEFF.]
What a Shocking Bad Hat! [=W. T. MONCRIEFF.]
What have I done? [=J. OXENFORD.]
What's in a Name? (Vic. 1835). [=W. T. MONCRIEFF.]
What! The Devil Again! [=W. H. MURRAY.]
Wheedling. [=J. LUNN.]
Where's Eliza? [=C. S. JAMES; see p. 330.]

p. 553] +Whitefriars; or, A Legend of Llandarff (Cardiff, 23/11/1838).
The White Lady. [=S. BEAZLEY. Original Music by Boiel-
dieu; arranged by Cooke.]
The White Squall. [Probably=J. T. HAINES.]
White Surrey. [=C. I. M. DIBDIN; see p. 295.]
Whitsun Eve. [Ascribed to E. R. LANCASTER.]
Who killed Cock Robin. [=C. J. MATHEWS. +C.G.
14/12/1829.]

p. 554] Who Pays the Piper? [=Bad Customers (UA).]
Who's the Rogue? [+8° 1801 (Songs, Choruses).]
Why did I marry? [The L.C. copy is a printed text of Barnaby
Brittle, of which this is an alteration.]
The Widow Barnaby. [Probably=T. H. REYNOLDSON.]
The Widow Bewitched. [=P. FARREN.]
The Widow's Choice. [=J. T. ALLINGHAM, Who Wins?]
Wife and Child. [=W. ST IVES.]
A Wife with Two Husbands. [=E. GUNNING; see p. 321.]
+The Wild Hag of the Mountain; or, The Fatal Glen of
Lorin (Panharmonion, 11/11/1831).

p. 555] The Wild Islanders. [=J. BYRNE.]
William the Conqueror. [=E. FITZBALL.]
William the Conqueror's Invasion of England. [=J. COURT-
NEY, The Invasion of England by William the Conqueror.]

p. 556] T. Wismar. 8° 1830.
The Wizard Priest. [=J. WALKER.]
Wolsey. [=J. F. SMITH; see p. 403.]
Woman. [=T. J. THACKERAY.]
Woman and Philosophy. [=J. PINKERTON.]
+D. A Woman's Heart (Qus. 3/1841).
Woman's the Devil. [=E. STIRLING; see p. 406.]
Woman's Will. [=E. L. SWIFT.]
The Wood Demon (Lyc. 1847). [=C. KENNEY and A. R.
SMITH.]
The Wooden Walls. [=A. CHERRY, Peter the Great.]
+P. The Woodman and his Ass; or, Harlequin in Fairyland
(Queen's, L'pool, 28/12/1835).
Worga. [=J. T. HAINES.]
The Wreck. [=A. V. CAMPBELL.]
The Wreck of the Leander Frigate. [=R. J. RAYMOND.]

p. 557] Yankee Doodle upon his Little Pony. [=N. LEE, Harlequin
and Yankee Doodle.]
The Young Courier. [=E. FITZBALL.]
+Young Heads upon Old Shoulders (Swansea, 18/7/1812).
The Young Prude. [=Belles without Beaux (UA).]
The Young Reefer. [=G. SOANE; see p. 404.]
The Young Scamp. [=E. STIRLING; see p. 407.]
Zameo. [=C. P. THOMPSON.]
Zangarotti. [=H. M. MILNER.]
+Zara; or, The Zingarian Girl (Strand, 22/7/1847).
Zohrab the Hostage. [=E. FITZBALL.]
+D. Zoleikha. 8° 1832.
Zophyrus. [=W. COOPER.]
Zorayda. [The L.C. copy is a printed text of M. G. Lewis,
Rich and Poor, altered.]

644   SUPPLEMENTARY NOTE

A few other plays of the period 1800–1850 are included (with a plus sign) in the 'Short-title Alphabetical Catalogue of Plays', vol. vi. These are: *The Advance Guard*; *The Ambassador*; *The Banished Lord*; *Courtship a-la-mode*; *The Casket of Gloriana*; *The Death of Darnley*; *The Death of General Abercrombie*; *The Errors of Ecstasie*; *Jinks, the Man that can't help it*; *King James I of Scotland*; *The Lion Chief*; *Lovers' Quarrels*; *The Old Church Porch*; *The Old Sailor's Ghost*; *Old Poz*; *The Organ Grinder*; *A Peep at the Danube*; *Peter the Emperor and Paul the Sailor*; *Sebastian of Portugal*; *Toads and Diamonds*; *Twelve at Night*; *Vincenzo, Prince of Mantua*; *Woman's Whims*.

INDEX OF PERSONS AND SUBJECTS

[A final volume in this series will present a general comprehensive index of all the English plays catalogued in this and the other Hand-lists. Consequently the present index is concerned only with persons and subjects.]